THE CAMBRIDGE HISTORY OF CHINA

General editors
DENIS TWITCHETT and JOHN K. FAIRBANK

Volume 11
Late Ch'ing, 1800-1911, Part 2

THE CAMBRIDGE
HISTORY OF
CHINA

Volume 11
Late Ch'ing, 1800–1911, Part 2

edited by
JOHN K. FAIRBANK
and
KWANG-CHING LIU

CAMBRIDGE UNIVERSITY PRESS
CAMBRIDGE
LONDON · NEW YORK · NEW ROCHELLE
MELBOURNE · SYDNEY

Published by the Press Syndicate of the University of Cambridge
The Pitt Building, Trumpington Street, Cambridge CB2 1RP
32 East 57th Street, New York, NY 10022, USA
296 Beaconsfield Parade, Middle Park, Melbourne 3206, Australia

First published 1980

Printed in the United States of America

Typeset by Western Printing Services, Avonmouth, England
Printed and bound by The Murray Printing Company, Westford, Massachusetts

Library of Congress Cataloguing in Publication Data (Revised)
Main entry under title:
The Cambridge History of China.
Vol. 11 edited by J. K. Fairbank and K. C. Liu.
Bibliography: p.
Includes index.
CONTENTS: v. 10. Late Ch'ing, 1800-1911, pt. 1.
v. 11. Late Ch'ing, 1800-1911, pt. 2.
1. China History. J. Twitchett, Denis Crispin.
II. Fairbank, John King, 1907– III. Liu, Kwang-Ching, 1921–
DS735.C3145   951'.03   76-29852
ISBN 0 521 22029 7 (v. 11)

GENERAL EDITORS' PREFACE

In the English-speaking world, the Cambridge histories have since the beginning of the century set the pattern for multi-volume works of history, with chapters written by experts of a particular topic, and unified by the guiding hand of volume editors of senior standing. *The Cambridge Modern History*, planned by Lord Acton, appeared in sixteen volumes between 1902 and 1912. It was followed by *The Cambridge Ancient History*, *The Cambridge Medieval History*, *The Cambridge History of English Literature*, and Cambridge Histories of India, of Poland, and of the British Empire. The original *Modern History* has now been replaced by *The New Cambridge Modern History* in twelve volumes, and *The Cambridge Economic History of Europe* is now being completed. Other Cambridge Histories recently undertaken include a history of Islam, of Arabic literature, of the Bible treated as a central document of and influence on Western civilization, and of Iran and China.

In the case of China, Western historians face a special problem. The history of Chinese civilization is more extensive and complex than that of any single Western nation, and only slightly less ramified than the history of European civilization as a whole. The Chinese historical record is immensely detailed and extensive, and Chinese historical scholarship has been highly developed and sophisticated for many centuries. Yet until recent decades the study of China in the West, despite the important pioneer work of European sinologists, had hardly progressed beyond the translation of some few classical historical texts, and the outline history of the major dynasties and their institutions.

Recently Western scholars have drawn more fully upon the rich traditions of historical scholarship in China and also in Japan, and greatly advanced both our detailed knowledge of past events and institutions, and also our critical understanding of traditional historiography. In addition, the present generation of Western historians of China can also draw upon the new outlooks and techniques of modern Western historical scholarship, and upon recent developments in the social sciences, while continuing to build upon the solid foundations of rapidly progressing European, Japanese and Chinese sinological studies. Recent historical events, too, have given prominence to new problems, while throwing into question many older conceptions. Under these multiple impacts the Western revolution in Chinese studies is steadily gathering momentum.

When *The Cambridge History of China* was first planned in 1966, the aim was to provide a substantial account of the history of China as a bench mark for the Western history-reading public: an account of the current state of knowledge in six volumes. Since then the out-pouring of current research, the application of new methods, and the extension of scholarship into new fields, have further stimulated Chinese historical studies. This growth is indicated by the fact that the History has now become a planned sixteen volumes, including the earliest pre-dynastic period, but which still leave out such topics as the history of art and of literature, many aspects of economics and technology, and all the riches of local history.

The striking advances in our knowledge of China's past over the last decade will continue and accelerate. Western historians of this great and complex subject are justified in their efforts by the needs of their own peoples for greater and deeper understanding of China. Chinese history belongs to the world, not only as a right and necessity, but also as a subject of compelling interest.

JOHN K. FAIRBANK
DENIS TWITCHETT

June 1976

CONTENTS

MAPS

MAP 1.   Ch'ing empire
– physical features

0 ————————— 500km
0 ————————— 300 miles
===== Trade Route
+++++ Grand Canal
ᨃᨃᨃᨃ Great Wall
ᨃ   Pass
░░░░░ Region of wind-borne loess

RUSSIAN

EMPIRE

kutsk

Baikal

Nerchinsk

Blagoveshchensk

Amur R.

Kiakhta

Argun R.

Great Khingan Mts.

Lesser Khingan Mts.

Tsitsihar

Ussuri R.

Urga

Kerulen R.

Harbin

Chiang-pai Mts.

Vladivostok

ONGOLIA

Gobi

esert

Liao R.

Mukden

40°N

Kalgan

Ku-pei-kou

KOREA

Ordos
Desert

Great Wall

Peking

Shan-hai
kuan

Lü-shun

Seoul

Tientsin

Wu-tai Mts.

Tai'uan

post-1855

Tsinan

Lanchow

Yellow R.

T'ai-hang Mts.

North
China
Plain

Grand Canal

Sian

Kaifeng

pre-1853

Tsin-ling Mts.

Huai R.

Nanking

Shanghai

30°N

Han R.

Soochow

Chusan Is.

Chengtu
Red Basin

Yangtze Gorges

Wuhan

Yangtze R.

Chien Tang R.

Ningpo

un-nan
lateau

Tungting L.

Poyang L.

Nan-ch'ang

Changsha

Kan R.

Wu-i Mts.

Foochow

Liu-ch'iu Is.

Kweiyang

Hsiang R.

Kweilin

Mei-ling

Amoy

Taiwan

20°N

West R.

Nanning

Canton

nan-fu

Red R.

Hong Kong

Hanoi

Macao

ANNAM
(VIETNAM)

Hainan I.

110°E

120°E

TABLES

PREFACE TO VOLUME 11

While generalizing is required in all thinking about history, it becomes a special problem in the case of China's history. 'China' is in fact one of the largest generalities used in modern speech. The term represents the largest body of people in one of the biggest land areas over the longest recorded time – a four-dimensional non-pareil. Just to think about 'China' or 'the Chinese' is to rise to a level of generality (measured in persons or years or acres) that in other fields of history would seem almost infeasibly high. Europe since the Minoan age is a smaller entity. To say, with our greater knowledge of Europe and comparative ignorance of China, that European history is more complex would be presumptuous. Until modern times the Chinese record was more extensive. Perhaps China's greater sense of unity produced more homogeneity than in Europe, or perhaps this is partly an illusion created by the traditional Chinese historians' primary concern for social order, the state and its ruling class.

In any case, China's historical record with its already high level of generality is now being studied in search of syntheses and unifying concepts to give peoples of today some image of China's past. This is urgently needed, but the difficulties are great: the public need for a generalized picture often coincides with a popular seeking for predetermined conclusions, in order to allocate blame and identify villains, or to acknowledge guilt and regret it, or to justify doctrines and reaffirm them, as the case may be.

This means that what the historian of China contributes to his history must be scrutinized with even greater care than usual, especially in a history of China written by outside observers. For example, modern Chinese history in the West has been in large part a history of foreign relations with China, the aspect of modern China most easily studied by foreigners. Of course the multiplicity of foreign influences on China since 1840 (or since 1514) is plain to see. It has even become customary to date modern times from the Opium War, a foreign invasion. But all such impacts from abroad formed only a small part of the Chinese people's day-to-day environment, in which the surrounding landscape and inherited ways remained dominant and changed only slowly. Is it not likely that foreign influences will in time bulk less large in the landscape of nineteenth-century China? Not because they will shrink in size or significance but simply because they will be overshadowed by the accumulated new knowledge about China's indigenous experience.

Volume 10 of this series begins not with the foreign commercial invasion and Opium War but with the view from Peking – the institutional structure of the Ch'ing empire in China and Inner Asia early in the nineteenth century. This is followed by Peking's growing domestic problems of administrative control and social order in the first half of the century. Similar signs of internal malaise as well as signs of rejuvenation appear in the accounts of the Taiping and the Nien rebellions and of the tortured success of the Ch'ing restoration. China's economy, and even her military institutions, shows the inner dynamics of an ancient yet far from stagnant society. In the face of unprecedented strains, millions of men and women knew how to survive. It is evident that by the end of the dynasty the eighteenth-century triumph of Ch'ing arms and governance in the Manchus' Inner Asian empire had actually set the stage for the expansion of the Han Chinese from China proper into the spacious borderlands of Manchuria, Mongolia, Sinkiang and eastern Tibet – a great secular migration consequent upon China's phenomenal population growth that began even before the eighteenth century.

The rise of the Canton trade – a two-way street – is only the best-known part of this great Han expansion in numbers, migration, trade and even investment. Part of this Chinese expansion had indeed already taken place overseas, parallel with the expansion of Europe. It occurred beyond the Ch'ing frontiers in that realm of maritime China which forms a minor tradition roughly half as old as the great tradition of the continental, agrarian-bureaucratic empire that dominated the official histories. Seafaring enterprise in the form of the junk trade from Amoy and Canton to South-East Asia (Nanyang, 'the southern seas') long antedated the arrival of the European colonial powers in that region. One has only to think of the Southern Sung navy taken over by the Mongols, of their expedition to Java in 1292, and of the early Ming expeditions across the Indian Ocean in the period 1405–33. Granted that the emperor's leadership of maritime China was foreclosed by the resurgence of Mongol power in the 1440s which pre-empted Ming attention, and by the eventual succession of the Ch'ing as another Inner Asian, anti-seafaring dynasty, the fact remains that in the South-East Asian colonies of the Spanish, Portuguese, Dutch, British and French the European rulers increasingly relied upon Chinese merchants and middlemen to handle retail trade and perform the tasks of licensed monopolists and petty tax collectors. These overseas Chinese (*Hua-ch'iao*, 'Chinese sojourners') became a special middle class in the European colonies, just as they became indispensable also to the rulers of Siam, where one of them indeed founded the Chakri dynasty that still reigns at Bangkok. Though unappreciated and sometimes denounced by Peking, the seafarers and entrepreneurs of maritime China thus participated in the commercial revolution of early modern times and the colonialism to which it gave rise in South-East Asia.

When this accelerating growth of international trade at length forced its way into China through the Tiger's Mouth (Hu-men, Bocca Tigris) below Canton, merchants of Canton, Swatow and Amoy both in legal trade and in the opium trade were among the prime movers in the subsequent growth of international contact. Despite the plethora of foreign commercial records and the present paucity of Chinese, we know that the foreign trade of China was a distinctly Sino-foreign enterprise – in fact, once the treaty ports were opened, the foreign firms' compradors handled most of the trade both into China from the ports and out of China through the ports. Hong Kong, Shanghai and the other places of trade became Chinese cities no matter what the foreign residents may have thought about their sovereignty, their treaty rights or the fire-power of their gunboats. It is almost equally true to say that Chinese participated in the foreigners' opening of China as to say that foreigners participated in China's commercial opening of herself. In the rapid growth of the East India Company's great staple trade in tea at Canton *c*. 1784–1834, the tea, after all, came from China. Taken together with the Chinese farmers or traders in far-off Sinkiang or Manchuria, the seafarers and entrepreneurs of maritime China bespeak the vitality of the Chinese people, especially since they received scant help from their own government.

If foreign trade was a two-sided process in which both Chinese and foreigners actively participated, there is also another consideration with which to appraise the foreign influence in late Ch'ing history: during the nineteenth century, foreign contact bulked larger and larger in the experience of almost every people. The great migration from Europe to the New World had long preceded the more modest movement of Chinese overseas in foreign vessels after mid-century. For the British public the Opium War was of less strategic relevance than the First Afghan War, the Boxer Uprising was only a spectacular incident during the long grind of the Boer War. For most peoples industrialization came from abroad; the centre of gravity in many aspects of change was seen to lie outside the country. International science and technology, like international trade and politics, increasingly contributed to the global life of a world society. In this perspective it seems only natural that outside influences should have played an unprecedentedly larger role in late Ch'ing history.

China's entrance into world society has now laid the basis for historical interpretations that are themselves an ultimate form of foreign influence. These interpretations align the Chinese experience with that of other peoples. This is done first with 'imperialism' and secondly with 'modernization'. These approaches are by way of analogy, seeking to find in China phenomena found universally elsewhere.

Both imperialism and modernization are terms of almost meta-historical scope that require precise definition and concrete illustration if they are to be of use to historians. In a general way imperialism implies foreign initiatives while modernization suggests domestic processes. In its economic aspect, imperialism in the case of China stopped short of colonialism. No plantation economy was developed by foreigners solely for an export market. Even the classic Marxist agent of disaster, the import of factory-made cotton textiles, did not destroy China's handicraft production of cloth; it was sustained into the second quarter of the twentieth century by the supply of cheaper machine-made cotton yarn that could be used by otherwise unemployed members of farming families whose weaving could not have fed them by itself but could nevertheless add a tiny bit to their meagre family incomes. The fact that in the 1930s perhaps 70 per cent of China's cotton cloth still came from handlooms indicates how strongly Chinese families felt compelled to make use of their unemployed labour power. Handweaving indexed their poverty. In thwarting the domination of factory-made cloth, it also suggests how China's people on the whole escaped becoming a mass market for foreign goods (with the exception of cigarettes and kerosene for illumination) simply by being too poor. This example may suggest how much more we need to know about the internal aspects of China's relations with the outside imperialists in the late Ch'ing.

The psychological impact of imperialism, though slow to accumulate, was less uncertain. As time goes on, imperialism as a theme in modern China's history may become more substantial in the realm of thought and psychology, conducive to the rise of nationalism, while it may stand up less well in the quantified field of economics. Chinese ideas of foreign exploitation are already more broadly and easily documented than such exploitation itself. The aggressive assertion of foreign privilege is the major fact in the record, and on this level the missionary vied with the merchant. The imperialism of warfare and gunboat diplomacy, treaty rights and the foreign presence, became very plain to all at the time and is clearly remembered in the national heritage today.

A more recent outsiders' view, the concept of modernization, as applied to China suffers from being a catch-all for the concepts of the social sciences developed mainly in the modern West. The effort of the social sciences to be objectively value-free may sometimes be contaminated by their being a culture-bound product of the West. If so, this should be a temporary problem that will be obviated by the growth of a world culture. More serious is the high level of generality inherent in the term modernization. We take it to be a prehension into unity of the ideas of progressive development exemplified in all the social sciences including history. Modern times see widespread growth which brings complexity, change and development in the analytic realms of the economy, the polity, the society and the culture. But the modernization process in each of these realms is defined in the terms of the discipline concerned. To posit a single principle at work in every realm across the board is a further act of faith. This may be a logical satisfaction and yet difficult to apply to the confused data of history. Do we really gain in understanding by promoting the adjective 'modern' to the status of an abstract entity, 'modernization'? The term may become a useful basket, like 'life', in which to carry a load of things largely unknown, messages undeciphered, mysteries unresolved. Like any term, once reified as a thing in itself, it may become a substitute for thought.

As the corpus of modern historical research and writing on China grows and develops, we should expect less demand for the over-arching generalizations that give preliminary structure to a new field of learning. The concrete experience and conscious concerns of the late Ch'ing era should receive major attention, as they do in many parts of this volume. While literature and the arts remain regrettably beyond our scope here, the history of philosophical and political thought gives us major insights into what happened and how. In brief, the late Ch'ing response to the West now begins to seem like only a minor motif; the major process was China's continued response to the Chinese past in the light of new conditions including the West. Stimulus, in short, is where you find it, and stimulus without response is no stimulus at all.

For example, the deterioration of the Grand Canal transport system to feed Peking roused an effort in the 1820s to revive the sea transport of government rice around Shantung, an institutional arrangement within the tradition of the statecraft (ching-shih) school of practical administrators. Only in the 1870s were steamships adopted to meet the problem. Again, the doctrinal basis for the self-strengthening movement, to defend China by borrowing Western technology, may be viewed as an application of traditional statecraft in a new context. Only in the 1890s, after many disasters, were ideas of evolutionary progress and social Darwinism smuggled into Confucianism as a necessary platform for the reform movement. And in the end, the principal struggle of the reformers was not against imperialism directly but against those Chinese traditions that had made imperialism possible. Late Ch'ing reformers and revolutionaries both accepted the ancient Confucian adage, 'If you can keep your own house in order, who will dare to insult you?' China's strength must come from within. For scholars trained in the classics, the chief source of inspiration for China's future was still her past. For today's historians of the late Ch'ing, this puts a premium on understanding China's great tradition as well as the nineteenth century. There is no substitute for our knowing what the generations before Sun Yat-sen actually had in mind.

Mary Clabaugh Wright (1917–70) left her mark on the history of late imperial China through her students and friends and in two books dealing respectively with the 1860s and the 1900s – the initial and final periods of the present volume. *The last stand of Chinese conservatism: the T'ung-chih Restoration, 1862–1874*, which developed from her Harvard dissertation of 1952, analysed the problems and policies of the Ch'ing regime comprehensively as few have done before or since. *China in revolution: the first phase, 1900–1913*, edited from a conference she organized and presided over in 1965, is the first all-embracing study of the subject that embodies the results of modern scholarship from half-a-dozen countries. From 1945 to 1959 Mary Wright built up the Chinese library of the Hoover Institution on War, Revolution and Peace at Stanford and then from 1959 until her untimely death was Professor of History at Yale University. Since this volume of the *Cambridge History of China* is so indebted to her pioneering work, we dedicate it to her.

JKF

October 1977   KCL

CHAPTER 1

ECONOMIC TRENDS IN THE LATE CH'ING EMPIRE, 1870–1911

There was little of the Chinese economy prior to the twentieth century that was not included within the agricultural sector or quite intimately connected with it.[1] The bulk of the following essay ought properly to be devoted to an analysis of the structure and development of Chinese agriculture in the nineteenth century and its implications for the rest of the economy. I have, however, while discussing agriculture first, given roughly equal attention to handicrafts, modern industry, trade and commerce, and the fiscal system. If these divisions are so obviously the customary ones, I can only plead my own limitations and the possible extenuation that – with honourable and increasing exceptions – the studies of China's modern economic history upon which I have had to rely for this survey are themselves conventionally descriptive works.

The treatment of material in all of the following sections is unavoidably selective. I have in each case focused on what was new or changing in the last five decades of the Manchu dynasty against a background which, until 1911 and long afterwards, remained a basically unaltered mix of the factors of production operating within a largely constant social context. This is not to imply that nothing of importance changed in the last century of imperial China. On the contrary, ideological and political storms uprooted the Confucian empire. Fundamental economic change and modern economic growth, however, did not come of their own momentum out of the late-Ch'ing economic system. They were pre-eminently the by-products of a new and possibly still tenuous political integration which itself was achieved only after decades of political strife, foreign invasion and civil war.

One must begin by reluctantly accepting that precise quantitative information of a global kind – as opposed to a fair amount of suggestive local and partial data – is not available and probably cannot be satisfactorily derived for pre-republican China. Nowhere is this more apparent

[1] The author gratefully acknowledges the support of the Committee on the Chinese Economy of the Social Science Research Council, and of the Center for Chinese Studies at the University of Michigan in the preparation of this essay.

than in the case of so fundamental a measure as national income. Table 1 reproduces, with modifications, the only attempt, of which I am aware, to estimate China's gross national product in the nineteenth century. The individual components were often arbitrarily arrived at, but it is doubtful whether substantial amounts of more reliable information can be assembled. These estimates roughly indicate the relative sizes in the 1880s of the several sectors of the economy.

TABLE 1

Estimated gross national product of China in the 1880s

Sector	Amount (1,000 taels)		%
Agriculture		2,229,941	66.79
Nonagriculture		1,108,816	33.21
mining	47,800		1.43
manufacturing*	128,000		3.77
construction	30,000		0.90
transportation	30,000		0.90
trade	220,000		6.59
finance	74,645		2.24
residential housing	164,000		4.91
government services	164,000		4.91
professional, gentry and other			
services	241,313		7.23
net income from abroad	11,258		0.34
Total		3,338,757	100.00

* almost entirely handicraft.

Source: Chung-li Chang, *The income of the Chinese gentry* (1962), 296. The principal shortcomings of this estimate, apart from the admittedly critical data question, are Chang's probable overstatement of the share of gentry services, and the much more serious reliance on 1887 official data for the area of cultivated land. As I suggest in the next section, these data and thus the share of agriculture should be adjusted upward by at least one-third. This I have done and, leaving Chang's other components unchanged, I have accordingly recalculated the percentages.

AGRICULTURE

While there were changes in detail and alterations in the size or quality of certain components, the technology and organization of Chinese agriculture differed little in 1911 from what it had been in 1870. (Even into the 1930s it remained largely unchanged.) The principal changes were: a slow but perceptible population increase unaccompanied by an equivalent extension of cultivated land; a resulting decrease – particularly in North China – in the size of the average farm; changes in the pattern of crops grown, partly in response to the increasingly adverse man–land ratio and partly in response to new external market opportunities; the absolute and relative decline of cotton spinning as a peasant handicraft and a partial restructuring of the sources of rural non-agricultural income in response to this decline; some differentiation of land-holding patterns in the immediate hinterlands of the growing treaty ports from those of the bulk of the rural interior of China; and a completion of the process already long under way by which the distinction between various legal forms of land tenure was dissipated.

No useful demographic data for the last half of the nineteenth century are of course available. The official estimates for the 1840s put China's population at a little more than 400 million persons; these, it has been argued, while not accurate in detail are relatively good data.[2] The Taiping Rebellion and the other great mid-century uprisings not only resulted in substantial population losses, especially in central China, but also produced a breakdown of the refurbished *pao-chia* system which had collected the reasonably reliable population data for the period 1776–1850. 'The century between 1851 and 1949, despite the availability of various figures, is practically a demographer's vacuum.'[3]

There are, nevertheless, sufficient qualitative indications from which to assert, if not to measure, a slowly increasing population from the 1870s until the end of the dynasty. Migrations of population from provinces to the west and north which had not been so severely afflicted gradually repopulated the Yangtze valley provinces that the civil wars had ravaged. The last four decades of the Manchu dynasty were internally relatively peaceful and, compared to mid-century, prosperous. While the wars with France in 1884–5 and with Japan in 1894–5 were politically and diplomatically of great significance, they had no major demographic effect. The great famine of 1877–8 in North-West China and lesser but still serious famines in 1892–4 and 1900 unquestionably resulted in temporary population losses. Such crises, caused by drought and floods, had been endemic in the past and were experienced again in the twentieth century, for example in 1920–1, 1928, 1931 and 1935. They are inherent components of the demographic pattern characteristic of many 'underdeveloped' countries which combines a high but widely fluctuating death-rate and a high but relatively stable birth-rate to produce slow but substantial population increments.

But, how large an increment? C. M. Chiao and J. L. Buck have estimated from birth- and death-rates observed in 4,216 farm families from four provinces in 1924–5 that the rural population of China might possibly have grown at an average rate of 1.4 per cent per annum between the 1860s and

[2] Ping-ti Ho, *Studies on the population of China, 1368–1953*, 47–64.   [3] *Ibid.* 97.

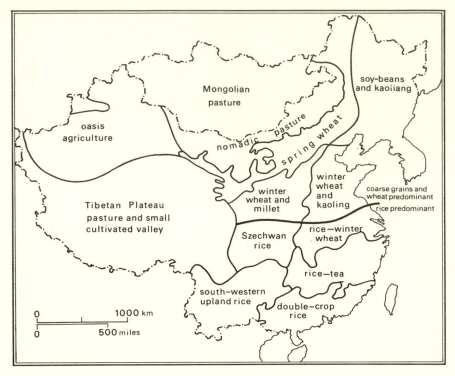

MAP. 2   Major crop areas

the 1920s.[4] Such a rate of increase, if uninterrupted, would have resulted in
a doubling of the population during these seven decades, and on the face
of it appears too high as an actual long-term average although it might
have been valid in some areas for shorter periods. In 1934, the National
Agricultural Research Bureau of the Ministry of Industry produced, from
retrospective and thus tenuous data assembled by its crop reporters, an
estimate of changes in the rural population and the area of farm land
between 1873 and 1933 which I reproduce in table 2. A population increase
of 17 per cent for the forty years 1873–1913, or an annual average of slightly
less than 0.5 per cent, is suggested. Assuming a total population of
between 350 and 400 million in 1873, by 1913 this total would have increased
to between 410 and 468 million. Bearing in mind that the mid-century
population was somewhat more than 400 million, that the Taiping and
other civil wars resulted in severe population losses, and that the population of China in 1953, after many years of war and civil war, was enumerated at 583 million in the closest thing to a real census that China has ever

[4] C. M. Chiao and J. L. Buck, 'The composition and growth of rural population groups in
China', *Chinese Economic Journal*, 2.2 (March 1928) 219–35.

TABLE 2

Index numbers of changes in China's rural population and area of farm land, 1873–1933 (1873 = 100)

	Population	Farm land
1873	100	100
1893	108	101
1913	117	101
1933	131	101

Source: Department of Agricultural Economics, National Agricultural Research Bureau, Ministry of Industries, *Crop reporting in China*, 1934, 48–53.

experienced, these estimates for 1873 and 1913 are at least not unreasonable.

The National Agricultural Research Bureau's respondents, as table 2 indicates, reported that the farm area in their several localities showed no increase comparable to the slow but continuing population growth which occurred. The resultant worsening of the man–land ratio is reflected in the historical data on average farm size shown in table 3, collected by J. L. Buck's field investigators for his monumental land utilization study. Buck's respondents overwhelmingly attributed the reported decreases in average

TABLE 3

Changes in the size of farms, 1870–1930

Regions, areas and locations	Number of locations reporting	Average crop area per farm (hectares)			
		1870	1890	1910	1930
China	55	1.37	1.35	1.06	0.92
wheat region	29	1.75	1.77	1.32	1.10
rice region	26	0.67	0.81	0.77	0.72
Wheat Region Areas					
spring wheat (Kansu, Tsinghai)	2	0.48	0.51	0.66	0.71
winter wheat–millet (Honan, Shansi, Shensi)	8	1.14	1.28	0.97	0.81
winter wheat–kaoliang (Anhwei, Honan, Hopei*, Kiangsu, Shantung)	19	2.19	2.18	1.53	1.26
Rice region areas					
Yangtze rice–wheat (Anhwei, Chekiang, Honan, Hupei, Kiangsi, Kiangsu)	15	0.77	0.99	0.84	0.79
rice–tea (Hunan, Kiangsi)	6	0.42	0.42	0.76	0.74
Szechwan rice (Shensi, Szechwan)	2	0.82	0.76	0.64	0.55
double-crop rice (Fukien)	1	0.58	0.54	0.55	0.53
south-western rice (Kweichow)	2	—	0.52	0.48	0.36

* Hopei province was, of course, called Chihli in the late Ch'ing period.
Source: John Lossing Buck, *Land utilization in China. Statistics*, 288.

farm size to increases in the population of their areas. In North China (Buck's winter wheat–kaoliang areas) the decline in average farm size was more striking than in central China (the rice–wheat and rice–tea areas). The difference is attributable to the much greater demographic losses from the Taiping Rebellion in the provinces south of the Yangtze River and the consequent temporary fall in the man–land ratio in Central and South China. As population migrated to these then relatively less-crowded provinces from more crowded areas, the man–land ratio rose and average farm size after 1900 slowly declined.

While it is certain that rural living standards between 1870 and 1911 did not improve, there is no conclusive evidence that population growth and declining average farm size were accompanied by a drastic secular fall in the peasant standard of living. The semi-annual official reports from the provinces to Peking on the quality of the summer and autumn harvests do indicate a definite downward trend in the course of the nineteenth century. It is reasonable to expect that some deterioration occurred during the catastrophic rebellions of the 1850s and 1860s as table 4 suggests. A continued decline after 1870, however, is not convincingly confirmed by the numerous reports of local crop conditions which appear annually in the *Reports and returns on trade* by the Imperial Maritime Customs. My suspicion is that the higher proportion of poorer harvests reported in the last decades of the dynasty in part reflects the efforts of the provinces to resist Peking's importunate demands for increased tax remittances, which are described below in the discussion of government and the economy. The depopulation attributable to the rebellions, moreover, could be called a Malthusian safety valve which temporarily reduced the inexorable pressure of population on land.

Conditions of individual farmers and of spatially separate localities of course differed widely, with the difference between survival and misery often depending upon uncertain weather, the rapacity of the local officials and the presence or absence of civil war and banditry in the locality. Overall, however, total crop production between 1870 and 1911 probably increased adequately to support the larger population. This increment was not due to any major changes in farm technology or organization. No important new crops or seed varieties (like corn and early-ripening rice earlier in the dynasty) were introduced in the second half of the nineteenth century. The middle decades of civil war, moreover, had seen a substantial destruction of capital stock which was only gradually replaced. Irrigation, water storage and control, and grain storage facilities were not extended or improved beyond their eighteenth-century levels. The increase in crop production was apparently the result mainly of a shift by farmers to crops

which yielded a larger amount of food or income per unit of land and at
the same time required more labour for their cultivation. Crop shifts of this
kind in the early twentieth century, as the man–land ratio continued to

TABLE 4

*Percentage of chou and hsien in nine provinces reporting above normal,
normal and below normal harvests, 1821–1910*

Number of reports*		Above normal	Normal	Below normal
1821	1,114	42.99	54.30	2.69
1825	1,192	46.47	51.67	1.84
1830	1,321	39.64	61.54	1.51
1835	1,229	20.17	65.58	14.23
1840	1,304	25.07	67.02	7.89
1845	1,306	29.24	63.93	6.81
1850	1,019	22.27	72.32	5.39
1855	979	14.09	65.67	20.22
1860	752	20.21	59.04	24.73
1865	1,087	5.79	53.81	40.38
1870	1,255	4.86	45.01	50.11
1875	1,308	6.19	53.66	40.13
1880	1,309	7.79	52.94	39.26
1885	1,246	6.26	49.51	44.22
1890	1,309	5.27	45.37	49.35
1895	1,243	3.94	45.29	50.76
1900	1,190	4.28	42.85	52.85
1905	1,198	4.00	43.24	52.75
1910	1,126	4.61	37.74	57.63

* For eight of the nine provinces both summer and autumn reports are included; the number of
chou and hsien reporting is thus about half the number of annual reports
Source: Calculated from data in Li Wen-chih, comp. *Chung-kuo chin-tai nung-yeh shih tzu-liao
ti-i-chi, 1840–1911* (Source materials on the history of agriculture in modern China, 1st
collection, 1840–1911), 761–9, which are based on reports submitted in response to the
following edict: 'An edict to the Hu-pu. Hereafter, in reporting the harvest results of
the several provinces, use the following categories; eight *fen* [i.e., 80 per cent of a
theoretical maximum] is to be taken as a rich harvest, six to seven *fen* as a normal harvest,
and five *fen* or less as a poor harvest.' *Ta-Ch'ing Kao-tsung shun-huang-ti shih-lu* (Veritable
records of the Ch'ien-lung Emperor of the Ch'ing dynasty), 339. 41a–b, 14 June 1749
(vol. 22, p. 5151 of Taipei reprint, 1964).

worsen, are shown in the data on trends in crop acreage between 1904–9
and 1924–9 collected by J. L. Buck's investigators and summarized in
table 5. These indicate a progressive substitution of corn, sweet potatoes
and sesame for barley, kaoliang and millet as food crops, and also an
increase in such cash crops as cotton to supply the expanding mills of
Shanghai and Tientsin. For the period 1870–1911, unfortunately, not even
such imperfect although suggestive data are available; but if changes of
this kind could occur amidst the political instability and civil war of the

early Republic, they are not implausible in the relative stability of the late-Ch'ing decades. Some partial clues are provided by an examination of trends in the exportation of agricultural products between 1870 and 1911.

TABLE 5

Trends in crop acreages between 1904–9 and 1930–3

	Number of localities reporting	Estimated percentage of total crop area*			
		1904–9	1914–19	1924–9	1930–3
Crops whose acreage increased or was unchanged					
broad beans	7	9	9	9	8
corn	22	11	14	16	17
cotton	29	11	14	18	20
opium	13	14	3	11	20
peanuts	18	9	8	11	11
rapeseed	5	15	21	27	28
rice	17	40	41	37	40
sesame	7	4	8	10	9
soy-beans	7	8	9	10	8
sweet potatoes	18	10	11	12	13
wheat	29	26	27	27	27
Crops whose acreage decreased					
barley	10	24	23	20	19
indigo	12	10	7	2	—
kaoliang	14	26	23	20	16
millet	15	22	18	17	17
sugar cane	10	7	6	5	6

* in the reporting localities
Source: Buck, *Land utilization*, 217.

In value terms, tea was China's most important single export until 1887 when it was overtaken by silk. The proportion of tea to total exports fell steadily from 54 per cent in 1871 to 18 per cent in 1898 and 11 per cent in 1906. While the decline in the absolute quantity of tea exported was far less precipitous, it does suggest that tea acreage did not increase during the four decades under consideration. The exportation of raw and manufactured silk as measured by both quantities and values increased throughout the four decades. This suggests the likelihood that additional land was devoted to growing mulberry and oak trees. In North China and Manchuria the leaves of oak trees fed the worms from whose silk 'pongee', an increasingly important export fabric, was woven.

From 1888 to 1919, with the single exception of 1899, China exported more raw cotton than it imported. This completely reversed the import surplus shown between 1870 and 1887 (except 1874). At first glance it

might appear that the growing exportation of raw cotton is a strong
indication that the total cotton crop increased significantly in the last two
decades of the Ch'ing. But matters were not in fact so simple. The increase
in cotton exports was accompanied by a steady rise in raw cotton prices
and by a simultaneous growing inflow of relatively inexpensive machine-
spun yarn from India and Japan. The conjunction of these three trends
suggests that cotton production did not expand or did not expand sufficiently to meet both domestic and export demand, that the resulting higher
domestic prices of cotton and yarn induced weavers to purchase the
cheaper imported commodity, and that in turn a reduced domestic demand
diminished the inducement to increase raw cotton production.

One crop which definitely expanded in acreage during the last decades of
the nineteenth century was opium. In value terms opium was China's
largest single import until the mid-1880s. Opium and cotton goods
together made up about two-thirds of China's imports in the 1870s and
early 1880s; by 1898 the share of the two had fallen to about 50 per cent.
This decline was entirely due to a decrease in the quantity (although not
the value, which continued to rise) of opium imported, while cotton goods
imports increased rapidly. The principal reason for the fall in the quantity
of opium imports was the steady spread of domestic opium cultivation.
Unfortunately no data are available with which to measure even roughly
the area of land newly planted with poppy to replace the imported article.
The significant price rises per unit at the very end of the Ch'ing and in the
first years of the Republic were caused by market speculation in reduced
quantity of the drug as the first step towards its *de jure* if not *de facto*
suppression. The legal import trade was abolished at the end of 1917, while
efforts to suppress domestic cultivation subsequently varied in success
with the morals and financial needs of the local warlords in whose territories the poppy was grown.

Again, judging from data on the quantity and value of exports between
1879 and 1915, it appears possible that there was a substantial increase in
crop acreage of soy-beans, rapeseed, sesame and peanuts. Before the 1890s
the trade in these commodities was negligible. From the turn of the century,
the value of bean products and vegetable oils exported shot quickly
upward, the oils going largely to Europe where they were used chiefly in
soap manufacture, and the beans and bean cake as well as oil to Japan. The
chief producing and exporting area was Manchuria; the flow of population
from North China to Manchuria after the Russo-Japanese War was
possibly related to an important expansion of soy-bean cultivation. Moreover, efforts to suppress the opium crop in North China led farmers to
increase their planting of beans, sesame and peanuts as a substitute cash

crop. On the other hand, important changes in domestic consumption patterns were taking place simultaneously which may suggest that the new bean and oil exports represented not so much an increased crop as a diversion to export of products hitherto consumed at home. From the 1890s there was a rapid increase in imports of kerosene, which replaced the more expensive vegetable oils used to make candles for illumination and other purposes. The remarkable growth in bean and oil exports, then, probably overstates the extent to which cultivation patterns were altered before 1900, although Buck's data give a strong indication, as we have seen, that the acreage of these and other cash crops did increase from the early twentieth century.

Only a very crude estimate of the production of major crops in a typical year at the end of the nineteenth century is possible. Data in the Kuang-hsu edition (1899) of the *Collected statutes* (*Ta-Ch'ing hui-tien*) on the area of land under cultivation – with some adjustments the official figure for 1887 is 847,760,554 *mou* – are imperfect in detail and in any case represent a substantial understatement of the actual cultivated area. The underlying unit of measurement in many localities was a 'fiscal' *mou* used to convert different grades of land to a single standard; some land reclaimed after 1712 had remained unregistered; and the property of the more powerful local elite was not always fully reflected in the tax rolls. The precise degree of under-registration is not known, but judging from J. L. Buck's 1929–33 agricultural survey findings, an upward adjustment by one-third would be quite conservative. Cultivated land (which I take as equivalent to the crop area) in the late-nineteenth century was then perhaps 1,130,344,579 *mou*. No comprehensive nineteenth-century data are available for the proportions of the total crop area planted in individual crops. If, however, the averages of Buck's 1929–33 percentages and those for 1931–7 by the National Agricultural Research Bureau are adjusted for the changes between 1904–9 and 1930–3 shown in table 5, an approximation of the situation in the last decades of the dynasty is possible. Based on these estimates, table 6 presents at least a plausible guess as to the output of major crops in the late-nineteenth century.

The fate of cotton spinning, the most important single rural handicraft in the nineteenth century, is discussed in the following section. In the relatively 'developed' lower Yangtze area (and possibly in Kwangtung as well), where commerce and manufacture were most advanced and where the impact of foreign trade was most substantial, the post-Taiping decades saw an increase in absentee landownership, representing the investment of commercial profits by successful merchants, brokers and compradors. Absenteeism in this sense is to be distinguished from the fact that the great majority of the rural elite did not of course reside in the peasant villages in which they owned land; their normal habitat was the rural town, at the level of the hsien city or lower. One form which this development took was the growth of the landlord bursary (*tsu-chan*) by means of which individual owners, primarily urban businessmen, entrusted their lands and tenants to the management of the bursary owner and received a proportionate share of the profits after taxes and other expenses were met. It is

TABLE 6

Estimated annual production of major crops, c. 1900

	Percentage of crop area	Crop acreage (*mou*)	Typical yield per *mou* (piculs)	Output (piculs)
Rice, unhusked	30.2	341,364,190	3.89	1,327,906,699
Wheat	26.3	297,280,735	1.39	413,220,222
Kaoliang	12.5	141,293,125	1.73	244,437,106
Millet	11.6	131,120,020	1.64	215,036,833
Barley	10.2	115,295,190	1.47	169,483,929
Soy-bean	6.7	75,733,115	1.39	105,269,030
Corn	4.2	47,474,490	1.87	88,777,296
Cotton, lint	2.4	27,127,500	0.27	7,324,441

Sources: Buck, *Land Utilization,* 217; Ta-chung Liu and Kung-chia Yeh, *The economy of the Chinese mainland: national income and economic development, 1933–1959*, table 30, p. 130, table A–9, p. 300.

impossible to estimate the extent of this phenomenon, but enough cases have been found by Muramatsu Yūji to suggest that in Kiangsu at least it was more than incidental.[5] The bursary owners tended to be well-placed members of the rural elite (gentry) who were able to call upon official assistance (even to the extent of the arrest and imprisonment of delinquents) to collect tenant rents. While rural class relations were never the proper subject for a pastoral idyll even under the best Confucian landlord, absenteeism in the late nineteenth century introduced an increasing element of harshness which became intolerable in the twentieth.

The official Ch'ing land records of 1887 still record the existence, in addition to private land (*min-t'ien*), of substantial acreages especially in North China and Manchuria of banner land (*ch'i-ti*), military land (*t'un-t'ien*), imperial manors (*chuang*) and the like. These reflect the intention of the early Manchu rulers to superimpose a land system corresponding to

[5] See Muramatsu Yūji, 'A documentary study of Chinese landlordism in the late Ch'ing and the early republican Kiangnan', *BSOAS*, 29.3 (1966) 566–99, and Professor Muramatsu's numerous studies of the *tsu-chan* cited therein.

the Manchu political and social structure upon that of conquered China. In reality, by the late nineteenth century little remained, apart from differential rates of land tax, of these earlier distinctions. The combined effects of population growth, inadequate official stipends, and the preponderant influence of the underlying Chinese system of private landownership had in practice almost entirely homogenized the various legal forms of land tenure. Banner land as well as private land was farmed by Chinese tenants in small, scattered plots which by one or another subterfuge were freely rented, mortgaged, bought or sold.

The land held under some form of official tenure, bursary land and private land in general were not normally farmed as contiguous estates with hired agricultural labour. The continued rarity of 'capitalist' commercial farming is the first of several aspects of late-Ch'ing agriculture which remained constant alongside the several changes that I have recounted. Examples can be cited of large landholdings by officials, wealthy gentry and monopoly merchants in excess of 10,000 *mou* throughout the nineteenth century; holdings of this size, however, were quite unusual. Ownership of land in late-Ch'ing China was skewed, but there were few large agricultural holdings comparable to the great estates of Europe and other parts of Asia or the giant ranches and commercial farms of the United States. The landowner normally ranged from the owner-farmer cultivating perhaps 20–30 *mou* in North China and 12–15 *mou* in the south, to some two million local elite families whose median holdings were perhaps 100–50 *mou*, most of which was normally rented to tenants.[6] Tenancy, as in the twentieth century, was much more common in the south (the 'rice region') than in the north (the 'wheat region'); perhaps, again as in later decades, 50 per cent of farming families could be classified as tenants or part-owners. Some signs of increasing numbers of tenancies can be observed in districts which had suffered prolonged famine and in areas near the major commercial centres, but there is little evidence that land tenure patterns changed radically in the last four decades of the dynasty.

Rents were paid either in money or in kind; if the latter, they were commonly 50 per cent of the major crop. Reported cash rents in the 1880s vary from 0.6 taels to 2.66 taels per *mou*, approximately 5 to 10 per cent of the value of land in these localities. (Compare the National Agricultural Research Bureau's estimate of average cash rents as 11 per cent of land

---

[6] There are no survey data describing nineteenth-century land tenure or utilization patterns comparable even to the admittedly inadequate twentieth-century reports. My comments are based in part on the results of an 1888 questionnaire to local informants compiled by George Jamieson for the Royal Asiatic Society: 'Tenure of land in China and the condition of the rural population', *Journal of the North China Branch of the Royal Asiatic Society*, NS, 23 (1889) 59–117.

values in the 1930s.) This suggests that, after deductions for taxes and other costs, the return on investments in land, while relatively secure so long as political stability was maintained, was only one-half as large as the 10 to 20 per cent which could be realized from commerce or moneylending. The comparatively low rate of return probably limited any tendency to increasing concentration of landownership. The real burden of tenancy depended upon other stipulations of the landlord–tenant contract in addition to rent. Individual examples of better and worse terms are available for the nineteenth century – labour service, short-term leases, rent deposits and the like – but we lack systematic evidence from which to conclude that the late-nineteenth-century situation was a progressively worsening one, rather than a perpetuation of the same wretched existence, for the numberless poor.

One piece of evidence – Professor Muramatsu's discovery that landlord bursary income from rents increased sharply between 1905 and 1917 – does suggest that the local elite were able to pass on to their tenants much of the burden of the increased taxation of the dynasty's last decade. These additional levies, which are discussed later in this essay, were assessed on the provinces in order to obtain funds for the Boxer indemnity payments. Given the historical ability of influential landowners to evade their proportionate shares of the ordinary tax burden (most commonly by paying none or only part of the 'extras' which had over time become attached to nominal land tax quotas), it is not unlikely that owner-farmers as well as the tenants of larger landlords ultimately paid a disproportionate part of the added taxation.

It is the overall stability of the agricultural system rather than any significant departures up or down from the traditional norms that is most remarkable. The equilibrium was satisfied at a very low level of subsistence for the great majority of the millions of farming families who constituted 80 per cent of China's population. The hazards of flood, famine and epidemic were compounded by the absence of inexpensive means of bulk transportation and of an effective central government which could channel funds and food from surplus to deficit areas. Few peasants could realistically expect ever to be better off than their fathers or grandfathers had been. Yet after the great Taiping and Nien uprisings no major peasant revolts threatened the Ch'ing government or the elite-dominated rural society. One might suggest that the absence of a substantial peasant-based revolutionary movement (the role of the omnipresent secret society was ambiguous – as often as not it was controlled by or in cooperation with the local elite) may be taken as an indication that 'restoration' and 'self-strengthening' were remarkably effective in suppressing traditional forms of domestic discontent – if not anti-dynastic nationalism and foreign political and economic incursions. The stability, in a narrower sense, of patterns of agricultural organization and land utilization was the consequence less of political conservatism than of the constraints of the available technology and of the social values which motivated the population.

Very large estates, as I have noted, were not common. Moreover, the average land actually cultivated by an individual farming family, owner or tenant, was very small; beyond a certain point larger owners found it preferable to let their excess land rather than farm it with hired labour. Twentieth-century data show a high correlation between the size of the farm household and farm size, an indication that the unit of cultivation was close to the minimum subsistence level. Miniature cultivation was aggravated by the fact that farms tended to be broken up into several non-adjacent parcels usually of different qualities or types of land. Considerable land was wasted in boundary strips, excessive labour time was used to travel from parcel to parcel, and rational irrigation practices were impeded. The rarity of latifundia, the tiny family farm, and parcelization of the typical holding, were all in part the consequence of traditional inheritance practices – in particular of the absence of primogeniture. For elite and peasant alike, the death of the head of the family was usually followed by the equal division of its holdings among all surviving sons who commonly established themselves as separate households. *Fen-chia* ('dividing the family'), as the process was called, might be resisted for a generation or more, but the elite ideal of the large extended family did not often survive the inevitable tensions. Hence, as in the forest primeval, individual oaks sprang up, matured, aged and decayed while the forest itself continued magnificently to dominate the countryside. Parcelization was obviously the outcome of successive efforts to provide each heir with roughly equivalent amounts of the several types of land (paddy, upland, orchard and so on) which had constituted the patrimonial farm.

Ownership of a substantial acreage, before or after *fen-chia*, did not imply management of that land as a unit. Local elite families would farm with hired labour only a portion of their holdings. In addition to the inadequacies of rural credit facilities, to the poverty of management techniques themselves, and to the unstable market for cash crops, there were limits on the quantity of land which would yield greater profits from direct cultivation than from tenant rents. These limits were set by the immense but uneven labour requirements of the existing farm technology. The potential employer of large quantities of farm labour was faced with high supervisory costs and diminishing returns from non-family labour which was used intensively but only at peak seasonal periods. Only improved seeds, more

and better fertilizers and expanded irrigation – that is, significant technological changes which did not occur – would have fully justified large-scale
farming to supply a distant market.

The agricultural sector of the Chinese economy in the last decades of the
Ch'ing dynasty was thus characterized by a factor mix in which land and
capital were in short supply and the superabundance of labour was subject
to some diminishing returns. It was, however, if not for the long run at
least for the purposes of any middle-term prediction, in a stable equilibrium
with no endogenous economic reason why it should not continue to reproduce itself. It is a tribute to the traditional technology that so vast a
population and so high a culture in its upper strata could be supported –
even if for the majority the level of subsistence was low indeed. The many
centuries of basic investment of immense quantities of human labour in
altering the land – by terracing, irrigation, flood control and drainage – had
made possible perhaps from as early as the seventeenth century an output
of 2.3 metric tons of rice per crop hectare. This is an important benchmark
which represents the theoretical maximum yield of pre-modern agricultural
technology (that is, without major current inputs of improved seeds,
fertilizers, pesticides and so on). China's average rice yield per crop hectare
reached only 2.47 metric tons in the 1930s and 2.54 metric tons in the years
1955/6–1960/1. In the latter period India's yield was no more than 1.36
metric tons.[7] But the gap between stability and stagnation is narrow. The
equilibrium of traditional agriculture had been reached at a very low level
of per capita output of which a very high proportion was consumed by the
agricultural producers. Only a small quantity of marketable surplus was
available either as industrial raw material or to feed the non-farm sector.
Conversely, the effective demand for urban manufactured products was
limited. Thus the immediate possibilities either of extensive industrialization or of agricultural development were narrowly constrained by the
disabilities of the agricultural sector.

HANDICRAFT INDUSTRY

The simplistic indictment of 'foreign capitalism' by some contemporary
Chinese historians for having progressively 'crushed' and 'exploited'
domestic handicraft industry from the mid nineteenth century onward is
belied by the actual state of the Chinese economy as late as the 1930s. In the
middle of that decade, even in the cotton textile industry which allegedly
suffered most severely from the 'incursion of foreign capitalism', 61 per
cent of the cotton cloth produced in China (in square yards; if the unit of

[7] See Shigeru Ishikawa, *Economic development in Asian perspective*, 69–77.

measurement were yards the proportion would be 73 per cent) was woven by handicraft methods.[8] Anyone who would claim that the Hunan or Szechwan peasant in the 1930s dressed in Naigaiwata cottons, smoked BAT cigarettes, and used Meiji sugar has a big case to prove. In 1933, the output of handicrafts accounted for an estimated 68 per cent of the total value of industrial output. Of course the relative share of handicrafts was greater in 1870 or 1911, prior to or in the early stages of the development of the small modern industrial sector which began in the 1890s, than it was in the 1930s. And in some important handicraft industries, notably cotton spinning, a sharp decline occurred from the nineteenth century to the twentieth. On both theoretical and empirical grounds, however, there is reason to believe that the total domestic and export demand for handicrafts did not decline in the twentieth century, and *a fortiori* that handicraft industry as a whole was not seriously undermined between 1870 and 1911. But to reject the crudest formulations is not to deny either that significant structural changes in the handicraft industrial sector took place in these four decades or that the strain and dislocation occasioned by these developments adversely affected substantial parts of the population.

Handicraft industry in mid-nineteenth-century China was carried on either in handicraft workshops, predominantly urban in location but present also in rural areas, or in individual households both in urban and rural locations. The distinction between these two forms of handicraft is sometimes quite arbitrary as peasant weavers, for example, in addition to the weaving performed by household labour, might accumulate sufficient funds to purchase several looms which were operated with hired labour; or urban craftsmen might similarly employ non-kin workers to supplement the labour of family members in milling rice or ginning cotton. 'Handicraft workshops' or 'manufactories' (*shou-kung-yeh kung-ch'ang*) were relatively large-scale shops as yet unequipped with power machinery. These enterprises, essentially removed from the household nexus and using the labour of several households, included such undertakings as salt wells and refineries in Szechwan, copper mines in Yunnan, pottery kilns like that at Ching-te-chen in Kiangsi, rice and wheat milling in cities throughout China, and the calendering and dyeing of cotton cloth in Kiangsu. No measure is or ever will be possible of the absolute extent of this extra-household manufacturing.[9] There can be no doubt, however, that it was

---

[8] Yen Chung-p'ing, *Chung-kuo mien-fang-chih shih-kao, 1289–1937* (Draft history of the Chinese cotton industry, 1289–1937), 311.

[9] P'eng Tse-i, comp. *Chung-kuo chin-tai shou-kung-yeh shih tzu-liao, 1840–1949* (Source materials on the history of handicraft industry in modern China, 1840–1949), 2. 382–90, lists 132 references in eighteenth- and early nineteenth-century writings to handicraft workshops; this is, of course, neither a controlled sample nor an exhaustive count.

vastly overshadowed both in employment and in output by the handicraft production of individual households, either ancillary to farming in rural China or performed by full-time urban and semi-urban craftsmen.

The most important household handicraft in rural China was the spinning and weaving of cotton. Because of its significance in the economy of the late-Ch'ing period, I shall first discuss developments in the handicraft cotton textile industry in some detail. The history of handicraft production in general during this period can then be assessed in the light of the fate of cotton textiles. From the Yuan dynasty onward cotton culture and manufacture had spread rapidly, cotton cloth becoming the principal daily article of clothing for all except the very wealthy. While cotton cultivation was fairly widely distributed, the principal producing areas were in the Yangtze valley provinces. It was in this region that cotton handicrafts were most concentrated and highly developed. Large areas in the Yangtze delta were better suited to growing cotton than food crops, and in the relatively humid climate of Kiangsu yarn of greater tensile strength and evenness could be spun. From Kiangnan (the area south of the lower reaches of the Yangtze River) and the districts around Shasi in Hupei, for example, large quantities of baled raw cotton and woven piece goods were carried by water and on the backs of porters to Manchuria and North China, to Szechwan via the Yangtze, to Yunnan and Kweichow in the south-west, and to the southern coastal provinces. It was more profitable for Kiangnan peasants to concentrate their productive resources on growing cotton and on weaving (and on spinning only what was required by that weaving) rather than to spin themselves all the cotton that they grew. Thus spinning by rural households for their own consumption with supplies from the Yangtze valley provinces and with local raw cotton was carried on to varying degrees throughout China. And locally woven cloth supplemented that which came from Hupei and Kiangnan.

But only in the leading cotton-producing areas had the handicraft production of cotton textiles developed into a major industry serving other than an immediate local market. From the weaving districts in southern Hupei, for example, cloth was brought by peasant weavers or petty merchants to the daily piece-goods market in Shasi. The wholesale merchants who purchased in this market graded the cloth by quality and stamped each grade with a well-known 'chop' (trademark) which was accepted as a guarantee of quality in the markets of Yunnan and Kweichow to which the goods were sent. Cloth from Hupei reached northern Yunnan via Szechwan, first by water on the Yangtze and its tributaries, then on the backs of porters who carried loads as large as 117 pieces of cloth weighing 220 pounds, and then by pack animal on the Yunnan mountain roads. Kweichow was reached mainly via Hunan employing the Tungting Lake and the Yuan River which flows into it. This was not, by contemporary standards, a petty trade either in size or in the distances traversed. As late as 1895, by which time there had already been radical changes in the structure of the handicraft cotton industry, more than 200,000 bales of raw cotton and 300,000 bales of piece goods were being imported annually into Szechwan largely from Hupei. And some 3,200,000 pieces of cloth were reaching northern Yunnan each year from Shasi. Similarly, China south of Amoy, North China and Manchuria were supplied mainly from Kiangnan. Moreover, substantial quantities of hand-woven cotton cloth were exported from Canton to England and the United States. Until 1831 England purchased more 'nankeens' (cloth manufactured in Nanking and other places in the lower Yangtze region) each year than she sold British-manufactured cloth to China.

Spinning and weaving in the cotton regions for the most part were carried on by individual rural households, to a small extent on a nearly full-time basis but more often in addition to the production of food crops upon which the family was chiefly dependent. Yarn was either spun in the household, or obtained in exchange from the merchants who purchased the cloth which the peasants wove. The income from textile handicrafts formed a larger part of the total income of poorer farmers with the smallest farms than it did of the more affluent. Preparation of the warp prior to weaving, for example, was commonly undertaken in small peasant households to supplement meagre agricultural incomes. For the cotton regions as a whole, however, maintenance of the minimum living standards of the dense rural population was critically dependent upon the market for raw cotton and cloth. The calendering and dyeing of cotton cloth tended to be concentrated in market towns and cities which also were the distributing centres for the finished product. These finishing processes were often controlled by the larger cloth merchants and carried out by hired labour, usually paid on a piece-work basis, in 'handicraft workshops' owned by these merchants or, as in Soochow, by intermediary 'contracting agents' (pao-t'ou) to whom the workers paid a monthly fee from their piece-work earnings for the use of the plant and equipment. In general, before the last quarter of the nineteenth century the cloth merchants exercised no similar direct control over the weaving of the cloth which was, as I have stated, usually executed on their own account by peasant households. In the urban areas handicraft manufacture was still under relatively strict guild supervision; the individual master craftsman and not the handicraft workshop was the dominant form of industrial organization.

The very unusual comprador Cheng Kuan-ying offered one version of the changes which occurred in the cotton textile handicraft industry in the second half of the nineteenth century:

Cotton is grown in the coastal regions, and spun into yarn and woven into cloth. In addition to supplying local needs, the cloth and yarn were shipped in considerable quantities to the western and northern provinces. But when foreign yarn and cloth began to be imported, the population responded to their lower price and high quality and one after another bought and used them. Thus half of the profits of spinning and weaving in the southern provinces was usurped. Now, in the treaty ports and the cities and towns of the interior, only twenty or thirty per cent of the people wear native cloth while seventy or eighty per cent wear foreign cloth.[10]

Foreign merchants and consular officials in late nineteenth-century China would have been amused to read Cheng's warnings to his countrymen; their reports in contrast were full of repeated complaints about the difficulty of penetrating the Chinese market, especially in the interior provinces. The mercantile community pointed particularly to restrictions on foreign residence in the interior and to the burden of the likin (*li-chin*) transit tax. The more perceptive of the consuls, however, recognized that the strength of the handicraft weaving industry was the principal obstacle to clothing every Chinese in Lancashire cottons.

Cheng Kuan-ying and the foreigners in the treaty ports, in fact, shared the truth between them. Foreign imports of cotton yarn and cloth began to increase significantly after the 1858–60 treaties opened additional treaty ports, including three on the Yangtze. This growth was facilitated by the newly gained right to inland steam navigation in China, by the transit pass system which permitted an additional one-half of the import duty to be paid on foreign goods in lieu of likin, and by the opening of the Suez Canal in 1869 which lowered shipping costs from Europe. Table 7 shows the annual quantity and value of cotton goods imports for the period 1871–1910. Cotton yarn and piece goods in 1871 made up about one-third of China's imports by value. While in succeeding years they fluctuated around that proportion of total imports, from the 1880s until 1920 (the peak year) imported cotton manufactures grew by leaps and bounds. The quantity of yarn imports increased twenty-four times – from 97,451 to 2,363,000 piculs (*tan*) – if the average annual amounts for the two decades 1871–80 and 1901–10 are compared. After 1913 a decline began as domestic machine-spun yarn progressively replaced imported yarn. While the imports of cotton piece goods exceeded yarn in value in every year except 1898, 1899 and 1903, their growth – a twofold increase between 1871–80 and 1901–10, from 11,463,010 to 21,442,000 pieces – was not nearly so

[10] Cheng Kuan-ying, *Sheng-shih wei-yen* (Warnings to a prosperous age), 7.20a–b.

TABLE 7
Quantity and value of cotton yarn and cloth imports, 1871–1910

	Yarn			Cloth		
	1,000 piculs*	1,000 haikwan taels†	Average value per picul (haikwan taels)	1,000 pieces‡	1,000 haikwan taels†	Average value per piece (haikwan taels)
1871	70	1,877	26.81	14,439	24,877	1.72
2	50	1,372	27.44	12,241	21,435	1.75
3	68	3,130?	46.03 ?	8,989	16,202	1.80
4	69	1,969	28.54	9,763	16,301	1.67
5	91	2,747	30.19	10,720	17,315	1.62
6	113	2,839	25.12	11,870	17,377	1.46
7	116	2,841	24.49	11,117	15,959	1.44
8	108	2,521	23.34	9,158	13,509	1.48
9	138	3,191	23.12	12,772	19,409	1.52
1880	152	3,648	24.00	13,561	19,735	1.46
1	172	4,228	24.58	14,931	21,818	1.46
2	185	4,505	24.35	12,159	18,201	1.50
3	228	5,242	22.99	11,500	16,805	1.46
4	261	5,584	21.39	11,229	16,557	1.47
5	388	7,871	20.20	15,706	23,623	1.50
6	383	7,869	20.55	14,041	21,181	1.51
7	593	12,591	21.23	15,267	24,457	1.60
8	683	13,496	19.76	18,664	30,942	1.66
9	679	13,019	19.17	14,275	23,116	1.62
1890	1,081	19,392	17.94	16,561	25,629	1.55
1	1,211	20,984	17.25	17,601	32,307	1.84
2	1,304	22,153	16.99	16,359	30,555	1.87
3	982	17,863	18.19	12,498	27,275	2.18
4	1,160	21,397	18.45	13,343	30,708	2.30
5	1,132	21,209	18.74	13,437	31,865	2.37
6	1,621	32,010	19.75	18,919	47,233	2.50
7	1,571	34,430	21.92	16,914	44,233	2.62
8	1,959	39,295	20.06	15,524	38,324	2.47
9	2,745	54,941	20.01	19,419	48,524	2.50
1900	1,488	30,187	20.29	15,964	45,419	2.85
1	2,273	49,012	21.56	16,688	50,640	3.03
2	2,448	54,794	22.38	22,958	72,752	3.17
3	2,738	67,736	24.74	19,272	60,884	3.16
4	2,281	59,516	26.09	18,704	64,568	3.45
5	2,554	67,209	26.32	35,760	114,244	3.19
6	2,541	65,141	25.64	28,734	87,587	3.05
7	2,273	57,515	25.30	18,193	61,401	3.37
8	1,823	46,173	25.33	16,906	64,725	3.83
9	2,406	62,464	25.96	21,196	74,827	3.53
1910	2,282	62,831	27.53	17,013	67,852	3.99

* piculs or *tan* of 133.33 lbs

† the haikwan tael was first used in 1874; 1871–3 values are the estimated equivalents in haikwan taels of values given in local taels in the customs returns

‡ of varying sizes, but commonly 40 yards long and 36 inches wide; cotton items measured in dozens or yards – perhaps 1 or 2 per cent of the total in square yards – rather than pieces are not included here

Source: Yang Tuan-liu and Hou Hou-pei, *Liu-shih-wu-nien lai Chung-kuo kuo-chi mao-i t'ung-chi* (Statistics of China's foreign trade during the last sixty-five years) tables 4, 9; China. Inspectorate-General of Customs, *Decennial reports . . ., 1922–1931*, I.113, 182.

spectacular. The importation of piece goods did, however, continue to grow until the 1920s and was cut sharply only when the Nanking government regained tariff autonomy. Paradoxically, the very success of yarn imports in the last four decades of the Manchu dynasty indirectly came to be the major obstacle to the equally rapid development of cloth imports. Yarn imports had a critical effect upon the structure of China's cotton textile handicrafts.

The average values per picul of imported yarn and per piece of imported cloth given in table 7 indicate a falling trend in yarn prices from the mid-1870s until almost the end of the century. Cloth prices also declined in the 1870s but began to rise again in the late 1880s and more sharply than the later increase in yarn prices. The major factor behind the appearance of cheaper yarn was the entry into the Chinese market on a large scale of the products of Bombay spinning mills which replaced the more expensive English yarn. From the 1890s Indian yarn was supplemented by increasing inflows of machine-spun yarn from Japan. The decline in the price of yarn was gradual; it extended over some two decades. It is all the more significant in that over the whole period 1871–1910 the gold value of the haikwan tael was itself steadily falling.

While imported machine-spun yarn was becoming cheaper, the price of Chinese raw cotton was rising. This price increase was a consequence of large exports of raw cotton to Japanese mills from the early 1890s onward, while the cotton crop increased little if at all before the spectacular growth of the modern textile industry in China during and after World War I. Together with the limited capacity of a fragmented and technologically backward agricultural sector to respond quickly to export demand, the importation of cheaper foreign yarn itself, which weakened the demand for native handspun, reduced the farmer's incentive to increase his raw cotton acreage. 'The most curious feature in connection with the native cotton industry', reported an English mission to China from Blackburn, Lancashire in 1896-7, 'is the high price of the raw material in comparison with other agricultural produce.'[11] Increasingly the handicraft weaver turned to imported machine-spun yarn, at least for his warp and sometimes for his weft as well.

In the 1870s and 1880s South China, Kwangtung in particular, was the main market for imported yarn, absorbing over half of the total. This proportion, however, fell steadily to about a fifth of total yarn imports. By the 1890s two regions, (1) North China and Manchuria and (2) the middle and upper Yangtze valley provinces of Anhwei, Kiangsi, Hupei, Hunan

[11] Blackburn Chamber of Commerce, *Report of the mission to China of the Blackburn Chamber of Commerce, 1896–7*, Neville and Bell's section, 212.

and Szechwan, together with Yunnan and Kweichow, were each receiving about 30 per cent of the total and thus constituted the major markets for imported yarn. The Kiangnan area, where cotton handicrafts were concentrated, absorbed annually about 10 per cent of yarn imports with large fluctuations from year to year. It is evident that the principal markets for imported machine-spun yarn were those regions where cotton growing and handicrafts were least developed. Cheap imported yarn made possible the economical development of handicraft weaving in districts which previously had purchased cloth or relatively expensive raw cotton from Kiangnan or Hupei. Marginal handicraft spinning declined and cloth, woven locally with warps of imported yarn and wefts of domestic handspun, competed with pure handspun cloth and foreign piece goods in such areas as Szechwan, for example, where it was reported that 'Indian cotton yarn is killing what little local cultivation of cotton there was, and, when woven, is encroaching on home-spun cloths and to a much less degree on imported grey shirtings.'[12]

The most obvious consequences of the increasing inflow of foreign yarn was thus a geographical dispersion of the handicraft weaving industry which in the first half of the nineteenth century had been concentrated in the major cotton-growing provinces. While the older weaving centres were hurt at first, in order to compete in their former markets they too had to adopt machine-made yarn. From the late 1890s Japanese yarn began to be used in large quantities for warp threads in the Shasi and Hankow areas. Although imported yarn did not win a large market there, Kiangnan handicraft weavers in the early twentieth century became the major purchasers of the output of the growing cotton mills of Shanghai. The adoption of machine-made yarn, moreover, strengthened the handicraft weaving industry as a whole. Cloth produced with a mixture of imported and handspun yarn was particularly suited in price and durability to the contemporary Chinese market. Spinning and weaving for household consumption with domestic raw cotton continued to be important in many areas of rural China, but a significant part of spinning for the market was displaced first by imported yarn and then by machine-made yarn from Chinese- and foreign-owned mills in the treaty ports.

While weaving continued to be primarily an individual household handicraft, in some areas by the turn of the century other forms of industrial organization had appeared. These changes were facilitated by the supply of cheaper machine-made yarn and also by improved foot-treadle wood looms and iron-gear looms introduced from Japan which increased the weaver's daily output. One estimate records the establishment of 142

---

[12] *Blackburn report*, F. S. A. Bourne's section, 5–6.

handicraft weaving workshops in the period 1899–1913, 69 of these in Kiangsu where they were supplied with Shanghai-made yarn, 15 in Shantung, 14 in Chihli (Hopei), 9 in Szechwan, 7 each in Shansi, Fukien and Kwangtung, 6 in Hupei, 4 in Manchuria, 3 in Chekiang and 1 in Kweichow. Table 8 indicates the size and equipment of these establishments.

TABLE 8

Capital, looms and workers in 142 handicraft weaving workshops, established 1899–1913

	Number of workshops for which data given	Total	Average	Largest	Smallest
Capital (Ch. $)	67	660,220	9,854	70,000	200
Number of looms	37	3,307	89	360	12
Number of workers	96	14,972	156	1,264	5

Source: P'eng Tse-i, comp. *Chung-kuo chin-tai shou-kung-yeh shih tzu-liao, 1840–1949* (Source materials on the history of handicraft industry in modern China, 1840–1949), 2. 369–76.

A *verlag* type of weaving, in which cloth merchants put-out yarn to rural weavers some of whom had abandoned their farming and wove for a piece-work wage the patterns stipulated by their merchant employer, also developed in a number of places alongside rural weavers who wove on their own account. No data are available to indicate the actual extent of this putting-out system, some notable examples of which were in Kao-yang and Pao-ti in Chihli (Hopei), Wei-hsien in Shantung and Hsia-shih in Chekiang. In the first three of these four examples, putting-out developed fairly rapidly from the first decade of the twentieth century until the mid-1920s. It flourished especially during and immediately after World War I, but declined sharply thereafter. For those people who could no longer rely on agricultural income as a cushion against fluctuating demand, rural weaving of this type was an inherently precarious occupation. It was an industry which produced for a non-local market but lacked the modern organization and financial facilities to respond to inevitable change.

The main reason for the much slower growth of cloth than of yarn imports was the extent and strength of the handicraft weaving industry which, as I have stated, was increased by the adoption of machine-made yarn. Relatively little imported cloth was used in rural areas; its principal sale was to the wealthier craftsmen and merchants in the cities and towns. The British consul in Amoy reported in 1886:

It is well known already that the many millions of lower-class Chinese toiling and moiling throughout the 18 provinces, and in huge territories beyond them.

do not wear foreign-made cloths, but homespun. Ask a Chinaman why this is, and he tells you that the poor wear suits of native cotton, because such clothing lasts three, four, or five times as long as foreign cloth, because it wears less easily, and because it is much warmer in winter. Why is it warmer? Because, he says, the yarn of which the native fabric is made is quite different from the foreign, and warmer by nature. While, therefore, the well-to-do merchant is wearing out three or four suits of handsomely finished *yang-pu*, the mechanic, the field-hand, the porter, and the boatman are and must be content with one suit of coarser but, in fact, better material.[13]

And the combination of a machine-made warp with a handspun weft made an even better cloth to compete with foreign piece goods. 'No doubt the common shirtings are being superseded by native cloth woven by hand from imported yarn', the Blackburn mission acknowledged, 'and for this there seems no help.'[14]

On the assumption that the average annual raw cotton crop in the decade 1871–80 was 7 million piculs and that it was approximately the same size in 1901–10, I have attempted to estimate the sources of the yarn and cloth consumed in an average year in these two decades. Table 9 summarizes this estimate. It will be seen immediately that the total consumption of cotton yarn increased with the population growth from the first period to the second. The handicraft spinning of yarn, however, which had a near monopoly in the first period, declined drastically both in absolute terms and as a proportion of the total yarn supply. Output fell by 2.4 million piculs, so that only half as much handspun yarn was produced in an average year in 1901–10 as in 1871–80. From 98 per cent of the total yarn consumed, handspun fell to 42 per cent. Handspun yarn was replaced by both domestic and imported machine-spun products. While in the first period there were as yet no modern spinning mills established in China, by 1901–10 Chinese- and foreign-owned mills in and near the treaty ports produced nearly 18 per cent of the total yarn consumed, in absolute terms an output approximately equal to the entire increase in total yarn consumption from 1871–80 to 1901–10. But far more important was the growth of imported yarn which by 1901–10 was nearly equal in quantity to the handicraft output. From 2 per cent of the total in 1871–80 it had increased to 40 per cent in 1901–10; in absolute terms, it was twenty-four times larger in the later period than in the earlier.

Total consumption of cloth, whether measured in yards or in square yards, also increased as the population grew. The output of domestic weaving mills, non-existent in 1871–80, was still barely noticeable in

[13] *Report on the native cloth in use in the Amoy consular district* (Foreign Office, miscellaneous series, 1886, no. 19), 4.
[14] *Blackburn report*, F. S. A. Bourne's section, 36.

1901–10; the great expansion was to come only from the early 1920s. Imported cotton piece goods, while they increased from the first period to the second, did so only to a moderate degree as compared with imported yarn. From 11 per cent (yards) and 19 per cent (square yards) of the total consumption in an average year in 1871–80 cloth imports grew to 16 and 26 per cent in an average year in 1901–10. The contrast with the quite remarkable increase in yarn imports is entirely due to the fact that the handicraft weaving industry held its own very well in the face of foreign competition from the earlier decade to the later.

TABLE 9

Sources of estimated yarn and cloth consumption, 1871–80 and 1901–10

| | 1. Cotton yarn 1871–80 | | 1901–10 | |
	tan	%	tan	%
Domestic mills	—	—	1,055,040	17.98
Imports	97,451	1.96	2,363,000	40.27
Handicraft	4,882,381	98.04	2,449,715	41.75
Total	4,979,832	100.00	5,867,755	100.00

| | 2. Cotton cloth 1871–80 | | | |
	yds	%	sq. yds	%
Domestic mills	—	—	—	—
Imports	414,805,000	11.40	376,165,000	18.92
Handicraft	3,224,960,440	88.60	1,612,480,220	81.08
Total	3,639,765,440	100.00	1,988,645,220	100.00

| | 1901–10 | | | |
	yds	%	sq. yds	%
Domestic mills	25,200,000	0.57	24,494,400	0.97
Imports	721,400,000	16.23	654,200,000	25.87
Handicraft	3,699,890,434	83.20	1,849,945,217	73.16
Total	4,446,490,434	100.00	2,528,639,617	100.00

Source: Albert Feuerwerker, 'Handicraft and manufactured cotton textiles in China, 1871–1911', *Journal of Economic History*, 30.2 (June 1970), 338–78.

The relative position of handicraft cloth declined slightly, but the absolute amount of cloth woven increased from 3.2 US billion yards in an average year in 1871–80 to 3.7 US billion yards in an average year in 1901–10. This was a creditable growth which shows the strength of this sector but which would certainly have been larger in the absence of foreign cloth imports. Some of those many peasants who had once engaged in spinning as an ancillary occupation undoubtedly turned to weaving as a replacement for their lost employment, but the most generous comparison of the labour lost by the 2.4 million picul decline in handspun yarn with that which could be absorbed by the increment of 600 or 700 million yards of handwoven cloth indicates that only 10 to 20 per cent of the total could have been accommodated. One cannot but conclude that among the peasant households in the regions where cotton spinning had been important, many were unable either to find urban employment for some of their family members or to increase their production and marketing of cash crops. For them the always precarious equilibrium between income and necessary expenditure was profoundly shaken.

This certainly is one source of the indictment of the 'incursion of foreign capitalism' to which I referred at the beginning of this section. No other handicraft industry was as important a supplement to rural incomes as cotton spinning and weaving. Although many other handicrafts maintained themselves or expanded in the last half of the nineteenth century, from the undoubted disruption of handicraft spinning the broader and unjustified claim has been advanced that the whole of the traditional handicraft sector was undermined by foreign imports and domestic factory products. There is also a second source which helps to account for the sometimes vitriolic tone of the indictment. Foreign capitalism, it is argued, not only crushed and exploited native handicrafts; it was even more culpable because it short-circuited the normative progression that should have taken place, according to the Chinese reading of Marx on European capitalism, from commodity production by individual households through handicraft workshops to modern factory industry. In China, handicraft workshops and the putting-out system were prevented by foreign capitalism from playing the role they had allegedly played in Europe as the critical intermediary stage to the full-scale development of capitalism. In China – the evidence supports the fact although not necessarily the interpretation – handicraft workshops appeared in substantial numbers only after modern industries had been brought forth directly or indirectly by foreign investment, and then only as ancillaries to the mechanized factories. Thus both handicraft and modern industry in late nineteenth- and early twentieth-century China were subservient to foreign capitalism.[15]

Certain handicraft industries unable to compete with imported products, for example native iron and steel production in Hunan and Kiangsi, had nearly disappeared by the end of the nineteenth century. Others expanded in response to export demand during all or part of the four decades from 1870 to 1911. Raw silk from 1887, when it replaced tea, was China's most important single export. While the proportion of silk to total exports

[15] See, for example, Fan Pai-ch'uan, 'Chung-kuo shou-kung-yeh tsai wai-kuo tzu-pen-chu-i ch'in-ju hou ti tsao-yü ho ming-yun' (The fate of Chinese handicraft industry after the incursion of foreign capitalism), Li-shih yen-chiu, 1962. 3, pp. 88–115.

declined, the actual quantity of silk exported increased throughout the period. Some of the raw silk was reeled in steam filatures, accounting for 40 per cent of the total exported in 1899. This was a relatively late development which became dominant only in the twentieth century, and in any case the steam filatures were hardly one step removed from handicraft workshops. The Commissioner of Customs at Chefoo, Shantung, reported in 1912:

The reeling of wild silk for export from the Manchurian cocoon is a comparatively modern industry, introduced in the seventies, since when it has developed considerably. Steam filatures, of which there are now three in existence, have, so far, not proved a success; but the foot-reel of foreign pattern has long been generally adopted, in place of the native hand-reel, with excellent results. There were 40 filatures at work during 1911; they employ over 14,000 hands, and their annual output is 14,000 piculs. No improvement in processes can be recorded.[16]

A preliminary reconnaissance of the contemporary literature records at least 415 handicraft reeling filatures, mainly in Kwangtung, Szechwan and Shantung, in the period 1892–1913.[17] Silk weaving was performed entirely on handlooms and was a major industry in South and Central China. The exportation of silk piece goods increased fairly steadily from the 1870s until the early 1920s when the competition of rayon fabrics began to be felt.

Handicraft tea processing, on the other hand, probably reached its maximum in the mid-1880s, after which Chinese exports of tea which had increased steadily from the opening of the treaty ports declined sharply. This fall resulted largely from the competition of Indian and Ceylon teas produced in colonial circumstances in which, in contrast to China, the exporters had sufficient control over production to maintain quality standards. In the case of tea, and of silk as well, the only overall data available are for exports. There is, however, no indication in contemporary writings that domestic demand declined in the late Ch'ing period, and with the population growth already postulated earlier in this chapter this is unlikely to have been the case. Thus the relative export success of silk and the growth and then decline of tea exports taken together, while they do not suggest a new flourishing of handicraft industry, contradict with equal force any assumption that handicraft was in mortal crisis at the end of the Manchu dynasty.

Oil pressing, rice milling, mining by native methods, together with silk weaving among the larger handicrafts, were little affected by imported or domestic manufactured goods in the nineteenth century. Oil pressing in

[16] China. Inspectorate-General of Customs, *Decennial reports . . ., 1902–1911*, 2.229–30.
[17] P'eng Tse-i, *Chung-kuo chin-tai shou-kung-yeh shih tzu-liao*, 2.356–66.

handicraft workshops in fact expanded rapidly from the 1890s in response to the demand for soy-bean oil by European soap manufacturers and for bean, bean cake and oil in Japan. The use of vegetable oils for lighting was, however, steadily supplanted by kerosene imports from the 1890s. Such minor handicrafts as the production of firecrackers, fans, bamboo furniture, Chinese medicines and agricultural tools – commodities for which there were no import substitutes – were not affected at all. The ginning of cotton for export in handicraft workshops with imported Japanese foot-treadle gins expanded in the port cities. Moreover, several new industries developed, for example, cotton knitting and the production of matches in handicraft workshops. Much of this growth of handicrafts at the turn of the century occurred in the form of handicraft workshops established in urban areas. There were apparently no comparable new developments in the rural areas apart from the putting-out organization of weaving already discussed. A slowly growing rural population, deprived in the course of the nineteenth century of a significant part of its income from cotton spinning, thus, perhaps increasingly, saw the departure of one or more family members for temporary or permanent employment in the workshops, factories and shops of the cities and towns. In 1911, however, this was still a minor trend.

MODERN INDUSTRY

Even for the small modern industrial sector which gradually appeared in the last part of the nineteenth century, the quantitative data that can be assembled are at best only gross approximations; information on output before 1912 is, for example, almost completely lacking. This is surprising since these enterprises were located primarily in the treaty ports, were recorded in the English-language press either because of their foreign sponsorship or because of their novelty if the entrepreneurs were Chinese, and are reflected in the documents of the Ch'ing officials who promoted many of them. The most recent and probably the best estimates that have been made suggest that prior to 1895 approximately 103 foreign-owned industrial enterprises, most of them small firms, were inaugurated in China. They and the Chinese-owned firms to be discussed below were often differentiated from handicraft industries only by the fact that they employed some power-driven machinery. In a strict sense manufacturing by foreigners was illegal under the treaties; but it existed nevertheless, for the most part in the Shanghai foreign concessions with a smaller number at other treaty ports. Prior to the 1880s the Chinese government did not interfere with the establishment of these petty foreign factories. When, however, Li Hung-chang and other officials began to promote their own manufacturing enterprises, they were able until 1895 to secure Peking's support to prevent foreigners from undertaking such major ventures as cotton textile mills. The estimated number and capital in 1894 of these foreign industrial firms are shown in table 10.[18]

TABLE 10

Estimated number and capitalization of foreign-owned industries in China in 1894*

Type of firm	Number	Capital (Ch.$)
Shipyards: construction and repairs	12	4,943,000
Tea processing	7	4,000,000
Machine silk reeling	7	3,972,222
Processing of exports and imports (other than tea and machine silk)	19	1,493,000
Other light manufacturing	39	3,793,000
Electric power and waterworks	4	1,523,000
Total	88	19,724,000

* Includes a small number of firms based in Hong Kong

Source: Sun Yü-t'ang, comp. *Chung-kuo chin-tai kung-yeh shih tzu-liao, ti-i-chi, 1840–1895 nien* (Source materials on the history of modern industry in China, 1st collection, 1840–1895), I. 242–7. Admittedly based on incomplete data.

From 1895 to 1913, following the legalization of foreign industry in the treaty ports by the Treaty of Shimonoseki, at least 136 additional foreign-owned manufacturing and mining enterprises were set up, with initial capital investments in excess of Ch.$100,000. These included 40 joint Sino-foreign firms which for all practical purposes were under foreign control. (All foreign-owned mines regardless of the size of their capitalization have been included in the above figure.) The total initial capitalization of these firms was Ch.$103,153,000, and some of their characteristics are shown in table 11.

While the establishment of the English, French, German and Russian firms was fairly evenly distributed over the two decades, all but two of the Japanese enterprises were begun in 1904 and later – evidence of Japan's increasing economic penetration of Manchuria after the Russo-Japanese War. Coal mining was the biggest field of investment, and Britain the largest investor. The high proportion of Sino-foreign mining enterprises reflects the influence of the Ch'ing government's mining regulations

[18] The currency unit given as Ch. $ in this section is the *yang-yuan* or 'foreign dollar', commonly the Mexican silver dollar which had considerable currency in the treaty ports. These were gradually supplemented by Chinese silver dollars. Until 1933, both the dollar and the tael were used as units of account. One dollar was valued at approximately 0.72 taels.

TABLE 11

Nationality, industry, location, size of initial capitalization of foreign and Sino-foreign manufacturing and mining firms established in China, 1895–1913

| | Number of firms | | | | Initial capitalization (Ch.$1,000) | | | |
	1 Foreign	2 Sino-foreign	1 + 2	Percentage of total	1 Foreign	2 Sino-foreign	1 + 2	Percentage of total
Nationality								
England	28	9	37	27.21	25,465	24,216	49,681	48.16
France	4	2	6	4.41	2,986	1,609	4,515	4.38
Germany	9	3	12	8.82	6,534	1,147	7,681	7.45
Japan	35	14	49	36.03	19,829	6,501	26,330	25.53
Russia	9	8	17	12.50	3,866	2,782	6,648	6.44
United States	6	2	8	5.88	2,551	689	3,240	3.14
other	5	2	7	5.15	3,028	1,950	4,978	4.83
Total	96	40	136	100.00	64,259	38,894	103,153	100.00
Industry								
mining	10	22	32	23.53	18,533	31,436	49,969	48.44
engineering and shipyards	7	0	7	5.15	2,895	0	2,895	2.81
electric power and water works	16	3	19	13.97	10,772	742	11,514	11.16
spinning and weaving	12	4	16	11.76	10,325	2,190	12,515	12.13
foodstuffs	34	5	39	28.68	15,126	2,022	17,148	16.62
other	17	6	23	16.91	6,608	2,504	9,112	8.83
Total	96	40	136	100.00	64,259	38,894	103,153	100.00

									Average capital (Ch. $1,000)
Location									
Kiangsu	33	11	44	32.35	18,501	5,121	23,622	22.90	
Chihli	7	6	13	9.56	4,645	24,309	28,954	28.07	
Hupei	8	2	10	7.35	3,576	1,609	5,185	5.03	
Shantung	5	1	6	4.41	3,503	92	3,595	3.49	
Manchuria	37	16	53	38.97	18,680	5,332	24,012	23.28	
other	6	4	10	7.35	15,354	2,431	17,785	17.24	
Total	96	40	136	100.00	64,259	38,894	103,153	100.00	
Size of initial capitalization									
less than 100,000	2	5	7	5.15	120	288	408	0.40	58
100,000–249,999	32	15	47	34.56	5,021	2,213	7,234	7.01	154
250,000–499,999	30	7	37	27.21	11,623	3,132	14,755	14.30	399
500,000–999,999	17	6	23	16.91	12,887	4,088	16,975	16.46	738
1,000,000–4,999,999	14	5	19	13.97	20,622	7,541	28,163	27.30	1,482
more than 5,000,000	1	2	3	2.21	13,986	21,632	35,618	34.53	11,873
Total	96	40	136	100.00	64,259	38,894	103,153	100.00	758

Source: Calculated from Wang Ching-yü, comp. *Chung-kuo chin-tai kung-yeh shih tzu-liao, ti-erh-chi, 1895–1914 nien* (Source materials on the history of modern industry in China, 2nd collection, 1895–1914), I. 2–13.

which, prior to 1902, required 30 to 50 per cent of the capital in any mining venture to be provided by Chinese investors. Of the 32 mining enterprises, 9 were British, representing a capital of Ch.$37,930,000 out of a total in this sector of Ch.$49,969,000 and representing a similar proportion of the total direct British investment in industry. Britain and Japan accounted for all of the firms under 'Engineering and shipyards', and for a very high proportion under each of the other categories, giving them together 86 out of 136 firms and Ch.$76,000,000 out of the Ch.$103,000,000 total initial capital. These foreign and Sino-foreign firms were, apart from the coal mines which were located primarily in Chihli and Manchuria, concentrated in Shanghai, the northern treaty ports and Manchuria. From 1906 to 1913, 53 firms including mines were inaugurated in Manchuria, largely by Japanese investors. The average size of the initial capital of the 136 enterprises was Ch.$758,000.

The data are even less satisfactory about Chinese-owned manufacturing and mining enterprises at the end of the Ch'ing dynasty (other than the joint Sino-foreign firms included above). There were, first, about 19 government-owned arsenals and shipyards, the largest of which were located in Shanghai (established by Tseng Kuo-fan and Li Hung-chang in 1865), Nanking (Li Hung-chang, 1865) and Hanyang (Chang Chih-tung, 1890). In addition to manufacturing munitions and a small number of steamships, the government arsenals were generally equipped with machine shops for the production and repair of tools and parts. A number of them operated training programmes for technicians and, as at the translation bureau of the Shanghai Arsenal, produced compilations and translations which served as textbooks for late-nineteenth-century Chinese students of science and engineering.

Secondly, a number of official and semi-official mining, smelting and textile enterprises had been undertaken from as early as 1872. Of these pioneering ventures, the largest and best-known, such as the Kaiping Coal Mines, the Hanyang Ironworks and its coal and iron mines (Hanyehping), Chang Chih-tung's Hupei Textile Mill and Li Hung-chang's Shanghai Cotton Cloth Mill, gradually passed out of the purview of the officials who had sponsored them and into the hands of private Chinese investors, or under foreign control in the case of Kaiping. No satisfactory estimate has been made of the size of the investment represented by the arsenals; and the data concerning the *kuan-pan* (official-managed), *kuan-tu shang-pan* (official-supervised and merchant-managed) and *kuan-shang ho-pan* (official and merchant jointly managed) varieties of official and semi-official firms are not always clearly distinguished from those purporting to describe manufacturing and mining enterprises established by private Chinese entrepreneurs (*shang-pan*, merchant-managed). The distinctions between semi-official and private undertakings of this type were in any case largely formal ones and perhaps of secondary significance as I shall indicate below. A recent search of the contemporary literature has yielded information about 75 manufacturing firms other than the arsenals referred to above (for example, silk reeling, cotton ginning, cotton spinning, flour milling, matches, paper mills) and 33 coal and metal mines established between 1872 and 1894 in which private investment played a greater or lesser role. Many of these were short-lived and often they were small, being distinguished from handicraft workshops only by their employment of some steam or electric power.[19]

From 1895 Chinese-owned manufacturing enterprises, like the foreign-owned, increased in number. But the total growth of the industrial sector in this period of China's early industrialization was minute in absolute terms and modest when compared to the relatively large spurt of new enterprises which began production in the period 1918–22. Ch'ing government efforts, after the disasters of the Sino-Japanese War and the Boxer Uprising, to promote industry by such measures as the creation of a Ministry of Commerce (later reorganized as Agriculture, Industry and Commerce) in 1903 and the promulgation of a 'Company Law' in 1904 may have contributed to this limited expansion. Certainly the burgeoning anti-imperialist nationalism of provincial merchants and gentry was a factor. The principal force behind the establishment of new firms, however, was the manifest profitability of the first few enterprises undertaken in most industrial sectors and especially in the manufacture of consumers' goods to be marketed in the treaty-port areas. Successful foreign- and Chinese-owned firms were earning annual returns on the initial market value of their capital investments of 10 per cent or more in the first decade of the twentieth century. The total market, however, was severely limited by the low level of effective demand in the bulk of rural China. Consequently successive firms entering any particular industry, after the first few pioneers, faced a situation of increasing risk and uncertainty. This risk was reinforced by the fact that many of the pioneer firms had been established on the initiative of important provincial officials, or with the aid of official funds, or with official support in such forms as partial tax exemptions or the monopoly of certain markets. Thus the Shanghai Cotton Cloth Mill (began production 1890, reorganized 1894) and the Hanyehping Coal and Iron Co. (began production 1894, reorganized 1896) were under Sheng Hsuan-huai's

[19] Sun Yü-t'ang, comp. *Chung-kuo chin-tai kung-yeh shih tzu-liao, ti-i-chi, 1840–1895 nien* (Source materials on the history of modern industry in China, 1st collection, 1840–1895), 2.1166–9, 1170–3.

direction as *kuan-tu shang-pan* enterprises and were dependent on the backing of the provincial leaders, Li Hung-chang and Chang Chih-tung respectively. But even such nominally private (*shang-pan*) enterprises as Chang Chien's Ta-sheng Cotton Mill (began production 1899) and the Chou Hsüeh-hsi's premier Chee Hsin Cement Co. (began production 1907) owed their initial success to the official support which their sponsors, because of their own official ties, were able to obtain – from Chang Chih-tung and Liu K'un-i in the former case and from Yuan Shih-k'ai for Chee Hsin. Given a limited market, the lack of a modern banking system which could systematically channel savings into industrial investment, a central government whose financial resources were severely limited, and competition from imported goods and foreign-owned factories in China, it is perhaps not surprising that some regional officials and the entrepreneurs who were associated with them attempted to establish limited but protected industrial empires for their mutual profit. Few purely private ventures could expect success.

The link between economic success and political power, which had characterized such monopolies as that of the Cohong or the salt merchants of an earlier period and was manifest again in Kuomintang China in the 1930s and 1940s, was not broken during the era of China's early industrialization.

Between 1895 and 1913, according to a recent estimate, at least 549 Chinese-owned private and semi-official manufacturing and mining enterprises using mechanical power were inaugurated. Their total initial capitalization was Ch.$120,288,000. This estimate excludes arsenals, mints and also apparently a relatively small number of purely official undertakings. Some of the characteristics of these 549 firms, which include all with an initial capital of Ch.$10,000 or more for which data could be found and about which there is more information than for the enterprises started before 1895, are given in tables 12–14.

The peak years for the establishment of modern industry during the two decades surveyed were 1905–8. In this four-year period, 238 firms with a total initial capitalization of Ch.$61,219,000 began operation. Much of the machinery installed came from abroad, which is reflected in the fact that annual imports of tools and machinery in 1905–8 were more than double the annual value in 1895–1904. Machinery imports continued to grow after 1908, but the number of new enterprises opened fell sharply until the much larger industrialization spurt of 1918–22. These trends perhaps suggest increased capital investment in the privileged established firms combined with an increasing difficulty in entering the limited market for new firms. They may also reflect a shift of venture capital to provincial railway projects inspired by the nationalist 'rights recovery' activities of the last years of the dynasty.

TABLE 12

Number and initial capital of Chinese-owned manufacturing and mining enterprises inaugurated 1895–1913, by industry

Industry	Number of enterprises	Percentage of total	Initial capital (Ch.$1,000)	Percentage of total	Average capital (Ch.$1,000)
Coal mining	42	7.65	14,508	12.06	345
Metal mining and smelting	39	7.10	7,565	6.29	194
Metal working	15	2.73	2,787	2.32	186
Public utilities (water and electricity)	46	8.38	21,600	17.96	470
Cement	3	0.55	2,620	2.18	873
Bricks, tiles	12	2.19	651	0.54	543
Pottery	7	1.28	772	0.64	110
Glass	10	1.82	3,429	2.85	343
Matches	26	4.74	3,444	2.86	132
Candles, soap	18	3.28	805	0.67	45
Cotton ginning	3	0.55	280	0.23	93
Cotton spinning	19	3.46	10,454	8.69	550
Cotton weaving and dyeing	27	4.92	1,261	1.05	47
Silk reeling	97	17.67	11,584	9.63	119
Wool weaving	7	1.28	5,215	4.34	745
Hemp weaving	4	0.73	1,000	0.83	250
Other weaving	6	1.09	732	0.61	122
Rice milling	9	1.64	1,012	0.84	113
Flour milling	53	9.65	8,622	7.17	163
Oil pressing	28	5.10	4,752	3.95	170
Cigarettes, tobacco	20	3.64	1,378	1.15	69
Other foodstuffs	15	2.73	3,111	2.59	207
Paper	14	2.55	5,929	4.93	424
Printing	6	1.09	1,160	0.97	193
Leather tanning	11	2.00	4,608	3.83	419
Other	12	2.19	1,009	0.84	84
Total	549	100.00	120,288	100.00	219

Source: Calculated from Wang Ching-yü, *Chung-kuo chin-tai kung-yeh shih tzu-liao*, 2. 869–920.

In both numbers and initial capital the bulk of these new industries was concentrated in such light manufacturing fields as textiles (160 firms or 29.14 per cent of the total, with a capitalization of Ch.$30,246,000 or 25.14 per cent of the total) and the processing of foodstuffs (125 firms or 22.76 per cent; Ch.$18,875,000 or 15.69 per cent). Mines accounted for 14.75 per cent of the firms and 18.35 per cent of the initial capitalization. Their relative importance reflects again the considerable success of the late-Ch'ing 'rights recovery movement' which accomplished the cancellation of a substantial number of foreign mining concessions during the first decade of the twentieth century, although sometimes at the price of clearly excessive compensation payments. The 46 electric power plants or water-works were established in the larger cities in all the provinces of China proper with the exception of Shensi, Kwangsi and Kweichow. They varied greatly in size and were most often to be found in the treaty port cities of the Yangtze valley and south-east coastal provinces.

TABLE 13

Number and initial capital of Chinese-owned manufacturing and mining enterprises inaugurated 1895–1913, by location

Location	Number of enterprises	Percentage of total	Initial capital (Ch.$1,000)	Percentage of total
Anhwei	18	3.28	1,868	1.55
Chekiang	29	5.28	4,346	3.61
Chihli (other than Tientsin)	34	6.19	11,951	9.94
Tientsin	17	3.10	4,219	3.51
Fukien	19	3.46	1,461	1.21
Honan	12	2.19	1,890	1.57
Hunan	24	4.37	3,968	3.31
Hupei (other than Wuhan)	9	1.64	1,937	1.61
Wuhan	28	5.10	17,240	14.33
Kiangsi	13	2.37	2,383	1.98
Kiangsu (other than Shanghai)	70	12.75	13,510	11.23
Shanghai	83	15.12	23,879	19.85
Kwangsi	5	0.91	1,424	1.18
Kwangtung (other than Canton)	68	12.39	5,038	4.19
Canton	16	2.91	5,791	4.81
Kweichow	1	0.18	79	0.07
Manchuria	44	8.01	4,922	4.09
Shansi	10	1.82	3,038	2.53
Shantung	20	3.64	4,614	3.84
Shensi	1	0.18	405	0.34
Szechwan	19	3.46	2,248	1.87
Yunnan	5	0.91	1,671	1.39
Other	4	0.73	2,406	2.00
Total	549	100.00	120,288	100.00

Source: Same as table 12.

With the exceptions of silk reeling, which after 1900 was increasingly performed in steam filatures, iron mining at Ta-yeh for export to Japan, and to a lesser extent oil pressing, these Chinese-owned modern industries were not engaged in processing raw materials for export. Only three modern cotton ginning plants, for example, are recorded. Much export processing continued to be primarily a handicraft industry, although supplemented by the output of foreign-owned processing plants. Cotton weaving and dyeing, even in the urban areas, remained also at the handicraft stage or were performed in small plants with minimal power-machinery in the vicinity of the new cotton spinning mills.

Many of these new manufacturing enterprises were, in fact, small. Of the 160 firms in the textile line, 97 were steam silk filatures of which 54 were very small plants located in Kwangtung. The 21 filatures located in Shanghai were each several times larger than those in the south, but the average initial investment for all 97 was only Ch.$119,000. Of the 549 enterprises, 303 had initial capitals of less than Ch.$100,000. The average capitalization of the remaining 246 Chinese-owned firms (capitalized at Ch.$100,000 and over) was Ch.$432,000 compared with an average investment of Ch.$758,000 for the 136 foreign and Sino-foreign enterprises in table 11.

TABLE 14

Initial capitalization of Chinese-owned manufacturing and mining enterprises, inaugurated 1895–1913

Size of initial capitalization (Ch.$)	Number of enterprises	Percentage of total	Initial capital (Ch.$1,000)	Percentage of total	Average capital (Ch.$1,000)
10,000– 49,999	214	38.98	5,899	4.90	28
50,000– 99,999	89	16.21	7,052	5.86	79
100,000–249,999	104	18.94	17,731	14.74	170
250,000–499,999	85	15.48	29,901	24.86	352
500,000–999,999	40	7.29	27,980	23.26	700
1,000,000 and over	17	3.10	31,725	26.37	1,866
Total	549	100.00	120,288	100.00	219

Source: Wang Ching-yü, *Modern industry,* 2. 1041.

Chinese-owned enterprises could of course locate in the interior, if they wished, as well as in Shanghai and other treaty ports. Of 468 non-mining enterprises, 239 were located in treaty-port cities and 229 in places other than treaty ports. As the foreign-owned non-mining firms were all located in the treaty ports, and marketed their products primarily in these places, the existence of Chinese firms in inland locations suggests that there was some degree of complementary as well as competition between the markets served by foreign industries in China and Chinese-owned enterprises. However, Chinese-owned modern manufacturing firms in the treaty ports had much larger initial capitalization and average size than the inland firms, as table 15 indicates. The four cities of Shanghai, Wuhan, Tientsin and Canton, as may be seen from tables 13 and 15, were the most important manufacturing centres. Shanghai, for example, led in at least the following industries: metal working, cotton textiles, silk reeling, flour milling, oil pressing, printing, candles and soap.

The foregoing data are of value only in suggesting gross trends. It is likely that some firms were either omitted or counted more than once, that a proportion of those undertaken failed during the period under consideration, and that the initial capital may have been overestimated in some cases (or quickly increased in others). It would therefore be misleading to take a simple sum of the number of firms and the magnitude of their capitals under the several categories discussed above as the absolute magnitude of China's nineteenth-century industrialization. The best that can be said is that by the end of the Ch'ing dynasty there were perhaps 500–600 foreign and Chinese mining and manufacturing enterprises employing mechanical power, and that the total capitalization of these firms was in the vicinity of Ch.$200,000,000.

TABLE 15

*Number and initial capitalization of treaty-port and inland Chinese-
owned manufacturing firms, 1895–1913*

	Number	Percentage of total	Initial capital (Ch.$1,000)	Percentage of total	Average capital (Ch.$1,000)
Inland enterprises	229	48.93	33,158	33.76	145
Treaty-port enterprises	239	51.07	65,057	66.24	272
Shanghai, Wuhan, Tientsin, Canton	144	30.77	51,129	52.06	355
Other treaty ports	95	20.30	13,928	14.18	147
Total	468	100.00	98,215	100.00	210

Source: Same as table 12.

Among these firms, it is estimated that 116 Chinese-owned enterprises and 40 foreign-owned employed 500 or more workers each, with a total of 130,985 in the former and 109,410 in the latter. The 500 employee cut-off point is arbitrary, of course, but if it is adopted these 240,395 workers may be considered the extent of the 'modern' labour force in China in the period 1900–10.

Some part of the investment in the nineteenth-century foreign factories was held by Chinese shareholders resident in the treaty ports, principally compradors of foreign trading firms or merchants dealing in silk, tea and imported yarn and cloth. This was especially true of the foreign-owned coastal and riverine steamship lines and of banks, insurance companies and goods warehouses which are not included in the data on manufacturing firms in table 10. But it was also the case in silk reeling, electric light and power utilities and, after 1895, in the newly established cotton textile mills. One recent study has identified 130 large Chinese shareholders who had invested in 44 foreign firms between 1860 and 1900.[20] Another sample, for 1896–1910, lists 78 Chinese investors, individuals and firms, in 17 foreign-owned factories mainly in Shanghai. Of these firms, 6 were cotton mills and 2 flour mills.[21] The total size of the investment by Chinese in foreign enterprises reflected in these two samples cannot be estimated. But such investment does testify to the availability of funds (often the profits of participation in foreign trade) in the treaty ports if there were prospects of substantial profits. The special status of foreigners and their concessions in the treaty ports provided the needed assurance. When Chinese entrepreneurs could give similar guarantees of potential profit, some of those who had invested in foreign firms also put their 'comprador capital' into Chinese-owned ventures. The special privileges of the *kuan-tu shang-pan* enterprises, and of others formally in the private sector but dependent in varying degrees on official favours, were intended to provide precisely this assurance.

But, as I have already stated, the overall prospects for modern manufacturing industry in late-Ch'ing China were limited. The institutions – a modern banking system in particular – for channelling non-treaty-port savings into industry did not exist. The central government was ideologically and politically incapable of establishing and guaranteeing the framework of legal, commercial and educational institutions without which modern enterprise could not thrive. Nor was it able, in the absence of tariff autonomy and in view of the special privileges foreigners had exacted, to provide protection for 'infant' Chinese-owned firms against competition from imports and the products of foreign firms in China. And, above all, it would have required a basic reorganization of the agricultural sector to provide the raw materials for industrial growth, food for an expanded urban population, and a sufficient market for increased output. The late-nineteenth-century Chinese economy was admittedly poor: the technology of Europe's industrial revolution was just beginning to appear in the coastal cities, and the rural population lived with an increasingly adverse man–land ratio and an agricultural technology which over the centuries had been exploited to the limits of its potential. But it was not an absolute shortage of capital which constrained China's early industrial development.

[20] Wang Ching-yü, 'Shih-chiu shih-chi wai-kuo ch'in Hua ch'i-yeh chung ti Hua-shang fu-ku huo-tung' (Investment by Chinese merchants in the foreign firms which invaded China in the nineteenth century), *Li-shih yen-chiu*, 1965. 4, pp. 39–74.

[21] Wang Ching-yü, comp. *Chung-kuo chin-tai kung-yeh shih tzu-liao, ti-erh chi, 1895–1914 nien* (Source materials on the history of modern industry in China, 2nd collection, 1895–1914), 2.1065.

As of 1912, manufacturing firms registered with the Ministry of Agriculture and Commerce reported a total capitalization of Ch.$54,804,000. In
the same year, traditional banks (*ch'ien-chuang*, 'money shops') and pawnshops registered with the ministry were capitalized at a total of
Ch. $164,854,000.[22] The resources of the economy, limited as they were,
remained sterilized in traditional vessels which only fundamental political
change could shatter.

DOMESTIC AND FOREIGN COMMERCE

The economy of late-Ch'ing China was, at its given level of technology,
characterized by a high degree of commercial development. Goods and
traders moved extensively throughout the country and, to a limited extent,
the domestic economy had developed links with the world market. At the
most basic level, the peasants of every rural area bought and sold regularly
at the periodic markets of the standard market towns which served their
groups of villages. Here such agricultural surplus as they produced and the
products of handicraft manufacture were exchanged for other local commodities or for goods manufactured in the treaty-port cities or imported
from abroad which, in small quantities, had flowed down through successive levels of the marketing system to the final consumer. These thousands
of basic markets, of which Skinner estimates there were 63,000 early in the
twentieth century,[23] were linked in turn to two higher level markets –
intermediate and central – and ultimately to the great trading cities of the
coast such as Tientsin, Shanghai and Canton.

At each level the markets were populated by itinerant pedlars, local
merchants and agents of firms from all markets except the basic ones. At its
upper levels – the central markets and above – the marketing system interpenetrated with the administrative hierarchy of the Ch'ing government.
The rural central markets and the urban city and regional markets were the
loci of the officially regulated merchant middlemen and the merchant
guilds (*ya-hang*) through whom the bureaucratic elite regulated and taxed
the commerce of the empire. Also in these upper markets were found the
exchange banks (often operated by families from Shansi province and
hence known as 'Shansi banks') through whose drafts large sums were
transferred from one upper level market to another. Other types of 'native
banks', such as the money shops (*ch'ien-chuang*) which advanced funds to
local merchants – usually on personal security and occasionally on the
security of designated goods – and also changed money from one local

---

22 *Ibid.* 2.1017.
23 G. William Skinner, 'Marketing and social structure in rural China, part II', *JAS*, 24.2
   (February 1965) 227.

currency standard to another, were also located in the upper level markets. In the basic markets, barter was not unknown and the financial institutions were limited to the local moneylender and the petty 'shroff' or money-changer.

The discreteness of the 63,000 rural basic markets and the structure of the marketing hierarchy as a whole were closely related to the degree of development of the means of transportation. The upper level markets were located on or at the termini of the principal water and, in North China, overland routes by which goods and persons were transported, while the basic markets were situated on the progressively less accessible feeder trails and waterways. The intricate and highly developed periodic marketing structure continued to flourish not only in late nineteenth-century China but well into the twentieth century as well, as a result of the relative absence of two critical changes: (1) improved transportation at the local level, which would make intermediate and higher level markets as easily avail-able to the peasant as his traditional basic market; and (2) a linking of the higher level markets to industrial centres within and outside China by superior steamship and railway communications with a consequent increase in the inflow and outflow of commodities, which in turn would decrease the self-sufficiency of the households which traded at the basic markets.

Certainly the bulk, perhaps as much as three-quarters, of all the trade in nineteenth-century China consisted of small-scale local trade. This was confined to the basic and intermediate market levels by high transport costs, by the profits of multitudinous middlemen at each successive level of the marketing system, and to some extent too by the relative self-sufficiency in basic grains of much of rural China.

'For the most part, trade takes to the water when it can', the Com-missioner of Customs at Lungchow noted in 1892.[24] This observation was applicable both to short-haul grain shipments within major producing regions (for example, from the Hunan districts bordering the Tungting Lake to the major markets of Hsiang-t'an or Changsha) and to the thousand-mile trip from the rice surplus province of Hunan to the deficit regions in the Yangtze Delta. Nevertheless the total amount of long-distance shipping of such a bulky, low-priced commodity as grain was very small. Even in the early twentieth century, the total freight and marketing cost of bringing rice by junk from Anhwei to Shanghai was almost double the original price of the rice in the Anhwei village where it was produced.[25] The long-

[24] China. Inspectorate-General of Customs, *Decennial reports . . ., 1882–1891*, 661.
[25] Amano Motonosuke, *Chūgoku nōgyō no sho mondai* (Problems of Chinese agriculture), 2.241–7, gives a meticulously detailed account of each item of cost from Anhwei to Shanghai.

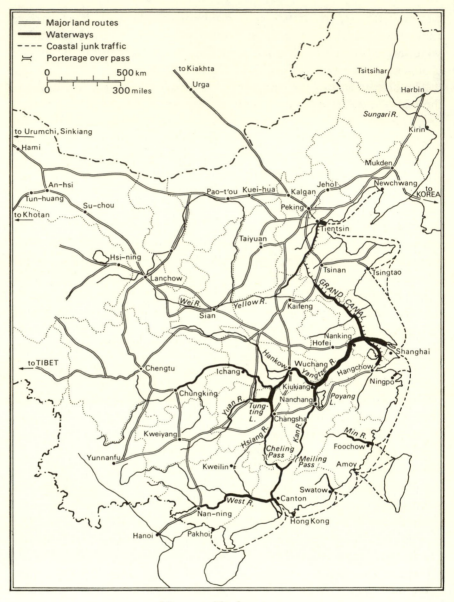

MAP. 3   Trade routes

distance trade – between higher level markets, but of course originating or terminating ultimately at the basic level – consisted for the most part of commodities with a relatively high value per ton whose production was favoured by the resources or climate of a particular region: raw cotton and cotton textiles from Kiangnan; salt from the brine wells of Szechwan or the coastal evaporating pans of Kiangsu; opium from Yunnan, Kweichow and Szechwan; sugar from Kwangtung and Fukien; copper and lead from Yunnan; teas from the middle and lower Yangtze valley; and silk from Chekiang, Kiangsu, Kwangtung and Szechwan. These products could bear the high freight and handling markup because of their higher values in relation to weight – in the case of tea for example, which was worth perhaps ten times as much per picul as an equivalent weight of rice, this might be 15 or 20 per cent between Anhwei and Shanghai. There were no alternative sources of supply, and they were consumed in disproportionate amounts by the wealthier residents (the gentry) of the towns and cities for whom the question of price was relatively less important.

In Central and South China in particular the major rivers and their branches and tributaries were the arteries and capillaries of commerce. A twentieth-century estimate, which appears applicable to the late Ch'ing as well, suggests that there were at least 4,000 miles of waterways suitable to steamer traffic, 15,000 miles more which could be navigated by steam launches, and an additional 27,000 miles open to 'native craft' of all kinds. Perhaps 25,000 miles of Yangtze waterways were ultimately navigable from Shanghai – by ocean steamer to Hankow, then by light-draft steamer to Ichang where goods were repacked and loaded on to junks, thence through the Yangtze rapids with the aid of trackers to Chungking;[26] from Chungking on progressively smaller junks via the upper Yangtze and its tributaries to northern Szechwan and to Kweichow, and by stream and porter into Yunnan. In the smallest streams the vessels may have been no more than bamboo rafts turned up at the bows; or maybe they were flat-bottomed skiffs, drawing perhaps nine inches of water fully loaded, whose crewmen were often in the water lifting and shoving. While the West River from Canton was navigable by steamer only to Wuchow on the Kwangsi border, thousands of junks on that stream and its tributaries carried goods further into and out of Kwangsi, Kweichow and Yunnan. A third major trade route (by which teas and silks were brought to Canton before the opening of Shanghai) proceeded via the North River from Canton, by porter over the Cheling or Meiling passes in the Nan-ling Mountains to the headwaters of the Hsiang and Kan rivers in Hunan and

[26] Chungking was first reached by small steamship in 1898. Regular steamer service began in 1908.

Kiangsi respectively, and then through the Tungting and Poyang lakes to the Yangtze. The necessity for overland porterage over the Nan-ling Mountains and the limited hinterlands of Ningpo, Foochow and Amoy favoured the development of Shanghai as the major foreign trade port, and the Yangtze as the principal route into the interior of China.

From Hankow, junks could proceed north-westward on the Han River into Shensi. To some extent also the Grand Canal continued to link the lower Yangtze valley with the North China plain. But North China was much less served with navigable waterways than the south. Here the large-wheeled North China carts and pack animals moved over dust and mud tracks, which constant traffic in the loess regions of Honan, Shansi and Shensi had sometimes cut down ten or more feet below the surface of the surrounding countryside. The major traditional trade routes from Peking followed a difficult course overland to Shansi, and via Kalgan across Mongolia to Kiakhta on the Russian border, with branches westward to Shensi and Kansu. Where water routes were not available, as in much of North China, the movement of goods was slow and expensive.[27] Overland freight costs by cart, wheelbarrow, pack animal or on the backs of porters are estimated to have been two to five times higher per ton mile than freight charges by junk.

The nineteenth-century commercial system, in spite of its high level of traditional development, was of course not yet a 'modern' market economy. While a few high-value commodities, as I have indicated, might have been carried by water throughout the empire, it would be incorrect to speak of a national market even for these. Commerce tended to be contained within a large number of hierarchically arranged cells, as a result of friction created by certain factors. These were a bimetallic silver–copper standard with multiple local currencies, high-cost transportation (in money and time), the comparative rarity of credit advances against commodities, the absence of a commercial banking system for the mutual clearing of indebtedness, and the omnipresence of numerous petty middlemen with vested interests in the traditional structure of trade. Each cell bustled with petty commerce and, to use Sol Tax's phrase, 'penny capitalism', but they were connected only by a traffic of semi-luxury goods and the outflow of silver and some grains in the form of taxes to the administrative hierarchy above.

---

[27] The distribution of stations on official routes suggests that most official travel was by horse overland. For the travel of government officials the Ch'ing statutes provided for the maintenance of 1,634 land stations, 92 water stations and 54 land and water stations throughout the empire. At each stage in the journey these stations provided horses, carts, sedan chairs or boats as needed, as well as lodging and food. Official documents were carried overland among some 15,000 postal stations. See Kono Michihiro, 'Shindai Santōshō no kansei rikujō kōtsūro' (Official overland communication routes in Shantung in the Ch'ing dynasty), *Shirin*, 33.3 (May 1950) 317–36.

Foreign observers in the second half of the nineteenth century, after the establishment of the likin tax in 1853 to finance the suppression of the Taiping rebels, were wont to see this levy on internal trade (which admittedly was sometimes capriciously administered) as the principal obstacle to their own trade and to the commercial integration of China.[28] But compared with freight and handling markups of 15 to 100 per cent, it appears unlikely that the common likin rate of 2 per cent at each tax station had more than a small effect on the total amount and direction of internal trade. The British, as I have stated earlier, found it difficult to sell Lancashire cloth in the interior of China because domestic handicraft weaving offered effective competition. The marketing structure and size of China's domestic commerce were constrained not primarily by burdensome official exactions, but by the limitations of pre-modern transportation and communications.

By the end of the Manchu dynasty in 1911, there was a small but noticeable change in the commercial system at its outer fringes. While, as I shall argue, it remained essentially intact, it is, after all, common sense that the late-Ch'ing economy was influenced by the progressive opening of treaty ports and the expansion of foreign trade. The trade data compiled by the foreign-administered maritime customs are almost the only substantial long-term historical statistics for modern China. But even these generally excellent data have shortcomings. To 1887, imports from Hong Kong were not included, and free on board and cost, insurance and freight values were not used so that export values were understated while imports were overstated. Moreover, the trade was measured in silver haikwan (maritime customs) taels in an era when silver was steadily declining in terms of gold with the result that the recorded value of the trade was inflated as compared with its gold value or its actual quantity. Table 16 presents values in current haikwan taels and index numbers of China's foreign trade for the period 1870–1911.

In current haikwan taels the total volume of trade increased more than sevenfold from 1870 to 1911. As already indicated, silver values inflate the actual growth of trade: in terms of quantity, imports increased 312 per cent and exports 307 per cent during these four decades. The growth of total trade measured in current values was relatively slow until the 1890s, with the most rapid increase coming in the first decade of the twentieth century. The quantity indices indicate that the growth of imports was fairly steady

---

[28] The Chinese, of course, were irritated by the fact that foreign goods could, to a degree, escape the likin if covered by 'transit passes' obtained by payment of half of the regular import duty. It should be remembered, however, that these passes were valid only so long as the goods remained in their original packaging and were transported to the destination stated on the pass. In effect, it was possible that the tax on goods under pass was only delayed until they reached the final consumer.

TABLE 16

Values and index numbers of China's foreign trade, 1870–1911

(All indices: 1913 = 100)

	Value in current haikwan taels (1,000)				Indices of value of total trade		Indices of quantity		Net barter terms of trade (import prices/ export prices)
	Net imports	Exports	Total	Trade balance	Current values	'Real' values*	Imports	Exports	
1870	63,693	55,295	118,988	− 8,398	12.2	—	25.9	33.3	76.5
1871	70,103	66,853	136,956	− 3,250	14.1	—	28.1	39.4	75.9
1872	67,317	75,288	142,605	+ 7,971	14.6	—	27.9	43.3	71.1
1873	66,637	69,451	136,088	+ 2,814	14.0	—	27.3	39.1	70.8
1874	64,361	66,713	131,074	+ 2,352	13.5	20.7	31.5	40.1	62.8
1875	67,803	68,913	136,716	+ 1,110	14.0	21.0	33.8	42.2	65.3
1876	70,270	80,851	151,121	+ 10,581	15.5	21.6	36.3	42.8	54.4
1877	73,234	67,445	140,679	− 5,789	14.5	21.9	36.1	40.8	65.2
1878	70,804	67,172	137,976	− 3,632	14.2	20.5	34.9	41.4	66.3
1879	82,227	72,281	154,508	− 9,946	15.9	22.0	40.8	43.2	63.9
1880	79,293	77,884	157,177	− 1,409	16.1	23.7	36.2	47.2	69.7
1881	91,911	71,453	163,364	− 20,458	16.8	23.3	40.8	43.5	72.8
1882	77,715	67,337	145,052	− 10,378	14.9	21.3	36.4	45.9	76.7
1883	73,568	70,198	143,766	− 3,370	14.8	22.0	35.0	47.2	75.1
1884	72,761	67,148	139,909	− 5,613	14.4	21.1	34.5	50.6	83.6
1885	88,200	65,006	153,206	− 23,194	15.7	23.1	40.5	47.6	83.3
1886	87,479	77,207	164,686	− 10,272	16.9	24.2	35.3	54.2	91.4
1887	102,264	85,860	188,124	− 16,404	19.3	28.4	41.6	41.2	62.4
1888	124,783	92,401	217,184	− 32,382	22.3	34.3	50.3	43.6	62.7

1889	110,884	96,948	207,832	— 13,936	21.3	31.4	44.0	45.2	63.0
1890	127,093	87,144	214,237	— 39,949	22.0	32.4	54.8	42.0	59.8
1891	134,004	100,948	234,952	— 33,056	24.1	35.5	60.8	47.9	56.1
1892	135,101	102,584	237,685	— 32,517	24.4	34.9	59.9	49.8	58.8
1893	151,363	116,632	267,995	— 34,731	27.5	38.8	59.4	57.2	67.0
1894	162,103	128,105	290,208	— 33,998	29.8	40.3	45.3	60.1	91.1
1895	171,697	143,293	314,990	— 28,404	32.4	45.6	45.8	66.3	96.4
1896	202,590	131,081	333,671	— 71,509	34.3	47.6	53.2	56.4	91.0
1897	202,829	163,501	366,330	— 39,328	37.6	47.6	49.7	61.6	85.7
1898	209,579	159,037	368,616	— 50,542	37.9	45.1	51.3	63.4	91.2
1899	264,748	195,785	460,533	— 68,963	47.3	50.9	69.2	62.5	68.5
1900	211,070	158,997	370,067	— 52,073	38.0	43.7	49.5	54.9	82.3
1901	268,303	169,657	437,960	— 98,646	45.0	55.5	62.5	59.8	85.4
1902	315,364	214,182	529,546	— 101,182	54.5	56.1	70.9	65.1	82.6
1903	326,739	214,352	541,091	— 112,387	55.6	54.0	65.1	59.8	85.5
1904	344,061	239,487	583,548	— 104,574	59.9	60.6	69.2	64.0	94.1
1905	447,101	227,888	674,989	— 219,213	69.3	62.5	96.6	62.5	89.8
1906	410,270	236,457	646,727	— 173,813	66.4	66.4	95.3	64.6	83.2
1907	416,401	264,381	680,782	— 152,020	69.9	67.2	88.7	67.1	84.3
1908	394,505	276,660	671,165	— 117,845	68.9	62.7	72.7	73.0	101.4
1909	418,158	338,993	757,151	— 79,165	77.8	70.1	77.1	92.9	105.1
1910	462,965	380,833	843,798	— 82,132	86.7	85.0	79.2	102.9	111.7
1911	471,504	377,338	848,842	— 94,166	87.2	82.3	80.9	102.1	111.7

* Total trade in current values divided by index of wholesale prices

Sources: Yang Tuan-liu, *Statistics of China's foreign trade,* tables 1–3; Nankai Institute of Economics, *Nankai index numbers, 1936,* 37–8; and Chi-ming Hou, *Foreign investment and economic development in China, 1840–1937,* 194–8, for pre-1904 terms of trade.

(the great spurt in 1905-6 was a direct consequence of the Russo-Japanese War and should be discounted) while exports, which were relatively stationary in the 1890s, increased rapidly in the last few years of the dynasty. Bean and bean product shipments, primarily from Manchuria, account for much of this export spurt. If the pre-1888 trade data are adjusted to measure imports at cost, insurance and freight values and exports at free on board values, and an allowance is made for opium and others 'smuggled' from Hong Kong, China's foreign trade probably showed an export surplus from 1870 to 1887. From 1888 to 1900, imports moderately exceeded exports by an annual average of 40,876,000 haikwan taels. After 1900, the import excess became substantially larger, the average annual excess for 1901-11 growing to 121,377,000 haikwan taels. Part of this adverse trade balance was offset by remittances homeward by overseas Chinese, and up to 1900 by a small net export of gold and silver. The remainder was financed by an inflow of capital – including investment in industry after 1895 as described above, and loans to the Ch'ing government which I shall discuss later.

Opium, mainly from India, ranked as the most important single Chinese import until 1890 when it was surpassed by cotton piece goods. Cotton cloth and yarn together after 1890 accounted for about one-third of China's imports by value. The cotton trade and its effect on the Chinese economy have already been discussed in connection with the handicraft industry. Cereals and other foodstuffs were imported largely to supply the large coastal cities in quantities which appear to have fluctuated with localized harvest supply conditions rather than the general quality of the harvest; this trade reflects both the growth of these cities and the heavy transportation and marketing costs for domestic grains grown outside their immediate hinterlands. The percentage distribution of China's principal imports is given in table 17, and exports are shown in table 18.

Silk and tea, which had been China's most important exports before the Treaty of Nanking, continued to occupy this position until the end of the Ch'ing dynasty. Their combined relative position in the export trade was, however, a diminishing one. Tea exports fell largely because of the inability of exporters in China to enforce quality standards among producers and middlemen in the face of growing Indian and Japanese competition. While the large absolute quantities of silk piece goods exported suggest the continued strength of a major rural handicraft industry, the new importance of bean oil, leather, flour, egg and egg products, and to a lesser extent ginned cotton exports, reflects the establishment from the turn of the century of numerous small handicraft workshops in the larger and medium-sized urban centres.

TABLE 17

Percentage distribution of China's principal imports, 1870–1910

	Total value (HK taels 1,000)	Total %	Opium %	Cotton piece goods %	Cotton yarn %	Cereals, flour %	Sugar %	Tobacco %	Coal %	Kerosene %	Metals and minerals %	Machinery* %	Railway† materials, vehicles %	All other %
1870	63,693	100	43.0‡	28.0	3.0	0.04	0.1	—	0.09	—	5.8	—	—	19.97‡
1880	79,293	100	39.3	24.9	4.6	0.1	0.4	—	1.2	—	5.5	—	—	24.0
1890	127,093	100	19.5	20.2	15.3	9.6	0.9	—	1.6	3.2	5.7	0.3	—	23.7
1900	211,070	100	14.8	21.5	14.3	7.0	3.0	0.5	3.1	6.6	4.7	0.7	—	23.8
1910	462,965	100	12.0	14.7	13.6	7.7	4.8	2.0	1.8	4.7	4.3	1.5	3.8	29.1

* Not recorded separately before 1886   † Not recorded separately before 1903   ‡ Estimated
Sources: Yang Tuan-liu, Statistics of China's foreign trade, table 5, pp. 15–25, table 9, pp. 43–8; Yu-kwei Cheng, Foreign trade and industrial development of China, 19.

TABLE 18

Percentage distribution of China's principal exports, 1870–1910

	Total value (HK taels 1,000)	Total %	Tea %	Silk, silk goods %	Seeds, oil %	Beans %	Hides, leather, skins %	Raw cotton %	Wool %	Coal %	Eggs, egg products %	Flour %	All other %
1870	55,295	100	49.9	38.8	1.2	1.2	—	0.5	—	—	—	0.3	8.1
1880	77,884	100	45.9	38.0	0.1	0.2	0.5	0.2	0.4	—	—	0.2	14.5
1890	87,144	100	30.6	33.9	0.6	0.4	1.4	3.4	1.6	—	—	0.3	27.8
1900	158,997	100	16.0	30.4	2.5	1.9	4.3	6.2	1.9	—	—	0.8	36.0
1910	380,833	100	9.4	25.4	8.4	5.6	5.3	7.4	2.5	1.5	1.1	1.4	32.0

Sources: Yang Tuan-liu and Hou Hou-p'ei et al., Statistics of China's foreign trade, table 4, pp. 4–14, table 8, pp. 3–42; Yu-kwei Cheng, Foreign trade, 19.

Hong Kong's large nominal share in China's foreign trade, combined with the lack of data before 1932 on goods shipped from and to Hong Kong, prevent an accurate statement of the proportions of trade with each foreign country. Table 19 presents an unadjusted percentage distribution of China's foreign trade for selected years, 1871–1911, while table 20 represents H. B. Morse's estimate for the Imperial Maritime Customs of the distribution of trade, which treats Hong Kong as a Chinese port and apportions its imports and exports among the several major trading countries. The United Kingdom was China's most important trading partner until the end of the nineteenth century – and on into the twentieth century if the entire British empire is considered. British predominance in the import trade is most notable, and as already indicated is accounted for by cotton piece goods from Lancashire and yarn and opium from India. The total British share, while it remained the largest, was a declining one. From the 1890s Japanese trade, spurred on by the provisions of the Shimonoseki Treaty and by Japan's post-1905 role in Manchuria, grew rapidly. The American and Russian shares in China's trade were also in general increasing ones.

Two general observations about the foreign trade which has just been described are pertinent here. First, although it was a growing commerce, as late as 1913 China's world trade per head of population (in US dollars: imports, $0.94; exports, $0.67; total, $1.61) was the *lowest* of eighty-three countries for which League of Nations data were compiled. It is possible that the 1913 population of China was overstated in these estimates; but even in the unlikely case that per capita foreign trade was double the figures given above, China would still be near the very bottom of the list of eighty-three. Professor Kuznets' studies have indicated that a negative correlation is to be expected between a country's size and its foreign trade as a proportion of national income. In the case of China this size factor was reinforced by an economic system with substantially autarchic economic cells, sustained by a relatively unchanging transport system.

The second observation is that, by and large, the inland distribution of foreign goods and, to a somewhat lesser extent, the assembly of exports were dominated by Chinese merchants and operated through the traditional channels of trade. 'There is at present not a single Western merchant engaged in the cotton-goods import trade in the whole Yang-tze Valley, except in Shanghai: English capital has been withdrawn from ports like Hankow, and has never been invested in the new ports like Ch'ung-king', reported the Lancashire mission to China of 1896–7.[29] Eleven large Chinese dealers in Hankow regularly bought imported cloth and yarn in Shanghai

[29] *Blackburn report*, F. S. A. Bourne's section, 70–1.

TABLE 19

Percentage distribution of China's foreign trade with principal trading partners, 1871–1911

	Imports from					Exports to				
	1871–3	1881–3	1891–3	1901–3	1909–11	1871–3	1881–3	1891–3	1901–3	1909–11
Hong Kong	32.5	36.2	51.2	41.6	33.9	14.7	25.4	39.3	40.8	28.2
Great Britain	34.7	23.8	20.4	15.9	16.5	52.9	33.3	11.3	4.8	5.1
Japan*	3.7	4.9	4.7	12.5	15.5	1.7	2.4	7.2	12.5	15.9
United States	0.5	3.7	4.5	8.5	7.1	14.1	12.4	9.8	10.2	9.0
Russia	0.2	0.2	0.6	0.8	3.5	3.3	7.3	8.6	5.5	12.5
Germany†	—	—	—	—	4.2	—	—	—	—	3.1
France†	—	—	—	—	0.6	—	—	—	—	10.7
Others	28.4	31.2	18.6	20.7	18.7	13.3	19.2	23.8	26.2	15.5
Total	100.0	100.0	100.0	100.0	100.0	100.0	100.0	100.0	100.0	100.0

* includes Taiwan from 1895   † included in 'Others' before 1909–11

Source: Yen Chung-p'ing et al., comps. Chung-kuo chin-tai ching-chi shih t'ung-chi tzu-liao hsuan-chi (Selected statistics on China's modern economic history), tables 7–8, pp. 65–6.

through their agents. They then resold the goods to Hankow retailers and to merchants from lower level markets in Hunan and Honan who came to Hankow for their supplies. In 1896, there were five European firms in Chungking; only one of these dealt in imported cotton goods, China's most important import, and that was in a small way. The cotton trade in Chungking was in the hands of twenty-seven Chinese firms who, together with three firms in Chengtu and one in Chia-ting, each August sent their

TABLE 20

Percentage distribution of China's foreign trade (including Hong Kong) with principal trading partners, 1899–1905

	Imports from			Exports to		
	average 1899– 1903	1904	1905	average 1899– 1903	1904	1905
Great Britain	20.13	23.92	23.53	8.60	7.72	6.97
British Dominions, etc.	28.33	26.54	23.81	13.98	12.49	12.44
(total British empire)	(48.46)	(50.46)	(47.34)	(22.58)	(20.21)	(19.41)
Japan*	18.26	18.06	16.13	12.70	15.51	14.03
United States	10.95	9.20	18.11	12.92	16.09	15.47
Russia	2.54	4.31	3.49	13.59	13.24	14.83
Germany	5.50	5.90	5.08	3.39	4.05	4.41
France	0.80	0.56	0.46	19.35	16.97	16.52
Others	13.32	11.51	9.40	15.47	13.93	15.33
Total	100.00	100.00	100.00	100.00	100.00	100.00

* includes Taiwan
Source: Calculations by H. B. Morse in China, Inspectorate-General of Customs, *Returns of trade and trade reports, 1906*, pt I, p. 46.

agents (often partners of the several firms) to Shanghai where they resided until May while they purchased and shipped cloth and yarn to Chungking. Lower level markets in Szechwan were supplied by local merchants who bought on credit from the Chungking dealers. In South China, agents or partners of firms in such relatively small centres as Linanfu in Yunnan bought directly from British importers in Hong Kong, the goods being shipped via Haiphong and entering China at Mengtze. While in the 1860s and into the 1870s branches of foreign firms, especially British, handled much of the importation of cotton goods into such ports as Hankow, these branches in the smaller treaty ports – which were the urban markets for large regional trading areas – were unable to develop permanent direct ties with rural Chinese distributors even at the central market level, not to speak of intermediate or basic markets. The Chinese firms with whom they dealt in Chinkiang or Hankow were located at the apex of the traditional marketing structure and had the advantage of local know-how and long-standing connections with lower level markets. Increasingly firms like those in Chungking mentioned above preferred to buy directly in Shanghai or Hong Kong where the selection of goods was larger and where they might benefit from competition among importers and frequent auction sales. Chinese and foreign steamship companies on the Yangtze were highly competitive and offered as favourable terms to Chinese merchants as to foreign. And, moreover, the Chefoo Convention of 1876 formalized the right of Chinese shippers transporting imported goods to obtain transit passes and thus nominal equality of taxation with the foreigner. It is perhaps only a small exaggeration, regarding the importation and distribution of the major staples of commerce, to describe the foreign trading firms in China as having been gradually transformed into Shanghai and Hong Kong commission agents serving the established Chinese commercial network. For some proprietary goods or those representing an advanced technology, networks of Chinese agents under direct foreign supervision were established from about the turn of the century. Some of the increasing Japanese trade after the Sino-Japanese War was also distributed by direct methods. But the bulk of the distribution of imports remained in Chinese hands.

The Chinese demand for imported goods was thus a limited one, and beyond the treaty ports this demand was supplied almost entirely through the traditional Chinese marketing system. On the export side the situation was similar, but there are indications of a somewhat greater foreign participation. The inability of foreign exporters in the treaty ports to exercise any quality control in the assembly of the annual tea crop was a major factor in the relative decline of China teas in foreign markets in the face of Indian, Ceylonese and Japanese competition. On the other hand, foreigners played a direct role at least in the earlier development of the supply of such new exports as hog bristles, hides and leather, and eggs and egg products.

The stability of the traditional marketing system was, as I have stated, directly related to the technology and cost of transportation. By 1911 steamships and steam launches and the railroad had penetrated the interior of China only to a very limited extent. In 1865, the Ch'ing government prohibited the traffic of foreign steam launches in inland waters which had been tolerated during the Taiping Rebellion. But foreign- and Chinese-owned steam shipping among the treaty ports including those on the Yangtze, which was permitted by the treaties, expanded from the 1870s. In 1874, 17 American, 11 British and 6 Chinese steamers were carrying freight on the Yangtze River and between Shanghai and other treaty ports. By 1894, 26 vessels owned by the China Merchants' Steam Navigation Co. and at least 51 owned by two British companies were in service on these routes. Smaller Chinese-owned steam launches were also beginning to ply between the treaty ports and inland cities not open to foreign traffic. The spread of the steam launch is apparent from the falling average tonnage of Chinese-owned steam vessels registered with the Imperial Maritime Customs: 1882, 737 tons; 1892, 247 tons; 1900, 35 tons. In 1898, in 'compensation' for China's refusal to accept Great Britain's offer of a loan, the British government forced Peking to permit foreign-flag steamers to trade at the inland ports from which they had been excluded since 1865. By 1903, 614 Chinese and foreign steamers had registered for inland trade, a number which increased to 977 in 1909, 1,030 in 1910 and 1,130 (936 Chinese and 194 foreign) in 1913. These small river steamers brought cheaper and more rapid transportation to the traditional trade routes on the tributaries of the Yangtze and West rivers (360 of the total in 1909 were registered at Shanghai, 72 at Hankow and 277 at Canton), but they remained vastly overshadowed in numbers and total tonnage by the thousands of junks and rafts of all sizes which continued to carry the bulk of the inland trade.[30]

Similarly, although 9,244 kilometres of trunk and branch railway lines had been completed by 1912 (including 288 kilometres before 1895), the railway had only a limited impact upon the late-Ch'ing economy and commercial system – as opposed to its very considerable political consequences for the ultimate fate of the Manchu dynasty. China's pre-1912 railways affected the economy and marketing system little not only because their total mileage was, after all, extremely small, but also because the bulk of this track was opened only in the last few years of the dynasty. Moreover, such consequences as the railway did have in the first years of the Republic were seriously distorted by endemic civil war which commandeered railway lines for troop transport, diverted revenues to the maintenance of warlord armies, and neglected repairs to the roadbed and rolling stock.

With minor exceptions such as the 199 kilometres from Peking to Kalgan which were built by Chinese engineers largely with the profits of the Peking–Mukden line, China's pre-republican railways were financed

---

[30] Even in the very unlikely case that the average tonnage of the 1,130 inland steamers of 1913 was as high as 100 tons (the 1900 average for Chinese-owned steamers was 35 tons), the total tonnage would be only 113,000. In September 1941, in the three provinces of Kiangsu, Chekiang and Anhwei, 118,292 junks and sampans of all sizes (*min-ch'uan*), totalling 850,704 tons and with crews of 459,178 persons, had registered with the boatmen's associations established by the Wang Ching-wei government. I have no data on the number and tonnage of junks in the late-Ch'ing period, but it is improbable that they could have been smaller than the 1941 figures for three provinces alone. See Mantetsu Chōsabu, *Chū-Shi no minsengyō* (The junk trade of Central China), 134–5.

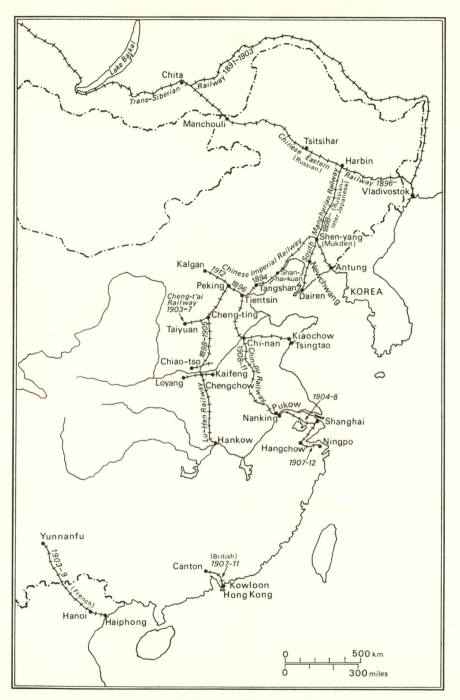

MAP. 4 Railway building, late Ch'ing

mainly by foreign loans and constructed by foreign concessionaires. The Chinese Eastern Railway in Manchuria (1,481 kilometres) and the South Manchurian Railway mainline from Harbin to Dairen (944 kilometres) were completely Russian undertakings with only a thin veneer of Chinese participation; and the Shantung railway from Kiaochow to Tsinan (394 kilometres) was a German financed and operated line. Slightly more than one-third of the total railway mileage in 1912 was in Manchuria, and un-questionably the railway was important for increasing the export of Manchurian soy-beans and for the steady growth of cotton goods imports in the first decade of the twentieth century. Harbin was in effect created by the Chinese Eastern Railway, and such ports as Newchwang and Chin-wangtao which lacked navigable waterways in their hinterlands were dependent on the railway. The major trunk lines within China proper – the Peking–Hankow railway (1,215 kilometres) and the Tientsin–Pukow rail-way (1,009 kilometres) – ran from north to south and provided links between the North China plain and the Yangtze valley where only the inadequate Grand Canal had served before. While these two parallel lines were possibly to some degree an uneconomical duplication, in general the routes of the lines completed in this first spurt of railway construction were well located to open new territories as in Manchuria, and to com-pensate for the absence of navigable waterways in North China. A radial network, centring perhaps at Hankow, would have been theoretically more desirable, but in 1906 when the Peking–Hankow line was completed it was not possible to foresee the duplication of lines for political reasons as in Manchuria in the 1920s, the delay of several decades before Hankow was connected with Canton, and the failure to build westward to Szechwan before 1949. At the end of the Ch'ing dynasty the comment of the customs commissioner at Shasi in Hupei applied to all except the few major centres in North China and Manchuria which were connected by rail: 'Shasi has no railway communication, and, being the centre of a most extensive system of natural and artificial waterways, can dispense with any for many years.'[31]

Though it may be contrary to the more common view, it does appear that the foreign merchant in late-Ch'ing China increasingly served rather than controlled the Chinese commercial system. The actual process of importing and exporting, however, which was conducted primarily at Shanghai and Hong Kong, remained almost completely in foreign hands until the 1920s. The principal link between the foreign merchant who spoke no Chinese and his customer or supplier from Chungking or Hankow who spoke no English was the comprador. While nominally employees of

[31] Decennial reports . . . , 1902–1911, I.292–3.

foreign firms, many compradors were traders on their own account in the goods handled by their employers. Their role in purchasing from Chinese dealers in exports and in arranging credit for buyers of imports provided unique opportunities to influence the flow of trade inward and outward and to profit therefrom. Many of the original investors in Chinese-owned shipping, financial and manufacturing enterprises were men who had grown wealthy as compradors of the leading foreign firms in Shanghai. The increase in the number of Chinese- and Japanese-owned export–import houses after 1911 (the Japanese apparently made greater efforts than the British or Americans to acquire some competence with the Chinese language) reduced the overall significance of the compradors as the link between foreign trade and the Chinese marketing system. In a somewhat truncated form, however, the institution lingered on.

Continued foreign dominance of the export–import process in the treaty ports was sustained by the role of foreign banks in China in financing foreign trade. From 1848, when the Oriental Banking Corporation established an office in Shanghai, the British enjoyed for forty years a virtual monopoly of modern-style banking in China. The two most important British-controlled firms were the Chartered Bank of India, Australia and China, whose first Chinese branch was opened in 1857, and the Hongkong and Shanghai Banking Corporation, which was established in 1865. German, Japanese, Russian, French and American competitors began to appear in the 1890s. Most of the advances of the foreign banks for financing imports and exports were made to foreign firms; direct loans to Chinese merchants were limited. Short-term credits were, however, allowed to 'native banks' which in turn loaned funds to Chinese merchants. In effect, the foreign banks by virtue of their monopoly of the financing of foreign trade also controlled the foreign exchange market. They were the channel through which the flow of silver to and from China took place, and they determined the fluctuating gold price of silver. Until 1935 the official exchange rate in the Shanghai market was based on the daily quotations of the Hongkong and Shanghai Bank.

The first Chinese modern bank, the Chung-kuo t'ung-shang yin-hang (known before 1911 as the Imperial Bank of China), was established by Sheng Hsuan-huai in 1896, but no Chinese bank played a significant role in the financing of foreign trade until the Hu Pu Bank established in 1904 had evolved into the Bank of China in the Republican period. Between 1896 and 1911 sixteen modern-style Chinese banks were opened (of which only seven survived up to the 1930s). All their main offices and branches were located in the larger cities; and they maintained only small and indirect connections with the trade of the interior in the form of short-term advances to inland 'native banks'. Modern commercial banking did not begin to penetrate the traditional marketing system until the 1920s and 1930s, while its total influence was meagre at best even after World War II. The bulk of local commerce in late-Ch'ing China, to the degree that it depended upon external credit at all, continued to be financed by old-style banks – one further indication that, other than in the major treaty ports, the structure of trade and the institutions which facilitated it had not changed greatly by 1911 from what they had been half a century before.[32]

GOVERNMENT AND THE ECONOMY

The consequences of the Ch'ing political system for the Chinese economy have often been stated in terms of excessive and capricious taxation, omnipresent corruption, and a general disdain for commerce and the merchant. These are not matters simply to be disregarded – the ideological posture of 'exalting agriculture and disparaging commerce' in particular requires examination that I cannot give it here (see chapter 8). The fact is, however, that within the constraints of the traditional technology, as earlier sections of this chapter have demonstrated, late-Ch'ing China was possessed of a complex, commercialized, 'developed' economy. Over the span of two centuries it had been able to support a growing population, had facilitated the 'pacification' of immense territories beyond the boundaries of China proper, and until the late eighteenth century (with the exception of the Rebellion of the Three Feudatories in 1673–81) had seen an unusually lengthy era of internal peace, relative prosperity and effective rule. In modern terms the tax burden on the population, while sometimes capriciously administered, was light. Depravity found its place in China as in other societies, but much of what appeared to the treaty-port observer as 'corrupt' represented the foreigner's inability to understand the informal but institutionalized *lou-kuei* ('customary exactions') which interpenetrated the highly rationalized fiscal system set forth in the official statutes of the dynasty. If the merchant was devalued in the official ideology and sometimes inordinately pressed for 'contributions' to the government, this does not negate the fact that he might be rich. The average annual profit of the Liang-Huai salt transport monopoly in the eighteenth century was perhaps 5 million taels, which was shared by thirty principal transport merchants and some two hundred lesser dealers; an additional profit of 2 million taels was divided annually among some thirty factory merchants. The merchant

---

[32] A substantial decline in the position of the Shansi banks from about 1900 is, however, to be noted. The semi-official modern banks established after 1896 absorbed much of their transfer business and the deposits of public funds upon which they had depended.

might also be powerful, in particular within the rural marketing structure where the local elite in and out of office invested in commerce or usury through the merchant's auspices. In addition a merchant might be fortunate. His sons and grandsons, with ample leisure and strict instruction – and perhaps a purchased initial degree – might themselves enter the political elite. In short, for the maintenance, extension and prosperity of the traditional economy at a relatively constant level of per capita output, the ideology and administration of the state were at least neutral factors and almost never, except in recurrent periods of dynastic decay, major obstacles.

If, however, one's point of reference is economic development – either in the sense of increasing per capita national product or in the sense of industrialization (that is, the rapid growth of a modern manufacturing sector with or without an immediate increment in per capita product), then undoubtedly the late-nineteenth-century Chinese government was incapable of supplying positive assistance. Ideology, traditional fiscal practices, and the patterns of revenue and expenditure, were all obstacles to suitable action.

In the first spurt of industrialization in the more 'backward' countries of Europe, Russia in the 1890s for example, as Professor Gerschenkron has shown,[33] the state budget substituted for deficient market demand and capital supply, which were sharply limited by the poverty of the agricultural sector. A similar role was played by the credit-creating operations of the industrial banks in less 'backward' countries such as Germany and France. Neither alternative was available in late-Ch'ing China. As we have seen, apart from the important role of modern foreign banks in financing international trade, the pre-1911 banking system of China was almost entirely limited to transfer banks of the Shansi bank type and to local 'native banks'. The directors of China's first modern bank, the semi-official Imperial Bank of China, were primarily concerned with gaining control of the lucrative transfer of government funds between the provinces and Peking. When this project failed, they turned completely to conventional commercial banking. Neither of the two relatively small government banks established later (the Bank of Communications founded in 1908; and the Hu Pu Bank founded in 1904 and reorganized as the Ta-Ch'ing Bank in 1908) was intended to make industrial loans.

The failure of the Ch'ing government to promote a modern banking system which could foster industrial investment ultimately stemmed from the same causes which made it unable to invest in economic development from its own budget. In brief, the fiscal system of the central government like other aspects of its administration was quite superficial. Even in

[33] Alexander Gerschenkron, *Economic backwardness in historical perspective*.

normal times the imperial bureaucracy, although highly centralized in its formal organization, did not penetrate very deeply into Chinese society, including those aspects of society which constituted the economy. The central government normally confined its economic role to claiming its share of a relatively fixed economic product and to providing the internal order and external defences which would permit that product to be reproduced from one year to the next. This was of course in accordance with the main stream of the Confucian political ideology. But at various times in the two millennia of empire the more activist Legalist strain in the Confucian–Legalist ideological amalgam which supported the imperial system had been drawn upon for departures from economic passivity, notably in the 'reforms' of Wang Mang and Wang An-shih. Such departures, however, were perhaps particularly difficult for the ultra-conservative Manchu dynasty, always conscious of its foreign origin and determined to demonstrate its mandate by upholding Confucian orthodoxy. Thus as land under cultivation increased (until about 1800) and as the population grew slowly and unevenly (except for probable losses during the mid-nineteenth-century rebellions), the total economic product of course grew in size. But for the central government, economic growth by the accretion of more units of roughly the same mix of factors of production was not an opportunity to increase its revenues and its participation in the economy. In 1712 the official rates for the most important imperial revenue, the land tax, were fixed in perpetuity by the K'ang-hsi Emperor; the provincial quotas due to Peking were to be raised only as new land was opened to cultivation and added to the tax rolls, increments which the provinces rarely recorded in their reports to the capital.

However, as we shall see, it is evident that provincial and local tax collections retained their flexibility and flourished with the increasing size of the national product. Yet from the point of view of possible economic development as opposed to maintenance of an economic equilibrium, these new resources were completely neutralized. It remained an ideological possibility, even though remote, within the central government bureaucracy that Legalist *raison d'état* might be revived and motivate programmes for economic development. To a limited extent this was done by the 'self-strengtheners' of the late nineteenth century, such as Li Hung-chang, Chang Chih-tung and Sheng Hsuan-huai, by the 'reformers' of 1898, and by the late-Ch'ing reform movement after 1901. But local administration was pre-eminently the home of the Confucian 'general will' until nearly the end of the dynasty. This was broader and more diffuse than the interests of the bureaucratic state *per se*, and reflected the preoccupation of the local elite with maintaining unchanged a society that was truly theirs. These people had been educated in and sustained by the Confucian ideal of rule by moral example. Although the 'general will' was increasingly penetrated by anti-imperialist nationalism after 1900, this did not extend to an acceptance of the fiscal burdens of economic development. No effective initiatives for economic change could be expected here. Hence my attention in what follows to the disabilities of the central government – a weak branch to be sure, but none other offered even a foothold.

The statutory receipts recorded by the Peking government did not change significantly between 1712 and the third quarter of the nineteenth century. (For selected years the total central government receipts were: 1725, 36,106,483 taels; 1753, 39,767,292 taels; 1812, 43,343,978 taels; 1841, 38,600,750 taels. Land tax supplied 75 to 80 per cent of the total. Provincial and local collections, however, continued to increase notwithstanding the freezing of land tax rates by the K'ang-hsi Emperor. Three principal devices were utilized to enlarge actual collections beyond the nominal quotas due to the central government. The first was a 'meltage' fee (*hao-hsien*), in theory assessed to compensate for remittances in silver of less than the required purity and for losses in melting and casting silver ingots. In practice these losses were minimal; the meltage fee was in fact a tax increase beyond the rates sanctioned by K'ang-hsi. In 1724, this surtax received formal imperial recognition and in part was remitted to Peking for payment to officials as an annual bonus to 'foster their honesty' (*yang-lien*), that is to compensate for inadequate salaries. The bulk of the collection, however, remained outside Peking's control. Secondly, local officials added a conventional sum for expenses of collection to the bill submitted to taxpayers. The third device was the relative freedom with which local magistrates set the exchange rates between nominal assessments in grain or silver and the number of copper cash per picul of grain or tael of silver which they would accept in full payment of the tax due.

In the mid-nineteenth century two major sources of revenue were added to the traditional land tax, salt gabelle and customs duty. The establishment of the foreign-operated Imperial Maritime Customs after 1854 regularized the collection of duties on foreign trade and channelled these receipts to the Peking government rather than to the provinces. The second new impost, in contrast, was almost entirely outside Peking's control. This was the likin (*li-chin*) which was originally instituted by provincial officials to finance their campaigns against the Taipings. It was first levied in 1853 in Kiangsu as an internal transit tax on grain passing through the Grand Canal. By 1862 it had been applied to nearly all commodities and had been adopted by nearly every province. In some cases likin was collected not only along the route of transit but also as a production tax at the point of origin or as a sales tax at the destination. The rate varied widely, from 1 to 10 per cent *ad valorem*, with the most common rate about 2 per cent at each tax barrier. Of the likin collections on merchandise reported annually by the provinces to the Hu Pu (Board of Revenue), only about 20 per cent was disposed of by the central government, the balance remaining under the *de facto* control of the provinces. The unreported collection, of unknown size, was also of course retained locally.

In addition some small and temporary increases in receipts from the salt gabelle and miscellaneous taxes were realized as a result of constant prodding by the Hu Pu in the 1870s and 1880s to meet the costs of a continuing series of crises: rebellion in Central Asia, the Ili dispute with Russia, the Sino-French War, floods and famines. The nearly doubled imperial revenue of the 1880s and 1890s as compared with mid-century receipts was, however, almost entirely accounted for by maritime customs duties and likin. For the immediate financing of such emergencies as Tso Tsung-t'ang's military expeditions and 'pacification' of the north-west, to which the traditional fiscal system was incapable of responding rapidly, the government was forced to turn to foreign loans (see chapter 4). Before 1894 nine loans totalling 40 million taels were concluded, mostly for military expenses. These funds were advanced by foreign firms in the treaty ports, not by foreign governments. By the outbreak of the Sino-Japanese War 33 million taels in principal and interest had been repaid, largely from maritime customs revenue.

Table 21 shows estimates of Peking's revenue from all sources and of the major items of expenditure in a typical year in the early 1890s. The revenue figures do not represent actual remittance of tax receipts to the capital; they are the amounts reported to the Hu Pu yearly (in two instalments). They were then stored in money or in kind in the several provincial treasuries to await allocation by the Hu Pu. No composite budget of income and expenditure was prepared by the central treasury. (One of the unrealized projects of the reformers was the establishment of a regular national budget.) Rather, items of recurring expenditure had gradually come to be charged piecemeal against the yields of specific taxes in particular provinces. Eventually one part of the reported total was retained by the provinces to cover local civil and military expenses for the ensuing period, a second portion was remitted to Peking (or elsewhere at the direction of the Hu Pu), and in some cases a third part was transferred as grants-in-aid to other provinces. The fiscal system was oriented to short-range operations and the weight of traditional practices made it incapable of responding rapidly to emergency needs. As a result of the Taiping and other mid-century rebellions Peking's control of the revenue sources of the empire had been weakened and the fiscal system was severely strained. In contrast to the last seventeen years of the dynasty, however, with the assistance of new revenues the government's civil and military expenditures until 1894 were met without major borrowing from abroad, and the normal income was stretched to amortize the costs of the relatively modest foreign loans that were made. Little, of course, was realized from the substantial investment in a modernized navy and foreign-style armies, as the meagre results of the pre-1895 *yang-wu* (foreign matters) military and industrial projects testify.

TABLE 21

Estimated annual revenue and expenditure of the central government
in the early 1890s (K'u-p'ing or treasury taels)

Revenue	
land tax	25,088,000
grain tribute	6,562,000
salt gabelle (including salt likin)	13,659,000
likin on merchandise	12,952,000
maritime customs (1893)	21,989,000
native customs	1,000,000
duty and likin on domestic opium	2,229,000
miscellaneous taxes, sale of degrees, 'contribution', etc.	5,500,000
Total	88,979,000
Expenditure	
central government administration, imperial household, stipends to Manchu garrisons	19,478,000
maritime customs administration	2,478,000
public works	1,500,000
modernized armies, coastal defence	8,000,000
defence of Manchuria	1,848,000
civil and military administration of Kansu and Central Asia	4,800,000
Northern Fleet	5,000,000
Southern Fleet	5,000,000
railway construction	500,000
grants-in-aid to Kwangsi, Kweichow and Yunnan	1,655,000
Provincial administration, provincial troops	36,220,000
Principal and interest payments on foreign loans	2,500,000
Total	88,979,000

Source: George Jamieson, *Report on the revenue and expenditure of the Chinese empire.*

As already noted, the revenue reported annually to Peking represented only a portion of the total tax collection of the empire. The share of the potential fiscal resources of the country which the central government could control was largely inelastic. It had no chance to increase revenue from the growth of foreign trade, because tariff rates could not be changed without the unanimous consent of the treaty powers, and it had only a limited ability to manipulate the salt gabelle and various minor taxes. Several estimates of total national tax revenues have been made; while none is more than an intelligent guess so far as the absolute total is concerned, collectively they are strong evidence that the total annual tax collection at all levels in the last decade of the Manchu dynasty was more than twice the amount reported to Peking. A recent examination of the provincial *Ts'ai-cheng shuo-ming-shu* (Descriptions of financial administration), which are the reports of the Financial Reorganization Bureaux set up by imperial decree in each of the provinces in 1909, suggests that the total tax revenue for 1908 was 292 million taels.[34] H. B. Morse in his account of revenue and expenditure in *The trade and administration of the Chinese empire* offers a minimum total of 284,154,000 taels for the early 1900s apportioned as follows: imperial administration, 99,062,000 taels; provincial administration, 142,374,000 taels; local administration, 42,718,000 taels. Finally, the imperial 'budget' for 1911 prepared by the Tzu-cheng yuan (Consultative Assembly) estimated total central and provincial income at 301,910,297 taels (including, it may be noted, likin collections of 44,176,541 taels which should be compared with the 12–15 million taels reported annually by the provinces, and non-tax revenues of 92 million taels). In contrast to Meiji Japan, where the land-tax revision of 1873 brought the major revenue sources of the country under the direct control of the new central government, the late-Ch'ing government was ideologically and politically incapable of extending its control of the revenue.

If we assume that total collections in the latter part of the dynasty were about 250 million taels and that Peking's share came to 100 million taels, what part of the national income was available for government expenditure? Only the crudest estimate is of course possible in the absence of reliable national income data. If Chang Chung-li's 'rough estimate of the annual gross national product in the 1880s' is adjusted for its understatement of the agricultural product, GNP in the late-nineteenth century may have been about 3,338,757,000 taels (see table 1 above). Total government revenue would then come to 7.5 per cent of GNP and the Peking government's share to 3 per cent.[35] These proportions are, as I have acknowledged, subject to a very wide margin of error. With this caveat in mind, it is instructive to note that proportions of this general order of magnitude for the share of government consumption in GNP are also to be found in several Western European countries and in the United States in the mid-nineteenth century.[36] Economic development in these less 'backward'

---

34 Yeh-chien Wang, *Land taxation in imperial China, 1750–1911*, 73–83.
35 Government revenue or expenditure in my estimate includes some part of the share which Chang attributes to gentry services.
36 Simon Kuznets, *Modern economic growth: rate, structure, spread*, 236–9.

countries was set in motion without any major direct assistance from the government budget.

The contrast with China of course lies in the greater quantity and quality, within the Western governments' total consumption, of expenditures for health and education and for general administrative, legislative and adjudicative services (including commercial and marketing services) which fostered a climate in which the private sector could profitably invest in new enterprises. China's problem was thus not only that a manifestly small proportion of GNP was subject to government control, and that only 40 per cent of even that total was available to the central authorities. Of equal and perhaps greater consequence was the fact that almost all of the increase in central government expenditure was for military purposes, mainly to suppress internal rebellion but also in response to a number of minor external crises. This was so even though this expenditure doubled in the course of the nineteenth century – compare table 21 with the examples cited of annual receipts for selected earlier years. Government services, such as they were, were not significantly augmented; nor was there any important departure from their traditional limitation, which was the maintenance of order and the collection of taxation with which to support the emperor and his bureaucracy. Perhaps the Ch'ing government – aroused now by anti-imperialist nationalism – after 1900 was ideologically prepared to do more. But both political weakness and fiscal stringency kept actual expenditures on such items as the new school system and industrial promotion to a low level.

After 1895 the triple demands of indemnity payments, servicing large foreign loans, and military expenditure wrecked the rough balance between income and outlay which Peking had precariously maintained until that time. Even as the prevalent ideological note was changing from 'exalt agriculture and disparage commerce' to 'enrich the nation and strengthen its military power', the imperial government was without the facilities to reverse the largely passive economic role it had hitherto assumed, even if it had wanted to do so. And despite the rise of nationalism, conservative resistance to change including modern economic growth remained strong until the end of the dynasty.

Between 1894 and 1911 the Ch'ing government contracted for loans from foreign lenders amounting to 746,220,453 *k'u-p'ing* taels. Of this total 330,587,160 taels was accounted for by loans for railway construction which were to be repaid from the revenue of the lines themselves. While the several contracts granted the foreign mortgagees *de facto* operating privileges and handsome commissions on the purchase of material, repayment of principal and interest on the railway loans did not represent a direct burden on the ordinary budget of the central government. Relatively small amounts were borrowed for industrial purposes (25,517,349 taels), to finance telegraph lines and equipment (5,452,783 taels), and for miscellaneous uses (647,812 taels). The industrial loans consisted mainly of advances by Japanese creditors to the semi-official Hanyehping Coal and Iron Co. Hanyehping was unable to repay these loans and fell deeper and deeper into debt to the lenders, thus providing the pretext for the inclusion of formal recognition of Japanese control over the company in the Twenty-one Demands of 1915.

Apart from the large sums for railway construction, the funds were borrowed principally for the military costs of the Sino-Japanese War (119,838,648 taels) and to finance the large war indemnity which China was required to pay to the victor (263,176,701 taels). These totals include several short-term advances; the seven major long-term military and indemnity loans are shown in table 22. Payment of principal and interest on these loans required an annual outlay of some 20 million taels in addition to the normal annual expenditure summarized in table 21. From where did these funds come? All but two of the loans in table 22 were entirely secured on the maritime customs revenue. The Arnhold Karberg loan of 1895 was secured as a first charge on the salt likin of Kiangsu and as a second charge on the customs revenue. The 1898 Anglo-German loan was secured on the unencumbered portion of the customs revenue (which in view of the earlier loans was small in 1898) and on the revenue of seven salt and likin collectorates in the Yangtze basin which were placed under the supervision of the Inspector-General of Customs. This, however, is only the beginning of the matter. Customs revenue between 1890 and 1900 remained fairly stable at about 22–3 million taels per annum. Its allocation to service the foreign debt left the Hu Pu with a substantial deficit in its regular accounts – at least 16,700,000 taels in 1900 according to the Board's estimate. Ultimately the loan payments were made by increasing salt prices several times, reducing some salaries and emoluments, raising the tax on domestic opium, increasing market taxes and other miscellaneous levies, enlarging slightly the likin remitted to Peking, and so on – all traditional measures, and each the result of a protracted negotiation with the provincial authorities. The payments were made as scheduled, but until 1902 the fiscal system was in chaos. Of some interest is an attempt to float a public domestic loan – China's first – in 1898: 100 million taels of 'Sincerity Bonds' paying 5 per cent and redeemable in twenty years were offered. Perhaps as much as 10 million taels' worth of bonds were sold before cries of extortion by the local elite and merchants brought the experiment to a close. There was little public confidence in the 'full faith and credit' of the Ch'ing government and no banking system to absorb government bonds at a huge discount as was so often done in the Republican era.

TABLE 22

Military and indemnity loans, 1894–8

	Face amount (in *k'u-p'ing tael equivalents*)	Underwriter	Security
7% Silver Loan of 1894	10,000,000	Hongkong and Shanghai Bank	maritime customs
6% Sterling Loan of 1895	18,653,961	Hongkong and Shanghai Bank	maritime customs
6% Gold Loan of 1895	6,217,987	Arnold, Karberg & Co. (for National Bank für Deutschland)	Kiangsu salt likin/ maritime customs
6% Gold Loan of 1895	6,217,987	Cassel Bank	maritime customs
4% Gold Loan (Franco-Russian) of 1895	98,968,370	Syndicate of Paris and St Petersburg banks	maritime customs
5% Sterling Loan (Anglo-German) of 1896	97,622,400	Hongkong and Shanghai Bank Deutsch-Asiatische Bank	maritime customs
4½% Gold Loan (Anglo-German) of 1898	112,776,780	Hongkong and Shanghai Bank/Deutsch-Asiatische Bank	likin/salt likin/ maritime customs
Total	350,457,485		

Source: Hsu I-sheng, *Chung-kuo chin-tai wai-chai shih t'ung-chi tzu-liao, 1853–1927* (Statistical materials on the history of China's foreign loans, 1853–1927), 28–31.

On top of the annual requirements for the service of the loans listed in table 22, from 1902 at least an equal amount had to be found to meet the annual Boxer indemnity payments. In the last years of the dynasty, loan service and Boxer payments together came to 46–7 million taels per annum. Part of the added outlay was obtained from increased customs revenue collections after the 1902 tariff revision and from the receipts of native customs stations placed under the Inspectorate of Customs by the Boxer protocol. It is instructive, however, that three-quarters of the Boxer payments until the fall of the dynasty were met by regular annual remittances by the provinces of land tax, salt and likin funds above the quotas shown in table 21. The extraction by Peking from the provinces – in spite of strong protests and without the inconclusive bargaining of 1895–1901 – of more than 18 million taels annually which had previously been outside its control was of course only possible in the extraordinary circumstances of a *de facto* occupation of North China by foreign armies. But this and the other funds raised more fitfully are evidence that the late-Ch'ing economy was not without some potential for savings. The missing factors were both the ideological sanction and the political power to mobilize this potential for productive investment.

A total of 476,982,000 taels in principal and interest was paid between 1895 and 1911 to foreign creditors on account of the Boxer indemnity and the three loans (Russo-French, two Anglo-German) from which the war indemnity to Japan was met. This represented a large net drain on China's available resources. (If the four military loans were included, payments would rise to 547,552,066 taels, but let us allow that military expenditure is an essential service and does not represent a net loss of resources in the sense that an indemnity does.) The sum of 476,982,000 taels is one-and-a-half times as much as the total amount borrowed from foreign lenders for railway construction before 1912. It is more than twice the size of the total initial capitalization of all the foreign, Sino-foreign and Chinese-owned manufacturing enterprises established between 1895 and 1913. Apart from the growth of maritime customs revenue in the dynasty's last decade, this enormous outflow of funds from the Chinese economy came ultimately from increased taxes on the population levied by local collectors and remitted to the central government for payment to foreign creditors.

The Ch'ing did not fall, however, primarily because the populace rose up against excessive taxation. Quite the contrary. By 1911 both its political and its fiscal resources were equally superficial and superfluous. When the Peking government after 1900 slowly began to break through the ideological resistance to engaging in 'national development' in its various aspects, it not only lacked the political control required (though it set out to get it); it was also saddled with foreign debts which pre-empted the fiscal resources with which it might have got started. But the process of acquiring these debts had been the blunt, educative instrument which had led the government to begin to broaden its objectives. So there is, perhaps, in all of this an element of tragic inevitability.

Slowly and on a very small scale, the 'traditional' Chinese economy had begun to change in the second half of the nineteenth century. The changes were not, however, of the kind to encourage the expectation either that the economic system would be radically restructured ('modernized', 'industrialized') with the mere passage of a few decades, or that the basically unaltered economy had a capacity to continue the growth along traditional lines which it had displayed until about 1800. The plain facts are that by the mid-nineteenth century, if not earlier, China's economy had reached the limits of development possible with the technology (mechanical and organizational) at its disposal, and that by 1911 very little new ('advanced', 'modern') technology had been imported and adopted or generated internally. Neither the state nor the private sector, moreover, was ideologically and fiscally competent to promote 'economic development' as a priority policy.

On the other hand, in spite of sectoral and local strains, by the end of the Ch'ing dynasty there was little to suggest that this economic system was in mortal agony, ripe to be overthrown and discarded. Much of the population lived close to – but still at a distance from, it is important to state – a minimum level of subsistence. Social disorder and class conflict were endemic. But rather than being symptoms of fundamental systemic malignancies, this turbulence seems to have oscillated in scope and intensity with the occurrence of temporary and largely random crises exogenous to the economic system itself: flood and drought, seasonal crop failures, banditry and civil war, foreign incursions, official corruption. Eventually, in the absence of technological advancements, the inexorable pressure of population on land could be expected to threaten the viability of the whole economy. A confrontation of this magnitude was, however, not yet on the agenda at the beginning of the twentieth century. In 'normal' years the population, rural and urban, could be provided for, however poorly.

As it happened the ideological and political components of the *ancien régime* collapsed and were discarded earlier than those that may be properly described as economic. When new political forces turned consciously to the task of economic development, they perhaps overconfidently assumed that the traditional economy too had been substantially undermined in the revolutionary century before 1949. They thought there was nothing inherent in the basic values or structure of the Chinese economy which would prevent rapid economic growth once the onerous fetters on the people's strength had been removed. That hope continues to haunt Peking.

CHAPTER 2

LATE CH'ING FOREIGN RELATIONS, 1866–1905

THE CHANGING CONTEXT

A new era dawned in Chinese foreign relations after 1861. Western belligerence had given way to moderation, and Chinese resistance to accommodation. Defeat in the two wars and the Anglo-French occupation of Peking climaxed by the burning of the Summer Palace in 1860 had shocked the more pragmatic Ch'ing officials into a realization that a new international situation had set in and that the contemporary Westerners were basically different from the barbarians who had disturbed China in earlier times. There was a growing feeling that 'the West wind is blowing East', and that it could not be stopped. It was therefore imperative that China accept this reality, however unpleasant. The more progressive scholars and statesmen resolved to honour China's treaty obligations, to modernize her diplomatic practice, to create Western-style industry and enterprises, and to employ foreigners to help manage the new situation. As a result, a proto-foreign office was established in 1861, a text on international law was translated in 1864, an imperial audience was granted to foreign diplomats without the kotow in 1873, and diplomatic missions were established abroad after 1876. By 1880 China had taken her place in the family of nations and learned to struggle for survival in a world of social Darwinism just like any other state. In form, the Confucian universal empire (*t'ien-hsia*) had been metamorphosed into a nation-state (*kuo-chia*), but in spirit the old Middle Kingdom world view still lingered. Torn between tradition and modernity, China went to war to defend Vietnam and Korea in the 1880s and 1890s, partly to fulfil her tributary obligations and partly to exert her suzerainty in the manner of Western colonial powers. When the wars were lost, the tribute system was shattered in theory as well as in practice, marking the total disintegration of the imperial tradition of foreign intercourse.

On the Western side, there was also a change of attitude, policy and power relationships among the leading states. Foreign governments and traders in the early 1860s were on the whole satisfied with the concessions of the recent treaties. Britain in particular had decided to curb her nationals' adventurous, expansionist tendencies lest she be drawn into administering a tottering Ch'ing empire. The Mutiny of 1857 in India, which demonstrated the extreme difficulty of governing Hindus and Muslims, was a sufficient lesson to London that Britain should not seek additional territorial possessions in the East. The new emphasis was to obtain political influence, economic privileges and strategic security without the burden and expense of a colony.[1] Hence British policy after 1861 was to support Chinese political stability and maintain British commercial pre-eminence by peaceful means – a marked departure from the forceful approach that had characterized the earlier confrontation. This policy of moderation, along with the rising assertiveness of other powers and the growing independence of other foreign diplomats in Peking, signalled the beginning, however imperceptible at the time, of the gradual decline of British domination of Western relations with China. While Britain continued to be paramount until the end of the century, she was slowly losing the indisputable position of leadership she had once commanded. During the generation after 1870, British interests were in fact threatened by Japan's extension of influence to Formosa (Taiwan) and acquisition of the Liu-ch'iu (Ryūkyū) and Bonin Islands, by Russian activities in Sinkiang, by the French annexation of Indo-China, and finally by the Japanese detachment of Korea which opened the door to the 1898 'Scramble for Concessions' in China.[2]

Late Ch'ing foreign relations must be examined both in the global context of intensified imperialism and shifting power configurations among the leading Western states and Japan, and also against the background of the progressive decline of Manchu rule and the disintegration of the imperial tradition of foreign intercourse.

FOREIGN RELATIONS, 1866–75

As China began a diplomatic modernization, Robert Hart, the young Inspector-General of Customs, and Thomas Wade, chargé d'affaires of the British legation, promoted the idea of 'progress', and under their influence the first Chinese mission was sent abroad.

The Pin-ch'un Mission, 1866

On 6 November 1865 Robert Hart submitted a memorandum to the Tsungli Yamen entitled 'Observations by an outsider' ('Chü-wai p'ang-

---

[1] Ronald Robinson, John Gallagher and Alice Denny, *Africa and the Victorians: the climax of imperialism*, 6, 8, 10–11, 471.
[2] L. K. Young, *British policy in China, 1895–1902*, 5, 7–13.

kuan lun'), in which he stressed the advantages of railways, steamships, telegraphs, mining and Western diplomatic practices. Tactfully he implied that acceptance of his advice would make China strong while rejection might turn her towards international servitude. 'The view of an outside observer is neither unconsidered nor coercive. What the foreign nations will demand in the future does not aim at hurting China; they merely hope that peace and friendship with her may be maintained.' Diplomatic representation abroad was considered by Hart as of 'paramount importance', because it would enable China to bypass the headstrong diplomats in Peking and make direct representations to foreign governments which were more fair-minded. This move would help China to preserve her independence and also 'constitute a tie which should bind her to the West so firmly and commit her to a career of improvement so certainly as to make retrogression impossible'.[3] Prince Kung found Hart 'quite capable of making vigilant examination of Chinese and foreign situations', but felt that his views could not be implemented for the moment.[4]

Following the Hart memorandum, Thomas Wade also presented to the Tsungli Yamen in 1866 a communication called 'A brief exposition of new ideas' ('Hsin-i lueh-lun'), expounding the usefulness of railways, telegraphs, mining, schooling, Westernized army training, and diplomatic representation. Wade warned that foreigners today were different from the barbarians of the past such as the Hsiung-nu, and unless China recognized this fact and sought progress along Western lines her fate would be sealed. In particular, diplomatic representation abroad would bring great benefits, for mutual communication would create a warm feeling between governments and forestall troubles. 'Even if [China] should be embroiled in a quarrel with a certain country, if she was in the right, other nations would of course come forward to assist her with good offices, if not with armed assistance.' Wade urged that China should not look to the past for guidance but to the future.[5]

As a consequence of these promptings, the Tsungli Yamen decided to send an informal exploratory mission to Europe under the guidance of Hart during his furlough in 1866. The mission was headed by Pin-ch'un, a 63-year-old ex-prefect and Hart's secretary for Chinese correspondence. Though Pin-ch'un was given a temporary third class civil service rank to

[3] Chinese text in Ch'ing-tai ch'ou-pan i-wu shih-mo (Complete record of the management of barbarian affairs). T'ung-chih period (hereafter IWSM-TC), 40.14-22. See also Robert Hart, 'Notes on Chinese matters', in Frederick W. Williams, Anson Burlingame and the first Chinese mission to foreign powers, 285.

[4] IWSM-TC, 40.10b.

[5] Chinese text in IWSM-TC, 40.22b-31b. The original English text is lost, but H. E. Wodehouse made a free translation from the Chinese text; see his 'Mr. Wade on China', The China Review, 1.1 (July-Aug. 1872) 38-44, and 1.2 (Sept.-Oct. 1872) 118-24.

add dignity to his mission, Prince Kung made it clear that it was not a formal diplomatic mission, but only an information-gathering junket to the West. Being unofficial, it would obviate touchy questions of protocol and avoid the high cost of a regular embassy. The mission visited London, Copenhagen, Stockholm, St Petersburg, Berlin, Brussels and Paris, and its novelty insured it a gracious welcome everywhere. Upon their return, members of the mission recorded detailed descriptions of what they had seen. Unfortunately, their observations were mainly limited to Western social customs, tall buildings, gaslights, elevators and machines; only in passing did they touch upon political institutions. The mission neverthe-less signified China's first effort towards dispatching embassies abroad, but establishment of regular legations had to wait until 1877.

The Burlingame Mission and the Alcock Convention

While Western governments followed a 'Cooperative Policy' at Peking in the 1860s, foreign traders and Old China Hands in the treaty ports increas-ingly clamoured for a more aggressive policy – to lay open all of China to Western commerce and promote 'progress' through adoption of railways, telegraphs, mining and other modern enterprises. Their pronouncements and the memoranda of Hart and Wade aroused fear in the Tsungli Yamen that the British were about to make new demands during the forthcoming treaty revision scheduled for 1868. The Yamen anxiously polled the power-ful provincial authorities for their views on issues that were likely to arise.

Tseng Kuo-fan, the leading statesman and governor-general at Nanking, suggested that China temperately but resolutely rejects all foreign demands regarding railways, telegraphs, inland navigation, transportation of salt in Chinese waters, and opening of warehouses, as these activities would harm the livelihood of the Chinese people. Mining, however, was potentially profitable and China might avail herself of foreign tools in the initial phase of operations. He believed that China should open diplomatic missions abroad when suitable men and funds were available, but he showed no concern about missionary activities, believing that their alternating periods of success and decline – according to the funds available – made them relatively ineffective and harmless.[6] Similar views were expressed by Li Hung-chang, governor-general of Hunan and Hupei, who was in touch with Tseng. Li attempted to calm the court's anxiety by pointing out the difference between treaty revision and peace negotiations: the former implied mutual discussion without the forcible imposition of one nation's demands upon the other; failure to reach an agreement would not bring

[6] *IWSM-TC*, 54.1–4, 18 Dec. 1867.

hostilities, whereas failure in the latter might. Hence in the forthcoming treaty revision there would be room for a dispassionate exchange of views without the risk of war.[7]

The Tsungli Yamen's fears were, in reality, unfounded as London looked without favour upon the Old China Hands' push for hasty 'progress' in China. In August 1867, Lord Stanley, the foreign secretary, assured Minister Rutherford Alcock in Peking that 'We must not expect the Chinese, either the Government or the people, at once to see things in the same light that we see them; . . . we must lead and not force the Chinese to the adoption of a better system.'[8]

The Tsungli Yamen, not having diplomatic agents in London, had no inkling of the British policy, but common sense suggested the application of the old principle of playing off the barbarians against one another. Prince Kung and Wen-hsiang invited the retiring American minister, Anson Burlingame, who had offered to act as if he were China's envoy if needed, to join a roving diplomatic mission to dissuade European and American governments from forcing the pace of Westernization in China. Burlingame readily accepted: 'When the oldest nation in the world, containing one-third of the human race, seeks, for the first time, to come into relations with the West, and requests the youngest nation through its representative, to act as the medium of such change, the mission is one not to be solicited or rejected.'[9]

Accompanied by a Manchu and a Chinese co-envoy,[10] Burlingame led the mission to the United States in May 1868. His eloquence and charm captivated the Americans and, after a flattering interview with President Andrew Johnson, he signed a treaty with Secretary of State Seward on 28 July 1868. It committed the United States to a policy of noninterference in the development of China, and stipulated the sending of Chinese consuls and labourers to the United States and reciprocal rights of residence, religion, travel and access to schools. Though Burlingame acted on his own authority, without the prior approval of the Chinese government, Peking was too grateful to disown the treaty.

In London, the mission was received by Queen Victoria. Lord Clarendon, foreign secretary, assured Burlingame on 28 December 1868 that provided China observed her treaty obligations faithfully, she was 'entitled to count upon the forebearance of foreign nations' and that Britain had 'neither a desire nor intention to apply unfriendly pressure to China to induce her Government to advance more rapidly in her intercourse with foreign

[7] *Ibid.* 55.6–10, 31 Dec. 1867.
[8] *China correspondence*, no. 5 (1871), document 2, p. 8.
[9] *Foreign relations of the United States*, 1868, 1.494.
[10] Chih-kang and Sun Chia-ku.

nations than was consistently with safety, and with due and reasonable regards for the feelings of her subjects.'[11] Alcock was informed of this assurance and was instructed to act accordingly in his forthcoming negotiations for treaty revision.[12]

Having secured the British promise, Burlingame moved on to Berlin, where he obtained from Bismarck a pledge that the North German Confederation would deal with China in whatever manner Peking considered in its best interest. After all these successes, Burlingame contracted pneumonia at St Petersburg and died on 23 February 1869. The mission, however, continued on to Brussels and Rome and returned to China in October 1870.

Burlingame's mission was successful in its immediate objective for it did commit Western powers to a policy of restraint in the forthcoming treaty revision, yet, in the long run, it encouraged the growth of conservatism in China. The mandarins, who spent 160,000 taels on the mission, came to believe that foreigners could be managed at a price and became more complacent and less responsive to outside stimuli.

During the prolonged discussion of treaty revision, the British mercantile community vigorously promoted the opening of all China and demanded new concessions on telegraphs, railways, mining, inland navigation and residence. Alcock firmly resisted their pressure and conducted the negotiations in a spirit of moderation and conciliation. In this he was strongly supported by Clarendon and by the influential under-secretary of the Board of Trade, Louis Mallet, who, in a lengthy position paper on 19 May 1869, favoured a 'safe course' in China to consolidate the position already gained, and the use of moral influence, moderation and patience to achieve future developments.[13] On 4 June 1869 Clarendon practically authorized Alcock to accept any arrangement satisfactory to the Chinese and 'wait for a more favourable and complete revision of Treaties' in the future: 'Her Majesty's Government are content that you should agree to accept what you can obtain at once.'[14]

The actual negotiations were conducted as between equals, without military threats, for the first time since the Opium War. The resultant Alcock Convention of 23 October 1869 allowed China to establish a consulate at Hong Kong; to increase the import duty on opium by 2.5 per cent *ad valorem* and the export duty on silk by a fraction over 1 per cent; and to

[11] *China correspondence*, no. 1 (1869). Correspondence respecting the relations between Great Britain and China, document 1, The Earl of Clarendon to Mr Burlingame, 28 Dec. 1868.
[12] *Ibid.* document 2, Clarendon to Alcock, 30 Dec. 1868.
[13] *China correspondence*, no. 5 (1871), Correspondence respecting the revision of the Treaty of Tientsin, document 107, p. 355.
[14] *Ibid.* document 117, Clarendon to Alcock, 4 June 1869.

qualify the most-favoured-nation arrangement so that the British must accept the conditions under which certain rights were granted other powers, if they wished to claim the benefits of those rights. Other provisions included the opening of Wenchow and Wuhu and the closing of Kiungchow on Hainan which was useless; an additional 2.5 per cent transit duty on British textile imports at the port of entry; foreign navigation on inland waterways in traditional Chinese boats owned by foreigners; steam navigation on Poyang Lake; a conditional and qualified right of foreign temporary residence in the interior; and Chinese assent to adopt a written code of commercial law. All in all, the terms of the convention demonstrated mutual concessions.

The Tsungli Yamen was of course proud of this first equal agreement and considered it final when both sides signed it. Ratification by London was regarded as a formality, since no previous treaties with foreign powers were unratified. Therefore, the Yamen urged the court to approve the convention quickly, especially in view of the growing British mercantile hostility towards the agreement.[15]

Alcock himself was highly satisfied with the results of his work. To Clarendon he proudly stated: 'I believe it [the Convention] will be found to secure advantages far in advance of the objects contemplated in the XXVII [or revision] Article of the Treaty.' That he could have achieved these results, Alcock acknowledged, was due in no small part to the mediatory service of Robert Hart: 'I believe it was mainly through his active intervention that they [the Yamen ministers] were at last led to see the expediency, if not advantage, of ceding many points previously insisted upon, and offering me terms I felt justified in accepting.'[16] With pride Alcock proclaimed that 'We are no longer dictating conditions of peace, but negotiating for reciprocal advantages upon an equal footing'.[17]

However, the British mercantile communities, both at home and in China and Hong Kong, scorned Alcock's diplomacy and scoffed at the idea of treating China 'as a country entitled to the same rights and privileges as civilized nations'.[18] They strenuously opposed the terms of the convention, especially the Chinese consul at Hong Kong, whom they saw as a revenue officer and a spy. Numerous memorials were sent to Parliament arguing against the ratification of the agreement.[19] Reinforcing the mercantile

15 *IWSM-TC*, 68.14–14b, 23 Oct. 1869.
16 *China correspondence*, no. 1 (1869), Alcock to Clarendon, 28 Oct. 1869.
17 *China correspondence*, no. 5 (1871), p. 360, Alcock to Medhurst, 1 April 1869.
18 Stanley F. Wright, *Hart and the Chinese customs*, 382.
19 Texts of these memorials may be found in *China correspondence*, no. 4 (1870), no. 6 (1870). They were presented by merchants and others in London interested in trade with China, and Chambers of Commerce from Glasgow, Leith, Edinburgh, Dundee, Manchester, Macclesfield, Shanghai, Foochow and Hong Kong.

opposition were unfavourable foreign attitudes. Except for the American chargé d'affaires, Dr S. Wells Williams, who praised the convention as 'a victory of peace', most other diplomats were cool and non-committal.

In the face of such adverse reactions, Alcock defended the agreement forcefully, pointing out that 'no country or Western government has ever before made such liberal concessions to foreign trade' and that China had granted greater religious toleration and a more moderate tariff than most European states.[20] Yet these arguments could not outweigh the combined force of strong mercantile opposition and lukewarm foreign attitudes. Lord Granville, foreign secretary after Clarendon, decided that ratification of the convention would increase rather than decrease misunderstanding and friction, and accordingly rejected it on 25 July 1870. This was an act undoubtedly detrimental to both Chinese and foreign interests.

The Tsungli Yamen felt betrayed in its trust in foreign goodwill and friendly international relations. The feeling was common among its negotiators that foreigners only took but never gave and that the minute a treaty slightly unfavourable to them was negotiated they disowned it. According to Thomas Wade who succeeded Alcock as minister, Wen-hsiang was 'thirsting for revenge because of the discredit and inconvenience our rejection of the Convention has occasioned, . . . the difficulties of the legation are infinitely multiplied by the rejection of the Convention of 1869'.[21] Yet in its report to the court on the British rejection of the agreement, the Yamen was surprisingly mild and devoid of bitterness:

It is true that in foreign political systems, the government's authority is weak while the merchants' influence is strong. . . . We have told him [Wade] in sharp, reproving language that if the new agreement is not implemented, Chinese and foreign traders and people will have no faith in future transactions, etc. . . . We [the Yamen] suspect that the large items wanted most by foreigners such as telegraph lines, railways, transportation of salt, and mining have been rejected by China, and even those items agreed to [made them feel] that their gains cannot compensate for their losses. Hence their dilatory tactic.[22]

The restraint exhibited by the Yamen was obviously part of a double-barrelled tactic. To the Chinese it played down the importance of the rejection of the convention,[23] but to the foreigner it played up the dire consequences of British bad faith. Clearly, there was no point in the Yamen

[20] *China correspondence*, no. 10 (1870), Memorandum by Sir R. Alcock on 'Further memorials respecting the China Treaty Convention', 3 May 1870, p. 9.
[21] Nathan A. Pelcovits, *Old China hands and the Foreign Office*, 104, citing FO, 17/654, 16 May 1873.   [22] *IWSM-TC*, 79.40–40b, 21 Jan. 1871.
[23] Apart from the Yamen report just cited, there was a conspicuous absence of reference to the British rejection of the Alcock Convention in court documents such as the *Veritable records* (*Shih-lu*) and the *Tung-hua lu*, and works of leading statesmen such as Tseng, Tso, Li, Wen-hsiang, Wo-jen, Shen Pao-chen, Feng Kuei-fen and Wang Chih-ch'un.

publicizing the failure of its policy of international conciliation, but demonstration of disappointment to foreigners served the purpose of putting them on the defensive.

It would be an overstatement to suggest that the rejection of the Alcock Convention ended a decade of goodwill between China and foreign powers, and gave rise to a wave of anti-foreignism in the 1870s. Anti-foreign riots had occurred before 1869, while Chinese disappointment following the British rejection was limited to a small circle of officials without much public awareness. Pragmatic officials such as Tseng Kuo-fan and Li Hung-chang continued to behave responsibly in their foreign dealings. Anti-foreign riots were mostly instigated by gentry who knew little about the British rejection. Hence it is hard to establish a direct link between the rejection and anti-foreignism; but it is certain that the British action confirmed the Chinese view that foreigners were greedy in nature and fickle in behaviour. If the Burlingame Mission heightened Chinese complacency, the rejection of the Alcock Convention reaffirmed Chinese suspicion of foreign trustworthiness. Both events had an adverse effect on Sino-Western relations.[24]

The Tientsin Massacre, 1870

Even as Burlingame was touring the United States, inviting missionaries to 'plant the shining cross on every hill' in China, anti-Christian activities broke out across the country. Christianity, as a heterodox faith, was antithetical to Confucianism, and its practice of mixed congregations ran counter to Chinese custom and aroused rumours of immoral and perverted behaviour (see volume 10, chapter 11). Missionary protection of Chinese converts and the construction of churches in disregard of time-honoured concepts of geomancy (feng-shui) irritated Chinese sensibilities.[25] Anti-Christian tracts appeared frequently and eruption of anti-missionary activities under gentry instigation was common. These activities elicited a ready reprisal from foreign representatives who felt, as did Rutherford Alcock, that failure to act would result in a 'serious loss of prestige and influence, on which everything depends in the East'. Thus in August 1868, when a mob in Yangchow plundered and set fire to the new missionary station of the China Inland Mission, Alcock sent Consul W. H. Medhurst

[24] Mary C. Wright, The last stand of Chinese conservatism: the T'ung-chih restoration, 1862–1874, 299: 'As the recapture of Anking and the founding of the Tsungli-yamen had symbolized the beginning of the Restoration, so the rejection of the Alcock Convention and the Tientsin Massacre symbolized its end.'
[25] For an excellent study of the missionary problem, see Paul A. Cohen, China and Christianity: the missionary movement and the growth of Chinese antiforeignism, 1860–1870, chs. 3–7.

and four ships to Nanking to force Governor-general Tseng Kuo-fan to cashier the Yangchow officials and pay compensation. Again, in November 1868, when a mob in Taiwan attacked foreign merchants in an effort to break the camphor monopoly, British interpreter John Gibson and Lieutenant T. P. Gurdon blew up the Chinese military installations at Anping and exacted 40,000 taels. Such actions produced quick results but invariably inflamed public feeling and aroused xenophobia. Even London found the Alcock–Medhurst action contrary to British policy and condemned the Gibson–Gurdon move as 'reprehensible' and 'rash and inexcusable'.[26]

In 1870, Tientsin was the site of a major anti-Christian riot. It is not by chance that Tientsin was the scene of the outburst, for it had twice been occupied by foreign troops – during the negotiations of the Treaties of Tientsin in 1858, and the Conventions of Peking in 1860. Even after the peace settlement, portions of the Anglo-French forces remained in Taku until 1865. The presence of foreign troops was always a cause of irritation, and additional fuel came from the French seizure of the imperial villa[27] in Tientsin in 1860 for use as a consulate. In 1869, the church and orphanage of Notre Dame des Victoires was constructed on the site of a razed Buddhist temple. As few Chinese would send orphans to the foreign establishment, the nuns offered a premium for each child, thereby encouraging rascals, known as 'child brokers', to kidnap children. The offer of a premium and the high mortality rate – the nuns were particularly interested in baptizing sick and dying children – inevitably aroused suspicion. Rumour spread that behind their high walls and closed gates, the foreigners bewitched the children, mutilated their bodies, and extracted their hearts and eyes to make medicines.

In 1870, Ch'ung-hou, superintendent of trade for the northern ports, inspected the orphanage and found no truth in the wild charges. Then the truculent French consul, Henri Fontanier, and his chancellor suddenly appeared armed with pistols and demanding justice for the nuns. Angry at the sight of the mob which the magistrate had been unable to disperse, Fontanier fired a shot which missed the magistrate but killed his servant. In retaliation the mob killed Fontanier and his assistant, and burned the church and orphanage. Ten nuns, two priests, two French officials and three Russian traders were killed, and four British and American churches were destroyed. This crisis summarily dispelled a decade of goodwill and cooperation. Foreign gunboats quickly anchored off Tientsin, and strong

[26] John K. Fairbank, 'Patterns behind the Tientsin massacre', *HJAS*, 20.3–4 (Dec. 1957) 482–3, 488, 501.
[27] Known as the 'Sea-viewing Pavilion', or 'Wang-hai lou'.

protests from seven foreign ministers were lodged with the Tsungli Yamen, demanding redress and punishment of the rioters.

The court appointed its most venerable servant, Tseng Kuo-fan, now governor-general of Chihli, to investigate the case. Ill and aged, Tseng accepted the strenuous assignment only to find the situation far knottier than he had anticipated. The French chargé d'affaires demanded the lives of the vigorously anti-foreign General Ch'en Kuo-jui and the Tientsin prefect and magistrate, while conservative Chinese officials and literati clamoured against any concession or appeasement. In this precarious situation, Tseng showed great integrity and courage. Rather than cater safely to public sentiment he risked his political future with the candid recommendation that the absolute truth of the case be established. He advised the court that Britain, the United States and Russia be indemnified first to dissociate them from the French cause. Tseng then visited the orphanage and learned first-hand from the children there that they were not kidnapped but had been sent by their families voluntarily. He asked the court to restore the reputation of the nuns by issuing a proclamation denying the rumours of cruel treatment of the children.

For the settlement of the case, Tseng recommended dismissal of the taotai, the Tientsin prefect and the district magistrate; capital punishment for fifteen chief instigators and banishment for twenty-one others. If this did not satisfy the French, Tseng stated, greater punishment might be imposed.

The conservatives immediately condemned Tseng as a traitor. The Hunan Association in Peking burned his calligraphy which had adorned its wall, and Grand Secretary Wo-jen ridiculed the idea of bargaining with the French about the penalty. The court, too, found Tseng's recommendations hard to accept. At this juncture, Li Hung-chang, governor-general at Wuchang, submitted a more palatable solution, suggesting capital punishment of eight and exile of twenty. Li was transferred to Tientsin to take over the investigation and Tseng was sent to Nanking as governor-general. Overwhelmed by a sense of personal inadequacy and hounded by the conservatives' accusations, Tseng lapsed into despondency. He wrote to friends, 'I fear public criticism without, and am conscience stricken within.'

French bellicosity in China was providentially tempered by the outbreak of the Franco-Prussian War in Europe. Li Hung-chang speedily settled the case, agreeing to pay a compensation of 400,000 taels, to send a mission of apology, to banish the Tientsin prefect and magistrate, and to sentence eighteen rioters to capital punishment and twenty-five to hard labour on the frontier. The apology mission, led by Ch'ung-hou, reached

France only to find the French government too involved in the Prussian War to receive it. The Tsungli Yamen then ordered Ch'ung-hou to return home. When he had reached New York, however, Ch'ung-hou was summoned back to France, where the provisional president, M. Thiers, received him at Versailles on 23 November 1871 and announced that France was not interested in decapitating the Chinese wrongdoers, but in securing lasting peace and order. The case was officially closed with Thiers' acceptance of the letter of apology from the Chinese emperor.[28]

The Audience Question, 1873

Even though foreign diplomats took up residence in Peking in 1861, they were continuously denied audience with the boy emperor. Prince Kung received them in his capacity as semi-regent and explained that an audience was inadvisable during the emperor's minority. Though they agreed that there was little point in demanding a meeting with a five-year-old emperor, the foreign representatives argued that repeated delay of the audience was an act of unfriendliness. Chinese postponement was due, of course, to the knowledge that foreigners would not perform the kotow, thus denying the myth of China's universal overlordship and the ancient tributary practice.

The Tsungli Yamen's tactics put off but did not solve the question of audience. Therefore, during the secret discussion of treaty revision in 1867, the Yamen solicited views on the question from leading provincial authorities. The majority were content to sidestep the issue until the emperor's majority. Li Hung-chang declared that contact with Prince Kung was sufficient access to the throne and that foreign representatives could gain nothing through personal audience with the emperor. As to the ceremonies for audiences following the emperor's majority, he suggested foreign ministers should be allowed to perform such rituals as they would before their own rulers. Tseng Kuo-fan asserted that just as the K'ang-hsi Emperor (1662–1722) had treated Russia as an enemy state on an equal footing rather than as an inferior, dependent state, the court should also regard foreign ministers as envoys from enemy states of equal status exempt from Chinese customs. A number of conservative officials, however, argued that China should not change her institutions and practices to suit the convenience of foreigners.

In 1872 the emperor reached his majority and was married, but no foreign diplomats were invited to the celebration; this avoided protocol problems. In February 1873, he inaugurated his personal rule and foreign

[28] Knight Biggerstaff, 'The Ch'ung-hou mission to France, 1870–71', *Nankai Social and Economic Quarterly*, 8.3 (Oct. 1935) 633–47.

representatives renewed their demand for an audience. Unable to defer the issue longer, the Tsungli Yamen conducted protracted discussions with the diplomats as to the proper rituals and finally agreed that foreign representatives should simply bow instead of kotow during the audience.

On Sunday 29 June 1873, the foreign diplomats convened at 5.30 a.m. but were not received by the T'ung-chih Emperor at the Pavilion of Violet Light until 9.00 a.m. The Japanese foreign minister, Soejima Taneomi, who was in Peking to exchange ratifications of a treaty of 1871, took this opportunity to demonstrate his mastery of Western diplomacy and assert Japanese equality with the Western powers by insisting that his ambassadorial rank entitled him to precede the Western ministers. He was therefore received first, followed in order of seniority by the Russian, American, British, French and Dutch ministers and the German interpreter. They laid their credentials on a table before the emperor, who expressed, through Prince Kung, his amicable feelings towards the foreign sovereigns represented there. The audience, for which Western diplomats had waited twelve years, took no more than half an hour.[29] It was an anticlimax, the more so when the foreign representatives later learned that the pavilion in which they had been received was also used for the reception of tributary envoys.[30]

The Margary Affair, 1875

The great depression in Europe in the early 1870s, brought on partly by the tariff war there, adversely affected the China trade, which declined steadily after 1872. To brighten trade prospects, the British revived a scheme to open a back door to interior China by constructing a railway and trade route from Burma to Yunnan and the upper Yangtze.

Captain Richard Sprye, a retired Indian army officer, had first proposed the idea in 1858 as a means to counter the Russian advance from the northwest and the American move across the Pacific. London was unimpressed but Sprye, undaunted, repeated the proposal to each new foreign secretary. Lord John Russell, foreign minister in 1859, remarked, 'Captain Sprye is a visionary who indulges in the wildest notions . . . there is a certain degree of interest attaching to his schemes but they are impracticable.'[31] The foreign office believed that such a back-door thrust would create troubles without a compensating commercial benefit. In 1874, the idea was revived

---

[29] British parliamentary papers, China, no. 1 (1874): Correspondence respecting the audience granted to Her Majesty's minister and the other foreign representatives at Peking by the emperor of China.

[30] Such as in 1839–43, 1845–8 and 1864. See John K. Fairbank, ed. The Chinese world order: traditional China's foreign relations (hereafter CWO), 262.

[31] Pelcovits, Old China hands, 115, citing FO 17/470, 22 Nov. 1859.

as Lord Salisbury, the only high official to fancy the project, became head of the India office in the Disraeli ministry. He ordered the Indian government to survey the proposed route and requested the foreign office to instruct the minister in Peking to seek Chinese permission for the entry of an exploratory mission from Burma.

Though sceptical of the commercial possibilities of such a route, Thomas Wade found the Chinese government readily assented to his request and agreed to let a British vice-consul, 28-year-old Raymond Augustus Margary, travel up the Yangtze River to meet the mission. Aware of the hostility to foreigners of guerrilla bands in the Chinese–Burmese border area, and despite warnings from local Chinese officials, Margary ventured on to Bhamo on the frontier to await the mission from Burma. There, on 21 February 1875, Margary was ambushed and killed.

Though international law relieves the host country of responsibility when a foreigner exposes himself to danger at his own risk, the British government obdurately held the Chinese government responsible and instructed Wade to obtain redress. The ambitious Wade demanded an investigation of the murder, an indemnity for the bereaved family, another expedition, and trial of the acting governor-general of Yunnan and Kweichow in whose jurisdiction the incident took place. He also raised the extraneous issues of audience procedure, transit dues, better etiquette in the treatment of foreign diplomats, and an apology mission to Britain. Peking agreed to an investigation and an indemnity but frowned on the other questions. Wade then impetuously withdrew his legation to Shanghai and, amidst rumours that he had entered into a pact with the Russian minister engaging a British army from India and a Russian force from Ili, he threatened to break off relations.

To avoid a rupture, on 29 August 1875 the court authorized the dispatch of an apology mission to Britain headed by Kuo Sung-tao, and sent Robert Hart to Shanghai to persuade Wade to resume discussions. When Hart tactfully intimated that Kuo might initiate settlement proceedings in London, excluding Wade from all claims to credit, the British minister agreed to meet with Li Hung-chang at the summer resort of Chefoo. On 13 September 1876, the Chefoo Convention was concluded to settle the Margary case. Part I dealt with the dispatch of an apology mission to Britain and the payment of 200,000 taels to the bereaved family. Part II provided for the preparation of an etiquette code for the Chinese government and foreign diplomats. Part III dealt with the opening of four new ports and the limitation of likin-free areas to treaty ports. However, the British government failed to ratify this convention until 1885 due to opposition from: (1) the United States, Germany, France and Russia, who criticized Britain's unilateral action; (2) the British mercantile community, which sought complete abolition of the likin; and (3) the Indian government, which protested against the increase in the opium tax.

The most significant outcome of the Margary incident was the dispatch of the mission of apology, which became the first resident Chinese legation abroad. Kuo Sung-tao, a progressive sixty-year-old friend of Li Hung-chang, was given the title of vice-president of the Board of War prior to his departure for Britain. After the presentation of the emperor's letter of apology to Queen Victoria on 8 February 1877, he set up the Chinese legation in London. In the next two years, other legations were established in Paris, Berlin, Spain, Washington, Tokyo and St Petersburg. By 1880 China had belatedly taken her place in the family of nations.

China's slowness in reciprocating the Western practice of diplomatic representation may be attributed to several causes. Institutionally, she had never dispatched permanent, resident embassies abroad but only *ad hoc* missions, which were sent out either in times of strength and prosperity to spread the prestige of the Son of Heaven and to bring outlying states into the tributary system, or in times of weakness and disorder to beg for peace or alliance with barbarian tribes. Psychologically, the majority of mandarins eschewed foreign affairs as beneath their dignity, and foreign assignment as a form of banishment. Burlingame's two associates had fared badly after their return: one was sent to an obscure post in western China, and the other to the Mongolian frontier, as if they had been contaminated by their foreign trip. To the question 'Who among men of rectitude today excels in foreign affairs?' a grand secretary replied: 'Do men of rectitude care to engage in foreign affairs?'[32] The censors, the Hanlin scholars and the conservative gentry and officials repeatedly proclaimed that historically barbarians were transformed by Chinese ways, not the Chinese by barbarian ways. They promoted conservatism against modernization and condemned foreign association as disgraceful. So powerful was the conservative atmosphere and the psychological inertia that it had taken China more than fifteen years to overcome this barrier and reciprocate the Western practice of diplomatic representation.

ACCELERATION OF IMPERIALISM IN FRONTIER AREAS AND TRIBUTARY STATES

The last three decades of the nineteenth century were a period of accelerated foreign imperialism in China. Europe, experiencing 'a generation of

[32] Immanuel C. Y. Hsu, *China's entrance into the family of nations: the diplomatic phase 1858–1880*, 202.

materialism', was propelled by the forces of nationalism, evangelism and capitalism into heightened activity in Asia, Africa and the Middle East. Industrialization created a need for raw materials and overseas markets, and Social Darwinism sanctioned expansion as a struggle for survival among nations. Religious fervour fired devotees with the sense of a divine mission to evangelize the heathen. And to all this was added the proud, self-righteous feeling of racial superiority, expressed as the 'White Man's Burden'.[33]

Epochal events of the 1860s – the end of the Civil War in the United States, the Meiji Restoration in Japan, the rise of the Third Republic in France, and the unifications of Italy and Germany – liberated energies for action abroad. The completion of the Suez Canal in 1869 further facilitated European expansion, and newly modernized nations – notably Japan and Germany – joined the imperialist ranks. In contrast, China under the Empress Dowager Tz'u-hsi made little headway in self-improvement and regeneration; after a brief upsurge during the T'ung-chih period (1862–74), dynastic strength steadily declined. Taking advantage of China's weakness, foreign powers nibbled away the frontier areas and tributary states.

Formosa (Taiwan) and Liu-ch'iu (Ryūkyū)

Japan had been a tributary state of China for a time during the Ming period (1368–1643), when the shogun Ashikaga Yoshimitsu accepted tributary status in order to enrich his coffers from trade. After the middle of the sixteenth century, however, nationalistic Japanese statesmen found such relations humiliating and discontinued official contact with China. After the establishment of the Ch'ing dynasty in 1644, official relations were still not resumed; the Manchu rulers, unlike the Ming emperors, never attempted to bring Japan into the tribute system.

With the opening of China and Japan in the mid-nineteenth century, Japanese traders began to arrive in Shanghai on British and Dutch ships. By 1870, the Meiji government had decided to establish official relations with the Ch'ing dynasty and sent Yanagiwara Sakimitsu to Peking to seek a treaty. The Tsungli Yamen, though inclined to permit trade, was reluctant to sign a formal treaty. Conservative officials opposed treaty relations with a former tributary state because it might set a precedent for other tributaries such as Korea and Annam (the Chinese name for Vietnam). They cited further the past records of Japanese piracy along the China coast and the Japanese arrival at the time of the Tientsin Massacre as proof

---

[33] Carlton J. H. Hayes, *A generation of materialism, 1871–1900*. William L. Langer, *The diplomacy of imperialism, 1890–1902*.

of their desire to take advantage of China. On the other hand, progressive officials like Li Hung-chang and Tseng Kuo-fan favoured treaty relations. Li said that Japan, though a tributary state of the Ming, was never a Ch'ing tributary; thus her status was basically different from that of Korea and Annam. That Japan sought official relations without an introduction by, or the aid of, a Western power, showed her independence and goodwill, and China should not begrudge her the request. Furthermore, the existence of large Chinese communities in Japan, China's importation of a considerable quantity of copper from Japan annually, and Japan's very proximity, led Li to recommend the establishment of equal treaty relations. Tseng concurred in these views and stressed, in addition, the reciprocal nature of Sino-Japanese trade as opposed to the largely one-sided Sino-Western trade. He approved of treaty relations but recommended withholding most-favoured-nation treatment.

On the strength of these recommendations, the court authorized the conclusion of a commercial treaty with Japan on 24 July 1871, which provided, among other things, for (1) nonaggression towards the other's territorial possessions; (2) a mutual offer of good offices in case of conflict with a third power; (3) mutual consular jurisdiction; (4) trade under a tariff in treaty ports only; and (5) no appointment of Japanese merchant consuls in China.

In 1873, the Japanese foreign minister Soejima Taneomi came to Peking, ostensibly to exchange ratifications, but actually to participate in the T'ung-chih audience and to determine China's position on the Formosa incident. By capitalizing on this incident, which concerned the killing of fifty-four shipwrecked Ryūkyūan sailors by Formosan aborigines late in 1871, Japan attempted to assert her exclusive right to speak for the Ryūkyūans. The question of Ryūkyū's status, which had been ambivalent for two-and-a-half centuries, was thus thrust to the fore.

Ryūkyū (Liu-ch'iu in Chinese) had been a regular tributary of China since 1372. During the Ch'ing it paid tribute every other year and, with Korea and Annam, was one of the three most important tributary states. In 1609, unknown to China, the Satsuma *han* (feudatory) of Japan subjugated Liu-ch'iu, putting the northern part under its direct administration and leaving the southern part to the Liu-ch'iu king. As a vassal, Liu-ch'iu paid tribute annually to Satsuma and periodically to the shogunal court at Edo (Tokyo). Eager to reap the benefits of the mainland trade, however, Satsuma directed Liu-ch'iu to continue its tributary relations with China. Satsuma determined Liu-ch'iu's royal succession but allowed Chinese investiture missions to confirm the legitimacy of a new king's rule. During the Ch'ing period a total of eight such missions visited Liu-ch'iu, the last in

1866, and during their stays Satsuma took great care to remove evidence of the Japanese presence. Although members of the Chinese missions could not fail to note traces of Japanese influence, the Ch'ing court officially knew nothing of Liu-ch'iu's double status and treated it as an exclusively Chinese tributary state.[34]

Thus, when Soejima asserted the right to speak for Liu-ch'iu in 1873, the Tsungli Yamen pointedly told him that as the islands were a Chinese tributary and Formosa part of China, the killing of sailors of one by aborigines of the other was no business of Japan. Moreover, as China had never interfered in the internal affairs of the aborigines, she could not be held responsible for their behaviour. Soejima argued that sovereignty over a territory was evidenced by effective control; since China did not control the Formosan aborigines, they were beyond her jurisdiction and any action by Japan to chastise them would not violate Chinese jurisdiction. The Japanese government then decided to send an expedition, and in April 1874 the Office of the Formosan Expedition was formed, with Ōkuma Shigenobu as director and Saigō Tsugumichi as commander of the expeditionary force. This move was in keeping with the Meiji foreign policy of expansion along Western imperialist lines, and served to divert domestic demands for representative assemblies and satisfy the clamour of ex-samurai for an expedition to Korea.

Faced with the Japanese invasion, Peking ordered Shen Pao-chen, director of the Foochow Dockyard, to defend Formosa. Shen found effective defence impossible – for example, the guns cast by the Nanking Arsenal could only fire salutes and would burst when real explosive shells were used. An early attempt at settlement failed when Saigō refused to honour the agreement and on 10 September 1874 the home minister, Ōkubo Toshimichi, arrived in Peking to direct negotiations.

Ōkubo repeated the argument that absence of effective Chinese administration on Formosa proved that China lacked sovereignty, and the Japanese landing, consequently, could not be construed as an invasion of Chinese territory. Prince Kung insisted that Sino-Japanese relations be governed, not by the general principles of international law, but by the treaty of 1871, which specifically stipulated nonaggression against each other's territorial possessions. Ōkubo retorted that the treaty concerned only Chinese–Japanese relations, not the Formosan aborigines who were beyond Chinese jurisdiction. A diplomatic impasse ensued and the British minister, Thomas Wade, offered to mediate. The case was finally settled when China agreed to pay half a million taels ($US750,000) of which

[34] Robert K. Sakai, 'The Ryūkyū (Liu-ch'iu) Islands as fief of Satsuma', and Ta-tuan Ch'en, 'Investiture of Liu-ch'iu kings in the Ch'ing period', in *CWO*, 112–34, 135–64.

100,000 taels was for the Ryūkyūan victims and 400,000 taels for the purchase of Japanese barracks constructed on Formosa. In addition, China agreed not to condemn the Japanese action – a concession which implied recognition of Japan's claim to sovereignty over Ryūkyū. China's willingness to pay for being invaded – as the British minister in Japan, Sir Harry Parkes, sarcastically described it – was a blatant revelation of her weakness and an invitation to further foreign encroachment. In 1879 Japan annexed Liu-ch'iu and renamed it Okinawa Prefecture.

The Ili Crisis, 1871–81

Ili, or Kulja in Russian, was a Chinese prefecture (*fu*) governing nine cities in northern Sinkiang near the border of Russian Turkestan (see volume 10, chapter 2). The Ili valley was not only agriculturally and minerally rich but also strategically important – its Muzart Pass controlled communication with southern Sinkiang. Possession of Ili facilitated control of all Sinkiang, and Western military experts described Ili as the fortress of Chinese Turkestan. A place of such importance naturally attracted the attention of strong neighbours. In 1851 the Russians had secured the Treaty of Kulja which allowed them to establish consulates and conduct duty-free trade at Ili and Chuguchak (Tarbagatai) on the Mongolian border. The Ili trade grew rapidly and the continuous expansion of the Russians in Central Asia brought them ever closer to Ili. Taking advantage of a Muslim rebellion in Sinkiang in the 1860s, the Russians were ready to move into this important area.

The Muslim Rebellion in Sinkiang had its roots in the corrupt local Ch'ing administration (see chapter 4). Since its conquest under the Ch'ienlung Emperor in 1759, Sinkiang had been governed as a military colony under the direction of a military governor at Ili, aided by a number of assistant military governors, imperial agents and some 21,760 troops at various key points. The high officials and officers were nearly all Manchus and bannermen, who ruled the populace – mostly Turki-speaking, turban-wearing Uighur Muslims – through local chieftains known as begs. The Manchu conquerors treated the subject Muslims as uncivilized aborigines, levying heavy taxes and exacting forced contributions to support their own unbridled extravagance. Muslim discontent inspired revolt, and the former hereditary and saintly rulers, or khojas, banished by the Ch'ing to Khokand, were ever anxious to re-establish themselves. The khojas of the Āfāqī line of the Makhdūmzāda family had once ruled Kashgaria (southern Sinkiang) before the Ch'ing conquest. They encouraged their co-religionists in Sinkiang to revolt, while they themselves organized

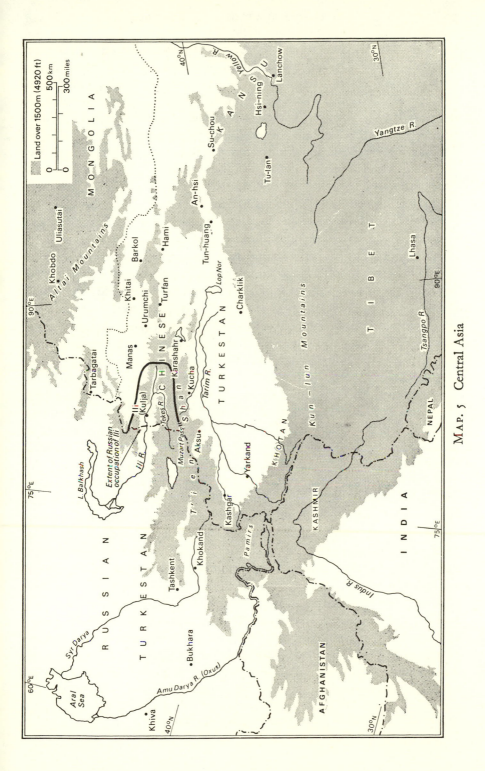

MAP. 5 Central Asia

invasions. During the century following the Ch'ing conquest, no less than a dozen uprisings and invasions took place. In 1864, amid the dynastic decline and a Muslim rebellion in North-West China, the Muslims in Sinkiang struck again. The local Ch'ing administration was too weak to suppress them, while the central government in Peking was too preoccupied with the Taiping, the Nien and other rebellions to undertake punitive measures (see volume 10, pages 74ff, and below, chapter 4).[35]

During the disorder, Ya'qūb (Yakub) Beg (1820–77), a Khokandian general, entered Sinkiang in 1865, and through a series of military and political manipulations established himself by 1870 as the ruler of Kashgaria and part of the northern Sinkiang. The British in India, with a view to blocking the extension of Russian influence, encouraged his empire-building and sent missions to cultivate friendship and supply arms.

The Russians viewed these developments with concern. They considered Ya'qūb's empire to be an extension of British influence, which when viewed in the larger context of Anglo-Russian rivalry in the Near East and Central Asia, took on added political significance. Moreover, the turmoil in Sinkiang had adversely affected the Russian trade and created unrest among the Kazakhs and the Kirgiz and other minorities in Russia. The Russian army, the bureaucrats and the bourgeois press all clamoured for a permanent occupation of Ili, but the government decided to occupy it only until Chinese authority was re-established in Sinkiang and then return it in exchange for new trade routes to Western China and certain 'rectifications of the border'.[36] In July 1871 General K. P. von Kaufman, the first governor-general of Russian Turkestan, sent troops to occupy Ili.

St Petersburg tried to create the impression that the Russian stewardship of Ili was an act of kindness to China during a period of disorder, but it was obvious that Russia believed the effete Ch'ing could never recover Sinkiang. To perpetuate disorder and prolong their occupation of Ili, the Russians signed a commercial treaty with Ya'qūb in 1872; the British followed suit a year later. Both countries granted him recognition in exchange for trade privileges.

Before they could reach Ya'qūb, the Ch'ing had to suppress the Muslim Rebellion in Shensi and Kansu. In 1866 the court appointed Tso Tsungt'ang governor-general of Shensi and Kansu with the specific assignment of suppressing the rebels there. However, before he assumed command, he was transferred to fight the Nien. After pacifying the Nien Rebellion in 1868, Tso assumed his earlier assignment, and by efficient leadership, good

[35] Immanuel C. Y. Hsu, *The Ili crisis: a study of Sino-Russian diplomacy, 1871–1881*, 18–22.
[36] A. L. Narochnitskii, *Kolonial'naia politika kapitalisticheskikh derzhav na dal'nem vostoke, 1860–1895* (The colonial policies of the capitalist powers in the Far East, 1860–1895), 207, 210–13.

strategy and hard campaigning, crushed the rebellion in these two provinces in 1873. Just as Tso's army was poised to strike into Sinkiang, the Formosan crisis with Japan arose as noted earlier, and China's weakness as revealed in the settlement pointed to the urgent need for coastal defence. The nation faced the vexing problem of whether it could support a bold naval programme simultaneously with a costly Sinkiang campaign. A grand debate ensued.

Maritime defence versus frontier defence

Prince Kung and Wen-hsiang were the first to express alarm at the inadequacy of the coastal defence after a decade of self-strengthening. They warned: 'If we continue to drift along passively and do not eagerly seek to improve ourselves and forge ahead, trouble in the future will be even more difficult to meet.' High officials on the coast proposed the creation of a navy consisting of forty-eight ships, divided into three squadrons and stationed on the North, Central and South China coasts. The threat of Japan, they felt, was more immediate than that of Russia. Li Hung-chang, leading spirit of this group, boldly asked the court to cancel the Sinkiang campaign and shift its funds to naval defence.

The advocates of maritime defence advanced five arguments: (1) frontier defence was not as important and urgent as maritime defence because of Peking's proximity to the coast and Sinkiang's distance from the capital; (2) financial exigency and the uncertainty of victory in Sinkiang compelled re-examination of the advisability of that campaign; (3) the barren land of Sinkiang was not worth the high cost of recovering it; (4) surrounded by strong neighbours, Sinkiang could not be effectively defended for long; and (5) to postpone its recovery was not renunciation of territory conquered by former emperors, but simply a sensible way of preserving strength for the future.

Many other officials, however, while not disputing the importance of naval defence, argued that it should not be undertaken at the expense of frontier defence. If China failed to suppress the Sinkiang rebels, the Russians would continue their advance, and the Western powers might attack along the coast in response. Russia was a greater threat than Japan or the Western powers because of her common frontier with China – Russia could reach China by land as well as by sea, whereas Japan and the Western countries could reach her only by sea. They compared the Russian trouble to a sickness of the heart, and the Western threat to that of the limbs. Tso Tsung-t'ang, leader of this group, stressed that Western powers usually fought only for commercial privileges, whereas Russia sought both commercial and territorial concessions.

The advocates of frontier defence also presented five arguments: (1) Sinkiang was the first line of defence in the north-west: it protected Mongolia, which in turn shielded Peking; (2) the Western powers posed no immediate danger of invasion, but the Russian advance in Sinkiang was a prevailing threat; (3) the funds for frontier defence should not be shifted to coastal defence, since the latter had already been allocated its own standing fund; (4) the land conquered by the dynastic forefathers should not be given up; and (5) strategic spots such as Urumchi and Aksu should be recovered first. Tso warned that to halt the campaign now was to invite foreign domination of Sinkiang.[37]

The arguments of both groups were cogent and well reasoned. But there was no immediate trouble along the coast, while there was a rebellion in Sinkiang and a Russian occupation of Ili. Thus, though not giving up the naval programme, on 23 April 1875 the court appointed Tso imperial commissioner to conduct the Sinkiang campaign.

Tso absorbed himself in an elaborate preparation for the campaign and decided on the strategy of 'proceeding slowly but fighting quickly'. By early 1876 he was ready to strike, and in March moved his headquarters to the advanced post of Su-chou. General Liu Chin-t'ang struck hard and fast into Sinkiang, and by November had conquered its northern half. Ya'qūb, still established in southern Sinkiang, grew apprehensive and sent an emissary to London in late spring 1877 to seek British mediation, indicating his willingness to accept the status of a tributary to China. But Tso's army moved faster than discussions in London. Ya'qūb was soundly defeated and driven to suicide on 29 May 1877. His sons carried on the fight, but internecine strife precluded any effective resistance. By the end of 1877 all of Sinkiang had been recovered except for the small enclave of Ili, still under Russian occupation.

Having re-established the imperial authority in Sinkiang, China had fulfilled the Russian condition for the return of Ili. But as the Russian minister in Peking repeatedly postponed discussion of the issue, the Tsungli Yamen charged its recently established legation in Russia to negotiate for the return of Ili. The mission head, Ch'ung-hou, was given the title of imperial commissioner first class, which meant an ambassador authorized to act as he saw fit.

Ch'ung-hou and the Treaty of Livadia

The Russians were determined to make the most of the Ili situation. The government had been under pressure from the industrialists and business-

---

[37] Immanuel C. Y. Hsu, 'The great policy debate in China, 1874: maritime defense vs. frontier defense', *HJAS*, 25 (1965) 212–28.

men in the central provinces and the Urals to secure new trade routes to Mongolia, Kansu and Shensi, where British and American goods and competition were nonexistent. Such trading possibilities and mining rights in Western China where precious metals abounded were said to be enough to relieve the economic crisis in Russia, which was evident during 1873–6. Under the direction of the minister of war, a special committee was called to formulate her policy in China. It decided to demand, as the price for the return of Ili, the right of Russian caravans to enter the interior of China, cession of the Tekes valley and the Muzart Pass, amnesty for the population of Kulja, and several other conditions. However, General Kaufman's proposal to ask for a large indemnity to pay for the construction of the Central Asian railway was rejected.[38]

Ch'ung-hou (1826–93), a compliant Manchu noble of no great ability, was totally unprepared for his mission. Ignorant of the intricacies of international diplomacy and Ili's geography, he arrived in St Petersburg where Russian flattery apparently overwhelmed him and disarmed his vigilance. Moreover, he seemingly feared the awesome Russians and was eager to return home to tend to urgent family affairs. Ch'ung-hou hastily negotiated the Treaty of Livadia, which returned Ili to China in name but ceded seven-tenths of the area to Russia, including the strategic Tekes valley and the Muzart Pass. It awarded to Russia an indemnity of 5 million roubles, the right to consulates in seven key places, and navigation on the Sungari River to Petuna in Manchuria. When these terms were telegraphed to Peking, the astonished Tsungli Yamen cabled Ch'ung-hou not to sign the treaty. His curious reply was that the treaty had already been negotiated and the texts copied out; no change or renegotiation was possible. On 2 October 1879, on his own authority, he signed the treaty and returned home without imperial authorization.

Chinese officialdom received the news with consternation. The Tsungli Yamen insisted that this way of restoring Ili to China was worse than none. Tso Tsung-t'ang feared that the fruits of his arduous Sinkiang campaign were about to be snatched away by Ch'ung-hou's stupidity. He urged the court: 'We shall first confront them [the Russians] with arguments . . . and then settle it on the battlefields.'[39] On the other hand, Li Hung-chang, never sympathetic to the Sinkiang campaign or the policy of pressing Russia for the return of Ili, was only superficially critical of the treaty and did not advocate its rejection: 'The present mission of Ch'ung-hou had its origin in an imperial edict endowing him with full powers to act as he saw

[38] Narochnitskii, *Kolonial'naia politika*, 227, 231–3.
[39] Tso Tsung-t'ang, *Tso Wen-hsiang kung ch'üan-chi* (Complete collection of Tso Tsung-t'ang's papers), *Tsou-kao* (Memorials), 55.38.

fit. We cannot say that he had no power to negotiate a treaty settlement. If we give assent first and then repudiate it later, we are at fault.'[40]

Li was in the unpopular minority. The prevailing sentiment among scholars and officials was for war to avenge the humiliation, regardless of whether or not the country was ready for it. Countless memorials poured into the court demanding severe punishment of the signatory and rejection of the treaty. The most eloquent of these came from a young librarian of the Supervisorate of Imperial Instruction, Chang Chih-tung (1837–1909), who announced: 'The Russians must be considered extremely covetous and truculent in making the demands and Ch'ung-hou extremely stupid and absurd in accepting them . . . . If we insist on changing the treaty, there may not be trouble; if we do not, we are unworthy to be called a state.' He demanded that Ch'ung-hou be decapitated to show China's determination to reject the treaty, even at the price of war. Because he spoke the mind of the literati and officials, Chang gained immediate fame.[41]

The court appointed Marquis Tseng Chi-tse, minister to Britain and France and son of Tseng Kuo-fan, as head of a second mission to Russia to renegotiate the treaty. Meanwhile, Ch'ung-hou's death sentence met with strong protests from the representatives of Britain, France, Germany and the United States, who could not remain indifferent to the inhumane treatment of a brother diplomat. When Queen Victoria sent a personal plea to the empress dowager, Ch'ung-hou was given a reprieve on 26 June 1880, but kept in prison to await the outcome of the second mission. Dissatisfied with this partial concession, Russia refused to deal with Tseng until Ch'ung-hou was granted a full pardon.

Irritated by China's actions, Russia sent twenty-three warships to China as a naval demonstration. War seemed imminent; there was great fear of a Russian naval attack along the coast in concert with an army thrust from Siberia through Manchuria to Peking. The court did not intend to precipitate a clash, but was pushed by literati-official sentiment into taking a stronger position than it wanted. To prepare for the eventuality of war, it installed several Hunan army officers of Taiping fame in key positions, and through Robert Hart invited Charles Gordon to China to help with defence.

Gordon, former leader of the Ever Victorious Army, had been secretary to the viceroy of India since the spring of 1880; but finding the life of a desk officer 'a living crucifixion', he resigned, and two days later received the telegraphic invitation from Hart. Gordon seized the opportunity, and

40 *Ch'ing-chi wai-chiao shih-liao* (Historical materials concerning foreign relations in the late Ch'ing period, 1875–1911), 17.16–19 (hereafter *WCSL*).
41 *WCSL*, 18.18–22b, 16 Jan. 1880. For a study of the life of Chang Chih-tung, see William Ayers, *Chang Chih-tung*, and Daniel H. Bays, *China enters the twentieth century*.

after meeting with Li at Tientsin agreed that China should not drift irresponsibly into war. He warned that as long as Peking was the seat of government China could not afford to fight any first-rate power, for the Taku forts could easily be taken, rendering Peking indefensible. If China must fight, he said, the court should be moved to the interior and be prepared for a long war of attrition. Such blunt counsels were unwelcome in the belligerent atmosphere of Peking, but Gordon made a powerful case for the inadvisability of war. Li used him both to discourage the war party from a disastrous venture and to show Russia that China did not lack friends in her hour of need.[42]

Marquis Tseng and the Treaty of St Petersburg, 1881

As Gordon was counselling for peace in China, Marquis Tseng was preparing himself for the mission to St Petersburg. To avoid his predecessor's mistakes, he thoroughly planned his diplomatic strategy and studied the maps of Ili. Determined to hold firm on the boundary issue, bargain on the question of trade, and be conciliatory on monetary compensation, Tseng set out for Russia with assurance from the British foreign office of unofficial assistance, and the British ambassador at St Petersburg was instructed by London to offer him advice.

The Russians, who secretly feared war at this point, ostensibly refused to open negotiations at St Petersburg, insisting on moving the site to Peking as punishment for China's bellicose attitude. The Ch'ing court urged Tseng to use all means to keep the negotiations in Russia. The Russians finally acquiesced but negotiations progressed slowly. The Russians were in no position to wage a distant war, due to their depressed economy following the Turkish War of 1876–7 and their international isolation after the Congress of Berlin in 1878. The St Petersburg government was further restrained by fear of revolution at home, and concern that the adverse effect of war on trade might goad Europe and America into taking sides with China. Moreover, the liberal and the conservative press as well as a group of sinologists also urged a peaceful course of action.[43] The government wanted peace but could not find a graceful exit from the predicament. After nearly half a year of fruitless arguments, the tsar finally decided to end the dispute by agreeing to return all of Ili, including the Tekes valley and the Muzart Pass, except for a few villages in the western part for the settlement of those Muslim refugees who refused to return to China. The number of Russian consulates was reduced to two (Turfan and

[42] Immanuel C. Y. Hsu, 'Gordon in China, 1880', *Pacific Historical Review*, 23.2 (May 1964) 147–66.
[43] Narochnitskii, *Kolonial'naia politika*, 235–6. The sinologists included V. Vasil'ev, M. I. Veniukov and V. Radlov.

Su-chou), and the indemnity, dignified under the name of 'military compensation', was increased to 9 million roubles (about 5 million taels). These terms were incorporated in a new agreement, the Treaty of St Petersburg, on 24 February 1881.

The peace settlement, generally considered a Chinese diplomatic victory, left behind two important consequences. First, the thought of having won a round from a powerful Western state stimulated Chinese self-confidence and conservatism, in spite of Tseng's warnings against pride, optimism and arrogance. The literati, who irresponsibly expressed their chauvinistic views (ch'ing-i), were encouraged to believe that the victory resulted from their war cries, and became overconfident of their ability to untangle China's problems in foreign relations.

The second significant outcome was the new status of Sinkiang. Traditionally known as the Western Region (Hsi-yü), Sinkiang had never been an integral part of China but had remained a frontier area held by her when she was strong, lost when she was weak. After the Treaty of St Petersburg, the court accepted the recommendation of Tso Tsung-t'ang and turned Sinkiang into a regular province in 1884, with Liu Chin-t'ang, the brilliant young general who contributed much to its reconquest, as its first governor. This institutional innovation constituted a milestone in Chinese frontier history.[44]

The Sino-French War over Annam (Vietnam), 1883–5

Following the settlement of the Ili crisis, there arose the problem of French encroachment in the tributary state of Annam. Known in ancient times as Vietnam, Annam first came under Chinese influence in the third century BC, and its northern part was conquered during the reign of Han Wu-ti (140–87 BC) in 111 BC. Its Chinese name was derived from the An-nan ('south-pacifying') protectorate established during the T'ang dynasty (AD 618–907) to govern the area. Though independent after the fall of the T'ang, Vietnam remained under strong Chinese cultural and political influence, and was an important tributary state during the Ming and Ch'ing periods.

Western influence reached Vietnam with the Jesuits in 1615, but church work progressed slowly in this predominantly Confucian state. The French East India Company made an unsuccessful attempt to trade, but French influence began to rise by the end of the eighteenth century, when Nguyên Phúc Ánh, the lone survivor of the *ancien régime* overthrown in 1788, regained control of the country with the aid of French officers. He was

[44] Hsu, *The Ili crisis*, 189–96.

installed as Emperor Gia-Long of the Nguyên dynasty, which lasted from 1802 until 1945.

Gia-Long and his successors were conservative Confucianists, who countenanced xenophobic riots against missionaries and converts. Louis Napoleon, eager to build a French Indo-Chinese empire and pose as a champion of Catholicism abroad, sent troops to Saigon in 1859 to punish anti-missionary aggressors. A treaty, imposed on Vietnam in 1862, secured for the French an indemnity of $US4 million and the rights to trade, to propagate religion and to control Vietnamese foreign relations, as well as cession of three provinces in the south known as Cochin China. In 1874 a new treaty was signed which confirmed French possession of Cochin China and direction of Vietnamese (now called by the French Annamese) foreign relations, and authorized French navigation on the Red River in Tongking in the north. This document reduced Annam to a French protectorate, though nominally recognizing her independence. China, preoccupied with the Formosan crisis and the Margary murder case, took no positive action to stop the French advance but refused to honour the treaty of 1874 on the grounds that Annam was a Chinese dependency.[45]

The French intensified their activities in Annam, and by 1880 had stationed troops in Hanoi and its port Haiphong and established fortresses along the Red River. The Annamese government, to counter the French advance, strengthened its ties with China by sending tribute and by seeking the aid of the irregular Chinese Black Flag Army, which was established along the Sino-Annamese border. By 1882, the Black Flag Army had begun engaging French troops, and in the following year the Ch'ing court also quietly dispatched regular troops into Tongking.

Li Hung-chang, governor-general at Tientsin, warned against challenging France before the completion of the Chinese naval and coastal defence programme. He argued that China should fight only if attacked, but, as even this could prove disastrous, he favoured a quick settlement through negotiations. Prince Kung, head of the Tsungli Yamen and still the leading member of the Grand Council, agreed that China should not prematurely challenge a first-rate Western power.

The rise of the Ch'ing-i Party

The cautious attitude of Li and Prince Kung was attacked and ridiculed by a coterie of young officials who were brilliant scholars but who had little practical experience in or genuine knowledge of foreign and military affairs. By fervid memorials championing a belligerent course of action,

[45] For details of French activities see John F. Cady, *The roots of French imperialism in Eastern Asia*, ch. 16.

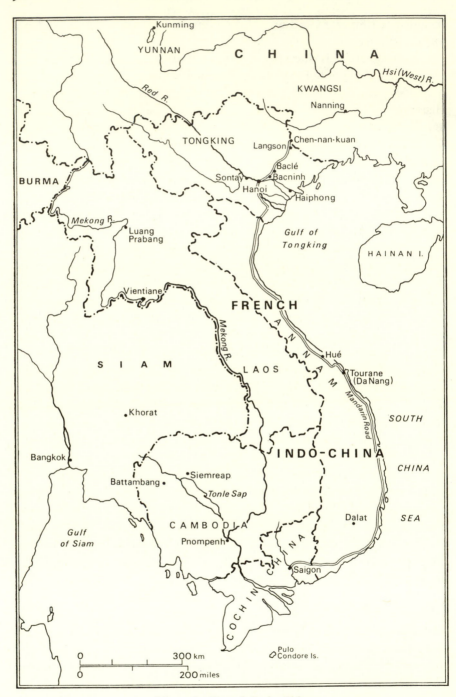

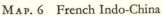

MAP. 6 French Indo-China

they won public acclaim and imperial attention. Calling themselves the party of the purists (Ch'ing-liu tang), they belittled France as a 'spent arrow', and condemned appeasement as encouraging greater demands from the insatiable enemy. War was won, they insisted, more by the human qualities of courage and virtue than by weapons, and Li Hung-chang was contemptuously compared to the notorious Sung traitor Ch'in Kuei (AD 1090–1155).[46]

Just as the Ch'ing-liu Party emphasized China's moral strength, so did Li stress her material weakness. But Marquis Tseng demonstrated a balanced grasp of the situation. Based on his understanding of France's domestic politics and international position, Tseng concluded that France could not afford a far-flung war. He warned Li against timidity in dealing with the French because: (1) they despised the weak and respected the strong. The more determined China was to fight, the greater the likelihood of peace. Indecision, procrastination and compromise could only lead to French gains, which would be difficult for China to recover later; (2) the French aspired after the coal mines in Kwangtung and the gold deposits in Yunnan; ceding Annam would not satisfy their appetite but would weaken China's southern defensive frontier; (3) the loss of Tongking would encourage Britain and Russia to covet Tibet and Korea; (4) the political instability in France and her isolated position in European politics would not permit her to wage a foreign war. For these reasons, Tseng warned against too much caution and urged a strong stance.[47]

The Ch'ing court vacillated between war and peace. Honour demanded the defence of a tributary, yet fear argued against fighting a leading Western power. A report from Robert Hart's agent in London, J. D. Campbell, led the court to believe that the French troops in Annam would not precipitate a full-scale war, and that the opening of Hanoi and the Red River to trade and navigation would remove the basic cause of contention. The court therefore instructed Li Hung-chang to open negotiations with the French minister. The first agreement, which would have made Annam a joint protectorate of China and France, was rejected by Paris, which then dispatched an expedition to Annam. Defeat of the Chinese troops in Tongking and fear of a French attack on China proper caused the empress dowager angrily to dismiss Prince Kung and four other members of the Grand Council and to order Li again to seek a settlement. The subsequent arrangement between Li and the French naval captain, F. E. Fournier, in 1884 called for Chinese recognition of all French treaties with Annam,

---

[46] Lloyd E. Eastman, 'Ch'ing-i and Chinese policy formation during the nineteenth century', *JAS*, 24.4 (Aug. 1965) 604–5.
[47] Hsiao I-shan, *Ch'ing-tai t'ung-shih* (A general history of the Ch'ing period), 3. 1070–1.

withdrawal of Chinese troops from Tongking, and a French promise of no demand for indemnity, no invasion of China, and no undignified reference to China in any future treaties with Annam. The agreement so inflamed the Ch'ing-liu Party that forty-seven memorials reached the court demanding Li's impeachment. Thus harassed, Li failed to report to the court the date stipulated by the Li–Fournier agreement for the withdrawal of Chinese troops from Annam.[48]

Having received no orders to withdraw, the Chinese troops in Tongking rejected French demands that they evacuate, and hostilities were renewed. Paris accused China of bad faith and sent an ultimatum on 12 July 1884 demanding a large indemnity and the immediate execution of the Li–Fournier agreement. Fearful of a French attack, the court at Peking transferred two leaders of the Ch'ing-liu Party to key defence positions: Chang Chih-tung became governor-general at Canton, and Chang P'ei-lun was put in charge of the Fukien fleet. On 23 August French ships under Admiral Courbet launched an attack at Foochow and, within an hour, sank or damaged eleven Chinese warships and destroyed the Foochow Navy Yard, built with French aid after 1866. Chang P'ei-lun was among the first to flee. His report to the court was so distorted with florid language that Peking thought that China had won a naval battle, but when the truth was learned, Chang was exiled to the frontier and the court declared war on France.

The peace settlement

The empress dowager supported war for three months, from August to November 1884, but in December she vacillated again as a result of her distress over the indecisive military outcome in Tongking, the French blockade of Taiwan, and the effort to stop tribute grain shipments from South China. The expected aid from Britain and Germany did not materialize; and there was also the threat of renewed Russian activities on the northern frontier and a Japanese advance in Korea. The desire for peace was reciprocated in France, where unstable political conditions and the difficulty of supporting a distant war began to weigh on the government. Peace arrangements were made secretly in Paris by Hart's London agent J. D. Campbell, and a major defeat suffered by French troops at Langson provided Peking with a face-saving opportunity to pursue peace and further dampened the war spirit in France. In June 1885, Li Hung-chang and the French minister in China concluded a formal agreement: China recognized all the French treaties with Annam, and France evacuated

<hr>

[48] Lloyd E. Eastman, *Throne and mandarins: China's search for a policy during the Sino-French controversy, 1880–1885*, chs. 4–5.

her troops from Taiwan and the Pescadores. No indemnity was paid, but China had expended in excess of 100 million taels and incurred debts of some 20 million taels.[49]

The indecision and vacillation of the court had proved disastrous. A firm war policy might have deterred French aggression and a persistent policy of peace might have spared the Fukien fleet and the Foochow Navy Yard. But ineffective leadership resulted in the destruction of both and the loss of the tributary status of Annam. The Ch'ing-liu Party must be held largely responsible by their emotional espousal of an unrealistic position.

The loss of Annam signalled the failure of the twenty-year-old self-strengthening movement. The limited diplomatic, military and techno-logical modernization had not strengthened the country to a point where it could resist foreign imperialism. China's weakness prompted the British to emulate the French and detach Burma by invasion in 1885. A treaty secured from China in 1886 reduced Burma to a British protectorate but permitted her to continue to pay tribute to Peking once every ten years. With the loss of these tributary states in the south, the fate of the leading tributary in the north-east, Korea, now hung in a delicate balance.

JAPANESE AGGRESSION IN KOREA

Korea, regarded by the Chinese as a valuable 'outer fence' of North China, was a leading tributary state during Ming and Ch'ing times. The Yi dynasty (1392–1910) annually sent three regular tribute missions to the Ming and four to the Ch'ing, and numerous smaller embassies. From 1637 to 1894, 507 Korean missions visited Peking and 169 Chinese missions travelled to Korea.[50] Living under the political and cultural shadow of China, Koreans modelled their institutions and way of life on the Chinese and described relations with China as 'serving the great' (*sadae*), as dis-tinguished from their more equal 'neighbourly relations' (*kyorin*) with Japan. Since 1637 Korea had maintained virtually no foreign intercourse other than tributary relations with China and occasional exchanges of delegations with Japan; she was known to Westerners as the Hermit Kingdom.

The opening of Korea

With the opening of China and Japan, Korea came under increasing Western pressure for trade, religious propagation and diplomatic relations.

---

[49] Shao Hsun-cheng, *Chung-Fa Yueh-nan kuan-hsi shih-mo* (A complete account of Sino-French relations concerning Vietnam [until 1885]).
[50] Hae-jong Chun, 'Sino-Korean tributary relations in the Ch'ing period', in *CWO*, 90–111.

But the Korean court had proscribed Christianity as a heterodox faith in 1786 and, apart from caring for the shipwrecked, refused any contact with the West. This intransigence intensified after the Taewŏn'gun (Grand Prince), father of the minor king Kojong, became regent in 1864. In February 1866, he renewed the persecution of Christians, which resulted in a massacre of foreign priests. In October, the French minister in China, without authorization from Paris, sent a punitive mission to Korea. The French forces captured Kanghwa at the river entrance below Seoul, but suffered a defeat outside the city and withdrew. In August of the same year, an American merchant ship, the *General Sherman*, arrived at P'yŏng'yang to demand trade with threats and gunfire. Behaving like a pirate, the ship was finally burned and its crew killed after it ran aground during low tide. In 1871 the state department authorized Frederick F. Low, minister in China, to investigate the case. He was accompanied by five naval ships. Refused negotiations off Kanghwa Island, the American expedition forced its way up the Han River leading to Seoul. When Korean shore batteries opened fire, the Americans retaliated, bombarding Kanghwa in full force. They then withdrew for lack of authorization to fight. The Koreans concluded they had won battles with both the French and the Americans.

The Tsungli Yamen, aware of China's inability to defend Korea, began in 1867 to advise Korea to reach an accommodation with the West. By 1879–80 the Chinese were urging Korea to enter treaty relations with the West in order to counter the rising influence of Japan.[51] Japanese relations with Korea, handled by the feudal lords of Tsushima during the Tokugawa period (1603–1867), came under the direct control of Tokyo after the Meiji Restoration in 1868. Missions dispatched to Korea to announce these political changes and revise relations were rejected by the Taewŏn'gun, who scorned Japanese modernization and viewed the assumption of the title 'Imperial Highness' by the Japanese emperor as improper.

In response to this insult, Japanese leaders decided to dispatch a punitive mission in 1873. This move would: (1) provide an outlet for disgruntled samurai and shift attention from domestic problems; (2) win for Japan a leading position in Asia by successfully challenging China's supremacy in Korea; (3) forestall British and Russian advances; and (4) revenge the failure of Hideyoshi's invasions of Korea in 1592 and 1597. However, Japanese leaders returning from the West reversed this decision on the grounds that the country's backward domestic conditions did not allow for a foreign venture.

Nevertheless, a surveying team, accompanied by gunboats, was dis-

---

[51] For a study of changing Chinese attitudes, see Mary C. Wright, 'The adaptability of Ch'ing diplomacy: the case of China's involvement in Korea', *JAS*, 17.3 (May 1958) 363–81.

patched in 1875. When attacked at Kanghwa Bay, the Japanese returned fire and destroyed the Korean forts. Following this victory, Tokyo sent six more ships to Korea and an emissary to Peking[52] to determine the Chinese response. The Tsungli Yamen, then involved in the Margary affair, timidly responded that Korea was tributary to China but had always been allowed complete freedom in her domestic and foreign affairs. Thus encouraged, Japan pressed for the opening of Korea, and the Ch'ing court, anxious to avoid a clash, instructed Korea to enter into negotiations. On 24 February 1876, the Japanese–Korean Treaty of Kanghwa was signed, stipulating: (1) recognition of Korea as an independent state on an equal footing with Japan; (2) exchange of envoys; (3) opening of three ports; and (4) Japanese consular jurisdiction in these ports. By not protesting Korean independence, China defaulted her claim to suzerainty.

Japan's action in Korea, followed by her annexation of the Liu-ch'iu (Ryūkyū) Islands in 1879, led to the Chinese decision that Korea should be opened to the West to check Japanese influence. Peking put Li Hung-chang in charge of Korean affairs to begin the opening of Korea to Western commerce and diplomacy. In 1882 he sent Ma Chien-chung and Admiral Ting Ju-ch'ang to Korea to introduce Commodore R. W. Shufeldt of the United States for treaty negotiations. On 22 May 1882, an American–Korean treaty was signed; the two countries agreed to exchange diplomats, to establish consuls at trading ports, and to treat each other as equals. The United States recognized Korean independence, but Korea issued a separate statement declaring her position as a dependency of China.[53] In subsequent years Korea signed agreements with Britain, France and Germany and, albeit tardily, began some modernization after the Chinese fashion.

Domestic insurrections and international politics[54]

After King Kojong began his personal rule in 1873, his queen of the influential Min family (and so called 'Queen Min') gained increasing power, which she exercised to support reform and to employ Japanese officers to train the Korean army. The Taewŏn'gun, determined to curtail her influence, capitalized on the discontent of dismissed soldiers and, in 1882, incited them to attack the palace and the Japanese legation. Queen Min narrowly escaped, while the legation was burned, seven Japanese officers

[52] Mori Arinori.
[53] Had this statement been included in the treaty, the US Senate would have refused ratification.
[54] For China's involvement in Korea during this period, see Wang Hsin-chung, *Chung-Jih chia-wu chan-cheng chih wai-chiao pei-ching* (The diplomatic background of the Sino-Japanese War).

were killed and the minister fled home; the Taewŏn'gun returned to power. Admiral Ting and Ma Chien-chung, arriving to investigate the situation, quickly took steps to prevent Japanese punitive action by arresting the Taewŏn'gun and sending him to China for detention. Acting on Ma's advice, the Korean king reached a settlement with Japan, agreeing to pay an indemnity of $US550,000, to send an apology mission, and to allow Japan to station troops and construct barracks at the legation. The establishment of Japan's right to send troops to Korea marked a significant victory for Japanese diplomacy.

After the insurrection of 1882, Li Hung-chang initiated positive efforts to strengthen China's position in Korea. China and Korea signed a commercial treaty, giving China extraterritoriality, and the Chinese granted loans and gifts of foreign-style guns to the Korean government. Li appointed a Chinese commercial agent to supervise Korean trade and assigned Yuan Shih-k'ai to train the Korean army. Paul George von Möllendorf, formerly in the Chinese customs service and then German consul at Tientsin, became customs commissioner and foreign affairs adviser in Korea. Six Chinese battalions were stationed in Korea to maintain order and guard against Japanese aggression.

Following 1882 the struggle mounted between pro-Chinese and pro-Japanese Koreans. The government was dominated by Yuan Shih-k'ai and the pro-Chinese groups, but the Japanese minister Takezoe Shin'ichirō sought to promote friendship and guide the pro-Japanese group led by Kim Ok-kyun. In 1884, when China, at war with France, withdrew three battalions from Korea, the pro-Japanese group attempted a coup on 4 December. Their troops broke into the palace, captured the king, and killed pro-Chinese officials. Yuan Shih-k'ai's forces soon overwhelmed the rebels and rescued the king, but Kim, the chief instigator, escaped to Japan.

Tokyo immediately dispatched an expedition and a high emissary (Inoue Kaoru) to Korea, demanding an indemnity, an apology and funds to reconstruct the legation. Another envoy, Itō Hirobumi, was sent to confer with Li Hung-chang who, preoccupied with the French war, compromised readily and agreed to a Sino-Japanese Tientsin Convention on 18 April 1885, which stipulated: (1) China and Japan would withdraw their troops from Korea within four months; (2) neither would train Korean troops, but would urge Korea to engage instructors of a third nationality; and (3) each would notify the other before dispatching troops to Korea, and upon the restoration of order would withdraw the troops at once. This agreement virtually reduced Korea to a co-protectorate of China and Japan, eliminated China's claim to exclusive suzerainty, and confirmed Japan's right to send troops to Korea.

Meanwhile, international rivalry intensified as Russia took Port Lazareff on the north-eastern coast of Korea and Britain seized Port Hamilton, an island in the south. Japan, recognizing the Western threat to her interests in Korea, adopted the policy of encouraging China to strengthen her control, thus curtailing other influences and ensuring that Japan would have only China to deal with in future Korean affairs. Unaware of this scheme, Li Hung-chang proceeded to strengthen China's grip by appointing Yuan Shih-k'ai Chinese Resident in Korea to direct all commercial and diplomatic affairs and supervise the domestic administration. Yuan quickly dominated the court, the customs, the trade and the telegraphic service, and became the most powerful man in Korea from 1885 to 1893. This period of Chinese supremacy in Korea coincided with rapid economic and military growth in Japan, and by 1894 Japan had modernized sufficiently to challenge China.

The already tense situation was exacerbated by the assassination in Shanghai of the pro-Japanese Korean leader, Kim Ok-kyun, in March 1894 by another Korean; his corpse was transported to Korea for mutilation as a warning to traitors. The Japanese considered the incident a direct affront, and though the foreign minister Mutsu Munemitsu argued that the killing of one Korean by another in China did not legally concern Japan, feelings ran high and secret societies such as the Genyōsha agitated for war. These groups encouraged the Tonghak Insurrection as an excuse for sending troops to Korea.

The Tonghak Insurrection, 1894

The Tonghak movement, originally religious in nature, became political as a result of official persecution. Its founder, Ch'oe Che-u (1824–64), a frustrated scholar distressed by official oppression and the progress of Christianity, established a cult of 'Eastern Learning' (Tonghak) which purported to be a mixture of the quintessence of Buddhism, Confucianism and Taoism. The Korean government banned it as heterodox and in 1864 Ch'oe was arrested, tried and decapitated. Forced to go underground, the sect gradually attracted men with political ambitions. In 1892, the Tonghaks petitioned for the lifting of the ban, but this was refused and their organization was ordered to be dissolved.

Shortly afterwards, the Tonghaks, aided by Japanese of the Genyōsha society, capitalized on a mass protest against official corruption to stage a rebellion. When the court requested Chinese aid, the Japanese minister encouraged Yuan to take positive action and implied that Japan had no intention of intervening. Li Hung-chang was lured into believing that Japan would not wage war, whereas Tokyo was fully prepared to act, and no sooner had the Chinese helped to crush the Tonghaks than 8,000

Japanese troops appeared. The Japanese demanded reform of the Korean internal administration, but, under instruction from Li, the Korean government responded that reform would be carried out after the withdrawal of Japanese troops.

The outbreak of war

Determined to find a diplomatic solution, Li hoped to win Western sympathies and force Japan into a peace settlement. When Russia failed to honour an understanding to intervene on China's behalf, Li turned to Britain for mediation. London had not anticipated this rapid turn of events and was caught without a suitable policy. Lord Rosebery, who took over the government after Gladstone in March, 'did not want an active situation in the Far East'.[55] What finally emerged was a mild innocuous proposal which called for a simultaneous withdrawal of Chinese and Japanese troops and the creation of a neutral zone around the Korean capital. The Japanese rejected the proposal as they also ignored an American plea for peace. Li's diplomatic efforts delayed China's military preparations; only when all hope of a settlement had faded did he authorize the dispatch of reinforcements to Korea. The Japanese learned of the convoy of reinforcements and on 25 July 1894 sank the British chartered steamer *Kowshing*, drowning 950 Chinese soldiers.[56] On 1 August China and Japan both declared war.

The war was, in effect, a contest between the two after a generation of modernization. On land, the Japanese defeated Li's Anhwei Army at P'yŏng'yang, set up a puppet government under the Taewŏn'gun, and declared Korea independent. At sea, although China boasted the larger fleet, not all of her ships were mobilized. Only Li's Peiyang fleet fought the Japanese; the Nanyang fleet and the two other provincial squadrons at Canton and Foochow remained 'neutral' for self-preservation. Furthermore, the Chinese ships, larger in tonnage than the Japanese, were older and slower and no match for the new and fast Japanese fleet. The two navies met on 17 September 1894 off the Yalu River in the Yellow Sea. Confusion plagued the Chinese forces from the first as the captain of the flagship countermanded the orders of his superior, Admiral Ting, regarding the fighting formation. When the first salvo from the flagship caused the bridge to collapse, wounding Admiral Ting and his British adviser, the flotilla was leaderless. A German adviser who was an army officer, assumed command but was ineffectual. After five hours of exchange, the Chinese

[55] Young, *British policy*, 16.
[56] The *Kowshing* was a British steamer chartered by the Chinese. Its sinking aroused some feeling in Britain but it was soon mollified by Japanese promise of reparation for the ship and assurance of the safety of British interests in China. See Young, *British policy*, 16.

had lost four ships and suffered casualties in excess of a thousand men. The Japanese lost but one ship.

The surviving Chinese ships retreated to Port Arthur and then to the naval base at Weihaiwei. In November the Japanese occupied Dairen (Ta-lien) and Port Arthur from the landward side, rendering the cannon in the forts ineffectual. In February 1895, the defeat was completed when the Japanese took Weihaiwei from the rear and turned the guns in the forts on the Chinese ships in the harbour. Admiral Ting committed suicide and his subordinates surrendered (see chapter 4).

This humiliating defeat after thirty years of self-strengthening exposed Li to severe criticism. His defence, that victory was impossible when only the Peiyang fleet and the Anhwei (Huai) Army opposed the might of the entire Japanese nation, was unable to save him from dismissal and disgrace.

The peace settlement

In November 1894, Prince Kung, reappointed head of the Tsungli Yamen, initiated a peace move by requesting the American minister to mediate, indicating that China was willing to pay an indemnity and recognize the independence of Korea. The Japanese, who by now had taken Port Arthur and Dairen and were threatening Manchuria and Liaotung, considered these concessions insufficient but intimated their willingness to negotiate. The Ch'ing court sent Chang Yin-huan, a minister of the Tsungli Yamen and vice-president of the Board of Revenue, to Hiroshima in February 1895 for a meeting with Itō and Mutsu but the Japanese refused to accept him, insisting that his powers were insufficient to negotiate a settlement. After the defeat of the Peiyang fleet, the court, desperate for peace, appointed Li Hung-chang as envoy first class to Japan.

The Japanese proposal for the peace settlement was a synthesis of the demands of various elements in the country. The army insisted on cession of the Liaotung peninsula; the navy demanded Taiwan (Formosa) as a base for operations in South Asia. The Progressive Party suggested Japanese control of Shantung, Kiangsu, Fukien and Kwangtung and the Liberals urged cession of Manchuria. The treasury proposed a large indemnity. The formula that ultimately emerged emphasized the independence of Korea, an indemnity, the cession of territory, and commercial and navigational privileges.

At the negotiations at Shimonoseki, Li stressed that China and Japan should recognize their common cultural and racial backgrounds, as well as their similar interests as Asians in an age of Western imperialism, and not exploit each other. Li attempted to use his age – seventy-three *sui* – to gain a psychological advantage over his younger opponents but to no avail.[57] At this critical point, Li was shot by a Japanese fanatic. Though the wound was not fatal, the incident proved very embarrassing to the Japanese government, which feared that it might provoke the Western powers to intervene on China's behalf. The Japanese emperor sent his personal doctor to treat Li and the government voluntarily declared an armistice and reduced the indemnity sought from 300 to 200 million taels. The foreign minister, Mutsu, noted that 'the misfortune of Li is also the fortune of the Great Ch'ing Empire. From now on peace terms will be more easily arranged, and the Sino-Japanese war will be terminated.'[58] On 17 April 1895, the Treaty of Shimonoseki was signed. It provided for: (1) recognition of Korean independence and termination of tribute to China; (2) an indemnity of 200 million taels; (3) cession of Taiwan, the Pescadores and the Liaotung peninsula; (4) the opening of Chungking, Soochow, Hangchow and Shasi to trade; and (5) the right of Japanese nationals to open factories and engage in industries and manufacturing in China.

Chinese reaction was severely critical. Li was accused of selling out the country. Chang Chih-tung, governor-general at Nanking, opposed ratification of the treaty and, on several occasions, provincial graduates who were gathered in Peking for the metropolitan examinations petitioned the court to reject the treaty and continue the fighting (see chapter 5).[59] But despite this opposition, the court exchanged ratifications on 8 May 1895.

Chinese leaders on Taiwan offered strong resistance to the cession of their island which, made a province after the French war, had made considerable progress in modernization under its first governor (see chapter 4).[60] Declaring their independence on 25 May they proclaimed Taiwan a republic and offered the presidency to the incumbent governor. Pressure from the Ch'ing representative, Li Ching-fang, son of Li Hung-chang, and the efforts of Japanese troops finally overcame the local movement in October 1895 and Taiwan was transferred to Japanese control.

In any reappraisal of the war, China's defeat appears inevitable. In the first place, the war pitted Japan, which had become a modern state in which nationalism bound the government and people together in a common purpose, against China, where government and people by and large formed separate entities. The Japanese war effort mobilized the consolidated might

[57] Li's tactics are revealed in the minutes of his conversations at the peace talks at Shimonoseki: 'Ma-kuan i-ho Chung-Jih t'an-hua lu', in Cheng Yen-sheng, *Chung-kuo nei-luan wai-huo li-shih ts'un-shu* (A historical series on China's internal disorder and external trouble), vol. 5.
[58] Li Shou-k'ung, *Chung-kuo chin-tai shih* (China's modern history), 464-5.
[59] The petition on 30 April 1895 contained 1,200 to 1,300 signatures.
[60] Liu Ming-ch'uan.

of the entire nation while the Chinese people were hardly affected by the conflict and the government relied almost entirely upon the Peiyang fleet and Anhwei Army of Li Hung-chang. Secondly, China had no clear demarcation of authority, no unity of command, and no nationwide mobilization. Conflicting advice from the Tsungli Yamen, provincial authorities, and irresponsible Ch'ing-liu officials rendered the court indecisive. Li, in charge of diplomatic and military affairs in Korea, had no authority to decide policy matters or to control ships and troops outside his area (see chapter 4).

Thirdly, corruption at court and in the Peiyang command doomed the Chinese effort from the start. The dowager's use of many million taels from naval funds to construct the Summer Palace (I-ho yüan), her trust in the eunuchs, and the general degeneration of public morality contributed to the defeat. Irregularities were rampant in the Peiyang command where Li chose his subordinates for their personal loyalty and willingness to work rather than for their uprightness. Many officers curried favour with the chief eunuch, Li Lien-ying, and embezzled public funds to make presents to him, who then protected their irregularities. For all its outward show the Peiyang fleet was weak. Knowing its weakness, Li had wanted to exhaust diplomatic means before deciding to fight.

Fourthly, Li's diplomacy was limited by his lack of understanding of international politics, his overconfidence in his personal powers of persuasion, and his reliance on the antiquated policy of playing off the barbarians against one another. When Russia failed to intervene on China's behalf, Li turned to Britain and the United States, but neither could effectively check Japan.

THE THREATENED 'PARTITION OF CHINA'

The triple intervention

On 23 April 1895, Russia, France and Germany sent a joint note to Tokyo warning that Japanese possession of the Liaotung peninsula would menace Peking, render illusory the independence of Korea, and threaten the general peace in East Asia. Russia, fearful of the Japanese presence on the Asiatic mainland, and herself interested in the ice-free ports of Dairen and Port Arthur, had instigated the intervention. Count Witte, minister of finance, stated that 'it was imperative not to allow Japan to penetrate into the very heart of China and secure a footing in the Liaotung peninsula'.[61]

---

[61] Sergei Iul'evich Witte, *The memoirs of Count Witte*, trans. and ed. by Abraham Yarmolinsky, 83.

Russia therefore decided to seek preservation of the *status quo ante bellum* in Liaotung and to take whatever action might be necessary, including bombardment of Japanese ports, to secure Japanese acquiescence. Russia was joined by France, her partner in the Dual Alliance, and Germany, who was anxious that Russia remain occupied in the East so as to reduce her pressure on Europe. To give teeth to the admonition, Russia recalled her warships from Chinese and Japanese harbours, declared Vladivostok a war zone and gathered troops there. Britain followed a policy of noninvolvement, primarily because Liaotung was not an area of direct British concern and the prime minister, Rosebery, feared the use of force against Japan.[62]

Before the conclusion of the peace treaty, Itō and Mutsu had recognized the possibility of a European intervention and urged that Japan refrain from territorial acquisitions on the mainland. But the military had insisted on the cession of land as essential to the victory. Now faced with the triple intervention, Japan had three alternatives: (1) to reject the warning at the risk of war; (2) to call an international conference on the Liaotung question; or (3) to accept the position of the three powers. On 24 April 1895, the imperial conference favoured the second course of action, but the foreign minister, Mutsu, demurred for fear that the Western powers would use the conference as an occasion to alter the other peace terms. The Japanese government finally decided to return Liaotung to China for 50 million taels. The powers reduced the sum to 30 million taels, and on 4 November 1895, Li Hung-chang and Hayashi Tadasu, the Japanese minister in China, signed a formal agreement retroceding Liaotung.

The Russians won the gratitude of the Chinese by their intervention, and by their offer of loans to pay to the Japanese an indemnity amounting to 100 million taels in the first year of payment. With an annual revenue of 89 million taels, the Ch'ing court was hardly in a position to pay such an indemnity. In 1895 Peking borrowed 400 million francs from a Franco-Russian banking consortium at 4 per cent interest. Later in 1896 and 1898, China twice borrowed £16 million at 5 per cent and 4.5 per cent respectively from a British–German consortium.

The Sino-Russian Secret Alliance

Impressed by Russian offers of friendship, leading Chinese officials advocated an alliance with Russia as a safeguard against future Japanese and Western aggression. Li Hung-chang, who had shown pro-Russian leanings in the debate of 1874 and the Ili crisis of 1878–81, was disappointed at Britain's failure to help China during the war. It prompted him to seek a

[62] Young, *British policy*, 17–18.

Russian alliance as the cardinal principle of future Chinese diplomacy. Eventually, the empress dowager, too, sanctioned the alliance.

On Russia's part, Count Witte welcomed the alliance in the hope of winning a concession to extend the Trans-Siberian Railway across Manchuria to Vladivostok. The Manchurian route would save 350 miles, much time and money, and would further Witte's policy of peaceful penetration of China. Witte met with opposition from the Asiatic department of the foreign office, and from the governor of Amur province who felt the project would arouse opposition from other powers and possibly precipitate a partition of China. But Witte won the tsar's support and Cassini, Russian minister to China, was instructed to explain to Li Hung-chang that such a railway would facilitate Russian troop movement for the defence of China. Though some discussion took place, no formal agreement was reached, despite the report in the British *North China Daily News* of a 'Cassini Convention'.

Negotiations for the railway concession and a Sino-Russian alliance finally materialized at the coronation of Nicholas II in 1896. When a middle-ranking official was authorized to attend the coronation, Cassini quietly protested that someone of Li Hung-chang's rank might be more appropriate to the occasion. The tsar himself is said to have telegraphed the empress dowager that Li's appointment would be more agreeable to him. So Li, at seventy-four *sui* and who had been in disgrace, was appointed imperial commissioner first class and set out on his first trip to the West to attend the coronation of the tsar and to visit the rulers of Britain, France, Germany and the United States. Witte related in his *Memoirs*, 'I . . . desired to prevent him [Li] from visiting any other European country before his arrival in Russia, for it was clear to me that while in Europe Li Hung-chang was bound to become the object of various intrigues on the part of the European statesmen.'[63] Therefore the tsar dispatched his confidant, Prince Ukhtomski, to 'intercept' Li at Suez and escort him to Odessa.

At St Petersburg, Witte impressed upon Li that to render to China armed assistance in an emergency, Russia needed the shortest possible railway route from her European section to Vladivostok. Such a route, through northern Mongolia and Manchuria, would increase the productivity of the land it traversed and would not arouse Japanese opposition because it would link Japan with Europe. Li secretly welcomed the project and reported to Peking that it would benefit China and Russia alike by blocking future British and Japanese advances. Witte and Li agreed on three principles:

(1) China would grant to Russia permission to construct a railway from

[63] Witte, *Memoirs*, 87.

Chita to Vladivostok, which would be operated by a private firm – the Chinese Eastern Railway Corporation.

(2) China would cede a strip of land sufficient for the building and operation of the railway, within which the corporation would have complete authority, including the right to maintain police. The railway might be redeemed by China after thirty-six years at 700 million roubles, but would pass free to her after eighty years.

(3) China and Russia agreed to defend each other against any Japanese attack on China, Korea or Russian possessions in East Asia.

It was rumoured that Li accepted a Russian bribe of $US1.5 million and at least a first payment to him seems to have been made. Witte denied it, but even if a fact, the bribery was not decisive in Li's thinking for he had come to Russia for the explicit purpose of concluding an alliance. Li, committed to the policy of playing off the barbarians – using Russia against Japan in this case – proudly announced that the treaty would give China peace for twenty years. But the peace lasted less than two years.

The scramble for concessions

After the triple intervention, Germany sought a naval base in China as her reward, citing the fact that all other major powers had bases in East Asia: Britain in Hong Kong, France in Tongking, and Russia in Vladivostok. The Chinese refused. But in 1897, the kaiser visited Russia and obtained a somewhat vague consent from the tsar to the German occupation of Kiaochow in Shantung. The Germans then capitalized on the murder of two German missionaries in Shantung (in November 1897) to seize Kiaochow and compel the Chinese to sign a ninety-nine-year lease and a concession for two railways in Shantung. Encouraged by this, the Russian foreign minister Muraviev won the tsar's support (over the protest of Witte) for a plan to occupy Port Arthur or Dairen. In December 1897, the Russians seized the two ports on the pretext of protecting China from the Germans, and in the following March compelled China to grant them the right to lease Port Arthur and Dairen for twenty-five years and to construct a South Manchurian Railway from the Chinese Eastern Railway to the ports and then west to Ying-k'ou (Newchwang) and east to the Yalu River. Witte later admitted having bribed the Chinese negotiators, Li Hung-chang and Chang Yin-huan, for their collusion. The Russians now held the Liaotung peninsula which China had reacquired from Japan three years earlier at the cost of 30 million taels!

The scramble for concessions now began in earnest. The British secured the lease of Weihaiwei for twenty-five years and the Hong Kong New

Territories for ninety-nine years,[64] and a promise that China would not transfer the Yangtze valley to any other power, thus making it a British sphere of interest.[65] Japan obtained a similar nonalienation commitment for Fukien province. The French leased Kwangchow Bay for ninety-nine years and established a sphere of influence in Kwangtung-Kwangsi-Yunnan. Only Italy, whose demand was rejected, failed to obtain a concession, while the United States was too preoccupied with the Spanish War and the Philippine Revolution to take any action. The threatened partition of China precipitated the reform movement of 1898 domestically (which is a large subject in itself; see chapter 5) and it also led to the declaration of the Open Door policy by the United States.

The Open Door policy

Although Britain claimed a sphere of special interest in China, she sought to promote the policy of an open door for trade wherever other powers had special influence. As a party to the scramble for concessions, Britain could hardly promote the idea alone and turned to the United States, the only major power with a 'clean' record, for support. In 1898 and again in 1899 the British minister in Washington approached the state department to suggest a joint sponsorship of a movement for equal commercial opportunity in China. The Americans, however, showed little interest until after the end of the Spanish War and the annexation of the Philippines. Then, A. E. Hippisley, a British commissioner of Chinese maritime customs, convinced his American friend, W. W. Rockhill, of the soundness of the proposal. Rockhill, a former minister in China, was adviser on Far Eastern affairs to the secretary of state, John Hay. The latter delivered to Britain, Germany, Russia, France, Italy and Japan in September 1899, a note prepared by Rockhill presenting the idea of equal commercial opportunity in China. It contained three main points, all of which added up to the preservation of the treaty system:

(1) Within its sphere of interest or leasehold, a power would not interfere with any treaty port or with the vested interest of any other power.

(2) Within its sphere of influence, no power would discriminate against nationals of other countries in matters of harbour dues or railway rates.

(3) Within each sphere of influence, the Chinese treaty tariff should apply and the Chinese government be allowed to collect customs duties.

No power committed itself to the note, each making its acceptance con-

[64] Young, *British policy*, 70–1. Five long cabinet meetings were held before the decision was made.
[65] *Ibid.* 91. The British readily admitted to having a sphere of interest in China but not a sphere of influence.

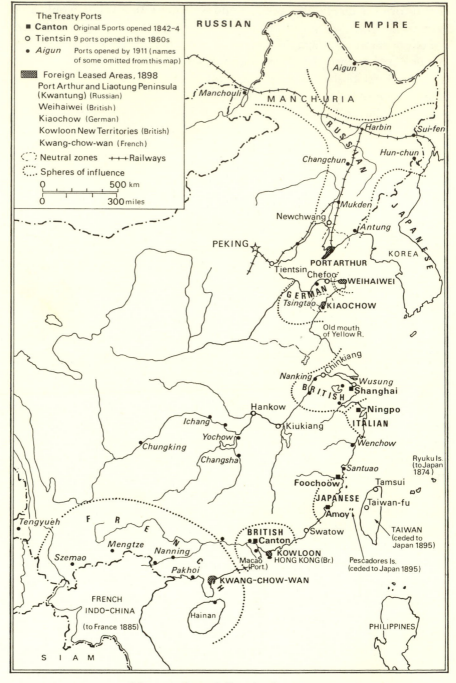

The Treaty Ports
- ■ **Canton** Original 5 ports opened 1842–4
- ○ **Tientsin** 9 ports opened in the 1860s
- ● *Aigun* Ports opened by 1911 (names of some omitted from this map)

▨ Foreign Leased Areas, 1898
Port Arthur and Liaotung Peninsula (Kwantung) (Russian)
Weihaiwei (British)
Kiaochow (German)
Kowloon New Territories (British)
Kwang-chow-wan (French)

⌐ Neutral zones   ┼┼┼ Railways
⌐ Spheres of influence

0   500 km
0   300 miles

RUSSIAN   EMPIRE

Aigun

Manchouli   M A N C H U R I A

                    Harbin   *Sui-fen*

RUSSIAN

Changchun   *Hun-chun*

                    Mukden

PEKING   Newchwang   *Antung*

                                  KOREA

Tientsin   **PORT ARTHUR**
            Chefoo   ▨**WEIHAIWEI**

G E R M A N
    Tsingtao ▨**KIAOCHOW**

            Old mouth
            of Yellow R.

                    Chinkiang
Nanking   *Wusung*
    B R I T I S H   ■**Shanghai**
                    ■**Ningpo**
Hankow   **ITALIAN**
Ichang   ○Kiukiang
            Yochow
Chungking   *Wenchow*
        Changsha
                        Ryuku Is.
                        (to Japan
                    Santuao 1874)
            Foochoow   *Tamsui*
                    JAPANESE
Tengyueh F R E   **Amoy** Taiwan-fu
                            TAIWAN
    Mengtze *Nanning* **BRITISH**   (ceded to
                    ■**Canton**   Japan 1895)
Szemao   ○Swatow
            KOWLOON   Pescadores Is.
        Pakhoi Macao**HONG KONG**(Br.) (ceded to Japan 1895)
            (Port.)
            ▨**KWANG-CHOW-WAN**

FRENCH
INDO-CHINA   Hainan
                            PHILIPPINES
(to France 1885)

S I A M

MAP. 7   Imperialism in the 1890s

tingent upon that of the others, but Hay nevertheless announced on 20 March 1900, that their assent was 'final and definitive'. Only Japan challenged this statement. On 3 July 1900, during the Boxer Uprising when the Open Door principle appeared threatened, the United States issued a second note, expanding the provisions to include the preservation of Chinese territorial and administrative integrity. A mere statement of intention, it did not solicit a response from the other powers.

The Open Door was a declaration of principles, not a formal policy of the United States government, which had neither the will nor the power to enforce it. However, the partition of China did subside after the declaration, not in response to the American call, but because the imperialists feared rivalry and conflict among themselves. The resultant equilibrium saved the Ch'ing empire from immediate collapse.

THE BOXER UPRISING

At the end of the Hundred Days reform (see chapter 5) the coup d'état of September 1898 restored the reactionary Manchus to power at the expense of both radical and moderate Chinese. Jung-lu and other conservatives such as Yü-lu and Ch'i-hsiu entered the Grand Council, and the grand secretary Kang-i gained increasing favour with the empress dowager. These men advocated a policy of hard resistance and, under their influence, the empress dowager resolved to grant no more concessions to foreign powers. When the Italians demanded cession of Sanmen Bay, Fukien, in February 1899, she ordered that the demand be resisted and saw the new policy vindicated when the Italians backed down in October. On 21 November 1899, she instructed the provincial authorities to entertain no more illusions of peace: 'It behooves our governors and governors-general throughout the country to unite forces and act in unison... With a country such as ours... what indeed is there to fear from any strong invader? Let us not think of making peace, nor rely solely upon diplomatic manoeuvres.'[66]

The flight of the court to Jehol in 1860 in the face of an Anglo-French invasion, defeat at the hands of the French and then the Japanese, and the foreign scramble for concessions in 1897–8 gave the dowager ample reasons for her resentment of foreigners. Foreign sympathy for the reform effort of 1898, foreign meddling which facilitated the escape of the reformers K'ang Yu-wei and Liang Ch'i-ch'ao, and the activities of these fugitives in Japan to continue the cause of reform compounded her antipathy. Now the foreign ministers in Peking openly disapproved of her plan to depose

[66] Chester C. T'an, *The Boxer catastrophe*, 32, with minor changes.

the Kuang-hsü Emperor and name the son of Prince Tuan as heir apparent. Humiliated and frustrated by their inability to resist this foreign interference with their plans, the empress dowager and Prince Tuan transferred their support to a major anti-foreign uprising, the Boxer movement.

Background of the Boxer movement

Anti-foreign sentiment permeated not only the court but also the scholars, the officials, the gentry and the people at large. Half a century of foreign humiliation had deeply wounded their pride and self-respect. The presence of haughty foreign ministers and consuls, and aggressive missionaries and traders, reminded them constantly of China's misfortune. A growing sense of injustice combined with larger social, economic, political and religious factors brought about a vast anti-foreign movement.

The Treaties in Tientsin in 1858 and the Conventions of Peking in 1860 had allowed foreign missionaries to propagate Christianity freely in the Chinese interior. But they had great difficulty in winning converts among the Chinese, who resented the invasion of Christianity under the protection of gunboats. Some missionaries adopted the practice of offering monetary subsidies or other amenities to their converts, and interceding with the magistrates on behalf of their converts in legal disputes. The Tsungli Yamen summed up the protective power of the missionaries in a report to the court: 'During the several decades since we have handled church cases, never once have we come across an instance in which the missionaries reprimanded or punished the converts.'

The gentry were particularly anti-foreign and regarded Christianity as a socially disruptive, heterodox sect. As self-appointed guardians of Confucian propriety, they resented the inroads of any foreign religion or philosophy and were particularly offended by the Christian converts' failure to perform traditional rituals and participate in local festivals. The gentry were not infrequently secret instigators of anti-mission riots. Folklore and rumour portraying the atrocities perpetrated by foreigners behind high church and convent walls inflamed Chinese antipathy, and Christianity became a basic cause of anti-foreignism (see volume 10, chapter 11).

The scramble for concessions in 1897-8 precipitated a sense of imminent national extinction on the part of patriotic Chinese. K'ang Yu-wei warned of the danger of becoming a second Burma, Annam, India or Poland, and the progressives proposed national salvation through radical institutional reforms. The reactionary and the ignorant, however, advocated the extermination of the foreigners. An estimated one thousand incidents occurring in Shantung after the German occupation of Kiaochow and countless incidents erupting in other parts of the country, all testify to the tremendous public anger over foreign encroachment.

The influx of foreign imports and the fixed customs tariff seem to have depressed the Chinese economy. The difficulty of life had increased during the mid-century rebellions as famine drove many to banditry. Many of the destitute who had at first blamed their misfortunes on the Taipings ultimately shifted their hatred to foreigners for having inspired the rebels with Christian ideology. In the post-Taiping era foreign products appeared increasingly in Chinese urban markets, and during the self-strengthening period (1861–94) foreign-style enterprises and industries as well as foreign capital were introduced.

Foreign railways also threatened the traditional transport systems. The Grand Canal and the Hankow–Peking land route could not compete with the railways now being built, and thousands dependent upon these transportation systems for their livelihood feared unemployment. By the end of the nineteenth century, China seemed beset by village poverty, rising unemployment and general hardship in popular livelihood. Many Chinese attributed all this to foreign influence and economic domination and, not surprisingly, deep hostility developed towards foreigners.

Economic hardships were compounded by natural disasters in 1898 when the Yellow River burst its banks inundating hundreds of villages in Shantung, and similar floods occurred in Szechwan, Kiangsi, Kiangsu and Anhwei. These disastrous floods were followed by a severe drought in North China in 1900. Victims of the natural calamities, and superstitious scholars and officials blamed the foreigners, who, they insisted, had offended the spirits by propagating a heterodox religion. Foreigners were accused of damaging the 'dragon's vein' (*lung-mai*) in the land by constructing railways, letting out the 'precious breath' (*pao-ch'i*) of the mountains by opening mines, and generally interfering with the natural (though mysterious) functioning of the topography, thus adversely affecting the harmony between men and nature. In this atmosphere of superstition, extreme economic hardship, and public resentment of the foreign presence, a major anti-foreign movement erupted in 1900.

The origin of the Boxers

'Boxers' was the English name for a Chinese secret society called the I-ho ch'üan, or the 'Righteous and Harmonious Fists' after the old-style calisthenics practised by its members. The I-ho ch'üan was an offshoot of the Eight-trigram sect (Pa-kua chiao), which was associated with the White Lotus sect, an anti-Ch'ing secret cult which had fomented the rebellion of 1796–1804. The I-ho ch'üan first received official notice in an edict of 1808 and, despite official prohibition, continued to carry on its activities in Shantung, Honan, Kiangsu, Anhwei and Chihli provinces. In the 1890s this traditionally anti-dynastic organization also took on an anti-foreign cast, vowing to kill foreigners and their Chinese collaborators.

The Boxers consisted of several uncoordinated groups, such as the Ch'ien Fists, the K'an Fists and the K'un Fists, each under its own leaders. The groups were usually organized into units of twenty-five, each under a leader with complete authority. The method of instruction differed with each group, but on the whole it was short and simple, completed within a day. The Boxers called their head 'Old Teacher' and lesser leaders 'First' and 'Second Elder Brothers'. Foreigners were 'Primary Hairy Men' (*ta mao-tzu*), Chinese Christians and those engaged in 'foreign matters' were 'Secondary Hairy Men' (*erh mao-tzu*), and those who used foreign goods were 'Tertiary Hairy Men' (*san mao-tzu*). All 'Hairy Men' were to be exterminated.[67]

The Boxer pantheon included both legendary and historical figures. Central to the Boxer programme, and of primary appeal to the superstitious populace, was the practice of magic arts. Through charms, incantations and rituals they invoked supernatural powers which they claimed granted them immunity to bullets, the power to fly, and the aid of divine generals and soldiers in battle. Being anti-foreign they shunned the use of guns and preferred old-style swords and lances.

Though some leading Boxers became pro-dynastic in the autumn of 1899, not all the groups shared this spirit with equal conviction. One band continued to hold to the 'anti-Ch'ing, revive-Ming' objective while other groups, being largely bandits, held no views on the matter. When the Boxers were summoned by the court to Peking in the summer of 1900, the pro-Ming band attacked the foreign legations but also secretly gathered forces in a futile attempt to overthrow the Manchu court.[68] The various Boxer groups were united, however, in their determination to destroy the foreigners and their Chinese collaborators.

Court patronage of the Boxers

In the 1890s a group of Boxers known as the Big Sword Society (Ta-tao hui) became particularly active in Shantung where it was secretly encouraged by Governor Li Ping-heng. Li held the Christians responsible for the

---

[67] This account of the Boxers is based on Lao Nai-hsuan, *I-ho ch'üan chiao-men yuan-liu k'ao* (Inquiry into the origins of the Boxer sect; 1 *chüan*, 1899), in Chien Po-tsan *et al.* eds. *I-ho t'uan* (The Boxers), 4.433–9. Cf. Immanuel C. Y. Hsu, *The rise of modern China*, 465–7.
[68] Li Shou-k'ung, *Chung-kuo chin-tai shih*, 589. Victor Purcell, *The Boxer uprising*, chs. 9 and 10.

riots that were being stirred up by the Boxers. He maintained that the Christians, 'with the support and protection of the missionaries, bullied and oppressed the common people'. He recommended that the Boxers be pacified rather than suppressed. When two German missionaries were killed in 1897, providing the excuse for the German occupation of Kiaochow, Li was dismissed under foreign pressure. Yü-hsien was then appointed in March 1899 as governor and he, too, patronized the Boxers and the Big Sword Society, ordering his subordinates to ignore the petitions and complaints of the missionaries and their converts. Under his aegis, the Boxers raised the banner of 'support for the Ch'ing and extermination of the foreigners' (*fu-Ch'ing mieh-yang*). The governor subsidized the Boxers, invited them to train his own soldiers and renamed them the I-ho t'uan as a form of officially sanctioned militia (*t'uan-lien*). Emboldened by official support, the Boxers increased their attacks on missionaries and converts while Yü-hsien continued to report to the court that 'there is absolutely no such thing as maltreatment of the Christians'. The court accepted this position and its pronouncements assumed a more antiforeign tone.[69]

When in December 1899 foreign pressure forced the court to remove Yü-hsien, he came to Peking where he convinced Prince Tuan, Prince Chuang and Grand Secretary Kang-i of the wisdom of supporting the Boxer forces. These reactionaries recommended the idea to the empress dowager, who in her frustration readily embraced it. Yü-hsien was named governor of Shansi and his successor in Shantung, Yuan Shih-k'ai, was admonished to refrain from punishing the Boxers. But Yuan refused to comply and succeeded in suppressing the Boxer movement in Shantung.

The court continued to favour the Boxers and on 12 January 1900, decreed that people drilling themselves for self-defence should not be considered as bandits. 'When peaceful and law-abiding people practise skill and calisthenics for the purpose of defending themselves and their families, or when they combine in village communities for the mutual protection of the rural population, this is only a matter of mutual help and collective defence.'[70] This edict and a similar one in April further encouraged Boxer activities, and in May the Boxers led a major uprising in Kao-lo village, Chihli. The governor-general, Yü-lu, aware of the dowager's secret patronage of the Boxers, proffered no chastisement and the court undertook no punitive measures. The Boxers became more daring, destroying railways and telegraph lines as symbols of the foreign enslavement of China.

In May 1900 the court considered organizing the Boxers into a militia

[69] T'an, *The Boxer catastrophe*, 46, 59. [70] *Ibid.* 60-1, with minor changes.

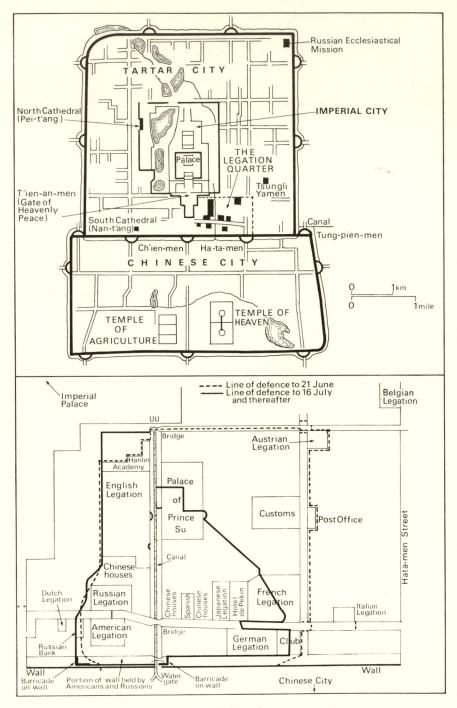

MAP. 8   Peking in 1900

but the plan was blocked by Yü-lu and Yuan Shih-k'ai. Impressed by reports of the Boxers' spiritual powers, however, the dowager summoned them to Peking. She commended their leaders and ordered all court attendants, including the women, to learn their art. Princes and nobles now engaged Boxers to guard their residences and some of the regular army joined the Boxers.

The rising tide of anti-foreignism prompted the foreign diplomats to call up troops from the ships off Taku on 28 May. Though the Tsungli Yamen attempted to limit the number of guards to thirty for each legation, the first detachment, arriving in Peking on 1 and 3 June, consisted of seventy-five each Russians, British and French, fifty Americans, forty Italians and twenty-five Japanese.

Encouraged by yet another favourable court decree of 29 May, the Boxers cut the railway line between Peking and Tientsin on 3 June. Chang Chih-tung, governor-general at Wuchang, and Sheng Hsuan-huai, director of railway and telegraphs, pleaded unsuccessfully with the court to suppress such activities. As the court was completely dominated by the reactionaries, foreign diplomats began to fear for the safety of foreigners in Peking. The British minister requested help from Admiral Seymour at Tientsin, and on 10 June an international force of 2,100 men left Tientsin by train. Half-way between Tientsin and Peking, the Boxers attacked the foreign expedition and blocked its progress to Peking. Telegraph lines between the two cities were cut, isolating the foreign community of Peking. On the same day, Boxers burned the British summer legation in the Western Hills, and on 11 June the chancellor of the Japanese legation was killed by troops of the reactionary Muslim general Tung Fu-hsiang.

On 13 June the court announced that the embassies were adequately protected and there was no need for more foreign troops in Peking. Governor-general Yü-lu and General Nieh Shih-ch'eng were ordered to resist the advance of Admiral Seymour, and the commander of the Taku Forts was alerted against a surprise attack. Beginning on 13 June large groups of Boxers swarmed into Peking, burning churches and foreign residences, killing Chinese converts, and dragging officials into the streets for public humiliation. They exhumed the bodies of missionaries, including the early Jesuits, made attacks on the legation guards, and on 20 June killed the German minister, Clemens von Ketteler. At Tientsin, the Boxers rampaged all over the city and, facing such disorder, the foreign forces occupied the Taku Forts on 17 June. Meanwhile, the Seymour expedition fought its way back to Tientsin.

Prince Tuan, Kang-i and the empress dowager now agreed that an all-out attack on the legations was necessary to expunge the humiliations of half a century. On 16 June, at the first of four imperial councils called to deliberate on the question, Yuan Ch'ang, a director of the Court of Sacrificial Worship, opposed the plan to attack, pointing out the falsity of the Boxer claim of immunity to firearms. The dowager retorted: 'If we cannot rely upon the supernatural formulae, can we not rely upon the hearts of the people? China has been extremely weak; the only thing we can rely upon is the hearts of the people.' The meeting was indecisive, but a decree was issued to recruit the 'young and strong' Boxers into the army.

At the second imperial council of 17 June, the dowager revealed an alleged four-point demand from the foreign powers: designate a special place of residence for the emperor; allow foreign ministers to collect provincial revenues; and permit them to direct Chinese military affairs. The fourth point, which she did not disclose, was said to be 'restore the emperor to power'. This four-point demand, actually fabricated by Prince Tuan, goaded the dowager into declaring that China should 'fight to the death' against any foreign action. The third council of 18 June was again indecisive, but on 19 June word arrived that the foreigners had demanded the surrender of the Taku Forts. The dowager called the fourth imperial council on 19 June to announce the break-off of diplomatic relations. She was determined to fight the powers with the help of the Boxers and over-ruled attempts by the Kuang-hsu Emperor to postpone the decision. On 21 June, an ambiguous but rather favourable report on the fighting at Taku and Tientsin arrived and the court confidently declared war on the foreign powers.[71]

The court now formally ordered the provincial authorities to organize the Boxers to oppose the foreign invasion. At Peking, the Boxers were officially subsidized and Prince Chuang, Kang-i and Prince Tuan assumed official command of Boxer bands. These bands, together with the government troops under General Tung Fu-hsiang, launched attacks on the legations and the Northern (Roman Catholic) Cathedral. Prince Chuang offered rewards for the taking of foreign captives while Kang-i declared: 'When the legations are taken, the barbarians will have no more roots. The country will then have peace.' By the attacks, made with the full approval of the dowager, the reactionaries sought to vent their wrath on the barbarians, rid the capital of the foreign menace, destroy evidence of court support for the Boxers, and stimulate support among the people. Within the legations the 450 guards, 475 civilians (including 12 diplomatic ministers), and 2,300 Chinese Christians, offered stiff resistance to the Boxers who, wearing wild, loose-hanging hair, carrying 'magic weapons', and moving in prescribed

[71] Hsiao I-shan, *Ch'ing-tai t'ung-shih*, 4.2196–8.

steps, resembled legendary witches. Peking was gripped in the pande-
monium of a witches' sabbath.

Alarmed by these developments, the foreign powers resolved to dispatch troops to China. Britain in particular was concerned with the future
of the Yangtze valley as her sphere of interest. The foreign office received
in early July a number of suggestions as to the proper course of action.
H. B. Morse, who later became a historian, proposed 'throwing a screen of
British and German troops between the valley and the rebellion'. Byron
Brenan, consul-general at Shanghai then on leave in London, recommended that Duke K'ung, a lineal descendant of Confucius, be considered
as a possible candidate for the throne should the allied military intervention
drive the court out of Peking, leaving behind a state of anarchy.[72]

Independent action of South and East China

Even before the formal declaration of war, it was clear that the court was
following a disastrous course of action. Li Hung-chang, now governor-
general at Canton and probably the only man capable of reversing the tide,
refused to act, declaring that Jung-lu, with his numerous troops, should
act to remove the reactionaries from control.[73] The provincial authorities,
unable to change court policy, were yet anxious to protect their jurisdiction
from the Boxer disruption and foreign punitive action.

When the court issued the declaration of war on 21 June, the leading
provincial authorities – Li Hung-chang at Canton, Liu K'un-i at Nanking,
Chang Chih-tung at Wuchang and Yuan Shih-k'ai in Shantung – collectively refused to recognize it, insisting that it was a *luan-ming*, an illegitimate
order issued without proper authorization of the throne. They suppressed
the declaration and, together with the governor-general of Fukien and
Chekiang, entered into an informal pact with the foreign consuls at
Shanghai, stating that they would protect foreign lives and property and
suppress the Boxers within their jurisdiction, and the foreign powers
would refrain from sending troops into their regions. Hence, the whole of
South-East China was exempt from the Boxer catastrophe and foreign
invasion.

The provincial leaders justified their actions on the grounds that the
Boxers and reactionaries had seized control of the court and issued illegitimate orders; that war with several foreign powers was insanity; and that
the lives of foreigners in the legations must be saved. They urged the court
to assign well-disciplined troops to protect the legations, and to continue

[72] Young, *British policy*, 171.
[73] Hsiao I-shan, *Ch'ing-tai t'ung-shih*, 4.2203.

to honour the foreign debts. They appealed to Jung-lu but he refused to cooperate.

Sheng Hsuan-huai suggested that Yuan Shih-k'ai march his troops from Shantung to Peking to rescue the dowager and the emperor from the clutches of the undesirable elements. Yuan declined, stating: 'Without authorization, if I should lead my troops northward to save the foreign ministers, I am afraid that I would be defeated first on the way. It is really difficult for me to comply.' Liu K'un-i, attempting to absolve the dowager of guilt, notified foreign consuls that the hostilities were 'beyond the expectations of the imperial court'. Meanwhile, the court decreed on 3 July that provincial authorities should purge the word 'peace' from their mouths.

On 14 July, foreign troops took Tientsin and threatened to march on Peking and, on the same day, thirteen south-eastern provincial authorities urged the court to suppress the Boxers, protect foreigners, compensate them for losses sustained in the disturbances, and send a letter of apology to Germany for the death of von Ketteler. Under these pressures, the court became somewhat conciliatory for a short time. The Tsungli Yamen invited foreign diplomats and their families to move to the Yamen for safety, pending arrangements for their return home. Li Hung-chang was ordered to instruct Chinese diplomats abroad to inform their respective governments that their representatives in Peking were safe. On 19 July, the Yamen again offered to send the foreign ministers to Tientsin under military escort but the foreigners, feeling the Yamen could not ensure adequate protection, preferred to remain in the legations to await relief. During this brief conciliatory period (14–26 July), the Yamen sent supplies to the legations and the attacks were suspended.

The policy of war and extermination was reaffirmed, however, with the arrival of the reactionary Li Ping-heng in Peking on 26 July. Five high officials who dared to counsel peace were executed and Yuan Shih-k'ai was moved to describe the situation as 'hopeless'.

Foreign reinforcements reached Taku in late July but mutual jealousy and dissension delayed their departure for Peking until 4 August. This international force of 8,000 Japanese, 4,800 Russians, 3,000 British, 2,100 Americans, 800 French, 58 Austrians and 53 Italians decisively defeated the Boxers and government forces, and on 14 August, arrived in Peking to relieve the besieged legations. The legations had held out for nearly two months, thanks in large part to Jung-lu, commander-in-chief of the Peiyang forces, who, afraid to oppose the dowager, had launched a noisy but only half-hearted attack on the quarter.

As the allies advanced the dowager, the emperor and a small entourage fled Peking. The emperor had wanted to remain to negotiate a settlement but the dowager forced him to accompany her. After a long and arduous flight, the court was re-established in Sian on 23 October. The Boxer catastrophe which had swept North China, Inner Mongolia and Manchuria, killing 231 foreigners and many thousands of Chinese Christians, was over at last.

The peace settlement

In the aftermath of the Boxer Uprising, Li Hung-chang was called upon to negotiate a peace settlement. He had earlier been summoned by the court to Peking on 18 June 1900, but, alarmed by the dowager's patronage of the Boxers, he delayed his departure from Canton. On 8 July, he was appointed governor-general of Chihli and superintendent of trade for the northern ports, posts which he had held previously from 1870 to 1895, and only then did he sail for Shanghai.[74] Arriving there on 21 July, he was thoroughly discouraged by the situation in Peking and refused to go north. On 7 August, the court appointed him plenipotentiary to negotiate with the foreign powers but still Li hesitated to go to Peking for he believed that the court would not agree to the measures that he saw as necessary to attain peace – namely, suppression of the Boxers and protection of the foreigners in Peking.

Li was somewhat consoled when the powers did not declare war on China but sent an expeditionary force merely to suppress the rebels. And, when Russia offered to withdraw her troops and civilians to Tientsin in preparation for negotiations, and to set a tone of moderation at the conferences to forestall excessive demands by the other powers, Li agreed to go north. He requested that Prince Ch'ing and Jung-lu be assigned to join him in the negotiations, and when the court complied, he went north under Russian protection, arriving in Tientsin on 18 September. When the powers declared Jung-lu unacceptable as a negotiator because of his part in the legation attacks, Li petitioned that he be allowed to go to Sian. Li hoped that Jung-lu, who joined the Grand Council on 11 November, would check the still strong influence of Prince Tuan and Kang-i.

Meanwhile the allied representatives in Peking refused to open negotiations before 'the return of the court', by which they meant 'the return of the emperor to power'. They hoped to use this demand as leverage to gain satisfaction of their other demands. The dowager refused, however, stating that she feared unacceptable terms would be imposed on her, and indicated that the court would return only *after* the peace settlement. The south-eastern provincial leaders now attempted to shift allied attention to

[74] He did so against British advice which urged him to stay in Canton. Young, *British policy*, 175.

the issue of punishment for guilty ministers. They put pressure on the court to accept the demand for punishment of nine pro-Boxer ministers, Governor Yü-hsien and General Tung Fu-hsiang. The court reluctantly agreed to punish the ministers but reserved judgment on General Tung. The powers insisted that Tung be punished, and Liu K'un-i and Yuan Shih-k'ai pressed Jung-lu for action, stressing that no wise statesman 'would love a single man against the public opinion of the nation, let alone against the interests of the people'.[75] On 3 December 1900, the court finally relented. In attributing guilt, no mention was made of the two chief culprits: the empress dowager and Jung-lu.

At Peking the allied negotiators had difficulty agreeing on terms. Germany demanded severe punishment, and the kaiser spoke of even the destruction of Peking. He sought to ensure that 'no Chinese will ever again even dare to look askance at a German'.[76] Because of von Ketteler's murder, the German field marshal, Count von Waldersee, was named commander-in-chief of the allied forces in China. Britain supported Germany in an attempt to check Russia while the Russians ingratiated themselves with the Chinese in the hope of gaining concessions in Manchuria, which they had occupied during the turmoil. The Japanese competed with the Russians in an attempt to win Chinese goodwill; France declared she had no designs on China and the United States announced the second Open Door note supporting 'Chinese territorial and administrative entity'. After prolonged debate, a joint note of twelve articles was announced on 24 December 1900, and reluctantly accepted by the Chinese court on 16 January 1901. The final settlement consisted of the following main features.

(1) Punishment of the guilty. The allies had originally demanded the death penalty for twelve officials, including Princes Chuang and Tuan, Kang-i, Yü-hsien, Li Ping-heng, Hsu T'ung and General Tung Fu-hsiang. In the final settlement, Prince Chuang was ordered to commit suicide, Prince Tuan to be banished to Sinkiang for life imprisonment, and Yü-hsien to be executed. General Tung was stripped of appointment. Kang-i, Hsu T'ung and Li Ping-heng, already dead, received posthumous degradation. In the provinces, a total of 119 officials received penalties ranging from capital punishment to mere reprimand.

(2) Indemnity. An indemnity of £67.5 million, or 450 million taels was levied with payment to be completed in thirty-nine years at 4 per cent annual interest, and with the maritime customs, likin, native customs and salt gabelle as security. To help meet the payment, the existing tariff was to

[75] T'an, The Boxer catastrophe, 139, 141.
[76] H. B. Morse, The international relations of the Chinese empire, 3.309.

be increased and hitherto duty-free merchandise to be taxed. The breakdown of the indemnity was as follows:[77]

Country	taels	percentage of total
Russia	130,371,120	29.00
Germany	90,070,515	20.00
France	70,878,240	15.75
Britain	50,620,545	11.25
Japan	34,793,100	7.70
United States	32,939,055	7.30
Italy	26,617,005	5.90
Belgium	8,484,345	1.90
Austria	4,003,920	0.90
Others	1,222,155	0.30

(3) Other important stipulations.

    (a) Apology missions to Germany and Japan.

    (b) Establishment of a permanent legation guard.

    (c) Destruction of the Taku and other forts between Peking and the sea.

    (d) Prohibition of the importation of arms for two years.

    (e) Stationing of foreign troops in key points from Peking to the sea.

    (f) Suspension of official examinations for five years in some forty-five cities where the Boxers had been active.

These items were formalized in The Boxer Protocol of twelve articles and nineteen annexes, and signed by Li Hung-chang, Prince Ch'ing, and the representatives of eleven powers on 7 September 1901. The allied troops evacuated Peking on 17 September, but the court did not return until 7 January 1902.

Russia in Manchuria

The peace settlement did not resolve the question of the Russian occupation of Manchuria. Under the pretext of suppressing the 'rioters' and restoring order, 200,000 Russian troops had swept into Manchuria, taking Aigun on 23 July 1900, Tsitsihar on 30 August, and Mukden (Shen-yang, the subsidiary Ch'ing capital) on 1 October. On 30 November, Admiral Alexeiev, Russian governor-general of the Liaotung peninsula, coerced the

---

[77] Actually, the indemnity far exceeded the losses sustained by the allies. The actual American private claims were only $2 million, which had been paid by 1905. In 1908 the United States government returned to China $10,785,286, while retaining $2 million for possible future adjustments, and in 1924 the rest of the indemnity was waived. The refund was specified by Washington to be used for educating Chinese students in the United States. To prepare these students for schooling in America, Tsing Hua College (later Tsing Hua University) was established in Peking, where many American teachers were employed. Remissions of the indemnity funds by other countries followed suit: Britain, 1922; Russia, 1924; France, 1925; Italy, 1925, 1933; Belgium, 1928; the Netherlands, 1933. Many writers in China have viewed the Boxer refunds as a form of cultural imperialism – a subject clearly in need of re-examination.

Manchu military governor of Mukden, Tseng-ch'i, into signing a 'provisional agreement' which virtually pre-empted Chinese rule in Manchuria. The Ch'ing court refused to recognize the agreement, which they insisted Tseng-ch'i had no authority to sign. Negotiations then opened in St Petersburg, and on 16 February 1901 the Russians proposed a twelve-article treaty (to replace the Alexeiev–Tseng agreement), which returned Manchuria to China in name, but, in effect, legalized the occupation of Manchuria by Russian troops disguised as 'railway guards'. The agreement prohibited China from sending arms to Manchuria or granting anyone railway and mining privileges there without Russian consent. It stipulated that China pay for the occupation and for damages to the Chinese Eastern Railway and granted Russia the right to construct a railway from the said line to the Great Wall.

The Russian action aroused the apprehension of the other powers. The Japanese minister in Peking warned Prince Ch'ing that any concession on the Russian occupation of Manchuria would lead to the partition of China. Britain and Germany admonished the court not to sign a separate treaty with Russia before the conclusion of a general agreement with the allies in Peking, and the United States, Austria and Italy urged China to resist the Russian demands. Count Witte, meanwhile, threatened that rejection of the proposal would lead to Russian incorporation of Manchuria. The dilemma of the court was intensified by the conflicting advice of leading officials. Li Hung-chang, his pro-Russian leanings now evident, advised signing the treaty to avoid a perilous break with Russia, while Chang Chih-tung and Liu K'un-i vigorously opposed the treaty.

Caught between conflicting advice and diverse international pressures, the court was incapable of reaching a decision. But after repeated admonitions against signing from the Chinese ministers in London and Berlin, and particularly from the minister in Tokyo, who stressed that Russia would not dare take action in Manchuria in face of the combined opposition of Britain and Japan, the court finally rejected the Russian treaty on 23 March. Facing international opposition, the Russians took no direct action but merely issued a statement that, as much as they would like to evacuate Manchuria, the realities of international politics did not permit them to do so at the moment. Li continued to support a separate settlement through direct negotiation and attempted to offer concessions in Manchuria to Russia in exchange for troop evacuation, but Count Witte refused his proposals. Thus rejected, old, weak and ashamed, Li Hung-chang died suddenly on 7 November 1901, at the age of seventy-eight.

Li's work was carried on by Prince Ch'ing and Grand Councillor Wang Wen-shao. As the international situation was unfavourable to Russia, she ultimately signed an agreement with China on 4 April 1902 promising to evacuate Manchuria in three stages at six-monthly intervals. On her part, China agreed to protect the Russian-dominated Chinese Eastern Railway. The first evacuation took place on schedule, but when the second stage was due in April 1903, the Russians did not leave but resorted to the subterfuge of disguising their troops as 'railway guards'. In addition, they demanded new monopolistic rights and re-occupied the evacuated cities of Mukden and Newchwang, sowing the seeds of war with Japan.

Repercussions of the Boxer Uprising

The Boxer movement developed out of the combined forces of the reactionary Manchu court, the conservative officials and gentry, and the ignorant and superstitious people. It was an unreasoned outburst of emotion and anger against foreign imperialism, possessing an inherent patriotic element. Marxist and other historians today consider it a primitive form of patriotic peasant uprising, with the right motive but the wrong methods.

The Boxer Uprising and its final settlement had many significant consequences:

(1) The allied occupation of Peking and the Russian advance into Manchuria sharpened international rivalry and caused the powers to fear conflict among themselves and the subsequent end of equal economic opportunity in China. There developed a general international desire to reduce tension and maintain the *status quo* in China. The United States issued the second Open Door note on 3 July 1900, in an effort to 'preserve Chinese territorial and administrative entity and safeguard for the world the principle of equal and impartial trade with all parts of the Chinese Empire.' And on 16 October, Britain and Germany signed an agreement (to which other powers were invited to adhere) stipulating that the signatories would refrain from seizing Chinese territory. This stalemate on imperialistic activities prevented an immediate break-up of the Ch'ing empire, but its international position fell to an unprecedentedly low point.

(2) The Boxer Protocol infringed severely upon Chinese sovereignty. The prohibition on arms importation, the destruction of the Taku and other forts, the stationing of foreign troops in the legation quarter, and the right of foreign powers to deploy troops from Peking to the sea, all compromised China's powers of self-defence. The suspension of government examinations in many parts of the country was a blatant interference with the internal administration of China.

(3) The indemnity of 450 million taels together with its accrued interest

would have amounted, if fully paid, to 982,283,150 taels, more than twice the original sum. As the payments had to be made in foreign currencies, China suffered additional losses in the exchange, especially during the years when the value of silver sharply declined. The outflow of such a large amount of capital inhibited, if not incapacitated, China's economic growth.

(4) Foreign ministers in Peking thenceforth constituted a powerful diplomatic corps that sometimes functioned above the Manchu court as a super-government.

(5) The barbarous Boxer conduct made China appear uncivilized to the world, while the brutal demonstration of foreign power created an image of invincibility and superiority that shattered Chinese self-confidence and self-respect. The Chinese attitude of disdain and hostility towards the foreigner often became one of fear and toadying.

(6) Although the Manchu court attempted some half-hearted reforms towards a constitutional government in an effort to survive, many Chinese, viewing the Manchu leadership as bankrupt, turned to revolution. Dr Sun Yat-sen's advocacy of a forceful overthrow of the Ch'ing received increasing sympathy and support. His image changed from that of a disloyal rebel to that of a patriotic revolutionary as the pulse of revolution quickened, precipitating the ultimate fall of the Manchu dynasty in 1911.

THE EFFECTS OF THE ANGLO-JAPANESE ALLIANCE AND THE RUSSO-JAPANESE WAR

Origins of the Alliance

The Russian occupation of Manchuria, with all its serious international ramifications, must be viewed in the larger context of European power politics. At the turn of the century, Europe was caught in a precarious balance of power between the Triple Alliance (Germany, Austria-Hungary and Italy) and the Dual Alliance (France and Russia), with Britain maintaining her 'splendid isolation'. The tension generated by the rivalry between the two camps and the fear that the two, being defensive alliances, might join in a continental league against Britain, resulted in a stalemate among the powers, prompting them to direct their attention towards Asia and Africa. From this perspective, the Russian encroachment in Manchuria was not merely an isolated case of violation of Chinese sovereignty, but a serious disruption of the existing international order. Japan, in particular, was concerned with her position in Korea and Manchuria, and the United States feared for the future of the Open Door in China. Britain felt threatened about her influence in Peking and her position south of the

Great Wall. On the other hand, France supported the Russian advance and Germany secretly encouraged Russia's eastward expansion to divert her focus from Europe. Clearly, a new era of international relations was unfolding, leading to an unprecedented East–West alignment.

Britain was at the crossroads. Her policy of 'splendid isolation' had left her no friends, and the Boer War, absorbing 250,000 British soldiers for two-and-a-half years (October 1899–May 1902), exposed the weaknesses in her imperial defences and the dangers of her isolation policy. In order to protect her empire and preserve her pre-eminence in world leadership, Britain was forced to emerge from isolation and search desperately for an ally. The first choice was Germany. London had hoped that the Anglo-German Agreement of October 1900, which pledged the maintenance of the *status quo* in China, would check the Russian advance in Manchuria, but Germany later excluded Manchuria from the pact in an apparent move to avoid antagonizing Russia. Repeated British attempts to seek an alliance with Germany met with no success, obliging London to look for other alternatives. France was out of the question because of her role in the Dual Alliance, while the United States adhered to her traditional policy of 'no entangling alliances', and having recently fought the Spanish War, was in no mood for an overseas venture to defend the Open Door. Japan thus became the only possibility, the more attractive because of her naval power and well-known antipathy towards Russia.

In 1901 the British Admiralty reckoned that the combined Russian–French naval forces in the 'China seas' outnumbered those of Britain by nine to four in battleships, but alignment with Japan would give Britain a superior ratio of eleven to nine in battleships and a preponderance of cruisers, obviating the need to draw ships from her European fleets. Apart from military considerations, Britain was concerned with possible Russian domination of Peking through their control of Manchuria, and the penetration of Russian economic influence (through Belgian capital in building the Peking–Hankow Railway) into the Yangtze valley – a traditional British sphere of interest. Also disturbing was the intensification of Russian activities in Tibet leading to the dispatch by the Dalai Lama of two missions to Russia in 1901–2.[78] If unchecked, the Russian southward thrust might threaten the security of India. With traditional fears thus revived, Britain found it imperative to ally with Japan in order to block the Russian advance and maintain her pre-eminence in Asia. With a far-flung empire, being isolated in European politics, and facing new Russian threats, Britain could hardly do otherwise. Negotiations with the Japanese

[78] Liu Yen, *Chung-kuo wai-chiao shih* (Chinese diplomatic history), enlarged by Li Fang-ch'en, 268–9.

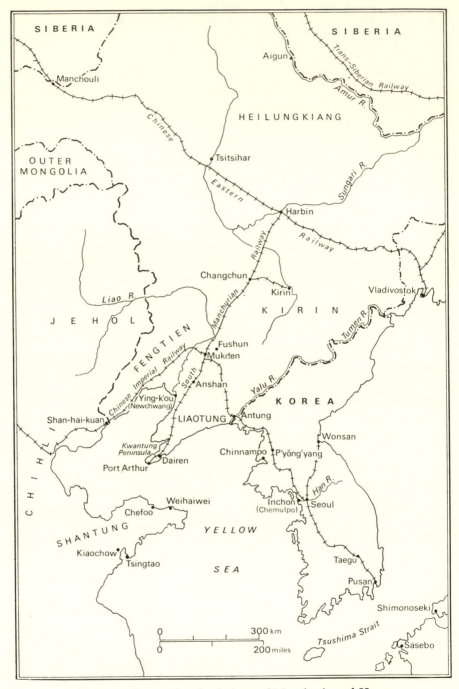

SIBERIA

SIBERIA

Manchouli

Aigun

Trans-Siberian Railway

Amur R.

HEILUNGKIANG

Chinese

OUTER MONGOLIA

Tsitsihar

Eastern

Sungari R.

Harbin

Railway

Railway

Changchun

Kirin

Vladivostok

Liao R.

K I R I N

Tumen R.

J E H O L

F E N G T I E N

Manchurian

Fushun

Mukden

Anshan

South

Yalu R.

K O R E A

Chinese Imperial Railway

Ying-k'ou
(Newchwang)

Shan-hai-kuan

LIAOTUNG   Antung

Wonsan

Kwantung
Peninsula

Chinnampo   P'yŏng'yang

Dairen

Port Arthur

C H I H L I

Han R.

Weihaiwei

Chefoo

Inchon
(Chemulpo)   Seoul

SHANTUNG

Y E L L O W

Kiaochow

Taegu

Tsingtao

S E A

Pusan

Shimonoseki

0   300 km
0   200 miles

Tsushima Strait

Sasebo

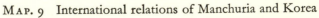

MAP. 9   International relations of Manchuria and Korea

minister in London proceeded swiftly in order to block any possible Japanese agreement with Russia, which would seriously jeopardize British interests in Asia.

For Japan, antagonism with Russia had been prevalent ever since the Triple Intervention of 1895. Alliance with Britain, the foremost Western power, was a dream beyond expectation, for it would elevate Japan's international status instantly, signify her coming of age as a great power, and serve as an effective shield against Russia. A powerful group led by the prime minister Katsura Tarō (a protégé of Yamagata Aritomo), the foreign minister Katō Takaaki, his successor Komura Jutarō, and minister to Britain Hayashi Tadasu, strongly favoured such a course of action, and they had the support of the elder statesmen Yamagata, Saigō Tsugumichi and Matsukata Masayoshi. But the influential former premier and elder statesman Itō Hirobumi, doubted British sincerity in abandoning the traditional policy of isolation and feared that the alliance would make Japan bear the brunt of fighting Russia, a task which he thought too onerous for his country. He preferred, instead, a rapprochement with Russia since the questions of Korea and Manchuria concerned mainly Japan and Russia, not Britain. His arguments evoked a sympathetic response from the other elder statesman, Inoue Kaoru, but Yamagata and his military group believed that any rapprochement with Russia could only be temporary and ultimately Japan would have to fight Russia for supremacy in Korea and Manchuria. Needless to say, the conflicting views in foreign affairs among the Japanese leadership were related to rivalry in domestic politics: Itō wanted to prevent the military from dominating the affairs of state, while the military wanted to deny Itō the chance of returning to political power.

In opposing the cabinet's stand, Itō had become something of a nuisance to Katsura. Katsura was anxious to rid himself of a political rival and an opportunity presented itself in October 1901 when Itō was invited by Yale University to receive an honorary doctor-of-law degree during its bicentennial celebration. After the event, Itō, with the encouragement of Inoue, went to Europe with the intention of visiting Russia in a private capacity to initiate negotiations. With Itō out of the country, Katsura ordered Hayashi to proceed with the alliance negotiations in London as fast as possible. When Itō reached Paris, Hayashi appeared with a draft treaty of the alliance. Itō was so discouraged that he thought of returning home, but in the end decided to proceed to Russia as planned. He asked Hayashi to temporize in London for a while. In Berlin he received word from Tokyo that negotiations for the alliance had gone too far for Japan to withdraw. Still undaunted, Itō continued his trip to Russia, where he proposed: (1) a mutual guarantee of Korea's independence; (2) a mutual promise not to use its territory for strategic purposes against each other; and (3) Russian recognition of Japan's freedom of action in Korea, in exchange for Japanese acknowledgment of Russia's paramount interests in Manchuria. The Russian government would not accept these conditions. It refused to give Japan a free hand in Korea and it insisted on freedom of action for Russia in Manchuria as well as in the rest of China.[79] Itō left Russia without reaching an agreement, but he still did not give up the idea of rapprochement. On the way home, in Berlin, he cabled Tokyo to warn again of the unreliability of Britain and proposed a postponement of the signing of the alliance pending further negotiations with Russia. The cabinet, however, was in no mood to risk losing a sure alliance with Britain for a dubious chance of reconciliation with Russia. On the recommendation of the privy council the emperor approved the Anglo-Japanese Alliance in December 1901. Itō accepted the decision with grace but urged that the alliance be used, not to confront Russia but to put pressure on her to reach an agreement based on the principle of *Man-Kan kōkan*: a quid pro quo of Japanese acceptance of Russian dominance of Manchuria for Russian recognition of Japanese dominance of Korea, in short, a 'Manchuria–Korea exchange'.

The Anglo-Japanese Alliance was formally concluded on 30 January 1902. In the preamble the contracting parties called for the maintenance of the *status quo* and general peace in East Asia through the preservation of the independence and territorial integrity of China and Korea, and equal opportunity for all nations in these two countries. The signatories declared that they would take necessary measures to safeguard their interests in these two countries if threatened by foreign aggression or domestic disturbances. They pledged neutrality if either became involved in a war with another power, and agreed to use their influence to prevent other powers from joining the war; but if another power joined the war against one of the signatories, the other signatory would come to its aid. Thus, Japan was given a free hand to fight Russia; if France should intervene on the side of Russia, Britain would come to Japan's rescue.

Impact of the Alliance

The immediate reaction of Russia and France was to extend the applicability of the Dual Alliance to East Asia, but it was merely a symbolic move. American sympathy was with Japan. President Theodore Roosevelt considered her a defender of the Open Door and China's territorial integrity, and even saw Japan's complete control of Korea as in the best interests of

---

[79] Ch'en Fu-kuang, *Yu-Ch'ing i-tai chih Chung-O kuan-hsi* (Sino-Russian relations during the Ch'ing dynasty), 331.

peace in East Asia.[80] To him the Chinese were weak, befuddled and easy prey of the strong, while the Japanese signified a rising power in the East. 'What nonsense to speak of the Chinese and the Japanese as of the same race!'[81] The president looked to Japan to block the Russian advance in Manchuria and was pleased to see her position strengthened through the British connection.

China reacted with a mixture of relief, shame and fear. Initially, there was a feeling of relief because the alliance was directed against Russia in favour of the preservation of China and Korea. A sense of shame followed because the foreign pledge for China's independence and territorial integrity put her into the same category as Korea and emphasized the fact that China's fate was not in her own hands but in those of her would-be protectors. Finally, there was fear that Japan would ultimately replace Russia as the chief imperialist in Manchuria. The joint memorial of the elder statesmen Chang Chih-tung, governor-general of Hu-Kwang, and Liu K'un-i, governor-general of Liang-Kiang, dated 16 February 1902, expressed these feelings of relief and anxiety when they informed the court that it was the activities of Russia in Manchuria that had aroused the resentment of Japan and Britain, and prompted them to form the alliance 'with the primary purpose of dealing with Manchuria'. However, they warned: 'If we can follow them [Britain and Japan] and hold firm, it will be good for Manchuria, but if we fall into the Russian trap and cause Japan and Britain to lose their rights, they would undoubtedly seek compensations from us.'[82] Two days later, in a telegram to Liu K'un-i and Yuan Shih-k'ai, now governor-general of Chihli, Chang expressed great concern over the implications of the alliance. Referring to the first article on the British and Japanese declaration to intervene in Chinese and Korean domestic disturbances, he questioned the meaning of 'disturbances'. Did it mean that they could send troops to China at will just as Japan did in Korea during the Tonghak Insurrection? Painfully he proclaimed: 'To rely on others for preservation and to be placed along with Korea is most disheartening. Our country has fallen to such a state of weakness that I have nothing more to say!'[83]

Yuan Shih-k'ai was even more emphatic in his analysis of the alliance. No country in the East, he informed the court, had a better army than Japan and no country in the West had a better navy than Britain. The com-

[80] Marius B. Jansen, *Japan and China: from war to peace, 1894–1972*, 79–80.
[81] Michael H. Hunt, *Frontier defense and the open door: Manchuria in Chinese-American relations, 1895–1911*, 78, 81.
[82] *WCSL*, 152.10b–12a.
[83] Chang Chih-tung, *Chang Wen-hsiang kung ch'üan-chi* (Complete collection of Chang Chih-tung's papers), 178.15.

bination of the two created a new power bloc affecting not only the balance in East Asia but the entire world, and they did so to protect their own national interests without any real intention of preserving China and Korea. Yuan asked, why should Britain and Japan exert themselves at great expense for the benefit of China? Therefore, the Chinese should expect no benefits from the alliance. On the contrary, the alliance forebode trouble for China should she ever relax her vigilance. Soberly he warned, 'There is no greater shame for China than to rely on the alliance of other countries for the preservation of her territory!' In the face of such humiliation, Yuan urged the court to strengthen the country through an immediate institutional reform, rapid army training, development of resources, and promotion of modern education.[84]

Despair prevailed among Chinese officialdom because of the country's total inability to do anything about the situation. It was clear that if the Anglo-Japanese Alliance led to a Russo-Japanese understanding, China would be the loser, and if it led to a war, Chinese territory would be the battleground, and China would be at the mercy of the victor. There was also a growing fear of the rise of Japan as the chief menace to China.[85] Chang Chih-tung found the Japanese becoming increasingly overbearing, employing the tactics of 'sweet talk but vicious action'.[86] He saw through the hollowness of the reference to the Open Door in the Anglo-Japanese Alliance and was very concerned about the ultimate Japanese designs. Yet he continued to regard Japan as a lesser evil than Russia on the grounds that it was preferable for China 'to seek the aid of a nearby state in order to ward off aggression by a distant foe'.[87]

Britain had hoped that the alliance would have a steadying effect on Japan, making her neither too belligerent nor too conciliatory towards Russia, thus lessening the chances of war. She saw no objection to an agreement between Japan and Russia provided she was kept informed of the negotiations and it did not violate the stipulations of the alliance. The Japanese government believed that an agreement with Russia was preferable to war, but the military doubted that any enduring agreement was possible and feared that Russian military power in the East would steadily increase after the completion of the Trans-Siberian and Chinese Eastern railways.

In Russia a series of conferences were held between November 1902 and

[84] Wang Yen-hsi and Wang Shu-min, comps., *Huang-ch'ao Tao-Hsien-T'ung-Kuang tsou-i* (Memorials of the Tao-kuang, Hsien-feng, T'ung-chih, and Kuang-hsu periods of the Ch'ing dynasty), reprinted in Taipei, 1968, 16.18.
[85] Li Kuo-ch'i, *Chang Chih-tung ti wai-chiao cheng-ts'e* (Chang Chih-tung's foreign policy proposals), 323–6.
[86] Chang Chih-tung, *Chang Wen-hsiang kung ch'üan-chi*, 180.35b.   [87] *Ibid.* 85.21b.

April 1903 to deliberate on East Asian policy. The finance minister, Witte, was attacked by an influential group led by the tsarist confidant, Bezobrazov, for involving Russia in the expensive work of railway building in Manchuria without providing adequate security against Chinese hostility or foreign intervention. This group controlled a timber-cutting concession in North Korea which they proposed should be exploited for profit and strategic purposes – using the concession as a military shield against Japanese penetration of southern Manchuria. Witte was rapidly losing influence with the tsar and his policy of peaceful penetration of Manchuria was discarded. The tsar decided that Russia should exploit the timber concession and halt the military evacuation of Manchuria until China accepted new conditions. In an attempt to turn Manchuria into a 'Yellow Russia',[88] St Petersburg decided to demand that China should agree not to cede or lease territory in Manchuria to any other power, nor, without consulting Russia, open any new areas to foreign trade or consular residence. No foreigners, other than Russians, were to be employed in any administrative capacity in Manchuria; the Russo-Chinese Bank was to continue to collect customs dues at Newchwang; and all rights secured by the Russian subjects in Manchuria were to be preserved by them.

On 18 April 1903 these demands were presented to the Chinese government which promptly communicated them to the interested foreign powers. Encouraged by Britain, Japan and the United States to reject the demands, the Chinese government informed St Petersburg that no new conditions could be discussed until the evacuation of Manchuria was completed in accordance with the convention of April 1902. A set of modified conditions proposed by Russia in September was also rejected, and on 8 October 1903, the date set for the final withdrawal of Russian troops from Manchuria, China concluded revised commercial treaties with the United States and Japan, opening Mukden, Antung and Tatungkow to foreign trade and residence. In retaliation for this direct challenge to their demands, the Russians re-occupied Mukden. Earlier, in August 1903, the tsar had created a viceroyalty of the Far East, vested with independent powers of war and diplomacy after the fashion of the viceroyalty of the Caucasus created in 1845, treating Manchuria as if it were a territory to be absorbed like the Caucasus.[89]

Meanwhile, Japan had entered into negotiations with Russia. The general terms proposed were: (1) preservation of the independence and territorial integrity of China and Korea; (2) maintenance of equal com-

---

[88] Ch'en Fu-kuang, *Yu-Ch'ing i-tai chih Chung-O kuan-hsi*, 338–9.
[89] Wu Hsiang-hsiang, *O-ti ch'in-lueh Chung-kuo shih* (A history of the Russian imperialist aggression in China), 220.

mercial opportunity in those two countries; (3) mutual recognition of the existing legal rights of Russia and Japan in Manchuria and Korea, and of the right to send forces to protect these interests and deal with internal disturbances; and (4) recognition of the exclusive right of Japan to advise and assist Korea in carrying out internal reforms. It was clear that Japan now assumed an interventionist position in Manchuria.

On 28 July 1903 the Russian government agreed to open discussions and the Japanese proposals were delivered on 12 August. In their counter-proposals, delivered on 3 October, the Russians insisted that Manchuria was outside the scope of discussion. As far as Korea was concerned, while recognizing Japan's paramount interests there, they demanded mutual respect for Korea's independence and territorial integrity, a neutral zone north of the thirty-ninth parallel, and no fortification of the south coast. In short, Russia denied Japan's right to intervene in Manchuria while granting her a less than complete control of Korea. Although Russia later abandoned the neutral zone demand, the differences between the two sides were too vast to be bridged. The Japanese concluded that war was inevitable.

The Russo-Japanese War

The decision for war was made in Tokyo after very sober assessments of the differences in the size, military preparation and financial resources of the two countries. It was felt that Japan could win early battles to achieve a position of strength from which to launch a peace settlement. General Kodama Gentarō, chief of staff, informed the throne: 'There is a good chance that Japan will win six out of ten victories on the battlefield. If that is the case, we can expect some country to step forward to offer its good offices to negotiate peace.'[90] The country in question was the United States, for President Roosevelt was sympathetic with Japan's role in bearing the brunt of fighting Russia and defending the Open Door in Manchuria, since the Chinese themselves could not do it and the United States would not do it due to public apathy.[91] To exploit fully the president's goodwill, Japan sent his former Harvard classmate, Kaneko Kentarō, to Washington. On 6 February 1904 Japan broke off negotiations with Russia and started hostilities a day later. On 10 February Russia and Japan declared war against each other.

The Ch'ing court was in a dilemma as to China's status in the war, which was fought in Manchuria. Even before the diplomatic impasse, Yuan Shih-k'ai advised the court on 27 December 1903 that 'if we make common cause with Russia, the Japanese navy would attack our Southeast;

---

[90] Jansen, *Japan and China*, 81.   [91] Hunt, *Frontier defense and the open door*, 78–81.

if we make common cause with Japan, the Russian army would invade our Northwest. Not only would China be placed in a dangerous position but the entire globe could be endangered. In case of a breakdown in Russo-Japanese negotiations, we should proclaim neutrality.'[92] On 7 January 1904 the Japanese minister in China informed Peking that his government desired that China remain strictly neutral in the event of a Russo-Japanese War. On 22 January Yuan again impressed upon the court the importance of neutrality, since China lacked the capacity to prevent the war from taking place in her territory. The defence of Manchuria, he pointed out, would require hundreds of thousands of men and even the defence of key points would take sixty to a hundred thousand, when China at best could mobilize only twenty to thirty thousand soldiers, whose munitions were in short supply because of the prohibition of arms importation by the Boxer Protocol.[93] Other officials such as Ts'en Ch'un-hsuan, governor-general of Liang-Kwang, however, advocated joining with Japan against Russia in an attempt to recover Manchuria.[94] But this was clearly an impractical suggestion. At the outbreak of the war, Yuan again urged the court to proclaim neutrality 'to settle people's minds'.[95] Only then did the court make the announcement, at the same time appealing to the belligerents to respect the imperial tombs at Mukden and Hsingking and not usurp the sovereignty of China in Manchuria: 'The territorial right of Manchuria must remain Chinese regardless of who wins and who loses; neither country should occupy (the area).' Japan agreed to honour China's neutrality and disclaimed any postwar territorial ambitions, but Russia refused to regard Manchuria as a neutral territory or discuss its future status.[96] Chinese public opinion became deeply resentful of the Russian arrogance and also critical of the timid Ch'ing attitude.

Earlier, on 6 February, the German ambassador in Washington suggested to Roosevelt that the United States propose to the various powers that they cooperate to maintain the neutrality of Chinese territory south of the Great Wall. Roosevelt objected that such a proposal would leave Russia free to operate in Mongolia and Sinkiang and that the dispatch of an international force for the purpose of protecting North China might provoke Chinese hostility. But Washington did send notes to the powers asking them to urge Japan and Russia to 'respect the neutrality of China and in all practicable ways her administrative entity'. The neutral powers as well as Japan and Russia agreed to this on the understanding that Manchuria be excluded.

The war itself hardly needs recounting here. Suffice it to say that by

[92] WCSL, 179.4b.   [93] Ibid. 181.3–5.   [94] Ibid. 181.16–17.
[95] Ibid. 181.18.   [96] Ibid. 181.27; 182.5, 7b.

spring 1905 the Japanese had taken Port Arthur, driven the Russians from southern Manchuria, landed in the Sakhalin Islands, and completely defeated the Russian navy, including the near-total destruction of the Baltic Fleet in the Straits of Tsushima. Militarily and financially exhausted, Japan asked Roosevelt to use his good offices to bring about a peace conference, which was held at Portsmouth, New Hampshire.

The Chinese were deeply concerned about the peace terms and how they would affect the future of their country. Sun Pao-ch'i, minister in Berlin, recommended that China take the initiative in opening Manchuria, Mongolia and Sinkiang to foreign commerce, as a means of preserving her sovereignty and forestalling future Russian designs.[97] The court asked for suggestions from the provinces and Chang Chih-tung's response of 24 July 1905 represented the consensus of most officials: 'It is utterly impossible that Japan would return to China all the special privileges she has seized in Manchuria. But if she takes too much she would violate her earlier pledge and incur the jealousy of European powers. This she would not do. [In saying] she is for China, Japan is in fact for herself, for a strong Japan needs the preservation of China. Russia only wants to deceive China and swallow her up; it is purely a case of hurting us and benefiting themselves . . . . Hence, regardless of the final peace terms, whatever rights Japan obtains in the East are far preferable to Russian [gains].'[98] Clearly, Chinese attitudes had changed from 'anti-Japanese, pro-Russian' after the Sino-Japanese War to 'pro-Japanese, anti-Russian' after the Russo-Japanese War.

Chang Chih-tung also recommended the complete opening of Manchuria to foreign commerce and residence, introducing British and American influence to counter the Japanese, and the employment of foreign advisers, including the Japanese, to govern the area. With the presence of these foreigners, he concluded, Manchuria could no longer be governed in the old way and her special status should be ended.[99]

The peace treaty, signed on 5 September 1905, provided for: Russian recognition of Japan's political, economic and military pre-eminence in Korea; the mutual withdrawal of troops from Manchuria within eighteen months; and the return of Manchuria to China except for the leased territory of Liaotung and the southern section of the Manchurian railway, which Russia agreed to transfer to Japan subject to China's approval. Russia agreed to cede to Japan the southern half of Sakhalin and the adjacent islands. Both Japan and Russia had the right to station troops in

[97] *Ch'ing Kuang-hsu ch'ao Chung-Jih chiao-she shih-liao* (Historical materials on Sino-Japanese negotiations during the Kuang-hsu period), 68.25, 24 June 1904.
[98] *WCSL*, 190.12b–15b.
[99] Chang Chih-tung, *Chang Wen-hsiang kung ch'üan-chi*, 85.23–b.

Manchuria to protect their respective railways, but not more than fifteen soldiers per kilometre. On 23 December 1905 China and Japan signed a 'Secret Protocol of 16 Articles' in Peking, which ratified the transfer of the Liaotung leasehold and the South Manchurian Railway to Japan. In addition it opened sixteen ports and agreed on a joint Sino-Japanese exploitation of the forest on the southern side of the Yalu River. Japan gained far more than was specified in the Portsmouth treaty, as a compensation for the 'generous' terms for Russia. She had in fact replaced Russia as the chief imperialist in Manchuria.

Japan's emergence as a great power and her renewal of a closer alliance with Britain in 1905 ushered in a new chapter in the international relations of East Asia. It did not end the rivalries of the powers in China but it did remove the fear of territorial partition which had threatened the moribund Ch'ing empire since 1895. Had Russia been victorious, she would most likely have annexed Manchuria and perhaps Mongolia, provoking the other powers to demand territorial compensation. But in defeat, Russia turned her attention to the Balkans where she collided with Austria-Hungary and Germany, setting the stage for World War I. Japan, now firmly established in southern Manchuria, was in a position eventually to threaten the independence and territorial integrity of China. But, in 1905, the return of Chinese administration in Manchuria, even though circumscribed by the special privileges of Japan and Russia, ensured that Manchuria would remain Chinese. On 20 April 1907 the Ch'ing court took measures to end the special political status of Manchuria as a frontier homeland of the Manchus and instituted the regular provincial system there, with Hsu Shih-ch'ang as governor-general and concurrently imperial commissioner, assisted by three civil governors who replaced the military governors in the provinces of Fengtien, Kirin and Heilungkiang.[100]

Equally notable was the rise of a constitutional movement in China under the impact of the Russo-Japanese War. The famous scholar-turned-industrialist, Chang Chien, proclaimed that 'the victory of Japan and the defeat of Russia are the victory of constitutionalism and the defeat of monarchism'. On 1 September 1906 the Ch'ing court was obliged to announce its intention of establishing a constitutional government, but its insincerity alienated it further from the people and gave new impetus to the revolutionary movement. China's unhappy vicissitudes in her foreign relations since the 1860s had paralleled the decline of the Ch'ing dynasty.

[100] For details of the status of Manchuria and its reorganization, see Robert H. G. Lee, *The Manchurian frontier in Ch'ing history*, 152 *et seq.*

CHAPTER 3

CHANGING CHINESE VIEWS OF WESTERN RELATIONS, 1840–95*

INTRODUCTION: TRADITIONAL VIEWS OF FOREIGN RELATIONS

China's invaders in the nineteenth century left a more extensive record than anything we are as yet aware of from the Chinese side. After all, success makes a good story. Exploits and impressions on the expanding frontier of the international trading world were variously recorded by travellers, diplomats, missionaries, journalists and others in a flood of correspondence, articles and books now available in Western libraries and archives. The Chinese who suffered invasion, on the other hand, had little but oddities, fears and disasters to record. The story of the foreign intrusion on the whole was unpleasant and humiliating. Moreover, it was known directly to only a few of the ruling class, literati and officials, while the commoners, especially those who worked with foreigners, were not accustomed to writing down their views and experiences for posterity. Consequently in examining Chinese views of the West we are obliged to rely primarily on upper-class writings by scholars who were thoroughly indoctrinated in the Chinese classical teachings and therefore least likely to depart from traditional attitudes towards foreigners.

In addition, China's perception of Western relations during the Ch'ing period was influenced by certain considerations peculiar to the ruling Manchus, who came from an area that differed significantly from China proper. The economy of Manchuria, for example, was semi-nomadic, based originally on a mixture of hunting, fishing and animal husbandry that was fundamentally different from the sedentary and agricultural economy of China. The Manchus therefore paid particular attention strategically to the nomadic societies of Mongolia, Sinkiang and Tibet, which shared certain basic characteristics with Manchuria. Although the Western impact from the coast would have constituted a severe challenge to any Chinese dynasty, the Manchu preoccupation with the northern nomadic region handicapped their efforts to deal with the Westerners who came to China from the south-

---

* The authors wish to acknowledge a heavy debt to Professor Kwang-Ching Liu who has supplied much helpful information, not all of which is specifically noted. They also wish to thank Professors Hao Chang and Richard B. Rice for helpful suggestions.

east. In addition, culturally the Manchus were a non-Sinic people. That they clearly recognized a difference between themselves and the Chinese was abundantly evident throughout their dominion in China. Being aliens themselves, the Manchus were not in a comfortable position to advocate nationalism when China faced the Western invasion in the mid-nineteenth century. Instead, they had their own dynastic interests at heart.

However, as the nineteenth century progressed, these Manchu elements became increasingly insignificant because of the gradual sinicization of the Manchus. They had adopted traditional Sino-Confucian institutions increasingly in the seventeenth century, and their sinicization accelerated after the Yung-cheng reign began in 1722. This trend was evident in the Ch'ien-lung Emperor's celebrated 1793 edict to the king of England, in which he forbade the residence of a Western representative inside China, and told the English that 'there is nothing we lack'.[1] It is not surprising, then, to find that in coping with the problem of Western incursion during the nineteenth century the Manchus relied heavily on Chinese culturalism.

By 1800 the Manchus had firmly adopted the Chinese world view. This Chinese world order was a set of ideas and practices elaborated and perpetuated by the ruling elite of China over many centuries.[2] At the heart of this order was the universal pre-eminence of the Son of Heaven (*t'ien-tzu*) who presided over *t'ien-hsia* 'all under heaven', a term that was often used to embrace the whole world including everything outside of China. For the Chinese, China was not viewed as a part of Asia, much less of the 'Far East'; it was Chung-kuo, or the Middle Kingdom, that embodied civilization itself. These Sinocentric ideas originated from the fact that China's superior size, power, history and resources all made her the natural centre of the East Asian world. The relations of the Chinese with non-Chinese peoples were coloured by this concept of Sinocentrism and an assumption of Chinese superiority.

The Chinese tended to think of their foreign relations as an extension of the principles of social and political order that were manifested internally within China. Accordingly, China's foreign relations were hierarchic and nonegalitarian, like the Chinese society and state. In theory, the Chinese world order should have been hierarchic in several respects – China was internal, large and high, while the non-Chinese 'barbarians' were external, small and low. At the same time, the ideas of inclusiveness and impartiality were also important. On his part the universal ruler should give largesse and hospitality to all in order to 'show nothing left out'. In doing so, a

[1] Ssu-yü Teng and John K. Fairbank, *China's response to the West*, 19.
[2] For this topic we draw heavily on John K. Fairbank, ed. *The Chinese world order* (hereafter *CWO*). For a perceptive analysis of transition of this world view in modern China, see Joseph R. Levenson, *Confucian China and its modern fate: the problem of monarchical decay*.

policy of impartiality should be adopted. All foreigners, near or far, were to be treated equally. The non-Chinese peoples were expected in theory to participate in the Chinese world order by observing the appropriate procedures and ceremonies in their contact with the Son of Heaven. These practices constituted what foreigners called the tribute system.

There were of course discrepancies between theory and practice concerning the Chinese world order. When the non-Chinese peoples refused to conform to this scheme, coercion might be used. Indeed, militarism can easily be found in the classical Confucian tradition. An old saying quoted in the *Tso-chuan* says, 'It is virtue by which the people of the Middle Kingdom are cherished; it is by severity that the wild tribes around are awed'.[3] This militant attitude continued in the later dynasties, as evidenced by the Ming emperor Yung-lo's aggressive determination to bring the whole known world into the framework of the Chinese system. At times when there was no war it was felt important to collect intelligence, analyse it, and test the results of the analysis so as to ascertain the other party's strength and intention. This was in keeping with the ancient classic on the art of war, the *Sun Tzu*: 'If you know yourself and know your adversary, a hundred battles will be a hundred victories.'

But the *Sun Tzu* hastens to add that to be victorious in all one's battles is not supreme excellence; supreme excellence consists in breaking the enemy's resistance without fighting. Actually, in the long history of China's relations with non-Chinese ethnic groups, pacifism generally prevailed, for lack of regard for physical coercion was deeply imbedded in the Confucian tradition. Confucius says, 'By indulgent treatment of men from a distance, they are brought to resort to him [the king] from all quarters.'[4] Mencius went further by declaring that 'those who are skilful in fighting should suffer the highest punishment'.[5] From the former passage a Chinese term for appeasement, *huai-jou yuan-jen* ('to cherish men from afar') was formed, and along with this a *chi-mi* or 'loose rein' policy (as when a rider controls a horse) was frequently used in dealing with stronger 'barbarians'. (The early decades of the mid-nineteenth century treaty system could be viewed in this perspective.) Often in the Han and T'ang dynasties, Confucian literati had warned that the strength of the government and of the people would be exhausted by a policy of military expansion. This pacific foreign policy was a reflection of the established order in China that from Han times onwards esteemed the triumph of literate culture (*wen*) over brute force (*wu*). Yet while the Confucian tradition tends, on balance, to be more

---

[3] James Legge, trans. *The Chinese classics. The Ch'un Ts'ew with the Tso Chuen*, 196.
[4] James Legge, trans. *The Chinese classics. The doctrine of the mean*, 409.
[5] James Legge, trans. *The Chinese classics. The works of Mencius*, 305.

pacific than militant concerning foreign policy, it was by no means one-sided. This ambivalent attitude was manifest in China's views of Western relations from 1840 to 1895.

INITIAL RESPONSE AND INERTIA, 1840–60

Traditional statecraft and the new strategy proposals

The early nineteenth century saw the emergence of revived interest in the school of statecraft or 'learning of practical use to society' (*ching-shih chih yung*). This school of thought, stressing the importance of social participation and this-worldly activism, reflected the ideal of Confucian humanism. On the one hand, it rejected the Neo-Confucian trend towards metaphysical speculation as being 'empty', and, on the other hand, it despised the practice of textual criticism as being pedantic and useless. It had flourished in the seventeenth century but, mainly due to the repressive policy of the Ch'ien-lung Emperor towards the literati class, was overshadowed by the school of scholasticism in the eighteenth century.[6]

The re-emergence of the statecraft school in the nineteenth century was evidenced by the revitalization of the Modern Text School of classical learning, which laid stress on one's emotional need for moral commitment to bring peace and prosperity to state and society in a practical way. An important scholar in this intellectual revival was Chuang Ts'un-yü of Wu-chin, Kiangsu (1719–88). Through his grandson Liu Feng-lu (1776–1829), who studied the classics under him, the *ching-shih* school gained momentum, for Liu exerted both direct and indirect influence on a group of young scholars during the early nineteenth century. They included the prolific writers Kung Tzu-chen and Pao Shih-ch'en, and the frontier experts Yao Ying and Hsiao Ling-yü. This group also included Lin Tse-hsu and Huang Chueh-tzu, who were to play important roles in the Opium War, and Wei Yuan and Feng Kuei-fen, who later were noted as reformers primarily interested in the problems arising from China's relations with the West. Of these men Wei Yuan and Kung Tzu-chen had especially close ties with Liu Feng-lu.

In the preface to *Huang-ch'ao ching-shih wen-pien* (Collection of Ch'ing dynasty writings on statecraft), Wei Yuan set forth two basic approaches of the statecraft school: emphasis on the present, and stress on the importance of practical application. What were the pressing problems of China during this time? In the first decades of the nineteenth century, a major

---

[6] For a brief account of the intellectual trends in early Ch'ing, see Liang Ch'i-ch'ao, *Intellectual trends in the Ch'ing period* (*Ch'ing-tai hsueh-shu kai-lun*), trans. by Immanuel C. Y. Hsu, I and II.

concern of the *ching-shih* literati was the problem of domestic administration, resulting from the slow process of dynastic decline in general and the White Lotus Rebellion in particular (see volume 10, chapter 3). These problems involved rebel-suppression techniques and general reform of grain transport and the salt gabelle. As the rebellion drew to a close, the *ching-shih* scholars paid increasing attention to frontier problems, especially those concerning Inner Asia. A case in point was Wei Yuan (1794–1857), who began his frontier interests when he was in his twenties. In 1830 his plan to make a personal tour of Sinkiang with General Yang Fang aborted, a missed opportunity he regretted for the rest of his life. However, he continued his investigation of the northern frontier, completing at least eight studies.[7] Other statecraft scholars continued such investigations, as evidenced by Chang Mu and Ho Ch'iu-t'ao in the fifties and Tseng Chi-tse and Chang Chih-tung in the seventies and eighties.

The maritime frontiers, to be sure, had sometimes caused concern. The coastal harassments of the Sino-Japanese pirates in the sixteenth century and the threats of Koxinga's forces from Taiwan during the seventeenth century were worrying, yet before the mid-nineteenth century China's overriding concern had been the Inner Asian frontier. With the mounting Western incursion from the south-east coast, however, the second quarter of the nineteenth century saw a significant reorientation in the focus of Chinese statecraft – from Inner Asia to the maritime world, whence came 'barbarians' with a new technology.

The statecraft writer Pao Shih-ch'en declared as early as 1826 that the British would soon pose a serious threat to China from the coast, but his view in this respect remained ambivalent; he wrote later that the relief of people's sufferings was far more important than maritime defence. The early writings on maritime defence naturally focused on the Kwangtung coast. Kuan T'ien-p'ei, who was to be killed during the Opium War, compiled the *Ch'ou-hai ch'u-chi* (First collection of papers relating to preparation for maritime defence) around 1836, and similar studies were completed by Liang T'ing-nan, Yü Ch'ang-hui and Li Fu-hsiang after the war.[8]

The overriding concern of some statecraft literati-officials was to understand the maritime West. But how? For Commissioner Lin Tse-hsu, an effective way was through translation. When he was in Canton in 1839, he ordered the translation of foreign newspapers from Canton, Macao, Singapore and India. Wei Yuan later suggested the establishment of an official translation institute. Kuo Sung-tao's 1859 memorial proposed the

[7] Wang Chia-chien, *Wei Yuan tui hsi-fang ti jen-shih chi ch'i hai-fang ssu-hsiang* (Wei Yuan's knowledge of the West and his ideas regarding maritime defence), 6.
[8] Ch'i Ssu-ho *et al.* eds. *Ya-p'ien chan cheng* (The Opium War), 4.461; 6.491, 535.

creation of an official school for the teaching of foreign languages.[9] (This approach was to be used during the fifties by some pragmatic officials on the coast, such as Ho Kuei-ch'ing, Lao Ch'ung-kuang and Hsueh Huan.) Besides newspapers, information was gathered on Western history, geography, law and political conditions. Under Commissioner Lin's sponsorship, passages of international law from Vattel were translated. Later, Liang T'ing-nan wrote a book, *Ho-chung-kuo shuo* (On the United States), which spoke highly of the American political system. Impressive as these works might be, it was the study of world geography that was to have the most considerable influence.

The interest in world geography appeared on the surface to be directed towards obtaining knowledge of the unknown Western world, and indeed of the entire globe. But when we consider the urgent needs of the times, it can be seen as a movement to strengthen China's own knowledge and ability. In other words, a segment of Chinese officials and literati of the period, after a war with a barbarian state of Western Europe, urgently sought to understand the enemy and discover what kind of place Europe was. It was necessary to seek correct answers. Under this pressure, there was a surge of interest in world geography.

The data on Europe in Chinese gazetteers and historical works were extremely scanty. This was especially true of materials concerning the powerful countries of nineteenth-century Europe, since earlier knowledge of world geography had all come from the pens of Catholic missionaries, and even among these works there were only three illustrated geographies. Before the 1840s Chinese authors had produced three fairly reliable reference works: Ch'en Lun-chiung's *Hai-kuo wen-chien lu* (Heard and seen in maritime countries; published in 1730), Wang Ta-hai's *Hai-tao i chih* (Little-known account of the seas and islands; 1760) and Hsieh Ch'ing-kao's *Hai-lu* (Records of the seas; 1820). Lin Tse-hsu consulted the *Hai-lu* to get an understanding of the situation in Britain.[10]

After 1840 Chinese literati began gradually to pay more attention to the subject of world geography, and by 1861 more than twenty-two books had been written.[11] Commissioner Lin Tse-hsu championed such study. Under his auspices, passages from Murray's *Cyclopaedia of Geography* were translated into Chinese in 1841 under the title of *Ssu-chou chih* (A gazetteer of

[9] Kuo T'ing-i *et al. Kuo Sung-tao hsien-sheng nien-p'u* (A chronological biography of Kuo Sung-tao), 1.132–4.

[10] Chung-yang yen-chiu-yuan chin-tai-shih yen-chiu-so, comp. *Chin-tai Chung-kuo tui Hsi-fang chi lieh-ch'iang jen-shih tzu-liao hui-pien* (Compendium of materials on modern Chinese understanding of the West and of the various powers; hereafter *HFJS*), 145.

[11] Some of these twenty-two works were collected in the geographical series *Hsiao-fang-hu chai yü-ti ts'ung-ch'ao* (Geographical series of Hsiao-fang-hu studio, preface 1894). Some were published separately. Seven are now lost except for their titles.

four continents). A pioneer and comprehensive work was Wei Yuan's *Hai-kuo t'u chih* (Illustrated treatise on the maritime kingdoms) which had its origins in Lin. The materials on foreign countries gathered by Lin were turned over to Wei in 1841, who compiled them into a large work of fifty *chüan* in 1842 and published it in the following year. This was the first significant Chinese work on the West.[12] Yao Ying was similarly interested in world geography. Unlike Commissioner Lin Tse-hsu and Wei Yuan, Yao acquired his knowledge of foreign countries from the British prisoners of war whom he captured while serving as a *taotai* on Taiwan during the Opium War. Another noted study on this subject entitled *Ying huan chih-lueh* (A brief survey of the maritime circuit) was compiled by Hsu Chi-yü, governor of Fukien, and was published in 1848.

With regard to their motives for writing, these men expressed the intention of making a rigorous pursuit of knowledge and of guiding the efforts of their fellow countrymen. Wei Yuan stated that his most important motive was to understand completely the situation of foreigners. Whether concerning the making of war or the conduct of peace negotiations, his central idea was to study the advantages the foreigners enjoyed and then to see how these advantages might be turned to use in subduing them. Because of this the *Hai-kuo t'u-chih* contains not only the geography of the various countries but, at the same time, as complete a treatment as possible of the techniques of shipbuilding and weapons production in foreign countries. Wei held that all his fellow countrymen should study the geography of foreign countries. Hsu Chi-yü's *Ying huan chih-lueh* was more systematic. Because Hsu was in charge of commercial affairs at Foochow, he could combine his official duties with his writing. He thus compiled the book from foreign sources by working daily over a five-year period. Yao Ying avowed that his motive in writing came from his anger over the treatment of China at the hands of foreigners. His hope was that he could bring Chinese, both young and old, to a true knowledge of other countries. Finally, he wanted to save China from disgrace, and by emphasizing maritime and frontier defence avoid China's conquest by a foreign nation.[13]

These scholars, especially Wei and Hsu, were thus instrumental in changing the Chinese geographical picture of the outside world. In so doing, they played a significant role, for they not only introduced new knowledge of the West, but also began to dissolve the Sinocentric view by showing that China was in reality not the 'Middle Kingdom'.

[12] For Lin Tse-hsu, see Ch'i Ssu-ho *et al. Ya-p'ien chan-cheng*, 6.506. For Wei Yuan, see articles by Jane K. Leonard and Peter M. Mitchell in *MAS*, 6.2 (1972) 151–204.

[13] Yao Ying, *Tung-ming wen hou-chi* (Supplement to Yao Ying's collected essays), 8.10b–11. Hsu Chi-yü, *Ying huan chih-lueh* (A brief survey of the maritime circuit), preface. Wei Yuan, *Hai-kuo t'u chih* (Illustrated treatise on the maritime kingdoms), preface. Also Fred W. Drake,

Impressed with British military power, some were interested in the superior Western weaponry and the need for China to emulate it. This new interest was epitomized in the popular saying *ch'uan-chien p'ao-li* (strong ships, powerful cannon). In the years 1821–61 at least sixty-six men supported the view that China must procure such warships and guns, and these included the Tao-kuang Emperor, high government officials and eminent scholars.[14] All of them advocated shipbuilding and arms research. Lin Tse-hsu also championed this programme. He purchased two hundred foreign guns to strengthen the Canton defences and ordered the translation of manuals on Western gun-making. For political reasons, however, he stopped short of advocating publicly the emulation of Western armament.

Wei Yuan, on the other hand, was more straightforward. In January 1843, he finished the first draft of his *Hai-kuo t'u chih*, in which he advocated the building of a shipyard and an arsenal at Canton, and the hiring of French and American engineers to carry out construction and to teach ship navigation and the operation of weapons. He also suggested adding a section to the imperial military examinations for naval officers so that those able to construct ships and weapons could enter public service, and those in the ranks who could pilot ships and operate weapons could gain promotion. He suggested that all naval officers be required to advance by these routes. These were pioneer ideas in the military history of modern China.[15]

Excluding the reprints of traditional works on weapons and munitions, the period produced twenty-two new works on Western arms – seven about the production of guns and cannon, and six on mines and bombs. Two works dealt with gun emplacements, and another two, the production of gunpowder. The remaining five works were on offensive and defensive artillery tactics. Most of these twenty-two works were finished between 1840 and 1850, with the latest appearing before 1860.[16] The relative values

---

China charts the world: Hsu Chi-yü and his geography of 1848.

[14] The names of forty-five are listed in Wang Erh-min, *Ch'ing-chi ping-kung yeh ti hsing-ch'i* (The rise of the armaments industry in the late Ch'ing period), 35. The others are: the Tao-kuang Emperor, Lu K'un (governor-general of Kwangtung and Kwangsi), I-liang (governor-general of Liang-Kiang), Chi-erh-hang-a (governor of Kiangsu), Ho Kuei-ch'ing (governor-general of Liang-Kiang), Chou T'ien-chueh (governor-general of grain transport), Kuei-liang (grand secretary), Hua-sha-na (president of the Board of Civil Appointments), Shen Chao-lin (president of the Board of War), Chin Ying-lin (sub-director of the Court of Judicature and Revision), Hsueh Shu-t'ang (junior metropolitan censor), Liu Ch'eng-chung (provincial censor), Yin Keng-yun (provincial censor), and the following gentry: T'ang I, Fang Hsiung-fei, Hsiao Ling-yü, Hsia Hsieh, Liang T'ing-nan, Wu Min-shu, Hsu Nai and Feng Kuei-fen.   [15] Wei Yuan, *Hai-kuo*, 2.2a–b.

[16] Ting Kung-ch'en, Kung Chen-lin (two works), Wang Chung-yang, Liang Chang-chü (two) and Hsi-la-pen wrote about guns and cannon; Huang Mien (two), Ting Shou-ts'un, P'an Shih-ch'eng, Lin Tse-hsu and Kao Pang-che about mines and bombs; Huang Mien and Yeh Shih-huai about gun emplacements; and Ting Shou-ts'un and Ch'en Chieh-p'ing about gunpowder. The remaining five authors were Chin Ying-lin, Chang Huan-yuan, Yü Ch'ang-hui, Hsu Nai-chi and Ch'i Yuan-fu. For a fuller account of these works, see Wang Erh-min,

of these writings varied, but they all demonstrate the intention of the Chinese literati to make an intensive effort to study Western military technology. In addition, more than ten authors investigated or wrote about Western warships in this period. The most detailed explanation was the *Huo-lun-ch'uan t'u-shuo* (Illustrated treatise on the steamship) by Cheng Fu-kuang.[17] All of these reactions were directly stimulated by Western contact, which resulted in the Chinese making real demands upon themselves. Collectively, these studies were for the purpose of, as Wei put it, 'learning the superior techniques of the barbarians in order to control the barbarians'.

Meanwhile, until China was able to use its own military strength, various temporary methods for controlling barbarians were suggested. One policy was the use of trade (*yung shang chih i*). Under the tribute system China as the host country customarily looked upon foreign relations and trade as one and the same thing. In fact, China did not even recognize the existence of foreign relations with the Western countries but only of 'barbarian affairs', in essence another name for trade. Some literati of the period, therefore, naturally thought of using trade to meet the necessities of foreign relations. In their treatment of traders from far-off countries, the Chinese had very early used the method of opening or closing markets in order to control them. It was not the intention of China to refuse trade absolutely, and this ultimate recourse was, therefore, not often used, although stoppages of trade had been used with increasing frequency to put pressure on the East India Company at Canton. In the 1840s Chinese officials tended to underestimate the true strength of the Western powers, and therefore used this policy too often. Failing at the same time to make a reasonable estimate of their own strength and state of preparedness, they invited the disaster of warfare. Trade stoppage was mainly used by Hsu Kuang-chin and by Yeh Ming-ch'en, successive governors-general at Canton, who were the most important advocates of the policy.[18]

The basic hypothesis of Sino-foreign trade, as the Chinese understood it, was that the foreigners could not give up their trade and so it could be used

Ch'ing-chi ping-kung yeh ti hsing-ch'i, 206-8; Wei Yuan, *Hai-kuo*, 87.2; *HFJS*, 229, 301-2, 418-19, 432, 435, 439, 875-904.

[17] Wei Yuan, *Hai-kuo*, 84.1b-6; 85 (this *chüan* is Cheng Fu-kuang's *Huo-lun-ch'uan t'u-shuo* or *Illustrated treatise on the steamship*). Hsieh Ch'ing-kao and Yang Ping-nan, *Hai-lu* (Records of the seas), 1.75. *HFJS*, 248-9, 860. *Shih-liao hsun-k'an* (Historical materials published thrice-monthly), 38.398b. *Ch'ing-tai ch'ou-pan i-wu shih-mo* (Complete record of the management of barbarian affairs), Tao-kuang (hereafter *IWSM-TK*) 59.48b; 63.38b-39. Wang Wen-t'ai, *Hung-mao-fan Ying-chi-li k'ao-lueh* (Short account of the red-haired English barbarians), in Wang Ch'ao-tsung, comp. *Hai-wai fan-i lu*, 6b. Wang Ta-hai, *Hai-tao i chih* (Little-known account of the seas and islands), in *Hai-wai fan-i lu*, 7a-b. Hsu Chi-yü, *Ying huan chih-lueh*, 7.48b-49.

[18] *IWSM-TK*, 80.25.

to make them surrender.[19] What was the value of this policy in fact? Modern sovereign states have used it continually, and it seems to be a necessary part of national sovereignty. But in the ancient tradition of trade with China under the tribute system, a trade boycott was only one device for manipulating the barbarian. The basic strategy was to use the lure of trade and profit to meet the foreigner's desires and thus to appease him and avoid military conflict. After the Opium War and the opening of the treaty ports, Chinese officials still thought in this way. Ch'i-ying's idea of extending equal trade opportunities to all the powers was the best evidence of this use of trade as a positive inducement to peaceful behaviour. Trade expansion, then, would have some positive value for the policy of using trade to control foreigners.[20]

As this time-honoured policy did not work as effectively as expected during the mid-nineteenth century, the strategy of using the people to control the barbarians (*yung min chih i*) was also advocated. This concept harks back to the ancient idea that 'Heaven sees as the people see', that the sanction for government is the tacit acquiescence of the populace. Popular opposition that can overthrow government can also be used to oppose invaders. This policy was most clearly suggested by Hsu Kuang-chin as governor-general of Liang-Kuang, and by Sheng-pao, an imperial commissioner,[21] but the number of those who discussed the policy was rather large, and its influence was widespread. The real aim was to use the public sentiment of the masses to oppose foreigners entering China, and it was first used to oppose the arrival of foreign merchants in the treaty ports. Later it was gradually applied in the interior to oppose the propagation of Christianity, frequently resulting in serious diplomatic complications. This policy reflected two of the literati's basic beliefs: the first was that foreigners feared the common people, whenever they were aroused against them (they often were by Chinese officials), and so it was possible to use popular sentiment to control the barbarians.[22] The second belief was that the people were loyal, given to group action, impetuous and easily incited, and thus could be used to oppose the foreigners.[23]

By the same token, the foreigners could be manoeuvred into opposing one another. This was the policy of using barbarians to control barbarians (*i i chih i*). As early as the sixth century BC, the Chinese had already deve-

[19] *Shih-liao hsun-k'an*, 36.340. IWSM-TK, 80.4a–b. Hsu Chi-yü, *Sung-k'an hsien-sheng ch'üan-chi* (Complete works of Hsu Chi-yü), 1.36b.

[20] Hsiao Ling-yü, *Yueh-tung shih-po lun* (On foreign trade and shipping in Kwangtung), 2b, in *Hsiao-fang-hu chai yü-ti ts'ung-ch'ao* (hereafter HFHC), 2nd supplementary series, pt 9.

[21] *Shih-liao hsun-k'an*, 36.340. IWSM, Hsien-feng (hereafter IWSM-HF), 34.22.

[22] Hsu Chi-yü, *Sung-k'an*, 1.31b–32.

[23] Wang Erh-min, 'Ch'i-ying wai-chiao' (The diplomacy of Ch'i-ying), *Ta-lu tsa-chih*, 30.10 (1965) 330–3.

loped the concept that the 'security of the Son of Heaven lay in [using] the surrounding barbarian states' (*t'ien-tzu shou tsai ssu-i*). This concept easily led to the idea of using foreigners to control foreigners.[24] Beginning in the Former Han dynasty when China was first involved with the Inner Asian area, both the theoretical discussions of scholars and the actual conduct of foreign relations showed the importance of the policy of 'using barbarians to control barbarians'. In the Opium War period the idea was proposed anew. Lin Tse-hsu advocated allowing the merchants of all other foreign countries except England to trade with China as a method of subduing England. During the war, Juan Yuan had suggested using America to control England, but the imperial negotiator I-li-pu disapproved. In the discussions which followed the war, Wei Yuan proposed a Chinese alliance on land with Russia to threaten British India, and even Vietnam, Burma and Nepal, and an alliance by sea with France and the United States to form a joint offensive strategy against Britain. It was only later, when Ch'i-ying was responsible for foreign affairs at Canton, that people came forward to oppose this policy. The opposition rested on two arguments. First, it was reasoned that although China had used the policy of 'using barbarians to control barbarians' from ancient times, it had always been necessary for China herself to be truly strong before the policy could be effective. In the present circumstances, America and France were separated from China by a great distance, and China had no power to control them. Secondly, supposing that America and France would help China, it could not be guaranteed that they would win. And should they win, then China would be faced with an even greater problem of control.[25]

In the 'using barbarians' policy of this period, there was no effort to influence the far-off countries of Europe and America. The Chinese officials and literati were not so far-reaching in their ambitions. The policy was aimed only at those British, American and French officials and merchants who came to China. It proposed to use the lure of trade with China to put the various countries in a state of mutual pressure, enmity and even warfare. The policy rested upon China's offering the advantages of trade to all sides. Thus it can readily be seen that the policy of 1840 and the policy of 'using barbarians to control barbarians' advocated by Li Hung-chang and Chang Chih-tung in the world of power politics and imperialist rivalry after 1870, are quite different. Of the three policies, 'using trade', 'using the

[24] Lei Hai-tsung, 'Ku-tai Chung-kuo ti wai-chiao' (Diplomacy in ancient China), *She-hui k'o-hsueh*, 3.1 (1941) 1-4. Hsia Hsieh, *Chung-hsi chi-shih* (A record of Sino-Western affairs), 1.19b. Li Hung-chang, *Li Wen-chung kung p'eng-liao han-kao* (Li Hung-chang's letters to friends and colleagues), 10.35.

[25] *IWSM-TK*, 21.21-2b; 24.36-7b. Wei Yuan, *Hai-kuo*, 2.1a-b. Wang Erh-min, 'Ch'i-ying wai-chiao',

people', and 'using barbarians', the last had the deepest and most far-reaching influence.

Misunderstanding and inertia

As the meeting of China and the West was a cultural conflict in the broadest sense, it is little wonder that the response to this new situation produced much misunderstanding and often inadequate methods. Two well-known examples are when England sent Lord Macartney to China in 1793 and Lord Amherst in 1816. The Chinese did not have a serious grasp of British national power or prestige, and they one-sidedly emphasized the requirements of the minute rites of the imperial tribute system, forcing the foreigners to accept the Chinese scheme of things. Thus two opportunities to establish normal bilateral diplomatic relations with Britain were lost. Under the tribute system China forced the foreigners to maintain trade contact only at Canton, and this policy was in the end self-defeating.

The Chinese misunderstanding of the Westerner was evident in their physical images of him. His very outward appearance was a source of wonderment: white skin, red hair, blue deep-set eyes, high-bridged noses, beards, tall stature and tight-fitting clothes. All these things caused strange reactions and led to misunderstandings of which the Opium War period has left many records. Wang Chung-yang, a literatus of the period, wrote a poem to describe his impressions. He pictured the British as having the beaks of eagles, the eyes of cats, red beards and hair, and long legs which could not be bent, making it impossible for them to run or jump. Their green eyes could not stand daylight so that at noonday they feared even to open them.[26] Yü-ch'ien, governor-general of Liang-Kiang, described clearly in several places how the British could not bend their waists or legs so that if they were struck, they would immediately fall over.[27] Admittedly, a few gentry members questioned these prevailing views. For example, the literatus Hsiao Ling-yü presented contrary evidence based on what he had actually seen – foreigners nimbly climbing mountains and crossing rivers. Pao Shih-ch'en made the common-sense judgment that the British were born and grew up on land and that he therefore could not accept the common belief that the British, once they disembarked from their ships, were unable to do anything.[28] Nevertheless, the physical difference between

[26] A Ying, comp. *Ya-p'ien chan-cheng wen-hsueh chi* (Literary writings concerning the Opium War), 191.
[27] *Shih-liao hsun-k'an*, 38.399.
[28] Hsiao Ling-yü, *Ying-chi-li chi* (On England), 1b, in *HFHC*, 2nd supplementary series, pt. 11. Pao Shih-ch'en, *An-Wu ssu-chung* (Four collections regarding peaceful government of Kiangsu), 35.10b. Arthur Waley, *The Opium War through Chinese eyes*, gives fascinating Chinese accounts of the war.

Chinese and Westerners did constitute a misunderstanding in Chinese minds.

Relations between China and the outside began with trade. It was commonly believed in China that foreigners needed large quantities of such Chinese products as silk, tea and rhubarb. From a superficial understanding of the situation, a segment of the Chinese literati drew some rather absurd conclusions which were firmly believed, widely disseminated and mutually reinforcing. That foreigners needed tea and rhubarb was widely known and that foreigners imported these two products was obvious. In the Opium War period many firmly believed that the foreigners needed tea and rhubarb so much that if the supply were cut off, they would become blind and subject to diseases of the intestines. Although several enlightened literati-officials, such as Huang En-t'ung, postwar governor of Kwangtung, and Wei Yuan, argued that foreigners wanted Chinese tea because of its superior taste and not as a question of life or death,[29] the misconception about the importance of tea and rhubarb prevailed. In fact, it was so widely embedded in Chinese minds that at least twenty citations from works of the period express this over-confident fantasy. Furthermore, among those subscribing to the concept were some practical-minded statecraft literati-officials, such as Commissioner Lin Tse-hsu, Pao Shih-ch'en and Hsiao Ling-yü.[30]

Behind these misjudgments lay a deep-rooted intellectual-institutional inertia. The Treaty of Nanking, for example, was regarded by the Tao-kuang Emperor as a device that would 'permanently prevent further troubles from happening' (*yung tu hou-huan*). Nor did the grand councillors provide the much needed impetus for change. Mu-chang-a and Sai-shang-a were not talented, the Neo-Confucianist Ch'i Chün-tsao was conservative and belligerent, the moralist Wang Ting committed suicide, and the practical-minded P'an Shih-en was too old to be vigorous and finally retired in 1849. Actually, the political atmosphere at Peking was so apathetic to politics after the Opium War that one could find in the restaurants and tea-shops signs saying: 'Don't talk about current affairs' (*mien-t'an shih-shih*).[31]

Provincial leaders were no better. Their programmes to deal with this

---

[29] Huang En-t'ung, *Fu-i chi-lueh* (Brief account of the pacification of barbarians), 2. Wei Yuan, *Hai-kuo*. 2.5b.

[30] Huang Chün-tsai, *Chin-hu ch'i-mo* (Seven works of Huang Chün-tsai), 2.2. *Shih-liao hsun-k'an*, 38.402b. *IWSM-TK*, 4.30; 5.25b-26; 9.6. *IWSM-HF*, 62.44b. Hsia Hsieh, *Chung-Hsi*, 3.21b-22. Chin Ying-lin, *Ch'ih-hua t'ang wen-ch'ao* (Essays written at the Ch'ih-hua t'ang), 12.3. T'ang I, *Yu-ts'un wen* (Essays of T'ang I), 4.13b-14. Hsiao Ling-yü, *Yueh-tung*, 1b. Yeh Chung-chin, *Ying-chi-li-kuo i-ch'ing chi-lueh* (A brief account of the condition of the English barbarians), 3b, in *HFHC* 2nd supplementary series, pt 11. Pao Shih-ch'en, *An-Wu*, 35.9.

[31] Ch'i Ssu-ho *et al.* *Ya-p'ien chan-cheng*, 5.529; 6.240, 459-62.

new situation were tradition-oriented, stressing the training of soldiers to swim, preparation for setting fires to attack the enemy, and restoration of military positions on the coast which had been destroyed during the war. Ch'i-ying, governor-general of Liang-Kwang, submitted a copy of an essay on military strategy written by a noted official of the T'ang period some eleven centuries before. Other governors-general on the coast, such as Ch'i-shan, Yang Kuo-chen, I-liang, Niu-chien, Pi-ch'ang and Li Hsing-yuan, were all indifferent to change. Liu Yun-k'o and Ho Kuei-ch'ing were exceptions, but even Liu was only a half-hearted reformer. This political-institutional inertia was also manifest in the coastal governors and high military commanders.[32]

China's inertia can also be seen in the views held by some political leaders towards the West. From the earliest Sino-Western contact, it was generally believed that these foreign relations were solely economic and not political and thus high officials should not be involved. For example, on 17 August 1842, Ch'i-ying planned to meet personally with the British in the negotiations for peace then under way, but the Tao-kuang Emperor ordered that it was better not to do so. Again on 8 May 1846, the imperial commissioner Sai-shang-a proposed a method for dealing with outsiders: cutting off all channels through which foreigners could even request interviews from Chinese officials.[33] Diplomatically, this was truly a 'closed door' foreign policy.

An alternative policy was that of bellicosity. Although Commissioner Lin Tse-hsu did not intend an all-out war with Britain, his hard-line policy was popular among many scholar-officials during this period, including the statecraft writers Pao Shih-ch'en and Yao Ying, and such high officials in the capital as Wang Ting, Li T'ang-chieh and Ch'i Chün-tsao. Less prominent scholars were also attracted by Lin's policies. Tsang Shu-ch'ing, a provincial graduate (*chü-jen*) of 1832, organized a militia force of some 10,000 men in his home province of Kiangsu during the war. For this effort he was granted the title of magistrate after the Treaty of Nanking was signed. But Tsang declined the honour, maintaining that it was shameful to receive an award after the success of an appeasement foreign policy.[34]

In such circumstances, it was no surprise that Wei Yuan's proposal of 'learning their superior techniques from the barbarians' was not heeded. Although a humble beginning in Western studies was made during the 1840–60 period, Chinese views of Western relations were limited by misunderstanding and intellectual-institutional inertia. Refusing to take foreign

[32] *Ibid.* 6.382–3, 386–7, 403–9, 420, 422.
[33] *IWSM-TK*, 58.33; 75.28.
[34] Ch'i Ssu-ho *et al. Ya-p'ien chan-cheng*, 2.569; 5.531; 6.543. Wang Chia-chien, *Wei Yuan hai-fang*, 130.

realities into account, China did not develop a nation-wide sense of urgency until more intense shocks stunned the Middle Kingdom. The net result was that China, in her striving for modern defences, largely 'lost' the two decades following the Opium War.

THE IMPACT OF WESTERN POWER AND WEALTH, 1860-95

Chinese recognition of a 'changed situation'

After 1860 a segment of the literati realized that China was facing a new situation the like of which she had not seen in thousands of years. Huang En-t'ung called this situation *pien-tung* (change), and Li Shu-ch'ang referred to it as *pien-tuan* (a turning point, lit. changed event). Wang T'ao termed it *ch'uang-shih* (an unprecedented event), and Ting Jih-ch'ang, Jui-lin, Tseng Chi-tse and Li Tsung-hsi named it *ch'uang-chü* (an unprecedented situation). But the most common term was *pien-chü* (a changed situation) which was used by Hsia Hsieh, Hsueh Fu-ch'eng, Wang T'ao, Li Hung-chang and Prince Kung (I-hsin) in the sixties, Cheng Kuan-ying in the seventies, and K'ang Yu-wei and other statecraft scholars in the eighties.

Although later statesmen and historians may, with good reason, regard the Opium War as an epoch-making event, the great majority of the literati-officials in late Ch'ing were unaware of the changing situation until after 1860. The available sources indicate that between 1840 and 1860 there was only one scholar, Huang Chün-tsai, a licentiate (*hsiu-ts'ai*) from Yang-chou, who explicitly wrote in 1844 that the advent of the Westerners constituted a great *pien-chü*.[35] But after 1861 many gentry members realized the importance of the event.

We find at least forty-three individuals from 1861 to 1900 who commented on the significance of this great change. The earliest was the prolific writer Wang T'ao who in 1864 marvelled at the convergence of Westerners on China. Huang En-t'ung, former governor of Kwangtung, recognized in 1865 that China was already facing a change greater than any in hundreds of years. Ting Jih-ch'ang claimed in 1867 that the expansion of contact between China and the West was a change greater than any which had occurred in a thousand years. Li Hung-chang stated in 1872 that the invasion of the East by Westerners was the greatest change to take place in three thousand years. In the Kuang-hsu reign, Tseng Chi-tse called it the greatest change in five thousand years, and Chang Chih-tung wrote

---

35 Huang Chün-tsai, *Chin-hu*, 4.3. Kuo Sung-tao also regarded 1840 as a turning point in Chinese modern history, but he did not make this remark until 1876. Kuo Sung-tao, *Yang-chih shu-wu wen-chi*, 11.1.

that no greater change had been seen from ancient times to the present.[36] In fact, the change was so enormous that it could not be understood on the basis of past experience. Indeed, it was simply unprecedented.

A letter from Li Hung-chang to Shen Pao-chen in 1862 stated that the mingling of Westerners with Chinese was well under way, and that the situation was unalterable. Wang T'ao wrote in a similar fashion two years later: 'The foreigners, coming from all corners of the earth, are now convergent on China. This is indeed an unprecedented event – an enormous *pien-chü* under heaven.' He later asserted that this changed situation would continue until the whole world became a large, congenial community. Before his diplomatic mission to Europe, Tseng Chi-tse in the early seventies was immensely impressed by the fact that so many Western ships were converging on China. Hsueh Fu-ch'eng marvelled equally at the fact that all maritime countries of the world, thanks to the steamship, were finally becoming neighbouring states.[37] Other far-sighted literati who made similar remarks in the sixties and seventies included Hsia Hsieh, Jui-lin and Kuo Sung-tao.

The advent of the West, according to these open-minded individuals, ushered in great changes in various ways. For one thing, the new situation posed a diplomatic problem for China. The reformer Feng Kuei-fen aptly pointed out in the early sixties that whereas China would soon suppress her internal rebellions, she could not expel the Westerners who were definitely in China to stay. Consequently, as Hsia Hsieh and Huang En-t'ung contended in the mid-sixties, the maintenance of peace with people coming from afar was an important task for the Chinese government. The great attention that China paid to her relations with the West in the ensuing decades prompted Li Shu-ch'ang, China's minister to Japan, to observe as a commonplace in 1884 that China had just entered a new era in her long history of dealing with the outside world.[38]

The new situation was also characterized by the military superiority of the West. The ominous foreign threat caught China unprepared not only because of the direction from which it came but also because of its indisputable military strength. Yang Ch'ang-chün, a high official, pointed out in

[36] Wang T'ao, *T'ao-yuan ch'ih-tu* (Wang T'ao's letters), 7.2. Ch'i Ssu-ho *et al. Ya-p'ien chan-cheng*, 5.409. *IWSM*, T'ung-chih (hereafter *IWSM-TC*), 55.25. Li Hung-chang, *Li Wen-chung kung ch'üan-chi* (Complete papers of Li Hung-chang), *Tsou-kao* (Memorials), 19.45. Tseng Chi-tse, *Tseng Hui-min kung i-chi* (Collected papers of the late Tseng Chi-tse), *Wen-chi* (Essays), 3.1. Wang Erh-min, *Wan-Ch'ing cheng-chih ssu-hsiang shih-lun* (Studies on the history of political thought in the late Ch'ing period), 215.

[37] Li Hung-chang, *P'eng-liao*, 1.9. Wang Tao, *Ch'ih-tu*, 7.2, 17b–18. Li En-han, *Tseng Chi-tse ti wai-chiao* (Tseng Chi-tse's diplomacy), 38. Hsueh Fu-ch'eng, *Yung-an ch'üan-chi* (Complete works of Hsueh Fu-ch'eng), *Hai-wai wen-pien*, (Collection of essays written overseas), 3.8.

[38] Hsia Hsieh, *Chung-Hsi*, 17.18. Ch'i Ssu-ho *et al. Ya-p'ien chan-cheng*, 5.409. Li Shu-ch'ang, *Cho-tsun-yuan ts'ung-kao* (Li Shu-ch'ang's writings), 5.6.

1874: 'The Western powers have dominated the four seas with their strong ships and powerful cannon for more than thirty years. They are further competing with one another for technological improvements. This is an unprecedented situation.' In the same vein, Li Hung-chang stated that the awesome military power of the West was demonstrated by its devastating cannon which could destroy China's strongest positions, leaving coastal and inland strongholds defenceless. In addition, this military superiority was facilitated by the fast communication provided by steamships and telegraphs. He thus concluded that the West was the most powerful enemy that China had ever faced during the past several thousand years.[39]

The heart of the change, according to many, lay in the fact that the West was not a nomadic power, but rather a maritime one. Li Hung-chang's memorial of 1874 stated: 'China's frontier problems usually occurred in the Northwest where the strength of China equalled that of the invaders. Besides, there was a demarcation line [in the Great Wall] between China and the foreign land. But today our southeast coast of more than ten thousand *li* is open to foreigners for commercial and missionary purposes. They even intrude inland including the capital. . . . This is indeed a changed situation which we have not seen during the past several thousand years.' Chou Sheng-ch'uan, an army commander, fully shared Li's view.[40]

The enlightened officials frequently attributed the changed situation to political imperialism. Huang En-t'ung wrote in 1865: 'As soon as England opened up China and signed treaties with us, the United States and France followed. All of them acquired special privileges from us. Even the smaller countries tried to follow their suit. This was indeed a change from the last several hundred years.'[41] Many saw the situation worsen as time progressed. Both Prince Kung and Li Hung-chang pointed out in the late sixties and early seventies that foreigners not only were active on the coast but also made intrusions inland, even to the capital. These Westerners, said Li, 'profess peace and friendship, but what they really want is to seize and possess China. If one country creates trouble with us, others will stir up conflict. This is a truly unprecedented change in the past several thousand years.' Other high officials, such as Yang Ch'ang-chün and Wang Wen-shao, held similar views.[42]

Political imperialism intensified as the nineteenth century progressed. Tsou Ch'eng was keenly aware that encirclement by foreign powers was an unprecedented change. He maintained that China had only to pay special attention to the north-west frontier in the T'ang and Sung times, and to

[39] *IWSM-TC*, 99.32, 34.
[40] *IWSM-TC*, 99.32; Chou Sheng-ch'uan, *Chou Wu-chuang kung i-shu* (Writings of the late Chou Sheng-ch'uan), 1.1.
[41] Ch'i Ssu-ho *et al. Ya-p'ien chan-cheng*, 5.409.   [42] *IWSM-TC*, 99.14, 32, 34, 52

the north-east frontier during the Ming dynasty. By the late nineteenth century, however, China found herself in a situation where foreign intrusion came from *all* directions. Ting Jih-ch'ang shared the same sense of urgency. He pointed out in a memorial in 1874 that China was completely surrounded by foreign enemies. France, based in Annam, posed threats to Kwangsi, Yunnan, and Kweichow; Great Britain, after having colonized India, was threatening Szechwan and Yunnan. Russia was a powerful country looming large in the north, threatening Sinkiang, Kansu, Shensi and Manchuria. The seven provinces on the south-east coast were constantly under the threat of invasion from the maritime West. He concluded that China in her long history had never faced invasions from both the land and the sea.[43]

The *pien-chü*, for some reformers, was also characterized by economic encroachment by the West. In the sixties Hsia Hsieh and Li Tsung-hsi discussed the consequential ramifications of Sino-Western trade, and the merchant-reformer Cheng Kuan-ying remarked that China's large-scale trade with the West was an unprecedented event in Chinese history. In 1867 Ting Jih-ch'ang marvelled at the wonders of the Western machines. During the seventies many literati-officials, such as Li Hung-chang and Wu Yun, maintained that a new era had dawned in China because of the introduction of steamships and railways. Indeed, many gentry members in the ensuing decade regarded the introduction of technology as the heart of the changed situation. For Hsueh Fu-ch'eng, the advent of Western technology constituted 'a most wonderful phenomenon in the universe'.[44]

The new situation reminded some of the literati-officials of the great change which had taken place in Chinese history with the fall of the Chou dynasty and the rise of the Ch'in; they were aware that the expansion of Sino-Western relations was a new starting point comparable to that ancient turning point in 221 BC. The tempo of change accelerated after the seventies, and many reformers were aware of this fact. For instance, in 1874 Ting Jih-ch'ang compared the Western invasion to a fierce fire, sweeping and destructive. Chang Yü-chao observed in the early eighties that the speed of the change was extremely fast, and the nature of the change was unprecedented.[45]

Many literati-officials thus recognized the dawning of a new era, but

[43] Wang Erh-min, *Cheng-chih ssu-hsiang* 209. Lü Shih-ch'iang, *Ting Jih-ch'ang yü tzu-ch'iang yun-tung* (Ting Jih-ch'ang and the self-strengthening movement), 233.
[44] Cheng Kuan-ying, *Sheng-shih wei-yen tseng-ting hsin-pien* (Warnings to a prosperous age, rev. edn), 2.41. *IWSM-TC*, 55. 25. Wu Yun, *Liang-lei-hsuan ch'ih-tu* (Wu Yun's letters), 8.18–19. Ko Shih-chün, comp. *Huang-ch'ao ching-shih-wen hsu-pien*, 116.5. Hsueh Fu-ch'eng, *Hai-wai wen-pien*, 3.8.
[45] Lü Shih-ch'iang, *Ting Jih-ch'ang*, 240; Chang Yü-chao, *Ch'ien-t'ing wen-chi* (Chang Yü-chao's writings), 2.5.

what did they consider to be the theoretical basis of this change? Being the products of a Confucian society, they looked to tradition for answers – and they found them. Indeed, traditional thought did not lack a belief in and sensitivity to change. The most important classic on this subject is the *Book of changes* (*I-ching*). One of its central ideas, that an exhausted situation leads to change and this change then leads to success (*ch'iung tse pien, pien tse t'ung*), was frequently quoted by the experts on Western affairs, including Wang T'ao, Ting Jih-ch'ang, Cheng Kuan-ying and Kuo Sung-tao. Indeed, the term *tzu-ch'iang* or 'self-strengthening', which referred to the various efforts to emulate the West from 1860 to 1895, was derived from this classic. Tseng Kuo-fan commented: 'The two important elements of the *I-ching* are timing and situation. They are controlled by an unknown cosmic force and are free from the interference of man.'[46]

The term *yun-hui*, derived from a Neo-Confucian cosmology developed by Shao Yung, refers to a mystically predestined change. It suggests that a mystical power exists which man is incapable of opposing and which asserts itself unpredictably and brings with itself momentous changes in the world of man and in the world of nature. Since all great historic changes could be seen to fit the application of this concept, many reformers came to describe the new situation after 1860 as *yun-hui*. Some maintained that *yun-hui* could be regarded as a manifestation of heaven's decree and was therefore irresistible. Yen Fu elucidated this idea most clearly. He said that China was experiencing the greatest change since the Ch'in period, and the reasons for the change were unknown. But if he had to name one, it was *yun-hui*. Once the force of *yun-hui* was at work, even a sage could not alter its course. Many reform-minded scholars, such as Wang T'ao, Cheng Kuan-ying and T'ang Chen, predicted that *yun-hui* would soon lead the world into a large, uniform community where all peoples would mingle freely.[47]

A segment of the literati boldly asserted that they were not alone in advocating change, for they claimed that the Confucian sages, had they lived in the nineteenth century, would have acted in a similar manner. In this connection Kuo Sung-tao mentioned the ancient sages Yao and Shun; P'i Hsi-jui named the Neo-Confucian masters Chu Hsi, Ch'eng Hao and Ch'eng I; Wang T'ao, Li Hung-chang and Cheng Kuan-ying implied that Confucius himself would have changed with the times had he lived in the nineteenth century; and Yen Fu held the boldest view of them all, for he asserted that the sages, being the products of *yun-hui*, could not have resisted

---

[46] Tseng Kuo-fan, *Tseng Wen-cheng kung shu-cha* (Tseng Kuo-fan's letters), 8.25.
[47] Ch'üan Tsu-wang, ed. *Sung Yuan hsueh-an* (Records of Sung and Yuan scholars), 9.5–6. Li En-han, *Tseng Chi-tse*, 38–9. Yen Fu, *Yen Chi-tao shih-wen ch'ao* (Yen Fu's poems and essays), 1.1. Wang T'ao, *T'ao-yuan wen-lu wai-pien* (Additional essays of Wang T'ao), 7.16–17. Cheng Kuan-ying, *I-yen* (Easy words), 1.1–2. T'ang Chen, *Wei-yen* (Warnings), 1.13.

change even if they so desired. Accordingly, a sage, being able to foresee the trend of the *yun-hui*, would have acted in concert with it.[48]

Many literati recognized the changing nature of the times, but what was the message of the change? They maintained that the advent of the West provided China with a golden opportunity. In 1864 Wang T'ao opined that heaven had caused the Western nations to converge on China, not to weaken China but to sharpen her like a knife being ground on a whetstone, thus making her a rich and powerful country. This was because, he later explained, China had the opportunity to employ the service of the Westerners in China.

According to Kuo Sung-tao, the new situation was like a double-edged blade. It could harm or benefit China, depending on whether China was able to utilize the situation to her own advantage. Indeed, many reformers, including Hsueh Fu-ch'eng and Ting Jih-ch'ang in the sixties, and Li Hung-chang and Cheng Kuan-ying in the seventies, urged their fellow countrymen to take advantage of this heaven-provided opportunity.[49]

The reformers thus realized that China was facing a significant change and that such change provided a challenging opportunity for the country. The question remained, how should China respond to this situation? Kuo Sung-tao said, 'In order to accommodate the change, we must have an understanding of the foreigners; in order to seize the opportunity, we must study the foreign methods.'[50] How, then, could China understand the foreigners and where should she begin to study the foreign methods?

In search of peaceful foreign relations

Skilful diplomacy, according to the reformers, had a paramount role in China's understanding of the West. Kuo Sung-tao argued that China's effort in war preparations, either defensively or offensively, was irrelevant to the situation. Hsueh Fu-ch'eng, Ting Jih-ch'ang and Wang T'ao all held that China must discard her traditional way of dealing with the outside world in order to seek new approaches. If China handled her foreign relations properly, there would be no need for her to use military power.[51]

After the establishment of the Tsungli Yamen in 1861 (see volume 10,

---

[48] Kuo Sung-tao, *Wen-chi*, 28.12. Wang T'ao, *Wai-pien*, 11.11–12. Li Hung-chang, *P'eng-liao*, 15.3–4. Cheng Kuan-ying, *I-yen*, 1.2. Yen Fu, *Yen Chi-tao shih-wen ch'ao*, 1.1.

[49] Wang T'ao, *Ch'ih-tu*, 7.3, 34. Kuo Sung-tao, *Wen-chi*, 12.20.

[50] Kuo T'ing-i, *Kuo Sung-tao*, 2.484.

[51] *Ibid.* 2.528. Hsueh Fu-ch'eng, *Ch'ou-yang ch'u-i* (Initial discussion concerning Western affairs) in his *Yung-an ch'üan-chi* (Complete works of Hsueh Fu-ch'eng), 21. Lü Shih-ch'iang, *Ting Jih-ch'ang*, 348. Wang T'ao, *Wai-pien*, 3.25. For an account of the changes made in China's conduct of foreign relations as a result of Western influence, see Immanuel C. Y. Hsu, *China's entrance into the family of nations: the diplomatic phase, 1858–1880.*

chapters 5 and 10), the training of diplomats and interpreters was stressed. Actually, as early as 26 February 1859 Kuo Sung-tao's memorial had recommended the establishment of an interpreters' school, with emphasis on the teaching of Western languages. Also, in 1861 Feng Kuei-fen stressed the urgency of learning Western languages. But such proposals did not materialize until 1862, when the Interpreters' College or T'ung-wen kuan was established in Peking. This school was the result of a joint memorial of Prince Kung and Wen-hsiang in 1861, in which they also recommended that young, intelligent Manchu boys be selected to learn foreign languages. The T'ung-wen kuan offered courses in English, French, Russian and German. To boost the spirit of the school, the grand councillor, Wen-hsiang, received its first student, encouraging him to study hard in order to understand the West. In time, the school produced a number of distinguished diplomats.

On the provincial level, Li Hung-chang took a similar position. With the help of the two noted reformers, Kuo Sung-tao and Feng Kuei-fen, Governor Li founded the Kuang-fang-yen kuan at Shanghai in 1863. Similar institutions were established at Canton in 1864 and at Foochow in 1866. These language schools gradually became centres of Western learning in general. By 1867 astronomy and mathematics were introduced in the curriculum of the T'ung-wen kuan, and by 1879 courses on physics, chemistry, physiology and international law were added.[52] The school gradually took on the appearance of a small liberal arts college.

Meanwhile, there emerged a group of specialists on foreign affairs in the treaty ports, beginning with those who served as Shanghai taotai during the fifties and sixties, men such as Wu Chien-chang, Hsueh Huan, Wu Hsu, Yang Fang, Ting Jih-ch'ang and Ying Pao-shih. Compared with such early treaty-port mandarins as Ho Kuei-ch'ing and Lao Ch'ung-kuang (see volume 10, chapter 5), they were more knowledgeable about the West. However, they could not be compared with the foreign affairs experts in the seventies and eighties, who included Kuo Sung-tao, Tseng Chi-tse and Ma Chien-chung, all of whom had the opportunity to observe the Western societies personally. This first-hand knowledge of the West was treasured by enlightened officials. Ting Jih-ch'ang memorialized in 1867 to advocate the establishment of regular legations abroad. For him, an important function of Chinese diplomats was to employ secretly the service of Westerners who had the technological knowledge of modern weaponry. Ten years later, China set up her first resident legation abroad under Kuo Sung-tao in London. Kuo set forth two goals for a Chinese diplomat. First, he should learn the good aspects of the host country in order to benefit China.

[52] Kuo T'ing-i, *Kuo Sung-tao*, 1.133-4, 234-5.

Secondly, every effort should be made to maintain a peaceful relationship between China and the state in which he was stationed.[53]

The best way to understand the West, as the reformers saw it, was through peace, not war. In the capital, the chief advocates of a peaceful foreign policy were Prince Kung and Wen-hsiang, who bore the responsibility of dealing with the European invaders. They believed that the Westerners sought trade, not territory. China's aim was therefore to appease the invaders with commercial privileges and to control them through material inducements. This was in line with the time-honoured *chi-mi* or 'loose rein' policy. There were others who shared this view, among whom Kuo Sung-tao (1818–91) was probably the most outstanding. During the Hsien-feng period, he had conceived a philosophical rationale for a conciliatory foreign policy (see volume 10, chapter 9). In answering Senggerinchin's question in 1858 as to the priority of fighting against the Nien in eastern Honan or against the Westerners around Tientsin, Kuo replied that since the Nien constituted a serious rebellion, they should be dealt with by military campaigns; as Westerners were interested only in trade, they should be dealt with peacefully instead of belligerently. When the general was indeed preparing for a war against the Anglo-French forces the next year, Kuo wrote to him seventeen times opposing such a move. After Senggerinchin and other generals were defeated in 1860, Kuo became increasingly anti-belligerent. He denounced those scholars who from the Southern Sung era on had advocated war while ignoring reality. During the Ili crisis, Kuo wrote from London arguing that China should avoid fighting Russia. After his retirement, he reiterated this peaceful policy both to the court and to the high provincial officials. In the same vein, he criticized China's warlike policy during the Sino-French War.[54]

Several high provincial officials were in favour of a peaceful foreign policy, and Li Hung-chang was the most influential of them all. Throughout the latter half of his life, Li devoted much of his efforts to keeping the peace and never spoke lightly of going to war. In 1870 he stated that on the evidence of China's historical experience, China could not wage foreign wars over an extended period of time. However, it was possible to maintain peace for a long time. Going further in 1871 he argued that even if China should achieve victory in a hundred wars, this could not be compared with a foreign policy which achieved victory without war. He lamented the fact that both Lin Tse-hsu and Senggerinchin, acting in a precipitate manner, provoked foreign wars which almost led to the col-

[53] Lü Shih-ch'iang, *Ting Jih-ch'ang*, 223. Kuo T'ing-i, *Kuo Sung-tao*, 2.714.
[54] Kuo T'ing-i, *Kuo Sung-tao*, 1.130, 139; 2.624, 851, 863–4, 898–900. For Kuo's manuscript on pacification, see Lien-sheng Yang, 'Historical notes on the Chinese world order', in *CWO*, 22–3.

lapse of the dynasty. In his correspondence with the Tsungli Yamen in the late seventies and early eighties concerning the Ili and Annam crises, Li staunchly advocated a peaceful policy.[55]

Tseng Kuo-fan, who died in 1872, wholeheartedly supported this pragmatic foreign policy. Echoing Kuo Sung-tao's view, in 1870 he denounced the scholars who during the previous seven hundred years had uttered empty words and advocated foreign wars. He asserted that the best way to handle foreign affairs was that of *chi-mi*, a policy that, according to Tseng, was a self-evident truth. His brother Tseng Kuo-ch'üan had a similar view. He maintained that the guiding principles in handling foreign relations were softness (*jou*) and patience (*jen*). Thus in 1883 he was opposed to the policy of war against France.[56] This foreign policy based on peace was shared by many other reform-minded literati-officials.

One way to maintain peace was to see to it that provisions in the treaties were properly honoured. This was the reason why Ting Jih-ch'ang, the Shanghai taotai, rejected the Chinese merchant's petitions to ban foreign cotton-goods shops in Shanghai in 1864. In the same vein, Kuo Sung-tao through strenuous efforts persuaded the populace of Ch'ao-chou to permit the entry of foreigners to that city in 1866. In a public letter addressed to the gentry Kuo explained that although Chinese were entitled to refuse any illegal request from the West, they should honour the treaties which opened that city as a treaty port. He ended the letter by citing the example of Yeh Ming-ch'en, who had been captured by the British troops because of his refusal to honour the treaties. Ting Jih-ch'ang, knowing that he was assigned to assist Kuo in handling this crisis, wrote in 1866, 'If Westerners abide by the treaties whereas we do not, then the injustice (*ch'ü*) rests with us.'[57]

This peaceful approach should not be construed as one of total submission. On the contrary, it was a positive policy. For, according to Ting Jih-ch'ang, this was the only way that China could protect her interests in accordance with the treaties. In 1864 Ting, as Shanghai taotai, skilfully and firmly rejected several extra-legal requests from foreigners, including the American desire to buy real estate inside the city of Shanghai, the British insistence on steamship traffic between Shanghai and Soochow, and the French request to install cable lines between Shanghai and Woosung. Ting clearly declared his principle: in foreign affairs, those provisions included

55 Li Hung-chang, *P'eng-liao*, 10.27b–28; 11.10. Kuo Sung-tao, *Kuo shih-lang tsou-shu* (Kuo Sung-tao's memorials), 12.37b–38. Li Tsung-t'ung and Liu Feng-han, *Li Hung-tsao hsien-sheng nien-p'u* (Chronological biography of Li Hung-tsao), 1.252.
56 Tseng Kuo-fan, *Shu-cha*, 33.10. Weng T'ung-ho, *Weng T'ung-ho jih-chi p'ai-yin-pen* (A typeset edition of the diary of Weng T'ung-ho), 4.1259–60. Kuo T'ing-i, *Kuo Sung-tao*, 2.900.
57 Lü Shih-ch'iang, *Ting Jih-ch'ang*, 65–8, 98. Kuo T'ing-i, *Kuo Sung-tao*, 1.397. *IWSM-TC*, 41.32.

in the treaties would be implemented; matters not included would be prohibited.[58]

One important way to maintain peaceful relations with the West, according to some high officials, was to treat all foreigners honestly. The sixties saw the formation of a foreign-policy theory based on sincerity, which is an important ingredient of Confucianism. Confucius said, 'Let his words be sincere and truthful, and his actions honourable and careful; such conduct may be practised among the rude tribes of the South or the North.'[59] This was the guiding principle of the reformers in the period following the Anglo-French occupation of Peking in 1860. Citing the quick withdrawal of Western forces from Peking in accordance with the treaties (see volume 10, chapters 5 and 9), Prince Kung and Wen-hsiang maintained that the Westerners were not the same as other foreigners in Chinese history who tried to gain territory from China. By using sincerity to keep them in bounds and thus tame their nature, China could advance her own interests.[60]

Tseng Kuo-fan, in a letter to Li Hung-chang in 1862, wrote that although it was extremely difficult for China to handle her foreign affairs, she had no need to seek fundamental principles outside the system Confucius had laid down. To be specific, China's policy towards barbarian peoples should be one of *chung* (faithfulness), *hsin* (trust), *tu* (sincerity) and *ching* (seriousness). He further explained that *tu* meant generosity and *ching*, carefulness. He added, '*Hsin* simply means honesty, yet it is particularly difficult to put this idea into practice. Therefore, the first step for us to take is to carry out this principle as thoroughly as we can.'[61] Tseng was not alone in emphasizing these four words of Confucius. In 1864 Wang T'ao also suggested to Ting Jih-ch'ang a foreign policy using these four principles. Kuo Sung-tao suggested to the throne in 1876 that these four terms should form the basis of China's foreign policy.[62] Tseng further elucidated this idea later on: 'It is true that the lack of sincerity is reflected in one's failure to keep promises or to live up to the treaty provisions. It is equally important, however, to be sincere in manner and in trival matters.' If one did not like a person, Tseng continued, this feeling should be reflected by his outward behaviour; to act otherwise would be insincere. By the same token, if peace were restored between China and foreign countries, China should treat foreigners fairly.[63]

[58] Lü Shih-ch'iang, *Ting Jin-ch'ang*, 69–79.
[59] James Legge, trans. *The Chinese classics, Confucian Analects*, 295.
[60] *IWSM-HF*, 71.17b–18. [61] Tseng Kuo-fan, *Shu-cha*, 18.17a–b.
[62] Wang T'ao, *Ch'ih-tu*, 7.16. *Ch'ing-chi wai-chiao shih-liao* (Historical materials concerning foreign relations in the late Ch'ing period, 1875–1911), 8.16.
[63] Tseng Kuo-fan, *Shu-cha*, 30.49.

Kuo Sung-tao had a similar view in 1861. He maintained that throughout Chinese history, China controlled foreigners by four different methods: virtuous behaviour, strategical design, awe-inspiring reputation, and benevolent actions. The crucial point was that the principle of sincerity was essential to all of these four categories. This diplomacy of sincerity was the cornerstone of Kuo's foreign policy theory during the rest of his life. Another scholar who shared a similar view in the early sixties was Feng Kuei-fen. He said that since peaceful negotiation had succeeded, Chinese should treat foreigners with frankness and faithfulness, and stop all unfriendly and suspicious activities at the same time. Some officials, such as Tseng Chi-tse, continued to expound the idea of sincerity and faithfulness in the seventies.[64] In certain respects this 'good faith' foreign policy coincided with the Western policy of respect for treaties, but China did not derive it from the West. From a very early time this kind of belief had been an element of Chinese statecraft.

'To seize the opportunity'

Besides advocating a peaceful foreign policy, the enlightened men of the day recognized that China must seize the opportunity of *pien-chü* to make herself strong militarily. This view led to Western-style training at Tientsin, establishing the Peking Field Force, using Western arms against the Taipings, and building arsenals and steamships (see volume 10, chapters 9 and 10). But the proponents of self-strengthening did not pursue these military programmes indiscriminately or irrespective of cost. In fact, they carefully followed certain principles. First, since they initially presumed that Westerners would be unwilling to teach Chinese their military secrets, China should learn them secretly. In discussing ammunition manufacturing and shipbuilding, the correspondence between the Tsungli Yamen and Li Hung-chang in 1864 put great emphasis on how to learn the foreigner's military secrets without ever arousing suspicion and provoking resentment.[65]

Secondly, these high officials insisted that in pursuing the military self-strengthening programmes, China should always retain her administrative integrity. This attitude was demonstrated by Li Hung-chang's suspicion of the training of Chinese troops by Western officers in 1862, by the insistence of Prince Kung and Tseng Kuo-fan on the Chinese control of the Lay-Osborn Flotilla in 1863 (see volume 10, chapter 9), and by Ting Jih-ch'ang's

---

[64] Kuo T'ing-i, *Kuo Sung-tao*, 1.187. Wang Chia-chien, *Wei Yuan hai-fang*, 155. Li En-han, *Tseng Chi-tse*, 39.

[65] Chung-yang yen-chiu-yuan chin-tai-shih yen-chiu-so, comp. *Hai-fang tang* (Archives on coastal defence), *Chi-ch'i chü*, 1.6. We are indebted to Professor Kwang-Ching Liu for this information as well as for much of the following discussion of reform.

effort to curb the power of British and French officers in training the Anhwei Army in 1864. Thirty years later, Li Hung-tsao and Jung-lu stood in opposition to the training of Chinese troops by Western officers for fear that China could not maintain firm control of the Westerners. Finally, the reformers tried to integrate technology into the civil service examination system. In the early sixties, Feng Kuei-fen, Li Hung-chang and Ting Jih-ch'ang urged that, to acquire the outstanding skills of the West, it would be necessary to change the examination system to include sections for the selection of men of modern talent. This proposal represented the most basic and progressive thinking of the time, but it had meagre results.[66]

The self-strengthening movement was China's response to the crisis in relations with the West. The term 'self-strengthening' was originally used in the *Book of changes* to describe the nature of heaven as enduring and strong, and to remind mankind not to cease its efforts to strengthen itself so that it might be in harmony with this disposition of heaven. In the Southern Sung dynasty, Tung Huai applied this concept to the relations between China and the Inner Asian peoples. He argued that if China could strengthen herself, then she need not fear these barbarians.[67] The modern meaning of self-strengthening lies in this general concept. At least thirty-nine writers discussed the quest for self-strengthening before 1895.

The self-strengthening movement inevitably involved *yang-wu* or Western affairs. The meaning of *yang-wu* changed over time. It was first used by a censor in July 1840, with the same general meaning as *i-wu* or barbarian affairs, referring to simple matters related to foreign affairs and foreign trade.[68] After 1860 it still often referred to the management of relations with the West (including Russia but not necessarily Japan). Gradually it came to mean government business involving relations with Westerners as well as Western methods and machines. In its narrow sense, however, the term suggested the adoption and use of Western technological knowledge. In other words, the concrete programmes for seeking strength usually involved a period of imitating Western methods. This may be called the *yang-wu yun-tung*, or Westernization movement. While self-strengthening was the goal of the literati-officials, Westernization in the narrow sense was the concrete programme for achieving it. Although self-strengthening in theory included reform of internal affairs, its major emphasis was actually the imitation of Western technology.

---

[66] Lü Shih-ch'iang, *Ting Jih-ch'ang*, 41–5. Li Tsung-t'ung and Liu Feng-han, *Li Hung-tsao*, 2.711–13.

[67] *I-ching (Book of changes)*, 1.5. *Sung-shih* (History of the Sung dynasty), 414.10. For a major study of Ch'ing policy in the 1860s, see Mary C. Wright, *The last stand of Chinese conservatism: the T'ung-chih restoration 1862–1874*.

[68] *IWSM-HF*, 22.29.

During the 1860-80 period there emerged a new awakening of cultural consciousness. It prompted discussions which placed more emphasis on ideas, attitudes and even institutions. This awakening was the realization of the need for reform (*pien-fa*), not so much real internal reform as adjustment of Chinese institutions in the face of the alien technological and economic challenge. In practice, the innovations introduced were superficial and haphazard. The new organizations established in the name of self-strengthening were invariably called *chü* or 'bureau', originally meaning an agency of a temporary nature, established to meet special exigencies. The designation *chü* now came to imply a more respectable long-term status that was meant by the founders to be part and parcel of a long-range reform. Yet *chü* did not have the stable situation of regular bureaucratic establishments. Such agencies as the China Merchants' Steam Navigation Company depended for security on the power of their official patrons and were vulnerable to attack by other officials.

Originally *pien-fa* (lit., change of method) indicated the advocacy of radical change in administrative institutions as urged by a minority wing of traditional scholars and officials who wrote on statecraft. From Wang An-shih of the Sung to Ku Yen-wu of the early Ch'ing or Kung Tzu-chen of the early nineteenth century, reform thinking of a comparatively basic nature had cropped up at long intervals. Beginning in the 1860s, the term *pien-fa* was sometimes employed for a modern, active adaptation of Western institutions. In the eyes of many officials this was indeed a serious matter. To such conservatives as Wo-jen, modifying China's institutions in order to facilitate the introduction of Western technology was not only degenerate but also radical. Yet basic changes in such institutions as the examination system or the training of armies were precisely what the few Westernizing officials originally had hoped for. Li Hung-chang termed his 1864 recommendation regarding changes in the military system as *pien-fa*, although he also used less offensive phrases such as 'accommodation' and 'changing plans'. In advocating the adjustment of the sacrosanct examination system to Western technology, Ting Jih-ch'ang made the boldest proposals – four of his projected eight categories in the examinations were to be associated with things Western, namely, current affairs, military expertise, natural sciences, and foreign languages and foreign affairs.[69]

In formal presentations to the throne in 1874, Li Hung-chang spoke of reform when he memorialized on the subject of maritime defence, citing the *Book of changes* and explaining fully the meaning of his request for change. He concluded that 'under the present circumstances if we desire to reinforce maritime defence there is no other way except *pien-fa* and the

[69] Lü Shih-ch'iang, *Ting Jih-ch'ang*, 347.

utilization of able men'. In a letter to the scholar, Wang K'ai-yun, in January 1881 he stated even more clearly: 'With regard to internal affairs, *pien-fa* is necessary.'[70] In the same period, sensitive officials and literati such as Kuo Sung-tao in 1875, Hsueh Fu-ch'eng in 1879, and Wang T'ao in the early 1880s discussed reform in specific terms. The fact that reform ideas made so little headway at the time was a measure of the obstacles they confronted. In the decades of the seventies and even eighties, China's leaders and writers, merely using bold phrases, actually compromised with the insurmountable institutional and political obstacles, yet tried nevertheless to seize the golden opportunity provided by the *pien-chü*.

This new cultural consciousness was suggested by the term 'Western learning' (*Hsi-hsueh*), which was only slowly gaining circulation and respectability. The idea of Western learning spawned many other concepts. The meanings of 'Western learning' and 'new learning' (*hsin-hsueh*) were similar, but the term 'new learning' was popular only after 1894. Western learning included all the various kinds of knowledge imported from Europe or America, by foreigners as well as Chinese. Since it was different from China's ancient traditional scholarship, by contrast it was called 'new learning'. From this contrasting of Chinese and Western, old and new, an attitude of cultural discrimination and selectivity naturally came into being, which included explaining the content of Western learning, analysing its special characteristics, and weighing its value.

The movement for adopting Western learning made manifest progress after 1860. As previously stated, translation of Western-language newspapers had been recognized as early as the 1840s as a method of obtaining foreign information. After 1851 this effort expanded to include the translation of books. If we consider only those translations carried out under official auspices, then the publications of the Kiangnan Arsenal and the Peking T'ung-wen kuan were still considerable. Many of these were the work of John Fryer and W. A. P. Martin, who were in the employ of the Ch'ing government. If we add the translations done privately by Western missionaries, the volume is greatly increased. All these translations formed an important bridge for conveying Western learning. That these translations were widely disseminated in official circles is beyond doubt.

We may cite a few examples. The new edition of Wei Yuan's *Hai-kuo t'u-chih* published after 1852 included materials from approximately twenty translated works of the period. Chao Lieh-wen collected the entire set of *Hsia-erh kuan-chen* ('The Chinese serial') published by Western missionaries

---

[70] Kwang-Ching Liu, 'The Confucian as patriot and pragmatist: Li Hung-chang's formative years, 1823–1866',. *HJAS*, 30 (1970) 34–6. *IWSM-TC*, 25.10. Li Hung-chang, *Tsou-kao*, 24.12. Li Hung-chang, *P'eng-liao*, 19.43.

in Hong Kong (in all, thirty-three issues published between August 1853 and May 1858) and lent it to his official and literati friends, including the Hanlin scholar Wu Chia-shan and the *taotai* Teng Sui-fan. In 1874, the same year that a German work on coastal defence was translated into Chinese and published, four governors-general and governors – Li Hung-chang, Li Tsung-hsi, Liu K'un-i and Ting Pao-chen – in separate memorials used the theory set out in this work.[71] The Kiangnan Arsenal's translation centre made the greatest contribution of the period. From 1868 when translation began until June 1879, a total of ninety-eight works were published, forty-five other works were translated but not published, and the translation of thirteen other works had not yet been completed. Sales had reached 31,111 items. This suggests the scale of diffusion of Western learning in the period.

A further step in this diffusion came with the establishment of Western-style schools. Official schools were established to study language, technology, telegraphy, mining, shipbuilding, naval warfare and land warfare. In addition, there were private schools run by foreign missionaries. The direct offering of knowledge about Western science and technology reached a new level. The spread of Chinese curiosity regarding Western science, especially among the literati and merchants in the treaty ports, was evidenced by their letters to John Fryer, editor of the periodical *Ko-chih hui-pien* ('The Chinese scientific magazine', 1876–92).[72]

Finally, in this diffusion process we may cite the importance of journeys abroad by officials and literati for travel or on diplomatic missions, by students such as those who joined the Chinese Educational Mission to the United States, and the Foochow Shipyard programme to England and France for the purpose of studying in foreign countries. These activities led to a deeper reception of Western learning. Their breadth of influence was enhanced by the travel memoirs and other writings of those who went abroad. Beginning with Pin-ch'un in 1866, Chinese officials and literati travellers started a good tradition, and thereafter those who went abroad gathered notes on what they saw, heard and felt, and wrote it up in diaries

[71] Suzanne Wilson Barnett, 'Wei Yuan and Westerners. Notes on the sources of the *Hai-kuo t'u-chih*', *Ch'ing-shih wen-t'i*, 2.4 (1970) 1–20. Chao Lieh-wen, *Neng-ching-chü jih-chi* (Chao Lieh-wen's [holograph] diary), 1.105. Li Hung-chang, *Tsou-kao*, 24.16a–b. Li Tsung-hsi, *K'ai-hsien Li shang-shu cheng-shu* (Li Tsung-hsi's political papers), 6.56. Ting Pao-chen, *Ting Wen-ch'eng kung i-chi* (Collected papers of the late Ting Pao-chen), 11.11. *IWSM-TC*, 100.24b–25. Through a close study of Yen Fu's translations of works by Western political and social thinkers, Benjamin Schwartz, *In search of wealth and power: Yen Fu and the West*, is a principal work on the late Ch'ing attempt to profit from Western thought.

[72] Chang Ching-lu, *Chung-kuo chin-tai ch'u-pan shih-liao ch'u-pien* (Materials on the history of publication in modern China, 1st collection), 23–5. San-pao Li, 'Letters to the editor in John Fryer's *Chinese Scientific Magazine*, 1876–1892: an analysis', *CYCT*, 4.2 (Dec. 1974) 729–77.

or poems. From 1866 to 1900 such writings about experience in foreign countries totalled more than 158 separate works by sixty-one individuals.[73] These diaries and poems were widely disseminated in published form and must have had some influence on officials and gentry. These publications were partly responsible for pushing institutional reform one step further. Whereas the *pien-fa* programme was sporadic during the sixties and seventies, it became a widespread movement in the 1885–95 period.

Commerce, industry and agriculture received increasing attention after the seventies. In 1879, Hsueh Fu-ch'eng in his proposals regarding foreign policy argued that in such changing times the function or means (*yung*) of policy should be trade, but industrialization should be the substance or aim (*t'i*).[74] The non-military aspects of industrialization slowly gained popularity, and during the last quarter of the nineteenth century the reform-minded officials looked to the construction of industries for civilian needs such as maritime transport, mining, textile manufacturing, railways, the minting of currency, and iron and steel manufacturing, all of which would employ Western machinery. The modernization of agriculture was also discussed. Cheng Kuan-ying mentioned it in the seventies and Tso Tsung-t'ang implemented it in Kansu from 1877 to 1881. More writings were published in the 1892–5 period, such as those of Ch'en Chih and Sun Yat-sen, which laid stress on the Western methods of breeding and irrigation, the use of agricultural machines and chemical fertilizer, and the usefulness of holding agricultural fairs. In 1895 and 1896, academic associations for agricultural studies, under the leadership of Sun Yat-sen and Chang Chien, were established in Canton and Shanghai, and a journal devoted to modern agriculture was published.[75]

At the heart of these efforts to learn economics from the West lay the burning desire to make China a rich and strong country. The slogan, to enrich the state and to strengthen the army (*fu-kuo ch'iang-ping*), was widely popular in the sixties and seventies. From the mid-seventies, however, there emerged a trend of thinking that stressed the importance of enriching the people (*fu-min* or *li-min*). This new idea can be traced back to 1875 when Kuo Sung-tao, in writing to Prince Kung, maintained that the government should encourage the people to engage in modern shipping and manufacturing, for the wealth of the state and the wealth of the people were inseparable. Cheng Kuan-ying, Wang T'ao and Li Hung-chang also dis-

[73] Of these 158 works all but about 20 can be consulted in *Hsiao-fang-hu chai yü-ti ts'ung-ch'ao*.
[74] Hsueh Fu-ch'eng, *Ch'ou-yang*, 10b.
[75] Tso Tsung-t'ang, *Tso Wen-hsiang kung ch'üan-chi* (Complete collection of Tso Tsung-t'ang's papers), *Shu-tu* (Letters), 19.59b–60. Ch'en Chih, *Yung-shu, Nei-p'ien* (Internal section), 2.2b–3. Sun Wen (Sun Yat-sen), *Kuo-fu ch'üan-chi* (The complete works of the national father), 5.4–5. Wang Erh-min, *Cheng-chih ssu-hsiang*, 136–7.

cussed the idea, but it was Ma Chien-chung who dwelt on it most systematically and convincingly in 1890.[76]

Although policy-oriented essays had traditionally called for protecting the people and looking after the convenience of the people, they seldom went beyond calls for reducing corvée and taxes, or providing rest for the people, and, in any case, were not often put into practice for any extended period. This traditional thinking formed only the remote background for the modern concept of enriching the people. This new idea of *fu-min*, however, recognized that the nation and the masses are intimately related, and that the wealth of the masses is the foundation of the nation's strength. In other words, if the nation is to be strong, all its people must be enriched and strengthened, for wealth and power are related.

THE AMBIVALENCE OF FOREIGN POLICY VIEWS, 1860–95

Some Chinese views of the West were less rational, constructive and pleasant. These were often belligerent, emotionally charged and occasionally xenophobic. This irrational or ideological anti-Western attitude was in the main attributable to the literati-officials' deep commitment, intellectually and emotionally, to the Chinese cultural tradition, although it was Western imperialism that precipitated the attitude. At the same time there emerged, however slowly and vaguely, a consciousness of China as the entity to be positively cherished – not so much xenophobic and culturally minded as rational and nationalistic.

The rise of anti-foreignism

Although anti-foreignism had its roots deep in the early history of China's relations with the outside world, it did not become a significant force to reckon with until after 1860 when Western pressures intensified. There was a wide spectrum of anti-foreignism. On the one hand, there were those who hated foreigners but did not object to the emulation of the West in order to fight back. On the other hand, some were indiscriminately opposed to everything foreign, be it Christianity or modern technology.

The rejection of Western technology

Since anti-missionary movements have been discussed elsewhere (see volume 10, chapter 11), we are here concerned mainly with opposition to the introduction of Western technology. The reasons for such opposition

[76] Kuo T'ing-i, *Kuo Sung-tao*, 2.480–2. Ma Chien-chung, *Shih-k'o-chai chi-yen* (Ma Chien-chung's essays and discourses), 1.1.

were numerous. The most fundamental one was that there was no need for China to pattern herself on the West. For one thing, the anti-foreign literati believed that Western technology, being specious in nature, was not essential to China, because popular sentiment (*min-hsin*) was more important than weaponry in making a strong country. What the barbarians feared in China, the grand secretary Wo-jen asserted, was the public sentiment of her masses rather than her cannon and warships. The emulation of the West, which was useless in defeating the enemy, would at the same time lead to the deterioration of popular support of the government. How could a government last long, he asked, if it lost the mandate of the people? He thus proposed that the fundamental programme should be directed to boosting popular morale rather than to imitating the barbarians' techniques. History, he contended, clearly showed that techniques could not strengthen a nation in time of weakness.[77]

Some scholar-bureaucrats believed specifically that China did not need to acquire Western-style weaponry for maritime defence. Liu Hsi-hung cited Russia and the United States as examples. The latter defeated Britain without the benefit of a navy, and the former, with only a token naval force, successfully challenged the British hegemony. Other critics were more concerned with China's presumed cultural superiority and implied that military techniques were often acquired at the cost of culture and good government. To illustrate this point, they mentioned the barbarians on China's northern frontier who, though strong in cavalry, none the less were culturally inferior and weak in organizing a polity.[78]

Whereas the reformers extolled their programmes as being practically useful, the anti-foreign literati-officials, stressing Confucian moral principles, were squarely anti-utilitarian. They persistently argued that what China should pay special attention to was the time-honoured Confucian principles of propriety, righteousness, integrity and a sense of shame. Indeed, to be virtuous was the very means of awing the barbarians. If the Confucian scholars, they continued, were encouraged to learn from the barbarians, they would lose their sense of shame. In the final analysis, these barbarian-oriented literati, being shameless and unpatriotic, would be of no use to China no matter how skilfully they had mastered the Western way.[79] Therefore, moral exhortation was fundamental, and its influence far-reaching. In contrast, they thought the utilitarian approach was superficial and near-sighted. It is not surprising, then, to find that Weng T'ung-ho, one of the tutors to the Kuang-hsu Emperor, often lectured the young

[77] Chung-kuo k'o-hsueh yuan *et al.* comps. *Yang-wu yun-tung* (The 'foreign affairs' movement; hereafter *YWYT*), 1.134, 277–83. *IWSM-TC*, 44.25; 79.1–2.
[78] Lü Shih-ch'iang, *Ting Jih-ch'ang*, 351.
[79] Lu Pao-ch'ien, 'Wo-jen lun' (On Wo-jen), *CYCT*, 2 (1971) 257–70, esp. 260. *YWYT*, 1.121.

monarch on the significance of distinguishing righteousness from profit. The desirability of making such a distinction led many literati-officials to oppose various self-strengthening programmes in the seventies and eighties, particularly the construction of the railway from Tientsin to T'ung-chou in 1889.[80]

The conservatives gave other reasons why it was not necessary for China to engage in *yang-wu*. A perusal of Chinese history, they maintained, showed that in all the prosperous times China did not learn from the barbarians. Why, then, they asked, must China emulate the West in the nineteenth century in order to be wealthy and strong? Furthermore, they asserted that even if China had to excel herself in science and technology, she still could avoid learning them from the Western barbarians. This was, they thought, because China had the best experts in these fields, and what the government needed to do was to look for such talent within China herself.[81]

For some literati-officials, what was good for the West was not necessarily beneficial to China, because there existed different conditions and values in each society. One such difference was population. The West, experiencing a labour shortage due to a smaller population, was in need of machines. The introduction of machinery in an overpopulated China would simply worsen the unemployment. Another example was railways. The desirability of building railways depended on the military strength of a country. The West, being strong, could take advantage of railways for quick transportation. China, being unable to defend her railways in time of war, would suffer from them, for the enemy would use them to facilitate his military manoeuvres in China.[82]

The anti-foreign gentry further argued that China could not successfully learn from the barbarians even if it was necessary for her to do so. For example, military know-how was too important for a country to share with others. The grand secretary Wo-jen said in his memorial of 1867 that the barbarians were always wicked and it was by no means certain whether they would wholeheartedly teach military techniques to China. By the same token, neither would the West sell its best armaments to China. Yü Yueh, a noted scholar, and Wang Ping-hsieh, who was at one time on Li Hung-chang's staff, argued along these lines. What China got from the West was outdated and obsolete, they insisted, for no country would be foolish enough to invite self-defeat. Li Yuan-tu, another scholar, wrote

[80] Wang Ping-hsieh, *Wu-tzu-ch'i shih wen-chi* (Wang Ping-hsieh's essays), 6.40b. Weng T'ung-ho, *Jih-chi*, 4.1577, 1580.
[81] *IWSM-TC*, 47.24–5.
[82] Lü Shih-ch'iang, *Ting Jih-ch'ang*, 351–3.

that only the determined could subdue the cunning, and only decisiveness could thwart plotting; but under no circumstances could one expect the disciple to outmanoeuvre the teacher.[83]

Some conservatives boldly claimed that modern technology was ineffective. Wang K'ai-yun, a celebrated scholar from Hunan, wrote that the steam-powered warships, depending entirely on coal energy, would be useless if the supply of coal was cut off. Besides, they were less manoeuvrable in rivers, and totally useless in warfare waged on land. Similarly, a gun must be light and mobile in order to be effective, but the Western-style guns were too heavy to move. In time of prosperity, they said, China could have afforded to toy with these useless novelties for the sake of curiosity, but she definitely should not squander money in time of financial distress.

The Confucian cosmological myth assumed mutual interaction between the cosmic and the human worlds. The conservatives claimed that the introduction of things Western – mines, railways, telegraph lines and church buildings – adversely affected the cosmic order, including the *feng-shui* or geomantic 'spirits of wind and water', which played a role in the growth of crops and the prosperity of people. Thus they often cited unusual astronomical phenomena, such as comets, as heavenly warnings that something was wrong in the human world. They also asserted that natural calamities, such as drought, flood, earthquake and fire, in the palace were concrete indications that the orderly geomantic forces had been obstructed and disturbed.[84]

It was further asserted that although Western technology benefited China in certain ways, its shortcomings far outweighed its merits. For one thing, it was harmful in the long run, as Yü Yueh pointed out, because it quickly consumed natural resources which were limited in supply. In the seventies, Liu Ping-chang, governor of Kiangsi, cited this reason for opposing modern mining. Others focused on the socio-political ramifications. Wang Ping-hsieh, for example, claimed that the introduction of Western technology would deepen social injustice, because the rich by using machines would be richer, while the poor becoming jobless would be poorer.[85]

Such social injustice had political consequences which concerned a great number of people. Officials of various ranks in the capital and provinces, such as the grand councillor Weng T'ung-ho, the activist censor T'u Jen-shou, Governor Wang Wen-shao, and the candidate for prefect Yang

[83] *IWSM-TC*, 47.24–5. Wang Ping-hsieh, *Wen-chi*, 6.29. Lü Shih-ch'iang, *Ting Jih-ch'ang*, 353.
[84] Wang K'ai-yun, *Hsiang-ch'i lou wen-chi* (Collection of essays of Wang K'ai-yun), 2. Weng T'ung-ho, *Jih-chi*, 4.1575.
[85] Lü Shih-ch'iang, *Ting Jih-ch'ang*, 358–9; Wang Ping-hsieh, *Wen-chi*, 5.5.

T'ing-hsi, all pointed out the possibility of political rebellions. Among the unemployed, the weak would become burglars, the strong, bandits and rebels. Thus, they concluded, the *yang-wu* effort, which was motivated by seeking profits for China, would lead to open rebellions. The cultural and political anti-foreignism of the early Kuang-hsu period thus accorded with the view of the senior Neo-Confucian scholar, Wu T'ing-tung (d. 1873): undertakings that were motivated solely by profit would end in a most unprofitable way.[86]

The fear of imperialism

In many ways, Chinese anti-foreignism grew out of the fear of Western imperialism. A large number of literati-officials, such as the Hanlin scholar Yin Chao-yung and the political advisers Wang Ping-hsieh and Hsueh Fu-ch'eng, held that the Westerners were adopting a policy of *ts'an-shih* – a steady encroachment on China not unlike a silkworm's gnawing away of a mulberry leaf. Before foreigners could colonize China, however, they would first exploit her economically, disturb her social order, interfere with her legal processes, and finally make her sink morally. According to them, the purpose of foreigners' coming to China was to familiarize themselves with Chinese geographical and social conditions in order to carry out their political aggression. Otherwise, they asked, why were the foreign missionaries not satisfied to worship God in their own lands? Western political encroachment on China, they maintained, was gradual but steady. For example, the issue of the Christian missionary movement, which was not mentioned in the Treaty of Nanking, figured prominently in the Treaties of Tientsin sixteen years later. They reasoned in the sixties that Western powers would apply pressure on China for more privileges during the ensuing treaty revisions.

The Chinese fear of Western political aggression was by no means limited to the coastal areas, for it was also clearly evidenced by the widespread anti-Christian placards in the interior. One such placard in Hunan in 1862 mentioned the miserable fate of Africa and India in the wave of Western expansionism, and lamented that China would soon follow suit. Similar placards were seen in Szechwan and Kwangsi during the sixties and seventies.

These anti-foreign sentiments were further inflamed by the arrogance and seemingly odd behaviour of foreign diplomats, merchants and missionaries. In 1880 some officials petitioned in Peking that China should prevent foreigners from constructing a high building in that city because, they maintained, it would be used for military intelligence purposes. A

[86] *IWSM-TC*, 100.29. Lü Shih-ch'iang, *Ting Jih-ch'ang*, 357.

local gentry member in Chungking in 1887 accused a French bishop of building a fortress-like church and having a style of life comparable to that of a Chinese emperor. What made things worse was that these foreign activities and privileges were often supported by gunboat diplomacy which reinforced Chinese anti-foreign feelings. This use of naked force on the part of the Western powers produced strong resentment even among such enlightened high officials as Tseng Kuo-fan and Li Hung-chang.

The anti-foreign literati insisted that foreigners, after having 'squeezed' the Chinese economy and indoctrinated the Chinese people, would finally use the barbarian-oriented Chinese to overthrow the Chinese government and thus 'swallow up' China. In this way China would suffer the fate of Java and the Philippines. They pointed out that the pro-Western Chinese merchants in the treaty ports cooperated with foreigners in order to evade taxes, and that Chinese Christians, who had refused to pay their share for the maintenance of Confucian temples, would soon refuse to pay any taxes. Wang Ping-hsieh worried that Chinese Christians, being loyal first of all to their religious leaders, would be unfaithful to the Son of Heaven and thus disobedient to Chinese laws.[87]

The anti-Christian literati pointed out that Christianity harboured and encouraged rebellious activities. This was an old theme from the mid-seventeenth century when the noted anti-Christian anthology, the *P'o-hsieh chi* (An anthology of writings exposing heterodoxy), was compiled. After Christianity was officially prohibited in 1724, it became associated in many minds with one of the most dreaded of secret cults, the White Lotus (see volume 10, chapter 3). In 1845, one year after the prohibition was lifted, Liu Yun-k'o, governor-general of Fukien and Chekiang, reminded the court of this very problem.[88]

Other literati, such as Wang Ping-hsieh and Ch'en Pao-ch'en, maintained that just as the T'ai-p'ing religion gave impetus to the Yellow Turban Rebellion in Han times, and the White Lotus sect constituted a strong anti-dynastic force during the Yuan, Ming and Ch'ing periods, so Christianity would lead to more internal disturbances in China. To these anti-Christian literati, the vicious nature of the religion was unmistakably demonstrated when certain Christian doctrines exerted considerable influence on the ideology of the Taiping rebel movement. Christianity was also widely identified with anti-dynastic secret societies in the fifties and

[87] Lü Shih-ch'iang, 'Wan Ch'ing Chung-kuo chih-shih fen-tzu tui Chi-tu-chiao tsai Hua ch'uan-chiao mu-ti ti i-chü, 1860–1898' (Chinese intellectual's suspicion and fear of the Christian missionaries in the late Ch'ing period, 1860–1898), *SFLS*, 3 (Feb. 1975) 148. Lü Shih-ch'iang, *Chung-kuo kuan-shen fan-chiao ti yuan-yin, 1860–1874* (Causes behind the Chinese gentry-officials' hostility towards Christianity, 1860–1874), 130.

[88] Ch'i Ssu-ho *et al. Ya-p'ien chan-cheng*, 6.383.

sixties. As Wang Ping-hsieh saw it, with the spread of Christianity the seeds of domestic disturbances had been sown.[89]

Accordingly, the anti-foreignists called for China to put an end to Western political aggression as soon as possible. If China continued to allow foreigners to stay, the situation would soon deteriorate to such an extent that even the sages would be unable to do anything about it. From this perspective anti-missionary movements were good omens, for they indicated that China's political consciousness remained high. The day when there were no such anti-foreign riots would be the time, they predicted, of China's complete subjugation.[90]

At the same time there existed irrational and blind anti-foreignism. Many believed the ancient saying, 'If he be not of our kin, he is sure to have a different mind.'[91] Thus, the foreigners, being called 'devils' and compared to animals, were believed to have killed Chinese for various purposes of alchemy and witchcraft. In order to put an end to such barbaric behaviour, Prince Ch'un (I-huan) in 1869 proposed a six-point programme to expel the barbarians. Having realized that his aim could not be accomplished, he memorialized in 1874, advocating the abandonment of all things foreign. He suggested that the court, to set a good example for the people, should discard the useless Western goods.

This type of emotional hatred of foreigners and things foreign was clearly evidenced by Wo-jen's insistence on resigning his appointment in the Tsungli Yamen in 1867. On his first day in office, he intentionally fell from his horse. Using this alleged injury as a pretext, he stopped going to his office. Although the court extended his sick leave several times, Wo-jen insisted that he still could not walk. After he was permitted to resign, however, he suddenly 'recovered' completely from his injury. A similar case was Teng Ch'eng-hsiu who was appointed to the same yamen in 1884. He declined the appointment immediately, claiming that he knew nothing about barbarian affairs. Instead, he asked the throne to assign him a military post, since he was willing to fight to death on the battlefield. Hsu T'ung's behaviour also gives eloquent testimony to this kind of irrational anti-foreignism. He was reported to have hated the sight of a Western-style building and to have remarked that he preferred the destruction of his country to reform. It was thus no surprise that he later became one of the chief firebrands responsible for the outburst of the Boxer movement.[92] The

[89] Lü Shih-ch'iang, Fan-chiao, 25, 117, 171-3. Lü Shih-ch'iang, 'I-chü', 8-9. Wang Ping-hsieh, Wen-chi, 6.6-14.
[90] Lü Shih-ch'iang, 'I-chü', 148-9.
[91] Legge, The Chinese classics, The Ch'un Ts'ew with the Tso Chuen, 355.
[92] For the intellectual background of Wo-jen and Hsu T'ung, see Hao Chang, 'The anti-foreignist role of Wo-jen, 1804-1871', Papers on China, 14 (1960) 1-29.

Boxer holocaust of 1900 climaxed the long history of China's xenophobia. The Boxers, being anti-foreign, rejected the use of Western-style weapons and preferred traditional swords and spears.

The belligerent foreign policy views

Another form of anti-foreignism was bellicosity. The irresponsible advocacy of war had been very popular during the Southern Sung period (1127–1279) when China, being militarily weak vis-à-vis the nomads of the north, faced the possibility of the destruction of her civilization. The military realism of Han times (206 BC – AD 222) and the cosmopolitan spirit of the T'ang dynasty (618–907) gave way to conservative bellicosity. This tradition re-emerged in the latter half of the nineteenth century. The literati-officials' advocacy of war against Russia, France or Japan was reminiscent of the 'hollow belligerence' of their Southern Sung counter-parts, who could wield the writing brush but had little idea of actual warfare.

Bellicosity in the late Ch'ing stemmed partly from the literati's resent-ment over the wars of 1840, 1860 and 1884. The grand secretary Wo-jen memorialized in 1867: 'The barbarians are our enemies. They had a military invasion in 1860, occupying our capital and disturbing the gods of our dynasty. . . . All the literati have been hating them. How can we for one day forget this enmity and shame?' When China was at war with the Anglo-French forces in 1860, many officials in Peking advocated a warlike policy. Ch'üan-ch'ing suggested that Chinese forces should simultaneously attack foreign warships at Taku, Teng-chou and Hong Kong, and Hsueh Shu-t'ang enumerated five reasons why China would win the war. Many princes and high officials petitioned the emperor to direct the war per-sonally. General Sheng-pao put it more simply. There was no reason why the Celestial Empire should give in, for the court might simply reject all foreign demands. If the West insisted, what the emperor needed to do was to give orders to fight, and then his generals would capture the barbarian soldiers and kill their leaders. It was further suggested that if China were defeated on the coast, she should move her capital from Peking to Shensi in order to continue the war.[93]

During the Tientsin Massacre crisis of 1870 a number of officials in the capital, especially the censors and young officials of the Six Boards, were militant in spirit. They maintained that the people, who hated the bar-barians and were familiar with the local situation, should be permitted to fight against the foreign aggressors. The people, armed with moral strength and outnumbering the enemy, could easily defeat Western ships and

[93] *IWSM-TC*, 47.25. Weng T'ung-ho, *Jih-chi*, 1.48, 56.

cannon. According to Prince Ch'un, it was easy for China to defeat the foreigners, for the local forces could handle the attack of a few Western warships, and the central government could crush a massive foreign attack.[94]

The bellicosity of literati-officials was evident during the several decades following the Opium War, but it remained inactive until the seventies, which saw the rise of a politically active group called the Ch'ing-liu tang or 'purists', who staunchly advocated a belligerent foreign policy. While the pragmatic reformers emphasized China's material weakness, these young, pedantic and inexperienced officials stressed her moral strength. Their leader was the powerful conservative Li Hung-tsao (1820–97), a grand councillor and imperial tutor, who in the early eighties, as Kuo Sung-tao put it, at once 'advocated war with Japan in the east and with France in the west'.[95]

Chang Chih-tung was a distinguished member of this group. During the Ili crisis of the late seventies, he persistently urged the court to adopt a strong, militant position towards Russia. Having listed ten reasons for the repudiation of Ch'ung-hou's treaty of 1879 (see Chapter 2), he argued that war preparations should be actively pursued, including the hiring of Western mercenaries. When the Sino-French War loomed on the coast in 1883, Chang once again urged the throne to discard indecisiveness and be ready to fight even if China was inferior to France in military strength. Why? Because 'China's coastal defense can never be strengthened', he argued, 'unless we have a fight [against France]; but the experience of fighting can never be obtained unless we take the risk of being defeated.'[96] In like manner, other Ch'ing-liu tang members, such as Chang P'ei-lun, Teng Ch'eng-hsiu, Ch'en Pao-ch'en, Huang T'i-fang, Wu Ta-ch'eng, Sheng-yü, Liu En-fu and Li Tz'u-ming, also championed a bellicose course of action in China's foreign relations, especially towards Russia, Japan and France. They belittled Russia as being backward, France as being weak, and Japan as being poor.

The views of these 'purists' of the war party were shared by other literati-officials. Wang Ping-hsieh, for instance, in the early eighties evaluated China's foreign policy along similar lines. The best policy, he asserted, was to wage a total war against the barbarians and exterminate

---

[94] *IWSM-TC*, 39.1–12.26.

[95] Kuo T'ing-i, *Kuo Sun-tao*, 2.889. For a general view of this group of officials, see Yen-p'ing Hao, 'A study of the Ch'ing-liu tang: the disinterested scholar-official group, 1875–1884', *Papers on China*, 16 (1962) 40–65.

[96] Chang Chih-tung's letter to Chang P'ei-lun, in *Chung-Fa chan-cheng* (Sino-French War), ed. by Shao Hsun-cheng *et al.*, 4.518–19. For Chang's views on the Ili crisis, see Li Tsung-t'ung and Liu Feng-han, *Li Hung-tsao*, 1.252, and Li Kuo-ch'i, *Chang Chih-tung ti wai-chiao cheng-ts'e* (Chang Chih-tung's foreign policy proposals), 43.

them completely; the next best was to utilize barbarians to control barbarians; and the worst policy was to take a defensive posture. As to the emulation of barbarians, he continued, it was unworthy to be called a policy at all. He went further to set forth detailed military strategies for warfare. For example, Chinese troops should never be gathered together in large numbers in order to avoid attack from the barbarians' powerful cannon. But, as he did not have a genuine knowledge of foreign affairs, most of his military proposals were far from practical. A case in point was his suggestion that China should dig ditches on the coast area so as to check the mobility of Western cavalry.[97]

Admittedly, these bellicose views did not always prevail, nor was China victorious in her foreign wars. Moreover some of the war advocates, such as Chang P'ei-lun and Wu Ta-ch'eng, were discredited on the battlefield. Yet the bellicose conservatives must be held mainly responsible for the Ch'ing espousal of an unrealistic policy and an emotional cause. After all, they helped to precipitate the Sino-French, the Sino-Japanese and the Boxer wars. Without denying the sometimes crucial factor of court politics, the instincts and psychology behind its warlike policies must be recognized.

The persistence of culturism

In addition to anti-foreignism, China's foreign policy views were equally influenced by the literati-officials' strong, intellectual commitment to Chinese culture, especially orthodox Confucianism. In his famous declaration against the Taipings, Tseng Kuo-fan called his fellow scholars to join him in defending the Chinese cultural heritage in the tradition of Confucius and Mencius. The Manchu court, in an effort to perpetuate the identity of state and culture, similarly promoted Confucianism by emphasizing the importance of the civil service examination system. It was this cultural consciousness that lent support to the anti-reform movement in Hunan in 1898 (see chapter 5).

This cultural consciousness was manifest in the conservatives' view of diplomacy. Wang K'ai-yun, after learning of Kuo Sung-tao's mission to London, wrote to Kuo in 1876 suggesting that Kuo should spread Confucianism to Britain, which had not been graced by a visit of any Confucian scholars. Similarly, a noted scholar of the Hanlin Academy was suspicious of Tseng Chi-tse's competence in diplomacy because Tseng, who failed to pass the civil examination, was not Confucian-minded at all.[98] Why, then, was Confucianism so closely intertwined with foreign policy

[97] Wang Ping-hsieh, *Wen-chi*, 6.29b–30, 41b.
[98] Lü Shih-ch'iang, *Ting Jih-ch'ang*, 357. Li En-han, *Tseng Chi-tse*, 75–6.

views? While Confucianism includes various complicated ideas, two of them are especially relevant to this issue.

Civilization versus barbarism

An important idea in Confucianism was the distinction between civilization and barbarism (*hua i chih pien*). The Confucian scholar-official did not think in terms of *Chinese* civilization. For him, there was only civilization and barbarism, and what was not civilized was barbaric. Civilization was, indeed, an empire without neighbours.[99] Thus China was not a state but the locus of civilized society *in toto*. This idea of civilization versus barbarism was in Confucius' mind when he commented on Kuan Chung, the celebrated minister of Ch'i. Although Confucius belittled Kuan in other aspects, he praised him for his ability to protect Chinese civilization from barbarian invasion: 'But for Kuan Chung, we should now be wearing our hair unbound, and the lapels of our coats buttoned on the left side.'[100] With this view in mind the early Ch'ing patriot Wang Fu-chih had commented that while the fall of Han and T'ang represented only dynastic changes, the Mongols' conquest of Sung meant the destruction of civilization itself, embodied in the teachings of such Confucian sages as Yao, Shun, Yü and T'ang.[101]

This distinction between Chinese (*Hua*) and barbarians (*i*) was mainly one of culture. Some eminent Chinese historians defined barbarians as those who did not follow the paths of humanity and righteous conduct and were cut off from the wisdom of the sages. This Chinese concept of barbarians can be traced to China's long experience of encounters with the nomads on China's northern frontier. These Inner Asian people were thought to be greedy, deceitful and unpredictable. Since this was the background against which China started her relations with the West, it was no wonder that the majority of the gentry literati viewed Westerners as barbarian. Wang Ping-hsieh provided a good example. The Ch'ing authorities in the sixties enlisted foreign officers to fight against the Taiping and Nien rebellions, and Wang called this event *Hui-ho chu-shun*, referring to the Uighur Turks' assistance to the T'ang court in suppressing the An Lu-shan Rebellion during the mid-eighth century. By the same token, in commenting on the Tientsin Massacre of 1870, Li Tz'u-ming wrote that China's relationship with the West was like the one between China and the barbarians from the tenth to twelfth centuries when the Sung dynasty was facing the menace of the barbarian Liao in the north.[102]

99 Vadime Elisseeff, 'The middle empire, a distant empire, an empire without neighbors', *Diogenes*, 42 (Summer 1963) 60-4.
100 Legge, *The Chinese classics, Confucian Analects*, 282.
101 Lü Shih-ch'iang, *Fan-chiao*, 15.   102 Wang Ping-hsieh, *Wen-chi*, 6.40. *CWO*, 295.

This idea of regarding Westerners as barbarians was revealed most markedly in the opposition of some literati-bureaucrats to the establishment of the Tsungli Yamen. The Ch'ing court had not established a foreign office before 1861, because China's foreign relations were in the main based on the tribute system which was already handled by various state organs. The Li-fan yuan (Mongolian Superintendency) dealt with Russian and northern frontier affairs. After learning of the imminent establishment of the Tsungli Yamen, Li Tz'u-ming argued that it was not in accordance with the *t'i-chih* or fundamental structure of the imperial order. Instead, he suggested that a new department in the Li-fan yuan be created, with Prince Kung as the head, in order to handle relations with the West.[103]

Similarly, many literati viewed Sino-Western relations in the context of the tribute system and regarded foreign affairs as beneath their dignity. The grand councillor Yen Ching-ming stated that men of rectitude did not care to engage in foreign affairs. After Kuo Sung-tao was appointed as China's minister to Britain in 1875, many of his friends were disheartened. Li Ho-nien and Feng Yü-chi urged him not to go to the barbarian land, and Li Tz'u-ming lamented this fact in his diary: 'Kuo Sung-tao stands out for his learning and literary talents, but he should not have accepted the mission to the West! I am truly regretful for him.'[104] During the late seventies Li continued to denounce China's dispatching of diplomats abroad.

Yet, in the opinion of a large segment of the Confucian scholars, it was these very barbarians who were threatening the existence of civilization. The Treaty of Tientsin, which permitted Western missionaries to go inland, alarmed many gentry members. Hsia Hsieh, for example, worried that this would be the beginning of the end of the sages' teachings. One placard in Hunan lamented in 1862, 'China, with a several-thousand-year civilization of propriety and righteousness, will soon be changed into barbarian status. What a pity!'[105]

Wang Ping-hsieh wrote in the sixties that although political disturbances happened in all times, the crisis that China then faced was a crucial one, for it might lead China to sink into barbarism. Foreign influence was thus more dangerous than flood or wild beasts. Could a man, he asked, face a more distressing situation than this? When the curriculum of the T'ung-wen kuan was to include more than astronomy and mathematics, many

[103] Li Tz'u-ming, *Yueh-man-t'ang jih-chi* (Li Tz'u-ming's diary), entry of TC 6/6/3, recalling his suggestion in 1861.
[104] Kuo T'ing-i, *Kuo Sung-tao*, 2.499, 526. *Pei-chuan-chi pu* (Supplement to collected epigraphs), comp. by Min Erh-ch'ang, 13.15.
[105] Cited in Lü Shih-ch'iang, *Fan-chiao*, 21-2. For Hsia Hsieh's view, see his *Chung-Hsi*, 16.6.

literati-officials, including Wo-jen, Li Tz'u-ming and Yang T'ing-hsi, were opposed to this Western learning for fear that the Confucian scholars, the vanguard of civilization, would be barbarianized.[106]

Man versus beast

The Confucian scholars were also imbued with the idea of a distinction between man and beast (*jen ch'in chih pien*). The Confucian teachings hold that an individual can be called a man only if he acts morally. He should behave in accordance with the 'nature' of man, being compassionate, able to distinguish right from wrong, and having a sense of shame. In particular, he should follow the teachings of the sages, including the cardinal principle of the three bonds (*san-kang*). These are the verities by which man as man must live. A beast, on the other hand, is cruel, opportunistic and preoccupied with the satisfaction of physical drives or wants. If an individual is characterized by these attributes, then he is morally less than human – indeed, he is a beast.

As both barbarism and animality were beyond the domain of civilization they were often used interchangeably. The Chinese in remote antiquity seem to have indulged in comparing barbarians with various kinds of animals. Barbarian tribes, referred to by *ti, man* and other terms, were often written in characters with animal radicals. China's traditional relations with the northern nomads were based partly on this myth. Just as the bone-and-stick policy compared barbarians to dogs, so the *chi-mi* policy compared them to horses or cattle. But strictly speaking, a beast was worse than a barbarian, for a barbarian was civilizable but a beast was beyond redemption.

Accordingly, the Confucian scholars put great emphasis on living up to *ming-chiao*, the Confucian moral code. The sacred core of their values and beliefs was the Confucian doctrine of the three bonds governing the hierarchic relation between ruler and minister, parent and son, and husband and wife. Li Hung-tsao, the powerful conservative, provided a good example of how a culture-minded scholar observed the proper parent–son relationship. On 13 August 1866, his mother died. He asked the court for a twenty-seven-month leave of absence in order to observe the mourning period, as specified by the Confucian tradition. On 18 August the two empresses dowager, in view of Li's important official duties as a grand councillor and an imperial tutor, granted him a one-hundred-day mourning period after which Li was to resume his duties but did not have to participate in the regular morning audiences. Five days later, Li repeated his petition, pointing out that it was particularly important for a

[106] Wang Ping-hsieh, *Wen-chi*, 6.31b–32. *IWSM-TC*, 47.24–5. *YWYT*, 6.153–4.

high official to observe the teachings of the sages. If he deviated from them, Li continued, he would not be worth being called a son – nor a man for that matter.

Another edict from the court on 28 August denied his request, but granted him further special privileges which included that during the ensuing twenty-seven months he would not be asked to wear court costumes, nor was he required to take part in the morning audiences, court festivals and ceremonial occasions. Three days later, Li petitioned again, insisting on his original request. Not to observe the full mourning period, he maintained, would not only make him a 'sinner' against the sages' teachings (*ming-chiao tsui-jen*), but also impair the imperial prestige. When his third attempt again failed to convince the court, Li used sickness as his excuse for not resuming his public service when the official hundred-day leave came to an end. Not until 26 November 1868, when the Confucian mourning period of twenty-seven months ended, did he 'recover' from his alleged illness and start to perform his official duties. Li's insistence on adhering to Confucianism was all the more remarkable, because the woman for whom he insisted on mourning was only his adoptive mother. When his own mother died in 1877, he observed another twenty-seven-month mourning period.[107] He was widely acclaimed among conservative officials, including Wo-jen, Hsu T'ung, and a host of censors, for his strict observation of the Confucian tradition.

This distinction between man and beast, many tradition-minded literati-officials believed, would soon come to an end because of the influence of the Westerners who did not observe the Three Bonds. A Westerner, they argued, was more loyal to his religious leader than to his political leader, and his belief in the Christian dogma of virgin birth was tantamount to an open repudiation of his father. In the same way as Mencius, in denouncing Mo Ti and Yang Chu, said that the one who did not respect his ruler and father was like a beast, so these scholars maintained that a Westerner was similar to an animal. Actually, their writings frequently referred to the Westerner as having the nature of dogs and sheep.[108]

A closer examination, these moralists went on, showed that a Westerner was in fact worse than a beast. For one thing, a beast, however unfilial it might be to its father, had affection towards its mother, but Jesus even refused to recognize his own mother. Besides, the anti-Christian literature vividly described the sexual perversions and promiscuity attributed to Christians (see volume 10, chapter 11). One pamphlet asked rhetorically, 'Are they not really worse than beasts?' Finally, the Westerners were not

[107] Li Tsung-t'ung and Liu Feng-han, *Li Hung-tsao*, 1.147–54, 241; 2.414.
[108] Wang Ping-hsieh, *Wen-chi*, 6.7b–9b, 11. Lü Shih-ch'iang, *Fan-chiao*, 31. *IWSM-HF*, 7.24.

only unfilial to their parents but also destroyed their ancestors' graves by mining and constructing railways and telegraph lines. All in all, as a Westerner was worse than a beast, the Hunanese scholar Wang K'ai-yun compared him to matter (*wu*), an entity without feeling or life. One anti-foreign tract warned in the sixties that, hard as it might be to believe, many Chinese were following such degenerate Western religious practices and technological programmes.[109]

The influences of conservatism

Although conservatism in the late Ch'ing was attributable partly to political factors, the great majority of the literati-officials were imbued with moral-ideological considerations. This Chinese culturalism combined with pedantic bellicosity had unique features. After all, the bolder proposals for self-strengthening had been blocked or long delayed in their acceptance, and even such as Wang K'ai-yun and Wang Hsien-ch'ien, who approved of the objectives, were not willing to 'change institutions'. After 1884 Chang Chih-tung changed his attitude from conservatism to the pursuit of *yang-wu*, yet his programme to cope with the changing times included the time-honoured Confucian principle of 'rule by virtuous men'.

Conservatism was evident not only among the officials in the capital but also among the governors and governors-general in the provinces. Some of them, such as Ts'en Yü-ying, Shen Pao-chen, Wen-pin and Li Ping-heng, were actively anti-foreign, while others such as Wang Wen-shao, Liu K'un-i and Li Han-chang were very lukewarm regarding Western technology. Liu Ping-chang, one of Li Hung-chang's former commanders, openly opposed the introduction of Western learning while serving as governor-general of Szechwan 1886-94. Chinese cultural inertia was also manifest in the slowness with which some of the important books on reform received imperial attention. Wei Yuan's *Hai-kuo t'u chih*, which was first published in 1843 and revised in 1847 and 1852, was not presented to the emperor until 1858. In that year Wang Mao-yin proposed that an official edition be reissued, but his proposal was not adopted. A similar case was Feng Kuei-fen's essays, *Chiao-pin-lu k'ang-i* (Straightforward words from the Lodge of Early Chou Studies), published in 1861; it was not until 1889 that Weng T'ung-ho presented it to the Kuang-hsu Emperor for perusal.[110]

[109] Wang Ping-hsieh, *Wen-chi*, 6.8-13b. Paul A. Cohen, *China and Christianity: the missionary movement and the growth of Chinese antiforeignism, 1860-1870*, 51. *Hai-fang tang, Tien-hsien*, 212. Kuo T'ing-i, *Kuo Sung-tao*, 2.857.
[110] Wang Chia-chien, *Wei Yuan hai-fang*, 176. Wang Chia-chien, *Wei Yuan nien-p'u* (Chronological biography of Wei Yuan). 82. Weng T'ung-ho, *Jih-chi*, 4.1630.

The conservative officials, especially the censors, attacked the pragmatic reformers at all levels. Naturally, they criticized the most influential ones including Prince Kung, Tseng Kuo-fan and Li Hung-chang. Nor did the reformers of secondary importance escape such slander. For example, those that Li Tz'u-ming defamed included the foreign affairs experts Ma Chien-chung, Li Feng-pao and Ch'en Lan-pin, and the entrepreneurs Tong King-sing, Hsu Jun and Sheng Hsuan-huai, all of whom he termed traitors and 'mean men' (*hsiao-jen*). Another example was Ting Jih-ch'ang. Because of his dealings with foreigners at Shanghai in 1864, and his involvement in the Ch'ao-chou crisis of 1866 and the Tientsin Massacre of 1870, he became increasingly unpopular among the conservatives. Their criticism led to his early retirement from his governorship of Fukien in 1878 at the age of fifty-five. Liu Ming-ch'uan, the first governor of Taiwan, pursued a bold modernization programme on that island from 1885, but conservative officials effected his removal in 1891.

No reformers were attacked as fiercely as Kuo Sung-tao. In 1876 when he went to Britain as minister, the literati satirized him for leaving the land of the sages to serve the foreign devils. His fellow townsmen, being ashamed of his conduct, tried to destroy his house. Actually, he had planned to write a book on self-strengthening and modern diplomacy but abandoned the idea later for fear of further conservative criticism. When his diary, which praised Western civilization, was published by the Tsungli Yamen in 1877, the court was prevailed upon to order the printing blocks to be destroyed. Kuo, who abounded with moral courage, at first refused to give in. In his reports from London, he praised Western technology, political institutions and educational systems. For these and other reasons, he was impeached time and again as a betrayer of both the dynasty and the Chinese cultural heritage. He finally succumbed to the pressure and resigned in 1879, cutting short a promising diplomatic career. After returning, he went straight into retirement in his native province of Hunan. Liu K'un-i recommended that Kuo be assigned to work in the Tsungli Yamen, but this recommendation did not materialize due to the opposition of the two powerful conservative grand councillors, Li Hung-tsao and Ching-lien.[111]

Prince Kung, in reviewing the slowness with which the self-strengthening programmes proceeded, pointed out that the conservatives' objection was an important factor. His remark was borne out by the history of China's railway development. The small Shanghai–Wusung line, opened by foreigners in 1876, was purchased the next year by Chinese officials who promptly had it torn up. Ting Jih-ch'ang's railroad construction plan aborted in 1877 due to the opposition of conservative critics. Liu Ming-

[111] Kuo T'ing-i, *Kuo Sung-tao*, 2.507, 554, 665, 666, 865.

ch'uan memorialized in 1880 to construct a railway from Peking to Ch'ing-chiang-p'u, and Li Hung-chang supported his proposal. However, the arguments of the traditionally minded censors and Hanlin scholars convinced the court, which finally abandoned the plan. The controversial project to build a railway from Tientsin to T'ung-chou had a similar abortive fate in 1889.[112] Other self-strengthening programmes, such as mines, telegraphs, steam shipping and technological schools, encountered similar opposition.[113]

The emergence of a national consciousness

Although nationalism as a widespread movement did not occur in China until the nineties, nationalism as a state of mind had its beginnings in the sixties and seventies. The anti-foreign feelings of many enlightened individuals, especially those on the coast (such as Wang T'ao and Cheng Kuan-ying), were motivated not so much by cultural considerations as by nationalistic sentiments. The emergence of a scattered national consciousness was evident in both the political and the economic fields. In officialdom, the awareness of national sovereignty and the adoption of the theory of balance of power in international affairs were unmistakable indications of political nationalism. In the treaty ports, the idea of engaging in commercial rivalry with the West was the cornerstone of mercantile nationalism. In both cases, however, the emergence of a national consciousness began with the gradual break-up of the time-honoured Sinocentrism.

The disintegration of Sinocentrism

This concept gradually lost its influence on the minds of the gentry-literati during the latter half of the nineteenth century. The first indication was that the great majority of the reform-minded gentry members stopped comparing foreigners to animals. It was a common practice, during the forties and fifties, for the literati-officials, including such noted reformers as Lin Tse-hsu and Kung Tzu-chen, to write the names of Western states in characters with animal (usually dog) radicals, but this practice was significantly reduced after the seventies. Except for certain clichés like *chi-mi*, Kuo Sung-tao's collected works, including volumes of prose, poetry and memorials, do not contain a single comparison between foreigners and animals.

---

[112] *IWSM-TC*, 98.19-20. Li Kuo-ch'i, *Chung-kuo tsao-ch'i ti t'ieh-lu ching-ying* (China's early railway enterprises), 37-45, 54-6, 76-8.

[113] See, for example, Weng T'ung-ho, *Jih-chi*, 2.992. *Chiao-t'ung shih* (History of transport and communications), *Hang-cheng pien* (Shipping), 1.149, 184. Li En-han, *Tseng Chi-tse*, 22-3. Kuo T'ing-i, *Kuo Sung-tao*, 2.844. *IWSM-TC*, 48.12-14.

Another indication of diminishing Sinocentrism was that, with time, the term *i* (barbarian) was less frequently used. (The term was barred from official documents by the British Treaty of Tientsin.) Wei Yuan wrote in the fifties that Westerners, being polite, righteous and knowledgeable, should not be called *i* at all. They were, as Wei put it, 'marvellous men' and 'good friends'. The enlightened thinkers used various terms to refer to the West: Huang En-t'ung called it *yuan* (far-away land), Ting Jih-ch'ang termed it *wai-kuo* (foreign states), and many others, such as Prince Kung, Ting Jih-ch'ang and Hsueh Fu-ch'eng, named it *Hsi-yang* (Western ocean). A host of anti-foreign writings in the forties and fifties referred to Westerners as *i*. However, when these works were reissued during the seventies and eighties, they were referred to as *yang* (foreigners).[114]

The Westerners, being neither animals morally nor barbarians culturally, thus became the equals of the Chinese. This Chinese awakening of international consciousness was evidenced in the discussion of historical parallels. In 1861 Feng Kuei-fen suggested a clear analogy between the Eastern Chou period (770–221 BC) and the contemporary world. By 1894 more than a dozen others, including Cheng Kuan-ying, Ma Chien-chung, Tseng Chi-tse, Wang T'ao, P'eng Yü-lin, Ch'en Ch'iu and Chang Chih-tung, had made similar observations. They maintained that during the periods of the Spring and Autumn Annals (772–481 BC) and Warring States (403–221 BC), the Chinese world was made up of a conglomeration of separate states and principalities that resembled the multistate system of the late nineteenth century.[115] This idea implied that China was not the Middle Kingdom but rather a state among equal states, like the state of Chin in late Chou. Such an analogy, however unconscious it may have been, helped to put aside Sinocentrism and usher China into the new world she now faced.

As we have seen, some progressive literati-officials, particularly the leaders of the self-strengthening movement, maintained that China should seize the changing times and learn from the West. Feng Kuei-fen, Ho Kai (Ho Ch'i) and Hu Li-yuan provided a rationale for this policy. In proposing reform guidelines, Feng Kuei-fen named two principles. The first

[114] Wang Chia-chien, *Wei Yuan hai-fang*, 38. Ch'i Ssu-ho *et al. Ya-p'ien chan-cheng*, 5.409; 6.508–9. *Hai-fang tang, Chi-ch'i chü*, 1.4.

[115] Feng Kuei-fen, *Chiao-pin-lu k'ang-i* (Straightforward words from the Lodge of Early Chou studies), 2.66a–b. Cheng Kuan-ying, *I-yen*, 2.12. Ma Chien-chung, *Shih-k'o*, 2.9a–b. Tseng Chi-tse, *Tseng Hui-min kung i-chi, Wen-chi*, 5.1. Wang T'ao, *Wai-pien*, 4.21a–b. P'eng Yü-lin's preface to Cheng Kuan-ying, *Sheng-shih wei-yen*. Ko Shih-chün, comp. *Huang-ch'ao ching-shih-wen hsu-pien* (Collection of Ch'ing dynasty writings on statecraft, continued), 101.9b. Ch'en Ch'iu, *Ching-shih po-i* (Broad suggestions on statecraft), 4.8b. Wang T'ao, ed. *Ko-chih shu-yuan k'o-i* (Assigned writings of students of the Shanghai Polytechnic Institute), (1892 series), 1.6, 14, 19, 20. 29b. Ch'en Chih, *Yung-shu*, 8.1b–2.

was *fa hou wang* or the emulation of the recent (not ancient) kings, and the second was *chien chu kuo* or the learning of things from other states. These states, which existed side by side on an equal basis and were wealthy and strong, provided excellent examples for China to emulate. There was no need for China to feel embarrassment in doing this, Ho Kai and Hu Li-yuan maintained, because of the cyclical nature of history. Just as China was strong in the past, so it became weak in the modern period. On the other hand, since the West was weak in the past, it naturally turned out to be strong later.[116]

Other Sinocentric terms were also called into question. One of these was *t'ien-hsia* or 'all under heaven', the all-embracing Chinese world. Cheng Kuan-ying argued that this term did not truthfully describe China, since China was only one nation among the family of nations. Unless the Chinese kept this realistic idea in mind, he added, China would not be psychologically prepared to accept the idea of international law.[117]

Economic nationalism

As trade was the main reason for the Western presence in China, it is no surprise that Chinese nationalism, arising from trade relations, developed early in the treaty ports. The old problem of trade policy had faced China since 1840, but now foreign trade began to concern the very life pulse of the country. The old government attitude of having little regard and responsibility for trade now changed to one of genuine distress among enlightened officials. The policy of 'using trade to control barbarians' had lost its value. In its place arose a new concept of the government's economic prerogative and a new stratagem of 'using trade as a weapon'. The traditional phrase *li-ch'üan* or material prerogatives (to be distinguished from the modern term *ch'üan-li* or rights) originally applied to the official management of such matters as revenue, the salt monopoly and canal transport. But after 1862 when Li Hung-chang and Ting Jih-ch'ang saw that the economic life of Shanghai was very much in the hands of foreigners, the term was employed to mean the administrative authority of the government over economic and financial matters which the foreigners sought to control.[118] Later, when Li established the China Merchants' Steam Navigation Company and the Shanghai Textile Mill, his most important goal was the recovery of *li-ch'üan* or economic control.

In the same vein, Ting Jih-ch'ang, having refused the requests of Russia, Britain and the United States to operate telegraph lines, insisted in

[116] Li Kuo-ch'i, *Chang Chih-tung*, 130-1.
[117] Cheng Kuan-ying, *Sheng-shih wei-yen*, 4.8.
[118] Liu, 'Confucian as patriot and pragmatist', 39.

the sixties and seventies that such modern enterprises should be managed by China. Kuo Sung-tao wrote from London in 1877 that the right to strike silver dollars was, to his surprise, the *li-ch'üan* of a sovereign state. Having seen the damaging effects of the foreign silver dollars on China's economy, he urged China to recover this *li-ch'üan*. Even before 1895, there was a strong feeling that mining rights should not fall into foreign hands. The merchants in the treaty ports, led by Tong King-sing and Hsu Jun, were also sensitive to this issue.[119]

According to some nationalistic thinkers, another *li-ch'üan* had been lost to foreigners through their domination over the Imperial Maritime Customs Service. In order to recover this *li-ch'üan*, Cheng Kuan-ying suggested that Chinese should be appointed as vice-commissioners of customs with a view to replacing the Western commissioners within ten years. China could not compare with Japan in this respect, Cheng continued, for the Japanese had already replaced the foreigners as Japan's commissioners of customs. For Teng Ch'eng-hsiu, Robert Hart's tenure as the inspector-general of the customs was most reprehensible. He therefore proposed that this post should be filled by two persons, one being a Chinese and the other a foreigner. Tseng Chi-tse also wrote to the Tsungli Yamen in 1886, urging the removal of Hart. Ch'en Chih fiercely attacked Hart in the early nineties, accusing him of corruption, unduly protecting foreign merchants, and interfering with Chinese tariff regulations. He also called for the replacement of Hart by a Chinese.[120]

In view of the Western economic encroachment on China, the enlightened high officials and patriotic merchants in the treaty ports soon began to talk of economic competition (*shang-chan*, lit., commercial warfare) with the foreigners. The term *shang-chan* first appeared in 1862 in a letter written by Tseng Kuo-fan, but at that time it was used only occasionally. Ting Jih-ch'ang, as Shanghai taotai, promised in 1863 to reduce the tax on Chinese junks in order to compete with foreign ships in the Newchwang–Shanghai bean trade. He wrote to Li Hung-chang the following year suggesting that Chinese merchants should be encouraged to buy and build steamships. Equipped with modern means of maritime transport, Chinese merchants would outcompete the foreign trader, for they were more familiar with the local markets. The motivation of the Westerner's coming to China, Ting continued, was mainly to seek profit. If he could not get profit, he would naturally leave China. In this way, it would not be

[119] Lü Shih-ch'iang, *Ting Jih-ch'ang*, 252–3. Kuo T'ing-i, *Kuo Sung-tao*, 2.645. Li En-han, *Wan-Ch'ing ti shou-hui k'uang-ch'üan yun-tung* (The movement to recover mining rights in the late Ch'ing period), *passim*. Yen-p'ing Hao, *The comprador in nineteenth century China: bridge between East and West*, 112–20. *Chiao-t'ung shih, Hang-cheng pien*, 1.147.

[120] Cheng Kuan-ying, *Sheng-shih wei-yen*, 3.4. Li En-han, *Tseng Chi-tse*, 306, 318.

necessary for China to expel foreigners by force. Li Fan in 1876 stressed to the emperor the importance of helping and protecting trade and in doing so he used Tseng Kuo-fan's term *shang-chan*. Hsueh Fu-ch'eng in 1879 asserted that Sino-foreign competition in trade could not be avoided.[121]

China's spirit of commercial rivalry with the West was evidenced by the efforts to establish steamship enterprises on the coast. Yung Wing and Hsu Tao-shen, with this patriotic view in mind and supported by the Tsungli Yamen, tried to set up a joint-stock steamship company at Shanghai in 1868. Although this project aborted for lack of capital, the China Merchants' Steam Navigation Company was inaugurated in 1873. Li Hung-chang, the promoter, declared that the aim of this enterprise was to rival the Western steamship companies. Tong King-sing and Hsu Jun, the company's managing directors, were extremely conscious of *shang-chan*. Their report to the shareholders in 1874 mentioned three favourable factors vis-à-vis the foreign shipping concerns. First, the Chinese company could rely on the imperial tribute rice for Peking as freight; secondly, its administrative costs were low; and thirdly, it could easily get freight from the native merchants. In order to prevent foreigners from subscribing to shares in the company, it was stipulated that names of shareholders and their native towns be registered on the share certificates which could not legally be sold to a foreigner.[122]

Among those who discussed the subject of *shang-chan*, Cheng Kuan-ying's treatment was the most complete, and he became the most important proponent of the concept. By the late 1870s Cheng had already discussed competition in the fields of trade and maritime transport. In subsequent editions of his work *Sheng-shih wei-yen* (1884–93) he put increasing emphasis on the necessity of using trade as a weapon. While high officials were preoccupied with military self-strengthening, Cheng ascribed to commerce and industry a primary role in coping with the changing times. He contended that since the strength of the West stemmed from wealth which in turn came from commerce and industry, it would be more useful for China to learn and wage *shang-chan* than *ping-chan* (military confrontation).

Cheng stated that a Western country used as weapons not only cannon but also trade. Actually, the entire nation was behind this policy, for both diplomatic negotiations and military confrontations aimed at expanding trade. Yet, although Western states had used trade as a weapon to colonize some areas, this strategy, by virtue of its being peaceful and slow, hardly alarmed the victims. Accordingly, China, like so many other countries,

[121] Tseng Kuo-fan, *Shu-cha*, 17.44a–b. Lü Shih-ch'iang, *Ting Jih-ch'ang*, 56–62. *Hai-fang tang, Chi-ch'i chü*, 1.4–5. *YWYT*, 1.165. Hsueh Fu-ch'eng, 'Ch'ou-yang', 10b.
[122] *Chiao-t'ung shih, Hang-cheng pien*, 1.139, 144, 147.

was quick to react to the Western military invasion but was slow to do so against the Western economic encroachment. In fact, China, having an unfavourable balance of trade, was severely harmed by her commercial relations with the West. Such an economic drain was, Cheng claimed, more damaging than losing territories and paying war indemnities. Given the sinister nature of the foreign economic invasion, how should China fight back?

Cheng asserted that China had to catch up with the West in three key areas. In order to nurture true talent, it was essential to reform the examination system and to establish technological and professional schools. To utilize natural resources, mining and the modernization of agriculture were most important. To promote commerce, the government needed to reform the tax system and abolish the likin tax on local trade. At the operational level, commercial warfare was to be fought on two fronts – increasing Chinese exports and decreasing Chinese imports. For the latter, he proposed that China should manufacture modern goods and cultivate poppy fields. For the former, he called for the improvement of the process of producing tea and the establishment of more silk filatures. The basic approach, however, was the elevation of the merchant's social status, which was theoretically at the bottom of the existing social structure. Specifically, a merchant should be treated as a member of the gentry and have access to the officials.

All in all, Cheng concluded, if Chinese merchandise could compete successfully with that of the West, the foreign merchants would be forced to lose money and would naturally go home. In contrast to the controversial and expensive programmes of military self-strengthening, *shang-chan* was an easier and more effective way to rival the West. To support his argument, Cheng cited Japan's modern history. At first, Japan, like China, suffered from foreign exploitation. But since Japan had revitalized her commerce and industry and competed with the West in earnest, she was able not only to avoid the harmful aspects of trading with the West but in fact to benefit from it. The world at this time, as Cheng saw it, was a world of commercial rivalry,[123] and Cheng was one of the first reformers in modern China to advocate mercantile nationalism. We may argue that the significance of Cheng's intellectual outlook lay in his economic interpretation of world history in general and of Western society in particular.[124]

[123] Liu Kwang-Ching, 'Cheng Kuan-ying *I-yen*: Kuang-hsu ch'u-nien chih pien-fa ssu-hsiang' (Cheng Kuan-ying's *I-yen*: reform proposals of the early Kuang-hsu period), *Ch'ing-hua hsueh-pao*, NS, 8.1–2 (1970) 373–425. Cheng Kuan-ying, *Sheng-shih wei-yen*, 2.35b–43. Cheng Kuan-ying, *Sheng-shih wei-yen hou-pien* (Warnings to a prosperous age: a sequel), 1.1; 2.37b; 4.56b–57; 7.19; 8.32; 8.53.
[124] For the socio-economic and intellectual milieu of Cheng's time, see Yen-p'ing Hao, 'A

Shang-chan was a strategy of warfare analogous to the policy of 'using agriculture as a weapon' (*keng-chan*) of the Legalist thinker Shang Yang (d. 338 BC). To be effective, however, the use of commerce as a weapon in the late nineteenth century required a broader framework that included the exchange of goods in foreign trade, trade regulations, maritime customs tariffs, treaties, the establishment of consulates, and the sending of diplomatic missions abroad.

The concept of national sovereignty

Economic nationalism was reinforced by political nationalism, which was most clearly seen in the awareness of national sovereignty. In order to keep this sovereignty, the policy of the balance of power was believed to be most useful. As trade and negotiations between China and the foreign powers daily became more frequent after 1860, the Chinese gradually assimilated the Western concepts of national sovereignty and the equality of states each having equal sovereignty. Under the treaties, however, China's sovereignty was impaired. The treaties lacked equality and reciprocity, and China stood on the disadvantaged side. Furthermore, in their negotiations, foreigners conducted themselves in accordance with the treaties to maintain the rights they had already obtained, and if there were further advantages to be gained, they always grasped them. China was often unable to use the treaties for her purposes and was, on the contrary, restrained by them. The recognition of this situation eventually aroused feelings of humiliation which were then transformed into concrete reflections and rational efforts to win equality for China in international affairs.

The issue that drew Chinese attention earliest and most intensively was that of extraterritoriality. A quarter of a century after it had been instituted in the 1840s, Wen-hsiang in 1868 told the British minister, Rutherford Alcock, that if foreigners would give up this right, then merchants and missionaries could live anywhere in the interior of China, but that if they sought to preserve it, the Chinese government would use all its power to limit foreigners and the troubles surrounding extraterritoriality to the treaty ports. When Kuo Sung-tao was China's minister in London, he reminded the throne in 1877 of the urgent need to abolish this right, and he discussed the issue with Lord Salisbury the next year. In the mid-eighties, his successor, Tseng Chi-tse, urged the Tsungli Yamen to face up to this issue positively. In an article entitled 'China, the sleep and the awakening', he called for the Chinese to get rid of extraterritoriality as soon as possible.

"new class" in China's treaty ports: the rise of the comprador-merchants', *Business History Review*, 44.4 (Winter 1970) 446-59.

In fact, Cheng Kuan-ying had criticized the Westerners' legal rights before 1881.[125]

Although China had accepted the idea of extraterritoriality, at first it did not have a specific name for it in Chinese. One of the first scholars to name it was Wang T'ao who used the expression *o-wai ch'üan-li*, or 'extra-ordinary rights'. However, it was Huang Tsun-hsien's term, *chih-wai fa-ch'üan*, or 'the legal right to govern aliens', that has become the standard expression. In the early nineties, Ch'en Chih also discussed this issue. All o them, enumerating the detrimental effects that extraterritoriality inflicted on China, called for its abolition in the name of justice and righteousness.[126]

It was this slow-burning desire that prompted some reformers to re-examine the Chinese legal system. Kuo Sung-tao in 1877, Ho Kai and Hu Li-yuan in 1887, Cheng Kuan-ying in 1892, and Sung Yü-jen in 1895 maintained that traditional Chinese law was unfair and too severe in punishment. Besides, the law could not be strictly enforced because of the interference of powerful gentry members. Under such circumstances, they argued, even the Chinese could not tolerate it, and naturally foreigners did not want to subject themselves to Chinese law. They thus proposed the improvement of the conditions of prisons, the abolition of decapitation and corporal punishment, and the substitution of labour for imprisonment. Only after China reformed her legal system, they concluded, could she expect to be treated equally by the Western powers.[127]

The second issue in connection with China's sovereignty was that of regulated tariffs. In 1878, thirty-three years after the establishment of the first treaty tariff, the censor Li Fan discussed the low import-tariff duties and their detrimental effects on China's economy. In the eighties, Tseng Chi-tse protested to the British minister, Thomas Wade, concerning further British intervention in Chinese customs regulations. In discussions with Japan's minister to China in 1889 about the unequal treaties to which both China and Japan were subjected, Tseng stated that obtaining tariff auto-nomy should be the first step for both countries in order to restore national sovereignty. Cheng Kuan-ying commented on this topic several times between 1884 and 1892. He argued that a sovereign state, regardless of its

---

[125] Robert Hart, *These from the land of Sinim, essays on the Chinese question*, 68–9. Wang Chia-chien, 'Wen-hsiang tui-yü shih-chü ti jen-shih chi ch'i tzu-ch'iang ssu-hsiang' (Wen-hsiang's knowledge of world affairs and his ideas regarding self-strengthening), *SFLS*, 1 (1973) 219–39. Wang T'ao, *Wai-pien*, 3.24b. Kuo T'ing-i, *Kuo Sung-tao*, 2.682, 758. Li En-han, *Tseng Chi-tse*, 306.

[126] Wang T'ao, *Wai-pien*, 3.25–6. Huang Tsun-hsien, *Jih-pen kuo-chih*, 7.21–3. Ch'en Chih, *Yung-shu*, 7.4b.

[127] Kuo T'ing-i, *Kuo Sung-tao*, 2.683–4. Ho Ch'i and Hu Li-yuan, *Hsin-cheng chen-ch'üan* (The true interpretation of new policies), 11. Cheng Kuan-ying, *Sheng-shih wei-yen*, 4.8; Sung Yü-jen, *Shih-wu lun* (On current affairs), 3b, 8b–9.

size and strength, should first of all have the right to control its tariff rates. He explicitly advocated that China should adopt a protective tariff.[128]

Another important question related to national sovereignty was the most-favoured-nation privilege. This was first granted in the British Supplementary Treaty of the Bogue in 1843. Thereafter it became a universal feature in the treaty system, with great injury to Chinese rights. In 1879, during talks in England between Tseng Chi-tse and the Brazilian minister to England, Tseng complained that the most-favoured-nation principle was not in accordance with international law and explained how China was urgently seeking to have it removed from the treaties. In the same year Hsueh Fu-ch'eng in his treatise, 'Proposals on foreign affairs', discussed both the most-favoured-nation privilege and extraterritoriality. He considered them to be the two articles in the treaties which were most harmful to China, and advocated that means be found to get rid of them. These opinions, set forth in the very first essay of Hsueh's manuscript, were forwarded by Li Hung-chang to the Tsungli Yamen for consideration.[129]

The importance of international law (the principles for conducting foreign affairs among the sovereign states) was also gradually realized. Although before the Opium War Commissioner Lin Tse-hsu had ordered the translation of excerpts on international law from Vattel's treatise, there was no complete text of the law of nations in Chinese. W. A. P. Martin started to translate Henry Wheaton's *Elements of international law* in 1862, and the Tsungli Yamen, after careful editing, published it two years later. Prince Kung and Wen-hsiang thought highly of it, and three hundred copies were distributed to the local authorities for reference. Armed with this new knowledge, Prince Kung in 1864 successfully forced the Prussian minister to release a Danish ship which had been detained in Chinese territorial waters. Another example was the use of references from Wheaton in settlement of the Margary Affair in 1875.[130]

After Martin was appointed president of the T'ung-wen kuan in 1869, he and some of his Chinese and Manchu colleagues translated various other works, including Johann Kapur Bluntschli's *Droit international codifié*, Theodore D. Woolsey's *Introduction to the study of international law*, and *Le manuel des lois de la guerre* compiled by the Institut de Droit International. These books influenced some officials. One of them was Kuo Sung-tao,

---

[128] *YWYT*, 1.116. Li En-han, *Tseng Chi-tse*, 304, 306–7. Cheng Kuan-ying, *Sheng-shih wei-yen*, 3.1b–3b; 4.9.

[129] *YWYT*, 1.165. Tseng Chi-tse, *Tseng Hui-min kung shou-hsieh jih-chi* (Tseng Chi-tse's holograph diary), 2156–7. Hsueh Fu-ch'eng, 'Ch'ou-yang', preface and 1b–2b.

[130] *IWSM-TC*, 27.25–26b. *Li Hung-chang chih P'an Ting-hsin shu-cha* (Li Hung-chang's letters to P'an Ting-hsin), 13.

who made favourable comments on international law in January 1877 on his way to Britain. During the Ili crisis, he memorialized in 1880 suggesting that Ch'ung-hou's punishment, being too severe, should be made in accordance with the principles of international law. Similarly, Li Hung-chang, citing international law, maintained that even when war broke out between two countries, their diplomats should not be insulted.[131]

While translated books were exerting influence among Chinese official-dom, merchant-scholars in the treaty ports acquired their knowledge of international law directly from Westerners. One case in point was the comprador-reformer Cheng Kuan-ying.[132] In the 1870s, he had such high regard for international law that he treated this topic in the very first essay of his book on reform, I-yen. In subsequent editions Cheng further elucidated the principles and usefulness of international law.

Ma Chien-chung studied international law in France in the seventies and, after returning to China, provided valuable advice to Li Hung-chang concerning international affairs. Before the Sino-French War formally started in 1884, Li dispatched Ma to Shanghai to arrange the sale of the fleet of the China Merchants' Steam Navigation Company to the American house of Russell and Company in accordance with international law. The arrangement was successful, for these steamships were not damaged during the war and were repurchased by the Chinese after the conflict, as originally arranged. Other literati, including Liang Ch'i-ch'ao, Ch'en Ch'iu and T'u Ju-hsueh, also made comments on this subject in the late eighties and early nineties.[133] In order to enforce international law, Ch'en Ch'iu proposed in 1893 that a world organization, consisting of all states, be established. He predicted that his proposal would materialize in thirty years.[134]

Balance of power

The importance of national sovereignty was thus recognized, but how a state, especially a weak one, could maintain its sovereignty was another issue. The answer, according to some enlightened literati-officials, lay in the proper use of the principle of the balance of power. An excellent example of survival of a small state among the strong and large states, they

[131] Li En-han, Tseng Chi-tse, 35. Kuo T'ing-i, Kuo Sung-tao, 2.574, 863. Li Hung-chang, P'eng-liao, 19.14.
[132] For Cheng Kuan-ying's reform ideas against his background as a comprador-merchant, see Yen-p'ing Hao, 'Cheng Kuan-ying: the comprador as reformer', JAS, 29.1 (Nov. 1969) 15–22.
[133] Chiao-t'ung-shih, Hang-cheng pien, 1.154–5. Wang Erh-min Cheng-chih ssu-hsiang, 195, 208. The Association for International Law Studies was established by Pi Yung-nien and T'ang Ts'ai-ch'ang at Changsha in 1898.
[134] Ch'en Ch'iu, Ching-shih po-i, 4.17.

maintained, was the tiny state of Yen in the Spring and Autumn period (722-481 BC). Other examples included Belgium and Switzerland in the late nineteenth century. Accordingly, they urged the adoption of this policy by China as well as her tributary states, such as Korea and Annam (Vietnam).

In 1878 Ma Chien-chung, who was studying international law in Paris, set forth in detail the Western balance of power theory, the history of its development, and its pragmatic value. The term *chün-shih* (balance of power) was first used by Ma in a letter from Paris meant to be submitted to the Tsungli Yamen (presumably by Li Hung-chang). A powerful advocate of this policy was Li Hung-chang himself, who in the seventies wrote that the advent of the Japanese, however unpleasant, could be viewed as a force to check the Western influence in China. In the eighties, in order to prevent foreigners from encroaching further, he tried to keep a delicate balance of Western influences in China. After 1895 this policy continued to have advocates among scholar-officials; one notable example was Chang Chih-tung.[135]

Li Hung-chang quickly adopted this principle in his foreign policy towards Korea. By 1879 he had decided to throw Korea open to Western trade and diplomacy. In a letter to a high Korean official, Li pointed out the usefulness of the Western theory of checks and balances, as demonstrated by the history of Turkey, Belgium and Denmark. Korea, facing Japanese encroachment, should emulate these countries. Korea was probably not a match for Japan, Li continued, but Japan's influence on Korea would be checked by the Western powers if Korea decided to open herself to Western trade.[136] In 1880, Ho Ju-chang, the Chinese minister to Japan, tried to impress on a visiting Korean official in Tokyo that 'Western countries have a system of balance of power (*chün-shih*)' which would ensure peace if Korea should enter into treaties with Western countries.[137] This indicates how concepts of the Western international system were being adapted for the purposes of a new Ch'ing Korean policy. In the decade prior to the Sino-Japanese War many other literati-officials, including Sheng Hsuan-huai and other statecraft scholars, suggested that Korea should emulate the small European countries of Belgium and Switzerland, whose independence, thanks to the principle of the balance of power, was guaranteed by the great powers.[138]

[135] Ma Chien-chung, *Shih-k'o*, 2.10b-11b; Li Hung-chang, *P'eng-liao*, 6.42; Li Kuo-ch'i, *Chang Chih-tung*, 126-213.

[136] Li Hung-chang, *Li Wen-chung kung i-chi* (Writings of the late Li Hung-chang), 5.18-19.

[137] The Korean envoy, Kim Hong-jip, replied that he had seen the term *chün-shih* in *Wan-kuo kung-fa* (Martin's translation of Wheaton's *Elements of international law*). See Kuksa p'yŏnch'an wiwŏnhoe, ed. *Susinsa kirok* (Records of diplomatic envoys), 177.

[138] Li Kuo-ch'i, *Chang Chih-tung*, 135.

Tseng Chi-tse generally shared Li Hung-chang's advocacy of the opening of China's tributary states to the trade and diplomacy of Western powers. In 1883, when tension between China and France had mounted but before any military confrontation, Tseng urged the court to adopt the policy of balance of power concerning Annam. This 'open door' policy, as Tseng put it, was like 'throwing out a lamb in order to provoke a fight among the tigers'.[139] As none of the tigers was strong enough to prey on the lamb, it was hoped the lamb would survive.

It was also recognized that the balance of power could maintain peace among sovereign states, each having equal sovereignty. A few Chinese literati got this idea from the Congress of Berlin in 1878, which had prevented a war between the great powers by forcing Russia to surrender much of her conquests. Ma Chien-chung, for example, wrote from Paris, stating that there were many countries, large and small, in Europe; although all of them were sovereign states, peaceful relations among them were maintained by a balance of power. Could China benefit from this policy by making alliances with strong sovereign states? Ma's answer was affirmative. In the late seventies he cited examples to show that cooperation and the making of alliances formed the most effective policy for the management of foreign relations. In the same period, reflecting their adoption of the theory of making alliances, Cheng Kuan-ying advocated an alliance with the United States, and Chang Huan-lun advocated an alliance with Britain.[140]

CONTINUITY AND CHANGE IN CHINESE VIEWS OF WESTERN RELATIONS

Chinese views of Western relations kept changing during the 1840–95 period, with a quickened tempo after 1860. Generally, foreign policy views changed from a 'closed door' policy in the forties to the 'good faith' policy based on the Confucian principle of sincerity during the sixties. However, modern diplomatic skills, especially the idea of international law, were stressed during the ensuing two decades. Power politics, particularly the concepts of balance of power and alliance with strong countries, prevailed during the eighties and nineties. Meanwhile, the mid-sixties saw the emergence of a national consciousness which grew stronger with time.

[139] *Ibid.* 134.
[140] Ma Chien-chung, *Shih-k'o*, 13b–14b. Cheng Kuan-ying, *I-yen*, 2.13a–b. Chang Huan-lun's proposal is referred to in Tseng Chi-tse, *Tseng Hui-min kung shih-hsi jih-chi* (Diary of Tseng Chi-tse's diplomatic mission to the West), 1.8b. See also Banno Masataka, 'Furansu ryūgaku jidai no Ba Ken-chū – gaikō oyobi gaikōkan seidō ni tsuite no futatsu no ikensho' (Ma Chien-chung during his days of study in France – two proposals regarding foreign relations and the foreign service system), *Kokkagakkai zasshi*, 84.5 and 6 (1971) 257–93.

While the principle of using trade to control the barbarians was popular in the 1840-60 period, it gave way to the more dynamic concept of 'commercial warfare' in the sixties and seventies. Altogether, these changes in foreign policy views represented a metamorphosis from a Confucian and idealistic attitude to one of pragmatism.

Trying to understand and emulate the West, the pragmatic literati-officials had a changing conception of the outside world which became sophisticated slowly but steadily. It started with the world-wide geographical study by Wei Yuan and Hsu Chi-yü in the forties and fifties, and changed to the military emulation effort made in the name of self-strengthening after 1860. After the mid-seventies, however, commerce and industry were emphasized by such merchant-entrepreneurs as Cheng Kuan-ying and Tong King-sing, and Western political and educational institutions were discussed by foreign affairs experts such as Kuo Sung-tao and Ma Chien-chung.

What role did the West play in the Chinese state and society in general? It was first assumed that its impact could be marginally absorbed into the Chinese polity and social order without changing the fundamental Chinese scheme of things. By 1860 the Westerners were still treated as a nuisance to be brushed off. In the end, however, Western affairs became a focal point of nation-wide concern.

Changes in the use of key terms give eloquent testimony to this progress in understanding the West. Affairs in connection with the West were in the main called 'barbarian affairs' (*i-wu*) before the sixties, 'Western affairs' (*yang-wu*) and 'Western learning' (*Hsi-hsueh*) in the seventies and eighties, and 'new learning' (*hsin-hsueh*) in the nineties. The first term was Sino-centric; the second and third were rather neutral in value judgment; while the last unmistakably implied approval. The change in attitude of some scholar-officials also illustrates this point. The leading advocates of self-strengthening, such as Tseng Kuo-fan, Li Hung-chang and Prince Kung, were all anti-foreign when they first confronted the Westerners. Their attitude became more and more flexible and realistic as their understanding of the West deepened.[141]

In spite of all these changes, the power of conservatism remained strong. Success in the introduction of things Western into China depended in large measure on the extent to which they were compatible with this tradition. Accordingly, the armament industry was easily accepted, yet mining and railway construction, which undermined the geomantic practices, encountered difficulties. Christianity, which challenged the

141 Hao Yen-p'ing, 'Yu shou-chiu tao ko-hsin' (From conservatism to reform), *Ta-lu tsa-chih*, 20.7 (April 1960) 26-7.

authority of Confucianism, was most vehemently opposed. In addition to the conservatives, many literati-officials who championed Western learning were at the same time anti-Christian. They included, among others, Wei Yuan, Hsu Chi-yü, Ting Jih-ch'ang, Hsueh Fu-ch'eng and Shen Pao-chen. This culturalism, namely the literati-officials' strong emotional and intellectual commitment to Confucianism, was markedly different from earlier anti-foreignism, which had stemmed partly from the physical differences between Chinese and Westerners. It is thus difficult to draw a clear-cut line between the conservatives and the Westernizers. Modernization in some senses meant Westernization. Many literati-officials accepted the *yang-wu* movement because it was modern, in the hope that it could save China from destruction. But then some rejected it because it was Western, in the fear that it would replace Confucianism. Faced with the problem of how to save China and at the same time remain Chinese, they held an ambivalent attitude.

This ambivalence was further demonstrated by the way in which some reform-minded gentry members defined China's cultural relations with the West. For them, China must learn from the West, yet Western learning was not important in a fundamental way. Trying to make sense of Western learning, they first used the dichotomy of *tao* (principle) versus *ch'i* (instruments) in the seventies and eighties. Wang T'ao and Cheng Kuan-ying, for example, classified Western technology in the category of *ch'i*, reserving the more valuable category of *tao* for Chinese learning. After the seventies a more dynamic dichotomy was employed. This was the noted *t'i* (substance) and *yung* (application) concept, namely 'Chinese learning for the essential principles, Western learning for the practical applications'. Admittedly, Chang Chih-tung and his fellow supporters of this concept theoretically misapplied the Neo-Confucian dualism, for *t'i* and *yung*, as correlative aspects of a given entity, are inseparable. Yet this approach had psychological significance, for it facilitated China's modernization without losing her cultural identity. Its dubious validity notwithstanding, it symbolized China's ambivalence towards the West.

A similar approach was to find the sanction for modernization within Chinese tradition, following the time-honoured practice of *t'o-ku kai-chih* or finding in antiquity the sanction for reform. The reform-minded argued that their self-strengthening programmes were in line with China's ancient tradition which emphasized change, technology and the use of talented aliens. They further alleged that Western sciences and institutions had originated in ancient China. Thus the more China changed, the closer she might come to her tradition – a view that retains its vitality even today.

CHAPTER 4

THE MILITARY CHALLENGE:
THE NORTH-WEST AND THE COAST

CH'ING ARMIES OF THE POST-TAIPING ERA

By the end of the Nien War in 1868, a new kind of military force had emerged as the Ch'ing dynasty's chief bulwark of security. Often referred to by historians as regional armies, these forces were generally described at the time as *yung-ying* (lit. 'brave battalions'). In the late 1860s, such forces throughout all the empire totalled more than 300,000 men. They included the remnants of the old Hunan Army (Hsiang-chün) founded by Tseng Kuo-fan, the resuscitated Hunan Army (usually called Ch'u-chün) under Tso Tsung-t'ang, and the Anhwei Army (Huai-chün) coordinated by Li Hung-chang. There were also smaller forces of a similar nature in Honan (Yü-chün), Shantung (Tung-chün), Yunnan (Tien-chün) and Szechwan (Ch'uan-chün).[1] These forces were distinguished generally by their greater use of Western weapons and they were more costly to maintain. More fundamentally they capitalized for military purposes on the particularistic loyalties of the traditional society. Both the strength and the weakness of the *yung-ying* were to be found in the close personal bonds that were formed between higher and lower officers and between officers and men. In this respect they differed from the traditional Ch'ing imperial armies – both the banner forces and the Green Standard Army.

The original Ch'ing banners had been composed of companies of 300 men supported by imperial stipends and grants of land. But to prevent Manchu princes and imperial officials from developing personal military power, the Ch'ing emperors had arranged in the early eighteenth century

[1] On the banner and Green Standard forces, see Wei Yuan, *Sheng-wu chi* (Chronicle of the sacred dynasty's military campaigns) and Lo Erh-kang, *Lü-ying ping-chih* (A treatise on the Green Standard Army). The *yung-ying* figure is from a memorial dated Jan. 1866 in Tseng Kuo-fan, *Tseng Wen-cheng kung ch'üan-chi* (Complete collection of Tseng Kuo-fan's papers; hereafter TWCKCC), *Tsou-kao* (Memorials), 23.35. On the Shantung Army see *Shan-tung chün-hsing chi-lüeh* (Brief record of military campaigns in Shantung), 4a.8, and Ting Pao-chen, *Ting Wen-ch'eng kung i-chi* (Collected papers of the late Ting Pao-chen), 1.4, 37b; 4.9, 16. On the Honan Army, see Yin Keng-yun *et al. Yü-chün chi lüeh* (A concise history of the Honan Army), 1.3.11; 5.10.10b–11; 12.22.5–6. The Yunnan Army originated with Ts'en Yü-ying's campaigns against Muslim revolts in that province; see Wang Shu-huai, *Hsien-T'ung Yun-nan hui-min shih-pien* (Muslim revolts in Yunnan during the Hsien-feng and T'ung-chih reigns), 224–8.

that the higher commanders of banner forces above the company level were to be rotated from garrison to garrison every three to five years.[2] The Green Standard forces, totalling some 600,000 men in the mid-nineteenth century, were positioned in tiny contingents as a constabulary or in the larger 'direct commands' (*piao*) of the top provincial civil and military officials. But these commands were only relatively large. For example, in the strategic Shensi–Kansu military area the 40,000 men were divided into thirteen *piao*, while in Chihli outside Peking 12,000 men were distributed among seven *piao*.[3] Although the Green Standard troops were hereditary soldiers, even their middle-ranking officers would stay with a given unit of troops usually between three and five years and never in their native province, in accordance with the law of avoidance. This inhibited the growth of long-term relationships between officers and men and especially between commanders and low-ranking officers in the local contingents. A task force pulled together from several Green Standard commands for a specific occasion seldom performed well: 'the men were not accustomed to their officers, while the officers were at loggerheads with each other'.[4]

The merit of the *yung-ying* had lain in the close personal ties between officers and men. Army commanders (*t'ung-ling*) personally chose the commanders of the various battalions under them. Each battalion commander (*ying-kuan*) responsible for some 550 men would personally choose his company officers (*shao-kuan*) who would in turn choose their platoon officers (*shih-chang*). The 10 or so common soldiers who formed a platoon were usually chosen by the platoon officer himself. Tseng Kuo-fan in 1868 extolled this system of personal relationships throughout the organization: 'Although rations came from public funds, the *yung-ying* troops were nevertheless grateful to the officers of the battalion for selecting them to be put on the rolls, as if they had received personal favours from the officers. Since in ordinary times there existed [between the officers and the troops] relations of kindness as well as mutual confidence, in battle it could be expected that they would see each other through hardship and adversity.'[5] As long as the throne's authority over civil and military appointments was not diminished – including the control of high provincial positions and the granting of the coveted Green Standard titles and posts to the *yung-ying*

[2] Cp. Robert H. G. Lee, *The Manchurian frontier in Ch'ing history*, 24–31. Richard J. Smith, 'Chinese military institutions in the mid-nineteenth century, 1850–1860', *Journal of Asian History*, 8.2 (1974) 136–41. Chang Po-feng, comp. *Ch'ing-tai ko-ti chiang-chün tu-t'ung ta-ch'en teng nien-piao, 1796–1911* (Chronological tables of Manchu generals-in-chief, lieutenants-general, imperial agents, etc., in various areas under the Ch'ing, 1796–1911).
[3] Lo Erh-kang, *Lü-ying ping-chih*, 92–100, 126–36, 162–4, 206–7.
[4] *Ibid.* 179–81, 213–20, 237–44. Chiang Chung-yuan, *Chiang Chung-lieh kung i-chi* (The papers of the late Chiang Chung-yuan), 1.2, 4.
[5] *TWCKCC, Tsou-kao*, 28.18b–19.

commanders and officers – the Ch'ing court could make these new armies serve its purposes within China (see volume 10, chapter 9). But in an age of continuous progress in weapons, tactics and auxiliary services, could armed forces that drew their principal strength from particularistic loyalties cope with China's new external challenge?

During the 1860s Peking approved (and even initiated) a number of training programmes – usually with the support of European powers, who hoped to see the Ch'ing dynasty become strong enough to defend the treaty ports and trade routes. But only minimal benefits resulted.

The dynasty did not intend to abandon the banner and Green Standard forces. Worthless and costly though they were, their maintenance seemed more important than the improvement of the *yung-ying*. For example, one notable effort was directed towards the banner armies at Peking itself. The Western-armed Peking Field Force (Shen-chi ying), founded in 1862 by Wen-hsiang and others, was drilled by some 500 bannermen who had been trained in the use of modern small arms by British officers at Tientsin, as arranged by the commissioner of trade, Ch'ung-hou (see volume 10, chapter 9). At first only some 3,000 strong, the Peking Field Force grew considerably in 1865, after Prince Ch'un, the Empress Dowager Tz'u-hsi's brother-in-law, was appointed the prince-minister in charge. At the throne's order, a total of 30,000 men from various banner units at Peking were detached for training with the new force. The power of reviewing the merits of troops and officers had meanwhile been transferred from their original commanders to Prince Ch'un.[6]

But the Peking Field Force did not grow further. Nor did Prince Ch'un make full use of the opportunity for Western training. In 1865–6, he agreed to send two contingents of 500 men each from the banner infantry to be drilled in the use of Western weapons at Tientsin, but he resisted the suggestion by Ch'ung-hou, Prince Kung's protégé, that mounted bannermen should also receive Western training. Fearful that these individuals might 'neglect the skills they practised in the past', he merely allowed a few of them to undergo a brief period of instruction at Tientsin. In 1869–70, the British training programme, now manned by only three foreign instructors (headed by Major Brown, who had served under Gordon in the Ever Victorious Army) was terminated. The Peking Field Force with its 30,000 men guarded the Ch'ing capital,[7] but in 1870, when

---

[6] Hsi Yü-fu *et al.* comp. *Huang-ch'ao cheng-tien lei-tsuan* (Classified compendium on the governmental documents of the Ch'ing dynasty), 331.8–9.

[7] Chung-kuo k'o-hsueh yuan *et al.* comps. *Yang-wu yun-tung* (The Western affairs movement; hereafter *YWYT*), 3.475–79, 484–91, 497–8. The total strength of the Peking Field Force's core contingents seems to have been kept at 6,000 men. As late as 1881–2, Japanese intelli-

war with France seemed imminent in the wake of the Tientsin Massacre, some 25,000 men of Li Hung-chang's *yung-ying* force had to be summoned to bolster Chihli's defences. Li's forces were authorized to be stationed at points half-way between Taku and Peking, up to such towns as Yang-ts'un and Ho-hsi-wu.[8] Peking's safety now depended on the loyalty of the Han Chinese.

Elsewhere in the empire, banner garrisons that had declined continued to be replenished and financed. But plainly there was no revival of Manchu power. In Canton, Ch'ing officials, conforming with Peking directives, accepted separate British and French offers to drill the Ch'ing troops in the use of modern arms. Beginning in 1863, with equipment purchased by provincial authorities, 360 bannermen were trained by the British and 300 by the French. Coordinated by a Manchu officer, 531 local Green Standard troops also underwent drill by the British. The training programmes at Canton were terminated, however, only three years later, when the disillusioned foreign consuls wanted the European instructors withdrawn.[9]

Meanwhile, Manchu officials were hard put to it to restore the banner garrisons at their statutory locations. In 1867, in Ili and four other centres in Sinkiang, only 150 banner soldiers had survived the Muslim revolts; they had to be transferred to Inner Mongolia for resettlement. In the twelve garrisoned cities of China proper, the bannermen and their families, living in their segregated quarters, were as demoralized as those that remained in Manchuria – indigent, addicted to opium, and regularly shortchanged by their superiors in their imperial stipends.[10]

Since banner strength could not easily be revived, the Ch'ing court sought to strengthen the Green Standard Army, over which the boards of War and Revenue still retained control. Ch'ung-hou's British training programme at Tientsin actually drilled more Green Standard troops than bannermen, and out of the former had arisen the Tientsin 'foreign arms and cannon corps' of 500 men, which proved valuable during the Nien War. Meanwhile, Liu Ch'ang-yu, the former Hunan Army commander who became governor-general of Chihli in 1863, had proposed giving new training to some 150,000 Chihli Green Standard troops without over-

gence found that the force's own command (*pen-pu*) consisted of only 3,500 infantry, 2,000 cavalry and 500 gunnery troops. See Fukushima Yasumasa, comp. *Rimpō heibi ryaku* (Military preparedness in neighbouring countries) 1.21b–22.

[8] Wang Erh-min, *Huai-chün chih* (History of the Anhwei Army), 354–5. Li Hung-chang, *Li Wen-chung kung ch'üan-chi* (Complete papers of Li Hung-chang; hereafter *LWCK*), *Tsou-kao* (Memorials), 17.10b.

[9] *YWYT*, 3.459–70, 481. In the mid-1860s, the Ch'ing government employed foreign instructors to train banner and Green Standard forces in two other cities: Foochow (from mid-1865 to 1866); and Wuchang (from early 1866 to mid-1868); see *ibid.* 471–2, 482, 492–4.

[10] *Huang-ch'ao cheng-tien lei-tsuan*, 333.11. Lee, *Manchurian frontier*, 123–5.

hauling the traditional command structure. Troops from the tiny *hsun* out-posts were organized into 'battalions' of 500 men each for the purpose of periodic drill in all of the seven centres in the province, but the troops were allowed to return to their posts during the long intervals in between drills.[11]

In 1866, Prince Kung secured imperial approval to give governor-general Liu more financial support. Troops from the large *piao* commands were to be detached to serve in six centres under Liu's coordination. The reorganized force was now designated *lien-chün*, or the 'retrained [Green Standard] forces'. The Board of Revenue at first allocated 100,000 taels from the Tientsin maritime customs for the new training programme's munitions needs. But in January 1867, Lo Tun-yen, president of the board, who belonged to the court faction opposing Prince Kung, memorial-ized to attack the plan – criticism which Tz'u-hsi must have welcomed, for an edict drastically pared down the new programme's revenue.[12] It was not until after the traumatic experience of the Nien cavalry invasion of Chihli in 1868 and the subsequent appointment of Tseng Kuo-fan as Chihli governor-general that further plans were made for the *lien-chün*. Arriving at Peking at a time when the Sino-British treaty revision aroused a heated foreign policy debate at court, Tseng found, as he reported to Li Hung-chang, that 'Prince Kung emphasized peace, while Prince Ch'un empha-sized war and defence; the general opinion sided with Prince Ch'un'. Both Manchu factions so trusted Tseng that he was given a free hand to make adjustments in the Green Standard system. Tz'u-hsi herself discussed this with Tseng.[13]

Tseng adapted his *yung-ying* formula to the Green Standard Army, although he was inhibited (perhaps by his own conservatism as well as by his political position) from bringing up more basic issues of reform. He recommended in 1869–70 that the newly created battalions should remain intact, their troops and officers to be chosen from the larger Green Standard commands of the provinces. Moreover, the quality and per-formance of the troops and lower-level officers so detached should be reviewed by new battalion officers, each in charge of approximately 550 men as in the *yung-ying* system. In the greatest departure from tradition,

---

[11] Wang Erh-min, 'Lien-chün ti ch'i-yuan chi ch'i i-i' (The origins and significance of the retrained Green Standard contingents), *Ta-lu tsa-chih*, 34.7 (April 1967) 216, summarizing Liu Ch'ang-yu's memorial.

[12] *Ch'ing-tai ch'ou-pan i-wu shih-mo* (Complete record of the management of barbarian affairs), T'ung-chih (hereafter *IWSM-TC*), 43.10. Liu Ch'ang-yu, *Liu Wu-sheng kung i-shu* (Papers of the late Liu Ch'ang-yu), 12.3, 21b, 31–7. *Ta-Ch'ing li-ch'ao shih-lu* (Veritable records of successive reigns of the Ch'ing dynasty), T'ung-chih (hereafter *CSL-TC*) 193.18b–19.

[13] *TWCKCC*, *Shu-cha* (Letters), 27.2. Tseng Kuo-fan, *Tseng Wen-cheng kung shou-hsieh jih-chi* (Tseng Kuo-fan's holograph diary), 2.2856, entry of 27 Feb. 1869.

Tseng wanted the battalion officers to have authority to replace troops found to be undesirable, with new recruits from among the natives of Chihli, including those who had never been in the register of hereditary Green Standard families.[14] The battalion officer himself was to be chosen by a high Green Standard officer – the general-in-chief or brigade general. Under the law of avoidance, the generals and in fact all Green Standard officers down to the second captains had to be natives of other provinces. While the retrained Green Standard troops and officers could not enjoy the native-place ties that characterized most *yung-ying* units, Tseng hoped that the middle-grade officers of the *lien-chün* could at least serve longer terms and could establish rapport with the brigade generals or generals-in-chief who were given the additional title of *t'ung-ling*, commanders of the *lien-chün*. The regulations drafted by Tseng and approved by the throne in April 1870 provided for a pay scale for the *lien-chün* officers and men, which was higher than that of their counterparts in the usual Green Standard units. But Tseng refrained from recommending the overhaul of the entire Green Standard system so as to reduce the number of worthless troops. He hoped that revenue for the *lien-chün* could come from new sources.[15]

Actually, the throne, during the preceding four years, had approved the proposals of other provincial officials that Green Standard troops in certain provincial commands be reduced so that the funds saved could be applied to the pay and weapons of the remaining Green Standard troops. Tso Tsung-t'ang, governor-general of Fukien and Chekiang until 1867, had begun reorganizing the Fukien Green Standard forces on this basis, and Ting Jih-ch'ang, governor of Kiangsu, with imperial sanction had reduced in 1869 the number of his 'governor's direct command' (*fu-piao*) from 1,600 to 1,000.[16] (See volume 10, page 503.) Ting was seriously interested in transforming the 1,000 men under his personal command into a nucleus for the general reform of the Green Standard Army in Kiangsu – a plan left unrealized when Ting himself had to leave in 1870 to mourn the death of his mother.

Having found in Tseng Kuo-fan's proposals the hope that the Green Standard system could as a whole be saved and improved, the throne in 1871 ordered each province to reduce its existing *yung-ying* forces to less than 8,000 men, except in such strategic provinces as Kiangsu and Chihli.[17]

[14] *TWCKCC, Tsou-kao*, 28.19b, 36.   [15] *Ibid.* 28.20b; 29.13, 16, 18b–19.

[16] Tso Tsung-t'ang, *Tso Wen-hsiang kung ch'üan-chi* (Complete collection of Tso Tsung-t'ang's papers; hereafter *TWHK*), 14.17; 19.16–21. Lü Shih-ch'iang, *Ting Jih-ch'ang yü tzu-ch'iang yun-tung* (Ting Jih-ch'ang and the self-strengthening movement), 186–7. *Huang-ch'ao cheng-tien lei-tsuan*, 325.4b, 8–10.

[17] Liu Chin-tsao, ed. *Ch'ing-ch'ao hsu wen-hsien t'ung-k'ao* (Encyclopaedia of the historical records of the Ch'ing dynasty, continued), 202.9, 505. Kwang-Ching Liu, 'The limits of regional power in the late Ch'ing period: a reappraisal', *Ch'ing-hua hsueh-pao*, NS, 10.2 (July 1974) 217.

While this guideline concerning the *yung-ying* was only loosely followed, the loyal provincial administrators now found convenient formulas to accommodate the vested interests of the Green Standard Army in each province. Some provinces (Kiangsu, Chekiang, Fukien and Kwangtung) followed the precedents set by Tso Tsung-t'ang and Ting Jih-ch'ang, and reduced the troops of certain commands which, at least in theory, raised the pay of the remaining Green Standard troops. Other provinces (Shantung, Honan, Shansi and Hunan) adopted *in toto* Tseng's regulations for Chihli and organized *lien-chün* battalions out of the Green Standard personnel – a method for which the Board of War indicated its preference in 1873.[18] The court did not object to the infiltration of the Green Standard system by *yung-ying* officers. As part of the dynasty's system of conferring recognition, many *yung-ying* officers since the 1850s had been given the brevet status of Green Standard officer. More of them were now allowed to fill actual Green Standard vacancies from second captain up to provincial general-in-chief, posts still controlled by the Board of War and, in the case of high commanders, by the throne itself.

While Tseng's *lien-chün* formula infused some new elements into the Green Standard Army at all levels, large amounts of deadwood undoubtedly remained. In the late seventies and eighties the number of Green Standard troops was still around 400,000, costing annually more than 6 million taels to maintain.[19] From the dynasty's standpoint, this large expenditure was not a total waste, for the retrained Green Standard forces, equipped with comparatively modern arms and deployed in revolt-prone areas of the provinces, maintained general internal tranquillity in the remaining years of the century.[20] But for large-scale campaigns such as the Muslim wars in Shensi, Kansu and Sinkiang, to say nothing of conflicts with European powers or Japan, the *yung-ying* continued to be the only instrument that could possibly be effective.

Yet the organizational principle of the *yung-ying* remained incompatible with modern military practice. For all the interpersonal rapport between its troops and officers, the *yung-ying* hierarchy gave the middle- and upper-level officers a status which could place them above direct participation in combat. It was extremely difficult to get the battalion or even company officers to participate in rigorous training, especially in Western-style drill. Ever since 1862–3, Li Hung-chang had hoped that his officers 'would learn

[18] *Huang-ch'ao cheng-tien lei-tsuan,* 326.6b–8.
[19] Memorial dated Jan. 1884 of Prince Kung and other Tsungli Yamen ministers, *YWYT,* 526. See also Chang P'ei-lun, *Chien-yü chi* (Memorials of Chang P'ei-lun), 6.10.
[20] See Lo Erh-kang, *Lü-ying ping-chih,* 72–3 (nn. 70–3). The uses of *lien-chün* in suppressing local revolts are now more fully documented in *Kung-chung-tang Kuang-hsu ch'ao tsou-che* (Secret palace memorials of the Kuang-hsu period, 1875–1908), e.g., 2.302, 664, 667; 3.172, 318, 323, 399, 445, 518, 753.

one or two secret methods from the Westerners',[21] but apart from conferring officer status on a few men originally trained by foreign drillmasters in the Ever-Victorious Army (for example, Lo Jung-kuang and
Yuan Chiu-kao), Li's method was merely for Western instructors to drill
the troops in his 'foreign arms corps'. The few Westerners who remained
with the Anhwei Army after 1864, including the Frenchman who became
a Ch'ing subject, J. Pennell, were unable to provide widespread and systematic instruction to either officers or men. Apparently the Chinese had
reservations about the applicability and overall utility of Western tactics.
Charles G. Gordon noted in 1864 that Ch'ing officers admired the foreign-
style infantry square, 'but thought it unlikely their men would stand'. The
Chinese 'allow of our superiority in Artillery, but think they are far in
advance in infantry'. Moreover, while *yung-ying* officers acknowledged the
value of Western artillery, they were disinclined to learn artillery drill.
Gordon noted that they were reluctant even to learn to 'shout their words
of command'.[22]

Could the Chinese accept Western help and yet remain self-reliant? On the
other hand, could the *yung-ying* forces do without foreign training and yet
acquire the essential discipline and skills demanded by modern warfare?
This dilemma is revealed in the history of the training programme at Feng-
huang-shan (twenty-five miles from Shanghai), initiated by Gordon himself in May 1864 immediately after the disbandment of the Ever-Victorious
Army.[23] Enthusiastically endorsed by the British minister and his consul in
Shanghai, the Feng-huang-shan training programme received 'verbal
assurances' of support from the Tsungli Yamen and was welcomed by Li
Hung-chang initially because of the faith he reposed in Gordon. To
Gordon, Li entrusted in June 1864 1,300 of the Anhwei Army troops
under two or three of his best officers.

The British interest in this programme was many-faceted. Gordon, who
did not regard centralized leadership of the decayed Manchu government
as feasible, thought that the British should help to develop a Chinese army
'through the Futais [governors], not through the Peking govt. who are a
very helpless lot'.[24] Minister Bruce, while not entirely in agreement with
Gordon on Ch'ing politics, none the less believed in rendering military
assistance to the Chinese. But it was the attitude of Harry Parkes, the

[21] Ssu-yü Teng and John K. Fairbank, *China's response to the West*, 69.
[22] Gordon Papers (British Museum), Add. MSS. 52,389, 26 Aug. 1864; 52,393, 'Confidential
memo on the imperialist sphere' (1864).
[23] For details see Richard J. Smith, 'Foreign training and China's self-strengthening: the case of
Feng-huang-shan, 1864–1873', *MAS*, 10.2 (1976) 195–223.
[24] Gordon Papers, Add. MSS. 52,389, 19 June 1864.

British consul at Shanghai, that put Li Hung-chang on his guard. Parkes wanted primarily to train Chinese troops who could defend Shanghai against possible further unrest in that area. He was also jealous of the French, who still maintained a small camp for training Chinese troops near Shanghai (troops who were not returned to the Chinese authorities until mid-1865). Li imputed to Parkes the intent of 'taking over our military authority and squandering our financial resources'.[25]

In late 1864, however, Gordon abandoned the training programme to return to England. Li had to accept Parkes' nominee as Feng-huang-shan's new drillmaster – Lieutenant Jebb of the British Army. In an agreement dated November 1864, Parkes accepted Li's *quid pro quo* that a commander of the Anhwei Army, P'an Ting-hsin, should have complete control over promotion and demotion of Chinese officers and troops, as well as their pay and equipment. The programme was to be financed from the maritime customs revenue. Jebb's duties were confined to drill and instruction, including the supervision of fifteen foreign staff members, also paid by the Chinese. Jebb proved, however, to be a bad choice, frequently absent from the camp and, when on duty, rigidly insistent on adherence to 'the Queen's Regulations and the Drill Book'.[26] When, in June 1865, Li was ordered by the throne to send troops and artillery to Chihli to guard its border against the Niens, he had no hesitation in pulling an entire battalion out from Feng-huang-shan, together with a 300-man artillery corps under training there, to be dispatched to the north under P'an Ting-hsin. Consul Parkes protested vehemently. Although Li agreed to replace the 850 men taken from Feng-huang-shan with other Anhwei Army troops, he no longer had, by this time, any faith in the Feng-huang-shan programme and repeatedly rejected requests for its expansion.

The camp's subsequent history was marked by Sino-Western friction as well as the exposure of the weaknesses of both the foreign instructors and the Anhwei Army itself. In July 1865 Lieutenant Jebb was transferred back to England, and Ting Jih-ch'ang, the Shanghai *taotai*, quickly manoeuvred to get W. Winstanley, a former subordinate of Gordon's, to replace him. The British consul's insistence on appointing a regular British officer was overruled by the legation in Peking. Winstanley was apparently reasonable and conscientious but he lacked sufficient authority, and his mediocre foreign instructors did little to inspire confidence among the troops. The *yung-ying* officers, for their part, behaved scandalously. Although the com-

[25] *IWSM-TC*, 25.27. Li none the less believed, in July 1864, that with Gordon in charge of the training programme, 'there will be no great trouble in the future'; *LWCK*, *P'eng-liao han-kao* (Letters), 5.21.

[26] Ting Jih-ch'ang, 'Ting Chung-ch'eng cheng-shu' (Political papers of Governor Ting), 7.10b–11. Alfred E. Hake, *Events in the Taiping Rebellion*, 526–7.

pany officers always appeared in parades and displays, they seldom participated in the actual training. Moreover, they and their superiors profited by withholding fifty Mexican dollars per company from the stipends of the men and lower officers on each pay day. Winstanley praised the adeptness of the troops in infantry, howitzer and rocket drills. But as in the banner and the Green Standard establishments, many *yung-ying* troops and officers at Feng-huang-shan were habitual opium-smokers. The troops were also unruly trouble-makers.[27] On occasion they showed resentment against foreigners: training had to be suspended in the aftermath of the Tientsin Massacre (June 1870). But after the routine was resumed, the wrath of the men turned against their corrupt *yung-ying* superiors, indicating the limitations of the system's rapport between troops and officers. Mutiny broke out twice in 1872, provoked by the officers' abuses of power including unjust punishment ordered by a battalion commander.[28] In May 1873, after having spent nearly 1.5 million taels over a nine-year period, the programme was abruptly terminated despite vigorous protest from the British consul. Once envisaged by a British officer as the 'Aldershot of China', Feng-huang-shan was never actually designed to train officers, but it did teach a considerable number of Anhwei Army troops to use modern weapons.

By the early 1870s, the Ch'ing forces undoubtedly had acquired the capacity to suppress rebellion in most areas of China proper. But it remained questionable as to whether they could stand up to foreign invaders on the coast or even deal with rebels in the difficult terrain of the North-West or Central Asia.

THE MUSLIM REVOLTS AND THEIR INTERNATIONAL IMPLICATIONS

The great Muslim revolts in the Ch'ing empire during the third quarter of the nineteenth century are particularly difficult to study because of the paucity of firm documentation on the Muslim side. The several Islamic revolts varied in the intensity of their ethno-religious consciousness, as well as in their circumstances and geographic location. In China proper, the rebellions in Yunnan (1856–73, also known as the Panthay Rebellion) and in Shensi and Kansu (1862–73, also known as the Tungan Rebellion) shared a background of community feuds. These resulted from the Muslim minority leading a distinctive life in their separate villages or urban

---

[27] Ting Jih-ch'ang, *Fu-Wu kung-tu* (Official papers of the governor of Kiangsu), 50.8. FO 228: 453 and 492, Winstanley's reports, 20 Nov. 1868 and 13 Jan. 1870.
[28] FO 228: 524, Winstanley's memo, 6 Jan. 1873.

quarters, where they maintained their religious practices and special customs. The Muslim revolt in Sinkiang, however, was characterized principally by a foreign invasion – the return from Kokand of a Makhdūm-zāda khoja, a descendant of the pre-Ch'ing Islamic rulers of Altishahr, where the tombs of his forebears near Kashgar were still the centres of faith. The turmoil in Sinkiang also led to the Russian occupation of the Ili area and to a lively Anglo-Russian rivalry, at least for a few years, over Ch'ing Turkestan.

Although the Muslims in China proper never had a clear, culturally sanctioned basis for their allegiance to the imperial authority at Peking, they had been in China for many centuries. Their literature, while retaining special reverence for their supreme deity, nonetheless subscribed to the Confucian *san-kang*, the human obligations to monarch, parent and husband.[29] Traditionally, the Muslims had been treated comparatively well by the Ch'ing emperors; Muslims took the state examinations and many of them served in the civil and military bureaucracy, although seldom in high positions. Beginning in 1762, however, severe discriminatory laws against them were decreed by the throne. Theft and robbery committed by Muslims in Shensi and Kansu were, for example, punishable by exile to Yunnan and Kweichow, and sometimes by the lifelong wearing of the cangue – much heavier penalties than that of light flogging dealt out to other Chinese in comparable cases.[30] These anti-Muslim laws preceded by some two decades the first outbreak of serious Muslim revolts under the Ch'ing; and these revolts, in turn, exacerbated the suspicion of the Ch'ing officials regarding the mosque-centred communities. As life became more difficult in the early nineteenth century, the Han Chinese increasingly looked upon the Muslims as competitors in landowning and in trade. When disputes between Han and Muslim were brought to court, adjudication was seldom fair towards the latter. The Han Chinese officials were themselves prejudiced, while the Manchu officials generally took the side of the Han Chinese.

Yunnan

The Muslim Rebellion in Yunnan that broke out in 1856 was an expansion of bloody community feuds that had flared up in the 1840s. The rebellion there must, however, be viewed not simply as a Muslim revolt, but as a general breakdown of order in this most south-western province of China. It began with prolonged fighting between Han and Muslim Chinese over

29 See *inter alia* Chin T'ien-chu, *Ch'ing-chen shih-i* (Resolving suspicions regarding Islam), 1b, 4–5, 17b, 19–21, 25–8.
30 Wang Shu-huai, *Hsien-T'ung*, 45–52.

the control of a silver mine in central Yunnan. Armed feuds between the majority communities and the Muslim minorities began to spread. In 1856, with the encouragement of a paranoid Manchu judicial commissioner, at least two or three thousand Muslims were massacred in Kunming, the provincial capital. In many counties of Yunnan, the Han gentry now organized military corps (*t'uan-lien*) to 'exterminate' Muslims, while the Muslims also organized themselves and began to occupy cities and take the lives of officials. In the general upheaval, Tu Wen-hsiu (1828–73), a Muslim of Han background who had had literary training, established in 1856 in Ta-li, western Yunnan, the kingdom of P'ing-nan ('pacification of the south') with a military and civil bureaucracy composed of both Han and Muslim Chinese and with himself as commander-in-chief (*ta yuan-shuai*) as well as sultan. A rival Muslim faction, commanded by Ma Ju-lung (1832–91), whose forebears had been officers of the Green Standard Army and who was himself a military *sheng-yuan*, occupied much of southern and central Yunnan but surrendered to the Ch'ing in 1862 and helped the latter to fight Tu Wen-hsiu.[31]

Ma Ju-lung's capitulation had the blessing of Ma Te-hsin (1794–1874), a respected religious leader, who had visited Mecca and Constantinople and who in his lifetime wrote more than thirty works in Chinese on Islam. In doctrine, Ma Te-hsin identified himself with the *Fuṣūṣ al-ḥikam* of Abn al-'Arabt, a thirteenth-century classic of Sufism, which summarizes the teachings of the prophets culminating in Muḥammad, and emphasizes the mystic approach to the Oneness of Being. Yet Ma also argued that the Islamic reverence for the lord (*chu-tsai*) was entirely compatible with the Neo-Confucian concepts of *li* and *ch'i*.[32] Ma Te-hsin served briefly as acting governor-general at Kunming in 1863 and helped to reconcile many Muslims to Ch'ing rule; nevertheless, he himself was to be assassinated at the instigation of Ch'ing officials at the end of the Yunnan Rebellion.

Tu Wen-hsiu's 'Panthay Kingdom' aroused some interest on the part of the French and British, who had by the mid-1860s established themselves in Cochin-China and in Lower Burma respectively. In 1867, when a French mission headed by a naval officer, Duart de Lagrée, visited the turncoat Ma Ju-lung (who was serving as the brigade general in Kunming), he found that a French priest was already helping the Ch'ing to manufacture ammunition for the modern arms Ma had at his disposal. De Lagrée's deputy, Francis Garnier, arrived at the rebel capital of Ta-li in February 1868, but was rudely refused an audience with Tu, the sultan. At that very

---

[31] *Ibid*. 136–84. Wellington K. K. Chan, 'Ma Ju-lung: from rebel to turncoat in the Yunnan rebellion', *Papers on China*, 20 (1966) 86–118.

[32] Ma Te-hsin, *Ta-hua tsung-kuei* (Destiny of the universe), foreword, author's preface, 1.15–24, 36–40; 2.1–2. Wang Shu-huai, *Hsien-T'ung*, 109–27.

moment, a delegation from British India, under Captain Edward B. Sladen, was at Bhamo, on the upper Irrawaddy, preparing for the overland journey to western Yunnan. A high Panthay official received Sladen very politely at a border town and talked about commerce with Burma. Yet Sladen's request for a visit to Ta-li was rejected.[33]

The extant documentation on Tu's administration shows that he was lording it over a Chinese-style bureaucracy, having declared that the three religions of Yunnan – Islam, Confucianism and the primitive cults of the Yunnanese tribes – were all to be honoured. Tu's forces dominated, at one time, nearly half of Yunnan's territory. He appointed Han Chinese to most civil offices and to at least one-third of the military positions. By 1871, however, his forces were pressed by the armies of the able new Chinese governor, Ts'en Yü-ying, who had modern weapons and even French drillmasters. In that year, Tu authorized a bizarre tribute mission to England. In April 1872, his envoy Liu Tao-heng offered to the Queen, in the name of the Panthay sultan, four large boxes containing pieces of Yunnan marble, symbolizing the land Tu ruled and his submission to Britain as a vassal. By then, Tu's cause was all but lost, and the Duke of Argyll, the secretary of state for India, could only suggest that the gift be deposited in a London museum, with a statement that it had no political significance.[34]

Shensi and Kansu

In any overview of the Muslim revolts in the Ch'ing empire of this period, the rebellions in Shensi and Kansu must be regarded as of crucial importance. For this mountainous loessland with its river valleys and caravan routes commanded Peking's principal gateway to Sinkiang, the frontier area which the Ch'ing emperors had worked so hard to win. Through the windblown Kansu corridor, moreover, the Chinese Muslims enjoyed comparatively easy contact with the vast Islamic world beyond, and could especially have some influence on the events in Sinkiang. An excess of population over resources, high taxes and the transfer of many of the select Green Standard forces to meet urgent needs in eastern China, had all weakened the two provinces of Shensi and Kansu in the 1860s as bastions of defence in China's north-west. Moreover, since the late eighteenth century Kansu had been the centre of a vigorous, activist Chinese school of

[33] Huang Chia-mu, *Tien-hsi hui-min cheng-ch'üan ti lien-Ying wai-chiao* (The diplomacy of the Muslim regime in Yunnan towards a British alliance), 25–37, 88–113.

[34] Pai Shou-i, ed. *Hui-min ch'i-i* (The Muslim uprisings; hereafter *HMCI*), 1.8; 2.106, 111–31. Wang Shu-huai, *Hsien-T'ung*, 118, n. 22. Huang Chia-mu, *Tien-hsi*, 164–89, citing India Office archives. Cf. T'ien Ju-k'ang, 'Yu-kuan Tu Wen-hsiu tui-wai kuan-hsi ti chi-ko wen-t'i' (A few problems regarding Tu Wen-hsiu's foreign relations), *Li-shih yen-chiu*, 1963. 4, pp. 141–50.

Sufism. This last factor, together with the sturdiness that resulted from horseback riding and the practice of related martial skills, made the Tungans (the Chinese Muslims of Shensi and Kansu, including those who migrated to Sinkiang) among the most stubborn rebels the Ch'ing ever encountered.

Like the Yunnan Muslims, the Tungans were Chinese-speaking. Their original Central Asian blood had been diluted by the custom of allowing their men to marry non-Muslim women and the practice of expanding the Islamic community by adopting Han Chinese children. More so than in Yunnan, however, contacts with Central Asia constantly reinforced their religious faith, which was guarded by the akhunds in each of the autonomous mosque-centred communities. Sufi tarikats such as the Naqshbandiyya and Qādiriyya were introduced into North-West China from Central Asia. Claiming their special links to God, the shaykhs of these tarikats sometimes performed 'wonders' (*kirāmāt*) like curing illnesses, restoring fertility to people, and foretelling events. Once accepted by the people as a saint (*walī*), the religious leader's authority became indisputable. Following his death, the tomb of such a saint would become a holy place. In the 1870s, the British traveller, H. W. Bellew, visited the tomb near Kashgar of the saintly founder of the Āfāqiyya, a branch of the Naqshbandiyya. After the Āfāqī khojas were driven out of Sinkiang by the Ch'ing forces in the mid-eighteenth century, the tomb of the Āfāqī founder continued to attract numerous pilgrims.[35] From their haven in Kokand, the Āfāqī khojas for three generations fomented unrest and waged holy wars to recover Altishahr (see volume 10, chapters 2 and 8). One of them was to do so again in the 1860s.

Meanwhile a Sufi practice known as the *dhikr-i jahrī* (vocal recollection) was introduced among the Naqshbandiyya of Kansu by Ma Ming-hsin, an eighteenth-century Chinese Muslim who had travelled to Bukhara and to the Arabian peninsula. Ma was converted to the vocal spiritual exercise, which was supposed to dispel all thoughts from the mind except the remembrance of God. After returning to his native Kansu, he began preaching in 1761–2 among the Salar Turks in Hsun-hua, in the extreme east of present-day Tsinghai, not far from the Kansu capital of Lanchow. His followers were identified by a phrase they used, *Che-ho lei-yeh*, almost certainly the transliteration of Jahriyya, the 'vocal' tarikat. Within two decades, this New Teaching (*Hsin-chiao*) (in dispute with the Old Teaching of earlier Chinese Naqshbandiyya, which was for 'silent recollection' of

[35] See Saguchi Tōru, *Jūhachi-jūkyūseiki Higashi Torukisutan shakaishi kenkyū* (A study of the social history of Eastern Turkestan in the 18th and 19th centuries), 534–8. Henry Walter Bellew, *Kashmir and Kashgar: a narrative of the journey of the embassy to Kashgar in 1873–1874*, 321–7.

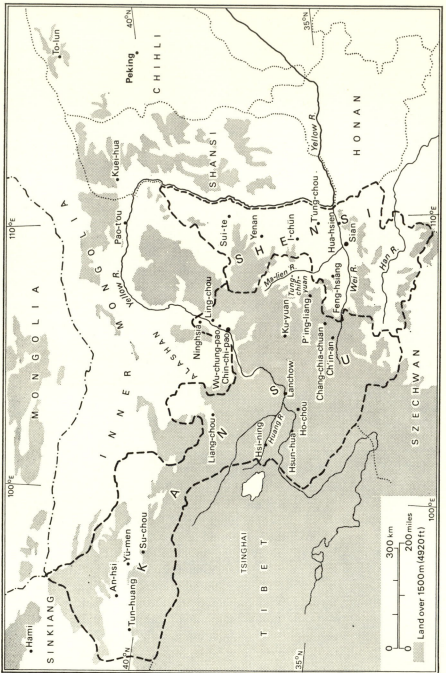

MAP. 10   The Muslim Rebellion in Shensi and Kansu 1862–73

God) led to a revolt against the Ch'ing authorities. Defeated and executed, Ma was regarded as a saint (*sheng-jen*) by his followers, who had to go underground. By the time the great Muslim Rebellion of Shensi–Kansu broke out in 1862, his mantle had descended to Ma Hua-lung, of Chin-chi-pao (in that part of Ninghsia under Kansu provincial jurisdiction). A devotee of the vocal school, Ma Hua-lung predicted future events, cured illnesses, and helped those who 'wished to have an heir to have one'. His followers willingly underwent whipping upon confession of wrongdoing. Ma was said to have sent out deputies (*hai-li-fei* or khalīfa) and teachers (*man-la* or mullā) to Urumchi in Sinkiang and even to K'uan-ch'eng-tzu in Manchuria.[36]

The Muslim revolt in Shensi and Kansu was, however, not just a religious movement. Like the revolt in Yunnan, the Tungan Rebellion was a large-scale community conflict – the coalescence of the persecuted mosque-centred communities for the purpose of survival. The revolt in Shensi was catalysed by a Taiping expedition into that province in April 1862, which reached the vicinity of Sian in mid-May. Stopped by the Ch'ing troops there, the Taipings moved rapidly eastward and entered Honan at the end of May, leaving the communities on both banks of the Wei River in turmoil. With official encouragement local armed corps were formed by the Han Chinese, and this effort was paralleled by the Muslims. In Wei-nan county a Muslim force, said to be 3,000 strong, was organized by Hung Hsing, a Chinese Muslim who had served as a runner (*ya-i*) of the county yamen.[37] In late May, in nearby Hua-hsien, large-scale Han–Muslim conflict was set off by the Han Chinese burning a Muslim village. Armed feuds between Han and Muslim spread immediately along the Wei valley. After Chang Fei, the imperially appointed commissioner of local defence, was murdered by a Tungan leader, proclamations appeared declaring that all Muslims were 'to be killed without further inquiry' (*ko-sha wu-lun*). Whether or not the proclamation was officially authorized, it pushed the Muslims towards an organized rebellion.[38]

Muslim tradition identifies the leaders of 'eighteen great battalions' (*shih-pa ta-ying*) in Shensi. At least three of the eighteen were akhunds

[36] Shan Hua-p'u, 'Shen-kan chieh-yü lu' (Legends of the Shensi–Kansu calamity) in *HMCI*, 4.311. Saguchi Tōru, *Jūhachi-jūkyūseiki*, 559–79. Joseph Fletcher, 'Central Asian Sufism and Ma Ming-hsin's New Teaching', in Chieh-hsien Ch'en, ed. *Proceedings of the Fourth East Asian Altaistic Conference*, 75–96. *TWHK, Tsou-kao* (Memorials), 38.35b, 63–4.

[37] Chu Wen-ch'ang (Wen-Djang Chu), 'T'an yu-kuan hsi-pei hui-luan ti liang-ko wen-t'i' (Two problems relating to the Muslim Rebellion in the north-west), *Ch'ing-hua hsueh-pao*, NS, 5.1 (1965) 135–7, 141.

[38] Tung-a chü-shih (pseud.), 'Ch'in luan chien-wen chi' (Diary of what I saw and heard during the Shensi calamity), in Ma Hsiao-shih, *Hsi-pei hui-tsu ko-ming chien-shih* (Brief history of the Muslim people's revolution in the north-west), 93–6.

(religious leaders). The rebels initially developed three centres: one in the prosperous market towns near T'ung-chou, at the eastern end of the Wei valley; one north of Sian, and another further west around Feng-hsiang, towards the Kansu border.[39] The rebels' early success was due to incredible Ch'ing weaknesses. Ying-ch'i, the Shensi governor, ensconced himself in Sian with Green Standard troops and local corps, but was unable to break a Muslim blockade that all but shut off the city's food supplies. In August 1862, Sheng-pao, notorious for his arranging the surrender of Miao P'ei-lin and other dissidents (see volume 10, chapter 9), was appointed imperial commissioner to rescue Sian. But Sheng-pao failed to arrange Muslim surrenders and his military inaction as well as gross corruption caused his removal in January 1863.

The Ch'ing began to win only with the arrival of To-lung-a (1817–64) as imperial commissioner. Originally a Manchu banner officer, To-lung-a had, through the patronage of Hu Lin-i, risen to be a commander of the Hunan Army (the force under him being identified as the Ch'u-yung).[40] In 1861, To-lung-a helped Tseng Kuo-ch'üan to recover Anking from the Taipings and, on his own, captured Lu-chou in 1862. His *yung-ying* force proved to be equally effective against the Muslims. In March 1863, his battalions captured two market towns that formed the principal Tungan base in eastern Shensi. He broke the blockade around Sian in August and pursued the Muslims to western Shensi. By the time of his death in March 1864, in a battle against Szechwanese Taipings who invaded Shensi, he had broken the back of the Muslim Rebellion in that province. A great many Shensi Muslims had, however, escaped to Kansu, adding to the numerous Muslim forces which had already risen there.

While the rebellion in Shensi was clearly provoked by Han gentry and officials, in Kansu it seems that the Muslims had taken the initiative, with the New Teaching group under Ma Hua-lung playing a large role. As early as October 1862, some Muslim leaders, spreading the word of an impending Ch'ing massacre of Muslims, organized themselves for a siege of Ling-chou, a large city only forty-odd miles north of Ma Hua-lung's base, Chin-chi-pao. Meanwhile, in south-eastern Kansu, Ku-yuan, a strategic city athwart a principal transport route, was attacked by the Muslims. Governor-general En-lin, in Lanchow, saw no alternative to a policy of reconciliation. In January 1863, at his recommendation, Peking issued an edict especially for Kansu, reiterating the principle of nondiscrimination towards the Muslims. But as in Shensi, both Han and Muslim local corps

[39] Shan Hua-p'u, 'Shen-Kan', in *HMCI*, 4.311–12.
[40] Unless otherwise indicated, our summary of events in Shensi and Kansu relies on Wen-Djang Chu, *The Moslem Rebellion in northwest China, 1862–1878*, and Kuo T'ing-i (Ting-yee Kuo), *Chin-tai Chung-kuo shih-shih jih-chih* (Chronology of events in modern Chinese history).

were multiplying and in conflict, and within four years all of Kansu, except for the provincial capital and a handful of other cities, had been occupied by Muslim forces.

Ma Hua-lung's religious-military network was based in four areas: Chin-chi-pao itself; Hsi-ning in eastern Tsinghai where many of the Salar minority had been converted to the New Teaching; and two areas in southern Kansu – Ho-chou (close to Tsinghai) and Ch'in-an (not far from Shensi and near a New Teaching centre, Chang-chia-ch'uan).[41] An able Chinese intendant of the Ninghsia circuit, Hou Yun-teng, rallied enough Green Standard and banner troops as well as local corps to defend Ling-chou for a year. But in December 1863 Ma Hua-lung's troops, led by his son and other devotees of the New Teaching, occupied not only Ling-chou (where 100,000 Han Chinese are said to have been massacred) but also the Chinese and Manchu cities of Ninghsia prefecture. Apparently at this time Ma assumed a Chinese-style title: 'Grand Marshal (*ta tsung-jung*) in Charge of Military Affairs of Ninghsia Prefecture, the Two Rivers and Other Areas' – the two rivers referring to the Yellow River and a major tributary.[42] With this authority, Ma appointed the prefects and magistrates in the area under his control, but to his growing number of followers he was a *sheng-jen* (saint), with special ties to God and capable of wondrous acts.

There were, of course, numerous rebel leaders in Kansu who did not adhere to the New Teaching. Out of more than seventy Muslim leaders who were active in Kansu between 1862 and 1866 and whose names have appeared in historical studies,[43] twenty have been identified as Ma Hua-lung's partisans. These included New Teachings missionaries as well as a number of middle-ranking officers of the Green Standard Army. Among the remainder, including eleven leaders who had recently come from Shensi, a number had allied themselves with Ma or received supplies from him. As compared with the Yunnan rebels, there were very few genuine turn-coats like Ma Ju-lung among the Shensi or Kansu Muslim leaders. Muslim surrenders often proved to be ruses. In mid-1864, Lei Cheng-kuan, a Hunan Army officer who had come with To-lung-a to Shensi and now fought in Kansu, captured both Ku-yuan and P'ing-liang, with the result that government highways were re-opened between the Wei River and western and central Kansu. Ho Ming-t'ang, a Shensi Muslim rebel and an akhund, surrendered to Lei, but in September when Shensi Muslims again

[41] See *inter alia* the petition of 1863 from gentry members of the Kansu–Ninghsia border to the throne through the Censorate, cited in Ma Hsiao-shih, *Hsi-pei hui-tsu*, 34.

[42] Lo Cheng-chün, *Tso Wen-hsiang kung nien-p'u* (Chronological biography of Tso Tsung-t'ang), 5.23. The tributary of the Yellow River is believed to be the Huang (Mathews' *Chinese-English Dictionary*, no. 2289), which links Hsi-ning in Tsinghai with south-western Kansu.

[43] The two works mentioned in n. 40 above, and Ma Hsiao-shih, *Hsi-pei hui-tsu*.

besieged Ku-yuan, Ho arranged to have the city gates opened from within, allowing his co-religionists to win (and incidentally to drive out a faction of Kansu Muslims who had also capitulated to Lei). An extant Muslim document relates that before every battle Ho would read from scripture and pray aloud: 'We rely on the Lord; we protect our religion as we go into battle, always with the help of the True Lord.'[44] In February 1865 Ku-yuan was lost again to the Ch'ing forces but Shensi rebels, under Ho, won it back in October – along with cities south-eastward to the Shensi border.

Without the aid of a genuine and powerful turncoat, the Ch'ing officials resorted to arranging 'surrenders' that actually left the territory in the hands of the rebels. The major case is that of Ma Hua-lung himself. In 1864–5, Peking directed two of its best Manchu commanders to attack Ma's base at the Kansu–Ninghsia border. The commanders were Tu-hsing-a, who was given principal charge of the campaigns in Kansu, and Mu-t'u-shan, formerly a cavalry officer under To-lung-a but now the Ninghsia general-in-chief. Year-long sieges of the two cities of Ninghsia prefecture were not successful and Mu-t'u-shan favoured accepting the proposals for peace put forward by Ma Hua-lung's lieutenants. Only after Tu-hsing-a, who adamantly opposed the idea, was transferred to be general-in-chief in Mukden did Mu-t'u-shan carry out his policy of accommodating Ma Hua-lung. Ma turned over to the Ch'ing forces 26 cannon, more than 1,000 foreign arms (*yang-ch'iang*), and more than 10,000 swords and spears. In return, Mu-t'u-shan memorialized the throne to clear Ma of his record as a rebel: 'Ma Hua-lung is very much trusted by the Muslims in Kansu. If he should be sent out to different places to try to persuade the Muslims, . . . they everywhere would surrender without a fight.'[45] An edict of May 1866 approved Ma's surrender and Ma even adopted a new loyalist name, Ma Ch'ao-ch'ing. He continued, however, to consolidate and expand his influence, without having to worry about Ch'ing attacks.

Meanwhile, effective Ch'ing rule in Kansu was collapsing. The Muslim revolt spread to the Kansu panhandle west of the Yellow River. In February 1865, a Muslim Green Standard officer in Liang-chou (now Wu-wei) crushed a rebellion and gained control of the city, and in March there were Muslim riots at Yü-men ('The Jade Gate'), which soon spread to An-hsi farther to the north-west. Kansu Muslims briefly took over strategic Su-chou in April and succeeded more permanently in December.

---

44 'Chi-shih' (Journal of events; fragment originally written in sinicized Arabic, translated by P'ang Shih-ch'ien into Chinese), in *HMCI*, 3.240 and plate facing p. 1.
45 Cited in Chu, *The Moslem Rebellion*, 64.

Some Muslims had returned to Shensi and that province was again in danger. Meanwhile, Sinkiang, which had felt the impact of the events in Shensi and Kansu as early as 1863, was in the throes of numerous revolts in its several regions and of invasion from beyond the Ch'ing empire's boundaries.

Sinkiang

In Sinkiang, the rebellious message from Chinese Muslims touched off a variety of reactions – as diverse as the area was ethnically and linguistically, and as segmented as its geography and historical tradition. Ch'ing administration there had many weaknesses, and until 1860 the dynasty was barely able to maintain order in Altishahr against the periodic jihad (holy war) of the Āfāqī khojas and their Turkic-speaking followers (see volume 10, chapters 2 and 8). Han Chinese migration into Sinkiang had been increasing, but this development, too, added to the potential for conflict: the Chinese settlers, whether Muslim or non-Muslim, constituted a minority in the view of the Turkic-speaking inhabitants and could, moreover, become subversive against Sinkiang's Ch'ing rulers. In this most northwestern territory of the Ch'ing empire, Chinese and non-Chinese had also to confront the emergence of Russia as the dominant factor in Central Asian trade and politics. Meanwhile Sinkiang, in those days when new mountain passes through the Pamirs and Karakoram were still being eagerly explored, was considered by British India to be all too close to its northern frontier.[46]

News of the Muslim revolt in China proper may have prompted as early as March 1863 a Muslim uprising in the Ili region, which the Ch'ing troops were able to put down very rapidly. In May of that year, fighting broke out between Muslims and Han Chinese in Khitai, in north-eastern Sinkiang, where Han farmers and traders were numerous and where the Ch'ing authorities, who encouraged the new settlers, had been heavy-handed in taxing the Muslims. In June, a separate revolt began at Kucha, in northern Altishahr, under the leadership of Rāshidīn Khoja – no relative of the Makhdūmzāda khojas. The revolt spread as far east as Karashahr and in the west approached Kashgar. Rāshidīn Khoja established his capital at Aksu and adopted the title of King of Turkestan. But in July, in Yarkand, where the Rāshidīn lineage did not command respect, a local rebel seized power over the city. In quick succession, a beg (native official)

---

[46] Our study of Islam in China and particularly of events in Sinkiang has benefited immensely from the manuscript of Professor Joseph Fletcher's current historical survey of Ch'ing Inner Asia. We are also grateful to Professor Lanny Bruce Fields of the State University of New York at Albany for insights gained from his *Tso Tsung-t'ang and the Muslims: statecraft in northwest China, 1868–1880*.

of the Kirghiz tribesmen occupied Yangi Hısar, only about thirty miles south of Kashgar; and in southern Altishahr, a Turkic-speaking leader set himself up as King of Khotan.

Meanwhile, in Urumchi, the Ch'ing bastion in eastern Sinkiang, T'o Ming, a Tungan akhund from Kansu,[47] said to be a partisan of Ma Hua-lung, was engineering a coup among the Ch'ing garrison forces. Following the pattern of Kansu Muslim revolts, T'o Ming won the devotion of So Huan-chang, a lieutenant-colonel of the Green Standard Army in Urumchi. So's forces had warred against the Han Chinese settlers' armed corps that feuded with the Muslims at Khitai. In July 1864 So led a mutiny in which the Manchu general-in-chief was killed, and won control of the Chinese city of Urumchi. T'o Ming now assumed the title of a Muslim king (*Ch'ing-chen wang*) with So as his commander-in-chief (*ta yuan-shuai*). T'o Ming's forces captured several cities along the Manas River, and in October Urumchi's Manchu city also succumbed. Sinkiang Tungans, who were trusted neither by the Ch'ing nor by the Turkestanis, responded with risings in Kur Kara Usu and in Turfan. In December, one of T'o Ming's generals occupied the latter city.

In November 1864, Ili, the seat of the Manchu military governor of all Sinkiang, was in turmoil. Led by Mu'aẓẓam Khan, a Taranchi who had been a hakim beg (principal native official), the rebels, mostly from the Turkic-speaking populace but including some Charhars, besieged the two main Manchu cities in Ili, Hui-ning and Hui-yuan. Ming-i, the Ili garrison commander, had just returned from Tarbagatai, where he had concluded a boundary agreement with the Russians. He and Ming-hsu, the military governor, sought aid from the Russian governor of West Siberia.[48] Preparing for a long siege, they even got their request relayed to the Russian minister in Peking through the Tsungli Yamen – but all to no avail. The Ch'ing troops defended the two cities valiantly for eighteen months, but were finally overcome in March 1866. Tarbagatai fell in April of the same year, after it had been under siege by local Muslims led by an akhund and assisted by the Kazakhs. Thus the Barkol–Hami area was the only part of Sinkiang that remained in Ch'ing hands, and even this region was subject to Muslim raids and riots.

In southern Sinkiang, meanwhile, the drama of Jahāngīr's holy war (see volume 10, chapter 8) seems to have been re-enacted, only to result in the rise of a skilful usurper who was perhaps also devout. The Manchus had lost control of Kashgar as early as mid-1864, but two other groups fought

[47] T'o Ming (T'o Te-lin) is believed to have come from Ho-chou, Kansu, and to have visited Chin-chi-pao before arriving in Sinkiang. Kuo T'ing-i, *Chin-tai Chung-kuo*, 1.449.
[48] Immanuel C. Y. Hsu, *The Ili crisis: a study of Sino-Russian diplomacy*, 27.

for control of the city. Ṣiddīq Beg, the Kirghiz chief leading one of the two groups contending for power at Kashgar, called on Kokand for help in early 1865. The result was, however, not direct Kokandi intervention, but the return of one of Jahāngīr's sons, Buzurg Khan. He came with only about sixty men, led by a general who had served in the Kokand Army – Ya'qūb Beg (c. 1820–77). Despite the smallness of his force, large numbers in the Kashgar region rallied to Buzurg Khan's standard, for a large part of the population still actively identified itself with the Āfāqī saintly heritage. Soon Buzurg Khan was strong enough to eliminate both rival groups that sought control in Kashgar. Subsequently, when the city was attacked by Rāshidīn Khoja of Aksu and a new ruler of Yarkand, the two potentates were defeated by an army organized by Ya'qūb Beg. Buzurg Khan was properly enthroned before Ya'qūb moved his force in April to nearby Yangi Hisar and defeated an isolated Manchu force.

Ya'qūb Beg, as it happened, was not only an able commander but also a master manipulator of power and of the religious sanction for it, the two being inseparable in Islamic Turkestan. Buzurg Khan soon felt very insecure in the company of his ambitious general and made plans to oust him. But Ya'qūb had meanwhile befriended the shaykh who kept prayerful watch over the Āfāqī tomb, and the latter refused the khoja's request that Ya'qūb be excommunicated. The scheming general now forced the khoja to move to Yangi Hisar, where he was a virtual prisoner for eighteen months. In 1867, the khoja was compelled (or persuaded) to leave Alti-shahr, ostensibly for a trip to Mecca. Ya'qūb Beg assumed power in Kashgar under the title of Badawlat (The fortunate). At the same time he declared his determination to carry on a religious war against the Tungans under T'o Ming; for, although also Sunnis (orthodox Muslims), they were believed to be of the Shafi'ite school of law and not the Hanafite school, to which Kashgar's religious authorities adhered.[49] Since T'o Ming's kingdom had been extending its influence westward from Turfan, Ya'qūb could justify his efforts in 1867–8 to consolidate Kashgar's control of the Tarim basin by subduing the ruler of Khotan, Mufti Ḥabīb Allāh, and that of Aksu and Kucha, Rāshidīn Khoja, for both potentates had enlisted the Tungans in their armies and welcomed Tungan support in other cities. Ya'qūb also arranged for the emir of Bukhara to confer on him the religious title of Atalïq Ghāzī (Father warrior of the faith). He thus gained a measure of legitimacy, strengthened by his instituting the strict interpretation of Islamic laws in the cities he governed. He also founded many new and land-endowed madrasas (religious schools).

---

[49] Tsing Yuan, 'Yakub Beg (1820–1877) and the Moslem rebellion in Chinese Turkestan', *Central Asiatic Journal*, 6 (1961) 145–8.

That Ya'qūb was probably a genuinely devout warrior is further indicated by his venture into Eastern Turkestan to attack the Tungan-controlled cities. It seems that he succeeded in 1869 only in taking Korla. But by the end of 1870, he had occupied Karashahr, Turfan and Urumchi itself. In this last feat, Ya'qūb enlisted the help of a non-Muslim Chinese, Hsu Hsueh-kung, a 'militia headman' (*t'uan-t'ou*) of the Han settlers in eastern Sinkiang. With the aid of Hsu and of disgruntled former supporters of T'o Ming, Ya'qūb's forces captured Urumchi in December. T'o Ming capitulated and fled to Manas, where he died after an illness. Ya'qūb's victory was, however, costly. According to one account, his expeditionary force, some twenty thousand strong in 1867, had been reduced by half after the campaigns in eastern Sinkiang.[50] But the expedition had important repercussions. In June 1871, Russian troops swept across the border and occupied the Ili area, forestalling any plans Ya'qūb might have had to conquer western Zungharia.

The Russian occupation of Ili must be seen in a larger perspective. For it signifies that Sinkiang was no longer just a part of Central Asia, as in Jahāngīr's day. Sinkiang now lay at the crossroads of three empires – Ch'ing, Russian and British. The first two, especially, had a large stake in her future, and for the moment Russia was ensuring that Ya'qūb's Islamic enthusiasm did not lead him to support other states in Turkestan which she was bringing under her control. During the years that saw Ya'qūb's rise to power, Kokand, Bukhara and Khiva were all making their last stand for independence. Russia took Tashkent in 1865 and Samarkand, belonging to the emirate of Bukhara, in 1868. The trend was to continue: Khiva finally capitulated in 1873 and the city of Kokand became Russian three years later. Meanwhile, the British, whose trade with Sinkiang was still small, had other reasons to be uneasy about Russian designs. The British were worried partly because they were ignorant – as indeed the Russians were also – of the infeasibility of large-scale military movement through the Karakoram mountain range. But with the Indian Mutiny still fresh in mind, the British were even more concerned about the potential unrest in India which might be sparked off by the Russians having access through native agents to the discontented border tribes between Kashmir and Afghanistan. Britain wanted Sinkiang in non-Russian hands, as part of a belt of buffer areas against the Russian empire.[51]

Ya'qūb Beg was not unaware of his precarious position, but what he could do, for himself or for the other Muslim states in Turkestan, was limited. He sent envoys to both India and Russia as early as 1868, discussing

---

[50] Ma Hsiao-shih, *Hsi-pei hui-tsu*, 61–2. Yuan, 'Yakub Beg', 149.
[51] G. J. Alder, *British India's northern frontier 1865–95: a study in imperial policy*, 15–48, 303–5.

prospects for trade and soliciting recognition for his kingdom. In 1872, with Russian troops now in Ili, he found it necessary to conclude with a Russian official a commercial agreement which did not confer diplomatic recognition. As Russian trade flourished under the low 2.5 per cent import tariff stipulated, Ya'qūb showed his resentment by putting misbehaving Russian merchants in confinement and arbitrarily seizing their goods. More cautiously, he began to work for the support of Britain and of the Islamic states beyond Central Asia.

Ya'qūb probably had been in touch with the Ottoman sultanate in the late 1860s, but it was not until 1873 that the Sublime Porte's recognition of his kingdom was made public. He was made an emir and in the same year the sultan-caliph sent him a gift of three thousand rifles, thirty cannon, and three Turkish military instructors. Meanwhile, exploratory visits to Kashgar by R. B. Shaw in 1868 and by D. T. Forsyth and others in 1870 had aroused British enthusiasm for Ya'qūb's regime. Forsyth was sent to Kashgar again in 1873, when he presented Ya'qūb with several thousand old-style muskets from British India's arsenal. Early in 1874 he concluded with the emir a commercial treaty that also conferred diplomatic recognition upon the new Kashgarian state. In London, Sir Henry Rawlinson wrote in a new 1875 edition of his *England and Russia in the East* that it would be easier for Britain to 'instigate a great anti-Russian Mahommedan [*sic*] movement north of the Oxus' than for Russia to stir up Muslim India.[52] But Sir Henry's proposal was never put to the test. Not Russia but China put an end to Ya'qūb's kingdom.

CH'ING VICTORIES IN SHENSI AND KANSU

Before imperial China's forces could get to Sinkiang, they had first to over-come the Chinese Muslims in Shensi and Kansu. In 1867, when Ya'qūb Beg established his khanate in Sinkiang, Tso Tsung-t'ang was still only recruiting his new Hunan Army (*Ch'u-chün*) and making the financial and transport arrangements for the defeat of the Tungans in China proper. The Shensi–Kansu campaign was to take him nearly seven years, 1867–73, while the actual war in Sinkiang waged by his forces took only two years, 1876–7 – not counting the long preparation period.

After Tso arrived in Shensi in July 1867, he had to be absent from the area for ten months on account of the Nien War. In the interval, Liu Tien, Tso's deputy as imperial commissioner for the Shensi–Kansu campaign, was able to clear southern Shensi of the Muslim rebels who had returned

[52] Cited in V. G. Kiernan, 'Kashgar and the politics of Central Asia, 1868–1878', *The Cambridge Historical Journal* 11.3 (1955) 328. See also Hsu. *The Ili crisis*, 34–5.

from Kansu. The Shensi Muslims now entrenched themselves in Tung-chih-yuan, a fertile plain in south-eastern Kansu, where their 'eighteen great battalions' continued to dispatch raids in every direction. Further north, meanwhile, the New Teaching leader Ma Hua-lung, ever since his 'surrender' to the Ch'ing early in 1866, had built up Chin-chi-pao as an economic as well as military base. Ma's followers included many Muslim merchants long in the trade between Kansu and Pao-t'ou in Inner Mongolia, employing caravan routes as well as rafts, made of inflated hides, that navigated the eastward great bend of the Yellow River. Ma himself owned two trading firms and he invested in the businesses of many of his followers. He was so situated as to be able to control the entire trade between Mongolia and southern Kansu.[53] His interest was, however, religious and military. He purchased firearms from as far as Kuei-hua city (the present Huhehot) and he forwarded them to the New Teaching centres elsewhere in Kansu. Ma also traded with the Shensi Muslims at Tung-chih-yuan, selling horses and munitions and buying grain. When Tso returned to Shensi in November 1868, he was convinced that Ma Hua-lung not only had connections in Sinkiang but had designs on Mongolia 'both north and south of the great desert'.[54]

Tso's preparations for his offensive in Kansu were nearly complete. From Hunan, his veteran officers had recruited a new force totalling some 55,000 men. In addition, Tseng Kuo-fan had transferred to Shensi in 1867 the only unit of his Hunan Army that was not disbanded – about 10,000 men under Liu Sung-shan, one of Tseng's best generals. The throne had also assigned to Tso's command 10,000 men from the Szechwan Army (Ch'uan-chün) under Huang Ting; 7,000 men of the Anhwei provincial army (Wan-chün) under Kuo Pao-ch'ang; and 6,500 men of the Honan Army (Yü-chün) under Chang Yueh. These forces all had experience in fighting the Taipings or the Niens, and they included a total of 7,500 cavalry, reinforcing the 5,000 mounts Tso himself procured.[55] However, apart from employing Manchu officers from Kirin to instruct his cavalry, Tso seems to have paid little attention to the training of his forces. He appreciated the fact that Liu Sung-shan's troops were adept in tactical formations and in sharpshooting. But from his own experience in the Taiping Rebellion, Tso was convinced that the two essentials for victory were courageous men and ample rations. He had briefly tried Western drill

53 Nakada Yoshinobu, 'Dōchi nenkan no Sen-Kan no Kairan ni tsuite' (A study of the Muslim Rebellion in Shensi and Kansu during the T'ung-chih period), *Kindai Chūgoku kenkyū*, 3 (1959) 132. *TWHK, Tsou-kao*, 30.66–7; 37.64. *TWHK, Shu-tu* (Letters), 10.36; 11.32b.
54 *TWHK, Wen-chi* (Essays), 1.18. *TWHK, Shu-tu*, 10.23b–26; 52; 11.10b.
55 Chu, *The Moslem Rebellion*, 105; Ch'in Han-ts'ai, *Tso Wen-hsiang kung tsai hsi-pei* (Tso Tsung-t'ang in the north-west), 51–2.

on his troops late in the rebellion, but found that 'command words cannot be used for large formations of soldiers'. Although Tso equipped his troops with Western firearms, somehow he came to think that target practice 'twice a day for ten days' was sufficient before the troops were sent to battle.[56] Fortunately, in his forthcoming offensive in Kansu he was to engage in a war that, despite the more difficult terrain, chiefly involved attacks on stockades and walled cities – not altogether different from the Taiping Rebellion. However, Tso did value the large siege guns, which a few of his veteran officers had learned how to use.

Tso had also been assured of a solution to his financial and logistical problems. In war-torn Shensi and Kansu, food was scarce and prices extremely high. Tso laid down the rule that his forces would go into major battle only when there were three months' supplies on hand.[57] Not only munitions but also large amounts of grain had to be brought to Shensi and Kansu from other provinces. To finance his supplies, Tso plainly had to depend on Peking's agreement to the formula adopted by many dynasties of the past: 'support the armies in the northwest with the resources of the southeast'. In 1867, five provinces of the south-east coast were asked by the throne to contribute to a 'Western expedition fund' (*Hsi-cheng hsiang-hsiang*) totalling 3.24 million taels annually. The arrangement came under the Ch'ing fiscal practice of 'interprovincial revenue assistance' (*hsieh-hsiang*), but at a time when these provinces were already assessed for numerous contributions to meet the needs of Peking or of other provinces.[58] Tso resorted, as early as 1867, to a stratagem that would compel the provinces to produce their quotas for his campaigns. He requested and obtained the throne's approval for his arranging lump-sum loans from foreign firms, guaranteed by the superintendents of customs at the treaty ports and confirmed by the seals of the provincial governors involved, to be repaid by these provinces to the foreign firms by a fixed date. In May 1867, Tso's agent in Shanghai, Hu Kuang-yung (*c*. 1825–85), obtained a foreign loan of 1.2 million taels in this fashion. But in December of the same year, when Tso requested a further foreign loan of 2 million taels under a similar arrangement, the court objected to the high interest rate Hu Kuang-yung quoted and merely approved half of the proposed loan. The superintendents of customs at four treaty ports were instructed to lend Tso the other million, without charging interest.[59] Tso was, for the time being, not encouraged to negotiate for more loans from foreign firms. Instead, to

[56] *TWHK, Shu-tu*, 11.45; 14.48, 55; 16.27b. *TWHK, P'i-cha* (Comments on petitions), 1.34–5.
[57] *TWHK, Tsou-kao*, 39.17.
[58] Chu, *The Moslem Rebellion*, 112–19. Liu, 'The limits of regional power' 204, nn. 58–9.
[59] *CSL-TC*, 220.26b–27; 244.19–29.

meet his needs, the court soon raised the 'Western expedition fund' to an annual total of 6.24 million, increasing the quotas of the original five provinces and asking two other provinces also to contribute. Most provinces did not deliver their quotas fully and promptly. Nonetheless Tso did receive from the provinces an average annual total of 4 million taels (computed for the entire period from Tso's initial appointment to the Shensi-Kansu post in September 1866 to February 1874).[60]

In 1867, even before his arrival in Shensi, Tso had set up two bureaux for military supplies, in Shanghai and Hankow. At Sian, he established an office to distribute supplies to the war areas and another to maintain communications with other provinces. Munitions procured in Shanghai were carried by foreign-owned steamships to Hankow, where these and other supplies were forwarded by junks on the Han River to the Shensi border and overland to Sian. Rice purchased in Szechwan was carried by boat on the Chia-ling River to a depot in Shensi. For the armies in hilly northern Shensi, grain was supplied from Shansi or from Kuei-hua in Inner Mongolia. Munitions for northern Shensi and Ninghsia were brought first to Kuei-hua via Tientsin. Tso intended his transport system not to be a burden on the localities along the route. His agents and troop convoys accompanied each shipment, and every carrier or cart-driver was supposed to be paid. Once within the boundaries of Shensi, the county magistrates were to provide enough carriers and carts to relay the cargo from one county to another. Payments made by the magistrates were to be reimbursed.[61] Altogether this system of supply was a remarkable demonstration of Tso's capacity for organization, and it must have worked somehow, since the war in Kansu did proceed.

Tso early on announced a principle regarding his war against the Muslims. He would be glad to accept a rebel leader's surrender provided it was genuine – that is, if the latter would turn over his weapons, horses and grain, and, in addition, accept Tso's plans for the resettlement of himself and his followers. Tso publicized the oft-repeated imperial injunction: 'The only distinction is between the innocent and the rebellious, there is none between Han and Muslim.' But Tso also made it a principle not to grant pardon to any active adherents of the New Teaching, which he compared with the White Lotus heterodoxy intent on subversion.[62] In a province where both the Muslim and the Han had been decimated by communal wars, atrocities by government troops, and pestilence in the wake of famine, Tso's campaign against the Tungans was a harrowing test

[60] Chu, *The Moslem Rebellion*, 113–14.
[61] Ch'in Han-ts'ai, *Tso Wen-hsiang kung*, 59–63.
[62] Chu, *The Moslem Rebellion*, 127–8. *TWHK, Tsou-kao*, 32.10b; 38.63b.

of will between the Confucian scholar-commander and the Islamic akhunds turned warriors. Tso was to find that his *yung-ying* troops were not always loyal and dependable. He was barely able to maintain morale among them. It was kept sufficiently high only because of the adequate rations Tso provided and the promise of loot at the wealthy Muslim strongholds – as well as the awareness among the forces at large that the European rifles and siege guns of Tso's select battalions must eventually prevail.

Moving westward from Shensi, Tso's two major objectives were Ma Hua-lung's strongholds around Chin-chi-pao and the Shensi Muslims' rural base in south-eastern Kansu at Tung-chih-yuan. Victory in the latter area was comparatively easy, for the Shensi Muslims' eighteen great battalions had neither centralized leadership nor defensible redoubts; the few big cities near their 4,500 square miles of productive land had been occupied by Kansu Muslims who did not always aid their Shensi co-religionists. Between mid-February and early April 1869, Tso's forces swept through Tung-chih-yuan, reportedly taking more than twenty thousand lives. Large bands of Shensi Muslims now moved off in all directions. Several leaders temporarily occupied towns northward towards Chin-chi-pao. Ma Hua-lung accepted some of them and their forces into his command. Others he presented with camels and advised to go elsewhere.[63] One Shensi band crossed the Yellow River and entered Ninghsia. They reached the territory of the Mongol prince of the Alashan banner and ransacked his villa and ancestral tombs – causing Peking to send troops in haste to that area from other points in Inner Mongolia.[64] Most of the Shensi leaders, however, remained in Kansu with their bands of fighting men, chiefly in or near the towns north-east and south-west of Lanchow.

While it was comparatively simple to conquer Tung-chih-yuan, the subduing of the Kansu Muslims' own strongholds was far more difficult. The complex problems Tso faced in operating against the four main rebel centres of the Kansu area (Chin-chi-pao, Ho-chou, Hsi-ning and Su-chou) are indicated by the history of the Chin-chi-pao campaign, the plans for which were laid down in late 1868.[65] Three main forces were to join in the attack. Liu Sung-shan, returning from the Nien War in Chihli, was to cut across northern Shensi from Honan to approach Chin-chi-pao from the east; the forces of Chang Yueh, of the Honan Army, who had been in Shansi guarding the Pao-t'ou area, were to cross Inner Mongolia and move

---

[63] *TWHK, Tsou-kao*, 31.16b; *TWHK, Shu-tu*, 10.32, 52b.
[64] *CSL-TC*, 261.24; 262.17–19; 263.10b–11; 276.23. N. Prejevalsky, who travelled through Alashan and Ordos in 1871, noted the effects of the Tungan raids in both areas; see his *Mongolia, the Tangut country, and the solitude of northern Tibet* (E. Delmar Morgan, trans.), 1.198, 210, 238n., 259.
[65] *TWHK, Shu-tu*, 10.19, 26, 36b.

southward on the west bank of the Yellow River; and Tso's other forces
were to occupy such cities as P'ing-liang and Ku-yuan in Kansu and
approach Chin-chi-pao from the south. The plan eventually worked, but
not before Tso's own forces experienced crises and reverses.

The most serious crisis was internal, for in March and April 1869, at the
same time as the victory at Tung-chih-yuan, two alarming mutinies occurred
in the best forces under Tso's command. In late March, after Liu Sung-shan
had cut through northern Shensi and approached the Kansu–Ninghsia
border, a mutiny took place at Sui-te (about seventy-five miles north-east
of Yenan), where he had left behind 4,500 troops to guard a supply depot.
Several hundred troops, including those who later confessed to being
members of the Elder Brothers Society (Ko-lao hui), robbed the grain
depot and took control of Sui-te city. Among the mutineers were as many
as four company officers, also said to be Elder Brother members.[66] The
revolt was quickly suppressed after Liu himself hurried back to Sui-te in
early April, but meanwhile an apparently unrelated mutiny had broken out
in I-chün in central Shensi, eighty miles north of Sian, involving the murder
of a *t'ung-ling* commander. Again the several hundred rebellious soldiers
included members of the Elder Brothers Society. Four company officers
and a battalion officer who joined them were also said to be members. The
mutineers were captured, however, by Tso's loyal forces. Tso personally
executed five of the ringleaders. He believed that the Elder Brothers
Society had originated in Szechwan and Kweichow but had affected the
Hunan Army through surrendered Taipings who were natives of these
two provinces, or through 'disbanded mercenaries' (*san-yung*) of other
provinces who had come to Shensi for adventure. He hoped that such
'venomous and devilishly elusive creatures' were very few among his
forces.[67] However, the Elder Brothers Society was long to persist in Tso's
armies, as an underground mutual aid group performing both legal and
illegal deeds.

Interrupted by the mutinies and their aftermath, operations against
Chin-chi-pao were not resumed until mid-August. Liu Sung-shan, advanc-
ing from northern Shensi, reached the vicinity of Ling-chou in early
September. Ma Hua-lung probably had no illusions about his own power
as compared with Tso's. He wrote to Tso and negotiated for peace, but his
overture was firmly rejected.[68] In November, Ling-chou was occupied by
Liu Sung-shan; Tso's forces in the south, having captured such cities as
Ku-yuan, moved continuously northward. Resistance stiffened, however,

[66] *TWHK*, *Tsou-kao*, 31.22.
[67] *Ibid.* 31.2, 23, 27, 28–9. *TWHK*, *Shu-tu*, 10.35; cf. 11.29.
[68] *TWHK*, *Shu-tu*, 10.55b; 11.7, 10b. *TWHK*, *Tsou-kao*, 33.2–3, 17.

as more and more of Ma's New Teaching devotees from Kansu, including Shensi Muslims who had once occupied Tung-chih-yuan, joined the war. Tso was soon to face what one of his admiring biographers has described as 'the greatest disaster of his entire career.'[69]

Moving southward from Ling-chou, Liu Sung-shan had to fight his way through hundreds of fortified villages, enclosed by hills on three sides and by the Yellow River in the west. The rural defenders, who possessed fire-arms, were also Ma's staunchest devotees. Liu had to advance slowly, and on 14 February 1870, he met his death under 'cannon fire'.[70] Although his able nephew and former staff officer, Liu Chin-t'ang (1844–94), managed to hold his force together, its forward movement came to a halt. It happened that at this very juncture, a far-flung counter-offensive on Ma Hua-lung's part was producing spectacular results. Employing the Shensi Muslims whom he had harboured or aided, in early January Ma had launched cavalry raids on several parts of Shensi. A few days before Liu Sung-shan's death, Ch'en Lin, a Shensi Tungan, had blocked off Liu's supply line in northern Shensi. Another Shensi Muslim, Ma Cheng-kang, now led his cavalry to the Wei valley itself.[71] On 15 February he passed east of Sian and crossed the Wei River to the very area where the Tungan Rebellion had started eight years before.

In Kansu, south of Chin-chi-pao, Tso's forces, which had advanced to within nearly fifty miles of this redoubt, had met defeat two days before Liu's death. The defeat now turned into a rout, and the Ch'ing expedition had to retreat to Ku-yuan. The series of reverses so alarmed Peking that in March it issued an edict ordering Li Hung-chang to bring his famous army from Hupei to Shensi and to take charge of the war in that province.[72]

Tso's military situation was still viable, however. For despite the fact that he was fighting far from the source of his supplies and despite the many weaknesses of his army system, Tso had, thanks to his elaborate planning and to Peking's backing, acquired in Kansu resources that could match Ma's. The Tungans who broke Tso's cordon and returned to Shensi appear to have totalled less than 4,000 and were repulsed by the cavalry Tso sent back to Shensi as well as by forces of that province.[73] Liu Sung-shan's death was a great blow, but the *yung-ying* system, its injustice and corruption notwithstanding, retained its cohesiveness whenever rapport was unimpaired between commander and officers and between

[69] W. L. Bales, *Tso Tsungt'ang: soldier and statesman of old China*, 246–7.
[70] *TWHK, Tsou-kao*, 34.60–1.
[71] The movement of Shensi Muslims from south-western Kansu to aid Chin-chi-pao is noted in Kuo T'ing-i, *Chin-tai Chung-kuo*, 528–33.
[72] *CSL-TC*, 277.1–3.
[73] *TWHK, Shu-tu*, 11.2b, 23b. *TWHK, Tsou-kao*, 35.1–2, 21.

officers and men. It was fortunate that Liu Chin-t'ang could step so easily into his uncle's shoes. Tso's immediate appointment of Liu as commander of the 'Old Hunan Army' (Lao Hsiang-chün), confirmed by Peking's edict in March 1870, added to the youthful commander's prestige. His supplies from northern Shensi were still blocked. But the problem of food was solved by grain received at Wu-chung-pao (north of Ling-chou) from rafts that came down the Yellow River, a route which had been opened by Chang Yüeh.[74]

As early as 10 March, the young Liu was pressing towards Chin-chi-pao again. Meanwhile, under a Szechwan commander experienced in cavalry warfare, Hsu Chan-piao, Tso's forces in south-eastern Kansu returned to the perimeter of that city, even before Li Hung-chang arrived in Shensi in June (only to depart the next month for a new task in Chihli). By September, several Ch'ing forces were closing in on Ma's stronghold, establishing direct contact with Liu Chin-t'ang, who was henceforth assured of grain and munitions from Tso's headquarters in Kansu.

The slow war of attrition eventually starved out Ma Hua-lung's base. By September 1870, Liu Chin-t'ang had reduced all but a score of the 500-odd forts around Chin-chi-pao. Krupp siege guns shipped to Kansu from Shanghai were now sent to Liu along with an officer who had served Tseng Kuo-fan as a gunner. The shells failed to breach Chin-chi-pao's heavy walls (said to be thirty-five feet thick), but in October Liu Chin-t'ang built a high gun position from which he bombarded the city over its walls.[75] Chin-chi-pao's dwindling number of inhabitants were now surviving on grass roots and flesh from dead bodies. In January, Ma Hua-lung finally surrendered to Liu Chin-t'ang, turning over his armoury, which included 46 cannon, 293 gingalls, 1,030 shotguns and 180 foreign arms. Tso stayed Ma's execution and bade him persuade Kansu Muslims elsewhere to surrender, too. However, no major leaders came forth to surrender, and when 1,200 more foreign arms were found secretly hidden in Chin-chi-pao, Tso ordered that Ma and his adult male relatives be executed. Some 800 of Ma's staff and officers and 1,000 troops were massacred. A total of 14,000 able-bodied inhabitants who survived (including as many as 11,000 Muslims from Shensi) were moved to the vicinity of P'ing-liang. Those women, children and aged men who were without support, totalling 20,000, were sent to refugee camps also in southern Kansu. Ch'ing troops were permitted to take whatever treasure they could find. Marauders in northern Shensi, of Han extraction, who had surrendered to Liu Sung-shan

74 CSL-TC, 276.7; 282.15 (line 6). TWHK, Shu-tu, 11.1b. TWHK, Tsou-kao, 35.41 (lines 8–9). Maps in Bales, Tso Tsungt'ang, 240, 248.
75 TWHK, Shu-tu, 11.21, 27. TWHK, Tsou-kao, 36.65b; 37.12–13, 59.

in 1869, were encouraged to move to Chin-chi-pao with their families, making it a Han Chinese city.[76]

With the death of Ma Hua-lung, Tso believed that no other Tungan leader could bring together Muslim rebels of diverse origins into a large movement. None the less, strong rebel centres still existed in several parts of Kansu and adjacent Tsinghai. Meanwhile, Peking was greatly disturbed by news from both Inner and Outer Mongolia. In July, several hundred Muslim cavalrymen from Kansu raided Inner Mongolia near To-lun. At the same time, a larger Muslim group (who originated in the Kansu corridor and who had pillaged and burned Uliasutai the preceding year), found its way between the deserts and came to tribal territories only a few days away from Urga in early October. Mongol and Manchu troops moved across the steppes to defend To-lun and Urga. Even Green Standard *lien-chün* troops in Chihli were dispatched by imperial order to the latter city. The two Muslim bands seem to have been defeated by November 1871, four months after the Russian occupation of Ili.[77]

Tso believed that his priority was to clear Kansu of the remaining rebel centres. Capitalizing on the victory over Ma Hua-lung, he distributed a proclamation proscribing the New Teaching but promising pardon to those who had been 'inflamed and misled' by it, implying, however, that the pardon would not include the khalifas and mullas. This policy, approved by the throne for the Kansu jurisdiction,[78] was to have a tangible effect in the Ho-chou campaign, which began in September 1871. Ch'ing armies advanced slowly to within thirty miles of Ho-chou by November, but in February 1872 were driven back by the rebel leader who had won control at that city, Ma Chan-ao, an Old Teaching Muslim. At a fortified town upon a wide river, Tso's forces met a crushing defeat, notwithstanding the new rifles they employed. However, even in victory Ma Chan-ao decided to negotiate for peace, to make the best of a situation that was ultimately hopeless. He told his followers that given the devastated condition of Kansu, should the war continue 'not only will the enmity of the Han people further deepen, the Muslim people will also not have a place to live'. Hence it was better to surrender after a victory than after a defeat.[79]

[76] *TWHK, Shu-tu*, 11.33. *TWHK, Tsou-kao*, 37.60; 38.3–5. Ch'in Han-ts'ai, *Tso Wen-hsiang kung*, 79.

[77] *CSL-TC*, 293.17; 309.22–3; 312.10–11; 313.1, 11; 315.6; 319.12b; 320.12; 321.16. While in Urga in Dec. 1870, Prejevalsky heard of the Tungan raid on Uliasutai. He reported that a Russian detachment had been sent to Urga and remained for more than a year; see his *Mongolia*, 1.16, 62.

[78] For Tso's proclamation, see *HMCI*, 4.1 (plate). Following the precedent of the Ch'ien-lung reign, the throne did not approve the proscription for all the empire, as recommended by Tso; *CSL-TC*, 310.15b–16.

[79] Ma Hsiao-shih, *Hsi-pei hui-tsu*, 46–7.

He was to turn over to Tso 4,000 horses and 'more than 10,000 firearms and spears', but he obtained Tso's pledge that the Muslim majority in Ho-chou should continue to live in that county, while the Han Chinese were for once to move out. By June, the Han Chinese in Ho-chou, along with some 2,000 Shensi Muslims, had been resettled elsewhere. Ma Chan-ao and other erstwhile rebel leaders were eventually absorbed into the local garrison under a Green Standard officer, while Tso's forces watched them from nearby cities.[80]

Tso Tsung-t'ang moved into his governor-general's seat at Lanchow in August 1872. In view of the Russian occupation of Ili, he had dispatched a force in December 1871 to Su-chou, the strategic city just beyond the narrow neck of Kansu towards Sinkiang. Under Hsu Chan-piao, this force of 6,500, including cavalry, had been able by the summer of 1872 to establish firm positions near rebel-held Su-chou. But Tso concentrated first on Hsi-ning, 120 miles north-west of Lanchow, especially because in 1872 it was under the control of Shensi Muslim leaders, including Pai Yen-hu who had been Ma Hua-lung's partisan and now had more than 10,000 seasoned Muslim fighters at his disposal. The task of attacking Hsi-ning was undertaken by Liu Chin-t'ang in August. It took Liu three months to penetrate the difficult and well-defended terrain into Hsi-ning, but he prevailed at last. He annihilated the 10,000 Muslim partisans, but Pai Yen-hu escaped. Ma Kuei-yuan, the 'Muslim gentry leader' of Hsi-ning who protected the New Teaching, was tracked down in the Tsinghai Salar territory.[81]

All this time Tso had in fact been preparing for the crucial assault on Su-chou, where under the New Teaching commander Ma Wen-lu (originally from Hsi-ning) numerous Tungan leaders had gathered. To add to Hsu Chan-piao's forces, Tso sent to Su-chou 3,000 men from his own Hunan Army in December 1872, and at his request both Sung Ch'ing and Chang Yueh of the Honan Army were ordered by the throne to join the campaign. Chin-shun, the recently appointed general-in-chief at Uliasutai, also participated. Tso had his hands full arranging finances and supplies, including the establishment of a modest arsenal at Lanchow where Lai Ch'ang, a Cantonese and a talented army officer with some knowledge of ordnance, began manufacturing extra shells for the German siege guns.[82] Tso was obsessed with the organization of the war, yet both conscience and policy called for making arrangements for the livelihood of 'good Muslims', with a view to removing the root causes of communal conflict.

[80] *TWHK, Tsou-kao*, 41.5–10, 36, 61–4.
[81] *Ibid.* 42.50–1; 43.24–5.
[82] *TWHK, Shu-tu*, 13.23, 32. Gideon Ch'en, *Tso Tsung-t'ang: pioneer promoter of the modern dockyard and the woollen mill in China*, 51–3.

There were, at this time, only some 20,000 Shensi Muslim refugees left in Kansu. They could not go home, because even this small number was not welcome in Shensi. Tso ensured that they were given land in rural areas around P'ing-liang and two other cities further south, isolated from Han Chinese communities. Kansu Muslims that had to be evicted from certain cities were sent to similarly designated areas near Lanchow. The rules were strict: inhabitants were to organize themselves in a *pao-chia* framework, the headmen of the decimal units to be selected by officials; trade was permitted, but whoever made a trip to the city had to carry a permit issued by the county magistrate, and those who desired to visit another province must apply to the circuit intendant for a passport; the New Teaching practices were forbidden. The segregated settlers were allocated land where irrigation was available, each family's acreage varying with its size. Tools and seeds were provided. Refugees unable to work or to find homes were to receive continued relief.[83]

In the meantime, the encirclement of Su-chou was completed, after Sung Ch'ing's 3,000 infantry and 500 cavalry arrived in mid-1873. The total Ch'ing force, under six commanders, was soon over 15,000 strong. In mid-September, Tso himself was on the scene, with his arsenal manager, Lai Ch'ang, who also was an expert gunner. The Krupp guns now bombarded the heavy walls, their fire being coordinated with mines that exploded under the walls. On 24 October, the Ch'ing forces entered the city and Ma Wen-lu surrendered. Tso memorialized that on 12 November, 5,400 native Muslims and 1,573 Muslims who had come to Su-chou from elsewhere were executed. To his quartermaster at Sian, Tso reported his plan that the aged, the young and women among the Muslims in Su-chou were to be resettled in southern Kansu, along with surviving Muslims from two other principal cities in the Kansu corridor. 'Their seed will no longer remain in these three prefectures, and one need not worry about collusion between Muslims inside and outside the Chia-yü Pass.' Tso wrote that the reduction of Su-chou was the 'most perfect feat of my military career over decades; it is regrettable that on the very next day the several armies were in dispute over the division of the spoils'.[84]

THE RECONQUEST OF SINKIANG

Having cleared Kansu of rebellious Muslims, Tso Tsung-t'ang expected to proceed to Sinkiang to confront Ya'qūb Beg and the Russians. As early as February 1874, Tso, with imperial authorization, had asked Chang Yueh

[83] Chu, *The Moslem Rebellion*, 149–55. Ch'in Han-ts'ai, *Tso Wen-hsiang kung*, 78.
[84] *TWHK, Tsou-kao*, 43.65, 85b–86; 44.5b–8. *TWHK, Shu-tu*, 13.34b–35.

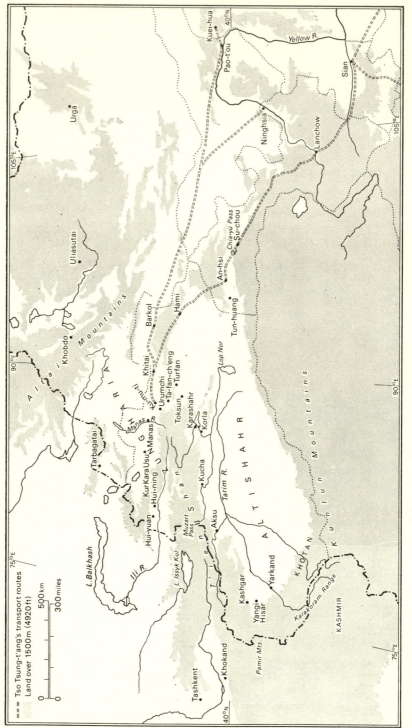

MAP. 11   The Ch'ing reconquest of Sinkiang 1876–8

== = Tso Tsung-t'ang's transport routes
Land over 1500m (4920ft)

500 km
300 miles

Tashkent
Khokand
Pamir Mts.
Kashgar
Yangi
Hisar
Yarkand
KASHMIR
Karakoram Range
KHOTAN
Kun Lun Mountains
ALTISHAHR
Aksu
Kucha
Tarim R.
Muzart Pass
T i e n   S h a n
L. Issyk Kul
Ili R.
L. Balkhash
Hui-yuan
Hui-ning
KurKara Usu
Manas
Manas R.
D Z U N G A R I A
Tarbagatai
Altai Mountains
Khobdo
Uliasutai
Urga
105°E
105°E
75°E
Korla
Karashahr
Toksun
Turfan
Ta-fan-ch'eng
Urumchi
Ku-mu-ti
Khitai
Barkol
Hami
Lop Nor
Tun-huang
An-hsi
Su-chou
Chia-yü Pass
Ninghsia
Lanchow
Sian
Pao-t'ou
Kuei-hua
Yellow R.
40°N
90°E
90°E
75°E
40°N
105°E

to proceed to Hami to begin an agricultural colony (*t'un-t'ien*) there.[85] Yet Tso himself was not given authority to direct the expedition to Sinkiang until more than a year later, in May 1875, and his main force, under Liu Chin-t'ang, did not leave Su-chou for Sinkiang until April 1876. It was the political decision made in Peking and the large funds that were put at Tso's disposal that enabled him to make the costly logistical plans that eventually brought a total force of more than 60,000 men to Ch'ing Turkestan. Tso's was the last great expedition of imperial China into the 'Western Region'. He himself compared his feat with the campaigns of the Han and T'ang dynasties.[86] It was, moreover, a war of the ethnic Chinese, as compared with the expeditions of the mid-Ch'ing period or of the T'ang. Tso paved the way for Sinkiang to become a Ch'ing province and enabled more Han Chinese settlers to go there. Yet despite his triumph – and the eventual Russian withdrawal from all but a strip of the Ili area – Russia was long to dominate Sinkiang economically.

Since the dynasty had in the past entrusted the military garrisons in Sinkiang chiefly to bannermen, in August 1874 it appointed Ching-lien as 'imperial commissioner for Sinkiang military affairs'. Ching-lien was the military lieutenant-governor of Urumchi who had recovered Khitai, the city further east. Tso, as governor-general of Shensi–Kansu, was merely authorized to arrange for transport of supplies for Ching-lien.

Circumstances and tradition had pointed to the recovery of Sinkiang as an unavoidable task. There was, for one thing, the beginning of unrest in Mongolia, under Tungan stimulus. Recent research has shown that after the sporadic Muslim raids into Mongolia (for example, in 1872, when a force from Su-chou invaded Khobdo and burnt the Yellow Temple that was the pride of the city), 'big armed bands of Mongol bandits appeared, in imitation of the Tungans'.[87] If Ya'qūb Beg or the Russians were allowed to be in possession of Sinkiang, disturbances were likely to spread to Mongolia. The question of whether the dynasty should avoid the costly venture of recovering Sinkiang was re-opened only after October 1874, when the Taiwan crisis (created by the landing of Japanese troops there five months earlier) was settled. Li Hung-chang suggested in a memorial in December that Ya'qūb could be recognized as a Ch'ing tributary vassal and that the large expenditure for the projected reconquest of Sinkiang could be saved for coastal defence (see chapter 2). Yet the Manchu statesman Wen-hsiang, while as anxious as anyone for the build-up of a new Ch'ing navy, none the less supported Tso Tsung-t'ang's view that a

[85] *TWHK, Tsou-kao*, 45.19, 79.
[86] Tso Tsung-t'ang, *Tso Wen-hsiang kung chia-shu* (Tso Tsung-t'ang's letters to his family), 6.58b.
[87] C. R. Bawden, *The modern history of Mongolia*, 154, 174. Ma Hsiao-shih, *Hsi-pei hui-tsu*, 54.

Sinkiang campaign must be urgently pursued. Wen-hsiang argued that if Sinkiang was left alone even for a few years, the rebels there 'would wax in strength: they could breach the Chia-yü Pass and threaten Shensi, Kansu and the interior, or they could move by the northern route, and the Mongol tribes would then migrate through the Great Wall: the shoulders and back of Peking will be broken'. Wen-hsiang also believed that Tso's armies had been battle-tested in Kansu and there was a good chance that they would go on to win in Sinkiang.[88]

This last consideration must have prompted the court to entrust the Sinkiang campaign to Tso, but then the wherewithal for the expedition had to be provided. In his capacity as governor-general at Lanchow in charge of transport and supplies for the Sinkiang campaign, Tso had obtained imperial approval in late 1874 to raise a loan of 3 million taels from foreign firms through his Shanghai agent under an arrangement similar to that for the loans he obtained in 1867–8. Tso explained that although in the last years of the war in Kansu, the annual revenue assistance under the 'Western expedition fund' had been increased to a total of more than 7 million, he was actually receiving only 5 million per year and he needed the 3 million loan mainly to pay debts to Chinese merchants. Now that he was actively planning the logistics of the Sinkiang campaign, he proposed in January 1876 a loan of 10 million taels from foreign firms to complete his preparations. Despite the opposition of his friend Shen Pao-chen, whom Tso had nominated to be in charge of the Foochow Navy Yard and who as governor-general at Nanking was now one of the two imperial commissioners for coastal defence, the throne authorized Tso to negotiate for a loan of 5 million taels from foreign sources while ordering the Board of Revenue to grant him immediately 2 million taels (which in fact came out of funds earmarked for coastal defence). At the same time the throne ordered twelve provinces to deliver to Tso a total of 3 million taels – adding up to the large amount he wanted. The 5 million loan was eventually arranged in 1877 from the Hongkong and Shanghai Banking Corporation, repayable in seven years and guaranteed by the customs at Canton, Foochow, Shanghai and Hankow.[89] For the three-year period from 1875 to the end of 1877, when the Sinkiang campaign was largely completed, Tso received a total of 26.7 million taels, averaging 8.9 million per

[88] Wen-hsiang's views expressed in a crucial court conference were confided by the elder statesman to Li Yun-lin, a Peking official. See Li Yun-lin, *Hsi ch'ui shih-lueh* (Brief record of events on the western frontier), 2–3, and also Lo Cheng-chün, *Tso Wen-hsiang kung nien-p'u,* 7.36b–37.

[89] Chu, *The Moslem Rebellion*, 119–22. The Hongkong Bank floated bonds in the treaty ports to raise the 5 million taels. Robert Hart wrote in Oct. 1877, 'Govt. pays the go-between (Hu-Kwang-Yung) 15% interest: he pays the bank 10%: the Bank pays the public 8%.' See John K. Fairbank *et al. The I.G. in Peking*, 1.251.

year. In 1878, the court approved a further loan Tso proposed for 3.5 million taels, half from the Hongkong Bank and half from Chinese merchants. To finance the completion of the war, Tso was to receive in the four years 1878–81 interprovincial revenue assistance totalling 25.6 million taels, or an average of 6.4 million per year.[90]

This interprovincial revenue assistance – totalling 52.3 million taels over a seven-year period – was the single most crucial factor behind Tso's victories in Sinkiang. Yet his success must also be ascribed to his planning and strategy, as well as his handling of complex logistics. Tso decided early on that his first objective should be eastern Zungharia. The Tungans were active there, and Tso hoped to draw Ya'qūb Beg out for a decisive battle, away from his bases in Altishahr. For this purpose, Tso needed first of all to get sufficient supplies to the two cities in north-eastern Sinkiang – Barkol and Khitai. To transport grain and munitions over the desert route between the Kansu corridor and these cities, Tso employed at one time 5,000 wagons, 29,000 camels and 5,500 donkeys and mules. Grain supply was an especially difficult problem. Chang Yueh's projected military-agricultural colony in Hami, although reported in 1875 to have reclaimed 19,000 *mou* of land, turned out to be unproductive. The price of grain in Kansu itself was very high to start with. Tso's experience showed that transporting grain through the forbidding desert traverse between Su-chou and Hami and thence over the jagged mountains to Barkol, could mean the loss en route of two-thirds of the amounts supplied. Tso found that a cheaper way to get grain to northern Sinkiang was to purchase as far away as Kuei-hua or Pao-t'ou, as well as at points in Ninghsia, and have the grain carried by camel over a northern route across the steppe directly to Barkol. Tso's armies obtained grain from this source in the crucial summer months of 1876.[91]

Tso's victory in the Sinkiang War must also be ascribed to the fact that he now made increasing use of European weapons or their Chinese imitations. He distributed to his forces European-made rifles, of which at one time he kept 15,000 in reserve. By 1876, the equipment of the Ch'ing forces in Sinkiang included repeating rifles, steel cannon using twelve- or sixteen-pound shells, Krupp needle guns and a European cannon 'that could hit as far as several *li*, especially good for assaulting cavalry and

---

90 Immanuel C. Y. Hsu, 'The late Ch'ing reconquest of Sinkiang: a reappraisal of Tso Tsung-t'ang's role', *Central Asiatic Journal*, 12.1 (1968) 56–8.

91 Ch'in Han-ts'ai, *Tso Wen-hsiang kung*, 92, 127. Chu, *The Moslem Rebellion*, 189. TWHK, *Tsou-kao*, 48.69. TWHK, *Shu-tu*, 15.53b, 16.27; 17.1, 39. That Tso's *t'un-t'ien* experiment did not meet his military needs is documented in Wang Hung-chih, *Tso Tsung-t'ang p'ing hsi-pei hui-luan liang-hsiang chih ch'ou-hua yü chuan-yun yen-chiu* (A study of the planning and transmission of food and funds in Tso Tsung-t'ang's suppression of Muslim Rebellion in the north-west), 96–7.

infantry formations'. Tso's arsenal at Lanchow, besides manufacturing cartridges and shells (some of which did not prove to be entirely satisfactory), even succeeded in 1875 in producing four 'steel rifle-barrelled breechloaders', witnessed by a Russian official. Some of Tso's forces still employed old-style light mortars (*p'i-shan p'ao*), but they seem to have discontinued the use of gingalls.[92]

Tso's victories in Sinkiang owed as much to the weaknesses of his opponents as to his own strength. The Tungans in Urumchi, after their subjugation by Ya'qūb Beg in 1870, had attempted an insurrection two years later. They were again defeated, however. Pai Yen-hu, remembered in Sinkiang legend as an akhund, arrived in northern Sinkiang in 1874, along with Tungan remnants from Su-chou and Tun-huang. He created for himself a base not far from Urumchi, but, like the Sinkiang Tungans, at that juncture declared his allegiance to Ya'qūb Beg.[93] Ya'qūb himself had meanwhile been training his troops with European methods under Turkish instructors. His total army was estimated by a Russian officer who visited Altishahr in 1876–7 to be 45,360 strong. From the new British firm, the Central Asian Trading Company, Ya'qūb had been buying some modern arms. He also had an arsenal which could manufacture 'percussion firearms'. Morale among his forces was low, however. Many recruits had been inducted involuntarily. Desertion, even among the elite Andijani cavalry, was frequent. The hakims of the oasis cities in Altishahr, who were responsible for producing the recruits, were also arbitrarily assessed lump sum payments at irregular intervals, beyond the annual taxes. Discontent was reported among the populace and their headmen and officials.[94]

Even the Russians aided the Ch'ing forces. As early as 1875, a Russian official, while visiting Tso at Lanchow, had offered to supply his forces in northern Sinkiang with grain to the amount of 5 million catties (one catty equals 1.33 pounds) at a very reasonable price. In mid-1876, 3 million catties were delivered at Khitai – not an inconsiderable help, in a period when grain was almost unavailable in the local markets.[95] Meanwhile, under Liu Chin-t'ang and the Manchu general Chin-shun, Tso's offensive in Sinkiang had started.

[92] *TWHK, Shu-tu*, 14.49; 15.41–2; 16.31; 17.14, 15b, 36; 18.26. P. Piassetsky, *Russian travellers in Mongolia and China* (J. Gordon-Cummings, trans.), 2.156–7.
[93] A. N. Kuropatkin, *Kashgaria: historical and geographical sketch of the country; its military strength, industries and trade* (Walter E. Gowan, trans.), 179. Nakada Yoshinobu, 'Ḍōchi nenkan no Sen-kan', 142, n. 13. Lo Cheng-chün, *Tso Wen-hsiang kung nien-p'u*, 6.36b, 44; 7.23b–24. *TWHK, Shu-tu*, 15.59; 16.65b. *TWHK, Tsou-kao*, 49.5b–6.
[94] Kuropatkin, *Kashgaria*, 197–206, 243, 249–50. Louis E. Frechtling, 'Anglo-Russian rivalry in eastern Turkestan, 1863–1881', *Journal of the Royal Central Asian Society*, 26.3 (1939) 483, citing British archives.
[95] *TWHK, Shu-tu*, 15.34; 16.10b; 17.5. Hsu, 'The late Ch'ing', 59.

In a belt of towns north of Urumchi, the Sinkiang Tungans made their last stand as a cohesive group. The heavily walled city of Ku-mu-ti, fifteen miles north-east of Urumchi, was attacked by Liu Chin-t'ang's big German guns. Tso reported that 6,000 Muslims were killed and 215 captured; only a few, including Pai Yen-hu, escaped. The very next day, on 18 August, Urumchi fell without resistance. But at Manas, the siege staged by Chin-shun's less well-equipped force was unsuccessful for nearly two months, until early November. Their city walls battered, several thousand Tungans finally marched out of the gates and were annihilated.[96]

Ya'qūb Beg himself had meanwhile come east to Turfan with some 15,000 men. A force he dispatched to help defend Ku-mu-ti and Urumchi arrived too late and was easily defeated. Tso, who directed battles from his headquarters at Su-chou, noted in a letter to a colleague: 'The Andijani chieftain [Ya'qūb Beg] has fairly good firearms. He has foreign rifles and foreign guns, including cannon using explosive shells [k'ai-hua p'ao]; but his are not as good nor as effective as those in the possession of our government forces. His men are not good marksmen, and when repulsed they simply ran away.'[97]

Ya'qūb built fortifications at Ta-fan-ch'eng, which commanded the northern approaches to the pass between Urumchi and Turfan. But in April, after the snow on the T'ien Shan foothills melted making operations again possible, Liu Chin-t'ang attacked Ta-fan-ch'eng and reduced it in four days.[98] More desertions from Ya'qūb's army ensued and his officials in such oasis cities as Aksu, especially those who had been begs or hakim begs under Ch'ing rule before 1867, now contacted the Ch'ing forces and offered their services. From Su-chou, Tso wrote to Chang Yueh, who was to leave Hami on an invasion of Turfan, saying it was good policy to treat the inhabitants of southern Sinkiang well. 'The Andijanis are tyrannical to their people; government troops should comfort them with benevolence. The Andijanis are greedy in extorting from the people; the government troops should rectify this by being generous.' To Liu Chin-t'ang, Tso wrote that the two chief enemies to catch were Ya'qūb Beg and Pai Yen-hu along with their 'diehard partisans' (ssu-tang). Tso did not find fault with the indigenous inhabitants of Altishahr. After the short Ta-fan-ch'eng campaign, Liu Chin-t'ang was reported by the Russians to have 'acted very judiciously with regard to the prisoners whom he took . . . . His treatment of these men was calculated to have a good influence in favour of the Chinese.'[99]

96 TWHK, Tsou-kao, 49.3–4, 58b.
97 Kuropatkin, Kashgaria, 180–1. TWHK, Shu-tu, 17.11b.
98 TWHK, Shu-tu, 18.9b. TWHK, Tsou-kao, 50.35.
99 Kuropatkin, Kashgaria, 182, 247, 254. TWHK, Shu-tu, 18.22b, 34.

The denouement for Ya'qūb Beg's regime now came swiftly. On 26 April, Chang Yueh entered Turfan, and on the same day Liu Chin-t'ang took Toksun, forty miles to the west. Ya'qūb retreated to Korla and there he died a few days later, under circumstances that remain a mystery. His kingdom quickly disintegrated, while his sons fought over the succession. Ch'ing forces now re-won one oasis town after another. Pai Yen-hu appeared in at least two short battles, but as usual escaped. In December Kashgar was recovered, and Ya'qūb Beg's eldest son as well as Pai Yen-hu retreated into Russian territory. By January 1878, the Ch'ing forces had recovered all of Sinkiang except Ili, still under Russian occupation.[100] The diplomatic crisis over this issue called for a military posture and Tso's forces were long to remain in Sinkiang. Tso himself moved his head-quarters to Hami in June 1880, and in November he left for Peking by order of the court for counsel on war and peace (see chapter 2).

As early as July 1877, Tso had recommended to the throne that Sinkiang be made a province. Even then he had found that Chinese traders, farmers and discharged soldiers were repopulating eastern Sinkiang, and he believed that a regular provincial administration, as opposed to mere dependency status, could bring more order to the area and prevent aggression.[101] Tso's proposal, though modified as to detail, was realized in 1884, when Liu Chin-t'ang became Sinkiang's first governor (serving 1884–91). Peking's most tangible motive was to reduce the cost of maintaining large *yung-ying* armies in Sinkiang, which even after the Ili crisis cost as much as 7.9 million taels annually. The conversion of Sinkiang into a province pre-supposed the reduction of existing troops there to only 31,000 men. They were to be placed under the Green Standard framework and maintained by interprovincial revenue assistance pared down to an annual total of 4.8 million taels (30 per cent of this amount was to be delivered to Kansu, supposedly to cover expenses incurred in that province on behalf of Sinkiang, such as the forwarding of military supplies). Meanwhile, the tax system in Sinkiang was to be reorganized in the hope that the province might eventually be fiscally self-sufficient.[102]

Administratively, Sinkiang was to have a governor residing at Urumchi, and was to be divided into twenty-six counties (*chou* or hsien) and ten sub-prefectures (*t'ing*), six prefectures, and four circuits. A cadastral survey was completed in 1887. From the 11.4 million *mou* of arable land, the tax-in-

---

[100] For the minor clashes with different Muslim groups in Sinkiang in 1878–9, including border raids supposedly inspired by Pai Yen-hu and other Tungans, see Kuo T'ing-i, *Chin-tai Chung-kuo*, 641–57.
[101] *TWHK*, *Tsou-kao*, 50.77.
[102] See Josephine Nailene Chou, 'Frontier studies and changing frontier administration in late Ch'ing China: the case of Sinkiang, 1759–1911' (University of Washington, Ph.D. dissertation, 1976), chs. 6 and 7.

kind to be collected would amount to 20 million catties of grain and 13.9 million catties of hay; total cash levies were set at only 57,952 taels. The begs and hakim begs of the old era were retained under the new system as village heads (*hsiang-yueh*) or as yamen clerks (*shu-li*). They were actually tax collectors and 'in their tyranny over the populace were no different from the begs of the old days'.[103] The collection of likin was also instituted, but this was given up in 1892 because the annual yield had been only slightly over 20,000 taels. Under the treaty of St Petersburg (1881), Russian merchants in Sinkiang enjoyed 'temporary' duty-free status and in fact conducted the bulk of the trade to and from Sinkiang. Since they were exempt from likin, to collect it at all merely encouraged all other merchants to cooperate with the Russians. The hard-won new Chinese province had to be managed tactfully, not least to counter Russian influence that was now backed by military power more formidable than that of Ya'qūb Beg had been.

LI HUNG-CHANG AND COASTAL DEFENCE

As governor-general of Chihli from 1870 to 1895, Li Hung-chang was the principal proponent of China's defence preparations in the coastal areas. Some four-fifths of all Ch'ing government projects undertaken in the name of self-strengthening from 1872 to 1885 were launched under his aegis.[104] Among these was the Peiyang (Northern Sea) Navy, by far the best among the several Ch'ing fleets. Li was also the untitled but acknow-ledged head of the Anhwei Army, apparently the best army in the empire. Li's power was not preponderant, however. Not only did he have to work within the treaty system guarded jealously by foreign powers, he also had to live with the complexities of factional politics at Peking and among the provincial officials, to say nothing of the caprice of the Empress Dowager Tz'u-hsi. Li's activities were further constrained by a cumbersome fiscal system and the vested interests at many levels. His tenure in Chihli was not really secure. When Tso Tsung-t'ang returned from Sinkiang in 1881, Prince Ch'un apparently entertained the idea of having him appointed governor-general in Li's place.[105] The compromises Li had to make in order to keep himself in power unquestionably affected the quality of his innovative programmes; yet without these compromises there would have been no such programmes at all.

A principal source of Li's value to the dynasty and its security lay of

---

[103] Tseng Wen-wu, *Chung-kuo ching-ying Hsi-yü shih* (History of China's management of the Western Region), 364.
[104] For a list of Li's major undertakings, see K. H. Kim, *Japanese perspectives on China's early modernization*, 4–12.
[105] See Liu, 'The limits of regional power', 199, n. 35.

course with the large *yung-ying* forces he founded. By 1871, the Anhwei Army numbered nearly 45,000 troops, of which 13,500 were stationed in Chihli. The rest were located, as directed by the throne, in Shansi (3,000), Hupei (3,500), Kiangsu (4,500) and Shensi (20,000). In subsequent years, Li's troops continued to serve as the major defence force not only in Chihli, but also in several other provinces, in each case under the control of the top official of the province. During the Sino-French War of 1884–5, the Anhwei Army fought in both Tongking and Taiwan; and in the conflict with Japan in 1894–5, Li's troops saw action on every major front.[106]

The Anhwei Army and its problems

Soon after arriving in Chihli in 1870, Li began to integrate Chihli's Western-trained military forces into his own military organization, hopeful of putting these local resources to more effective use. He began with the 6,000 or so Green Standard *lien-chün* troops of the province, attempting to provide them with the same kind of drill and instruction as were available to his own men. He also secured the appointment of Anhwei Army commanders as high officers of the province's Green Standard system, in each case with Peking's approval. Ch'ung-hou's foreign arms and cannon corps, which Li inherited, was given retraining. Li refortified Taku and built a strategic walled city fronting the river ten miles from the estuary. He also expanded the Tientsin Arsenal, having been allocated funds for the purpose from the Tientsin maritime customs.[107]

Li seems to have left the training of the Anhwei Army troops to two or three high commanders (*t'ung-ling*) in Chihli, among whom Chou Sheng-ch'uan (1833–85) was the most energetic and conscientious. A veteran of the Taiping and Nien wars, Chou in the 1870s commanded the best-equipped detachment of the Anhwei Army, with usually more than 10,000 men under him. Like Li, Chou placed great emphasis on modern weapons. Quite knowledgeable about them, he repeatedly recommended that Li purchase Krupp cannon, Remington, Snyder and other modern rifles, Gatling guns and the like. His petitions to Li and instructions to his own troops indicate his awareness of the need not only to acquire and to keep in good condition new Western weapons, but also to provide systematic training in their use.[108]

[106] *Ibid.* 201–2, n. 49. Wang Erh-min, *Huai-chün chih,* 356–61.
[107] Stanley Spector, *Li Hung-chang and the Huai Army,* 169–71. Liu, 'Limits of regional power', 203, n. 52. *LWCK, Tsou-kao,* 17.52; 26.38–41.
[108] Chou Sheng-ch'uan, *Chou Wu-chuang kung i-shu* (Writings of the late Chou Sheng-ch'uan; hereafter *CWCK*), *Chüan-shou* (Introductory section), 34–5, 38b, 40b, 49b; 4.3b–4, 10; *Wai-chi* (Supplement), 1.7.

Unlike some other *yung-ying* commanders, Chou was also convinced of the advantages of Western-style instruction and drill. He not only produced manuals, but often personally supervised the drill of his troops, and he continually exhorted his battalion and company officers to take part in it, too. Money rewards and 'badges of merit' (*kung-p'ai*) were recommended for superior marksmanship; poor performance was punished. Ch'a Lien-piao, one of several Anhwei Army officers whom Li had sent to Germany for training during the 1870s, received Chou's special praise for expertise in Western drill.[109]

Although Chou did not want to employ Western instructors for his force, he often solicited foreign advice. Yet he reacted defensively, at times defiantly, to foreign criticism. He was sceptical, for example, of much of Gordon's military advice when the Victorian hero returned to China during the Ili crisis of 1880, and he even took to task the German officers that Li employed in the 1880s for knowing too little of night fighting and the advantages of prone firing. At times, Chou clearly misunderstood the point of foreign advice – for example, when he characterized Gordon's advocacy of mobile, guerrilla-like tactics as laughable. Yet his charge that Gordon underestimated the importance of sophisticated technology seems fair enough.[110] Chou, like Li, had a sustained interest in applied sciences (especially medicine) and modern means of communication, including the telegraph and railway.

At least by contemporary Chinese standards, the battalions under Chou's command constituted a first-rate force. Japanese, German, British and American accounts of his troops are basically favourable.[111] Yet several times during the early 1880s Chou himself remarked that the force had declined, that after twenty years it had lost its sharpness and acquired a 'twilight air'. The problem lay not so much in equipment as in the *yung-ying* system for the selection and promotion of officers. The experienced officers, Chou complained, lacked vigour, while the new ones lacked knowledge. Although Chou repeatedly admonished his battalion and company officers to participate in drill as strenuously as their troops, the officers continued to resist such involvement. It was, they felt, degrading. Chou's own writings as well as independent foreign observations note this crucial

[109] *CWCK*, 1.2.24; 2.2.1–2, 13; 4.19–24, 26b–27, 32–3, 37; *Wai-chi*, 1.11–23, 44. On the students sent to Germany for military training, see Wang Erh-min, *Huai-chün chih*, 203.

[110] *CWCK*, 1.2.2, 14–18, 34–47; 4.26b–34. On Gordon's new tactical ideas, see *North-China Herald* (hereafter *NCH*) 11 Sept. 1880.

[111] Fukushima Yasumasa, *Rimpō heibi ryaku*, 3.45b–46. Mark Bell, *China, being a military report on the northeastern portions of the provinces of Chihli and Shantung; Nanking and its approaches; Canton and its approaches; etc.*, 2.4, 57–9. Captain Trotter, 'Some remarks on the army of Li Hung-chang', War Office, 33/4 (1880), 127–30.

and persistent problem, but little apparently could be done to remedy it.[112] Chou's officers sought identification with the Ch'ing bureaucracy – even the Green Standard bureaucracy – yet they lacked a sense of professional pride as military personnel.

The essential problem with Chou's army was simply that it remained *yung-ying*. Almost invariably he resisted suggestions by German advisers to modify any detail regarding its structure. Although aware of the universal conscription systems of France and Germany, Chou believed that they were unsuitable to Chinese conditions. His concession to the idea was to suggest that the fifty labourers (*ch'ang-fu*) kept by each battalion of the *yung-ying* armies be given the chance of becoming soldiers.[113] Chou lauded the paternalism and interpersonal rapport that characterized the Anhwei Army. In fact, he had staffed his detachment with many of his own relatives. And although he himself greatly admired the skill and knowledge of foreign-educated officers such as Ch'a Lien-piao, Chou seldom recommended them for the Green Standard titles and offices so coveted by the *yung-ying* officers. There was apparently no objective standard by which Chou and Li made these special recommendations.[114]

Chou's force was comparatively free from the common evils of opium-smoking, gambling and exploiting the populace, but he did have occasion to warn his men and officers regarding morals and morale.[115] The efficiency of the Anhwei Army's training programme must have suffered by the involvement in valuable but non-military tasks. In the seventies and early eighties, Chou's force was frequently involved in construction work, in land reclamation and the establishment of agricultural settlements (*t'un-t'ien*), and in famine relief.[116]

Meanwhile, the Anhwei Army continued to be subject to the vagaries of Peking's fiscal policy. Li Hung-chang's incessant struggle against declining revenues has been amply documented. During the seventies, the entire Anhwei Army's annual income averaged well above 3 million taels, but by the late eighties and early nineties, the yearly average had dwindled to less than 2.5 million.[117] The high price of arms forced Li to continue paying his men (and theoretically the officers, too) at three-quarters of the rate given in the army's original regulations, leaving one-quarter in permanent arrears, to be paid upon retirement. Peking did put pressure on the pro-

[112] *CWCK*, 1.1.19b; 1.2.41b–42; 2.2.22b; 4.36–7; *Wai-chi*, 1. 14b, 18b–21, 23b, 36–7. Bell, *China*, 2.57, 197. Trotter, 'Some remarks on the army of Li Hung-chang', 129.

[113] *CWCK*, 2.2.16b–17; 4.32b–47.

[114] *CWCK*, *Chüan-shou*, 33b, 49, 56; 2.2.1–8, 13; *Wai-chi*, 1.50b. Wang Erh-min, *Huai-chün chih*, 146–7.

[115] See Chou's army song, *CWCK*, *Wai-chi*, 1.50–52. For specific problems, see *ibid*. 37, 39, 41.

[116] *CWCK*, *Chüan-shou*, 31b–56.

[117] Spector, *Li Hung-chang*, ch. 7. Wang Erh-min, *Huai-chün chih*, 275–90.

vinces to see that they delivered to Li, at least at the reduced level, the allotments for the Anhwei Army stationed in Chihli. But Peking also sought to oversee certain details of the army's expenditures. The force was subject to the regulations concerning 'preparing detailed reports on expenditures' (*tsao-ts'e pao-hsiao*) as required by the Board of Revenue, and for a long time the latter refused to consider transport, fuel and the wages of each battalion's *ch'ang-fu* labourers as legitimate disbursements.[118] Despite his being in charge of the empire's best army, Li plainly still looked to Peking for its financial support and consequently had to make all kinds of compromises. It was within this framework, as well as that of the *yung-ying* institutions themselves, that Li made his effort to build a modern navy.

Building a navy

Li's ideas on naval defence crystallized during the 1874 policy debate. Although he still felt that the navy was not quite as important as the army, his proposals reflect a heightened concern with the pressing needs of coastal security, including the safety of Korea, so close to Manchuria and North China. One obvious need was the rapid acquisition of modern war-ships. Li recognized that China's two major shipyards at Shanghai and Foochow were incapable of producing suitable vessels even at prohibitive cost. With the throne's support, he began to purchase ships from abroad. Initially, Robert Hart was his intermediary. In April 1875, Li ordered four gunboats from England through Hart, and in 1877 he ordered four more. But he began to view Hart as a competitor for the control of China's naval programme (see volume 10, chapter 10). Li ordered vessels through indi-viduals other than Hart, and Hart filled orders for provincial administrators other than Li. Both men sought to coordinate arms-buying, each for his own reasons, but neither was successful.[119] Li had never regarded as politically feasible only one naval command for the entire China coast. In the mid-1870s he argued against the Tsungli Yamen's proposal to create a commander-in-chief (*t'ung-shuai*) in charge of the coastal and Yangtze provinces, even though he was the most likely candidate for the position. It was his fate to bear the main burden while grappling with a fragmented military and naval system.

During the seventies and early eighties, Li at Tientsin, the southern commissioner at Nanking, and officials in Fukien and Kwangtung, all became involved in ship-buying. The result, predictably, was chaos. Four

118 Wang Erh-min, *Huai-chün chih*, 284–9. *CWCK*, 2.2.15. *LWCK*, *Tsou-kao*, 25.46.
119 John L. Rawlinson, *China's struggle for naval development, 1839–1895*, 68–81. Stanley F. Wright, *Hart and the Chinese customs*, 467–78.

distinct fleets developed: one each under the northern and southern commissioners, one at the Foochow Navy Yard, and one under the governor-general at Canton. There were also a number of old-style water forces, including the so-called Yangtze Navy (Ch'ang-chiang shui-shih). The arms, ships and training of these naval forces differed greatly not only from area to area, but also within a given jurisdiction. Moreover, lacking central government guidelines (in spite of Hart's suggestions), provincial officials were often duped by unscrupulous arms dealers. Even Li Hung-chang did not escape manipulation. Armament merchants from Europe and America busied themselves around his yamen, his commanders and his foreign advisers.[120]

Li's financial resources were not as large as many had thought. Of the 4-million-tael annual 'maritime defence fund' (*hai-fang ching-fei*) promised by the throne in 1875, by late 1877 Li had received a total of less than 2 million taels, owing to the greater pressure put on the provinces to supply funds for Tso Tsung-t'ang's expedition to Sinkiang. With the cooperation of the southern commissioner, especially Shen Pao-chen, Li none the less was able to expand his fleet. Shen yielded to Li four British gunboats originally ordered by the southern command. In the aftermath of Japan's annexation of Liu-ch'iu in 1879, as well as the Russian naval threat during the Ili crisis, Li obtained imperial approval in 1880–1 to order from Germany the construction of two Stettin-type ironclad battleships and a steel cruiser. They were to be financed from several sources: whatever was received from the 'maritime defence fund'; a million taels to be transferred from the China Merchants' Steam Navigation Company in payment for previous government loans; 600,000 taels donated by the salt merchants of southern Anhwei; and 'borrowing' from maritime customs revenue set aside for diplomatic missions.[121] The German ships, ordered in 1881, did not arrive until after the Sino-French War. Meanwhile, Li planned a large dockyard at Port Arthur (Lü-shun) at the southern tip of Manchuria. Port Arthur and Weihaiwei in Shantung were to serve as his naval bases.

In 1882, the Ch'ing empire could boast some fifty steam warships, about half of them Chinese-built. Li controlled a dozen vessels – eight small gunboats and two 1,350-ton cruisers ordered through Hart from Armstrong and Company in Britain, and two products of the Foochow Navy Yard. The American naval officer, Commodore Robert Shufeldt, whom Li had apparently considered placing in charge of his Peiyang squadron for a time in 1881, praised the British ships he inspected: 'Every modern appliance

---

[120] Chester Holcombe, *China's past and future*, 79–81. William Manchester, *The arms of Krupp 1587–1968*, 150–1.
[121] Rawlinson, *China's struggle*, 71, 73–7. *LWCK, Tsou-kao*, 37.32–4; 40.52–6.

in the art of naval warfare has been placed on these new ships – guns with large calibre and high velocity, moved by hydraulic power, machine guns, electric lights, torpedoes and torpedo boats, engines with twin screws, steel rams, etc., etc. Indeed, the material of this squadron is complete, yet it is evident that in order to be really effective, it needs an intelligent personnel and a thorough organization.'[122]

Li was not unaware of the problem of personnel. His support of the Chinese Educational Mission of 1872 to Hartford, Connecticut, was based in part on the hope that it would provide Western-trained military and navy men. Li was reconciled to the Tsungli Yamen's wish to withdraw the mission in 1881 partly because, contrary to the Burlingame Treaty of 1868, Annapolis and West Point would not admit Chinese for training. In 1876, Li had added an electric torpedo works to the Tientsin Arsenal. During the same year, he sent seven Anhwei Army officers to Germany to learn 'the art of war'. But for Chinese naval officers, the best source in the 1870s was the cadets trained by the Foochow Navy Yard. Although the Kiangnan Arsenal had a small programme of shipboard training, the 'ship and shore' training at Foochow was considered more thorough.[123]

By the autumn of 1873, four cadets from the Foochow shipyard's department of practical navigation had qualified as captain or mate, four more were on a cruise from which they would return with similar ratings, and six others were expected to qualify by the following spring. A year later, fourteen graduates of the engine-room department had been appointed to Foochow-built ships, and seven other qualified engineers awaited assignment. Li was anxious to tap this pool of experts trained by foreigners in China. In 1877, on the recommendation of Li and Shen Pao-chen, the first group of thirty Foochow students was sent to Europe for further training (see volume 10, page 541). Upon their return to China in 1879 and 1880, all obtained important positions on naval vessels or at the Foochow Navy Yard. Several entered Li Hung-chang's service.

After 1875, the Foochow Navy Yard had declined, partly because far fewer foreign personnel were now retained. After the transfer of its first two commissioners, Shen Pao-chen and Ting Jih-ch'ang, the administration of the shipyard fell into less capable hands. Soon it was criticized for incompetence, sloth and corruption. Operating funds were curtailed, reflecting diminished interest on the part of both Peking and provincial officials. An edict of mid-1881 cited a report to the effect that after years of

[122] Letter from Shufeldt to Senator Aaron A. Sargent, 1 Jan. 1882, cited in Paul H. Clyde, comp. *United States policy toward China: diplomatic and public documents 1839–1939*, 163.
[123] Rawlinson, *China's struggle*, 85. Knight Biggerstaff, *The earliest modern government schools in China*, 46–9, 177–8.

expensive training Chinese naval students still did not know how to navigate a ship. Although such accusations were often inspired by conservatism or factional jealousy, the quality of some of the Foochow cadets who returned from Europe did not evoke confidence. Li Hung-chang himself described them as 'more than enough in refinement and elegance but not sufficiently military in spirit'.[124]

Li now sought a more reliable source of Western-trained Chinese naval officers. In 1880–1, he founded his own naval academy (*shui-shih hsueh-t'ang*) at Tientsin. The first dean of the academy was Yen Fu, a Foochow graduate who had received further training at Greenwich and who later gained fame as a great translator of Western works on political thought. Foreign instructors at the new academy included three officials detached from the maritime customs and a young American, L. C. Arlington. In 1882, Li obtained through Hart the services of William Lang, a British naval officer who had assisted in bringing to China some Armstrong ships ordered by Li in the 1870s. Lang served Li for nearly two years as chief inspector (*tsung-ch'a*) of the northern squadron, but he was not attached directly to the Tientsin Naval Academy. As a kind of 'vice-admiral' under Admiral Ting Ju-ch'ang, a former Anhwei Army cavalry officer, Lang's chief task was to train the existing personnel on board Li's warships.[125]

The Tientsin Naval Academy resembled the English division of the Foochow Navy Yard in basic curriculum and structure (see volume 10, pages 532ff). It had two departments – one for deck officers, opened in 1881, and the other for engine-room officers, started in 1882. In the hope of attracting talented individuals who might otherwise succumb to the lure of the examination system, Li emphasized in the academy's public announcement that China's new warships offered young men of upper-class family new opportunities to enter officialdom. Referring to the Foochow graduates, he pointed out that 'scions of respectable families . . . have studied . . . and were made captains. Some are now second- or third-rank officials and have been decorated.'[126] The first students at the new academy graduated after only three years. They continued their training on board ships which were put on alert by the Sino-French War. Although the Peiyang fleet was barely involved in this conflict, Lang was forced by British neutrality to withdraw from China's service. His temporary successor, a German named Siebelin, was totally incompetent. Lang did not resume his work for the Chinese navy until early 1886.

[124] *Ibid*. 249. L*WCK*, *P'eng-liao han-kao*, 19.41.
[125] Fairbank, *The I.G. in Peking*, 1.537–8.
[126] Cited in Rawlinson, *China's struggle*, 92.

THE SINO-FRENCH WAR AND ITS AFTERMATH

The Sino-French War of 1884–5 was the first external test of China's new military and naval programmes of the past two decades. China did not fare well. In two years of sporadic fighting on land and sea, the Chinese suffered heavy losses in funds, manpower, *matériel* and prestige. In the end, China lost her traditional claim of suzerainty over Annam (the Chinese name for Vietnam), and had to allow French commercial penetration into her southern interior provinces (see chapter 2).

France's victory was, however, far from decisive.[127] For over a year prior to China's 'unofficial' declaration of war in 1884, Liu Yung-fu's 'Black Flag' forces effectively harassed the French in Tongking, at times fighting behind entrenched defences or else laying skilful ambushes. In late June 1884, led by Wang Te-pang, one of Tso Tsung-t'ang's former officers, *yung-ying* troops participated in defeating the French near Baclé after three days of heavy fighting. In early August, forces directed by Liu Ming-ch'uan, the famous Anhwei Army commander, repulsed an assault by Admiral Lespès aimed at the Keelung forts on Taiwan, and in October the French suffered another serious setback near Tamsui. In 1885, the Chinese defeated French forces at Chen-nan-kuan on the China–Annam border (23 March), and went on to recapture the important city of Langson and other points in Annam during the next two weeks. In the eyes of some, China was on the verge of victory when peace negotiations forced the cessation of hostilities on 4 April 1885.

In fact, however, China's diplomatic and strategic situation was extremely unfavourable. Relations with both Russia and Japan were strained over China's position in Korea, and there were rumours that the French were planning to assist the Japanese in operations against China herself in the north.[128] Moreover, China laboured under severe administrative and logistical handicaps. While Peking's policy-makers continued to be of two minds, at the provincial level the civil and military authorities were totally confused. This confusion was especially obvious at Foochow, where on 23 August 1884 a 'modern' Chinese-built fleet of eleven ships was destroyed by the French in less than an hour. Following this Foochow debacle, incompetent leadership, poor training and lax discipline in the southern (Nanyang) fleet based in Kiangsu made a fiasco out of the attempt to break Admiral Courbet's blockade of Taiwan.

Even China's successes in land war were somewhat hollow. Liu Yung-

[127] See *inter alia* Lloyd E. Eastman, *Throne and mandarins: China's search for a policy during the Sino-French controversy 1880–1885*, 48–50, 87–90. Kuo T'ing-i, *T'ai-wan shih-shih kai-shuo* (A general account of Taiwan history), 169–74.
[128] Eastman, *Throne and mandarins*, 198–200.

fu's limited victories in Tongking, for example, resulted partly from the dash and pluck of the Black Flags in irregular warfare, but these encounters were also characterized by French indecisiveness, logistical difficulties, tactical errors and simple lack of preparation. When the French launched a concerted offensive at Sontay on 13–16 December 1883, the Black Flags received 'a terrible, if not mortal, blow'. At the occupation of Bacninh by the French four months later, Liu Yung-fu reportedly withdrew without a fight.[129] And even at Langson, often touted as a major Chinese victory, France's defeat seems to have been due less to the efficiency and training of Ch'ing forces than to their overwhelming numerical superiority, and also to French supply problems. Eyewitness accounts indicate that General Negrier's forces were extremely short of ammunition and other supplies, owing to the mass desertion of the French 'coolie corps'. According to one Western observer considered by other foreigners to be sympathetic to the Chinese, Ch'ing forces in the Langson area were well-armed but extremely ill-trained and poorly-led.[130] Victories were won in spite, rather than because, of China's military system, and Chinese casualties were almost invariably much higher than those of the French. Only on Taiwan were Chinese forces able to hold their own man-for-man against the French, thanks largely to the astute preparations by Liu Ming-ch'uan and the tactical ability of a few Anhwei Army officers.[131]

Li Hung-chang has often been blamed for the naval disasters of the Sino-French War. Critics argue that he might have saved the Foochow fleet if he had been willing to send Peiyang ships southward immediately upon request. Both he and the southern commissioner, Tseng Kuo-ch'üan, were warned against being 'province-minded' during the war. But Li's concern with the defence of the north was justified, as even Chang Chih-tung realized – especially in the light of heightened Japanese activities in Korea. Moreover, the French, for their part, had in fact contemplated attacking the north. That they refrained from such a course was due in part to Li's forces there.[132] While Li obviously was not anxious to test his fleet against the French, he did not lack patriotism. China's complex international situation and the entire Ch'ing administrative system militated against a rapid and unified response to the French challenge.

[129] Henri Cordier, *Histoire des relations de la Chine avec les puissances occidentales*, 2.481 ff. *NCH*, 22 May 1885. Henry McAleavy, *Black flags in Vietnam: the story of a Chinese intervention*, 230–1.
[130] *NCH*, 22 May 1885. James G. Scott, 'The Chinese brave', *Asiatic Quarterly Review*, 1 (1886) 226–44.
[131] Liu Ming-ch'uan, *Liu Chuang-su kung tsou-i* (Liu Ming-ch'uan's memorials; hereafter *LCSK*), 3.5, 9–11.
[132] Rawlinson, *China's struggle*, 115. Eastman, *Throne and mandarins*, 166 (n. 5). Chang Chih-tung, *Chang Wen-hsiang kung ch'üan-chi* (Complete collection of Chang Chih-tung's papers; hereafter *CWHK*), 7.13b–14. Cf. Clyde, *United States policy*, 180.

The Navy Yamen and the Peiyang Navy

Despite the belief of some literati-officials that China actually won the land war against France in 1884–5, the deficiencies of the Chinese navy were exposed with glaring clarity. Many called for new efforts, including more centralized coordination. As early as 1870, the elder statesman Tseng Kuo-fan had proposed that naval steamships be put under a single command.[133] In 1885 this idea became suddenly feasible, at least in name. In October 1885, a Navy Yamen was created in Peking, with Prince Ch'un as the principal minister of naval affairs (*tsung-li hai-chün shih-wu ta-ch'en*) and Prince Ch'ing (I-k'uang, 1836–1916) and Li Hung-chang as associate directors (*hui-t'ung pan-li ta-ch'en*). The organization of this 'Chinese Admiralty' was comparable to that of the Tsungli Yamen, with, eventually, six other officials appointed as assistant ministers, but the thirty secretaries serving in nine groups were predominantly Manchus.[134] Prince Ch'un himself seems at this point to have been converted to the cause of self-strengthening. But the Navy Yamen must be viewed as primarily a device by the empress dowager and her favourites to divide with Li Hung-chang the funds which Peking was able to extract from the provinces, ostensibly for an unimpeachable purpose.

In the background was a major event in court politics that took place in April 1884. Acting on a censor's attack on Prince Kung and the Grand Council regarding the responsibility for military reverses in Tongking, Tz'u-hsi, by an edict issued as regent, dismissed the entire Grand Council and replaced them with five new members, headed by Prince Li (Shih-to). Prince Kung was also removed from the Tsungli Yamen along with three other members, its leadership now passing to Prince Ch'ing. It was not appropriate for Prince Ch'un, as the young emperor's father, to serve in the Grand Council or the Tsungli Yamen, but a further edict from Tz'u-hsi required that 'Prince Ch'un be consulted in all important matters of the Grand Council'.[135] Prince Ch'un had among his advisers Sun Yü-wen, an astute and corrupt official of Hanlin Academy background who had gained the trust of Tz'u-hsi and was soon appointed to the Grand Council, serving until 1895, four years after the death of Prince Ch'un himself.[136]

Although siding with the 'war party' during the Ili and the Annam crises,

[133] Wang Chia-chien, 'Ch'ing-chi ti hai-chün ya-men' (The Navy Yamen of the late Ch'ing period), *Chung-kuo li-shih hsueh-hui shih-hsueh chi-k'an*, 5 (1973) 2. Referring to Tseng's plan, Li Hung-chang wrote to him in 1871 that it 'is not feasible at present, therefore the court's intention is to set it aside'; *LWCK, P'eng-liao han-kao*, 11.1.

[134] Wang Chia-chien, 'Ch'ing-chi ti hai-chün ya-men', 14–18.

[135] Wu Hsiang-hsiang, *Wan-Ch'ing kung-t'ing shih-chi* (True account of palace politics during the late Ch'ing), 134–5, 145.

[136] *Ibid.* 131. Chang Ch'i-yun *et al.* eds. *Ch'ing-shih* (History of the Ch'ing dynasty), 6.4902.

Prince Ch'un had shown little interest in naval matters in the past. He had been buying Western munitions for the Peking Field Force, but it was not until early 1881 that he began to show an ambivalent interest in railways and machine-worked mines.[137] His – and Tz'u-hsi's – decision to create the Navy Yamen was undoubtedly influenced by Li Hung-chang's three-week sojourn in Peking in September 1885, when the plan was thrashed out.

Li badly needed funds to maintain and to build up his fleet and related facilities. Although he had signed an agreement with Itō Hirobumi on Korea in April, Li was convinced that a confrontation with Japan over China's closest tributary state was only a matter of time. Prince Ch'un also could see the importance of Korea, but he knew, too, that Prince Kung, his half-brother and political opponent, had incurred Tz'u-hsi's wrath in large measure by opposing the dowager empress's desire for luxurious gardens and palaces. Li had been receiving in the early 1880s only about 600,000 taels annually from the provinces for the 'maritime defence fund'.[138] He saw in the Navy Yamen, with its imperial backing, a device that would compel the provinces to deliver more funds for naval purposes, in addition to the demands of imperial construction work. Li saw no alternative to entering into a grand collusion, as it were, with the throne itself.

The throne now put pressure on the provinces to forward to the Navy Yamen the full amount of 4 million taels annually of the old 'maritime defence fund', even, as the edict stated, at the cost of reducing Green Standard and *yung-ying* troops and getting rid of naval war-junks and worthless old steamships. In addition, a new system of 'maritime defence contributions' (*hai-fang chüan*) was announced. Ranks and offices were openly sold for the purpose, and officials were encouraged to 'repay imperial kindness' (*pao-hsiao*) with funds which could bring them promotion or even forgiveness for past delinquencies.[139]

Tz'u-hsi's priorities were first the rebuilding of the many-pavilioned gardens around the Three Lakes (San-hai) west of the palace, in the centre of Peking, and then the new summer palace outside the city to the northwest. As early as June 1885, she had ordered four wealthy Manchu grandees, including the hapless Ch'ung-hou, to 'assist in the construction work' – that is, to make money donations. Those four and several others together produced 240,000 taels. In January 1886, an edict openly sought funds for the San-hai construction work from the Canton Hoppo and, as a

[137] *YWYT*, 1.117–18. Li Kuo-ch'i, *Chung-kuo tsao-ch'i ti t'ieh-lu ching-ying* (China's early railway enterprises), 57–8.
[138] *LWCK*, *P'eng-liao han-kao*, 20.60. Pao Tsun-p'eng, 'Ch'ing-chi hai-chün ching-fei k'ao-shih' (The truth about late Ch'ing naval funds), *Chung-kuo li-shih hsueh-hui shih-hsueh chi-k'an*, 1 (1969) 21.
[139] Pao Tsun-p'eng, 'Ch'ing-chi hai-chün', 28–31.

'loan', from the Navy Yamen itself. Prince Ch'un wrote to Li Hung-chang in December that 'the Peking Field Force and the Navy Yamen' together had produced 750,000 out of the 2,200,000 taels raised to date, but the work for the lake gardens still required more funds. The prince suggested that Li should arrange more funds. He hoped Li's office would help to arrange a foreign loan of 700,000 taels 'in the name of either a [naval] academy in Peking or some project of your headquarters'. Li could only comply, but he apparently added 227,000 taels to the loan for the purpose of his own fleet. Arranged by Wu T'ing-fang, who was then managing Li's railway project in northern Chihli – a plan which received the Navy Yamen's blessing – the loan was provided by the Tientsin agent of Berliner Handels Gesellschaft. A total of 5 million marks at 5.5 per cent interest was to be repaid over fifteen years from the maritime customs revenues of Tientsin, Newchwang and Chefoo.[140] Li finally surrendered his principle of not raising funds through foreign loans – but only at Peking's behest.

Meanwhile, Li received annually from the Navy Yamen (some of it delivered directly to Tientsin but for the Yamen's account) his share of about 1.5 million taels. He also received smaller, irregular payments from the Yamen to meet special needs. He bought two new British and two German cruisers in 1886–7, ordered through Tseng Chi-tse and Hsu Ching-ch'eng, ministers to Britain and Germany respectively. (Li Feng-pao, former minister to Germany, was accused of receiving a large personal commission while ordering Li's first three German vessels and had been dismissed in 1884.)[141] In 1888, when the new cruisers arrived, Li reorganized his fleet under a set of Regulations for the Peiyang Navy (*Pei-yang hai-chün chang-ch'eng*). This document combined British naval practices, *yung-ying* institutions, and Green Standard terminology. Admiral Ting was to be assisted by two post captains, with the rank of *tsung-ping* or brigade general, each in command of a 7,430-ton ironclad. The cruisers, ranging from 2,300 to 2,850 tons, were entrusted to captains bearing the title of *fu-chiang* or colonel. The captains, while required to obey the admiral, all had complete authority on board their vessels and over the deputies in charge of finances and provisions (*chih-ying wei-yuan*) as well as students in training.[142] With a total of two ironclad battleships, seven cruisers, six gunboats and six torpedo boats, it was an impressive fleet.

However, Li found it impossible to expand his fleet further, even though

[140] *CSL*, Kuang-hsu (hereafter *CSL-KH*) 209.1b; 221.10b–11. Prince Ch'un's letter is printed in *LWCK*, *Hai-chün han-kao* (Letters concerning the Navy Yamen), 2.22b–23; see also 2.36. Charles J. Stanley, *Late Ch'ing Finance: Hu Kuang-yung as an innovator*, 58.
[141] Pao Tsun-p'eng, 'Ch'ing-chi hai-chün', 26–8. Rawlinson, *China's struggle*, 139. *YWYT*, 3.12.
[142] *Pei-yang hai-chün chang-ch'eng* (Regulations of the Peiyang Navy) in *YWYT*, 3.195–264; see also 200, 203, 206, *et passim*.

he was aware that Japan was buying ships of a newer, improved model. The difficulty was financial, for Tz'u-hsi now turned to her plan for the new summer palace north-west of Peking to be named the Garden to Nourish Harmony (I-ho yuan). The exact amount she took for this purpose from the maritime defence funds is difficult to determine. But we find Prince Ch'un writing to Li in November 1888, requesting that he approach the governors-general and governors of several provinces to raise a total of 2 million taels, to be deposited with foreign firms at Tientsin, the interest on which would be used to further construction of the summer palace.[143] This was, however, merely the beginning, for in March–June 1891 the throne approved memorials from the Navy Yamen itself, openly recommending that disbursements for the Garden to Nourish Harmony be met from 'maritime defence donations' and from funds earmarked for diplomatic missions. The emperor himself had, as early as March 1888, proclaimed in an edict that his wish was to please the imperial 'mother' by providing her with suitable surroundings for rest and enjoyment, as the Ch'ien-lung Emperor had done for his mother.[144] Imperial ethics apparently allowed for such juggling of funds for filial purposes.

Meanwhile, the Peiyang Navy continued to receive an annual total of around 1.3 million taels in 1889–90, barely enough to maintain its existing fleet, installations and personnel. In 1890, the Port Arthur naval base, equipped with a 400-foot stone dock supplied with steam power and commanding a harbour dredged to twenty-five feet deep, was completed at a total cost of over 3 million taels (the principal work was done by a French firm). Henceforth, however, Li was not able to add a single ship to his fleet. Apparently because of the increased demands of the empress dowager and the numerous sycophants who profited from the building of the summer palace, the Navy Yamen had recommended to the throne that 'all procurement of ships and weapons be suspended'.[145]

Inadequate funding was, however, not the only difficulty confronting Li's navy. While raising funds and protecting his own power, Li was also seeking a solution to the growing need for qualified persons. With the decline of the Foochow Navy Yard, Li's naval academy at Tientsin emerged as the leading source of trained naval officers of low rank. In 1888, Li reorganized the academy with the assistance of Lang, who had

[143] This request and the disposition of the 2 million taels the provincial officials actually produced is discussed in Wu Hsiang-hsiang, *Chin-tai shih-shih lun-ts'ung* (Studies in modern historical events), 1.151–70, and in Pao Tsun-p'eng, 'Ch'ing-chi hai-chün', 38–42.
[144] *CSL-KH*, 252.1; 294.9; 296.8.
[145] *LWCK, Tsou-kao*, 71.3; 74.33; 76.50; 78.53 (line 1). Spector, *Li Hung-chang*, 231. Wang Chia-chien, 'Lü-shun chien-kang shih-mo' (The establishment of the Port Arthur naval base), *CYCT*, 5 (June 1976) 261.

returned to China in early 1886. The revised regulations for the academy suggest a willingness to bring Chinese naval training abreast of modern Western practice. Entrance requirements were tightened, the course of study was expanded to six years and nine months (including twenty-seven months on board training ships), and regular examinations were scheduled. The regulations also included elaborate stipulations concerning rewards and punishments, promotions, and naval etiquette. Graduates were awarded the status of candidate for sub-lieutenant (*ch'ien-tsung*).[146] 'Ship and shore' training facilities were provided at Port Arthur, Weihaiwei, Taku and other points on the north coast.

Arrogance and fondness for intrigue characterized some of China's top naval personnel, however. Considerable strain existed between senior officers of Foochow background and officers from other areas. Lang's invaluable work was resented by some high officers, whom the British captain described as 'ignorant and envious men'.[147] This tension, together with the ambiguity of Lang's status in the Chinese service, led to an incident which resulted in his resignation in 1890. Lang's departure was extremely unfortunate. Not only did it prompt the exclusion of Chinese students from British naval schools, but it also led to a decline of standards within the Peiyang Navy. Hart bitterly lamented Lang's resignation, although acknowledging that Lang's own inflexibility had got him into trouble.[148]

Meanwhile, officials elsewhere were attempting to improve naval training – invariably with resources even more limited than those of Li. At Canton, Governor-general Chang Chih-tung established in 1887 the Kwangtung Naval and Military Officers' Academy (Shui-lu-shih hsueh-t'ang), based on an already-existing training school begun in 1881 at Whampoa by Governor-general Chang Shu-sheng, a former Anhwei Army commander. Although in theory Chang Chih-tung felt that naval and military training were of equal importance, in practice he placed greater emphasis on the navy because of Kwangtung's coastal location. The nautical part of the Whampoa academy, modelled after the Foochow school and the Tientsin naval academy, drew some of its early faculty and students from both institutions. Wu Chung-hsiang, who had served for ten years as proctor at Foochow and had helped Li Hung-chang set up the Tientsin academy, became the first director of the naval division of Chang Chih-tung's

146 See Rawlinson, *China's struggle*, 158–63. Fairbank, *The I.G. in Peking*, 1.473–4.
147 Rawlinson, *China's struggle*, 165. A. E. J. Cavendish, 'The armed strength(?) of China', *Journal of the Royal United Service Institution*, 42 (June 1898) 720.
148 *NCH*, 6 June, 4 July and 15 Aug. 1890; Fairbank, *The I.G. in Peking*, 1.797, 801. Cf. Yao Hsi-kuang, *Tung-fang ping-shih chi-lueh* (Brief account of war in the East), in Shao Hsun-cheng *et al.* eds. *Chung-Jih chan-cheng* (The Sino-Japanese War; hereafter *CJCC*), 1.62–3.

academy. Although the naval division began with over seventy students in 1887 and subsequently at least thirty-seven pupils were transferred from Foochow, by 1893 a total of only twenty-five cadets remained. Financial limitations may have accounted in part for the sharp fall in the subsidized enrolment, but Chang's dual emphasis on Chinese studies as well as naval techniques must have been distracting to many students. Each day at the academy, cadets were required to read from the classics in order to 'strengthen the root'. While Li Hung-chang's academy at Tientsin would not allow students to take the civil service examinations, Chang Chih-tung would permit his cadets to do so. Chang's transfer in late 1889 was nonetheless a serious setback to the academy. His successor, Li Han-chang, thwarted plans for its expansion, and in 1892–4, the notorious conservative Kang-i, governor of Kwangtung, intentionally destroyed the programme. During Kang-i's tenure the Naval and Military Officers' Academy at Canton was closed, the foreign staff dismissed, and the modern vessels of the Kwangtung flotilla permanently anchored.[149]

At Peking, near the summer palace, the so-called K'un-ming Lake Naval Academy, founded in 1887 to justify the Navy Yamen's expenditure, prepared some forty Manchu students for further training at the Tientsin Naval Academy. The Nanyang Naval Academy, established as late as 1890 by Tseng Kuo-ch'üan in Nanking, was less of a mockery. Modelled on the Tientsin Academy, the Nanyang school was meant to provide officers for the Nanyang fleet. It was reported that its entrance requirements were strict, its curriculum comprehensive, and its instructors (several of them graduates of the Tientsin Academy) competent. But it failed to attract good students and its funds were apparently short. Its first batch of cadets did not graduate until after the Sino-Japanese War.[150]

Liu Ming-ch'uan on Taiwan

In 1885 the Ch'ing court took another step towards strengthening the empire's coastal domain. On 12 October, the very day that the inauguration of the Navy Yamen was announced, an edict decreed that Taiwan, hitherto part of Fukien province and governed by a taotai (circuit intendant), was to be made a separate province with Liu Ming-ch'uan as its first governor. A former Anhwei Army commander, famous for his part in the defeat of the Taipings and the Niens, Liu had been responsible for the

---

149 William Ayers, *Chang Chih-tung and educational reform in China*, 108–13. Biggerstaff, *The earliest modern government schools*, 54–7. Cf. Rawlinson, *China's struggle*, 91.
150 Pao Tsun-p'eng, *Chung-kuo hai-chün shih* (History of the Chinese Navy), 232–6. Biggerstaff, *The earliest modern government schools*, 58–60. NCH, 18 Nov. 1892; 12 Jan. 1894.

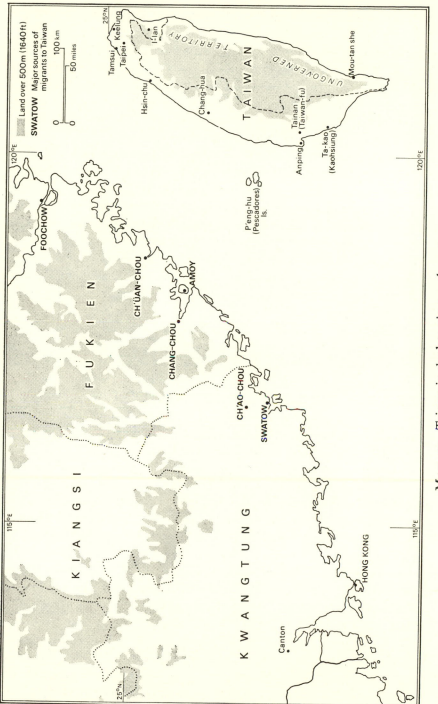

MAP. 12   Taiwan in the late-nineteenth century

defence of Taiwan during the French invasion of 1884–5. In 1884, he had been made governor of Fukien residing on Taiwan. Now he was to be governor of the Ch'ing empire's twentieth province. (The Fukien governor-ship was to be taken up concurrently by the governor-general of Fukien and Chekiang, whose seat was in Foochow.) Liu was to have sole responsi-bility for the administrative personnel on Taiwan and especially in the military field.[151] Belatedly, the Ch'ing court acknowledged the strategic importance of Taiwan and its economic potential.

For nearly two centuries after the Ch'ing conquest of Koxinga's descend-ants on Taiwan in 1683, this island, which the Portuguese called Formosa, was to the Manchus a frontier area too dangerous to abandon. It harboured dissidents who could turn it once more against the dynasty. Peking, how-ever, was not able to enforce the regulations restricting emigration of Chinese from the mainland to Taiwan. The Ch'ing record there since the mid-eighteenth century was one of corrupt but minimal government, punctuated by periodic suppression of uprisings. The shelling of Keelung by British ships during the Opium War and the opening of Tamsui and Ta-kao (the present Kaohsiung) as treaty ports in the early 1860s barely began to awaken Peking to the importance of the island. The episode of Japanese invasion in 1874 did, however, convince a few statesmen of the urgent need to strengthen its defences. Shen Pao-chen, imperial commis-sioner during the crisis of 1874, spent a year on Taiwan, where he installed coastal batteries and planned a machine-worked coal mine at Keelung. Ting Jih-ch'ang, governor of Fukien 1875–7, gave considerable attention to Taiwan matters and made a tour of the island in the winter and spring of 1876–7. He witnessed the first machine excavation of coal from the Keelung mines and it was thanks to him that a thirty-mile telegraph line between Taiwan-fu (Tainan) and Ta-kao was laid in 1877. Ting had ambitious plans for making Taiwan a naval base in South China, and for the construction of a north–south railway on the island to help the movement of troops in wartime. These ideas, though approved in principle by the throne, were not given financial encouragement from any quarter, least of all from the governor-general of Fukien and Chekiang, who controlled Fukien finances. Ting inspected the Green Standard forces on the island and found evidence of flagrant corruption, including a large number of 'troops' that existed only on the rosters. On his recommendation, at least ten Green Standard officers on Taiwan were dismissed, including the brigade general and a colonel. Ting himself was, however, disillusioned about the chance of his innovative ideas being carried out on Taiwan. Since 1875, he had been attacked by literati-officials even more viciously than Li Hung-chang

[151] *CSI-KH*, 215.5. *LCSK*, 6.4.

had been, especially for his views on the need for ironclad battleships and in favour of Western studies. Pleading illness (which was genuine), Ting tendered his resignation from the Fukien governorship, and it was accepted by the throne in April 1878.[152]

Ting's vision for Taiwan was now assumed by Governor Liu. Taking office in the aftermath of the French war, Liu was given more financial support than had been granted to Ting. The maritime customs revenues of Tamsui and Ta-kao (and their respective 'outports', Keelung and Anping), amounting in 1886–9 to 450,000 taels annually and slightly more thereafter, were allocated to maintaining the armies on Taiwan. In 1885, the throne gave Liu another 800,000 taels annually for a limited period of five years. This amount was made up by 440,000 from the Fukien treasury and the Foochow customs and 360,000 from the customs at Shanghai, Kiukiang, Hankow, Ningpo and Canton.[153] Liu's overall revenue was still not abundant, considering his ambitious plans. He was praised by foreigners of the time as a 'phenomenal Chinese official', although the record of his five years of governorship was, in the words of a judicious modern scholar, 'a mixed one at best'.[154]

A disciple of Li Hung-chang regarding the importance of armament, Liu immediately placed large orders in Europe through European and American firms for cannon and rifles. Before Liu's time, Shen Pao-chen, Ting Jih-ch'ang and others had already equipped the forts on Taiwan and the Pescadores with artillery. In the three years beginning 1886, Liu added thirty-one new Armstrong guns to the emplacements on Taiwan and the Pescadores. Some two-thirds of the guns were of nine- to twelve-inch calibre. He also bought ten thousand breechloading rifles and planned an arsenal near Taipei, spending by 1886 over 20,000 taels on the construction of the works, and 84,000 taels on machinery, metal and more rifles and cartridges. With some three hundred employees working under a German engineer, the new arsenal supplied Liu's forces with shells and cartridges, and its machine shop proved extremely valuable when, in 1887, work began on Liu's plan for railways on Taiwan.[155]

As early as 1886, Liu made plans for telegraph connections between

[152] Lü Shih-ch'iang, *Ting Jih-ch'ang*, 229, 283–319. *YWYT*, 1.121, 131. Huang Chia-mu, 'Chung-kuo tien-hsien ti ch'uang-chien' (The first installation of telegraphs in China), *Ta-lu tsa-chih*, 36.6 and 7 (combined issue, April 1968) 179–80.

[153] *LCSK*, 6.1b, 3b; 8.16b, 18b. Cf. Lin Tung-ch'en (Lin Tō-shin), *Taiwan bōeki shi* (History of trade and commerce in Taiwan), 186.

[154] James W. Davidson, *The island of Formosa past and present: history, resources, and commercial prospects*, 247. William M. Speidel, 'The administrative and fiscal reforms of Liu Ming-ch'uan in Taiwan, 1884–1891: foundation for self-strengthening', *JAS*, 35.3 (May 1976) 458.

[155] William M. Speidel, 'Liu Ming-ch'uan in Taiwan, 1884–1891' (Yale University, Ph.D. dissertation, 1967), 165–6, 170–2.

Taipei and Tainan and sea cables linking Taiwan, the Pescadores and Foochow – all considered militarily indispensable. Under contract with the German firm of Telge and Company and the British firm of Jardine, Matheson and Company respectively, both lines were completed in 1887 – five years after Li Hung-chang had founded the Imperial Telegraph Administration at Tientsin.[156]

As in the days when he fought the Taipings and the Niens, Liu Ming-ch'uan, the non-literati commander, was not only receptive to Western weapons, but was also eager to provide his troops with Western-style drill. Liu considered the Green Standard troops on Taiwan to be the worst in the Ch'ing empire. With a nominal quota of 14,000 men, their actual number was only 4,500 in 1884–5. Liu started a retraining programme, selecting new officers from the skilled marksmen in the ranks. Neither was Liu satisfied with the *yung-ying* armies on Taiwan. He memorialized in 1885 that the Hunan and Anhwei armies had become 'strong crossbows, the strength of which has been spent'. He considered fresh training absolutely necessary, especially now that breechloading firearms had been introduced. 'Unless the sights of the firearms are set accurately, the aim cannot be gauged for either distance or height: to have a rifle would then be the same as having none.'[157]

In late 1885, there had been sixteen Hunan Army (Ch'u-yung) battalions on Taiwan, under Liu Ao, formerly one of Tso Tsung-t'ang's commanders, who served as the Taiwan taotai 1881–5. Liu Ming-ch'uan now took control of Liu Ao's Hunanese force, as well as ten battalions of the Anhwei Army which he himself had brought to Taiwan. Replenishment of the Anhwei Army, chiefly from Liu Ming-ch'uan's native Ho-fei, gave him a total by 1888 of forty-three battalions or about 22,000 men. Two European instructors drilled his troops.[158]

Liu realized that he could not rely on the 800,000-tael annual revenue-assistance for more than the stipulated five years. He saw a chance, however, of producing revenue by making the real owners of agricultural land pay more taxes. This reform called first of all for a cadastral survey, which was never carried out on a province-wide basis during the Ch'ing dynasty except in newly created Sinkiang and Taiwan. Having in mind the entrenched vested interests in rural China, Li Hung-chang had remarked categorically in 1870, after he became governor-general of Chihli, 'a cadastral survey for an entire province is certainly impossible to accom-

[156] Samuel C. Chu, 'Liu Ming-ch'uan and the modernization of Taiwan', *JAS*, 23.1 (Nov. 1963) 47–8.
[157] *LCSK*, 2.11–14, 20.
[158] Speidel, 'The administrative and fiscal reforms', 450, n. 46. Speidel, 'Liu Ming-ch'uan', 168, 177–8. Kuo T'ing-i, *T'ai-wan shih-shih kai-shuo*, 202.

plish'.[159] However, Liu Ming-ch'uan set out in 1886 to do just that, with the result that the estimated income from Taiwan's land tax was raised from 183,366 to 674,468 taels by 1888.

Two years before this date, Liu had created Tax Assessment Bureaux (Ch'ing-fu chü), one in Taipei and one in Tainan, to compile family-by-family landholding registers. He was actually capitalizing on the island's two centuries of pioneering settlement by immigrants from across the Formosa strait. A comparatively small number of men (some say 40,000 in all Taiwan) had since the early eighteenth century secured patents from the government for the reclamation of large tracts of land.[160] However, few of these patent-holders actually engaged in reclamation themselves. Instead they divided each tract among several developers, who, in turn, rented it to tenants. As the immigrants came in greater numbers and the land value increased, many developers actually became large absentee landlords – living in the cities and receiving 40–60 per cent of the crop produced by the tenants. Such landlords were known on Taiwan as *hsiao-tsu hu* (lit., small-rent households): they were supposed to pay to the patent-holders (who were honoured as *ta-tsu hu*, or big-rent households) some 10 per cent of the crop on the land originally received. According to tradition, only the patent-holder paid the land tax. Since the Ch'ing bureaucracy on Taiwan was notoriously ineffective, patent-holders often evaded paying the moderate taxes due. Liu Ming-ch'uan was aghast to find, for example, that the entire county of Tamsui produced only 780 taels of land tax annually! Many patent-holding families had, moreover, declined, and the *hsiao-tsu hu*, who were often very large landlords with gentry status, paid no taxes at all.

At least in northern Taiwan, Liu won the cooperation of the local gentry leaders and carried out the tax reform smoothly. The *hsiao-tsu hu*, being the actual landowners, were given the deeds and assessed annual taxes on their land. The theoretical validity of the original patent remained, but the *hsiao-tsu hu*'s annual payments to the patent-holders were reduced by 40 per cent. The new system was accepted in northern Taiwan as early as 1888. In central and southern Taiwan, however, reform encountered resistance partly because of abuses in the land survey. In 1888, there was a serious uprising in Chang-hua, led by Shih Chiu-tuan, a local landowner.[161] Although the new taxes eventually prevailed in the central plain, Liu

[159] *LWCK, P'eng-liao han-kao*, 10.35b.
[160] This account of Liu's land-tax reform and its background is based on Speidel, 'The administrative and fiscal reforms', 452–4. Ramon H. Myers, 'Taiwan under Ch'ing imperial rule, 1684–1895: the traditional economy', *Journal of the Institute of Chinese Studies of the Chinese University of Hong Kong*, 5.2 (Dec. 1972) 383–6. Edgar B. Wickberg, 'Late nineteenth century land tenure in Taiwan', in Leonard H. D. Gordon, ed. *Taiwan: studies in Chinese local history*, esp. 86–8.   [161] See Speidel, 'The administrative and fiscal reforms', 454 (n. 64).

Ming-ch'uan found it necessary to compromise with the even more entrenched interests in southern Taiwan, agreeing to a formula under which some patent-holders retained their ties to the land while sharing with the *hsiao-tsu hu* the payment of the newly assessed land tax.

Meanwhile, Liu sought to tap the island's commercial resources. He imposed a variety of likin taxes, many of which had, however, to be given up because of foreign merchants' opposition. He taxed camphor at each distillery in the hills, although he had to allow foreign merchants to export it likin-free. Such sources of income, together with the maritime customs and the retained portion of the land tax (that is, *p'ing-yü*, the 'weight differential' in the silver to which the taxes collected in copper were converted), gave Taiwan under Liu Ming-ch'uan a total revenue of 2.12 million taels even when the interprovincial revenue assistance ceased after 1889.[162]

With these still limited resources Liu pursued many plans for improvement, such as railways, shipping, coal mines, a school of Western learning, and foreign instruction for his armies. But unfortunately at a time when all China should have been preparing for defence against Japan, Liu's forces had to be employed in the densely wooded mountains of Taiwan, fighting 'ferocious savages'.

Conflict between the Taiwanese aborigines and the Han settlers was no doubt inevitable. As the immigrants increased to an estimated 2.5 million by the 1880s, there was naturally a struggle for the arable land of the lower hills, where the aborigines were destroyed, displaced or subdued. The time-serving Ch'ing officials who were willing to come to Taiwan had never developed a satisfactory 'mountain policy'. Conflict between settlers and 'savages' was perpetual, and the latter, who bought firearms and were adept at defending the mountain passes, often swept down on the plains to kill in vengeance.[163] Partly to facilitate the war against them and partly to gain access to camphor and timber, Liu built a road from the east coast to the west, through the mountains, ending in Chang-hua. As the war intensified, hundreds of Ch'ing troops and several of the best Anhwei Army officers lost their lives to disease in the malarial areas. Altogether Liu conducted forty campaigns against the 'savages' during his tenure on Taiwan. Despite the use of machine guns and field pieces, his forces suffered major defeats – for example in 1889 near I-lan, when 273 officers and men were lost, including Liu's own nephew. The morale of the Ch'ing troops was low,[164] there was little loot awaiting them in the wilderness –

162 *LCSK*, 8.21b–22; cf. 20b.
163 See *inter alia* Davidson, *The island of Formosa*, 114, 135 ff., 252.
164 Speidel, 'Liu Ming-ch'uan', 288–94.

which made this aborigine war altogether different from the campaigns against the Taipings, the Niens or the Muslims.

Governor Liu was both conscientious and innovative. In 1885, he impeached the *taotai* Liu Ao for corruption and so antagonized the bureaucratic and landowning interests in the Tainan area. To attract civil servants of higher quality to Taiwan, he proposed to the throne in 1886 that, as in Sinkiang, officials who served with merit for longer than three years should be given priority for promotion when they returned to the mainland. Liu had to choose his prefects and magistrates from the list of candidates for Taiwan posts prepared by the Board of Civil Appointments. In 1888, however, he requested that in view of the special circumstances on Taiwan, for a period of ten years the county magistrates there should be chosen at the governor's recommendation and especially from among persons experienced in the cadastral survey. The board felt a ten-year suspension of the rules was too long, but the throne let him choose his county magistrates for three years.[165]

Like Li Hung-chang, Liu set up special agencies called 'bureaux' (*chü*) to take charge of his new undertakings. In 1889, however, the court emphatically reiterated an 1885 edict, asking the provinces to reduce the number and personnel of such bureaux, and for those which were really indispensable, to report their finances regularly to the Board of Revenue.[166] When the court's policy was really focused on the palace gardens of Peking, Liu's innovations could hardly receive imperial support. Even Li Hung-chang's China Merchants' Steam Navigation Company had to repay in the 1880s the government loans received in the 1870s.[167]

By 1890, Liu Ming-ch'uan, like Ting Jih-ch'ang before him, was losing hope. Even his remarkable cadastral survey was attacked by censors, on the grounds that it had provoked rebellion in 1888.[168] Liu had established a Commercial Affairs Bureau (Shang-wu chü, known in English as the Formosan Trading Company), financed by both Taiwan government capital and private subscriptions, especially from Chinese in Singapore. Although it owned two new British-built steamships in 1888, it steadily lost money in competition with foreign firms and even with the China Merchants' Steam Navigation Company. In 1888 Liu reorganized the famous coal mine at Keelung as a government agency – The Keelung Government Colliery (Chi-lung kuan mei ch'ang). Yet it lacked working

[165] *LCSK*, 6.5b; 9.17b, 23. For the imperial rescript on Liu's further memorial of 1889, see 9.23b.
[166] *CSL-KH*, 276.13–14.
[167] See Albert Feuerwerker, *China's early industrialization: Sheng Hsuan-huai (1844–1916) and mandarin enterprise*, 133, table 11.
[168] Speidel, 'Liu Ming-ch'uan', 405, n. 14; also *LCSK*, 1.20.

capital, and Liu was ready to accept an investment of 1.4 million taels by a British merchant, on the understanding that for twenty years the enterprise would have a monopoly of machine extraction of kerosene as well as coal on Taiwan. Peking, however, refused to approve. To salvage the Keelung mines, in June 1890 Liu put a new proposal to the throne: that the mines be worked by a group of Chinese merchants, headed by a Cantonese. The Taiwan government would furnish one-third of the enlarged capital and receive a corresponding share of the profits. It was a measure of Liu's loss of standing in Peking – and also perhaps of the decline in influence of his patron, Li Hung-chang – that he was severely criticized by the Tsungli Yamen as well as the Board of Revenue for reviving a proposal already rejected by the court: it was suspected that foreigners were behind the investors. An edict of October 1890 punished Liu Ming-ch'uan by 'dismissal from his post while retaining its duties' (*ko-chih liu-jen*).[169]

In June 1891, when Liu resigned as governor of Taiwan, he had perhaps one consolation. Ever since 1880 he had championed railways for China, and in 1887 he had obtained the throne's approval to construct railways on Taiwan. Under 'government supervision and merchant operation' (*kuan-tu shang-pan*), a million taels had been raised by Liu's commercial bureau from Overseas Chinese. The work had proceeded very slowly, but in June 1891, 15 miles of the 20-mile track between Taipei and Keelung had been laid, and two years later, under Liu's successor Shao Yu-lien, a 42-mile track between Taipei and Hsin-chu was also completed.[170] It was a slow start, but in 1894 there were only 319 miles of railway in all China, including Taiwan. In Chihli, it had taken Li Hung-chang two decades to build a railway of 257 miles.

Military academies and their problems

China's first academy to train personnel for land war, the Tientsin Military Academy (*wu-pei hsueh-t'ang*), was not established until 1885, five years after the founding of the naval academy there. This tardy start is hard to understand – especially in the light of Li Hung-chang's efforts in the seventies to send Chinese military trainees to both Europe and the United States.[171] The American general, Emory Upton, had suggested to Li as early as 1875 that a Chinese military academy be established, but Li rejected as too

169 Chu, 'Liu Ming-ch'uan', 40-2, 44-6. Huang Chia-mu, *Chia-wu chan-ch'ien shih T'ai-wan mei-wu* (Coal mining in Taiwan prior to the war of 1894), 223-35. *CSL-KH*, 288.89.
170 Chu, 'Liu Ming-ch'uan', 50. Cf. H. B. Morse, *The international relations of the Chinese empire*, 3.77-8.
171 On the failure to get Chinese students into West Point, see US Department of State, *Foreign relations of the United States*, 1875, pt 1, 227-8, and Holcombe, *China's past and future*, 82-3.

expensive Upton's proposal for nine 'professors and instructors' from the United States Army and a six-year programme of instruction in the English language. In 1880, Gordon also urged Li to set up a military academy, but only in 1884 did he seriously pursue the idea, evidently because of the Sino-French War, the arrival in China of some German military instructors, and the changing attitude of some of his own commanders, notably Chou Sheng-ch'uan.[172]

Delay in establishing a military academy was undoubtedly due to the resistance of most *yung-ying* officers to the injection of new elements into their units. The new-style navy threatened fewer vested interests, although Li's early naval officers were said to have very quickly developed a prejudice against newly trained cadets. Even Chou Sheng-ch'uan indicated that while he favoured a Chinese military academy on the Western model, he felt nonetheless that it was 'not necessary to train many commanders (*chiang-ling*)'.[173] Chou was basically satisfied with the Anhwei Army's command structure, and he knew that many veteran officers would resist personnel changes.

Li's initial proposal for an academy was very modest. He planned to train only about one hundred lower officers and some troops selected from the Anhwei Army and the *lien-chün* battalions, together with some civil functionaries (*wen-yuan*) who were 'willing to learn about military affairs'. The compressed curriculum consisted of astronomy, geography, science, surveying, drafting, mathematics, fortifications and military drill and operations. Half a dozen German officers began teaching at the school. Instruction was primarily in German, with the help of translators drawn from the Peking Interpreters' College (T'ung-wen kuan) and elsewhere. Li expected the students to complete their education in one year (it actually took two), after which they would return to their original units to impart their newly acquired knowledge to their comrades. In all, about 1,500 'cadets' were trained in this way from 1885 to 1900. Most served only as instructors; only a few became officers.[174]

In the spring of 1887, Li added a five-year programme designed to produce officers. Applicants were limited in age to between thirteen and sixteen, and were required to have had a Chinese education appropriate for their years. This qualification was tested by an entrance examination. Forty

[172] Peter S. Michie, *The life and letters of Emory Upton*, 290–8, 309–10. *YWYT*, 3.552. Wang Chia-chien, 'Pei-yang wu-pei hsueh-t'ang ti ch'uang-she chi ch'i ying-hsiang' (The Peiyang Military Academy: its creation and influence), *SFLS*, 4 (April 1976) 319–20.

[173] Wang Chia-chien, 'Pei-yang wu-pei hsueh-t'ang', 324, 339 (n. 18), 341 (n. 36). Biggerstaff, *The earliest modern government schools*, 85.

[174] Biggerstaff, *The earliest modern government schools*, 61–2. Wang Chia-chien, 'Pei-yang wu-pei hsueh-t'ang', 7–8. *LWCK*, *Tsou-kao*, 53.42–4; 74–23. Cavendish, 'The armed strength(?) of China', 717.

students were accepted initially. Each had to pledge to be at the academy for five consecutive years and not to take the civil service examinations or get married. Leave was granted for mourning a parent, but only for a short period.[175] The five-year course was comparatively rigorous: the first three years included a foreign language (German or English), arithmetic, algebra, geometry, mechanics, astronomy, natural science, geography, map-making, Chinese history and the classics; the last two included gunnery, military drill, fortifications and other technical subjects. Periodic examinations tested proficiency, determined class standing, and provided the basis for progress reports to the throne. This general approach was also followed at Li's military training schools at Weihaiwei and Shanhaikuan, which may be considered extensions of the Tientsin programme.[176]

Like the Tientsin naval academy, the military academy was financed by the dwindling Peiyang 'maritime defence fund'. Though plagued by poor and corrupt management, difficulties with foreign instructors, the language barrier, and problems with students, many important figures in China's early twentieth-century history were trained there.[177]

The only other military academy established prior to 1894 was the military division of Chang Chih-tung's Kwangtung Naval and Military Officers' Academy. In 1885 Chang had begun using German instructors in his newly organized *yung-ying* force – called the Kwangtung Victorious Army (Kuang-sheng chün). One or two of these German officers taught in the military school, but Chinese instructors did most of the teaching. Chang was apparently satisfied with their instruction, for he later selected graduates to serve as officers in his Self-Strengthening Army (Tzu-ch'iang chün), organized in Nanking in early 1896, and engaged instructors from the school to teach at his Hupei Military Academy (*wu-pei hsueh-t'ang*), founded at Wuchang later the same year.[178]

On the eve of the Sino-Japanese War, China appeared, to undiscerning observers, to possess respectable military and naval forces. Praise for Li Hung-chang's Anhwei Army and other Chinese forces was not uncommon, and the Peiyang Navy elicited considerable favourable comment.[179] When war between China and Japan appeared likely, most Westerners thought China had the advantage. Her army was vast, and her navy both out-

---

175 *NCH*, 13 April 1887.

176 *Ibid*. Biggerstaff, *The earliest modern government schools*, 63. Wang Chia-chien, 'Pei-yang wu-pei hsueh-t'ang', 8.

177 Wang Chia-chien, 'Pei-yang wu-pei hsueh-t'ang', 9–19. Holcombe, *China's past and future*, 84–5.

178 Ayers, *Chang Chih-tung*, 110–13 (esp. n. 42). Biggerstaff, *The earliest modern government schools*, 64–5.

179 See *inter alia*, Anon. 'The Chinese and Japanese armies', *Journal of the Military Service Institution of the United States*, 15 (1894) 255–9. *NCH*, 6 June 1890, 29 June, and 27 July 1894.

numbered and outweighed Japan's. The German general staff considered a Japanese victory improbable. In an interview with Reuter, William Lang predicted defeat for Japan. Lang thought that the Chinese navy was well-drilled, the ships were fit, the artillery was at least adequate, and the coastal forts were strong. Weihaiwei, he said, was impregnable. Although Lang emphasized that everything depended on how China's forces were led, he had faith that 'in the end, there is no doubt that Japan must be utterly crushed'.[180]

THE DISASTER OF THE SINO-JAPANESE WAR

The illusion of China's military and naval superiority was quickly dispelled by Japan's rapid thrust into Korea, Manchuria and China proper. Unlike the Sino-French War with its vacillations of policy on both sides, the Sino-Japanese War was dominated from the outset by Japan's systematic campaign that aimed at nothing less than the capture of Peking. The outcome starkly dramatized the failure of China's military preparations and the effectiveness of Japan's. Since 1868, Japan's army and navy building had both benefited from and contributed to modernizing change in other sectors of her society. By 1872, conscription had been introduced stimulating the further growth of national consciousness, while a centralized system of military and naval education sent officers abroad and established schools at home. In 1878, an independent general staff was created, and in 1883, a staff college. Close cooperation was ensured between the army and navy.[181]

Foreign advisers and instructors, including the Englishman John Ingles and the German Jacob Meckel, did much to bring the Japanese armed forces to a high state of efficiency. Meckel helped to reorganize the war ministry, refine the general staff, improve military education, and develop logistics and medical services. He also helped to restructure the army into divisions and taught the Japanese 'the demands of full-scale mobilization, which included a strategic railway network, a new conscription act, and improved staff exercises'. Thus he achieved far more in Japan than his approximate counterpart in China, Constantin von Hanneken. Ingles also was able to do more than his counterpart Captain Lang.[182]

[180] NCH, 21 Sept. 1894. Rawlinson, China's struggle, 162, 169. Ernst Presseisen, Before aggression: Europeans prepare the Japanese army, 140–1.
[181] Aritomo Yamagata, 'The Japanese army', in Shigenobu Ōkuma, ed. Fifty years of new Japan, 1.209. Richard J. Smith, 'Reflections on the comparative study of modernization in China and Japan: military aspects', Journal of the Hong Kong Branch of the Royal Asiatic Society, 16 (1976) 11–23.
[182] See Presseisen, Before aggression, esp. chs. 3 and 4. T. A. Brassey, ed. The naval annual, 1895, 91. Frederick T. Jane, The imperial Japanese navy, 36. Alfred Vagts, Defense and diplomacy: the

Even prior to the declaration of war, the Japanese had shown at Sŏnghwan (in Chinese: Ch'eng-huan), Korea, in late July, that Japan's 'generals knew how to command, and that the army organization worked smoothly, even in a country unprovided with good roads'. Throughout the war, reports from French, English and other foreign observers repeatedly praised the Japanese for their strategic and tactical acumen, effective training, discipline, valour, *esprit de corps*, and the excellence of their transport, commissariat and medical facilities. China did not simply lose the war through weakness; Japan won it through strength.

After August, the Japanese offensive in Korea moved rapidly.[183] On 10 August the Japanese fleet harassed Port Arthur and Weihaiwei in order to cover troop transport; the Chinese navy failed to respond to the challenge. In little over a month, Japanese troops had captured the key city of P'yŏng'yang (16 September), taking this heavily defended outpost in a single day and driving the Chinese forces under Yeh Chih-ch'ao and others of the Anhwei Army across the Yalu River. On the very next day the Japanese fleet decisively defeated the Chinese near the mouth of the Yalu (see chapter 2). This victory, brilliantly engineered by Admiral Itō Sukenori, destroyed several Chinese ships and gave the Japanese command of the seas, allowing them to land their armies at will and to devise especially bold campaign plans.

During October the Japanese drove into Manchuria, defeating the Chinese at Chiu-lien-ch'eng and Feng-huang-ch'eng, near the Yalu. In early November, they captured Chin-chou and the heavily fortified Chinese position at Dairen (Ta-lien) Bay, where they acquired large stores of military supplies, including 621 rifles, 129 guns, over 33 million rounds of small-arms ammunition, and nearly 2.5 million rounds of cannon shells.[184] The loss of Dairen Bay greatly facilitated Japanese operations against the supposedly 'impregnable' Chinese naval base at Port Arthur,

soldier and the conduct of foreign relations, 185. Wang Shu-huai, *Wai-jen yü Wu-hsu pien-fa* (Foreigners and the reform movement of 1898), 89 (n. 28).

[183] The following sketch of the war is based primarily on Yao Hsi-kuang, *Tung-fang ping-shih*, in *CJCC*, 1.1–108. *Nisshin sensō jikki* (Actual record of the Japan–Ch'ing War), Chinese translation of excerpts in *CJCC*, 1.218–86. Japan, Imperial General Staff, *History of the war between Japan and China*, vol. 1. E. Bujac, *Précis de quelques campagnes contemporaines*, vol. 2, *La Guerre sino-japonaise*. Kuo Sung-p'ing, 'Chinese reaction to foreign encroachment' (Columbia University, Ph.D. dissertation, 1953). Cheng Ch'ang-kan, *Chung-Jih chia-wu chan-cheng* (The Sino-Japanese War of 1894). Liu Feng-han, 'Chia-wu chan-cheng shuang-fang ping-li ti fen-hsi' (An analysis of the strength of both belligerents during the war of 1894), *Chung-kuo i-chou*, 829 (14 March 1966) 13–16, 830 (21 March 1966) 11–14. N. W. H. DuBoulay, *An epitome of the China-Japanese War, 1894–1895*. Richard Wallach, 'The war in the East', *Proceedings of the United States Naval Institute*, 21.4 (1895) 691–739. For Japanese works consulted, see the bibliographical essay for this chapter.

[184] Vladimir (pseud. for Zenone Volpicelli), *The China-Japan War compiled from Japanese, Chinese, and foreign sources*, 215, 223, 231. Yao Hsi-kuang, *Tung-fang ping-shih*, in *CJCC*, 1.34–6. *Nisshin sensō*, in *CJCC*, 1.246–56.

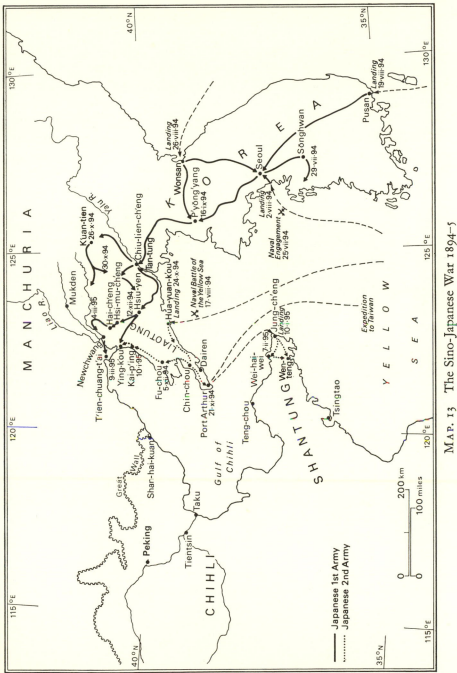

MAP. 13 The Sino-Japanese War 1894–5

Japanese 1st Army
Japanese 2nd Army

40°N
35°N

130°E
125°E
120°E
115°E

Landing
19·viii·94
Pusan

Landing
26·viii·94
Wonsan

Songhwan
29·vii·94

Seoul

K O R E A

P'yŏng'yang
16·ix·94

Landing
2·viii·94

Naval
Engagement
25·vii·94

Kuan-tien
26·x·94

Chiu-lien-cheng

Yalu R.

30·x·94

Mukden

Hai-ch'eng
4·iii·95
Hsi-mu-ch'eng
12·xii·94
Hsiu-yen

Han-tung

Hua-yuan-kou
Landing 24·x·94

Naval Battle of
the Yellow Sea
17·viii·94

L I A O T U N G

Newchwang

T'ien-chuang-t'ai
9·iii·95
Ying-kou
10·i·95
Kai-p'ing
10·i·95

Fu-chou
5·xi·94
Chin-chou

Dairen

Port Arthur
21·xi·94

Y E L L O W

Expedition
to Taiwan

S E A

M A N C H U R I A

Liao R.

Wei-hai-
wei 7·ii·95
Jung-ch'eng
Wen-
teng Landing
10·i·95

Teng-chou

Tsingtao

S H A N T U N G

Gulf of
Chihli

Great Wall

Shan-hai-kuan

Taku

Tientsin

Peking

C H I H L I

35°N
40°N

120°E
125°E
115°E

200 km

100 miles

0

which fell on 21 November 1894. This not only gained for Japan the best dockyard in East Asia, but also severely demoralized Chinese military forces and threw Peking into a panic.

In Manchuria during late November and early December the Japanese then captured several important positions, including Fu-chou, Hsi-mu-ch'eng and Hai-ch'eng. The loss of Hai-ch'eng, on 13 December 1894, was especially serious. Not only did it hinder communications and fragment Chinese military strength, it also made Mukden itself vulnerable. Throughout the remainder of the war, Ch'ing forces repeatedly attempted to retake Hai-ch'eng, often at great cost, but never with success.

In early January 1895, the occupation of Kai-p'ing facilitated communications between the First and Second Japanese Armies, and gave Japan control over all inland and coastal routes to China from the Liaotung Peninsula. Later in the month, the Japanese began attacking Shantung as part of a large pincer movement aimed at Peking. They bombarded Teng-chou in a diversionary attack on 18 January, invaded Jung-ch'eng two days later, and finally captured Weihaiwei after a fortnight of sometimes heavy fighting. The Weihaiwei campaign provided, in the words of a French observer, a 'remarkable example' of close cooperation between land and naval forces. Japan 'exhibited all the methods of modern warfare by land and sea; dashing assaults on the forts, skilful handling of guns and ships, [and] daring torpedo attacks which strewed the harbour with sunken hulls'.[185]

The fall of Weihaiwei was a crushing blow to the Chinese. What was left of the Peiyang fleet was destroyed or taken by the Japanese, and Admiral Ting Ju-ch'ang and several other military and naval commanders committed suicide. From Shantung the way was now open for a quick advance on Peking. In the midst of Chinese peace overtures, the fighting continued in both Shantung and Manchuria. During the latter half of February, Ch'ing forces under Sung Ch'ing (including large detachments of the Anhwei Army) and others battled furiously for the recovery of Hai-ch'eng. Although at times outnumbered by the Chinese by more than two to one (about 60,000 to 25,000), the Japanese held the city tenaciously, inflicting heavy losses. The Chinese achieved a few tactical successes, but not major victories.[186]

During the first two weeks of March, Japanese land forces in Manchuria took Newchwang, Ying-k'ou and T'ien-chuang-t'ai. Soon thereafter, the Japanese also began the invasion of Taiwan, capturing P'eng-hu island in

---

[185] Lieutenant Sauvage, *La Guerre sino-japonaise 1894–1895*, 204. Vladimir, *The China-Japan War*, 303–4. *Nisshin sensō*, in *CJCC*, 1.269–75.

[186] *Nisshin sensō*, in *CJCC*, 1.275–8. DuBoulay, *An epitome*, 63–5. Sauvage, *La Guerre*, 220–7.

the Pescadores on 25 March. At the time of the signing of the Treaty of Shimonoseki (17 April 1895), Japan was poised for a two-pronged attack on Peking from southern Manchuria and the Shantung peninsula. Although the Chinese had reportedly massed from 150,000 to 200,000 troops in northern Chihli, it is unlikely that they could have held Peking.

From beginning to end, the Sino-Japanese War had been an unmitigated disaster. In the peace negotiations, China's most effective bargaining point was not the remaining strength of her military and naval forces, but rather Japanese guilt over the wounding of Li Hung-chang by a Japanese fanatic.[187]

[187] Yao Hsi-kuang, *Tung-fang ping-shih*, in *CJCC*, 1.90–108. DuBoulay, *An epitome*, 62, 70–1 Sauvage, *La Guerre*, 229. *Nisshin sensō*, in *CJCC*, 1.281–5.

CHAPTER 5

INTELLECTUAL CHANGE AND THE REFORM MOVEMENT, 1890-8

BACKGROUND – ASPECTS OF THE WESTERN IMPACT

In China in the 1890s there began an intellectual ferment which not only generated a movement for political reform but also ushered in a new era of socio-cultural change. This ferment, to be sure, owed a great deal to indigenous developments within the Chinese cultural tradition in the late nineteenth century. In Confucianism the reactions against the vogue of Han learning continued to reverberate among Chinese scholars, and there was a revival of interest in Buddhism and classical non-Confucian philosophies. All these developments, however, were more or less outgrowths of the intellectual changes that had already begun in the early nineteenth century.[1] What transformed these indigenous developments into an intellectual ferment was the change provoked by Western expansion.

This had two primary aspects. The obvious one was the coercion and exploitation that Western nations imposed on China – imperialism. The other, a transformative one, was the variety of changes brought to China through contact with the West. The 1890s saw new developments in both areas.

By 1890 China had had to confront half a century of imperialist expansion, but now imperialist aggression entered a new and climactic stage. In the wake of China's humiliating defeat by Japan, the Western powers, spearheaded by France's claim to a 'sphere of influence' in South and South-West China in the early summer of 1895, began a frenzied 'scramble for concessions'. At the height of this scramble, with Germany at Kiaochow, and Russia at Port Arthur, China was threatened with imminent dismemberment. An unprecedented atmosphere of crisis was created, and a pervasive fear of 'being cut up like a melon'.

This coincided with a new development in the Western transformative impact in China, which had been steadily at work ever since the early 1840s. Its single most striking consequence in the late nineteenth century was undoubtedly the socio-economic transformation that took place in the principal treaty ports. There, to begin with, Western expansion generated

[1] Hao Chang, *Liang Ch'i-ch'ao and intellectual transition in China, 1890-1907*, 7–34.

a sustained, cumulative economic growth which resulted in a more or less 'modern' sector of the economy in those cities closely bound up with the external world market. Related to this economic development was a process of social change which led to the emergence of such new groups as the comprador-businessmen, salaried professional workers and an urban proletariat. Furthermore, due to the 'demonstration effect' of Western institutions of all kinds and growing communications with the outside world, a process of social mobilization inevitably set in among the local populace, slowly eroding their traditional attitudes and commitments while making available new values, new expectations and new patterns of behaviour.

Yet despite this local transformation, throughout the late nineteenth century economic development and social change remained largely confined to the treaty ports. Outside these small and isolated enclaves, the social and economic structure of traditional China was little affected. The Chinese gentry still enjoyed their traditional elite status and remained the dominant social group in the empire. In short, Western expansion, while creating a new society in the treaty ports, failed nevertheless to extend its transforming effect to inland China.

The same, however, cannot be said about the Western *cultural* impact on China. Here the turning point came during the 1890s, when Western ideas and values for the first time spilled over from the treaty ports on a large scale, providing a decisive impetus to the intellectual ferment that emerged among gentry-literati in the middle of the decade. To understand the significance of these important changes we must take a broad look at the cultural impact of the West on China in the preceding decades.

It is an important but often overlooked fact that for almost half a century after 1840 the influx of Western learning was slow and its impact on the Chinese gentry-literati superficial, especially when compared with the fast growth and transforming effect that Western culture achieved in nineteenth-century Japan. While Western learning rapidly became the focus of national attention in Japan after the middle of the century, in China it was confined for decades to the treaty ports and to a limited number of government officials concerned with the management of the so-called 'Western affairs' (*yang-wu*, see chapter 3). The penetration of Christian missionaries into inland China in the decades after 1860 produced little in terms of intellectual communication; indeed, it actually created socio-cultural conflicts that widened the psychological chasm between China and the West. The majority of Chinese gentry-literati still lived in the mental universe of their own tradition.

This imperviousness to Western culture on the part of the gentry-literati is not surprising when one recalls that up to the 1890s their education was still oriented to the civil-service examination system and to the Confucian learning which formed its foundation. That the West for so long left no mark on such a central cultural institution is in itself both a significant reflection of, and an important factor in, the intellectual insulation of most Chinese gentry-literati from the outside world.

The indifference of Chinese gentry-literati to Western culture can be seen in several areas. After the Kiangnan Arsenal was established in 1865, its translation bureau's publications had a very limited sale. According to one estimate, from the mid-1860s until the mid-1890s, the bureau sold about 13,000 copies.[2] This indifference of the Chinese reading public was in striking contrast to the situation in Meiji Japan, where Fukuzawa Yukichi's *Seiyō jijō* (Conditions in the West) sold 250,000 copies (including private copies) almost immediately after publication in 1866.[3] Further evidence of indifference may be seen in the lack of success of the modern schools which the Ch'ing central government and various provincial governments set up between 1861 and 1894, schools designed to offer training in Western languages, technological expertise and military discipline and organization. None of them had much influence, largely because the Chinese literati would not attend them.[4]

There is no better reflection of this intellectual insularity than the fact that up to the 1890s Western knowledge had little place in the curricula of local academies (*shu-yuan*). This situation again differed markedly from late-nineteenth-century Japan. An American who went to teach at one typical secular school in Japan in 1870 was impressed by the prominent place accorded to Western learning and the school's sizeable collection of Western books.[5] Yet had he visited a typical Chinese academy even twenty years later, he would have found scarcely any evidence of Western influence. Liang Ch'i-ch'ao studied at two such large and famous academies in Canton in the late 1880s. In neither school did he find a trace of Western learning; the curriculum was still dominated by traditional Confucian studies. And this was in Canton – a treaty-port city where Western influences presumably went deeper than in other areas of China. Although few monographic studies have been done on the late Ch'ing academies, all the available material suggests that Western learning was by and large barred from their curriculum prior to the educational reforms which began in 1895.[6]

[2] Chien Po-tsan *et al.* eds. *Wu-hsu pien-fa* (The reform movement of 1898; hereafter *WHPF*), 2.18.
[5] This has been documented by R. P. Dore and others.
[4] Knight Biggerstaff, *The earliest modern government schools in China*, 1–93.
[5] R. P. Dore, *Education in Tokugawa Japan*, 2.
[6] Ting Wen-chiang, *Liang Jen-kung hsien-sheng nien-p'u ch'ang-pien ch'u-kao* (The first draft of a documentary chronological biography of Mr Liang Ch'i-ch'ao), 1.11–14.

Further evidence may be found in an educational bibliography which was put out by no less outstanding a scholar-official than Chang Chih-tung in the mid-1870s and which became popular later in the century. It made no mention whatsoever of Western learning. When we look at the writings of such respectable Confucian scholars of that period as Chu Tz'u-ch'i, Ch'en Li, Chu I-hsin and Wang K'ai-yun, it is also surprising that their attention was almost exclusively concentrated on traditional Confucian scholarship. Inconclusive as all these separate pieces of evidence may be, together they point to the existence of a wide cultural gulf between the Westernized treaty ports and the intellectual world of Chinese gentry-literati throughout most of the nineteenth century.

Gradually over the decades, however, this gulf began to be bridged by the slow infiltration of Western thought, which culminated in a wide dispersal of Western ideas and values among Chinese gentry-literati at the end of the century. More important, this spread of Western thought was accompanied by a significant change in attitude towards it on the part of the gentry-literati. Until the 1890s, what little Chinese interest there was in Western learning was largely concentrated on technical knowledge (*i*). But at the end of the century, if we may judge from a popular contemporary bibliography of Chinese literature on Western learning, Chinese scholarly attention was increasingly attracted to Western political experience and knowledge (*cheng*) and to Western religious thought (*chiao*).[7]

The growing acceptance of Western knowledge and values among the gentry-literati fostered the penetration of Western ideas from the periphery to the centre of the Chinese cultural tradition. This penetration brought about a significant fusion of Western thought with indigenous intellectual trends, which eventually gave rise to the intellectual ferment of the mid-1890s. This ferment, of course, can be understood only in the context of the general sense of urgent need for change stimulated by the stepped-up imperialist aggression. But the post-1895 atmosphere of national crisis served only as a catalyst which facilitated changes that had begun in the early 1890s.

One such development was the intellectual activity of Christian missionaries in the 1890s. Between 1860 and 1900, the proselytizing efforts of the Christian churches, both Protestant and Catholic, met with little success. In fact, in view of the leading role the Chinese gentry-literati played in the frequent anti-Christian incidents in late-nineteenth-century

---

[7] Liang Ch'i-ch'ao, *Hsi-hsueh shu-mu-piao* (A bibliography of Western learning), in Chih-hsueh hui, comp. *Chih-hsueh ts'ung-shu ch'u-chi* (Works of substantial learning, 1st series), 1896, *ts'e* 9–10.

China, it would seem that the Christian missionaries did little to bridge the cultural gap between themselves and the Chinese social elite. But some missionaries were not simply religious agents spreading Christian gospel; they also played the role of what Albert Feuerwerker has aptly called 'cultural brokers', purveying Western secular ideals and knowledge among educated Chinese. In this secular capacity they relied mainly on three institutions: schools, private associations and newspapers. The latter two were especially important as instruments for their cultural activities in the 1890s.

These endeavours took a great stride forward in 1887 when the Society for the Diffusion of Christian and General Knowledge Among the Chinese (SDK), popularly known in China as the Kuang hsueh hui, was established. Although the SDK was not entirely a creation of Christian missionaries, the latter took the initiative in founding it. They provided the driving force in promoting its activities, especially after 1891 when the energetic Welsh missionary, Timothy Richard, took over as general secretary of the organization. Under his vigorous and imaginative leadership the society not only greatly expanded its activities but adopted a new approach, aiming its efforts primarily at persuading the Chinese elite of the value of Western culture.[8] This proved to be very successful, achieving a degree of influence on the Chinese elite that was unprecedented since the beginning of large-scale missionary activities in China in the 1860s. Among the government officials and gentry-literati responsive to the SDK's efforts, the impact of the society was felt in two areas. First, the very establishment of the SDK as a voluntary association geared to intellectual-political goals set an organizational model which proved to be very appealing among many reform-minded literati. Secondly, the intellectual impact of the SDK stemmed from the latter's publication of a large variety of writings and translations dealing with Western learning and current world affairs, including some very popular books such as the translation of Robert MacKenzie's *History of the nineteenth century* and a *History of the Sino-Japanese War*.

Among the publications of the SDK, the *Wan-kuo kung-pao* (The Globe Magazine) was by far the most popular. This monthly had its origin in a magazine first entitled *Chiao-hui hsin-pao* (The Church News) founded by the American missionary Young J. Allen in 1868. Changed to its later title after 1874, this magazine became not only a channel for spreading Christian beliefs and Western secular knowledge but a forum for social criticism and

---

[8] Wang Shu-huai, *Wai-jen yü Wu-hsu pien-fa* (Foreigners and the reform movement of 1898), 9–25, 33–46.

public proposals.[9] Thus in its orientation and format, the *Chiao-hui hsin-pao* marked a break with the then existing newspapers in China, which were either geared to the treaty-port business world or to Christian church communications. Suspended in 1883 the publication of *Wan-kuo kung-pao* was revived in 1889, now under the sponsorship of the SDK. With Young J. Allen still as its editor, the magazine retained its prior orientation and format, concentrating on presenting, in literary Chinese, Western knowledge and information about current world affairs. In the course of the 1890s its circulation grew rapidly, up to some four thousand copies. Thus as cultural brokers, Christian missionaries were finally able to make their influence widely felt in the intellectual world of the gentry-literati – something they had never achieved in their religious capacities as Christian proselytizers prior to 1890.[10]

The contribution of the *Wan-kuo kung-pao* to the intellectual ferment of the reform period should be gauged by the kind of influence it had on contemporary Chinese literati. In the first place, the use of newspapers and magazines as vehicles of social criticism and public discussion undoubtedly set an example for the new socio-politically oriented Chinese journalism that was to emerge in the latter part of the 1890s. Further, *Wan-kuo kung-pao* and other SDK publications also proved to be a powerful leaven for the ferment of new ideas and values. An authoritative bibliography on Western learning of the time listed many SDK publications and strongly recommended *Wan-kuo kung-pao* as the source of new knowledge.[11] True, the missionaries' intellectual influence was not always explicit and direct. For in making public proposals and social criticisms in *Wan-kuo kung-pao* and elsewhere, missionaries usually stopped short of challenging in any overt way the imperial institution of China. Yet the socio-political information and ideals which they publicized in their writings were often pregnant with radical implications which their reform-minded Chinese readers were only too happy to draw. In this way the missionary publications did more to stimulate the ideal of political reformism than to provide its content.

Another development was the publication of political writings in the early 1890s by a number of reform-minded Chinese scholars, most notably

9 Adrian A. Bennett and Kwang-Ching Liu, 'Christianity in the Chinese idiom: Young J. Allen and the early *Chiao-hui hsin-pao*, 1868–70', in John K. Fairbank, ed. *The missionary enterprise in China and America*, 159–96. See also Adrian A. Bennett, comp., *Research guide to the* Chiao-hui hsin-pao (*The church news*), *1868–1874; Research guide to the* Wan-kuo kung-pao (*The globe magazine*), *1874–1883*. After 1889 the English title was *The review of the times*.
10 Wang Shu-huai, *Wai-jen*, 40-4. Richard H. Shek, 'Some Western influences on T'an Ssu-t'ung's thought', in Paul A. Cohen and John E. Schrecker, eds., *Reform in nineteenth-century China*, 194–203.
11 Chi-yun Chen, 'Liang Ch'i-ch'ao's "missionary education": a case study of missionary influence on the reformers', *Papers on China*, 16 (1962) 111–12.

Sung Yü-jen, Ch'en Ch'iu, T'ang Chen, Cheng Kuan-ying, Ch'en Chih and Ho Ch'i (Ho Kai). In many respects their reformist thought was not innovative when compared with that of the preceding three decades. Their concern with national wealth and power and their ideas on administrative and educational reforms, commercialism and industrialism were either echoes or further elaborations of similar ideas which had been more or less in the air since the 1860s. Even some of their most daring proposals for the drastic change of such institutions as the civil-service examination system had already been foreshadowed in the writings of Christian missionaries.

In the area of political thinking, however, the reformist writings of the early 1890s featured ideas which decisively distinguished them from those of the previous decades. Almost all of these reformist thinkers had moved in varying degrees towards accepting the Western ideal of political participation. This is clearly seen in their espousal of the parliamentary institution and what some of them called the polity of constitutional monarchy (chün-min kung-chu) – ideas which had been only vaguely adumbrated in a marginal way in the reformist thought of the 1870s and 1880s but were now of central importance. To be sure, the political participation they envisaged was still limited. For Sung Yü-jen it was still conceived vaguely in the traditional terms of broadening the communication between the emperor and officialdom. In the views of T'ang Chen, Ch'en Chih and Ch'en Ch'iu, members of the 'discussion chamber' should be drawn from officialdom as well as from the social elite of gentry-literati. Cheng Kuan-ying and especially Ho Ch'i and Hu Li-yuan conceived of a much broader participation in a parliament. Still their idea of participation was not yet fully democratic, since participation was to be limited to those having status and wealth; besides, the emperor was allowed to retain considerable power in the making of all policies. Behind the willingness ot these reformist thinkers to circumscribe political participation was their more or less shared realization that social conditions in China were not yet ready for the full implementation of democracy.[12]

Furthermore, most of them saw political participation under a constitutional monarchy as more of a means than an end, for their overriding concern was how to achieve national wealth and power in a time of rampant imperialism. In their search for the Western secrets of national strength, they went beyond the previous emphasis on technological ingenuity and commercial-industrial resourcefulness. The Western key to national development, they now discovered, lay primarily in the capacity for united will

[12] Sung Yü-jen, Ts'ai-feng chi (Miscellaneous notes on world customs), in Chih-hsueh hui, Chih-hsueh ts'ung-shu ch'u-chi, 1.6a-b, 13a-14a. WHPF, 1.55-8, 177-80, 198-201, 228, 245-7. See also Lloyd E. Eastman, 'Political reformism in China before the Sino-Japanese War', JAS, 27 (Aug. 1968) 695-710.

and collective action across the barrier between the ruler and the ruled. This capacity was particularly developed in the West thanks to the unique institution of parliament which, according to Ch'en Chih, was able to 'combine the monarch and the people into one body, and channel the ruling and the ruled into one mind'.[13] Thus with these early reformers there began a tendency, which later became very pronounced among modern Chinese intellectuals, to assimilate democracy into nationalism and to view the former as no more than an ingredient in the latter.

Not all of these reform-minded intellectuals, however, were dominated by this instrumental conception of political participation. For instance, Ho Ch'i and Hu Li-yuan, whose writings became very popular in the treaty ports in the late 1890s, were inclined not only to prize democracy as a means to national wealth and power but also to see its value in intrinsic terms. For in their writings one sees the Mencian moral rhetoric of anti-despotism grown into a glorification of popular sovereignty as the universal principle of government. In this view the traditional political order stood condemned as much for lack of moral legitimacy as for political ineffectiveness.[14] Whether on moral or on political grounds the important fact is that all these early reformers in varying degrees were willing to see the Chinese polity reorganized along lines other than the traditional.

This willingness signalled a significant new departure for the reformism of the late Ch'ing; hitherto reformist thinking had been predicated on the assumption of the legitimacy of the traditional polity and on the presupposition that adequate innovations could be carried out within the framework of the traditional political order. Now its legitimacy was questioned and the possibility of organizing the polity on a different base was considered. In contemporary parlance, Western learning was the source of knowledge not only for technical arts but for political ones as well.

In view of their wide-ranging critique of the institutional order of the traditional state, it is interesting to see that these reformers in general stopped short of criticizing the religio-ideological foundation of the old order – namely, Confucianism. In fact some of them, like Ch'en Chih, Ch'en Ch'iu and especially Sung Yü-jen, went out of their way to defend Confucianism and to uphold the validity of the Confucian ideological order (*kang-ch'ang ming-chiao*). As Ch'en Chih observed, in China a defective political institution was combined with a sound moral ideological order. For most of these reformers this moral-ideological conservatism underlay and tempered the radicalness of their political reformism.[15]

---

[13] *WHPF*, 1.245.
[14] Ho Ch'i and Hu Li-yuan, *Hsin-cheng chen-ch'üan* (A true interpretation of new policies), 5.42b–61b.   [15] Sung Yü-jen, *Ts'ai-feng chi*, 1.14a–b, 15a, 23a–b, 24b, 26.

Here again Ho Ch'i and Hu Li-yuan stood out as exceptions. They wrote in Hong Kong, where Ho in fact was a leading citizen with British degrees in law and medicine and an English wife. Unlike most other reformers, whose enthusiasm for Western constitutionalism and the parliamentary system was limited by their loyalty to Confucianism, the relentless attack on the traditional polity by Ho and Hu from a Western liberal standpoint reflected the radicalness of their moral-ideological outlook. In their polemical writings, published in the late 1890s, they went beyond criticizing the dominant trends of Confucianism and cast doubt on the relevance of the Confucian classics as a whole to the practical needs of China as a country. Their radical views, which attacked Confucianism in all but name, came to a head in their open challenge to the sanctified Confucian doctrine of the 'three bonds'. Such a doctrine, which enjoined authoritarianism as the organizing principle of state and family, ran counter to their professed egalitarian beliefs and hence had to be rejected as a viable ideological foundation of state and society. Clearly, in their view China was saddled with a moral-ideological order as defective as were its political institutions and technological culture.[16]

Such a critical view of Chinese tradition in all these areas meant that the reformers felt the need to learn from Western civilization about all the three major problems China faced – technological (*i*), political (*cheng*) and moral-religious (*chiao*). This broadened conception of the value of Western learning certainly represented a significant departure from the emphasis on the commercial and industrial arts, which had dominated the view of Western learning among the advocates of the self-strengthening movement. Inevitably a new view of the relationship between Western learning and the Chinese cultural heritage was made possible by the now heightened prestige of Western learning.

It must be remembered that the metaphysical dualism of the orthodox Neo-Confucian world view saw everything in the world, animate or inanimate, as invariably a fusion of principle and material force. The latter receives its essential nature from the former, while the former takes concrete shape and substance in the latter. In this way the two are thought to be inseparable. Neo-Confucianism expresses this ontological dualism in different formulations, a popular one being the dichotomy of *tao* (way) versus *ch'i* (instrument or vessel), or alternatively substance (*t'i*) versus function (*yung*).

In the theoretical framework of Neo-Confucianism, although the realm

---

[16] Ho Ch'i and Hu Li-yuan, *Hsin-cheng chen-ch'üan*, 5.9b–15, 19–23, 42b–61b. Cf. Paul A. Cohen, 'Littoral and hinterland in nineteenth century China: the "Christian Reformers"', in John K. Fairbank, ed. *The missionary enterprise in China and America*, 197–225.

of *tao* is given logical priority over that of *ch'i*, that priority does not necessarily connote higher value. But in its more popular nineteenth-century
formulations, the dichotomy of *tao* versus *ch'i*, consciously or unconsciously,
was charged with valuational overtones. This was certainly true of the
dichotomy used by some Chinese scholars in their attempt to make sense of
Western learning. After 1860, those who saw the significance of Western
learning in the framework of the *tao–ch'i* combination tended to construe
it under the category of *ch'i*, while reserving the category of *tao* for
Chinese learning. Thus, Western learning was given a value – but only an
instrumental and a secondary one, whereas traditional Confucian learning
was still regarded as the lofty locus of intrinsic and basic values. But now,
along with the recognition of value in Western political ideals and institutions, there was a marked tendency in some of the reformist writings of the
early 1890s to emphasize the inseparability of *ch'i* from *tao*. If Western
learning is found to have the value of instrument, there must also be some
tao in it, since inherent in the *ch'i* of anything is a *tao*. Clearly implicit in
this line of thinking was an inclination to prize the West as the source
not only of instrumental and secondary but also of essential and central
values.[17]

Although these reformist thinkers shared an awareness of the need for
change in the central political institutions of China, their common political
ideas were not the result of any concerted intellectual effort. Isolated from
one another, they reached the same conclusions by coincidence. Although
the publication of their writings in the early 1890s contributed to the
changing intellectual climate in the decade, their aggregate impact was far
less than that of an intellectual and political movement started at the time
by a group of young Cantonese scholars whose leader was K'ang Yu-wei.

K'ANG YU-WEI AND THE EMERGING INTELLECTUAL FERMENT

K'ang Yu-wei (1858–1927) was a Cantonese scholar who came from an
intellectual background very unusual for his time. Born into a scholar-
official family with a Neo-Confucian tradition, he developed an image of
himself as a Confucian sage and hence had a strong sense of moral mission
beginning very early in his childhood. Later in his youth his sense of
mission was given a heightened social orientation under the profound
influence of his teacher, Chu Tz'u-ch'i, a prominent Confucian scholar in
Kwangtung, who emphasized the centrality of moral-political purpose in
Confucian learning.

[17] Onogawa Hidemi, *Shimmatsu seiji shisō kenkyū* (Studies in political thought of the late Ch'ing),
75–111.

Meanwhile, K'ang was also exposed to other intellectual influences through his extensive reading of non-Confucian philosophical and religious literature. Mahayana Buddhism left a particularly strong impression on him. Its image of the Bodhisattva as a suffering saviour was combined with the Confucian ideal of the sage to intensify his sense of mission and social concern, while its spiritual teachings deepened his existential sensibilities.

K'ang's mental horizon was further broadened when trips to Hong Kong and Shanghai drew his attention to Western learning. In the early 1880s he began to read all the books about the West that he could find. In the meantime, living as he did in an area near Canton and in Hong Kong, he naturally became keenly aware of the repeated Western aggressions that China suffered in the nineteenth century. In 1884, at the beginning of the Sino-French War, he was in Canton where he personally experienced all the tensions and fears that attended the imminence of a foreign attack. This direct experience of the power and militancy of the Western nations inevitably lent a special urgency to his study of Western learning. His fervent interest in the subject soon led him to discover a new intellectual world that was to have a transforming effect on his mental outlook.[18]

Thus, by the early 1880s K'ang had been exposed to a variety of intellectual influences outside the Neo-Confucianism of his family tradition – non-Confucian classical Chinese philosophies, Mahayana Buddhism and Western thought, both Christian and secular. By the mid-1880s these influences had begun to crystallize into two central concerns that were to remain dominant throughout his life. One was an existential yearning for a new world in which the chaos, suffering and injustice that he saw everywhere would be replaced by moral harmony and spiritual bliss. This 'universalistic' concern with the human condition was obviously influenced by his study of the spiritual literature of Confucianism, Taoism, Mahayana Buddhism and Christianity, and it impelled him to begin fragmentary efforts at formulating in the 1880s a sometimes vague, sometimes contradictory, but always bold and earnest *Weltanschauung*, to make sense of the new world that was opening before him.

In addition to K'ang's universalistic spiritual concern was a more particularistic concern with China's growing national crisis. This manifested itself in his fervent interest in secular Western learning, especially in Western forms of government, and was reflected in 1886 in his petition to Chang Chih-tung, then governor-general at Canton, to promote the translation of Western books on government. K'ang's patriotism finally led him

[18] Richard C. Howard, 'K'ang Yu-wei (1858–1927): his intellectual background and his early thought', in Arthur F. Wright and Denis Twitchett, eds. *Confucian personalities*, 303–5.

to a daring political act. In the late autumn of 1888, when he was in Peking to take the metropolitan examination, he defied the court's long-standing prohibition against a non-official literatus memorializing the court directly and submitted a stirring memorial to the emperor calling for 'changing the established laws'. Beyond this bold call, his ideas on concrete approaches to reform were vague and general. But a burning sense of how the national integrity was threatened by Western aggression permeated the memorial.[19]

From the very beginning, K'ang saw the threat of Western expansion as not simply socio-political but cultural and religious as well. In addition to the national crisis, China was also caught in a spiritual crisis in which Western Christianity threatened to engulf it. At stake was thus not only China, the *kuo* (state), but Confucianism, the *chiao* (faith). To meet the challenge of Western expansion, it was therefore as important to protect the faith (*pao-chiao*) as to protect the state (*pao-kuo*). Eventually these twin goals formed the core of K'ang's reform programme, which he spelt out in a series of memorials and political writings submitted to the Kuang-hsu Emperor between 1895 and 1898.

The thrust of K'ang's political programme was a series of institutional reforms which, if carried out, would amount to a 'revolution from above'. The first step in this programme was the establishment of a Bureau of Government Reorganization (Chih-tu chü) directly under the emperor and staffed by reform-minded officials. This office would be charged with planning for and carrying out institutional reform. An important part of this programme would be the building of a modern navy and army. For this purpose the traditional military examination system, which focused on testing skills in archery and swordsmanship, would be abolished in favour of modern military academies modelled on Prussian and Japanese military schools. These academies would then produce professional officers who would serve as the core of new standing armies to replace the now effete forces of the Ch'ing government.

More important than military reform in K'ang's programme for government reorganization were his plans for economic development and the rationalization of public finance. Half of the twelve offices to be set up under the Bureau of Government Reorganization were to deal with these two tasks. Emphasis on the state's responsibility for promoting industry, commerce, agriculture, mining and modern transportation was a persistent theme of K'ang's reform proposal.[20]

Underlying these ideas of institutional change was K'ang's acceptance of

[19] *WHPF*, 2.123–31.
[20] T'ang Chih-chün, *Wu-hsu pien-fa shih lun-ts'ung* (A collection of articles on the reform movement of 1898), 154–78.

the political ideal of national wealth and power. Nowhere was his commitment to this goal more clearly reflected than in his recommendation to the Ch'ing court that the Petrine reform of Russia and the Meiji reform of Japan be taken as the models for China.[21]

Another cluster of K'ang's reform proposals recommended a drastic renovation of cultural-educational institutions. These proposals suggested that special measures be taken by the Chinese government to fortify Confucianism as the national religion in order to counter the influx into China of alien faiths, especially Western Christianity. In this direction K'ang recommended the formation of a government ministry of religion to establish and oversee a nation-wide system of Confucian churches, and the replacement of the traditional system of counting time by dynasty and reign with a system using the year of Confucius' birth as the basic point of reference.[22]

According to K'ang, this religio-ideological defensiveness should be coupled with a heightened cultural responsiveness to Western secular knowledge and ideals. The latter goal could be achieved partly by translating Japanese books about the West on a massive scale and partly by sending students abroad to acquire Western knowledge. But the most important step in the direction of assimilating Western culture was drastic educational reform, beginning with the elimination of such important categories of the traditional examination system as the eight-legged essays and the old-style military tests. In their place, tests based on specialized Western knowledge would be introduced. K'ang hoped that these renovations would lead to the eventual abolition of the examination system and the establishment of a nation-wide school system.

Part of the purpose of this educational reform was doubtless to provide China with the literate and skilled citizenry so essential for national development. Another part must be sought in K'ang's acceptance of the Western ideals of popular sovereignty and constitutional government. A constitutional monarchy, for K'ang as well as for some other early political reformers, had the important function of increasing the political participation of people outside the government and therefore strengthening the bonds between the rulers and the ruled. In this context, democracy was prized as an effective means of achieving national solidarity and political cohesion. But K'ang's conception of a constitutional and parliamentary government was not solely conceived in these utilitarian terms. He also saw democracy as a political ideal destined to be realized in all future

[21] Richard C. Howard, 'Japan's role in the reform program of K'ang Yu-wei', in Jung-pang Lo, ed. *K'ang Yu-wei: a biography and a symposium*, 288–302.
[22] T'ang Chih-chün, *Wu-hsu pien-fa shih lun-ts'ung*, 168–9.

human societies. For this goal as well as the nationalistic goal of collective wealth and power, an educated citizenry was essential.[23]

As far as K'ang's political programme was concerned, constitutional monarchy and national wealth and power emerged as his two guiding ideals. These ideals, coupled with his concern for promoting Confucianism, lay behind the two overriding goals of his reformism – protecting the state and protecting the faith. His reformism was buttressed by a comprehensive ideology based on his radical interpretation of Confucianism, which K'ang developed mainly from his contact with a major trend of late Ch'ing thought, the New Text School. In the years between 1890 and 1898 he spelt out his interpretation in a number of writings which rocked the intellectual world of the Confucian literati to its foundation.

His first major piece of radical interpretation of Confucianism was *Hsin-hsueh wei-ching k'ao* (An inquiry into the classics forged during the Hsin period), which he published in 1891. This work was intended to discredit the School of Empirical Research (K'ao-cheng hsueh), then known as the School of Han Learning (Han hsueh), which had been popular among Confucian literati since the seventeenth century. K'ang was not the first to exert himself in this direction; since the late eighteenth century, quite a number of Confucian scholars had attempted to dispute the claim of the School of Empirical Research to the time-honoured title of Han learning on various textual and philological grounds. For them 'true' Han learning lay not with the School of Empirical Research, which could trace its intellectual lineage to the dominant trend of Confucian learning in the Later Han dynasty, namely the Ancient Text (Ku-wen) School, but with the New Text (Chin-wen) School, the mode of Confucian thought that had prevailed during the Former Han dynasty. In this way a long-forgotten intellectual controversy dating from Han times was revived during the late Ch'ing among Confucian scholars (see volume 10, chapter 3).

Building as he did on the groundwork laid by the late Ch'ing scholars of the New Text School, especially by a contemporary scholar of that school, Liao P'ing, K'ang set forth the provocative thesis that the intellectual fountainhead of the School of Empirical Research, the Ancient Text version of Confucian scholarship, could all be proven by textual criticism to be a forgery; therefore, the true Han learning – the authentic teachings of Confucianism – was the preserve of the New Text School.[24]

K'ang's purpose was to discredit the socio-moral indifferentism of Han learning as a deplorable deviation from the original teachings of Confucius and, more important, to reaffirm political concern and institutional reform

[23] Onogawa Hidemi, *Shimmatsu seiji shisō kenkyū*, 75–111.
[24] Hao Chang, *Liang Ch'i-ch'ao*, 48–52.

as the central orientation of Confucianism, which he believed to lie at the core of the New Text exegetical interpretation. This interpretation was presented in 1898 in his second major work of reform ideology, *K'ung-tzu kai-chih k'ao* (Confucius as institutional reformer).

In K'ang's view, Confucius was above all a great innovator, not only as the prophet-like founder of the Confucian religion but also as an institution-building 'king'. Drawing on certain cryptic interpretations of the New Text School, he maintained that Confucius, shortly before his death, received a mandate from heaven to devise new institutions for a forth-coming new dynasty. In K'ang's terms, Confucius was a 'sage-king' (*sheng-wang*) or an 'uncrowned king' (*su-wang*), intent on institutional reform (*kai-chih*). But what did institutional reform mean in K'ang's scheme? In the original literature of the New Text School, *kai-chih* was a broad but vague concept with strong religio-mystical overtones more suggestive of ritual changes than of institutional innovation in its modern sense. K'ang's ideal of *kai-chih*, on the other hand, had all the modern connotations of institutional change, as clearly reflected in his reform programmes. Through his interpretation of Confucianism, he sought cultural sanction for his reform of the foundation of traditional China's polity.

Institutional reform, in K'ang's view, was not only desirable but indeed inevitable, since he saw historical change as linear progress. This con-ception was implicit in his portrayal of Confucius as a messianic, forward-looking 'sage-king' who viewed history as a unilinear development through determinate stages towards an ideal future. Although K'ang apparently derived this linear conception of history mainly from his reading of Western thought, he spelt it out in a framework borrowed from the New Text School – the doctrine of three ages. As he interpreted this doctrine, Confucius saw human history as inexorably developing from the age of disorder (*chü-luan shih*), through the age of approaching peace (*sheng-p'ing shih*), to the final age of universal peace (*t'ai-p'ing shih*), or, as K'ang later put it in another scheme, through the age of small peace (*hsiao-k'ang*) towards the final age of great unity (*ta-t'ung*). Each of the three ages had its appropriate political system: absolute monarchy for the age of disorder; constitutional monarchy for the age of approaching peace; and republican government for the age of universal peace. As history pro-gresses through the three ages, changes of institutions inevitably occur. In brief, institutional changes are inherent in the progress of history.[25]

K'ang's conception of history as unilinear progress through determinate stages also involved the belief that historical progress would eventually

[25] Hsiao Kung-chuan, 'K'ang Yu-wei and Confucianism', *Monumenta Serica*, 18 (1958), 88–212.

consummate itself in the ideal society of great unity. This millennialism in his thinking was a reflection of that universalistic, spiritual concern which had preoccupied him since his early youth. As articulated in the ideal of 'great unity', this universalistic concern was fed by both a fervent moral quest for an ideal human community and a profound existential revolt against the suffering that K'ang believed pervaded human societies everywhere. The result was his vision of a universal moral community where suffering would evaporate and happiness prevail. According to K'ang, human suffering, although of various kinds, all stemmed from one basic source – man's inveterate egoism and his accompanying tendency to make a distinction between himself and others. Out of these human tendencies grew the ubiquitous social inequalities which shackled every part of human life. In depicting his universal human community of the future, K'ang emphasized the elimination of social inequality and discrimination of any kind. This radical social levelling would involve the abolition of almost all existing human institutions, including state, private property and family. In this sense K'ang's utopian world of 'great unity' is pervaded by a radical egalitarianism and universalism.[26] This bespoke the syncretic nature of K'ang's world view.

The very concept of 'great unity' was derived by K'ang from Confucian utopianism. In content it bore considerable resemblance to the Confucian ideal of *jen*, in that both symbolized a yearning for a universal moral community of organic oneness. Yet K'ang's social and moral radicalism went beyond the acceptable limits of Confucianism. The family, for example, occupied such a central place in Confucianism that the ultimate realization of *jen* would result in a moral *gemeinschaft* which was seen as an extension rather than a transcendence of family. To the extent that the ideal of great unity involved the transcendence of such a vital social institution as the family, K'ang's social utopianism owed at least as much to Mahayana Buddhism, Christianity and Mohism as to Confucianism.

K'ang's utopian ideal of universal moral community, though made known among his disciples and close associates, was not publicized during the 1890s. Furthermore, in the framework of his developmental view of history, this universalistic ideal was relevant only for the distant future. Thus, his overriding goal was still a national community of wealth and power; the operative part of his ideology was still his radical interpretation of Confucianism centred around the ideal of institutional reformism. In brief, although K'ang envisaged a universal community as his ultimate goal and hence could not himself be regarded as a nationalist, the visible part of his ideology included a large element of nationalism.

[26] Hao Chang, *Liang Ch'i-chao*, 52–7.

In any case that part of his ideology publicized during the 1890s had a significant impact on the gentry-literati. It embraced a set of Western political values which K'ang shared with a number of other contemporary reformist thinkers, the difference being that K'ang expounded these values in an ideological framework which not only accommodated them in a total interpretation of Confucianism but also linked them with important indigenous trends in late Ch'ing thought. Presented in terms of familiar traditional issues, the Western political values exerted a much greater appeal than they would have had otherwise. Although K'ang's radical interpretation of Confucianism scandalized many of his contemporaries, the new thought achieved considerable impact. Even if many of the Chinese gentry-literati still abhorred Western learning, they could not ignore it. To the extent that K'ang's ideas drew the attention of a large number of Chinese scholar-officials to Western thought, it provided a powerful stimulus for change in the intellectual climate of the 1890s.

K'ang's reformist ideology had momentous implications, both political and intellectual. Politically, its call for institutional reforms implied a questioning of the political effectiveness of government. More important, the advocacy of such Western political ideas as popular sovereignty, political participation and constitutional government joined with the more or less similar views of other political reformers to pose a challenge to the legitimacy of the traditional political order. As these new political values spread to wider and wider circles of public consciousness, China faced not only administrative breakdown but also the beginning of a process of political disintegration that culminated in the Revolution of 1911.

Equally significant were the intellectual implications which flowed from K'ang's radical interpretation of Confucianism. To be sure, in the course of its long development Confucianism had been subject to a variety of different interpretations, but these had seldom been allowed to extend to its fundamental socio-political values and beliefs. The fact that K'ang had brought these central values and beliefs into question already implied that Confucianism was waning as the focus of Chinese faith. The implication was all the more serious when K'ang went so far as to tamper with the long-accepted image of Confucius and the inner core of Confucian values. A disturbing question occurs to anyone who reads K'ang's provocative interpretation: what is the true identity and character of Confucianism? The emergence of this question had the ominous consequence of transforming Confucianism from what so far had been the unquestioned centre of faith into an ideology, the basic character of which was problematic and debatable. For many, this question inevitably came as a shock. It struck the intellectual world of the Chinese gentry-literati, in Liang Ch'i-ch'ao's words, 'like a volcanic eruption and earthquake'.

THE REFORM MOVEMENT

The mere publication of K'ang's reformist ideology undoubtedly acted as a powerful stimulus to intellectual change. The impact became all the greater when he used it to inspire and organize a reform movement. The foundation of this movement had been laid when K'ang set up a private school in Canton, the Ch'ang-hsing Academy, where he taught a small group of devoted young scholars. Innovative at the time, its curriculum still maintained a Confucian format, but actually was a sharp departure from contemporary Confucian schools. It consisted largely of K'ang's own radical interpretation of Confucianism and an emphasis on the study of the teachings of Mahayana Buddhism, non-Confucian Chinese trends of thought, and Western learning; one primary purpose was to imbue its students with K'ang's political consciousness and reformist ideals. Little wonder that many of these students later became dedicated political activists. One of them, Liang Ch'i-ch'ao, became K'ang's chief assistant in his campaign for institutional reform.[27]

Although K'ang in 1888 had memorialized the court on the need for reform, his drive for change in the form of a sustained and large-scale movement did not begin until 1895. His immediate occasion for resuming this campaign was China's defeat in the Sino-Japanese War, which produced a greater impact on the public consciousness than any of the defeats China had previously suffered at the hands of foreign powers. In the first place, the disaster cost China materially much more than had her previous setbacks. In addition to being forced to open more treaty ports and to pay a staggering indemnity, she had to give up her claim to suzerainty over her last important tributary state, Korea, and to cede large areas of her own territory, Taiwan and the Liaotung peninsula, to Japan. Such enormous sacrifices, coming as they did after more than twenty years of loudly proclaimed 'self-strengthening' reforms, seemed particularly shocking and ominous. Finally, the profound sense of loss was compounded by a feeling of humiliation, particularly poignant because the Chinese had traditionally despised Japan as a backward state far inferior to China in both culture and power.

In the spring of 1895 K'ang and his disciple, Liang Ch'i-ch'ao, were in Peking for the metropolitan civil-service examination. When China was

[27] *Ibid.* 41–7.

forced in April of that year to conclude the humiliating peace treaty with Japan at Shimonoseki, K'ang immediately seized the occasion to mobilize his fellow examination candidates to protest against the peace treaty and to petition the court for reform. The result was a dramatic mass petition against the peace treaty. Thirteen hundred candidates signed the stirring memorial drafted by K'ang, urging the court to repudiate the peace treaty and initiate reform. All these protests and petitions went unheeded. Yet an atmosphere of public concern was created, encouraging K'ang to go further in his campaign.[28]

This reform campaign took on a much broader scope than it had when K'ang first launched it single-handed in 1888. At that time his efforts had not gone beyond petitioning the emperor and lobbying high officials in the court. K'ang now continued his new attempt to get reform initiated from above by following the sensational mass petition with two further bold calls for reform, which he made to the court in the early summer of 1895. At the same time K'ang and his followers made an important strategic decision: they coupled their attempts to petition the court with efforts at winning support from below. Underlying these attempts was the reformers' long-range vision of establishing in China a constitutional government and a participant polity. For the attainment of these goals, mere reforms from above were far from adequate; they must be supplemented with 'development from below'.

To promote this, K'ang and his associates created new organizational and propaganda instruments. The most important organization was the study society (*hsueh-hui*), which performed two significant functions. First, it carried out the all-important integrative function of inducing intellectual consensus and organizational solidarity without which the formation of a modern state is impossible. Secondly, its more specific task was the education and mobilization of the literati-gentry. Much as K'ang and his friends desired to see 'development from below', they knew that the Chinese population, given its general lack of education, was not yet prepared to undertake such a task. Before general education and popular enlightenment materialized, much would depend on the leadership of the 'middle class' of Chinese society – the gentry degree-holders. On the one hand, this class constituted the local elite, better educated and more capable than the masses of the people. On the other, as compared with the officials, the gentry were better qualified to lead the populace because of their social proximity to and greater contact with them. Herein lay the strategic importance in

---

[28] T'ang Chih-chün, *Wu-hsu pien-fa jen-wu chuan-kao* (Draft biographies of participants in the reform of 1898), 334.

Chinese society of the gentry, who, as Liang Ch'i-ch'ao put it, 'because of their familiarity with the condition of the people, can serve as the channel between the high and the low'.

But unfortunately, the gentry were not yet prepared to play the mediating role and to supply the enlightened leadership for the general populace, since they either lacked political motivation or had little information about national and world situations. Furthermore, they had little civic spirit and few organizational skills in their background. To overcome these deficiencies, the young reformers looked to the study society as the best instrument for their education and mobilization.

These societies were to be organized on the basis of two principles – locality and intellectual specialty. They were to be set up first at Peking and Shanghai, with branch societies following later in every province, prefecture, county and town. Meanwhile, for the purpose of educating gentry-officials in the new knowledge, societies were to be formed throughout the country for each specialized discipline. In this way the reformers envisaged a nation-wide network of study societies to stimulate 'development from below'.[29]

Another new institution which the K'ang-Liang group used to promote its movement was the newspaper, which they realized was a powerful instrument for spreading new knowledge and ideals as well as for promoting an intellectual consensus among the people. While K'ang's efforts to petition the court for reform were unsuccessful, his endeavours to promote 'development from below' by means of the study society and the newspaper, in spite of official suppression and social resistance, were milestones in the social and cultural development of modern China.

K'ang's first organizational experiment in forming a study society was the establishment of the Society for the Study of Self-Strengthening (Ch'iang hsueh-hui) in Peking in August 1895. Although K'ang was the motive force behind the society, it was Ch'en Chih, then a minor official in the central government, who served as its official manager. At first, the society was quite successful, bringing together not only many reform-minded scholar-officials in the capital, but also some Westerners, including the British minister Nicolas R. O'Conor, and the missionaries Timothy Richard and Gilbert Reid. More significantly, its membership roster included a number of high-ranking officials in the Ch'ing government: governors-general in the provinces such as Chang Chih-tung, Wang Wen-shao and Liu K'un-i; and prominent figures in the court such as Weng T'ung-ho, Sun Chia-nai and Li Hung-tsao.[30] Many donations of money

[29] T'ang Chih-chün, *Wu-hsu pien-fa shih lun-ts'ung*, 222–7.
[30] *Ibid.* 334.

put the society on a sound financial basis. Its members convened regularly every ten days and listened to public speeches on current affairs.

Liang Ch'i-ch'ao was appointed secretary. When a daily newspaper, *Chung-wai kung-pao* (Sino-foreign gazette), was published under the society's sponsorship, Liang and another of K'ang's students, Mai Meng-hua, served as its editors. This 'newspaper' usually consisted solely of an essay written by Liang or Mai about current affairs, but occasionally it also featured some writings borrowed from the SDK publications. To facilitate its circulation among the scholar-officials in Peking, it was distributed free of charge along with the palace gazette. At the height of its popularity in the capital, it had a circulation of three thousand copies.

Meanwhile, K'ang, considering Shanghai 'a focal link between south and north, where so many gentry-literati converge', established a branch of the Society for the Study of Self-Strengthening there in the autumn of 1895. It received substantial funding from Chang Chih-tung, then the acting governor-general at Nanking, and also managed to publish its own daily called *Ch'iang-hsueh pao* (Self-strengthening journal) which, like the *Chung-wai kung-pao*, was distributed free.[31] Thus the months following the tumultuous spring of 1895 saw some new and significant stirrings among scholar-officials – efforts not only to arouse a general consciousness of national crisis but also to organize and channel this consciousness into a directed and coordinated movement for change.

These organizational efforts, however, soon met with suppression from the government. Chang Chih-tung withdrew his financial backing from the Shanghai branch of the society and banned its newspaper because it outraged provincial authorities by dating years from Confucius' birth rather than the reign period of the Ch'ing dynasty. Apparently Chang saw in this practice an ominous implication of disloyalty to the Ch'ing. Meanwhile, the society in Peking also felt the deadening hand of the government, despite the considerable support it enjoyed at a high level. In February 1896 a censor accused the society of illegally forming an association which might encourage among literati the dangerous practices of unrestrained political discussion and public criticism. This impeachment, once brought forward, could not go unheeded by the court. Since 1652 it had been the established Ch'ing policy to ban private proposals and petitions against government policies and the forming of private societies. Acting on the censor's impeachment, the government proscribed the society, thereby closing it down barely five months after its foundation.[32]

Although the disbandment of the Ch'iang hsueh-hui and the reform

[31] T'ang Chih-chün, *Wu-hsu pien-fa shih lun-ts'ung*, 249.
[32] *Ibid.* 16, 227–9.

newspapers at both Peking and Shanghai was a setback for the fledgling reform movement, new opportunities soon emerged elsewhere. In the spring of 1896, shortly after the Shanghai branch of the society was banned, its remaining funds and some additional money pooled from private sources were used to found a newspaper. Wang K'ang-nien served as manager, and Liang Ch'i-ch'ao was invited to be chief editor. This was the beginning of the famous *Shih-wu pao* (Chinese progress) which started to circulate from Shanghai in August 1896. In the following spring, an affiliated paper was founded at Macao. At first called the *Kuang Shih-wu pao*, it later became *Chih-hsin pao* (The China reformer). These two newspapers kept the reform movement alive in the lower Yangtze valley and on the south-east coast.[33]

The soul of the *Shih-wu pao* was in the articles by Liang Ch'i-ch'ao. He was a devoted student of K'ang Yu-wei, and naturally many of his writings bore the strong imprint of K'ang's influence. A close examination, however, reveals that Liang's writings did not simply popularize K'ang's ideas but developed them to the point where nationalism and democratization were made more central in the reform platform.

Like K'ang and many other reform-minded scholars of the time, Liang reacted strongly against the technological orientation of the self-strengthening movement. Learning from the experience of the Meiji reform in Japan, he argued that, to revitalize China as a nation, political reform was even more important than the introduction of Western technology. If political reform were successfully carried out, military and technological innovation would automatically follow, while mere technological innovations unaccompanied by political change would result in a sheer waste of effort, as had been amply shown in the self-strengthening movement. In other words, Liang's reform programme asserted the primacy of political reform over technological change.

Liang insisted that the key to political reform in China was a total remodelling of educational institutions. This involved essentially the abolition of the civil-service examinations and the establishment of a nation-wide school system. A primary aim of this new approach would be to spread literacy and useful knowledge among the populace and, equally important, to provide a political education based on a knowledge both of China's cultural tradition and of the political ideals and experience of the West. From these new institutions, Liang hoped, there would emerge a citizenry which was intellectually competent as well as politically conscious.

At the heart of Liang's educational approach were two central ideas,

[33] *Ibid.* 231–43, 249–50.

namely *pien* (change) and *ch'ün* (grouping). Influenced by K'ang Yu-wei's philosophy of history and by Social Darwinism which was being introduced into China at the time, Liang conceived change primarily in the sense of unilinear progress. In Liang's thinking this kind of change, however, was governed by a new political awareness summed up in the omnibus idea of *ch'ün*. This term expressed the need for establishing associations among the gentry-literati to mobilize and organize them for social and political action. Significantly, in addition to the ideal of association, the concept *ch'ün* also involved certain broader political ideals that entailed a profound devaluation of China's traditional political institutions. The ancient monarchy, according to Liang, was oriented primarily to maintaining the dynastic regime in power and hence often was purely repressive. Such a repressive order could not maintain China as a viable state in the modern world of imperialist aggression and international competition. To begin with, it would inhibit the generation of energy and vitality in the populace, the collective dynamism so essential to the survival and development of the nation. Secondly, the repressive monarchy prevented communication – not only between the rulers and the ruled, but also among the different sectors of the society. Lacking this communication, traditional China was as deficient in national solidarity as it was in national dynamism.

Underlying this indictment of the traditional political order was obviously a new conception of political community, one strongly influenced by nationalism and by the Darwinian image of a world dominated by relentless international rivalry and struggle. During this period Liang never explicitly identified this conception with nationalism. In fact, as a close follower of K'ang Yu-wei, he still professed his belief in K'ang's universalistic ideals. Yet the ideal of nationalism was just beneath the surface of his political writings.

But nationalism, while important, was not the sole determinant in Liang's vision of the new political community, for accompanying his pragmatic evaluation of the traditional political order was his concern for moral legitimacy. The traditional institution of kingship was not only politically ineffective; it was also morally reprehensible. Liang envisaged the state as a corporate entity which should belong to all members of the community – not only to the rulers, but also to the ruled. Hence the community should be the summation of the interests and wills of all its members. Domination of the populace by an individual ruler or ruling family would be nothing less than a flagrant manifestation of moral selfishness and hence could only result in the degeneration of community. This new conception of community bespoke a moral commitment to a Rousseau-like ideal of popular sovereignty and general will. In brief, the new political community Liang envisaged as the ultimate goal of political reform embodied in itself not only dynamism and solidarity but democracy as well.[34]

Centred on this new ideal of political community, Liang's reformism, in ultimate terms, aimed at no less than a radical transformation of the traditional political order of China. The propagation of these radical ideals soon made political reformism the focus of the growing intellectual ferment. As the ferment spread, the reform movement gradually lost the unambiguous unitary character which it had when it started under the sole leadership of K'ang Yu-wei. To be sure, K'ang's reform programme and ideology still represented the most publicized and visible part of the movement. Underneath, however, there were other currents significantly different from K'ang's thought. Thus, reformism as an intellectual movement may be best seen as a spectrum. At the more moderate end was often found the type of thinking represented by such scholar-officials as Ch'en Pao-chen and Huang Tsun-hsien, who agreed with K'ang on the need for institutional changes but did not necessarily share his radical interpretation of Confucianism. The intellectual stance of some in this moderate wing did not differ substantially from the attitude of such advocates of self-strengthening as Chang Chih-tung and Li Hung-chang. On the other hand, at the more radical end were views hardly distinguishable from and in some respects even more radical than the contemporary revolutionary movement. Against this background two figures deserve special attention, for they played leading roles in the increasingly broad and variegated intellectual ferment that developed around the reform movement.

One was Yen Fu, who in his youth had studied in England for two years and hence belonged to that small minority of Chinese who not only knew a Western language but had also seen the West at first hand. During the years 1895 to 1898 he had published a series of essays in a newspaper in Tientsin, expressing his own views on China's national crisis and its need for reform. In 1897 he was one of the founders of a new Chinese daily in Tientsin, the *Kuo-wen pao*, soon to become the most important newspaper in North China, and a weekly magazine, the *Kuo-wen hui-pien*, to spread new knowledge and publicize reformist viewpoints. During the same years he also began his translation enterprise and completed his translation-commentary on Huxley's *Evolution and ethics*, which he called *T'ien-yen lun* (On evolution). Yen Fu's writings and translations soon had an important impact on the reading public. His *T'ien-yen lun*, a resounding success after its publication in 1898, had had influence even prior to publication, since both K'ang Yu-wei and Liang Ch'i-ch'ao had read the text and became Yen's admirers before it appeared in print.

[34] Hao Chang, *Liang Ch'i-chao*, 73–120.

By the standard of his time, Yen Fu's political attitude was quite moderate, since what he recommended was no more than gradual institutional reform and policy innovations. But this was combined with a radical intellectual attitude which looked forward to a future when China would undergo a thorough cultural transformation. Both his political gradualism and his intellectual radicalism stemmed from his basic Social Darwinian outlook, which he derived mainly from reading Spencerian philosophy.

The Spencerian idea that evolution is inevitably a slow, cumulative process which cannot proceed by leaps and bounds deterred Yen from any belief in the miracle of drastic transformation. Practically, this meant that China should not go through institutional changes until its people were ready; a long process of education was needed to transform them physically, intellectually and morally. What Yen Fu aimed at was no less than a complete change of values in the future.

Yen Fu's cultural radicalism grew out of his burning nationalistic concern – how to achieve collective wealth and power so that China could survive in a world of rampant imperialism. Couched in a Social Darwinian framework, his collectivistic concern led him to believe that the key to collective wealth and power must be sought in a distinctive Western vision of the cosmos. This pictures the universe as an 'inexhaustible storehouse' of energy and force, inexorably engaged in a constant process of evolution from the 'homogeneous and simple' to the 'heterogeneous and organized'. This picture is as true of the universe at large as of the human world, where energy is generated and evolution is fuelled by the struggle for existence. In this sense struggle is not only inevitable among human beings, given the earth's limited resources and teeming life, but, as the spring of dynamism and progress, it is also a blessing for the world.

This vision of reality exhilarated and engrossed Yen Fu since it projected such ideals as struggle, dynamism and progress which he held dear. These basic Darwinian values and world views also led him to admire Western liberal ideals. In Yen Fu's mind the success of modern Western civilization lay in the miracle that in the West the energy of human individuals could not only be released but also fused to generate collective dynamism. The modern Western ethos was a unique, happy combination of public spirit and raw energy. According to Yen Fu's study of Western thought and his observation of England, this combination could be created only in the context of a free society and democratic institutions. His belief in liberalism and democracy was part and parcel of his acceptance of the Social Darwinian ideal of collective dynamism.

Thus in terms of both world view and basic values, Yen Fu was an unreservedly ardent admirer of Western civilization – which led him to unrelenting criticism of Chinese tradition. While he saw an overflow of collective energy in the modern West, he saw only an atrophy of dynamism and public spirit in the Chinese tradition. As he emphasized, in comparison with the modern West, China was weak because in the past Chinese sages had done little to foster the energies and capacities of the people, and dynastic rulers had done everything to suppress them. It is not surprising then that he almost completely refuted the indigenous trends of thought in his own time, not only attacking the mechanistic requirements of the examination system but dismissing likewise all the current schools of Confucianism as intellectual waste. The remedy to China's ills lay only in Western ideas and values.[35]

Another influential figure but of a very different intellectual stamp was a young Hunanese scholar, T'an Ssu-t'ung. The son of a high government official and a member of the Chinese gentry-literati, T'an Ssu-t'ung had a largely Confucian education. Later, in his early adult life, through his own intellectual search he was exposed to the influences of Western learning, Christianity and Mahayana Buddhism, and he also felt the impact of the revival of non-Confucian classical philosophies, most notably Mohism, in the late nineteenth century. Such diverse intellectual influences led to the formation of an eclectic intellectual outlook which he spelt out in a provocative philosophical tract, *Jen-hsueh* (On humanity), written in 1896–7. Although this tract was not published until the early 1900s, its contents were made known before publication to his close friends including Liang Ch'i-ch'ao.

At the core of *On humanity* lies a world view which yearns for a universal community on earth. Such a community would be full of vitality and dynamism, constantly developing towards a better future. It would also be a moral *gemeinschaft* characterized by radical egalitarianism and an unimpeded flow of feeling. This utopian vision owed as much to the religious universalism and moral idealism of Mahayan Buddhism, Neo-Confucianism, Christianity and Mohism, as to the ethos of dynamism of the industrial-commercial societies in the modern West. Conspicuously muted, however, was the idea of nationalism which had begun to be a striking feature in the thought of so many of T'an's contemporaries.

From such a vision of the world T'an brought forth a radical critique of Chinese tradition. Like Yen Fu, he attacked the traditional monarchy which he depicted as a despotism of the darkest kind, repressing both human ability and feeling. But unlike Yen Fu, whose attack on the traditional institutions was confined to the political order, T'an extended his attack also to the central social institution of traditional China, the family.

---

[35] Benjamin Schwartz, *In search of wealth and power: Yen Fu and the West*, 42–112.

This is evident in his unreserved challenge to the core of the traditional moral and social order – the Confucian doctrine of three bonds (*san-kang*). These most sacred of all human relationships included those of ruler and subject, father and son, and husband and wife. All three were based on the authoritarian principle of absolute one-sided domination. For T'an the two family relationships of father–son and husband–wife were as corrupting and inhibitive as the political relationship of ruler–subject. All three, in T'an's mind, constituted one single perverse and repressive order under which the traditional world could only wither and degenerate.

To establish a viable human community on earth, T'an thus called for the ripping apart of the stifling net of three bonds and thereby destroying China's traditional social-political order as a whole. Unlike K'ang Yu-wei or Yen Fu, T'an recommended no methodical reform programme and gave no indications in his *On humanity* as to how to implement his vision by concrete and specific steps. Yet throughout the tract he used highly emotional language starkly conveying the twin notes of total negation and total release. Out of these grew a mystique of revolution.[36]

So far we have seen that although the intellectual ferment of the reform movement contained a broad spectrum of ideas, it was chiefly marked by a radical trend which reflected two primary concerns. One was the widespread demand for national wealth and power. The other was a search for religio-moral meaning, manifested mainly in the thinking of K'ang Yu'wei and T'an Ssu-t'ung. Both concerns fed radical thinking that struck at the ideological foundation of the traditional political order. Thus it is no surprise that, in the years following 1895, ideological discord gradually emerged not only between the radical reformers and the conservative scholar-officials but also between the radical and the moderate reformers. This ideological discord finally came into the open in Hunan in the latter part of 1897.

REFORM IN HUNAN

After the Ch'ing court clamped down on K'ang Yu-wei's campaign in Peking in early 1896, the reform movement had to confine its activities to ideological propaganda in Shanghai and Macao in order to gain public support. But new developments were meanwhile under way in Hunan, which soon brought the centre of the reform movement to the capital, Changsha, and thus gave it a chance of success at the provincial level.

The reform in Hunan at this time must be understood against the background of two major developments in the Chinese state and society in the latter half of the nineteenth century. The first was the increase of power on

[36] T'an Ssu-t'ung, *T'an Ssu-t'ung ch'üan-chi* (The complete works of T'an Ssu-t'ung), 56–90.

the part of the governors and governors-general in the aftermath of the mid-nineteenth-century rebellions and the various efforts at economic-technological development and institutional change undertaken by many of these provincial officials, each in his own area of jurisdiction, to cope with the international crisis that China faced. These renovative efforts over the three decades after the early 1860s constituted the bulk of the so-called self-strengthening movement.

The second major development was the increase of power of the local elite. Philip Kuhn has shown how their power grew through their organization of local defence forces during the years of the mid-nineteenth-century rebellions. There are indications that this increase in power also led to the heightened involvement of gentry in public functions of a non-military nature. Much of this was simply an extension of their traditional public activities in a time of weakened government. But in some provinces it was also related to commercialization directly or indirectly stimulated by contact with the West. These indigenous developments combined to give a greater role to the gentry in the politics of their home towns and provinces.[37]

Consequently, in the latter part of the nineteenth century the political role of the gentry expanded at the same time that the power of provincial officials increased. A coincidence of activism on the part of both led to the beginning of a reform movement in Hunan in the 1890s. In the first place, Hunan was blessed with a succession of two able and enlightened scholar-officials at the apex of the provincial hierarchy from the early 1890s. Wu Ta-ch'eng who served as governor from 1892 to 1895 had already made some start in educational, economic and military renovation. Reform was more vigorously pushed on a broader scale when Ch'en Pao-chen took over as governor in late 1895. In his efforts to promote provincial reform he had the help of a forward-looking son, Ch'en San-li, who had many friends among the reform-minded literati of the younger generation. He was also assisted by two high officials in the provincial administration, Huang Tsun-hsien and Chiang Piao.

Huang was a Cantonese scholar-poet and veteran diplomat who had served in Japan, the United States, England and South-East Asia. From his long service overseas, he developed strong reformist leanings and also became a leading expert on foreign affairs, especially on Japan. During the 1890s his *Jih-pen kuo-chih* (History of the Japanese state) and his historical poems on Japan had been an important source of information on Meiji reform for the Chinese literati. Since 1895 he had been very active in reform politics. He was a member of K'ang Yu-wei's Society for the Study of

---

[37] Philip A. Kuhn, *Rebellion and its enemies in late imperial China: militarization and social structure, 1796–1864*, 189–225.

Self-Strengthening in Shanghai. After it was disbanded, he was one of the few instrumental in establishing the *Shih-wu pao* with Liang Ch'i-ch'ao as its chief editor. Beginning in the summer of 1897, he served as salt intendant for Hunan and also for a short while after that as the acting judicial commissioner of the province. In these capacities he was not only a zealous champion of reform. His first-hand knowledge of the outside world, especially his perception of the rise of Meiji Japan, was also a major source of inspiration and ideas for the institutional innovations that were to be launched in Hunan after 1895.[38]

Chiang Piao was Hunan commissioner of education from 1895 to 1897. Although he had entered officialdom by way of the regular civil service examinations, he developed an intellectual outlook not bound by traditional Confucian scholarship. After passing the metropolitan examination, Chiang Piao studied at the T'ung-wen kuan in Peking and later visited Japan. He participated in the Society for the Study of Self-Strengthening in Peking in 1895 and became an active promoter of new learning after going to Hunan.[39]

In addition to having a reform-minded provincial administration, Hunan was also under the jurisdiction of the governor-general of Hu-Kwang, Chang Chih-tung, a vigorous and persistent promoter of technological and institutional innovations, who gave substantial backing to important aspects of the reform movement such as the newspaper and the study society. Equally significant at this time was the enthusiasm for reform shown by many influential leaders of the provincial gentry. They not only gave fervent support to the government's reform efforts. In fact in many important directions they took the initiative. Thus when the reform started in earnest in Hunan in 1895, it was a joint enterprise of both the government and the provincial elite. This cooperation from the Hunanese gentry was indeed remarkable in view of the fact that in the late nineteenth century Hunan was a well-known citadel of gentry conservatism. Even the early 1890s still saw waves of Hunan-based anti-foreignism sweeping through the Yangtze valley. As late as 1892 an attempt to build a telegraph line in Hunan had caused a riot among the local populace.[40] The winds of change were obviously blowing strong in Hunan as the 1890s wore on.

From the beginning, technological and economic innovations were a striking aspect of the reform movement. At the governor's initiative, electric lights were introduced and macadamized roads constructed in

---

[38] Wu T'ien-jen, *Huang Kung-tu hsien-sheng chuan-kao* (A draft biography of Huang Tsun-hsien), 1–223.

[39] T'ang Chih-chün, *Wu-hsu pien-fa jen-wu chuan-kao*, 181–2.

[40] *Hu-nan chin-pai-nien ta-shih chi-shu* (A chronicle of major events in Hunan in the last one hundred years), 137–8.

Changsha. A mining bureau was set up in the provincial government, and a telegraph line was established between Changsha and Hankow.[41] More significant than these government-sponsored projects were enterprises undertaken by prominent local gentry on their own initiative. In late 1895, a match factory was founded by two gentry leaders, Wang Hsien-ch'ien and Chang Tsu-t'ung, with encouragement from the governor. In 1896, Wang Hsien-ch'ien, Hsiung Hsi-ling and other provincial gentry with widespread local support raised a fund to establish a steamship line that aimed to link Hunan with Hupei. In the winter of the same year, Wang and Hsiung got a loan from the government to set up the Pao-shang-ch'eng Manufacturing Company. They even petitioned the governor to construct a railway through Hunan to link Hankow with Canton.[42]

While the reform movement in ensuing years continued to inspire new endeavours in the industrial-commercial field, innovations were also undertaken on other fronts. To begin with, there was the endeavour to organize militia and to change a local academy at Changsha into a new-style military school as the foundation for further military improvement. More significant, however, were some institutional innovations attempted largely under the guiding hand of Huang Tsun-hsien. These involved an effort to set up a special training programme for officials which provided them with technical expertise and knowledge of current affairs. The purpose was to prepare government officials for leading roles in provincial reforms. Huang also drew up some new regulations with the aim of improving the judicial procedures and prison system. The core of Huang's legal and administrative reform lay in the establishment of a Bureau of Protection and Defence (Pao-wei chü) modelled on the modern police bureaux which Huang had seen in Japan and Western countries. Appended to this bureau was a new reformatory which aimed not only to penalize criminals but also to re-educate the dregs of local society. Both institutions were meant as improvements over the traditional *pao-chia* system in order to strengthen organization and order at the grass-roots level of local society. However, the Bureau of Protection and Defence, according to Huang's design, was not entirely a government organization but again a joint enterprise where both government officials and gentry-literati participated on a governing board to oversee its operations.[43]

Most significant and also fateful in the Hunan reform movement was a

[41] *Ibid.* 126–9. See also Onogawa Hidemi, *Shimmatsu seiji shisō kenkyū*, 281–4.
[42] Onogawa Hidemi, *Shimmatsu seiji shisō kenkyū*, 281–3. Charlton M. Lewis, 'The reform movement in Hunan (1896–1898)', *Papers on China*, 15 (1961) 62–90. Cf. also Charlton M. Lewis, *Prologue to the Chinese Revolution: the transformation of ideas and institutions in Hunan province, 1891–1907.*
[43] *Hu-nan chin-pai-nien ta-shih chi-shu*, 137–8. Wu T'ien-jen, *Huang Kung-tu*, 156–96.

series of cultural-educational innovations. The official who spearheaded them was the commissioner of education, Chiang Piao. In the school curriculum he stressed the value of new Western knowledge and the maintenance of a balance between it and the study of China's cultural heritage. In keeping with this policy, a knowledge of current world affairs was required for the various examinations held at the prefectural level, in addition to the traditional Confucian subjects. This made the *Wan-kuo kung-pao*, the translation of Robert MacKenzie's *The nineteenth century: a history*, and other SDK publications required reading for the examination candidates.

Chiang Piao's emphasis on new learning also led him to experiment with a revision of curriculum in one local citadel of practical Confucian learning, the Chiao-ching shu-yuan (Academy for Critical Examination of the Classics) at Changsha. He recommended the inclusion of three subjects of new learning – geography, mathematics and foreign languages – to supplement the two cardinal subjects in the Neo-Confucian curriculum: the doctrinal study of Confucian classics and the practical study of public affairs.[44]

Chiang Piao also introduced the first Hunan newspaper, installed in the Chiao-ching shu-yuan under his auspices. Published every ten days, it began in the spring of 1897 under the name of *Hsiang-hsueh hsin-pao* or *Hsiang-hsueh pao* (Hunanese study), and later grew into a major regional vehicle for reformism and for spreading new knowledge.

Chiang Piao resigned his post in the autumn of 1897. The educational innovations he had undertaken were by and large within the ideological bounds of the self-strengthening movement, but by the time of his departure, the cultural and educational reforms were already taking a more radical turn.

The first important development in this new phase was the creation of a new school – the School of Current Affairs (Shih-wu hsueh-t'ang) – in the autumn of 1897. The school was another project launched jointly by the gentry and the provincial government. Both the proposal and the funding for creating such a school came from the provincial gentry while the managing director and the vice-director of the school were appointed by the governor. The appearance of this new school apparently aroused widespread enthusiasm among the local populace since as many as four thousand youngsters were reported to have come to Changsha to take the initial entrance examination. Only forty were eventually admitted into the school for the first year.

Although the school in its format was intended as a sharp departure from

44 *Hu-nan chin-pai-nien ta-shih chi-shu*, 113, 138-9.

the traditional academy, the curriculum it offered was on the whole a balanced one. The prominence of Western learning, which ranged from natural sciences and history to legal and political studies, was combined with a heavy dose of courses on the Confucian classics in particular and on the Chinese cultural heritage in general. In fact, in his statement announcing the entrance examination for the school, Governor Ch'en Pao-chen still emphasized the centrality of Chinese learning as the guiding principle of education. Thus when first projected, the school seemed to be no more than another self-strengthening enterprise.

However, when the choice of teaching staff for the division of Chinese studies was made, the school began to take on a radical character. Again at the recommendation of Huang Tsun-hsien, Liang Ch'i-ch'ao was invited to be the chief lecturer. Three other young Cantonese scholars were invited to be Liang's assistants: Yeh Chueh-mai, Han Wen-chü and Ou Ch'ü-chia, all of them K'ang Yu-wei's disciples. Liang and his assistants arrived at Changsha in the autumn of 1897.

That year also marked the rise of other persons in Hunan who were ideologically sympathetic with Liang's party. In the spring of that year a young Hunanese scholar, T'ang Ts'ai-ch'ang, an avid student of Western learning and New Text Confucianism, joined the *Hsiang-hsueh pao* as its chief editor. Later in the autumn, T'ang's close friend, T'an Ssu-t'ung, came back from Nanking and he too plunged into the reform movement. After Liang arrived in Changsha to assume his teaching duties at the newly opened academy, both T'an and T'ang assisted him by giving lectures to the students. Meanwhile, P'i Hsi-jui, a renowned Hunanese scholar of the New Text persuasion, also came back from Kiangsi to support the rising reform movement. All these people made their appearance in Hunan, it must be remembered, at a time when Chiang Piao was succeeded by a fervent advocate of K'ang Yu-wei's New Text teachings, Hsu Jen-chu, as the new commissioner of education.[45] The arrival of this constellation of people was bound to open a new phase in the reform movement in Hunan.

The new phase began with the teaching by Liang and his assistants at the School of Current Affairs. In keeping with his emphasis on the primacy of 'political studies' (*cheng-hsueh*), Liang's instruction consisted mainly of interpreting the two Confucian classics, the *Ch'un-ch'iu* (Spring and Autumn Annals) and the *Mencius* in terms of such Western political ideas as popular rights and egalitarianism. Liang tried to instil this sort of political radicalism in his students not only by means of lectures but also by writing comments on the students' notes which he required them to submit regularly. One prominent theme in the comments was the depiction of the

45 T'ang Chih-chün, *Wu-hsu pien-fa jen-wu chuan-kao*, 183–6.

political tradition of imperial China as a shameful record of moral depravity and political robbery.

Liang and his colleagues not only tried to propagate these radical ideas among students within the school but attempted to disseminate them to the outside world by surreptitiously reprinting and distributing many thousands of abridged editions of Huang Tsung-hsi's seventeenth-century tract against despotism *Ming-i tai-fang lu* (A plan for the prince) supplemented with interpretive comments by Liang and his friends.

The political radicalism of Liang and his colleagues also contained a surprising note of anti-Manchu racialism. In Liang's written comments on the students' notes he sometimes made explicit references to the strictly tabooed fact that the Manchus had committed horrendous atrocities during their conquest of China in the seventeenth century. Furthermore, he and his associates also reprinted and distributed thousands of copies of Wang Hsiu-ch'u's *Yang-chou shih-jih chi* (An account of ten days in Yang-chou), a banned and lurid description of outrageous brutalities the Manchus had allegedly perpetrated at Yangchow. In doing this the reformers made themselves virtually indistinguishable from the contemporary revolutionaries, since this anti-Manchu account and Huang Tsung-hsi's *A plan for the prince* were also used by the revolutionaries as major propaganda for a number of years before their own pamphlets on revolution were published in the early 1900s.

Liang's radical political attitude was further evidenced in a daring memorial he submitted to Governor Ch'en Pao-chen in the wake of the German occupation of Kiaochow in the winter of 1897, suggesting that Hunan, if necessary, should declare its independence from the central government at Peking. This proposal was a reflection of Liang's exasperation with the ineptitude of the Ch'ing court in coping with the growing aggression of foreign powers, which threatened to partition China. If the central government could not be motivated to carry out reform, Liang argued, then the only way to prevent national subjugation by foreign powers was to follow the example of Satsuma and Chōshū in late Tokugawa Japan: to secede from the central government.

Liang's reference to the Japanese experience was not accidental. It reflected the fact that Liang came to join the reform movement in Hunan with the model of Satsuma and Chōshū very much in his mind. In an article he published in the daily newspaper *Hsiang-pao* he openly urged the Hunanese gentry to learn from the experience of late Tokugawa Japan. The Meiji Restoration was a success, as Liang noted, mainly because changes were first successfully carried out in the four feudal domains of Satsuma, Chōshū, Tosa and Hizen, and then spread to the rest of Japan.

This experience should be very instructive for China, given her vast size and long-standing problems. So to follow Japan's model, Liang emphasized, efforts should be made first to effect changes in the limited area of a few provinces and then to change China as a whole. In Liang's view, Hunan at that time provided the best environment for such a regional reform. To bring it about the Hunanese should even consider the possibility of taking the revolutionary action of secession from the central government. Liang was obviously drawing the lesson from the Japanese example that regional autonomy could be made to serve the purpose of nationalism.[46]

The propagation of these revolutionary ideas soon created a climate of political agitation in the new school that tended to radicalize the reform movement. This was carried further when the Southern Study Society (Nan-hsueh hui) was established in the winter of 1897. By this time the reformers as a group seem to have split into two wings: the radicals and the conservative-moderates. The protagonists of the new society, except for a few sympathetic officials in the provincial government, were mostly those young Cantonese and Hunanese gentry-literati who had joined the reform movement in its later stage. Conspicuously absent from the list of participants were some of the provincial gentry-literati who had hitherto been involved in the major technological innovations of the reform movement, such as Wang Hsien-ch'ien and Chang Chu-t'ung. Thus, unlike the founding of the School of Current Affairs, which represented the joint efforts of enlightened provincial officials and the moderate reformist gentry, the Nan-hsueh hui was from the beginning largely the creation of the radical wing of the reformist gentry-literati with the support of some provincial officials.

As conceived by these radical young reformers, the Southern Study Society was to play an even more central role than the School of Current Affairs in their drive for provincial reform. The importance they attached to the Society followed from their conception of the crucial functions of study societies in general: the education and organization of the gentry. In short, the Southern Study Society was seen as an indispensable vehicle to promote gentry power (*shen-ch'üan*) in Hunan and other southern provinces. The latter goal now had a central place in the radical reformers' political programme. In the first place, gentry-power was regarded as an essential stepping-stone to the gradual achievement of popular participation and sovereignty. Furthermore, in view of the leading role of the gentry in Chinese society, the promotion of gentry power was also seen as a pre-

[46] Hao Chang, *Liang Ch'i-chao*, 125–8.

liminary step to the development of the national power of China. Given such a political programme on the part of the radical reformers, the Southern Study Society was bound to have a top priority on their agenda.

The crucial functions ascribed to the Southern Study Society no doubt explain the eagerness with which the gentry-literati established study societies in Hunan at this time. A contemporary newspaper in Tientsin, *Kuo-wen pao*, reported in the early summer of 1898 that 'forests of lecture halls' had sprung up throughout the province. This was probably a journalistic exaggeration, but at least thirteen societies outside the Southern Study Society can be identified in these years. None of them compared with the Southern Study Society in size; at its height it probably had more than 1,200 members.

More significant than its large membership was the way the society was organized and the wide range of its intended activities. Theoretically it was a private voluntary association, but because of government involvement in its founding and operations, it took on a semi-official character. An important indication of this was the political privileges its members enjoyed. For example, they could make proposals about local public affairs which, if found valid and useful, could be submitted, through the channel of the society, to the governor and other high provincial officials for implementation. Furthermore, members, in studying current problems, could ask the government for access to the public files. All this suggests that the Southern Study Society was an organization more public than private, and at least closely affiliated with, if not formally a part of, the government.

The semi-official character of the society and its activities suggests that in the minds of the participants it was meant to be more than a voluntary organization. As P'i Hsi-jui, a prominent speaker at meetings of the society, noted in his diary, the elaborate regulations were intended to lay the groundwork for a provincial assembly controlled by the local gentry. This possibility was reinforced by Liang Ch'i-ch'ao's remarks about the society shortly after its closure: 'Though nominally a study society, Nan-hsueh hui had all the makings of a local legislature.' Liang, in fact, regarded the Nan-hsueh hui as the keystone of the whole reform movement in Hunan.[47]

In addition to functioning as a preparatory organization for self-government, the Southern Study Society also engaged in cultural activities such as the establishment of a library and the daily newspaper *Hsiang pao*, which

[47] Wang Erh-min, *Wan-Ch'ing cheng-chih ssu-hsiang shih-lun* (Studies on the history of political thought in the late Ch'ing period), 101–33. P'i Hsi-jui, 'Shih-fu-t'ang wei-k'an jih-chi' (P'i Hsi-jui's hitherto unpublished diary), *Hu-nan li-shih tzu-liao*, 1 (1958) 80.

began circulation in January 1898. Along with the *Hsiang hsueh-pao*, *Hsiang pao* became a primary medium through which the ideas and activities of the Hunan reform movement were publicized. Radicals such as T'ang Ts'ai-ch'ang, T'an Ssu-t'ung, I Nai and Fan Chui controlled these two newspapers. T'ang in particular was a central figure on their editorial boards.

In intellectual outlook T'ang was close to both K'ang Yu-wei and T'an Ssu-t'ung. Like K'ang, he was an avowed follower of the New Text School, believing in the centrality in Confucianism of the ideals of historical progress and institutional change. Though not as systematic as T'an in articulating his ideas, he had much the same intellectual outlook and a critical attitude towards Chinese tradition, especially its political order. Like T'an, he denounced the monarchy as the most blatant manifestation of human egoism and hailed democracy as the order of the future. Just as in the cases of K'ang and T'an, underlying T'ang's moral and political radicalism was an eclectic mind not only influenced by a variety of traditional ideas but also bearing the deep imprint of the West. With this eclectic background and radical outlook, T'ang, together with T'an Ssu-t'ung and other young Hunanese scholars, transformed the *Hsiang hsueh-pao* and *Hsiang pao* into a fertile field for sprouting new ideas.[48]

With the emergence of these new cultural institutions in late 1897 and early 1898, the reform movement grew increasingly radical. This alarmed both the conservatives and also those gentry-officials who until then had been strong supporters of many reform programmes. The result was a split within the ranks of the reformers. Moderates now joined forces with the conservative gentry-officials to attack the radicals and tried to check their zeal. The split finally broke into a stormy ideological struggle in the spring of 1898.

The attack mounted by the alliance of conservatives and moderates reached its height in the early summer when Wang Hsien-ch'ien and other leaders of the provincial gentry organized Changsha students in three local academies to draw up a Scholars' Compact of Hunan (Hsiang-sheng hsueh-yueh). In it they tried to present a united ideological position against what they considered the dangerous heresy then raging in the province. For them there was at stake no less than the basic values and beliefs of Chinese civilization. To defend these values and beliefs against the growing heresy, they saw themselves following the hallowed tradition of Mencius and Han Yü. Just as Mencius defended Confucius' teachings against the heresies of

---

[48] T'ang Chih-chün, *Wu-hsu pien-fa jen-wu chuan-kao*, 189–97. See also T'ang Ts'ai-chih, 'T'ang Ts'ai-ch'ang ho shih-wu hsueh-t'ang' (T'ang Ts'ai-ch'ang and the School of Current Affairs), in *Hu-nan li-shih tzu-liao*, 3 (1958) 98–108.

Yang Chu and Mo Ti, and Han Yü against the heresies of Buddhism and Taoism, they were now pledging themselves to protect Confucianism against the heresies of the K'ang-Liang group.[49]

According to these Hunanese gentry, the first and foremost among the dangers of these heresies was the unveiled criticism of the Chinese political tradition in general and of the Manchu regime in particular. Equally appalling to them was K'ang Yu-wei's radical interpretation of Confucianism. Against all this the Hunanese gentry reactions were violent. Some resorted to wholesale denunciations; others like Yeh Te-hui engaged in point-by-point rebuttals. All were marked by a vehemence very different from the tolerance that normally characterized doctrinal disagreements within the Confucian tradition.[50]

This difference was not accidental. The traditional penchant for tolerance of doctrinal differences sprang from the fact that intellectual disagreements among Confucian scholars over the centuries usually took place well within the framework of a shared belief in the central values and institutions of the tradition. What the Hunanese gentry found in the thought of the K'ang-Liang group were challenges to their fundamental beliefs. To begin with, K'ang's *An inquiry into the classics forged during the Hsin period* denied in one breath the validity of both the Neo-Confucian orthodoxy and the popular School of Han Learning. Moreover, in his *Confucius as an institutional reformer*, K'ang went further to assert not only the justifiability but also the inevitability of changing the sacred political institution of the monarchy within the framework of Confucianism. To prove further the politically subversive implications of K'ang's interpretations the Hunanese pointed to a general practice among the K'ang-Liang group of dating their letters and writings from Confucius' birth instead of from the start of the current reign of the Ch'ing emperor. In the eyes of most of the Hunanese gentry-literati this amounted to denying the legitimacy of the dynasty.

Even more shocking was the radical reformers' open advocacy of the Western ideals of people's rights and egalitarianism. To the majority of gentry, the propagation of these ideals was a frontal challenge to the sacred core of their values and beliefs – the Confucian doctrine of three bonds. This doctrine had two striking characteristics: authoritarianism, since the three bonds were relations of unconditional domination, and inviolability. In the orthodox Confucian world view, the human order was inseparably fused with the cosmic order; thus the three bonds as the core of the human order were seen as inherent in the cosmic order and the universal

[49] *Hu-nan chin-pai-nien ta-shih chi-shu*, 142–5. See also Su Yü, *I-chiao ts'ung-pien* (Collection of writings for upholding sacred teachings), 5.14–18b.
[50] Su Yü, *I-chiao ts'ung-pien*, 3.30–4; 4.1–83.

tao. This Confucian cosmological myth still controlled the moral and social thinking of the majority of Chinese gentry-literati.

The new thought of the 1890s challenged the doctrine, both indirectly and directly. The indirect challenge arose when the spread of Western physical sciences and Social Darwinism brought with them the growing acceptance of a naturalistic world view. Inevitably this would gradually erode the Confucian cosmological myth which assumed the imbeddedness of human society in the cosmos. Shorn of this myth, the doctrine was bound to lose much of its traditional sacredness and persuasiveness.[51]

The new thought also directly undermined the moral legitimacy of the three bonds. T'an Ssu-t'ung's philosophy unreservedly assaulted the doctrine, but his *On humanity* was not published until after 1900 and its influence was confined to the limited circle of his close friends. The publicized frontal challenge to the doctrine came only with the propagation of the Western liberal ideals of popular rights and social equality.

That these liberal ideals contradict the doctrine of three bonds is obvious. While people's rights denied the authoritarian relation between the sovereign and his subjects, the ideal of social equality clashed with the authoritarian tenor of the doctrine as a whole. Not surprisingly, many Hunanese gentry-literati denounced the egalitarian ideal as an outright negation of the particularistic ethics and the principle of superordination and subordination, both of which they saw as the heart of the old social and moral order. This denunciation was set forth most succinctly in a letter written to a friend by a conservative Hunanese, Tseng Lien: 'The proposal that we should change [after the model of the] barbarians began with reference to technology, and then to politics and then to moral teachings. In this way, the bonds between ruler and subject, father and son, husband and wife became completely destroyed. Once these bonds were gone, all the people on earth would look upon their relatives and superiors in the same casual way as duckweeds float past each other in water. . . . Once the moral principles that govern the ruler–subject and father–son relationships were brazenly ignored, troubles would begin within one's own door . . . and servants and actors would presume to place themselves above officials and scholars.'

For Tseng, as for many of his fellows, the acceptance of the ideal of social equality literally meant that the world was turned upside down. Little wonder that these ideals were decried by almost all Hunanese gentry who denounced the new thought, even though the radical reformers never openly attacked the doctrine *in toto*. For the majority of gentry-scholars, no

[51] Li Che-hou, *K'ang Yu-wei T'an Ssu-t'ung ssu-hsiang yen-chiu* (A study of the thought of K'ang Yu-wei and T'an Ssu-t'ung), 51.

longer was just one Confucian value or one traditional institution in jeopardy, but the sacred core of the whole moral and social order. To them, the influx of Western thought was threatening the very identity of Confucianism and Chineseness.[52]

The ideological attack on the new thought of K'ang and Liang was not an isolated movement. While it raged in Hunan in the spring and summer of 1898, anti-radical campaigns were also under way elsewhere. Censors submitted impeachments to the court denouncing K'ang Yu-wei's heretical teachings and reform activities, and a scholar-official, Wang Jen-chün, published refutations of K'ang's reform ideology in the Shanghai newspaper, *Shih-hsueh pao* (Journal of substantial study).[53] But the most powerful rebuttal outside Hunan came from a group of eminent scholar-officials centred around Chang Chih-tung.

In the spring of 1898 Chang Chih-tung published his *Ch'üan-hsueh p'ien* (Exhortation to study), in which he agreed with the Hunanese gentry's basic arguments but went deeper. From late spring to midsummer, Chang's book appeared in instalments in the *Hsiang hsueh-pao* and lent strong ideological support to the crusade against the radicals.

In Chang's view K'ang's ideology was summed up in the three slogans he put forward as the goals of his movement: protecting the state, protecting the faith, and protecting the race. But for Chang the formulation of these goals as separate entities was mistaken. There should be only one goal – protecting the state – the attainment of which automatically would entail the other two.

It is easy to see why, in Chang Chih-tung's mind, protection of the race depended upon protection of the state, but to understand why he considered the protection of the faith reducible to that of the state, an examination of his conception of 'state' is necessary. It must be remembered that Chang defined his own idea of protecting the state mainly to refute K'ang's. In K'ang's thought, at least as reflected in the preamble and governing regulations of the Pao-kuo hui (The Society for Preserving the State), *kuo* clearly referred to the corporate entity which embraced the total population of the geographical area of China. In Liang Ch'i-ch'ao's political writing, especially in his idea of *ch'ün*, the definition of *kuo* as the collective whole of the total population in a clearly demarcated geographical area was set out even more clearly. This corporate conception of *kuo*, however, had no place in the political thought of Chang Chih-tung, who identified *Chung-kuo* completely with the specific dynastic house of the Ch'ing. To protect the state meant first and foremost to protect the Ch'ing dynasty.

[52] Su Yü, *I-chiao ts'ung-pien*, 4.1-83; 5.12-13, 14-18b.
[53] T'ang Chih-chün, *Wu-hsu pien-fa shih lun-ts'ung*, 251; Su Yü, *I-chiao ts'ung-pien*, 3.14-25.

Thus in his definition of loyalty (*chung*) he specifically emphasized the Ch'ing dynasty as the rightful focus of people's loyalty by citing fifteen policies that the Ch'ing had implemented in the past as indications of its 'benevolent government' (*jen-cheng*). These policies of benevolent government distinguished the Ch'ing from Western nations and all previous Chinese dynasties including the Han and T'ang and fully justified its claim on the people's loyalty. Implicit in Chang's thinking is the notion that loyalty directed merely to *Chung-kuo* without specifying the Ch'ing, as K'ang and Liang had done, was dangerously misplaced.

Chang's definition of loyalty, in the last analysis, was still determined by his commitment to the Confucian doctrine of three bonds. This doctrine, institutionalized as the core of imperial Confucianism, tied it closely to the central institutions of monarchy and family. Herein lay a striking feature of Chinese cultural and political tradition – the fusion of polity and religion, which, in Chang Chih-tung's terms, was put as 'the combination of ruler and teacher' (*i-chün chien-shih*) or 'the mutual support of polity and religion' (*cheng-chiao hsiang-wei*). From this standpoint naturally Chang refused to consider the protection of the faith as separate from the protection of the state. He would, of course, consider K'ang Yu-wei's attempt to promote Confucianism outside the established political framework as heretical. For in Chang's view the very effort to protect the faith, quite apart from the substantive tenets of K'ang's interpretation of Confucianism, had the dangerous implication of dissociating religion from the state and thus undermining the sacred doctrine of three bonds.

Chang's disagreement with K'ang, however, went even deeper for he disputed K'ang's basic approach to protecting the state, the idea of political reformism (*pien-fa*). Ostensibly Chang was an ardent advocate of *pien-fa* and considered himself an admirer of Western politics (*Hsi-cheng*). On the surface he agreed with K'ang and Liang on the priority of studying Western politics over Western technology (*Hsi-i*). But in fact *cheng* and *fa* in Chang's comprehension had very different connotations. For him *cheng* essentially meant bureaucratic administration while *fa* referred to government policies and administrative rules. Chang's idea of *pien-fa* then boiled down to no more than a further extension of the administrative reformism of the self-strengthening movement and the statecraft tradition. Chang's premise was that *cheng*, understood in the sense of fundamental political value or institution, fell in the sanctified realm of the doctrine of three bonds and so was also part of the sage's way (*sheng-tao*). The latter, in the famous dictum of Confucianism, 'stemming from Heaven, is unalterable in as much as Heaven is eternal'.

Chang Chih-tung's commitment to the basic socio-political values of

Confucianism not only shaped his stance on the issue of political reformism, it also determined his attitude towards Western thought in general. He had been a zealous advocate of Western learning and his *Exhortation to study* went to great lengths to argue the significance of Western knowledge. Yet Chang's whole argument was predicated on an 'order of priority' (*hsun-hsu*), according to which the study of Western knowledge, however important, must be subordinate to that of Chinese learning and its core in the Confucian classics. For in the latter were stored the governing principles of the moral and institutional tradition, which not only gave a sense of identity and direction to China as a nation and people; they were also the verities which man as man must live by.

Thus Chang Chih-tung on the one hand urged the Chinese to be 'open-minded' (*chih-t'ung*) towards Western knowledge; on the other, he urged them to combine this 'open-mindedness' with a 'sense of the fundamental importance' (*chih-pen*) of Confucian teachings. In this way, the two could be made to complement each other. This understanding was the basis of Chang's famous dictum: 'Chinese learning for the fundamental structure, Western learning for practical use'.[54]

In substance Chang was reaffirming no more than the ideological position of the self-strengthening movement, ostensibly staking out a middle ground between radicals and conservatives, whose rancorous and divisive struggle he felt was splitting the country. But Chang's middle ground was in fact more of a reaction against the radicals than the conservatives. For the thrust of his position was to defend the central values and institutions of Chinese tradition against the onslaught of rising radicalism not only in Hunan but in many other parts of China as well.

Thus the publication of Chang's *Exhortation to study* in the midst of the intellectual disputes in Hunan signalled the beginning of a new phase in the ideological conflict in China. First, the centre of conflict was being shifted from that between the advocates of self-strengthening on the one hand, and the conservatives on the other, to that between the former and the radical reformers. Secondly, the ideological conflict thus far had taken the form of policy debates within government circles. But now the new disputes spread outside the government and raged among the gentry-literati at large. Finally, up to 1890 the policy debates, whether between Prince Kung and Wo-jen in the 1860s or between the advocates of self-strengthening and the Ch'ing-liu tang in the 1870s and 1880s, by and large had taken place within a consensus on basic values among all the participants. The controversy of the late 1890s, however, was no longer contained by such a consensus. In fact it was precisely certain basic values that

[54] Chang Chih-tung, *Ch'üan-hsueh p'ien* (Exhortation to study), 3.80.

were at issue. Thus in both depth and scope the intellectual disputes of the reform era marked a break with the past and foreshadowed the ideological conflicts that were to rage in China after 1900.

In the spring of 1898 Hunan was the storm centre. As the spring drew to a close the emerging ideological discord finally flared into political struggle and social conflict. Many Hunanese provincial gentry now responded to the call of such leaders as Wang Hsien-ch'ien and Yeh Te-hui and rallied behind them to stir up local sentiment against the radicals. To exert social pressure on the provincial government, some of them individually sent letters of protest to the governor or the educational commissioner; others acted as a group. In the summer of 1898, a public petition in the name of the Hunanese gentry as a whole was presented to the governor. It denounced the radical reformers as dangerous heretics and requested the expulsion of Liang Ch'i-ch'ao and his friends from the School of Current Affairs. Gentry-scholars sympathetic with the young radicals fought back by petitioning the provincial government to reorganize the conservative-dominated local academies, whereupon Wang Hsien-ch'ien and his followers mobilized students in certain academies to reinforce their attack.[55]

In addition to organized protest, the Hunan gentry also resorted to popular propaganda and outright social ostracism. For instance, students at one local academy printed and distributed placards and handbills to mount a smear campaign against the School of Current Affairs. One Hunanese radical reformer, Fan Chui, an active member of the Southern Study Society and also a writer for the *Hsiang pao*, was evicted from his home county by the local populace.[56] At the height of the storm, riots against the radical reformers were reported. The campaign against new thought now took on a character reminiscent of anti-Christian incidents in the late nineteenth century.

Meanwhile political pressure was also coming from the office of the governor-general at Wuchang to support the anti-radical campaign in Hunan. Until the spring of 1898 Chang Chih-tung had ordered government offices and academies throughout Hupei to subscribe to the reform newspapers in Hunan. But now, horrified by the radical thinking and activities that were spreading in Hunan, he ordered subscriptions to be stopped, and he and his close adviser, Liang Ting-fen, sent notes to warn the Hunan officials of these radical trends. Meanwhile, some Hunan gentry were also trying to get Peking to control the radicals. Acting on reports from Hunan, censors memorialized the court demanding strong measures against the K'ang-Liang party. Tseng Lien, the conservative gentry-

---

55 Su Yü, *I-chiao ts'ung-pien*, 5.12–13. *Hu-nan chin-pai-nien ta-shih chi-shu*, 151–2.
56 Su Yü, *I-chiao ts'ung-pien*, 5.1. *Hu-nan chin-pai-nien ta-shih chi-shu*, 151–2.

scholar, citing Liang Chi-ch'ao's radical teachings and activities in Hunan as evidences of treason, even asked the court to put K'ang and Liang to death.[57]

Thus from spring to summer 1898, as pressure mounted to counter the radicalization of the reform movement, most of the reformers were compelled to leave the province. In early August, under pressure, Governor Ch'en Pao-chen memorialized the court to burn the blocks and ban reprinting of K'ang Yu-wei's provocative *Confucius as a reformer*. The attempts of radical scholar-reformers to carry out cultural innovations in Hunan ended in complete failure, even though some activities continued through the summer.

The reason for the failure of the Hunan reform must be sought in the radicalization of the movement in its later stage. From beginning to end it had the full support of provincial government authorities. This particularly auspicious environment inspired the young radicals with high hopes of achieving drastic political changes, first regionally and then throughout the country. The driving force in the radicalization was this province-to-centre approach, the model for which was the Japanese experience of the Meiji Restoration, when some feudal domains like Chōshū and Satsuma spearheaded the whole political development that led to Japan's national rejuvenation. The idea of using the Japanese model, however, turned out to be ill-conceived. The provincial authorities of Hunan did not have the kind of independent power that the Japanese feudal lords of Chōshū and Satsuma had had. They could not carry out comprehensive local reforms independent of the central government. Without autonomous regional power to back them, the radical reformers ran afoul of powerful conservative forces at the local level, which eventually brought the movement to a halt.

At the root of this contrast lay the difference between the social and political structure of Ch'ing China and that of Tokugawa Japan. Feudalism in the Tokugawa society and polity gave many feudal domains in Japan a great deal of autonomy, which made possible successful regional reforms in outlying areas as a foundation for later nation-wide political transformation. The development from region to centre, however, was hardly possible in the centralized bureaucratic empire of the Ch'ing. To be sure, the political structure of China in the late nineteenth century has been generally seen as decentralized, largely because of the emergence of so-called regionalism in the provinces. This picture, however, has been over-

[57] *Hu-nan chin-pai-nien ta-shih chi-shu*, 162–4. Huang Chang-chien, *Wu-hsu pien-fa shih yen-chiu* (Studies on the history of the reform movement of 1898), 371–405. Tseng Lien, *Ku-an chi*, 12.1–19b.

emphasized. In the first place, as recent studies suggest, even at the height of 'regionalism', the Ch'ing court still maintained a good many institutional controls under which the governors-general and governors had only limited leeway rather than autonomous regional power.[58]

Furthermore, regional power was restricted by the ideological authority which the central government still maintained intact, and until mid-1895 the Western impact failed to penetrate the intellectual world of the gentry-literati in any significant way. Confucian values and beliefs, at least in their Neo-Confucian orthodox form, inculcated an intense loyalty to the emperor and a belief in the inviolability of the imperial system, so that the ideological authority of the central government was still an important check on regional power and independent innovation.

In addition to these institutional and ideological restraints from above, there was also a powerful social force from below to limit regional innovation, namely, the gentry. In the Ch'ing era, the gentry were a social elite as well as a power elite at the local level. In their home districts or provinces they undertook important public activities with the sanction of government. Indeed, local administration would have been crippled without their participation.

This local power elite constituted a strong centripetal force because of their close identification with the imperial court, based on both practical and ideological considerations. To begin with, their elite status was largely dependent upon the civil-service examination system of the central government. Furthermore, the imperial bureaucracy provided an institutional framework in which they could gain access to power and wealth. Thus, prestige, economic interests and power tied the gentry to the political centre of the empire with a bond that their local attachments could hardly loosen.

These ties of interest were reinforced by the ideological tie of orthodox Confucianism centred around the doctrine of three bonds. Apart from enjoining a personal loyalty to the emperor, the doctrine also implanted a religio-cosmological belief in the institutional sacredness of kingship. Bound by these ideological ties, the gentry became not just a powerful social force making for political integration of the empire; they also acted as stout guardians of the traditional socio-political order.

As indicated before, after the middle of the nineteenth century, the power of the local elite grew along with that of governors and governors-general. This gave the so-called regionalism in the late Ch'ing a dual character that must not be overlooked. As long as the gentry remained

---

[58] Kwang-ching Liu, 'Nineteenth-century China: the disintegration of the old order and the impact of the West', in Ping-ti Ho and Tang Tsou, eds. *China in crisis*, 1.1.109–12.

loyal as shown above, the regional power of the governors and governors-general could not go very far. Conservative gentry could check the regional officials' autonomy and they could also curb the officials' capacity for innovation. This was what happened in Hunan in the three years after 1895.

For much of the late nineteenth century, the Hunan gentry, as the Chinese gentry elsewhere, remained a conservative and centripetal social force. It was thus not surprising that they should repeatedly come into conflict with movements that threatened radical change to Chinese society. In the 1850s and 1860s the Hunan gentry organized powerful military forces to defend the central government against the Taipings in order to preserve the traditional order. In the three decades after 1860 it was also the Hunan gentry who resisted most vigorously the spread of Christian missionaries inland. True, things changed considerably in Hunan in the years following 1895. But for the majority of the gentry-literati involved in the reform movement this meant only that they began to accept what many governors and governors-general had proposed for decades, namely the self-strengthening type of changes. In the meantime it must not be forgotten that most of these gentry-literati also shared the other side of the concept of change held by advocates of self-strengthening, namely change predicated on the immutability and sacredness of the central values and institutions of the Chinese tradition. Thus when the reformers undertook changes that threatened these central values and institutions, the Hunan gentry immediately withdrew their cooperation and mounted a relentless attack on the reformers. The defeat of the reformers in Hunan meant that although changes had started towards the end of the nineteenth century they had not gone far enough to alter the basic socio-political orientation of the gentry, as they were to do in the 1900s. The political order in China was still buttressed by the cultural support of Confucianism and the social support of its local elite. This identification of the dominant social and cultural forces in the provinces with the institutional foundation of the state made radical reform on the regional level extremely difficult, and by the same token made the Japanese-inspired province-to-centre approach to reform a forlorn hope.

THE DEBACLE OF 1898

While the reform movement was being aborted in Hunan, it was revived in Peking in the early spring of 1898. The immediate occasion for this resurgence was again the deepening crisis on China's foreign front. In November 1897 Germany moved into Shantung to occupy Kiaochow Bay and the port of Tsingtao. Russia followed by sending gunboats into Port Arthur in December. Their efforts to dominate Shantung and Manchuria respectively as their 'spheres of influence' precipitated the general scramble for concessions in early 1898. This spasm of territorial seizures threatened to partition China into a congeries of foreign colonies. Under the shadow of imminent dismemberment, a new wave of alarm swept across the land.

The sense of an impending national doom drove K'ang Yu-wei back to Peking to resume his campaign for reform in the winter of 1897. Beginning in early 1898 K'ang again petitioned the Ch'ing court for reform. Unlike his previous petitions, the new appeals soon drew positive responses from the court, which spearheaded a series of unexpected and fateful developments in the spring and summer of 1898, carrying K'ang Yu-wei close to power and his reform movement almost to success. These developments took place because of new alignments of power in the central government centred around the two principal figures in the court: Empress Dowager Tz'u-hsi and the Kuang-hsu Emperor.

Tz'u-hsi in 1889 had officially announced her retirement but she continued to pull the strings. All memorials still had to be sent to I-luan-tien, the empress dowager's residential palace, for her perusal. She might allow Kuang-hsu to handle day-to-day administration, but on important matters such as appointment to the Grand Council and the six boards she retained decision-making power. According to Weng T'ung-ho's diary, when he went to the palace for imperial instructions during such crises as the Sino-Japanese War and the scramble for concessions, he was often received not by the emperor alone but by him together with the empress dowager, who usually had much to say on both foreign and domestic affairs.[59]

In retirement, Tz'u-hsi's authority rested on several factors. As empress dowager, she was the official mother of the emperor. In the name of parental status she wielded an authority which the emperor could hardly resist under a dynastic tradition officially committed to ruling in accordance with filial piety. Also bearing on Tz'u-hsi's authority was the fact that unlike the T'ung-chih Emperor, who legitimately inherited the throne from his father (the Hsien-feng Emperor), Kuang-hsu was not a legitimate heir to T'ung-chih but owed his position entirely to Tz'u-hsi's will and manoeuvres. Growing up under her shadow Kuang-hsu inevitably became conditioned by the fear that if the empress dowager could make him she could also break him.

More importantly, Tz'u-hsi's power also stemmed from the fact that the majority of high officials in the court owed their positions to her patronage and were personally loyal to her. The composition of the Grand Council in the period from the inauguration of Kuang-hsu's nominal rule in 1889 to

59 Kung-ch'uan Hsiao, 'Weng T'ung-ho and the reform movement of 1898', Ch'ing-hua hsueh-pao, NS, 1.2 (April 1957) 111–245. WHPF, 1.508.

his fall from power in 1898 may serve as an illustration. A brief look at the dynastic history of the Ch'ing indicates that in almost every instance when a new emperor came to power a major shake-up in the Grand Council took place. It is therefore significant that the Kuang-hsu Emperor's assumption of power in 1889 involved no such shake-up. In fact, for four years after 1889 the five grand councillors were the same as those appointed in the last few years of Tz'u-hsi's regency. Starting with 1893 new names began to be added to the original roster. From that year until September 1898 altogether ten new councillors were appointed; some served continuously throughout the period, some only temporarily. While most were officials who had risen through Tz'u-hsi's patronage, none were close to the emperor except his tutor and trusted adviser, Weng T'ung-ho. But even Weng owed his prominence chiefly to the empress dowager and he was reported to have said in 1889: 'Without [the empress dowager], how could [we] have come this far?' In short, those high officials who helped the emperor make important decisions were mostly, if not all, the empress dowager's men. This largely accounts for Tz'u-hsi's power during her so-called retirement.[60]

While compelling Kuang-hsu's loyalty and obedience, Tz'u-hsi's power inevitably generated resentment and hence created strains and conflicts, which were aggravated by other differences between the two. First, in age: in 1895 Kuang-hsu was twenty-four, Tz'u-hsi sixty. Another divergence was in intellectual background and outlook. To be sure, Kuang-hsu had received a largely traditional education, but as soon as he began to 'assume power' in 1889, he was exposed to a new source of ideas, at first largely under Weng T'ung-ho's influence. In that year, for instance, on Weng's recommendation the young emperor became interested in *Chiao-pin-lu k'ang-i* (Straightforward words from the Lodge of Early Chou Studies), a collection of essays on reform written around 1860 by Feng Kuei-fen, who emphasized the usefulness of Western learning accepted within the frame-work of 'the moral principles and ethical teachings of China'. Very soon, however, his interest in the new learning grew beyond what Weng T'ung-ho could approve. For three years, from 1891 to 1894, he studied foreign languages in the palace under foreign teachers from the T'ung-wen kuan. In 1894 he read some of the writings of such political reformers as Ch'en Chih and T'ang Chen. In 1895 Sun Chia-nai, another of his tutors, reported that the emperor was studying with him Timothy Richard's popular trans-lation of Robert MacKenzie's *The nineteenth century: a history*.[61]

[60] Fu Tsung-mou, *Ch'ing-tai chün-chi-ch'u tsu-chih chi chih-chang chih yen-chiu* (A study of the organization and functions of the Grand Council in the Ch'ing period), 529-683.

[61] Wang Shu-huai, *Wai-jen*, 53. *WHPF*, 1.509-12.

Partly perhaps because the empress dowager grew alarmed over Kuang-hsu's deepening addiction to the new thought, she decided in 1895 to stop his tutorial studies except for those of traditional Chinese learning. But this prohibition in fact did not prevent him from pursuing his fervent interest in Western learning. Inevitably the emperor's intellectual outlook varied considerably from that of the empress dowager.

Out of the discord that gradually emerged after 1889 between the two rulers, there grew a factional rivalry in the palace as well as the government. Much of its development is still shrouded in mystery: it is thus easy for historians to distort its significance and nature. First of all it must be remembered that, in the maelstrom of faction-ridden court politics, the rivalry between the two rulers was only one growing current. In studying the court politics of this period, one must therefore guard against the danger of interpreting all factional struggles solely in terms of this rivalry. One must also resist the temptation simply to identify the factional rivalry between the two rulers with the ideological conflict between conservatives and reformers. For the fact is that the empress dowager, as the real power in the court, naturally commanded the allegiance of the majority of officials. In her faction were thus men of a variety of political outlooks and per-suasions, including both conservatives and moderates. It is true that most officials on the emperor's side were inclined towards reform. But they, such as Weng T'ung-ho and Wang Min-luan, were not necessarily more reform-minded than, say, Li Hung-chang and Jung-lu, who were usually identified as important members of the empress dowager's faction. In fact, the rivalry between the emperor and the empress dowager did not become ideological until early in 1898.

Moreover, until then, the so-called emperor's faction was only an amorphous, small group representing scattered pro-emperor sentiments. Although a number of those who made known their sympathy for the emperor, such as Wen T'ing-shih and Wang Min-luan, were close to Weng T'ung-ho, the emperor's sympathizers did not always have close mutual relationships, nor had any deliberate efforts been made to band them together as an organized faction. Moreover, the dividing line between the two factions was not as sharply drawn then as it came to be after the spring of 1898. Weng T'ung-ho, for instance, while widely regarded as the leading figure in the emperor's faction, had never opposed the empress dowager. Until the very end of his service in the summer of 1898, he considered his main purpose was to mediate rather than to create discord between the two rulers. In his case a pro-emperor position clearly did not involve an anti-empress dowager posture.[62]

[62] Kung-ch'uan Hsiao, 'Weng T'ung-ho', 111–243.

The situation began to change, however, when K'ang Yu-wei came back to re-open his campaign for reform in the winter of 1897. In the spring and summer of 1898 the scattered pro-emperor sentiments gradually crystallized into a fully fledged faction, and the factional rivalry became ideologically charged and eventually polarized the court around the issue of radical versus moderate reform. Controversial as K'ang Yu-wei became after his bold and sensational appeals for reform in 1895, there were still several officials in the court who were impressed by K'ang's patriotic dedication and intellectual resourcefulness and so recommended him to the emperor. But the high official who was, more than any other, instrumental in introducing K'ang Yu-wei into the 'emperor faction' was Weng T'ung-ho.

In his early years at court, Weng's political viewpoint was no different from that of the conservative majority. In the late 1880s, however, he became interested in Western affairs and leaned towards reform. This significant change in outlook had a decisive impact on the young emperor. The defeat of China by Japan in 1894 reinforced Weng's views, and thereafter he became a fervent advocate of reform.

Weng's strong reformist leanings inevitably drew his attention to K'ang Yu-wei's campaign. Zealous as Weng was for reform, his outlook was still more or less along the lines of the self-strengthening movement, a far cry from the radical reformism K'ang embraced. That is why Weng expressed misgivings when he first learned of K'ang's unorthodox and provocative view of Confucianism published in his *An inquiry into the classics forged during the Hsin period*. But, as Hsiao Kung-ch'üan has suggested, Weng's interest in K'ang and his later recommendation of him to the emperor may not have been entirely motivated by ideological considerations. He was, after all, an ambitious high official involved in a power struggle with such other eminent reform-minded officials as Li Hung-chang and Chang Chih-tung. To Weng, then, reform was not only an ideal but also a prize of high power value. K'ang with his resourcefulness in ideas of reform might serve as a valuable ally who could conceivably help Weng to outwit his opponents in reform-mongering at court.[63]

Furthermore, K'ang's heterodox views of Confucianism and his radical ideas of institutional change were made known only gradually in the 1890s. K'ang Yu-wei did not appear to be as radical in the mid-1890s as in 1898. In fact, most of his 'far-out' views were publicized only in the spring and summer of 1898. Before that time his reform programme still looked reconcilable with the moderate reformism of those like Weng, Sun Chia-nai and Chang Chih-tung, who were impressed by K'ang's intellectual grasp

[63] *Ibid.*

and courageous political stand. When the full extent of K'ang's radicalism became known, Weng and some others became alarmed and moved away from K'ang's stand. But Weng had recommended K'ang to the emperor and they were already in direct communication.

Shortly after K'ang arrived in Peking in the winter of 1897 but before his renewed appeal for reform reached the emperor, the latter ordered an interview to be arranged at the Tsungli Yamen between K'ang and such high officials as Li Hung-chang, Jung-lu and Weng T'ung-ho. At this interview, on 24 January 1898, K'ang boldly declared that 'the institutions of the ancestors' needed to be changed and that the 'laws and governmental system' of China should be done away with. Even Weng felt dismayed at K'ang's talk, which he described in his diary as 'unrestrained to the extreme'.[64]

Meanwhile, K'ang submitted to the emperor three memorials to follow up his reform proposals of 1895. Unlike the previous memorials, these three reached the emperor. They openly proposed the promulgation of a constitution and the establishment of a national assembly. More important, they now spelt out K'ang's specific and concrete ideas for the policy innovations necessary to carry out his ideal of institutional reform. First of all, the government must consciously take Meiji Japan and Petrine Russia as models. To follow these models, the emperor should take three important steps. First, he should assert his power as emperor and make known his resolve for reform. Secondly, an office should be set up at the palace gate to short-circuit the sluggish bureaucratic channels so as to elicit ideas and detect talents directly from below. Finally, to bypass the whole existing bureaucracy, a Bureau of Government Reorganization should be established in the palace to lay out the blueprints for institutional reforms and to carry them out. Altogether K'ang's strategy was a bold call to strip the whole court and bureaucracy of power and concentrate it all in the hands of the emperor and his reform advisers. For all practical purposes, it was a declaration of war on the whole Ch'ing official establishment.

Kuang-hsu's response to K'ang's memorials was apparently enthusiastic; for as soon as K'ang's first memorial reached him, he ordered the Tsungli Yamen to submit to him K'ang's writings on reform. Thereafter, when K'ang submitted his reform proposals to the court, he accompanied them with his *A study of the political reforms in Meiji Japan*, *An account of the reforms of Peter of Russia*, and other assorted writings on the politics and histories of modern European countries. Thus in the early spring of 1898, well before K'ang had his first personal audience with the emperor, an outline of his ideas was already at the latter's disposal.[65]

[64] *Ibid.*   [65] T'ang Chih-chün, *Wu-hsu pien-fa shih lun-ts'ung*, 154–221.

Meanwhile, K'ang continued his drive to mobilize the scholar-officials for his cause by organizing study societies among them. On 5 January 1898, he set up a Kwangtung Study Society (Yueh hsueh-hui) at Peking among the people who came from his own native province – Kwangtung. Two months later came the establishment of the Fukien Study Society (Min hsueh-hui), the Szechwan Study Society (Shu hsueh-hui), and the Shensi Study Society (Kuan hsueh-hui), all organized by reform-minded scholar-officials from these different provinces. Meanwhile, K'ang and his friends formed two other associations: the Economic Study Society (Ching-chi hsueh-hui) and the Awaken to Shame Society (Chih-ch'ih hsueh-hui).

The resumption by K'ang, Liang and their associates of the campaign for reform, as in 1895, coincided with the holding of triennial metropolitan examinations. Thousands of candidates now thronged Peking. With German and Russian aggression in Shantung and Manchuria respectively, the capital was charged with tension and indignation. K'ang again thought of mobilizing these candidates and gentry-officials in the capital to 'form a great society to vent national indignation'. Thus K'ang, along with a reform-minded censor, Li Sheng-to, organized the Society for Preserving the State (Pao-kuo hui), which held its first meeting on 12 April. Under its influence, three other societies of a similar nature but more restricted in scope, the Protect Chekiang Society (Pao-Che hui), Protect Yunnan Society (Pao-Tien hui) and Protect Szechwan Society (Pao-Ch'uan hui), were established in Peking.[66]

Modelled on the Ch'iang hsueh-hui, the Pao-kuo hui was meant to be a nation-wide rather than a local organization, with headquarters at Peking and Shanghai but with affiliates eventually in every district, prefecture and province in the country. What made the Pao-kuo hui different from the Ch'iang hsueh-hui was the new rhetoric of nationalism in which the goals of the society were spelt out. The motivating force behind the Ch'iang hsueh-hui had been the dawning national consciousness. Yet this was somewhat muted by the conventional language of patriotism in which the preamble and announcements of the Ch'iang hsueh-hui were couched. The goal of the society, for instance, was still 'self-strengthening' (*tzu-ch'iang*), a term in vogue since the 1860s. In the preamble of the Pao-kuo hui, however, such conventional patriotic language was replaced by a new rhetoric. The goals of the society were the protection of national rights (*kuo-ch'üan*), national territory (*kuo-ti*) and the national creed (*kuo-chiao*). The appearance of these new terms clearly showed the significant growth of nationalism in China in the three years since 1895.

[66] *Ibid.* 256–61.

The Pao-kuo hui, however, turned out to be no more successful than its predecessor, although it looked a lot more impressive in membership. While the Ch'iang hsueh-hui had only 30 members, the Pao-kuo hui had 186. But it did not enjoy the kind of support the Ch'iang hsueh-hui had had from the upper echelon of government. No prominent names appeared on its roster. Furthermore, it had hardly got started when conservatives began to attack it. K'ang's emphasis on national interest rather than on that of the Manchu dynasty horrified many as potentially subversive. Very soon a pamphlet, *A rebuttal of Pao-kuo hui*, was circulated. Censors moved to impeach the society. An anti-Pao-kuo hui movement was organized. Under this attack, even K'ang Yu-wei's original co-sponsor, Li Sheng-to, backed out and joined the impeachment to protect himself. Meanwhile most of the examination candidates had left the capital after the outcome of the metropolitan examination was announced in mid-April. Thus after holding only three meetings and lasting about one month, the Pao-kuo hui rapidly faded away.[67]

The fate of this body indicated the degree of hostility and suspicion that was developing around K'ang Yu-wei's campaign for reform in Peking in the late spring and early summer of 1898. The frenzied ideological struggle between the followers of K'ang and their opponents, as seen above, was also reaching its zenith in Hunan at this time, and a principal tactic of the opponents was to take their case to the central government, making all kinds of accusations against the reformers, based on their reports of the latter's activities in Hunan. Consequently, to many officials in the central government, K'ang Yu-wei and his associates were now *proven* to be a dangerous group. When K'ang, with all his unorthodox views and radical politics, suddenly gained access to the emperor and became embroiled in the power struggle within the palace, the atmosphere grew tense indeed.

The K'ang-Liang group's petition for reform suddenly bore fruit when, on 11 June, the Kuang-hsu Emperor issued an edict announcing reform as the national policy of the country. On 16 June, K'ang was summoned to the palace for his first personal audience with the emperor. During this audience, which lasted for hours, K'ang emphasized that what China needed was an across-the-board institutional change. As he promised the emperor, 'After three years of reform China could stand on her own. From then on China would daily make progress and outstrip all the other countries in terms of wealth and power.' Following the audience, the emperor gave K'ang a special appointment in the Tsungli Yamen with the exceptional privilege of presenting memorials straight to the emperor

[67] *Ibid.* 256–60. T'ang Chih-chün, *Wu-hsu pien-fa jen-wu chuan-kao*, 344–50. John Schrecker, 'The Pao-kuo hui: a reform society of 1898', *Papers on China*, 14 (1960) 50–64.

without going 'through channels'. With this direct line of communication established between the emperor and K'ang, the reform movement entered a new phase well known as the 'Hundred Days'.

These hundred days from 11 June to 21 September saw a quick succession of more than a hundred decrees issued by the emperor, trying to force through reforms on an unprecedented scale. Until late August most of these decrees dealt with the economic, military and cultural-educational spheres. In both the economic and military spheres the edicts represented an intensification of the self-strengthening movement. In the economic sphere, greater efforts were to be mounted by the state to promote agriculture, commerce and industry. For this purpose a spate of innovations was decreed: a bureau of agriculture, industry and commerce to be established at the capital with branch offices in every province; a mining and railway office in the central government; regulations to reward technological developments; post offices at the capital and other commercial centres; and monthly budgetary reports to rationalize government finance. As for military reforms, emphasis was placed on training modern armed forces, strengthening naval forces, and organizing *pao-chia* and the militia system, all to be undertaken by the provincial governments.

The cultural-educational innovations went significantly beyond the accomplishments of the self-strengthening movement and represented the culmination of educational reform already under way in a piecemeal fashion since 1896. Two of the most important planned innovations were a radical revamping of the civil-service examination system, including the replacement of the traditional requirements for good calligraphy and stereotyped eight-legged essays with new requirements for essays on current affairs and for a knowledge of 'substantial studies' (*shih-hsueh*); and the establishment of a Metropolitan University at the capital and of various high and primary schools in every province plus military and technical schools.

Beginning in late August the emperor further intensified his drive for reform and began to remodel the government structure. A number of offices in the central government and several provincial offices under the governors and governors-general were abolished. The important boards and offices in the central government were also ordered to do away with their existing administrative rules and to compile new ones. New councillors were to be appointed in the government to determine policies. On 13 September, the Kuang-hsu Emperor announced his determination and readiness to 'open his palace for discussing changes of government structure'.[68]

All the policy innovations decreed during the Hundred Days were based

[68] T'ang Chih-chün, *Wu-hsu pien-fa shih lun-ts'ung*, 178-216. Huang Chang-chien, *Wu-hsu pien-fa shih yen-chiu*, 1-305.

on proposals made by reform-minded gentry-officials of both moderate and radical persuasion. Most of the ideas for these proposals originated either directly or indirectly from K'ang Yu-wei, who not only submitted a series of memorials about the general directions and approaches of the reform prior to 11 June, but continued after that date to spell out his ideas in concrete policy proposals presented in twenty-one memorials to the emperor.

Not all of K'ang's proposals, however, were acted on in the reform edicts issued during the summer of 1898. His recommendations regarding military and cultural-educational reforms were almost all adopted. Most of his proposals concerning economic innovations, except his recommendation for the abolition of the grain tribute and likin systems, were also translated into reform edicts. But his recommendations for changes in political institutions, where he suggested the promulgation of a constitution, the establishment of a national assembly, and the announcement of joint rule by the emperor and people, were not put forward in the emperor's decrees. However, the emperor's announcement in mid-September of his readiness to discuss fundamental changes of political institutions showed his receptivity to these possibilities. Thus, as the summer wore on, Kuang-hsu's drive for reform became increasingly radical and threatened to culminate in a drastic recasting of the whole political structure of the empire.[69]

This trend towards radicalization not only ran counter to the ideological stand of the majority of government officials, it also ran afoul of the vested interests of almost the whole of officialdom. The revamping of the examination system threatened the career opportunities of the vast number of literati in the empire. The announced policies of abolishing many offices in the government and of changing the existing administrative rules of the bureaucracy threatened the immediate interests of many incumbents. Military reform would involve reduction and disbanding of many existing military forces. The appointment of young reformers to strategic, though minor, posts in such important offices as the Grand Council and Tsungli Yamen, plus the new rules of memorialization by which literati and officials could bypass the regular bureaucratic channels and present proposals directly to the emperor, all tended to upset the power position of high officials in the court. At the top, the reform programme defied the empress dowager's authority and directly menaced her powers and the fortunes of her most trusted eunuchs. Finally the breathtaking pace of the reform drive and its increasing radicalization created a general atmosphere of apprehen-

[69] T'ang Chih-chün, *Wu-hsu pien-fa shih lun-ts'ung*, 154–221.

sion and insecurity in which the reform movement could be easily seen as an indiscriminate dismantling of the whole existing order. Thus, the Hundred Days polarized the whole court into an irreconcilable opposition between the emperor and a small group of radical young reformers on the one side and the empress dowager and the whole of officialdom on the other.

The conflict between the two sides broke into the open almost as soon as the Hundred Days' reform got under way. On 15 June, four days after reform was proclaimed to be the national policy, Weng T'ung-ho, who had helped the emperor draw up the imperial edict, was dismissed from the court into retirement under pressure from the empress dowager's faction. From then on, while the emperor and the radical reformers were busy issuing edicts, the empress dowager and her powerful faction quietly consolidated their power. On the day of Weng's dismissal, Jung-lu, her trusted protégé, was appointed acting governor-general of the metropolitan province, Chihli, in command of all the armed forces in North China. Meanwhile, a decree was issued by which a personal audience with the empress dowager, as a gesture to acknowledge gratitude and to pledge loyalty, was made compulsory for any ranking official in the government who received a new assignment.

In the ensuing two months the conflict continued to escalate. In early September, the emperor went so far as to order at one stroke the dismissal of the two presidents and four vice-presidents of the Board of Ceremony. Meanwhile, four young scholars with strong reformist leanings, Yang Jui, Lin Hsu, Liu Kuang-ti and T'an Ssu-t'ung, were appointed by the emperor to be secretaries in the Grand Council to help in its deliberations and to innovate policies. With such bold moves to assert authority and capture power, the stage was set for a final showdown.

This came on 21 September, when the empress dowager staged a successful coup d'état which stripped the Kuang-hsu Emperor of power and forced him into solitary seclusion. On the same day she also announced her return to power to 'give instruction on administration' (hsun-cheng), and thus began her third regency, which lasted for another decade until her death. Meanwhile, in late September she launched a purge which led to the dismissal and arrest of many literati and officials who were directly or indirectly involved in K'ang Yu-wei's movement. Six young reformers were executed, including the radical Hunanese scholar, T'an Ssu-t'ung and K'ang Yu-wei's younger brother, K'ang Kuang-jen. K'ang Yu-wei himself managed to escape the purge by fleeing to Hong Kong with the help of British officials, while Liang Ch'i-ch'ao escaped on a Japanese gunboat to Japan. On 26 September, the empress dowager revoked all the important policy innovations that the Kuang-hsu Emperor had announced during the Hundred Days.

LEGACIES OF THE REFORM ERA

The reform movement thus proved to be as much of a failure at the capital as it had been in the provinces. Paradoxically, the empire, while centralized enough to prevent radical changes at the regional level, was not centralized enough at the apex of the imperial government to be able to undertake a concerted drive for comprehensive institutional change. The failure of the reform movement, however, not only revealed a glaring inability on the part of the Chinese political system for comprehensive innovation. It also reflected how the political leadership was unable to renovate the system and undergo the self-transformation necessary in China's time of crisis.

But the reform movement must not be counted a complete failure. Underlying it from the beginning was an intellectual ground swell. As the political effort unfolded after 1895, the feeling and attention it aroused fed back to deepen and broaden this groundswell. Eventually, while the reform movement failed to achieve its political goal, the intellectual changes it induced had a long-range nation-wide impact on the society and culture of China.

First of all, they ushered in a new phase of Chinese culture – the era of ideologies. As seen above, the reform era witnessed an intellectual ferment brought about by the large-scale influx of Western thought into the world of the Chinese gentry-literati. Thus started the disintegration of established world views and institutionalized values that raised the curtain on the cultural crises of the twentieth century. From the beginning the cultural crisis was accompanied by a frantic search which led many Chinese intellectuals to look deep into their past and also beyond their civilization's horizon for intellectual reorientation. So the upshot was a plethora of ideologies that inundated China from the late 1890s. The advent of these new ideologies and the concomitant intellectual changes of unprecedented magnitude owed much to the new instruments of change that mushroomed in the years after 1895. One such instrument came from the reshaping of traditional academies (shu-yuan) to create new schools. Almost from their first appearance in the tenth century, academies had served as important centres of the gentry-literati's intellectual activities. During the centuries that followed it was largely in the academies that Neo-Confucianism flourished and maintained its intellectual vitality. In the late Ming, they also played an important political role in providing independent centres from which some Confucian scholars could carry on political protest and criticism of the court on a collective basis.

After the early Ch'ing put the academies under government financial control and banned lectures and discussions of a socio-political nature, they lost their intellectual vitality and political significance. But their continued importance as educational institutions for the elite was reflected in their vast number – at one estimate, about 4,500 in the nineteenth century. In Kwangtung alone, by another estimate, there were 411 academies during the Ch'ing period.[70] Their educational function, however, was reduced largely to routine preparation for civil-service examinations. A few academies founded early in the nineteenth century, such as the Hsueh-hai t'ang at Canton and the Ku-ching ching-she at Hangchow, saw some revival of Confucian scholarship. But the winds of change that blew strong in the treaty ports after the 1840s hardly touched the embalmed intellectual life in most academies.[71]

A significant change came only in the 1890s. Restructured academies and new schools began to be set up by gentry-literati, at first sporadically and then after 1895 in increasing numbers. Pioneering in this educational reform were a number of provincial officials such as Chang Chih-tung, Sheng Hsuan-huai, Liao Shou-feng and Chiang Piao.[72] Even more important than these local efforts were a number of memorials submitted to the court in 1896 by Ch'ing officials asking for the general establishment of new schools. Most outstanding was the memorial of Li Tuan-fen, a ranking official in the court and a close associate of K'ang and Liang, who suggested that the reshaping of traditional academies through curriculum revision was the most practical way to set up new schools. This proposal was accepted by the court and decreed as a government policy.[73] In response, old-style academies in many areas throughout the empire were reported to have made the suggested changes, and significant efforts were also made to set up new schools. Thus in the two years from 1896 to 1898 a spate of educational reforms swept across the empire, culminating in the all-out efforts during the Hundred Days' reform to revamp the examination system and establish an empire-wide school system. With the empress dowager's coup d'état, educational reform was stopped, but no attempts were made to reverse changes already made. In this way the basic educa-

[70] Liu Po-chi, *Kuang-tung shu-yuan chih-tu* (Institutional history of the local academies in Kwangtung), 78–9, 337–430. Tilemann Grimm, 'Academies and urban system in Kwangtung', in G. William Skinner, ed. *The city in late imperial China*, 475–98.

[71] Hsieh Kuo-chen, 'Chin-tai shu-yuan hsueh-hsiao chih-tu pien-ch'ien k'ao' (Changes in the institutions of academy and school in the modern period), in Hu Shih *et al.* eds. *Chang Chü-sheng ch'i-shih sheng-jih chi-nien lun-wen-chi* (A collection of essays in celebration of Chang Yuan-chi's seventieth birthday), 281–322.

[72] For Chiang Piao's educational reform, see Onogawa Hidemi, *Shimmatsu seiji shisō kenkyū*, 276–81. For Liao Shou-feng, see *WHPF*, 2.375–81. See also Sheng Lang-hsi, *Chung-kuo shu-yuan chih-tu* (The academy system in China), 223–30.

[73] *WHPF*, 2.292–6.

tional reforms after 1900 and the abolition of the examination system in 1905 had their beginnings after 1895.

The heart of educational reform lay in curriculum revision. Its main purpose was of course to accommodate Western learning, and a prominent tendency in the revision was to accept Western knowledge under the category of 'substantial studies' (*shih-hsueh*). This had been a principal category in Confucian intellectual culture. It referred to studies with practical significance for the central moral and social concerns of Confucianism. Over the centuries *shih-hsueh* had been repeatedly invoked by Confucian scholars as a controlling category to draw the line and refute what they considered devoid of 'substance' and therefore worthless. The fact that in the new curriculum Western knowledge was given a prominent place under the category of *shih-hsueh* indicated the recognition of 'Western thought' as having a place on the traditional scale of intellectual values.

Curriculum revision in many old respectable academies thus led to a significant spread of Western learning in the late 1890s. To be sure, it was in most cases non-political and technical, consisting of mathematics, science, world geography and history, or Western languages. But the K'ang-Liang group put greater emphasis on Western political experience and ideals than on specialized technical knowledge. K'ang and Liang also directly involved themselves in carrying out educational innovations. In the small private school K'ang Yu-wei founded at Canton in 1891, the Ch'ang-hsing hsueh-she, an essential part of the education was to fuse the Confucian ideal of social responsibility with Western political values so as to foster the students' political consciousness.[74]

This politically oriented educational programme was later inherited by Liang Ch'i-ch'ao, who in his propaganda for reform stressed the importance of Western political ideals and experience as distinguished from Western technical knowledge. With this ideal of political education in mind, he urged the model of a college of political studies (*cheng-chih hsueh-yuan*) upon his friends who engaged in the local reform of academies at Hangchow and in Shensi. He also pursued this idea when he offered private instruction at Shanghai in 1896–7. Later in Hunan his programme of political education was mainly responsible for the creation of a radical intellectual atmosphere in the Shih-wu hsueh-t'ang. Many students of that school later became political activists and figured prominently in the post-1900 reform and revolution.

The voluntary association known as the study society was not an

[74] Liang Ch'i-ch'ao, 'Nan-hai K'ang hsien-sheng chuan' (A biography of K'ang Yu-wei), in *Ying-ping-shih ho-chi, Wen-chi* (Collected works and essays from the Ice-drinker's Studio, collected essays), 3.64–7.

entirely new instrument. Over the centuries the formation of societies among scholars for literary purposes had been commonplace. During the late Ming, associations (*she*) among some scholar-officials voiced political criticism and engaged in factional struggles. But from the late seventeenth century the trend turned decisively against associational activities, largely owing to the strict Ch'ing government ban on forming gentry-literati associations with political orientation.[75] When the Ch'iang hsueh-hui in 1895 inaugurated a sudden growth of associational activities, the memory of voluntary organizations among Confucian literati under the Sung and Ming was certainly one source of inspiration. But the immediate impetus came mainly from the West. The intensive activities of the SDK among the official-literati must have impressed upon them the potential effectiveness of such a society as an instrument of change. Meanwhile knowledge of the West showed the important contribution that voluntary associations had made to Western progress. One contemporary popular discussion of the function of the study society typically saw it as a key to rapid cultural development in modern Europe.

Altogether in the three years from 1895 to 1898, seventy-six study societies were reported. Gentry-literati were responsible for the establishment of about two-thirds of them. Significantly these elite societies were not all concentrated in the few large coastal cities. They were to be found in ten provinces and thirty-one different cities – twenty-five of them inland. Thus these societies were largely gentry-sponsored and also nationwide in distribution. Scattered as they were, they became important institutional media to supplement the new schools and revamped academies in spreading new thought. The latter spread new values and knowledge among many youngsters of gentry-literati background, while the societies reached mainly adults.[76]

A rough breakdown of these societies according to their announced goals is also revealing. Among them was one devoted to the religio-ideological purpose of promoting Confucianism; more than thirty aimed either to study traditional Confucian learning in the new practical spirit or to study Western sciences and to translate Western books; fifteen promoted social reforms (such as the anti-opium movement, anti-footbinding or women's education); and twenty-three sought to arouse the patriotism and

---

[75] Frederic Wakeman, Jr, 'The price of autonomy: intellectuals in Ming and Ch'ing politics', in *Daedalus*, 101.2 (Spring 1972) 35–7. See also Chang Yü-fa, *Ch'ing-chi ti li-hsien t'uan-t'i* (Constitutionalist groups of the late Ch'ing period), 6–23.

[76] The total number of societies recorded here is computed on the basis of those societies reported in the *Shih-wu pao*, *Hsiang-hsueh pao*, *Chih-hsin pao* and those listed by Chang Yü-fa, T'ang Chih-chün and Wang Erh-min. See Chang Yü-fa, *Ch'ing-chi ti li-hsien t'uan-t'i*, 199–206. Also Wang Erh-min, *Wan-Ch'ing cheng-chih ssu-hsiang shih lun*, 134–65, and T'ang Chih-chün, *Wu-hsu pien-fa shih lun-ts'ung*, 222–70.

political consciousness of the gentry-literati. To be sure, among these last only a few like the Pao-kuo hui and others founded at Peking in the spring of 1898 stated their goals explicitly in the rhetoric of nationalism. But all of these twenty-three societies clearly owed their origin to an acute sense of national crisis. Even in the case of non-political societies such as those devoted to introducing Western knowledge and improving social customs, a heightened consciousness of national need gave the principal impetus to their formation. In this sense the emergence of these study societies was clearly an index of the spread of nationalism among the upper class.[77]

The growing number of scholars banding together in study groups also evidenced certain trends broader than the emergence of national consciousness in Chinese society. China's social tradition had been on the whole dissociationist in the sense that, outside kinship bonds, people had distrusted one another and generally avoided public associations. Now, however, the gentry-literati were resorting to organizational activity outside the contexts of kinship or bureaucracy. Much as in a Western associationist society, they were forming small, autonomous and voluntary groups for concrete purposes. In this sense study organizations among the gentry-literati broke with the dissociationist tradition of late imperial China and began a new trend which was to characterize many social groups in twentieth-century China.[78]

Since many of the societies were organized for political action, they also represented a tendency towards greater political participation. The gentry-literati's commitment to the Confucian ideal of public service and their role as a social elite had always moved them towards political participation, but it had been confined within the bureaucratic framework. The study societies after 1895, however, fell completely outside the bureaucracy. A few, like the Ch'iang hsueh-hui, Nan hsueh-hui, and Pao-kuo hui, were organized explicitly with the Western ideal of democratic participation in mind. Even in other cases where democratic participation was not a conscious guiding purpose, the societies bespoke an increasing willingness on the part of scholars to resort to collective action and to become involved in politics.

Still more important than the new schools and the study societies as instruments of change were the newspapers and magazines that emerged during the years of the reform movement. To be sure, by the 1890s the modern press was no longer a novelty in China. By the mid-1890s there were about a dozen newspapers published in the chief port cities, mostly in

---

[77] Wakeman, *The price of autonomy*, 55–67. Chang Yü-fa, *Ch'ing-chi ti li-hsien t'uan-t'i*, 199–206. Wang Erh-min, 'Ch'ing-chi hsueh-hui hui-piao', 134–65.

[78] Masao Maruyama, 'Patterns of individuation and the case of Japan: a conceptual scheme', in Marius B. Jansen, ed. *Changing Japanese attitudes toward modernization*, 459–531.

Hong Kong and Shanghai.[79] From 1895 the public press in China, however, underwent a drastic expansion and a new development. Between
1895 and 1898 about sixty newspapers came into existence. Such an
expansion was unprecedented, presaging a new turn in national development. But it is significant that a good number of papers were now found
outside the treaty ports, not only in lower Yangtze cities like Soochow,
Wusih and Hangchow, but also in a number of inland cities like Hankow,
Changsha, Kweilin, Chungking, Chengtu and Sian.[80]

No figures exist to indicate the exact circulation of these newspapers.
Most of them were small and probably confined to local or regional areas.
Only five, *Shih-wu pao, Chih-hsin pao, Hsiang pao, Hsiang-hsueh pao* and *Kuo-
wen pao*, all run by people closely related to the reform movement, could
claim a large regional or nation-wide circulation. The largest was the *Shih-
wu pao*, which sold more than 10,000 copies at its height. The nation-wide
impact of *Shih-wu pao* can be measured by the number of its distribution
agencies. When the newspaper began publication in the autumn of 1896 it
had agencies in nineteen cities scattered throughout nine provinces. The
number finally grew to sixty-seven in fifteen provinces as well as in Chinese
communities in South-East Asia and Japan. Even in inland cities like Sian,
Lanchow, Chengtu and Chungking, it had two or three agencies. In brief,
it penetrated almost all the provinces of China proper.[81]

The wide circulation of *Shih-wu pao* and other reform newspapers was
due partly to official patronage by provincial and prefectural governments.
Officials in at least eleven provinces were reported to have ordered the
purchase and study of the principal reform newspapers by the subordinate
offices and institutions in their administration.[82] But the most important
reason for the widespread appeal of the newspaper was that many of these
reformer-journalists, unlike the journalists of the earlier treaty-port press,
were themselves members of the gentry-literati. Because of their elite background, these newly emerging newspapers carried greater weight than the
treaty-port press not only among the educated public in general but more
particularly among the members of the gentry-literati. Chang Chih-tung
probably expressed the general attitude when he recommended *Shih-wu pao*
to his subordinates on the grounds that the reform newspapers, being

---

79 Roswell S. Britton, *The Chinese periodical press, 1800–1912*, 1–85.
80 This rough estimate of the total number of newspapers published between 1895 and 1898 is
made on the basis of those reported in the *Shih-wu pao, Chih-hsin pao* and *Hsiang-hsueh pao*, plus
the list of newspapers recorded in T'ang Chih-chün's study in *Wu-hsu pien-fa shih lun-ts'ung*,
227–70, and Chang Ching-lu, *Chung-kuo chin-tai ch'u-pan shih-liao pu-pien* (Materials on the
history of publication in modern China, first collection), 65–84.
81 The total of *Shih-wu pao*'s distribution agencies is computed from lists in each issue of the
newspaper.
82 T'ang Chih-chün, *Wu-hsu pien-fa shih lun-ts'ung*, 236.

founded by gentry-officials (*shen-kuan*), were 'the first healthy and useful newspapers since the beginning of journalism in China'. In Chang's view the involvement of gentry-officials was the distinctive feature of the reform newspapers as against the treaty-port newspapers, which, being operated by foreign merchants and commercially oriented, were 'quite naturally despised by gentry-literati'.[83] As Chang's attitude indicates, the newspapers that emerged in the period of the reform movement were clearly the beginning of a new kind of press – an elite press as distinguished from the earlier treaty-port press.

This elite press, following the model of the missionaries' *Wan-kuo kung-pao*, was markedly different from the treaty-port press in both format and content. The treaty-port press generally devoted large sections to local and commercial news and, in the case of the missionary-sponsored papers, to Christianity. Even in such a progressive treaty-port newspaper as Wang T'ao's *Hsun-huan jih-pao*, the local news of Canton and Kwangtung province still occupied an important place and the commercial section was 'generally twice the size of the other sections'. In contrast, the reform newspapers had two principal sections. One was devoted to news concerning imperial edicts on important government policies, domestic news about other parts of the country, and important international events. Another section was devoted to editorial articles that were largely socio-political essays on national affairs. Conspicuously absent were the commercial and local news so prominent in the treaty-port papers. The elite newspapers were inclined to direct their concern to what happened to their country as a whole and to how their country stood in comparison with other countries. This pattern showed a trend clearly identifiable as nationalism.[84]

Indeed this nationalism was perhaps the leading feature of the burgeoning elite press. Almost every major newspaper professed in its opening statement that its publication was primarily a response to national crisis. Even such a small specialized newspaper as the *Wu-hsi pai-hua pao* (Wusih vernacular news) stated its goal to be that of promoting the vernacular for the purpose of national wealth and power.[85] As Liang Ch'i-ch'ao observed, the purpose of a newspaper was first and foremost to facilitate intellectual communication so as to bring about national integration.

The rise of these newspapers marks the beginning of what may be called elite nationalism in China. Nationalism as a state of mind in isolated cases could of course be traced to earlier decades. Men like Wang T'ao, Kuo Sung-tao and Ma Chien-chung all had a nationalist pattern of thinking, but

83 Chang Chih-tung, *Ch'üan-hsueh p'ien*, 2.16a–b (pp. 111–17).
84 Britton, *The Chinese periodical press*, 1–85.
85 *WHPF*, 4.542–5.

nationalism as an intellectual movement and as a widespread consciousness appeared clearly only after 1895; for schools, study societies and, above all, the elite press, made it possible.[86]

As a vehicle for nationalism the elite press was permeated with a new consciousness of the need and obligation to participate in politics. The inference was that by political participation China as a nation could head in a new direction and change for the better. The commercial orientation and foreign ownership of the older treaty-port press had led its newspapers generally to avoid publishing polemical writings of socio-political signifi-cance, whereas after 1895 the new elite press joined the new schools and study societies as a powerful instrument for spreading a new political consciousness.

These three institutions reinforced each other. Just as the principal reform papers reported the creation of new institutions like newspapers, new-style schools and study societies, so in the new-style schools and societies newspapers were read and discussed. In the Yü-lu Academy at Changsha, for example, the chancellor, Wang Hsien-ch'ien, urged the students to read the *Shih-wu pao*. One society, Kung-fa hsueh-hui, made it a principal purpose to study both domestic and foreign newspapers. Another study society, Chiao-ching hsueh-hui, for instance, grew out of the estab-lished academy, Chiao-ching shu-yuan. Meanwhile the Nan hsueh-hui announced that one of its goals would be to promote educational reform. This sort of feedback among the three institutions greatly reinforced their overall impact. They created an intellectual excitement that reached far and wide among educated Chinese.

This amounted to the beginning of a modern public opinion in China. Even though Confucianism had encouraged social responsibility, its moral idealism did not always lead to a practical interest in national affairs, while the Ch'ing government had banned public discussion of politics. Such political awareness as did exist occasionally among scholar-officials could not easily be communicated. Consequently the new institutional channels, once established, could rather quickly begin to aggregate and articulate individual views and create something like the public opinion in a modern society – a momentous new development after 1895.

Another important heritage of the reform era was the birth of a new social group – the Chinese intelligentsia.

Their distinguishing characteristics lay not so much in their class back-ground or social status as in the novel outlooks and patterns of behaviour

[86] Paul A. Cohen, 'Wang T'ao and incipient Chinese nationalism', *JAS*, 26.4 (Aug. 1967) 559–74. Cf. Paul A. Cohen, *Between tradition and modernity: Wang T'ao and reform in late Ch'ing China*.

they shared and in the distinctive socio-cultural roles they played in the modern transformation of China. One can best see this by comparing the new intelligentsia with the old gentry-literati. First the gentry-literati for the most part were a local elite rooted in their home towns who discharged important functions in their local communities. By contrast, the new intelligentsia were largely free-floating intellectuals who tended to congregate in the urban centres and had little relationship with the local areas from which many of them or their families had originally come. Typically, K'ang, Liang and many of their colleagues were natives of Kwangtung but their principal scenes of action were elsewhere, in places like Peking, Shanghai and Changsha.

Further, to the extent that the gentry-literati had engaged in political-organizational work, these activities were in the context of either government bureaucracy or their local society. True, for many centuries after the turn of the second millennium AD the gentry-literati had sometimes got involved in other political-organizational activities: private Confucian academies formed major foci of such activities under the Sung and Ming; voluntary associations organized among gentry-literati, especially those that cropped up in connection with the famous Tung-lin and Fu-she movements, flourished for a while in the seventeenth century.[87] Yet all these social trends died out. Certainly by the late nineteenth century the Chinese gentry-literati had for a long time engaged in very few such activities. In contrast, the modern intelligentsia's political-organizational activities took place largely outside the contexts of bureaucracy or local society. In the cities their activities centred around schools, newspapers and voluntary associations, and so set the pattern for later generations. Small in number, scattered in the large cities, and cut off from the local communities of their home counties, the Chinese intelligentsia, as they first emerged in the reform era, were certainly marginal men in Chinese society. Yet in China as elsewhere in the modern world, marginal men were often people particularly sensitive to change and often themselves became agents of change.

The intelligentsia were also set apart from the gentry-literati by the kind of relationship they had with government. The gentry-literati and the traditional Chinese state had had a sort of symbiosis. Despite the strains and conflicts that often existed, powerful ties of both interest and ideological belief usually bound the gentry-literati to the state. The Chinese social elite inclined in general to be more of a supporter than a critic of the government. On the other hand, no such ties have existed between the Chinese intelligentsia and the modern governments. On the whole they have made

[87] Hsieh Kuo-chen, *Ming Ch'ing chih chi tang-she yün-tung k'ao* (A study of parties and societies during the transition from Ming to Ch'ing), 145–255.

more political demands on the government than the gentry-literati did and their political support has been much more contingent. Consequently their relationship with the state, more often than not, has been one of tension rather than symbiosis. Here again the first generation of the Chinese intelligentsia proved to be typical. K'ang Yu-wei, Liang Ch'i-ch'ao, Yen Fu and other members of the intelligentsia were not necessarily revolutionary opponents of the government, yet a sense of alienation and critical consciousness was an essential part of their political stance.

In their relations with the Chinese cultural tradition, there was also a striking difference between the old and new groups. The Chinese gentry-literati had felt self-sufficient within their own cultural tradition. For them this tradition was the only intellectual source on earth that could provide the wisdom and the norms to orient the human mind and social action. Consequently they were endowed with a heightened pride in their own cultural heritage and a singularly strong sense of intellectual continuity with the past. If the gentry-literati sometimes felt troubled by their relations with the political authority, their sense of cultural identity was seldom in question. By the beginning of the reform era, however, fifty years of contact with Western civilization had greatly expanded the cultural horizon for many educated Chinese but at the same time it had given them a feeling of alienation from their own tradition. As cultural symbols of various sorts flooded into China from outside, the Chinese intellectuals lost their mental bearings in the modern world. Thus the Chinese intelligentsia were born not only with an expanded cultural horizon but also with a deeply troubling problem of cultural identity, which the gentry-literati had rarely known in the past.

In all these relationships with society, state and cultural tradition, the reform era saw the presence of new social types who were markedly different from the old gentry-literati. Their emergence, along with a novel intellectual climate, new institutional instruments of change, and a burgeoning public opinion, constituted the principal legacies of the reform era.

CHAPTER 6

JAPAN AND THE
CHINESE REVOLUTION OF 1911

The modern transformations of China and Japan were inextricably inter-related. With the advent of steam navigation both countries found isolation untenable, and the appearance of Western gunboats in the harbours of each had significance for the other. Cultural ties and a shared written language meant that the response of either country was quickly accessible to the other, and observation of the process of challenge and response invited reflection and appropriation. China's crisis with the West preceded that of Japan by a good decade and a half; Japan became fully involved with the international order in 1860, the same year that the Ch'ing Summer Palace was consumed by flames kindled by the British-French expedition. There-after the determination of Japanese leaders to preserve national unity against the foreigner drew reinforcement from the ruinous disunity of China in the 1860s. Soon Japan's drive for modernization provided encouragement and a warning for China. By the turn of the century Japan's leap to international equality had made its institutions the natural focus of learning for a generation of young Chinese.

The rapid shift of images each country held of the other during these years provides a field for analysis that is only now becoming fruitful. In Japanese eyes the Chinese changed from the thoughtful, introspective sages who peopled the paintings of the Tokugawa artists to the hapless rabble the print makers of 1895 showed in full flight before Japan's modern troops. Eventually they became the awkward, self-conscious students who drew the hoots of street urchins for their hair and dress in early twentieth-century Tokyo. In Chinese eyes the Japanese, remembered as dwarfs who had troubled the serenity of the late Ming, returned as modernized neigh-bours who offered to lead them into a bright new future that in fact turned out to contain a new Asian imperialism. At mid-century a Japanese govern-ment pronouncement warned that Westerners should be treated with as much respect as if they were Chinese, but on the eve of the Sino-Japanese War Japanese leaders were warning their countrymen against uncritical acceptance of the Western scorn of Chinese weakness. Chinese leaders first praised, then came to fear, Japanese achievements, and warned that the

Japanese should be regarded as even more dangerous than Westerners. Then, as the urgency of modernization became apparent, Japan's modernized institutions nevertheless became the objects of study, and Japan itself a breeding ground for revolution in China. Since China and Japan interacted so importantly in their respective modern histories, it is useful to look at both sides of the relationship.

THE OPENING OF CHINA AS A WARNING TO JAPAN

China's contribution, however unwitting, to the modernization of Japan provides an appropriate beginning for this discussion. Its dimensions were several. There was the importance of the news of danger, and of direct observation and experience in China. Experience in the West itself brought to Japan a sense of competition with China. Less central, though significant, was the benefit of Chinese translations from the West.

Scholars agree on the importance of the sense of alarm that gripped mid-nineteenth-century Japan at the approach of the Western world, and it is clear that the news from China provided an important part of that consciousness. Already in the 1830s the appearance of the American ship *Morrison* in Japanese waters led to grossly inaccurate stories that that mighty Englishman, whose influence was thought to permeate the Canton area, was on his way to deal with the Tokugawa government. In 1838 the daimyo Tokugawa Nariaki predicted that Japan would be the first object of Western attack; China was too large, and the Ryūkyū Islands and Korea too small, to attract the warships. After reports of the Chinese defeats came in, proving him wrong, the impact was great. 'This concerns a foreign country,' the shogunal minister Mizuno Tadakuni wrote to a subordinate, 'but I think that it should provide a good warning for us.'[1] Soon Dutch and Chinese traders brought Chinese publications to Nagasaki.

Wei Yuan's works circulated widely in Japan, where they were accessible to all who were literate. His *Hai-kuo t'u chih* (Illustrated treatise on the maritime kingdoms) appeared in many Japanese editions. Wei Yuan's discussion of the wisdom of learning from the West in material and technological respects, and his assumption that such steps could be reconciled with orthodoxy in moral and political concerns, was congenial to many of his Japanese readers. Sakuma Shōzan, who read Wei after he had already

---

[1] For Nariaki, memorial of Tempō 10, 6/22 (1 Aug. 1839), in *Mito han shiryō* (Mito han historical materials), *bekki jō*, 98. For Mizuno, Nihon Shiseki Kyōkai, *Kawaji Toshiakira Monjo* (Kawaji Toshiakira documents), 8 (1934) 318–19. Both are cited in Tadashi Yoshida, 'Sakuma Shōzan as an advocate of "Eastern morality, Western science" ', in *Princeton Papers in East Asian Studies*, 1 *Japan* (1972) 54. The first report of the Chinese defeats came via a Dutch vessel to Nagasaki in 1840.

submitted a recommendation on coastal defence to his lord, was struck by the resemblance between his thought and that of Wei Yuan. 'When the English barbarians were invading the Ch'ing empire', he wrote, 'I submitted a plan in a memorial. Later I saw the *Sheng wu chi* of the Chinese writer Wei Yuan . . . . Wei and I were born in different places and did not even know each other's name. Is it not singular that we both wrote lamenting the times during the same year, and that our views were in accord without our having met? We really must be called comrades from separate lands.'[2]

As news from China increased in quantity and quality in mid-century Japan, it became an important element in the mounting sense of crisis that pervaded the land. The information made available by Wei Yuan made it possible for Yoshida Shōin to make a connection between the braves demobilized after the Opium War and the disorders in Kwangtung. Such news influenced the power elite profoundly. Its full import was delayed by the confusing nature of reports about the rebellions in China. They came from a variety of sources, some from Korea through accounts of the daimyo of Tsushima, others from China through merchant ships, from Nagasaki through Dutch reports, from a Japanese active for several years on the China coast, and from Chinese publications carried by a Cantonese who sailed with Perry. Japanese reports of the Taiping Rebellion began with stories of Ming revival and English support for the Ming partisans. Gradually, more accurate and official Chinese accounts permitted readers to make an association between Christianity, rebellion and the enormous losses of life and property. In the 1860s direct accounts from Japanese who got to Shanghai were further reinforced and confused by fictional narratives of epic battles between Ming partisans and Ch'ing armies. Many such accounts drew on the old Koxinga tradition of supporting their heroes, but more and more related Chinese disasters to foreign intervention and conquest.[3]

The most important result of the Japanese perception of Chinese

[2] For a discussion of Japanese editions and influence of the *Hai-kuo t'u-chih*, see Wang Chia-chien, 'Hai-kuo t'u-chih tui-yü Jih-pen-ti ying-hsiang' (The influence of the *Hai-kuo t'u-chih* in Japan), in *Ta-lu tsa-chih*, 32.8 (April 1966) 242–9. Translations came out in 1854 and continued into the early Meiji period. For its impact on Shionoya Tōin (1810–67), an influential Confucian who edited one of the early Japanese editions, see R. H. van Gulik, 'Kakkaron: a Japanese echo of the Opium War', *Monumenta Serica*, 4 (1939) 478–545. Sakuma Shōzan's admiration did not however extend to Wei Yuan's discussion of guns. 'It is', he noted, 'for the most part inaccurate and unfounded. It is like the doings of a child at play. No one can learn the essentials of a subject without engaging personally in the study of it. That a man of Wei's talent should fail to understand this is unfortunate.' Quoted in Ryusaku Tsunoda, William Theodore deBary, and Donald Keene, eds. *Sources of the Japanese tradition*, 614.
[3] For the course and sequence of Japanese intelligence about Taiping successes, see Ichiko Chūzō, 'Bakumatsu Nihonjin no Taihei Tengoku ni kansuru chishiki' (Japanese knowledge of the Heavenly Kingdom of Great Peace in late Tokugawa times), in Kaikoku Hyakunen Kinen Bunka Jigyōkai, ed. *Meiji bunkashi ronshū* (Essays in Meiji cultural history), 453–95.

disasters was the resolve not to repeat the Chinese experience. First-hand observation of that experience began to be collected by Japanese who travelled to Shanghai in the 1860s, and it provided significant reinforcement for views of crisis and response. The first ship sent to Shanghai was the *Chitose Maru* which went in 1862, and since its passengers, all commissioned by their political authorities, included Bakufu, Chōshū, Saga, Owari and Ōmura samurai as well as merchants, their travel records, supplemented by those of others who travelled beyond Shanghai to Europe, provided important documentation of the direct impact in Japan of the state of affairs along the China coast.[4]

For numbers of Japanese the forest of foreign masts in Shanghai harbour was convincing proof of the impossibility of continuing the old patterns of seclusion.[5] Equally impressive to many was the evidence of Western superiority and arrogance in the arrangements for the defence of Shanghai, and the apparent fear with which the Chinese regarded the Westerners. Out of this came a heightened conviction of the need to prepare for resistance to the West through acquisition of Western arms. The China coast, and especially Shanghai, also served as an entrepot for the arms and equipment that provided the military strength of the Bakufu and its enemies. The Japanese branches of China coast trading firms, like Jardine, Matheson and Company, especially at Nagasaki, provided access to steamers and small arms for Satsuma, Chōshū and Tosa. Numbers of important Restoration leaders – Takasugi Shinsaku, Godai Tomoatsu, and Gotō Shōjirō among them – found direct access to military *matériel* in Shanghai.

The same firms, and the same route, conveyed some of these men to Europe. Itō, Inoue, Mori, Godai, Terajima and others first experienced the West through the prism of their brief Shanghai encounters. Their letters home reported their pleasure in the distinctions Europeans were beginning to draw between the determined reforms of Japan and the more uncertain course of events in China. European discernment of Japanese efficiency and Chinese failure encouraged them. From early on one begins to see in such reactions the inception of a desire to stand with the West and not with the East, to dissociate themselves and their country from the overtones of weakness and ineffectiveness that accompanied the term 'oriental'. A few

---

[4] *Ibid.* 481–6, details the early missions, passengers and sources.
[5] Thus Inoue Kaoru's biographer notes that 'When he reached Shanghai, and saw from the deck of his ship the hundred or so warships, steamships, and sailing vessels in the anchorage, and the busy scene of ships entering and leaving the harbour, he was completely taken aback. For the first time the Marquis realized the need of developing a navy in order to carry out exclusion, and for the first time he saw the full meaning of Sakuma Shōzan's teachings and the inadequacy of simple exclusionist thought.' Inoue Kaoru kō denki hensankai, *Seigai Inoue kō den* 1.90–1.

decades later this desire found its classic formulation in an essay by Fukuzawa Yukichi in 1885. In an editorial written in the aftermath of the failure of reform in Korea and the defeat of China by France, he called on his countrymen to 'part with Asia'. Shortly afterwards the point was emphasized by foreign minister Inoue Kaoru in a memorandum which argued that Japan had no alternative to the establishment of a 'Western-style empire on the edge of Asia'. All such arguments were based on the importance of avoiding identification with the disastrous course of nineteenth-century China.[6]

A final, and seldom noted, benefit for Japan of China's prior contact with the West is interesting for the contrasts it offers to the later relations between the two. Early translations of Western books into Chinese contained important character-compounds that made their way into Japanese 'modern' thought. By the end of the century these compounds were so widely accepted in Japan that during the subsequent importation of Japanese words into China many Chinese assumed they were indebted to Japan for this vocabulary as for so much other terminology. The infusion was particularly important in the publication of translations of international law with their need for approximations of terms like 'rights' and 'sovereignty'. But these remained relatively few in number in comparison with the flood of Japanese words that later entered the Chinese language. Nor was there at any time in the early self-strengthening movement a Japanese student in China for the study of modernization.

MEIJI JAPAN IN CHINESE THINKING

During the second half of the nineteenth century the image of Japan held by influential Chinese leaders gradually changed to one of grudging admiration. Early approval and even admiration of Japanese institutional changes and technological efforts can be seen in some of the writings of Feng Kuei-fen. Li Hung-chang thought well of late-Tokugawa moves for military reform. Separated as these reforms were from a full-scale and unified national movement, they seemed to combine tradition with technology, and contributed logically to thoughts of a common front against the West. These attitudes survived the early years of the Meiji Restoration. After his appointment as governor-general of Chihli in 1870 Li Hung-chang, according to one authority, was 'impressed by Japan's comparative success in dealing with the West . . . and by the large funds which Japan

---

[6] Marius B. Jansen, 'Japanese views of China during the Meiji period', in Albert Feuerwerker, Rhoads Murphey and Mary C. Wright, eds. *Approaches to modern Chinese history* (hereafter *AMCH*), 163–89.

was reported to have raised for arsenals and steamships. Li felt that China should befriend Japan, and perhaps even send officials to reside in that country, with a view to preventing her from siding with the Western nations.'[7] Then, as the Japanese used the outrages inflicted by Taiwanese aborigines on Ryūkyūan fishermen as an excuse to claim the Ryūkyū Islands in 1874 and to move against Taiwan, Li and his colleagues began to see in Japan a possible source of danger. The Meiji changes now began to seem too completely emulative of the West.

In a fascinating colloquy with Mori Arinori, who came to Peking after the resolution of the dispute in 1875, Li expressed surprise and shock at Japan's willingness to cut herself off from the cultural tradition of East Asia. In the Japanese foreign office's official English transcript of the interview, Li is quoted as saying, 'I think very highly of almost everything that has recently been done in your country, but there is one thing I cannot so well appreciate: that is the change of your old national costume into the European fashion . . . . The costume is one of those things that recall the sacred memory of the ancestors and ought to be kept on with reverence by the posterity forever.' In response Mori assured him that 'If our ancestors were still living they would without doubt do exactly what we have done . . . about a thousand years ago they adopted the Chinese costume as they then found it better than the one they had.' 'You might', Li countered, 'with wisdom have adopted the Chinese costume . . . it is very convenient . . . and can be made entirely out of the materials produced in your own country.' But, noted Mori, 'None of your ancestors four hundred years ago could have willed the change of their costume that took place afterwards at the commencement of the present dynasty [i.e. the wearing of the queue]. Change is change, and moreover this change of yours was forced upon you despite your disliking it.'[8] But while Li warned Mori against excessive Westernization and spoke darkly of the danger of foreign loans, in a memorial of December 1874 he cited these with other measures as basis for the observation that Japan's 'power is daily expanding, and her ambition is not small'. And by 1885 he wrote that 'In about ten years, Japan's wealth and power will be considerable. She is China's future disaster, not our present anxiety.' And at the end of those ten years, when Li's prophecy had come true and he himself appeared before Itō Hirobumi to sue for peace at Shimonoseki, he still strove for some way to 'be brothers instead of ene-

---

[7] Kwang-Ching Liu, 'Li Hung-chang in Chihli: the emergence of a policy, 1870–1875', in *AMCH*, 74.

[8] I am indebted to Professor Hayashi Takeji, formerly of Tōhoku University, for the English text of the discussion. A Japanese version appears in Kimura Kō, *Mori Sensei den* (Biography of Mori), 102, and the exchange is also quoted by Sanetō Keishū, *Chūgokujin Nihon ryūgaku shikō* (Draft history of Chinese students in Japan), 64–5.

mies . . .. A thing which is detrimental to one of us must also be so to the other . . .. It is quite time the yellow race should prepare against the white.'[9]

Ironically, however, it was the war with Japan in 1894–5 that was pivotal for Chinese attitudes towards Meiji modernization. In China, as elsewhere, the war was accepted as a test of the effectiveness of the modernization steps taken in both countries, and the success of Japanese arms and the contrast between united effort in Japan and sectional responsibility in China left little room for doubt as to which was the more effective pattern of organization. The shock of defeat by Japan was greater than was the now-accustomed aggression by Western powers. Consequently the onus for defeat was not borne entirely by Japan. It was shared in good measure by the Manchu dynasty and by Li Hung-chang. Soon the Japanese defeat was eclipsed by the new Western demands; the European powers that intervened in 1895 to act ostensibly as guarantors of Chinese territorial integrity against Japanese demands soon proceeded after 1897 to walk off with the booty they had protected. The indignation this aroused in China led directly to the Hundred Days reforms of 1898. (See pp. 318ff.)

Meiji Japan held a very special place in the minds of the Confucian reformers of late Ch'ing times. Its success in introducing institutions of representative government on a basis of largely traditional ideology, and its ethos of national service rather than of personal or sectional gratification, seemed to suggest a pattern which could be followed by any country seeking modernization. It is significant and appropriate that key figures in the reform circle were important in introducing to Chinese readers and leaders, the facts and applicability of the Meiji achievements. Thus Huang Tsun-hsien (1848–1905) arrived in Tokyo with the first resident Chinese Minister, Ho Ju-chang, as counsellor of legation in 1877. Huang formed numerous contacts with Japanese literary men, and wrote a history of Japan. This work, completed only after a period as consul-general in San Francisco, was finished in 1887, but it was not circulated until the time of the Sino-Japanese War and was published only in 1897 as *Jih-pen kuo-chih*. It was Huang who invited Liang Ch'i-ch'ao to come to Shanghai as editor of a journal of the Society for the Study of Self-Strengthening, and who stood sponsor to both T'an Ssu-t'ung and Liang in Hunan. His history of Japan came to the attention of the Kuang-hsu Emperor in 1898, at a time when its author was serving in Hunan.[10]

[9] Ssu-yü Teng and John K. Fairbank, *China's response to the West*, 119–20. The 1895 talks were recorded in English. See Morinosuke Kajima, *Diplomacy of Japan 1894–1922*, 202.

[10] Joseph R. Levenson, *Liang Ch'i-ch'ao and the mind of modern China*, 23–5; and Noriko Kamachi, 'Huang Tsun-hsien'. The next significant Chinese study of Japan's modernization was Tai Chi-t'ao (Tai Ch'ien-chou 1890–1949), *Jih-pen lun* (On Japan), published 1928. A Japanese translation of this perceptive book is in *Chūgoku* (China), nos. 56–63 (July 1968 – Feb. 1969).

K'ang Yu-wei, the leading figure among the reformers, made good use of Japanese examples in his arguments. The Meiji constitution seemed to him a success and a significant element in Japan's strength. K'ang recommended the Japanese example in his first memorial to the emperor in 1888, and he stuck to his argument thereafter. In 1898 he urged the emperor to 'adopt the methods of Russia and Japan with which to fix the policies of the empire', and to 'take the Meiji government as the model of administration'. As the summer of 1898 proceeded, K'ang made less mention of Peter the Great and more of Meiji; it was now vital for China to liberalize her rules and broaden participation in government. Japan, he pointed out, was 'geographically near to us and her governmental forms and social institutions are similar to ours'. Later K'ang repeated and developed these arguments in longer studies of Russia and Japan for the emperor. Nevertheless, his advocacy remained more general than specific. He approved of the search for new models, and he approved particularly of Japan's constitutional reorganization. True Confucian principles, he thought, required the democratization of Chinese institutions.[11] But although K'ang admired what the Japanese admired, there is little reason to think that Meiji nationalism or social structure were his goals. Before 1911 he tended to reserve higher praise for the German example, which seemed to combine freedom with the discipline he felt China needed.

Predictably, the Meiji leaders found much to approve of in the reform movement of 1898. They themselves were at this point keenly concerned about Western imperialist expansion in China, and anxious to assist Chinese resistance. Foreign minister Ōkuma Shigenobu contributed a rationale for government policy with his 'Ōkuma Doctrine' under which Japan, long a recipient of China's culture and spirit in the past, would now repay that debt by holding the West at bay to provide the time necessary for China to reorganize under new leadership. Itō Hirobumi visited Peking during the Hundred Days, and was granted an audience by the emperor. After the empress dowager's coup against the reformers, the leaders of the reform movement received Japanese protection. K'ang had English pro-

[11] See Kung-chuan Hsiao: 'The case for constitutional monarchy: K'ang Yu-wei's plan for the democratization of China', *Monumenta Serica*, 24 (1965) 1–83; 'Weng T'ung-ho and the reform movement of 1898', *Ch'ing-hua hsueh-pao*, NS, 1.2 (April 1957) 111–245 (for dates of memorials mentioned above, see p. 159, and nn. on pp. 228–9); 'The philosophical thought of K'ang Yu-wei: an attempt at a new synthesis', *Monumenta Serica*, 21 (1962) 129–93; and 'In and out of utopia: K'ang Yu-wei's social thought', *The Chung Chi Journal* 7.1 (Nov. 1967) and 8.1 (May 1968). Professor Hsiao has brought together many of his writings in *A modern China and a new world: K'ang Yu-wei, reformer and utopian, 1858–1927*. Professor P'eng Tse-chou *Chūgoku no kindaika to Meiji Ishin* (The modernization of China and the Meiji Restoration), incorporating and adding to his articles published since 1970, provides the most inclusive treatment of the reform movement and Japan.

tection as far as Hong Kong, and there boarded a Japanese vessel which took him to asylum in Japan. Liang Ch'i-ch'ao, who fled to the Japanese consulate at Tientsin, proceeded to Japan on a Japanese gunboat.

The reformers were soon established as leading figures in the growing Chinese community in Japan. Their contacts tended to be with highly placed, upper-class Japanese. Ōkuma Shigenobu personally received K'ang Yu-wei, and corresponded with him thereafter. So did Prince Konoe Atsumaro. Inukai Ki and other leaders of the parliamentary movement prided themselves on friendship with their distinguished Chinese guests. As a growing student movement began to swell the Chinese community in Japan the reformers, with their intellectual and moral prestige, stood to benefit. Liang Ch'i-ch'ao especially came into his own as a publicist and spokesman for the Chinese community. He was the central figure in the establishment of a school headed by Hsu Ch'in for Chinese youths, while his advocacy of constitutional monarchy, often with arguments familiar to the Japanese setting, brought on a vigorous journalistic war with the partisans of republicanism.

At the same time the Japanese example bulked large in the governmental reforms that the dynasty undertook in the years after the Boxer Rebellion. After the Ch'ing court returned to Peking in 1902 the empress dowager accepted the rationale for administrative and educational reforms set forth in a series of memorials submitted by Chang Chih-tung and Liu K'un-i (see chapter 7). Military reforms included schools designed to train a generation of professional army officers. Japanese instructors gradually came to outnumber European, and Chinese cadets were sent in increasing numbers to military schools in Japan. The Japanese armed forces also provided the model for the administrative structure of the new Chinese armies. Legal reforms meant new law codes drawn from German and especially Japanese practice, and a number of Japanese legal scholars of later eminence began their careers as consultants and advisers in Chinese employ.

The Japanese example was particularly central to plans for constitutional institutions, especially after the Japanese defeat of Russia. Between 1906 and 1911 study missions to Japan and Europe heard the same sort of cautious advice from Itō Hirobumi that Itō had earlier heard from his German mentors. The missions concluded that the Ch'ing constitution should be conferred by the court. In 1908 the empress dowager's announcement of a nine-year programme of preparation for constitutional government, like many of the substantive proposals that accompanied it, was taken directly from the Japanese experience of 1881–90 (see chapter 7).

CHINESE STUDENTS IN JAPAN

No other reforms approached the long-range significance of the changes in education. In China's switch from classical to modern thought, from traditional to Western standards and emphases, Japan played a role of critical importance. The denigration of foreign learning in China had made it controversial to send even Yung Wing's small party of students to the United States in 1872 and had forced their return and the abolition of the educational mission in 1881. But during the decade that followed the Japanese victory over China, this attitude gave way to an emphasis on overseas study so strong that it became not only advantageous but finally even critical to one's success in official preferment. Japan seemed to offer the most inviting, most economical, and least subversive source for such training. The Chinese student movement to Japan in the first decade of the twentieth century was probably the largest mass movement of students overseas in world history up to that point. It produced the first generation of leaders of Republican China.[12] In size, depth and impact it far eclipsed Chinese student movements to other countries. It thus becomes possible to say, with a recent survey, that 'the period from 1898 to 1914 saw a major Japanese influence on the course of Chinese history'.[13]

The movement of students began after the Sino-Japanese War. The first thirteen students came to Japan in 1896. A special school was set up for them in the Kanda district of Tokyo. They had no knowledge of Japanese, and their early instruction was chiefly in language. Four of them left within the first weeks. Tedium, unpalatable food, and real or fancied abuse discouraged them. Seven finished the course, however, and became the first of the corps of Japan experts who began to produce usable Chinese textbooks on Japanese and guides to study in Japan.

The next round of European imperialist advances in China, beginning with the German seizure of Kiaochow in 1897, brought new urgency to the study of modern institutions at the same time that it made Japan more acceptable as an avenue for Westernization. With the failure of the Hundred Days in 1898, as we have noted, the leading reformers and many of their disciples fled to Japan for shelter. As the Manchu court experimented with the obscurantist tides that led to the Boxer disaster of 1900, reform-minded

---

[12] The authoritative works here are those of Sanetō Keishū: *Meiji Nisshi bunka kōshō* (Cultural interchange between China and Japan in the Meiji period); *Chūgokujin Nihon ryūgaku shikō*; and esp. *Chūgokujin Nihon ryūgaku shi* (History of Chinese students in Japan). The 1960 edn of the last-mentioned work is used throughout this chapter; statements noted are from pp. 140 and 110–11.

[13] John K. Fairbank, Edwin O. Reischauer, Albert M. Craig, *East Asia: the modern transformation*, 631.

viceroys like Chang Chih-tung and reform-frustrated intellectuals like K'ang Yu-wei and Liang Ch'i-ch'ao continued to raise the esteem in which they held study in Japan.

Already in his *Exhortation to study*, Chang Chih-tung had pointed out that the Japanese had translated much of what was necessary from the West, and that since their language was closer and easier for Chinese students to master, Japanese books should be used. And he strongly endorsed study abroad. 'To study in the West for one year is better than reading Western books for five years ... to study in a Western school for one year is better than to study for three in Chinese schools.' Japan, however, had particular advantages and lessons to offer. 'As a country for overseas study the West is not like Japan. Japan is nearby and inexpensive for travel, so that many can go; as it is close to China, students will not forget their country. Japanese writing is similar to Chinese, and can readily be translated. Western learning is extremely varied, and the Japanese have already selected its essentials. The customs and conditions of China and Japan are comparable, and it is easy for students to conform to them. It is best to be able to concentrate one's efforts on a small number of concerns.' And as for the lesson to be learned, 'Japan is only a small country, and how did it rise? It was because men like Itō, Yamagata, Enomoto, and Mutsu were students in the West twenty years ago.'[14]

The first group of students was thus followed by others. In 1899 there were over a hundred in Japan. Emissaries from Chang Chih-tung were making surveys of study facilities. A study guide prepared under his direction was completed in 1898 and republished in 1899 and 1900, and it remained a standard guide thereafter. Chang now began sending small numbers of military specialists for study as well. Nor was enthusiasm limited to officials. Liang Ch'i-ch'ao summarized the advantages of the Japanese language: its sounds were few in number, and all of them existed in Chinese; its grammar was uncomplicated, much of its vocabulary was related to Chinese; and 60 to 70 per cent of the language was written in Chinese characters.

Leading Japanese also began to see the significance of such a movement for their own country. Scholars like Ueda Mannen and diplomats like Ōtori Keisuke began to write and speak to their countrymen about the opportunities and responsibilities that were coming with the education of their neighbours. This was also the climate in which Ōkuma Shigenobu worked out his 'Doctrine' of Japan's return of its historic obligations to its mainland neighbour. Ueda and other educators called for moves to prepare special educational programmes for Chinese students and the establishment

[14] Quoted in Sanetō Keishū, *Chūgokujin Nihon ryūgaku shi*, 41.

of special language schools so that they could be ready for university-level work within two or three years of their arrival in Japan. Conscious also of popular ambivalence and possible insults to the Chinese, he argued for special funds to erect adequate dormitory facilities to avoid possible embarrassment, exploitation and 'corruption' of the students. Vacation tours to important parts of Japan should also be laid on to acquaint the students with all aspects of Japanese life.[15]

In China, meanwhile, the Boxer disaster and the failure of obscurantist anti-foreignism brought new prominence for reform-minded viceroys like Chang Chih-tung and Liu K'un-i and new urgency to their message of educational and institutional reform. The emphasis on education abroad and the number of publications about Japanese educational opportunities rose rapidly. There now began to be a link between Japanese study and bureaucratic employment. Related to this, and ultimately the most important development of all, was the reform and final abolition of the system of civil service examinations in 1905. Instead of a grounding in the classics, study abroad was to become the basic requirement for entrance into government service.

The effect on the number of students in Tokyo was immediate. By the end of 1905 estimates of Chinese students in Japan rose to between eight and ten thousand, and for 1906, the peak year, from six to twenty thousand. So great a discrepancy in the estimates suggests the difficulties of counting in a setting in which statistics for passports, visas and school or course registrations are unreliable. Sanetō, the foremost student of this educational migration, using conservative contemporary estimates, arrives at these totals:

Chinese students in Japan

1901	280
1903	1,000
1904	1,300
1905	8,000
1906	8,000
1907	7,000
1908	4,000
1909	4,000
1912	1,400
1913	2,000
1914	5,000

At its peak the student tide included entire families, as fathers accompanied their sons, and young Chinese girls as well as women with bound feet came to learn. Only a minority of those who came were prepared for formal

[15] See excerpts in *ibid.* 45.

work or able to gain admittance to it, so that the numbers of graduates of Japanese schools, while still considerable, are much smaller than the numbers in residence:[16]

Chinese graduates in Japan

1901	40
1902	30
1903	6
1904	109
1905	15
1906	42
1907	57
1908	623
1909	536
1910	682
1911	691
1912	260
1913	416
1914	366
1915	420

Few educational structures would have been equipped to cope with this human tide. Japan's certainly was not. In response to the influx of Chinese students a variety of steps were taken to provide some guidance. Many special schools were established. The Seijō Gakkō, which began as a military preparatory school for Japanese cadets, accepted Chinese students and educated many. Other schools which played important roles were the Nikka Gakudō, established in 1898, the Kōtō Daidō, in 1899, the Tōa Shōgyō, in 1901, the Kōbun Gakuin, in 1902, and especially the Tokyo branch of the Dōbun Shoin, also established in 1902. The Kōbun Gakuin, for instance, included Huang Hsing, Lu Hsun and Ch'en Tu-hsiu among its total of 7,192 Chinese students, of whom 3,810 completed its course. Many private institutions, and especially Waseda, opened new international divisions to cater for their new students. Women's schools were also opened to prepare future mothers for modernity. Opening ceremonies, often graced with eloquent references to the mothers of Mencius and George Washington, would have reassured Chang Chih-tung of the advantages of study in the 'Eastern Country'.[17]

Despite such efforts, it cannot be doubted that the majority of the students fared poorly. Most of them were as ill-prepared for study in Japan as Japanese institutions were to receive them. Many attended cram courses and arrangements that stressed economy of time and concentration on the

[16] Figures from *ibid.* charts facing p. 545. He finds no basis for estimating student numbers for 1909–12 and 1915. A breakdown of graduates by schools (pp. 138–40) shows that institutions range from the imperial universities to private girls' higher schools. For the period 1901–39, Sanetō lists a total of 11,966 Chinese graduates.

[17] For schools, specialties and dates, see *ibid.* 64–79.

crises of the hour. The majority were not enrolled in regular schools at all. Their stays consequently became shorter, and their restlessness and dissatisfaction were transmitted directly to their families and friends in China. Yet a movement of such dimensions, which produced the first generation of leaders of republican China, has to be considered of pivotal importance in the experience of the elite of this whole generation. Communications between Tokyo and China were so easy and unstructured that the impact of life abroad went far beyond those persons registered in the Japanese schools. The quality of the experience and of the influences to which the students were exposed is thus of the greatest interest and importance.

The Chinese experience in Japan can be sampled in the memoirs and autobiographies of the students. It is also documented in the surveys and reports compiled by both Chinese and Japanese authorities, and is reflected in the numerous student publications.[18] The trip often began with encouragement from someone already gone or going. Students often returned home to encourage others to follow their example. Once they had arrived in Tokyo, the Kanda section became their home. Students put their impress upon its lodgings, business establishments and restaurants. Special shops for printing, food and even pawnshops catering for Chinese students came into existence. New publishing houses like Fuzambō began as enterprises designed to provide the translations from Japanese, and the journals and textbooks that were needed. Barbers toiled to bring the queue into some sort of conformity with the laws of modernization, and achieved a pompadoured compromise that became known as the Fuji hairdo.[19] As local organizations in China funnelled more students into Japan, provincial organizations sprang up in Tokyo to harbour and guide them as they arrived. While students came from all parts of China, the future revolutionary centres, Kwangtung, Hunan, Kiangsu and Chekiang, were best represented.

The experience was often full of contradictions and ironies. These can

---

[18] Sanetō has in preparation a catalogue of Chinese diaries. By 1902 there were already 57 diarists of trips to Japan from China; one official inspector, Li Tsung-t'ang, recorded his impressions for nine trips to Japan during this period, *ibid.* 313, 425. After 1906 the Chinese government issued a monthly bulletin of instruction for study in Japan. There was also a number of novels, of which *Liu-tung wai-shih* (Unofficial history of study in Japan) is the best known. It has been studied by Sanetō Keishū in *Nihon bunka no Shina e no eikyō* (The influence of Japanese civilization on China), of which there is a Shanghai edn of 1944, *Jih-pen wen-hsueh tui Chung-kuo ti ying-hsiang* (Chang Ming-san, trans.)

[19] See the recollections of Sun Po-ch'un (1891–), who studied in Tokyo from 1905 to 1914 and, after a period of teaching in Peking and in the Chinese foreign service, returned to Tokyo as instructor in the Foreign Language University and Tokyo Metropolitan University: 'Kajuku, Dōbun Shoin, Minposha: Nihon ni ikiru ichi Chūgokujin no kaiso' (Family tutorial, Dōbun Shoin, the *People's Tribune*: the recollections of a Chinese resident in Japan), *Chūgoku* 30 (May 1966) 24–33, and esp. 'Ryūgakusei: Gakkō kyōiku, bempatsu no koto' (Overseas Chinese students, school education, queues), *Chūgoku*, 31 (June 1966) 28–33.

be detected in the account of the anarchist Ching Mei-chiu, who first came to Japan as a student in 1903. His first night in a Japanese inn was full of surprises. 'There was a special quality about Japan. To begin with, the inns were built of wood and you had to take your shoes off before coming into the room. Here we had crossed the seas and gone abroad to study in order to prepare for a future restoration, yet once in Japan the first thing we had to do was go back to antiquity.'[20] Students could be expected to receive instruction leaflets warning them how to behave in Japanese society. Traffic moved to the left, one did not shout or raise one's voice, one should not stand idling in the street, should spit only into spittoons, be meticulous about separate slippers for toilets and halls, treat maids with dignity, offer seats on crowded street cars to the old, the young and females, be careful about one's valuables, keep one's clothes clean, never ask another's age, and never eat too much Japanese rice, which was hard to digest.[21]

The actual educational experience, nominally the purpose of all this, was often unrewarding. Japanese lecturers and writers delighted in assuring the students that their country faced the same situation that Japan had in the early Meiji period. Their examples were replete with instances of Japanese who had travelled abroad for foreign learning. Exponents of each field of specialization were prepared to offer assurances that its findings were vital to the success of the Restoration government.

NATIONALISM AND ITS REPERCUSSIONS

The central lesson most students seem to have learned was the importance of nationalism. Their experience of Japan tended inevitably to supplement their provincial consciousness with an increased sense of Chinese identity. In Kanda a national organization began to take shape under the consciousness of Chinese nationality and distinctiveness. The Chinese Student Centre in Kanda played an important unifying role. Shortly before the Revolution of 1911 the American-sponsored YMCA, also in Kanda, was able to exploit its independence of Japanese ties to eclipse the earlier student centre or *kaikan*, which was Japanese sponsored. But both organizations served as meeting places. Both helped to fuse provincialism with nationalism. Provincial consciousness was never lost, and most students' primary

---

[20] Ching went on to ruminate about Han dynasty customs, when Chinese too sat on the floor, and suggested that these still prevailed in Japan together with the exaggerated code of civility. *Ryūnichi kaiko – Chūgoku anakisuto no hansei* (Recollections of a sojourn in Japan – half a life of a Chinese anarchist); this is a trans. by Ōtaka Iwao and Hatano Tarō of the Japan portions of Ching's *Tsui-an* (Record of a 'crime').

[21] Sanetō Keishū, *Chūgokujin Nihon ryūgaku shi*, 192–5, reproduces such a pamphlet, 'Rules for students abroad', and notes that contemporary Chinese novels sometimes described returned students as quiet and decorous.

memberships were in provincial groupings. A careful study of revolutionary organization shows that recruiting and reporting were done through provincial divisions in Tokyo. But the student meeting places, like the revolution, merged regional affiliation with national awareness.[22]

Japan served to strengthen the students' consciousness of nationality in many ways. Condescension and discrimination certainly played an important part. The long-sustained Japanese admiration of China and the Chinese had not survived the vainglory of the Sino-Japanese War, which government and people alike saw as a struggle between civilization and medievalism. The victory over China, coming as it did after long decades of patience in the face of unequal treatment by the West, produced a jingoism that affected all parts of Japanese society and consciousness. Popular prints, popular fiction, popular poetry and exultant songs, all acted to instil and reinforce a sudden burst of cheap and claptrap patriotism. Chinese students who came to Japan were inevitably among its first targets. Their country had been found weak, unprepared and non-modern. 'At the time of the war against China', Kōtoku Shūsui put it, 'the patriotism of Japanese developed to extremes that had never been known before. They despised the Chinese, they scorned them as effeminate, and they were hateful to them. Nor did it end with words; from white-haired elders to little children, everybody was full of bloodthirsty intentions toward the four hundred million.'[23] The students were thus treated to a good deal of derision and contempt. Street urchins focused on their queues and followed them with shouts of 'chan chan bōzu'.

The setting was one to remind Chinese constantly of their weakness and failure. A Chinese novel about student life depicted even the Japanese coolies turning back from their rickshaw shafts to ask Chinese student customers if they realized that Japan was defeating Russia, and to ask them whether that did not make them jealous.[24]

Predictably, one effect of this was to irritate students into having their queues cut off, adopting Western dress, and passing for modern. Ching Mei-chiu describes his first attempts at conversation, by scribbling phrases in Chinese, with Japanese students at his school. ' "Why don't you cut your hair?" they asked; "we call it a pig tail." ' Overcome with shame, he

[22] Shelley Hsien Cheng, 'The T'ung-meng-hui: its organization, leadership, and finances, 1905–1912' (University of Washington, Ph.D. dissertation, 1962) 116–17. Note also the provincial ties described in K. S. Liew, *Struggle for democracy: Sung Chiao-jen and the 1911 Chinese Revolution*, 40, 59. Sanetō Keishū, *Chūgokujin Nihon ryūgaku shi*, 515, notes that the Student Centre took over the mechanics of exporting Japanese books to China after 1902.
[23] Kōtoku Shūsui, *Teikokushugi* (Imperialism), 35. An Iwanami bunko reprint of the famous work of 1901.
[24] *Shang-hsin jen-yü* (Wounded to the soul), a polemical novel by Meng Yun-sheng, published 1906. Sanetō Keishū, *Chūgokujin Nihon ryūgaku shi*, 213.

headed straight for a barber and indicated with gestures his wish to have his queue cut.[25]

These attitudes of disparagement came to be associated with the very term for China. 'Shina' as a term went back to T'ang times, when it had entered Chinese usage through Buddhist writings of Indian origin. Although used a good deal in late Tokugawa and Meiji times by Japanese, it alternated with 'Ch'ing', and the Sino-Japanese War was still referred to as the war with the 'Ch'ing'. Thereafter Japanese used 'Shina' increasingly, and early in the student movement Chinese students seem to have been attracted to it through its mildly subversive overtones of avoiding reference to the dynasty. But as 'Shina' became associated with hooting children who ran after Chinese in the streets, it carried overtones of Chinese weakness. Chinese resentment became sharp later in the century, after republican disasters and the Twenty-one Demands. But the Meiji experience began this process.[26]

Japan made a more positive contribution to Chinese nationalism through example. The last decade of the Meiji period was one of surging pride in the national achievements evident in the alliance with England and the victory over Russia. Japanese nationalism made its impress upon even profoundly unpolitically minded students. A young diarist from Honan recorded little interest in his lectures or surroundings, but showed his astonishment at Japanese patriotism. The stories of General Nogi's loss of his sons at Port Arthur won his admiration, and he wrote that even Japanese girls were so patriotic that very few of them married Chinese students.[27] Liang Ch'i-ch'ao, describing the scene at Ueno as relatives and friends arranged festive send-offs for young men entering the army, described a banner inscribed with three characters 'grant death in battle'. 'On seeing this I was astonished and respectful,' he wrote, 'unable to put it out of my mind.' Japan had a 'Yamato damashii' or Yamato spirit; nothing was more urgent for China than to develop a 'China damashii'. Liang went on to stress the identification of self and country as the most urgent need, so that common people would feel possessive about their country. Participation would only follow identification. When a work appeared by a

[25] Ching Mei-chiu, *Tsui-an*, 34.
[26] Kuo Mo-jo, for instance, was to write in 1936, 'Japanese call China "Shina". Originally it didn't have a bad meaning, and they say it comes from the sound Ch'in. But when you hear it from the mouth of Japanese it sounds worse than "Jew" from the mouth of a European.' Quoted by Sanetō Keishū, *Chūgokujin Nihon ryūgaku shi*, 224, who gives a long discussion and apology for the use of the term. Takeuchi Yoshimi, in the pages of *Chūgoku*, 16 (March 1965) 34–6, also warns against the use of 'Shina'. In 1930 the Nationalist government secured Japanese government agreement to abandon the use of the word in official communications.
[27] Sanetō Keishū, *Meiji Nisshi bunka Kōshō*, 277–336, for the diary of a young man whose name is known only from the phonetic symbols Sokoman. For Nogi, see 317.

Japanese legal scholar, Hozumi Yatsuka, *Kokumin kyōiku: aikokushin* (The spirit of patriotism in national education), it was promptly translated and issued by the Peking University Press as a textbook. Numerous other Japanese works and biographies dealing with patriotism also quickly found Chinese translations.[28]

Since the student movement served as a breeding ground for Chinese nationalism, it was natural for student numbers to grow or decline along with political indignation or setbacks. As the figures show, student numbers declined rapidly after 1906, although they remained impressive. Another reason for the decline was an increasing dissatisfaction with the quality of education that many were getting in Tokyo. To some observers this seemed appropriate to the quality of those to be educated; in fact Japanese periodicals began to speculate that superior Chinese students were being sent elsewhere, with only the less qualified coming to Japan. There may have been some grounds for this idea; the United States made its first remission of Boxer funds for the education of Chinese students available in 1908, while Japan did not do the same until 1924. Chinese government surveys and representatives began to express alarm over the disruptive influences inherent in an uncontrolled flood of inadequately prepared students in Japan, and Ch'ing regulations began to prescribe criteria for the selection of students and courses and to discourage short courses. Japanese educational authorities cooperated with these regulations in order to manage their guests. This in turn aroused waves of student indignation against their government and against their Japanese hosts. The quality of schooling probably improved, as the figures of school graduates indicate, but so did the intensity of student organization and disaffection. In 1907 agreements were worked out to open up the best Japanese state higher schools to Chinese students on a regular schedule, and during the next two years over 460 Chinese students were enrolled in them. In June 1911 the Chinese government scheduled the establishment of a preparatory school in Peking to prepare students for the Japanese special higher schools. There was also a rise in the number of Japanese teachers going to China, both to open their own schools and to teach in Chinese schools.[29]

The misgivings of observers and authorities in Tokyo and Peking grew as students became increasingly self-conscious, emotional and vigilant. Each affront to them served to heighten their nationalism, and also served to inconvenience and usually alarm their hosts and sponsors. In 1902

[28] Sanetō Keishū, *Chūgokujin Nihon ryūgaku shi*, 512–13.
[29] *Ibid.* 106–7 for the 1907 agreements. For Japanese teachers in China, 96. By late Ch'ing, Japanese teachers there numbered about 600, and even in 1909, long after the tide had ebbed, 311 out of 356 foreign teachers invited by Chinese schools were Japanese. Cost must of course have been a major factor in this.

Chang Ping-lin and others scheduled a rally to honour the last Ming emperor, but it was, at the last minute, ruled out by Japanese authorities. That same year the Chinese minister Ts'ai Chün decided to refuse to provide the guarantees necessary for nine private students to be enrolled at the Seijō preparatory military academy. When a group of students refused to leave the legation until the minister met them, the legation called in Japanese police to arrest them, thereby providing the students with the charge that Chinese authorities were availing themselves of Japanese police assistance in ejecting their own nationals from buildings immune to such interference. Since the students had already heard rumours that Ts'ai Chün had memorialized Peking to warn of revolutionary leanings among their number, their indignation was at white heat. Wu Chih-hui, arrested and deported, tried to commit suicide by leaping into the moat as he was taken past Kajibashi in Tokyo. Liang Ch'i-ch'ao joined the fray by denouncing the minister as an 'enemy of civilization' in his journal *Hsin-min ts'ung-pao* (The new people miscellany). Of fourteen Japanese newspapers surveyed by Sanetō all but two, which were neutral, supported the students. After extensive mediation efforts by Japanese official and private quarters a compromise was worked out liberalizing the provisions regarding guarantees for students. At the same time the Chinese legation appointed a new official as student supervisor. Shortly afterwards, the minister was replaced and the nine students entered Seijō.[30]

The following year the Chinese government transferred its military students to a newly established preparatory school for the Japanese military academy. It also responded to the urging of the new Chinese minister that 'Japanese military education stresses loyalty and patriotism and subordination to superiors . . . and contains no dangers of unbridled indiscipline or opposition to government'. It set up regulations under which a hundred students between the ages of eighteen and twenty-two would be selected for military education with government sponsorship. At the same time, a University of Tokyo professor, Terao Tōru, sponsored a school to enable privately supported students to follow a military education despite the Peking government's ban on this kind of school.[31]

In 1903 Chinese students organized a successful opposition to the inclusion of Chinese minorities and of Fukienese products in an Osaka Exhibition under the theme of the 'Races of Man'. Osaka merchants joined in the protest. So far, none of these issues had involved a Chinese-Japanese confrontation. Since the prevailing tide of Japanese sentiment during these years was anti-Russian (Professor Terao, indeed, was one of the 'seven jingoes' who agitated vigorously for war), there was even less likelihood

[30] *Ibid.* 424-60.   [31] *Ibid.* 68-71.

of a confrontation over the next incident, which focused on resistance to Russia in April and May of 1903. This movement was provoked by the Russian refusal to withdraw from Manchuria on schedule, and by Russia's 'Seven Demands' on China, first denied and then admitted by the Russians (in a curious anticipation of the Twenty-one Demands of 1915), as they sought to make permanent their position in Manchuria. Chinese students gathered information from the Japanese press, which was alert to possible encroachments that would be permanently damaging to Japanese interests in Manchuria. The student demonstrations took place without apparent reference to Japanese supporters or incitation, and were in fact ultimately discouraged and stopped by the Japanese government for fear of diplomatic embarrassment. But they were undoubtedly congenial and welcome to Japanese popular opinion. Students organized themselves in the Kanda Student Centre, and formed first a Resist Russia Volunteer Corps and then a student army. Students, in scenes of intense emotionalism, signed announcements of their determination to die, and they commissioned representatives to return to China to urge Governor-general Yuan Shih-k'ai to declare war. Instead, they were advised by his underlings to return to their books. The Chinese government, with British and Japanese encouragement, rejected the Russian demands,[32] and after receiving representations from Peking, the Japanese foreign office warned the students that their activities were becoming a diplomatic embarrassment to Japan. At this point the movement was aborted and changed to an Association for Military Education, which was frankly revolutionary in intent. This series of events was important in the way it marshalled student support from all provinces by using the provincial journals and the central student organization at the Centre. Extremely important student figures, among them Huang Hsing and Ch'en T'ien-hua, also found an opportunity to further nationalist and anti-Manchu agitation.[33]

Hitherto, student activism had been nominally directed against foreign imperialism and slights to Chinese national dignity and sovereignty rather than against the Ch'ing. But it nevertheless showed an increasing tendency to oppose the Peking government. The ties with centres of discontent in Shanghai were close, and alarm spread quickly through China via the journals published by provincial groups in Tokyo. The fiery anti-Manchu pamphlet of Tsou Jung, *The revolutionary army*, first published in Shanghai

---

[32] For the development of the crisis as seen by the British, and the confidential leaking of the 'Seven Demands' by the Chinese Foreign Office to the English representative, see George A. Lensen, ed. *Korea and Manchuria between Russia and Japan 1895–1904: the observations of Sir Ernest Satow, British minister plenipotentiary to Japan (1895–1900) and China (1900–1906)*, 213–17.

[33] For a detailed analysis, Nagai Kazumi, 'Kyoga gakuseigun o megutte' (Concerning the student army to resist Russia), *Shinshū Daigaku kiyō*, 4 (Sept. 1954), 57–83.

in 1903 with a preface by Chang Ping-lin, also appeared concurrently in Hong Kong and Tokyo editions. Feng Tzu-yu credits it with a total of a million copies.[34] A recent analysis lists this work together with three others as the most important pamphlets of the revolutionary period; the others were Chang Ping-lin's attack on K'ang Yu-wei's reformism and the two tracts by Ch'en T'ien-hua written immediately after the Resist Russia Movement, *Meng hui-t'ou* (Wake up!) and *Ching-shih chung* (Alarm to arouse the age).[35]

The year 1905 brought the students into confrontation with Japanese educational authorities. In November of that year the Tokyo ministry of education issued a set of regulations entitled 'Problems in controlling students from the Ch'ing'. Of these, Articles 9 and 10 specified that schools should ensure that their students reside in appropriately authorized dormitories and maintain control over them, and that schools were to monitor student conduct, refuse to admit doubtful cases, and terminate the status of those who violated rules. The regulations represented Chinese as well as Japanese concern, for Chang Chih-tung had become sufficiently alarmed by evidence of student disorder and radicalism to warn that the tide of eight thousand or more students was full of revolutionary danger; 'Nine out of ten are intimidated,' he wrote, 'while the instigators and troublemakers do not number more than one in ten.'[36] The students quickly protested that the regulations constituted discrimination against them, since they denied to them alone the constitutional freedom enjoyed by Japanese, and they charged that the regulations were political in motivation. Soon the same provincial organizations and publications that had served to pump students into Japan began to pull them out of school in protest. Very large numbers returned home, and several thousand who did not go began a forty-day student strike. Resolution of the issue again included negotiations between the minister to Peking, Uchida Yasuya, and Chang Chih-tung.

While these negotiations were still in progress, the Japanese establishment began to weary of student unrest. On 7 December the *Asahi shimbun*

[34] Tsou Jung, *The revolutionary army: a Chinese nationalist tract of 1903*, intro. and trans. with nn. by John Lust, 152, 84.

[35] Shimada Kenji, *Chūgoku kakumei no senkusha tachi* (Forerunners of the Chinese revolution), 64. This work includes a Japanese translation of Ch'en's political novel *Shih-tzu-hou* (Roar of the Lion), 81–121. Shimada also, in *Shingai kakumei no shisō* (The thought behind the Revolution of 1911), gives a trans. of *Ching-shih-chung*, 83–144. See also Ernest P. Young, 'Ch'en T'ien-hua (1875–1905): a Chinese nationalist', in *Papers on China*, 13 (1959) 113–62. On the latter see also Shimada, *Chūgoku kakumei no senkusha tachi*, 61–79.

[36] Quoted in Nagai Kazumi, 'Iwayuru Shinkoku ryūgakusei torishimari kisoku jiken no seikaku: Shimmatsu ryūgakusei no ichi dōkō' (The nature of the so-called incident involving Ch'ing regulations for controlling overseas students: a movement among Chinese students in Japan towards the end of the Ch'ing), *Shinshū Daigaku kiyō*, 2 (July 1952) 31. Sanetū Keishū, *Chūgokujin Nihon ryūgaku shi*, 461–511, also provides detailed coverage of the struggle.

observed that the strike was caused by the students' misunderstanding of the regulations and their purpose. 'The strike of more than eight thousand Chinese students in schools in all parts of Tokyo has become a great problem', it began. 'It is based on flimsy grounds, on discontent growing out of an excessively narrow and one-sided interpretation of the Ministry's regulations by the students, and also derives from that self-indulgent and mean self-will that seems peculiar to Chinese nationals.' Ch'en T'ien-hua, who had hitherto taken little part in the strike, spent much of the night composing a testament in which he called upon his fellows never to forget those four characters (self-indulgent and mean); 'If the students are truly self-indulgent and mean, isn't China doomed?' Early the next morning he gave point to his words by committing suicide in the ocean at Ōmori. 'Never forget those four characters,' he had written in his testament, 'always work to make them inapplicable, work to build a country in which they have no place, study for your love of country.' In consequence almost two thousand students returned to China. As the strike deepened, Japanese Diet members and other leaders entered the discussion, and the student movement never regained its earlier élan. Inevitably, the residence requirements were relaxed, and by January 1906 the strike was beginning to wane.

   The strike provided the occasion for one of the few large-scale attempts to bring Chinese and Japanese students together. Although numerous personal friendships were formed, the great majority of Chinese students saw little of their Japanese counterparts in any social or informal sense. In January 1906 an effort was launched to form a Sino-Japanese Student Association. An opening meeting drew about 1,500 students, who heard addresses by Count Ōkuma, Viscount Aoki and similar luminaries. Ōkuma once again compared China to the Japan of forty years before, and pointed out the logic of study in Japan for Chinese students. Ma Hsiang-po called upon the Chinese students not to neglect their studies out of love of country, and not to neglect their love of country out of zeal for their studies.[37] Some students gained more meaningful and personal impressions. Lu Hsun said later, in praise of his mentor Professor Fujino, that his consideration in lending him notes and looking over his notebooks was so conspicuous that he was afraid other students would charge him with favouritism. But the more usual notes that emerge from Chinese recollections are a resentment at Japanese condescension and a consciousness of weakness. The weak and the strong, as Kita Ikki noted later, are seldom friends, and it seems clear that the recently weakened and the recently strengthened, in a relationship as complex as that of China and Japan, were not likely to be friends.

[37] Sanetō Keishū, *Chūgokujin Nihon ryūgaku shi*, 492.

The student movement continued to be an important source of stimulation, discontent and activism despite the moderate decrease in student numbers and their gradual restriction to more qualified and serious students. Throughout the last years of the Ch'ing dynasty, provincial and national organizations of Chinese students in Tokyo kept a vigilant eye on real and fancied insults to Chinese sovereignty and dignity. The Japanese were as often at fault in these matters as were other powers, even when they infringed on the dignity of Peking in the interest of revolutionaries presumably more congenial to student tastes. In the steady sequence of railway loans and spheres-of-interest rivalries the students found no lack of issues with which to maintain their political consciousness.[38]

INFLUENCE THROUGH TRANSLATION

The cultural importance of the migration to Japan was very great. As Kuo Mo-jo summarized it in the 1950s, 'We studied Western culture through Japan . . . . At the same time that the study of Japan broke the feudalistic conventions of the past, it served to further China's progress toward modernity.'[39] The student movement was motivated in the first instance by the desire to speed the acquisition of Western knowledge. Early student journals and newspapers had sections reserved for translation. As early as 1896 Liang Ch'i-ch'ao was calling China's translation effort too slow, and urging the use of Japanese translations. Soon Chinese were using Japanese compendia for more than Western knowledge. Indeed, one of the first Japanese works to be translated (in 1899) was a history of East Asia. By 1900 a group of Chinese students in Japan (who included two future prime ministers and two future ministers to Japan) had set up a translating and publishing organization. Within a few years enterprising publishers had put together an encyclopedic shelf of a hundred Japanese texts in translation. Kuo Mo-jo's recollections of his high-school books in Szechwan included translations from Japanese science texts. The search for the secrets of Japan's modernization led logically to translations of a good deal of Japanese modern history also, and lists of works translated in the early years of the twentieth century are surprisingly rich in biographical studies of Meiji leaders and political history. They include, also, current Japanese studies of politics, works like Kōtoku Shūsui and Ukita Kazutami on imperialism.

[38] See, on a railway issue, Nagai Kazumi, 'Kō-Setsu roji to Shimmatsu no minshū' (The Kiangsu–Chekiang railway and the people in late Ch'ing), *Shinshū Daigaku kiyo*, 11 (1957) 1–25, a study of resistance to the British loan for the Chekiang and Kiangsu railways in 1907–8, a movement which began with Tokyo meetings of students from the areas involved. For the loan negotiations, E-tu Zen Sun, *Chinese railways and British interests 1898–1911*, 61–8.

[39] Quoted in Sanetō Keishū, *Chūgokujin Nihon ryūgaku shi*, 245.

The turn to Japan was of particular importance because it came at a time when Chinese interests in outside literature were shifting from the purely technological to the institutional and political. With the twentieth century, Professor Tsien has noted, 'Changing interests were reflected in the translations, as the enthusiasms for natural and applied sciences of the past centuries shifted to the social sciences and humanities. This new emphasis exercised a great influence on the political and social development of China in the following years. From 1902 to 1904, almost half of the translated books were concerned with history and institutions. The interest in institutional reform and Japanese influence were dominant factors in translations during the early years of this century.' During the period 1880 to 1940 some 2,204 works were translated from Japanese, and of these nearly half were in the social sciences, history and geography. A study of trends in translation shows that in overall influence Japanese translations formed only 15.1 per cent of the total from 1850 to 1889, and 18.2 per cent from 1912 to 1940, but that they came to 60.2 per cent from 1902 to 1904.[40] This proportion very probably held for the remainder of that decade.

The Japanese influence affected translations into Chinese from Western languages in both the selections made and the vocabulary. The infusion of Japanese terminology into Chinese was massive. This held true at all levels. It was evident in popular translations of the romantic political novels of the 1880s like *Kajin no kigū* (Strange encounters with elegant females), and *Keikoku bidan* (A noble tale of statesmanship), both translated by Liang Ch'i-ch'ao, and went beyond these to the entire tide of new knowledge that swept into China. A recent survey estimates that over three-quarters of the new Chinese vocabulary of those decades was Japanese in origin, through Chinese-character compounds that had already become standard in Japanese usage. Japanese influence affected the form as well as the content of books. Modern printing in Japan is sometimes dated from the presses that Hepburn and his Japanese associate Kishida Ginkō procured in Shanghai in the 1860s. Half a century later Chinese students found new printing techniques in Japan, together with Western-style binding, that they utilized for their periodicals and translations and reimported to China.[41] The student movement thus made its impress on every aspect of the cultural and technological diffusion of knowledge and experience in late Ch'ing and early Republican China.

[40] Tsuen-hsuin Tsien, 'Western impact on China through translation', *FEQ*, 13.3 (May 1954) 318–19.
[41] Sanetō Keishū, *Chūgokujin Nihon ryūgaku shi*, 378, for estimates of vocabulary flow. The author sees 1905 as the turning point for use of Western-style bindings in student translations. Part of Kishida's diary of his 1867 trip to Shanghai appears with an introduction in *Chūgoku*, 24 (1965) 5–16.

JAPAN AND THE CHINESE REVOLUTIONARIES

To the intellectual and educational impact there was added a direct personal and political contact between Japan and the Chinese revolutionary movement. It is a contact that has been a good deal more noted in Western and Japanese scholarship than in Chinese studies. Its dimensions are increasingly apparent as a result of the publication of memoirs and source materials.[42]

There were many reasons for the Japanese and their government to maintain a direct interest in the state of politics in China. The danger of a Manchu collapse and of the partition of China was a constant theme in Japanese writings on national security and international politics after the Sino-Japanese War, and the heightened international competition and rivalry posed problems of affiliation and choice for the Meiji statesmen. It seemed to them that they also had to seize the opportunity to influence the course of events in China. Their natural preference was to do this through advice and assistance to the legitimate government. Proffers of aid through military missions and educational programmes constituted unimpeachable evidence that Japan had overtaken China in the race for modernity, and made real the sense of Japanese leadership in an Asian restoration. On the other hand, Japan had achieved its successes through emulation of and affiliation with the West, and a good many Japanese felt it in their true interests to continue to observe Fukuzawa's advice to be separate from Asia. This concern was maintained through at least the Russo-Japanese War, when a Chinese tie was avoided lest the West conceive of that struggle in racial terms. Thereafter Japan's full involvement in imperialist policies further reduced the urgency and attractions of an Asian stance.

Yet there was also a general opinion that an ultimate confrontation between East and West, yellow and white, was inevitable. This conviction was current in the last decade of the Meiji period, when a good deal of writing in the West about the inevitability of a racial struggle was quickly reported to the Japanese. To the extent that one shared this view, Japan's need to affiliate with China was clear. And, should the Chinese government prove incapable of response or inflexible in its assumptions of superiority, the Japanese would have to think about supporting an alternative regime.

This gloomy view of racial struggle and the fear of Western domination that characterized the entire Meiji period crossed most political positions. Shadings varied and tactics were many, but the root sense of kinship and

---

[42] Marius B. Jansen, *The Japanese and Sun Yat-sen*, and 'Japanese views of China', 163–89.

commitment to an Asian cause – expressed as 'common culture, common race' – was seldom denied. The year 1895 brought a solution for Japan's primary problems of independence and equality among the great powers, and thereafter it became possible to face the problem of Asia. The practical meaning of this step for Chinese reformers and revolutionaries was determined in good measure by the structure of Japan's leadership. The principal Meiji leaders, who were entering the status of *genrō* as the twentieth century began, were on the whole firm in their commitment to the path of affiliation with the West that had worked so well for them. Some of them, especially Yamagata Aritomo, were much concerned about a future clash between the races, but the responsibilities of power usually sufficed to keep their eyes and commitments on the side of the navies and industrial plants of the West. Yamagata's position overlapped with that of the military specialists, whose leader he was. The army leaders were particularly aware of China's lack of power to deter the West, and quick to take upon themselves responsibility for continental positions – in Korea, in Liaotung, in 'South Manchuria' – from which they could make up for their neighbour's weakness. Their concern with China's borders to the north and the Russian armies there made them keen to help train China's new armies. Individual officers like Fukushima Yasumasa became figures of romance and legend in their courageous individual efforts to reconnoitre the little-known interior of Central Asia.[43]

As against the power elite, there were men who were wary of Western ties, tired of their country's apparent second-class status in the international order, and articulate advocates of nationality and of Asia. Without the responsibility of power or the direction of national affairs, these Japanese could afford to be contemptuous of caution and diplomacy. As self-appointed guardians of the national conscience with access to communications, they were important heirs of the national reawakening that had followed the advocacy of emperor, nation and cultural nationalism. This category, or spectrum, included the nationalist societies that grew out of the era of party organization in the 1880s – Tōyama Mitsuru's Genyōsha of 1881 and Uchida Ryōhei's Kokuryūkai ('Black Dragon' or Amur Society) of 1901. As self-appointed advocates of nationalism and morality the nationalist leaders had ready access to men of wealth and power and to youths of courage and conviction. The government, which was working out a new orthodoxy of emperor and state, could neither contradict nor control them. From their ranks came activists in Korea, China and

[43] The official history of the Kokuryūkai (Amur or 'Black Dragon' Society), Kuzuu Yoshihisa *et al.* eds., *Tōa senkaku shishi kiden* (Stories and biographies of pioneer East Asian idealists), concludes with an extensive biographical honour role of East Asian pioneers.

Manchuria as well as agents of intimidation and propaganda in domestic politics.

Related to though not identified with these organizations were men like Arao Sei (Kiyoshi), who was convinced that Japan's economic future lay in the development of trading ties with China. Only in Asia, where Japan had the advantages of proximity and familiarity, could she expect to meet the challenge of the West. Well into the late 1890s sentiments of this sort were still minority opinions in a society that had so determinedly gone to school with the West, and this fact contributed to the zeal and sense of moral superiority with which the Asianists called their countrymen back to their proper mission. Arao went to Hankow in 1886 after having distinguished himself in army staff work. He set up an ostensibly mercantile establishment and assigned his men geographic sectors of investigation, thereby collecting information on all parts of China. While his overall thought was of a Japanese hegemony over much of Asia, when it came to China he argued that Japan's security was directly dependent upon that of her neighbours. Hence it was necessary for Japan to reform and strengthen the Ch'ing empire.[44]

The nationalist and Asianist movements intersected with the highest level of the elite in the person of Prince Konoe Atsumaro (1863–1904). With his impeccable social credentials, his international experience and early schooling in Germany, and his position as head of the House of Peers, Konoe was in a unique position to speak and act. He made it his mission to sponsor and emphasize the study of Asia and above all of China. He sponsored, subsidized and led the Tōa Dōbun Shoin (lit., 'East Asian common culture academy') which was established in 1898. Through its educational centres in China and research centres in Japan it made important contributions to the cultural exchange that was its mission. The year of its founding, 1898, was also the year Ōkuma set forth his 'Ōkuma Doctrine'. Konoe sensed in the contemporary imperialist seizures in China, and in Japanese public denigration of China's weakness, a dangerous trend to abandon China and join the West in the imperialist scramble. In a much-quoted article in *Taiyō* in January 1898 he called for close Sino-Japanese cooperation and association. The root causes of Western aggression were racial, he argued, and Japan had no choice but to oppose them and to assist China to do so. 'The survival of the Chinese people is by no means a matter of some one else's welfare,' he warned, 'it affects the vital interest of the Japanese themselves.' Japanese would have to study China, travel to

[44] Inoue Masaji, *Kyojin Arao Sei (Kiyoshi)* (Grand old Arao Sei), provides a biography. See also Akira Iriye, 'The ideology of Japanese imperialism: imperial Japan and China', in Grant K. Goodman, ed. *Imperial Japan and Asia: a reassessment*, 35.

China, and meet Chinese, and only then would they be able to adopt policies appropriate to the danger both countries faced.[45] Just as Konoe's activities intersected with those of the government in 1898, his efforts joined those of the nationalists in 1901. That date marked the founding both of the Kokuryūkai, an organization dedicated to establishing Japan on the Amur, and of Konoe's National United League on Russian Policy, the Kokumin Tairo Dōshikai.

Farther from power and influence, but still on the fringes of the power elite, were the Meiji liberals associated with the movement for peoples' rights (Jiyū minken undō). Many of them saw their struggle for political liberalism in Japan as related to those of other Asian peoples. Most of them, despite their use of Western liberal and constitutional thought, were vigorously 'Asian' in their resistance to the Western thrust. Early Jiyūtō (Liberal party) writers and editorialists were keenly aware of conditions in Korea, and wanted to sponsor liberalism there as well as in Japan. Ōi Kentarō developed a bizarre filibustering expedition to Korea for the sake of liberty in 1885, and during the same period Tarui Tōkichi, a founder of the East Asian Socialist Party (Tō Shakaitō) which was quickly banned by the Japanese police, wrote a tract (Daitō gappō ron) calling for the union of Japan and Korea in a state to be known as Great East (Daitō). For him, as for others, the war of the races was nearing so rapidly that there was no time for half-way measures. Asian solidarity had to be established. These schemes contained idealism and commitment as well as parochialism and arrogance, and they appealed to the best in Meiji universalism as well as the worst in Meiji particularism and chauvinism. Similarly, liberal theorists like Nakae Chōmin argued for associating the reform of China with that of Japan, and as early as 1881 Ueki Emori had organized a Rise Asia (Kōa) Society. Even after the mainstream of the movement for parliamentary liberalism drew closer to the Meiji government with the promulgation of the Meiji constitution in 1889, it was logical for its more radical wing, the twentieth-century socialists and anarchists, to maintain the Asian consciousness of their predecessors through a warm interest in China and the Chinese.[46]

The most striking examples of personal cooperation with Chinese revolutionaries were provided by Japanese of the liberal left. Miyazaki Tōten was acclaimed by Sun Yat-sen as 'a chivalrous hero. His insight is extensive, his ideals are out of the ordinary; he is one who hastens to

---

[45] A convenient and authoritative summary of the history and the contributions of the Tōa Dōbunkai and Tōa Dōbun Shoin can be found in Chūgoku, 21 (Aug. 1965) 7–22.
[46] Some of these matters are discussed in Jansen, 'Japanese views of China', 163–89. For Miyazaki's complete works see Miyazaki Ryūsuke and Onogawa Hidemi, eds. Miyazaki Tōten zenshū.

help another's need, his heart warm with benevolence and righteousness. He always laments the deterioration that has befallen the yellow race, and grieves because of China's increasing weakness.' Miyazaki and his brothers came out of the early liberal movement, experimented with Christianity, drank in the single-tax solution of Henry George, and devoted their lives to the service of the Chinese revolutionary cause.[47]

Because these themes of crisis, commitment and conscience were so basic to the Meiji scene, it is not surprising that men who devoted their lives to what their countrymen saw as high ideals, could find rapport at many points within the structure of the groups which have been sketched above. Some important contacts came by fortunate coincidence. For example, Ōkuma Shigenobu and Inukai Ki, leaders of the political party movement, were in office at a time when the crisis of imperialist advance in China triggered the reform movement of 1898. The launching of the life work of Miyazaki Tōten, the introduction of Sun Yat-sen to important Japanese supporters, the Hundred Days in Peking, the Kenseitō cabinet of Ōkuma and Itagaki, the founding of the Dōbunkai, the flight of Chinese reformers to Japan, and the beginnings of the student movement, all came in quick succession.

It has already been noted that the Chinese reformers, who were a natural elite among the political refugees, received the care and hospitality of high-ranking Japanese. Support for the escape of K'ang Yu-wei and Liang Ch'i-ch'ao to Japan was arranged at the highest levels of the Tokyo government. Intermediary for much of this, and privy to all of it, was the Dōbunkai head, Prince Konoe. K'ang met leading Japanese, enjoyed the hospitality of Count Ōkuma, and had a long talk with Konoe himself in which the latter contrasted for him the long preparation of the Meiji Restoration with the seemingly precipitate course of the Hundred Days. As always, Konoe emphasized his sense of common cultural and political concerns with China, and the need for an Asian Monroe Doctrine. It was the feeling of Konoe's group that K'ang was too prominent to be encouraged to stay in Japan for very long, however, and in the spring of 1899 secret foreign office funds were made available (via Konoe) for K'ang's departure for Vancouver, Canada. Liang Ch'i-ch'ao also met with Konoe and other highly placed Japanese. In 1899 Konoe himself travelled to China. There he had long talks with reform-minded officials. Chang Chih-tung remonstrated with him on the subject of Japanese sanctuary for K'ang and Liang, and the possible harm the latter's writing could do to Chinese students in Japan. Konoe deprecated the appeal and importance of the reformers, and preferred to turn to his favourite subjects of Sino-

[47] From Sun Yat-sen's foreword to Miyazaki's *Sanjū-sannen no yume* (Thirty-three years' dream).

Japanese cooperation and common concerns. A little earlier in Hong Kong, Konoe had met Miyazaki and Hirayama Shū, both the recipients of government funds, in order to acquaint himself with political currents in South China.[48]

Activist liberals like Miyazaki and Hirayama found their natural friends among the Chinese revolutionaries and not among Chinese reformers or Japanese peers. In 1900 Miyazaki's efforts to get K'ang Yu-wei and Sun Yat-sen to cooperate drew so much suspicion from K'ang that it ended in his arrest by the Singapore authorities, while Konoe, noting the stories of this in his diary, dismissed his countryman as a 'plotter'. Ties with the student movement also took time to develop. During the early years, when students were still carefully sponsored and academically oriented, Sun Yat-sen and his Japanese friends received relatively little support from Chinese students in Japan. But then as the number, variety and political intensity of students grew, revolutionary sentiments gained ground. At the same time, Japanese nationalism, turned as it was against Russia, did not immediately offend. Consequently the Chinese revolutionaries found the ground better prepared for their efforts among Japanese as well as among Chinese students.

Sun Yat-sen had fled to Japan after the failure of his first attempt at revolt in Canton in 1895. In Yokahama he cut his queue, grew a moustache and adopted Western clothes of Japanese cut. 'After the Japanese war,' he later recalled, 'when the natives of Japan began to be treated with more respect, I had no trouble, when I let hair and moustache grow, in passing for a Japanese.' From Japan he went to London where his detention and near extradition by the Chinese embassy, which he described in his widely read *Kidnapped in London*, made him famous. He returned to Japan in August 1897. He now made the acquaintance of Miyazaki and Hirayama. They had heard of his return to Japan from Sun's associates in China, where they had gone to investigate politics at the request of Inukai Ki. Sun very quickly established a magnetic influence over his new friends. Although they reported to Inukai, and indeed introduced Sun Yat-sen to him, their loyalty was to Sun and to the vision of a resurgent Asia they shared with him.

Their first cooperative project was a plan to aid the Filipino revolution of Aguinaldo, through the purchase and shipment of arms and the transport of a small group of adventurers. The project foundered, as did the over-age and overloaded ship on which the guns were sent, taking the lives

[48] Konoe's diary notations permit study of the network of his formal and informal relationships. He planned K'ang's visit on 16 Oct. 1898, met him 12 Nov. 1898, received funds for his use on 14 March 1899, was in Hong Kong in Oct. 1899, and met Chang Chih-tung on 4 Nov. 1899. *Konoe Atsumaro nikki*, vol. 2.

of several Japanese adventurers. In a second project, the Japanese tried to get Chinese revolutionaries and reformers together after the disastrous failure of the Hundred Days. This too came to nothing. Although reformers and revolutionaries were alike dependent upon Japanese sanctuary and in touch with the same Japanese – Miyazaki had met K'ang Yu-wei in Hong Kong and Hirayama had accompanied Liang Ch'i-ch'ao to Yokohama – the Chinese reformers had little confidence in the revolutionaries, whom they considered their cultural and social inferiors. Early schools that were established with the help of Inukai and Konoe quickly came under the control of reformers rather than revolutionaries. Meanwhile the adventurer-liberals among the Japanese gravitated towards the activist revolutionaries rather than towards the reformers. In 1900, the abortive revolt led by T'ang Ts'ai-ch'ang at Hankow had the nominal support of Chinese of both factions, but thereafter the divisions among Chinese anxious for change were permanent.[49]

In the late summer of 1900 Sun Yat-sen tried to stage a revolution in Kwangtung, placing the greatest reliance upon Japanese participation. The revolt was based upon the now Japanese island of Taiwan, and to some extent related to the expectation that Japan would take advantage of the Boxer disturbances in North China to move into South China. Amoy was, in fact, occupied for a time by Japanese troops in response to a staged anti-Japanese 'provocation'. Sun Yat-sen drew up a provisional government that had several Japanese in posts of responsibility. One of his associates rounded up secret-society members in Kwangtung, and began to lead them in the direction of Amoy to meet the hoped-for supplies of men and weapons from Japan. In initial engagements the rebels were everywhere victorious. But two weeks after the rising had begun Sun Yat-sen, realizing Japanese aid would not after all be forthcoming, sent word to abandon the attempt. Yamada Yoshimasa, a Japanese who carried this final message, fell into the hands of Manchu troops who killed him. As Sun wrote on his epitaph, 'he came forward and went to his death in battle for the cause of righteousness. Truly he sacrificed himself for humanity and became a pioneer of the new Asia.'[50]

After the failure of this revolt in 1900, Sun Yat-sen experimented unsuccessfully with sources of support from Indo-China, which the French

[49] See, for the early revolutionary movement and its vicissitudes, Hsueh Chün-tu, 'Sun Yat-sen, Yang Ch'ü-yun, and the early revolutionary movement in China', JAS, 19.3 (May 1960) 307–18. Yen-p'ing Hao, 'The abortive cooperation between reformers and revolutionaries (1895–1900)', Papers on China, 15 (1961) 91–114. Mary Backus Rankin, Early Chinese revolutionaries. Radical intellectuals in Shanghai and Chekiang, 1902–1911.
[50] Jansen, The Japanese and Sun Yat-sen, 82–104. It was the failure of the Waichow (or Hui-chou) revolt that brought Miyazaki to write his Thirty-three Years' Dream.

governor-general invited him to visit in 1903, and from the United States, where he tried to sway the Triad Society leaders. These failures, added to his earlier disillusionment with the lack of discipline and dependability among the secret-society members of South China who had provided the bulk of his earlier following, convinced him that he should recruit from among the Chinese students in Japan, and particularly from those in military schools. The dramatic growth of the student movement came during the years of Sun's wanderings in Indo-China and the United States. The rising tide of Japanese feeling against Russia was also important. Kokuryūkai members saw their nationalism related to Asian opportunities, and believed that, with the fall of the Ch'ing, Chinese control of Manchuria would lose its rationale. Consequently, as the official history of the organization put it, 'love of country and chivalry went hand in hand in the Japanese help of the South China revolutions'.[51] Meanwhile, the student volunteer army organized against Russia in 1903 produced additional recruits for the revolution. Huang Hsing, for example, returned to Hunan to attempt an insurrection. He began as an instructor in a Japanese language school, but in addition printed and distributed the revolutionary pamphlets of Ch'en T'ien-hua. Virtually every member active in the early stage of the revolutionary organization, the Hua-hsing hui, which he founded, had been or would become a student in Japan. Before the organization staged the insurrection that was planned for 1904, however, the Ch'ing authorities raided Huang's home and his Japanese school, and the principals barely made the dangerous and difficult trip back to Japan. In Tokyo Huang was soon contacted by some of the same Japanese who had assisted Sun Yat-sen. Like Sun, he accepted the argumentation of 'common culture and common race', and with his associate Sung Chiao-jen he provided an additional focus for Japanese encouragement and assistance.[52]

Sun Yat-sen returned to Tokyo when the student tide was at full flood in the late summer of 1905. His revolutionary programmes and slogans had now been worked out. What was lacking was a new organization, and this he built in cooperation with Huang Hsing, to whom his Japanese friends provided the introduction. After a series of planning meetings the T'ung-meng hui was formed on 30 July 1905, at the home of Uchida Ryōhei, the Kokuryūkai head. Some seventy persons were present, virtually all of them

---

[51] Quoted in Jansen, *The Japanese and Sun Yat-sen*, 111. For Sun's contact with students and his secret society ties, see Cheng, 'The T'ung-meng-hui', 36. See also Harold Z. Schiffrin, *Sun Yat-sen and the origins of the Chinese Revolution*, 300ff.

[52] Sung, however, never fully accepted the Japanese arguments. Noriko Tamada, 'Sung Chiao-jen and the 1911 Revolution', *Papers on China*, 21 (1968) 189. For Huang, the fullest source is Hsueh Chün-tu, *Huang Hsing and the Chinese Revolution*. The fullest treatment of Sun is that of Liew, *Struggle for democracy*.

Chinese students, representing seventeen of the eighteen provinces. The formal inaugural meeting was 20 August, this time at the residence of Sakamoto Kinya. Three Japanese – Miyazaki Tōten, Hirayama Shū and Kayano Chōchi – were full members, and Miyazaki was given powers of attorney in 1907 to negotiate for arms and supplies as Japanese representative of the organization. The T'ung-meng hui (Revolutionary Alliance or League) built upon the provincial organizations the students had formed in Tokyo; it added to these some of the techniques of oaths and secrecy of the traditional secret societies, and it did so in the name of the Three Principles that Sun Yat-sen had worked out through his reading in the West, together with Five Slogans, one of which called for Sino-Japanese friendship. The T'ung-meng hui thus represented in unique degree the visible product of China's search for nationalism and modernization through education in Japan.

The intellectual content of the League's propaganda and its political struggle with the reform persuasion represented by Liang Ch'i-ch'ao, are treated elsewhere (see chapter 9). Its leaders sometimes had a difficult task defending themselves against revolutionaries less persuaded of the benign course of Japanese opinion. Hu Han-min, writing in *Min pao*, found himself explaining and apologizing for some of the condescension and arrogance implicit in the 'favour' of Count Ōkuma and the more explicit disfavour of the Tokyo government.[53] Even these explanations proved inadequate after 1907, when the Japanese government chose to align itself formally with the imperialist powers in a series of agreements to arrange Asian boundaries and decided to ask Sun Yat-sen to leave Japan. His departure, like that of K'ang Yu-wei eight years earlier, was eased by secret foreign office money to ward off an open break or the wrath of his Japanese nationalist friends, but it deprived the revolutionaries of the use of their Tokyo base and gradually shifted the centre of T'ung-meng hui activities to other points on the fringe of China. In Sun's absence the centrifugal tendencies inherent in the provincial origins and intellectual diversity of the organization weakened its unity and vitality. But the more important trends inherent in the steady accretion of education, nationalism and discontent among young Chinese went on as before, to the ultimate benefit, though not the direct credit, of the revolutionary movement.

Direct Japanese influence declined as the revolution neared. Miyazaki, Kayano and other agents of the revolutionary party became the objects of government surveillance and distrust. So did their Chinese friends on their

---

[53] Shimada Kenji, *Shingai kakumei no shisō*, 193–4, discusses several speeches in which Ōkuma adopted a very hard line on China's need to take Japanese advice, and Hu Han-min's attempt, in *Min-pao*, to distinguish between the Japanese government and Japanese people.

secret visits to Japan. The image of a friendly Japanese government gradually changed to that of a particularly dangerous imperialist power, the more feared for its proximity and ease of access. The outbreak of revolution in 1911 found Sun Yat-sen travelling from America, not to China or to Japan, but to England in hopes of deterring a threatened Japanese intervention, while the Tokyo government itself was so unsure of its course that it succeeded in alienating almost all candidates for power in China. In Manchuria, Japanese army-backed adventurers launched their first attempt to set up a separate pro-Japanese buffer state. Elsewhere Sun Yat-sen's old friends were active but unable to deliver or guarantee the support of their countrymen. Kita Ikki, a socialist and nationalist, was close to Sung Chiao-jen, but he also managed to send daily cables to Uchida Ryōhei, the Kokuryūkai head, reporting on the political confusion. He later retired to write a thoughtful explanation of why Japanese bourgeois-imperialist society had failed in its great opportunity to establish a position of leadership and trust with a Chinese republic struggling to be born. Others, including Miyazaki and Kayano, were so close to Sun Yat-sen that they shared in his speedy eclipse after the failure of the revolutionary government. He himself, thrown back upon the hospitality of Japan after his brief moment of success, proved more willing to make promises with regard to Japanese interests in Manchuria than he had before.[54]

The Japanese also played a role in the longer and deeper intellectual revolution in modern China. As the Japanese government alternated between the repressive and imperialist emphases of Prime Minister Katsura (1901–6; 1908–11) and the milder interludes under Saionji (1906–8; 1911–12), intellectuals of the socialist left found an occasional opportunity to express their disenchantment with parliamentarianism in speech and publication. Miyazaki Tamizō, brother of Tōten, was a firm advocate of Henry George's single-tax theory, and published two articles in the revolutionary journal *Min pao*. There is no reason to doubt that such views and contacts contributed to Sun Yat-sen's views on the land problem.[55]

A more direct influence can be traced in the currents of anarchism. Works on Russian nihilism had been published in Japan as early as the 1880s, and Japanese radicals later related the founding of their ephemeral East Asian Socialist Party in 1882 to these works. After 1902 a growing interest in anarchism developed in Japan. A Waseda professor wrote an

[54] Jansen, *The Japanese and Sun Yat-sen*. George M. Wilson, *Radical nationalist in Japan: Kita Ikki, 1883–1937*, 45–53. For Kita's telegrams from China see Takahashi Masao, ed. *Nihon kindaika to Kyūshu* (Kyūshū and Japanese modernization), 4.424–80.

[55] Martin Bernal, 'The triumph of anarchism over Marxism, 1906–1907', in Mary C. Wright, ed. *China in revolution: the first phase, 1900–1913* (hereafter *CIR*), 116. Harold Schiffrin, 'Sun Yat-sen's land policy', *JAS*, 26.4 (Aug. 1957) 549–64.

influential work about the Russian revolutionary movement which empha-
sized a three-stage periodization of revolutionary literature, propaganda
and agitation, and assassination and terror. This had influence among
Chinese revolutionaries. The Russo–Japanese War further increased
Japanese interest in Russia, and popular novelists like Futabatei Shimei and
popular heroes of the war-like Hirose Takeo were deeply influenced by
Russian values and culture. The term and concept of anarchism entered
Chinese language and thought through Japanese translations in 1903.
During the same years the individual heroics of Russian revolutionaries
began to seem unusually appropriate models of emulation to Chinese
students. The emotionalism of the decade, shown in the isolated patriotic
suicides, the students' consciousness of themselves as a vanguard, and
their disgust with the tyranny of their government, all made the Russian
case seem relevant.

After the brief Revolution of 1905, a number of Russian refugees and
revolutionaries made their way to Nagasaki. Sun Yat-sen on his way to
Annam met them through introductions by the Kokuryūkai and Kayano.
The Miyazaki-Kayano group worked with the Russians to publish a
magazine called *Kakumei hyōron* (Revolutionary review) which was intended
to speed both the Chinese and Russian revolutions. Though it was soon
stopped by the Japanese police, the journal was produced in a climate of
vigorous left-wing publication in Japan. *Hikari* (The light), *Heimin shimbun*
(Commoners' press), *Chokugen* (Straight talk) and others indicated by their
titles the current of social criticism. All this coincided with a major turn
within the Japanese socialist movement as Kōtoku Shūsui made known his
shift to anarchism in 1906. For a time *Min pao* and *Kakumei hyōron* borrowed
from and advertised each other. *Min pao* came increasingly into the hands
of men like Chang Ping-lin and Chang Chi, who had an interest in
anarchism, even before Sun's expulsion from Japan. These men were by no
means pro-Japanese (Chang Ping-lin, indeed, tended to be highly critical of
Japanese culture and aspirations), nor were they pro-Western. But they
were like their Japanese counterparts in the general tide of radical intellectuals. Their denunciations of the evils of capitalist society and institutions and of the West, and their moral strictures and judgments, though
expressed in terms of anarchist radicalism, owed much to the philosophical
currents hostile to bourgeois materialism in their own tradition.

It is beyond the scope of this chapter to discuss the larger question of the
impact of Japan on modern Chinese liberal and revolutionary thought.[56]

---

[56] Bernal, 'The triumph of anarchism over Marxism' suggests some aspects of the problem. See
also Ishimoda Shō, 'Kōtoku Shūsui to Chūgoku' (Kōtoku Shūsui and China), in Takeuchi
Yoshimi, ed. *Ajia shugi* (Asianism), vol. 9: *Gendai Nihon shisō-taikei*, 384–410. On the Russian
and anarchist influences in the Chinese Revolution, see Don C. Price, *Russia and the roots*

The Chinese increasingly drew directly from Western sources in their ideological borrowing, and the specifically Japanese element that inhered in translations from the Japanese would be difficult to define. Yet it is clear that the streams of radical thought in the two countries cannot be considered in isolation. For members of the Chinese student generation in Japan the Japanese radicals were personal friends and moral giants. The diary of Ching Mei-chiu makes clear how significant it was for one important Chinese student to hear speakers like Kōtoku Shūsui and Ōsugi Sakae. Japanese radicalism played a large part in the Chinese environment in Tokyo.[57]

The Japanese influence was not of course decisive, but supplemented and reinforced the larger trends of change which the Chinese experienced. Nor, indeed, were the revolutionaries themselves decisive figures in making the first revolution; in the words of Mary Wright, 'they created a tradition rather than a revolution'.[58] It is difficult to measure the impact of Japanese contacts on the Chinese leaders personally. But it is often easy to recognize in that contact the most important experience in the lives of certain Japanese. The 'China rōnin', as Miyazaki and his friends were called, were known as such throughout their lives. For them the struggle to build a new East Asia was a cause that transcended personal or national boundaries. On both sides, however, the experience of internationalism proved difficult to accommodate in the rising tides of nationalist consciousness.[59]

of the Chinese Revolution, 1896–1911, and Michael Gasster, *Chinese intellectuals and the Revolution of 1911. The birth of modern Chinese nationalism.*

[57] For meetings and contacts, see the reminiscences of Takeuchi Zensaku, 'Meiji makki ni okeru Chū-Nichi kakumei undō no kōryū' (Interflow in the Chinese and Japanese revolutionary movements in late Meiji years), *Chūgoku kenkyū*, 5 (Sept. 1948) 74–95. However, it will also be seen from R. A. Scalapino and H. Schiffrin, 'Early socialist currents in the Chinese revolutionary movement: Sun Yat-sen versus Liang Ch'i-ch'ao', *JAS*, 18.3 (May 1959) 321–42, that the examples and arguments chosen are uniformly those from the West.

[58] Introduction, *CIR*, 45.

[59] A residence of Huang Hsing's in Tokyo became the headquarters of the post World War I student organization, the Shinjinkai, of which Miyazaki Tōten's son was a founding member. See Henry D. Smith, II, *Japan's first student radicals*, 59.

CHAPTER 7

POLITICAL AND INSTITUTIONAL
REFORM 1901–11

THE REFORM EDICT OF THE KUANG-HSU EMPEROR

When the allied forces seized Peking on 14 August 1900, the Empress Dowager Tz'u-hsi and the Kuang-hsu Emperor evacuated the capital and fled to Sian, where they arrived on 26 October. In early December, high-ranking officials in the capital and the provinces were ordered to submit memorials giving their ideas on governmental, military, educational, financial or any other reforms. On 29 January 1901, the emperor, under the direction of the empress dowager, issued an edict stating that while the three bonds and five relationships were eternal, the method of the government should be changed in accordance with the times. In this edict the deeply rooted evils of China were summarized as follows:

The weakness of China is caused by the strength of convention and the rigid network of regulations. We have many mediocre officials but few men of talent and courage. The regulations are used by the mediocre men as the means of their self-protection, and taken advantage of by the government clerks as sources of profit. The government officials exchange numerous documents but they never touch reality. The appointment of men of talent is restricted by regulations which are so rigid that even men of extraordinary talent are missed. What misleads the country can be expressed in one word, selfishness (*ssu*) and what suffocates all under heaven is precedent (*li*).[1]

The edict also asserted that China had learned from abroad only superficial words and phrases, not 'the fundamentals of the wealth and strength of the West'. It therefore ordered the high officials to consider and report 'what things should be kept as they are now and what should be changed among the court regulations, state precedents, civil administration, people's welfare, education, civil service examinations, military systems and financial administration and so on? What should be eliminated, and what should be combined together; what should be adopted from the outside, and what should be found within?' In response many high officials submitted opinions on institutional and administrative reform. In April 1901, the

---

[1] *Ta-Ch'ing li-ch'ao shih-lu* (Veritable records of successive reigns of the Ch'ing dynasty), Kuang-hsu (hereafter *CSL-KH*), 476.9.

government created the Bureau of Government Affairs (Cheng-wu ch'u) to examine these reform proposals and select those to be followed.[2] Thereafter, this bureau became the headquarters of the government reform programmes.

REFORMS IN EDUCATION

The chief objective of the Ch'ing reforms after the Boxer incident was the adoption of certain elements from the West. For this purpose it was necessary that government officials be versed in Western culture. The government therefore made the Hanlin academicians study Western learning. It called home students studying abroad to give them official appointments, and offered a special civil-service examination in public administration (*ching-chi t'e-k'o*) to those who were recommended by high officials in the capital and the provinces.[3]

Along with these makeshift measures, the government attempted an overall reform in the method of selecting officials. Ever since the seventh century, Chinese rulers had set written examinations by which men could qualify to be high-level civil servants. This system of examination (*k'o-chü*) had been an excellent institution and during more than a thousand years' of practice the system had become more and more complete. At the same time, however, it had fallen prey to formalism. Most of the questions asked in the examinations required one to choose certain phrases from the Confucian canon and to paraphrase and explain them. By Ming and Ch'ing times, each Confucian classic was supplied with official annotations, which became the accepted version for the examinations. Consequently the examination candidates tried to memorize the entire text of the classics as well as the official version of the annotations. The civil-service examinations became merely a test of memory and writing ability, requiring not logical and clear essays but essays in an elegant style, studded with parallel phrases and classical allusions. In addition, an essay had to consist of eight paragraphs, written in the so-called 'eight legged' (*pa-ku*) style. Even the handwriting had to be in the 'small, square style' (*hsiao-k'ai*).

Such had been the reality during the Ch'ing. It is no exaggeration to say that in China all students studied for the civil-service examinations. No wonder the products of the orthodox education were, in most cases, stereotyped, conventional men without capacity for creative thinking.

---

[2] *CSL-KH*, 481.4b.

[3] A valuable source book on Ch'ing educational reform is Shu Hsin-ch'eng, ed. *Chin-tai Chung-kuo chiao-yü shih-liao* (Historical materials on modern Chinese education); also the same author's recompilation, *Chung-kuo chin-tai chiao-yü shih tzu-liao* (Materials for the history of education in modern China; 3 vols. 1963). On the gentry's role in initiating schools. see Marianne Bastid, *Aspects de la réforme de l'enseignement en Chine au début du XXᵉ siècle*.

From such education how could one expect to secure the type of men required for a new age?

Plainly, a revision in the examination system was inevitable. In 1901 the Ch'ing government began by abolishing the eight-legged essays. Instead, plainer expositions of the *Four books* and *Five classics* and essays on Chinese history and government and on Western politics and scholarship were to be required, beginning with the provincial examinations in 1902.

Secondly, recognizing the need for a Western-style public school system, the government decided to convert the academies or *shu-yuan* into Western-style schools. Such schools had been advocated by Chang Chih-tung and Sheng Hsuan-huai ever since the Sino-Japanese War, and they had set up schools in Wuchang, Tientsin and Shanghai. However, it proved almost impossible to get students to go to these schools, because the strongest motive for education was still government office. Therefore to attract students to its new schools the government accepted their graduates as civil-service candidates.[4]

Study abroad was also encouraged by the Ch'ing government. The reason given was that there were not enough qualified teachers for the new schools that were to be built in China. It was costly to invite teachers from abroad; besides even if large sums of money were spent, good foreign teachers would be hard to get; therefore it was quicker to send Chinese students abroad. Studying in Japan was particularly encouraged. Compared with the West, travel to Japan and also living were much cheaper, the Japanese used the same written characters, and their manners and customs were closer to the Chinese (see chapter 6). In addition, it was felt that Western culture had been imported to Japan in almost its original shape, and so there was less need to take the trouble to go to the West.

Thus educational reform started with reform of the civil-service examinations, creation of new schools, and encouragement of study abroad. Following this line more and more new schools were opened, but their curricula and the required years of study varied greatly. Realizing the necessity of standardization, the government put out in 1904 a set of regulations for school administration modelled on the Japanese example. Under this system, schooling was divided into three parts – elementary, secondary and higher education. At the elementary level were the junior primary school (*ch'u-teng hsiao hsueh-t'ang*) for students seven to twelve years old (*sui*) and the senior primary school (*kao-teng*) for students aged twelve to sixteen. At the secondary level was the middle school (*chung hsueh-t'ang*) for students aged sixteen to twenty-one. For higher education there were to be the higher school (*kao-teng hsueh-t'ang*) for ages twenty-one

---

[4] See Wolfgang Franke, *The reform and abolition of the traditional Chinese examination system*, 53–67.

to twenty-four, the university (*fen-k'o ta-hsueh*) for ages twenty-four to twenty-eight, and finally the academy of sciences (*t'ung-ju yuan*). The graduates from the academy of sciences or university were to be given metropolitan or *chin-shih* degrees; graduates from higher school, provincial or *chü-jen* degrees; and graduates from middle school and senior primary school, licentiate or *sheng-yuan* (*hsiu-ts'ai*) degrees. This would make the graduates from the new schools qualified as candidates for regular official appointments.[5]

After setting up this system on paper, the government established in December 1905 a Ministry of Education (Hsueh Pu) as the central organ for educational administration. In the past, the Board of Rites had been in charge of the civil-service examinations as well as the traditional education related to them. However, the administration of some Western-style schools opened after the Sino-Japanese War had not been entrusted to the Board of Rites. A Metropolitan University (Ching-shih ta hsueh-t'ang) had been founded in 1898 and charged with administration of the new schools. But this Metropolitan University, really a combination of a university and a ministry of education, had not been able to function as the headquarters for school administration as the new schools increased too rapidly in number. Therefore, the Metropolitan University was now made the highest institution of learning and the Ministry of Education was created separately to take charge of the schools.[6]

When the government established this school system in 1904, it intended after 1906 gradually to decrease the number of recipients of degrees through the old civil-service examinations, and eventually to abolish the examinations after a sufficient number of new schools had been founded in all the provinces. The outcome of the Russo-Japanese War, however, accelerated this process, for the victory of Japan was taken as one of constitutionalism over autocracy. Many Chinese thought that constitutionalism was almost inevitable for China. But in order to run a constitutional government, the people must think and judge independently. For this purpose, the traditional education was quite unsatisfactory, and indeed rather harmful. During the Russo-Japanese War, more and more people advocated abolition of the civil-service examinations. In September 1905, when the victory of Japan became decisive, the government decided to do away with the examinations in the following year.[7]

[5] *CSL-KH*, 523.19b-20; Franke, *Reform and abolition*, 59-67; see also William Ayers, *Chang Chih-tung and educational reform in China*, ch. 7.

[6] See the account by Yü Ch'ang-lin reprinted in *Ch'ing-ch'ao hsu wen-hsien t'ung-k'ao* (Encyclopedia of the historical records of the Ch'ing dynasty, continued), 106.8648-50; also Chuang Chi-fa, *Ching-shih ta hsueh-t'ang* ([The predecessor of] Peking University), ch. 2.

[7] *CSL-KH*, 548.4-5; Ayers, *Chang Chih-tung*, 233-4.

It was indeed an epoch-making event when this system, which had lasted for about 1,300 years, was completely abolished. Thereafter, the new school graduates were to occupy the responsible posts in the government, replacing the traditional degree holders. It was also decided that graduates from foreign schools of the level of higher school or above were also to be eligible for *chin-shih* or *chü-jen* degrees, partly according to the results of examinations to be taken by them on their repatriation.[8]

What were the effects of these educational reforms? According to the statistics of the Ministry of Education, in 1904 the total number of schools was 4,222 and the number of students 92,169; in 1909, the number of schools was 52,348 and of students 1,560,270.[9] These numbers indicate an amazing development in school education. However, it is questionable whether any real change in the content of education accompanied it.

First of all, as a result of the difficulty in getting teachers who were qualified for the new education, it was unavoidable that the old curriculum was still used in most of the new schools. In 1909, 48 per cent of the teachers who taught in the junior grade elementary schools were traditional degree-holders who did not know anything about the new education. This shows how difficult it was to get new teachers for the new education.

Secondly, almost all the private schools were opened by gentry-literati, and most of the public schools were also founded on their initiative. The gentry class, however, was fundamentally opposed to the government policy to abolish the civil-service examinations, to build schools, and to encourage study abroad. There were good reasons for this. The gentry enjoyed their various privileges in their localities not because they had wealth or aristocratic lineage, but merely because they had passed the examinations. Abolition of the examinations meant the disappearance of their privileges. Moreover, since their sons had usually prepared for the examinations, their abolition would destroy the privileges which whole gentry families had enjoyed and looked forward to. For this reason the gentry-literati as a class were consistently opposed to abolition. After the Ch'ing government decreed it anyway, the gentry cleverly ceased their resistance, and instead found a new way of preserving their privileges by opening schools, which could bestow the degrees of *chin-shih*, *chü-jen* and *sheng-yuan* on their graduates. By sending the younger members of their families to the schools, the gentry hoped to maintain their privileges and so they were very eager to open schools, even spending their own money.

[8] See Y. C. Wang, *Chinese intellectuals and the West, 1872–1949*, 61, 63, 68–9.
[9] *Ti-san-tz'u chiao-yü t'ung-chi t'u-piao, Hsuan-t'ung yuan-nien* (Statistical charts and tables on education, the third issue, for 1909).

Thirdly, old elements were retained in the new system as much as possible. For example, a director for the final examination was appointed by the emperor from among high-ranking officials, and this officer presided over the examination together with the president of the Ministry of Education or the provincial governor or governor-general. Degrees were then bestowed upon those who passed. It is evident that this procedure was exactly the same as before. 'School' seemed only a different name for the old civil-service examination.

Confucianism was still considered the fundamental content of scholarship, and even in the new schools was not to be neglected.[10] On the first and fifteenth days of every month schools were to hold a ceremony of Confucian worship, while many school hours were to be spent in reading and lecturing on the classics. Take the case of the junior grade primary school, for example: out of thirty class-hours per week, twelve were for reading and lectures on the Confucian classics. First-grade students were to read forty words a day from the *Analects* and the *Classic of filial piety*; second-grade students were to read sixty characters a day from the *Analects*, the *Great learning* and the *Doctrine of the mean*; for the third grade, a hundred characters a day from the *Mencius*; for the fourth grade, a hundred from *Mencius* and the *Book of rites*; and for the fifth grade, a hundred a day from the *Book of rites*. Besides all this there was a two-hour class for self-cultivation or moral education, which was a kind of Confucian education. It is obvious that Confucianism was stressed; even the method of learning was the same as before.

Both in the auditorium and in the classrooms of a school the Yung-cheng Emperor's *Sacred edict with extended commentary* was to be posted. It was to be recited in unison on the first day of every month, and to be used as the text for teaching the official spoken language (Mandarin). These features indicate how the traditional mass education or indoctrination for the villages (the 'local lectures' or *hsiang-yueh* system) was now taken over by the new schools, while through standardizing the spoken language, a unification of national sentiment was to be attempted.

The government authorities were extremely cautious about anything new. For example, no foreign language was to be taught in the elementary schools, because of the fear that if children were taught a foreign language while very young, they might neglect traditional scholarship. Further it was thought that foreign terms should not be used, since their use would make it impossible to preserve the purity of the Chinese language and

[10] For regulations on the new schools of this period, see Chang Po-hsi *et al. Tsou-ting hsueh-t'ang chang-ch'eng* (Regulations concerning educational institutions as approved by the throne). An important study of the new schools is Su Yun-feng, *Chang Chih-tung yü Hu-pei chiao-yü kai-ko* (Chang Chih-tung and educational reform in Hupei).

carry on proper scholarship. For instance, such terms as *she-hui* (society), *ying-hsiang* (influence) and *hsi-sheng* (sacrifice) had been recently imported from Japan, but these modern terms had different meanings from the original Chinese connotations. Such terms as *t'uan-t'i* (groups), *kuo-hun* (national spirit), *p'eng-chang* (expansion) and *wu-t'ai* (stage, theatre) and *tai-piao* (representative) had come into popular use around this time, but it was felt that these were not beautiful because they were not originally in the Chinese vocabulary but had been made up by the Japanese.[11] So this kind of term also should not be used, lest the Chinese language fall into chaos.

It was emphasized that in learning the techniques of government and law from foreign countries, one should learn the whole rather than pay attention to small details. The administration explained that 'in order to achieve wealth and power for the nation, it is certainly necessary to learn politics and law from foreign countries. In these days, students often talk about people's rights or freedom.' However, these words express only one aspect of Western law and government. 'What the foreign countries call people's rights is a term parallel to obligations (*i-wu*); what is called freedom is parallel to law. The observation of law and obligations is the duty (*chih*) of servitors and subjects, while rights and freedom are to be enjoyed by them. Without law and obligations, how can there be rights and freedom?'[12] These remarks were specially enunciated because the government feared students might riot against it, making light of the emperor's authority and indiscriminately asserting their rights.

Women were not allowed to receive the new education for the following reasons: in China where segregation of men and women was strictly enforced in public, they should never be allowed to go to school together nor walk around the streets; it would be embarrassing if women read too many Western books and were misled to imitate foreign manners and customs; if such should happen, they would start to advocate freedom of marriage and disregard the authority of parents and husbands. In 1907, however, the necessity for the education of women was admitted and regulations were drawn up concerning normal schools and primary schools for girls.[13] Even so, the aim of the education of women was limited to producing good wives, wise mothers and some teachers. The equality of men and women and freedom of marriage were still denied as before. Consequently, boys and girls were to be in separate schools even for elementary education, and women were not to attend political meetings.

[11] 'Hsueh-wu kang-yao' (Guidelines for educational affairs), in *Tsou-ting hsueh-t'ang chang-ch'eng*, 1. 10.
[12] *Ibid.* 12b.
[13] See Li Yu-ning and Chang Yü-fa, comps. *Chin-tai Chung-kuo nü-ch'üan yun-tung shih-liao, 1842–1911* (Historical materials on the women's rights movement in modern China), 2.974–89.

In the junior grade primary schools, middle schools and higher schools, military drill was to be given. In the higher schools, a three-hour class in military science was added and the military systems of various countries and military history and strategy were to be taught. This military education was restricted to government schools, as were also political science and law. These subjects were not allowed at private schools, a fact which shows how far the government was suspicious of the people's motives.

Considering the above points, one wonders how far the government was really serious about the new education. Possibly the government leaders did not consider public school education really desirable but reluctantly adopted the new system because it had been demanded not only by constitutionalists like K'ang Yu-wei and Liang Ch'i-ch'ao but also by provincial governors. As stated in the school regulations sanctioned by the emperor (*Tsou-ting hsueh-t'ang chang-ch'eng*) of 1904, the aim of the new system was 'to create a people who honour Confucianism (*K'ung-chiao*), love the great Ch'ing empire, and are loyal to the great Ch'ing empire'.[14] It is not impossible to interpret 'the great Ch'ing empire' to mean China but it seems more likely that it meant the Manchu dynasty. Consider the fact that law, politics and military science were prohibited in private schools and that the goals of education were, as stated in 1906, to inculcate loyalty to the sovereign, veneration of Confucius, public-spiritedness (*shang-kung*), respect for military spirit (*shang-wu*), love of practicality (*shang-shih*) and 'loyalty to the sovereign' as the highest virtues. In other words, the Ch'ing government started school education rather reluctantly, forced by pressures from outside, and its aim was not to create a new people for an age of constitutionalism or a people who could enrich and strengthen the country, but only to create a people who would love the Ch'ing dynasty and stay loyal to the Ch'ing emperor.

The course of events went against the intentions of the Ch'ing government leaders, and the anti-Manchu movement spread among the students. In 1907, the government prohibited students from becoming involved in political affairs, or having mass meetings, and repeated this prohibition again and again. As a result, the anti-Manchu movement in schools within the country was generally kept down, but it grew among the students studying in Japan. In the reform programme promoted by the Ch'ing government after the Boxer incident, study in Japan was very much encouraged and so the number of Chinese students in Japan increased every year. By 1905 and 1906 it had reached around ten thousand (see chapter 6). In the freer environment of Japan, the Chinese students criti-

---

[14] 'Ko hsueh-t'ang kuan-li t'ung-tse' (General rules on the administration of all schools), in *Tsou-ting hsueh-t'ang chang-ch'eng*, 5. 8b.

cized the Ch'ing much more sharply, and the number of those who joined
the constitutional or the revolutionary movements increased every year,
particularly after the Russo-Japanese War. Facing this problem, Peking
sent an inspector of Chinese students to Japan in 1902, and in 1903 put out
regulations to prohibit students from discussing political affairs, publishing
newspapers or journals concerned with politics, or doing any other thing
that would affect public morale or disturb social order. The Chinese
government asked the Japanese government for assistance in controlling
Chinese students. Tokyo responded and in 1905 issued its 'regulations concerning public and private schools which accept Chinese students'. This
Japanese government action aroused bitter resentment among the Chinese
students in Japan.[15]

The Chinese government itself soon took more direct action instead of
relying on Japanese government help. In February 1906, a decision was
made that the students sent to Japan were to be limited to those who could
write good Chinese and were well versed in the Confucian classics. In
December, the Chinese minister to Japan was appointed controller of the
Inspectorate of Chinese Students in Japan, making possible closer supervision. But no matter how vigorously the Ch'ing government tried to control its students in Japan, the results were rather adverse. The tighter the
controls became, the stronger was the anti-Manchu feeling among the
students. Eventually, of course, the Chinese student body in Japan became
the nucleus of the anti-Ch'ing movement.

REFORMS IN THE MILITARY SYSTEM

One of the main Ch'ing reforms was aimed at reorganizing the corrupt and
degenerate old army and building a powerful new force. The regular army
had consisted of the banner forces (pa-ch'i) and the Green Standard (Lü-
ying) troops, but by the nineteenth century these forces, particularly the
Green Standard, were of no use. Consequently, the government had had to
recruit armies on a temporary basis to meet rebellions or wars with foreign
countries, and this temporary arrangement had become the regular method
(see chapters 6 and 9 in volume 10, and above chapter 4). After the rebellions were suppressed, some of the new armies were disbanded but most of
them were maintained and called at first 'brave battalions' (*yung-ying*) and
later called 'defence battalions' (*fang-ying*). (Names of armies proliferated
over the years even more rapidly than the armies themselves.) Yet the
Sino-French and Sino-Japanese wars showed that they were corrupt and
no longer effective.

[15] Sanetō Keishū, *Chūgokujin Nihon ryūgaku shikō* (rev. edn 1970), 461–3.

China's defeat in 1895 awakened the Ch'ing to the keen necessity of having well-trained troops with Western-style equipment. As a result, in North China Yuan Shih-k'ai, who had inherited from Li Hung-chang the leadership of the Peiyang Army, set out to organize a Newly Created Army (Hsin-chien lu-chün), while in the Yangtze area Chang Chih-tung organized his Self-Strengthening Army (Tzu-ch'iang chün). Both were in the Western style. The Boxer experience further indicated the need for this kind of army.[16]

In 1901, therefore, the Ch'ing government ordered the provincial governors to reorganize the army system in the provinces. At the same time, the government abolished the old-style military examinations and created military academies (wu-pei hsueh-t'ang) in each province. The graduates from these schools were to be appointed officers in the new army. Simultaneously a decision was made to eliminate 20 or 30 per cent of the Green Standard forces and semi-regular defence forces (fang-yung) during 1901. However, it was not possible to build an army equipped and trained in Western style (to be called the New Army, Hsin-chün), unless an effective central control were established. Otherwise, the New Army in the provinces would only strengthen the power of the provincial governors and threaten that of the central government. In 1903, therefore, the government set up in Peking the Commission for Army Reorganization (Lien-ping ch'u), as a central agency to recruit and train the New Army throughout the empire. It thus attempted to achieve central control over the New Army units which had already been recruited and trained in the provinces. In 1904, the government decided to reorganize the military system as a whole and to create thirty-six divisions of the New Army under the control of the Commission for Army Reorganization. In order to train the officers for the New Army, the government decided to send students to the Japanese Military Academy, and to set up a system of military schools which would start from primary military school and lead up to a military academy.

The thirty-six divisions of the New Army, each with 12,500 men including officers and soldiers, would total 450,000 men and compose the Regular Army. Besides this, Reserves for the First Call (Hsu-pei chün) and Reserves for the Second Call (Hou-pei chün) were to be organized. The

---

[16] On military reform beginning in 1901, see Ralph L. Powell, The rise of Chinese military power 1895–1912, chs. 4–7; Stephen R. MacKinnon, 'Yuan Shih-k'ai in Tientsin and Peking: the sources and structure of his power' (University of California, Ph.D. dissertation, 1971). For military reform in the 1895–1901 period, which provides essential background, see Liu Feng-han's two monographs, Hsin-chien lu-chün (The Newly Created Army [under Yuan Shih-k'ai, 1895–1900]) and Wu-wei chün (The Wu-wei Army [under Jung-lu and Yuan Shih-k'ai, 1899–1901]).

term of service in the Regular Army (Ch'ang-pei chün) was three years, after which men would return home and receive occasional drill and a small stipend for another three years. These men would be the Reserves for the First Call. As Reserves for the Second Call they would then serve another four years, receiving less drill and less salary. On completion of this term, men would return to civilian status released from further military duty.[17]

Conscription was regarded as the ideal, but for the time being it was decided to recruit soldiers on a voluntary basis. At the same time, qualifications for admission to the army were made more strict. Formerly, any volunteer could serve as a soldier regardless of his experience, family background, occupation or age. But now only men from twenty to twenty-five years old who were in good physical condition, resident in their native province and had families, were to be qualified as soldiers. Opium addicts and those who had committed crimes repeatedly in the past were excluded. By setting up these standards of recruitment for the thirty-six divisions of the New Army, the Commission for Army Reorganization on behalf of the central government tried to establish some control over it. However, the other existing armies were still under the control of the Board of War (Ping Pu). Accordingly, on the reorganization of the government in 1906, the Board of War and the Commission for Army Reorganization were merged into the Army Ministry (Lu-chün Pu) which headed all the land forces in the empire.

The Manchu T'ieh-liang was appointed president of the Army Ministry, and two other Manchus were appointed senior and junior vice-presidents. Thus the land forces came completely under Manchu command. Immediately after this reform, the Army Ministry annexed four divisions of the Peiyang Army under Yuan Shih-k'ai leaving him only two divisions (the Second and the Fourth). It was unprecedented for the central government directly to control the armed forces. It was also epoch-making that the Army Ministry now commanded four out of the six divisions of the Peiyang Army, which was the strongest in the empire.[18]

Encouraged by this success, the Ch'ing government pushed on with a policy of getting the control of all military forces into Manchu hands. In 1907, Chang Chih-tung, governor-general of Hupei and Hunan, and Yuan Shih-k'ai, governor-general of Chihli, were transferred to Peking to be grand councillors. The rank of grand councillor was certainly higher than that of governor-general, but their promotion meant that their military

[17] See Stephen R. Mackinnon, 'The Peiyang Army, Yuan Shih-k'ai, and the origins of modern Chinese warlordism', *JAS*, 32.2 (May 1973) 405–23.
[18] See Mackinnon, 'Yuan Shih-k'ai in Tientsin and Peking', 106–19.

forces were no longer under their direct command. These two men, who had commanded the strongest armed forces in the empire, were thus deprived of power under the façade of promotion.[19] Finally, in 1910, all six divisions of the Peiyang Army were taken under the direct command of the Army Ministry.

In 1908 the Kuang-hsu Emperor died, the infant Hsuan-t'ung Emperor (named P'u-i) was enthroned, and his father, the second Prince Ch'un (Tsai-feng), emerged as prince regent, the most powerful figure in the court. As soon as he assumed the post, Prince Ch'un created a New Palace Guard (Chin-wei chün) and entrusted its training to his brother Tsai-t'ao, and two other Manchus, Yü-lang and T'ieh-liang. In 1909, it was decreed that the emperor was the supreme commander of the army and navy, but that while the emperor was a minor, Prince Ch'un was to exercise supreme command over the military forces.

At the same time, the navy was organized and preparations were started to separate military administration from military command. The Naval Council (Hai-chün ch'u) was established in 1910, and the General Staff Office (Chün-tzu fu) in 1911, independent of the Army Ministry. Prince Ch'un appointed his younger brother Tsai-hsun as president of the Naval Council; and his other younger brother Tsai-t'ao as chief of the General Staff Office. Thus Prince Ch'un got all the military forces of the empire into the hands of himself and his blood brothers.[20] In this way the Ch'ing put the military forces first into the hands of Manchus, and then during the Hsuan-t'ung period, into those of imperial clansmen.

Meanwhile, however, from the very beginning of their military reforms the Ch'ing rulers had planned to retrain the banner forces and also train the members of the imperial clan and Manchu aristocrats to be military officers. In 1903 the government ordered Yuan Shih-k'ai and T'ieh-liang to instruct bannermen in Peking. This force later became the First Division of the New Army. Also in 1903, a Military School for Princes and Nobles (Lu-chün kuei-chou hsueh-t'ang) was founded to train the sons of Manchu princes and nobles as well as Manchu high-ranking officials to be army officers. In 1908, a Naval School for Princes and Nobles was founded for the same purpose. At the same time the government sent certain princes and nobles to Japan and Europe to observe their military establishments, and sent their sons to study military science in those countries.

The corruption of the banner forces in the late-Ch'ing era had been as bad as that of the Green Standard forces. But the government did not

19 See Daniel H. Bays, *China enters the twentieth century: Chang Chih-tung and the issues of a new age, 1895–1909*, 189–97.
20 Pao Tsun-p'eng, *Chung-kuo hai-chün shih*, 519–20.

curtail the banner forces through which many Manchus got their livelihood. For the Green Standard Army, on the other hand, since they consisted of Chinese, retrenchment was planned from early on. In 1901 the Green Standard forces were to be reduced by 20 to 30 per cent, and were to be reorganized into a police force (*hsun-ching*) by 1906; however, these plans did not work out. In 1907, it was decided to reorganize the Green Standard into the Reserve Forces (Hsun-fang ying, lit., patrol battalions): in peace time they would be assigned to maintain the peace by catching thieves and robbers, and in war time they would be mobilized as auxiliary forces to the New Army.[21]

Military reforms were planned as above described. But was it possible after all for the Ch'ing government to build military forces which would be at the same time both strong and loyal to the Ch'ing emperor? This indeed was a question much like the similar problem in education. Military reform met many difficulties. First, it had been taken for granted in China that only good-for-nothing fellows would become soldiers, and those who were recruited as troops on a temporary basis were usually uprooted peasants or vagabonds. For this reason, in recruiting the New Army it was impossible to enforce the regulations that disqualified opium smokers and those who had criminal records, and at the same time limit the qualified recruits to native residents with families. Unavoidably, such idealistic regulations were neglected, and, in reality, disbanded soldiers of the Green Standard and defence militia as well as uprooted peasants and vagabonds came into the New Army.

Secondly, army building was costly, and the Ch'ing government did not have enough money. The government had to rely on provincial governors for financial support. But provincial governors were reluctant to cooperate with Peking when it was attempting to centralize command over the armed forces. Powerful governors-general like Chang Chih-tung and Yuan Shih-k'ai increased the military forces under their command. As a result, the government was displeased with them and eventually deprived them of their military power. But in the meantime, minor provincial governors, though unable to behave like Chang Chih-tung or Yuan Shih-k'ai, could still sabotage the building of the New Army. As a result, when the Revolution of 1911 broke out the government did not have its planned thirty-six divisions but only twenty. However, it was not only the Chinese provincial governors who resisted the government's military reforms. Even the president of the Army Ministry, the Manchu T'ieh-liang, finally resigned from the War Ministry in 1910. He had been fighting effectively to cut down the influence of Chinese officials, but he resigned because he could not

[21] Powell, *Chinese military power*, 247–9.

follow Prince Ch'un's line of imperial clan-centrism. Dissatisfaction spread even among the Manchu officials.

Nevertheless, the New Army had a great influence in changing the traditional concept of the military among the Chinese. Nationalism was generated around the time of the Sino-French and Sino-Japanese wars and was invigorated through the experience of the Boxer incident, the Russian occupation of Manchuria, and Japan's victory over Russia. It was against this background that the government elevated military officials to the same rank as civil officials, created schools for officers, and sent many students to Japan for military training, while the emperor became the commander of all the forces of the empire. As a result, the general tendency to despise the military declined and volunteers to serve as military officers came even from the ranks of the gentry, who had never thought of such a possibility before. This was a great change. The shift in people's attitude towards military officers naturally changed their attitude towards the army. In the new system, it was no longer enough to excel in physical strength and military skill to be an officer, one had also to be good at scholarship. Military officer candidates were sent to study in Japan, where they were imbued with revolutionary thought. The recruitment of gentry as officers, together with the fact that soldiers were recruited from among the native population, led the provincial units of the armed forces to resist the centralization of the army just as the provincial governors did.[22] Consequently, when the Revolution of 1911 broke out, it was actually started by the New Army and most of the troops of the New Army sided with the revolutionaries. It was mainly the Reserve Forces, which had been reorganized from the Green Standard, that stood up for the Ch'ing government.

PREPARATIONS FOR CONSTITUTIONALISM

The Ch'ing government had started its reforms in education and the military in 1901, but it began to consider seriously the possibility of constitutionalism only after the Russo-Japanese War.[23] The outcome of this war gave a great impetus, for it was considered a victory of constitutionalism over autocracy. The Chinese like other peoples in Asia were awakened by the war, and the revolutionary movement was stimulated. Demands became louder that China should adopt constitutionalism in order to

---

[22] See Yoshihiro Hatano, 'The new armies', in Mary C. Wright, ed. *China in revolution: the first phase, 1900–1913* (hereafter *CIR*), 365–82.

[23] For the general background of the Ch'ing constitutionalist movement, see Chang Yü-fa, *Ch'ing-chi ti li-hsien t'uan-t'i* (Constitutionalist groups of the late Ch'ing period), chs. 1–6; Chang P'eng-yuan, *Li-hsien-p'ai yü hsin-hai ko-ming* (The constitutionalists and the 1911 Revolution), chs. 1–3.

become strong and wealthy. Since powerful provincial officials like Chang Chih-tung and Yuan Shih-k'ai joined the chorus, the Ch'ing government could not remain deaf to it. In December 1905, it sent five ministers headed by Tsai-tse to Japan, England, the United States, Germany and France to observe their governments and examine the possibilities for constitutionalism in China. The mission returned in July 1906, and every member recommended constitutionalism.[24] The Chinese envoys overseas also memorialized that a constitution, far from injuring the authority of the imperial household, would actually be the best means to maintain it. Thereupon the empress dowager and the emperor summoned Prince Ch'un, the grand councillors and grand secretaries, the ex-officio members of the committee of ministers, and Yuan Shih-k'ai to a conference at the new Summer Palace (I-ho yuan) to discuss the pros and cons of constitutionalism. At this imperial conference Prince Ch'ing and Yuan Shih-k'ai seconded the adoption of a constitution, but T'ieh-liang and Jung-ch'ing opposed it. It was finally decided after long discussion that constitutionalism should be adopted. On 1 September 1906, the Kuang-hsu Emperor, under the direction of the empress dowager, ordered the high-ranking officials in the capital and the provinces to begin preparations for it.[25] Thus the issue was decided and preparations were started.

Reforms in the administrative system

The first problem that the Ch'ing government took up after committing itself to constitutionalism was the reform of administrative institutions.[26] Immediately after the Boxer incident, the government had started a series of reforms including renovation of the corrupt officialdom and the reorganization of the outdated bureaucratic structure. But this effort had run into many difficulties.

The causes of corruption among many officials, and the outdated features of the bureaucratic system, were considered to be the following. First of all there was the system of contributions (*chüan-na*), especially including the purchase of official posts. As in previous eras, sale of office had been temporarily resorted to when the government needed extra revenue, but ever since the time of the Taipings it had become a permanent arrangement. As a result, among officialdom were many who had acquired

---

[24] See E-tu Zen Sun, 'The Chinese constitutionalist mission of 1905–1906', *Journal of modern history*, 24.3 (Sept. 1952) 251–68.

[25] *CSL-KH*, 562.8–9.

[26] On general institutional background, see Rinji Taiwan Kyūkan Chōsakai, ed. *Shinkoku gyōseihō* (Administrative laws of the Ch'ing dynasty), pt 1. A mine of information on late Ch'ing administrative reform may be found in Esther Morrison, 'The modernization of Confucian bureaucracy' (Radcliffe College, Ph.D. dissertation, 1959).

their post by money or by military merit. This was felt to cause a great deal of corruption.

Further, the routine work of government offices was not clearly understood by high-ranking civil officials, and minor functionaries or government clerks actually took charge of it. There were complex regulations concerning the form of official documents. Account books were peculiar to each office. It was impossible for high-ranking officials, who stayed at one post about three to five years at most, to master these regulations. As a result, they had no choice but to rely on the clerks who served year after year. These clerks were low in social status, and most of them did not receive any fixed salaries. They lived on fees which they collected from the people with whom they happened to have contact in the course of litigation or tax payments. Since there were no fixed quotas for their fees, these were a kind of bribe. The people suffered very much from the exactions of government clerks.

Also, there were many offices with few duties. In China, children were supposed to follow whatever precedent was set by the parents. For this reason government offices founded by previous emperors were kept going even when the times had changed and reorganization was necessary. In such cases the old offices were left unchanged and new ones were founded separately. For example, the Ch'ing government had as its office for central administration the Grand Secretariat staffed by four or six grand secretaries. During a campaign against the Mongols in 1729–30 the Yung-cheng Emperor had established the Grand Council near the palace in which the emperor had his office, in order to let the grand councillors, who were the emperor's most trusted officials selected from among the grand secretaries and presidents of the Six Boards, discuss secret military affairs. Thus the Grand Council began as a temporary organization and all posts in it were held concurrently. No official was exclusively appointed to such a post. However, the Yung-cheng Emperor did not abolish this office after the campaign was over and continued to consult the grand councillors on important state affairs. The emperors who succeeded Yung-cheng followed this practice. Thus after the Grand Council was established most of the functions of the Grand Secretariat were taken over by it, making the latter almost dispensable, yet it was not abolished. Indeed ever since the Ch'in unification, though many dynasties rose and fell in the course of history, each pretended to be the successor of the previous one, even in cases where it had conquered its predecessor with military force. In this way the bureaucratic organization of the Ch'in dynasty had been inherited from one dynasty to the next, with some modification, all the way down to the Ch'ing. In short, China's bureaucratic organization had not changed basically from the third century BC or at least from the early seventh century AD, down to the twentieth century. One evidence of this was the many titles of office inherited from the ancient past.

An even more serious defect was that the responsibilities of officials were not clearly defined. Ambiguity of responsibility was in many cases caused by the appointment of more than one president to one office. In the case of the Grand Secretariat, there were four or six grand secretaries, the grand councillors numbered between four and eight, and there were two presidents for each of the Six Boards or Ministries (Liu Pu). The number of ministers in the Tsungli Yamen created at the request of the Western countries in 1861 was not fixed, and there were as many as ten ministers in it, or even more as in the 1894–8 period. When there were so many top officials in one office, none of them would be willing to take responsibility. Naturally, each would try to shift responsibility on to the shoulders of others. Since the Chinese government had appointed plural presidents to many offices throughout its history, no doubt this was done to prevent ministers from monopolizing power as a threat to the throne. For the same purpose a Ch'ing governor-general and governor were mutually involved in such a way as to restrain each other so that local power could not be concentrated in the hands of a single official.

When the Ch'ing government began its reforms in 1901, it attempted to remedy these accumulated defects. First of all, a decision was made to simplify the forms of official documents in every office and to abolish the clerks. The system of selling official posts was abolished, although the practice actually continued in various forms. The posts of Director-General of the Yellow River Conservancy (Ho-tung ho-tao tsung-tu),[27] and of Commissioner of the Transmission Office (T'ung-cheng shih-ssu)[28] were abolished. The Supervisorate of Imperial Instruction (Chan-shih-fu)[29] was annexed to the Hanlin Academy. The posts of the governors of Yunnan, Hupei and Kwangtung were abolished.[30] These were all dispensable offices.

While abolishing certain titular offices, the government created new ones. First the Ministry of Foreign Affairs (Wai-wu Pu) was created by reorganizing the Tsungli Yamen which had been reluctantly set up in 1861 as a committee of the Grand Council. Thus it began as only a temporary

[27] This official was charged with the conservation of the Yellow River dikes in Honan province. But this could be taken care of by the governor of the province.
[28] This office, inaugurated in the Ming period, had been charged with inspecting memorials before transmitting them to the emperor. But many criticisms were raised and during the Ch'ing it existed merely as a titular office.
[29] This office was charged with the duties related to the heir apparent. Since the later Ch'ing emperors did not designate an heir apparent this post had become unnecessary.
[30] The offices of these governors were each in the same city as the office of a governor-general.

office, with concurrently appointed ministers, amounting to as many as
ten or more. Because of its informal status, the Western powers felt some
inconvenience in negotiating with the Tsungli Yamen and had demanded
its reorganization after the Ch'ing defeat in the Boxer incident. The
Ministry of Foreign Affairs was now made a permanent formal body with
a president and two vice-presidents. This was the beginning of the disintegration of the traditional structure of Six Ministries which had come
down from the Sui and T'ang dynasties. The new Foreign Ministry made a
seventh and moreover was placed higher in rank than the other six – really
a great change.

Another innovation soon followed when the government organized a
Ministry of Trade (Shang Pu) in 1903. In traditional China, the active
promotion of the people's welfare beyond the level of subsistence had not
been the proper business of the ruler, and the government was not often
engaged in promoting agriculture, industry or commerce. But now it was
accepted that the wealth of the nation was needed for strengthening the
military, and the promotion of agriculture, industry and commerce was
required for enriching the country.

In 1905, the Ministry of Police (Hsun-ching Pu) and Ministry of Education (Hsueh Pu, mentioned above) were set up. The attempt was to establish a Western-style police system, and in 1906 it was decided to recruit
policemen from among the Green Standard soldiers. The Ministry of
Police was changed to the Ministry of the Interior (Min-cheng Pu).[31]

Shortly after the declaration in 1906 of the programme to prepare for
constitutionalism, a further reform in government institutions was inaugurated on the following principles. First was the principle of the separation
of the three powers, executive, legislative and judicial. However, no legislative organ was to be introduced as yet; only the executive and judicial
organs were to be reformed at this time. Secondly, superfluous officials
were to be weeded out, and the responsibility of officials was to be
clarified.[32] As a result, the following reform measures were carried out.

(1) Offices with overlapping duties were combined. The Court of
Sacrificial Worship (T'ai-ch'ang ssu),[33] Banqueting Court (Kuang-lu ssu)[34]
and Court of State Ceremonial (Hung-lu ssu)[35] were annexed to the Ministry
of Rites; the old Board of War, the Commission for Army Reorganization
(Lien-ping ch'u) and the Court of the Imperial Stud (T'ai-p'u ssu)[36] were

---

[31] *CSL-KH*, 564.11–13.
[32] *Tung-hua hsu-lu* (The Tung-hua records, continued), Kuang-hsu, 202.12–14.
[33] The office in charge of the sacrifice at the imperial mausoleum.
[34] The office in charge of matters related to banquets given in the court.
[35] Supposedly in charge of ceremonies at state banquets.
[36] In charge of raising and training military horses.

combined to form the Army Ministry (Lu-chün Pu); the Board of Revenue (Hu Pu) and the Commission on Finance (Ts'ai-cheng ch'u) were reorganized into the Ministry of Finance (Tu-chih Pu). The Commission for Army Reorganization and the Commission on Finance had been created for the purpose of centralizing military and financial administration. Since ancient times, the offices in charge of military affairs had been the Board of War, and for financial affairs, the Board of Revenue, but they had now become dispensable. They were not abolished, but the unification of the Commission on Finance with the Board of Revenue, and of the Commission for Army Reorganization with the Board of War, was an unprecedented step in China, even though it may have seemed like a matter of course to casual observers.

(2) The central administrative organs were expanded. A Ministry of Posts and Communication (Yu-ch'uan Pu) was set up, and the Board of Punishments (Hsing Pu) was reorganized into the Ministry of Justice (Fa Pu) while its functions were limited to judicial administration.[37] In this way the number of ministries in the central government became eleven. Ever since the Sui and T'ang, the administrative organs of the central government had been the Six Ministries or Boards of Civil Appointments, of Revenue, of Rites, of War, of Punishments and of Works. When the Ministry of Foreign Affairs was added in 1901, and later the Ministries of Trade, of Police and of Education, the ancient Six Boards had still persisted regardless. But now as a result of the reform in 1906, only the Boards of Civil Appointment (Li Pu) and of Rites (Li Pu) retained their old names. The traditional establishment of the Six Boards had completely disappeared.

(3) A single headship was established in each ministry. This was a very important step. Previously under the Ch'ing, dual presidents had been appointed to head each board, usually one Manchu and one Chinese. This device let the Manchus and the Chinese check each other, but also tended to make the presidents irresponsible. Abolition of the dual presidency system clarified responsibility. At the same time it also implied that discrimination between Manchus and Chinese was to be ended. In the same spirit, in order to avoid concurrent appointments as much as possible, the concurrent appointment of ministry presidents to be grand councillors was abolished.[38]

(4) The Supreme Court of Justice (Ta-li yuan), the Audit Department (Shen-chi yuan) and the National Assembly (Tzu-cheng yuan) were created separately from the ministries. The authority of the Supreme Court of Justice was clearly separated from that of the Ministry of Justice, which

---

[37] This was provided for by the edict cited in n. 31 above.   [38] See nn. 31 and 32.

was purely an administrative body.[39] Previously, the courts and the judicial administration had not been separate. The Audit Department was to be independent of the ministries, since it was charged with auditing their accounts. Even though it had been decided that the matter of legislative organs was not yet to be touched upon, the necessity of inviting expressions of popular opinion was keenly felt and so the National Assembly was designed to be a tentative legislative organ preceding the future opening of the parliament. (Details of the National Assembly will be discussed below.)

Two important changes which the government attempted to include among the administrative reforms could not be realized. One was to reform the provincial bureaucracy, the other was to create a responsible cabinet. In general, there were many ambiguities in the Ch'ing local bureaucracy. For example, the relationships between provincial governors and the central government, and between governors-general and governors were not very clear. Possibly the Ch'ing government preferred not to clarify these relations. At any rate, since the time of the Taipings, the authority of governors-general and governors had increased. They were not closely controlled by the central government in military or financial administration. One aim of the Ch'ing reform was to reduce their power by placing them under the control of the central government ministries and commissions instead of leaving them as direct subordinates of the emperor who reported to him directly, parallel to the ministries at the capital.[40] This would have created a unitary regime with the provinces under the ministries instead of parallel with them under the emperor – a very basic change of administrative structure. Naturally, the high provincial officials opposed this move.

The demand for a responsible cabinet system was a natural consequence of one principle of the current reform, namely, to clarify responsibility. However, this would result in the abolition of the Grand Council, the Grand Secretariat and the Bureau of Government Affairs. Opinions against the adoption of a responsible cabinet system were based on the grounds that the general management of administration should be shared by a number of officials; otherwise, a single person could monopolize authority and might infringe upon the power of the throne. This view won, and no reform was made concerning the central executive organization.

Thus both the reduction of the power of the provincial governors and the adoption of the cabinet system,[41] two items on which the government had placed its highest priority in the reform effort, were not realized. A

[39] See n. 32.
[40] *CSL-KH*, 574.6–7; *Tung-fang tsa-chih* (The eastern miscellany), 4.8 (1907), 'Nei-wu' (Internal affairs), 401–24.
[41] *Ibid.* 5.1 (1908), 'Nei-wu', 10–13.

reform in the provincial administrative system was carried out in 1907 but the authority of the provincial governors was not reduced, nor were really substantial changes made, and the reform ended up with a mere alteration of the names of offices in local administration. Perhaps the only significant change was that District Courts (Shen-p'an t'ing) were established at various levels in the provinces in an attempt to set up an independent local judicial authority on the model of the Supreme Court of Justice in the central government.[42]

Another important event was a reform in the administration of the Three Eastern Provinces, called by foreigners Manchuria. Since this was the ancestral habitat of the Ch'ing dynasty, a special administrative system had been set up there. Now reforms were carried out to make the Manchurian administration the same as that in the other parts of China. The military governorship in Mukden (Sheng-ching chiang-chün) was abolished; instead, a governor-general of the Three Eastern Provinces (Tung-san-sheng tsung-tu) was set up in 1907 and governors were appointed over the provinces of Kirin, Fengtien and Heilungkiang.[43]

Although the Ch'ing government was unable to reduce the regional power of high provincial officials, it was successful in increasing the power of the Manchu officials in the central government. After single presidents had been appointed to head each government ministry, out of thirteen top officials, namely, the grand councillors and presidents of ministries, there were seven Manchus, five Chinese and one Mongol bannerman. A Mongol bannerman was, of course, Mongol in race, but he belonged to the Manchu camp. Therefore, as a result of the reforms in the central government, the ratio of top Manchus to Chinese turned out to be 8 : 5. Compared with the previous arrangement under which the numbers of Manchus and Chinese had been the same, the Ch'ing government had skilfully put the control of the central government further into the hands of Manchus under the fair principle of abolishing racial discrimination.

Another basic principle of reform had been to minimize concurrent appointments. Following this policy, Yuan Shih-k'ai resigned from all the posts he had held concurrently and his power was considerably reduced. As we have noted, the government promoted Chang Chih-tung and Yuan Shih-k'ai, the two Chinese governors-general who had amassed the most regional power, to be grand councillors, thus depriving them of their power in the provinces. Therefore, although there was no reform in provincial administration, the power of the Manchu officials in the central

[42] See n. 31.
[43] See Chao Chung-fu, 'Ch'ing-mo tung-san-sheng kai-chih ti pei-ching' (Background of the late Ch'ing reorganization of the government of the three Manchurian provinces), CYCT, 5 (June 1976) 313–35; Robert H. G. Lee, The Manchurian frontier in Ch'ing history, ch. 7.

government increased enormously, and the influence of the Chinese provincial officials was quite reduced in comparison.

During the Hsuan-t'ung period from 1908 to 1911, this tendency became even stronger. First of all, in January 1909 Yuan Shih-k'ai was forced to retire to Honan on the pretext of a foot ailment. Chang Chih-tung died nine months later. Thus, two formidable Chinese high officials were removed from the path of the regent, Prince Ch'un. Encouraged by this, he got the control of the land forces and navy into the hands of his two brothers, and finally in May 1911, in response to the demand of the Chinese that a responsible cabinet should be set up, he finally organized a cabinet. It was to be responsible to the throne. At the same time, the Grand Secretariat, Grand Council and Bureau of Government Affairs were abolished. The cabinet was to consist of one prime minister (*tsung-li ta-ch'en*), two deputy prime ministers (*fu ta-ch'en*) and the presidents of the Ministries of Interior (Min-cheng Pu), Finance, Education, Army, Navy, Justice, Agriculture, Industry and Commerce (Nung-kung-shang Pu), Posts and Communications (Yu-ch'uan Pu), Dependencies (Li-fan yuan), and Foreign Affairs, making thirteen members in all.[44] Out of the thirteen ministers in the cabinet, eight Manchus and only four Han Chinese were appointed; five out of the eight Manchus were members of the imperial clan. Prince Ch'un, having secured the military power for imperial clans men, now added the general control of the administration. This fact, however, reveals that by this time the prince regent actually felt he could not trust even Manchu officials except for his own clansmen. The appointment of this cabinet was the last desperate effort of the Manchu court as it faced collapse. Within less than a year after this imperial clan-centred cabinet was organized, the revolution started in Wuchang, and in less than another year, the Ch'ing government fell. The court had used the reform programme to achieve an increasing concentration of its steadily decreasing power.

The schedule for the preparation for constitutionalism and the 'Principles of the Constitution'

When the Ch'ing government announced its policy decision to adopt constitutionalism, critics urging more radical views began to demand that the government realize this aim immediately, and they soon compelled the government to respond to this demand in one way or another. In August 1908, the government therefore announced its plans for the preparations for constitutionalism and declared that in the ninth year, in 1916, the con-

[44] *CSL* Hsuan-t'ung (hereafter *CSL-HT*), 52.18-23.

stitution would be promulgated and the first elections for the parliament would take place, and that the parliament would be convened in 1917.[45]

At the same time the government issued the 'Principles of the Constitution',[46] which were modelled on the Japanese constitution promulgated in the Meiji era. The first two articles read: '(1) The emperor of the Ta Ch'ing dynasty shall reign over and govern the great Ch'ing empire with his majesty's unbroken line of succession for ages eternal. (2) The emperor shall be sacred and inviolable.'[47] In the Japanese constitution the emperor had been given great power, but in the 'Principles' the power of the Ch'ing emperor was to be even greater than that of the Japanese emperor. Almost nothing could limit the prerogative of the throne. The emperor was given the following powers: (a) the power to convoke and to dissolve the parliament was lodged in the sovereign; (b) laws which passed the parliament could not be put into practice without the sovereign's approval; (c) there was no regulation in the 'Principles' concerning the organization of a cabinet, but the right to appoint ministers belonged to the sovereign and the parliament could not interfere; (d) the judicial power belonged to the sovereign, and was to be exercised in the name of the emperor; (e) the parliament had no right to interfere in any military affairs. The sovereign had the prerogative to organize and command all the military forces of the empire and to decide on the size of the regular forces; (f) it was the sovereign's absolute authority to declare wars, to make peace, and to conclude treaties with foreign countries. These matters were not to be submitted to the decision of the parliament; (g) during a period of emergency the sovereign could proclaim martial law and restrict the rights of the people.

Once it became certain that constitutional government was going to be put into effect, criticism arose from intellectuals and especially from the constitutionalists, who had long advocated such a step but were not satisfied with the basic 'Principles' and the process of preparation. They ardently demanded an immediate inauguration of constitutional government. Under this pressure, the Ch'ing government in 1910 shortened the schedule by four years, and decided to promulgate the constitution in 1912, and to convene the parliament in 1913.[48] However, this concession was nothing more than throwing water on thirsty soil, and was far from adequate to calm the clamour for the immediate opening of parliament. In the meantime, in October 1911, the revolution burst forth.

[45] *CSL-KH*, 583.4–5; 595.1–2. *Ta-Ch'ing Kuang-hsu hsin fa-ling* (New statutes and decrees of the Ch'ing dynasty in the Kuang-hsu period) 2.25–32.
[46] *Tung-hua hsu-lu*, Kuang-hsu, 219.1–7.
[47] Translation adopted from Hsieh Pao-chao, *The government of China, 1644–1911*, 372.
[48] *CSL-HT*, 43.2–5.

Frightened by this, the Ch'ing government at its last gasp hurriedly announced in November 1911 the major 'nineteen articles' of the expected constitution.[49] In this document, in order to appease the revolutionary movement, the power of the sovereign was radically reduced and the authority of the parliament was increased in comparison with the 'Principles' of 1908. The main changes were as follows: (1) the constitution was to be drafted by the National Assembly and to be promulgated by the sovereign. The power to amend the constitution belonged to the parliament, and the sovereign could not interfere; (2) the prime minister was to be elected by the parliament and to be appointed by the sovereign. Imperial clansmen were not qualified to be prime minister. Whenever the prime minister was impeached by the parliament he was to dissolve the parliament or his cabinet was to resign in a body; (3) the emperor was to have direct command of the army and navy, but he could not use either of them to settle internal issues without the sanction of the parliament; (4) no treaty was to be concluded without approval of the parliament. If peace were to be made or war declared when the parliament was in recess, the act was to be laid before the parliament for approval at its next session. Needless to say, by the time these changes were announced, they had little practical significance.

The Provincial, the National and the Local Self-Government Assemblies

Once the Ch'ing government had decided to convene a parliament in 1917, it had to admit that the earlier it could listen to public opinion and reflect it in the government, the better it would be. Hence it convened the first meeting of the Provincial Assemblies (Tzu-i chü) in 1909, and of the National Assembly (Tzu-cheng yuan) in Peking in 1910. The Provincial Assembly was to be the antecedent of the eventual provincial legislature, and the National Assembly the antecedent of the parliament.

According to the regulations issued in 1908,[50] the Provincial Assembly was constituted roughly as follows.

(A) *Qualifications for voting.* (1) Must be a male twenty-five years of age or older, a permanent resident of the province, with at least one of the following qualifications: (a) one who had engaged in educational or other public service in the province during three full years; (b) a graduate of middle school or a higher educational institution in China or abroad; (c) a *sheng-yuan* (licentiate) or higher degree holder; (d) one who had once served as a civil official of the seventh rank or higher, or as a military officer of the fifth rank or higher; (e) one who owned 5,000 *yuan* or more worth of

[49] CSL-HT, 63.10; 65.9b, 11–18. The last reference gives the text of the 'Nineteen articles'.
[50] CSL-KH, 579.14–15; Ta-Ch'ing Kuang-hsu hsin fa-ling, 2.2b–24.

working capital or immovable property in the province. (2) Alternatively one could be a male twenty-five years of age or older who was not registered as a permanent resident of the province but who had lived in the province for two or more years and owned 10,000 *yuan* or more worth of working capital or immovable property.

(B) *Eligibility for election.* A male thirty years of age or older who was a permanent resident of the province or who had lived in the province ten or more years.

(C) *Number of assembly members.* 5 per cent of the fixed quota of *sheng-yuan* of each province. The Nanking region and Kiangsu province, which had higher land-tax quotas, were given nine and twenty-three members extra, respectively.

(D) *Permissible subjects of discussion.* (1) Matters that the provincial government might innovate or seek to reform. (2) Budget and balance of accounts of the revenue and expenditure of the province. (3) Matters related to taxation and public bond issues of the province. (4) Revision or repeal of regulations which affected only the province concerned. (5) Elections for members of the National Assembly. (6) Inquiries put by the National Assembly, governor-general or governor. (7) Disputes in a municipal council; matters petitioned or proposed by the Local Self-Government Assembly (Tzu-chih hui).

(E) *Relationship with the provincial governor.* (1) The governor-general and governor should be responsible for proclaiming and carrying out the resolutions of the Provincial Assembly in cases where they had no objection to the resolutions. Without the approval of the governor-general or governor, such resolutions were not to be put into effect. (2) In case the governor-general or governor was not satisfied with a resolution of the Provincial Assembly, he could order it to be reconsidered. (3) After further discussion, if no consensus were reached, the decision of the National Assembly should be sought. (4) The governor-general or governor had the right to convoke, suspend and dissolve the meetings of the Assembly.

Judging from these stipulations in the regulations, it seems that the Provincial Assembly was to be the gentry's organ for expressing their opinions, but it could hardly be considered a legislative organ. It was rather an advisory body for the provincial governors, because they were entitled to refuse the resolutions of the Provincial Assembly. Nevertheless, the presence of the Provincial Assembly may well have inhibited provincial governors from arbitrary exercise of their authority. Even before, a provincial governor could not afford to neglect the views of the eminent gentry and had to conduct himself carefully so as not to offend them – otherwise, he might provoke considerable trouble for himself. In this sense the Provincial Assembly may be regarded as merely a codification of what had been the actual practice. The fact that the Ch'ing government fixed the quotas for members of the Provincial Assembly as 5 per cent of the quotas for *sheng-yuan* in each province[51] suggests that the government had such an idea in mind. Anyhow, once this codification was achieved, the pressure of the local gentry on the provincial governors no doubt increased.

In 1909, the first elections for the Provincial Assembly took place in every province. In the results, many of those elected proved to be between forty and forty-five years old, and gentry members were a majority. However, the kind of gentry who had profound scholarship and high repute among the people rather refrained from participating in local politics and in the Provincial Assembly. Many of those elected were politically ambitious and were not always highly regarded.[52]

Thus the embryonic form of a legislative body at the provincial level came into being, and in 1909 the first session of the Provincial Assembly met in each province. The immediate result in many provinces was that the provincial governor and the Provincial Assembly came into conflict. The provincial governor was after all more powerful than the Assembly because of his veto power. But this only drove Assembly members to join the movement demanding the immediate opening of the parliament, which would not be a mere advisory body.

The National Assembly was created by the Ch'ing government to be a deliberative body, or an embryonic form of parliament. According to the regulations drawn up in 1909,[53] its main features were as follows.

(A) *Membership.* Its members were to consist of a hundred imperial nominees and a hundred representatives elected by popular vote. Among the imperial nominees, forty-eight were to be imperial clan members or Manchu nobility, thirty-two officials in active service, ten scholars and ten highest-level taxpayers. The representatives by popular vote were to be elected from among the members of the Provincial Assemblies and by their vote, subject to approval by the provincial governors.

(B) *Permitted subjects of discussion.* (1) The budget and the balance of accounts of the revenue and expenditure of the state. (2) Matters related to taxation and public bond issues. (3) Revision or repeal of laws. (4) Matters on which a Provincial Assembly and provincial governor had disagreed. (5) Any other matters submitted by the emperor.

(C) *Relations with the administrative authorities.* (1) The presidents of ministries or other high administrative organs could order reconsideration

---

[51] *Ibid.* 4b.
[52] For descriptions of the manner in which the elections were conducted, see Chang P'eng-yuan, *Li-hsien-p'ai*, 12–40.
[53] *CSL-HT*, 17.14–19; see also *Ta-Ch'ing Kuang-hsu hsin fa-ling*, 2.1–2b.

when they were dissatisfied with resolutions of the National Assembly. (2) After the reconsideration, if the two parties did not reach agreement, an imperial decision was to be called for. (3) When the National Assembly had questions about the decisions of the Cabinet or the Bureau of Government Affairs, it could request explanations. (4) In case the president of an administrative organ infringed upon the authority of the National Assembly or broke laws, the National Assembly could memorialize requesting an imperial judgment.

Evidently, the National Assembly did not have authority to supervise the government. Nor was the government obliged to carry out the resolutions of the National Assembly. Therefore, in a strict sense, the National Assembly was only a consultative body.

The election of members of the National Assembly started in 1909, and its first session was convened in October 1910 in Peking. From then on the National Assembly often got into conflict with the presidents of ministries and the provincial governors. As a result, several of the resolutions were not approved by the presidents of the relevant administrative organs and were scrapped by imperial decisions. For this reason, the National Assembly members also started to clamour for the immediate opening of the parliament.

Recognizing that constitutional government should be based on local self-government, the Ch'ing regime decided to promote it. The 'Regulations regarding self-government in cities, townships, and rural districts' ('Ch'eng-chen-hsiang ti-fang tzu-chih chang-ch'eng') were drawn up in 1908,[54] and the 'Regulations regarding self-government in prefectures, subprefectures, departments and counties' ('Fu-t'ing-chou-hsien ti-fang tzu-chih chang-ch'eng') in 1910.[55] Elections for the local assemblies began immediately. The eligibility for voting and election was limited as follows: the voter must be male, twenty-five years of age or over, with Chinese nationality, who had lived in the place for three or more years continuously, and who paid two *yuan* or more of regular tax or public donation. The directors (*tung-shih*) of the local council (*tung-shih hui*) were to be elected by the assembly concerned. On such an occasion, the number of votes cast by the assemblymen should correspond to the amount of property they owned. Property owners thus were especially privileged in local self-government. Among the assemblymen there was a considerable number of gentry members with lower degree status. Most of those who were elected to be presidents of assemblies and township or rural district directors were

---

[54] *Ta-Ch'ing Kuang-hsu hsin fa-ling*, 2.44–62.
[55] *Ta-Ch'ing Hsuan-t'ung hsin fa-ling* (New statutes and decrees of the Ch'ing dynasty in the Hsuan-t'ung period), 14.1–15.

gentry members. Indeed, late-Ch'ing local self-government was really government by the gentry. Nevertheless, strong pressures were put on this self-government system by the government bureaucracy. Prefects, department magistrates and county (hsien) magistrates had the authority to dissolve the local assemblies. The resolutions of the municipal councils could not be put into effect without the approval of these local government officials. The county magistrate could dismiss township or rural district directors and could disapprove of such self-government officers elected by the assemblies concerned. As a consequence this local self-government, much as in the case of the Provincial Assembly and the National Assembly, was essentially an auxiliary organ or advisory body for the government.

From olden times in China there had been a system of mutual guarantee groups such as *pao-chia* or *li-chia*, which functioned as auxiliaries to the government in maintenance of public order and tax collection. As a rule, the gentry were not involved in this system. However, the gentry might have considerable influence over such mutual guarantee groups as were still functioning; in any case over lineages and other communities in each locality. As a matter of fact, the local government administration was made possible only by the cooperation of these local communities, which were dominated by the gentry. Now in organizing local self-government as a basis for constitutional government, the Ch'ing could not, of course, afford to neglect the power of the gentry. Since the power which the local gentry had enjoyed was not authorized by law, government officials had been able sometimes to neglect the gentry, at least in theory. But now the authority of the gentry was stipulated and guaranteed by law. This was the actual content of the local self-government system projected in the late Ch'ing. Viewing this from another angle, it is possible to say that the Ch'ing government attempted to consolidate its rule by putting the gentry members under the control of the local officials while officially approving their domination in the locality, in other words, by formally incorporating their functions into the lowest level of government administration. In short, this local self-government of the late Ch'ing was an attempt on the part of the conservative Ch'ing government and of the similarly conservative local gentry members to preserve their political power in a changing world, by cooperating with one another for their mutual benefit.[56]

[56] See John Fincher, 'Political provincialism and the national revolution', in *CIR*, 185–226; Philip A. Kuhn, 'Local self-government under the republic', in Frederic Wakeman, Jr, and Carolyn Grant, eds. *Conflict and control in late imperial China*, 268–80.

FINANCIAL REORGANIZATION AND CENTRALIZATION

Ch'ing finance was so extremely chaotic that each ministry in the central government as well as each provincial government received almost no control from the centre. Centralization of financial administration was the essential first step if the government was to promote education, develop the military forces, and prepare for constitutional government.

The first attempt at financial reform after the Boxer incident was currency unification. At this time the currencies circulating in China included the traditional silver in bulk (*sycee*), copper cash and various kinds of foreign-minted dollars. In addition, after Chang Chih-tung opened a mint in Canton in 1889 to produce copper and silver coins by machine and it proved to be profitable, many provincial mints were opened and poured out coins. But there was no standardization of these. In fact since 1850 various kinds of currency had been in circulation without any uniform exchange rates fixed among them. To crown this chaos, official and private banks and money changers in every province as well as the foreign banks issued paper currency. Such a chaotic state of currency naturally inhibited the development of commerce. Demands for currency unification became more insistent among Western businessmen. As a matter of fact, the Sino-British commercial treaty of 1902 and the Sino-American and Sino-Japanese commercial treaties of 1903 required that the Ch'ing government unify the currency. Moreover, because of the drastic fall in the world silver price after the latter half of 1901, the import trade became very disadvantageous for China as a silver standard country. Also, China suffered from having to pay her foreign debts and indemnities in gold after the Sino-Japanese War.[57] Therefore, not only among Westerners but also among Chinese, there were proposals to adopt the gold standard and to attempt the standardization of the currency.

Realizing this was an urgent necessity, the Ch'ing government set up a Commission on Finance (Ts'ai-cheng ch'u) for this purpose.[58] Now currency reform was so closely related to the interests of foreign countries that progress would be difficult without their cooperation. Accordingly the Ch'ing government, together with the Mexican government which was still on the silver standard, asked the United States to cooperate on friendly terms in an effort to establish stable relations between the currencies of countries on the gold standard and those on silver. As a result, a Com-

[57] For background, see Frank H. H. King, *Money and monetary policy in China, 1845–1895*; Wei Chien-yu, *Chung-kuo chin-tai huo-pi shih, i-pa i-ssu – i-chiu i-chiu* (History of currency in modern China, 1814–1919).
[58] This was established in 1903 but amalgamated in 1906 with the Ministry of Finance (Tu-chih Pu).

mission on International Exchange was set up in 1903 and in the next year an American expert, Jeremiah W. Jenks, came to China to investigate currency conditions. Jenks recommended to the Chinese government the following plan: (1) China should adopt the gold standard immediately, but gold currency should not be circulated within the country but be used only as a reserve for currency and for foreign payments; (2) within the country, silver currency should be used as the standard currency; (3) the ratio between gold and silver should be 1:32; (4) in order to supervise the adoption of the new currency system, foreigners should be employed.[59]

Germany and France agreed to this proposal, but Britain and Russia opposed it. Within China, there were pro and con opinions, but because of strong opposition from Chang Chih-tung the proposals were shelved. The bases of Chang's opposition were as follows: (1) foreigners should not be allowed to meddle in Chinese financial or currency problems; (2) because copper cash was normally used in China, a silver standard would be enough, but a gold standard too much to adopt; (3) the actual ratio between silver and gold was 1:40; to make it 1:32 would deceive the people, allow up to 20 per cent profit from minting, and circulate a currency without substantial value; (4) the drop in the world silver price was disadvantageous for payment of China's indemnities and foreign loans, but advantageous for promoting exports and discouraging imports. It was not a problem for the Ch'ing empire when its prime objective was to enrich the country and strengthen the military.

When Jenks's proposals were turned down, opinion in the government settled on the idea of maintaining the silver standard for the time being even if gold might be adopted in the future. But there was still a controversy over the standard coin: whether it should be a silver coin of one Chinese ounce (*liang* or tael) or a silver coin of one *yuan* (equal to 0.72 of a *k'u-p'ing* or treasury tael), equivalent to about half a United States silver dollar. Chang Chih-tung advocated minting the silver tael on the grounds that tax payments were based on the tael and that silver dollars would not be able to compete with foreign silver dollars. Yuan Shih-k'ai agreed. Thereupon in 1905, the government decided to make the silver tael the standard coin for the time being, and to open a Central Mint at Tientsin and four other branches in order to manufacture silver taels exclusively, while prohibiting other mints from doing so. In practice, however, the controversy over adopting the silver tael or the silver dollar continued. Advocates of the former were mainly provincial governors like Chang

---

[59] Jenks's recommendations, translated in *Pi-chih hui-pien* 3.1–62, were published in *Report on the introduction of the gold-exchange standard into China* (US Senate document no. 128, 58th Congress, 3rd session, 1904).

Chih-tung and Yuan Shih-k'ai; supporters of the latter were officials of the Board of Revenue (later Ministry of Finance) and Chinese and foreign merchants. Because of the strong influence of Chang and Yuan up to 1908, the government decided again in 1908 to unify the currency system on a silver standard. But in 1909, when Yuan Shih-k'ai lost his position and Chang Chih-tung died, the supporters of the silver dollar suddenly became stronger. It was finally decided in 1910 that the silver tael system was to be abolished, and that the silver dollar was to be the standard coin, to be minted only at the Central Mint and its branches in Hankow, Canton, Yunnan and Chengtu.

Unfortunately this did not mean that previously issued silver currencies were withdrawn from use. The new silver dollar was merely added to the old system, serving only to increase the confusion, which continued to the end of the dynasty.

Also, there were provincial mints casting copper cash. Since cash were minted to raise funds, their quality tended to deteriorate and cause inflation. Since cash were most closely linked to the daily life of the people, this caused them a great deal of hardship. For this reason, when the Central Mint opened at Tientsin in 1905, the government started to mint only copper cash, because it was considered that the most urgent need of the day was to get the copper currency under control and perhaps even standardize the currency on a copper basis. But the government did not have enough funds to absorb the copper cash minted in the various provinces. It ordered the provinces not to mint any more cash and to close those mints that had not yet started operating. Since the provincial governors were not willing to follow this order, the abusive minting continued.[60]

Another cause of confusion was the paper currency. Towards the end of the dynasty, provincial governors and certain merchants operated official or private banks, and both they and money exchange shops issued paper currency without restriction, which also caused inflation and suffering among the people. In 1905 the Ch'ing government founded the Board of Revenue Bank (Hu Pu yin-hang) with 4 million taels of capital, to issue paper currency of high credibility in an attempt to curb this unlimited issuance of paper currency. However, even the paper notes issued by this bank were not backed by adequate reserve funds nor were they issued in fixed amounts. And so this issuance of paper currency by the Board of Revenue Bank merely added to the confusion. Thereupon the government

[60] Wei Chien-yu, *Chung-kuo chin-tai*, 179–81; Yang Tuan-liu, *Ch'ing-tai huo-pi chin-yung shih kao*, 283–361.

reorganized this bank as the Ta Ch'ing Government Bank (Ta-Ch'ing yin-hang) in 1908, with capital of 10 million *yuan*.

In 1910, in an attempt to centralize the paper currency, the government decided that thereafter only the Ta Ch'ing Government Bank should issue paper notes; at the same time, it fixed the amount of issuance and set up a reserve fund. Other sources were not allowed to issue paper notes, and those already issued were to be gradually retired from circulation. Of course, these plans did not work out. The amount of paper currency in circulation was estimated to be 650 million taels. If the Ta Ch'ing Government Bank were to issue the same amount of notes, it might have needed a reserve fund of 325 million taels, but it had only 10 million taels of capital.[61]

An attempt was also made to unify weights and measures. In China, weights and measures varied according to the province; even in one province they varied according to the locality; and even in the same locality they varied according to the purpose. As with the currency, this situation hindered the development of commerce. In August 1908, the Ch'ing government issued regulations specifying standards of length (*ying-tsao-ch'ih*), of volume (*ts'ao-hu*) and of weight (*k'u-p'ing* tael).[62] It decided to adopt the decimal system for weights and measures. According to the schedule issued, measures and scales used by government officials were to be adjusted to the new system within two years, and those used by private persons within ten years, but the government did not last long enough to see if these plans could be put into practice.

At the same time, the Ch'ing government made an attempt to centralize its financial administration. In provincial government finances, only regular revenue and expenditure were reported to the Board of Revenue. Extra revenue and expenditure were not reported although they had both greatly increased after the Taiping era. This non-reporting contributed to the disintegration of central influence over local administration in the late Ch'ing period. For this reason, after unifying the central financial administration by putting the Board of Revenue and the Commission on Finance together in 1906, the government ventured on an attempt to centralize financial administration nation-wide. But this naturally met strong resistance from the provincial governors.

Nevertheless, the following policy guidelines were drawn up in 1909:[63] (1) the authority to borrow from abroad was to lie exclusively with the Ministry of Finance. If any ministry of the central government or any

[61] Yang Tuan-liu, *Ch'ing-tai huo-pi chin-yung shih-kao*, 374-85; Wei Chien-yu, *Chung-kuo chin-tai*, 192-207.
[62] *CSL-KH*, 579.2-3; *Kuang-hsu cheng-yao* (Important policies of the Kuang-hsu reign), 34.43b-44; Meribeth E. Cameron, *The reform movement in China, 1898-1912*, 179.
[63] *Ta-Ch'ing Kuang-hsu hsin fa-ling*, 10.95-8.

provincial government were to contract a foreign loan, it needed the permission of the Ministry of Finance, in whose name the loan must be made; (2) hitherto, funds raised by the various offices of the central government had been left at the disposal of these offices. Hereafter, all such funds were to be reported to the Ministry of Finance; (3) since the official banks of various ministries were now issuing paper notes without any restriction, and since the state was responsible for these paper notes, the Ministry of Finance was authorized occasionally to investigate these official banks; (4) every province was spending money raised within the province without reporting it to the central government. Hereafter, all such money should be reported to the Ministry of Finance, which was authorized to investigate such matters.

In keeping with this policy, a decision was made that the Ministry of Finance should start in March 1909 to investigate the revenue and expenditure of every ministry and provincial government during 1908, and that a budget system be instituted from 1911. Accordingly, extensive studies were made of the fiscal realities in each province and the results were published.[64] In 1910, the Ministry of Finance compiled a proposed national budget for 1911, on the basis of budgets submitted by each province and ministry, and laid it before the National Assembly. The Assembly passed it with some amendments. According to the Chinese use of quotas up to this time, the amount of revenue was supposed to be always the same, while expenditures should be only as much as was available, and so there had been no need for budgeting. That China should adopt a budget system was therefore epoch-making – except that the exercise proved to be largely meaningless. This first budget was unworkable because the original proposals submitted by the ministries and provincial governments were irresponsible, all being based on a policy of 'minimum income, maximum expenditure'. Consequently the national budget made by the Ministry of Finance proved to be a 'red-ink' budget with 296 million taels of revenue and 376 million taels of expenditure. Inevitably this became an issue in the National Assembly, and an amendment was passed to make the revenue 301 million, and expenditure 298 million, in order to be in balance.[65] But of course this amendment had no firm basis. The Revolution of 1911 cut short the make-believe. Since revenues were not yet centralized, Peking had no single purse, nor any knowledge of actual income and expenditure. Budgeting remained a technical impossibility.

---

[64] *Ts'ai-cheng shuo-ming shu* (Reports on the financial administration), 23 reports each of several hundred pages, published *c.* 1911.
[65] See Wang Yeh-chien, *Land taxation in imperial China, 1750–1901*, 73–6.

OTHER REFORM PROGRAMMES

Compilation of new legal codes

China from ancient times had had laws corresponding to modern administrative law and a criminal code, but none or few corresponding to modern civil law or a commercial code. Again, judicial and administrative authority were not separate as in the modern West. But during the post-Boxer period, when the Ch'ing government positively attempted to enrich the nation and strengthen the military by adopting Western ways, it saw the necessity of revising the laws in accordance with the Western model. Ever since the government began to take the initiative in promoting industry and commerce, it had become apparent that civil and commercial codes were necessary; and at the same time the Chinese gradually came to realize the disadvantages of the unequal treaties and wished to get rid of extraterritoriality. But for this purpose, it was essential to revise the laws and judicial administration on the Western model. As a matter of fact, Britain, the United States and Japan demanded this in their treaties of 1902 and 1903. As a result of all this, in 1902 the Ch'ing government decided to start preparations for revision of the laws and judicial administration. An experienced official, Shen Chia-pen, as head of an office for this purpose began an examination of the current *Code of the Ch'ing dynasty (Ta-Ch'ing lü-li)*. As a result, in 1905 such cruel penalties as slow slicing, public exhibition of heads, and beheading of the corpse, and the penalty of tattooing were abolished. Physical punishments like flogging with the bamboo were replaced by fines. Collective responsibility and torture were also abolished.[66]

From 1906 onwards, the government invited Japanese legal specialists to help compile a new criminal code as well as civil and commercial codes, and in 1908 the draft of the new criminal code was completed. This was modelled on the Japanese criminal code, which was based on the German code; in it punishments were limited to the death penalty, imprisonment or fines. Thus all the previously existing physical punishments were abolished, while the new practices of suspension of sentence and release on parole were introduced. To the list of crimes were added new kinds of crimes related to foreign affairs, elections, transportation and communication, and public hygiene. The result in fact was a completely new criminal code rather than a revised edition of the *Code of the Ch'ing dynasty*. Naturally, much opposition arose against this draft code. When it was submitted to

---

[66] See Marinus J. Meijer, *The introduction of modern criminal law in China*, chs. 1–2 and L. S. Tao, 'Shen Chia-pen and modernization of Chinese law', *She-hui k'o-hsueh lun-ts'ung*, 25 (Sept. 1976) 275–90.

the high-ranking officials of the central and provincial governments for comment, the following points were most severely criticized: (1) according to the proposed draft, a crime committed by a person below sixteen years of age was not to be prosecuted – this age limit should be lowered; (2) death by hanging was too light a punishment for those who committed the crimes of injuring the imperial family, revolt, conspiracy or parricide; (3) penal servitude was too light a punishment for the crimes of excavating tombs, or destroying or abandoning or stealing a corpse; (4) it was not acceptable to apply the concept of legitimate self-defence to crimes committed against the ancestors; (5) it was not acceptable that adultery with women who do not have husbands should not be prosecuted.[67] In short, the draft of the new criminal code was criticized from the Confucian point of view. As a result changes were made to meet most of the above objections.

After these revisions the draft code was submitted along with supplementary regulations to the National Assembly for discussion. In the Assembly, various opinions were voiced but hardly any conclusions were reached. In the end, only the general provisions were passed, while the specific provisions and the supplementary regulations were suspended. In January 1911, however, on the grounds that if constitutional government were ever to be realized it was not possible to postpone the promulgation of the criminal code, the dynasty promulgated the general provisions, as well as the specific provisions and the supplementary regulations which had not been passed by the National Assembly. The government intended to submit them to the Assembly for approval at its next session.

Meanwhile, because the compilation of the new criminal code was so slow, the revised *Code of the Ch'ing dynasty* had been promulgated in 1910 as a temporary measure, under the title of *Current code as revised and approved* (*Ho-ting hsien-hsing hsing-lü*).[68] This was largely the same as the original code except for the parts revised in 1905 as above-mentioned, with some changes in terminology and simplification of the regulations in certain respects. It remained in force until 1928.

Along with the new criminal code, the government began to compile commercial and civil codes. The need for a commercial code was particularly urgent because it was a prerequisite for the development of commerce. As early as January 1904, the *Ordinance for the general regulation of merchants* (*Shang-jen t'ung-li*), *The company ordinances* (*Kung-ssu lü*) and other regulations had been drafted. Since these were all hastily made and not

---

[67] Meijer, *Modern criminal law*, chs. 3–5; *Ta-Ch'ing Kuang-hsu hsin fa-ling*, 19.25b–64.
[68] *Ta-Ch'ing hsien-hsing hsing-lü* (Current code of the Ch'ing dynasty), 26 *chüan*; Yang Hung-lieh, *Chung-kuo fa-lü fa-ta shih* (Chinese law: the history of its full development), 887–98.

satisfactory, the compilation of a new commercial code was started in 1908 with a Japanese adviser, but it was only partially completed. Apart from this, the Ministry of Agriculture, Industry and Commerce drafted a commercial code and put it before the National Assembly in 1910, but the dynasty fell before it was passed.

A large-scale compilation for the civil code began with a Japanese adviser in 1907, and a draft was completed in 1911. This was based on the Japanese civil code, which was modelled on the German one. However, the proposed draft was unpopular on the grounds that it neglected traditional Chinese customs; and in any case there was no chance to put it into practice before the dynasty fell.[69]

Elimination of bad customs

Along with the reforms in administration, justice, law and the military system, the Ch'ing government also launched a campaign against bad customs among the people. In 1902, the government came out against footbinding which was already under attack by missionaries and Chinese reformers.[70]

In 1906, the throne issued an edict to prohibit opium. Orders were issued to the following effect: (1) cultivation of poppy was to be gradually reduced and to be exterminated within ten years; (2) it was prohibited to take up opium smoking, to start opium dens, or to import opium; (3) officials who indulged must quit opium smoking within six months.[71] As to opium importation, the government negotiated with the British authorities and in 1907 the British agreed to reduce the amount of opium exported annually from India to China by 10 per cent of the average export for the past five years, and to continue such reduction provided that the Ch'ing government made progress in the prohibition of opium smoking during the next three years. In 1910, in the re-opened negotiations, the British were reluctant to promise to stop the export of opium within seven years. But under pressure from British opinion and the strong demands of the National Assembly and Chinese students for an immediate ending of the

---

[69] Shimada Masao, 'Shimmatsu ni okeru min shōritsu sōan no hensan ni tsuite' (On the compilation of the drafts for civil and commercial codes toward the end of the Ch'ing period), *Horitsu ronsō*, 34.6 (1962) 119–49; Thomas Mitrano, 'The Chinese bankruptcy law of 1906–1907: a case history', *Monumenta Serica*, 30 (1972–3) 259–337.

[70] *CSL-KH*, 492.9b; Li Yu-ning and Chang Yü-fa, *Chin-tai Chung-kuo nü-ch'uan*, 1.525–32.

[71] *Tung-hua hsu-lu*, 203.6–9; *CSL-KH*, 579.2b–3; Yu En-te, *Chung-kuo chin-yen fa-ling pien-ch'ien shih* (The historical evolution of anti-opium statutes and decrees in China), ch. 5; for background see Jonathan Spence, 'Opium smoking in Ch'ing China', in Wakeman and Grant, *Conflict and control*, 143–73.

opium trade, the British finally promised in 1911 to stop opium exportation from India to China by 1917.[72]

Abolition of discrimination between Manchus and Chinese

As alien rulers of China the Manchus, unlike the Mongols, had paid special attention to the treatment of Chinese and tried not to discriminate against them. However, if the Manchus with a population of only one-fortieth that of the Chinese and a somewhat lower cultural level were to maintain their position as rulers, some discriminatory treatment was unavoidable. For example, Manchu males could not marry Chinese women; the codes of decorum and punishment applied to the Manchus and Chinese were different; and certain official posts were open only to Manchus.

The Ch'ing court now tried to create harmonious relations between Manchus and Chinese by revising these regulations. In 1902 the ban on marriage between a Manchu male and Chinese female was lifted; in 1904 the posts of (Manchu) general-in-chief (*chiang-chün*) and lieutenant-general (*tu-t'ung*) as well as certain posts in the maritime customs were opened to Chinese. An administrative reform in 1906 opened the single presidency of the new central government ministries to either a Manchu or a Chinese, regardless of race. Whereas previously all Manchus had been provided with their livelihood, and did not engage in agriculture or commerce so that they could concentrate on military duties, in 1907 the government abolished this special treatment, gave them land, and ordered them to cultivate it to support themselves the same as the Chinese. Also in this year the code of decorum and punishment was made equal for the two races. Manchu officials were also ordered to stop calling themselves 'your slave' (*nu-ts'ai*) when speaking or writing to the emperor, and instead to use the term 'your servitor' (*ch'en*) just as the Chinese did.[73] All this cosmetic effort meant little, however, when Manchu-centrism was being strengthened in the military and administrative systems. During the brief Hsuan-t'ung period, political and military power was concentrated in the hands of the Manchu imperial clansmen, which played directly into the hands of the revolutionaries.

CHARACTERISTICS OF THE LATE-CH'ING REFORMS

When we review the political and institutional reforms made by the Ch'ing government after 1901, the following points are conspicuous. First, there

---

[72] 'Agreement relating to opium', 8 May 1911, in John V. A. MacMurray, comp. *Treaties and agreements with and concerning China, 1894–1919*, 1.861–6.
[73] *CSL-KH*, 492.9b; 576.1b; 579.2. *CSL-HT*, 30.26. Lee, *Manchurian frontier*, 144–5.

were many self-defeating contradictions among the reform plans. For example, while creating the National Assembly and Provincial Assemblies in order to widen the path for the expression of public opinion as part of the preparation for constitutionalism, the government put increasingly strict controls over all expression of thought. Once the Ch'ing had accepted the idea of constitutionalism, Chinese intellectuals began to demand the immediate opening of the parliament. Liang Ch'i-ch'ao formed the Cheng-wen-she (Political Information Institute) in Tokyo and promoted the movement for constitutionalism. The government was very suspicious of this influential movement. It issued a warning that students should con-centrate on their studies and not touch political affairs nor even make speeches in public. It also warned the gentry and the merchants against interfering in government affairs, saying that under the monarchical con-stitutions of various countries, sovereignty belonged to the throne; and that while 'expression of public opinion is allowed in government affairs, it is up to the imperial court to conduct government affairs and to determine which public opinions are to be adopted'.[74] In 1908, Liang's Cheng-wen-she was closed by government order. Thus the Ch'ing tried to limit thought even while reforming the imperial despotism.

Secondly, all the participants in the reform programmes sought their own interest. The reforms after 1901 were promoted mainly by Jung-lu, a Manchu grand councillor, and Chang Chih-tung, Liu K'un-i and Yuan Shih-k'ai, who were Chinese governors-general. After the death of Jung-lu in 1903, Prince Ch'ing (I-k'uang) took over his position. Thereafter the main promoters of reform were I-k'uang in the central government, assisted by his ally Yuan Shih-k'ai in Tientsin who took concurrent posts in Peking, and Chang Chih-tung and others in the provinces where they accommodated Chinese gentry sentiments concerning reform. Chang's influence diminished after the death of his colleague Liu K'un-i in 1902, and it might almost be said that after 1903 the reforms were carried through by the joint efforts of Prince Ch'ing and Yuan Shih-k'ai. However, around the time of the administrative reform in 1906, a powerful group of Manchus appeared who opposed Prince Ch'ing and Yuan. This group was led by T'ieh-liang, the president of the Army Ministry, and Jung-ch'ing, president of the Ministry of Education, backed by Prince Ch'un (Tsai-feng), the younger brother of the Kuang-hsu Emperor. Jung-ch'ing was a Mongol but he identified himself with the Manchus. For two years after 1906, the reform programmes were struggled over by the two groups, but gradually the circumstances turned against the group of Prince Ch'ing and Yuan Shih-k'ai. Finally in 1908, when the emperor and the empress dowager

[74] CSL-KH, 583.4b; Ta-Ch'ing Kuang-hsu hsin fa-ling, 2.25–32.

both died, and Prince Ch'un became the prince regent, Yuan Shih-k'ai was forced to retire to Honan. In 1909 Prince Ch'un dominated the scene. T'ieh-liang disliked him and left the government. In his stead, two brothers of Prince Ch'un, Tsai-hsun and Tsai-t'ao, and other imperial clansmen flocked around Prince Ch'un.[75]

What were the aims of the Manchu court in carrying out the reform, programme? Were the Ch'ing rulers really convinced of the necessity of reform? After the Boxer incident, reform was demanded not only by the constitutionalists like K'ang Yu-wei and Liang Ch'i-ch'ao, but also by Chinese provincial governors and by the foreigners too. In order to prevent the anti-Manchu forces from growing any larger and to keep the support of the Chinese provincial governors and the foreigners, the Ch'ing rulers had no alternative but reform, whether they liked it or not. In fact the government had no original reform plans of its own. All it wanted was to keep up appearances regardless of the actual contents.

Thus the Ch'ing government started its reforms in a negative posture, but in the course of time, particularly after the Russo-Japanese War, it became more and more serious about the reform effort. By this time, however, it was not for the sake of enriching the country and strengthening the military in order to defend China from the powers, as K'ang and Liang advocated. Rather it was a reform for the purpose of defending the Ch'ing government from the attacks of both Chinese and foreigners. In other words, it was reform for the sake of preserving the Ch'ing dynasty. For this purpose, it was necessary for the emperor to have supreme command over the army and navy, to reign over the empire with an allegedly unbroken line of succession for ages eternal, and to be sacred and inviolable.

The Chinese provincial governors also wanted to preserve the Ch'ing dynasty. That was why they cooperated with the empress dowager, Prince Ch'un and the high-ranking Manchu officials. However, their wish to preserve the dynasty was not based simply on their loyalty to the throne or their love for the Ch'ing. It was because they felt that without the dynasty their power would vanish. For this very reason, when the court tried to diminish the power of the Chinese provincial governors and centralize power in the hands of the Manchus, they naturally fought against it. Bitterness was added by the fact that before 1908 the Chinese governors had been servitors of the empress dowager, but then Prince Ch'un succeeded her and exercised the prerogative to control the officials of the empire even though his personal prestige was much less and his power more and more shaky. For this very reason, no doubt, the resentment of the Chinese provincial governors against the Manchu government grew more bitter

[75] See Hsiao I-shan, *Ch'ing-tai t'ung-shih* (A general history of the Ch'ing period), 4.2501–16.

than ever. Inept Manchu rulers were destroying China's Confucian monarchy.

It was the gentry members who gave social and economic support to the provincial governors during the late Ch'ing period. The gentry had originally been opposed to the reform effort, but once the decision, which they most opposed, had been made to abolish the civil-service examinations and announce constitutionalism, they rather suddenly changed their attitude and actively supported reform. There is little doubt that they acted to preserve their own interests rather than the Ch'ing government or China as a nation. For them, the new schools were equivalent to the old civil-service examinations. By opening schools, they could pass their privileges as gentry on to their children. Also, the basis of the constitutional regime of the future was supposed to be in the local self-government system. And this kind of local self-government was exactly what they desired. Therefore they willingly cooperated with this reform together with the provincial governors, and when the government later attempted to centralize power they opposed it along with the provincial governors. Yet whenever provincial governors took any action which seemed against their interest, the gentry members opposed the governors. It was for this reason that the provincial governors and the Provincial Assemblies often came into conflict.[76]

The reform programmes required large sums of money. The government started on its reforms without having enough funds. Inevitably it had to try to squeeze the necessary funds out of the provinces. In every province extra taxes in the form of compulsory contributions were imposed on the public under various names. It was the common people who found this most unbearable. For them it did not matter at all whether constitutionalism or autocracy or whatever was going on; after all, what they wanted was a peaceful life with less tax burden. Reflecting this desperate situation among the people, popular risings broke out almost every year in the late Ch'ing period in many localities. Meanwhile, the government, while coercing the governors to make contributions to finance reform on the one hand, gradually cut down the power of these same provincial governors on the other. Naturally the governors refused or sabotaged their assignments. As a result, the government was compelled to borrow money from foreign countries to carry out its reform programmes.

In 1911, the government made contracts with the Four-Power (British, American, German and French) Banking Consortium for a loan of £10 million for the purpose of developing Manchuria and for currency reform,

[76] For further discussion, see Chūzō Ichiko, 'The role of the gentry: an hypothesis', in *CIR*, 297–313.

and another loan of £6 million for the Hankow–Canton Railway. The former was to carry out the currency reform that had been planned in 1910, and the latter was for the nationalization of railways that had been privately projected or developed. This Canton–Hankow Railway loan turned out to be the torch that sparked off the Revolution of 1911. In 1898 the American China Development Company had acquired the right to build a Canton–Hankow Railway. However, the storm of the rights recovery movement, which arose all over China after the Boxer incident, swept over Kwangtung, Hupei and Hunan provinces in particular. In 1905 Chang Chih-tung, governor-general of Hunan and Hupei, as representative of these provinces, negotiated with the Development Company and succeeded in recovering the railway rights. As a result, the Hupei part of the railway came under the management of that province, whereas the Hunan and Kwangtung parts were put under private ownership.[77] After this the railway was built only very slowly, and eventually Peking decided to nationalize the Szechwan–Hankow and Canton–Hankow Railways on the not unsound grounds that privately owned companies could not operate effectively. For this purpose the government tried to borrow the necessary funds from the Four-Power Banking Consortium. Thereupon, fierce opposition flared up among the gentry members and merchants of the four provinces of Szechwan, Hupei, Hunan and Kwangtung. Even the provincial governors, who were obliged to suppress the agitation against this government action, were rather sympathetic towards the gentry and merchants. The agitation never calmed down and finally developed into the starting point of the revolution. The question may be asked whether the gentry and the provincial governors were against foreign loans as such. If they could have got such loans themselves, they would perhaps have had no objection.

In summary, the reform programme during the last five or six years, if not the entire last decade of the Ch'ing dynasty, may be viewed as attempts of the Manchu rulers, Chinese provincial governors and Chinese gentry members to preserve their power, or even to expand it. These elements often worked at cross-purposes. In the event, the reforms led to the fall of the dynasty.

[77] The latest work on this subject is En-han Lee, *China's quest for railway autonomy, 1904–1911.*

CHAPTER 8

GOVERNMENT, MERCHANTS
AND INDUSTRY TO 1911*

MERCHANTS AND MODERN ENTERPRISE: A REASSESSMENT

When the Ch'ing dynasty collapsed in 1911, there were about six hundred Chinese-owned manufacturing and mining enterprises run by machinery. Some 5,600 miles of railway track had also been laid. The amount of Chinese capital involved in these modern ventures was probably about $160,000,000.[1] This was sizeable, but represented only 6 or 7 per cent of the capital invested in agriculture.

Although the last decade of the Ch'ing saw an accelerated pace in these developments, especially in the building of railways, these several industries did not lead to any sustained economic growth. Little planning was done among their sponsors and managers to see that industrial developments were functionally integrated among themselves and with other sectors of the economy – credit facilities, capital formation, marketing, tax structure and the like. In any case, many of the necessary changes presupposed a nation-wide basis of operation and were therefore beyond the means of the provincial officials who dominated modern industry. (Even the far larger economic spurt between 1918 and 1922 failed to establish a trend towards sustained growth. In 1933, the Chinese modern sector, consisting of manufacturing, mining, banking and transport, accounted for only about 12 per cent of the nation's net domestic product.)[2]

The political rationale for industrialization

It was not for lack of trying that China's early industrial experiments ended with dismal results. Beginning with the building of shipyards and arsenals

---

* This chapter draws upon Wellington K. K. Chan, *Merchants, mandarins and modern enterprise in late Ch'ing China*. The author is grateful to Kwang-Ching Liu and Stephen R. MacKinnon for valuable comments, and Occidental College and the Haynes Foundation of Los Angeles for financial support.
[1] The dollar ($) cited here and subsequently is the Mexican or Chinese silver dollar, worth about 0.72 taels or 2 English shillings during the 1900s. Both taels and dollars were units of account.
[2] See Ta-chung Liu and Kung-chia Yeh, *The economy of the Chinese mainland: national income and economic development, 1933–1959*, 89; and Chi-ming Hou, 'Economic dualism: the case of China, 1840–1937', *Journal of Economic History*, 23.3 (1965) 277–97.

in the 1860s, leaders of the Chinese political and intellectual elite took a series of actions which clearly indicated their favourable attitude towards Western technology and industrial management. This new attitude, expressed by the slogan *tzu-ch'iang* (self-strengthening), launched a movement to borrow practical knowledge from the West in order to build a stronger China.[3]

Having such a popular goal, self-strengthening has had tremendous appeal to all patriots even down to the present day. But ideas as to how best to achieve this new strength varied over time and according to ideological temperament. Cultural purists wished to borrow only military hardware such as guns and gunboats. Yet the mere addition of modern military implements proved inadequate to counter Western encroachment. Even before the renewed European pressure that culminated in the humiliating Sino-French War of the mid-1880s, the Chinese leadership had begun to formulate policies for a broader self-strengthening programme.

One new source of information helped to refocus the continuing debate among scholar-officials on Western borrowing. In 1864, the maritime customs began to publish import and export figures from the treaty ports, and they showed unmistakably that China almost always had a trade deficit. Concern for this imbalance dated from the early nineteenth century, and critics had blamed it for the rising cost of silver in terms of copper cash. Now, with concrete maritime customs statistics, officials again raised the issue that the imbalance was draining the people's wealth, and that the nation was growing weaker as the people became poorer. Hsueh Fu-ch'eng, Li Hung-chang's adviser, even made the exaggerated claim in 1879 that 'the foreign merchants acquire a profit of about thirty million taels a year'.[4]

Hsueh and many other similarly concerned officials thus provided a rationale for promoting 'commercial affairs' (*shang-wu*). Since China could not refuse to accept foreign goods, she could only discourage imports by producing more of her own manufactures for both the domestic and foreign markets. Then, as the trade imbalance was reversed, the additional wealth would contribute to her strength. Once the link between wealth and power was established in this way, the pursuit of wealth became the motive for a new programme of self-strengthening. To provide ideological respectability, the proponents of this new programme turned to the Legalist strain of Confucianism which favoured maximizing state wealth and power. By recycling the old slogan, *fu-ch'iang* (wealth and power), several scholar-officials produced a new literature during the 1880s to

---

[3] See *Cambridge history of China*, vol. 10, ch. 10.

[4] Hsueh Fu-ch'eng, 'Ch'ou-yang ch'u-i' (Preliminary proposals concerning foreign affairs), in Chien Po-tsan *et al.* eds. *Wu-hsu pien-fa*, 1.154–6.

show their conversion: Ma Chien-chung's *Fu-min shuo* (Discussion on the wealth of the people), Ch'en Chih's *Fu-kuo ts'e* (Policies on enriching the state), Wang K'ang-nien's *Lun Chung-kuo ch'iu fu-ch'iang i-ch'ou i-hsing chih-fa* (Feasible paths towards China's search for wealth and power), and many others (see chapter 3).[5] Indeed, they promoted their new economic ideas so vigorously that communist historians have come to view them as spokesmen of an emergent capitalist class.[6]

However, these writers' main emphasis was on modern industry. They generally assumed that commercial enterprises could at best play a supporting role. In fact, foreign trade activities were by and large restricted to the treaty ports. Transport difficulties, the role of local fairs and regional markets, as well as ingrained notions among most merchants as to how business should be conducted, all contributed to keeping domestic commerce in its traditional mode.[7]

More importantly, influential officials who became major sponsors of modern enterprise were especially partial to industry. From the early 1870s, Li Hung-chang argued that guns and gunboats alone did not make a nation strong; their operation required the support of industry in manufacturing, mining and modern communications; industry would create new wealth – a further source of national strength.[8] Chang Chih-tung, too, realized the link between military power and economic development. Emphasizing his belies that the development of industry had to take precedence over commecer, Chang argued that 'all of the Western nations' wealth and strength were derived from coal and iron'.[9]

Thus the Chinese promotion of modern enterprise in the late nineteenth century was inspired by the political necessity of quickly achieving respectable national strength. This fundamental goal united government officials of various persuasions in a common commitment to industrialization.

[5] For a discussion of several of these writings see Chao Feng-t'ien, *Wan-Ch'ing wu-shih-nien ching-chi ssu-hsiang shih* (History of economic thought during the last fifty years of the Ch'ing period), 41–147.

[6] See, e.g., Mou An-shih, *Yang-wu yun-tung* (The Western affairs movement), 128.

[7] G. William Skinner, 'Marketing and social structure in rural China, part 1', *JAS*, 24.1 (Nov. 1964) 3–43.

[8] Li Hung-chang, *Li Wen-chung kung ch'üan-chi* (Complete papers of Li Hung-chang; hereafter *LWCK*), *P'eng-liao han-kao* (Letters to friends and colleagues), 13.21b. On Li's motives see Kwang-Ching Liu, 'Li Hung-chang in Chihli: the emergence of a policy 1870–1875', in Albert Feuerwerker, Rhoads Murphey and Mary C. Wright, eds. *Approaches to modern Chinese history* (hereafter *AMCH*), 68–104.

[9] Cited in Li Kuo-ch'i, *Chang Chih-tung ti wai-chiao cheng-ts'e* (Chang Chih-tung's foreign policy proposals), 12.

The merchants' changing roles and status

Having become obsessed with the idea that modern enterprise begets wealth, and that wealth begets power, official promoters in the late Ch'ing soon decided that industry was too important to be left in the hands of private entrepreneurs. Thus, with industrial development as the goal, these officials assumed successive new roles: first supervisors, then managers, then investors and finally, for some, official-entrepreneurs. In assuming these new roles, official promoters raised new questions about the status and function of merchants in Chinese society.

Changes in the nature of the merchant class had, however, predated the push for modern enterprise. During the eighteenth and the first half of the nineteenth centuries, the licensed salt merchants and the Hong merchants of Canton were among the most prominent commercial groups in China. Other major types included itinerant merchants (*k'o-shang*) in the thriving inter-regional trade in silk, tea, medicines and other regionally based products. The prominence in the various commercial cities of innumerable guild halls (*hui-kuan*) based on common geographical origins attested to the size and influence of the merchant community. But the Opium War and the Taiping Rebellion had upset both the trade monopolies and the economic basis upon which the inter-provincial trade was built.[10]

In the second half of the nineteenth century, new kinds of merchants with new entrepreneurial functions emerged. Best known was the comprador. First hired by the Hong merchants as purveyors, after 1842 the compradors gradually changed their roles to become stewards for foreigners, then business managers under contract and finally independent entrepreneurs trading with foreign merchants. The observation of Western business practices by compradors and comprador-merchants brought new economic ideas and new social attitudes into the Chinese merchant class.[11]

A second type of merchant was the trader-financier who was appointed to quasi-official positions to help the regular officials devise fiscal policies and raise miscellaneous taxes, often by ingenious improvisations that went beyond the imagination and expertise of the official's usual advisers (*mu-yu*). Having bought a brevet rank and title, a merchant could become adviser and valuable functionary to a high official and use his new connections to maximize profit in private or semi-official enterprises. One famous case was that of Hu Kuang-yung, a merchant banker who, during the 1850s and

---

[10] Peng Chang, 'Distribution of provincial merchant groups in China, 1842–1911'. P'eng Tse-i, 'Shih-chiu shih-chi hou-ch'i Chung-kuo ch'eng-shih shou-kung-yeh shang-yeh hang-hui ti ch'ung-ch'ien ho tso-yung' (The reconstruction of Chinese city handicraft and trade associations in the late nineteenth century and their functions), *Li-shih yen-chiu*, 1965, 1, pp. 71–102.
[11] Yen-p'ing Hao, *The comprador in nineteenth century China: bridge between East and West.*

1860s, built up an empire of native banks, pawnshops, pharmacies and silk and other commodity trading. Hu's success was the result of hard work, good fortune and venturesome spirit. More important, however, was his series of appointments as financial adviser and purveyor to Governor Wang Yu-ling and Governor-general Tso Tsung-t'ang (see chapter 4).[12]

After 1870, as officials began to sponsor industrial enterprises, a number of comprador-merchants were recruited to be managers in official enterprises. At the same time, more and more officials were appointed to help administer or to supervise each new enterprise. Some retained their official appointments but devoted most of their energy to the enterprises. Others made formal exits from the official world to devote all their time to private or semi-official business. Just as merchants purchased official titles, so officials and gentry swelled the merchant ranks. By 1900, so many had interchangeable official and merchant roles that entrepreneurial activity had become a respectable alternative to an official career. These developments gave rise to a new social stratum of 'gentry-merchants' (shen-shang) within the general merchant class, who became innovative entrepreneurs committed to economic modernization for both public and private reasons.

This influx of men of gentry and official background into merchant ranks facilitated an ideological reassessment of the latter's place in Chinese society. In 1897, the conservative censor Ch'u Ch'eng-po memorialized the throne condemning the traditional discrimination against merchants. A big landlord and a long-time associate of the reactionary Hsu T'ung, Ch'u advocated modern commerce and industry as the means to save China from Western imperialism. Another well-known conservative literatus, Wang Hsien-ch'ien, went even further. He claimed that if the platitudes uttered by officials could be separated from social practice, merchants and the proprietors of handicraft industry had actually been in the Chinese upper stratum since Ch'in and Han times. Wang concluded that if China were to become a modern capitalist society, the merchant class must lead the nation's industrial effort.[13] Reform-minded scholar-officials underwent similar conversions. Liang Ch'i-ch'ao, who had derided merchants for being 'subversive, manipulative and monopolistic', soon praised them for their resourcefulness and spirit of enterprise and urged them to cooperate with the government in large-scale trade and industry.[14]

On 22 April 1903, in announcing the establishment of the first national

[12] Charles J. Stanley, Late Ch'ing finance: Hu Kuang-yung as an innovator.
[13] Chang T'ing-chü, 'Wu-hsu cheng-pien shih-ch'i wan-ku-p'ai chih ching-chi ssu-hsiang' (The economic thought of the reactionary faction during the reform of 1898), Chung-kuo ching-chi, 4.6 (1936) 141-7.
[14] Liang Ch'i-ch'ao, Yin-ping-shih wen-chi (Collected essays of the Ice-drinker's Studio), 1.1b-11; 11.1-47b; 23.33-53.

Ministry of Commerce (Shang Pu), the throne declared that 'when by social convention industry and commerce have been thought of as matters of the least importance, the national economy and the people's livelihood have progressively grown weak .... We must now abandon all official habits [of feeling superior towards merchants]. We must unite and not permit any barrier (*ko-ai*) [between merchants and officials].'[15]

This imperial exhortation acknowledged a change in the state ideology. Probably because new industrial projects were eagerly sponsored by senior officials, their managers' modern skills assumed an aura of responsibility. Moreover, most managers, if they had no official background to begin with, soon became wealthy men with purchased official ranks and titles. Merchants, gentry and officials who formed a new social stratum of gentry-merchants did not, however, become a distinct bourgeois class at this time. In the large treaty ports, the number of gentry-merchants was so considerable that their common life-style, values and social and political orientations had become quite distinct. But they still lacked a broad unity of purpose and retained strong commitments to traditional native place and clan ties.[16]

OFFICIAL SPONSORSHIP OF MODERN INDUSTRY

Ever since the early Han dynasty there had been debates over state control of salt and iron; the Legalist preference for state involvement in major economic activities had been generally accepted. Though challenged by orthodox Confucians who idealized frugal, benevolent government and a self-regulating, self-sufficient economy, strong-minded emperors and pragmatic bureaucrats favoured the Legalists' interventionist thinking. Consequently, recurrent debates on this issue often dealt with the extent and the nature of state control but seldom with the need for control itself.[17] Former Ch'ing officials and scholars could think of promoting industry only within the framework of state supervision. Their ingrained notions of the state's prerogatives, reinforced by a newly acquired sense of national urgency, led officials to believe that modern enterprise was too important to leave to merchants. The merchants agreed, if only because they realized

[15] *Kuang-hsu ch'ao tung-hua lu* (The Tung-hua records of the Kuang-hsu reign), 29th year, 3rd month, pp. 27–8.

[16] For a somewhat contrary view, see Marie-Claire Bergère, 'The role of the bourgeoisie', in Mary C. Wright, ed. *China in revolution: the first phase, 1900–1913*, 229–5. Also Joseph W. Esherick, '1911: a review', *Modern China*, 2.2 (April 1976) 141–84.

[17] It is true that the state offered minimal regulations and that commerce operated independently of the state. (Gary G. Hamilton, 'Merchants and modernization: changing views of Chinese commerce', MS, Berkeley, December 1975.) However, the lack of clearly defined regulations did not mean absence of control but only that there were broad guidelines, mainly ideological, making up a perimeter beyond which merchants could not tread.

that state initiative, support and protection were essential for any large innovative undertaking, particularly one facing the competition of heavily financed foreign enterprises.

Li Hung-chang's style of leadership

In the 1860s, since the government-funded and managed arsenals and ship-yards (see volume 10, chapter 10) dealt directly with national defence, no private capital or management was sought. However, as official promoters moved into the wider field of profit-oriented industry during the 1870s, a new pattern of government–merchant cooperation had to be mapped out. Several factors made it impractical for the government to organize these industries as state monopolies. First, in spite of the long history of such monopolies, the Ch'ing government maintained them on only salt, copper and porcelain. Major items such as tea, sugar, grain, textiles and transport shipping, were mostly owned and managed privately. Secondly, modern enterprise required special management and technological skills beyond the competence of officials. Thirdly, and probably most important, the public treasury simply did not have large amounts of idle funds to convert into capital for large-scale industrial projects.

In 1872, when Li Hung-chang proposed the first of the non-military modern industries, the China Merchants' Steam Navigation Company, he did not intend it to be either a government monopoly or even a purely official enterprise. By adapting a bureaucratic term *kuan-tu shang-pan* (government supervision and merchant management) from the salt mono-poly, Li was clearly searching for some form of joint official and merchant effort which would incorporate features from the salt administration, the Western model of joint-stock companies and the traditional Chinese partnership companies. As a model, the salt administration was useful because it already had a tradition of co-opting wealthy merchants who provided capital and managerial skills while officials retained overall con-trol. The Western model was useful because modern enterprise required modern technology and some measure of Western-style management. Support from government funding would be only as loans. Private investors, putting up their own money and managing it under official sponsorship and supervision, would assume all the risks.[18] Beyond these general guidelines, however, neither Li nor any other official promoter had

[18] Li Hung-chang's several *kuan-tu shang-pan* operations are discussed by Albert Feuerwerker, *China's early industrialization: Sheng Hsuan-huai (1844–1916) and mandarin enterprise*. See Kwang-Ching Liu, 'Two steamship companies in China, 1862–1877' (Harvard University, Ph.D. dissertation, 1956), for details about the first years of the China Merchants' Steam Navigation Co.

a precise organizational formula in mind. *Kuan-tu shang-pan* remained loose and flexible, as became apparent when later supervisors like Sheng Hsuan-huai used the same term while changing the working relationship between officials and merchants.

Li's *kuan-tu shang-pan* operations also used the traditional Chinese form as a model. Instead of adopting the Western practice of holding share-holders' meetings in order to elect boards of directors and all the senior officers, they followed the traditional Chinese method of hiring a manager who was then given almost absolute control. The owners did not intervene on a daily or monthly basis, but once a year reviewed the business with the manager who, if unsatisfactory, could be dismissed.[19] All three major industries sponsored by Li during the 1870s – the China Merchants' Steam Navigation Company in 1872, the Kaiping Mining Company in 1877 and the Shanghai Cotton Cloth Mill in 1878 – had management features similar to those of a traditional company. First, they were all headed by managers of merchant background, even though all had purchased official titles and were given quasi-official status. Even Chu Ch'i-ang, who managed the China Merchants' Steam Navigation Company in the early months, was an official of merchant origin. Chu continued to operate a junk transport business while holding his official post.[20] When Chu was unable to raise sufficient private capital, he was replaced by two ex-compradors, Tong King-sing (T'ang T'ing-shu) and Hsu Jun, in 1873. Tong initiated the Kaiping mines with the help of two regular officials, Ting Shou-ch'ang, a former Tientsin taotai, and Li Chao-t'ang, the incumbent taotai of the Tientsin customs. The three set up the company's regulations and organizational structure. But hardly had the company begun to function when Ting and Li left the scene. Instead, Tong was joined by two other Cantonese merchants, Hsu Jun and Wu Chih-ch'ang.[21]

For the Shanghai Cotton Cloth Mill, Li obtained the service of another ex-comprador, Cheng Kuan-ying, to work with another merchant, P'eng Ju-tsung, who had made the original proposal for the mill. In 1880, after P'eng had left as a result of disputes with the other merchant investors, Li retained Cheng and appointed five other merchant managers to assist him in running the reorganized mill. Only Kung Shou-t'u, an expectant taotai put in charge of the mill's official relations, was primarily an official although with business experience.[22] All of these men were gentry-

[19] *Shina keizai zensho* (Complete economic studies of China), 1.185–7.
[20] For Chu Ch'i-ang's biography, see *Ch'ing-shih kao* (A draft history of the Ch'ing dynasty), *Lieh-chuan* (Biographies), 239.3, and Feuerwerker, *Early industrialization*, 108.
[21] Ellsworth C. Carlson, *The Kaiping mines, 1877–1912: a case study of early Chinese industrialization.*
[22] Yen Chung-p'ing, *Chung-kuo mien-fang-chih shih-kao, 1289–1937* (Draft history of the Chinese cotton industry, 1289–1937), 84–92.

merchants. They purchased official titles because the latter had become *sine qua non* for any merchant who wanted to gain admission to an official yamen to conduct business or seek official support. Most of them were also former compradors.

Secondly, while retaining his hold as sponsor and patron, Li allowed these merchant-managers much freedom of action as entrepreneurs. The China Merchants' competed successfully with its foreign competitors and increased its tonnage enormously in 1877 by taking over the fleet of Russell and Company. The Kaiping Mining Company greatly expanded its capital from merchant resources while Tong and Hsu were in charge. In the case of the faction-ridden Shanghai Cotton Cloth Mill, Li did not step in to order a drastic reorganization until it became clear that Cheng Kuan-ying's departure in 1884 had taken away the investors' support and the management's know-how. Thus, although Tong, Hsu, Cheng, Kung and the other gentry-merchant managers served at Li Hung-chang's pleasure, Li himself, much like the owner of a traditional company, did not as a rule interfere with their business activities. His protection against excessive official squeeze as well as his many timely and egregious loans of official funds benefited the companies far more than his increased opportunities for personal gain and patronage benefited him.

Thirdly, like the traditional company's passive owners, most shareholders in these early years did not question their powerlessness under management. The relative ease with which merchant-managers like Tong were able to raise merchant capital suggests that these shareholders made their investments out of loyalty to and trust in the manager. Whether the trust was warranted is a different matter. In 1884 Tong and Hsu were forced to relinquish their control over the China Merchants' to Li's appointed supervisor, first Ma Chien-chung and then Sheng Hsuan-huai, because it was found that they and others had diverted company funds into their own private business. In 1883–4, a financial crisis in Shanghai caused by the spread of Sino–French conflict led to many business failures, including those in which Tong, Hsu and Cheng were involved. When they could not repay the company funds, and when court censors began attacking Li Hung-chang for covering up their malpractices, they had to resign. Similarly, Cheng Kuan-ying had apparently made private use of the Shanghai Cotton Cloth Mill's capital which he had raised. This led to his resignation in 1884, as well as the mill's eventual reorganization and transfer to the control of Sheng Hsuan-huai.

Such managerial malpractices reflected traditional company procedures, which provided no independent auditor to check the manager's accounts. Financial irregularities of this sort were a constant feature of traditional enterprise, tolerated as part of the risk in any business investment, as long as both the company and the manager's private use of the company funds were doing well. This was analogous to the Chinese official's use or misuse of revenues on a personal basis. He, too, was tolerated as long as he could pay the tax quota.

Official supervisors versus merchant managers

Thus, around 1885, management control over two of these earliest three *kuan-tu shang-pan* operations was transferred to Sheng Hsuan-huai. Sheng came from an official family and was himself trained to be an official. A member of Li's personal staff (*mu-fu*), he had been assigned to the China Merchants' almost since its inception in 1873. Although he seems to have left the company to manage the Imperial Telegraph Administration (also a *kuan-tu shang-pan* concern) in 1882, Sheng's natural talent in financial management made him Li's logical choice as successor to Hsu and Tong. With Sheng serving as director-general (*tu-pan*), Li could exercise official supervision more closely. Not only did Sheng tolerate the considerable amount of nepotism and misuse of company funds which had already existed under Tong's administration, he increased those practices and also brought in more bureaucratic management. Little tonnage was added to the fleet, and the shipping company was barely able to maintain its profits by 'pooling agreements' with its two main competitors. This involved written agreements between the China Merchants' and the two British carriers, Jardine, Matheson and Company, and Butterfield and Swire, setting forth uniform freight rates and pooling all their earnings, which were then divided according to the mileage contributed by each company.[23]

As for the Kaiping Mining Company, Tong and his merchant associates had effective control over its general policy and finance until Tong's death in 1892, and they ran the mining company more in the manner of a traditional firm than of the Western joint-stock model they were supposed to emulate. As in his management of the China Merchants', Tong as chief manager (*tsung-pan*) was not above borrowing company funds to invest in other mines, native banks and speculative ventures on his own account. Shareholders' general meetings (*ku-tung ta-hui*) were indeed held, but only perfunctorily. There is no record of any published annual accounts even

---

[23] See Kwang-Ching Liu, 'British-Chinese steamship rivalry in China, 1873–1885', in C. D. Cowan, ed. *The economic development of China and Japan: studies in economic history and political economy*, 49–78, esp. 75 (n. 1) showing China Merchants' diminishing share of total earnings between 1884 and 1893 as its fleet stagnated while those of its two British competitors expanded.

though they were required by company regulations. Tong also practised nepotism by bringing his son into the company and promoting him to high positions. He also arranged for his own brother to act for him while he went on a trip to Europe in 1883. The fact remains that during his tenure, the Kaiping Mining Company expanded its operation each year until its coal production rose to about a quarter of a million tons. It made profits and suffered no direct charges of squeeze or corruption. Indeed, Tong enjoyed a reputation as an honest and effective manager. His indulgences in favouritism and other traditional practices should be judged within the cultural milieu in which he lived.

Tong King-sing's death in 1892 marked the beginning of gross corruption and creeping bureaucratization in the Kaiping mines. The new manager, Chang Yen-mao, was a Chinese bannerman and bureaucrat who owed his rise to his corrupt patron, Prince Ch'un. Under Tong's management, expansion of the plant and facilities was funded by new merchant capital. But since the merchants discontinued their support after Chang's takeover, the company turned to foreign loans, and a way was opened for foreign control which came after 1900.

These developments contrasted sharply with the earlier period when merchant-managers of these operations had comparatively little difficulty in raising sufficient capital from private sources. Soon after Tong and Hsu took charge in July 1873, the China Merchants' paid-up capital grew rapidly to almost half a million taels in 1874 and then to a million by 1880. Between 1881 and 1883, demand for the company's shares even exceeded supply, especially during 1882 when it quickly reached its authorized capital of 2 million taels.

There were at least two reasons for the China Merchants' popularity with private investors. First, Tong and Hsu were in actual control, especially between 1882 and 1883 while Sheng Hsuan-huai, Li's official representative, was temporarily reassigned elsewhere. Secondly, merchant investors who had adopted a wait-and-see attitude were impressed by the profit returns as well as by Li Hung-chang's benign patronage. Thus, the same period also saw merchants giving similarly generous support to Li's two other *kuan-tu shang-pan* companies. Between 1878 and 1882, Tong and Hsu raised a million taels for the Kaiping mines, while around 1880, Cheng Kuan-ying collected most of the 352,800 taels he raised for the Shanghai Cotton Cloth Mill.

Around 1883, however, merchant enthusiasm waned, and from then on, fewer and fewer of them invested in these and other government-sponsored enterprises. Several factors contributed to this trend. First, both the large size of the capital and the profitability of modern industry had made it a desirable target for official control. Secondly, officials like Sheng Hsuan-huai acquired experience in management and in arranging loans from the government. Thirdly, these same officials discovered other sources of capital besides government loans as more of their official friends invested their money and as their control over several companies allowed them to transfer funds from older and stronger establishments to newer and weaker ones. Finally, these officials shifted from their advisory, protective roles to become official managers in name as well as in fact. Managers of merchant background like Tong, Hsu and Cheng lost their posts, thus discouraging other merchant investors.

To cite just two examples: between 1887 and 1893, Sheng Hsuan-huai tripled the Shanghai Cotton Cloth Mill's capital to about a million taels by the use of government loans and the transfer of funds from the China Merchants' and an insurance company which he also controlled. Practically no new merchant capital was added. A second example is the Mo-ho Gold Mine sponsored by Li Hung-chang and the tartar-general of Heilungkiang in 1887. They appointed a typical official manager, Li Chin-yung. Li had minor degree status, experience of *mu-fu* service under Li Hung-chang, good merchant contacts and a reputation for business acumen. Between 1887 and 1889, he made repeated attempts among his many merchant friends in Shanghai and Tientsin to raise a rather modest 200,000 taels as the initial capital of the mine. He collected only 60,000 to 70,000 taels. Finally, the Heilungkiang provincial treasury had to grant him a loan of 30,000 taels, while one Tientsin merchant supplied the other 100,000 taels as a second loan after Li Hung-chang guaranteed its repayment.[24]

Although the lack of merchant participation was partially compensated by government capital and loans, official sponsors continued to seek new ways of attracting investors. One incentive was the opportunity for private investment by officials and their friends and relatives. It seems that those who invested were close friends and associates of those in charge. Sheng Hsuan-huai depended on the same small group of colleagues to provide him with private capital for his several enterprises – the Imperial Telegraph Administration from the early 1880s, the Hua-sheng Spinning and Weaving Mill, the Hanyang Ironworks and the Imperial Bank of China in the mid-1890s. On the other hand, the central government, spurred on by critical censors, often objected to the use of public funds for industrial ventures, and demanded the repayment of loans made earlier.

Yet public funds remained crucial to the financing of *kuan-tu shang-pan*

[24] Kung Chun, *Chung-kuo hsin-kung-yeh fa-chan-shih ta-kang* (An outline history of China's modern industrial development), 36–43; *LWCK, Tsou-kao* (Memorials), 69.40–42b gives a brief biography of Li Chin-yung.

enterprises. From the late 1880s, and prior to Li Hung-chang's political decline in 1895, Chang Chih-tung's textile and mining complexes had come to rival Li's. Sheng Hsuan-huai, whose middle-level official rank was never sufficiently powerful to protect his growing industrial network, had to depend first on Li, and later on Chang for political backing and for support to secure government loans. Since the court did not want local revenue to become excessively diverted to industry, new projects submitted to the court for approval invariably contained plans that promised to attract merchant participation. Chang Chih-tung's numerous proposals to the throne included such plans even though he distrusted the merchants and thought their mentality too outmoded to accept modern industry. These plans then became a convenient cover, for many provincial sponsors knew that once the project was approved, some amount of public funds from local sources could always be found. Through need and self-interest, the well-connected provincial officials in fact relied increasingly on govern- ment funds to keep their modern industries going. Consequently, the nature of *kuan-tu shang-pan* operations changed after the mid-1880s while the worsening bureaucratic practices were justified and consolidated.

By tapping government resources, Sheng Hsuan-huai, the most success- ful official-entrepreneur, came to control numerous *kuan-tu shang-pan* operations. Thus, in trying to find capital for his Imperial Telegraph Administration, Sheng depended heavily on provincial treasuries and on government loans which used existing telegraph lines as collateral. Merchant capital was available only for the commercially profitable lines running through the lower Yangtze and the south-east coastal areas.

A similar case is the Hanyang Ironworks which Sheng managed for Chang Chih-tung from 1896. Sheng had avoided the commitment that private investment would be found to replace the staggering 5,600,000 taels of official funds already spent on the ironworks. Nonetheless, Chang changed the status of the massive industrial plant from an official under- taking (*kuan-pan*) to a merchant operation under government supervision (*kuan-tu shang-pan*), because the central government had resolutely refused to commit any more public funds to it. Since 1894, Chang had been ordered by the court to invite merchants to undertake the enterprise. He stalled for about a year by pleading that he still needed more experiments to prove that the right kind of coal to make steel had been found, for he claimed that otherwise no merchants would step forward. On 16 October 1895, he informed the throne that the search for the right coal had been successful and the finished product had been offered a high price. He was now ready to invite merchants to take over, he stated, but in order that the merchants could have time to look over the plant and mine sites properly, he needed a further government appropriation to keep the ironworks running until the end of the year.[25]

By late 1895, Chang was under so much pressure from the court that he would accept Sheng's help on almost any terms, and Sheng offered to repay the government by means of a levy of one tael per ton of pig-iron produced. Sheng tried to raise a limited amount of capital from merchants to improve existing facilities, but this attempt failed. He complained that the merchants were hesitant because the success of the coal mines and iron smelting was in doubt. As part of the bargain which he had arranged with Chang Chih-tung, however, he was able to draw upon 1,900,000 taels of a separate government fund, earmarked for the Peking–Hankow Railway for the purchase of steel. By 1904, some 2 million taels were raised from two sources: the larger portion came from a transfer of funds from the China Merchants', the remainder from himself and the same official and gentry associates who were contributing to his other *kuan-tu shang-pan* ventures in banking, shipping, telegraphs and textiles.[26]

The transfer of one company's funds to another was a technique Sheng frequently employed. Some time between 1890 and 1891, on his own authority and despite his associate manager Cheng Kuan-ying's protest that the merchant investors had not been consulted, Sheng transferred some 300,000 taels from the China Merchants' to the Shanghai Cotton Cloth Mill. In 1896, Sheng ordered another massive transfer of funds to his new venture, the Imperial Bank of China – 800,000 taels from the China Merchants' and 200,000 taels from the Imperial Telegraph Administration. In both cases, these transfers amounted to 30 or 40 per cent of each company's total capital at the time.[27]

Chang Chih-tung's promise of merchant partnerships

As more merchants came to distrust official intentions, fewer and fewer from the late 1880s onwards were willing to risk investment in bureaucratically controlled enterprises. Officials responded by offering an alternative formula of merchant participation. Using new slogans which may all be subsumed under the widely used phrase *kuan-shang ho-pan* (official and merchant joint management), these officials promised more equitable partnerships between the state and the private investors.

From his base in Wuchang in the mid-Yangtze basin, Chang Chih-tung

[25] Chang Chih-tung, *Chang Wen-hsiang kung chi* (The papers of Chang Chih-tung), ed. Hsu T'ung-hsin, *Tsou-kao* (Memorials), 69.11b–13b.
[26] Sheng Hsuan-huai, *Sheng shang-shu Yü-chai ts'un-kao ch'u-k'an* (Collected papers of ministry president Sheng Hsuan-huai, 1st issue), 4.24–6.
[27] Cheng Kuan-ying, *Sheng-shih wei-yen hou-pien* (Warnings to a prosperous age: a sequel), 10.27a.

was the first major figure to apply the new slogan to industrial projects. Chang had been slow to accept the need for accommodation with the West, but he had changed his views from the early 1880s and had grasped the importance of building up industry. Chang considered his earliest industrial venture, the Hupei Cotton Cloth Mill of 1889, as a kind of *kuan-shang ho-pan* operation, even though the arrangements he made for it were quite different from all the other textile or textile-related industries he sponsored later under the same rubric. In 1888, while serving in Canton, he had come upon a novel way of raising sufficient capital to launch a weaving factory. To the throne, Chang cryptically recommended a policy of 'official promotion of merchant enterprise' (*kuan wei shang-ch'ang*).[28]

Chang's new method turned out to be the levying of a tax on the so-called *wei-hsing* merchants of Canton, who were licensed to run lotteries in which winners had to predict accurately the surnames of the successful candidates in each imperial civil-service examination.[29] In 1889, Chang committed them to an enforced contribution of 400,000 taels for that year and another 560,000 taels for 1890 in addition to their regular taxes. He informed the throne of these extra levies about a year later, when his new assignment as governor-general of Hu-Kwang forced him to request the throne's permission to move both funds and factory site from Canton to his new post. To justify this unusual method of raising capital for a cotton textile mill in the Hankow area from the Canton lottery merchants, Chang argued that regular merchant shares would be slow in coming, and that he hoped to find greater interest among the merchants once the enterprise became profitable. That Canton funds could be thus used for an undertaking in Hupei is a measure of the backing Chang enjoyed in Peking.

The lottery merchants' 'contribution' was in fact a kind of confiscation. Yet Chang saw in this unusual source of government revenue a means of taking complete control over the factory. Besides seeking imperial approval for the transfer of funds and factory site to central China, his memorial included a request to borrow some government funds; his successor as governor-general in Canton, Li Han-chang, would allow Chang to take away only slightly more than half of the promised revenue from the extra levy on local lotteries. The Hupei mill that was eventually established, although in name a merchant-official joint venture, actually acquired its 'merchant capital' by coercion.

Chang Chih-tung was not, however, against merchant cooperation whenever feasible. Though he had a low opinion of merchant capabilities

---

[28] Chang Chih-tung, *Chang Wen-hsiang kung chi, Tsou-kao*, 17.24–6; 19.3b–6; 29.30–31b.
[29] For details about this quaint form of lottery, see Hsi Pao-kan, comp. *Fo-shan chung-i hsiang-chih* (Gazetteer of Fo-shan), *chüan* 4.

and patriotism, he was realistic about the need for merchant support. In 1894, in an effort to expand the mill's capital, he promised 'guaranteed dividends' (*kuan-li*) of 15 per cent per annum to any new investor, and was apparently partially successful.[30] But he continued to withhold from the merchants any involvement in management responsibilities.

Management of the mill was headed by a member of his personal staff, Ts'ai Hsi-yung, and after Ts'ai's death in 1896 by Sheng Ch'un-i. Both had come from official backgrounds. Ts'ai, a graduate of the T'ung-wen kuan, had been a linguist on the staff of Ch'en Lan-pin, the Chinese minister to the United States, Spain and Peru from 1875 to 1881. In the early 1880s, having impressed Chang Chih-tung with his knowledge of the West and his ideas about self-strengthening, Ts'ai took up employment under Chang and soon became the chief architect and supervisor of his modern industrial, military and educational projects.[31] Little is known about his successor Sheng Ch'un-i, but he appears to have been less knowledgeable about modern enterprise. Sheng's takeover from about 1896 coincided with the beginning of Chang's increasing difficulty with his several industrial projects.

The Hupei Cotton Cloth Mill, however, had problems from the beginning. Although at first it was profitable, Chang used not only its profits but some of its capital as well to support his other enterprises which were suffering losses. The Hanyang Ironworks, until its reorganization in 1896, drew a total of 340,000 taels from the mill, and paid back only about 60,000 taels in freight and insurance. Similar untidy accounting between the mill and Chang's other industries, as well as bureaucratic waste and high interest on loans necessary for the mill to meet its own needs, added to the drain on the company. By 1902, when its losses forced Chang to turn it over to a private concessionaire, its loans from government sources amounted to at least 683,375 taels.[32]

Chang Chih-tung's second textile venture, the Hupei Cotton Spinning Mill had a more typical *kuan-shang ho-pan* history.[33] It began in 1894 when Chang was getting some merchant support for his older mill. Chang promised the throne that the merchant investors would be partners. He failed, however, to spell out in detail how the partnership would be carried out. Although he used such terms as *kuan-shang ho-pan* and *chao-shang chu-kuan* (inviting merchants to assist officials) to describe the new mode of official and merchant cooperation, his outline as presented to the throne for approval still looked very similar to *kuan-tu shang-pan* operations.

[30] Wang Ching-yü, comp. *Chung-kuo chin-tai kung-yeh shih tzu-liao, ti-erh chi, 1895–1914* (Source materials on the history of modern industry in China, 2nd collection 1895–1914), 1.573–4.
[31] Li Kuo-ch'i, *Chang Chih-tung*, 17.
[32] Wang Ching-yü, *Chung-kuo chin-tai kung-yeh shih tzu-liao*, 1.572.   [33] *Ibid.* 2.579–91.

Several merchants, however, responded positively. By 1887, they had contributed some 300,000 taels or half of the capital for this new mill. It seems that while Chang appointed a senior official to be director-general (*tu-pan*) and Sheng Ch'un-i as chief manager (*tsung-pan*), the merchant shareholders were given control of at least the machines and the company accounts. During 1897, however, when the mill became ready for production, Chang appointed Taotai Wang Ch'ang-ch'uan to be his resident representative on the site to supervise the mill. Already the merchant partners were getting uneasy over Chang's increasing interference. Wang's appointment as the official-in-residence turned their simmering unrest into open revolt. Wang responded by defending the government's right to participate in the management of the company, for the government had put up 50 per cent of the capital.

Their subsequent debate remains unclear. It seems that Chang negotiated for a compromise. It was rejected, and in July 1897 the merchants quit. According to Chang's version, the merchants wanted not only full management, but also an additional 200,000-tael loan. In return, the original government capital share of 300,000 taels would be turned into a loan at a predeterminate rate of guaranteed interest.[34]

Chang claimed he had agreed to these terms except for the additional loan of 200,000 taels; whereupon, the merchants decided to pull out. It was likely that Chang had insisted on some form of government control. To avoid such control would have been a major breakthrough for the merchants when contrasted with the position they held under the *kuan-tu shang-pan* formula. Indeed, officials and merchants would have reversed their roles. Under the *kuan-tu* operations, the officials who made use of merchant capital were ultimately in charge of the management. Under the new plan, as reported by Chang, the merchants would have been the ones to make use of the government capital and still have control over the management. As for the guaranteed interest on the official loan, this was very similar to the 'guaranteed dividend' which all private and official capital was promised, regardless of whether it was invested in the *kuan-tu* or any other type of enterprise.

In any case, by the summer of 1897 the spinning mill was changed into essentially a government operation. Half of the merchant investments were reimbursed outright. The other half were paid in bonds to mature a year later. This apparently created much ill-feeling. Chang Chien, a gentry promoter of modern enterprise who enjoyed official backing, reported that his effort at the same time to raise money for a private textile mill ran into great difficulty after the break occurred between Chang Chih-tung and the

34 Chang Chih-tung, *Chang Wen-hsiang kung chi*, *Kung-tu* (Official correspondence), 12.15b–16b.

merchants. Many private investors who had already pledged money to Chang Chien withdrew their support.[35] The Hupei Cotton Spinning Mill did not go on to make a profit. In 1902, it followed the way of the cotton cloth mill and was leased out to a private company.

Far from being deterred by these failures, Governor-general Chang attempted another large-scale operation in 1905 and 1906. This time, he openly acknowledged that the government had been wrong to intervene in the managerial process of modern industry, and he offered to sponsor reformed *kuan-shang ho-pan* companies whose management would be responsible to the shareholders. Chang also promised private investors that they would have a monopoly of production and marketing within Hupei and Hunan and a guaranteed profit of at least 5 per cent on their capital outlay during the first five years. Government control was to be limited to: first, official auditors making regular inspections of company books, and secondly, the government and the company getting together during the sixth year to decide on a reasonable annual rate of taxes.

Chang Chih-tung hoped that these generous terms would attract merchants to subscribe in force to his new joint-stock companies, and that little if any official funds would be needed. These hopes were dashed when the carpet factory, planned for an 800,000 taels capital, opened in 1906 with 300,000 taels of official funds and a mere 100,000 taels from private sources. Two years later, it was closed down for lack of working capital. Several other ventures, including a paper mill and glass, cement, needle, nail and leather factories, also failed after a very short existence. The general cause apparently was inexperienced and wasteful management. In the case of the needle and nail factory, it was opened in 1908 after having been equipped with the most modern machinery from Europe. The chief manager, however, did not possess any entrepreneurial background. Rather, he had once served as a tutor in Governor-general Chang's household, and probably owed his position to this connection. In 1910, after he had declared bankruptcy for the factory, he was indicted, convicted and imprisoned for having embezzled at least 50,000 taels of the company funds.[36]

Chang's promise of more equitable partnerships with the merchants remained only a promise. For one thing, Chang wanted everything to be near himself. His cotton cloth mill followed him from Canton to Wuchang. His iron smelting plant was located right next to his yamen, even though it was close to neither the coal nor the iron ore. Chang also could not

---

[35] Chang Chien, *Chang Chi-tzu chiu-lu* (Nine records of Chang Chien), ed. Chang Hsiao-jo, *Shih-yeh lu* (Record on industrial enterprise), 1.14.

[36] Wang Ching-yü, *Chung-kuo chin-tai kung-yeh shih tzu-liao*, 1.592, 613–20. *Hsiang-kang Hua-tzu jih-pao* (Chinese Mail, Hong Kong; hereafter *HTJP*), 1905: 6/2, 6/20.

delegate authority, but trusted only himself to maintain close supervision. Especially following the death of his assistant Ts'ai Hsi-yung in 1896, he had little faith in his official managers. Moreover, neither Ts'ai nor Sheng Ch'un-i appears to have been a capable manager.

Chang Chih-tung was also singularly unsuccessful in attracting any talented merchant to assist him. There was no comprador of distinction among his advisers. Probably this was inevitable, given his persistently low opinion of merchant ability. In this sense, Chang's approach to industrial development was in sharp contrast to Li Hung-chang's. Li attracted many good managers and administrators from both merchant and official ranks, and ably made use of their talents. On the other hand, the lack of assistants with the calibre of Sheng Hsuan-huai or Tong King-sing seriously contributed to the limited success Chang Chih-tung achieved as a promoter of modern industry.

Growing disenchantment

The growing reluctance of merchants to invest in officially sponsored modern enterprises during the late nineteenth century was due to more than their being given insufficient responsibility. When any of these companies failed, the provincial governments usually made official loans the priority claim on the company's remaining assets, leaving little for the merchant shareholders. In 1893, after having been in operation for more than ten years, the Silk Bureau in Chefoo went out of business. After it had met the government's claims fully, its official-managers offered the investors only 10 taels for every share for which they had paid 200 taels, and 20 taels if the additional 200 taels' second instalment had been paid up. Apparently this was done without much consultation with the investors, who according to Hsu Jun complained bitterly about these unfair proceedings. Hsu, who was no friend of Sheng Hsuan-huai, laid the blame on him, claiming that Sheng later took over the bureau and turned it into a profitable business. Hsu then commented: '[Official-managers] have strong authority, but lack a sense of obligation. How could they obtain the respect of others? There is nothing one can do. For [us merchants] to fight them would be like striking rocks with eggs. Truly we can do nothing.'[37]

One can cite more examples to show that officials themselves were well aware of the merchants' dissatisfaction. Governor-general Liu K'un-i, when asked to express his opinion on applying the *kuan-tu* formula to building railways, memorialized the throne in 1895 as follows:

If we restrict ourselves to the *kuan-tu shang-pan* formula, then nothing is achieved

[37] Hsu Jun, *Hsu Yü-chai tzu-hsu nien-p'u* (Hsu Jun's chronological autobiography), 73b.

except by the officials. When officials hold all authority and merchants are given none, this will not lead to success. When capital is collected from the merchants, and profit is distributed by the officials, then indeed the government has yet to acquire trust from those to whom investment invitations are extended. Moreover, even though enterprises such as the China Merchants' Steam Navigation Company and the Hua-sheng Cotton Spinning Mill have achieved commendable results, yet their management remains with the officials. Moreover, their profits have not been much. Merchants still feel they are set apart.[38]

Liu's analysis could also be applied to the *kuan-shang ho-pan* enterprises, for the two types were actually more or less the same.

Sheng Hsuan-huai was well aware of such complaints from merchants. Later in the same year in which Hsu Jun accused him of having unfairly treated the Chefoo Silk Bureau's investors, Sheng tried to work out a more equitable compensation for the shareholders of the Shanghai Cotton Cloth Mill after it had burnt down in October 1893. With the approval of Li Hung-chang, Sheng held back government claims on its 265,390 taels of official loans. He then offered to pay the merchants in cash from the mill's remaining assets and in the form of shares in the successor company – the Hua-sheng Spinning and Weaving Mill. As a result, the merchant share-holders received a cash refund at 20 per cent of their initial investment, and the rest in Hua-sheng shares. However, if Sheng had hoped that such apparent goodwill towards the merchant investors would bring them back with new capital for Hua-sheng, he was to be disappointed. The merchants remained sceptical, and since his small coterie of overworked business associates had access to only limited sources of capital, Hua-sheng remained under-capitalized. After a promising start, it ran consistently at a loss throughout its short existence to 1901. In that year, Sheng turned it into a private company after he had received the court's permission to declare all the company shares invalid, including those which had been issued in exchange for old shares of the Shanghai Cotton Cloth Mill.[39]

However, merchant sentiments towards merchant-official collaboration in modern industry were not totally negative, and this explains why this type of enterprise continued to be founded right up to the end of the dynasty and afterwards. If there was a good deal of disenchantment, there was also general awareness that official participation was needed in the face of foreign competition. Such a feeling of ambivalence was best exemplified by Cheng Kuan-ying, himself a merchant-manager in at least two of these enterprises. On the one hand, Cheng conceded that the merchants needed official protection because there was no commercial law or constitutional

[38] Cited in Li Kuo-ch'i, *Chung-kuo tsao-ch'i ti t'ieh-lu ching-ying* (China's early railway enterprises), 131.
[39] Hsu Jun, *Hsu Yü-chai tzu-hsu nien-p'u*, Sheng Hsuan-huai, *Sheng shang-shu Yü-chai*, 5.41–3.

guarantee to safeguard their rights and properties. He suggested, therefore, that the *kuan-tu shang-pan* or *kuan-shang ho-pan* formula was justifiable. On the other hand, Cheng felt that it was only a short-term solution; eventually a fair and enforceable law should be enacted to protect the merchants.

Cheng contended that bureaucratic corruption and administrative inefficiency had greatly reduced the profits of some firms and caused the failure of others. Referring to three profit-making *kuan-tu shang-pan* enterprises, the Imperial Telegraph Administration, the China Merchants' and the Kaiping mines, he exclaimed that if only they were run by merchants, 'their profits will know no bounds!'[40] Cheng also observed that the operations were too dependent on the whims of provincial official patrons. 'Even if one accepts the fact that Li Hung-chang is very enlightened and will not overtax merchant enterprises, the fact remains that Li cannot be the superintendent of trade for the northern ports forever.'[41]

Later on, writing in the early years of the republican era, Cheng became much more caustic towards the Ch'ing government's involvement in various industries. He accused the officials of 'inflicting losses on the merchants and promoting benefits for themselves' while they pretended to help the merchants. He recalled how the Imperial Telegraph Administration was nationalized during the late 1900s without proper compensation to its shareholders. He contrasted it with the Japanese government's policy where new and infant industries were given financial support and managerial personnel to tide them over their initial years. Cheng then related one specific case which he had learned of from a Japanese friend. The latter, who operated a copper company, was suffering such heavy losses during the first few years that he was about to declare bankruptcy. The government, however, stepped in to investigate, and after having dealt severely with those officers who were corrupt, helped the company with funds and management advice and general supervision. When it began to make a profit after a few years, the government relinquished all of its authority over the company and returned it to the merchant directors. Cheng implied that the Chinese government should have adopted such a model for its own industrial enterprises.[42]

Here, then, were widely disparate perspectives of what merchant-official collaboration ought to be. The merchants welcomed official encouragement and sponsorship. They would even accept, for the initial period at least, state control in the form of government loans and managerial direction. In contrast, Chang Chih-tung, Sheng Hsuan-huai and the other official sponsors had very different conceptions of official-merchant rela-

[40] Cheng Kuan-ying, *Sheng-shih wei-yen hou-pien*, 8.43–4.
[41] *Ibid*. 12.4a.   [42] *Ibid*. 8.56b–57.

tions in such a partnership. Because the state had little excess capital for these economic undertakings, the merchants' resources must be tapped and their capital coopted to work towards national goals. But modern enterprise, with all its usefulness in strengthening the Chinese nation vis-à-vis the West, was too important to be left solely in the hands of the merchants. Officials must retain control.

Given the state's traditional role in the Chinese economy, it would be hard to fault the officials' self-righteous perspective on state control. But in the process of maintaining such control, they went beyond Li Hung-chang's original vision of merely general supervision and aid. They went directly into management, and as official managers as well as private investors in their personal capacity, they had a natural tendency to confuse state and bureaucratic interests and to slide back from working for the nation to looking after their own personal interest. As more officials became involved in modern enterprises, these tendencies increased until they came to shape the style of industrial development in China.

CAMPAIGNS FOR PRIVATE ENTERPRISE

It would be hard to say whether bureaucratic control or under-capitalization was the more debilitating to the growth of modern enterprise during the late Ch'ing. The two issues were related. If sufficient capital were to be found – and it had to come from outside as well as inside the government – then something had to be done to ameliorate the stifling effects of bureaucratic control. Since 1873, appeals for public subscriptions of company shares led to poor results, for the merchants were wary of the official promoters' intentions.

After about 1900, however, a number of similar campaigns succeeded in raising large amounts of capital. A different climate of opinion allowed investors to pledge capital on the condition that the company would be privately managed (*shang-pan*). The central government, too, helped to raise public confidence by promulgating laws and regulations for incorporation of private companies. Even though these state measures often failed to work well in practice, they bolstered the private investors' claims to legal protection.

The biggest stimulus to the public's increasing support was, however, the rising political temper of the new century. Major groups of merchants in large cities formed their own associations to carry out political campaigns such as boycotts against foreign goods or to demand Chinese representation in the foreign-run Municipal Council of Shanghai.[43] These

[43] See, e.g., Mark Elvin, 'The administration of Shanghai 1905–1914', Edward J. M. Rhoads,

patriotic concerns about Western imperialism soon focused on the economic issue of foreign control over Chinese industry. Since the government seemed unwilling or unable to prevent foreign domination, politically conscious merchants and gentry now used this to justify their agitation for privately managed companies. These campaigns attained great size and strength because patriotism was reinforced by self-interest.

Private railways and economic nationalism

One campaign of great popularity was the movement to recover from foreign companies the rights in railway finance and construction.[44] Modern industry, though first promoted to make China strong, was being handed over to foreign capitalists because the state preferred to borrow money from foreign bankers and so maintain nominal state control over what in effect would be foreign-owned enterprises. Arguing in this manner, the activists among provincial gentry and merchants turned private management into a political issue. Their protest was no longer economic but political, a contest in which *shang-pan* was equated with preserving the nation's economic strength against foreign encroachment, while state sponsorship was seen as collusion with Western bankers. Complete, unfettered private management, free from state and foreign control, became an integral part of the rights recovery movement.

The Chinese state, however, had decided that railways, unlike a textile factory, were too strategic to be left to private entrepreneurs. During the 1890s, Chang Chih-tung, as the official supervising the first major Chinese railway, had argued passionately that railways affected the interest and sovereignty of the state. Private capital, he conceded, could supplement state or foreign loans, but the ultimate authority must remain with the officials.

The Canton–Hankow Railway provided the first major challenge to Chang's views. In 1904, merchant leaders of the Seventy-Two Guilds and the Nine Charitable Halls in Canton organized several well-attended meetings asking for the return to Chinese hands of the construction and financing rights for this railway. These rights had been given by the Chinese government to an American organization, the China Development Company. In Hankow, Chang Chih-tung supported, and probably even

'Merchant associations in Canton, 1895–1911', and Susan Mann Jones, 'The Ningpo *Pang* and financial power at Shanghai', all in Mark Elvin and G. William Skinner, eds. *The Chinese city between two worlds.*

[44] An equally popular movement similarly motivated and going on at the same time was the agitation to recover mining rights from foreign companies, see Li En-han, *Wan-Ch'ing ti shou-hui k'uang-ch'üan yun-tung* (The movement to recover mining rights in the late Ch'ing period).

instigated, a similar merchant and gentry-led recovery movement. The ostensible reasons for the flare-up of these local sentiments were the construction delays and the unauthorized sale of a controlling portion of the China Development Company's stock to a Belgian syndicate. The real motive, however, was genuine and increasing hostility towards foreign concessions and loans.

During 1905, control over the China Development Company was regained by another American company. But the campaign had acquired so much support from thousands of merchants, students and gentry attending dozens of vociferous meetings that the central government, fearing local insurrection, forced the Americans to accept a redemption agreement.

The Kwangtung provincial government tried to build the railway on its own by raising local taxes. After local gentry and merchant leaders agitated for private management, Governor-general Ts'en Ch'un-hsuan responded by arresting one gentry and one merchant leader. But this action backfired, early in 1906, by reactivating the thousands of students and shophands who had earlier joined in the many rallies of the rights recovery movement but had later withdrawn from the controversy over company funding and management. Now, by condemning the leaders of the smaller group advocating private management, Ts'en made their case against official control understandable and popular. Several more meetings followed, passing resolutions to deplore the governor's plans to levy surtaxes, organizing delegations of support to visit the imprisoned leaders, and making pledges to contribute money to fund a private railway company.[45]

Modern enterprises during the late Ch'ing had been unable to attract popular support through public subscription of shares because of their high cost. Since the 1870s, the several subscription efforts had been pricing their shares at 100 taels each. Since the average wage of a shophand at the time was $3 (or about 2.3 taels) per month – a sum sufficient to support a small family – 100 taels was a princely sum which only the very wealthy could afford. These meetings in 1906 attacked the traditional high price and argued that the huge sums required for railway building could come only from mass participation. Their decision was to offer a low-priced share payable in instalments. When they finally adopted $5 shares (about 4 taels), to be paid for in three instalments over twelve to eighteen months,

[45] *HTJP*, 1906: 1/9, 1/15; *South China Morning Post* (hereafter *SCMP*), 1906: 1/12, 1/15, 1/18. There is only sketchy documentation of these dramatic conflicts among officials, gentry and merchants, e.g., as collected in Mi Ju-ch'eng, comp. *Chung-kuo chin-tai t'ieh-lu shih tzu-liao* (Source materials on the history of railways in modern China), 3.1045–55. Ts'en Ch'un-hsuan said nothing about this episode in his autobiography *Lo-chai man-pi*. Much of the available record can be gleaned only from two contemporary newspapers, the *Hua-tzu jih-pao* and the *SCMP*, both of Hong Kong.

even penurious students could afford them. During February 1906, $1,648,788 was collected as first instalment payments. The campaign to raise $20 million as capital for a privately owned railway company was well under way.

This company, formally named the Kwangtung section of the Canton-Hankow Railway Company, petitioned Peking for *shang-pan* status. To keep up the pressure on the government, all the new pledges which kept pouring in from Cantonese merchants residing overseas, or from Hong Kong and other provinces, were conditional upon such a status.[46]

Neither the Peking nor the Canton authorities could go against such a powerful demonstration of popular support. In April 1906, Cheng Kuan-ying, the ex-comprador and industrialist, was elected by the organizing committee, composed of local guild and charitable hall leaders, to be the company's chief manager (*tsung-pan*). Official sanction of *shang-pan* status soon followed. By 21 June, Cheng was able to report that over $8.8 million had been received in first instalments. This was the largest amount of capital raised by any means in China up to this time.

But gaining private management rights did not end the controversy over control and direction of the company. During the next five years, the company was run as a *shang-pan* enterprise. But these five years were filled with continual crises. First, it was the legality of the elected officers. Cheng Kuan-ying's election as chief manager was challenged by some shareholders until he was forced to resign and was replaced by Liang Ch'eng, an official who had just completed his service as Chinese minister to Washington. Factionalism among the shareholders followed. A pervading sense of distrust among the directors led to a system of checks and balances, dividing up areas of responsibility so that the chief manager did not even have the authority to coordinate, much less to manage, the entire enterprise.[47]

All this contributed to the shareholders' militancy and public disenchantment. When allegations were made that the company accounts were not properly kept, and that corruption was rife among the officers, the provincial government had an opportunity to reassert control. In 1911, the central government nationalized all private and semi-private railways, partly because the Canton railway, like the other major private railway between Hankow and Szechwan, was a failure. At the time of the takeover, the Canton company had received some $16 million in paid-up capital, about $10 million of which had gone to build a mere forty-five miles of track. Inefficiency such as this, together with public disclosure of embezzlement by its officers, totally discredited this *shang-pan* company. National-

46 *SCMP*, 1906: 3/2, 3/4, 3/7, 3/10, 4/14. *HTJP*, 1906: 3/3, 3/5, 3/10, 3/19.
47 Cheng Kuan-ying, *Sheng-shih wei-yen hou-pien*, 9.46b–47, 61a–b, 74a–b.

ization brought forth protest. But most protesters were more agitated over the 60 per cent cash reimbursement of their capital than over the demise of private management.

The Shanghai–Hanchow–Ningpo Railway's record as another *shang-pan* company during the same years is strikingly similar.[48] In late 1907, after mounting a massive, at times violent, campaign, the local gentry and merchant leaders in Chekiang recovered the rights of construction from a British company, and raised capital by selling $5 shares to be subscribed in five annual instalments. The Chekiang Railway Company, one of the two provincial companies building a railway to traverse the south bank of the lower Yangtze, was soon hit by corrupt practices, shoddy engineering work, management squabbles and declining public support. T'ang Shou-ch'ien, a scholar-official with a reputation for being progressive, had been elected chief manager in 1905 on account of his persistently outspoken leadership in the rights recovery movement. Complaints that T'ang was crafty, unbending and arrogant were countered by praise of his championship of the constitutional movement and his ability to stand up to government encroachment.

In 1909, T'ang Shou-ch'ien offered to resign in order to appease his critics. But this action only provided his partisans with a chance to show their strength by raising a vigorous campaign to retain him. After he was thus reconfirmed, T'ang's abrupt dismissal a year later by an imperial decree once again raised doubts about the efficiency of private management if it could only be attained through mass ownership. Politically minded owners, who bought shares in order to resist Western economic imperialism, were prone to seize on their newly acquired rights as shareholders to intervene in company affairs, especially in matters involving the relationship between a private company and the state. The result was to politicize the mass-supported private management.

T'ang's dismissal in 1910 led massive shareholders' meetings in Shanghai to decide that no one, not even the emperor, could legally dismiss a company officer who had been properly elected. They cited Article 77 of the Company Law, promulgated by Peking a few years before, giving the rights of election and dismissal of company officers to each company's

---

[48] Largely on the foreign interest aspects of this railway, are E-tu Zen Sun, 'The Shanghai-Hangchow-Ningpo railway loan of 1908', *FEQ*, 10.2 (1950) 136–50; Madeleine Chi, 'Shanghai-Hangchow-Ningpo railway loan: a case study of the rights recovery movement', *MAS*, 7.1 (1973) 85–106; and En-han Li, 'The Chekiang gentry-merchants vs. the Peking court officials: China's struggle for recovery of the British Soochow-Hangchow-Ningpo railway concession, 1905–1911', *CYCT*, 3.1 (1972) 223–68. For contemporary accounts and documents see Mo Pei, ed. *Chiang-Che t'ieh-lu feng-ch'ao* (The storm over the Kiangsu–Chekiang railway), throughout the monthly journal *Tung-fang tsa-chih* (The eastern miscellany; hereafter *TFTC*), and Mi Ju-ch'eng, comp. *Chung-kuo chin-tai t'ieh-lu shih tzu-liao*, 3.999–1009.

board of directors. More meetings were held throughout September, some turning into mass demonstrations. One in Ningpo was attended by over ten thousand people. Backed by these popular expressions of support, the company approached the Chekiang governor, Tseng Yun, and the provisional provincial assembly (Tzu-i chü). The latter opined that no government could ignore its own statutory laws, especially at a time when the throne was encouraging constitutional government. Governor Tseng finally consented to transmit the resolution officially to Peking. The assembly had threatened to stop all its official business.

But the Ministry of Posts and Communications (Yu-ch'uan Pu) had already replied on 24 September, reiterating Chang Chih-tung's standard argument that railways involved rights of sovereignty (*kuo-ch'üan*), hence even those railway companies with *shang-pan* status remained tied to the government in a special relationship. Thus each of the chief and associate managers of the railway companies, after being elected, received their formal appointments from the ministry. The Yu-ch'uan Pu concluded that railway companies were 'state-controlled companies' (*kuan-chih kung-ssu*), and that the dismissal order would stand.[49]

The Chekiang Company's shareholders responded by sending a delegation to Peking, but the ministry's senior vice-president insisted that Article 77 was inoperative because T'ang owed his appointment ultimately to the emperor, who authorized it after the ministry had transmitted the wishes of the company shareholders. The emperor, therefore, had the authority also to remove him. At least for the railways, *shang-pan* was practically no different from *kuan-tu shang-pan* for the state retained the power to choose the senior officers.

A more crucial issue for both the Kwangtung and Chekiang railways was that of managerial style. Although Liang Ch'eng and T'ang Shou-ch'ien had very different personalities, both in the end involved their companies in bureaucratic practices. Liang fell prey to waste and inefficiency and finally doctored the company accounts for his personal benefit. T'ang championed the cause of provincial gentry interests and brought the company into conflict with central authority. As more became known about these two companies' mismanagement, more and more people came to view *shang-pan* not as a right to be won for the public good, but as a licence to enrich or to confer political power on company directors and managers. The Chekiang Railway Company retained its fuzzy *shang-pan* status for a while but in 1911 it too was taken over by the state. That neither railway became an enterprise truly run by merchants reflected the well-nigh

[49] *TFTC*, 'Chung-kuo ta-shih chi' (Major events in China), 7.9 (1910) 67–70; 7.10, 75–7; 7.11, 87, 94–5.

impossibility for major industry in late Ch'ing China to develop independently of bureaucratic connections.

The Mou-hsin Mill as a private enterprise

A few modern enterprises were able to avoid either official sponsorship or comprador management. They sprang from the resources of traditional merchants who had come to realize that machinery could be utilized for greater profit and higher productivity. The first successful venture of this kind was the Mou-hsin Flour Mill.[50] Begun in 1901, this mill owed its origin to two brothers, Jung Tsung-ching and Jung Te-sheng of Wusih in Kiangsu. Although the family had some minor official affiliations, the Jungs were not members of the gentry or official class. The father, a government clerk, sent the elder son, Tsung-ching, to a blacksmith's shop to be an apprentice and the younger one to school. The latter preferred to learn a trade; ultimately, both spent three years as apprentices in two local banks (ch'ien-chuang) in Shanghai.

Upon completing their apprenticeship, Te-sheng took up a clerical post in a government office, while Tsung-ching continued to work in a Shanghai bank. During 1897–8, while in Shanghai together, the senior Jung and the two brothers decided to invite a few friends to open a local bank of their own. The father died soon after the bank was opened, and as it was making little profit the other investors sold all their shares to the Jung brothers. In about 1900, the brothers became interested in flour milling. Jung Te-sheng had discovered that although there was a growing market for flour, it was still tax exempt because flour was regarded as an imported item strictly for foreigners' consumption. There was little competition, only four mills having been founded: one each in Tientsin and Wuhu, and two in Shanghai of which one was American-owned and the other owned by Sun To-shen who was a son of Grand Councillor Sun Chia-nai. The Jung brothers, however, were complete strangers (wai-hang) to modern industry, not knowing what machinery was needed and how much the whole operation would cost. None of the mills they approached would allow them to inspect its plant. They made inquiries at one foreign firm importing American machinery, and were told that they would need some 80,000 taels for machinery alone in order to start a small-sized factory. Finally, they found some British-made motors to run four French-made stone grinders. Altogether, these cost them less than 20,000 taels.

[50] For Mou-hsin's early years and the Jung family background, see Ch'en Chen and Yao Lo, *Chung-kuo chin-tai kung-yeh shih tzu-liao, ti-i-chi* (Source materials on the history of modern industry in China, 1st collection), 1.372–6, 381–2.

This was a far larger sum than the Jung brothers could put together. Fortunately, a family patron, Chu Chung-fu, stepped in to help. Chu had just lost his minor official post, and was looking around for some suitable investment. He, together with a friend, now contributed half of the new company's 30,000 taels of capital. The two Jung brothers provided one-fifth or 6,000 taels, while several of their relatives made up the remaining 9,000 taels.

The total of 30,000 taels, however, was found to be inadequate even before the mill was launched. In 1902, the Jung brothers turned over practically all of their bank's profit of 10,000 taels to the mill, making themselves the largest partners. In the following year, they increased their shares further when new profits from their bank allowed them to buy all of Chu's shares. Chu had decided to give up his partnership, for he was leaving Shanghai in order to take up another official post. Reorganization of the mill followed. The paid-up capital was increased to 50,000 taels with the help of other friends. The name of the company was changed from Pao-feng to Mou-hsin. As they completed these arrangements, the Russo-Japanese War began. There was an increased demand for flour, and the mill started to make money.

With success, the company decided to try something better than the original stone grinders. In 1905, it acquired six new British steel grinders at a bargain price. The model was new and the British exporters were anxious to try them out in China. They turned out to be a great success, for the improved and increased product in 1905 yielded to the mill a profit of 66,000 taels for that year. This profit, together with more earnings from the bank, was again ploughed back into the mill. On 11 January 1905, when the Mou-hsin Flour Mill became the fourth enterprise to register with the central government as a private corporation of limited liability, it had already announced its intention to raise its capital to 60,000 taels.[51]

The Jung brothers then tried to branch out into another field of modern enterprise. In 1906 and 1907, they invited friends and relatives to set up a cotton mill in their home town of Wusih. The investment capital came from their flour mill profit for these years. The market for cotton fell, however, following the end of the Russo-Japanese War. Faced with an uncertain future, they quickly withdrew and transferred their money back to the flour mill. They then waited until 1915 before they launched a second, and this time successful, venture into the cotton spinning industry. Meanwhile, their flour enterprise continued to prosper. In 1908, they established a second factory in Wusih. It was expanded in 1910 and again in 1914. With

[51] Nung-kung-shang pu t'ung-chi ch'u, *Nung-kung-shang pu t'ung-chi piao, ti-i-tz'u* (Statistical tables of the Ministry of Agriculture, Industry and Commerce, 1st issue), 5.1b.

the outbreak of World War I, flour imports ceased and Jung's mills, branching into Shanghai and Hankow, grew by leaps and bounds until they averaged 8,000 bags a day in 1914. By 1929, the Jung brothers controlled some twelve factories, which turned out 100,000 bags a day, representing one-sixth of China's total flour output produced by machine-run factories.

The Jung brothers were the first traditional merchants to make a successful switch into modern industry with a bare minimum of official sponsorship and financial support. They had no comprador experience, and built up their mill from money they had saved from their local bank, as well as from the mill's profit which they ploughed back consistently.

They were, however, not without some help from bureaucratic sources. First, Chu Chung-fu's funds were crucial in that initial period when the brothers had very limited resources. More important, Chu's participation probably gave the venture the needed lift of prestige and assurance so that the Jung brothers could persuade their friends and relatives to put in their investments.

Secondly, they ran into bureaucratic opposition while building their plant. Local gentry, supported by officials, complained about its tall chimney which, by the rules of geomancy, might bring calamity upon the community. Although available records do not tell what role Chu, a minor official, played in the negotiations that followed, it would be safe to assume that he helped considerably in drawing up the final settlement, which allowed the plant to be built with only a few restrictions. Thirdly, there was the minor bureaucratic background of the Jung family itself. Both the father and the younger brother had been minor bureaucrats for some time. The money they so acquired presumably made up some, if not most, of their initial investment in the local bank and then in the flour mill. After these 'bureaucratic influences' are taken into account, one must conclude that the success of the Mou-hsin Flour Mill represents a new departure for traditional merchants. However, Mou-hsin had rather insignificant capital – tens of thousands of taels as opposed to the 2 or 3 million taels of the larger textile mills supervised or managed by officials. In the political context of the time, it was just not possible to attract a large amount of capital or run a large modern enterprise without close official cooperation.

The only true exceptions were a small number of large modern enterprises founded at this time in Hong Kong by overseas Cantonese merchants. The three major ones were The Sincere Company opened by Ma Ying-piao with $25,000 in 1900, the Wing On Company by Kuo Lo and his brother Kuo Ch'üan with $150,000 in 1907, and the Nanyang Brothers Tobacco Company by Chien Chao-nan and his brother Chien Yü-chieh with

$100,000 in 1906. Both The Sincere Company and Wing On were depart-
ment stores modelled on similar ones in Australia where Ma and the two
Kuo brothers had first made their money. The Chien family had business
connections in Japan, Vietnam, Thailand, Singapore and other parts of
South-East Asia. Thus all of them owed their entrepreneurship to forces
outside the traditional society. It was not until 1912 that The Sincere
Company opened a branch in Canton, then a second one in Shanghai two
years later. The other two companies followed until all three became major
private enterprises during the 1920s. However, their initial success in the
last years of the Ch'ing took place outside the Chinese political order.[52]

New administrative regulations and legal codes

The idea that privately managed enterprise had a role to play in the industrial development of the nation led to efforts for official protection of
private entrepreneurial activities. New government bureaux at the capital
drew up administrative regulations and laws to define merchant status, to
incorporate private companies, to establish patent rights and bankruptcy
proceedings, and so on. The first comprehensive regulations, published on
21 January 1904, were 'General Rules for Merchants' (Shang-jen t'ung-li) in
nine articles and 'Company Law' (Kung-ssu shang-lü) in 131 articles. These
were followed by laws on company registration (1905), bankruptcy (1906)
and patent rights (1906).[53] Of these the Company Law was by far the most
significant, for it recognized five broad types of commercial and industrial
enterprises: (1) partnerships of two or more persons with unlimited
liability; (2) similar partnerships with limited liability; (3) joint-stock companies of seven or more shareholders with unlimited liability; (4) similar
joint-stock companies with limited liability; and (5) sole proprietorships
with unlimited liability. In 1904, a bureau was established to register these
companies.

The result was impressive. Some 272 companies with a combined
authorized capital of approximately 100 million taels registered with the
bureau between 1904 and 1908. This figure was, however, exaggerated, for
probably only half or less of the authorized capital was ever paid up. Nor
were all the companies modern enterprises. Out of the 272 companies, 44
were traditional single-owner pawnshops, local banks, Chinese pharma-

52 Sincere Co., Hsien-shih kung-ssu erh-shih-wu chou-nien chi-nien tse (The Sincere Co.: twenty-fifth
anniversary). Wing On Co., Hsiang-kang Yung-an yu-hsien kung-ssu erh-shih-wu chou-nien chi-nien lu
(The Wing On Co. Ltd. of Hong Kong: twenty-fifth anniversary). Chung-kuo k'o-hsueh
yuan Shang-hai ching-chi yen-chiu so et al. Nan-yang hsiung-ti yen-ts'ao kung-ssu shih-liao
(Historical materials concerning the Nanyang Brothers Tobacco Company).
53 Nung-kung-shang pu, Nung-kung-shang pu hsien-hsing chang-ch'eng (Current regulations of the
Ministry of Agriculture, Industry and Commerce).

ceutical companies or other wholesale and retail trading firms. The bulk, 153 out of 272, however, consisted of modern joint-stock companies with limited liability. They represented a predominant share of the total capital accumulation. Indeed, they made up practically all of China's modernized enterprises by 1908.[54]

The Ch'ing government also initiated elaborate systems of official awards. The first regulations emphasized engineering and craftsmanship skills. Adopted as part of the 'Hundred Days reform' in 1898, they were probably never acted upon. A second set, published in 1903, aimed at investors and promoters. But these too proved ineffective, for the smallest amount an individual was allowed to invest or promote in order to win an award was half a million Chinese dollars. At such a high figure, very few could qualify. Moreover, the status of 'adviser (*i-yuan*), fifth class' would have been downright demeaning to anyone who had the social prestige to raise such an amount in the first place. However, between 1906 and 1907, a comprehensive system of awards was finally set up. Three categories were offered: first, to mastercraftsmen and inventive mechanics; secondly, to promoters of industry at greatly scaled down amounts of capital raised; and thirdly, to investors, including investiture in a life peerage for really outstanding contributors.

The actual number of awards handed out remained small. As the *Tung-fang tsa-chih* pointed out, Chinese entrepreneurs did not want brevet ranks or empty titles, but real and effective means of protection from the government.[55] Since both ranks and titles could still be bought, and were in fact bought by merchants in large numbers, these awards were hardly awe-inspiring. Worse than that, the sums required were still too high. To become a baron (*nan*), third class, one had to invest $10 million. Little wonder, then, that no one was created a life peer. But though the whole system of awards was ineffectual, it still showed the central government's positive attitude towards modern industry and its willingness to adopt the Western practice of encouraging merchants by official recognition.

PEKING AND THE PROVINCES: THE CONFLICT OVER LEADERSHIP

The awards, like the legal codes, emanated from Peking. These were central government functions. They made the local merchant more aware of Peking and enhanced the latter's ability to direct national economic

[54] Calculated from data in the *Nung-kung-shang pu t'ung-chi piao, ti-i-tz'u, ts'e* 5; also its *ti-erh-tz'u* (2nd issue), *ts'e* 5.
[55] *TFTC*, 'Shang-wu' (Commerce), 2.1 (1905) 2–3.

policies. Whereas before 1900 the central government had not developed new institutional means to lead industrial development, thereafter Peking tried to move against provincial domination by building new institutions and launching new programmes.

Regional direction of industrial growth laboured under inherent limitations. First, provincial officials usually rotated from post to post. The efforts of industrial promoters were often repudiated by those who succeeded them. Secondly, although the central government failed to finance large industries of its own, it retained the authority to approve how provincial revenues were to be distributed. Once the central government had given its sanction, however, the actual disbursements and all the patronage that went with them were arranged under the provincial leaders' authorization. This diffused the authority between the central and provincial governments and made it impossible to follow priorities on the national level so that industries could develop in an orderly manner. On the other hand, given the progressively worsening quality of their personnel during the late Ch'ing, the ministries in Peking probably could not have done better than the provinces did.

New ministries at the capital

The rudimentary commercial code for merchants and companies was the product of fundamental reform in the central bureaucracy. First, the traditional Six Ministries (Liu Pu) were streamlined and new ones added (see chapter 7). Secondly, there was a new ideological commitment to acquire new areas of management and assert central government authority. Thus in the area of commerce and industry, Peking organized a new ministry, set up branch bureaux in the provinces, and encouraged merchants to form chambers of commerce.

The notion of a ministry of commerce had been expressed by prominent treaty-port merchants like Cheng Kuan-ying ever since the 1880s, but it received no serious consideration until Sheng Hsuan-huai took an interest in about 1902. Sheng's concern reflected not only his understanding that a modern economy required national direction, but also his own uneasy relations with the provincial leaders of industry. Although successful as an official supervisor of several major companies, Sheng had never been high enough in the official hierarchy to have an independent power base either in the provinces or at Peking. He had begun his career under Li Hung-chang, and when Li's power declined after 1895, Chang Chih-tung was his new patron. But Chang preferred to keep his industrial projects under close supervision, which made his patronage often unreliable. In 1902,

Sheng was a vice-director of the Imperial Clan Court and associate imperial commissioner for negotiating commercial treaties, a middle-rank central-government official. He suggested launching a new central ministry to direct industrial and trade affairs.

Sheng's proposal coincided with similar recommendations by two Manchu princes. The second Prince Ch'un, the emperor's half-brother, and Tsai-chen, the son of Prince Ch'ing, had just returned from separate tours overseas, evidently impressed by the Chinese merchants who had entertained them. Although there was some opposition led by Grand Councillor Jung-lu, it petered out when he died in April 1903. Five months later, the Ministry of Commerce (Shang Pu) was officially launched.[56]

At first, morale was high in this new ministry. In official ranking, it was placed above the six traditional ministries and second only to the foreign office. It was given a broad jurisdiction, and authorized to take over all the major commercial and industrial programmes which had been set up among the traditional ministries and agencies. It also planned to set up bureaux directly responsible to it in the provinces. The president was Tsai-chen. His father, Prince Ch'ing, was writing up a general reform of state finance for the newly formed Committee on Finance (Ts'ai-cheng ch'u). It was even rumoured that Prince Ch'ing intended to put this powerful committee under the new ministry. The press reported that Peking bookstores were denuded of books on industry and international commerce; bureaucrats had bought them all up to prepare themselves for the new ministry's staff entrance examinations.

But the Ministry of Commerce failed to live up to these expectations. Where conflicts occurred, it did not succeed in getting the other ministries or agencies to give up their jurisdiction. For example, the imperial commissions for commercial affairs, for commercial treaties and for railways all went on as before, independent of the new Shang Pu.[57] The ministry was, moreover, poorly financed; its major source of income was the interest on maritime customs deposits before they were disbursed for the Boxer indemnity payments. Since the rate of interest, as well as the length of time most deposits stayed in the bank, varied from year to year, the ministry spent more time making up new funding proposals than on new industry programmes.[58] Most crucial to the ministry's failure, however, was the inept leadership of Tsai-chen and his associates. Tsai-chen had acquired

---

[56] News about the preparations of the ministry appeared regularly in the *HTJP*, see e.g., 1903: 3/23, 5/7, 7/18, 8/8, 9/26, 10/10, 10/31, 11/13, 12/30.

[57] Ch'ien Shih-fu, comp. *Ch'ing-chi hsin-she chih-kuan nien-piao* (Chronological tables of the newly established offices of the late Ch'ing period), 68, 71.

[58] For some of these proposals, see *HTJP*, 10/10/1903; 1904: 2/9, 7/6, 8/13; 1905: 2/24, 5/31; 1909: 10/16, 11/8; also *TFTC*, 'Chi-tsai' (Reports and documents), 6.9 (1909) 430.

great notoriety as a dissolute and corrupt man. In May 1907, he was forced to resign over allegations that he had accepted from another official a high-priced singing girl for himself and a large bribe of 100,000 taels for his father Prince Ch'ing.[59] Wu T'ing-fang, a British-trained barrister and diplomat who had helped with the ministry's organization and regulations, stayed for just four months as its senior vice-president in 1903. Wu was able and honest, while his replacement for the next three years, Ch'en Pi, was another official with a reputation of corruption.

In the general overhaul of 1906, the Shang Pu was drastically reorganized. Its jurisdictional claims over railways, shipping, telegraphs and the postal service went to a new Ministry of Posts and Communications (Yu-ch'uan Pu). Since these communication industries accounted for most of the capital – especially from foreign loans – available for development at the time, the reorganized ministry, renamed Ministry of Agriculture, Commerce and Industry (Nung-kung-shang Pu), was left with little to manage. In 1907, it tried to retrieve its jurisdiction over the China Merchants' Company. The Yu-ch'uan Pu claimed, however, that shipping should be under its jurisdiction. The Nung-kung-shang Pu argued that the company was under merchant management and therefore within its sphere. They finally allowed the Yu-ch'uan Pu to supervise the company's transportation policies, such as operating routes, and the Nung-kung-shang Pu to supervise its business operations.[60]

It is still not clear why responsibility for directing the nation's modern enterprises was gerrymandered into two ministries. The chief beneficiary appears to have been Yuan Shih-k'ai, who assumed various degrees of control over the Yu-ch'uan Pu between 1907 and 1911. Thus, until Sheng Hsuan-huai became its president in 1911, the ministry was headed by a series of Yuan's protégés, Ch'en Pi, Hsu Shih-ch'ang and T'ang Shao-i; while its powerful railway department was at all times headed by another protégé, Liang Shih-i. This was not a simple clash between central and provincial interests. In September 1907, both Yuan and Chang Chih-tung, recalled to the capital from their provincial posts, were appointed grand councillors. Possibly by concentrating the communication industries – at this time mostly railways – into one ministry, the central government was aiming at a new concerted effort in railway development. Railway management had a special appeal for Peking – not only because of its economic and strategic importance, but also because of the large foreign loans needed to finance construction.[61] Probably Yuan and Chang were moved to the

[59] See Shen Yun-lung, 'Chang-wo wan-Ch'ing cheng-ping chih I-k'uang' (Prince Ch'ing: wielder of political power towards the end of the late Ch'ing period), in his *Hsien-tai cheng-chih jen-wu shu-p'ing*, 2.73–4.   [60] TFTC, 'Chi-tsai', 5.10 (1908) 93.
[61] See En-han Li, 'Chekiang gentry-merchants vs. Peking Court Officials'.

Grand Council partly to make use of their long experience and interest in railways. In 1908, Chang was also appointed director-general of the Canton–Hankow and Szechwan–Hankow railways. However, if Peking had hoped to seize the initiative in railway management, its tactics failed again. Neither Yuan nor Chang could hold the provincial gentry and prominent merchants in line.

Responses from the provinces

Provincial governors were understandably hostile to the new plans to set up ministerial branch offices in provincial territory. However, since Peking had no additional resources to use, provincial government leaders responded by offering token compliance in a variety of ways. As the ministries tried to impose their new agencies at the provincial level, the provinces pushed forward their own institutions and offered to put them under Peking's nominal control. For example, early in 1904, with the court's approval, President Tsai-chen proposed to set up an entirely new bureaucratic network of Commercial Affairs Bureaux (Shang-wu chü) to serve his Ministry of Commerce in the provinces. Provincial authorities responded that their commercial affairs bureaux already existed to perform such functions. In fact, Chang Chih-tung had started the first such bureau in 1896 to plan modern economic policies, but had soon used it to raise industrial capital and secure loans. Chang's example was followed in other provincial capitals until these bureaux came to be generally disliked by the merchants. For some time in 1903 and 1904, the two major bureaux in Canton and Shanghai were forced to shut down because of their unpopularity.[62]

During the summer of 1904, the ministry succumbed to the provincial wishes. In August, the existing commercial affairs bureaux were formally designated to be the ministry's branch offices to direct all commercial and industrial development in the provinces. Each would be headed by a commissioner for commercial affairs (shang-wu i-yuan) selected by the governor-general and governor, but approved and appointed by the ministry. The commissioner would have the rank of prefect or expectant circuit intendant (taotai) and must be conversant with commercial and industrial affairs, make periodic reports, compile statistics, conduct investigations, and provide protection to local and returned merchants. He was allowed direct access to the ministry in writing, but a copy of his reports must go to the offices of the governor-general and the governor.[63] The ministry thus got

---

[62] Chang Chien, Chang Chi-tzu chiu-lu, Cheng-wen lu (Political record), 1.19a–b. Wang Ching-yü, Chung-kuo chin-tai kung-yeh shih tzu-liao, 1.596–7.
[63] Ta-Ch'ing Kuang-hsu hsin fa-ling (New statutes and decrees of the Ch'ing dynasty in the Kuang-hsu period), 16.36–7.

only the face-saving device of appointing the commissioners, while the provinces kept the actual power by selecting their own candidates and receiving copies of their reports to the ministry.

This arrangement led to the opening of many more bureaux. By the end of 1908, forty-four commissioners had been appointed, but the ministry soon discovered that they were not responsive to its instructions. The following administrative manoeuvres between Peking and the provincial capitals showed both the ministry's plight and its ineffectiveness. By late 1904, the ministry was already complaining to the throne that the provinces were choosing commissioners of commercial affairs who had no knowledge of commerce and industry. 'Although many governors-general and governors are conscientious in selecting good men [for the posts], many others regard them as routine appointments [for anyone on their staff].'[64] It requested the throne to order the governors-general to be more careful. This showed the difficulty. To enforce its directives upon a non-complying provincial government, a central government ministry had to resort to imperial authority. The ministry's founders had hoped it would be able to accomplish more in the provinces than the traditional ministries had, but unfortunately the new ministry arrived on the scene at a time when the central government was becoming more dependent on the provinces for new sources of revenue to pay off national debts.

In the summer of 1905, the Ministry of Commerce complained again to the throne that the branch bureaux did not carry out its orders. While the ministry had taken the initiative in settling many bankruptcy claims made on defaulting local banks in Kiangsu, Kiangsi and Shantung, it had been largely excluded from one case in Shanghai, and other provinces had 'refused even to acknowledge receipt of letters from us for the last four to seven months. As for our telegrams, they were met with similar delaying tactics.'[65] Some time later a contributor to the ministry's *Commercial Gazette* expressed the general frustration: in trying to protect merchants, the ministry could do nothing unless the provincial governors-general and their subordinates enforced its policies.[66]

However, these conflicts between the central and provincial bureaucracies were often beyond the control of the governors and governors-general. After all, Peking still retained effective control over appointments, dismissals and reassignments of all regular provincial officials. Especially during the last few years of the Ch'ing, most provincial governors were in fact hand-picked by the corrupt Prince Ch'ing and owed him favours and

[64] *TFTC*, 'Shang-wu', 1.11 (1904) 119–20.
[65] *TFTC*, 'Shang-wu', 2.9 (1905) 88–90.
[66] Wang Yu-ling, 'Shang-pu chih tse-jen' (The responsibility of the Ministry of Commerce), *Shang-wu kuan-pao*, 7 (1906) 1–4.

loyalty. Much provincial non-compliance was due to the complex relations between governors, the clerks and tax collectors of the permanent staff, and the provincial and local gentry who controlled economic enterprises and even public functions like taxation. It was the gentry and minor bureaucrats at all levels – not merely the governors or their official associates – who were the real beneficiaries of the growth of regional and local power.[67]

In 1907, the reorganized Ministry of Agriculture, Industry and Commerce tried again to control the bureaux, which had been reorganized into Bureaux for Agricultural, Commercial and Industrial Affairs (Nung-kung-shang-wu chü), with a rearrangement of departments to correspond with those in the ministry. In 1908, more progress was made when the new bureaux were put on the same level as the provincial salt or police administrations, and headed by regular officials with the title of 'intendant for the encouragement of industries' (ch'üan-yeh tao, 'industrial taotai'). By imperial decree, the intendant was responsible to both the parent ministry and the Ministry of Posts and Communications. Presumably, as a regular and senior provincial official, he was no longer selected entirely by the provincial authorities. By the end of 1908, nine intendants had been appointed.

While this seems to have been a victory for the Ministry, there is no evidence that after 1908 it had any great impact on the provinces. Several factors may account for this. First, it lost a good deal of its zest or sense of mission. The new president succeeding Tsai-chen in 1907 was another imperial clansman, P'u-t'ing, who served without much political backing or imagination to the end of the dynasty. Secondly, during these last years, the court was preoccupied with its own factional struggles, which apparently led senior provincial officials to identify their interests more and more with the provinces in which they held office. For example, Chou Shan-p'ei, a Chekiangese, was the intendant for industry in Szechwan from October 1908 to the summer of 1911. When the crisis came over railway nationalization, he opposed the central government's policy.[68]

Finally, Peking's failure in industry was only part of a further deterioration of central authority over the provinces. The throne, by permitting expression of popular sentiment through representative assemblies in the provinces, had hoped to bring the local gentry and gentry-merchants more to its side. But the result was to unbalance even further an already tenuous

[67] For an analysis of the growth of regional and local power in the hands of government clerks and local gentry, see Kwang-Ching Liu, 'The limits of regional power in the late Ch'ing period: a reappraisal', Ch'ing-hua hsueh-pao, NS, 10.2 (1974), 207–23 (Chinese text and nn., pp. 176–207).

[68] See Chou Shan-p'ei, Hsin-hai Ssu-ch'uan cheng-lu ch'in-li chi (An eyewitness account of the struggle for the Szechwan railway in 1911).

relationship between the gentry elite and the regular bureaucracy. The authority of provincial government became so eroded that when the Revolution of 1911 came, most governors simply had to follow the gentry's lead or run for their lives.

THE EMERGENCE OF ENTREPRENEURIAL OFFICIALS

The failure of both the *kuan-tu shang-pan* and *kuan-shang ho-pan* experiments to attract merchant investment in modern enterprise resulted from the inability of official promoters like Li Hung-chang and Chang Chih-tung to convince investors that their interests would not be sacrificed by official managers. By the 1900s, the merchants' response was loud and clear: leave us our unless we are full partners. On the other hand, the inability of private individuals or groups to set up large-scale enterprises at this time demonstrated that merchants by themselves were still too weak and disunited to lead China to industrialization. In the end, with the official promoters unwilling or unable to relinquish control, a partial way out was found in new arrangements which totally eschewed government sponsorship or left it purely *pro forma*.

The key was the emergence of official-entrepreneurs. The late Ch'ing reappraisal of the role of commerce and industry had already made modern enterprise ideologically respectable. Officials who at first did little more than exercise general supervision, began to invest their own money, took on managerial functions and ended up making entrepreneurial decisions. This metamorphosis from official to official-entrepreneur was exemplified most clearly by Sheng Hsuan-huai. But Sheng kept his management of industrial enterprises subsidiary to his dominant concern for success in the world of officialdom. He favoured bureaucratic manipulation at the expense of sound business practice. He was successful in those enterprises where he clearly enjoyed a monopoly or massive official subsidies; he often failed where there was competition.[69]

The main reason for preferring sound business practices was that by the 1900s, some official-entrepreneurs had begun to raise most or all of their capital from themselves or their friends, doing it in their private individual capacities, without formal government sponsorship. Since profit and loss now affected them personally, it became easier to separate their bureaucratic functions from their entrepreneurial roles. As managers and owners who were also directly in charge of, or in a position to influence, government policy, they no longer required formal official sponsorship to protect their

[69] For a different interpretation of Sheng's priorities, see Nakamura Tadashi, 'Shimmatsu seiji to kanryō shihon: Sei Sen-kai no yakuwari o megutte' (Late Ch'ing politics and bureaucratic capital, with reference to Sheng Hsuan-huai's role), in *Chūgoku kindaika no shakai kōzō*, 34.

enterprises from official exploitation. Two middle-rank officials, both taotais of Shanghai, seem to have pioneered this development when they quietly joined with merchants to invest in the Hua-hsin Spinning and Weaving Mill in Shanghai around 1890. Li Hung-chang, whose Shanghai Cotton Cloth Mill had monopoly rights over that entire region, could have protested, but he remained silent. He had presumably given his unofficial blessing, for the two officials involved, Taotais Kung Chao-yuan and Nieh Ch'i-kuei, together with a gentry-merchant banker, Yen Hsin-hou, were Li's protégés.[70]

The Hua-hsin Mill, after some initial losses, went on to become a profitable venture during the 1900s. Nieh Ch'i-kuei, who had been promoted to a governorship, then bought out the mill's other shareholders and gave it to his two sons to run. There is strong evidence that Nieh used official funds rather than his own to pay for his initial shares. Such a transfer by officials of public funds into private capital was quite common. Hua-hsin's radical departure from the usual *kuan-tu* or *kuan-shang ho-pan* arrangements gave the word *kuan* a new meaning: instead of 'government' or the 'corporate body of officialdom', it now meant an individual official. Thus Hua-hsin was in fact a private enterprise in which official and merchant shareholders collaborated as individuals. It needed no formal official ties because the officials among its investors assured it of official protection.

In the following decade, official-entrepreneurs, by combining roles as investor, manager and official sponsor, were able to provide modern enterprise with state protection without its stultifying control.

Chou Hsueh-hsi and Chang Chien as official-entrepreneurs

Chou Hsueh-hsi, whose father, Chou Fu, rose from provincial governor of Shantung to governor-general of Liang-Kiang and then of Liang-Kwang during the 1900s, began his official career under Yuan Shih-k'ai around 1900. Impressed by Chou's skill in economic affairs, Yuan promoted him rapidly, from expectant to substantive taotai, then salt commissioner, and finally in 1907 as Chihli's provincial judicial commissioner. In 1906, as part of his general duties to supervise Chihli's industrial development, he headed a committee set up to organize a mining company, and then became its chief manager.[71]

[70] On the Hua-hsin Mill and the Nieh family, see the compilation taken from the company archives and eyewitness accounts, *Heng-feng sha-ch'ang ti fa-sheng fa-chan yü kai-tsao* (The origin, development and reconstruction of the Heng-feng Spinning Mill), and Nieh Tseng Chi-fen, *Ch'ung-te lao-jen pa-shih tzu-ting nien-p'u* (Chronological autobiography of Nieh Tseng Chi-fen at age eighty).

[71] For Chou's biography, see Chou Shu-chen, *Chou Chih-an hsien-sheng pieh-chuan* (An unofficial

The structure of the Lanchou Official Mining Company Ltd. was a blend between a private corporation and a government-supervised enterprise. Probably because litigation was still going on between the Chinese government and the British-controlled Kaiping Mining Company nearby, Chou decided to call it a *kuan-tu shang-pan* enterprise with the state contributing a portion of its capital. However, there was to be no official supervisor or director-general (*tu-pan*), the title used for the head of a *kuan-tu* organization since the 1880s. Instead, control of the company rested in a board of fifteen directors, two of whom would be the chief manager (*tsung-li*) and the associate manager (*hsieh-li*). To ensure effective control, each manager was required to hold at least 2,000 shares, while each of the other thirteen directors and the two additional auditors were to hold at least 1,000 shares.[72] At 100 taels a share, this meant that these seventeen officers held a minimum of 19,000 shares or 1,900,000 taels. As the company's capital at its opening in 1908 was 5 million taels (three-fifths of which were paid up), this represented close to 40 per cent of all shares. When the government's shares of 500,000 taels or 10 per cent were added, the officers and the government together held a theoretical majority at shareholders' meetings.

The major investors also had the right to multiple votes – one vote for every 50 shares up to a total of twenty-five votes. Moreover, only those who had invested 5 shares, or 500 taels, might introduce proposals, and those with 50 shares, or 5,000 taels, might vote on resolutions. Thus, small investors who bought fewer than 5 shares had no voice. Chou's formula made certain that the number of major investors would be kept small and that they alone would decide on policies and run the company. Although we have only a partial list of the seventeen original directors and officers, the nine names that we have show that they were all officials serving under Yuan Shih-k'ai, that they were Chou's friends and that they shared common geographical origins like Anhwei (Chou's native province) or Honan (Yuan Shih-k'ai's).

The Chee Hsin Cement Company, Chou's other major industry, was structured and managed in much the same way as the Lanchou mines.[73] As a private corporation, however, Chee Hsin did not have any state capital,

biography of Chou Hsueh-hsi) and Howard Boorman, ed. *Biographical dictionary of Republican China*, 1.409–13.

[72] Carlson, *Kaiping mines*. Chou Shu-chen, *Chou Chih-an hsien-sheng pieh-chuan*, 33–40.

[73] The primary sources on Chee Hsin are the compilation of the company archives Nan-k'ai ta-hsueh Ching-chi hsi, *Ch'i-hsin yang-hui kung-ssu shih-liao* (Historical materials on the Chee Hsin Cement Company) and Kan Hou-tz'u, comp. *Pei-yang kung-tu lei-tsuan hsu-pien* (Categorized collection of documents from the office of the Commissioner of Trade for the northern ports, continued), *chüan* 19. A recent study in English is Albert Feuerwerker, 'Industrial enterprise in twentieth-century China: the Chee Hsin Cement Company', in *AMCH*, 304–41.

only a 400,000-tael loan from the Tientsin Official Bank which the company later repaid. The company, consistently making good profits, was never without adequate funding. Chou raised the authorized 1 million taels within the first year. His support came largely from the same group of associates who were supporting his mines. In 1912, each company share was split into two. The company then requested an additional capital of $1\frac{1}{2}$ million taels for development and expansion. To ensure the continued domination of the small group of officers, half of the new shares were reserved for the original stockholders, with options to buy in amounts according to the size of their holdings. The other half was offered, not to the general public, but to the provincial government of Chihli and the various provincial railway companies which used the company's products. But the company files show no investment from these sources in the later years. It is likely that the entire $1\frac{1}{2}$ million taels were absorbed by the same shareholders and their friends. Similarly, when the company asked for another 300,000 taels shortly thereafter to set up a northern branch of the factory, it was specifically limited to the old shareholders. The latter apparently managed to meet the calls for new capital because they ploughed back most of their dividends and bonuses.

Chou Hsueh-hsi went on to found other enterprises. In 1909 he organized the first waterworks company in Peking. Between 1911 and 1920 he ventured into banking, glass works and textiles. The Lanchou mines continued to prosper after it amalgamated with the larger Kaiping mines, while Chee Hsin expanded and eventually dominated the entire country's cement market.

Chou owed his success to efficient management, consistent ploughing back of profits by large shareholders, and the ability of himself and other major shareholders, as Yuan's officials, to offer the companies political protection. In 1916, following Yuan's death and the split up of the Peiyang clique, Chou joined the Anfu clique, offering his economic resources in return for continued political support.

Chang Chien, on the other hand, was a different kind of official-entrepreneur. While Chou Hsueh-hsi retained his official post, Chang left office entirely. The decision did not come easily; he had spent most of his adult life sitting for the state examinations, and won the much-coveted first place among the *chin-shih* graduates in 1894 only after several failures. Chou and Chang also differed in their search for financial and managerial backing. Chou turned to his official colleagues, while Chang appealed to merchants.

In 1895, while on home leave from his official post in Peking because of his father's death, Chang was approached by Chang Chih-tung to organize a modern cotton spinning mill. His home district, T'ung-chou (Nan-t'ung), was a major cotton growing area with a long tradition in the handicraft spinning and weaving industries. There had been local opposition to an earlier attempt by Sheng Hsuan-huai to set up a modern mill there. Chang was chosen not only because, as a local notable, he would be better able to counteract any renewed opposition, but also because Chang Chih-tung was looking to the local merchants to fund the new plant.[74]

Chang Chien took up his assignment probably without any idea what it would be like to organize and run a modern enterprise. He had permission to set up a private company, and the two local cotton goods merchants whom he had befriended offered to help organize a committee of six merchant directors to raise capital. His initial plan to build a mill with private funds alone does not mean that he had any ideological objection to state funding. Chang had had many years' experience in public finance while serving as private secretary to several officials; he accepted the general view that modern industry should be managed under official support and direction. Indeed, Chang's own strict moral scruples led him to the traditional wisdom that official supervision could only do good so long as the officials in charge were capable and upright. When his merchant directors discovered that they could not raise sufficient money, Chang seized upon an offer of government-owned machinery to make up the balance. When some merchants protested that this would open the way for bureaucratic interference, Chang responded self-righteously that he, being an upright official, 'could counter any such moves'.[75]

Fortunately, this simplistic attitude towards merchant-official partnership did not stay with him for long. During the next few years, as he tried desperately to raise sufficient capital for the Dah Sun Mill, he learned that his unsullied reputation and good intentions were not enough to warrant the merchants' trust. He also learned that promises of support made by his official friends were circumscribed with qualifications, or often not delivered. In the words of his son, who wrote a biography of him, 'At the top, the governor-general expressed support, yet at the lower levels, all the officials wanted to ruin his enterprise.'[76] The difficulties he encountered made Chang sensitive to the problems merchants and officials faced while trying to build a modern industry. They taught him the social and economic

---

74 On the founding of the Dah Sun (Ta-sheng) Mill, Chang Chien's own accounts are in his *T'ung-chou hsing-pan shih-yeh chih li-shih: Ta-sheng sha-ch'ang* (A history of the industries established at T'ung-chou: The Dah Sun Cotton Spinning Mill), and *Chang Chi-tzu chiu-lu, Shih-yeh lu*, 1.14–18. One recent study is Samuel C. Chu, 'Chang Chien and the founding of Dah Sun', *Ch'ing-hua hsueh-pao*, NS, 2.1 (1960) 301–17.
75 Ch'en Chen and Yao Lo, *Chung-kuo chin-tai kung-yeh shih tzu-liao*, 1.353.
76 Chang Hsiao-jo, *Nan-t'ung Chang Chi-chih hsien-sheng chuan-chi* (A biography of Mr Chang Chien of Nan-t'ung), 1.72.

restraints under which he had to operate. And they helped him decide to leave the official world altogether. The rigidity and servility of the bureaucracy disgusted him; he came to realize that in some ways entrepreneurial activities well done were truer to the Confucian calling, for modern enterprise provided work and helped the people's welfare. This explains why, as he transformed himself into a successful entrepreneur, he branched out from cotton mills into land reclamation, river conservancy, modern education, and fisheries.

The Dah Sun Mill's original plan was to raise 600,000 taels for a middle-sized spinning plant. But the committee of six directors in T'ung-chou and Shanghai ran into problems almost immediately. Governor-general Chang Chih-tung was replaced by Liu K'un-i, who reneged on the tax exemption promised earlier. The end of the Sino-Japanese War led to a sharp rise in the price of raw cotton. New foreign mills were being opened in Shanghai, driving the financially weaker Chinese mills to near bankruptcy. Two of Chang's directors resigned, and two others urged him to postpone the project. Chang's response, however, was to invite new directors and to expand the mill's proposed capital to 1 million taels by accepting Liu K'un-i's offer of 500,000 taels' worth of government-owned looms and spindles. The switch from private management to a presumed joint official-merchant venture led two more directors to quit.

Finally a compromise was struck. Chang and his remaining merchant directors agreed to accept only half of the government machinery for 250,000 taels. Private funds would make up another 250,000 taels for a spinning and weaving mill of reduced size. But the merchants continued to do poorly in raising their share of the capital. Eventually, only 170,000 or 180,000 taels were collected, and more money had to be accepted as government loans before the mill was opened in 1899. These loans did not come easily. Chang described how he continually had to plead with his official friends. He avoided default only after Governor-general Liu personally authorized additional government loans.

Chang Chien's experience, therefore, offered no easy model for others to follow. The eventual success of Dah Sun was due to his sound management and hard work. But it owed even more to Chang's official connections, which provided him with the needed funds, however reluctantly, and which allowed him to continue calling it a *shang-pan* operation even though more than half of its funds came from official sources in the form of fixed and circulating capital and loans. Consequently, Chang, as an official-entrepreneur, was able to coopt government capital and use it without state supervision.

A perspective

Despite many progressive officials' good intentions and their ingenious accommodation to modern management techniques, late Ch'ing China failed to build up a strong industrial base. By 1911 China had several modern industries – in textiles, mining, iron foundries, shipping and railways. But they were widely scattered, functionally unintegrated and sometimes controlled by competing provincial groups. Official domination and state control have often been singled out as causes for China's failure, But the key was not these two factors alone, but how control and domination were exercised. Meiji Japan, at a comparable stage of industrial development, depended heavily on forceful state efforts, but the Japanese government sold most of its state-run factories to private entrepreneurs by the early 1880s.[77] In contrast, the Chinese officials refused to relinquish control and became even more involved in industrial management as they blended official justification with self-interest.

At first, Li Hung-chang's *kuan-tu shang-pan* formula had required merchants to invest their own capital and to run modern enterprises at their own risk and under his general supervision. Li saw in such an arrangement a means to tap the private capital necessary if China were to start a full range of modern industry. The merchants' favourable response suggests that they saw Li's offer as an equitable exchange, providing freedom from excessive official squeeze in return for overall supervision. But even Li's power was not sufficient to protect his enterprises from the influence of other segments of the bureaucracy. Meanwhile, his own representatives in these enterprises, such as Sheng Hsuan-huai, became increasingly ensnared by conflicts of interest between national goals and personal gain. They encroached more and more upon the rights of managers of genuine merchant background. Then, as the merchants were in many cases unwilling or unable to provide adequate capital, provincial government funds were utilized with increasing frequency. This provided official supervisors like Sheng with the opportunity to turn themselves into actual managers and to transform state supervision into bureaucratic control.

Chang Chih-tung's exploitation of new terms such as *kuan-shang ho-pan* to suggest more equitable partnerships with the merchants did not change this trend of increasing bureaucratic involvement. Chang, unlike Li, did not have an open mind about the merchants' spirit of enterprise or their concern for the national welfare. He was also reluctant to delegate authority freely to either his official subordinates or competent merchant leaders.

---

[77] Thomas C. Smith, *Political change and industrial development in Japan: government enterprise, 1868–1880.*

The various industrial projects he sponsored had even less merchant support.

By about 1900, this apparent lack of success in industrial development, coupled with its total domination by provincial officials, encouraged the central government to try to take the lead in developing a national policy for commerce and industry. For many reasons, all major enterprises had been sponsored by senior provincial officials. Internal disorder and general trends during the downswing of a typical dynastic cycle in the late nineteenth century provided the regional leadership with money, military power and talent. Moreover, they had greater access to, and were more familiar with, Western skills and practices. But regionally based developments had to operate under a number of inherent weaknesses. First, there was neither coordination of policies nor a set of uniform principles. Secondly, provincial officials were frequently reassigned, and many a struggling company failed because their successors could no longer support them. Thirdly, only two or three 'regions', for reasons of accessibility to Western influence, the presence of able officials, and some abundance of commercial wealth, participated in the development of modern enterprise.

The central government's efforts to challenge this provincial domination were a step in the right direction. But its efforts at major institutional reforms, such as the introduction of a centralized ministry of commerce with branch offices in the provinces, encountered vigorous opposition not only from the provincial officials, gentry and gentry-merchants, but also from parts of its own bureaucracy. The several ministries squabbled with each other over jurisdictional claims.

Consequently, industrial development remained at the provincial level. But it was up against the pervading merchant mentality which favoured commerce over industry. For most Chinese merchants were really traders who did not understand the slower growth patterns of industrial enterprise. They were easily swayed by the fluctuating ups and downs of the marketplace, which offered them quick and short-term profits.

Privately run railways turned out to be the only major experiment during the late Ch'ing which had an opportunity to capture a broad base of financial support. Between 1906 and 1908, a few provincial railways achieved success because they were able to rouse a truly popular movement to support them. In Canton, Hong Kong, Hangchow, Shanghai and Ningpo, literally tens of thousands of factory workers, students and shophands took out millions of their own silver dollars to organize provincially based railway companies. They had been politically activated by the rights recovery movement which demanded that foreign bankers return the financing and construction rights over these railways. Since there was widespread belief that the Chinese government colluded with the Western powers because of its need for foreign loans, private management became an integral part of these campaigns.

But these railway companies, too, failed. By 1911, state control over them was again attempted, just before the dynasty's own demise. In any case, even if the dynasty's central authority had been stronger, it is doubtful whether a sufficiently large pool of capital for a full range of modern industry could have been secured from a citizenry only recently awakened to these opportunities. Moreover, the record of the railway companies indicates that merchant and gentry shareholders who were motivated by political causes to make investments tended towards factionalism, and that such business politics were as harmful to efficient management as was bureaucratic control. Government-merchant relationships seldom ran smoothly when they were unequal partners, with no legal safeguards for the merchants. China in 1911, despite the Western challenge and influence, still lacked the institutional basis on which modern industry could develop with private initiative and capital.

CHAPTER 9

THE REPUBLICAN REVOLUTIONARY
MOVEMENT

Between the autumn of 1911 and the spring of 1912 a series of events occurred in China that has come to be known as the Revolution of 1911. Its most prominent feature was the fall of the Ch'ing dynasty and the replacement of the empire by a republic. Although analysts of the revolution have clashed on many issues,[1] only recently has the very significance of the revolution been questioned. One leading scholar has found that there was so little social reform that the revolution was 'a sham';[2] another finds that the old ruling class maintained itself much as it had in previous dynastic transitions and that the Revolution of 1911 was therefore merely another 'dynastic revolution'.[3] As a result of such challenges to older interpretations, the nature of the Revolution of 1911 has become a matter for hot debate.

Among the wealth of new ideas that have emerged from recent controversies, two provide the points of departure for this chapter.[4] One is that the revolution encompassed not only the political change from dynasty to republic but also a variety of social changes, including the appearance of new social groups and the transformation of old ones.[5] The revolution is therefore best understood as the 1900–13 phase of the twentieth-century social revolution, not merely as the 1911–12 phase of political change. Secondly, within this broader concept the importance of the revolutionaries is far less than what it was in older interpretations.[6] This was a revolution bigger than all its leaders, 'a revolution without real leadership'.[7] In this view the revolutionary movement is important less for what it contributed to the events of 1900–13 than for the revolutionary tradition it created. In

[1] For these controversies among Chinese writers on the revolution see Winston Hsieh, *Chinese historiography on the Revolution of 1911: a critical survey and a selected bibliography*. For a report and papers of a conference in Wuchang, October 1961, see Hu-pei sheng che-hsueh she-hui k'o-hsueh hsueh-hui lien-ho hui, ed. *Hsin-hai ko-ming wu-shih chou-nien lun-wen chi* (A collection of articles on the fiftieth anniversary of the Revolution of 1911).
[2] Jerome Ch'en, *Yuan Shih-k'ai*, 92.
[3] Chūzō Ichiko, 'The role of the gentry: an hypothesis', in Mary C. Wright, ed. *China in revolution: the first phase, 1900–1913* (hereafter *CIR*), 297–313.
[4] For the new ideas and recent controversies see 'Introduction: the rising tide of change', in *CIR*, 1–63, and Philip C. Huang's symposium in *Modern China*, 2.2 (April 1976) 139–226.
[5] *CIR*, esp. 1–3, 24–44.   [6] *CIR*, 45–8.   [7] *CIR*, 53.

brief, then, current interpretations lean towards the paradox that the Revolution of 1911 was a bigger phenomenon than used to be thought, but that the actual achievements of the revolutionaries were less.

Recent scholarship has posed the problem of determining how much of a revolution occurred, who was responsible for what did occur, and what place this period occupies in China's entire history of revolution. A tentative answer might begin with recognition that a variety of protest movements came together temporarily in 1911–12. Some were revolutionary and some were not, but for a combination of reasons that we shall try to elucidate, all found it suited them at that moment to favour or at least to accept the replacement of the Ch'ing dynasty by a republic. A fragile coalition whose members had differing aims, interests and social backgrounds emerged from a society in enormous flux, a society in which some old ties had been broken but others only strengthened, and in which some new ways were in full flower while others were at many different points of germination and growth. By 1911, in other words, there was no longer one China. The clashing interpretations may obscure the fact that there was social revolution in some parts of China but a rejuvenation of traditional authority and class relationships in others, and many gradations in between. It is not simply that each interpretation has part of the truth, but that during the 1900–13 period Chinese society split and began to re-unite along new lines. The year 1911 was not the major turning point in a history of modern democracy as represented by some older interpretations, but it was the culmination of nearly two decades of extraordinary ferment that left China more radically changed than had any other two decades in many centuries. The changes, however, were strikingly uneven, partly because the revolutionaries were only one active force among many between the early 1890s and 1913. The revolutionary movement helped to convert what had been, since the 1860s, a relatively mild split between reformist and anti-reformist gentry into a sharp cleavage, as a result of which the former found more in common with the revolutionaries than they did with the anti-reformist gentry. Temporarily at least, gentry status came to be less of a unifying force than political and ideological affiliation. The new cleavage divided an essentially urban Westernizing China from a largely rural traditional China, and it promoted new alignments and alliances that began to transcend old ties of kinship, class and native place; examples include chambers of commerce and political parties. The cleavages, alignments, interests and sentiments that grew out of the revolutionary movement shaped Chinese life for decades thereafter. It is in this sense that the 1900–13 period represents the first stage of China's revolution.

EARLY COALITIONS: THE REVOLUTIONARY MOVEMENT
BEFORE 1905

In the early 1890s there was still a fundamental unity in China. The issue that produced the deepest division – how much to borrow from the West in order to resist it – had created no serious attempt or even inclination to overturn the traditional system. It was assumed that the purpose of borrowing techniques from abroad was to defend Chinese culture. This common assumption far outweighed all disagreements.

In the middle of the decade consensus was punctured by the first pin-prick of revolution. On the initiative of Sun Yat-sen a small organization was formed to overthrow the Ch'ing and found a republic. It promoted an uprising in 1895 which, although a failure, marked the beginning of armed revolution.

Another current flowed into the revolutionary movement in the late 1890s from within the traditionalist camp. Japan's victory in 1894–5 convinced many reformers that the self-strengthening movement had been a failure and that a more far-reaching effort was needed. After the failure of the reform movement of 1898, one wing became more radical and from then on, chiefly under the guidance of Liang Ch'i-ch'ao, followed an unsteady course between revolution and reform.

Both groups, the republican revolutionaries and the radical reformers, sought supporters among the overseas students. Between 1902 and 1905 the students' number grew to about eight thousand, sufficient to be noticed by both the government and its opponents and to constitute the most numerous, vocal and active of all Chinese revolutionaries.

None of these groups was a well-organized or cohesive unit, but all had in common a desire to define and defend a Chinese nation, to make it strong and prosperous even if that could be done only at great cost to the traditional civilization. Occasionally they tried to work together. But for the most part they went their separate ways, while the Ch'ing government retained the political initiative. For the first decade of its existence, then, the revolutionary movement was an inchoate affair that had no decisive impact on events.

Sun Yat-sen and the Society to Restore China's Prosperity, 1894–1903

Sun Yat-sen was mainly responsible for the founding of China's first avowedly revolutionary organizations. Born in Hsiang-shan hsien near Macao, Kwangtung in 1866, Sun went to Hawaii in 1879 and spent most of his formative years among Overseas Chinese and in Western schools in

Hawaii and Hong Kong. He was decisively influenced by his overseas environments. His village childhood shaped him relatively less. He was a Westernized Chinese who spoke English, adopted Christianity, earned a medical degree, and lived much of his life either on the foreign fringe of China, in Hong Kong and treaty ports such as Shanghai, or on the Chinese fringe of foreign lands, in Chinese communities in the United States, Japan and South-East Asia. From his thirteenth birthday to his forty-fifth, Sun spent only about four years in China. Foreigners were among his closest associates and supporters. Sun early came to admire the West and Japan, especially for the strength and efficiency of their governments, their level of technology and economic development, and the sense of energy and movement that permeated their societies.

Inspired by his exposure to foreign life and an acquaintance with nineteenth-century Chinese reformist thought, Sun drew up a reform proposal that he attempted to present to Li Hung-chang in 1894. The content of the proposal was routine for its time. Sun stressed the need to develop Western education, promote commerce, and encourage the growth of science and technology, especially for their application to agriculture. Most of what Sun wrote had been said for thirty years or more by Chinese reformers, and none of it was meant to be revolutionary. It is of interest, first, that Sun's mild and commonplace thinking of mid-1894 turned revolutionary only a short time thereafter; secondly, that he felt that the most powerful official in China should give a personal hearing to a young doctor who was only two years beyond his medical training. The sharp turn in Sun's thinking has never been clearly explained, but his attempt to bring his ideas right to the top suggests that, however moderate his ideas, Sun had no taste for moderate actions. When one effort to reach the top failed, Sun resolved on another. Whatever the reasons for his sharp turn in 1894, the incident suggests the sense of personal mission that was to characterize his entire life.

Frustrated by his failure to receive a hearing from Li Hung-chang, Sun decided to return to Hawaii. There he organized China's first modern revolutionary society, the Society to Restore China's Prosperity (Hsing-Chung hui). Two months later, in January 1895, he went to Hong Kong and joined some old friends and acquaintances to found another branch of the society. This branch represented an alliance between Sun and Yang Ch'ü-yun, a revolutionary who was even more Westernized than Sun and who became the nominal head of the branch. Available documents do not prove that the Society to Restore China's Prosperity immediately put itself on record as being opposed to the dynasty and in favour of a republic; but indications are strong that Sun and at least a few of the more educated among the twenty-odd who joined in Hawaii were already committed to a republican revolution.[8] For the time being, however, the organization's programme stressed the foreign threat to China and the inability of the weak and corrupt Ch'ing to resist imperialism. This patriotic appeal remained the core of revolutionary sentiment for at least the next nine or ten years.

The groups in Hawaii and Hong Kong were small and weak. Insufficiency of funds plagued them constantly. The original membership amounted to no more than a few dozen and never exceeded several hundred. With only a few exceptions the members came from the Canton area, and approximately two-thirds of them lived outside China proper; their contact with their 400 million countrymen was limited almost entirely to kinship relations and a few loose ties with secret societies. Their structure was so weak that they had only occasional contact with each other. They were not the disciplined and well-organized elite groups we have come to associate with modern revolutions. But they were a new element in Chinese politics. The members were nearly all poor and rather uneducated. Almost half were merchants and about a quarter were labourers. The influential educated few had received a predominantly modern education. Several, including Sun, had some classical Chinese training, but none of them could be considered a traditional literatus. On the contrary, the Society to Restore China's Prosperity represented a cross-section of what were still commonly regarded as lower class people.

The planning for an uprising began in March 1895, when China and Japan were still at war. Although a peace treaty was signed in April, circumstances still seemed propitious for revolt several months later. The terms of peace, highly unfavourable to China, were particularly resented in the Canton area. Large numbers of demobilized soldiers roamed the countryside, some resorting to banditry. Discontent spread to all levels of society, gentry as well as peasants. Secret societies found their ranks growing, and small uprisings became more frequent.

Christian missionaries and their Chinese converts were prominent among Sun's supporters. Under cover of a few small front organizations (an 'agricultural association' and a Presbyterian congregation in Canton), the Hsing-Chung hui stockpiled weapons, recruited among the demobilized troops and sought contacts with secret societies and local militia. Sun had

[8] For this controversy see the discussion in Harold Z. Schiffrin, *Sun Yat-sen and the origins of the Chinese Revolution*, 26–35, 42–4. Questions concerning the society's founding date and other circumstances are examined in Chang Yü-fa, *Ch'ing-chi ti ko-ming t'uan-t'i* (Revolutionary groups of the late Ch'ing period), 152–65; see 180–205 for an exhaustive analysis of the society's membership. See also Lilia Borokh, 'Notes on the early role of secret societies in Sun Yat-sen's republican movement', in Jean Chesneaux, ed. *Popular movements and secret societies in China, 1840–1950* (hereafter *PMSS*), 138–9.

become intrigued with secret societies at least as early as 1886, and their potential for large-scale anti-government action never ceased to attract him. Their appeal was probably due mostly to the wide network of branches they had and the fact that they, like his own followers, represented primarily the 'outsiders' or 'low-prestige groups' in Chinese society. Secret-society members included wandering labourers, uprooted peasants, discharged soldiers and others who had lost their means of livelihood, as well as bandits, pirates, thieves, smugglers and other less savoury or more desperate people. Especially in hard times, however, they also attracted scholars who had failed the civil-service examinations and even some gentry, merchants and other well-to-do or prestigious individuals. These people often became leaders of secret societies. It was precisely such leaders who joined the Society to Restore China's Prosperity. Thus, Sun's contact with the secret societies gave him access to people of varied social background, although he did not acquire a large number of followers.

Neither the paucity of his followers nor their slack organization and shallow roots in China troubled Sun Yat-sen. He assumed that anti-dynastic feeling was so strong and widespread that a slight nudge would set it in rapid motion. His strategy was to win a foothold on the mainland and establish an enclave from which the revolutionaries might then fan out and ignite a regional or nation-wide uprising. But their allies in China were too few and unreliable, and problems of bringing in men and supplies from neighbouring places such as Hong Kong proved insoluble. Preparations lagged in 1895, the rising was postponed, an arms shipment was intercepted, the plot was discovered by Canton authorities, the troops from Hong Kong were arrested, and the plot collapsed without a shot being fired, at least not by the revolutionaries.

Sun narrowly escaped, hiding first in the home of a Christian minister and then making his way to Hong Kong and eventually to Japan. There he cut off his queue, symbolically severing his ties with Manchu China, and began to disguise himself as a Japanese. (This act was more symbolic than he could know. Already considerably removed from his ancestral heritage by his lengthy experience abroad, Sun was not to touch Chinese soil again for more than sixteen years, except for one day in December 1907 when he investigated a revolt on the Tongking–Kwangsi border.) Together with two of his lieutenants, Ch'en Shao-pai and Cheng Shih-liang, Sun founded a small branch of the Hsing-Chung hui in Yokohama. Leaving Ch'en in charge in Japan, where he was aided by a Japanese Christian Sun had met in Hawaii, and sending Cheng back to Hong Kong to cultivate secret-society contacts, Sun set out for Hawaii, the United States and Europe. Thwarted in China, he hoped to promote the revolution from abroad.

In London in 1896 there occurred a bizarre incident that illuminates Sun Yat-sen's methods of appealing to foreigners and his instinct for heroics. For reasons that are not yet fully clear, although it has been persuasively suggested that he took a carefully considered risk, Sun went to the Chinese legation. There he was held prisoner for twelve days while preparations were made to send him back to China and a surely dire fate. At the eleventh hour two Englishmen who had been Sun's teachers came to his aid, and he was released amid great publicity. Quick to grasp the opportunity, Sun fed the reporters' hunger for interviews and then wrote letters to the major English newspapers to thank them and the British public and government. His letters to the newspapers reveal traits that were to characterize his career – his belief in appealing to the best instincts of Westerners, and his efforts to persuade Westerners that he was seeking to do for his country what Westerners of goodwill would do if they could. The entire incident, he wrote, was further confirmation 'of the generous public spirit which pervades Great Britain, and the love of justice which distinguishes its people . . . . Knowing and feeling more keenly than ever what a constitutional Government and an enlightened people mean, I am prompted still more actively to pursue the cause of advancement, education, and civilisation in my own well-beloved but oppressed country.'[9]

Sun also wrote a short autobiography and a little book entitled *Kidnapped in London*, which he wrote in English and later disavowed. It was not published in Chinese until 1912.[10] Sun's emphasis on his foreign audience could hardly be more clearly revealed than in this incident. Almost immediately he was an international celebrity, and he squeezed every last ounce of publicity out of it. Whatever he did, even going to church, he did in view of the press whenever possible. He cultivated a wide range of personal contacts, including Russian revolutionaries as well as English missionaries. He published articles such as one in the *Fortnightly Review* in which he called for 'the entire overthrow of the present utterly corrupt regime, and the establishment of good government and a pure administration by native Chinese with, at first, European advice, and, for some years, European administrative assistance'.[11] During the eight months following his sensational release from the Chinese legation, Sun represented himself as something like a secular missionary, the leader of a movement that would bring to China the benefits of modern Western political culture and also pave the way for Western commercial development.

All Sun asked in exchange was that Britain allow him to return to Hong Kong and that the powers observe a 'benevolent neutrality'. His requests

[9] Schiffrin, *Sun Yat-sen*, 126.   [10] Hsieh, *Revolution of 1911*, 16.
[11] Schiffrin, *Sun Yat-sen*, 131.

were refused. England still considered that her interests were best served by adhering to a five-year banishment order issued by the governor of Hong Kong shortly after Sun's 1895 plot. Sun gave no sign that he was discouraged, and indeed he was too excited by his experience in London and the favourable publicity he was receiving to feel anything but optimistic. Deciding to prepare himself for bigger things, he spent most of the next five months reading in the British Museum Library. It was probably in this period that Sun became acquainted with most of the Western thought that he later attempted to mould into a programme for the Chinese revolution. In particular he became fascinated with the ideas of Henry George, who was then very much in vogue among English intellectuals such as the Fabian socialists. Meanwhile, his London adventure was making him known to potential allies in Japan and elsewhere. Sun's heightened reputation helped him to raise money among the Overseas Chinese in Canada on his way back to Japan in the summer of 1897. When he reached Japan Sun found the most favourable response he had yet received, this time from a group of Japanese expansionist adventurers. Through them he met prominent Japanese politicians and came to think of Japan as a 'natural ally' of China. Sun adopted a Japanese name, Nakayama (in Chinese, Chung-shan, lit. 'central mountain'). He applied himself to learning Japanese and assiduously cultivated his new contacts. Since no aid had come from Europe, Sun had turned to another, closer, foreign source (see chapter 6, page 368).

Attempts at cooperation: Sun, K'ang Yu-wei and Liang Ch'i-ch'ao

Together with his new comrades Sun plunged into an extraordinary variety of activities. With the Japanese serving as intermediaries he began by renewing his efforts to cooperate with K'ang Yu-wei, Liang Ch'i-ch'ao and other reformers. Those efforts had begun early in 1895 and continued intermittently for about a year and a half. One reason for their failure had been K'ang's rise to a high position and his belief that more could be accomplished by a reformist emperor following the examples of Peter the Great and Meiji Japan than by revolutionaries such as Sun. By 1898, however, Sun had gained perhaps a little stature while K'ang had lost a great deal. Since K'ang had now been branded an outlaw by the Ch'ing court, there seemed to be new possibilities for cooperation following the end of the 1898 reforms.

That movement had brought together people of many viewpoints and had stretched traditionalism to its limits. One faction, perhaps best exemplified by T'an Ssu-t'ung's call for 'complete Westernization', went beyond those limits. In 1898 T'an was almost alone in holding such ideas, but soon after his execution in that year other reformers moved closer to the position he had held. One, a degree-holder named Pi Yung-nien, promptly joined Sun. Liang Ch'i-ch'ao had before 1898 already spoken approvingly of 'the political authority of the people' and 'people's rule' exercised through representative institutions. Until the failure of the 1898 reform movement he believed that such democratic changes could occur through reform from above. By the end of 1898 he had founded a news-paper in Tokyo. Soon he spoke of popular 'rights' instead of merely the people's 'authority', and he argued that instead of waiting for them to be granted by the court 'rights can only be secured by each citizen's struggling for them, without giving way a single inch'.[12] Liang had become a revolutionary, and he was now chief spokesman for those young scholar-gentry who, cut adrift by the failure of the 1898 reforms, had come to believe that tradition was stagnant and radical policies necessary.

Sun Yat-sen recognized and welcomed the opportunity to broaden the revolutionary movement. Cooperation between Sun and Liang reached joint publication of an anti-Manchu periodical late in 1899, and when Liang went to Hawaii that December Sun gave him a letter of introduction to his brother. Unluckily for Sun, Liang had gone to Hawaii on the instructions of K'ang Yu-wei, to carry out an assignment for the Society to Protect the Emperor (Pao-huang hui) which K'ang had founded in July. Liang was torn between, on the one hand, his ties with K'ang and all his mentor stood for and his own doubts about Sun's potential, and, on the other, his radical tendencies. He tried to explain that despite his belief in anti-Manchuism it was best for the time being to pursue the goal of popular government in the name of the emperor; once the empress dowager had been eliminated, he said, the emperor could become president of a republic.

No evidence exists of any reply by Sun Yat-sen to this suggestion. Liang continued on his wobbly path. He wrote prolifically, joined a secret society in Hawaii in order better to cultivate the Overseas Chinese, spoke in favour of assassination in 1900, and even as late as October 1904 praised Russian terrorists: 'Great is the dagger! Holy the bomb!'[13] When the Boxer movement broke out in the spring of 1900, the Society to Protect the Emperor decided that its opportunity had come to rescue the captive monarch. Feverish preparations for an uprising began, aimed at creating a government in the south that would be headed by the Kuang-hsu Emperor. To Sun Yat-sen these circumstances seemed to offer yet another chance to unite the anti-Ch'ing forces, and despite his disillusionment with Liang he

12 Philip C. Huang, *Liang Ch'i-ch'ao and modern Chinese liberalism*, 26, 28–30, 60.
13 Don C. Price, *Russia and the roots of the Chinese Revolution, 1896–1911*, 134.

once again explored the possibility of cooperation with K'ang. But K'ang stayed aloof, and the efforts came to nothing. In August an uprising at Hankow, led by T'ang Ts'ai-ch'ang and supported by K'ang, collapsed. The Society to Protect the Emperor then continued its work in exile, cutting heavily into Sun's support among the Overseas Chinese.

Sun resumed his labours. He retained the support of some former gentry reformers such as Pi Yung-nien and Shih Chien-ju, and he also sought to work with Cantonese gentry, secret societies in central as well as southern China, Li Hung-chang and other important officials, and foreigners such as the governor of Hong Kong and even Filipino rebels. Although all of these efforts fell far short of their goals, and some of them were so unrealistic as to be fanciful, they dismayed authorities in Peking. Sun's most intensive efforts coincided with the Boxer Uprising, foreign invasion and the Hankow uprising supported by K'ang and Liang. Alarmed by the prospect of an alliance uniting all its enemies, and worried most of all that the upper classes were beginning to sympathize with the rebels, the Ch'ing government felt compelled to introduce far more drastic reforms than it had previously contemplated. Thus the indirect results of Sun Yat-sen's flurry of revolutionary activity may have been far greater than the direct results.

The direct results were rather slight. By mid-1900 Sun had attracted enough support to encourage him to promote another uprising. Once again his target was Canton, but this time he decided first to launch his campaign further to the east, establish a base of operations (at Waichow, or Hui-chou), and then move on to Canton. In other respects the uprising was much like the one in 1895: the participants were mainly secret-society men together with numerous Chinese Christians (possibly 30 per cent of Sun's original force) and a handful of Japanese and Westerners; the strategy was to use a small force to spark a general rebellion; the major stumbling block was obtaining weapons and shipping them inland to the fighting men; repeated delays and shifts of plans permitted information leaks and gave the government time to prepare for the uprising. Within two weeks after fighting began in October the Ch'ing had gained the upper hand. A few days later Sun gave the order to disband the revolutionary forces and headed once again for Japan, there to reflect on his second failure.

Sun felt encouraged because a fundamental point in his strategy seemed to have been vindicated. The Waichow campaign saw a small band of revolutionary fighters grow quickly into a sizeable force. The populace in Kwangtung at first merely withheld support from the government, but their neutrality soon turned into active support for the revolt. Thousands joined, and as peasants swelled the revolutionary ranks it became easier to obtain food and supplies, gather intelligence, set ambushes for Ch'ing reinforcements, and defeat larger and better-equipped units. This, however, was as far as the embryonic guerrilla tactics developed. Local support for the revolutionaries was due largely to local issues, and Sun's men carried out only a minimal and short-run ideological and organizational effort. There was no sustained attempt to enlarge upon local issues, cultivate latent anti-Manchu or anti-imperialist sentiments, circulate new political ideas, or begin to establish an organization that would be independent of or at least distinct from existing ones such as secret societies. The political thought Sun is said to have absorbed in great quantities during his studies in England in 1897 was not evident in 1900. The revolution, at this stage, was a traditional jacquerie or putsch more than a twentieth-century revolution.

To an observer more objective than Sun, therefore, the outlook for his movement might have appeared quite dim after the failure of 1900. In retrospect, one is as much impressed by the ease with which the revolt was suppressed as by its initial successes. Considering the unstable conditions of 1900, and keeping in mind that this instability was the product of more than a century of internal troubles as well as many decades of foreign exploitation of China, the achievements of the revolutionaries seem small in comparison with the size of their opportunity. Either scholars have exaggerated the extent of dynastic decline, or the revolution in 1900 was a very weak movement indeed.

Sun Yat-sen's reputation had fallen to the point where other revolutionaries dismissed him with epithets such as 'uncultured outlaw', 'romantic thief' or illiterate 'tough guy'. The young Hunanese leader, Sung Chiaojen, expressed a commonly held view: Sun, he said, is capable only of making a lot of noise. Sun, however, recalled that after his 1900 failure people stopped thinking of him in such unflattering terms; 'the progressive elements were actually sympathetic with me in my misfortunes'.[14]

For several years Sun changed his strategy rather little. His preference for basing his movement on appeals to secret societies, Overseas Chinese, Japanese and Westerners remained as strong as ever. Sun made his headquarters in Japan until September 1903, but he travelled from one Overseas Chinese community to another to raise funds, seek adherents and probe for foreign backing. In Hanoi he founded a small branch of the Society to Restore China and met the French authorities to explore the possibility of obtaining aid. The French had been interested in Sun for some time. Four

[14] Li Chien-nung, The political history of China, 1840–1928, trans. Ssu-yü Teng and Jeremy Ingalls, 183. For varying characterizations of Sun, see K. S. Liew, Struggle for democracy: Sung Chiao-jen and the 1911 Chinese Revolution, 24, and Chün-tu Hsueh, Huang Hsing and the Chinese Revolution, 35–6.

months before the Waichow uprising he had met the French minister in Tokyo and asked help to obtain weapons and military officers. According to the minister, Sun promised in return to give France 'all that we would ask'. Sun is reported to have said in June 1900: 'We are not the enemies of foreigners. Far from it. On the contrary, we make an appeal to their understanding for the regeneration and transformation of our fatherland.'[15] The French continued to watch Sun's activities closely. In 1903 they met him again and reported to the Minister of Colonies that Sun had offered France 'the most alluring economic advantages and a sort of protectorate over the new state that he dreams of organizing'.[16] But France still offered no aid.

By late 1903 Sun had failed to reassemble even the fragile organization he had put together for the 1900 uprising. Secret societies, Overseas Chinese, and foreigners had proved to be a flimsy coalition that provided only the most shaky foundation for a revolution. Sun noticed the potential mass support in the countryside; but his vaguely outlined programme had little meaning to rural people, and he created no relationship with them apart from the unreliable secret societies. Sun's failures and the death or defection of some of his closest collaborators temporarily quashed his usually buoyant spirits. 'When I reached Tokyo [in July 1903]', Sun wrote to a friend, 'I searched everywhere for old comrades [but] there was not one to be seen, and I was deeply disappointed.'[17] He stayed in Tokyo for only a few weeks and then, discouraged, left for Hawaii to resume his wandering quest for support among the Overseas Chinese.

The student movement, 1901–5

By 1901, in addition to the attempted rebellions and the foreign invasion of 1900, the Ch'ing court was faced with rapidly spreading alienation among the Chinese upper class. Since 1895 allegiance to traditional thinking had been so badly shaken that some of the more Western-oriented were even prepared to accept colonization by the West in order to promote change in China. Such despair and resignation were less common than active criticism of the Ch'ing government and outright official disobedience to edicts from Peking. Its call to war in 1900 was ignored in the larger part

---

[15] Ministère des Colonies, Indo-Chine: Relations Extérieures, B-11 (36) carton 33 (1906–9), Document no. 2. Dispatch from Foreign Minister to Minister of Colonies, 28 July 1900, reporting a conversation of 7 June 1900.

[16] *Ibid.* Document no. 4. Dispatch from governor-general of Indo-China to the Minister of Colonies, 26 February 1903. On Sun's relations with the French see also J. Kim Munholland, 'The French connection that failed: France and Sun Yat-sen, 1900–1908', *JAS*, 32.1 (Nov. 1972) 77–95.

[17] Sun Wen (Sun Yat-sen), 'Tzu-chuan' (Autobiography), in *Kuo-fu ch'üan-chi* (The complete works of the national father), 1.36.

of China. Meanwhile, even during the reactions of 1898–1900, some provincial authorities had quietly managed to continue reforms such as sending students abroad.

One major result of the Ch'ing reforms after 1901 was to bring into existence the very social groups and organizations that would later be instrumental in overthrowing the dynasty. These included a rising merchant class newly organized into chambers of commerce, a new military and a new intelligentsia. The new intelligentsia was the first to form and become active. It was an offshoot of the reformist gentry who emerged in 1895. Like them the new intelligentsia came primarily from upper-class backgrounds and had received at least some traditional education. Both groups regarded foreign imperialists and reactionary officials as their enemies. Both felt deeply concerned about China's fate and determined to lead the country's regeneration. But the new intelligentsia was younger, and it developed a new outlook as a result of study abroad.

For a brief period in the early 1900s one man played a vital role in the development of both the reformist gentry and the new intelligentsia. With one foot in each camp, Liang Ch'i-ch'ao was living proof of how close to each other the reformist and radical intellectuals stood. Following the failure of the 1898 reforms, Liang had fled to Tokyo and founded a newspaper in which he began to introduce to his readers a wide variety of new ideas. No sooner did Liang himself excitedly gulp down Western and Japanese writings of all sorts than he relayed them to his readers in a vivid, lively and appealing style. He also founded several schools. His writings fired the imaginations of an entire generation. By 1903 Liang was calling for the most radical social, cultural and political changes, and the literate youth were considerably influenced by him.

Other young Chinese followed Liang's example. As early as 1900 journals, similar to Liang's newspaper, published translations of Western and Japanese works and began to include editorials about China's problems and how to solve them. The Chinese students' heroes were the men of the American and French revolutions – Washington, Danton, Robespierre, Napoleon – but they also sought out the revolutions' intellectual roots in Rousseau and Montesquieu; they even went back to the Greeks on occasion, but they soon turned chiefly to Rousseau and to nineteenth-century writers such as Darwin and Mill and finally to Herbert Spencer. Ideas of 'progress', 'struggle for existence' and 'survival of the fittest' began to dominate the students' thinking.

The atmosphere of change and growth in Japan also favoured the emergence of an increasingly radical group of Chinese intellectuals. Japan had shown that it was possible to throw off foreign domination and earn the powers' respect. In 1902 England had even accepted Japan as an ally. Chinese students poured into Japan during a time of mounting war fever. The students' sensitivity to the Russo-Japanese War was sharpened by the fact that it was fought on Chinese soil to decide which imperialist power would dominate that particular part of China, while the Chinese government watched helplessly. With Japan's victory over China in 1894–5 and China's humiliation in 1900 fresh in their minds, the students' admiration for Japan's success was mixed with outrage at China's impotence and shame. Student journals were filled with attacks on imperialism, attacks on the Manchus for permitting imperialism, and exhortations to promote the martial and patriotic spirit that the students found so admirable in the Japanese. They condemned their own people's lethargy, selfishness and ignorance, and they called for unity, personal sacrifice for the national good, and the expulsion of all foreigners from Chinese soil.

Underlying all of the students' demands was a new but somewhat contradictory sense of nationhood. It combined pride in China's past with a conviction that the Chinese people would have to be fundamentally changed in order to create a strong and modern Chinese nation. Thus Liang Ch'i-ch'ao's series of articles on 'A New People' was among the most popular of the day, for here Liang struck a note that gave the past its due but also looked ahead to a new future. It adroitly made the same criticisms of China that foreigners made, but did so in a way that saved Chinese self-respect.

Liang found in Chinese culture 'an independent spirit which . . . is really the fundamental basis of nationalism'. China's 'special characteristics which are grand, noble, and perfect, and distinctly different from those of other races', he said, should be preserved in such a way that they could renew themselves. 'It is like a tree: unless some new buds come out every year, its withering away may soon be expected.' Such rejuvenation could be furthered by selecting from 'the methods followed by other nations in becoming independent', characteristics that 'we originally lacked'. Liang set himself apart from nineteenth-century reformers who had sought to borrow only the superficial features of Western civilization. They had grafted 'branches onto our withered trunk' while neglecting such roots as 'the people's virtue, the people's wisdom, and the people's vitality'. The deepest root of all was what Liang called 'public morality', the principle that 'what is beneficial to the group is good, and what is detrimental to the interests of the group is bad'. China's most serious deficiency was that 'among our people there is not one who looks on national affairs as if they were his own affairs'.[18]

[18] See William Theodore DeBary, Wing-tsit Chan and Burton Watson, eds. *Sources of Chinese*

Having addressed himself to one contradiction in his generation's thinking – the conflict between its ties to Chinese culture and its determination radically to change that culture, Liang had identified a second contradiction. A major factor preventing the Chinese from taking an interest in national affairs was their identification with their own particular localities and provinces. The students were no exception to this conflict, but they struggled to resolve it.

Chinese students who went to Japan were sponsored either by their provinces, the central government or private sources. The most common of the three was provincial sponsorship. When the students reached Japan they grouped themselves into provincial organizations and tended to associate primarily with their fellow provincials. They lived together and published journals with names like *Chekiang Tide*, *The Hupei Student World* and *Kiangsu*. Some groups even organized provincial independence or 'self-government' movements (see chapter 6, pages 348ff.).

While the students' provincial loyalties remained very strong, however, they also regarded their provincial organizations as building blocks for a new Chinese nation. The students deplored China's lack of unity mainly because their country was in an international 'struggle for existence', as the Hupei students put it. Kiangsu youth explained that in modern countries 'it is essential to depend on the intelligence and courage not of individuals, but of the whole country . . . . It is not strange that we have not won battles of war and commerce and have remained poor and weak.' China's weakness was due to 'the lack of national cooperation', and the Hupei student magazine said in its very first issue: 'National cooperation must be brought about step by step, built on smaller units of cooperation. Love of country must therefore start from love of the home province.'[19] The Hunan students agreed: 'If we want to plan for China we must plan for Hunan.'[20]

Committed to national unity and sensitive to the divisiveness inherent in provincial loyalties, the students moved quickly to form national groups and to unite provincial ones. As early as 1900 organizations such as the Determination Society (Li-chih hui) were founded to promote contact among provincial groups. Others, such as the Youth Society (Ch'ing-nien hui), dedicated themselves to 'nationalism' (*min-tsu chu-i*) or the recovery of

tradition, 757–9. For examples of Liang's influence see Y. C. Wang, *Chinese intellectuals and the West, 1872–1949*, 223–4; Mao Tse-tung in his autobiography told to Edgar Snow, *Red Star over China*, 137, 139–40; and Kai-yu Hsu, *Chou-En-lai*, 12.

[19] The foregoing are all quoted by Yoshihiro Hatano, 'The new armies', in *CIR*, 366.

[20] Quoted in Charlton M. Lewis, 'The opening of Hunan: reform and revolution in a Chinese province, 1895–1907' (University of California, Ph.D. dissertation, 1965), 165. See also Charlton M. Lewis, *Prologue to the Chinese Revolution: the transformation of ideas and institutions in Hunan province, 1891–1907*. Cf. Edward J. M. Rhoads, *China's republican revolution: the case of Kwangtung, 1895–1913*, 47–8.

'national sovereignty' (*kuo-ch'üan*). Some of these organizations were made up almost entirely of men from a single province, but by 1903 sentiment was growing among the students to form a national organization that would transcend provincial lines.

In the next two years, this sentiment produced meagre results. In the spring of 1903, for example, in protest against Russia's occupation of Manchuria, Youth Society members organized a Volunteer Corps to Resist Russia. Revolutionaries in Shanghai published the *Russian Alarm* and *Warning Bell Daily* to protest against Russian policy and criticize the Ch'ing for failure to resist. Under the command of one Volunteer Corps member who was studying at a Japanese military academy, two hundred others held daily drills; meanwhile, two leaders journeyed to Tientsin to ask Yuan Shih-k'ai, governor-general of Chihli, to act against Russia and accept their aid in the enterprise. When these efforts failed, the most radical of the students went underground and continued their attempts to promote a militant patriotism. New publications adopted names such as *Twentieth Century China* and the *Flag of China* instead of provincial names. Old publications were converted: for example, the *Hupei Student World* became the *Voice of China*. New groups took names such as the Society for China's Revival (Hua-hsing hui) or the Patriotic Society (Ai-kuo hui) that suggested a national orientation, and their programmes spelt out national objectives.

Founded by Huang Hsing, a Hunanese who had just returned to China after a year in Japan, the Society for China's Revival was one of the first and most important of the revolutionary organizations that attempted to reach far beyond provincial borders. Although most of its members came from Hunan and its purpose was, in Huang's words, 'to capture Hunan province as a revolutionary base', Huang stressed that 'one province cannot fight the rest of the nation'. Therefore he prepared to 'seek cooperation from the people of other provinces whenever possible so that when the time comes, concerted action can be taken'.[21] Members were drawn from at least eight provinces besides Hunan, and the Society for China's Revival forged links with other groups in five provinces (Kwangsi, Szechwan, Hupei, Kiangsi and Chekiang) and two major cities (Shanghai and Nan-

[21] Hsueh, *Huang Hsing*, 18. For a summary of these groups' activities see Chang Yü-fa, *Ch'ing-chi ti ko-ming t'uan-t'i*, 251–6; for materials on these and other pre-1905 revolutionary activities see Chung-hua min-kuo k'ai-kuo wu-shih-nien wen-hsien pien-tsuan wei-yuan-hui, ed. *Ko-ming chih ch'ang-tao yü fa-chan* (The leadership and development of the revolution), vols. 1–3. For student periodicals, see *ibid.* 2.499–763; and Chang Nan and Wang Jen-chih, *Hsin-hai ko-ming ch'ien shih-nien chien shih-lun hsuan-chi* (Selections from opinions expressed in periodicals and newspapers during the decade before the 1911 Revolution), series 1 (1901–4), series 2 (1905–7). Complete files of the *Russian Alarm* (73 issues, 15 Dec. 1903 to 25 Feb. 1904) and most of the 338 issues of the *Warning Bell Daily* (29 Feb. 1904 to 30 Jan. 1905) are in the Kuomintang archives in Taiwan.

king). Its original membership was almost exclusively made up of students, but with a strenuous effort it managed to attract some soldiers stationed in Hunan and neighbouring provinces. It also sponsored an auxiliary organization for the express purpose of making contacts with the Ko-lao hui (Elder Brothers Society) and other secret societies. Significantly, the auxiliary's name was Society against the Common Enemy (T'ung-ch'ou hui); the Society for China's Revival had no programme apart from anti-Manchuism to offer its secret society allies. Huang and some friends established a Japanese language school to serve as a cover for their activities, which proceeded to gather momentum steadily during most of 1904.

Similar efforts were under way in other parts of China. In Hupei, a student revolutionary named Wu Lu-chen who had graduated from a Japanese military academy returned home to serve in the government's New Army (Hsin-chün). He then used his influence to obtain positions in the military for some of his comrades and to agitate among the troops. His friends held meetings at schools in various parts of the province, where they preached revolution and distributed copies of radical journals and tracts. By the summer of 1904 they had a thriving organization, which they called the Institute for the Diffusion of Science (K'o-hsueh pu-hsi so) in order to masquerade as a study society. The group learned that Huang Hsing was planning a revolt for the autumn of 1904, and arrangements were made to coordinate action in Hupei with Huang's in Hunan.

An ambitious plot was designed for simultaneous uprisings in six cities in Hunan, and it was hoped these could be coordinated with similar efforts in Hupei, Szechwan, Kiangsi, Nanking and Shanghai. It cannot be determined precisely how far these plans got, although they at least chose a date (the empress dowager's seventieth birthday, which fell on 16 November 1904); but in late October government agents learned of the plot and promptly acted to crush it. Huang and other leaders scattered and most made their way to Japan after several more haphazard attempts at small uprisings and several more narrow escapes. By this time Huang Hsing and the others were prepared to consider a different approach to carrying out a revolution in China.

Many other revolutionary groups flourished and withered between 1903 and 1905. Some of the students in Japan returned to China. In Shanghai a group of them joined a student strike and organized a Society for the Education of a Militant Citizenry. Its secret declaration of principles expressed fear that if Ch'ing rule continued the Chinese 'may vanish from the face of the earth'. Expressing the mood of desperation and activism that pervaded the student writings of this time the declaration said that 'it is better to struggle to the death than do nothing'.[22] True to its principles the society formed an assassination squad, began to make bombs, and sent members to seek contacts with secret societies and other organizations such as the Society for China's Revival.

Out of these efforts grew one of the few organizations that survived until 1912, the Restoration Society (Kuang-fu hui). Like the others it attempted to unite intellectuals and secret-society members against the Manchus, and it was also a provincial society that sought to reach beyond its own borders. Founded by students and a few older prominent intellectuals from Chekiang, the Restoration Society also drew recruits from Anhwei and Kiangsu and had its original base in Shanghai. Strongly influenced by anarchist ideas, it suffered from poor organization and ineffectual leadership. The students' efforts to mobilize a reliable secret-society fighting force never got very far, and the Restoration Society achieved a reputation chiefly for an impetuosity that resulted in at least two sensational assassination plots and several abortive uprisings.

The divided movement and the growth of anti-Manchuism

The number of students in Japan increased from about a hundred in 1901 to about eight thousand in 1905. Small clusters of students were active in China, especially in the relative safety of larger cities, particularly those such as Shanghai that offered the additional shield of foreign settlements. Still others were in Europe and America. Although contacts existed among the dozens of small student organizations, and the students read each other's publications, there was little successfully coordinated activity. Their efforts to grow beyond their provincial groups and to carry the revolution into China had failed. Ch'ing alertness and strength was far greater than they had anticipated. Like Sun Yat-sen they had seen the need for allies or at least for greater numbers than their own following provided, and they had sought to meet that need by tapping the potential that the secret societies seemed to offer; but, like Sun, their efforts had miscarried. The students could only inveigh from a distance, divided among themselves, separated from other revolutionary groups and from the people of China. Frustrated by failure, they turned more to the printed page than to the field of battle, but their writings called for renewed and immediate

---

[22] Mary Backus Rankin, *Early Chinese revolutionaries: radical intellectuals in Shanghai and Chekiang, 1902–1911*, 29–30. For a basic source on the Restoration Society see T'ao Ch'eng-chang, 'Che-an chi-lueh' (A brief account of the revolts in Chekiang), in Ch'ai Te-keng *et al.* eds. *Hsin-hai ko-ming* (The 1911 Revolution; hereafter *HHKM*), 3.3–111. For an analysis, see Chang Yü-fa, *Ch'ing-chi ti ko-ming t'uan-t'i*, 289–300, 463–528, including a list of 271 known members.

violent action. In one of the most popular pamphlets of the time, for example, Ch'en T'ien-hua wrote:

Kill! Kill! Kill! . . . Advance *en masse*, kill the foreign devils, kill the Christian converts who surrender to the foreign devils! If the Manchus help the foreigners kill us, then first kill all the Manchus. If those thieving officials help the foreigners kill us, then first kill all the thieving officials. . . . Advance, kill! Advance, kill! Advance, kill![23]

The Chinese government's response forced the hotly anti-imperialist students to consider some difficult choices. By appealing to nationalism as well as domestic reform Peking hoped to deflect revolutionary sentiment. Once again, and in a more imaginative fashion than when it supported the Boxers in 1900, the Ch'ing court was attempting to turn discontent in China against the foreign imperialists instead of itself. An anti-imperialist rights recovery movement was backed up by the foundation of military academies and the dispatch of more students to Japan for further military training, all for the purpose of creating the New Army. In January 1904 an imperial edict approving the formation of chambers of commerce made it plain that the objective was to resist foreign economic domination.[24] Critics of the government reconsidered their position. Travelling in the United States in 1903, Liang Ch'i-ch'ao had begun to think that revolution and republicanism would not cure China's ills. Impressed by the vigour of the Ching reforms, Liang decided in 1905 that the Chinese people could only attain self-government after a period of 'enlightened absolutism'. K'ang Yu-wei and Liang now argued that imperialism was the most immediate threat to China and all should rally against it by supporting Ch'ing policy.

Although the effect of all this on the students cannot be determined very precisely, it is plain that student opinion was divided and that only a minority favoured anti-Manchu revolution. For most, anti-imperialism came first, and if they opposed the Ch'ing it was likely to be because of its appeasement of the West and Japan. Between 1903 and 1905, however, a growing segment of the students moved towards a position closer to Sun Yat-sen's, in which anti-imperialism was muted, Western-style reforms emphasized, and anti-Manchuism intensified.

An outstanding example of youth's anti-Manchuism was a tract, *The revolutionary army*, written by a nineteen-year-old from Szechwan, Tsou Jung, with a preface by Chang Ping-lin, a distinguished classical scholar

[23] Quoted in Joseph W. Esherick, *Reform and revolution in China: the 1911 Revolution in Hunan and Hubei*, 48.
[24] Cited by Rhoads, *China's republican revolution*, 68, 62.

whose hatred for the Manchus was deeply rooted in the thought of the Ming loyalists. The collaboration between Tsou and Chang illustrates how the revolutionary movement brought about unexpected alignments.

Tsou's text included a wide-ranging indictment of Ch'ing rule and, in the most inflammatory language, called for a revolution 'to wipe out the five million barbarian Manchus, wash away the shame of two hundred and sixty years of cruelty and oppression, and make China clean once again'. Although he stated plainly that China was 'doubly enslaved', by the powers as well as by the Manchus, his wrath fell almost entirely on the latter. Furthermore, Tsou's pamphlet was full of admiring references to the French and American revolutions, German and Italian unification, and individual leaders such as Washington and Mazzini and thinkers such as Rousseau. In his concluding prescription for China's future, he confessed: 'I have carefully imitated the principles of American revolutionary independence.'[25]

Tsou's fiery prose and Chang's preface enraged the Ch'ing authorities. After months of strenuous effort they were unable to persuade officials of the Shanghai International Settlement, where Tsou Jung's tract was published, to extradite the authors. Shielded from the full wrath of the Ch'ing by foreigners, Chang and Tsou were finally tried by a mixed Sino-Western tribunal which, to the Manchus' intense frustration, in May 1904 sentenced Chang to three years in jail and Tsou to only two. The victory was a hollow one for the Chinese government, which had sought harsher penalties and had been humiliated by foreign interference, but it temporarily stymied the revolutionary movement in Shanghai.

Tokyo, with its growing concentration of Chinese students, soon became the centre of revolutionary propaganda. There, where it was safer to express anti-Manchuism than anti-imperialism, student writings gradually changed their focus. Instead of concentrating on anti-imperialism, Ch'ing appeasement, and the need to create a new and more militant Chinese people, the students began to dwell on the shortcomings of the Manchus. China's ills came to be blamed mostly on the alien dynasty. Anti-Manchu propaganda intensified precisely at the time when disunity was a major problem to the students. One tactical reason for this change was the need for a broad revolutionary movement, embracing secret-society members and Overseas Chinese as well as young intellectuals, soldiers, labourers and the small but growing numbers of merchants, especially in the treaty ports. The issue was how a movement for an essentially political

---

[25] See Tsou Jung, *The revolutionary army: a Chinese nationalist tract of 1903*, introd. and trans. with nn. by John Lust, 123 (a slightly different translation). The original Chinese text is also available in *HHKM*, 331–64.

revolution could adjust to the startling fact that a social revolution was beginning. New social groups and classes were being born and the old transformed. Anti-Manchuism was one idea all could accept with little or no reservation, whereas some felt ambivalent about anti-imperialism and others were indifferent. This is partly because imperialist penetration of China was uneven. Merchants who suffered from foreign discrimination in the treaty ports and villagers whose lives were disrupted by missionaries or foreign-soldiers might naturally be more hotly anti-imperialist than secret-society members who had a long tradition of anti-Manchuism but little or no contact with foreigners – we have come to think of secret societies as anti-*Western*, but they were basically anti-*foreign* and sometimes were even led by Chinese Christians against the Manchus. Overseas Chinese were at least as sensitive to the Manchus' inability to protect them from discrimination in Hong Kong, Singapore, Hanoi and San Francisco as they were to Western imperialism; in any case, they could more safely voice anti-Manchu sentiments than criticize the British, French or Americans.

In short, many blamed China's plight more on Manchu weakness than on foreign aggression. All Chinese could see the Manchus' inadequacies and all were affected by them. Anti-imperialism could not command such unanimous support, especially among the radical intellectuals and merchants, both of whose hostility to imperialism was mixed with admiration and envy, while their hostility to the Manchus was undiluted.

Moreover, Western imperialism appeared to be receding in 1904–5. Britain and France were preoccupied in Europe, and Russia was being humbled by Japan. Japanese imperialism now presented a greater threat than Western domination, but since Japan had become the students' major refuge they were in no position to make an issue of it. The revolutionaries in Tokyo would soon minimize the possibility of foreign intervention in the event of rebellion in China, and they would prefer to discuss the virtues of republican government rather than the evils of imperialism. They hoped that by giving more prominence to anti-Manchuism than to anti-imperialism they might avoid antagonizing the powers and possibly gain their sympathy, an attitude in accordance with that of Sun Yat-sen.

By 1905 the revolutionary movement confronted both promise and peril. Revolutionaries still feared foreign aggression, but still more to be feared was the growing vigour of the Ch'ing government. Although Peking's record was mixed, on the whole it was showing far more vitality than anyone would have expected in 1900, with no sign of slowing down. The court was taking an occasional strong stand against the imperialists, with due caution, while its domestic reforms were going beyond the very things it had refused to tolerate in 1898. The dynasty was gaining new support, even from such modern-minded patriots as Liang Ch'i-ch'ao.

Such trends threatened the revolutionary movement with extinction, but other trends offered hope. Thanks to the Ch'ing reforms the student movement had grown, and new opportunities existed for educated people simultaneously to pursue careers and promote revolution; for example, to work in the reforming bureaucracy and the New Army and to subvert them. There were new careers in teaching and journalism, professions that only a few years earlier had hardly existed. Educational reforms created a demand for teachers who had some foreign learning. Young writers who got their first experience on student journals in Japan returned to China and joined the rapidly growing Chinese press. In many cities they found a heightened public spirit that expressed itself in civic reforms such as anti-opium and anti-gambling campaigns, new schools, experiments in municipal government, and anti-foreign demonstrations. Educated youth, working as teachers and journalists and preaching radical ideas, found like-minded people in chambers of commerce and among local officials, police and soldiers. In brief, the students could see many potential allies. Their past failures to unite among themselves and with secret societies and others in the hinterland had taught them the need for a broader movement. As one student leader put it in 1905, the revolutionary current was like a small canal that had grown into a big river. A stream begun by human effort had become a natural stream. It was time for further effort: 'Open up the mountain in order to reach the spring and tap its water.'[26] They had retained their optimism and determination.

THE REVOLUTIONARY ALLIANCE, 1905–8

The summer of 1905 was a turning point for China. One of the major reasons for the change in course was Japan's victory over Russia, which came at a time when both the Chinese government and its revolutionary opposition were open to exploring unfamiliar paths. To each side, Japan's experience pointed a different way.

In what seemed to the Chinese and other Asians like a wink of an eye, Japan had transformed itself into a modern nation and world power. It had markedly altered international relations, especially in Asia, and it had won the admiration of the world. The Chinese court observed that the Japanese had achieved these remarkable feats while adopting a constitution and establishing a parliament but without entirely abandoning their traditions. Indeed, there were grounds for believing that the Japanese had managed

[26] Liew, *Struggle for democracy*, 48.

to strengthen national solidarity by reviving the ancient emperor institution that expressed it. Peking was sufficiently impressed to study Japanese constitutionalism and to begin to imitate it.

The revolutionaries found additional lessons in Japan's experience. Asians could conquer Westerners, earn their respect, and even incite them to revolution. Their curiosity about the outside world now thoroughly aroused, Chinese students looked everywhere for ideas and information. They sensed a new trend in the world and found evidence for it in Russia, Turkey, Poland and many other places as well as Japan. What impressed the students most was other people's militancy, especially the Japanese martial spirit. (Similarly, Liang Ch'i-ch'ao's observation of Japanese solidarity had inspired his call for a 'public morality'.) A strong sense of common national purpose, it seemed, could compensate for a lack of natural resources and a late start in modernization. A widespread popular devotion to national goals, the Chinese students felt, was exactly what their countrymen lacked, and without it China would remain at the mercy of more unified countries. Solidarity was also precisely what their own movement lacked. Buoyed with fresh hope and new confidence, they moved once again to amalgamate. In August 1905, after a decade of rather haphazard and uncoordinated activity, the separate strands of the movement bound themselves into a single anti-dynastic organization, the Chinese [Revolutionary] Alliance (Chung-kuo t'ung-meng-hui).[27] It became the means whereby the revolutionaries gained recognition as serious contestants for political power during the next two to three years.

The Revolutionary Alliance represented an attempt first to unify the student organizations and secondly to bring them together with Sun Yat-sen and his following. Although this much was only imperfectly and temporarily achieved, it represented a markedly greater degree of unity than had previously existed in the movement. About a thousand members joined in the first year of the organization's existence, and a large majority came from student groups. The founders' hope of going on to a third level, a nation-wide anti-Ch'ing coalition, was frustrated. Unity was fragile from the very first, and by 1907 it began to crumble. In 1908 the Revolutionary Alliance virtually ceased to function. Although it revived in 1910, at the time of the 1911 uprisings that toppled the dynasty, Revolutionary Alliance membership was less than ten thousand. At the height of the

---

[27] The T'ung-meng hui's official seal gave its English name as 'The China Federal Association'. See Marius B. Jansen, *The Japanese and Sun Yat-sen*, illus. facing p. 119. The revolutionaries considered but finally decided against including either the words 'anti-Manchu' or 'revolutionary' in the organization's name; see Feng Tzu-yu, 'Chi Chung-kuo T'ung-meng hui' (An account of the China Revolutionary Alliance), *KMWH*, 2 (1953) 148. The document shown in Jansen, however, indicates that Sun sometimes included the word 'revolutionary'.

organization's operations it may have had more members, and it surely had a great many more sympathizers, but even a revolutionary leader estimated that a majority of the students in Japan favoured constitutional monarchy.

The founding of the Revolutionary Alliance in 1905 brought the revolutionary movement into a new stage for which the Alliance served more as a symbol than as a propelling force. It was the umbrella organization for a movement that was too diverse and too far-flung to fit under one umbrella. When a wide anti-Ch'ing coalition fleetingly came into existence in 1911, the Revolutionary Alliance was only one element in it and probably not the most important. But at least during the period 1905–8 it was the major source of the revolutionaries' arms, money and ideas, and it was the chief object of Ch'ing retaliation and foreigners' interest. By friend and foe alike the Revolutionary Alliance was frequently referred to simply as 'the revolutionary party'.

Formation of a new revolutionary front

While the Chinese students in Japan were coming to recognize their need for greater unity, Sun Yat-sen had been travelling to Chinese communities in Hawaii and the United States. In his search for support from secret societies Sun went so far as to join the American branch of the Triad Society in 1904. He succeeded only in raising enough money to cover his travelling expenses. He received some encouragement from Chinese Christians and Westerners, particularly missionaries, but most Overseas Chinese favoured the Emperor Protection Society of K'ang Yu-wei and Liang Ch'i-ch'ao more than they did Sun and other revolutionaries.

Early in 1905 Sun's plummeting hopes were suddenly revived. On his way back to Japan Sun met Chinese students in Europe. After some heated debate with them Sun acknowledged that he had neglected the students and had relied too heavily upon secret societies. He declared himself persuaded that students, especially those who infiltrated the New Army, could tip the balance in favour of revolution. The students and Sun agreed to organize a new revolutionary party in which students and secret societies would have equal weight. Elated by Sun's change of attitude towards them, one student recalled, 'we excitedly sent a letter to Tokyo to report this affair and to ask each of our comrades to join eagerly when Sun arrived in Japan'.[28] Sun's elation was probably tempered by the fact that all but fourteen of the sixty students he recruited during his five-and-a-half months in Europe dropped out by the time he left.

[28] Chu Ho-chung, 'Ou-chou T'ung-meng hui chi-shih' (True account of the Revolutionary Alliance in Europe), *KMWH*, 2 (1953) 257.

Among the students in Japan there were sharp differences of opinion, but few were strongly opposed to the idea of uniting behind Sun. Despite his failures Sun had the highest reputation of any single revolutionary leader. Sun's major asset was his foreign expertise. At a time when the students were worried about the threat of foreign intervention against a revolution, they sought a leader who might make their movement acceptable to foreigners. Sun's Western education and his range of experience and contacts, particularly in Japan and the West, were matched by no other revolutionary. Foreign leaders took Sun seriously enough to watch his career closely, and some of them occasionally went out of their way to meet him. He was not received by the president and secretary of state of the United States, as K'ang Yu-wei and Liang Ch'i-ch'ao were, but he did share with his two rivals the distinction of being the only 'rebels' excluded from the amnesty granted by the Manchus on the empress dowager's seventieth birthday (1904). Thus he was one of China's three top public enemies, and he was the only avowed revolutionary of the three. His personal integrity and dedication to republicanism and modernization were unquestioned. No other revolutionary matched his capacity to raise money among the Overseas Chinese. The students had more contacts than Sun in the interior of China, but the failures of 1904 had shown them to be insufficient. Much would have to be done outside China, and it would have to be coordinated with work on the Chinese mainland. Sun's contacts with secret societies might complement the students' organizations in China. All in all, he was the only person behind whom a highly diverse and far-flung revolutionary movement could hope to unite. (One student made the interesting suggestion that Sun's reputation might usefully serve to draw attention away from the revolutionaries who were doing the real work.[29] It cannot be determined how many had this view of Sun as a combination of figurehead and lightning rod.)

Sun landed in Japan on 19 July 1905, to find that his Japanese friends (see chapter 6, page 370) had already established close relations with Huang Hsing, Sung Chiao-jen, Ch'en T'ien-hua and other Hunanese leaders of the Society for China's Revival. Issues remained, however, and since other organizations were to be included in the alliance, negotiations were complex. The basic issue was the small size and tight organization favoured by Sun, against a more broadly based and looser organization preferred by the students. One part of this question was whether older bodies such as the Society for China's Revival would retain their identity separate from the new Revolutionary Alliance. Another part concerned the role that the secret societies and the New Army would play and what relationship there

[29] Cited by Liew, *Struggle for democracy*, 43–4.

would be between them and the intellectuals. Sun stressed, as he had in his discussions with students in Europe, the revolutionary potential of the secret societies and the value of his contacts with them. Student leaders such as Sung Chiao-jen argued that the intellectuals formed the most important group in the revolutionary front. Sun agreed that the secret societies needed the leadership of the students, without which the revolution could be only destructive, but he insisted that it was through the power of the secret societies that intellectual leadership would be exercised. The students, however, seemed to agree with their friends in Europe who believed that intellectuals should concentrate on subverting the New Army, many of whose officers had studied in Japan and were sympathetic to the revolution. Once again Sun professed to be persuaded. It was finally agreed that both the secret societies and the New Army troops were essential to the revolution, but this compromise did not strictly govern policy. Although the revolutionaries tried to work with both groups, for several years after 1905 the secret societies continued to provide the manpower for the anti-Ch'ing movement. It was only after secret-society uprisings repeatedly failed that the New Army received a major share of the revolutionaries' attention.

Sun and the students also debated how authority would be structured and distributed. In the end Sun contented himself with the title *tsung-li* (director) and the appearance of centralized leadership, while the Revolutionary Alliance adopted an elaborate formal structure modelled on the government of the United States. In providing for federalism, checks and balances, and divided authority, Sun and his comrades even created legislative, executive and judicial departments, but this was only symbolic of their allegiance to modern republicanism. In this curious marriage of democratic structure and conspiratorial function, Western forms were little more than a facade. The functioning departments soon turned out to be provincial branches and other factions and sub-groups.

All but one of China's provinces were represented in the Revolutionary Alliance, and roughly three-quarters of the known original membership consisted of students in Japan. About a hundred members, many of them students, were recruited abroad. The Revolutionary Alliance was thus very different from Sun's first revolutionary society, which was made up overwhelmingly of Kwangtung people (of whom more than half lived abroad) and in which the largest occupational groups were merchants (42 per cent) and artisans (18 per cent). Kwangtung was also the home of more Alliance members than any other province, but Hunan was a close second, and the two provinces accounted for only one-third of the total membership. Two other large contingents came from Hupei and Szechwan; the remaining members were scattered among thirteen other provinces, five of which had ten members or less.[30]

The available membership rosters probably exaggerate the extent to which students dominated the Revolutionary Alliance. During its seven years of existence they remained its backbone and probably its largest component, but the Alliance was essentially a coalition in which no single element, not even the provincial student organizations, prevailed. Its diversity, at least in comparison with early Chinese revolutionary groups, was due to more than its broader provincial representation. The student organizations included older intellectuals such as Ts'ai Yuan-p'ei, Wu Chih-hui, Chang Ping-lin and Liu Shih-p'ei, many of whom had classical training and had even passed the traditional examinations. They represented a wide spectrum of ideas and were sometimes vigorously at odds with each other. Some, such as Wu and Chang, were bitter personal enemies. Some were suspicious of Sun while others were very close to him. Some worked closely with secret-society leaders, others with Westerners and Japanese, still others mainly with the students. Provincial associations cut across all these differences, and so did the primarily upper-class background of the membership, but in none of these respects was the Revolutionary Alliance a homogeneous organization. Sun Yat-sen's following, for example, represented primarily the Overseas Chinese, mostly small businessmen and shopkeepers but also including some larger entrepreneurs and a variety of labouring people. Many had contacts in China, particularly among the secret societies. While it was only a small number compared with the students and their allies, Sun's following was highly important. A major source of the organization's funds was the money Sun raised, especially among the Overseas Chinese. This gave Sun's followers a powerful voice, and his personal influence was heightened by their financial backing. In addition to the many small contributors there were a few wealthy individuals – some of them Sun's friends, some relatives or friends of students, and others not identified with any faction or group – who made heavy contributions. Above all, there was no unified command or strict discipline. The groups in the coalition often cooperated, but they did not merge. Each retained something of its own character. The students' numbers, therefore, did not mean that they controlled the Revolutionary Alliance.

---

[30] The Revolutionary Alliance membership list for 1905–6 may be found in *KMWH*, 2 (1953) 158–217. The most thorough studies of the Alliance are Shelley Hsien Cheng, 'The T'ung-meng-hui: its organization, leadership, and finances, 1905–1912' (University of Washington, Ph.D. dissertation, 1962) and Chang Yü-fa, *Ch'ing-chi ti ko-ming t'uan-t'i*, 301–462. Note also Ta-ling Lee, *Foundations of the Chinese Revolution, 1905–1912*.

Ideology and the 'revolution-reform debate'

The unity achieved by the revolutionaries in 1905, although decidedly imperfect and unstable, was a higher degree of unity than the ten-year-old movement had previously reached. Much of its cement was supplied by ideology, but this is only to say that in the realm of ideas the revolutionaries were somewhat less divided than they were otherwise. There was no widely accepted doctrine in the republican revolutionary movement. Rather, there was a lively and vigorous ferment of ideas that reached closest agreement on the Manchus' incompetence and exhaustion of their mandate. From near-unanimity on this issue, opinion in the movement became more divided when it came to questions of republicanism, land and other economic policy, social change and more specific policy problems.

Both the widening area of consensus and the sharpening points of ideological conflict help us to understand the character of the republican revolutionary movement and its place in China's modern history. The widening consensus embraced many so-called 'reformers' as well as revolutionaries. Although these two sides engaged each other in hot debate and with some malice, their exchanges revealed considerable areas of general agreement and some striking common assumptions. They also brought out differences among the revolutionaries that were as weighty as those between Liang Ch'i-ch'ao and Sun Yat-sen. Both sides, especially the revolutionaries (since Liang, only thirty-two years old in 1905, was virtually a one-man debating team), represented diverse points of view that usually diverged still further in the crucible of polemics. Neither side, and indeed probably not even any individual, was very consistent. On the contrary, in their near-frantic desire to find, absorb, integrate and apply new ideas, thinkers in this period were highly eclectic, contradictory, ambiguous and protean. Still, out of a welter of writings between 1905 and 1911 there emerged a body of ideas that had enough force to begin modern China's intellectual revolution and enough cohesion to provide ideological underpinnings for political and social revolution.

The main outlines of revolutionary ideology were provided by Sun Yat-sen. Sun may have lacked depth as a thinker, but his ability to gauge others' moods, to reconcile his own ideas with theirs, and to express himself graphically and simply, often compensated for the insufficiencies of his thought. Impatient with detail, frustrated by complexities, but above all overwhelmingly preoccupied with the practical chores of financing and otherwise making revolution, Sun left the task of elaborating revolutionary ideology to others. As they filled in his outlines and added their own ideas, some of them leaped far beyond him. Others, of course, from the very beginning rejected Sun's framework in part or completely. In the same way that the entire movement outgrew Sun by spreading to a great variety of people and groups, so its ideas outgrew the Three People's Principles. However, Sun kept returning from repeated failures and periodic rebuffs to regain key positions in the movement, and his personal stamp remained evident in the revolutionary movement's anti-Manchuism and republicanism, its strategy and tactics (especially its conspiratorial style), and its struggle to reconcile its opposition to foreign domination with its search for foreign help and approval. Even in social and economic policy, where Sun's ideas were most controversial and least accepted in the republican camp, his influence was considerable. Sympathizers and critics alike, despite having staked out their own positions, continued to argue about what Sun had said and meant, to discuss the issues he had posed, and to use the terms he had coined.[31]

The core of revolutionary ideology was expressed in the oath, written by Sun and taken by all members of the Alliance, to 'drive out the Manchus, restore Chinese rule, establish a republic, and equalize land rights'. From 1905 onwards, these bare bones took on flesh and muscle through the labours of scores of writers in journals and pamphlets that were published all over the world. Tokyo remained the centre, but contributions came from Hong Kong, Singapore, Paris, San Francisco, Vancouver, Hawaii and, as the Ch'ing grip loosened, inside China. The leading publication was the *People's Report (Min pao)*, the official journal of the Revolutionary Alliance. It was first published in Tokyo in November 1905, and came out twenty-four times before it was suppressed three years later; in 1910 two additional numbers appeared. Its editorial board changed several times, and it remained open to a great variety of views. Other journals also thrived, especially from 1905 to 1907, and although the *People's Report* survived longer than any of them and also attracted more prominent revolutionaries to write for it, it was never the sole voice of the movement.[32] A good deal of contact was maintained among the various publications, including reprinting each other's articles and advertising each other's contents, but most went their individual ways. Some took stands that were directly at odds with basic Revolutionary Alliance policies, notably the *New Century (Hsin shih-chi)* magazine published in Paris and the

[31] For examples see Martin Bernal, *Chinese socialism to 1907*, 136–8, 152–60. Bernal's interpretation of early Chinese socialism differs in many respects from the views set forth in this chapter.
[32] Cf. Bernal's assessment of the *People's Report* (also translated as *People's Journal*) and its varying phases (*ibid.* 68–73, 107–97, 217–23). An invaluable guide to the journal's history, including its contents and the authors' pen-names, is Man-hua (T'ang Tseng-pi), 'T'ung-meng-hui shih-tai *Min-pao* shih-mo chi' (A history of the *Min-pao* in the era of the Revolutionary Alliance), *KMWH*, 2 (1953) 218–38; the same article is available in *HHKM*, 2.438–59. See also Michael Gasster, *Chinese intellectuals and the Revolution of 1911: the birth of modern Chinese radicalism*, chs. 3, 4 and 6.

Journal of Natural Principles (*T'ien-i pao*) issued in Tokyo; the former was dedicated to the anarchism of Kropotkin and Bakunin, the latter to its own variety of a classless, stateless society and to women's rights. Still another revolutionary periodical stressed anti-Manchuism and the preservation of traditional Chinese culture, another the introduction of foreign ideas, another the defence of China's borders against Western imperialism.

In 1905, however, the keynote was unity and nationalism. The students and Sun Yat-sen shared a sense of almost desperate urgency about their country's future. Compared with the West and Japan, by whose standards they had decided to measure China's progress, Chinese youth felt shamefully laggard. Now, at a mass meeting of students in Tokyo on 13 August 1905, Sun Yat-sen told them that China could move even faster than Japan.

Japan's pace seemed dizzying to the students; to hear China's leading revolutionary explain to them how they could go even faster was electrifying. Sun told them that their country possessed a unique combination of noble heritage, matchless human and material resources, models such as Japan and the United States from whom to learn, and Japanese friends and Chinese leaders like himself who understood Japan and the West and therefore knew what to avoid in borrowing from abroad as well as what to copy. Japan's modernization, he observed, had been guided by a small group of men. Thanks to the students, who were acquiring the skills needed to build a new China, their country would soon have equivalent leadership. As long as the Chinese revolutionaries stayed united, nothing was impossible. They could create the most modern and efficient form of government as easily as they could make the most modern and efficient locomotive. They could modernize their economy by applying the principles of Henry George. They could throw off foreign domination and attain full sovereignty by establishing a republic and thereby proving to foreigners that China was strong, resolute and progressive.

The themes Sun stressed – unity, sovereignty and national strength – suited the students' mood. They had accepted him mainly on the grounds that he understood the foreign threat and knew not only how to nullify it but even how to turn it into support for the Chinese revolution. He articulated with confidence the sense of special mission that the students felt: 'Everything can be managed by men of determination. What the ordinary people do not understand will have to be introduced by [such] men . . . . If in one transformation we can stir people's hearts, civilization will come in a hurry and in only ten years the word "independence" will be stamped on people's brains.'[33]

Sun had called upon the students to lead a crusade for national salvation.

[33] Quoted in Harold Z. Schiffrin, 'The enigma of Sun Yat-sen', in *CIR*, 465.

It was a call that future revolutionary leaders were to issue repeatedly and students to heed in decades to come. In this case it vastly overshadowed and even conflicted with the movement's other aims. The goals of republicanism and equal land rights, for example, expressed in the Alliance oath, were equivalent to the second and third of Sun's Three People's Principles, democracy (*min-ch'üan chu-i*) and socialism or, more literally, 'people's livelihood' (*min-sheng chu-i*). The populism and egalitarianism implicit in these principles ran counter to many of the students' habits and feelings, and perhaps to their upper-class backgrounds. Although they were strongly attracted to new ideas of democracy and social justice, they were even more strongly drawn to nationalism, perhaps because it appealed both to new patriotic sentiments and to older notions of solidarity and cultural superiority.

Whatever the reason, the second and third of Sun's three principles commanded much less support than the first, nationalism (*min-tsu chu-i*). Indeed Sun himself, however fond he was of equating his three principles with liberty, equality and fraternity, and with government of, by and for the people, had a pronounced elitist streak; like the students, he valued popular participation less than he did strong leadership. Like them too, he subordinated the ideals of democracy and social justice to the rapid transformation of China into a wealthy and powerful state. Democracy was to some extent an end in itself, and the Chinese revolutionaries were not indifferent to ideas of popular rights, checks and balances, and federalism. But they valued democracy more for its seeming association with national power. The strongest states were the democracies, and the one that was rising fastest to wealth and power, the United States, was a republic. Democracy and republicanism were primarily means of achieving a strong Chinese nation. Social justice was similarly both end and means but more the latter: socialism, the Chinese believed, meant an end to extremes of rich and poor and of privilege, but it also meant national solidarity. When either the second or third principle threatened to interfere with realization of the first, it could be compromised or softened. On several occasions, for example, 'equalization of land rights' was quietly shelved in order to appease landed interests or others whose support was deemed necessary to 'the national revolution'.[34]

While the Chinese worked out these ideas with one eye on the foreign

[34] The clearest example was an offshoot of the Revolutionary Alliance, its so-called Central China Branch (see below, pp. 518–20), which explicitly confined its aims to 'The two principles of overthrowing the Ch'ing government and establishing a democratic constitutional political system'. Chung-hua-min-kuo k'ai-kuo wu-shih-nien wen-hsien pien-tsuan wei-yuan hui, comp. *Wu-ch'ang shou-i* (The initiation of the righteous rising at Wuchang), 2nd collection, 1.5.

threat, they paid equal attention to foreign models. No characteristic of Chinese intellectual life in the decade or so before 1911 is more prominent than foreign influence. Chinese curiosity about foreign life and a tendency to adopt foreign ideas, growing slowly since about 1860 and accelerating rapidly since the 1890s, waxed to a near mania after 1905. At times, in their passion to learn about the West and Japan, Chinese youth neglected the problem of applying in China what they were learning. Revolutionary writers paid more attention to patriotic movements in Turkey, Poland and Portugal than to those in Canton and Shanghai. When they discussed democracy and social justice, which they did fervently, it was usually in terms framed by foreign thinkers and applicable more to foreign problems than to China's. They discussed constitutionalism, for example, primarily in terms of German political theory and Japanese practice. They wrote of Russian revolutionaries, the use of terror and the problem of political assassination, with little reference to the differences between Russia and China and between themselves and the Russian revolutionaries. Their avid discussions of anarchism and socialism were devoted more to explaining Western thought and political issues such as the prospects for the British Labour Party than to the problems of developing socialism in China. An occasional writer explored questions that were crucial to China, such as land nationalization and the relationship between land policy and tax policy, but even these discussions tended to reflect Western problems more than China's. For example, they were mostly in the context of whether or not state socialism was desirable, which the Chinese socialists discussed primarily as a political issue in Germany and Japan.

The Chinese were not simply admiring imitators. They saw much to criticize in Western life, and they foresaw severe economic and social crises in store for the industrialized nations. Indeed, in a fascinating reversal of Marx, they predicted that China would be able to build socialism more easily than industrialized states because class division was too pronounced in the latter. They envisaged, therefore, a relatively peaceful transition to a moderate form of socialism in China. Some of them, notably Sun, also suggested modifications of Western democratic practices that would have to be made if republicanism were to work in China. Still, on the whole they adopted foreign ideas rather uncritically and swallowed them with insufficient rumination. Some intellectual indigestion resulted, which contributed in turn to poor political planning and execution when the time came to establish their new government.

The Chinese revolutionaries felt a kinship with 'progressive' foreigners. Considering themselves to be democrats and socialists as well as nationalists, they felt part of a pioneering world-wide force. This is one reason why they paid such careful attention to revolutionaries abroad. By no means the least important appeal of republicanism and socialism to the Chinese was the conviction that those two doctrines were sweeping the world; the Chinese saw them as the newest and most 'advanced' ideas that would provide for national power, political unity and order, and social well-being. In their search for the new and the progressive, Chinese intellectuals frequently abandoned one idea for another or put together ideas that were not easily compatible. Their ideology developed a severely split personality in which a major conflict was the unspoken one of attitudes towards foreigners. They felt a kinship with foreign revolutionaries, and they also envied wealthy and powerful foreign states; they resented Western and Japanese imperialism, but they sought Western and Japanese aid. Dilemmas of this sort, inherent in a situation of partial imperialist domination, contributed much to the instability of the movement and its ideology. Revolutionaries dropped out, switched sides, changed ideas, and argued among themselves. Chang Ping-lin challenged the value of republicanism and its suitability for China; advocates of socialism argued about different degrees of nationalization; anarchists attacked all forms of organized authority; the *People's Report* mulled questions about the rights of the minority and of individuals in relation to majority opinion and the 'general will'. By 1907 these disagreements had erupted into factionalism and open strife. One major issue, political more than ideological, nevertheless had implications for Alliance ideology. Sun was accused by Chang Ping-lin and others of having accepted a large sum of money from Japanese sources and in other ways having neglected his Chinese comrades in favour of Japanese supporters. Another issue, also raised primarily by Chang and clearly related to the political issue, was whether the revolution had become too foreign-oriented at the expense of China's own culture and traditions. The Alliance had never spoken with one voice, but from 1907 onward its message was cacophonous, and a major point of discord was the relationship between the Chinese revolution and the outside world.

It is against this background of Alliance ideological ferment, vitality, growth, confusion and dissidence that the debate between the reformers and revolutionaries must be viewed. The debate was carried on mainly in the pages of Liang Ch'i-ch'ao's *Renovation of the people* and the *People's Report* between 1905 and 1907. After October 1907, when Liang's journal ceased publication, the debate continued in a less focused and systematic way in publications both in China and around the world.

Liang vigorously defended the Ch'ing efforts to introduce constitutional government, and at the same time he prodded Peking to move faster towards a more substantial democracy than its reforms intended. With still greater vigour he slashed at the revolutionaries, but his attack was selective. Liang's views on democracy and popular sovereignty, national power, industrialization and socialism were close to those of many revolutionaries; on these points they usually debated details or methods rather than fundamental aims and values. The crucial issues they debated in 1905–7 were whether these goals could be reached without first toppling the Manchus, whether they could be achieved speedily, and whether an anti-Manchu revolution would invite or forestall foreign intervention and control. Although they also debated different forms of socialism and whether China should be a constitutional monarchy or a republic, they discussed these matters with less heat than they argued the issue of whether or not continued Manchu rule could be tolerated.

Liang Ch'i-ch'ao's fundamental position was that an anti-Manchu revolution was dangerous and unnecessary. It was dangerous because it would introduce disorder that would make foreign intervention inevitable. It was unnecessary because the very reforms that the Manchus had begun would gradually modify their autocracy out of existence. Underlying these views was Liang's deep pessimism about China's ability to effect fundamental changes rapidly. A sensitive and protean man who was severely buffeted by the turbulent conditions of his time, Liang was unable to hold unswervingly to these views, but they were among the most consistent of his beliefs and he fought doggedly for them between 1905 and 1907.

The revolutionaries' position was that there was already considerable disorder and foreign presence in China and that the Manchus were responsible for it. The Manchus, who were themselves alien rulers, had permitted the powers to come in and had proved incapable of getting them out. Indeed, the Ch'ing had acquiesced in Western domination of China in order to maintain its throne. China's loss of its pre-eminence in the world was due not to traditionalism or overpopulation or any historical accidents, but to the failures of the Ch'ing government. Thus the revolutionaries blamed the invading imperialist powers less than those in China who had failed adequately to resist the invaders. *Min pao* writers minimized foreign aggressiveness in order to refute Liang and to support the revolutionaries' argument that the powers, despite having benefited from China's weakness and Ch'ing appeasement, would now welcome a more stable and progressive regime in Peking.

Liang hit very hard at the imminent threat of foreign domination, insisting that the powers were predators who would take advantage of the first opportunity to dismember China. He even came to oppose efforts to obtain foreign capital. Sun Yat-sen argued that Western and Japanese aid would be forthcoming in the effort to overthrow the Manchus and, subsequently, to move China ahead. He laboured ceaselessly to obtain such aid, and he remained convinced that the Chinese revolution could not succeed without assistance from foreigners. Supporters such as Hu Han-min, a leading *People's Report* writer, defended Sun's ideas, and the Revolutionary Alliance openly appealed for foreign help.

The Ch'ing government, which in its anti-foreignism had even urged secret societies to 'exterminate the barbarians' in 1900, was still pressing to 'recover sovereign rights'. Its reformist supporters considered that its efforts, even if insufficient, were preferable to the revolutionaries' appeasement. Indeed, when nationalism came to be concentrated against Japan in a 1908 incident, the revolutionaries did not take the lead. On the contrary, an intense popular outburst supported the government's seizure of a Japanese ship carrying contraband arms for the revolutionaries. Although many people were outraged at the government's failure to persevere in its resistance to imperialism, at least until 1909 they preferred to urge it to do more rather than think of overthrowing it.

Revolutionary Alliance spokesmen insisted that throwing off Manchu rule was the indispensable first step to effective resistance against imperialism and to building a modern country. Schiffrin has perceptively noted that the temporary deflection of revolutionary nationalism from anti-imperialism to anti-Manchuism was mainly a tactical shift in emphasis: 'It was not that the young nationalists forgot their anti-imperialist grievances, but that they despaired of winning such a clash and became reconciled to a holding action in foreign relations.'[35] It may be added that the revolutionaries' reluctance to attack the foreign powers directly did not prevent them from making their anti-imperialist point indirectly; when they vowed to end Manchu rule they also pledged to restore China to Chinese control.

In the heat of ideological debate, anti-Manchuism boiled over and obscured other topics. *People's Report* declared, 'The Manchu government is evil because it is the evil race which usurped our government, and their evils are not confined to a few political measures but are rooted in the nature of the race and can neither be eliminated nor reformed.'[36] Such blatant racism may have been primarily a propaganda tactic and not an ideological principle, but it contributed to an atmosphere of vituperation and hatred that interfered with reasoned discourse. Thus, ironically, as intellectuals played an increasingly prominent role in the revolution, reason gave way to passion. One of the students later summarized how his generation reacted to the various appeals they heard around 1905: 'While we got our mental food from Liang Ch'i-ch'ao, we drew our emotional nourish-

[35] Schiffrin, *Sun Yat-sen*, 298–9.
[36] Hu Han-min, 'Min-pao chih liu ta chu-i', *Min-pao*, (April 1906) 8.

ment from Dr. Sun Yat-sen and his sympathizers. Generally speaking, it is emotion that leads to action when a decisive hour comes; when that hour came in China, Dr. Sun, both dreamer and man of action, won a decisive victory over the new literati who stood for constitutionalism [i.e., constitutional monarchy].'[37] More intent upon winning a debate than unravelling the knotty problems of republicanism, land policy and the role of foreigners in China's modernization, the revolutionaries won an ideological skirmish but lost the struggle for leadership of a new China. Later, when the Ch'ing had fallen and anti-Manchuism had served its purpose, they had little else to offer the nation. To compound the irony, the reformers and revolutionaries who overlooked their common goals, interests and values before 1911 and behaved like bitter enemies, were to come together to overthrow the Ch'ing in 1911–12. The debates therefore demonstrate how far from readiness the anti-Ch'ing movement was before 1911.

The ideological debates of 1905–8 were oddly removed from life in China. Not only did they neglect the problems of the 80 per cent of the population who lived in the countryside, but they were also detached from the new movements that were growing in the cities. In addition to frequent and sometimes massive anti-foreign demonstrations there were many new organizations engaged in a great variety of reforms, some of which were beginning to develop from purely local activities into provincial or even nation-wide movements. These ranged from familiar reformist programmes such as anti-gambling, anti-opium and anti-footbinding campaigns to education associations, labour unions, railway-building and public works projects. In all of these activities there was new participation by people who until now had not been active in public life, especially women, youth and merchants. In 1905–8 the ideas held by the leaders of the revolutionary movement barely touched the concerns of their potential supporters. The leaders' thinking on questions of politics and economics was tangential to the activities of anti-foreign demonstrators and social reformers who were becoming increasingly vocal in their demands that the Ch'ing move more rapidly and decisively. Only in their accusations that the Ch'ing reforms were hypocritical devices aimed chiefly at strengthening the Manchu government could the revolutionary intellectuals make effective contacts with popular protest movements. The potential bonds that existed between the revolutionaries' professed dedication to nationalism, democracy and social welfare on the one hand, and the mounting public demand for national dignity, self-government and social reform on the other were not tightened. No organizational ties were created. The contact that was made

[37] Monlin Chiang, *Tides from the West: a Chinese autobiography*, 53.

was between ideas that reformers and revolutionaries agreed upon. What Liang Ch'i-ch'ao and his opponents on the *People's Report* argued about seems to have mattered little to activist groups such as the Canton Merchants Self-Government Society or the Nanchang Self-Government Association. Even local groups that were founded by Revolutionary Alliance members, such as the Kiukiang Reading Society and the Kan-chou Study Society in Kiangsi province, brought reformers and revolutionaries together in essentially non-ideological cooperation. A study of the revolutionary movement in Kiangsi has found that divisions that were clear and sharp in Tokyo were blurred in Kiangsi.[38]

The more important division in China was between those who were actively promoting substantial change and those who were not. In this respect the revolutionaries and reformers made similar contributions. Their debate circulated new ideas and developed a new vocabulary among the educated elite. The ideas concentrated on national solidarity, and the vocabulary was enriched by concepts of citizenship, equality, rights, representation, nationalization and public opinion. The meanings and implications of such words remained to be fully defined and absorbed, but in the decade before 1911 they became the common intellectual coin of a whole generation. The debates of 1905–8 pushed all but a few traditional ideas and thinkers into obscurity and brought to prominence a new intelligentsia. Their writings fed a growing demand for radical change. After 1910, as the Ch'ing finally demonstrated its incapacity to satisfy that demand, ideas of revolution and republicanism began to fall upon increasingly receptive ears.

Revolutionary strategy and the secret societies

The Revolutionary Alliance changed its military strategy remarkably little from the strategy that had failed before 1905. It still relied heavily upon secret societies for its military manpower and hoped to set in motion a nation-wide revolution by promoting an armed uprising in a single province such as Kwangtung.

Military victory was to be followed immediately by a three-stage sequence to build a republic. As each county (hsien) was liberated from Ch'ing rule, martial law would be introduced. Within three years at most the 'accumulated evils' of corruption, injustice, misgovernment and harmful old social customs such as footbinding were to be eliminated. Martial law would thereupon be revoked and provisional constitutions enacted in each locality. During an ensuing six-year period under these provisional constitutions

---

[8] Samuel Y. Kupper, 'Revolution in China: Kiangsi province, 1905–1913' (University of Michigan, Ph.D. dissertation, 1973), 95–6.

the power of local self-government was to be transferred to the people in each county, while a military government retained control over national affairs. The final step was to be the enactment of a national constitution and the holding of national elections, as a result of which martial law would disappear and republican government under the constitution would manage the country.

Scholars have given Sun Yat-sen credit for formulating 'the central idea of China's modern political revolution: the conception of political tutelage by a provisional government which would train the politically-inert Chinese populace for eventual participation in a constitutional democracy'.[39] If Sun originated the idea of tutelage, however, many others accepted its basic premise. Liang Ch'i-ch'ao also insisted that the Chinese people were not yet prepared to govern themselves. He called for a transitional period of 'enlightened absolutism' under Ch'ing stewardship. The essential difference was not the concept of tutelage itself but the identity of the tutor. Sun's major contribution was the idea of a provisional government. No one explained what qualifications a tutor in democracy needed or how they would be obtained. The intellectuals simply assumed that they were best equipped to manage China's transition to democracy. Sun's concept of a speedy but staged transition to constitutional government was relied upon heavily by Revolutionary Alliance writers in their debate with Liang. The two chief polemicists, Wang Ching-wei and Hu Han-min, saw tutelage as the answer to Liang's contention that revolution might lead to dictatorship under a military strongman.

Sun's military strategy proved difficult to execute. Without inland bases of its own, the Revolutionary Alliance could only react to events within China instead of taking the initiative. It was too far removed from the action, and its allies in the interior were too weak to sustain operations until the Alliance could reinforce and supply them. In the spring of 1907, for example, peasant rebels who were under heavy government pressure in south-western Kwangtung sent two representatives to Sun for assistance. After an aide investigated, Sun sent Huang Hsing and a Triad leader named Wang to oversee the campaign. It took Wang until early September to raise a substantial force of peasants and secret-society men and arrange to cooperate with two companies of rebellious troops. Wang quickly captured a key city and moved on to attack the prefectural seat in whose garrison Huang Hsing had meanwhile managed to obtain a position. But their attempt at a coordinated attack from within and without failed when Huang was unable to do his part. Wang then moved off and improvised an independent campaign that raised his force from five hundred to between

[39] Ssu-yü Teng and John K. Fairbank, *China's response to the West*, 226.

three and four thousand men, but after a battle that lasted for several days he ran out of ammunition and had to retreat. From his headquarters in Hanoi, two hundred miles from the action, Sun was unable to get supplies or reinforcements to his fighting men. About four months after it began the revolt in south-western Kwangtung collapsed. At least five, and perhaps as many as a dozen or more, uprisings failed for similar reasons between 1906 and 1908.

What exactly were those reasons? Manifestly the vast stretches of rough terrain posed a major obstacle to Sun's strategy of outside support. Geography alone made it unworkable. But there were more than miles, mountains, hostile troops, and police lying between the revolutionaries in Japan, Hong Kong, Hanoi and Shanghai on the one hand, and their potential allies and supporters in China on the other. There was also a vast social distance. The Alliance, although more diverse than any of its predecessors, was still made up largely of intellectuals. To create a national revolution they had to cross class lines. In Sun's strategy, secret societies were the bridges. But they could not quite carry the load.

In some respects the revolutionaries and the secret societies were natural allies. Branded as outlaws, both were composed of people who did not fit into the traditional social hierarchy, and both resented foreign domination.

The Revolutionary Alliance cooperated with secret societies primarily to gain access to dissatisfied, rebellious and, it was hoped, potentially revolutionary peasants. According to this interpretation peasant uprisings, already common in the nineteenth century, spread in the early 1900s. Most began as small movements in which local issues predominated, but grain shortages, inflation and higher taxes (often to pay for reforms such as new schools) became issues in so many areas as to be nearly nation-wide. Therefore, local rebellions might grow into wider movements. Secret societies, having local organization, and some peasant membership, were uniquely situated to direct such movements. Revolutionaries who looked for secret-society allies 'were seeking a short cut to local influence'.[40] They had devised no other means of securing popular support. The secret societies were not an ideal means but neither were they hopeless. They were expanding into the countryside in the 1900s and showing signs of growing coherence. At least in 1906 they were the most active and powerful antigovernment forces in China.

By 1906 uprisings were breaking out all across Central and South China. One of them, along the Hunan–Kiangsi border in December 1906, was so large that troops had to be sent from four provinces to suppress it. Miners and other workers joined throngs of peasants from an area of some eight

40 Rankin, *Early Chinese revolutionaries*, 129.

hundred square miles known as P'ing-Liu-Li (from P'ing-hsiang in Kiangsi and Liu-yang and Li-ling in Hunan). The insurgents' aims were mixed. In Kiangsi several revolutionary students attempted, without the knowledge of Alliance headquarters in Tokyo, to promote a mass movement by bringing intellectuals and secret-society people together in one organization. On the Hunan side of the border revolutionaries were less involved. Economic demands were central to the entire movement, but in other respects there was less unity. In Kiangsi the Manchus were attacked for appeasing foreigners. In Hunan there were old slogans such as 'sweep away the Ch'ing but protect the foreigners' and 'take from the rich to help the poor'. While tradition was evident in a group calling itself the 'Southern Restoration Army of the Great Chinese Empire', another hailed the 'government of the Republic of China' with its promise of liberty and the equalization of land rights.[41] Still, the uprising was under local leadership, provoked mainly by local issues, and the students were unable to create lasting ties with the secret societies.

For nearly two years the Revolutionary Alliance laboured to strengthen its relations with secret societies and, through them, with the Chinese people. It failed. Countless uprisings occurred, a few under Alliance direction, many more led by secret societies, but by far the greatest number with no discernible organization from above. The Kiangsi experience was typical. Although economic hardship deepened into famine, banditry and a rash of uprisings in the decade before 1911, the revolutionaries completely failed to connect their movement with the peasants. Instead, peasant disaffection found traditional types of protest. In Chekiang peasant revolts 'were almost always completely divorced from the revolutionary movement'.[42]

The failure of the student radicals to ally with the secret societies and, through them, with the masses, is not simply attributable to class prejudice. As Marxist scholarship confirms, neither the student radicals nor the secret societies represented a single class or a single point of view.[43] Some secret societies were not consistently anti-Manchu, nor consistently anti-foreign or anti-imperialist, and some were led by lower gentry, merchants, landowners or officials. Indeed, the weight of scholarly opinion suggests that the weaknesses of the secret societies were at least as important as the

[41] See Esherick, *Reform and revolution in China*, 62–3, where it is also pointed out that this proclamation was composed by students and 'virtually copied' from Sun Yat-sen's Three People's Principles. Cf. Lewis, *Prologue*, 185–96, and Kupper, 'Revolution in China', 78–93.
[42] Rankin, *Early Chinese revolutionaries*, 192.
[43] Li Wen-hai, 'Hsin-hai ko-ming yü hui-tang' (The Revolution of 1911 and the secret societies), in Hu-pei sheng che-hsueh she-hui k'o-hsueh hsueh-hui lien-ho hui, ed. *Hsin-hai ko-ming wu-shih chou-nien lun-wen-chi* (Anthology commemorating the fiftieth anniversary of the 1911 Revolution), 170–1, 180.

aloofness of the revolutionaries in accounting for their inability to work effectively together.[44]

Both the secret societies and the revolutionaries represented a broad spectrum of social background and discord as well as common interests. The problem was that neither represented the masses.

The radical intellectuals of this period claimed a special status because of their foreign education. They advocated 'tutelage' of the common people by 'men of determination', in itself evidence of such a claim, yet few revolutionaries went among the people. Most stayed in large cities abroad or, when in China, congregated in the foreign areas of major treaty ports. Unlike the traditional upper-class gentry, the modern intelligentsia did not have a base in villages and smaller cities such as hsien capitals. They were probably more cut off from the masses than traditional intellectuals had been. The frequency of gentry involvement in secret societies, for example, suggests that the traditional elite had less trouble establishing ties with commoners than did the modern elite, who found more in common with urban merchants, Overseas Chinese and foreigners than with Chinese peasants or *yu-min*. The divisions between traditional and modern, rural and urban, were becoming more glaring than the old division between gentry elite and masses.

Evidence for this comes from the Canton area and is supported by studies of Szechwan, Hunan, Hopei, Kiangsi, Shanghai and Chekiang. In the Canton delta the revolution saw two movements, one welling up in the countryside from largely spontaneous and traditional sources, and the other reaching out from the revolutionary movement in major cities. Between them, centred in towns and smaller cities, were the secret societies. The Triad Society, for example, confined its activities to marketing centres and their environs; it did not reach out to the peasantry in the countryside. 'People's armies' (*min-chün*) began to form in rural areas, villages and small towns. They originated as local militia, clan bands or community defence corps. Gradually they began to combine into larger units and to engage government troops. As they moved beyond villages and market towns towards larger urban centres (thereby becoming susceptible to mobilization for more than local objectives) secret societies provided the necessary means of organization, communication and coordination. Eventually, some of these 'people's armies' came into contact with the Revolutionary Alliance and cooperated with it in Canton and perhaps in other key cities.

[44] *Ibid.* 171-7, 182-4. See also: Jerome Ch'en, 'Rebels between rebellions – secret societies in the novel *P'eng-kung an'*, *JAS*, 32.4 (Aug. 1970) 807-22, John Lust, 'Secret societies, popular movements and the 1911 Revolution' in *PMSS*, 166, and Rankin, *Early Chinese revolutionaries*, 134-9.

By that time, however, many of the rural youth had returned to their homes.[45]

In Kwangtung, in short, the revolutionary movement was accompanied by a considerable upheaval in the countryside with which the revolutionaries were able to establish only temporary, loose, flimsy and generally minimal ties. In some cases those ties were created by revolutionaries going into remote areas to organize new groups or by rural youth coming to urban centres where they joined existing organizations, but far more often the ties were provided by secret societies. The Revolutionary Alliance offered no firm land policy that would attract peasants. Indeed it favoured the very modernization programme that peasants objected to financing. It also lacked the organizational ability to make the most of what limited ideological appeal it could muster. Thus the revolutionaries were never able to exploit fully the access to the masses that secret societies might have provided, or to find a better intermediary than the secret societies. Still less were they able to contact the masses directly.

When the revolutionaries did link up with a secret society they often failed to reach its general membership. In the movement's earlier days, the secret-society members who joined Sun's Society to Restore China's Prosperity and participated most actively in the first revolts were not the ordinary members so much as the leaders, people who were 'educated and rather well off'.[46] In Chekiang the two secret societies with which the revolutionaries worked closely were both headed by lower gentry, and one of them even published a newspaper. In these instances and others, to use Rankin's apt phrase, the revolutionaries treated the masses 'more like troops than disciples'.[47]

Both gentry and revolutionaries sought to use the secret societies for their own ends, as gentry had for centuries. The most revealing example was the Progressive Association (Kung-chin hui), set up in Tokyo in 1907 (probably around April) to unite secret societies in a wide area of the central Yangtze. It represented a protest by a sizeable Alliance faction against Sun's policy of concentrating on South China and against what its leaders saw as excessive concern with theory and excessive influence of intellectuals. About ninety Alliance men were among the original members, and the structure was modelled on the Alliance. The founders were strongly anti-Manchu but were less enthusiastic about the remainder of the Revolu-

[45] Winston Hsieh, 'Triads, salt smugglers and local uprisings: observations on the social and economic background of the Waichow Revolution of 1911', in PMSS, 146–7, and 'Peasant insurrection and the marketing hierarchy in the Canton delta, 1911', in Mark Elvin and G. William Skinner, eds. The Chinese city between two worlds, 119–41.
[46] Borokh, 'Notes on the early role of secret societies', 138–9.
[47] Rankin, Early Chinese revolutionaries, 231.

tionary Alliance programme, especially its land policy. The Progressive Association charter adopted the Alliance's first three points but converted the fourth, 'equalization of land rights', to 'equalization of human rights' – a clear example of how Revolutionary Alliance ideology failed to survive its voyage inland and failed to reach the masses. 'Land rights' were changed to 'human rights', the society leaders claimed, because 'human rights' would be more attractive to secret-society members. But peasants found 'human rights' mystifying. As one participant recalled, 'because the society abandoned the original slogan, it was impossible to attract the broad masses of peasants'.[48]

The change was intended to appeal even more to landowners than to peasants. Many Progressive Association leaders came from landlord families, and 'human rights' was less offensive to them than even vague 'land rights'. Furthermore, what they meant by 'human rights' was not what Alliance intellectuals meant. In the Kiangsi branch, for example, the Progressive Association adopted a Confucian code: ' "Equal human rights" meant correct behavior as defined according to the traditionally accepted norms of society.'[49]

Thus the republican revolutionaries' efforts to tap the potential in China for popular revolt led to no strong links with the general population. The republicans also found that they had to compromise with the gentry elite, who had their own ideas about revolution. The Progressive Association was the first clear hint of what later became a widespread attempt to combine an anti-Manchu republican revolution with preservation of the traditional social and economic order.

By early 1908 the Revolutionary Alliance had spent most of its energy. For about a year it had sponsored or participated in one uprising after another – a total of at least five and perhaps as many as eight, according to different interpretations – without any visible success. The government had little trouble in suppressing them. None promised to initiate the chain reaction that the revolutionaries intended. As their failures mounted the Alliance members fell to squabbling among themselves. Divisions that had been papered over in 1905 now shattered the facade of unity. The *People's Report*, under a new editor hostile to Sun Yat-sen, printed criticisms of republicanism and took on a pessimistic tone. Meanwhile, the Ch'ing government, regaining the initiative that the revolutionaries had seized in 1905-6,

[48] Wu Yü-chang, *The Revolution of 1911*, 93–4. For fuller discussion of the Progressive Association see Edmund S. K. Fung, 'The Kung-chin hui: a late Ch'ing revolutionary society', *Journal of Oriental Studies*, 11.2 (1973) 193–206, and Chang Yü-fa, *Ch'ing-chi ti ko-ming t'uan-t'i* (Revolutionary groups of the late Ch'ing period), 529–40, 617–56.
[49] Kupper, 'Revolution in China', 99–100.

stepped up its pressure on foreign authorities to ban or restrict the revolutionaries' activities in Japan, Hong Kong, Indo-China, the Shanghai International Settlement and other foreign sanctuaries. Inside China it cracked down on dissent. Revolutionary efforts continued, but coordinated activity became more difficult. Students, secret societies, older revolutionary intellectuals, and anti-Manchu gentry went their separate ways for about the next two years, until in 1910 new alignments began to form. Meanwhile Sun Yat-sen, expelled from Japan in 1907 and from Hanoi in January 1908, took refuge in Singapore. From there he resumed his travels to Chinese communities around the world, still pursuing the strategy he had formulated thirteen years before.

THE FALL OF THE CH'ING DYNASTY, 1908-12

By 1908 the Ch'ing regime had survived more than a century of rebellions and foreign pressure. Against the background of gigantic movements such as the White Lotus, Taiping and Nien, the small and scattered uprisings of 1895–1908 seem rather insignificant. The Ch'ing suppressed them quickly and easily. By contrast, incidents in 1911 that seem hardly different from those of 1895–1908 led to the fall of the dynasty. Support for the Ch'ing, little shaken by earlier uprisings, suddenly evaporated in 1911. A few small incidents developed rapidly into new patterns, larger movements, and finally a republic.

Manifestly crucial changes occurred between 1908 and 1911. But were those changes merely the final stages of a very long decay or a sudden turn in a new direction?

Tradition in general and the Ch'ing system in particular had been eroding for a long time before 1911, but with signs of periodic rejuvenation. Even Ch'ing failures, such as self-strengthening or the 1898 reforms, showed a stubborn persistence of traditional adaptability. The post-1901 reforms were another example. The Ch'ing in its last decade may have been the most vigorous government and lively society that China had during the 150 or 200 years before 1949. Ch'ing history was not simply a long process of decay.

In this perspective there was an abrupt change around 1911. The Ch'ing had allowed and even encouraged the growth of new interest groups. It had contributed to a new atmosphere and to the creation of new institutions. It had widened participation in public affairs and brought those affairs under public discussion. At least until 1908 it kept the new currents under enough control to prevent any serious threat to the established order. Most members of chambers of commerce, study groups, self-government associations and other new organizations remained loyal subjects. But they were beginning to see themselves as citizens. Their demands on the Ch'ing increased. By 1908 their expectations had grown astonishingly. Only twelve years before, for example, most Chinese literati had felt K'ang Yu-wei so radical that they supported the empress dowager against him. When the same Ch'ing leadership reversed itself and even went beyond what K'ang had attempted, the 'new gentry' soon decided that the court was not going far enough fast enough. In 1910–11 they pressed new demands which, when not met, led to widespread disaffection and a broader anti-Ch'ing coalition.

To paraphrase Lenin, what happened between 1908 and 1911 was that the more active part of the upper class ceased to want the old way, while the remainder of the upper class became unable to carry on in the old way. The missing element, according to Lenin's formula for a revolutionary situation, was the 'lower classes'. Although not altogether absent from the final anti-Ch'ing coalition, they were not present in sufficient numbers to produce a mass revolution. The decisive elements in the coalition of 1911 were soldiers, particularly those in the New Army, and the 'new gentry', especially those in provincial assemblies, self-government associations and investors' groups. The 'lower classes' were active in the coalition mainly through the New Army, but also in movements quite apart from the coalition. The revolutionary students also played their most direct role in the New Army, and perhaps also among the 'new gentry'. Their propaganda, including old copies of the *People's Report* and other journals, continued to circulate in the hinterland years after publication. Some of the students also joined with other revolutionaries in 1911 to reorganize themselves and enter the coalition they had helped to promote.

The meandering course of many years suddenly shifted and gathered force. An opposition that had been kept off balance by the Ch'ing reforms, divided both by the reforms and its own inner contradictions, and that was geographically dispersed and socially heterogeneous, had managed to survive until a nation-wide crisis pulled it together.

THE EMERGING COALITION

The New Army

Ch'ing military modernization had produced its first units of the New Army around 1894–5. By the early 1900s Ch'ing reforms were having an effect upon the social composition and general outlook of Chinese armies (see chapter 7, page 383). Hupei, for example, in 1905 established a new system of recruiting by means of written examinations. Concurrently, most of the illiterate soldiers were discharged. Thus the Hupei Army drew more of its manpower from the upper class. In other provinces, too, educated men formed a markedly higher proportion of the new armies than they had of old.[50] This greater willingness of educated youth to follow a military career was a change of first importance. A Chinese Communist leader recalled that in 1910–11, when he was a teenager in the P'ing-Liu-Li area, 'a majority of my schoolmates even went so far as to break with the traditional concept that "good men are no more used as soldiers than good iron is used for nails." They came to accept the idea that . . . death in battle was a glorious death. They considered it an honor to join the New Army.' Many ran off to join, including some under age who forged papers to get into the enlistment examinations.[51]

Equally novel was the New Army effort at education, especially to reduce illiteracy. Soldiers welcomed the opportunity to participate in study associations, and learning became a popular activity. A Hupei soldier recalled that in his unit everyone could read at about elementary school level and all the squad leaders were able to write.[52]

Unlike some old-style forces, New Army recruits were drawn from the communities in which they were garrisoned. Recruitment was more careful, including safeguards such as recommendations and guarantees from local leaders to ensure good behaviour. This made for more upper-class recruits. However, most troops, non-commissioned officers, and even lower commissioned officers probably continued to come from peasant

[50] General studies include Liu Feng-han, *Hsin-chien lu-chün* (The Newly Created Army) and the same author's *Wu-wei chün* (The Wu-wei Army); Ch'en Hsu-lu and Lao Shao-hua, 'Ch'ing-mo ti hsin-chün yü hsin-hai ko-ming' (The late Ch'ing New Army and the Revolution of 1911), in Hu-pei sheng che-hsueh she-hui k'o-hsueh hsueh-hui lien-ho hui, *Hsin-hai ko-ming wu-shih chou-nien lun-wen chi* (A collection of articles on the fiftieth anniversary of the Revolution of 1911), 147–65, Chang Yü-fa, *Ch'ing-chi ti ko-ming t'uan-t'i*, 110–19, 540–646; Edmund S. K. Fung, 'Military subversion in the Chinese Revolution of 1911', *MAS*, 9.1 (1975) 103–23. For Hupei, see Josef Fass, 'Revolutionary activity in the province of Hu-pei and the Wu-ch'ang uprising of 1911', *Archiv Orientální*, 28 (1960) 127–49 and 'The role of the New Style Army in the 1911 Revolution in China', *ibid*. 30 (1962) 183–91; Vidya Prakash Dutt, 'The first week of revolution: the Wuchang uprising', in *CIR*, 383–416; Y. Hatano, 'The new armies', in *CIR*, 365–82; J. Esherick, *Reform and revolution in China*, 143–53ff; and Edmund S. K. Fung, 'Li Yuan-hung and the Revolution of 1911', *Monumenta Serica*, 31 (1974–5) 151–71. For other provinces see Hatano, 'The new armies', 374–5, 377–8; Gavan McCormack, *Chang Tso-lin in northeast China, 1911–1928*, 15–27; C. H. Hedtke, 'Reluctant revolutionaries: Szechwan and the Ch'ing collapse, 1898–1911' (University of California, Ph.D. dissertation, 1968); William R. Johnson, 'The Revolution of 1911 in Yunnan and Kweichow' (University of Washington, Ph.D. dissertation, 1962); Winston Hsieh, 'The Revolution of 1911 in Kwangtung'(Harvard University, Ph.D. dissertation, 1969); and Donald S. Sutton, 'The rise and decline of the Yunnan Army, 1909–1925' (University of Cambridge, Ph.D. dissertation, 1970).

[51] Chang Kuo-t'ao, *The rise of the Chinese Communist Party*, 1.20.

[52] Li P'ei-chi, 'T'ung-meng hui yü pang-hui ti kuan-hsi tsa-i' (Random reminiscences regarding the Revolutionary Alliance's relations with the secret societies), in *Hsin-hai ko-ming hui-i lu* Reminiscences of the 1911 Revolution), 6.84.

families. Vagrant and bandit elements were more rigorously excluded. In contrast with earlier Chinese military forces, the New Army had good relations with the local people. For many Chinese their only contact with the revolutionary movement came through the New Army.

Returned student officers from Japan visibly furthered these tendencies. From the very beginning of the student migration to Tokyo military studies were highly popular. Military careers gained in prestige when the old route to a successful civil career was closed in 1905. To those who cared as much about their country as about their careers, military training could satisfy both concerns. Many young men felt that what China most needed and Japan could best teach was the way of the warrior. Revolutionary Alliance members intensively spread propaganda among these military students. Despite the government's frantic efforts to limit modern military training to the politically reliable, rosters of military schools in Japan bulged with the names of young Chinese radicals. When they went back to China to serve in the New Army they spread revolutionary propaganda.

Events in Hupei deserve close attention, since that is where New Army troops began the 1911 revolt. In that province Governor-general Chang Chih-tung had made a particularly intensive effort to build a modern army. But Chang was less effective than other officials – for example, Yuan Shih-k'ai in Chihli – in screening out revolutionary elements. Hupei had been a hotbed of revolutionary activity for at least five years before 1905, and military students were involved in it very early. Wu Lu-chen, for example, had been sent from a Hupei military academy for advanced study in Japan. After briefly interrupting his training to participate in T'ang Ts'ai-ch'ang's abortive uprising of 1900, he graduated from the imperial Japanese Military Academy in 1902. By that time he was a friend of Sun Yat-sen and an active revolutionary under cover. He rose to important posts in the New Army, including one in Peking. Other Hupei students also believed as early as 1904 that army support was essential to the revolution; some of them (later including Alliance members) enlisted purposely to work under cover for revolution. The Institute for the Diffusion of Science, a revolutionary group founded in June 1904 in Hupei, may have been the first attempt to unite students, soldiers and the secret societies.

After the failure of their attempt in 1904 to coordinate an uprising with Huang Hsing, the Hupei students took more than a year to regroup. From early 1906 a series of about thirty revolutionary organizations are recorded. These organizations' close involvement with the army – but not, despite similar names, with the T'ung-meng hui – is suggested by names like 'Army Revolutionary Alliance' (Chün-tui t'ung-meng hui) and 'Institute for the Restoration of Martial Spirit' (Chen-wu hsueh-she). As early as 1906 a high

Ch'ing official warned of growing Alliance activity in the New Army, including the use of revolutionary songs and vernacular writings to agitate troops. A Society for Daily Improvement (Jih-chih hui) is said to have been especially successful at organizing the rank and file, although it survived for less than a year (from early 1906 to January 1907). This began a trend from 1907 to 1910 away from an exclusively officer membership, until by 1911 the chief revolutionary group in the New Army consisted almost entirely of enlisted men.

In the autumn of 1908, revolutionary activity in Hupei nearly halted because its leader, a New Army soldier, was transferred to Szechwan. This suggests how thin was the organization. But the Hupei revolutionaries quickly regrouped. A major role was played by the Progressive Association. Late in 1908 its founder, Sun Wu, returned from Japan. He soon lost faith in the secret societies and turned to the New Army for recruits and allies. Meanwhile, the 'Army Revolutionary Alliance', the most logical potential ally for the Progressive Association, was succeeded by the 'Society for the Study of Popular Government' (Ch'ün-chih hsueh-she). The new name was revealing. In the summer and autumn of 1908 the government had cracked down upon groups that claimed the right to assemble openly for democratic purposes. Even Liang Ch'i-ch'ao's moderate Political Informa-tion Institute (Cheng-wen she) was suppressed. The Ch'ing, unfolding its own plans for constitutional government, refused to tolerate efforts to hasten or alter them. The founding of the Hupei society for the Study of Popular Government in the midst of all this can be viewed as an open and defiant challenge to the authorities.

The challenge presented itself less than a month after the empress dowager died. With her hand removed from the reins of power, the Hupei revolutionaries saw an opportunity for more brazenly open and wider-ranging political activity. Three members of the Society for the Study of Popular Government began to publish a newspaper that obtained wide circulation and carried the revolutionary message beyond army circles and beyond the Wuhan cities. When that Society was replaced by the Institute for the Restoration of Martial Spirit in September 1910, the latter also published a newspaper. Together with revolutionary classics such as Tsou Jung's *The revolutionary army*, a flood of newspaper propaganda was aimed at the rank and file. Returned students opened wine-shops, inns, tea-houses, general stores and other establishments as close as possible to army bar-racks. Many of these became fronts for local revolutionary bureaux. Most of the New Army, the Minister of War confided to an American military attaché, had turned anti-Manchu.[53]

[53] Chin-tung Liang, *The Chinese Revolution of 1911*, 17, citing the US Department of State.

Still, in 1910 the time was not yet ripe. The army could not act alone, and it was not quite ready even to try. In Hupei, organizations such as the Progressive Association and the Institute for the Restoration of Martial Spirit found cooperation impossible. In provinces other than Hupei the revolutionaries' success among New Army units varied. Until 1909 they gained fewer adherents in the north than in the south; from then on, Revolutionary Alliance members began to fill key posts in the Peiyang Army. Even in Canton, where revolutionary work had been going on for so long, preparations were still inadequate. For example, one of the most famous Alliance attempts to organize a mutiny in the New Army is now revealed to have been more a local riot than a revolutionary uprising: the ineptitude of local officials caused the Canton outburst of February 1910; the revolutionaries then merely tried (without success) to exploit an incident not of their own making.[54] Their problem in Kwangtung was that they lacked an organization among the enlisted men, although Alliance members were numerous among middle and lower officers.

In 1910 the revolutionaries redoubled their efforts and the government began to panic. It is not clear whether the revolutionaries were as successful as officialdom perceived them to be, but by the end of 1910 New Army disaffection had sharply intensified and Ch'ing authorities were reacting almost frantically. Army units were transferred back and forth or occasionally even demobilized; officers were frequently replaced or discharged; spying was stepped up; curfews were imposed and regulations generally tightened. The Institute for the Restoration of Martial Spirit decided to operate deeper underground and to seek allies. At the end of January 1911, its leaders met in Wuchang to found a new front organization, for which they chose the innocent name of Literary Institute (Wen-hsueh-she). Within a month about four hundred new recruits had joined. Nearly every battalion in the area was represented in the membership. The leaders resolved to continue publishing a newspaper and to send a copy to each army unit. Each of the Wuhan tri-cities had a branch office, and agents were sent out to other parts of Hupei and to several provinces in which Hupei troops were stationed. Some even went as far as Manchuria.

As the Literary Institute intensified its recruitment and propaganda campaign, it found itself competing with similar efforts by the Progressive

Foreign relations of the United States. Other sources, e.g. Fung, 'Military subversion', 114, suggest about a third of the Hupei New Army was revolutionary by 1911.

[54] Detailed discussion in Rhoads, *China's republican revolution*, 189–96. Contrast the older and more orthodox interpretation in Hsueh, *Huang Hsing*, 76–7 and Lee, *Foundations of the Chinese Revolution*, 189–92. On events in Hunan see Arthur L. Rosenbaum, 'Gentry power and the Changsha rice riot of 1910', *JAS*, 34.3 (May 1975) 689–715 and Esherick, *Reform and revolution in China*, 123–38.

Association. Although some revolutionaries in Hupei belonged to both organizations, they were unable to coordinate their efforts. The explanation offered by the leader of the Literary Institute suggested that the social changes claimed for the New Army in Hupei had not gone very far after all: 'We are lowly soldiers and they are either gentlemen clad in Western-style clothes or Mandarins in flowing robes and wide-sleeved jackets with superior wisdom and high reputations. They will never condescend to look at us and we cannot have anything to gain by hanging around them.'[55] It would require the help of intermediaries and an atmosphere of crisis before the friction between these groups was finally neutralized enough to permit some cooperation. The intermediaries would be provided by a splinter group of Revolutionary Alliance members in Shanghai. The government was already creating the crisis.

The new gentry and the assemblies

Border disputes in 1910 with Japan, Russia, Britain and France made Peking vulnerable once again to criticism of its weakness, and the constitutionalists in the provincial assemblies (see chapter 7, page 398) became more outspoken. Fifty-one of them from sixteen provinces gathered in Shanghai and formed a Federation of Provincial Assemblies. The Federation then sent a delegation of thirty-two to Peking to petition for the prompt convening of a parliament. This won several concessions from the government, including the formation of a provisional National Assembly and a shortening by three years of the transition period to full constitutionalism. Following three petitions in January, July and October 1910, a decree of 4 November promised to convene a parliament in 1913 (instead of 1917) and to promulgate a constitution before parliament opened. Still dissatisfied, the assemblymen pressed for a cabinet that would be responsible to them. But the government stiffened, and the reformers won no more concessions. As a result some of them lost faith in a peaceful transition to democracy and a few even began to think of revolution.

The decree of 4 November 1910 ordered the petitioners to disband but, led by members of the provisional National Assembly, many of them stayed in Peking and held discussions for another two months. Thus by early 1911, the petition movement had gone on for a full year and had moved from cautious and respectful requests for moderate changes to

---

[55] Liew, *Struggle for democracy*, 111. The extent to which class differences were decisive is especially difficult to determine in this case. Although progress had been made in overcoming them, the Society for Daily Improvement had been betrayed by a returned student from Japan. Successor organizations, according to Liew, 'became a little apprehensive of the reliability of overseas students'. *Ibid.* 112.

urgent demands for greater changes. These consistently stressed the same issues – the foreign threat to Chinese unity and sovereignty, the danger of economic crisis and revolution, and irresponsible government – but they used stronger language each time. Early in 1910 they had appealed to the authorities to mobilize popular support to prevent rebellion. A year later they were beginning to accept the idea of revolution. In July 1910 a constitutionalist newspaper editorial observed that while Europeans shed blood to create parliaments the Chinese had only poured ink, which was why Europeans succeeded while 'our ink has failed repeatedly'. Six months later this implied call to violence was made clearer with the demand that the constitutionalists should 'not waste valuable time by waging an empty war of tongues'.[56] In March 1911 the constitutionalists' chief spokesman, Liang Ch'i-ch'ao, called on all Chinese to 'join their strength in planning the overthrow of this bad government and in reconstructing a good government'.[57]

Liang found it impossible to join the revolutionaries he had fought so bitterly for the preceding eight years, but he now accepted the very views he had denied. He even argued that revolution would not expose China to the danger of foreign intervention and partition, an issue that he and the *People's Report* writers had debated with the most heat. Many of his reformist followers found themselves in a similar position. 'The constitutionalists were awakening from their beautiful dream of constitutional monarchy, . . . and their subsequent actions moved steadily from the temperance of the petitioning period to public opposition to the Ch'ing court.'[58] Ch'ing intransigence was unifying the opposition factions. Although unable to lead a revolution, nearly all would soon be ready to accept one. Of the reformist leaders only Chang Chien of Kiangsu had not moved from his original position. But once the revolution broke out he was to play a vital role in ending the Ch'ing dynasty.

By the spring of 1911 the balance of forces was shifting, and 'new gentry' were tipping the balance. Although the opposition was still too divided to challenge the government, the elements of a powerful anti-Ch'ing coalition were now in existence. In some New Army units 70 per cent of the men belonged to revolutionary organizations. In others, they had many sympathizers and fence-sitters but very few anti-revolutionary soldiers. Provincial assemblymen had returned to their homes filled with anger. Those

---

[56] P'eng-yuan Chang, 'The Constitutionalists', in *CIR*, 172–3.
[57] Ernest P. Young, 'The reformer as a conspirator: Liang Ch'i-ch'ao and the 1911 Revolution' in Albert Feuerwerker, Rhoads Murphey and Mary C. Wright, eds. *Approaches to modern Chinese history*, 248.
[58] Chang P'eng-yuan, *Li-hsien-p'ai yü hsin-hai ko-ming* (The constitutionalists and the 1911 Revolution), 111–13.

who had served in the provisional National Assembly (they were younger and more Western-oriented than the average provincial assemblyman) were especially militant. Merchants had been among the leading participants in anti-foreign demonstrations and boycotts, and they had supported both the revolutionary and constitutional movements. Many had been especially active in the petitioning of 1910; when it failed they shared the feelings of the assemblymen and, like them, were prepared to participate in the anti-Ch'ing movement though not to initiate it. Again like the assemblymen, they had new local organizations such as chambers of commerce that were beginning to merge to form larger provincial or even national associations. There was even a new type of 'commercial gentry' interested in Chinese economic growth, efficient administration, and freedom from foreign domination, combined with foreign-style reforms like railway development.

The revolutionary organizations

The catalytic elements in this potential coalition were the revolutionary organizations, who found themselves at a critical point in April 1911. Dissatisfaction with the strategy of seeking a base in South China had been smouldering for years and had intensified in 1910. For two years the Revolutionary Alliance had scarcely functioned. Its last uprising had been in 1908, and the *People's Report* had been closed down that October. Since 1907 there had been bitter internal feuding, severe shortages of funds, and even defections to the government side. Some leaders were driven to desperate schemes. Wang Ching-wei, for example, plotted to assassinate high-ranking Manchus and was jailed early in 1910. At about the same time another coup in Canton failed. A more fruitful plan finally came from members who proposed that the Alliance re-examine its entire strategy and shift its main sphere of operations to the central Yangtze. Comrades in Hupei, who had felt the same way for several years, responded favourably. After failing in the summer of 1910 to persuade Sun Yat-sen to call a meeting to reorganize the Alliance, several members decided to take action independent of Sun and set up a new agency to direct operations along the Yangtze. The plan infuriated Hu Han-min and provoked new squabbles among the revolutionaries.

Meanwhile Sun's faction persisted in its old pattern. After more than five months of careful preparation, in April 1911 it mounted yet another uprising in Canton at Huang-hua-kang. It collapsed within a few hours with the death of eighty-six revolutionaries, leaving the organization in South China decimated and morale at a new low. But while this failure ended the movement in the south, it only encouraged those who had

resolved to concentrate on Central China. At this precise moment the
Ch'ing regime itself precipitated the crisis that brought together the
divided revolutionaries and their potentially or mildly revolutionary allies.

THE BIRTH OF THE REPUBLIC

After nearly a decade of reform Peking had arrived at an insoluble dilemma.
The initiative it had managed to regain in 1908 was again slipping from its
hands. Challenges to its authority came from all sides. Its old military forces
were weak, the new, unreliable. The able and dedicated in its bureaucracy
were losing ground to the cautious and corrupt. The most talented of
China's educated sought new careers and left the old ones to the most
venal. The government's reforms opened opportunities for officials at local
levels to build local power. Its attempts to suppress criticism only provoked
more. Efforts to divide its opponents only scattered without eliminating
them. It easily crushed the Revolutionary Alliance uprising in Canton at
the end of April, but this success owed more to the revolutionaries' bung-
ling than to Ch'ing strength. The revolutionaries' ideas, less easily dealt
with, were infecting both the old educated elite and the new. In brief, the
Ch'ing came to see that its reforms were going out of control – the more it
reformed the less authority it had, but the less it reformed the less legitimacy it could claim. It tried to stop the trend selectively at first, refusing
some demands in 1910 but compromising on others. In 1911 it decided
that entirely new initiatives were required, which sealed its doom.

The Ch'ing chose its initiatives with inexplicable folly. Within two weeks
in May 1911 the court proclaimed a new cabinet, announced nationalization of the Szechwan–Hankow and Hankow–Canton railways, and
negotiated a foreign loan to build them. The cabinet was an undistinguished
group of thirteen that included only four Chinese; its heavy Manchu
majority was dominated by five incompetent members of the imperial clan.
Promptly labelled the 'royal' or 'clan' cabinet, it provoked widespread
anger and despair. Revolutionaries could claim it proved all they had said
about the Manchus' self-serving anti-Chinese policies. To the constitutionalists it was a clear rejection of their appeal for a cabinet responsible to
parliament. Even Chang Chien was openly critical; the country, he said,
was now 'rapidly disintegrating'.[59] Finally, the cabinet aroused the dis-
approval of a heretofore relatively quiet rival, Yuan Shih-k'ai, for it replaced one of Yuan's closest friends with one of his chief adversaries as
minister of communications. That post included railway administration,
and the cabinet's formation was closely related to the new nationalization

[59] Ch'en, *Yuan Shih-k'ai*, 82.

policy, of which Yuan also disapproved. Many others disapproved for similar reasons, suspicious of the effort to strengthen central government at the expense of local and provincial interests. But these political objections to railway nationalization were almost drowned by the protests of those who had invested in private railroad companies. These irate investors, mainly local gentry and merchants, were enraged a month later when Peking revealed its plan to reimburse them mostly with government bonds. The revolutionaries had always insisted that the Ch'ing reforms were designed only to strengthen the dynasty; now they had fresh ammunition and new targets. Peking was all the more vulnerable on this issue because its 1910 military budget was nearly eight times that of 1905. Foreign loans were paying for a vast expansion of the Ch'ing army.

While the widespread indignation at the foreign loans was often hypocritical, as pointed out in chapter 8, still the movement for rights recovery was a genuinely popular movement, and those who objected to the Ch'ing loans might also have objected to foreign loans to provinces. More importantly, the protest was not so much against the loans themselves as the manner in which the loan agreements were concluded. To many assemblymen, for example, the deeper issue was that they had not been consulted. This was the heart of the matter. What all the Ch'ing initiatives had in common was arbitrariness. The 1911 loan was not the first foreign loan the Ch'ing had concluded, but it came at a time when the anti-Ch'ing factions had had quite enough of government unaccountability.

Tyranny had expressed itself simultaneously in three different ways, offending racial sensitivities and patriotic feelings, democratic sentiments, and economic interests all at once. (Curiously enough, the three initiatives amounted to a contravention of the Three People's Principles.) From this perspective we may assess the revolutionaries' role in the Ch'ing last judgment. The regime was found wanting primarily because of its own errors, but the verdict was pronounced according to principles that the revolutionaries had done most to establish. The principles were not entirely clear or consistent, and some who defended them paid them lip service while prepared themselves to violate them, but they were the closest thing China had to a national consensus in 1911. Finally, the revolutionaries returned to the centre of events because, while various groups stood for one principle or another, only they stood for all. They were therefore in the best position of all the factions in the final anti-Ch'ing coalition to mediate conflicts of interest and bring rival groups together. And they found their closest allies among the constitutionalist reformers.

The Friends of the Constitution

The first response to the Ch'ing initiative in May 1911 was that of the constitutionalists. Some of them had been thinking, since the first elections, of trying to organize a political party. During the petition movement the idea gained favour, particularly after Liang Ch'i-ch'ao circulated among the assemblymen a proposal outlining the principles he thought should govern a party. Sun Hung-i, a member of the Chihli provincial assembly who had become the leader of the petitioners, pushed the idea further. In March 1911, he invited to Peking the chairmen of the provincial assemblies to discuss the means of 'destroying the government's customary disdain for its citizens, making foreigners respect us, and working out a thorough policy on which we can finally take a stand'.[60] It was in this atmosphere that the constitutionalists learned of the 'royal cabinet' and railway nationalization. Within ten days, forty of them, representing sixteen provinces, had gathered in Peking, nominally to hold a second meeting of The Federation of Provincial Assemblies but, in fact, to organize a party. Sixteen days later, on 4 June 1911, the Friends of the Constitution (Hsien-yu hui) came into being.

This society aimed at unifying the constitutional movement in order to press the government to call parliament immediately and to form a more representative cabinet. It hoped not to overthrow the government but to broaden its base of popular support. Its programme was a compromise; phrases such as 'respect constitutional monarchy' made it plain that the Chang Chien wing of the movement was still strong. Even with such concessions in the charter, Chang would not join, although some of his associates did. Chang was a staunch constitutionalist but an only slightly less steadfast monarchist, an outstanding example of the 'new gentry' whose modernism and traditionalism were almost but never quite in balance, whose progressivism and conservatism were so intermingled as to be scarcely distinguishable. It was men of this cast of mind, widely respected for their ability and honesty as well as their combination of past-, present- and future-mindedness, who eventually came to feel betrayed by the Ch'ing. They became the reluctant revolutionaries who made the revolution look respectable but also ensured that it would be minimal.

Chang Chien had slowed the more active constitutionalists but not stopped them. Leaders such as Liang Ch'i-ch'ao, Sun Hung-i, P'u Tien-chün (chairman of Szechwan's provincial assembly), T'ang Hua-lung

[60] Chang P'eng-yuan, *Li-hsien p'ai*, 117. This section relies also on the careful research of Chang Yü-fa (see n. 48 above). For the view that the elite joined the revolution mainly to hold it in check, see Young-tsu Wong, 'Popular unrest and the 1911 Revolution in Jiangsu (Kiangsu)', *Modern China*, 3.3 (July 1977) 321–44.

(Hupei chairman) and T'an Yen-k'ai (chairman of both the Hunan provincial assembly and the Friends of the Constitution) sharply disagreed with Chang, not only on the adequacy of the Ch'ing concessions but on the railway nationalization and foreign loan schemes. The factions other than Chang's among the constitutionalists had taken substantial steps towards unity. Some of them, especially the younger members of the new party, were in close contact with revolutionaries. Most important, the new society had created the nucleus of a national political organization. With headquarters in Peking and branches in all provinces but four – Heilungkiang, Yunnan, Kansu and Sinkiang – it was more capable than any other organization of initiating and carrying on a concerted effort. Its potential for united action was enhanced by its members' high status in Chinese life. Its cautiously worded programme allowed it to function openly. Its leadership retained public respectability and legitimacy. The heads of the branches were all chairmen and vice-chairmen of provincial assemblies, members of high standing with the old elite who also could claim a mandate conferred by election to office. Officers of the Friends were also provincial assemblymen or members of the provisional National Assembly. All had some modern education as well as traditional learning. They shared values, attitudes and interests, including investments in modern enterprises like railroads. By the late spring of 1911 they had been acting in concert for at least a year and a half. When they returned to their home provinces in early June, they were in a mood and position to play active roles in national affairs.

The Central China branch of the Alliance

For the revolutionaries the Ch'ing initiatives could hardly have been better timed. Demoralized after the Canton failure of April 1911, they were groping for a new strategy. Disunity had plagued them for three years, with no end in sight. In the crucial Wuhan area non-cooperation between the Literary Institute and the Progressive Association made efficient action impossible. But two days after the government's first decree on railway nationalization the two bodies met to explore ways of lessening their competition. Revolutionary Alliance representatives attempted to guide the parleys. Agents scurried back and forth between Tokyo, Shanghai, Wuhan and Hong Kong in a renewed effort to unify the revolutionary movement. On 1 June the two Hupei groups agreed to cooperate. Although more than three months passed before the details were worked out and a joint command established, the advocates of an uprising in Central China intensified their efforts, led by students from Hunan and Hupei.

Sun Yat-sen's supporters, meanwhile, remained opposed to the Yangtze idea, convinced it would be five years before an effective uprising could be mounted. Sun himself, once again circling the globe to solicit funds and promises, was not involved in the discussions. From mid-1910 until his arrival in New York on 17 February 1911, Sun was in Hawaii, Japan, Malaya and Europe. Tired of seeking the support of Sun's faction and with sarcastic references to his 'wandering about', the Hunan–Hupei activists decided to go their own way. All along the Yangtze they rallied revolutionary groups, bringing together early leaders of the student movement such as the Hunanese Sung Chiao-jen (who had been instrumental in founding the Revolutionary Alliance in 1905), later converts such as Ch'en Ch'i-mei (who had studied in Japan 1900–2 and joined the Alliance in 1906), and still newer participants (including people from the lower Yangtze provinces and from as far away as Shansi). The reorganization of 1911 gathered momentum from May to July, culminating in yet another new organization to unify the sprawling revolutionary movement.

The new agency, although named The Headquarters for Central China of the Revolutionary Alliance (Chung-kuo t'ung-meng-hui chung-pu tsung-hui), was set up in direct violation of the Alliance's constitution: it ignored the requirements that a new branch must have its leader appointed by the head of the Alliance and its rules approved by the parent organization's leaders (the Central China branch had no leader but instead a 'temporary' five-man secretariat or general affairs council (*tsung-wu hui*) to direct its activities); collective leadership was clearly provided for in a rule that action required unanimous agreement of the five; and 'equalization of land rights' was muted in order to ally with the Hupei groups, especially the Progressive Association. Since the Central China leaders had objected to Sun's over-bearing leadership, these provisions declared their independence from him.[61] Although explicitly associated with the Alliance, the Central China branch plainly retained freedom of action. Its activities in August and September concentrated on cementing relations between the Literary Institute and the Progressive Association, working out a common strategy, and circulating revolutionary literature in the Yangtze region.

Sung Chiao-jen persuaded his comrades in the Central China branch leadership to devote two years to preparation for a vast uprising in 1913. A complex plan was worked out that would secure Central China for the revolution, with Hupei as the hub of a campaign stretching to Shensi and Shansi in the north, Nanking and Shanghai in the east, Hunan in the south,

[61] The rules, members and declaration of the Central China branch may be found in Chung-hua-min-kuo k'ai-kuo wu-shih-nien wen-hsien, *Wu-ch'ang shou-i*, 1.2–11. See also Edmund S. K. Fung, 'The T'ung-meng-hui Central China Bureau and the Wuchang uprising', *Journal of the Institute of Chinese Studies of the Chinese University of Hong Kong*, 7.2 (1974) 477–96.

and Szechwan in the west. Agents went to work in all of these places. From their headquarters in Shanghai, Sung and others fired off newspaper articles like machine-gun bullets. The torpor of 1910 had vanished, and 1913 soon began to seem too far off. Once the two Hupei groups had established their joint command and arranged a division of labour, pressure mounted for immediate action.

The crisis in Szechwan

Substantial but cautious protests against the Ch'ing initiatives of May had been promptly voiced by Szechwan gentry. But these protests were repeatedly brushed aside. When details of the nationalization and foreign loan plans became known, they intensified. The Ch'ing court announced compensation terms that outraged investors in Szechwan, who felt with justification that the terms offered to them were the least satisfactory among the four provinces involved. Peking stubbornly refused to negotiate. Petitions and rallies did not budge the provincial authorities who, on the contrary, even interfered with the investors' communications with each other.[62]

In this atmosphere the Friends of the Constitution, which in Szechwan was 'popularly referred to as the "people's party" ',[63] adjourned and sent its leaders back to their home provinces. P'u Tien-chün, chairman of the Szechwan provincial assembly, lost no time. Under his leadership a Railway Protection League (Pao-lu t'ung-chih hui) was formed at a meeting of more than two thousand people in Chengtu on 17 June. The league quickly set up branches in many parts of the huge province and contacted local groups ranging from guilds and chambers of commerce to peasant associations and secret societies. It proposed to call a 'citizens' convention' (kuo-min ta-hui) in Peking in order to bring direct pressure on the government 'according to the practices of foreign nations'.[64] It published three newspapers. In brief, it conducted a remarkable campaign to unite a broad section of the population in what was at first a purely peaceful and relatively moderate protest.

Peking remained totally unmoved. Its intransigence was symbolized by the remark that if it accepted Szechwanese demands 'everyone would argue with the government over things and imperial decrees would not be carried out'.[65] Peking's determination to rule by decree rather than consultation or compromise provoked the league to more radical steps. An

---

[62] This incident and related events are discussed in rich detail by Hedtke, 'Reluctant revolutionaries', 193–227.
[63] Ibid. 188.   [64] Ibid. 208.   [65] Ibid. 215–16.

escalating conflict was thus set in motion that culminated in a decision by railway investors on 1 September to refuse to pay taxes. A confrontation could no longer be avoided.

In the summer of 1911, therefore, a widespread popular protest movement swept Szechwan. It concentrated increasingly on Ch'ing arbitrariness and foreign penetration. Its leaders were new gentry, especially the provincial assemblymen. The Szechwan assembly, instead of mobilizing upperclass support for government policies as Peking had optimistically hoped, became the centre of militancy. Its 127 members were upper class (35 held higher degrees and another 74 lower degrees), rather young (average age about forty-two) and actively reform-minded. Only 4 were known to be Alliance members, but there were probably others who leaned towards revolution, and many were followers of Liang Ch'i-ch'ao. A good number had commercial investments and worked with merchants, not only in business ventures but also in the general management of local affairs. (Of the 13 directors of the railway company, 7 were close associates of P'u Tien-chün.) These enterprising young gentry, having now joined with merchants and students to claim a larger role in government, used the provincial assembly as their stage. Peking sternly warned that assemblies 'only advise local officials, who are under the control of the supreme sovereign'.[66] But Szechwan assemblymen insisted on a much wider range of activity. They demanded a voice in local tax policy, the right to inspect local schools, and the convening of a National Assembly. They even published a newspaper, financed by business and educational circles in Szechwan as well as assemblymen and edited by P'u Tien-chün himself. Its major purpose was to publicize the need for constitutional government and reform of provincial administration, but it carried articles on a wide range of political reforms.

At first glance one may view the Szechwan crisis as essentially economic. Szechwan had recently been singled out for subjection to a new land tax to help pay the expenses of other provinces. Much of the early debate about what stand to take against Peking focused on the adequacy of government bonds as compensation, and whether to demand more satisfactory reimbursement or to insist on provincial ownership of the railways. Assembly members at first did not protest against the government's plan to finance the railway with a foreign loan; indeed some welcomed the additional funds as a spur to construction. But this seemingly overwhelming concern with economic questions was matched by political concerns. The foreign

[66] 'Constitution building in China', *North China Herald*, 9 Sept. 1910, p. 598. Between 15 July and 23 Sept., the *North China Herald* published in eleven parts a detailed study of the Manchu constitution. The last three, 9, 16 and 23 Sept., dealt with local–central government relations and provincial assemblies.

loan, for example, was criticized because the court had acted without first consulting the National Assembly. Later, charges of 'selling out to foreigners' were made, and political issues came to overshadow economic ones. The struggle over railways was revealed to be part of a deeper political contest between central and provincial authority. The Railway Protection League's combination of economic and political purposes was evidenced by the slogans 'railways should be under commercial management' and 'all affairs of state should be open to public discussion'. Taken from 1898 reform edicts of the Kuang-hsu Emperor, these slogans showed that the protesters were traditional enough to seek the imperial aura. In Chengtu, altars were placed on streets all over the city and incense was burned in reverence to Kuang-hsu. Presumably the slogans revealed the K'ang–Liang reformist orientation of League members. They did not intend to overthrow the dynasty, but they sought a new distribution of political power and new representative institutions.

These political objectives, amplified in an anonymous publication 'A discussion of Szechwanese self-protection', were seized upon by the governor-general, who wired Peking that the railway issue was a pretext behind which was hidden an independence movement. He then proceeded to jail P'u Tien-chün and nine other League members. This provoked mass demonstrations in the provincial capital the very same day (7 September 1911). Protests and uprisings then erupted all over the province. A number of counties declared independence, and some even established revolutionary governments.

The sudden occurrence of so many outbursts seems attributable mainly to secret societies connected with Szechwan gentry in general and the Railway Protection League in particular. A handful of Revolutionary Alliance agents may also have played a part.

Within a week Szechwan was in chaos, the authorities in utter confusion. The court belatedly agreed to provide full compensation to railway investors, but demonstrations continued. Peking transferred troops from Hupei under Tuan-fang as imperial commissioner and instructed him to restore order by force if necessary. Tuan-fang moved too slowly but his forces, heavily influenced by revolutionaries, might not have helped in any case. By the end of September events were beyond the control of either the authorities or the original protest leaders.

Local militia, their ranks now swollen with angry peasants, destroyed police and tax offices, opened jails, looted warehouses, and cut telegraph wires. There is irony and pathos in this, for the peasants would have suffered most from the tax plan of the Szechwan railway builders. Impoverished and wretched, peasants lashed out against the authorities at

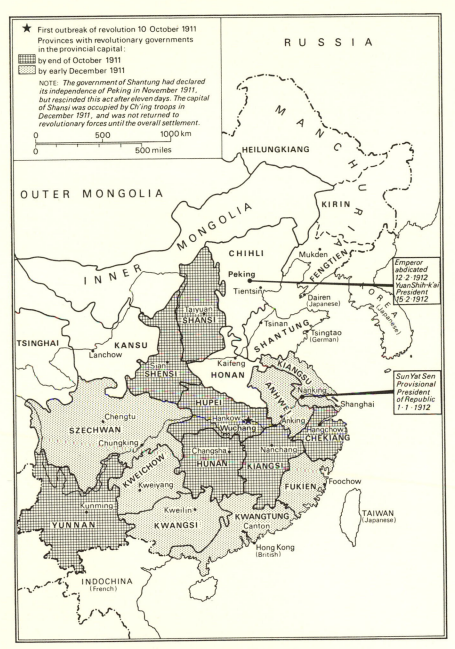

MAP. 14   The Revolution of 1911

hand. They had their own grievances and, before long, their own leaders. Revolutionary Alliance and secret-society men led some militia groups, but they were soon shunted aside by peasants, bandits and smugglers. Old-style provincial forces (*hsun-fang tui*), assigned to restore order, also joined the rioters. Armed bands of as many as a hundred thousand overwhelmed government forces, which by early October were concentrating on holding the provincial capital and a few other cities.

Thus by the time Hupei erupted in October, Szechwan had been in flames for weeks. The Wuchang uprising, however, has been traditionally regarded as the spark of China's Revolution of 1911. It was there that a new revolutionary provincial government was first proclaimed, and this proclamation led to fourteen more between 10 October and 27 November. The Szechwan protests became anti-dynastic only after the Wuchang revolt.

The crisis in Hupei: revolution and moderation

The transfer of troops from Hupei to Szechwan created a sense of urgency among the revolutionaries in Wuhan. Further transfers would remove the very men they were counting on as the backbone of an uprising. Revolutionary Alliance leaders were willing to forget about 1913 and act quickly, but not as quickly as desired by the Literary Institute and the Progressive Association. These groups were trying to decide what to do when an accident on 9 October forced their hand. They had just learned to their chagrin that Alliance leaders Huang Hsing (then in Hong Kong) and Sung Chiao-jen (in Shanghai) both wanted to wait. Huang hoped for simultaneous uprisings in several provinces at the end of October and Sung was similarly pessimistic about an immediate success in Wuhan alone. Sun Yat-sen, travelling in the United States, was unaware of the plans. The Hupei leaders, huddling in Wuchang to revise their scheme in the light of this disappointment, suddenly learned that an explosion had occurred at one of their Hankow ammunition stations. The police were closing in. After a moment of indecision and near panic, the Wuchang conclave resolved to strike. But its call to arms came too late for many of its followers who had already fled or been arrested. The Wuchang office itself was raided before many of the leaders could escape. Troops and agents loyal to the government seemed to be everywhere. Turncoats appeared among the revolutionaries. Frantic now, Literary Institute men in various army units tried to rally their forces. In one afternoon of desperate consultation on 10 October, a handful of enlisted men hastily improvised a plan for that evening and then unhesitatingly struck. They killed their officers and headed immediately for the largest arsenal in the vicinity, which was guarded by a company from the same battalion. This company joined its comrades, and the company commander, who is said to have sympathized with republicanism, was persuaded to take charge of the small rebel band of about three hundred. Under his leadership the insurgents regrouped, swelled their ranks to about four thousand New Army soldiers, and attacked the local headquarters where the governor-general had massed his forces. Fighting raged through the windy, intermittently rainy night. By early morning Ch'ing authority in Wuchang had been broken. That afternoon the revolutionaries formed a military government for Hupei and had the audacity to speak for all of China and proclaim a republic. They also adopted a new calendar, changing the year designation from Hsuan-t'ung three (i.e., the third year of the reign of the Hsuan-t'ung Emperor) to Chung-hua (China) 4609 (i.e., the 4,609th year since Huang-ti, the mythical founder of the Chinese state).

These events set in motion others that over the next four months ended Ch'ing rule and launched the Republic of China. In the course of those four months, men who took the initiative on the afternoon of 10 October surrendered power to men who fought against them that same night. Sergeant Hsiung Ping-k'un, who rallied his forces on 10 October, and company commander Wu Chao-lin, who took charge that crucial evening, yielded to men such as Li Yuan-hung and T'ang Hua-lung, who represented the old order as much as they did the new.

Li was an army colonel with modern training who commanded a brigade in Wuhan. Stationed there since 1896, he had tried repeatedly to stamp out revolutionary activity in that vicinity. Despite his efforts, some of his own men joined the uprising on 10 October. Li fought back at first; he is even said to have killed a revolutionary who asked him to change sides. When the tide turned in favour of the insurgents he attempted to hide, but the revolutionaries sought him out. Convinced that they needed a leader whose name would impress both Chinese and foreigners, they simply turned to Li as the highest-ranking officer available. The only other qualification they demanded was that their candidate be Chinese rather than Manchu. On the morning of 11 October, Li was brought out of hiding and offered the post of military governor in the new regime. Still wearing his queue, Li replied that the revolutionaries had made enough trouble and should return to their barracks before Ch'ing reinforcements annihilated them. They then dragged him to the provincial assembly where they formed their government and issued declarations in his name. Still he would not budge. For two days the troops coaxed, cajoled and threatened him. On at least two occasions would-be assassins among them had to be forcibly restrained. The new government sent telegrams to local officials in Hupei, to other provinces, and to the foreign consuls, proclaiming the steps they had taken and signing Li's name. Meanwhile they consolidated their control of the Wuhan tri-cities. Li finally weakened. Impressed by the revolutionaries' achievements and confronted now with a choice between assuming the governorship or being executed as a traitor, he grudgingly agreed to serve. When Alliance leaders including Huang Hsing and Sung Chiao-jen arrived in Wuhan about two weeks later, Li was not replaced.

One decisive argument against replacing Li was that a change in government leadership might make foreigners question the new regime's stability. The Hupei revolutionaries were deeply concerned about the attitude of the foreign powers, and they quickly made conciliatory gestures. Among their earliest resolutions was one to honour all foreign treaties concluded by the Ch'ing regime and to meet all obligations included therein. Notes to this effect were sent to all foreign consulates on 13 October, although the revolutionaries stipulated that they would not recognize any agreements made with the Ch'ing from that day forward. The notes also guaranteed the protection of foreigners' rights and property and expressed the hope that friendly powers would cooperate with China in the interests of world peace and human happiness.

The Hupei revolutionaries' zeal to present an appearance of stability and continuity helps to explain the role played in the revolution by the Hupei provincial assembly and its chairman, T'ang Hua-lung. When the troops took Li Yuan-hung to the assembly in order to form their government, choose their leaders, and decide upon their policies, they were in effect acknowledging its power to give legitimacy to their acts. For the same reason they turned to the assembly chairman. When Li was made military governor, T'ang was elected head of the civil administration. T'ang was a *chin-shih* of the same year as provincial assembly chairmen P'u Tien-chün of Szechwan and T'an Yen-k'ai of Hunan. Like them, he had studied in Japan, become a follower of Liang Ch'i-ch'ao, and been active in groups such as the Friends of the Constitution. One of the most militant constitutionalists, T'ang was also among the first to support the revolution. Unlike Li he did not have to be persuaded; indeed, he claimed to have been a revolutionary long before October 1911. Others in Hupei had stronger revolutionary credentials than T'ang, but he was put in the highest civil post, probably for the same reasons of respectability that dictated the selection of Li Yuan-hung.

It seems, then, that non-revolutionary leaders rose to high positions in the new government in order to reduce its revolutionary appearance as much as possible, particularly to the foreign powers. The case of T'ang Hua-lung suggests that the revolutionaries, especially those in the New

Army who were new to politics and uncertain both of their political power and their social standing, were anxious to demonstrate their sobriety and sense of responsibility as well as their belief in representative institutions and constitutionalism. They thought they could do both by naming to high office a gentry man of well-known dedication to such principles. T'ang Hua-lung helped revolutionaries preserve continuity and an appearance of stability in the midst of their struggle to overturn Chinese politics. Thus political leadership after the revolution fell into much the same hands that held it before. In other provinces there was considerable dismay at the failure of the revolution in Hupei to bring forth new leadership, but many of the dismayed soon found events in their own provinces taking a similar route.

Enigmas of the revolution

We have arrived at the point in the history of the Revolution of 1911 when it seems to have swallowed the revolutionaries. This is the period when crucial questions about the revolution are most sharply posed. Unfortunately it is also the period for which the data have only recently begun to be collected, sifted and analysed, the period for which the evidence is still thinnest and most contradictory. It seems best here to identify issues and suggest possible lines of interpretation rather than firm conclusions.

Beginning with Hupei's action of 10 October, fifteen provinces declared their independence during the next seven weeks. In many of these provinces smaller units such as cities and hsien (counties) announced their autonomy before provincial authorities did so. Between the first secessions in October 1911 and the Ch'ing abdication on 12 February 1912, local and provincial regimes rose and fell frequently. A great variety of power relationships was worked out among New Army officers, provincial assembly leaders, former Ch'ing officials, merchants, secret-society leaders, members of the Revolutionary Alliance and other revolutionary party leaders. Few of these relationships remained stable for very long. The power of government had a new meaning in China and was exercised in new ways. Social standing and political influence were measured afresh. Many new and conflicting interests had rather quickly come into existence, in particular a multiplicity of private interests and a conception of the public interest that had not existed before 1900. The Ch'ing policies of 1911 had finally brought these growing interests together in a critical mass. But their very multiplicity created countless possibilities for different combinations. In analysing events in China during and immediately after 1911, the central problem is this complex interaction.

The most common pattern of interaction saw uprisings initiated by New Army soldiers who had been influenced by Revolutionary Alliance propaganda but who acted in concert with or were supported by gentry and assembly members. The most common outcome was a provincial regime headed by a military governor together with a civil administration dominated by the gentry and assembly. But the relations between military and civil authorities varied greatly. In some provinces merchants fitted into the military–gentry–assembly constellation of power. In others, former Ch'ing officials or Revolutionary Alliance men entered the diverse circle of the new ruling elite. Meanwhile vast areas of the countryside saw peasant uprisings fade out and old patterns of authority quickly re-established.

The very jumble and variety of the 1911–13 period make a significant point. As late as the 1890s there were clearly defined limits within which people thought and acted. By 1911 those limits were shattered. The history of China since 1911 has revolved around how a new framework for thought and action came into being. The shifting alignments of 1911–13, by their very variety and instability, were symptomatic of revolutionary change. The new forces were too numerous and too varied to be reconciled with each other and with the many survivals of the old order. But there was no going back. When Chang Chien accepted the end of the empire, he said 'each is the master of his will, and nothing in the world can limit this power'.[67] A different country from the pre-1900 China was coming into existence.

China's enduring problem of central–local relationships remained, but there were signs that a solution was to be sought along new lines. As early as November 1911, the provincial governments took steps to convoke a national assembly and create a national government. The Hupei leaders had announced a Han Chinese government and called on other provinces to rise up together with Hupei. Less than a month later Hupei called on the other revolutionary governments to send delegates to Wuhan to discuss the formation of a provisional central government. Similarly, soon after their provinces had declared independence, the military governors of Chekiang and Kiangsu called for a national conference ('in emulation of the Continental Congress of America') to be held in Shanghai. Thus by early November there were two efforts, one (in Shanghai) on the very heels of the other (in Hankow), to convene a national conference of 'independent' provinces.

Provincial separatism remained strong, but discussions went on continually until a new national government came into being in March 1912. The issues in late 1911 and early 1912 were the terms of abdication, the

[67] Marianne Bastid, *Aspects de la réforme de l'enseignement en Chine au début de XXe siècle*, 100.

location of the new capital, the role of the cabinet and the parliament, and the nature of the constitution and the federal system. These were over-whelmingly national issues. And they were debated by a wider public than had ever before participated in Chinese politics.

Perhaps, then, the 'traditional' forces that seemed to have swallowed up the revolution were not so traditional after all. To be sure, the old elite showed remarkable tenacity after 1900, but in comparison with its staying power over the centuries, it began to be rapidly transformed. The new gentry so prominent in the assemblies and in the new provincial and national regimes from 1911 on may have represented the substantial beginnings of a social revolution. As the New Army accepted partnership with them, it may have found the new gentry more radical than we have customarily assumed. The hypothesis that a real revolution occurred and that its leaders were the more radical of the moderates (the 'progressive constitutionalists') together with the more moderate of the radicals (the 'conservative revolutionaries') may turn out to be the most fruitful line of inquiry.[68]

The eclipse of the revolutionaries

In addition to their contribution to the New Army revolts and their participation in local and provincial regimes in late 1911, members of the Revolutionary Alliance and other avowedly revolutionary organizations were surprisingly active at the national level in 1911–12. Huang Hsing, for example, arrived in Hankow on 28 October and took command of the revolutionary forces. Others played leading roles in the vital negotiations that led to the Ch'ing abdication and the founding of the new national government. Even Sun Yat-sen returned to prominence at the end of 1911, though his idea of a three-stage transition to republicanism was ignored. In general, the revolutionaries played a larger part in what transpired in China between October 1911 and March 1912 than seems justified by their relative inactivity between 1908 and 1911. One source of their prominence was that they, among all the anti-Ch'ing forces, had the broadest appeal and the most comprehensive national programme. Having the most con-tacts, they were in the best position to serve as a rallying point or clearing house.

Nevertheless, the revolutionaries' prominence was short-lived – only the brief interlude between the provincial independence movements of October–November 1911 and the formation of a new government under

---

[68] See Chang P'eng-yuan, 'A typological hypothesis on the elites of the 1911 Revolution in China', *Journal of the Oriental Society of Australia*, 9.1 and 2 (1972–3) 32–8.

Yuan Shih-k'ai in March 1912. In those few months decisions affecting the nation could not be made without their consent, but they lacked the power to carry out policies. The revolutionaries could not be dispensed with but they could not dominate national politics any more than they could control local or provincial politics. When the time came to resolve the basic national issues, they had to yield to Yuan Shih-k'ai in the same way as Sergeant Hsiung Ping-k'un and Captain Wu Chao-lin had had to yield to General Li Yuan-hung and the Hupei chairman T'ang Hua-lung.

The chief parties to the discussions of national affairs in 1911–12 were the revolutionaries and Yuan Shih-k'ai. The court had turned to Yuan for help only four days after the Wuchang revolt began. Although it took him a month to obtain satisfactory terms as prime minister with wide powers, he sent an aide to negotiate with the revolutionaries in Wuhan about the beginning of November. The aide reported that his argument for constitutional monarchy left the revolutionaries totally unmoved, but they all spoke highly of Yuan.[69]

From about 8 November one revolutionary leader after another voiced support for Yuan. The question was not whether he would be president but whether he would support the revolution. Would he force the Manchus to abdicate, accept his mandate to rule from elected representatives of the republic rather than from the Ch'ing government, and respect republican institutions during his presidency? The provincial representatives meeting in Hankow affirmed that Yuan would be president if he would guarantee to support the republic. Negotiations and intermittent fighting went on simultaneously until 2 December, when a truce went into effect.

Opposition to Yuan's election was relatively small, but enough to delay an agreement. It came chiefly from a group of assemblymen at Shanghai who had refused to join the others in Hankow and who held out for a revolutionary president. Yuan, who was by now giving signs that he would accept the revolutionaries' conditions, had to bide his time while they worked out their internal disagreements. They finally did so with the election of Sun Yat-sen as provisional president on 29 December.

Agreement with Yuan did not follow until early February. A traditional interpretation has attributed this delay to perfidious scheming by Yuan. It is argued that Yuan held the Manchus' destiny so firmly in his hands that he had only to accept the revolutionaries' offer of the presidency, but he preferred to manoeuvre until he could make the presidency resemble a throne. Relying on his own military power, foreign support, and deft

---

[69] The aide, Ts'ai T'ing-kan, was impressed even more by the revolutionaries' youth than by their intransigent republicanism. Of the forty delegates with whom he met, Li Yuan-hung, at 48 *sui*, was the oldest. See Cyril Pearl, *Morrison of Peking*, 230–1.

political manipulation, Yuan hoped to manoeuvre the Manchus out of power and the revolutionaries into oblivion. This interpretation also brings out, however, that Sun's election as provisional president struck Yuan as a betrayal. Yuan was therefore reluctant to accept Sun's assurances that he would defer to Yuan as soon as the Manchus abdicated.

Recent scholarship has shown that Yuan's position in North China was much shakier than used to be thought.[70] He had many enemies at court, and he had to proceed very carefully in all his negotiations, especially those involving abdication. The military balance of power within China was actually against him. The revolutionary armies had considerable strength in the south and potential support in the north, while Yuan's own forces were not entirely reliable. His position was shaky also because of uncertainty about the foreign powers' intentions. It quickly became evident to all that Britain's role would be decisive, and the British chose to sail cautiously with the tide. They respected Yuan and were pleased to see him return to office, but they were also impressed with the wide support that the revolution had so quickly attracted. They preferred a constitutional monarchy under nominal Manchu control, but they were not prepared to intervene to promote it. Meanwhile the anti-Ch'ing forces controlled precisely those parts of China where British interests lay. Although the British did not intervene directly, it is clear that if they helped anyone, even unintentionally, it was the revolutionaries. Yuan himself later complained that British intervention was entirely responsible for the trend towards a republic. Although Yuan probably exaggerated Britain's role, it is clear that London was not helping him except towards presidency of a republic, which was what the revolutionaries also wanted. This was also the course that old friends among the constitutionalists, such as the influential Kiangsu provincial assembly chairman, Chang Chien, had been urging upon Yuan. Chang had finally taken his stand against the Ch'ing in November 1911. He then told Yuan that constitutional monarchy suited a small country like Japan but not a country as large and diverse as China.

Thus Yuan found himself compelled by circumstances to seek a compromise with the revolutionaries. All indications are that he did so. His own civilian advisers sympathized with the revolution, and the delegation he sent to Nanking was not only headed by T'ang Shao-i, who openly favoured a republic with Yuan as president, but even included the revolutionary leader Wang Ching-wei as an adviser. There were concurrent

[70] See Ch'en, *Yuan Shih-k'ai*, and the following articles: Stephen R. MacKinnon, 'Liang Shih-i and the communications clique', *JAS*, 29.3 (May 1970) 581–602, 'The Peiyang Army, Yuan Shih-k'ai, and the origins of modern Chinese warlordism', *JAS*, 32.2 (May 1973) 405–23; Masaru Ikei, 'Japan's response to the Chinese Revolution of 1911', *JAS*, 25.2 (Feb. 1966) 213–27; and Ernest P. Young, 'Yuan Shih-k'ai's rise to the presidency', in *CIR*, 419–42.

informal peace negotiations by military representatives of the two sides, and on 20 December both the political and military negotiating teams worked out agreements. The key point in each was that a republic would be established. The head of the northern delegation agreed to the republic but said that he would have to refer the agreement to Yuan and the cabinet for final approval, and the meeting thereupon adjourned. He then suggested to Yuan that the decision be made by the National Assembly. Yuan accepted this idea, and after much discussion at court he obtained on 28 December an imperial edict summoning the National Assembly. The agreements of 20 December, as one scholar has noted, 'were substantially the same as those upon which the North and South finally and openly agreed'.[71] Why, then, did the compromise take another two months to be worked out?

Possibly Sun Yat-sen and his followers delayed the settlement more than Yuan did. If Yuan's position was as shaky as suggested above, and if the powers were following Britain's lead in coming to favour a republic, the revolutionaries may have found themselves by mid-December in a stronger bargaining position than they had expected. Sun Yat-sen, travelling in the United States when the Wuchang revolt broke out, learned of it from a Denver newspaper and promptly took it upon himself to open negotiations with Western leaders. He reflected on China's international position and concluded that Britain was the key to it, not only because of her own power and interests in China but also because she was Japan's ally. London was therefore his first stop. He arrived there in late October and remained until 21 November. Correctly or not, he gained from the foreign secretary, Sir Edward Grey, the impression that Britain looked favourably upon the revolution and upon Sun personally, and furthermore that if Sun were to return to China and establish a formal government he could open discussions with London about loans. Sun's own account suggests that he was very optimistic about the new government obtaining British aid.

When Sun arrived in Hong Kong on 21 December, he discussed strategy with other Revolutionary Alliance leaders. Hu Han-min argued that the Ch'ing government had already lost its mandate and that the revolutionaries' major problem now was to defeat Yuan's army. Sun's best strategy was therefore not to go to Nanking, where he would find himself lacking the military power to challenge Yuan, but to remain in Canton and build up his army. Sun, however, wanted the Manchus' formal abdication, and for this purpose he thought Yuan could be useful. He also preferred a political solution to a military one. He was anxious to forestall foreign intervention and at the same time impress foreign and domestic observers with a peaceful and clear-cut transfer of authority. Sun was also convinced that the time

[71] Chün-tu Hsueh, *Huang Hsing*, 134.

had come for him to step in and exert personal leadership. He wanted to use Yuan to overturn the dynasty, but he reaffirmed to Hu that he still did not trust Yuan. His remarks to Hu seem to mean that he intended to challenge Yuan for political leadership.

This interpretation gains force in the light of Sun's subsequent actions. He proceeded forthwith to Shanghai where, in a heated discussion with revolutionary leaders, he argued insistently for a presidential system against those who preferred a cabinet or parliamentary system. The parliamentary system, Sun held, was not suitable to China's present unusual circumstances, for it would restrict too much the power of the leader: 'We cannot impose such a restrictive system on the man we single out to elect because we trust him.'[72] Two days later Sun allowed himself to be elected president of the Nanking provisional government.

It is entirely possible that the republicans decided to form a provisional government and choose a president only as a tactic to increase the pressure on Yuan. But the timing of the election, which came nine days after the agreements of 20 December and one day after Yuan obtained the court's consent to convene the National Assembly, suggests something more. In brief, Yuan had some justification for regarding Sun's 29 December election as 'a betrayal of promises and a tendency toward a permanent division of the country'.[73] Yuan's mistake, if any, may have been that he underestimated the republicans. In January they moved rapidly to inaugurate their provisional president, organize their government, address themselves to the foreign powers, decide tentatively upon a national flag (the final decision to await popular election of a parliament), and even to strike behind Yuan's lines.

This last requires some elaboration. Certain defeated Manchurian revolutionaries had gathered in Shantung and were preparing to launch a counter-attack. Sun Yat-sen blessed the effort, named one of the leaders (Lan T'ien-wei) military governor of Manchuria, and helped him to equip a substantial force including four ships. Late in January Lan was ordered north to re-open the struggle in Manchuria. After initial minor successes in early February, Lan reached stalemate. A truce was called when the Ch'ing abdicated on 12 February.[74]

Thus Sun was not idle during his brief sojourn as provisional president of the Chinese republic. And the republicans, although they continued to press their negotiations with Yuan and never undertook a full military campaign against him, did not merely allow themselves to be taken in by

[72] Hu Han-min, 'Hu Han-min tzu-chuan' (Autobiography), in *KMWH*, 3.428.
[73] Ernest P. Young, 'Yuan Shih-k'ai's rise to the presidency', 435.
[74] This incident is discussed in Masaaki Seki, 'The 1911 Revolution in Fengtien province' University of Washington, MA thesis, 1968), 106–9.

trickery. Many of them wanted Yuan from the very beginning, and if they did eventually succumb to the temptation to test their strength against him, they did not allow the test to go very far. When Yuan accepted their conditions towards the end of January and finally obtained the abdication three weeks later, the republicans were satisfied to accept him.

It seems reasonable to conclude that the revolutionaries had pressed matters until they found the limits of their power. They gained the leadership of China's interim government, and they conducted the negotiations that reunited the country under Yuan and the new republic. Their probe for greater power had revealed that they lacked the resources. Now they had no choice but to take their chances that the new republican institutions they had insisted upon creating would enable them to play a part in government affairs. In 1912 and 1913 they struggled with skill and courage to make the republic work. Western-style democratic institutions soon proved to be too foreign, too new, and too weak to carry the load that the revolutionaries had placed on them. And when a president of Yuan Shih-k'ai's ambition and ruthlessness chose to subvert the republic, its adherents saw no choice but to fight. A 'second revolution', this time against Yuan, broke out in 1913. Easily put down, it marked the end of phase one of the Chinese revolution.

CHAPTER 10

CURRENTS OF SOCIAL CHANGE

The forty years intervening between the quelling of the popular uprisings and the fall of the Ch'ing dynasty were not a period of total upheaval of the Chinese social order but rather of transformation within Chinese society. Novels written at the turn of the century by Liu E and Wu Wo-yao portray scholars and officials surrounded by new types of people whose growing influence had begun to hem them in: revolutionaries from the south, Boxers from the north, and powerful businessmen with foreign connections. Certain members of the upper class clearly perceived that a social evolution was taking place and identified the decade between 1894 and 1904 as a turning point during which change accelerated in irreversible fashion. 'In the last ten years things have changed more than in a whole century', commented Chang Chien near the end of 1904.[1]

Contemporary observers also noted that the most striking transformations in Chinese society during the Kuang-hsu and Hsuan-t'ung eras were occurring within the ruling classes, which were diversifying and becoming fragmented. Changes affecting the lower classes were much less evident. In contemporary accounts, the common people seemed to be still indifferent to change and only slightly worse off. In the streets of Shanghai in 1911 there was little difference in appearance between a modern factory worker and a labourer newly arrived from northern Kiangsu; there was a striking contrast, however, between the blue robes of scholars and the Western suits of businessmen, with their top-hats and motor-cars. To the passer-by this difference reflected the breadth of China's transition from the old to the new. However, if we are to elucidate the internal dynamic of China's social evolution at the end of the Ch'ing, we must, in the last analysis, look at the rural world which still contained some 95 per cent of the total population.

Earlier chapters in this volume have already discussed the economy, foreign relations and ideas of the West and of reform, as well as developments affecting the military, merchants, officials, gentry-literati, students and revolutionaries.

[1] Chang Chien, *Liu-hsi-ts'ao-t'ang jih-chi* (Diary from the cottage west of the willow), (25 Oct. 1904).

THE PRIVILEGED CLASSES

During the last quarter of the nineteenth century, the ruling class, which had remained relatively homogeneous since the establishment of Manchu domination under K'ang-hsi, was diversified by the addition of new categories.

On the eve of the major rebellions of the mid-nineteenth century, the social elite was composed essentially of active and retired officials, scholars with examination degrees or academic titles, and their extended families. At the provincial level they were joined by heads of large commercial concerns and banks, and at the local level, by wealthy landowners and merchants. Possession of civil or military degrees by one of its members was sufficient qualification for a family to be considered among the privileged classes, but there were several gradations that must be kept in mind. For appointment as a regular official one needed the degree of *chü-jen* (provincial graduate) or at least *kung-sheng* (imperial student), which was given for academic achievement. It was, of course, all the better if such degrees were accompanied by wealth which would enable the degree-holder to play an important social role. At a lower level the majority of *sheng-yüan* (government students), who formed the chief body of degree-holders, were still considered to be very close to commoners because their titles gave them only a few legal privileges.[2] Finally, within the local communities up to the provincial level, official degrees were not essential for membership in the ruling class if one were sufficiently wealthy and had a minimum of education. Nevertheless, in popular opinion and especially in the opinion of the upper class, degree status was taken as the badge of membership in the social elite. Families of merchants and landowners had not really made it into the upper class until they secured through purchase or examination this public proof of their status. Contemporary parlance reflected these general beliefs. The term *shen-shih* (lit., officials and scholars) is usually translated as 'gentry'. It refers to officials who had retired or were temporarily out of office and scholars in the local scene. But this term was often used by local gazetteers of the mid-nineteenth century to refer to local power-holders, including some who had no degrees.

The gentry elite: post-Taiping officials and degree-holders

The privileged class first experienced a change due to the expansion of traditional means of access to the status of scholar. In return for the con-

---

[2] Ping-ti Ho, *The ladder of success in imperial China: aspects of social mobility, 1368–1911*, 34–40.

tributions of different local communities to the repression of popular uprisings, especially that of the Taipings, examination quotas were greatly increased although there had been only meagre increases since the beginning of the dynasty. The total quota of civil *sheng-yuan* rose from 25,089 before the Taiping Rebellion to 30,113 in 1871; that of military *sheng-yuan* increased proportionately from 21,200 to 26,800.[3] Permanent increases, which were not continued after 1871, were augmented by temporary increases concurrent with the growing requirements of imperial military expenditure. Though they were numerous, temporary increases had very little cumulative effect because they applied to only one examination session and were equivalent to only 5 per cent of the permanent increases, or about 484 extra places. On the basis of these figures, and assuming each *sheng-yuan* had a further life expectancy of thirty-three years, we arrive at a constant total of approximately 910,000 graduates during the last quarter of the nineteenth century, compared to 740,000 before the Taiping Rebellion, which is an increase of 23 per cent. Of the total population, the percentage of graduates rose from 0.18 per cent to 0.24 per cent.[4]

Although the increase in the *sheng-yuan* quota was actually slight, the sale of official titles and posts was widespread. This practice had been in use since the Ming dynasty, was used widely by early Ch'ing rulers, less widely at the beginning of the nineteenth century, and was again widespread by the second half of the century. Earlier it had been used in order to diversify and balance bureaucratic recruitment, but this time the government's motives were entirely financial. Prices were often lowered by as much as 90 per cent in order to encourage sales. During the last thirty years of the nineteenth century, the total number of purchased titles rose to nearly 534,000 from its pre-Taiping total of 355,000.[5] After 1860, local officials between the fourth and seventh ranks who had purchased their positions outnumbered those who had gone through the regular route of examinations.[6]

If we include wives and children, who received the same legal privileges accorded to title-holders, the total number of family members benefiting from scholar status increased from 5,500,000 before the rebellion to 7,200,000 afterwards, while the total population dropped slightly and probably did not regain its 1850 level until after 1890. When we consider

---

[3] Chung-li Chang, *The Chinese gentry*, 88, 94.
[4] *Ibid.* 98–102.
[5] *Ibid.* 103–11.
[6] Ho, *Ladder of success*, 47–50. See also the detailed tables on local magistrates for the whole Ch'ing period in Li Kuo-ch'i and Chou T'ien-sheng, *Ch'ing-tai chi-ts'eng ti-fang-kuan jen-shih shan-ti hsien-hsiang chih liang-hua fen-hsi* (A quantitative analysis of the careers of prefects and magistrates in the Ch'ing dynasty), 206–347.

that a degree-holder's prestige was shared by his brothers, adult sons, and most distant relatives, who, although they did not enjoy identical legal privileges, did use his prestige to elevate themselves above the common level, the total number of privileged people is even larger.

Owing to its irregular distribution, the swelling of the official elite accentuated regional disparities. Before the Taipings the proportion of scholars and officials and their immediate dependants, in relation to the total population, varied from 0.7 per cent in Anhwei to 3.5 per cent in Szechwan. After the Taipings it varied from 0.6 per cent in Szechwan to 5 per cent in Chekiang.[7] The proportion dropped in Yunnan and Kweichow because of their poverty, which prevented them from being able to contribute money to the war. It dropped even further in Szechwan and remained stable in Kwangtung, but only because of rapid demographic growth, since these rich provinces had contributed substantial amounts and were therefore allowed to increase considerably the absolute size of their contingent of regular and purchased degree-holders. The proportion had risen almost everywhere, tripling in Chekiang and quadrupling in Shensi and Kansu. But here again, specific situations were quite dissimilar: the proportion rose in the provinces of the north-west because their overall population had dropped, while the wealth of the coastal provinces and those of the Yangtze valley enabled them to make up for the particularly unfavourable balance between their demographic and cultural level on the one hand, and their contingent of official degrees on the other. Thus the upkeep of a larger privileged class aggravated the problems of the poorer provinces while the disproportionate growth of the bureaucratic and scholar elite living along the Yangtze River and the coast gave them an overwhelming preponderance in absolute numbers.

The growth of the different levels in the hierarchy of the scholar class was also unequal. Before the Taipings, 125,000 of the 1,100,000 holders of degrees and official titles, or 11 per cent, had at least the degree of *kung-sheng* or higher and were thus truly upper class. Of the total group, 350,000, or 32 per cent, had purchased their titles; in the more influential category of officials and holders of official titles, the proportion was as high as 50 per cent. After the Taiping Rebellion, 204,000 of the 1,450,000 holders of official titles and degrees, or 14 per cent, obtained at least the degree of *kung-sheng* and thus entered the upper gentry. Of the total group, 530,000, or 36 per cent, had purchased their new status; among officials and holders of official titles, the proportion now ran as high as 66 per cent.[8]

The composition of the scholar class was therefore changing even as it

[7] Chang, *Chinese gentry*, 113–15.
[8] The figures and percentages given above are taken from Chang, *Chinese gentry*, 116–37.

grew in total size. Its growth was accompanied by the spectacular increase of 'irregulars' who had not achieved their status through the regular route of examinations.

This inflation of the traditional ruling class was a major phenomenon only until the end of the nineteenth century. Actually, the permanent increases in the examination quotas before 1871 had already reached the peak of their cumulative effect by that time. The number of temporary increases did not vary throughout the last years of the century. Military examinations were abandoned in 1901 and civil examinations in 1905, bringing to a close this ancient method of recruiting the ruling class. Though the sale of official titles and degrees continued, it ceased to have much appeal or importance as soon as people were given unlimited access to titles through examinations taken in the new schools (see chapter 7, pages 376–83).

The increase in numbers of the scholar class strained its cohesion and accentuated the differences, and even opposition, between title-holders with positions of responsibility and others who were unable to find jobs, and between those who had struggled through the regular path of examinations and those who had not. It affected the quality of the elite's capacity for leadership. It forced those with inferior degrees into an even lower position in the social spectrum and was a factor in their increasing poverty. It also diluted the legitimacy and effectiveness of a social hierarchy which had been originally founded on the privileges of the scholar class, and jeopardized a political order which had been sustained by the alliance between scholars and the imperial power.

New groups were forming within the ruling class throughout the latter half of the nineteenth century in response to the development of specialized technical functions. By the end of the century this change had overtaken in importance the growth of the elite through traditional means.

The new military

The modern necessities of war and defence promoted the rise of a privileged military class. From a simple professional group with relatively low status, the military was to become an influential social force. Two stages which partially overlap can be discerned in this change, corresponding to two rather different types of warfare.

The first group of these new officers originated from the repression of the popular movements which shook China to an unprecedented degree between 1850 and 1874. These were the men who organized militia, raised armies, and led them in combat against the Taipings, Niens and Muslims. Most of the early officers had already obtained official degrees prior to their mobilization;[9] the case of Hunan particularly illustrates this wide-spread militarization of the scholar class.[10] Soon afterwards, owing to the dictates of necessity and because younger leaders like Li Hung-chang began to attach more importance to competence than to either titles or Confucian orthodoxy, commoners began to outnumber them in the command of the new armed forces.[11] For these men, whether they originally held a degree or not, it was only their military achievements that brought them into local, and in some cases national, prominence. Such was the case of Liu Yü-hsun, originally a licentiate from Chung-chou in Kiangsi, who dominated Nanchang and the surrounding region for fifteen years at the head of a provincial army he had himself organized. Such was also the case of Liu Ming-ch'uan who rose from smuggling salt to leading an army in Anhwei, and finally to the governorship of the province of Taiwan (see chapter 4). However, it does seem noteworthy that most of these officers later entered civil service. Military service was simply a stepping-stone to power within the bureaucracy. The imperial practices of conferring civil ranks and titles in return for services, and checking local military leaders who had grown too powerful by consigning them to low-level positions in the civil service, did nothing to deter this opportunism. This was all the more true because the various *yung-ying* armies, in contrast to the banner troops and the Green Standard forces, the two 'regular armies' (*ching-chih chün*), were given no permanent statutory status and their officers did not possess official rank. Certain military leaders, like Liu Yü-hsun, declined positions offered to them out of preference for the gains their local authority assured both them and their particular clans. But all of the more powerful commanders and most of their subordinates sought out and accepted positions in the civil hierarchy; several of them became governors-general or governors. This indicates rather clearly that even as late as the end of the nineteenth century positions within the hierarchy of the civil officialdom were considered more valuable than military rank. However, the very fact that their history as soldiers either paved the way for or simply accelerated their climb to the highest reaches of civilian government gave new lustre to the armed forces and definitely prepared the way for the military to assume a new role in society.

[9] Until 1856 most of the officers of the Hunan Army were scholars. The proportion dropped sharply for commissions given after this date. Cf. Lo Erh-kang, *Hsiang-chün hsin-chih* (A new history of the Hunan Army), 55–64.

[10] Philip A. Kuhn, *Rebellion and its enemies in late imperial China: militarization and social structure, 1796–1864*, 146–51.

[11] Holders of official titles and degrees accounted for only 12 per cent of the military command of the Huai Army, and at most a third of the core of the Huai clique, that is the top commanders of the eleven army corps: Wang Erh-min, *Huai-chün chih* (History of the Huai Army), 184–5.

Actually, because of the fact that they sometimes lacked the prejudices of traditional scholarly education and because they were usually keenly aware of the need to maintain order and government, these officers and military leaders often became strong advocates of the introduction of Western technology. As a result of the initiatives of Tseng Kuo-fan, Li Hung-chang, Liu Ming-ch'uan, Kuo Sung-tao, Tso Tsung-t'ang, Liu Ch'ang-yu, Shen Pao-chen and their collaborators, the first modern large-scale enterprises were developed. The Anking Arsenal, created in 1861 by Tseng Kuo-fan, as well as the arms industry established thereafter were probably both simply a practical application of the *ching-shih* (statecraft) school's ideas about the use of any technique which might help to maintain the order and authority of the state. But with the spread of mining, means of communication and transport, and textile factories, it became clear that the basic concepts of *ching-shih*, in favour of protecting the public domain from encroaching private interests and ensuring that state-owned resources would not be used for individual profit, were overridden. Veterans of the repression of the popular movements thus played a pivotal role in the transition from the traditional function of the omnicompetent literati-official who, among other things, was able to assume military responsibilities, to the function of the technical expert, who gained political influence through his special competence.

Creating new armies and modernizing traditional troops also gave rise to another group of influential military men. In 1853 Tseng Kuo-fan introduced special training for the non-commissioned officers of his new Hunan Army, emphasizing endurance and discipline. This was later imitated by the Anhwei Army. The technical training of the officer corps along Western lines was begun in 1862 at Shanghai and Ningpo, where a few company commanders and their men were trained in the use of Western equipment and tactics by French and English military advisers (see chapter 4). In November of the same year an edict prescribing the development of similar training for high-ranking officers was issued in order to maintain Chinese control over the armed forces. Progress came slowly. The navy was the first to be emphasized; in addition to technical schools, a school for cadets was added to the Foochow Arsenal in 1867. Several of its students travelled to France and England to complete their training in 1875, 1877, 1882 and 1886. Other naval schools were opened in Nanking, Weihaiwei and Lü-shun (Port Arthur); Li Hung-chang founded another at Tientsin in 1881. As early as 1872 he sent a group of his army officers to Germany for further training. Several foreign advisers were employed in Chihli, Kiangsu and Kwangtung in the training of a small number of troops whose officers were then able to offer instruction in other provinces. Li Hung-chang founded the first military school at Tientsin in 1885. In 1887 Chang Chih-tung opened a combined naval and military school at Whampoa near Canton. Until the Sino-Japanese War, no more than a few hundred officers were educated in these schools. But with the dawn of the technological revolution called for by the widespread use of Western arms, the status of the soldier began to rise, making him an agent of technological progress.[12]

Only after 1895 did the number of these new officers begin to increase significantly. They also began to replace the older generation in the highest positions of command and at the head of fully modernized army corps. Emphasis was shifted from establishing modern naval defence to the transformation of ground forces, which brought with it more far-reaching and profound social consequences.

Until the Sino-Japanese War, those few troops who had been 'Western-trained' simply adopted foreign arms and drill. In December 1895, the throne approved the creation of two units which also borrowed the German system of military organization, training and tactics. These units were the Tzu-ch'iang chün (Self-Strengthening Army) of Chang Chih-tung and the Hsin-chien lu-chün (Newly Created Army) of Yuan Shih-k'ai. Many of the Self-Strengthening Army's recruits, who had been chosen and trained with particular care, knew how to read and write. This was without precedent in the Chinese Army and, as a result of the prestige given to education, conferred a certain level of social esteem on the military profession which it had previously lacked. From the ranks of Yuan Shih-k'ai's officers came five presidents of the republic or acting chief executives, one prime minister, and most of the warlords who shared the domination of North China after 1916. Those of humble origins, like Ts'ao K'un or Feng Kuo-chang, were educated by the army. Meng En-yuan, who remained functionally illiterate, was an exception to the rule. The new army officers were unique in their generally high level of education, which the ranking officers of the old army lacked, and in their technical understanding of Western methods of defence and strategy, neither of which were available to the scholars and civil dignitaries who had organized militia during the preceding generation.

The promotion of new officers was stepped up after 1901 owing to military reform. The Green Standard forces, which had been sorely tried by the Boxer Rebellion, were disbanded. New Western-type units with a regular army backed up by reserves were to be formed in the provinces,

---

[12] According to observations of foreign experts, Chinese holdings of Western arms in 1885 amounted to more than 200,000 rifles and repeating rifles, several hundred thousand percussion rifles, about 50 machine guns, and 1,200 guns of various bores: Archives of the French Ministry for Foreign Affairs, *Chine. Correspondance politique des consuls. Shanghai*, 12.211–15. Note on Chinese arms, 26 Aug. 1885.

equipped, trained and commanded in Western style, and made the basis of a modern army called the Lu-chün (Regular Army); such was the substance of a decree issued on 12 September 1901. Yuan Shih-k'ai took advantage of imperial decrees to strengthen the Hsin-chien lu-chün, which was designated after 1901 the Peiyang or Northern Army (Pei-yang lu-chün), and became the strongest military force in the whole of China, accounting in 1911 for more than a third of her total troops. Other new active units of the so-called New Army or Regular Army (Ch'ang-pei chün) were formed in Hupei, Kiangsu, Shansi, Shensi, Kiangsi, Kwangsi, Kweichow and Yunnan between 1901 and 1904 (see chapter 7, pages 383–8).

An imperial decree of 29 August 1901, abolishing traditional military examinations, eased the competition for the new officers, and on 11 September 1901, the throne called for the creation of military schools in each province and the establishment of national regulations for military education. By the end of 1903 nearly every province had its own military school. Yuan Shih-k'ai opened six of them at Paoting, offering diversified technical education to general-staff officers as well as recruits. Graduates of his school at Tientsin filled most of the faculty positions at other schools, along with German and, increasingly, Japanese instructors. The regulations on general education sanctioned on 3 January 1904, required students to perform military exercises and wear uniforms;[13] higher education was to include courses in military history, tactics and logistics. On 12 September 1904, military schools received special regulations consisting of twenty articles which had been prepared by the Commission for Army Reorganization (Lien-ping ch'u). Modelled closely on the Japanese system, it called for the creation of an educational hierarchy offering instruction from the level of higher elementary school to that of university education for general-staff officers. These regulations were not followed to the letter. The two schools for ranking officers which were to have been opened in Peking never materialized; the only education available at this level was at Paoting, under the aegis of Yuan Shih-k'ai, or abroad. The quality of instruction also varied greatly from one school to another. But the reform movement did succeed in creating additional provincial military schools and increasing the number of officers who were sent abroad to complete their education. In 1906 there was a total of thirty-five military schools with a combined enrolment of 6,307 students, as well as 350 midshipmen in the four naval schools of Weihaiwei, Nanking, Foochow and Whampoa, 691 officers and cadets in Japan, and 15 or so in Europe.[14] There were in 1911 nearly seventy institutions of military education. In addition to military techniques,

[13] Chang Po-hsi, Chang Chih-tung and Jung Ch'ing, *Tsou-ting hsueh-t'ang chang-ch'eng*, 1.14, 17b.
[14] Ralph L. Powell, *The rise of Chinese military power 1895–1912*, 235–6.

students acquired a certain amount of culture, some degree of proficiency in a foreign language, and basic scientific training. Military education quickly gained in social prestige. Chang Chih-tung had set an example in 1902 by requiring his subordinates to enrol their sons in the military schools of Wuchang and by sending three of his grandsons to a Japanese military school. The Military School for Princes and Nobles (Lu-chün kuei-chou hsueh-t'ang), which opened at Peking in 1906, was attended not only by members of the imperial clan, but also by children of illustrious former militia leaders like Liu Ming-ch'uan, and sons of presidents of ministries, governors and scholars. On the eve of the revolution, military schools were drawing their students from the highest levels of provincial society and there were even old-type civil degree-holders who enlisted as simple soldiers.[15] This development was also aided by the creation of a new hierarchy of military ranks, which provided titles and salaries similar to those of the civil bureaucracy.[16] The deaths of Li Hung-chang in 1901 and Liu K'un-i in 1902 – the last great commanders against the Taipings, opened the way for a new generation of provincial rulers whose authority rested more exclusively on military power. Yuan Shih-k'ai was definitely the prototype, but Chang Chih-tung, the scholar-official *par excellence*, also devoted the last years of his life to the formation of a modern army. To compensate for its weakening moral, social and political authority, the use of arms was seen as imperative by the throne as well as by the most ambitious men in the provinces. This general tendency to enhance the value of armed forces favoured the growth of an educated military staff who enjoyed social esteem and political influence.

In 1911 the Chinese armies, theoretically claiming approximately a million men, probably included only 600,000 actual combatants, of whom some 175,000 were in the modernized Regular Army and another 175,000 in the semi-modernized *hsun-fang tui*. The latter was a provincially funded territorial force, created in 1907 to absorb soldiers released from the Green Standard Army, the *yung-ying* forces and other miscellaneous troops. Among the banner troops which, together with 50,000 soldiers not as yet demobilized from the Green Standard battalions, completed the armed forces, 75,000 men had been trained in Western techniques.[17] Altogether there were nearly 70,000 officers; 10 per cent were of superior rank and 800 had

---

[15] Witness the accounts of Ch'en Hsiao-fen and Ho Sui in Chung-kuo jen-min cheng-chih hsieh-shang hui-i Hu-pei sheng wei-yuan-hui, ed. *Hsin-hai shou-i hui-i lu* (Reminiscences of the righteous beginnings of the 1911 Revolution), 1.68.

[16] General regulations bearing on this matter were published by decree on 20 Dec. 1904. *Ta Ch'ing Te-tsung ching-huang-ti shih-lu* (Veritable records of the Kuang-hsu Emperor of the Ch'ing dynasty), 537.14–14b. They were elaborated on 11 Nov. 1909. *Ta Ch'ing shih-lu Hsuan-t'ung cheng-chi* (Veritable records of the Hsuan-t'ung Emperor), 22.20–4b.

[17] For a discussion of various sources for these figures see Powell, *Chinese military power*, 288–98.

been educated in Japan. The general quality of these officers – even those of lowest rank – their level of education, and their competence in technical and scientific matters, was far superior to that of their counterparts in the old armies, and contrasted starkly with the general mediocrity of the civil bureaucracy. After 1895, high-ranking officers who had been trained in modern methods were more likely to remain in the army than to seek high-level civil placement. Military reform had helped to guarantee them valuable careers. In effect, the army outstepped the civil bureaucracy: its Westernized career-men were promoted far more quickly than civil servants who were experienced in foreign matters. But it was not only the hope of rapid advancement which gave the military profession its growing prestige; it also profited greatly from the dissemination of culture among the officer corps and the generally higher quality of the troops, which, in the eyes of Chinese public opinion with its traditional emphasis on education, gave it a very favourable image.

However, the emergence of the military as a socially influential group might be more precisely linked to the rising current of virulent nationalism since the Sino-Japanese War. Most obvious were the financial sacrifices agreed to after the defeat, which were necessary to modernize the army. But there was also the vision, inspired particularly by the examples of Germany and Japan and the doctrines upon which they were based, of an army which would at once defend and regenerate the nation. In his day, Tseng Kuo-fan had conceived of a disciplined army providing a good example to the populace, a conception promoted by the Commission for Army Reorganization in the texts it issued in 1904 and 1906. Tseng Kuo-fan, however, had relegated the political and moral leadership of the country entirely to scholars, who, according to the formula *yung ju-sheng ling nung* (use the Confucian scholars to lead the peasants), were to preside over an eminently civil social order according to the dictates of Confucian values. After the Sino-Japanese War, however, the army was exalted more and more as a model, and even a guide, for the nation. In accordance with suggestions in the press and numerous petitions,[18] an edict outlining the directives for public education issued in April 1906 included respect and promotion of military matters (*shang wu*). The cult of the military spirit was taken up by the majority of educational societies created after 1905, which were largely composed of gentry-literati. Their national federation, convened at Peking in 1911, adopted as its first recommendation the institution of national military education (*chün-kuo-min chiao-yü*), strictly and

[18] The reformist press played a pioneer role in this campaign, notably the *Hsin-min ts'ung-pao* (The new people miscellany), esp. articles by Fen Ho-sheng and Chiang Pai-li published in 1902.

properly organized, in all public and private schools.[19] These efforts were still quite limited in their practical effects; as late as 1911 the society had not been militarized on a large scale and few schools had actually formed veritable student troops. Be that as it may, military authority and prestige had been fortified by the general current of ideas: the army could now become in the eyes of the public a truly uplifting national institution.

Even if it were a symbol of national recovery, can this new officer corps really be considered an agent of national solidarity? The military had no real unity. Its origins were disparate, its training diverse, and numerous were the forces which divided it. In it were some men of very humble origins, like Chang Hsun, Ts'ao K'un or Liu Po-ch'eng. Chang Hsun, who in 1917 attempted an imperial restoration, rose through the ranks during the Franco-Chinese War, the Sino-Japanese War and the Boxer War. Ts'ao K'un, who became president of the republic in 1923–4, was able, thanks to the help of Yuan Shih-k'ai, to be among the first graduates of the military school at Tientsin. Liu Po-ch'eng, who was trained at the military school in Chengtu, Szechwan, later became a marshal of the communist forces. Others came from very rich and powerful families. Hsu Ch'ung-chih, whose grandfather was governor-general of Fukien and Chekiang, was a graduate of Shikan Gakkō (Army Officers Academy) in Japan, commander of the 20th brigade at Foochow in 1911, leader of Fukien province's revolutionary forces, and minister of war under Sun Yat-sen in 1925. There were also many sons of landowners and scholars of both modest and substantial means, *sheng-yuan* and even *chü-jen* with no money, who, due to lack of alternatives, took up military careers after the abolition of the examination system. Their numbers rose during the years preceding the revolution, especially among the troops of Central and South China. Among these were Chu Te, the future organizer of the Red Army, who in 1909 entered military school in Yunnan; Ts'ai O, an unsuccessful candidate for the *chü-jen* degree who became a disciple of Liang Ch'i-ch'ao, graduated from the best military schools in Japan, commanded the 37th brigade at Kunming in 1911, led the republican revolution in Yunnan, and organized resistance to the monarchy proposed by Yuan Shih-k'ai in 1915–16; and Chiang Kai-shek, the future head of the Nationalist government, who attended military school at Paoting and completed his education in Japan.

While rather strong ties of personal loyalty sustained by favours enabled Yuan Shih-k'ai to maintain his hold over the Peiyang Army, this was not the case with the southern officers whose command was divided among the provinces and changed hands often. The troops organized by Chang Chih-tung were far superior in their technical education to those of Yuan Shih-

19 *Chiao-yü tsa-chih* (The Chinese Educational Review), 3.6, *fu-lu* (Appendix), 2.

k'ai; their officers were all graduates of military school and often as many as half of the soldiers were literate. As a result of their far-reaching education in the military schools of the south, their many contacts established through study abroad, their literati origins, and the rather chaotic control exercised over them, the officers of the south were generally more open to ideas than their northern colleagues, and therefore more likely to be sympathetic to revolutionary action.[20] Most of the mutinies which occurred after 1908, including the one which brought down the empire, broke out among the southern troops, who were also the focal point of the revolutionaries' major successful efforts at propaganda. Openness to new ideas, although less widespread than in the south, was far from non-existent among the officers of the Peiyang Army, where there were many political study groups, one of which was frequented after 1909 by Feng Yü-hsiang, a future warlord.[21]

There was absolutely no solidarity among the various groups officering the different armies of China. Loyalty to the dynasty survived only among the older officers of the Peiyang Army, the banner troops, and the territorials (*hsun-fang tui*). Anti-Manchu sentiment, even though it was very widespread, provided no unity. Nor was the throne's effort to unify the various forces and centralize their command successful;[22] the officers of the territorial troops were jealous of the material privileges of the Regular Army; various factions were opposed to each other, sometimes on the basis of personal loyalties (the best example being the group around Yuan Shih-k'ai), sometimes provincial loyalties, and at others, loyalty to the same school.[23] The only faith in common among the new officer corps was a belief in military authority, rather than civil authority, a belief derived from an education based on German and Japanese doctrines at a time of declining political stability. This trait certainly distinguishes them most radically from the older elite.

[20] Witness the accounts of many who did not achieve historical celebrity, in Chung-kuo jen-min cheng-chih hsieh-shang hui-i ch'üan-kuo wei-yuan-hui wen-shih tzu-liao yen-chiu wei-yuan-hui, ed. *Hsin-hai ko-ming hui-i lu* (Reminiscences of the 1911 Revolution), 2.211–13, 281–301; 4.247–55. See also Ch'en Hsu-lu and Lao Shao-hua, 'Ch'ing-mo ti hsin-chün yü hsin-hai ko-ming' (The late Ch'ing New Army and the Revolution of 1911), in Hu-pei-sheng che-hsueh she-hui k'o-hsueh hsueh-hui lien-ho hui, ed. *Hsin-hai ko-ming wu-shih chou-nien lun-wen chi* (A collection of articles on the fiftieth anniversary of the Revolution of 1911; hereafter *HHWS*), 147–65.

[21] James E. Sheridan, *Chinese warlord: the career of Feng Yü-hsiang*, 43–4.

[22] For a description of these unavailing efforts after 1907, at a time when the death of Chang Chih-tung and the disgrace of Yuan Shih-k'ai made this task easier, see Powell, *Chinese military power*, 254–81.

[23] Alumni of the Shikan Gakkō thus formed a rather united circle: T'ao Chü-yin, *Pei-yang chün-fa t'ung-chih shih-ch'i shih-hua* (Historical anecdotes on the period of the Peiyang warlords), 1.22–5.

Products of Western contact

Other new groups were forming within the privileged classes in response to the exigencies of political and economic relations with other countries. The common cause behind their organization was *yang-wu* (Western matters), which included not only direct diplomatic relations but all dealings with the West. Although *yang-wu* was partially responsible for the new military organization, its main effect was the emergence of certain other social categories.

First were the specialists in official negotiations. The earliest professionals at *yang-wu* were interpreters; but with neither degrees nor official titles, as in the case of several Christians recruited for the job, they were assigned very minor roles. However, with the war of 1858–60 appeared young technicians in foreign relations such as Ma Chien-chung, a scholar from a well-known Catholic family in Shanghai who was educated by the Jesuits of Zikawei (Hsu-chia-hui) and who joined the staff of Li Hung-chang about 1875. Most of them were originally recruited because of their linguistic competence, but because of their greater understanding of foreign affairs and their insight into and experience of Chinese administration, they gained recognition as valuable negotiators.

Each seat of power in foreign affairs, in the major treaty ports and at Peking, was endeavouring to form its own group of experts. The largest of them was associated with the commissioner regulating commerce in the northern ports, the post held by Li Hung-chang from 1870 to 1895. Another gravitated around the Tsungli Yamen. While he was governor-general of Liang-Kwang, Chang Chih-tung maintained his group at Canton, shifting it to Wuchang when he took charge of Hu-Kwang in 1889. Another group, which was divided between Nanking and Shanghai, was under the commissioner for commerce in the southern ports (Nan-yang ta-ch'en), who was also governor-general at Nanking. Sometimes individuals passed from one group to another, such as Ch'en Ch'in, who left the Tsungli Yamen in 1870 to join Li Hung-chang. Yung Wing, the first Chinese graduate of an American university, served both Li Hung-chang and Chang Chih-tung.

These experts had various educational backgrounds. Ku Hung-ming (1857–1928), a Chinese born in Penang who became secretary and counsellor to Chang Chih-tung in 1880, was educated entirely abroad, first in Singapore and then in Edinburgh and Germany. Wu T'ing-fang, born at Canton into the famous 'Howqua' family of the Cohong epoch, spent part of his childhood in Singapore, studied law in London where he was the first Chinese to be admitted to the bar, and was already established in Hong

Kong as an influential lawyer when Li Hung-chang persuaded him in 1882 to join him in Tientsin. Lo Feng-lu, whose services Li Hung-chang recognized by recommending his appointment as minister to England, completed the education he had received at the Foochow Arsenal school with several years' study in Europe. Ts'ai Hsi-yung, a loyal assistant of Chang Chih-tung, served the diplomatic corps in the United States, Japan and Peru after his graduation from the Peking Interpreter's College (T'ung-wen kuan). Several others attended those rare schools which offered Western education before 1895, and were not therefore obliged to leave the country. Many others such as Shen Pao-ching, Sheng Hsuan-huai and Cheng Kuan-ying, who were economic managers under Li Hung-chang, acquired their expertise on the spot through their dealings with foreigners and the demands of business.

In fact, these technicians in Western affairs quickly assumed responsibility not only for the negotiations but also, to some degree, for the economic matters under discussion. They were likely to be given assignments overseeing foreign commerce, as customs taotai at Tientsin or superintendents of customs and concurrently circuit taotai at treaty ports. They were more often engaged in the management of modern official undertakings. The same men might be given responsibility successively for constructing an arsenal, administering a navigation company, setting up a textile factory, and directing a military school. Sheng Hsuan-huai is perhaps the most well-known among them.[24] Many others among the entourages surrounding Li Hung-chang and Chang Chih-tung pursued similar but less glorified and successful careers. Yang Tsung-lien, for example, whom Li Hung-chang installed as taotai at Hankow in 1870, was given responsibility for building a railway on Taiwan in 1882, directed the military school at Tientsin in 1885, founded a match factory in 1886, became taotai in Chihli, and then assumed responsibility for establishing an arsenal in Shansi. There was also Ts'ai Hsi-yung who in Canton organized a torpedo school in 1886, a naval school in 1887, and a mint in 1888, then at Hupei, a steelworks and the Hanyang Arsenal in 1890, the Wuchang mint in 1893, and in the same city, a cotton mill in 1892, a silk-spinning mill in 1894, the Self-Strengthening School (Tzu-ch'iang hsueh-t'ang), which offered a Western curriculum in 1895, and a military school in 1896.[25]

Similar to the official *yang-wu* experts, another group of businessmen emerged which specialized in marketing Western goods. Compradors

[24] For his biography see Albert Feuerwerker, *China's early industrialization: Sheng Hsuan-huai (1844-1916) and mandarin enterprise.*
[25] Chang Chih-tung, *Chang Wen-hsiang kung ch'üan-chi,* 47.22b–23.

were its first and foremost members. After the abolition of the Cohong system in 1842, these businessmen were indispensable as intermediaries between foreign firms and a market where language barriers, and the complexity of the monetary system, commercial institutions and customs, all opposed direct transactions. They were generally under contract with foreign merchants, which distinguished them from the licensed brokers (*ya-hang*), who were the traditional intermediaries of Chinese domestic commerce and were independent commission agents. The comprador acted as a Chinese proxy to a foreign firm: he hired and managed the native personnel, he was the treasurer, comptroller, financial officer, salesman and market researcher, and he assisted his foreign colleagues in all their dealings with the Chinese.

Most compradors were originally from around Canton. Because of their long experience with foreign trade, the Cantonese merchants did not hesitate to grant to their fellow townsmen the full financial guarantee required of compradors by their foreign bosses. They also provided agents who were highly competent in the tea trade, which was the principal export at the beginning of the treaty period. Cantonese compradors therefore helped to develop foreign business in other treaty ports and even Japan. But the growth in the export of silk, coupled with the decline in tea exports and the increasing importance of activities which had previously been marginal for foreigners, notably banking, encouraged the rapid rise of compradors in Chekiang and then Kiangsu. Most of them, who were originally from Ningpo and Soochow, began as silk merchants or as employees of Chinese banks (*ch'ien-chuang*) situated in Shanghai. At the beginning of the twentieth century, most compradors were still from Canton, but Shanghai, the most important commercial centre, was dominated by those from Chekiang and Kiangsu.[26]

Compradors were usually merchants who had already achieved some degree of success, and were therefore capable of obtaining guarantors when they were hired by foreign firms, although at the turn of the century there were some who had been promoted through the ranks after many years of service with the same company. At the same time, most of these compradors were merchants who had only recently become rich, and for whom employment with foreign firms offered the chance to perfect their talents and increase their personal wealth. In effect, they were distinguished from other merchants by the rapidity and magnitude of their earnings. To an annual salary of about 1,000 taels, they added commission, 'squeeze' and profits from their personal dealings, which were enhanced admirably by the wealth, relations, advice and protection which association with

[26] Yen-p'ing Hao, *The comprador in nineteenth century China: bridge between East and West*, 48–54.

foreigners procured. Compradors in charge of large Western firms accumulated several millions of taels; two examples are Hsu Jun, a comprador for Dent at Shanghai from 1861 to 1868, and Chu Ta-ch'un, a comprador for Jardine's at Shanghai at the turn of the century.[27] The total number of compradors grew from 250 in 1854, to 700 in 1870 and 20,000 in 1900.[28] The compradors' total income for the period from 1842 to 1894 was about 530 million taels.[29] This amount is rather low when compared with the income of the scholar-elite which is estimated to have been 645 million taels per annum near the end of the nineteenth century.[30] This is a considerable sum both in view of the number of people involved, and when compared with the total volume of foreign investment in China, which was estimated at 584 million taels in 1902.[31] Bankruptcies were, however, very frequent, and comprador assets fluctuated a great deal.

Compradors not only had the financial capacity but also were willing to invest in new sectors. They were the first to make large sums of money available for the founding of modern enterprises and played a decisive role in their launching. It has been estimated that they provided 30 per cent of the capital for the six steam-navigation companies in Shanghai between 1862 and 1873; 62.7 per cent of the capital needed to open coal mines between 1863 and 1886; 23.23 per cent of the capital needed by twenty-seven large Chinese cotton mills opened between 1890 and 1910; and 30 per cent of the capital needed by Chinese machine manufacturing during the same period.[32] In addition to their important financial participation, compradors also assumed responsibility for the promotion and management of new firms. They were innovative and skilful at taking risks and using Western business practices in order to succeed in their ventures. Because they were able to assure the prosperity of foreign firms, the government often asked them to provide technical management of official undertakings. But by the end of the nineteenth century they were beginning to initiate and head their own companies.[33] In this way they performed an important function in economic modernization.

Compradors were also unique in some features of their life-style and mentality. Because they were in such close contact with foreigners, they

[27] Wang Ching-yü, comp. *Chung-kuo chin-tai kung-yeh shih tzu-liao*, 959–60, 966–7.
[28] These estimates are taken from Hao, *The comprador in nineteenth century China*, 102, and concern 'major' compradors. Figures for 1870 and 1900 include both working compradors and former compradors who were still engaged in some kind of commercial activity.
[29] Hao, *The comprador in nineteenth century China*, 102–5.
[30] Chung-li Chang, *The income of the Chinese gentry*, 197.
[31] Charles Frederick Remer, *Foreign investments in China*, 69.
[32] Hao, *The comprador in nineteenth century China*, 120–36.
[33] Wang Ching-yü, *Chung-kuo chin-tai kung-yeh shih tzu-liao*, 1091–5, lists 105 companies with which thirteen of the most noteworthy compradors had been associated as promoters or large investors between 1878 and 1910.

willingly adopted Western dress, furnishings, pastimes and religious beliefs, and incorporated them, together with their Chinese habits, into a hybrid cultural *mélange* of which pidgin English is a good linguistic example. They were also able to abandon traditional values in order to give their sons an entirely Western education, to defend the notions of profit and economic development, and, in some cases such as Cheng Kuan-ying, to become advocates of institutional reform.

In addition to the compradors, another group can be distinguished whose boundaries are less well-defined: those who, without entering directly into the service of Western firms, endeavoured to reap a profit from foreign trade or the introduction of Western technology. Most obvious are those merchants who built their fortunes by producing exportable goods or distributing imports. For example, Hu Yuan-lung, a tea merchant from Ch'i-men in Anhwei, planted 300 hectares (5,000 *mou*) during the 1850s; then, faced with the sagging market for green tea, he converted entirely to black tea in 1876 and founded his own processing plants, thereby assuring both his personal prosperity and the reputation of his region for the production of tea.[34] Yeh Ch'eng-chung, the orphaned son of a small farmer from Chekiang, began his career by hauling and selling kerosene; when he died in 1899 he left 8 million taels.[35] Ku Hsing-i, who came from the family of a poor scholar, created a large grain business in Shanghai, profiting from the cargo-capacity of steamboats.[36] Native banks or *ch'ien-chuang* also flourished in Shanghai as intermediaries between the Chinese population and foreign banks, providing brokers with the credit necessary to purchase imported goods while they awaited resale to domestic distributors. There were 58 *ch'ien-chuang* in Shanghai in 1883, 82 in 1903, and 115 in 1908.[37] A few families dominated the banking business, establishing branches in all the treaty ports of the Yangtze valley. These were the Fangs, the Lis, and the Yehs of Ningpo, the Ch'engs of Soochow, and the Yens and the Wans of Tung-t'ing-shan.[38]

Certain of these merchants and financiers also entered industry. Thus in 1872, Ch'en Ch'i-yuan opened the first civil industrial concern financed with native Chinese capital – a steam-powered silk-spinning mill in the suburbs of Canton.[39] Until 1895, the number of financiers and merchants entering industry grew steadily. Many of them became the principal share-

[34] P'eng Tse-i, comp. *Chung-kuo chin-tai shou-kung-yeh shih tzu-liao, 1840–1949*, 2.104.
[35] Wang Ching-yü, *Chung-kuo chin-tai kung-yeh shih tzu-liao*, 954–6.
[36] *Ibid.* 958.
[37] Chung-kuo jen-min yin-hang Shang-hai-shih fen-hang, ed. *Shang-hai ch'ien-chuang shih-liao* (Historical materials on Shanghai native banks), 32, 94.
[38] *Ibid.* 730–51.
[39] Sun Yü-t'ang, *Chung-kuo chin-tai kung-yeh shih tzu-liao*, 957–65.

holders and administrators of businesses registered as foreign. In the Yangtze provinces and in Chihli they were active in official enterprises. Tea merchants, for example, furnished most of the initial capital for the Shanghai Cotton Cloth Mill (Shang-hai chi-ch'i chih-pu chü) in the early 1880s (see chapter 8). But after 1885 they concentrated their efforts, as had their associates in the southern provinces all along, in those sectors of private industry neglected by the government: silk, processing of food-stuffs, matches, paper and glass manufacturing, and the construction and upkeep of machinery. Most of these were small concerns with little mechanization, often almost indistinguishable from new forms of handi-craft enterprise in large workshops or in jointly financed groups of home-workshops, which enabled greater use of new technology and arose primarily at the instigation of merchants.[40] Combining new with tradi-tional activities assured large profits. Starting with an initial capital of 18,000 taels which he invested in a moneyshop at Ying-k'ou in 1888, Yeh Liang-ch'ing, a Cantonese merchant, accumulated more than 2 million taels by 1906, exercising a near monopoly on the export of soy products to Kwangtung, heading several native banks, factories producing soy-bean cakes and tobacco, timber yards and real estate companies, and investing heavily in banks and railways.[41]

This group of merchants and financiers engaged in new activities was certainly less unorthodox than the compradors. These businessmen were far less likely to assume foreign ways of life. Not only did they continue to purchase official titles and degrees, but they also encouraged their sons to study Confucian classics so as to pass the civil service examinations. Families in Ningpo and Soochow, for example, maintained a kind of division of labour among their members, some of them entering careers as officials, others entering into business. But traces of a new mentality began to appear during the last twenty years of the nineteenth century. Among the charitable operations financed traditionally by wealthy merchants were schools offering Western curricula and hospitals using Western medicine.[42] Tea merchants from Hunan and Hupei pressed Chang Chih-tung in 1891 to introduce courses in Western languages and commercial practices at the Liang-Hu Academy.[43]

In the years between 1870 and 1895, another group arose whose social style varied far less from traditional norms. These were simply stock-

[40] P'eng Tse-i, Chung-kuo chin-tai shou-kung-yeh shih tzu-liao, 2.331–449.
[41] Sasaki Masaya, 'Eikō shōnin no kenkyū' (A study of the Ying-k'ou merchants), in Kindai Chūgoku kenkyū, 1 (1958) 219–22.
[42] For example, the school in Shanghai to which Yeh Ch'eng-chung gave 200,000 taels, or the Kuang-chi Hospital founded in 1893 by Cantonese merchants.
[43] Chang Chih-tung, Chang Wen-hsiang kung ch'üan-chi, 97.23b–24.

holders in modern companies. The salt merchants of Hsuchow probably viewed their financial contributions to the Li-kuo-i coal mine in 1882 as an official levy,[44] but foreign businesses, whose capital during the nineteenth century was often 40–80 per cent Chinese, included, in addition to compradors and wealthy merchants, a sizeable percentage of small stockholders who were likely to be officials, scholars or employees in treaty ports.[45] Official enterprises also attracted investment from bureaucrats and scholars.

Until the Sino-Japanese War, the distinctions between the various groups involved with *yang-wu* remained relatively clear: technicians and experts, compradors and independent businessmen. This is reflected in the language of the time which designated the first group *shen* or *kuan* (officials or officially employed experts), the second group *mai-pan* (compradors), and the last group *shang* (merchants). However, these groups did collaborate as partners in official enterprises and, the last two especially, as partners in private enterprise. Mobility between the groups was frequent. Compradors were recruited among merchants and were likely to become independent businessmen again upon leaving their foreign employers. Compradors, such as T'ang T'ing-shu and Cheng Kuan-ying, and merchants, such as Chu Ch'i-ang, became official experts, and official experts, such as Yang Tsung-lien, became businessmen.

Taken together, these new social groups constituted only a fraction of the privileged class, which was able to accommodate them as new members at the same time that it gave older gentry families a chance to renew their past glory in an exclusively urban setting. These groups were too weak individually to give direction to the upper class; in order to exercise any political or ideological influence they were forced to attach themselves to one of the powerful provincial officials involved with *yang-wu*, like Tso Tung-t'ang, Li Hung-chang or Chang Chih-tung. They could advise, but leadership was always in the hands of those whose education and origins were more orthodox and traditional. However, one of the most striking indications of the social transformation taking place at this time is the fact that their sons were frequently given a business education rather than pushed into officialdom to aid the family's social ascent.[46]

[44] Sun Yü-t'ang, *Chung-kuo chin-tai kung-yeh shih tzu-liao*, 1115–18.

[45] Wang Ching-yü, 'Shih-chiu shih-chi wai-kuo ch'in Hua ch'i-yeh chung ti Hua-shang fu-ku huo-tung' (Investment by Chinese merchants in the foreign firms which invaded China in the nineteenth century), *Li-shih yen-chiu*, 1965.4, pp. 39–74. The author estimates the amount of Chinese capital invested in this manner at more than 40 million taels.

[46] This concern was most evident among compradors: see Hao, *The comprador in nineteenth century China*, 172–3, 221. However, it was also felt among simple merchants and even official managers: cf. Wang Ching-yü, *Chung-kuo chin-tai kung-yeh shih tzu-liao*, 929–30.

The new intelligentsia and entrepreneurs

The social spectrum spanned by the elite was changing perceptibly at the turn of the century as a result of modifications in the activities and functions of the literati.

A Western-style intelligentsia was emerging. It was concentrated in the treaty ports and maintained much less contact with the rural population than had former scholars. Its first representatives were men like Wang T'ao (1828–97), whose individual destiny was affected as much by national upheavals, the growing poverty of scholars, the fall of the Taipings and the spread of foreign presence and missionary activities, as by his own intellectual itinerary, which led him to become a pamphleteer-journalist living entirely off his writing.[47] Others, who were perhaps less brilliant, followed in his footsteps, men such as K'uang Ch'i-chao, a member of the educational mission to the United States, who founded the first Cantonese newspaper in 1886.

They were joined by scholars with more orthodox educational backgrounds such as Liang Ch'i-ch'ao and his friends, Mai Meng-hua and Wang K'ang-nien, who after the Sino-Japanese War renounced their traditional occupations to devote themselves to the propagation of new ideas. Engineers and technicians who had been educated in an earlier epoch joined them. Yen Fu, for example, one of the first graduates of the naval school at Foochow, found his true vocation in commentary on and translation of Western philosophy. Teachers and graduates of modern schools who had studied abroad increased in number, especially after the abolition of the examination system in 1905 had narrowed the chances of an official career. A number of traditional scholars re-enrolled in teachers' training schools, often abroad.[48] Liberal professions such as law and medicine began to appear in the larger cities. But many from among this new intelligentsia were forced to live on the modest salary of a job which gave them neither glory nor power.

The intelligentsia included social types unknown in traditional China, the most striking of which were professional politicians and revolutionaries. Sun Yat-sen is a famous example. However, his cosmopolitan youth kept him out of Chinese society, which he penetrated only through another generation of scholars, whose intellectual education led it to reject tradition. Behind heroes like T'ang Ts'ai-ch'ang, Tsou Jung and Huang

---

47 For a biography of Wang T'ao see Paul A. Cohen, *Between tradition and modernity: Wang T'ao and reform in late Ch'ing China*. For a biography of Yen Fu see Benjamin Schwartz, *In search of wealth and power: Yen Fu and the West*.

48 Martin C. Yang, *Chinese social structure: a historical study*, 296–315, gives examples of this process.

Hsing, were a multitude of others, many of whom had also studied abroad, who led precarious lives as agitators and clandestine pamphleteers, and who had broken with their families.[49] As opposed to the scholar-literati, the intellectuals were determined to discredit tradition rather than to preserve it.

Without completely abandoning their intellectual pursuits, many scholars of middle and high status began after 1895 to participate in modern economic activities. They built up their investments, but they also launched and managed all kinds of enterprises. This new social layer helped to make business an honourable and highly regarded occupation. Factories were opened by Ch'en Pi, Shen Yun-p'ei, Lu Jun-hsiang and Chang Chien, all of whom had completed metropolitan degrees.[50] Sun Chia-nai and Weng T'ung-ho, who were imperial preceptors, respectively had a son[51] and a grand-nephew[52] in business. Most of the *yang-wu* experts who had earlier administered the *kuan-tu shang-pan* (government supervision and merchant operation) enterprises became involved in big business on their own account, using skill (as did Sheng Hsuan-huai and Yen Hsin-hou), government purchases, official patronage and state funds.[53] Regular officials also willingly followed this route, bringing with them children and relatives. Chou Hsueh-hsi, a member of Yuan Shih-k'ai's entourage, is a good example. This evolution was no longer limited to the treaty ports. It moved inland into the most prosperous provinces, reaching even county seats where some retired official might have opened a brick factory. Of 386 factories employing more than twenty-five workers in the province of Kiangsu in 1912, 263 were outside Shanghai; of 95 companies with limited liability, 51 had their principal offices outside Shanghai.[54]

Merchants, members of the scholar elite, and bureaucrats began to be united in a new activity – the development of capitalist enterprise. Among the merchants, the comprador's uniqueness began to dwindle. In time, foreign personnel became more familiar with Chinese customs and Western

[49] Mary Backus Rankin, *Early Chinese revolutionaries: radical intellectuals in Shanghai and Chekiang, 1902–1911*, describes those of the lower Yangtze; for those of Hunan see Joseph W. Esherick, *Reform and revolution in China: the 1911 Revolution in Hunan and Hubei*, 46–65.

[50] Wang Ching-yü, *Chung-kuo chin-tai kung-yeh shih tzu-liao*, 926, 928, 934–43.

[51] *Ibid.* 927.

[52] Chiang-su sheng hsing-cheng kung-shu shih-yeh ssu, *Chiang-su sheng shih-yeh hsing-cheng pao-kao shu* (Report on Kiangsu province's economic administration), 5.52, 55, 58.

[53] Shao Hsun-cheng, 'Yang-wu yun-tung ho tzu-pen-chu-i fa-chan ti kuan-hsi wen-t'i' (The problem of the relationship between the Western affairs movement and the development of capitalism), in *Pei-ching-shih li-shih hsueh-hui ti-i ti-erh-chieh nien-hui lun-wen-hsuan-chi* (Selected papers from the first and second annual meetings of the Peking Historical Association), 258–280.

[54] Calculations based on the lists of names recorded in *Chiang-su sheng shih-yeh hsing-cheng pao-kao shu*, 3.2–51; 5.39, 69.

firms became more and more eager to deal directly with their partners, obviating the need for compradors. As transactions between China and the West multiplied, the functions and responsibilities of Chinese employees of Western firms diminished. They lost their basis of power and became simple executive agents. The Japanese Mitsui Co. was the first to drop the position of comprador in 1899; this example was followed in 1907 by the Yokohama Specie Bank. More and more compradors were utilizing their profits from foreign firms to create independent Chinese enterprises. Inversely, independent merchants, or 'national capitalists', often borrowed money from foreigners or sold factories to them. The distinction between private initiative or capital and official enterprises became blurred. Many official enterprises functioned with a larger part of capital provided by merchants. Moreover, if an official invested his money in official enterprises, can we then assert that this was different from investing it in private companies, and that he was therefore not a capitalist? (See chapter 8, page 425 *et seq.*) The bureaucracy never distinguished absolutely between state profit and personal profit, their attitude depended more on the outcome of the venture. If it failed, the bureaucrats would let the company shareholders absorb their personal loss rather than repay government loans themselves; if dividends were paid, as was frequently the case between 1900 and 1911, bureaucrats always considered that because they had invested their own money, any profit was theirs. Finally, even in their management, which was personally assumed more and more by bureaucrats instead of being delegated to merchants, official enterprises resembled private enterprises still more; so much so that these latter were able to obtain part of the bureaucratic fortunes and solicit protection from official circles. Companies which made use of official influence were distinguished more by their large size than by their specific nature. Certainly the growth of large-scale capitalism was favoured by a stronger association between bureaucrats and new economic activities.

At the beginning of the 1900s a new social stratum was emerging from the traditional elite. This social stratum was not yet identified by any particular name, but it was the subject of almost every allusion in contemporary texts to the *shen-shang*, a term often translated as 'gentry merchants' (see chapter 8, page 437). *Shen-shang* could mean official and scholar gentry on the one hand, and merchants on the other, as two different and juxtaposed categories distinct at the same time from the people (*min*) and officials in post (*kuan*); but this usage was becoming increasingly rare. Generally, if the term were applied to a group, it represented a global notion including both official and scholar gentry involved in business and merchants possessing literary degrees or official titles, as well as simple scholars and merchants associated with them. If applied to an individual it represented only the first two categories. We might translate it as 'business gentry'. Participation in business was indeed their common characteristic; but we must understand 'businessman' in its widest sense, including trade, banking, industry and all sorts of enterprises, provided they had capitalist characteristics. We must also keep in mind that it was applied to many different situations. There were people like Shen Tseng-chih, who had obtained his *chin-shih* degree and occupied official posts in various departments of the government. He made a good deal of money from sinecure posts, from scholarly work and from large landholdings; he also invested in banks and owned shares in railway construction. On the other hand there were others like Huang Tso-ch'ing, who acquired influence through his various business ventures and applied himself to obtaining official titles.

Business gentry formed the majority and most active and influential segment of the new gentry which manifested its collective existence by helping to organize 'the mutual defence of the south-east' (*tung-nan hu-pao*) during the Boxer War, and by inspiring and sustaining the court's reform movement after 1901. But it would be difficult to consider the two categories to be identical. In the ranks of the *shen-shang*, contemporaries included merchants such as the Shansi bankers, who despite their large-scale trade remained traditional, even in their economic views. On the other hand, we ought to include in this modern elite all partisans of reform, although some of them had no immediate ties with the world of business, whether they were still traditional scholar-officials (*shih-ta-fu*) who exploited the privileges of their status,[55] or intellectuals (*chih-shih fen-tzu*, a newly coined term) living in cities as writers or calligraphers, or even officers in the army.

Did this modern elite constitute a bourgeoisie? They certainly displayed many bourgeois characteristics, but they were still too bound by traditional economic and social forms to be called a bourgeoisie. In fact, the bourgeois elements were so intermingled with the others before 1905–6 that we can scarcely isolate them. Each individual was entangled in a network of familial, personal and professional relationships, where traditional principles contended with modern principles according to circumstance and temperament. Only during the last five years of the monarchy did a truly bourgeois class begin to emerge, that is, a group of modern or semi-modern entrepreneurs, tradesmen, financiers and industrial leaders, unified by material interests, common political aspirations, a sense of their col-

---

[55] The autobiographical novel of Liu O, *Lao-ts'an yu-chi* (The travels of Lao-ts'an), admirably evokes this type of character; English translation by H. Y. Yang and G. M. Taylor, *Mr. Derelict*. Harold Shadick, trans. *The travels of Lao Ts'an by Liu T'ieh-yun (Liu E)*.

lective destiny, a common mentality, and specific daily habits.[56] The personality of the Chinese bourgeoisie crystallized as a result of confrontations with imperial power and the foreign presence. As its economic power grew – the total capital invested in Chinese enterprises tripled between 1905 and 1911 – the bourgeoisie began to protest against ineffectual administration and the lack of protection by the government. It adopted an attitude of political opposition in local incidents, in the constitutional movement, and in the campaigns to reclaim China's sovereign rights. It supported nationalism with singular vehemence, demanding participation in the administration of the concessions, and of the maritime customs, in the elaboration of customs tariffs, and organizing boycotts and merchant militia to struggle against foreign domination.

However, the bourgeoisie as a class existed only at Shanghai and Canton, with a few elements in Tientsin, Hankow and other major treaty ports. It was aware of itself, as is evident in the name of *ch'i-yeh-chia* (entrepreneurs) by which its members referred to themselves with a nuance of pride.[57] But it was rarely perceived as such by contemporaries. It rarely acted alone and most often served as auxiliary to the much greater body of the modern elite from which it had predominantly come.

New social institutions

Certain institutions were linked to the transformations within the privileged classes. Ming and Ch'ing officials had commonly employed colleagues of their own class as private advisers (*mu-yu*, 'tent friends'), especially in law and finance. Now this custom met new needs. Private advisory teams (*mu-fu*), half-civil and half-military, were set up by high-level provincial officials responsible for the novel tasks of repressing the Taipings and dealing with foreigners. It was in such groups that the first *yang-wu* experts such as Hsueh Fu-ch'eng or Ma Chien-chung were brought together, and that part of the rising generation of business adepts such as Sheng Hsuan-huai and politicians such as T'ang Shao-i was first tried out. However, the next step taken by Tseng Kuo-fan, Li Hung-chang[58] or Chang Chih-tung in promoting such men or securing the service of other recognized experts, was to appoint them as *wei-yuan* (official deputies or specially commissioned officials) in charge of a new specialized task. Another device also borrowed

---

[56] This bourgeoisie, in the restricted sense of the term, is described by Marie-Claire Bergère, *La Bourgeoisie chinoise et la révolution de 1911*, 2–54.

[57] Chang Chien, *Chang Chi-tzu chiu lu* (Nine records of Chang Chien), *Chiao-yü lu* (Record on education), 3.20b.

[58] The *mu-fu* of these two personages is the primary subject of Kenneth E. Folsom, *Friends, guests and colleagues: the* mu-fu *system in the late Ch'ing period.*

from Ch'ing administrative tradition was the creation of non-statutory agencies or bureaux (*chü*). Most of the new official undertakings such as the arsenals, likin offices and industrial enterprises, were called *chü* and invariably headed by non-statutory officials identified as *wei-yuan*. T'ang T'ingshu (Tong King-sing) and Yung Wing both served in that capacity. The *mu-fu* as it developed in the latter half of the nineteenth century, and even more the expansion of the *chü* and *wei-yuan* system made room for a degree of expertise in administration and served as the principal channel between the old scholar elite and a new professional elite. But after the 1890s this informal organization, which in the case of the *mu-fu* consisted of provincial liaisons and strong allegiances to the official 'hosts' who unified and maintained each group, was replaced in its role as nursery for social transformation by institutions which were further removed from the Confucian tradition.

An increasing number of the modern elite had been educated at the new schools which offered Western curricula. Missionary schools focusing on religious instruction, whether they taught in Chinese as did the Catholics, or used foreign language and methods as did most Protestants, did not at first attract any notice at all among the elite. The effects of a new kind of education became evident only when schools were developed, first by the government and then by Protestant missionaries, which offered a half-Chinese, half-foreign education up to the secondary and higher levels, and where religious instruction gave way to general knowledge. Even though the Protestant missionary schools had 17,000 students and a few small colleges in 1890 they, like the several official institutions such as the T'ungwen kuan at Peking and the Foochow Arsenal schools, still produced only personnel who had to fight their way into a *mu-fu* in order to attain positions of some influence. Only with the reform movement after 1895 and the institution of a modern national school system in 1902, completed under the regulations issued in 1904, did modern schools become for ambitious young scholars an obligatory place of perfection capable of ushering them into a new world. However, even though school diplomas also conferred traditional academic degrees, it still seemed surer and easier, so strong was the hold of the examination system, to follow the traditional path in order to be assured of status. In bringing this double system to a close, the abolition of the old examinations on 2 September 1905 gave the modern schools a monopoly over the education of the elite.

There were altogether 35,787 modern schools in 1907, and 87,272 in 1912, with a total enrolment which rose from 1,006,743 to 2,933,387.[59] Despite the intentions of their founders, and because their programmes

[59] Marianne Bastid, *Aspects de la réforme de l'enseignement en Chine au début de XXe siècle*, 76.

were fragmented, unconnected with Chinese reality, and offered by teachers who were often ill-prepared, these schools did more to encourage protest and demands than to consolidate the imperial monarchy. Local efforts at ameliorating the quality and extent of education, and even the best results from the teaching of skills conducive to national development, succeeded only in alienating the new elite from the old regime and the rest of the population, without rallying them around any ideal other than a very mixed-up and often ambiguous nationalism. However, owing to the emphasis on group work and discipline, which varied greatly from the traditional academic emphasis on individual attainment, the modern schools succeeded in giving youth an awareness of its strength. Students discovered the power of collective action and used it to stage numerous strikes and protest movements.[60] This dynamism of educated youth was to play a socially determinant role in the Revolution of 1911.

The study societies (*hsueh-hui*) which flourished after 1895, as well as the many more specialized associations which were created during the last ten years of the monarchy in such areas as education, agriculture or the preparation of a constitution, are perhaps the best examples of the changing social mentality of the elite and were undoubtedly its most efficacious means of diffusion. They attracted those people who already exercised responsibility in the society, who were able to assume still more, and who were thus in a position most directly to effect change.

Study societies which blossomed in the wake of K'ang Yu-wei's Ch'iang hsueh-hui after the Sino-Japanese War were founded for political ends rather than academic ones, a fact which distinguished them from traditional scholarly organizations and was a violation of the law and particularly the interdiction which K'ang-hsi's Sacred Edict had imposed on scholars meddling with policy. They wrote by-laws outlining formal regulations whose rigour contrasted with the customary style of traditional groups, whether regional, familial, bureaucratic or even outside the orthodoxy. These juridical and structural characteristics were accentuated in associations of the 1900s, often with the support of the government itself; the regulations which it promulgated in 1906, for example, for educational societies called for a thorough hierarchical network running from the sub-prefectures to the provinces, with punctilious internal organization and procedures for debate. In the study societies of 1895–8, which totalled less than 10,000 members, the predominant ideal was that defined by K'ang Yu-wei: mobilize and educate scholars, affirming at once a national solidarity and a certain popular sovereignty. The national and populist conception of political legitimacy which they conveyed was definitely at odds

[60] *Ibid.* 84–94, 154.

with the proclaimed cosmological foundation of the imperial order which it was to confront, but these societies adhered to the Confucian idea of union with the prince and desired only to become instruments of collaboration with the imperial power.

However, after the failure of the Hundred Days reform, associations of the elite gradually became involved in combative and even radical political opposition. This evolution was consummated in 1904–5 by groups made up predominantly of students. Among other groups it was longer and more complex. Their associations fought a legal battle against bureaucratic tyranny. The official recognition which they sought and obtained did not enfeoff them as the government had hoped, being still confident in the traditional system, but rather helped to set them up as veritable political parties, spokesmen for the interests of whatever social group they represented. Actually, the same individuals were often at the head of educational societies, associations for the promotion of constitutional government or the defence of economic interests: men like Chang Chien, T'ang Shou-ch'ien or Hsu Ting-lin in Kiangsu, Chang Yuan-chi in Chekiang, Yang Tu or Lung Chang in Hunan, and Ch'en Hui-p'u in Kwangtung.[61] The numerical development of these associations gave them a representative nature and political existence independent of official favours. In 1909 the 723 educational societies accounted for 48,432 members. Far from being linked to professional criteria – teaching members were the minority – the membership reflected the total picture of the modern elite, from scholar-officials to industrial leaders. Education, wealth, administrative qualities and the collective responsibilities which they assumed marked them off conspicuously. They were an aristocracy of money and competence, determined to force the bureaucracy to effect reform.

Within these associations opinion was unified and formulated on a provincial scale as well as a local one. Once created, organizations were often carried by their own dynamic force much farther in defiance of imperial authority than their founders had initially intended.[62] The provincial assemblies elected in 1909 were an institutional expression of the autonomous political power demanded by the modern elite. During the last two years of the monarchy, they showed by their actions that they were a united force.[63] As a result of the provisions of the electoral law, 90 per cent of the representatives were degree-holders, but they were relatively

[61] On constitutional associations see Chang Yü-fa, *Ch'ing-chi ti li-hsien t'uan-t'i* (Constitutionalist groups of the late Ch'ing period), 365–78. On the composition of different associations and their overlaps, see Bastid, *Aspects de la réforme de l'enseignement*, 70–2, 163–5.

[62] On this phenomenon in connection with educational societies, *ibid.* 73–5, 172–3.

[63] The political aspects of their actions are described by P'eng-yuan Chang, 'The constitutionalists', in Mary C. Wright, ed. *China in revolution: the first phase, 1900–1913* (hereafter *CIR*), 144–73.

young, residing for the most part in large urban centres and often associated with modern enterprises.[64] Despite the low proportion of businessmen among their members, provincial assemblies actively represented the
interests of the modern elite, notably by their energetic defence of the
economic interests of private enterprise.[65]

Along with the general effect of new schools, public associations and
provincial assemblies, various more specific institutions helped to differentiate the new elite from the traditional elite. There were, for example, the
chambers of commerce (*shang-hui*). The first one was established at Shanghai
in 1902 under the name Commercial Office. An edict issued in January
1904 approved and regulated their creation throughout the country; in
1909 there were 44 general chambers of commerce (*shang-wu tsung-hui*) and
135 branch offices (*shang-wu fen-hui*). As organs of liaison between local
businessmen, chambers of commerce did not supplant the traditional commercial associations; on the contrary, guilds often affiliated with them.
Chambers of commerce therefore enhanced the growing amalgamation
and coordination of different business circles. Their role was originally
conceived as that of an administrative cog which was the official representative of the local business community in dealings with the imperial
government and foreigners. This resulted in their preference for directors
holding academic titles or official status and meant that they often met the
needs of entrepreneurs before those of ordinary shopkeepers.[66] But they
were quickly emancipated from the shadow of imperial functionaries and
became spokesmen for the entire business milieu, whose nature was
changing as it absorbed the traditional scholar elite and modern companies
developed.

On a still more modest scale, institutions like modern banks (*yin hang*),
as opposed to the traditional *ch'ien-chuang* and *yin-hao* (money shops), slowly
began to transform social habits, as did similar corporations with limited
liability, which were regulated by an edict in 1904. The structure of these
concerns perhaps increased the distance between executives and subordinates, and undoubtedly relations with clients deteriorated, but they did
encourage audacious initiatives because they guaranteed financial backing
without the fear of having to rely upon personal or family funds to cover
potential losses.

[64] Chang P'eng-yuan, *Li-hsien-p'ai yü hsin-hai ko-ming* (The constitutionalists and the 1911
Revolution), 28–40, 248–312.
[65] This phenomenon is described well for Hunan and Hupei by Esherick, *Reform and revolution in
China*, 99–105. For Kwangtung see Edward J. M. Rhoads, *China's republican revolution: the case
of Kwangtung, 1895–1913*, 155–71.
[66] These chamber of commerce details were quite striking in Canton where another active
organization had also been formed in 1899 by merchants in order to protect their common
interests, the Seventy-two Guilds. See Rhoads, *China's republican revolution*, 35–6, 80–1, 148–9.

The common trait among these various institutions which fashioned and symbolized the transformation of the elite, was that they were outside the traditional bureaucratic set-up and also that they divorced themselves from it. This could have been a consequence of the specialization of the personnel of *mu-fu* and *chü*, of the Western education received by the students of the new schools, or of the combativeness of the associations and chambers of commerce. These institutions enabled and incited their members to affirm their differences with the traditional order.

The beginning of the break-up

Diversification of the ruling class was accompanied by a marked decline in its coherence and cohesion. In addition to personal quarrels, confrontations were heated between the traditional and new elites. This was evident in the intellectual and political controversy which pitted partisans and adversaries of *yang-wu* against each other over the addition of a department of mathematics and sciences to the T'ung-wen kuan in 1867. The conflict grew more bitter during the 1870s. Each initiative and every project for modernization proposed by Li Hung-chang and his protégés brought numerous attacks. The so-called *ch'ing-liu tang* ('party of the purists') led the offensive. But official opposition was sustained and encouraged by local opposition to the introduction of machinery and modern economy. Magistrates frequently joined the elite to lead popular demonstrations such as the one opposing the opening of mines in Kaiping in 1878. The Sino-French War helped to bring the *ch'ing-liu* polemic to a close; many of its members then embraced reform. From then on the high-level administration was divided less over the principle of economic modernization than over its terms and conditions. One of the subjects required by the *chin-shih* examinations of 1888 was international commerce. In the debate over railway development opened by the Empress Dowager Tz'u-hsi in 1889, imperial counsellors, secretaries, ministerial presidents, governors-general, governors and censors admitted almost unanimously the necessity for railway construction.[67] But practical considerations blocked most economic initiatives until the Sino-Japanese War. Because they absolutely refused to let China sink further under foreign domination, the majority of scholarly and bureaucratic opinion within influential circles insisted on using only national resources, but they would eventually point out that these resources were too weak to sustain a major effort and that they were in danger of being depleted by a policy of unconsidered provincial railway investment. In effect, the potential social

[67] Relevant texts are assembled in Chung-kuo k'o-hsueh yuan *et al.* eds. *Yang-wu yun-tung,* 6.198–270.

repercussions of poorly conceived and badly controlled modernization looked disquieting to many officials. Particularly feared were the unemployment and impoverishment of the masses, and the immorality of enormous individual profits being acquired by a minority. Recommendations to the throne emphasized the same theme over and over again: 'go slowly', 'proceed by stages', 'examine things carefully before acting'. This extreme caution, inspired basically by the desire to master the human consequences of progress, succeeded in paralysing the entire effort. Rare were those predisposed to granting absolute priority to new forms of economic development, and approving, as did Liu Ming-ch'uan, domination by the merchant class.[68] We must also keep in mind that with the exception of the provincial capitals, a few bustling prefectures, and the treaty ports, the majority of literati were indifferent to these problems.

The defeat by Japan starkly accentuated these cleavages. In order to save the country, one faction of the scholar elite and the bureaucracy embraced the cause of reform. Dropping its Confucian scruples, this faction fought for the creation of modern enterprises and declared economic expansion an immediate national imperative. Antagonism was exacerbated between those members of the elite urging reform and the others, whom contemporary novelists cruelly denounced for their egoism, their meanness and their ignorance.[69] The traditional elite fought back not only with petitions, pamphlets and bureaucratic trouble-making, but also with violence, riots and destruction of factories and new schools.[70] They encouraged and supported the suppression of the Hundred Days reform.[71] In the northern provinces certain of them found common cause with the Boxers, whom they saw as adversaries of modernism.[72] However, the virulent hostility between the modern and traditional elites began to dwindle or rather to find other manifestations. Many of the scholars and officials who had abetted and enthusiastically imitated the initiatives of K'ang Yu-wei recoiled, in the spring of 1898, even before the Hundred Days, in the face of the inevitable consequences of his actions: the sup-

---

[68] *Ibid.* 6.249.
[69] One of the more famous portraits is a novel by Li Pao-chia, *Kuan-ch'ang hsien-hsing chi* (An exposé of officialdom), published serially in a Shanghai review between 1901 and 1905.
[70] Cf., e.g., the difficulties experienced by Chang Chien in 1896–8 when his proposal to open a textile factory was resolutely opposed by 300 of Nan-t'ung's elite. See Bastid, *Aspects de la réforme de l'enseignement*, 33. On reactions in Kwangtung see Rhoads, *China's republican revolution*, 35–6.
[71] Sergei Leonidovich Tikhvinskii, *Dvizhenie za reformy v Kitae v konts* xix *veka i Kan Iu-vei* (The reform movement in China at the end of the nineteenth century and K'ang Yu-wei), 257–80.
[72] An inquiry made in 1958 into survivors in the Tientsin region is very informative: Chung-kuo k'o-hsueh-yuan Shan-tung fen-yuan li-shih yen-chiu-so, ed. *I-ho-t'uan yun-tung liu-shih chou-nien chi-nien lun-wen chi*, 259, 263–4.

pression of scholarly hegemony and social hierarchies (see chapter 5).[73] In order to reiterate their attachment to the Confucian orthodoxy which legitimized them, they quite naturally sought support among their brothers who had remained loyal to tradition, while offering them, thanks to the formula *Chung-hsueh wei t'i Hsi-hsueh wei yung* (Chinese learning for the essential, Western learning for the application), the prospect of a certain adaptation and the means to palliate their loss of moral authority by the growth of their material and political power. In view of its immediate acceptance, the abolition of the examination system must not have seemed a threat to the privileges of the elite, but only a new set of criteria by which it was to be determined. The status of the elite depended thereafter on admission to modern schools, which explains the enthusiasm accompanying their creation among even the most traditional elements of the elite.

In the very last years of the monarchy, division among the new privileged classes grew from within and was actually more ideological than social. The distinction between moderates and revolutionaries does not really reflect distinctions between richer and poorer bourgeoisies, nor between national bourgeoisie and comprador bourgeoisie. Again, it does not fit very well with a distinction between a business-oriented bourgeoisie and an elite class still rooted in traditional structures. Nor does it allow consideration for the break between generations. The divergent choices made by the reformer Liang Ch'i-ch'ao, who was born in 1873, and the revolutionary Chang Ping-lin, born in 1868, both scholars with a classical education, can be explained only by differences in their personalities and individual experiences. The same must be true for Huang Hsing, the revolutionary from a gentry family of Hunan, and Li Hou-yu, a reformist businessman from Shanghai.

We should not overestimate the virulence of opposition within the privileged classes, since diversity of opinion often occurred within the same family, some of whose members might embrace new ways while others continued in traditional paths. Family solidarity remained generally strong. Hsu Hsi-lin, one of the leaders of the Restoration Society (Kuang-fu hui) in Chekiang, was protected for years by his cousin, who had been provincial governor.[74] Certain branches of the Li family of Chen-hai devoted themselves to bureaucratic careers, others exploited ancestral lands, others went to Shanghai to operate *ch'ien-chuang* and real estate companies, in which the rest of the family would invest capital.[75] Rather than a coalescence of families according to clearly polarized predominant interests, as was the

[73] Cf. Esherick, *Reform and revolution in China*, 17–18.
[74] Mary Backus Rankin, 'The revolutionary movement in Chekiang: a study in the tenacity of tradition', in *CIR*, 347–8.
[75] Chung-kuo jen-min yin-hang Shang-hai-shih fen-hang, *Shang-hai ch'ien-chuang shih-liao*, 734–7.

case with the 'conquering bourgeoisie' of western Europe, there was more often a wide variety of occupations within the same family coupled with a certain ideological openness and a basic sympathy to new concepts, even though their disparity was still rather poorly discerned.

It is evident that the gradual transformation giving rise to the modern elite did not uniformly affect traditional scholar families. Many of them fell into jeopardy during the last forty years of the monarchy and landed in obscurity and common poverty. Can we see in this a normal manifestation of the traditional mobility which has often been described,[76] and which assured within the framework of a rigid social hierarchy the continual renewal of the elite? Or had this phenomenon increased? Our present understanding makes it impossible to say. The fall of certain scholar families was certainly noted by contemporaries, but it is possible that this pattern is apparent in absolute figures due to the global post-Taiping increase in degree-holders, without being true in relative terms. We cannot determine whether the numerical growth of the privileged classes continued after 1900 nor whether the fall of one family was compensated as it had been before by the rise of another. However, statistical inquiry into the modern schools, through which most of the elite passed subsequently, seems to indicate that this was not so. In effect, because of the higher cost of the new education, the number of secondary-school students showed a net drop in comparison with the number from the old academies (shu-yüan), where scholars at a certain level had formerly received their further education.[77]

Rather than causing opposition at the national level between the different social strata composing the elite, the variability and the inegality of the process of change revived racial and regional differences and even antagonisms. The Manchus and the other national minorities were barely affected by the changes upsetting the Han elite. Some, especially Manchus and Mongols, were opposed to an evolution which could only erode their dominant position within traditional society. Others were too far removed from the centres of the new economic and intellectual life to feel its effects very strongly. In this way threads of interest, if not of culture, which linked the allogenic aristocracies to the Han gentry were loosening. Similar contrasts are evident between the maritime provinces where currents of modern change were widespread and inland provinces where change was less obvious. But even within the most advanced regions, the

[76] Particularly in Ho, *Ladder of success.*
[77] At the end of the nineteenth century there were more than 2,000 academies, with nearly 150,000 students. In 1909 there were 702 secondary schools attended by 72,000 students; by this date academies had completely disappeared. On the relative decrease of the educated elite see Bastid, *Aspects de la réforme de l'enseignement,* 83–5, 222–4, and Rhoads, *China's republican revolution,* 76.

new elites were perceptibly different; that of Chihli remained closely associated with the official apparatus whose initiatives had fostered its existence, around Li Hung-chang and then Yuan Shih-k'ai. In the provinces of the lower Yangtze the new ruling class, even though most of its members had previously been *shen-shih*, was breaking away more sharply from the traditional regime in its political and intellectual as well as economic outlook. In Kwangtung merchants prevailed over scholars in a modern elite which was more restricted but at the same time more inclined to radicalism, and in which Overseas Chinese played an important role. The bureaucratic groups rooted in common provincial origins, such as the natives of Anhwei patronized by Li Hung-chang, scholars from Kiangsu protected by Weng T'ung-ho, and associations (guilds) founded on similar geographic provenance (*pang* and *hui-kuan*), were gradually eclipsed by a new kind of provincialism concerned more specifically with the defence of interests of a certain territory and its inhabitants, rather than those of a cultural community. The more impersonal values of this new provincialism – allegiance to a vast territorial unity and its entire population, probably prepared the way for the rise of nationalism.[78] But in its earliest manifestations, notably the 'mutual defence of the south-east' which in 1900 separated the southern provinces from the north and its domination by the Boxers, this new provincialism generated antagonism. The local autonomy exercised by the modern elite in the years which followed led as well to bitter rivalries between counties and between provinces who were interested only in selfishly monopolizing public resources in order to better their own condition at the expense of others. Local autonomy sometimes even gave in to the allure of withdrawal, as if the security, modernism and harmony of a model city could disregard the prevailing national disorder and poverty.

However, the rupture presenting the most profound consequences was that which separated an urban elite, tainted by the West and seeking change, from a rural elite which had been its intellectual, political and social seed bed. The urbanization of elites is an age-old phenomenon. Even as early as the Sung, cities attracted scholars and rural landowners by their refined culture and their commerce. Visits to the city were frequent and the truly wealthy bought second homes or even moved there. This movement accelerated during the nineteenth century. Commercial growth increased the size and attractiveness of cities.[79] But the rural elite was then forced into the cities in search of alternative income sources such as usury, in order to make up their diminishing rental returns caused by partitions of

[78] Cf. John Fincher, 'Political provincialism and the national revolution', in *CIR*, 185–226.
[79] On the demography of several treaty ports see Wang Ching-yü, *Chung-kuo chin-tai kung-yeh shih tzu-liao*, 1173–4.

property, monetary instability, and the growing resistance of tenants. After the middle of the century the recurrent insecurity which reigned in the countryside motivated even the most well-to-do to install themselves in the cities. In this way, most of the elite who fled to Shanghai during the Taiping revolt had made it their principal place of residence.[80]

At the beginning of the twentieth century the urbanization of the elite took on particular significance. Their move to the city meant that they took up not only urban residence, but also urban preoccupations, which alienated them even more from rural problems.[81] After the abolition of the civil-service examinations, the acquisition of elite status demanded attendance at new schools. These were first opened in cities and their cost induced elite families to cease funding village schools.[82] In town, where the confrontation with the imperialist threat was more direct, the elite was far more interested in the modernization of the army and the development of industry and commerce than in the organization of militia and promotion of agricultural prosperity. Those who still owned land maintained relations with farmer-tenants through the offices of bursary, overseers and collectors. Within the ranks of the bureaucracy the practice of observing the full long periods of mourning for the death of parents gradually fell into disuse owing to earlier recall by the court, and this precluded those long sojourns on the family properties which had often helped to reinforce the officials' connections with their rural heritage. In this way the urban elite was slowly alienated from the countryside. Thus by its entire orientation, the elite world of the city stood in opposition to that of the countryside.

Despite this general trend, however, in 1910, at Changsha, Wang Hsien-ch'ien and Yeh Te-hui, two gentry members living in the city with large interests in modern business, were still in a position to manipulate a rice riot, which nevertheless had probably been caused by their own speculation (they were also traditional rice merchants), and managed to turn its fury against the symbols of urban reform – official schools, banks and police stations.[83] But the evolution continued, affirmed by transformations in attitudes and life-style. The rise of the women's liberation issue was one of the more striking manifestations of the new concerns among well-to-do urban circles. The first group to oppose the binding of feet was founded at Canton in 1894. This was followed by similar organizations in all the provincial capitals, to which women were admitted in their own names

---

[80] Muramatsu Yūji, *Kindai Kōnan no sosan: Chūgoku jinushi seido no kenkyū* (Landlord bursaries in modern times: studies of landlordism in China).

[81] Esherick, *Reform and revolution in China*, 66–9.

[82] The cost was double at the elementary level, and four or five times greater for higher levels. Bastid, *Aspects de la réforme de l'enseignement*, 84, 124, 150, 218, 222, 224.

[83] Esherick, *Reform and revolution in China*, 125–37.

alongside their husbands. After several petitions, an edict was issued in 1902 outlawing foot-binding. The practice declined quickly in cities, where diligent magistrates administered fines, but not in the countryside. Education of women was begun by missionaries shortly after the Opium War but for a long time remained elementary and principally religious and was disdained by wealthy families. The first non-missionary Chinese school for girls was opened at Soochow in February 1897 by Chiang Lan-ling, the mother of Hsu Mo, a future judge on the International Court of Justice at The Hague. Others were soon opened at Shanghai, Peking and Canton. Official statutes for the education of women were published in 1907. The following year the province of Kiangsu had 105 girls' schools with 4,455 students. Provincial assemblies promoted the cause of women's education. At the beginning of the republic the official statistics of the Ministry of Education listed 141,430 girls in school. Women were also sent to study abroad, originally at their own expense. In 1906, 13 went to the United States. The following year, competition for government scholarships was opened to them: of the 600 candidates for the United States, 31 were accepted, 3 of whom were women. In 1910, there were 150 women students in Japan.[84] If the younger generation was particularly active in the revolutionary movement, they were also desirous of awakening women's consciousness and arousing public opinion through literature and the press.[85] Their appeals did not fall on deaf ears. Freedom of marriage and the right of women to work began to be accepted within the wealthy families of large cities. In private schools elementary education became co-educational and at the secondary level women's programmes were similar to men's. Some men joined them in their demand for participation in political power.

As its most dynamic elements moved into the cities to perfect their educations or amass their fortunes, the traditional rural elite of the *shen-shih* found itself without leadership. Its intellectual prestige was endangered by the pre-eminence of Western learning, to which it adapted only with difficulty and which it could not really master. Its political influence was limited to the rural township (*chen*), rural district (*hsiang*) and the county. Owing to the legal basis which the institution of local councils gave to this influence, the rural elite were without doubt sufficiently strong to abuse it without fear of government reprisal; but now they possessed fewer connections in the upper echelons of power and less sway through whatever

[84] H. E. King, *The educational system of China as recently reconstructed*, 92–6.
[85] On this feminist propaganda, Chinese women showed themselves to be often ahead of the rest of the world, having, for example, founded the only daily newspaper in the world published and edited exclusively by women. Cf. Catherine Gipoulon, *Qiu Jin, femme et révolutionnaire en Chine au* xixème *siècle*, 233–44.

connections they had. They could barely bring efficient protection to their local community. Thus their former moral and social authority over the populace and their role as model and guide were depreciated by the imperial state whose power they had supported.

The present condition of research does not permit a precise numerical evaluation of the relative strength of the old and new groups within the ruling class. But there is evidence to suggest an order of magnitude and underline the importance of the transformation. For example, we can compare the total of 1,443,000 holders of official degrees or ranks at the end of the nineteenth century with the number of 300,000 who signed a petition circulated in June 1910 and drawn up by provincial assemblies demanding the immediate convocation of a parliament.

As it gradually broke up, the traditional scholar class ceased to identify itself with the imperial state. Even though its members still constituted a majority of the privileged classes, other elements had risen above the commoners and installed themselves in the upper class by means of business, the military and technology. But more important, the *shen-shih* no longer dominated society as the traditional specific social corps it had been. It was no longer united by attachment to the same political order, nor by the same Confucian ideology, nor by the defence of common legal privileges. An objective coalition did exist among the emerging bourgeoisie, the modern elite and the rural elite, in spite of their divergent interests. This was a coalition to defend vested positions. But there was nothing like that sentiment of solidarity and agreement on fundamental principles which had for centuries, despite unequal economic circumstances amidst its members, assured the cohesion of the scholar class and the stability of the imperial regime.

THE COMMON PEOPLE

A new group: industrial workers

Changes within the lower classes seem at first much less striking. Industrial workers were the only group to emerge as a new social category. They first appeared in Kwangtung and Chekiang where they worked in foreign-owned shipbuilding and repair yards, particularly at Hong Kong immediately after the Opium War. This first generation, which was made up primarily of urban specialized handicraft workers, helped with the technical education of a large proportion of the workers needed by the official enterprises and foreign industries which developed after 1860. When Tso Tsung-t'ang constructed the Lanchow Arsenal in 1872, he called for workers from Canton because of their well-known skill. It was also Cantonese workers who organized the first strike in Shanghai in 1868 at shipyards owned by S. C. Farnham and Company, a recently founded American firm.[86]

The growth of the industrial proletariat, which rose from about 100,000 in 1894[87] to 661,000 in 1912,[88] reflects above all the influx of unskilled labour into the workforce. Most of this labour was of rural origins, often recently arrived to swell the mass of urban poor, and included a large number of women and children. At first the workforce was hard to recruit and very unstable, especially in the mines. The Kaiping coal mines, which employed 1,000 workers during the 1880s, had gone to some expense to bring well-qualified and better-paid workers from Swatow and Canton, and also took on local peasants who were willing to work at the mines during winter but who left during the agriculturally important summer. These local workers went on strike in 1882 to demand pay equal to their southern co-workers.[89]

These problems of personnel management may partially explain the predominance of hiring practices handed down from the traditional organization of work and the neglect of free hiring, which was itself often handled through the offices of various intermediaries such as overseers or compradors. There were two basic systems: contracted apprenticeships and recruitment through 'work contractors' (*pao-kung-t'ou*). The first, which was descended directly from traditional guilds to the textile mills and machine-shops of Chihli and the middle Yangtze, had in fact been stripped of its traditional function. Apprenticeship had become nothing more than an excuse to justify the use of an under-age and under-paid workforce which was kept in quasi-servitude, with absolutely no guarantee of promotion to qualified employment. Recruitment by *pao-kung* (contract labour), which was more common especially at Shanghai and in the mines, was always characterized by the presence of an intermediary who had been given full responsibility by a company for the hiring of personnel. Workers were forced into financial and social dependence upon this intermediary throughout their employment with the company. This system, whose origins are similar to the practices of Western firms which gave the com-

---

[86] Wang Ching-yü and Nieh Pao-chang, 'Kuan-yü Chung-kuo ti-i-tai ch'an-yeh kung-jen ti tou-cheng tzu-liao' (Materials on the struggles of the first generation of Chinese industrial workers), *Ching-chi yen-chiu*, 1962.3, pp. 43–51.

[87] According to incomplete estimates of Sun Yü-t'ang, *Chung-kuo chin-tai kung-yeh shih tzu-liao*, 1201, a third of all workers were employed in foreign factories. The proportion was similar for the 60,000 labourers working in factories and mines employing more than 500 workers.

[88] Ch'en Chen and Yao Lo, *Chung-kuo chin-tai kung-yeh shih tzu-liao* (Source materials on the history of modern industry in China), 1.21. Wang Ching-yü, *Chung-kuo chin-tai kung-yeh shih tzu-liao*, 1183, estimates 240,000 labourers in factories and mines employing more than 500 workers between 1900 and 1910, of which 109,000 were in foreign enterprises.

[89] Sun Yü-t'ang, *Chung-kuo chin-tai kung-yeh shih tzu-liao*, 1245, 1248–9.

prador total responsibility for Chinese personnel and which go back especially to the customary hiring of unskilled agricultural and mine workers, kept workers in a nearly servile condition.[90] It also gave rise to cruel abuses: in Hunan in 1881, recruiting agents went into gambling places and got peasants drunk to encourage them to gamble; once they were no longer able to pay their debts, they were 'sold' to the mine, where they were forced to stay underground working until they died of exhaustion after several weeks or months.[91]

In certain cases the material conditions of workers were relatively favourable as industrialization got under way. Workers at the Kiangnan Arsenal in 1867 earned four to eight times as much as agricultural workers and coolies in the same region, from Mex. $0.10 to Mex. $0.20 for only eight hours work, for which they were paid directly. At that time the working day was eleven hours at the Nanking Arsenal, and eleven and a half at the Tientsin Arsenal, but there was one day off every two weeks, which was unheard of in traditional occupations. However, as hiring became easier the working day became longer, although the two-weekly day off also became widespread; around 1905 factories would frequently operate continuously, with two shifts each working twelve hours, between 300 and 320 days a year.[92] In addition, the depreciation of copper money and soaring prices of foodstuffs combined to substantially diminish the workers' buying-power: prices had on the average doubled while wages had risen only by 75 per cent. Workers were often limited to only one meal a day.[93] Even though by the 1880s some large concerns had opened small hospitals and begun paying meagre compensation for work-related accidents, which was a major advance at that time, and even though some owners had agreed to provide safer and more hygienic working conditions, workers in most factories and mines still laboured without any protection under incredibly unhealthy conditions.[94] The frequency and seriousness of accidents, the extent of work-related illness, and the poor sanitary conditions all recall the beginning of the industrial era in Europe. Draconian personnel policies, calling for fines and corporal punishment for the slightest mistakes, often allowed overseers to tyrannize workers.[95]

90 *Ibid.* 1232–3, 1244–6; Wang Ching-yü, *Chung-kuo chin-tai kung-yeh shih tzu-liao*, 1234–40. Jean Chesneaux, *Le mouvement ouvrier chinois de 1919 à 1927*, 94–108.
91 E-tu Zen Sun, 'Mining labor in the Ch'ing period', in Albert Feuerwerker, Rhoads Murphey and Mary C. Wright, eds. *Approaches to modern Chinese history*, 61–5.
92 Sun Yü-t'ang, *Chung-kuo chin-tai kung-yeh shih tzu-liao*, 1222; Wang Ching-yü, *Chung-kuo chin-tai kung-yeh shih tzu-liao*, 1198–261.
93 Wang Ching-yü, *Chung-kuo chin-tai kung-yeh shih tzu-liao*, 1245–54.
94 Sun Yü-t'ang, *Chung-kuo chin-tai kung-yeh shih tzu-liao*, 1237–41; Wang Ching-yü, *Chung-kuo chin-tai kung-yeh shih tzu-liao*, 1204–16.
95 Wang Ching-yü, *Chung-kuo chin-tai kung-yeh shih tzu-liao*, 1216–22.

The unskilled nature of industrial work and the high rate of turnover combined to impede united action. However, major companies did assemble large groups of workers in principal treaty ports: Shanghai, Canton and Wuchang together accounted for more than a third of the total. It was in these concentrations that the combativeness of labour was most vigorous. Between 1900 and 1910, Shanghai counted 76,000 workers in forty-six factories with more than 500 workers; Shanghai also sustained thirty-six of the forty-seven labour strikes recorded in this period.[96] The frequency of these strikes was thought by foreign capitalists to bode ill; most of them were movements of basic economic protest, primarily against low wages but also against generally abominable working conditions. They were spontaneous and often very violent, including the destruction of machinery. Foreign companies were more likely to be the targets of violence. This indicated not only deep hostility towards modern industrial practices similar to that in Europe at the beginning of the nineteenth century – a sentiment inherited from peasants and artisans by a recently formed proletariat – but also nationalist radicalism, which continued late-nineteenth-century anti-foreign popular movements and gave the labour movement a certain political significance.

It is evident from their chronological development that China's initial industrial strikes occurred in three distinct waves: 1898–9 (ten strikes), 1904–6 (fifteen strikes) and that which, beginning in 1909, immediately preceded and accompanied the fall of the imperial regime (twenty-four strikes). It is obviously tempting to assert a concordance between these labour movements and the major stages of political events: first, the break-in of the powers, the Hundred Days reform, and the outbreak of the Boxer Rebellion; next, recrudescence of the nationalist movement, with the anti-American boycott, the founding of the T'ung-meng hui, the anti-Manchu uprising in Hunan, and the rise of constitutionalism; finally, the republican revolution. However, only during the period 1904–6 does there appear to have been any direct relationship between workers' actions and political events. Dockers in Canton and labourers in Shanghai, Nanking and Wuhan did participate in the anti-American boycott; the Hua-hsin cotton mill went on strike to protest against a take-over by Japanese capitalists; 3,000 miners from P'ing-hsiang, Liu-yang and Li-ling participated in the anti-Manchu uprising in Hunan.[97] But even in these instances, the proletariat did nothing more than lend its support to political move-

[96] Calculations based on the data in Wang Ching-yü, *Chung-kuo chin-tai kung-yeh shih tzu-liao*, 1184–5, 1190, 1299–301.
[97] Chao Ch'in, 'Hsin-hai ko-ming ch'ien-hou ti Chung-kuo kung-jen yun-tung' (The Chinese workers' movement around the time of the 1911 Revolution), *Li-shih yen-chiu*, 1959.2, pp. 1–16.

ments which had been organized by other social groups. The coincidence of the other major waves of strikes with political effervescence seems to have been a result of precise economic conjuncture rather than of any intrinsic liaison: inflation and harvest crises during the last years of the monarchy gave rise to increased labour demands as well as other discontents.

Despite the vigorous solidarity manifested in most of the strikes, the Chinese proletariat of the early twentieth century was still profoundly marked by the same regional and professional rivalries which had afflicted traditional guilds. For example, strikes in a single company by workers who had come from the same province and who were specialists at the same tasks, were often ignored by the rest of that company's workforce.

In fact, skilled labour in large cities, particularly mechanics, carpenters and weavers employed by newer mechanized factories, continued to belong to handicraft corporations where they had received their technical education and been employed before entering big industry. In Shanghai naval carpenters and railway mechanics joined the same guilds as artisans. At the dawn of industrialization guilds were able to exercise enough influence to safeguard their interests, particularly regarding industrial use of skilled labour. Factories had to use them as agents for obtaining qualified workers, who were compelled to keep on paying dues to the guild. On the eve of the revolution, membership of a guild had become mostly customary, often in order to profit from its charitable works.

Unskilled labour was more likely to form *entr'aides* (*pang* or *pang-hui*) which were rather loose groups of jobless workers from the same area who banded together around a chief. The latter often served as intermediary for contract labour (*pao-kung*). In certain trades and certain regions the influence of secret societies was predominant: the Triad Society and its branches traditionally recruited large groups of miners and transportation workers. Secret societies dominated all trades in Canton and Hong Kong, where they organized what was nearly a general strike in 1884 in response to Admiral Courbet's attack on Foochow and Taiwan.[98]

Through the channel of secret societies quite a few workers also joined revolutionary organizations: in 1911 the T'ung-meng hui drew members from the crews constructing the railway between Szechwan and Hupei and from railway workers on the Shanghai–Nanking and Shanghai–Hangchow lines. However, even among these groups, worker participation was rather more individual than a collective action of the proletariat as such. None of these bodies specifically represented labour interests. Though organizations

---

[98] Sun Yü-t'ang, *Chung-kuo chin-tai kung-yeh shih tzu-liao*, 1244–8; Wang Ching-yü, *Chung-kuo chin-tai kung-yeh shih tzu-liao*, 1265–9. Wang Ching-yü and Nieh Pao-chang, 'Kuan-yü Chung-kuo ti-i-tai ch'an-yeh kung-jen ti tou-cheng tzu-liao', 43–51.

which were more strictly professional were being founded, such as the Association for Mechanical Study created in Canton in 1909 and the future seed of the Kwangtung Mechanics Union, their members included small employers as well as workers; their primary emphasis was the improvement of technical education through workshops and courses. The T'ang-shan club, opened in 1902 to Kaiping coal miners, railway workers and masons, offered facilities for reading, listening to music, and attending lectures. Skilled workers were more likely to create separate organizations based on class, for example the founding of a club for postal employees in Canton in 1906. But all of these groups were rather friendly gatherings and devoted primarily to spare-time activities, mutual aid, and training. There is no direct relationship between organized labour movements and these first labour associations.[99]

The industrial proletariat was too small and far too bereft of class consciousness to constitute an autonomous force within the mass of the people. Without doubt, strikes gave it the appearance of a distinct group and paved the way for its evolution. But owing to its youth, its mobility and the unskilled nature of the work mainly required of it, the proletariat succeeded only in suggesting the qualitative mutation which was to radically differentiate it from the social groups which nurtured it: impoverished peasants, skilled artisans, and urban masses. The role which it would collectively assume in popular movements had not yet crystallized.

Even when we increase the ranks of workers in new companies by considering employees of the modern tertiary or service industries, office workers, employees of various commercial and urban services such as customs, utilities and telecommunications, the number of people working directly with the most advanced economic and technical aspects of industrial production remains minimal in comparison with the total working population. Although the sources are inadequate for us to deduce an exact figure, it cannot have amounted to more than about 1 per cent, including families. This proportion of new to old is extremely low compared to that existing in the privileged class between the modern and traditional elites. It was not accompanied by the same degree of difference in material conditions or outlook. Industrial capitalism thus had far greater effect on the social organization of the ruling class than among the people.

Rural parvenus and peasant impoverishment

Movement is, however, discernible beneath the apparent invariability of

[99] Chesneaux, *Le mouvement ouvrier chinois de 1919 à 1927*, 181–5.

the rural situation. It is most difficult to identify both because documentary sources which would verify it are nearly always inaccessible and because it led to no radical modification of either relations or modes of production. It consisted primarily of slow shifts within an agrarian set-up that remained on the whole identical throughout the period.

A certain increase in the number of wealthy farmers is evident in several regions, specifically the provinces of the lower and middle Yangtze, Shantung, Fengtien, Kwangtung and Szechwan.[100] It seems to have been linked to commercial development and mobility of land ownership. However, commercial development covered several different factors, one of which was the extension of interior commercial expansion which had been enhanced during the eighteenth century by refinement of traditional methods of road and water transport and had become a source of urban wealth. In spite of the ravages of the large rebellions of the mid-nineteenth century, the effects of this expansion were still being felt in the Canton delta, southern Kiangsu and in the middle Yangtze valley, which was the centre of a very large grain trade. A vast system of regional markets had sprung up in western and central Shantung dependent on the Grand Canal, which had been opened to private transport by the government. This widening of markets was accompanied by urban growth and a more rigorous division of labour within the handicraft industry; it also stimulated the growth of specialized commercial agriculture in order to satisfy the growing needs of urban populations.[101] This type of agriculture in turn attracted wealth from the towns: city merchants bought farmland which they could manage directly through the intermediary of paid hands and at the same time established stores, handicraft workshops and pawnshops, in market towns. Thus farming, trade and the handicraft industry often went hand in hand and benefited from each other. Farmers who managed to increase their landholdings willingly converted to this type of commercial farming, the profits of which they would then invest in lucrative trades in market towns. Being seriously jeopardized around the middle of the nineteenth century by insecurity and natural disasters, this market economy of central and western Shantung was superseded after 1890 by commercial growth linked to treaty ports and railway transport. Mercantile activity shifted thereafter to the east along the coast, and no longer depended on the Grand Canal. These regions were in turn the site of a process of commercialization and specialization in agriculture, which this time undoubtedly increased the

---

[100] Li Wen-chih, comp. *Chung-kuo chin-tai nung-yeh shih tzu-liao ti-i chi, 1840–1911* (Source materials on the history of agriculture in modern China, 1st collection, 1840–1911), 638–40, 672–85.

[101] Ching Su and Lo Lun, *Ch'ing-tai Shan-tung ching-ying ti-chu ti she-hui hsing-chih*, 3–37.

drain of agricultural profit into urban investment and attracted little urban capital back into the countryside.[102]

In the Yangtze valley and the Canton delta, this second phase of commercial development associated with Western penetration and the growth of treaty ports started earlier and increased the effects of the first. In the north-east, on the other hand, the later process of commercial development acted alone.[103]

This increase in the mobility of landownership may have facilitated an increase in the number of wealthy farmers. Actually, the custom of dividing landholdings equally among all inheritors led to a periodic partitioning of property into less than viable units. A series of poor harvests, an increase in taxes, or unforeseen market fluctuations – all of which were regular occurrences during the last forty years of the monarchy[104] – were enough to force small landowners to sell their plots, often at low prices, in order to pay their debts and survive. Statistics are available for a few regions, and they indicate an obvious decrease in the price of land during the early twentieth century at the same time as agricultural prices were rising.[105] Profiting from the floods of 1910, one landowner from Anhwei acquired 9,000 *mou* of land; the pace of land sales always accelerated during difficult periods.[106]

However, the increase of some rural fortunes was not necessarily accompanied by a concentration of landownership. Several regions certainly experienced concentration, such as areas in Anhwei or Hunan where, following the defeat of the Taipings, certain military officers and officials secured large estates for themselves, but this phenomenon was not general nor always lasting.[107] Smallholdings were still predominant.[108]

Often, greater returns were the result of more efficient management and reflected the introduction of more profitable crops such as opium; greater efficiency also permitted some farmers to increase their acreage. Szechwan thus witnessed the growth of a category of wealthy tenant-farmers who themselves owned a little or no land at all.[109] In Shantung, new agricul-

---

[102] Ramon H. Myers, *The Chinese peasant economy: agricultural development in Hopei and Shantung, 1890–1949*, 184–257.

[103] Li Wen-chih, *Chung-kuo chin-tai nung-yeh shih tzu-liao ti-i chi*, 386–416, 469–82, 651–60.

[104] *Ibid.* 557–63.

[105] Myers, *The Chinese peasant economy*, 142. These figures concern sorghum-producing regions of Chihli and Shantung. This case was not general; cf. two adverse examples given by Li Wen-chih, *Chung-kuo chin-tai nung-yeh shih tzu-liao ti-i chi*, 276–7.

[106] Li Wen-chih, *Chung-kuo chin-tai nung-yeh shih tzu-liao ti-i chi*, 175–8.

[107] *Ibid.* 178–88.   [108] *Ibid.* 193–6, 629–60.

[109] Kubota Bunji, 'Shimmatsu Shisen no daidenko, Chūgoku kisei jinushi-sei tenkai no ichimen' (Wealthy tenant farmers in Szechwan province in the late Ch'ing period: an aspect of the development of the parasitic landlord system in China), in Tōkyō Kyōiku Daigaku Tōyōshigaku Kenkyūshitsu *et al.* eds. *Kindai Chūgoku nōson shakaishi kenkyū*, 247–96.

tural practices were successfully introduced by landlords on estates which usually did not exceed 500 *mou*. These 'managerial' landlords cultivated their own land with the aid of paid hands, and obtained yields 30 to 50 per cent higher than did small growers as a result of more intensive use of organic fertilizers and better farm implements. An increasing percentage of their profit was invested in commercial and financial activities rather than in the acquisition of more land.[110]

The development in southern Kiangsu of bursaries (*tsu-chan*), bureaux for the collection of farm rents and taxes from several owners' landholdings, most of whom were absentee landlords, allowed a few landlords who remained to augment their incomes by administering them. They afforded prosperity to an auxiliary or parasitic group within the agricultural economy. This group consisted of tax-collectors and surveyors, many of whom also held subaltern posts in a yamen and eventually used their double earnings to promote usury, small businesses or land buying.[111]

These various transformations, many of which were the continuation of slow secular evolution, resulted in the appearance of a novel rural oligarchy in various regions. This oligarchy had relatively few roots in the traditional scholar elite, most of whom had fled the countryside after the Taiping Rebellion and abandoned agronomy. Neither did it surpass very much the status of *sheng-yuan*, though *sheng-yuan* degrees and purchased *chien-sheng* titles were rather frequent among its ranks. It did not command the scholars' traditional cultural prestige, and scarcely assumed their traditional ritual functions within local communities, but it did request and obtain the direct help of government forces to defend its private interests. Rarely did it maintain troops at its own expense, but it knew well how to use to its own profit whatever militia were still active after the Taipings or had been reassembled due to fleeting crises.[112] This rural oligarchy was also able to appropriate large sections of public land in border areas and uncultivated zones of the eighteen provinces, which it systematically worked unconstrained by customary tenants' protections.[113]

The relative success of certain of these rural types during the reigns of Kuang-hsu and Hsuan-t'ung does not appear to have been supported by any substantial increase in agricultural production, even locally. Instead, if numerous contemporary accounts about the countryside's general poverty are accurate, the increase of particular personal fortunes was made at the

[110] Ching Su and Lo Lun, *Ch'ing-tai Shan-tung ching-ying ti-chu ti she-hui hsing-chih*, 41–81, 130–41.
[111] Muramatsu Yūji, *Kindai Kōnan no sosan: Chūgoku jinushi seido no kenkyū* (Landlord bursaries in Kiangnan in modern times: studies of landlordism in China), *passim*. On the growing importance of these categories in village societies in other regions see Myers, *The Chinese peasant economy*, 268–70.
[112] Li Wen-chih, *Chung-kuo chin-tai nung-yeh shih tzu-liao ti-i chi*, 287–96.
[113] *Ibid.* 214–33.

direct expense of small farmers. The gradual impoverishment of a majority of peasants dispossessed of their lands, constrained to cultivating insufficient plots by the caprices of partitioning, burdened by increases in rent and taxes, and no longer allowed to make up deficits with their own handiwork, seems to have been almost universally the case.[114] Present research does not allow us to measure this precisely, but the spread of rural poverty seems to have been behind many other characteristics of social evolution at the close of the empire: changing conditions within the handicraft trades, migration, emigration and the rise of a sub-proletariat.

Changing handicraft trades

A small number of destitute peasants entered the ranks of the industrial proletariat. Greater numbers of them enlarged the handicraft labour force which was also undergoing transformation. After considerable damage inflicted by twenty years of internal strife, handicraft trades were undergoing change in order to keep pace with foreign commerce and industrial competition. Incomplete statistics for fifteen cities in six different provinces during the years 1864-94 indicate that forty-three out of seventy-six handicraft corporations whose activities are listed were new.[115] Certain handicrafts had undergone serious decline: cotton hand-spinning furnished only 50 per cent of domestic consumption by 1905. This was also true for iron and steel foundries in Hunan and Shansi, which supplied interprovincial commerce and had practically disappeared by 1900 owing to increased competition from imported metals. But other sectors stimulated by export business and industrial progress were developing and even creating better means of transport. Silk-spinning greatly increased in Kwangtung, Chekiang, Szechwan, Shantung and Fengtien. Tea manufacturers prospered, although briefly, during the years 1870–80, in Chekiang, Fukien, Taiwan, Anhwei, Kiangsi and Hupei, comprising altogether nearly four hundred companies. Chinese specialities such as porcelain, fans and bamboo objects, were much in demand. Moreover, exporting encouraged the growth of silk-weaving, while developments in transport enhanced the manufacture of oil and flour and old-style coal-mining. Ying-k'ou had two oil mills in 1866, and thirty in 1895; rice mills in Wuhu grew from twenty in 1850 to over a hundred by 1900. Though it hit certain handicrafts very hard, the diffusion of industrial production activated others: because

---

[114] *Ibid.* 255–82, 301–85, 502–8, 908, 929.
[115] P'eng Tse-i, 'Shih-chiu shih-chi hou-ch'i Chung-kuo ch'eng-shih shou-kung- yeh shang-yeh hang-hui ti ch'ung-chien ho tso-yung' (The reconstruction of urban Chinese handicraft and trade associations in the late nineteenth century and their functions), *Li-shih yen-chiu*, 1965.1, pp. 72–3.

mechanical spinning lowered the production costs of durable cloth, it allowed a large increase in hand-weaving in centres traditionally known for their textiles; it even encouraged the rise of a similar handicraft industry in several regions which had not previously seen any textile manufacturing at all. During the very last years of the nineteenth century, handicraft manufacturing of matches, soap, cigarettes, glass and knitted goods developed rapidly.

This rise in handicraft production, which was particularly marked after the introduction of major mechanized industry, largely took the form of manufactories, extended workshops, or several home-situated workers grouped together and paid on a piece-work basis. This production utilized partially mechanized, or at least improved, tools such as the Japanese foot-treadle loom which was used widely by weavers in Chekiang after the 1880s. At the end of the nineteenth century there were no more than thirty handicraft manufacturers of cotton goods, but between 1901 and 1911 over three hundred were established.[116] During this period the government also attempted to encourage handicrafts by creating handicraft bureaux (*kung-i chü*) in every province, which were to open apprentice workshops, develop techniques, and furnish aid to particular enterprises. This effort produced rather substantial results in Chihli and Shantung.[117]

The capitalist drift within several handicraft trades brought about a change in relationships among owners, workers and apprentices which was reflected even in corporate organization. Trades which felt the most threatened carried specialization further and further, regulating ever more strictly the admission of apprentices and co-workers from elsewhere, production rates, sales and working hours, in order to contain competition and distribute shrinking profits as equitably as possible among a growing number of tradesmen. These measures undoubtedly enabled many artisans to survive, although precariously, but hindered both the accumulation of capital and initiative. Prosperous trades, where large workshops were developing, also encouraged a tendency towards separate organizations for workers and apprentices, even while such groups remained exclusive and subordinate to owners' associations.[118] The frequency of strikes demanding higher wages seems to have accelerated during the first decade of the twentieth century.[119]

[116] Fan Pai-ch'uan, 'Chung-kuo shou-kung-yeh tsai wai-kuo tzu-pen-chu-i ch'in-ju hou ti tsao-yü ho ming-yun' (The fate of Chinese handicraft industry after the incursion of foreign capitalism), *Li-shih yen-chiu*, 1962.3, pp. 88–115.
[117] P'eng Tse-i *Chung-kuo chin-tai shou-kung-yeh shih tzu-liao*, 2.505–74.
[118] P'eng Tse-i, 'Shih-chiu shih-chi hou-ch'i Chung-kuo ch'eng-shih shou-kung-yeh shang-yeh hang-hui ti ch'ung-chien ho tso-yung', 71–102; P'eng Tse-i, *Chung-kuo chin-tai shou-kung-yeh shih tzu-liao*, 2.28–41, 599, 602, 604, 611.
[119] P'eng Tse-i, *Chung-kuo chin-tai shou-kung-yeh shih tzu-liao*, 2.615–17.

Despite meticulous corporate protection and the development of manufactories, the outlook for the majority of handicraft workers had actually
often become quite tenuous by the turn of the century, because of their
dependence on a growing market which was still very poorly regulated and
for which industrial competition had greatly reduced profit margins. This
was aggravated by large increases in the cost of food and the depreciation
of the copper currency with which they were paid.[120] According to official
statistics, there were more than 13 million artisans in thirty trades in 1912.[121]
It seems that the number of handicraft workers had grown in the mid-
nineteenth century, absorbing full-time or part-time a fraction of the rural
manpower surplus, and making it harder than ever for tradesmen to be
assured of stable conditions. Nomadic artisans were more numerous; tea-
shops would always be full of penniless wandering workers in quest of jobs.
Bankrupt artisans found their way into the ranks of industrial labour and
the leadership of popular movements.

Migrations

Rural poverty, often supplemented by the ill-fortune of artisan trades,
sustained the flow of interior migrations. Great displacements of population particularly affected provinces of the lower Yangtze in the aftermath
of the Taipings and repopulated devastated regions of southern Kiangsu,
Anhwei, Kiangsi and northern Chekiang with settlers from Honan and the
crowded areas of Hupei, Hunan, northern Kiangsu and eastern Chekiang.
This continued at a slower pace until the end of the monarchy. In the space
of fifty years, more than a million peasants left the sub-prefecture of
Kuang-shan in Honan and settled in over sixty localities in southern
Kiangsu, northern Chekiang, Anhwei and Kiangsi.[122] Urban centres
especially attracted the inflow of immigrants; for example, the population
of Shanghai increased from 107,000 inhabitants in 1880 to 345,000 in 1900
and 1,250,000 in 1911. As they moved from one area to another, these
groups brought with them agricultural techniques and particular customs,
which often helped to strain relations or nourish conflicts between different
local groups.[123]

The most spectacular of these interregional migrations was without

---

[120] *Ibid.* 2.582–95.   [121] *Ibid.* 2.431.

[122] Li Wen-chih, *Chung-kuo chin-tai nung-yeh shih tzu-liao ti-i chi*, 166–72. Wang T'ien-chiang,
    'T'ai-p'ing t'ien-kuo ko-ming hou Su Che Wan san sheng ti t'u-ti kuan-hsi' (The agrarian
    relations in the three provinces of Kiangsu, Chekiang and Anhwei after the Taiping Revolu-
    tion), *Hsin chien-she*, 1963.8, pp. 46–54. Ping-ti Ho, *Studies on the population of China, 1368–1953*,
    153–8.

[123] Wang Ching-yü, *Chung-kuo chin-tai kung-yeh shih tzu-liao*, 1172–3. Ho, *Studies on the population
    of China*, 153–8.

doubt the colonization of Manchuria by peasants from northern provinces, especially Shantung and Chihli. After a long period of secrecy because of edicts which restricted the use of these territories by Manchus and banner troops, immigration to the cradle of the reigning dynasty rose continually throughout the nineteenth century and was slowly legalized. Repeated famines and natural disasters which afflicted Chihli and Shantung during the reign of the Chia-ch'ing Emperor led, in 1803, to the official authorization of 'temporary' immigration. Between 1786 and 1840 the population of Fengtien rose from 807,000 to 2,213,000; that of Kirin from 148,000 to 324,000; and Heilungkiang grew from 35,000 in 1771 to more than 136,000 in 1808.[124] In the face of Russian and then Japanese ambitions, the throne decided in 1860 to encourage colonization. One after another, the most fertile regions were officially opened to immigrants who had been forced out, in increasing numbers, from the provinces of northern China by rural unrest and poverty. When Fengtien, Kirin and Heilungkiang were broken up into ordinary provinces in 1907, all interdictions preventing Chinese immigration were annulled. Immigration was at that time between 300,000 and 400,000 arrivals per year. The population of Fengtien had grown to 10,696,000 by 1911, double its level of 1897; Kirin had grown to 3,735,000, five times its level of 1897; Heilungkiang counted 1,453,000 inhabitants.[125]

The relatively rapid development of mining, military industries, and commercial enterprises of all sorts, after 1880, imparted to these regions a particular physiognomy. Custom and tradition were far less important and fortunes were often acquired very quickly, but the burdens of taxation were also heavier as soon as the administration had put its fiscal network into operation, and the likelihood of economic survival was also slimmer in a milieu which provided no collective protection or solidarity. It was in northern Manchuria, among its hordes of illegal immigrants, ex-convicts, bandits, adventurers, displaced peasants and prospectors, all known by the generic term *Hung-hu-tzu* (Red Beards), that communities, organized on principles of absolute collectivism and egalitarianism, appeared spontaneously during the last years of the nineteenth century, illegally assuming veritable administrative and political functions. The most famous of these was the Zheltuga Republic, named after a tributary of the Amur, which brought together 20,000 people in 1885, arousing the curiosity of several European travellers oriented towards utopian socialism.[126]

[124] Chung-kuo k'o-hsueh yuan Chi-lin-sheng fen-yuan li-shih yen-chiu-suo *et al.* eds. *Chin-tai tung-pei jen-min ko-ming yun-tung shih* (A history of the people's revolutionary movement in the north-east in modern times), 8.

[125] *Ibid.* 158. Li Wen-chih, *Chung-kuo chin-tai nung-yeh shih tzu-liao ti-i chi*, 775–808.

[126] Mark Mancall and Georges Jidkoff, 'The Hung Hu-tzu of Northeast China', in Jean Chesneaux, ed. *Popular movements and secret societies in China, 1840–1950* (hereafter *PMSS*), 125–34.

While people from the central and northern provinces sought relief from their poverty through interior migration, citizens from the south looked overseas in the hope of upgrading their lives.

Officially authorized and encouraged after 1876, emigration to Taiwan attracted mostly inhabitants of a few prefectures of southern Fukien and northern Kwangtung; 200,000 to 300,000 people returned to the mainland when the island was ceded to Japan in 1895. During the latter half of the nineteenth century groups of Hakka from the Canton delta moved to less crowded areas in western Kwangtung, especially the Lei-chou peninsula and the island of Hainan.[127] A flux of temporary migration developed between Yunnan and Tongking, stimulated by the opening of a railway which in 1911 carried more than a million Chinese fourth-class passengers. But the majority of Chinese emigrants were from Kwangtung and Fukien; after 1840 they spread throughout South-East Asia, coastal areas of the Pacific, Cuba, the islands of the Indian Ocean and as far as South Africa. It is difficult to establish exact figures for this emigration, a notable part of which was only temporary. The number of Chinese residing abroad was estimated at two or three million in 1876, and about eight or nine million in 1908, most of them in South-East Asia.[128] These estimates do not differentiate between recently arrived immigrants and natural growth, which was probably rather high in certain Chinese communities of South-East Asia, such as Penang or Siam, for example, which had much earlier origins.

Emigration, which was forbidden for reasons of political security by laws which the government was incapable of enforcing, developed under the worst conditions. Between 1850 and 1875 foreign agents and navigation companies used dishonest and often violent means to recruit 1,280,000 'contracted' workers, who in fact were slaves and were used to supply manpower to plantations and mines in Cuba and South America (then deprived of the African slave trade) as well as in Malaya. These unfortunate people, packed together in warehouses and cargo ships, undernourished and cheated out of their promised meagre wages from the start, sustained a mortality rate from disease and suicide as high as 50 to 60 per cent. Denounced by Chinese and foreign opinion, abuses of the coolie trade forced imperial authorities and the foreign governments concerned to establish jointly certain controls over hiring practices and shipboard conditions. The Portuguese decision in 1875 to prohibit emigration under contract from Macao theoretically brought to a close the coolie trade, which internal wars in Latin America had already begun to deprive of its major market. Composed from that time onwards of entirely 'voluntary'

[127] Ho, *Studies on the population of China*, 163–6.
[128] Fukuda Shōzō, *Kakyō keizai ron* (On the Overseas Chinese economy), 80–1.

workers, emigration was still partly organized under contract systems; more than a million coolies were hired in this manner and shipped to European colonial possessions in South-East Asia, the Pacific and South Africa between 1875 and 1914.[129]

The imperial government was no more able to protect this Chinese contract labour from exploitation by its hosts than it was to protect the free emigrants, who grew by far the more numerous during the last quarter of the nineteenth century. Chinese authorities did, however, move from an attitude of indifference to a stance of concerned vigilance.[130] Under the influence of a few diplomats and high-ranking officials such as Ch'en Lan-pin, Kuo Sung-tao, Chang Chih-tung, Hsueh Fu-ch'eng and Huang Tsun-hsien, the government finally began to appreciate the economic and political importance of Overseas Chinese communities. Between 1869 and 1895 the establishment of consulates was negotiated in the principal areas of emigration. Imperial diplomacy defended Chinese nationals against measures intended to restrict Chinese emigration to the United States and Canada during the 1880s and Australia after 1890. It protested against the cruelties to which they were subjected. Traditional laws prohibiting emigration were officially abolished by an edict issued on 13 September 1893, and measures were taken for the issuing of passports and the exemption of Overseas Chinese from fiscal vexations of local officials once they returned home. These measures encouraged emigrants to return their savings and investments to China and facilitated constant exchange between the continent and Chinese communities abroad at a time when departures were increasing: Amoy registered 100,000 per year at the beginning of the twentieth century, while Singapore registered nearly 250,000 entries annually.[131] The yearly total of the funds sent home by Overseas Chinese for 1907 was reckoned to be 73 million taels. They also provided an important part of the capital of modern Chinese enterprises.

The return of money generated by emigration made possible the actual survival of a good many inhabitants of coastal prefectures; it stimulated industrialization around Canton, but also throughout the eastern provinces as far north as Manchuria; at the national level its volume greatly helped to make up a balance of payments that had been saddled with commercial deficits and foreign debt. But the particularly numerous and active

[129] Ch'en Tse-hsien, 'Shih-chiu shih-chi sheng-hsing ti ch'i-yueh hua-kung chih' (The flourishing Chinese contract labour system in the nineteenth century), Li-shih yen-chiu, 1963.1, pp. 161–79.
[130] On this new policy of the Ch'ing government see Michael R. Godley, 'The late Ch'ing courtship of the Chinese in Southeast Asia', JAS, 34.2 (Feb. 1975) 361–85.
[131] Li Wen-chih, Chung-kuo chin-tai nung-yeh shih tzu-liao ti-i chi, 941–2. Wang Ching-yü, Chung-kuo chin-tai kung-yeh shih tzu-liao, 1178–9.

wealthy merchants of Chinese communities in so-called Nanyang ('the southern seas'), that is, south-east Asia, went even further to encourage the modernization of the mother-country by furnishing much of its personnel and inspiration. Ch'en Ch'i-yuan, founder of the first steam-powered silk-spinning mills near Canton, Wu T'ing-fang, counsellor to Li Hung-chang, and Chang Pi-shih, a millionaire given responsibility by the throne to over-see policies of economic development after 1901, were all from Nanyang. Emigrants were better informed about Western matters, were convinced of the superiority of commercial careers, and were also attached more fiercely to the homeland and their national identities as a result of their defensive feelings aroused by a hostile environment. From them came cultural models which influenced the continent, such as the freedom of expression in the press or a system of education combining Western science with Chinese literary study, as practised in a school opened in Havana in 1886. Though the imperial government drew on the wealth and talent of its subjects abroad, reformist and revolutionary political movements which arose near the end of the monarchy also looked to foreign communities to provide material support and personnel which helped them to survive the persecution which they were experiencing in China itself. Of particular benefit was the support of secret societies, which had grown strong in foreign situations in order to provide organized defence of Chinese minorities; they were also traditionally hostile to the Manchu dynasty (see chapter 9).[132]

The economic, social and political impact of emigration overseas during the last thirty years of the monarchy greatly outweighed its demographic effects, which were important only in a few regions of south-eastern China.

The Growth of a Sub-proletariat

Internal migration and emigration among the lower classes did nothing to moderate a phenomenon which continued to rise throughout most of the country after the quelling of major popular insurrections, namely the development of a sub-proletariat. The widespread growth, in both rural and urban areas, of a population completely destitute, with no fixed liveli-hood, often with no regular place of residence, hardest hit by famines, natural disasters and epidemics, is most powerfully described by clear-sighted contemporaries.[133] They assign responsibility to the combined effects of agricultural difficulties, demographic growth, disbanding of

---

[132] These societies are studied in depth by Leon F. Comber, *Chinese secret societies in Malaya: a survey of the Triad Society 1800 to 1900*; W. P. Morgan, *Triad societies in Hongkong*; and Wilfred Blythe, *The impact of Chinese secret societies in Malaya. A historical study*.
[133] Li Wen-chih, *Chung-kuo chin-tai nung-yeh shih tzu-liao ti-i chi*, 935–8, 945–6.

troops after civil wars, and unemployment created by the introduction of technical means and modern enterprises, particularly affecting transport and textiles.

As a result of the precarious livelihood maintained by most farmers and rural artisans, the smallest accident, poor harvest, or tax surcharge was enough to swell the ranks of migrant paupers. Now a devastating series of natural disasters regularly desolated immense areas. Chihli and Fengtien were flooded in 1886, 1890 and 1893. Every year from 1886 to 1911, some sixty counties in Kiangsu and forty in Anhwei were plagued by either floods, wind, drought or insects. The worst damage was sustained by provinces along the Yellow River, where, by the thousands, the same villages were the victims of floods and drought year after year, leaving them neither the time nor the means to repair dikes and canals. Hydraulic works fell into disuse in many places not only because of administrative ineptitude and corruption, but also because of the exhaustion of local resources, which aggravated the problem by accentuating the effects of adverse weather conditions. The number of bankrupt starving peasants in the seventy or eighty counties of Szechwan stricken by drought in 1902 could be counted in hundreds of thousands.[134] Neither traditional village solidarity nor the government's feeble attempt at aid could any longer absorb the incredible number of people who had been stripped of all resources. The percentage of homeless displaced persons (*yu-min*) attained startling levels in many regions: 90 per cent in one county of Shensi, 33 per cent in one Yunnan village, and 25 per cent in another county in Hunan.[135] Not all localities were dealt the same blow; some, in the richer areas of the south, even enjoyed stable, though modest, prosperity; but the cumulative effects of wars and disasters tended for the most part to generalize and aggravate this process of impoverishment.[136]

Normally, the imperial government supported the interests of landlords; an edict issued in 1854 punished refusal to pay farm-rents by penalties equal to those reserved for tax evasion.[137] In cases of famine, official protection was given first to farmers and those who had fixed employment. Often rejected or cast aside by clans and other organized forms of village life, the poor also escaped to a large extent imperial networks of control: *pao-chia* (local police system) and *hsiang-yueh* (lecture systems) were even less

[134] Chung-kuo k'o-hsueh-yuan Shan-tung fen-yuan li-shih yen-chiu-so, *I-ho-t'uan yun-tung liu-shih chou-nien lun-wen chi*, 243. Li Wen-chih, *Chung-kuo chin-tai nung-yeh shih tzu-liao ti-i chi*, 720–2, 733–5, gives annual tabulations of natural disasters for the valleys of the Yellow River and the Yangtze.
[135] Kung-chuan Hsiao, *Rural China: imperial control in the nineteenth century*, 690. Chambre de Commerce de Lyon, ed. *La Mission lyonnaise d'exploration commerciale en Chine 1895–1897*, 79.
[136] Li Wen-chih, *Chung-kuo chin-tai nung-yeh shih tzu-liao ti-i chi*, 686–92.
[137] Hsiao *Rural China*, 391.

able to keep track of them than they were those citizens who were more well-provided. The novelist Lu Hsun has left us perhaps the most poignant description of the millions of sorry sights who crowded Chinese villages and cities in perpetual quest of a living. He has done this through the character of Ah Q who, in his meagre subsistence, was mocked and abused on all sides by the sometimes pitying and sometimes cruel contempt of rural and city dwellers alike.[138]

Among these all too vulnerable elements, from agricultural day-labour and coolies to migrants and beggars, and finally bandits, all social plagues found an easy prey – opium, gambling and prostitution were rampant.[139] But the rural and urban poor also provided secret societies and popular movements with troops which were easily mobilized. The Ko-lao hui (Elder Brothers Society) which was highly active in provinces along the Yangtze, drew most of its membership from bankrupt peasants and artisans, soldiers and 'braves' (*yung*) demobilized after the Taipings, and coolies and boatmen whose jobs had become otiose as the result of innovations in transportation; the Triad Society primarily attracted the agricultural sub-proletariat.[140] The predominance during the latter half of the nineteenth century of *hui-tang* (secret societies), with declared political and social pretensions, over *chiao-men* (sects), which were more specifically religious, seems to parallel directly the growth of an unemployed population of uprooted elements and social rejects, for whom *hui-tang* offered a kind of protection and security.[141]

Instability and precariousness therefore more aptly characterize lower-class conditions in Chinese society at the end of the monarchy than do models of continuous evolution. The overall result for groups and families seems to have been a downward mobility, degradation of the traditional structures which had sustained the life of the common people, and destruction of the relative economic safeguards which these structures had assured them.

To be sure, the prospect for simple folk was not universally gloomy. In a land as vast and varied as China, there were many examples of the *nouveaux riches* who had started with nothing; of simple coolies who became millionaires – like Yeh Ch'eng-chung; of industrious and clever farmers who managed to live quite well; and of prosperous and peaceful regions. Some

---

[138] Lu Hsun, *The true story of Ah Q*, trans. by Gladys Yang and Hsien-i Yang.
[139] Cf. texts cited by Hsiao, *Rural China*, 399–402.
[140] Wang I-sun, 'Hsin-hai ko-ming shih-ch'i tzu-ch'an chieh-chi yü nung-min ti kuan-hsi wen-t'i' (Problem of the relationship between the bourgeoisie and the peasants during the era of the 1911 Revolution), in *HHWS*, 118–21.
[141] Wang T'ien-chiang, 'Shih-chiu shih-chi hsia-pan-chi Chung-kuo ti pi-mi hui-she' (Chinese secret societies in the second half of the nineteenth century), *Li-shih yen-chiu*, 1963.2, pp. 83–100.

parts of the modern elite ascended from the ranks of the common people, along with another relatively wealthy intermediate category of land-owners, usurers, merchants and other middlemen. China's enormous population still comprised above all farmers with a regular occupation, owning small plots of land. This category was also subject to individual mobility (there are as yet no studies which would enable us to measure whether this rate was any higher than it had been during previous epochs); in many regions its means were shrinking, as in Shantung and Chihli where the average size of farms dropped 20 to 50 per cent (in one county) between 1870 and 1910;[142] in certain localities its loss of relative importance within the total population probably went hand in hand with its loss of absolute numbers. But within this category, the status, functions and occupations of its members changed only slightly. On the other hand, there was consider-able growth in the number of people no longer contained within the tradi-tional Confucian occupational classes (scholars, peasants, artisans, mer-chants) and also in the old organizational network and patterns of solidarity which characterized them. This group included factory workers and any-one not possessing *heng-ch'an* (stable property), so essential to traditional perceptions of society; people such as bankrupt peasants and artisans, wandering, migrant and vagabond workers of all kinds, disbanded troops and fallen scholars.

The traditional social system thus crumbled from both above and below. Not only did the upper classes undergo break-up and transformation, there was also the dramatic rise of a class of marginal commoners untouched by legal confines and driven by circumstance outside society's forms of control and patterns of order and respectability.

DYNAMICS OF SOCIAL CHANGE

Foreign impact versus internal factors

Among the many factors contributing to changes in Chinese society during the last forty years of the monarchy, the foreign intrusion, in various forms, was of primary importance. It was directly responsible for the emergence of new groups, such as compradors and *yang-wu* experts, as well as for the decline of certain activities such as hand-spinning and traditional water and overland transport in Central and North China. In many regions foreign commerce ushered in economic imbalances which brought about greater poverty and unemployment for some of the inhabitants. However, the foreign penetration seems to have influenced Chinese society far more pro-foundly by its indirect effects. The Western presence and the connections

---

[142] Myers, *The Chinese peasant economy*, 137–8.

with the rest of the world inspired new activities and modified certain established functions, triggering the growth of a group of modern businessmen and entrepreneurs, a military aristocracy, a landowners' oligarchy, and an urban intelligentsia, while the traditional corps of gentry-literati disintegrated and transformed itself.

It is important to note, however, that within the evolution of Chinese society at the end of the empire, the intellectual movement seems to have been a far more significant factor than imperialism in bringing about socio-economic change. Some Marxist historians' attempts to define the reformers of 1895–8 as 'representatives of the bourgeoisie' are not convincing, since China at that time had no bourgeoisie. On the contrary, it was these reformers who initiated or, shall we say, invented it. Gentry-literati such as Chang Chien who suddenly began to invest in and create modern enterprises after the Sino-Japanese War, were inspired by primarily political and ideological motives. Their actions were derived from a sort of intellectual conversion or contagion. Only after the rise of Chinese industry during the years 1905–11 did the lure of profit take the upper hand and economic gain become the primary motive. Chinese capitalism was characterized for a long time by a certain voluntary idealism.

Among the lower classes, anti-Christian and anti-Western propaganda seem to have fermented more active revolt than did the ravages of foreign economic exploitation. The population of areas where the effects of massive foreign activity were more tangible seem to have been less inclined to violent uprising than the inhabitants of regions far removed from foreign traffic. After 1870, most of the struggles against the Western presence broke out in localities which had been largely ignored by foreign commerce; the foreign presence in these areas sometimes amounted to as little as three or four missionaries.[143] The few incidents and boycotts occurring in Shanghai and Canton in more than forty years seem pale in comparison with the Boxer Rebellion.

However, can the intellectual movement and the practical power of its ideas be explained in purely psychological terms? Were they not also sustained by certain material conditions?

The nationalistic sentiment of the gentry-literati in 1895 would have been ineffective had it not been supported by advantageous economic change. In order to understand this change, Chinese historians have looked at the role played by the 'sprouting of capitalism' (*tzu-pen-chu-i meng-ya*) – nurtured by the development of a market economy since the sixteenth century – in the rise of a business bourgeoisie at the turn of the century.[144]

---

[143] Cf. Li Shih-yueh, *Fan-yang-chiao yun-tung* (The anti-Christian movement), 31–105.
[144] This discussion, during the years 1954–60, continued arguments which had been developed

But, in fact, in only a few local examples can we discern any direct link between traditional commerce and industrial capitalism. The larger rebellions of the mid-nineteenth century had in any case disrupted such an evolution, and the rise of handicraft production in large workshops accompanied rather than preceded the creation of factories. Most of the new elite came quite directly from the traditional ruling class of gentry-literati and officials, whose primary source of revenue had always been the land, even though they reaped growing profits from merchandising and money-trading. We then have to look at the ownership of land for further explanations.

Embittered relations on the land

The force behind the changes which shook Chinese society at the end of the imperial era perhaps lay more in the progressive deterioration of the agrarian situation and especially in landowners' relationships with their tenants.

Demographic growth was one of the principal causes of the dismantling of the 'feudal' relations which had long entrapped peasants. During the twenty years following the bloodshed of the civil wars of the third quarter of the nineteenth century, the population regained and surpassed its already high level of 1850. Although population increase in the lower Yangtze was definitely slowed down as a result of the Taiping wars, it seemed to accelerate in the plains of North China. The problem was not only that there were more people to feed, it was complicated by the fact that, judging from sources such as genealogies, the growth rate was relatively higher among the privileged strata.[145] This resulted in simultaneous and contradictory phenomena: exacerbated exploitation of tenants, loss of authority by landlords, and the spread of decadence and poverty.

Competition among farmers as well as the landowners' new needs combined to provoke increases in rents and greater surcharges. This change took place gradually and became ever more widespread. Once they had decided to establish residence in town, landlords no longer provided seed or tools; they ceased overseeing personally the harvest-time crop division and began to prefer fixed rents of grain or money; these practices were also

during the 1920s and 1930s on the nature of Chinese society: see Chung-kuo jen-min ta-hsueh Chung-kuo li-shih chiao-yen-shih, ed. *Chung-kuo tzu-pen-chu-i meng-ya wen-t'i t'ao-lun chi* (Collected papers on the problem of the incipiency of capitalism in China). It is summarily recapitulated by Albert Feuerwerker, 'China's modern economic history in Communist Chinese historiography', in Albert Feuerwerker, ed. *History in Communist China*, 229–34.

[145] A study done by Yung-teh Chow dealing with the first part of the twentieth century (*Social mobility in China*, 110–13) shows that the higher growth rate among the privileged class was the result of a lower infant mortality rate combined with a higher fertility rate. Sources

instituted by neighbours who had remained in the rural areas.[146] As protection against tenants' defaulting, a *ya-tsu*, or farmers' bond, came into widespread use, often amounting to as much as ten years' rent.[147] This was abolished on land which was redistributed after the Taipings, and perpetual tenure fell slowly into disuse. Landlords profited from fluctuations of currency and agricultural market prices to manipulate the rates of rent commutation in their own favour and to further market speculation. Increasing fiscal burdens as a result of military expenditure, the cost of modernization, and the multiplication of surtaxes imposed by official and private collectors, weighed heavily on small growers, the *hsiao-hu*, while large landowners, the *ta-hu*, used their influence to have themselves exempted. Immediately after the posthumous publication in 1876 of Feng Kuei-fen's optimistic writings on the reduction of land taxes in Kiangnan in the aftermath of the Taipings, T'ao Hsu, a scholar from Soochow, described in a pamphlet entitled 'Inquiry into rents' (*Tsu ho*) the hypocrisy and injustice of the reforms of 1863, which had benefited only an avid minority of families connected with the higher bureaucracy. He denounced excesses in rents, the unpitying tyranny exercised by *ta-hu*, and the decline of production and agricultural productivity which resulted from the manifold obligations placed on small farmers.[148] We can estimate that on the eve of the Revolution of 1911, the peasants' fiscal burdens had at least doubled, if not tripled, in comparison with the 1840s. The land tax, which was by then their lesser obligation, had increased by as much as 60 to 80 per cent. As a result of inflation, the actual global burden was, it is true, probably less than it had been prior to the Taipings.[149] In general, however, greater inequalities of assessment, more vexatious systems of collection, and accelerating growth of taxation after 1895 in order to finance wars, debts and reforms, combined to crush humble folk.

Perhaps one of the major factors, and as yet no concrete studies have been made, was the crumbling of a system of personal relations and social responsibilities capable of moderating antagonism and violent class conflict.

available for the nineteenth century allow us only to observe the difference in growth rates. They furnish insufficient information on fertility and infant mortality.

[146] Li Shih-yueh, *Hsin-hai ko-ming shih-ch'i Liang-Hu ti-ch'ü ti ko-ming yun-tung* (The revolutionary movement in the Hunan–Hupei area during the era of the 1911 Revolution), 35–41.

[147] Li Wen-chih, *Chung-kuo chin-tai nung-yeh shih tzu-liao ti-i chi*, 256–8. Shiraishi Hiroo, 'Shimmatsu Konan no nōson shakai – ōso kankō to kōso keikō' (Rural Hunan society in the late Ch'ing – the practice of *ya-tsu* and the tendency toward rent resistance), in *Chūgoku Kindaika no shakai kōzō* (Social structure in China's modernization), 1–19.

[148] T'ao Hsu's text can be found in an appendix to Tōkyō Kyōiku Daigaku Tōyōshigaku Kenkyūshitsu, ed. *Kindai Chūgoku nōson shakai shih kenkyū* (Studies in modern Chinese rural social history). See also in the same volume a study by Suzuki Tomoo, 'Shimmatsu gensoron no tenkai – "Sokaku" no kenkyū' (The development of rent reduction theories in the late Ch'ing period – a study of 'Inquiry into rents'), 199–246.

[149] See Wang Yeh-chien, *Land taxation in imperial China, 1750–1911*, 110–28.

This system, which had served to assure vertical integration in rural communities, tended to fall apart. Partial or total release from farm rents in cases of poor harvest, and help and various forms of protection extended to tenants and small growers by landlords or local elite, became more infrequent or more onerous. The absenteeism of landowners, which was the corollary of the urbanization of the elite, accentuated this evolution without being its sole cause, since those who remained in the villages certainly did not exhibit any greater Confucian benevolence. Their ruthlessness, especially when combined with their absence in the city, eroded any mutual confidence and moral authority they might have retained in their relations with tenant farmers. In effect, it made rapport more difficult and reduced the flexibility of the implicit bargaining by which reciprocal obligations were reckoned; it directed a blow at a central notion in the working of Chinese society, the *kan-ch'ing*, that is, the sense of reciprocity in human relations, or, rather, a feeling of mutual acceptance and individual duty among people of differing conditions. It was certainly not pure chance that so many educated Chinese at the end of the nineteenth century deplored the disappearance of *i-hsin*, the union or unity of hearts, and looked to the West to provide institutional palliatives for what they saw as the failure of traditional practices.

However, many landowning families of average or modest means, ruined financially by wars, bureaucratic exactions, or simply by the pressure of a surplus of mouths to feed, fell into decadence and destitution without being replaced in their local functions of collective responsibility as mediators between rural communities and exterior authorities. For many villages of North China at the beginning of the twentieth century, this poverty deprived them of spokesmen who could represent their interests in a literate yet forceful way, leaving them only one course of action – revolt.

Popular movements and their social efficacy

Certainly, the reigns of Kuang-hsu and Hsuan-t'ung were not marked by peasant insurrections comparable to those of the Taipings, the Nien and the Muslims. But these uprisings, whose scope certainly had no precedent in Chinese history, started an erosion of traditional rural society which other popular movements continued with varying degrees of impact. Between 1840 and 1911 the incidents never abated, although their vigour was irregular. After having reached a peak between 1850 and 1875, they slowed and then accelerated again at the end of the century. C. K. Yang has done a quantitative analysis of mass actions reported in the *Ta-Ch'ing li-ch'ao shih-lu* (Veritable records of the Ch'ing emperors), which indicates the following frequencies:[150]

Years	1836–45	1846–55	1856–65	1866–75	1876–85	1886–95	1896–1911
Number of incidents	246	933	2,332	909	385	314	653

The figures given in the *Shih-lu* still seem rather lower than what must have been the actual numbers, particularly for the years immediately preceding the Revolution of 1911. Investigations conducted at that time by the Shanghai magazine *Tung-fang tsa-chih* recorded 113 uprisings in 1909 and 285 in 1910.[151] Also of note is the fact that after the relative calm following the major insurrections, both the average duration of incidents and the number of participants increased. While North China, and particularly the province of Chihli, remained the principal site of unrest, its geographical distribution widened to include every province in China.[152]

Though there was nothing comparable to the Taipings, the last years of the empire still experienced the Boxer Rebellion, which raged for three years in the northern provinces, drew the monarchy into war against foreign powers, and was prolonged by recurrent agitation which reached as far as Manchuria and Szechwan. In Kwangsi, the revolt which had begun in 1898 as an ephemeral outbreak by the T'ien-ti hui (Triad Society), took on renewed vigour in 1900 and menaced neighbouring provinces in 1903. Several hundred thousand soldiers were needed to repress this uprising, which persisted until 1906. Throughout China from about 1890 onwards, the authorities were alarmed at the recrudescence of *min-pien* (popular revolts).[153]

What was the social significance of this popular turbulence? Pending new research, it seems that many of these movements took very specific forms, with neither avowed nor apparent social objectives: simple riots against missions, foreigners, Christians, Manchus or modern technology,

[150] C. K. Yang, 'Some preliminary patterns of mass action in nineteenth century China', in Frederic Wakeman, Jr, and Carolyn Grant, eds. *Conflict and control in late imperial China*, 190. Mass action classed under the rubrics 'Christian proselytism', 'Collective donation to government military expenses' and 'Local self-defence', have been subtracted from C. K. Yang's totals, retaining only those incidents showing characteristics of social protest or disturbance threatening public order.

[151] The list of incidents registered this way was put together by Wang I-sun, 'Hsin-hai ko-ming shih-ch'i tzu-ch'an chieh-chi yü nung-min ti kuan-hsi wen-t'i', 135.

[152] Yang, 'Some preliminary patterns of mass actions', 178–87.

[153] Various of these movements have been the subject of monographic studies. On the Boxer movement see: Chien Po-tsan, *I-ho t'uan* (The Boxers); Chung-kuo k'o-hsueh-yuan Shan-tung fen-yuan li-shih yen-chiu-so, *I-ho-t'uan yun-tung liu-shih chou-nien chi-nien lun-wen chi*; and Victor Purcell, *The Boxer uprising*. Other studies and a general bibliography are in Jean Chesneaux, ed. *Mouvements populaires et sociétés secrètes en Chine aux XIXe et XXe siècles*, and its English version (which is slightly different) *PMSS*.

and not against landlords, the rich or tax collectors. According to statistics established by C. K. Yang, disorders of this type represent between a quarter and a third of the incidents mentioned in the *Shih-lu* between 1876 and 1911. It was essentially from this category that arose the better organized agitation which was the most menacing to imperial security: the wave of anti-foreign riots of 1891 in the Yangtze valley,[154] and the Boxer Uprising.

In such movements, the rioters' social origins were very heterogeneous. Among the inciters and leaders were a number of gentry-literati, aspiring officials, yamen employees and elite landlords or merchants, alongside artisans, boatmen, pedlars, demobilized soldiers, geomancers or monks. In the ranks of the troops, working farmers made up a minority alongside coolies, vagabonds, outcasts or very young men, as in the Boxer troops. C. K. Yang's statistics claim that the *Shih-lu* identifies the social status of the leaders of more than a third of the incidents which it recorded in the reigns of Kuang-hsu and Hsuan-t'ung: 57 per cent of them belonged to the ruling class or were at least directly associated with it. They included gentry-literati, officials, noblemen, landlords, established merchants, officials' servants and government runners. Such a social recruitment of their leadership makes riots resemble more a civil war than a class war.

It is also true that the recurrent agitation at the end of the empire was fomented in large part by secret societies, whose membership was composite and whose aims were ambiguous. Though they offered opposition to the established order, they were also dependent upon it; they served to regulate the equilibrium of the traditional regime. Their members' separation from proper society was more often based on individual rupture, mishap, ambition or force of character, than on a foundation of common economic conditions. Secret societies bore all the characteristics of an elective fraternity. They recuperated and disciplined those who lived outside the official order, thus saving it from brutal collapse. Their integration within traditional society was manifested by their local features, their ideology of a return to a past golden age, their rituals, and their fictitious honorific titles. When the situation demanded, their leaders did not shy away from compromise or collusion with the authorities. At the end of the nineteenth century, many of the larger elite families in the Yangtze valley had at least one member in the Ko-lao hui who would protect his relatives from action by his fellow-members, and also could gain for the latter some leniency from the magistrates.

[154] On these riots see Guy Puyraimond, 'The Ko-lao-hui and the anti-foreign incidents of 1891', in *PMSS*. Also Edmund S. Wehrle, *Britain, China and the antimissionary riots, 1891–1900*, 19–44, and Charlton M. Lewis, *Prologue to the Chinese Revolution: the transformation of ideas and institutions in Hunan province, 1891–1907*, 16–39.

Much of the unrest at the end of the empire can therefore only with difficulty be considered manifestations of peasant war or class struggle in the strict sense. Still, we ought not to deny its economic and social roots, nor see it simply in the light of pure political opposition or simple insubordination. In reality, each of the riots against foreign missions was preceded by agricultural calamity or local economic disaster. In the summer of 1886 the price of rice in Chungking was exorbitant when angry crowds burned down the Protestant church. Several years of flooding and scarcity had plagued the population of the Yangtze valley when riots broke out in 1891. In Shantung from 1895 to 1898, natural catastrophes, famines and requisitions preceded the Boxers' insurrection. Very often, missions which were attacked had become particularly abusive landowners; having acquired vast holdings of land, some of which had been fraudulently extracted from the collective domains of clans or temples, they would allow only Christians to farm it and steadfastly refuse to participate in the common obligations of their locality. Chinese converts were reproached for having sold themselves in exchange for protection from the authorities and protection from poverty. The bands which threw themselves into the assault on missions as well as the bulk of the members of secret societies were composed of exactly those people who foresaw no possibility of finding such security. This category also produced the leaders of the most trenchant movements. The two main leaders of the Boxers, Ts'ao Fu-t'ien and Chang Te-ch'eng, were respectively a demobilized soldier and a Grand Canal boatman forced out of business by advances in steam navigation.

Most of the uprisings against foreigners opened menacingly, and sometimes violently, with attacks on the property of some local elite, who had been suspected of complacency regarding foreigners, or on the yamen. Though the Boxers' struggle was aimed primarily at foreigners, they also, despite their alliance with the throne, made social demands. Certainly, their social programme does not appear to have gone any further than the elementary redistribution of booty taken from the rich and the one slogan, 'protect the people', destined primarily to get easier food supplies from simple peasants. But this primitive social protest remained one of the permanent traits of their activity and was shared by those groups scattered throughout the countryside of the north and Szechwan after 1900, who continued the resistance. One of the characteristics of the anti-foreign and anti-Manchu popular uprisings at the end of the Ch'ing dynasty was not the absence of social content, but rather the fact that elementary economic antagonism took on political dimensions, owing largely to the influence of the secret societies.

All the same, foreigners and Manchus were only marginal causes of the

unrest which marked the end of the dynasty; nor were the popular movements caused solely by activities of secret societies. Mutinies, banditry,
pillage, food riots, tax-resistance agitations and movements of resistance to
farm rents were the particular manifestations of a general and endemic
unrest. It was often expressed through elementary protest and spontaneous
action. People might suddenly refuse to pay the rent after a bad harvest and
reinforce their refusal by beating up the landlord's overseer. Increasing
severity and avidity on the part of officials provoked other minor local
incidents: crowds might drive an official from a yamen because he had
passed a sentence deemed unjust or ordained surtax increases; workmen
employed on public works might strike to protest against an official's mis-
handling of their wages; prisoners might murder their gaoler because he
had abused or mistreated them.

Among the various modes of struggle, outright violence predominated.
It was directed against the machinery of order and oppression. Crowds
attacked yamens, prisons, rich people's homes, overseers, tax collectors and
usurers, shipments of merchandise, and public or private granaries; they
burned debt certificates and land and fiscal records. Riots developed slowly,
but once under way they were displays of strength which were sometimes
limited to individual brutalities but could go as far as the formation of
veritable troops, most often armed. Rioters were armed with whatever was
at hand in the country – spears, clubs, knives, some old rifles – but if the
riot was prolonged, they were likely to come up with supplies of munitions
(thanks to secret societies) or even soldiers. Magistrates and the local elite
were well aware that the people's endurance and patience were long-lasting;
but they also knew that it was possible with a concession at the right time
to nip a blossoming revolt in the bud. However, it appears that with the
last years of the nineteenth century they became less and less successful,
and their bargaining power began to dry up, particularly as there were more
people than ever who had absolutely nothing to lose and who lived by the
strength of their violence. Once a riot had begun, authorities were more
and more likely to resort to armed repression rather than to arbitration or
compromise, in order to disperse the crowds. But the use of force seemed
only to increase the violence.[155]

In addition to violence, social unrest after 1880 was characterized by its
political dimension. This trait stands out when we look at the geographical
distribution of the disorders recorded in the *Shih-lu*. The northern region
around Peking, the seat of imperial power, had the highest frequency of
disturbances; nearly half of all the incidents occurred in administrative

---

[155] Cf. the statistics of Yang, 'Some preliminary patterns of mass action', 205–6, on the methods
used to suppress and appease the trouble.

centres – Peking, provincial capitals, seats of prefectures and counties.[156] Even the most sporadic and elementary riots often exhibited this political dimension. For example, peasants would seize a yamen underling; or they would march on a city and attack the yamen; perhaps a destitute scholar might join a band of starving peasants looting granaries in villages of the south and post a poem calling for divine vengeance to be brought upon the emperor's head. Even though the pretext for a revolt might have been personal or private, such as increases in rent or feuds among clans, people would willingly attack the symbols of political power associated with the adversary.

Between the 1880s and the Boxer Rebellion, the political dimension of social agitation seems to have grown primarily because of the influence of secret societies. In effect, due to the disarray in which the lower classes found themselves after the failure of the large rebellions of the mid-nineteenth century – with displaced populations, shattered solidarities, disorganized rural communities, and the harshly reaffirmed authority of the privileged classes – secret societies became the only helpful structures for those powerless people who found themselves suddenly thrust into a hostile environment. They developed rapidly, fed equally by the mass of demobilized soldiers and the first unemployed victims of technological modernization. It was not by chance, for example, that the phenomenal extension of the Ko-lao hui in the lower and middle Yangtze valley during the last third of the nineteenth century occurred in the same region which had witnessed the repression of the Taipings, where demobilized soldiers were most numerous, and where steam navigation had extended most rapidly. Scattered as they were throughout the country, secret societies, true to their anti-dynastic faith, often inspired rioters to defy authority even when they were not themselves the instigators.[157]

However, at the beginning of the twentieth century, though there were no indications of a substantial diminution of their influence, secret societies no longer appear to have played such a determinant and indispensable role in politicizing social unrest. Actions undertaken jointly with revolutionaries showed some of this decline in the political stature of secret societies. But even more indicative was the development of fairly broad popular movements which challenged imperial authority without the assistance of secret societies, such as the trouble linked to the interdiction against the growing of opium, which lasted several months in Chekiang, Kansu, Kweichow, Manchuria and Shansi, from 1909 to 1911; or the revolts

---

[156] *Ibid.* 187.
[157] Wang T'ien-chiang, 'Shih-chiu shih-chi hsia-pan-chi Chung-kuo ti pi-mi hui-she' (Chinese secret societies in the second half of the nineteenth century), *Li-shih yen-chiu*, 1963, 2, pp. 93–7.

against the high cost of grain and land-tax increases in the central provinces during the same period; or again the agitation provoked by censuses and the financing of modern schools and reforms, which spread through all the provinces after 1906. Insurgents attacked public buildings, vilified the administration, took magistrates prisoner and sometimes executed them. At Lai-yang, in Shantung, in May–June 1910, a conflict which arose over supplementary fiscal exactions, for which the authorities were attempting to pin responsibility on the local elite, degenerated into a battle of unprecedented violence. More than forty thousand people participated and about a thousand were killed or wounded.[158]

Documentary sources suggest that all these disturbances were precipitated by economic factors, which added force to pre-existing discontent from other causes. Still, certain authors have suggested that far from reflecting a general worsening of living conditions, these social struggles were rather the manifestation of a difficulty in adapting to changes which were improving the overall situation.[159] They base their argument either on the relative feebleness of popular agitation during the reigns of Kuang-hsu and Hsuan-t'ung compared to the civil wars of the mid-nineteenth century, or on the theory that extreme poverty forces peasants to put all their energy into the struggle for physical survival, thereby leaving little capacity for revolt. It has been demonstrated, it is true, that in certain regions in Kwangtung, the development of commercial agriculture gave peasants greater independence vis-à-vis landlords, thus encouraging them to resist paying rents.[160] However, a general interpretation of this type ought to be based on detailed economic studies, which are lacking in this case. The state of contemporary research and available sources allow us only to affirm that, though certain farmers were able to improve their standards of living during the last decades of the empire, the proportion of the truly poor rose. This latter category supplied the popular movements with most of their members.

It remains true nonetheless that it was apparently due mainly to their political dimension that popular movements influenced social evolution. They highlighted the growing incapacity of the imperial political apparatus to maintain social order and wore down what strength it retained. The peasant movement at the end of the empire has been reproached for having scarcely transformed its objectives compared with earlier peasant uprisings,

[158] Chung-kuo shih-hsueh hui Chi-nan fen-hui, comp. *Shan-tung chin-tai shih tzu-liao* (Materials on the modern history of Shantung), 2.5–64. Ch'ai Te-keng *et al.* eds. *Hsin-hai ko-ming* (The 1911 Revolution), 3.465–79.

[159] Cf. Myers, *The Chinese peasant economy*, and the remarks of Albert Feuerwerker, *Rebellion in nineteenth-century China*, 74.

[160] Maeda Katsutarō, 'Shindai no Kanton ni okeru nōmin tōsō no kiban' (Basis of peasants' struggle in Kwangtung during the Ch'ing period), *Tōyō gakuhō*, 51.4 (March 1969) 1–38.

for having remained relatively insensitive to the general historical context of foreign penetration into China, for having abandoned the Western-inspired modernist innovations of the Taipings, and for not having been able to look at China from new perspectives.[161] It is true that except for those who rose with republican cooperation – though their political ideology was then dictated from outside and their ideas for rural land reform moderate – these popular uprisings never generated a programme comparable even to that of the Taipings. They never succeeded in delineating any kind of coherent 'revolutionary project'.

However, social evolution accelerated in the wake of this self-styled rebelliousness. The repeated assaults by popular forces shook the political apparatus which protected traditional relations of production, the exploitation of peasants by the elite. This was a primordial factor in the emergence of any revolutionary situation, when all social classes, including the elite, dropped their support of the ruling regime.[162] Actually, the elite reproached the imperial state for its impotence, but they profited from it and they laboured to perpetuate it, after the repression of the Taipings, by local extensions of their power and exactions. Disaffection and defiance on the part of the rural elite grew with a political system which no longer afforded them the necessary support. They also imperceptibly dropped the social conceptions and values of mutual support and collective responsibility which were inherent in this system. The *ssu* (private interest) overtook the *kung* (common interest), as noted by many gentry-literati at the end of the nineteenth century. This was an apparent regression, but this *ssu* was in turn to lead to another *kung*, that of national collectivity. Insecurity and fright at popular fury also encouraged many in the elite to undertake new occupations. This tendency spread through Central China after the wave of riots in 1891, then through the rest of the country following the Boxer Rebellion. This mutation of the elite, as well as their flight towards the cities, arose largely as a result of the pressure from below coupled with their instinct for preserving privileges. These deep-seated feelings are evident in the oft-expressed wishes of new businessmen and the modern elite to create jobs and eliminate the poverty and obscurantism of the masses. Paradoxically, the social premium put on technical expertise, such a distinctive trait of society at the end of the empire, owes perhaps more in the final analysis to the fists of the Boxers than to foreign gunboats or the objurgations of Liang Ch'i-ch'ao. These threatening fists made the establishment rush to new devices in order to keep its position.

---

[161] Cf. Jean Chesneaux, *Le Mouvement paysan chinois, 1840–1949*, 78–85.

[162] See particularly a study by Aleksandra Sergeevna Kostiaeva, *Narodnye dvizheniia v Kitae 1901–1911 gg.* (Popular movements in China, 1901–1911), 107–10.

Popular revolts also played an important role in the newer phenomena of social mobilization, which had touched all social classes by the last years of the monarchy. This did not affect social status or relations of production, but indicated changing attitudes about the place of individual action in society. Each riot was itself a form of social mobilization. More than this, through both imitation and defensive reaction, popular movements incited all social classes to coalesce in order to intervene collectively in public life. There were, for example, initiatives for the formation of self-defence groups, campaigns for the protection or multiplication of modern schools or popular instruction, boycotts and protest rallies in Peking or seats of provincial authority.

Popular insurrections saved the territorial unity of the empire, since foreign powers were dissuaded from their hope of dismembering China by their fear of mass uprisings, particularly their terrifying experience with the Boxers. But while they prevented the break-up of support for national unity, these movements led to the destruction of a traditional system with its interlocking codes of political, social and moral order under the aegis of the Son of Heaven.

The end of the empire did not witness the disappearance of traditional society, but rather its progressive dislocation. The scholar gentry splintered and broke from its ancient association with the monarchy. New privileged groups arose: a military caste, a modern elite including a business bourgeoisie, a landed oligarchy. Village communities lost their cohesion: organizations of mutual help and assistance among clans became more restrictive; displaced labourers crowding into cities (where they were ill-received by guilds) in their search for work became more numerous, as did those with neither means of support nor places to live. This dislocation was not only horizontal, but also vertical. The social structure began to give way little by little, weakened by forces arising from the lower reaches. The Taiping Rebellion marked the start of this breakdown, and its major effect was perhaps not so much that it tarnished the respect and confidence of the people for their masters, but rather that it modified the link between the imperial government and the traditional ruling class by encouraging the latter to assume greater local power. This served to strip the sovereign and his agents of their function as arbiters and regulators, thereby depriving them of their most efficacious means of holding power. Throughout the following decades, the harassment by popular revolts, the extension of foreign influence, and the manifest impotence of the political system to maintain social stability, further maimed the mechanisms of integration and articulation. The newly forming urbanized elite sought to found a novel political order and turned its back on the traditional world of the countryside, on its constraints as well as its solidarity.

Thus it was a disjointed social system whose structure was decapitated with the imperial abdication on 12 February 1912. Social transformations at the end of the Ch'ing dynasty were at once the cause and the consequence of weakening political authority. There is perhaps an obvious specificity in the particularly strict correlation between social phenomena and political phenomena, a specificity resulting from the traditional ways of organization in the Chinese world and from imperial Confucianism as a universal and all-inclusive system. Finally, the effects of the conjuncture were articulated through secular trends: foreign relations further enhanced commercial development, the social status of merchants, and the integration of the several regions within the empire. Along with natural disaster, they also contributed to the rising difficulties of the rural communities.

China in 1911 offered the double perspective of a disjointed society which was also the breeding ground for a host of new social forces, such as new armies, a modern elite, and revolutionaries, which coalesced in opposition to the dynasty in 1911. This new life could not be masked by the remaining outline of a society which had been slowly bereft of its soul and its spirit. Unsure of its identity, and based uncertainly on an extreme variety of regional conditions, Young China, as it was then called, was perhaps no more than froth on the surface. *Nouveaux riches*, young officers, vibrant intellectuals of the big cities – could they possibly have succeeded in putting an end to the monarchy had they not been aided by a long attrition of imperial power effected by popular pressure? But was it even the assault of Young China which finally brought about the abdication of the emperor? Was it not the pallor and then the effacement of political willpower in the highest echelon? As an urban uprising, the Revolution of 1911 has been interpreted as the offspring of unprecedented social changes after the opium wars, and as the brainchild of an urbanized elite which had turned its back on the old world of the agrarian empire and now looked to the West for new techniques of political organization and economic development. However, though the republic was now in the hands of the new elite, the downfall of the empire which gave birth to it had been the gradual achievement of profound movements within the whole countryside.

BIBLIOGRAPHICAL ESSAYS

I. ECONOMIC TRENDS IN THE LATE CH'ING EMPIRE, 1870–1911

No satisfactory synthetic treatment of China's modern economic history has been published in any language. A two-volume Hong Kong collection of photo-lithographed reprints of forty-six articles on modern economic and social history published in the People's Republic and Taiwan during 1953–67 gives some indication of the state of the field: *Chung-kuo chin san-pai-nien she-hui ching-chi shih lun-chi* (Collected articles on China's social and economic history in the last 300 years). Twenty-one important older articles originally published in the journal *Chung-kuo she-hui ching-chi shih chi-k'an* (Chinese Social and Economic History Review) between 1932 and 1949 have also been conveniently reprinted: *Chung-kuo chin-tai she-hui ching-chi shih lun-chi* (Collected articles on China's modern social and economic history).

Published sources for the economy in the late Ch'ing period include two large collections of documents photographically reproduced from the archives of the Tsungli Yamen and the Ministry of Foreign Affairs: Chung-yang yen-chiu-yuan chin-tai-shih yen-chiu-so (Academia Sinica, Institute of Modern History), *Hai-fang tang* (Archives on coastal defence), which cover the purchase of foreign weapons and the establishment of arsenals and machine shops, telegraphs and railways in the period 1861–1911; and *idem, K'uang-wu tang* (Archives on mining affairs) for the years 1865–1911.

Substantial quantities of raw data – more often consisting of excerpts from relatively inaccessible printed sources than of previously unpublished documents, and sometimes arranged under tendentious headings – were assembled and published in the first decade of the People's Republic. Li Wen-chih, comp. *Chung-kuo chin-tai nung-yeh shih tzu-liao ti-i chi, 1840–1911* (Source materials on the history of agriculture in modern China, first collection, 1840–1911) includes an extensive bibliography. The first two volumes of P'eng Tse-i, comp. *Chung-kuo chin-tai shou-kung-yeh shih tzu-liao, 1840–1949* (Source materials on the history of handicraft industry in modern China, 1840–1949) cover the late Ch'ing. On factory industry before World War I, see Sun Yü-t'ang, comp. *Chung-kuo chin-tai kung-yeh shih tzu-liao, ti-i chi, 1840–1895 nien* (Source materials on the history of industry in China, 1st collection, 1840–1895); and Wang Ching-yü, comp.

Chung-kuo chin-tai kung-yeh shih tzu-liao, ti-erh chi, 1895–1914 nien (Source materials on the history of modern industry in China, 2nd collection, 1895–1914). Documents on the history of railways are collected in Mi Ju-ch'eng, comp. *Chung-kuo chin-tai t'ieh-lu shih tzu-liao, 1863–1911* (Source materials on the history of railways in modern China, 1863–1911). But the most important single source on transportation and communications is National Government, Ministries of Communications and Railroads (Chiao-t'ung t'ieh-tao pu chiao-t'ung shih pien-tsuan wei-yuan hui), *Chiao-t'ung shih* (History of transport and communications). Microfilm and 'a grand table of contents' published in 1970 and available at Center for Chinese Research Materials, Washington, DC, provide access to the 23,776 pages of documents in this collection. Very detailed data on foreign loans appear in Hsu I-sheng, *Chung-kuo chin-tai wai-chai shih t'ung-chi tzu-liao, 1853–1927* (Statistical materials on the history of China's foreign loans, 1853–1927). Yen Chung-p'ing *et al.* comps. *Chung-kuo chin-tai ching-chi shih t'ung-chi tzu-liao hsuan-chi* (Selected statistics on China's modern economic history) draws on a wide range of sources which are carefully noted, but the compiler sometimes ignores the index number problem.

For foreign trade and much else the voluminous publications of the Chinese Maritime Customs are indispensable. These have now been made available on microfilm by the Center for Chinese Research Materials, Washington, DC. The trade statistics are usefully collated, with full reference to the original sources, in Hsiao Liang-lin, *China's foreign trade statistics, 1864–1949*.

The monographic literature is scanty. Probably the best place to begin is with the relevant sections of G. William Skinner *et al.* eds. *Modern Chinese society: an analytical bibliography* which covers publications in Western, Chinese and Japanese languages, dealing with the period 1644–1972.

Among many monographs on particular subjects, the following may be noted. On agriculture, in addition to the work of John Lossing Buck, see Dwight H. Perkins, *Agricultural development in China, 1368–1968*, a brilliant study showing how expansion of cultivated acreage and increased yields per acre enabled China's farmers to feed a growing population; and Amano Motonosuke, *Shina nōgyō keizai ron* (On the Chinese agricultural economy), a massive summary of the available data on the twentieth-century economy until 1949, but valuable for the previous century as well. A fair amount of scholarly attention has been given to modern manufacturing and mining, but little to handicrafts. Albert Feuerwerker, *China's early industrialization: Sheng Hsuan-huai (1844–1916) and mandarin enterprise* defines the nature of late-Ch'ing industrialization. On military industries, see Wang Erh-min, *Ch'ing chi ping-kung-yeh ti hsing-ch'i* (The rise of the armaments industry in the late Ch'ing period). On railways, Li Kuo-ch'i, *Chung-kuo tsao-ch'i ti t'ieh-lu ching-ying* (China's early railway enterprises). On steamships, Kwang-Ching Liu, *Anglo-American steamship rivalry in China, 1862–1874*. On mining, Ellsworth C. Carlson, *The Kaiping mines, 1877–1912: a case study of early Chinese industrialization*. Yen Chung-p'ing, *Chung-kuo mien-fang-chih shih-kao* (Draft history of the Chinese cotton industry) is the best available study of a single industry. The impact of foreign industrial investment is well-handled in Chi-ming Hou, *Foreign investment and economic development in China, 1849–1937*. On population, see Ping-ti Ho, *Studies on the population of China, 1368–1953*. The administration and size of the land tax are treated in Yeh-chien Wang, *Land taxation in imperial China, 1750–1911*, and the fiscally important salt monopoly in Saeki Tomi, *Shindai ensei no kenkyū* (A study of the Ch'ing salt administration). On the monetary system, see Yang Tuan-liu, *Ch'ing-tai huo-pi chin-jung shih kao* (Draft history of money and money markets in the Ch'ing period), and Frank H. H. King, *Money and monetary policy in China, 1845–1895*.

The several essays in three recent volumes of conference papers touch on many aspects of the late-Ch'ing economy: W. E. Willmott, ed. *Economic organization in Chinese society*; Mark Elvin and G. William Skinner, eds. *The Chinese city between two worlds*; Dwight H. Perkins, ed. *China's modern economy in historical perspective*.

2. LATE CH'ING FOREIGN RELATIONS, 1866–1905

The study of Chinese diplomatic history of the late Ch'ing period must be multi-archival, multi-lingual and inter-disciplinary. It must begin with documented studies in the several major languages, and be supplemented by consideration of the Chinese social, political, economic, intellectual and psychological milieu which set the stage for China's foreign relations. This approach, combining the methods of history and the social sciences, naturally contrasts with the research of the nineteenth and early twentieth centuries, when Europeans and Americans studying China were either sinologues concentrating on language and culture or foreign relations specialists employing only Western materials. Thus the pioneering work of H. B. Morse was based mostly on British sources, while Henri Cordier used primarily French materials, and Tyler Dennett relied mostly on American documents. Although their works led the way at the time, by today's standards they constitute essentially histories of British, French and American diplomacy concerning China. By relying so fully on their national sources, they not only ignored Chinese materials and Chinese perspectives but also failed to achieve a multi-archival approach even to Western sources. A new standard was set by William L. Langer's *The diplomacy of imperialism, 1890–1902* first published in 1935, but East Asian sources were still largely absent from its purview.

Since the 1930s, scholars have been able to avoid the old intellectual parochialism and to include the study of Chinese sources in their attempts to understand the Chinese perspective. When Chinese materials relating to Ch'ing foreign affairs became available in quantity in 1930, a new age of Chinese diplomatic history began. Under the influence particularly of T. F. Tsiang (Chiang T'ing-fu) a new generation of Chinese and Western scholars emerged, employing both Chinese and Western materials and gradually subjecting their researches to modern historical and social science standards. Their endeavours blossomed in the 1940s and 1950s, enhanced Western knowledge of China, and initiated a multi-archival approach to Chinese diplomatic history. The importance of Japanese scholarship on modern China was increasingly recognized. There has also been a clear effort to understand Marxist scholarship on China, which offers data and interpretations often unknown to non-Marxist scholars.

The principal Chinese documentary collections in this field are the following (though this is only a selection and it omits the papers of individual officials):

1. *Ch'ing-tai ch'ou-pan i-wu shih-mo* (Complete record of the management of barbarian affairs), T'ung-chih period, 1862–74, 100 *chüan*.

2. Wang Yen-wei and Wang Liang, comps. *Ch'ing-chi wai-chiao shih-liao* (Historical materials concerning foreign relations in the late Ch'ing period, 1875–1911), 218 *chüan* plus an introductory *chüan* and 24 *chüan* for the Hsuan-t'ung period (1909–1911).

3. *Ch'ing Kuang-hsu ch'ao Chung-Jih chiao-she shih-liao* (Historical materials concerning Sino-Japanese negotiations during the Kuang-hsu period, 1875–1908), 88 *chüan*.

4. Chung-yang yen-chiu-yuan chin-tai-shih yen-chiu-so, ed. *Ch'ing-chi Chung-Jih-Han kuan-hsi shih-liao* (Documents on Sino-Japanese–Korean relations, 1864–1911), 11 vols.

5. *Ch'ing Kuang-hsu ch'ao Chung-Fa chiao-she shih-liao* (Historical materials concerning Sino-French negotiations during the Kuang-hsu period), 22 *chüan*.

6. Chung-yang yen-chiu-yuan chin-tai-shih yen-chiu-so, ed. *Chung-Fa Yueh-nan chiao-she tang* (Archives on Sino-French negotiations over Vietnam), 7 vols.

7. *Ta-Ch'ing li-ch'ao shih-lu* (Veritable records of successive reigns of the Ch'ing dynasty), 4,485 *chüan*.

8. *Ch'ing-shih kao* (A draft history of the Ch'ing dynasty), 536 *chüan*; punctuated and indexed edn, *Ch'ing-shih* (Taipei, 1961–2, 8 vols.).

9. *Kung-chung-tang Kuang-hsu ch'ao tsou-che* (Secret palace memorials of the Kuang-hsu period), 26 vols.

10. Chung-yang yen-chiu-yuan chin-tai-shih yen-chiu-so, comp. *Chung-Mei kuan-hsi shih-liao* (Historical documents on Sino-American relations, 1805–74), 3 vols.

11. Shao Hsun-cheng *et al.* eds. *Chung-Fa chan-cheng* (The Sino-French War), 7 vols.

12. Shao Hsun-cheng *et al.* eds. *Chung-Jih chan-cheng* (The Sino-Japanese War), 7 vols.

13. Chien Po-tsan *et al.* eds. *I-ho t'uan* (The Boxers), 4 vols.

On the types, uses and transmission of Ch'ing documents, see John K. Fairbank and Ssu-yü Teng, *Ch'ing administration: three studies*; on court procedures and policies, Silas H. L. Wu, *Communication and imperial control in China: evolution of the palace memorial system*.

There are of course numerous series of published volumes of documentation giving the Japanese, Korean and European records of those countries' diplomatic relations, including their relations with China. For Japan see James

Morley, ed. *Japan's foreign policy, 1868–1941: a research guide*; also Kuo, T'ing-yee, comp., and James Morley, ed. *Sino–Japanese relations, 1862–1927: a checklist of the Chinese Foreign Ministry Archives.*

Since British policy played a leading role in late Ch'ing foreign relations, the available archives are of major value. In addition to the familiar published documents (such as the Parliamentary Papers including selections of China Correspondence, and Hansard's Parliamentary Debates) one may also consult the Foreign Office documents on China at the Public Record Office in London, especially: FO 17. China Political Correspondence, 1815–1905; FO 371. Political Correspondence, 1906–32; FO 228. China Consular Correspondence, 1834–1930; FO 405. Confidential Prints on China, 1848–1954; FO 233. Chinese Secretary's Office, Legation File; and FO 682. Chinese Secretary's Office, Legation File, 1839–1939. See also Hui-min Lo, *Foreign Office confidential papers relative to China and her neighbouring countries, 1840–1914, with an additional list, 1915–1937.* There has also been a massive reprinting, *British Parliamentary Papers*, China, 19th century, by the Irish University Press Area Studies Series in 42 vols.

In the United States the files have been made available on microfilm. In addition to the published *Foreign relations of the United States, 1866–*, there are available from the National Archives *China: dispatches, China: instructions* and *China: consular reports*, all microfilmed for the period 1844–1906. Dispatches, instructions and consular reports after 1906 may be seen in the National Archives, Washington, DC. See *Catalogue of National Archives Microfilm Publications.*

On Russian materials, which remain under-utilized, see *Krasnyi arkhiv, istoricheskii zhurnal* (Red archives, historical journal, 1922–41), 104 vols.; and Leonid S. Rubinchak, comp. and trans., Louise M. Boutella and Gordon W. Tgayer, eds. *A digest of Krasnyi Arkhiv: a historical journal of the Central Archive Department of the U.S.S.R.* 106 vols. See also entries in P. E. Skachkov, ed. *Bibliografiia Kitaia* (Bibliography on China); Sergei Leonidovich Tikhvinskii, ed. *Man'chzhurskoe vladychestvo v Kitae* (Manchu dominion in China); and G. V. Efimov, *Istoriko-bibliograficheskii obzor istochnikov i literatury po novoi istorii Kitaia* (Historical-bibliographical review of the sources concerning the literature on the modern history of China), 3 vols.

The following are among the more important recent secondary works. On the inauguration of diplomatic relations, see Masataka Banno, *China and the West, 1858–1861: the origins of the Tsungli Yamen*, and Immanuel C. Y. Hsu, *China's entrance into the family of nations: the diplomatic phase, 1858–1880.*

On the acceleration of imperialism in frontier areas see: John K. Fairbank, ed. *The Chinese world order: traditional China's foreign relations* for background information; T. F. Tsiang, 'Sino-Japanese diplomatic relations, 1870–1894', *Chinese Social and Political Science Review*, 17 (1933) 1–106; Immanuel C. Y. Hsu, *The Ili crisis: a study of Sino-Russian diplomacy, 1871–1881*; Li En-han, *Tseng Chi-tse ti wai-chiao* (Tseng Chi-tse's diplomacy); Lloyd E. Eastman, *Throne and mandarins: China's search for a policy during the Sino-French controversy, 1880–1885*; John F.

Cady, *The roots of French imperialism in Eastern Asia*; and Shao Hsun-cheng, *Chung-Fa Yueh-nan kuan-hsi shih-mo* (A complete account of Sino-French relations concerning Vietnam (until 1885)).

On Japanese aggression in Korea see: Hilary Conroy, *The Japanese seizure of Korea, 1868–1910: a study of realism and idealism in international relations*; and Wang Hsin-chung, *Chung-Jih chia-wu chan-cheng chih wai-chiao pei-ching* (The diplomatic background of the Sino-Japanese War); Lin Ming-te, *Yuan Shih-k'ai yü Ch'ao-hsien* (Yuan Shih-k'ai and Korea); C. I. Eugene Kim and Han-Kyo Kim, *Korea and the politics of imperialism 1876–1910*; Ching Young Choe, *The rule of the Taewŏn'gun, 1864–1873: Restoration in Yi Korea*; Marius B. Jansen, *Japan and China: from war to peace, 1894–1972*, ch. 4.

On the threatened partition of China and the Boxer Uprising see: John E. Schrecker, *Imperialism and Chinese nationalism: Germany in Shantung*; Victor Purcell, *The Boxer uprising*; Chester C. T'an, *The Boxer catastrophe*; Peter Fleming, *The siege at Peking*; Edmund S. Wehrle, *Britain, China, and the antimissionary riots, 1891–1900*; and L. K. Young, *British policy in China, 1895–1902*.

On Russian activities in Manchuria during 1900–5, see George A. Lensen, ed. *The Russo-Chinese War*, and Ch'en Fu-kuang, *Yu-Ch'ing i-tai chih Chung-O kuan-hsi* (Sino-Russian relations during the Ch'ing dynasty).

On the Anglo-Japanese Alliance, see Ian H. Nish, *The Anglo-Japanese Alliance: the diplomacy of two island empires, 1894–1907*.

On American involvement in Manchuria, see Michael H. Hunt, *Frontier defense and the open door: Manchuria in Chinese–American relations, 1895–1911*.

3. CHANGING CHINESE VIEWS OF WESTERN RELATIONS, 1840–95

Historical sources for the study of China's perception of Western relations during the late Ch'ing period are rich but scattered. The main source materials on the outspoken scholar-officials are their own writings. Some of these have been included in the massive documentary collections published under the auspices of the Chinese Historical Association, especially Ch'i Ssu-ho. *et al.* eds. *Ya-p'ien chan-cheng* (The Opium War), Shao Hsun-cheng *et al.* eds. *Chung-Fa chan-cheng* (The Sino-French War) and Chung-kuo k'o-hsueh yuan *et al.* eds. *Yang-wu yun tung* (The Western affairs movement). However, the most important primary source is still the official compilation *Ch'ing-tai ch'ou-pan i-wu shih-mo* (Complete record of the management of barbarian affairs). The recent publication, Chung-yang yen-chiu-yuan chin-tai-shih yen-chiu-so, comp. *Chin-tai Chung-kuo tui Hsi-fang chi lieh-ch'iang jen-shih tzu-liao hui-pien* (Compendium of materials on modern Chinese understanding of the West and of the various powers), is a comprehensive collection for the period 1821–61. The best annotated collection in English translation covering documents of the late Ch'ing period from 1839 is still Ssu-yü Teng and John K. Fairbank, *China's response to the West: a documentary survey 1839–1923*. For general observations on Chinese attitudes towards the West, consult Wang Erh-min's recent work,

Wan-Ch'ing cheng-chih ssu-hsiang shih-lun (Studies on the history of political thought in the late Ch'ing period).

The traditional Chinese world view, which significantly influenced China's conception of the West in modern times, can be seen in James Legge, trans. *The Chinese classics*, and in Naba Toshisada's well-known study, *Chūka shisō* (Sino-centrism). The authoritative study of this topic is John K. Fairbank, ed. *The Chinese world order: traditional China's foreign relations*. For the re-emergence of the statecraft school, which figured prominently in China's attitude towards the West, researchers will want to examine the important collection, Ho Ch'ang-ling, *Huang-ch'ao ching-shih wen-pien* (Collection of Ch'ing dynasty writings on state-craft) and its several sequels. A valuable study of one of the statecraft scholars is Wang Chia-chien, *Wei Yuan tui Hsi-fang ti jen-shih chi ch'i hai-fang ssu hsiang* (Wei Yuan's knowledge of the West and his ideas regarding maritime defence).

Mid-nineteenth-century Chinese recognition of a 'changed situation' among some scholar-officials is examined in Wang Erh-min, *Chung-kuo chin-tai ssu-hsiang shih-lun* (Historical essays on modern Chinese thought), chs. 2 and 6. But there was no consensus of opinion as to the best way of dealing with this unprecented situation. The spectrum of these views can be seen partly in the geographical series, *Hsiao-fang-hu chai yü-ti ts'ung-ch'ao* (Geographical series of Hsiao-fang-hu studio), and in Ko Shih-chün, comp. *Huang-ch'ao ching-shih-wen hsu pien* (Collection of Ch'ing dynasty writings on statecraft, continued), and Sheng K'ang, comp. *Huang-ch'ao ching-shih-wen hsu-pien*, two works with the same title but different content. China's first envoy to the West is the topic of the well-researched study, by Kuo T'ing-i *et al. Kuo Sung-tao hsien-sheng nien-p'u* (A chronological biography of Kuo Sung-tao); and Kuo Sung-tao's successor as minister to London is carefully examined in Li En-han, *Tseng Chi-tse ti wai-chiao* (Tseng Chi-tse's diplomacy). For the views of those enlightened officials who maintained that China had to seize the opportunity of the changed situation and make herself strong, see the multi-volume *Hai-fang tang* (Archives on coastal defence), and Kwang-Ching Liu, 'The Confucian as patriot and pragmatist: Li Hung-chang's formative years, 1823–1866'.

Hao Chang, 'The antiforeignist role of Wo-jen, 1804–1871', examines the intellectual background of a Neo-Confucian high official. Weng T'ung-ho, *Weng T'ung-ho jih-chi p'ai-yin-pen* (A typeset edition of the diary of Weng T'ung-ho) provides detailed information about conservatism at court. For the attitudes of a politically active group of young, pedantic and inexperienced literati-officials, see Yen-p'ing Hao, 'A study of the Ch'ing-liu tang: the disinterested scholar-official group, 1875–1884', and Lloyd E. Eastman, *Throne and mandarins: China's search for a policy during the Sino-French controversy, 1880–1885.* For sympathetic studies on key figures of conservatism see Lu Pao-ch'ien, 'Wo-jen lun' (On Wo-jen), in *CYCT*, and Li Tsung-t'ung and Liu Feng-han, *Li Hung-tsao hsien-sheng nien-p'u* (Chronological biography of Li Hung-tsao), on the powerful grand councillor and imperial tutor. The latter, co-authored by a grandson of Li Hung-tsao, contains many rare and previously unpublished documents, including Li's letters and diaries. The anti-Christian views are skilfully examined in Paul A. Cohen, *China and Christianity: the missionary movement and the growth of Chinese antiforeignism, 1860–1870*, which emphasizes the cultural incompatibility between Confucianism and Christianity; see also Lü Shih-ch'iang, *Chung-kuo kuan-shen fan-chiao ti yuan-yin* (Causes behind the Chinese gentry-officials' hostility towards Christianity, 1860–1874), which besides stressing the role of Western imperialism analyses the Confucian view of 'man, barbarian and beast'.

For the awareness of national sovereignty and the adoption of the theory of balance of power in international affairs consult: Lü Shih-ch'iang, *Ting Jih-ch'ang yü tzu-ch'iang yun-tung* (Ting Jih-ch'ang and the self-strengthening movement); Li Kuo-ch'i, *Chang Chih-tung ti wai-chiao cheng-ts'e* (Chang Chih-tung's foreign policy proposals); Banno Masataka, 'Furansu ryūgaku jidai no Ba Ken-chū – gaikō oyobi gaikōkan seidō ni tsuite no futatsu no ikensho' (Ma Chien-chung during his days of study in France – two proposals regarding foreign relations and the foreign service system). Mercantile nationalism in the treaty ports is emphasized in Paul A. Cohen, *Between tradition and modernity: Wang T'ao and reform in late Ch'ing China*, Yen-p'ing Hao, *The comprador in nineteenth century China: bridge between East and West*, and Wang Erh-min, *Chung-kuo chin-tai ssu-hsiang shih-lun*, ch. 5.

4. THE MILITARY CHALLENGE

Late Ch'ing military institutions are surveyed in Ralph L. Powell, *The rise of Chinese military power 1895–1912*, and in Richard J. Smith, 'Chinese military institutions in the mid-nineteenth century, 1850–1860'. The mid-nineteenth-century development is analysed in Philip A. Kuhn, *Rebellion and its enemies in late imperial China: militarization and social structure*. Kuhn goes beyond Lo Erh-kang's *Hsiang-chün hsin-chih* (A new history of the Hunan Army) in stressing the local defence forces or *t'uan-lien*. At a 'higher level of militarization', the concrete arrangements for the Hunan Army are discussed in Wang Erh-min's 1973 article 'Ch'ing-tai yung-ying chih-tu' (The 'Brave Battalion' system of the Ch'ing dynasty).

On the Green Standard Army, Lo Erh-kang, *Lü-ying ping-chih* is still standard. *Kung-chung-tang Kuang-hsu ch'ao tsou-che* (Secret palace memorials of the Kuang-hsu period) includes provincial reports on the deployment of 'retrained Green Standard forces' (*lien-chün*) to prevent or to suppress popular risings.

On foreign influence upon the Ch'ing armies, Richard J. Smith, *Mercenaries and mandarins: the Ever-Victorious Army in nineteenth century China* puts F. T. Ward and C. G. Gordon in historical perspective. See also the same author's 'The employment of foreign military talents: Chinese tradition and late Ch'ing practice'. Among contemporaneous Western writings, J. Lamprey, 'The economy of the Chinese Army' (1867), is perceptive though condescending. A series of competent foreigners wrote on Ch'ing military affairs, for example Emory Upton (1878), Mark Bell (1884), James Harrison Wilson (1887) and

A. E. J. Cavendish (1898), but they could not penetrate the political and fiscal background and organizational principles of the *yung-ying*.

On the Muslim rebellions in the north-west, W. L. Bales, *Tso Tsungt'ang: soldier and statesman of old China* differs from nineteenth-century Western writers in admiring Tso's generalship. The limitations of his sources led Bales into numerous errors, as pointed out in Wen-Djang Chu's monograph (1966) *The Moslem Rebellion in northwest China, 1862–1878*, which is the best book on the Ch'ing war against the Muslims in Shensi and Kansu. Like all of us, Chu had to use indirect sources regarding Tso's Muslim enemies. Pai Shou-i, the leading Chinese Muslim scholar, could produce in *Hui-min ch'i-i* only two short documents written by the Chinese Muslims in Shensi and Kansu. Chu's monograph, reinforced by Immanuel C. Y. Hsu's 1968 article, 'The late Ch'ing reconquest of Sinkiang: a reappraisal of Tso Tsung-t'ang's role', leaves no doubt that the Ch'ing dynasty, by coercing the provinces to produce 'inter-provincial revenue assistance', expended very large resources in the north-west campaigns, from 1868 at least until Sinkiang became a province in 1884. Study of China's *coastal* self-strengthening has usually neglected this Inner Asian perspective.

Opinions progressively in favour of coastal defence, 1840–94, are surveyed in a 1967 article by Wang Chia-chien, 'Ch'ing-chi ti hai-fang lun'. K. H. Kim, *The last phase of the East Asian world order: Korea, Japan, and the Chinese empire, 1860–1882* stresses Li Hung-chang's alertness to Japanese designs upon Korea as early as the 1870s. The difficulties and disasters of Li's naval effort are vividly described in John L. Rawlinson, *China's struggle for naval development 1839–1895*. Empress Dowager Tz'u-hsi's squandering of funds earmarked for coastal defence on palace gardens is carefully documented by Pao Tsun-p'eng (1969). Li's responsibility for China's defeat by Japan in 1894–5 is stressed by Liang Chia-pin (1975). Existing secondary works merely begin, however, to explore the court policies and entrenched institutions contributing to Li's deteriorating military capacity.

Among non-Chinese sources there are, for example, at least two French versions (Ferdinand Lecomte and Captain Armengaud) of how the Chinese won their surprise victory at Langson late in March 1885. James G. Scott, the British observer, provides concrete details in his 1886 article, 'The Chinese brave'. The Japanese wartime periodical *Nisshin sensō jikki* (Actual record of the Japan–Ch'ing War) remains the most detailed chronicle of the war, more valuable than the official histories compiled by the army general staff (Sambōhombu) in 1904–7 or by the naval general staff (Kaigun gunreibu) in 1905. At present, no one-volume military history, in any language, of either the Sino-French or the Sino-Japanese War, can be recommended.

Regarding Sinkiang and Taiwan as frontier areas, Owen Lattimore *et al. Pivot of Asia: Sinkiang and the Inner Asian frontiers of China and Russia* remains the best survey of the oasis scene and the various ethnic groups, Anglo-Russian rivalry, and the Russian policy of indirect domination through the Han Chinese. Tseng Wen-wu, *Chung-kuo ching-ying Hsi-yü shih* (History of China's management of the Western Region), reflects Han ethnocentrism but notes the weaknesses of the Chinese administration after Sinkiang became a province. Leonard H. D. Gordon, ed. *Taiwan: studies in Chinese local history* is an excellent brief introduction to the island's nineteenth-century situation. Kuo T'ing-i, *T'ai-wan shih-shih kai-shuo* (A general account of Taiwan history) is a mainlander's history which yet gives the early migrants full credit for developing the island.

For other works on China's military 'self-strengthening', 1860–94, see *Cambridge history of China*, vol. 10, 'Bibliographical essay 10', pp. 608–11.

5. INTELLECTUAL CHANGE AND THE REFORM MOVEMENT 1890–8

The reform movement of the 1890s is an under-researched subject. Its full-scale history is yet to be written in any language. The four-volume collection of materials compiled in the early 1950s by Chien Po-tsan *et al. Wu-hsu pien-fa* (The reform of 1898), still stands as the most useful introduction to research on this subject. Researchers will certainly want to consult the bibliography, which is still the most complete one available regarding the original sources.

The lack of a full-scale, systematic account in Chinese is somewhat compensated for by a number of collections of articles, by far the best of which is T'ang Chih-chün, *Wu-hsu pien-fa shih lun-ts'ung* (A collection of articles on the reform movement of 1898). The same author's *Wu-hsu pien-fa jen-wu chuan-kao* (Draft biographies of participants in the reform of 1898) is a convenient compendium of biographical information on many of the personalities involved. Huang Chang-chien, *Wu-hsu pien-fa shih yen-chiu* (Studies on the history of the reform movement of 1898) is a mine of information which, however, needs to be used critically. An analysis of the Western and Japanese influences on the reform movement is supplied by Wang Shu-huai, *Wai-jen yü Wu-hsu pien-fa* (Foreigners and the reform movement of 1898). The best study of the court politics of the reform era is Kung-chuan Hsiao, 'Weng T'ung-ho and the reform movement of 1898'. Kwang-ching Liu, 'Nineteenth-century China: the disintegration of the old order and the impact of the West', provides a general interpretation of the reform movement and its background.

As for the reform movement in Hunan, the most up-to-date treatment is in Charlton M. Lewis, *Prologue to the Chinese Revolution: the transformation of ideas and institutions in Hunan province, 1891–1907*. A good, comprehensive study of this subject together with a useful bibliography is Lin Neng-shih, *Ch'ing-chi Hu-nan ti hsin-cheng yun-tung* (The movement for new policies in late Ch'ing Hunan).

The best general discussion of the intellectual background of the reform movement is Onogawa Hidemi, *Shimmatsu seiji shisō kenkyū* (Studies in political thought of the late Ch'ing). For the intellectual stirrings prior to 1895, Paul A. Cohen, *Between tradition and modernity: Wang T'ao and reform in late Ch'ing China*, and Lloyd E. Eastman, 'Political reformism in China before the Sino-Japanese

War', *JAS*, 27.4 (Aug. 1968) 695–710, provide a good introduction. Kung-chuan Hsiao, *A modern China and a new world: K'ang Yu-wei, reformer and utopian, 1858–1927* offers the most comprehensive and detailed study of K'ang Yu-wei's thought. Richard C. Howard, 'K'ang Yu-wei (1858–1927): his intellectual background and his early thought', in Arthur F. Wright and Denis Twitchett, eds. *Confucian personalities*, and 'Japan's role in the reform program of K'ang Yu-wei', in Jung-pang Lo, ed. *K'ang Yu-wei: a biography and a symposium*, are useful for understanding the formation of K'ang's reformist outlook. Li Che-hou, *K'ang Yu-wei T'an Ssu-t'ung ssu-hsiang yen-chiu* (A study of the thought of K'ang Yu-wei and T'an Ssu-t'ung) is an illuminating study of two closely related minds within the reformist camp, in spite of the study's Marxist ideological straitjacket. For understanding the broad ideological spectrum of reformism see: Benjamin Schwartz, *In search of wealth and power: Yen Fu and the West*; Don C. Price, *Russia and the roots of the Chinese Revolution, 1896–1911*; and Hao Chang, *Liang Ch'i-ch'ao and intellectual transition in China*.

There has been little monographic study of the intellectual critics and opponents of reformism apart from Ch'en Ch'iu's pioneering essay, 'Wu-hsu cheng-pien-shih fan pien-fa jen-wu chih cheng-chih ssu-hsiang' (Political thought of the opponents of reform at the time of the coup d'état of 1898), *Yen-ching hsueh-pao*, 25 (1939) 59–106. Further use can be made of the following two sources: Chang Chih-tung, *Ch'üan-hsueh p'ien* (Exhortation to study); and Su Yü, *I-chiao ts'ung-pien* (Collection of writings for upholding sacred teachings), where the main arguments against reformism, especially those attacking the K'ang-Liang group, are presented.

A wealth of new and sometimes untested ideas, mainly from current research, is provided in the symposium volume edited by Paul A. Cohen and John E. Schrecker, *Reform in nineteenth-century China*. Though it is focused on a later period, stimulus may also be found in the conference volume edited by Charlotte Furth, *The limits of change: essays on conservative alterations in Republican China*.

6. JAPAN AND THE CHINESE REVOLUTION OF 1911

The impact of events in China on late Tokugawa Japan is treated by Ayuzawa Shintarō in Kaikoku Hyakunen Kinen Bunka Jigyōkai, ed. *Sakoku jidai Nihonjin no kaigai chishiki* (Japanese knowledge of the outside world during the era of seclusion). Pages 135–44 of this work, where he discusses the editions and influence of Wei Yuan's *Hai-kuo t'u-chih*, form the basis for Wang Chia-chien, 'Hai-kuo t'u-chih tui-yü Jih-pen-ti ying-hsiang' (The influence of the *Hai-kuo t'u-chih* in Japan), in *Ta-lu tsa-chih*, 32.8 (April 1966) 242–9. The impact on Shionoya Tōin (1810–67), an influential Confucian who edited one of the early Japanese editions, is discussed by R. H. van Gulik, 'Kakkaron: a Japanese echo of the Opium War', *Monumenta Serica*, 4 (1939) 478–545. For Sakuma Shōzan's ambivalent reaction to Wei Yuan's appreciation of technology, see excerpts quoted in Ryusaku Tsunoda, Wm. Theodore de Bary and Donald Keene, eds.

Sources of the Japanese tradition, 614. Japanese responses to the Taiping Rebellion are discussed by Ichiko Chūzō, 'Bakumatsu Nihonjin no Taihei Tengoku ni kansuru chishiki' (Japanese knowledge of the Heavenly Kingdom of Great Peace in late Tokugawa times), in Kaikoku Hyakunen Kinen Bunka Jigyōkai, ed. *Meiji bunkashi ronshū* (Essays in Meiji cultural history), 453–95, and less rigorously by Masui Tsuneo in *Taihei tengoku* (The Heavenly Kingdom of Great Peace). Etō Shinkichi, 'Nihonjin no Chūgoku-kan: Takasugi Shinsaku ra no baai' (Japanese views of China: the cases of Takasugi Shinsaku and others), in *Niida Noboru Hakushi tsuitō rombunshū* (Essays to commemorate Dr Niida Noboru), vol. 3: *Nihon hō to Ajia* (Japanese law and Asia), 53–71, discusses three important diaries of travellers to Shanghai.

The reformers' knowledge of Japan has attracted much scholarly attention. Richard C. Howard, 'Japan's role in the reform program of K'ang Yu-wei', in Jung-pang Lo, ed. *K'ang Yu-wei: a biography and a symposium*, 280–312, outlines the problem. For a survey of information about the Meiji Restoration that was available to the reformers, see P'eng Tse-chou (Hō Taku-shū), 'Kō Yū-i no hempō undō to Meiji ishin' (K'ang Yu-wei's reform movement and the Meiji Restoration), *Jimbun gakuhō*, 30 (1970) 149–93. More recently Professor P'eng has incorporated this as the opening section of his *Chūgoku no kindaika to Meiji Ishin* (The modernization of China and the Meiji Restoration). The same author's 'Ryō Kei-chō no Meiji Ishin kan to Chūgoku henkakuron' (Liang Ch'i-ch'ao's view of the Meiji Restoration and his arguments for reform in China), in Sakata Yoshio and Yoshida Mitsukuni, eds. *Sekaishi no naka no Meiji Ishin: gaikokujin no shikaku kara* (The Meiji Restoration in world history: as seen by foreigners), 61–114, is reprinted as pp. 193–262 of *Chūgoku no kindaika to Meiji Ishin*. On Huang Tsun-hsien see Noriko Kamachi, 'Huang Tsun-hsien (1848–1905): his response to Meiji Japan and the West', (Harvard University, Ph.D. dissertation, 1972). For Liang Ch'i-ch'ao and Huang Tsun-hsien, see: Joseph R. Levenson, *Liang Ch'i-ch'ao and the mind of modern China*, 23–5; George M. Wilson, 'Politics and the people: Liang Ch'i-ch'ao's view of constitutional developments in Meiji Japan before 1890', *Papers on Japan* (1961); and Philip C. Huang, *Liang Ch'i-ch'ao and modern Chinese liberalism*. Wang T'ao is the subject of Paul A. Cohen, *Between tradition and modernity: Wang T'ao and reform in late Ch'ing China*. Cheng Kuan-ying is discussed by Ichiko Chūzō in *Kindai Chūgoku no seiji to shakai* (Politics and society in modern China).

The influences on and content of the thought of K'ang Yu-wei can best be examined in a series of authoritative monographs by Kung-chuan Hsiao: 'Weng T'ung-ho and the reform movement of 1898', *Ch'ing-hua hsueh-pao,* (April 1957); 'The philosophical thought of K'ang Yu-wei: an attempt at a new synthesis', *Monumenta Serica*, 21 (1962); 'The case for constitutional monarchy: K'ang Yu-wei's plan for the democratization of China', *Monumenta Serica*, 24 (1965); 'In and out of Utopia: K'ang Yu-wei's social thought', *The Chung Chi Journal*, 7, 8 (1967–68); 'Economic modernization: K'ang Yu-wei's ideas in historical perspective', *Monumenta Serica*, 27 (1968); and 'Administrative modernization:

K'ang Yu-wei's proposals and their historical meaning', *Ch'ing-hua hsueh-pao*, 8 (1970). Many, but not all, of these have been brought together in the same author's *A modern China and a new world: K'ang Yu-wei, reformer and utopian, 1858–1927*, (1975). Jung-pang Lo has translated K'ang's autobiography and edited a series of essays about him in *K'ang Yu-wei: a biography and a symposium*, (1967).

Cultural interaction and the Chinese student movement in Japan have been the lifelong concern of Sanetō Keishū, whose most authoritative summary appeared in 1960 as *Chūgokujin Nihon ryūgaku shi* (History of Chinese students in Japan); tables and statistical data can be found there. Other works by the same author include *Meiji Nisshi bunka kōshō* (Cultural interchange between China and Japan in the Meiji period); *Chūgokujin Nihon ryūgaku shikō* (Draft history of Chinese students in Japan); and *Nihon bunka no Shina e no eikyō* (The influence of Japanese civilization on China), of which there is also a Shanghai translation of 1944, *Jih-pen wen-hsueh tui Chung-kuo ti ying-hsiang* (Chang Ming-san, trans.). Chinese sources not covered by Sanetō have been utilized in a recent monograph: Huang Fu-ch'ing, *Ch'ing-mo liu-Jih hsueh-sheng* (Late Ch'ing students in Japan), which emphasizes political as well as cultural activities of the students. Student journalism is discussed by Robert A. Scalapino in 'Prelude to Marxism: the Chinese student movement in Japan, 1900–1910', in Albert Feuerwerker, Rhoads Murphey and Mary C. Wright, eds. *Approaches to modern Chinese history*, 190–213. Recollections of former students include those of Sun Po-ch'un (1891–), 'Kajuku, Dōbun Shoin, Minpōsha: Nihon ni ikiru ichi Chūgokujin no kaisō' (Family tutorial, Dōbun Shoin, the *People's Tribune*: the recollections of a Chinese resident in Japan), *Chūgoku*, 30 (May 1966) 24–33, and 'Ryūgakusei: gakkō kyōiku, bempatsu no koto' (Overseas Chinese students, school education, queues), *Chūgoku*, 31 (June 1966) 28–33. Ching Mei-chiu's autobiography, *Ryūnichi kaiko – Chūgoku anakisuto no hansei* (Recollections of a sojourn in Japan – half a life of a Chinese anarchist), trans. Ōtaka Iwao and Hatano Tarō, appeared in Tokyo in 1966 (Peking edition, *Tsui-an* (Record of a 'crime'), 1924).

Discussions of student activities include, in addition to Sanetō, Nagai Kazumi, 'Kyoga gakuseigun o megutte' (Concerning the student army to resist Russia), *Shinshū Daigaku kiyō*, 4 (Sept. 1954) 57–83; and the same author's 'Iwayuru Shinkoku ryūgakusei torishimari kisoku jiken no seikaku: Shimmatsu ryūga-kusei no ichi dōkō' (The nature of the so-called incident involving Ch'ing regulations for controlling overseas students: a movement among Chinese students in Japan towards the end of Ch'ing), *Shinshū Daigaku kiyō*, 2 (July 1952) 31. Shimada Kenji, *Chūgoku kakumei no senkusha tachi* (Forerunners of the Chinese revolution), and *Shingai kakumei no shisō* (The thought behind the Revolution of 1911), translate and discuss a number of student revolutionary tracts including one of Ch'en T'ien-hua. Ernest P. Young, 'Ch'en T'ien-hua (1875–1905): a Chinese nationalist', *Papers on China*, 13 (1959) 113–62, focuses on Ch'en's testament and suicide. The impact and importance of the translation movement is discussed by Tsuen-hsuin Tsien, 'Western impact on China through translation', *FEQ*, 13.3 (May 1954) 318–19. Sanetō Keishū, *Chūgokujin Nihon ryūgaku shi*, 378, adds estimates of vocabulary flow.

The relationships between Japanese activists and Chinese revolutionaries are discussed in Marius B. Jansen, *The Japanese and Sun Yat-sen*, and 'Japanese views of China during the Meiji period', in Feuerwerker, Murphey and Wright, *Approaches to modern Chinese history*, 163–89. See also Ch'en Ku-t'ing, 'Sun Chung-shan hsien-sheng yü Jih-pen ch'ao-yeh p'eng-jen ti kuan-hsi' (Sun Yat-sen and his Japanese friends in and out of the government), in *Chung-Jih wen-hua lun-chi* (Collected essays in Chinese and Japanese cultures). There are bibliographies compiled by Nozawa Yutaka in *Shisō* (Thought) (1957), 79–93, and in a collection of articles in *Chūgoku* (Nov. 1966), both entitled 'Son Bun to Nihon' ('Sun Yat-sen and Japan'). Miyazaki Torazō's memoirs, *Sanjū-sannen no yume* (Thirty-three years' dream) were edited in 1967 with annotation by Etō Shinkichi; and also included in his works, *Miyazaki Tōten zenshū*, ed. Miyazaki Ryūsuke and Onogawa Hidemi. The earliest Chinese translation appeared in 1903. Kayano Chōchi, another close collaborator with Sun, published his account as *Chūka minkoku kakumei hikyū* (Private sources for the Chinese republican revolution) (1940). The diary of Konoe Atsumaro, founder of the Dōbunkai, appeared in Tokyo in 1968–9 as *Konoe Atsumaro nikki*, 6 vols. The Dōbunkai official records together with biographies of members and adherents can be found in Nakajima Masao, ed. *Taishi kaiko roku* (Memoirs concerning China), and a supplement, *Zoku Taishi kaiko roku*. In addition there is a biography of Arao Kiyoshi, *Kyojin Arao Sei* (*Kiyoshi*) (Grand old Arao Sei) by Inoue Masaji. The official history of the Kokuryūkai, with biographies of many of the China activists, is *Tōa senkaku shishi kiden* (Stories and biographies of pioneer East Asian idealists), ed. by Kuzuu Yoshihisa *et al.* For Kita Ikki see George M. Wilson, *Radical nationalist in Japan: Kita Ikki, 1883–1937*; Kita's messages from China are reprinted in Takahashi Masao, ed. *Nihon kindaika to Kyūshū: Kyūshū bunka ronshū* (Kyūshū and Japanese modernization: essays on Kyūshū culture), 4.424–80.

For Japanese government policy during the period of revolution see, in addition to the above: I. H. Nish, 'Japan's indecision during the Boxer disturbances', *JAS* 20.3 (May 1961) 449–61; Ichimata Masao, 'Yamaza Enjirō – Meiji jidai ni okeru tairiku seisaku no jikkōsha' (Yamaza Enjirō: A practitioner of the Japanese policy on the Asian continent in the Meiji era), *Kokusaihō gaikō zasshi*, 72.3 (Oct. 1973) 249–98; and Masaru Ikei, 'Japan's response to the Chinese Revolution of 1911', *JAS*, 25.2 (Feb. 1966) 213–27.

7. POLITICAL AND INSTITUTIONAL REFORM 1901–11

Ch'ing-t'ing chih kai-ko yü fan-tung (Reform and reaction at the Ch'ing court), compiled to commemorate the fiftieth anniversary of the founding of the Republic of China, offers important documentary sources on political and institutional reform. No comprehensive study in English has been published for almost half a century; see Meribeth E. Cameron, *The reform movement in China, 1898–1912*. The following three books provide a general history of Chinese politics during the period: Li Chien-nung, *Chung-kuo chin-pai-nien cheng-chih shih* (A political history of China in the last hundred years); Yano Jin'ichi, *Shinchō masshi kenkyū* (Studies in late Ch'ing history); and Rinji Taiwan kyūkan chōsakai, *Shinkoku gyōseihō* (Administrative laws of the Ch'ing dynasty).

On the constitutional movement see Chang P'eng-yuan, *Li-hsien-p'ai yü hsin-hai ko-ming* (The constitutionalists and the 1911 Revolution). Since Chang's study makes no particular mention of local self-government it may be supplemented with Teraki Tokuko's article, 'Shimmatsu Minkoku shonen no chihō jichi' (Local self-government in late Ch'ing and early republican China), *Ochanomizu shigaku*, 5 (1962). See also Chang Yü-fa, *Ch'ing-chi ti li-hsien t'uan-t'i* (Constitutionalist groups of the late Ch'ing period), which studies the personnel actively involved in the movement; and Samuel C. Chu, *Reformer in modern China: Chang Chien, 1853–1926*, which examines the personal role of one leader. From the People's Republic there are also interpretations of the constitutional issue by Hu Sheng-wu and Chin Ch'ung-chi, *Lun Ch'ing-mo ti li-hsien yun-tung* (On the constitutional movement in late-Ch'ing); and by Li Shih-yueh, *Chang Chien ho li-hsien-p'ai* (Chang Chien and the constitutionalists).

The military system of the late Ch'ing was outlined in 1930 by Wen Kung-chih, *Tsui-chin san-shih-nien Chung-kuo chün-shih shih* (History of Chinese military affairs in the last thirty years); and later in 1970 by Pao Tsun-p'eng, *Chung-kuo hai-chün shih* (History of the Chinese Navy). The system is discussed in further detail in three studies: Ralph L. Powell, *The rise of Chinese military power 1895–1912* and Liu Feng-han, *Hsin-chien lu-chün* (The Newly Created Army (under Yuan Shih-k'ai, 1895–1900)) and *Wu-wei chün* (The Wu-wei Army (under Jung-lu and Yuan Shih-k'ai, 1899–1901)). See also Jerome Chen, *Yuan Shih-k'ai, 1859–1916*.

Ch'en Ch'ing-chih has summarized the educational reform of the time in *Chung-kuo chiao-yü shih* (History of education in China), while the fundamental source materials are contained in the four-volume *Chin-tai Chung-kuo chiao-yü shih-liao* (Historical materials on modern Chinese education), edited by Shu Hsin-ch'eng and published in Shanghai in 1923. See also Wolfgang Franke, *The reform and abolition of the traditional Chinese examination system*; William Ayers, *Chang Chih-tung and educational reform in China*; and Su Yun-feng, *Chang Chih-tung yü Hu-pei chiao-yü kai-ko* (Chang Chih-tung and educational reform in Hupei).

On other aspects monographic work is scanty. For legal reform see Marinus J. Meijer, *The introduction of modern criminal law in China*; also Yang Yu-chiung, *Chin-tai Chung-kuo li-fa shih* (History of legislation in modern China) and Yang Hung-lieh, *Chung-kuo fa-lü fa-ta shih* (Chinese law: the history of its full development). On the currency system see Wei Chien-yu, *Chung-kuo chin-tai huo-pi shih* (History of currency in modern China); P'eng Hsin-wei, *Chung-kuo huo-pi shih* (History of Chinese currency); and Miyashita Tadao, *Chūgoku heisei no tokushu kenkyū: kindai Chūgoku ginryō seido no kenkyū* (A monographic study of the Chinese currency system; a study of the silver tael system of modern China). Two recent books illuminate the social aspects of reform or non-reform in the period 1901–11: Charlton M. Lewis, *Prologue to the Chinese Revolution: the transformation of ideas and institutions in Hunan province, 1891–1907*; and Joseph W. Esherick, *Reform and revolution in China: the 1911 Revolution in Hunan and Hubei*. Daniel H. Bays, *China enters the twentieth century: Chang Chih-tung and the issues of a new age* discusses the response of this statesman to nationalism and reformism.

8. GOVERNMENT, MERCHANTS AND INDUSTRY TO 1911

Chinese merchants during the late Ch'ing, and indeed at other times as well, left precious little record of their activities. For those who became involved with modern enterprise, the best sources are still the published writings of major officials like Li Hung-chang, Chang Chih-tung and Yuan Shih-k'ai. The comprador and industrialist Hsu Jun's remarkable *Hsu Yü-chai tzu-hsu nien-p'u* (Hsu Jun's chronological autobiography) details his several enterprises from the 1860s, but remains a rare exception. In English, Charles J. Stanley, *Late Ch'ing finance: Hu Kuang-yung as an innovator* is at best partial, covering only aspects of Hu's activities over one period of his life. Statistical data on numerous merchants, such as their ownership of companies, amount of investment, purchased ranks and titles, service on chambers of commerce, etc., are included in two records published by the late Ch'ing government: Nung-kung-shang pu t'ung-chi ch'u, comp. *Nung-kung-shang pu t'ung-chi piao, ti-i-tz'u* (Statistical tables of the Ministry of Agriculture, Industry and Commerce, 1st issue; 6 *ts'e*, 1909) and the *ti-erh-tz'u* (2nd issue; 5 *ts'e*, 1910).

Documents and studies relating to major official-entrepreneurs are far more abundant. Sheng Hsuan-huai's papers are collected in *Sheng shang-shu Yü-chai ts'un-kao ch'u-k'an* (Preserved papers of ministry president Sheng Hsüan-huai, 1st issue), and in *Sheng Hsuan-huai wei-k'an hsin-kao* (Unpublished letters of Sheng Hsuan-huai). Albert Feuerwerker, *China's early industrialization: Sheng Hsuan-huai (1844–1916) and mandarin enterprise* is the first systematic study of official participation in modern industry and how it affected industrial development in China during its crucial early phase. Two book-length case studies are Ellsworth C. Carlson, *The Kaiping mines (1877–1912)* and Ch'üan Han-sheng, *Han-Yeh-P'ing kung-ssu shih-lueh* (A brief history of the Hanyehping Co.).

Chang Chien's record in industry is equally well documented by his own writings: *Chang Chi-tzu chiu-lu* (Nine records of Chang Chien), and *T'ung-chou hsing-pan shih-yeh chih li-shih: Ta-sheng sha-ch'ang* (A history of the industries established at T'ung-chou: The Dah Sun Cotton Spinning Mill); by a lengthy biography by his son: Chang Hsiao-jo, *Nan-t'ung Chang Chi-chih hsien-sheng chuan-chi* (A biography of Mr Chang Chien of Nan-t'ung); and by recent studies, e.g., Samuel C. Chu, *Reformer in modern China: Chang Chien, 1853–1926*.

However, the documents on their industrial involvement as recorded by official-entrepreneurs tend to reflect the official ethos and not merchant perspectives. In order to get a more sympathetic view of the merchants, the researcher should make imaginative use of contemporary social novels such as Wu Wo-yao (Wu Chien-jen), *Erh-shih-nien mu-tu chih kuai hsien-chuang,* available in an abridged translation: *Vignettes from the late Ch'ing: bizarre happenings eye-witnessed over two decades,* Shih-Shun Liu, trans.

One merchant who spoke out intelligently and voluminously was Cheng Kuan-ying. His *Sheng-shih wei-yen hou-pien* (Warnings to a prosperous age: a sequel), less well-known than his shorter political treatise, *Sheng-shih wei-yen* (Warnings to a prosperous age), not only deals extensively with his several enterprises, but also expresses his views on the government's roles in economic development. Another contemporary source representing a merchant perspective is the *Hsiang-kang Hua-tzu jih-pao* (Chinese Mail of Hong Kong), published every two days, then as a daily newspaper, from 1864 to 1940.

During the late 1950s and early 1960s, historians from the People's Republic of China compiled several volumes of materials from company archives, each dealing with a major industrial or commercial enterprise whose beginnings went back to the late Ch'ing. They include: *Ch'i-hsin yang-hui kung-ssu shih-liao* (Historical materials on the Chee Hsin Cement Company); *Pei-ching Jui-fu-hsiang* (The Jui-fu-hsiang Company of Peking); *Heng-feng sha-ch'ang ti fa-sheng fa-chan yü kai-tsao* (The origin, development and reconstruction of the Heng-feng Spinning Mill); and *Nan-yang hsiung-ti yen-ts'ao kung-ssu shih-liao* (Historical materials of the Nanyang Brothers Tobacco Co.).

Complementing the individual company records are several large compilations of documents on a single industry like the Chung-kuo jen-min yin-hang Shang-hai-shih fen-hang, ed. *Shang-hai ch'ien-chuang shih-liao* (Historical materials on Shanghai native banks) and Mi Ju-ch'eng, comp. *Chung-kuo chin-tai t'ieh-lu shih tzu-liao, 1863–1911* (Source materials on the history of railways in modern China, 1863–1911). On the development of modern industry in general see the source materials cited on p. 603 above on the history of modern industry in China, 1st collection, 1840–95, comp. Sun Yü-t'ang, in 2 vols., and a 2nd collection, 1895–1914, comp. Wang Ching-yü, also in 2 vols.; also another series, confusingly given the same title, but without dates, compiled by Ch'en Chen and Yao Lo, numbered *ti-i-chi* (1st collection) and *ti-san-chi* (3rd collection), in 2 vols. each, and published in Peking in 1957 and 1961 respectively. These documents include not only official writings, but also short biographies of numerous merchants, translations of contemporary Western accounts, company reports and other sundry records which are not easily accessible.

These compilations from mainland Chinese historians, though duplicating some readily available records, have greatly increased the bulk of information about the men and the institutions that organized the early phase of modern enterprise in China. They have also contributed to a number of important studies in recent years: e.g., Albert Feuerwerker's chapter in this volume, and his 'Industrial enterprise in twentieth-century China: the Chee Hsin Cement Company' in Albert Feuerwerker, Rhoads Murphey and Mary C. Wright, eds.

Approaches to modern Chinese history; Susan Mann Jones, 'Finance in Ningpo: the "ch'ien-chuang", 1750–1880', in W. E. Willmott, ed. *Economic organization in Chinese society*, and her related article, 'The Ningpo *Pang* and financial power at Shanghai', in Mark Elvin and G. William Skinner, eds. *The Chinese city between two worlds*; and Wellington K. K. Chan, *Merchants, mandarins and modern enterprise in late Ch'ing China*.

Finally, a word should be said about the changing perspective on the Chinese merchant in recent historiography. A number of scholars have begun to de-emphasize the old stereotype of a merchant class oppressed by unsympathetic mandarin overlords. Instead, they now suggest that, for the last imperial era at least, close mutuality and even identity of interest existed between officials and merchants. For such a new view see Lien-sheng Yang, 'Government control of the urban merchant in traditional China', *Ch'ing-hua hsueh-pao*, 8.1–2 (1970) 186–209; Thomas A. Metzger, 'State and commerce in imperial China', *Asian and African Studies*, 6 (1970) 23–46; Yen-p'ing Hao, *The comprador in nineteenth century China*; and W. E. Willmott, ed. *Economic organization in Chinese society*.

9. THE REPUBLICAN REVOLUTIONARY MOVEMENT

For the non-specialist who wishes to examine the revolutionary movement in more depth or the entire revolution in more breadth, there are two books to begin with that place the revolution in historical perspective and illuminate its early years: Harold Z. Schiffrin, *Sun Yat-sen and the origins of the Chinese Revolution*, which takes Sun's life and the revolutionary movement up to 1905, and Charlton M. Lewis, *Prologue to the Chinese Revolution: the transformation of ideas and institutions in Hunan province, 1891–1907*. Marius B. Jansen, *The Japanese and Sun Yat-sen*, and K. S. Liew, *Struggle for democracy: Sung Chiao-jen and the 1911 Chinese Revolution* complete the survey of Sun's career and of the Hunan branch of the revolutionary movement. For further details on the Kwangtung and Hunan-Hupei areas of the revolution see Edward J. M. Rhoads' *China's Republican revolution: the case of Kwangtung, 1895–1913*, and Joseph W. Esherick, *Reform and revolution in China: the 1911 Revolution in Hunan and Hubei*. Mary Backus Rankin, *Early Chinese revolutionaries: radical intellectuals in Shanghai and Chekiang, 1902–1911* studies another region where the revolutionary movement had distinctive features and also bridges the gap between social-political history and intellectual history. The latter is also treated in Martin Bernal, *Chinese socialism to 1907* and Michael Gasster, *Chinese intellectuals and the Revolution of 1911: the birth of modern Chinese radicalism*. Other useful books include Chün-tu Hsueh, *Huang Hsing and the Chinese Revolution*, which makes excessive claims for Huang Hsing's import-ance but contains a good deal of valuable information; Ta-ling Lee, *Foundations of the Chinese Revolution, 1905–1912: the historical record of the T'ung-meng hui*, a curiously outdated and error-strewn book that nevertheless offers the only available general treatment of the Revolutionary Alliance, also useful as a convenient summary of older scholarship; and Wu Yü-chang, *The Revolution of*

1911: a great democratic revolution of China, valuable both as a personal memoir of the revolutionary movement and as an introduction to Marxist interpretations. For other interpretations and recent controversies see Mary C. Wright, ed. *China in revolution: the first phase, 1900–1913*, especially the editor's introduction, pp. 1–63; and 'A symposium on the 1911 Revolution', *Modern China*, 2.2 (April 1976) 139–226.

For specialists, the starting point is Winston Hsieh, *Chinese historiography on the Revolution of 1911: a critical survey and a selected bibliography*, which provides an inventory of primary and secondary sources, helpful comments on individual items, and a thoughtful essay on the entire historiography of the revolution. Scholars will wish to pay particular attention to the massive collections of documents and memoirs that have recently been published; see Hsieh, pp. 50–4 and 65–8. Another important guide to materials in Chinese is *Ch'ing-chi ko-ming yun-tung ch'i-k'an hsu-mu hsuan-chi* (The revolutionary movement during the late Ch'ing; a guide to Chinese periodicals) compiled by P. K. Yü, Yu-ning Li and Yü-fa Chang. It contains the tables of contents and inaugural manifestos of sixteen periodicals published between 1900 and 1911; there is also a brief introduction in English. For a valuable discussion of sources and issues see Marie-Claire Bergère, 'La Révolution de 1911 jugée par les historiens de la république populaire de Chine: themes et controverses', *Revue Historique*, 468 (Oct.–Dec. 1963) 403–36. For the issues that have emerged among Chinese specialists on the Revolution of 1911 see Hu-pei sheng che-hsueh she-hui k'o-hsueh lien-ho hui, *Hsin-hai ko-ming wu-shih chou-nien lun-wen chi* (A collection of articles on the fiftieth anniversary of the Revolution of 1911) which appeared too late for Professor Bergère to examine in her essay. A new and thoughtful guide is Edmund S. K. Fung, 'Post-1949 Chinese historiography on the 1911 Revolution', *Modern China*, 4.2 (April 1978) 181–214.

Another important source of articles by Chinese scholars is *Chung-yang yen-chiu-yuan chin-tai-shih yen-chiu-so chi-k'an* (Bulletin of the Institute of Modern History, Academia Sinica). Note vol. 2 (June 1971), a special number entitled 'Chung-hua Min-kuo chien-kuo liu-shih nien chi-nien' (In commemoration of the sixtieth anniversary of the founding of the Republic of China). The same institute's series of monographs are noted in Winston Hsieh's bibliography; among titles that must be added are Ch'i Ping-feng, *Ch'ing-mo ko-ming yü chün-hsien ti lun-cheng* (Controversies between the revolutionaries and constitutional monarchists in the late Ch'ing period); Chang Yü-fa, *Ch'ing-chi ti li-hsien t'uan-t'i* (Constitutionalist groups of the late Ch'ing period); the same author's *Ch'ing-chi ti ko-ming t'uan-t'i* (Revolutionary groups of the late Ch'ing period); and Huang Fu-ch'ing, *Ch'ing-mo liu-Jih hsueh-sheng* (Late Ch'ing students in Japan).

For the great wealth of material in Japanese, consult the bibliographic essay and footnotes to ch. 6 above and the bibliographies of monographs cited in this chapter by Bernal and Rhoads. Finally, there are several studies of related topics that are helpful for understanding the Revolution of 1911. These include Jerome Ch'en, *Yuan Shih-k'ai, 1859–1916*, 2nd edition; Edward Friedman, *Backward toward revolution: the Chinese revolutionary party*; Roger V. DesForges, *Hsi-liang and the Chinese national revolution*; George T. Yu, *Party politics in republican China: the Kuomintang, 1912–1924*; Don C. Price, *Russia and the roots of the Chinese Revolution, 1896–1911*; Ernest P. Young, *The presidency of Yuan Shih-k'ai: liberalism and dictatorship in early republican China*; and the study by Joseph W. Esherick already cited.

10. CURRENTS OF SOCIAL CHANGE

There are an infinite number of sources which might help to clarify Chinese social history at the end of the empire. Actually, the notion of social history may cover such an extensive field, including morals, attitudes, customs, organizational patterns of human groups and their relationships, even the evolution of economic circumstances, that almost any document, whether written, iconographic, architectural or even musical, can further our under-standing of the realities of Chinese society, its structures, movements, mechan-isms or self-images. We restrict ourselves here to written sources.

Quantitative data, so fundamental to the historiography of Western societies, are scanty, scattered and very fragmentary, particularly for the last quarter of the nineteenth century. Several series of land documents preserved in Japan have been the basis of important studies by Muramatsu Yūji, *Kindai Kōnan no sosan: Chūgoku jinushi no kenkyū* (Landlord bursaries in Kiangnan in modern times: studies of landlordism in China) and Amagai Kenzaburō, *Chūgoku tochi monjo no kenkyū* (Studies on Chinese documents on land). Except for these, archives of land documents and local government are as yet inaccessible to researchers outside continental China and largely ignored by historians of the People's Republic in their publications. Most available sources provide data which are essentially qualitative. Moreover, because almost all of them were produced by the ruling class and written in a style whose rigid formalism tended always to enclose the new in traditional categories, they are of inadequate help in studies of lower-class conditions and social movements. The massive collection of oral history to which historians of the People's Republic have devoted the last thirty years in an effort to correct this historical bias has unhappily produced little actual publication as yet.

Several collections conveniently assemble scattered materials and are therefore useful as points of departure: first are the compendia cited in the essays above to chs. 1 and 8, edited by Ch'en Chen, Sun Yü-t'ang and Wang Ching-yü respectively on modern industry, by Li Wen-chih on agriculture, by P'eng Tse-i on handi-crafts, and by Chung-kuo jen-min yin-hang Shang-hai-shih fen-hang on Shanghai native banks. To these must be added the large Japanese compilations of the end of the nineteenth century and the beginning of the twentieth such as: Nisshin Bōeki Kenkyūjo, *Shinkoku tsūshō sōran* (General survey of the foreign trade of the Ch'ing dynasty); Tōa Dōbun Shoin, comp. *Shina keizai zensho* (A comprehensive survey of China's economy); Negishi Tadashi, *Shinkoku shōgyō sōran* (General survey of commerce of the Ch'ing dynasty); Rinji Taiwan Kyūkan Chōsakai, *Shinkoku gyōseihō* (Administrative laws of the Ch'ing dynasty); official yearbooks (*nien-chien*) published after 1906 by the central government and certain provincial governments. Biographical dictionaries and collections, such as Fei Hsing-chien, *Chin-tai ming-jen hsiao-chuan* (Biographical notes on famous men of modern times), Chin-liang, *Chin-shih jen-wu chih* (Personalities of recent times), and Arthur W. Hummel, *Eminent Chinese of the Ch'ing period*, regrettably concentrate too much on the official class and its political and literary activities. The most instructive accounts can be found mainly in local gazetteers (*fang-chih*), private diaries, the press, and especially the realistic and satirical literature of the early twentieth century, notably that published bi-monthly in a review edited at Shanghai by the Commercial Press, *Hsiu-hsiang hsiao-shuo* (Illustrated stories), which published novels by Liu O, Li Pao-chia and Wu Wo-yao. Western sources (diplomatic and missionary archives and reports) provide a useful complement, but are rich in social information only for the period after 1895, when Chinese sources also become more eloquent.

Perhaps because the nature of available sources has discouraged historians, or because their attention has been focused on political or intellectual phenomena, or because *a priori* schemas have tied up research, we still know very little about the evolution of Chinese society during the last forty years of the monarchy. G. William Skinner's bibliography, *Modern Chinese society: an analytical bibliography*, is the most complete list of works on this subject. It shows that, except for several pioneering works principally by Chinese and Japanese authors, exploration is still very partial and fragmentary. There is not a single work which treats the question in-depth or in its entirety. However, the novice reader can discover the ground yet to be covered by comparing the somewhat idyllic description given in 1885 by G-Eugène Simon, *La Cité chinoise* (whose title was inspired by *La Cité antique* of Fustel de Coulanges), and Martin C. Yang, *Chinese social structure*, which analyses the society of the republican era. A number of articles in G. William Skinner, ed. *The city in late imperial China* and in Mark Elvin and G. William Skinner, eds. *The Chinese city between two worlds* are very valuable in defining the social landscape.

The privileged class is relatively the best studied, due to fundamental works on gentry-literati recruitment, mobility and fortune: Chang Chung-li, *The Chinese gentry*, and *The income of the Chinese gentry*, highlighted by Ho Ping-ti, *The ladder of success in imperial China*. The restricted analysis by Robert M. Marsh, *The mandarins: the circulation of elites in China, 1600–1900*, of the recruitment of those officials described in Hummel's biographical dictionary, has now been enlarged and modified by the statistical inquiries of Li Kuo-ch'i, *Ch'ing-tai chi-tseng ti-fang-kuan jen-shih shan-ti hsien-hsiang chih liang-hua fen-hsi* (A quantitative analysis of the careers of prefects and magistrates in the Ch'ing dynasty). The latter depicts geographic and social origins, as well as profiles of the careers of prefects and sub-prefects, on the basis of data supplied by local gazetteers. On compradors, there is the excellent monograph of Hao Yen-p'ing, *The comprador in nineteenth century China*; on merchants, Wellington K. K. Chan, *Merchants, mandarins and modern enterprise in late Ch'ing China*. Works concerning the accumulation of capital for modern enterprises also shed light on the emergence of novel social categories. Among these are the following articles: Shao Hsun-cheng, 'Yang-wu yun-tung ho tzu-pen-chu-i fa-chan ti kuan-hsi wen-t'i' (The problem of the relationship between the Western Affairs movement and the development of capitalism); Chang Kuo-hui, 'Chung-kuo chin-tai mei-k'uang ch'i-yeh chung ti kuan shang kuan-hsi yü tzu-pen-chu-i fa-sheng wen-t'i' (The relations between officials and merchants in modern Chinese coal-mining enterprises and the problem of the birth of capitalism); Wang Ching-yü, 'Shih-chiu shih-chi wai-kuo ch'in Hua ch'i-yeh chung ti Hua-shang fu-ku huo-tung' (Investment by Chinese merchants in the foreign firms which invaded China in the nineteenth century); and the collection edited by Tōkyō Kyōiku Daigaku, *Chūgoku kindaika no shakai kōzō* (Social structure in China's modernization). Marie-Claire Bergère, *La Bourgeoisie chinoise et la révolution de 1911*, describes the milieu of modern business in Shanghai at the time of the republican revolution. Ralph L. Powell, *The rise of Chinese military power, 1895–1912*, gives an overview of military evolution, completed by Wang Erh-min, *Huai-chün chih* (History of the Anhwei Army), which is very useful on the recruitment of the officer corps, and by Liu Feng-han, *Hsin-chien lu-chün* (The Newly Created Army (under Yuan Shih-k'ai 1895–1900)). There is, as yet, no monograph of this type on the modern army after 1901. The new intelligentsia has been the subject of numerous studies, notably: Y. C. Wang, *Chinese intellectuals and the West 1872–1949*; Mary Backus Rankin, *Early Chinese revolutionaries: radical intellectuals in Shanghai and Chekiang, 1902–1911*; and Michael Gasster, *Chinese intellectuals and the Revolution of 1911: The birth of modern Chinese nationalism*. Certain biographical studies also provide precious insight: on Westernization and the Chinese of the treaty ports, Paul A. Cohen, *Between tradition and modernity: Wang T'ao and reform in late Ch'ing China*; on feminism and the condition of women, Catherine Gipoulon, *Qiu Jin, femme et révolutionnaire en Chine au XIXème siècle*.

There are two solid studies on the conditions and struggles of workers at this time: Wang Ching-yü and Nieh Pao-chang, 'Kuan-yü Chung-kuo ti-i-tai ch'an-yeh kung-jen ti tou-cheng tzu-liao' (Materials on the struggles of the first generation of Chinese industrial workers); and Chao Ch'in, 'Hsin-hai ko-ming ch'ien-hou ti Chung-kuo kung-jen yun-tung' (The Chinese workers' movement around the time of the 1911 Revolution). As an introduction to the unjustly neglected world of artisans, there is Fan Pai-ch'uan, 'Chung-kuo shou-kung-yeh tsai wai-kuo tzu-pen-chu-i ch'in-ju hou ti tsao-yu ho ming-yun' (The fate of Chinese handicraft industry after the incursion of foreign capitalism), which touches primarily economic aspects, and P'eng Tse-i, 'Shih-chiu shih-chi hou-ch'i Chung-kuo ch'eng-shih shou-kung-yeh shang-yeh hang-hui ti ch'ung-ch'ien ho tso-yung' (The reconstruction of Chinese city handicraft and trade associations in the late nineteenth century and their functions).

Rural society has been most drastically neglected. The numerous works of

Muramatsu Yūji and Amagai Kenzaburō, two collections of which were cited above, contribute monumentally to the understanding of land organization, but are limited to the regions of southern Kiangsu, Chihli and Manchuria. The collection edited by Tōkyō Kyōiku Daigaku, *Kindai Chūgoku nōson shakai shih kenkyū* (Studies in modern Chinese rural social history), contains analyses of the agrarian situation in Hunan and Szechwan. Shantung, however, is the subject of the most rich and original work of all, a monograph by Ching Su and Lo Lun, *Ch'ing-tai Shan-tung ching-ying ti-chu ti she-hui hsing-chih* (The social characteristics of managerial landlords in Shantung during the Ch'ing period) which utilizes continuous series of private archives concerning agricultural production. Ramon H. Myers, *The Chinese peasant economy: agricultural development in Hopei and Shantung, 1890–1949*, contains in reality very little on the imperial period. Kung-chuan Hsiao, *Rural China: imperial control in the nineteenth century*, is the best work on the life of rural communities in that century, but considers primarily the problem of maintaining public order.

Paradoxically, the study of popular movements has claimed far more attention than the study of the peasant situation. For monographs concerning the principal movements of the period, see the notes accompanying this chapter. The collection of articles edited by Jean Chesneaux, ed. *Mouvements populaires et sociétés secrètes en Chine aux XIXᵉ et XXᵉ siècles* (the English edition of which is slightly different: *Popular movements and secret societies in China, 1840–1950*), deals especially with secret societies and contains a useful bibliography. Aleksandra Sergeevna Kostiaeva, *Narodnye dvizhenija v Kitae v 1901–1911 gg* (Popular movements in China, 1901–1911), is a solid study of the overall picture of peasant turbulence following the Boxers. The statistical analysis by C. K. Yang is a pioneering work which ought to be followed up ('Some preliminary patterns of mass action in nineteenth century China', in Fredric Wakeman, Jr and Carolyn Grant, eds. *Conflict and control in late imperial China*). Frederic Wakeman, 'Rebellion and revolution: the study of popular movements in Chinese history', *JAS*, 36.2 (Feb. 1977) 201–37, points out contemporary tendencies of historiography in this subject area.

Our understanding of the different social categories, especially of their changes and articulations, is therefore definitely deficient. This is reflected by differences of opinion about the respective roles of the gentry and the bourgeoisie in the 1911 Revolution, illustrated particularly by the articles of Chang P'eng-yüan, Ichiko Chūzō and Marie-Claire Bergère in Mary C. Wright, ed., *China in revolution: the first phase*. Regional studies, such as Charlton M. Lewis, *Prologue to the Chinese Revolution: the transformation of ideas and institutions in Hunan province, 1891–1907*, Edward J. M. Rhoads, *China's republican revolution: the case of Kwangtung, 1895–1913*, and especially Joseph W. Esherick, *Reform and revolution in China: the 1911 Revolution in Hunan and Hubei*, have since illustrated the repercussions of reforms and political movements on the process of social transformation, particularly in the ruling strata. Social incidences of educational reform are shown by Marianne Bastid, *Aspects de la réforme de l'enseignement en*

Chine au début du XXe siècle. These works suggest a specificity of social differentiation which owes at least as much, if not more, to cultural criteria and attitudes as to economic interests.

BIBLIOGRAPHY

CHINESE AND JAPANESE PUBLISHERS

Cheng-chung 正中 (Taipei)
Ch'eng-wen 成文 (Taipei)
Chia-hsin 嘉新水泥公司文化基金會 (Taipei)
Chikuma 筑摩書房 (Tokyo)
Commercial Press 商務印書館 (major cities)
Chung-hua 中華書局 (major cities)
Chung-yang wen-wu 中央文物供應社 (Taipei)
Ch'ung-wen 崇文書店 (Hong Kong)
Dai Nihon Kyōka Tosho 大日本教化圖書 (Tokyo)
Daian 大安 (Tokyo)
Hakubunkan 博文館 (Tokyo)
Hsueh-sheng 學生書局 (Taipei)
Heibonsha 平凡社 (Tokyo)
Hsin-chih-shih 新知識出版社 (Shanghai)
Iwanami 岩波書店 (Tokyo)
Jen-min 人民出版社 (Shanghai and other cities)
K'o-hsueh 科學出版社 (Peking)
San-lien 生活、讀書、新知三聯書店 (Peking, Shanghai)
Sao-yeh shan-fang 掃葉山房 (Shanghai)
Shen-chou kuo-kuang she 神州國光社 (Shanghai, Peking)
Shih-chieh 世界書局 (major cities)
T'u-shu chi-ch'eng 圖書集成 (Shanghai)
Wen-hai 文海 (Taipei)
Wen-hsing 文星 (Taipei)

WORKS CITED

A Ying 阿英 (Ch'ien Hsing-ts'un 錢杏村), comp. *Ya-p'ien chan-cheng wen-hsueh chi* 鴉片戰爭文學集 (Literary writings concerning the Opium War). 2 vols. Peking: Ku-chi 古籍, 1957
Alder, G. J. *British India's northern frontier 1865–95: a study in imperial policy.* London: Longmans, 1963

Amagai Kenzaburō. 天海謙三郎. *Chūgoku tochi monjo no kenkyū* 中国土地文書の研究 (Studies on Chinese documents on land). Tokyo: Keisō Shobō 勁草書房, 1966

Amano Motonosuke 天野元之助. *Shina nōgyō keizai ron* 支那農業経済論 (On the Chinese agricultural economy). 2 vols. Tokyo: Kaizōsha 改造社, 1940–2

Amano Motonosuke. *Chūgoku nōgyō no sho mondai* 中国農業の諸問題 (Problems of Chinese agriculture). 2 vols. Tokyo: Gihōdō, 1952–3

AMCH: Feuerwerker, Albert, Murphey, Rhoads and Wright, Mary C. *Approaches to modern Chinese history*

Anon. 'Chi-shih' 紀事 (Journal of events), originally written in sinicized Arabic; extant fragments, P'ang Shih-ch'ien 龐士謙, trans., in *HMCI*, 3.237–40

Anon. 'The Chinese and Japanese armies'. *Journal of the Military Service Institution of the United States*, 15 (1894) 255–9

Armengaud, Captain (Jean Louis). *Lang-Son: journal des opérations qui ont précédé et suivi la prise de cette citadelle*. Paris: R. Chapelot et Cie, 1901

Ayers, William. *Chang Chih-tung and educational reform in China*. Cambridge, Mass.: Harvard University Press, 1971

Bales, W. L. *Tso Tsungt'ang: soldier and statesman of old China*. Shanghai: Kelly and Walsh, 1937

Banno, Masataka. *China and the West, 1858–1861: the origins of the Tsungli Yamen*. Cambridge, Mass.: Harvard University Press, 1964

Banno Masataka 坂野正高. 'Furansu ryūgaku jidai no Ba Ken-chū — gaikō oyobi gaikōkan seido ni tsuite no futatsu no ikensho' フランス留学時代の馬建忠―外交及び外交官制度に就いての二つの意見書 (Ma Chien-chung during his days of study in France — two proposals regarding foreign relations and the foreign service system). *Kokkagakkai zasshi* 国家学会雑誌, 84.5 and 6 (1971) 257–93

Barnett, Suzanne Wilson. 'Wei Yuan and Westerners. Notes on the sources of the *Hai-kuo t'u-chih*'. *Ch'ing-shih wen-t'i* 清史問題, 2.4 (1970) 1–20

Bastid, Marianne. *Aspects de la réforme de l'enseignement en Chine au début de XXe siècle, d'après des écrits de Zhang Jian*. Paris and The Hague: Mouton, 1971

Bawden, C. R. *The modern history of Mongolia*. New York: Praeger, 1968

Bays, Daniel H. *China enters the twentieth century: Chang Chih-tung and the issues of a new age, 1895–1909*. Ann Arbor: University of Michigan Press, 1978

Bell, Mark. *China, being a military report on the northeastern portions of the provinces of Chihli and Shantung; Nanking and its approaches; Canton and its approaches; etc.*, 2 vols. Simla: Government Central Branch Press, 1884

Bellew, Henry Walter. *Kashmir and Kashgar: a narrative of the journey of the embassy to Kashgar in 1873–1874*. London: Trübner, 1875

Bennett, Adrian A. *Research guide to the Chiao-hui hsin-pao (The church news), 1868–1874*. San Francisco: Chinese Materials Center, 1975

Bennett, Adrian A. *Research guide to the Wan-kuo kung-pao (The globe magazine), 1874–1883*. San Francisco: Chinese Materials Center, 1976

Bennett, Adrian A. and Liu, Kwang-Ching. 'Christianity in the Chinese Idiom:

Young J. Allen and the early *Chiao-hui hsin-pao, 1868–70*', in John K. Fairbank, ed. *The missionary enterprise in China and America*, pp. 159–96. Cambridge, Mass.: Harvard University Press, 1975

Bergère, Marie-Claire. 'La Révolution de 1911 jugée par les historiens de la république populaire de Chine: themes et controverses', *Revue Historique*, 468 (Oct.–Dec. 1963) 403–36

Bergère, Marie-Claire. *La Bourgeoisie chinoise et la révolution de 1911*. Paris: Mouton, 1968

Bergère, Marie-Claire. 'The role of the bourgeoisie,' in *CIR*, 229–95

Bernal, Martin. 'The triumph of anarchism over Marxism, 1906–1907', in *CIR*, 97–142

Bernal, Martin. *Chinese socialism to 1907*. Ithaca: Cornell University Press, 1976

Biggerstaff, Knight. 'The Ch'ung-hou mission to France, 1870–71'. *Nankai Social and Economic Quarterly*, 8.3 (Oct. 1935) 633–47

Biggerstaff, Knight. *The earliest modern government schools in China*. Ithaca: Cornell University Press, 1961

Blackburn Chamber of Commerce. *Report of the mission to China of the Blackburn Chamber of Commerce, 1896–7*. Blackburn: North East Lancashire Press, 1898

Blacker, Carmen. *The Japanese enlightenment: a study of the writings of Fukuzawa Yukichi*. Cambridge University Press, 1964

Blythe, Wilfred. *The impact of Chinese secret societies in Malaya. A historical study*. London, Kuala-Lumpur, Hong Kong: Oxford University Press, 1969

Boorman, Howard L. and Howard, Richard C. *Biographical dictionary of Republican China*. 4 vols. New York: Columbia University Press, 1967–71. Vol. 5 index, 1979

Borokh, Lilia. 'Notes on the early role of secret societies in Sun Yat-sen's republican movement', in *PMSS*, 135–44

BPP: British parliamentary papers

Brassey, T. A., ed. *The naval annual, 1895*. Portsmouth: J. Griffin, 1895

British parliamentary papers. Various issues. London: various dates

Britton, Roswell S. *The Chinese periodical press, 1800–1912*. Shanghai: Kelly and Walsh, 1933

BSOAS: Bulletin of the School of Oriental and African Studies

Buck, John Lossing. *Land utilization in China*. 3 vols. Shanghai: Commercial Press, 1937

Bujac, E. *Précis de quelques campagnes contemporaines:* vol. 2, *La Guerre sino-japonaise*. Paris: Henri Charles-Lavauzelle, 1896

Cady, John F. *The roots of French imperialism in Eastern Asia*. Ithaca: Cornell University Press, 1967

Cameron, Meribeth E. *The reform movement in China, 1898–1912*. Stanford University Press, 1931

Carlson, Ellsworth C. *The Kaiping mines, 1877–1912: a case study of early Chinese industrialization*. 2nd edn. Cambridge, Mass.: Harvard University Press, 1971

Catalogue of National Archives Microfilm Publications. See US National Archives

Cavendish, A. E. J. 'The armed strength (?) of China', *Journal of the Royal United*

Service Institution, 42 (June 1898) 705–23

CCTW: Elvin, Mark and Skinner, G. William, eds. *The Chinese city between two worlds*

Ch'ai Te-keng 柴德賡 *et al.* eds. *Hsin-hai ko-ming* 辛亥革命 (The 1911 Revolution). 8 vols. Shanghai: Jen-min 1957; also cited as *HHKM*

Chambre de Commerce de Lyon, ed. *La Mission lyonnaise d'exploration commerciale en Chine 1895–1897.* Lyon: A. Rey et Cie, 1898

Chan, Wellington K. K. 'Ma Ju-lung: from rebel to turncoat in the Yunnan rebellion', *Papers on China*, 20 (1966) 86–118

Chan, Wellington, K. K. *Merchants, mandarins and modern enterprise in late Ch'ing China.* Cambridge, Mass.: Harvard University Press, 1977

Chang Ch'i-yun 張其昀 *et al.* eds. *Ch'ing-shih* 清史 (History of the Ch'ing dynasty). 8 vols. Taipei: Kuo-fang yen-chiu yuan 國防研究院 , 1961

Chang Chien 張謇 . *T'ung-chou hsing-pan shih-yeh chih li-shih: Ta-sheng sha-ch'ang* 通州興辦實業之歷史：大生紗廠 (A history of the industries established at T'ung-chou: The Dah Sun Cotton Spinning Mill). Nan-t'ung, 1910

Chang Chien. *Chang Chi-tzu chiu lu* 張季子九錄 (Nine records of Chang Chien). Chang Hsiao-jo 張孝若 , ed. 80 *chüan.* Shanghai: Chung-hua, 1931; Taipei: Wen-hai, 1965

Chang Chien. *Liu-hsi-ts'ao-t'ang jih-chi* 柳西草堂日記 (Diary from the cottage west of the willow). Original edn: 15 *ts'e* in Shanghai, Jen-min, 1962; and 4 *t'se* in Taipei, Wen-hai, 1967. 2nd edn complete: 12 *ts'e* in Taipei, Wen-hai, 1969

Chang Chih-tung 張之洞 . *Chang Wen-hsiang kung chi* 張文襄公集 (The papers of Chang Chih-tung). Hsu T'ung-hsin 許同莘 , ed. 150 *chüan.* Peking, 1919–21

Chang Chih-tung. *Chang Wen-hsiang kung ch'üan-chi* 張文襄公全集 (Complete collection of Chang Chih-tung's papers). 120 *ts'e.* Peiping: Wen-hua chai 文華齋, 1928; also cited as *CWHK*

Chang Chih-tung. *Chang Wen-hsiang kung ch'üan-chi* 張文襄公全集 (Complete collection of Chang Chih-tung's papers). Wang Shu-nan 王樹枏 , ed. 228 *chüan.* Peiping 1937. Taipei reproduction, Wen-hai, 1963

Chang Chih-tung. *Ch'üan-hsueh p'ien* 勸學篇 (Exhortation to study). 1898 preface; Kuang-hsu period edn. Taipei reproduction, Wen-hai, 1966

Chang Ching-lu 張靜廬 . *Chung-kuo chin-tai ch'u-pan shih-liao ch'u-pien* 中國近代出版史料初編 (Materials on the history of publication in modern China, first collection). Shanghai: Ch'ün-lien 羣聯 , 1954

Chang Ching-lu. *Chung-kuo chin-tai ch'u-pan shih-liao pu-pien* 中國近代出版史料補編 (Materials on the history of publication in modern China, supplementry collection). Shanghai: Chung-hua, 1957

Chang, Chung-li. *The Chinese gentry.* Seattle: University of Washington Press, 1955

Chang, Chung-li. *The income of the Chinese gentry.* Seattle: University of Washington Press, 1962

Chang, Hao. 'The antiforeignist role of Wo-jen, 1804–1871', *Papers on China*,

14 (1960) 1–29

Chang, Hao. *Liang Ch'i-ch'ao and intellectual transition in China, 1890–1907.*
Cambridge, Mass.: Harvard University Press, 1971

Chang Hsiao-jo 張孝若. *Nan-t'ung Chang Chi-chih hsien-sheng chuan-chi*
南通張季直先生傳記 (A biography of Mr Chang Chien of Nan-t'ung).
Shanghai: Chung-hua, 1930. Taipei reproduction, Wen-hsing, 1965

Chang Kuo-hui 張國輝. 'Chung-kuo chin-tai mei-k'uang ch'i-yeh chung ti kuan
shang kuan-hsi yü tzu-pen-chu-i fa-sheng wen-t'i' 中國近代煤礦企業中的官商
關係與資本主義發生問題 (The relations between officials and merchants in
modern Chinese coal-mining enterprises and the problem of the birth of
capitalism) *Li-shih yen-chiu* 歷史研究, *1964.3, pp. 117–44*

Chang, Kuo-t'ao. *The rise of the Chinese Communist Party.* 2 vols. Lawrence:
University of Kansas Press, 1971–2

Chang Ming-san 張銘三, trans. *Jih-pen wen-hsüeh tui Chung-kuo ti ying-hsiang*
日本文學對中國的影響 (The influence of Japanese literature on China).
Shanghai: Hsin shen pao k'an 新申報刊, 1944. See Sanetō Keishū, *Nihon
bunka no Shina e no eikyō* (q.v.)

Chang Nan 張枬 and Wang Jen-chih 王忍之. *Hsin-hai ko-ming ch'ien shih-nien
chien shih-lun hsüan-chi* 辛亥革命前十年間時論選集 (Selections from opinions
expressed in periodicals and newspapers during the decade before the 1911
Revolution). 2 series (*chüan*), each in 2 vols. Peking: San-lien, 1960, 1963

Chang P'ei-lun 張佩綸. *Chien-yü chi* 澗于集 (Memorials of Chang P'ei-lun). 6
chüan, 1918 preface. Taipei reproduction, Wen-hai, 1967

Chang, Peng. 'Distribution of provincial merchant groups in China, 1842–1911',
University of Washington, Ph.D. dissertation. Seattle, 1958

Chang, P'eng-yuan. 張朋園. 'The constitutionalists', in *CIR*, 143–83

Chang, P'eng-yuan. *Li-hsien-p'ai yü hsin-hai ko-ming* 立憲派與辛亥革命 (The
constitutionalists and the 1911 Revolution). Taipei: Commercial Press for
IMH, Academia Sinica, 1969

Chang, P'eng-yuan. 'A typological hypothesis on the elites of the 1911
Revolution in China'. *Journal of the Oriental Society of Australia*, 9.1 and 2
(1972–3) 32–8

Chang Po-fang 章伯鋒, comp. *Ch'ing-tai ko-ti chiang-chün tu-t'ung ta-ch'en teng nien-
piao, 1796–1911* 清代各地將軍都統大臣等年表 (Chronological tables of
Manchu generals-in-chief, lieutenants-general, imperial agents, etc., in various
areas under the Ch'ing, 1796–1911). Peking: Chung-hua, 1965

Chang Po-hsi 張百熙 *et al. Tsou-ting hsüeh-t'ang chang-ch'eng* 奏定學堂章程
(Regulations concerning educational institutions as approved by the throne).
5 *ts'e.* Nanking, 1904. Wuchang: Hu-pei hsüeh-wu ch'u 湖北學務處, Taipei
reproduction, Wen-hai, 1972

Chang T'ing-chü 張廷舉. 'Wu-hsu cheng-pien shih-ch'i wan-ku-p'ai chih ching-
chi ssu-hsiang' 戊戌政變時期頑固派之經濟思想 (The economic thought of
the reactionary faction during the reform of 1898). *Chung-kuo ching-chi*
中國經濟, 4.6 (1936) 141–7

Chang Yü-chao 張裕釗. *Ch'ien-t'ing wen-chi* 濂亭文集 (Chang Yü-chao's writings). 8 *chüan*. Soochow: Ch'a-shih mu-chien chai 查氏木漸齋, 1882

Chang Yü-fa 張玉法. *Ch'ing-chi ti li-hsien t'uan-t'i* 清季的立憲團體 (Constitutionalist groups of the late Ch'ing period). Taipei: IMH, Academia Sinica, 1971

Chang Yü-fa. *Ch'ing-chi ti ko-ming t'uan-t'i* 清季的革命團體 (Revolutionary groups of the late Ch'ing period). Taipei: IMH, Academia Sinica, 1975

Chang Yueh 張曜 *et al.* eds. *Shan-tung chün-hsing chi-lueh* 山東軍興紀略 (Brief record of military campaigns in Shantung). 22 *chüan* each with two or three parts. *c.* 1885. Taipei reproduction, Wen-hai, 1970

Chao Ch'in 趙親. 'Hsin-hai ko-ming ch'ien-hou ti Chung-kuo kung-jen yun-tung' 辛亥革命前後的中國工人運動 (The Chinese workers' movement around the time of the 1911 Revolution). *Li-shih yen-chiu* 歷史研究, 1959.2, pp. 1–16

Chao Chung-fu 趙中孚. 'Ch'ing-mo tung-san-sheng kai-chih ti pei-ching' 清末東三省改制的背景 (Background of the late Ch'ing reorganization of the government of the three Manchurian provinces). *CYCT*, 5 (June 1976) 313–35

Chao Erh-hsun 趙爾巽. *Ch'ing-shih kao* 清史稿 (Draft history of the Ch'ing dynasty). 536 *chüan*. Peiping: Ch'ing-shih kuan 清史館, 1928. Shanghai reproduction, Lien-ho shu-tien 聯合書店, 1942. See Chang Ch'i-yun *et al.*

Chao Feng-t'ien 趙豐田. *Wan-Ch'ing wu-shih-nien ching-chi ssu-hsiang shih* 晚清五十年經濟思想史 (History of economic thought during the last fifty years of the Ch'ing period). Peiping: Yenching University, 1939

Chao, Kang. 'The growth of a modern cotton textile industry and the competition with handicrafts', in Dwight H. Perkins, ed. *China's modern economy in historical perspective* (q.v.)

Chao Lieh-wen 趙烈文. *Neng-ching-chü jih-chi* 能靜居日記 (Chao Lieh-wen's [holograph] diary). Taipei: Hsueh-sheng, original photolithograph, 1964

Chen, Chi-yun. 'Liang Ch'i-ch'ao's "missionary education": a case study of missionary influence on the reformers'. *Papers on China*, 16 (1962) 66–125

Ch'en Chen 陳真 and Yao Lo 姚洛. *Chung-kuo chin-tai kung-yeh shih tzu-liao* 中國近代工業史資料 (Source materials on the history of modern industry in China). 4 collections (*chi* 輯) totalling 6 vols. Peking: San-lien, 1957–61

Ch'en Chih 陳熾. *Yung-shu* 庸書 (Commonplace writings). 1897, preface 1896, n. p.

Ch'en Ch'ing-chih 陳青之. *Chung-kuo chiao-yü shih* 中國教育史 (History of education in China). Taipei: Commercial Press, 1966

Ch'en Ch'iu 陳虬. *Ching-shih po-i* 經世博議 (Broad suggestions on statecraft). n. p., 1893

Ch'en Ch'iu 陳鍫. 'Wu-hsu cheng-pien-shih fan pien-fa jen-wu chih cheng-chih ssu-hsiang' 戊戌政變時反變法人物之政治思想 (Political thought of the opponents of reform at the time of the coup d'état of 1898). *Yen-ching hsueh-pao*, 25 (1939) 59–106

Ch'en Fu-kuang 陳復光. *Yu-Ch'ing i-tai chih Chung-O kuan-hsi* 有清一代之中俄關係 (Sino-Russian relations during the Ch'ing dynasty). Kunming: National Yunnan University, 1947

Ch'en, Gideon. *Tso Tsung-t'ang: pioneer promoter of the modern dockyard and the woolen mill in China*. Peiping: Yenching University, 1938; New York reproduction, Paragon, 1961

Ch'en Hsu-lu 陳旭麓 and Lao Shao-hua 勞紹華. 'Ch'ing-mo ti hsin-chün yü hsin-hai ko-ming' 清末的新軍與辛亥革命 (The late Ch'ing New Army and the Revolution of 1911), in *HHWS*, 1.147–65

Ch'en, Jerome. 'Rebels between rebellions – secret societies in the novel *P'eng-kung an*'. *JAS*, 39.4 (Aug. 1970) 807–22

Ch'en, Jerome. *Yuan Shih-k'ai, 1859–1916*. 2nd edn. Stanford University Press, 1972

Ch'en Ku-t'ing 陳固亭. 'Sun Chung-shan hsien-sheng yü Jih-pen ch'ao-yeh p'eng-jen ti kuan-hsi' 孫中山先生與日本朝野朋人的關係 (Mr Sun Yat-sen and his Japanese friends in and out of the government), in *Chung-Jih wen-hua lun-chi* 中日文化論集 (Collected essays in Chinese and Japanese cultures), pp. 1–19. Taipei: Chung-kuo wen-hua hsueh-yuan 中國文化學院, 1967

Ch'en Lun-chiung 陳倫炯. *Hai-kuo wen-chien lu* 海國聞見錄 (Heard and seen in maritime countries), 2 *ts'e*, 1793 preface. Taipei reproduction, Hsueh-sheng, 1975

Ch'en Ta-tuan. 'Investiture of Liu-ch'iu kings in the Ch'ing period', in *CWO*, 135–64

Ch'en T'ien-hua 陳天華. *Meng hui-t'ou* 猛回頭 (Wake up!). *c.* 1904, in *Ch'en T'ien-hua chi* 陳天華集 (Collected writings of Ch'en T'ien-hua), pp. 51–90. Shanghai: Chung-kuo wen-hua fu-wu she 中國文化服務社, 1946. See also *HHKM*, 2.144–70

Ch'en T'ien-hua. 'Ching-shih chung' 警世鐘 (Alarm to arouse the age), in Chung-hua min-kuo k'ai-kuo wu-shih-nien wen-hsien pien-tsuan wei-yuan hui 中華民國開國五十年文獻編纂委員會, comp. *Ko-ming chih ch'ang-tao yü fa-chan* 革命之倡導與發展 (The initial guidance and the development of the revolution); *Chung-kuo T'ung-meng hui* 中國同盟會 (The Revolutionary Alliance), vol. 6, pp. 143–71. 6 vols. Taipei: Cheng-chung, 1965. See also *HHKM*, 2.112–43

Ch'en Tse-hsien 陳澤憲. 'Shih-chiu shih-chi sheng-hsing ti ch'i-yueh Hua-kung chih' 十九世紀盛行的契約華工制 (The flourishing Chinese contract labour system in the nineteenth century). *Li-shih yen-chiu* 歷史研究 1963. 1, pp. 161–179

Cheng Ch'ang-kan 鄭昌淦. *Chung-Jih chia-wu chan-cheng* 中日甲午戰爭 (The Sino-Japanese War of 1894). Peking: Chung-kuo ch'ing-nien ch'u-pan she 中國青年出版社, 1957

Cheng Fu-kuang 鄭復光. *Huo-lun-ch'uan t'u-shuo* 火輪船圖説 (Illustrated treatise on the steamship). 1840. Reprinted in Wei Yuan, *Hai-kuo t'u-chih* (q.v., 1852 or later edn), *chüan* 85

Cheng Kuan-ying 鄭觀應. *I-yen* 易言 (Easy words). Shanghai: Chung-hua yin-wu chü 中華印務局, *c.* 1881

Cheng Kuan-ying. *Sheng-shih wei-yen tseng-ting hsin-pien* 盛世危言增訂新編 (Warnings to a prosperous age, rev. edn), 1892. Facsimile reproduction of 1910 reprint, Taipei: Hsueh-sheng, 1965

Cheng Kuan-ying. *Sheng-shih wei-yen hou-pien* 盛世危言後編 (Warnings to a prosperous age: a sequel). 15 *chüan*. Facsimile reproduction of 1910 edn, Taipei: Ta-t'ung 大通, 1968

Cheng, Shelly Hsien. 'The T'ung-meng-hui: its organization, leadership, and finances, 1905–1912'. University of Washington, Ph.D. dissertation. Seattle, 1962

Cheng, Yu-kwei. *Foreign trade and industrial development of China.* University Press of Washington, DC, 1956

Ch'eng Yen-sheng 程演生, ed. *Chung-kuo nei-luan wai-huo li-shih ts'ung-shu* 中國內亂外禍歷史叢書 (A historical series on China's internal disorder and external trouble). 98 works in 17 vols. Shanghai: Shen-chou kuo-kuang she, 1936

Chesneaux, Jean. *Le mouvement ouvrier chinois de 1919 à 1927.* Paris: Mouton, 1962. English translation: *The Chinese labor movement 1919–1927.* Stanford University Press, 1968

Chesneaux, Jean, ed. *Mouvements populaires et sociétés secrètes en Chine aux XIXe et XXe siècles.* Paris: Maspero, 1970

Chesneaux, Jean, ed. *Popular movements and secret societies in China, 1840–1950.* Stanford University Press, 1972; also cited as *PMSS*

Chesneaux, Jean. *Le Mouvement paysan chinois, 1840–1949.* Paris: Seuil, 1976

Chi, Madeleine. 'Shanghai-Hangchow-Ningpo railway loan: a case study of the Rights Recovery Movement'. *MAS*, 7.1 (1973) 85–106

Ch'i-hsin yang-hui kung-ssu shih-liao. See Nan-k'ai ta-hsueh Ching-chi hsi, Ching-chi yen-chiu so

Ch'i Ping-feng 丌冰峯. *Ch'ing-mo ko-ming yü chün-hsien ti lun-cheng* 清末革命與君憲的論爭 (Controversies between the revolutionaries and the constitutional monarchists in the late Ch'ing period). Taipei: IMH, Academia Sinica, 1966

Ch'i Ssu-ho 齊思和 *et al.* eds. *Ya-p'ien chan-cheng* 鴉片戰爭 (The Opium War). 6 vols. Shanghai: Shen-chou kuo-kuang she, 1954

Chiang Chung-yuan 江忠源. *Chiang Chung-lieh kung i-chi* 江忠烈公遺集 (The papers of the late Chiang Chung-yuan). 1873. Taipei reproduction, Hua-wen 華文, 1968

Chiang, Monlin. *Tides from the West: a Chinese autobiography.* New Haven: Yale University Press, 1947. Taipei reproduction, World Book Co., 1963

Chiang-su sheng hsing-cheng kung-shu shih-yeh ssu 江蘇省行政公署實業司, ed. *Chiang-su sheng shih-yeh hsing-cheng pao-kao shu* 江蘇省實業行政報告書 (Report on Kiangsu province's industrial administration). 10 *pien*. Soochow: Kiangsu provincial administration, 1914

Chiao, C. M. and Buck, J. L. 'The composition and growth of rural population groups in China'. *Chinese Economic Journal*, 2.2 (March 1928) 219–35

Chiao-t'ung shih. See next item

Chiao-t'ung t'ieh-tao pu chiao-t'ung shih pien-tsuan wei-yuan hui 交通鐵道部 交通史編纂委員會, comp. *Chiao-t'ung shih* 交通史 (History of transport and communications). 37 vols. Nanking: Ministry of Communications, 1930–7. Microfilm and a 'grand table of contents' published in 1970 are available at Center for Chinese Research Materials, Association of Research Libraries, Washington, DC

Chiao-yü tsa-chih 教育雜誌 ('The Chinese Educational Review'). Shanghai, etc.: Commercial Press, 1909–48

Chien Po-tsan 翦伯贊 *et al.* eds. *I-ho t'uan* 義和團 (The Boxers). 4 vols. Shanghai: Shen-chou kuo-kuang she, 1951

Chien Po-tsan *et al.* eds. *Wu-hsu pien-fa* 戊戌變法 (The reform of 1898). 4 vols. Shanghai: Shen-chou kuo-kuang she, 1953; also cited as *WHPF*

Ch'ien Shih-fu 錢實甫, comp. *Ch'ing-chi hsin-she chih-kuan nien-piao* 清季新設 職官年表 (Chronological tables of the newly established offices of the late Ch'ing period). Peking: Chung-hua, 1961

Chih-hsin pao 知新報 ('The reformer'). Thrice-monthly. Macao, 1897–1900

Chih-hsueh hui 質學會, comp. *Chih-hsueh ts'ung-shu ch'u-chi* 質學叢書初集 (Works of substantial learning, first series). 30 works in 38 *ts'e*. Wuchang: Chih-hsueh hui, 1897

Chin-liang 金梁. *Chin-shih jen-wu chih* 近世人物志 (Personalities of recent times). Shanghai, 1934; Taipei: Kuo-min 國民, 1955

Chin T'ien-chu 金天柱. *Ch'ing-chen shih-i* 清眞釋疑 (Resolving suspicions regarding Islam). 1738 preface. Chinkiang reprint: Ch'ing-chen ssu 清眞寺, 1876

Chin Ying-lin 金應麟. *Ch'ih-hua t'ang wen-ch'ao* 矛華堂文鈔 (Essays written at the Ch'ih-hua t'ang). 12 *chüan*, n.p., 1851

Ch'in Han-ts'ai 秦翰才. *Tso Wen-hsiang kung tsai hsi-pei* 左文襄公在西北 (Tso Tsung-t'ang in the north-west). Chungking, 1945. 3rd reprint, Shanghai: Commercial Press, 1947

Ch'in-ting ta-Ch'ing hui-tien 欽定大清會典 (Imperially approved Ch'ing dynasty compendium of institutions; also translated as 'Collected statutes of the Ch'ing dynasty'). Kuang-hsu edn. 100 *chüan*. Peking, 1899

China: consular reports. Microfilm for 1844–1906. Washington, DC: National Archives. See US National Archives, *Catalogue of National Archives Microfilm Publications*

China correspondence. Various issues and dates. See *British parliamentary papers*

China: dispatches. Microfilm for 1844–1906. Washington, DC: National Archives. See US National Archives, *Catalogue of National Archives Microfilm Publications*

China. Inspectorate-General of Customs. *Decennial reports on the trade, navigation, industries, etc. of the ports open to commerce ..., 1882–1891.* Shanghai: Imperial

Maritime Customs, 1893

China. Inspectorate-General of Customs. *Decennial reports on the trade, navigation, industries, etc. of the ports open to commerce . . . , 1902–1911.* 2 vols. Shanghai: Imperial Maritime Customs, 1913

China. Inspectorate-General of Customs. *Decennial reports on the trade, navigation, industries, etc. of the ports open to commerce . . . , 1922–1931.* Shanghai: Inspectorate General of Customs, 1933

China. Inspectorate-General of Customs. *Returns of trade and trade reports, 1906.* Shanghai: Imperial Maritime Customs, 1907

China: instructions. Microfilm for 1844–1906. Washington, DC: National Archives. See *Catalogue of National Archives Microfilm Publications*

Chine. Correspondance politique des consuls. Various issues. Paris: various dates

Ching Mei-chiu 景梅九. *Tsui-an* 罪案 (Record of a 'crime'). Peking: Kuo-feng jih-pao she 國風日報社, 1924. For Japanese trans., see Ōtaka Iwao and Hatano Tarō

Ching Su 景甦 and Lo Lun 羅崙. *Ch'ing-tai Shan-tung ching-ying ti-chu ti she-hui hsing-chih* 清代山東經營地主底社會性質 (The social characteristics of managerial landlords in Shantung during the Ch'ing period). Tsinan: Shan-tung jen-min ch'u-pan she 山東人民出版社, 1959. English trans. by Endymion Wilkinson, *Landlord and labor in Late Imperial China: case studies from Shandong.* Cambridge, Mass: Harvard University Press, 1977

Ch'ing-ch'ao hsu wen-hsien t'ung-k'ao. See Liu Chin-tsao

Ch'ing-chi wai-chiao shih-liao. See Wang Yen-wei and Wang Liang

Ch'ing Kuang-hsu ch'ao Chung-Fa chiao-she shih-liao 清光緒朝中法交涉史料 (Historical materials concerning Sino-French negotiations during the Kuang-hsu period). 22 *chüan.* Peiping: Palace Museum, 1933

Ch'ing Kuang-hsu ch'ao Chung-Jih chiao-she shih-liao 清光緒朝中日交涉史料 (Historical materials concerning Sino-Japanese negotiations during the Kuang-hsu period, 1875–1908). 88 *chüan.* Peiping: Palace Museum, 1932

Ch'ing-shih 清史 (History of the Ching dynasty). See Ch'ing-shih pien-tsuan wei-yuan hui

Ch'ing-shih kao 清史稿 (A draft history of the Ch'ing dynasty). See Chao Erh-hsun

Ch'ing-shih pien-tsuan wei-yuan hui 清史編纂委員會, comp. *Ch'ing-shih* 清史 (History of the Ch'ing dynasty). 8 vols. Taipei: Kuo-fang yen-chiu yuan 國防研究院, 1961–2

Ch'ing-tai ch'ou-pan i-wu shih-mo 清代籌辦夷務始末 (Complete record of the management of barbarian affairs). 80 *chüan* for the late Tao-kuang period (1836–50); 80 *chüan* for the Hsien-feng period (1851–61); 100 *chüan* for the T'ung-chih period (1862–74). Peiping: Palace Museum photolithograph, 1930; also cited as *IWSM*

Ch'ing-t'ing chih kai-ko yü fan-tung. See Chung-hua min-kuo k'ai-kuo wu-shih-nien wen-hsien pien-tsuan wei-yuan hui

Choe, Young. *The rule of the Taewön'gun, 1864–1873: Restoration in Yi Korea.*

Cambridge, Mass: Harvard University Press, 1972

Chou, Josephine Nailene. 'Frontier studies and changing frontier administration in late Ch'ing China: the case of Sinkiang, 1759–1911'. University of Washington, Ph.D. dissertation. Seattle, 1976

Chou Shan-p'ei 周善培. *Hsin-hai Ssu-ch'uan cheng-lu ch'in-li chi* 辛亥四川爭路親歷記 (An eyewitness account of the struggle for the Szechwan railway in 1911). Chungking: Jen-min, 1957

Chou Sheng-ch'uan 周盛傳. *Chou Wu-chuang kung i-shu* 周武壯公遺書 (Writings of the late Chou Sheng-ch'uan). Nanking, 1905. Taipei reproduction, Ch'eng-wen, 1969; also cited as *CWCK*

Chou Shu-chen 周叔楨. *Chou Chih-an hsien-sheng pieh-chuan* 周止菴先生別傳 (An unofficial biography of Chou Hsueh-hsi). Peiping: 1948 preface. Taipei reproduction, Wen-hai, 1966

Chow, Yung-teh. *Social mobility in China: status careers among the gentry in a Chinese community*. New York: Atherton Press, 1966

Chu Ho-chung 朱和中. 'Ou-chou T'ung-meng hui chi-shih' 歐洲同盟會紀實 (True account of the Revolutionary Alliance in Europe). *KMWH*, 2 (1953) 251–70

Chu, Samuel C. 'Chang Chien and the founding of Dah Sun'. *Ch'ing-hua hsueh-pao*, NS, 2.1 (1960) 301–17

Chu, Samuel C. 'Liu Ming-ch'uan and the modernization of Taiwan'. *JAS*, 23.1 (Nov. 1963) 37–53

Chu, Samuel C. *Reformer in modern China: Chang Chien, 1853–1926*. New York: Columbia University Press, 1965

Chu Shou-p'eng 朱壽朋, comp. *Tung-hua hsu-lu* 東華續錄 (The Tung-hua records, cont.). 64 *ts'e*. Shanghai: Chi-ch'eng 集成圖書公司, 1904

Chu Shou-p'eng, comp. *Tung-hua hsu-lu* 東華續錄 (Tung-hua records, continued [through the Kuang-hsu period]). 220 *chüan*. Shanghai: T'u-shu chi-ch'eng, 1909. Also entitled *Kuang-hsu ch'ao tung-hua lu*. Peking reproduction, Chung-hua, 1958

Chu Wen-ch'ang 朱文長 (Wen-Djang Chu). 'T'an yu-kuan hsi-pei hui-luan ti liang-ko wen-t'i' 談有關西北回亂的兩個問題 (Two problems relating to the Muslim rebellion in the north-west). *Ch'ing-hua hsueh-pao*, NS, 5.1 (1965) 125–41

Chu, Wen-Djang. *The Moslem Rebellion in northwest China, 1862–1878*. The Hague and Paris: Mouton, 1966

Ch'üan Han-sheng 全漢昇. *Han-Yeh-P'ing kung-ssu shih-lueh* 漢冶萍公司史略 (A brief history of the Hanyehping Co.). Chinese University of Hong Kong, 1972

Ch'üan Tsu-wang 全祖望, ed. *Sung Yuan hsueh-an*. See Huang Tsung-hsi

Chuang Chi-fa 莊吉發. *Ching-shih ta hsueh-t'ang* 京師大學堂 ([The predecessor of] Peking University). Taipei: National Taiwan University, College of Letters, 1970

Chūgoku 中国 (China). Tokyo: Chūgoku no Kai 中国の会, 1963–72

Chun, Hae-jong. 'Sino-Korean tributary relations in the Ch'ing period', in *CWO*, 90–111

Chung-hua min-kuo k'ai-kuo wu-shih-nien wen-hsien pien-tsuan wei-yuan hui 中華民國開國五十年文獻編纂委員會, comp. *Wu-ch'ang shou-i* 武昌首義 (The initiation of the righteous rising at Wuchang). 2nd edn, amplified. Taipei: Cheng-chung, 1961

Chung-hua min-kuo k'ai-kuo wu-shih-nien wen-hsien pien-tsuan wei-yuan-hui, comp. *Chung-hua min-kuo k'ai-kuo wu-shih-nien wen-hsien* 中華民國開國五十年文獻 (Documents concerning the founding of the Republic of China, compiled at its fiftieth anniversary). Series 1 in 16 vols., including *Ko-ming yuan-yuan* 革命遠源 (Early sources of revolution), 2 vols.; *Lieh-ch'iang ch'in-lueh* 列強侵略 (Aggression of the powers), 4 vols.; *Ch'ing-t'ing chih kai-ko yü fan-tung* 清廷之改革與反動 (Reform and reaction at the Ch'ing court), 2 vols.; *Ko-ming chih ch'ang-tao yü fa-chan* 革命之倡導與發展 (The leadership and development of the revolution), 8 vols. Series 2 in 5 vols., including *Wu-ch'ang shou-i* 武昌首義 (The initiation of the righteous rising at Wuchang), 1 vol.; *K'ai-kuo kuei-mu* 開國規模 (Arrangements at the founding of the Republic), 1 vol.; *Ko-sheng kuang-fu* 各省光復 (Restoration of the provinces), 3 vols. Taipei: Cheng-chung, 1961–6

Chung-hua min-kuo k'ai-kuo wu-shih-nien wen-hsien pien-tsuan wei-yuan hui, comp. *Ko-ming chih ch'ang-tao yü fa-chan* 革命之倡導與發展 (The leadership and development of the revolution). 8 vols. Taipei: Cheng-chung, 1964–5. See above

Chung-hua min-kuo k'ai-kuo wu-shih-nien wen-hsien pien-tsuan wei-yuan hui, comp. *Ch'ing-t'ing chih kai-ko yü fan-tung* 清廷之改革與反動 (Reform and reaction at the Ch'ing court). 2 vols. Taipei: Cheng-chung, 1966. See above

Chung-kuo chin san-pai-nien she-hui ching-chi shih lun-chi. See Ts'un-ts'ui hsueh-she

Chung-kuo chin-tai she-hui ching-chi shih lun-chi. See Ts'un-ts'ui hsueh-she

Chung-kuo jen-min cheng-chih hsieh-shang hui-i ch'üan-kuo wei-yuan-hui wen-shih tzu-liao yen-chiu wei-yuan-hui 中國人民政治協商會議全國委員會文史資料研究委員會 ed. *Hsin-hai ko-ming hui-i lu* 辛亥革命回憶錄 (Reminiscences of the 1911 Revolution). 6 vols. Peking: Chung-hua, 1961–3

Chung-kuo jen-min cheng-chih hsieh-shang hui-i Hu-pei sheng wei-yuan hui 中國人民政治協商會議湖北省委員會. ed. *Hsin-hai shou-i hui-i lu* 辛亥首義回憶錄 (Reminiscences of the righteous beginnings of the 1911 Revolution). Wu-han: Jen-min, 1957

Chung-kuo jen-min ta-hsueh Chung-kuo li-shih chiao-yen-shih 中國人民大學中國歷史教研室, ed. *Chung-kuo tzu-pen-chu-i meng-ya wen-t'i t'ao-lun chi* 中國資本主義萌芽問題討論集 (Collected papers on the problem of the incipiency of capitalism in China). 3 vols. Peking: San-lien, 1957–60

Chung-kuo jen-min yin-hang Shang-hai-shih fen-hang 中國人民銀行上海市分行 (Shanghai branch of the Chinese People's Bank), ed. *Shang-hai ch'ien-chuang shih-liao* 上海錢庄史料 (Historical materials on Shanghai native banks). Shanghai: Jen-min, 1960; second printing, 1961

Chung-kuo k'o-hsueh yuan Chi-lin-sheng fen-yuan li-shih yen-chiu-so 中國科
學院吉林省分院歷史研究所 *et al.* eds. *Chin-tai tung-pei jen-min ko-ming yun-tung
shih* 近代東北人民革命運動史 (A history of the people's revolutionary movement in the north-east in modern times). Ch'ang-ch'un: Jen-min, 1960;
Tokyo reproduction, Daian, 1964

Chung-kuo k'o-hsueh yuan chin-tai-shih yen-chiu-so 中國科學院近代史
研究所 *et al.* eds. *Yang-wu yun-tung* 洋務運動 (The Western affairs movement).
8 vols. Shanghai: Jen-min, 1961; also cited as *YWYT*

Chung-kuo k'o-hsueh yuan ching-chi yen-chiu-so 中國科學院經濟研究所 *et al.*
eds. *Pei-ching Jui-fu-hsiang* 北京瑞福祥 (The Jui-fu-hsiang firm of Peking).
Peking: San-lien, 1959

Chung-kuo k'o-hsueh yuan Shan-tung fen-yuan li-shih yen-chiu-so 中國科學
院山東分院歷史研究所 ed. *I-ho-t'uan yun-tung liu-shih chou-nien chi-nien lun-wen
chi* 義和團運動六十周年紀念論文集 (Articles commemorating the sixtieth
anniversary of the Boxer movement). Peking: Chung-hua, 1961

Chung-kuo k'o-hsueh yuan Shang-hai ching-chi yen-chiu-so 中國科學院上海
經濟研究所 . *Nan-yang hsiung-ti yen-ts'ao kung-ssu shih-liao* 南洋兄弟煙草公司
史料 (Historical materials of the Nanyang Brothers Tobacco Co.). Shanghai:
Jen-min, 1958

Chung-kuo Kuo-min-tang chung-yang wei-yuan-hui tang-shih shih-liao pien-
tsuan wei-yuan-hui 中國國民黨中央委員會黨史史料編纂委員會 comp. *Ko-
ming wen-hsien* 革命文獻 (Documents of the revolution). Collections (*chi* 輯)
1–60, each *chi* usually in one vol. but may include subdivisions. Taipei:
Chung-yang wen-wu, 1953–72; cited as *KMWH*, according to the consecutive (*tsung* 總) page numbers

Chung-kuo she-hui ching-chi shih chi-k'an 中國社會經濟史集刊 (Chinese social and
economic history review). Quarterly. Nanking: Academia Sinica, 1933–9

Chung-kuo shih-hsueh hui Chi-nan fen-hui 中國史學會濟南分會, comp. *Shantung chin-tai shih tzu-liao* 山東近代史資料 (Materials on the modern history of
Shantung). 2 vols. Tsinan: Jen-min, 1957

Chung-yang yen-chiu-yuan chin-tai-shih yen-chiu-so, 中央研究院近代史研究所,
comp. *Hai-fang tang* 海防檔 (Archives on coastal defence). Hardback, 9 vols;
paperback, 17 vols. Taipei: IMH, Academia Sinica, 1957

Chung-yang yen-chiu-yuan chin-tai-shih yen-chiu-so. *K'uang-wu tang* 礦務檔
(Archives on mining affairs). 8 vols. Taipei: IMH, Academia Sinica, 1960

Chung-yang yen-chiu-yuan chin-tai-shih yen-chiu-so, ed. *Chung-Fa Yueh-nan
chiao-she tang* 中法越南交涉檔 (Archives on Sino-French negotiations over
Vietnam). 7 vols. Taipei: IMH, Academia Sinica, 1962

Chung-yang yen-chiu-yuan chin-tai-shih yen-chiu-so, comp. *Chung-Mei kuan-hsi
shih-liao* 中美關係史料 (Historical documents on Sino-American relations,
1805–74). 3 vols. Taipei: IMH, Academia Sinica, 1968

Chung-yang yen-chiu-yuan chin-tai-shih yen-chiu-so, comp. *Chin-tai Chung-kuo
tui Hsi-fang chi lieh-ch'iang jen-shih tzu-liao hui-pien* 近代中國對西方及列強認識
資料彙編 (Compendium of materials on modern Chinese understanding of

the West and of the various powers). 2 vols. Taipei: IMH, Academia Sinica, 1972; also cited as *HFJS*

Chung-yang yen-chiu-yuan chin-tai-shih yen-chiu-so, ed. *Ch'ing-chi Chung-Jih-Han kuan-hsi shih-liao* 清季中日韓關係史料 (Documents on Sino-Japanese-Korean relations, 1864–1911). 11 vols. Taipei: IMH, Academia Sinica, 1972

Chung-yang yen-chiu-yuan chin-tai-shih yen-chiu-so chi-k'an 中央研究院近代史研究所集刊 (Bulletin of the Institute of Modern History, Academia Sinica). Taipei, Aug. 1969– ; also cited as *CYCT*

CIR: Wright, Mary C. ed. *China in revolution: the first phase, 1900–1913*

CJCC: Shao Hsun-cheng *et al.* eds. *Chung-Jih chan-cheng*

Clyde, Paul H., comp. *United States policy toward China: diplomatic and public documents 1839–1939*. Durham: Duke University Press, 1940

Cohen, Paul A. *China and Christianity: the missionary movement and the growth of Chinese antiforeignism, 1860–1870*. Cambridge, Mass.: Harvard University Press, 1963

Cohen, Paul A. 'Wang T'ao and incipient Chinese nationalism'. *JAS*, 26.4 (Aug. 1967) 559–74

Cohen, Paul A. *Between tradition and modernity: Wang T'ao and reform in late Ch'ing China*. Cambridge, Mass.: Harvard University Press, 1974

Cohen, Paul A. 'Littoral and hinterland in nineteenth-century China: the "Christian" reformers', in John K. Fairbank, ed. *The missionary enterprise in China and America* (q.v.), pp. 197–225

Cohen, Paul A. and Schrecker, John E., eds. *Reform in nineteenth-century China*. Cambridge, Mass.: Harvard University Press, 1976

Comber, Leon F. *Chinese secret societies in Malaya: a survey of the Triad Society from 1800 to 1900*. Locust Valley, NY: J. J. Augustin for the Association for Asian Studies, 1959

Conroy, Hilary. *The Japanese seizure of Korea, 1868–1910: a study of realism and idealism in international relations*. Philadelphia: University of Pennsylvania Press, 1960

Cordier, Henri. *Histoire des relations de la Chine avec les puissances occidentales*. 3 vols. Paris: F. Alcan, 1901–2

CSL: Ta-Ch'ing li-ch'ao shih-lu

CWCK: Chou Sheng-ch'uan. *Chou Wu-chuang kung i-shu*

CWHK: Chang Chih-tung. *Chang Wen-hsiang kung ch'üan-chi*

CWO: Fairbank, John K., ed. *The Chinese world order*

CYCT: Chung-yang yen-chiu-yuan chin-tai-shih yen-chiu-so chi-k'an

Davidson, James W. *The island of Formosa, past and present: history, people, resources, and commercial prospects*. London and New York: Macmillan, 1903. Taipei reproduction, Bank of Taiwan, 1972

DeBary, William Theodore, Chan, Wing-tsit and Watson, Burton, eds. *Sources of Chinese tradition*. New York: Columbia University Press, 1960

Des Forges, Roger V. *Hsi-liang and the Chinese national revolution*. New Haven: Yale University Press, 1973

Drake, Fred W. *China charts the world: Hsu Chi-yü and his geography of 1848*. Cambridge, Mass.: Harvard University Press, 1975.

DuBoulay, N. W. H. *An epitome of the China-Japanese War, 1894–95*. London: Harrison and Sons, 1896

Dutt, Vidya Prakash, 'The first week of revolution: the Wuchang uprising', in *CIR*, 383–416

Eastman, Lloyd E. 'Ch'ing-i and Chinese policy formation during the nineteenth century'. *JAS*, 24.4 (Aug. 1965) 595–611

Eastman, Lloyd E. *Throne and mandarins: China's search for a policy during the Sino-French controversy, 1880–1885*. Cambridge, Mass.: Harvard University Press, 1967

Eastman, Lloyd E. 'Political reformism in China before the Sino-Japanese War'. *JAS*, 27 (Aug. 1968) 695–710

Efimov, G. V. *Istoriko-bibliograficheskii obzor istochnikov i literatury po novoi istorii Kitaia* (Historical-bibliographical review of the sources concerning the literature on the modern history of China). 3 vols. Leningrad: Izd-vo Leningradskogo Universiteta, 1965–72

Elisseeff, Vadime. 'The middle empire, a distant empire, an empire without neighbors'. *Diogenes*, 42 (Summer 1963) 60–4

Elvin, Mark. 'The administration of Shanghai, 1905–1914', in *CCTW*, 239–62

Elvin, Mark and Skinner, G. William, eds. *The Chinese city between two worlds*. Stanford University Press, 1974; also cited as *CCTW*

Esherick, Joseph W. '1911: a review'. *Modern China*, 2.2 (April 1976) 141–84

Esherick, Joseph W. *Reform and revolution in China: the 1911 Revolution in Hunan and Hubei*. Berkeley: University of California Press, 1976

Etō Shinkichi 衛藤瀋吉. 'Nihonjin no Chūgoku-kan: Takasugi Shinsaku ra no baai' 日本人の中国観—高杉晋作らの場合 (Japanese views of China: the cases of Takasugi Shinsaku and others), in *Niida Noboru Hakushi tsuitō rombunshū* 仁井田陞博士追悼論文集 (Essays to commemorate Dr Niida Noboru), vol. 3: *Nihon hō to Ajia* 日本法とアジア (Japanese law and Asia), pp. 51–71. Tokyo: Keisō Shobō 勁草書房, 1970

Etō Shinkichi, ed. *Sanjū-sannen no yume* 三十三年の夢 (Thirty-three years' dream: Miyazaki Torazō's memoirs). Tokyo: Heibonsha, 1967. See also Miyazaki Ryūsuke and Onogawa Hidemi, eds. *Miyazaki Tōten zenshū*

Fairbank, John K. 'Patterns behind the Tientsin massacre'. *HJAS*, 20 (1957) 480–511

Fairbank, John K., ed. *The Chinese world order: traditional China's foreign relations*. Cambridge, Mass.: Harvard University Press, 1968; also cited as *CWO*

Fairbank, John K., ed. *The missionary enterprise in China and America*. Cambridge, Mass.: Harvard University Press, 1974

Fairbank, John K., Bruner, Katherine Frost and Matheson, Elizabeth MacLeod, eds. *The I.G. in Peking: letters of Robert Hart, Chinese Maritime Customs 1868–1907*. 2 vols. Cambridge, Mass.: Harvard University Press, 1975

Fairbank, John K., Reischauer, Edwin O. and Craig, Albert M. *East Asia: the modern transformation.* Boston: Houghton Mifflin, 1965

Fairbank, John K. and Teng, Ssu-yü. *Ch'ing administration: three studies.*
Cambridge, Mass.: Harvard University Press, 1960

Fan Pai-ch'uan 樊百川. 'Chung-kuo shou-kung-yeh tsai wai-kuo tzu-pen-chu-i
ch'in-ju hou ti tsao-yü ho ming-yun' 中國手工業在外國資本主義侵入後的
遭遇和命運 (The fate of Chinese handicraft industry after the incursion of
foreign capitalism). *Li-shih yen-chiu* 歷史研究, 1962.3, pp. 88—115

Fass, Josef. 'Revolutionary activity in the province Hu-pei and the Wu-ch'ang
uprising of 1911'. *Archiv Orientálni,* 28 (1960) 127—49

Fass, Josef. 'The role of the New Style Army in the 1911 Revolution in China'.
Archiv Orientálni, 30 (1962) 183—91

Fei Hsing-chien 費行簡. *Chin-tai ming-jen hsiao-chuan* 近代名人小傳
(Biographical notes on famous men of modern times). Shanghai: 1916;
Taipei: Wen-hai, 1966

Feng Kuei-fen 馮桂芬. *Chiao-pin-lu k'ang-i* 校邠廬抗議 (Straightforward words
from the Lodge of Early Chou Studies). 2 *chüan.* Wu-hsien, Kiangsu: the
Feng family, 1884

Feng Tzu-yu 馮自由. 'Chi Chung-kuo T'ung-meng hui' 記中國同盟會
(An account of the China Revolutionary Alliance). *KMWH,* 2 (1953) 145—57

FEQ: Far Eastern Quarterly. See *JAS*

Feuerwerker, Albert. *China's early industrialization: Sheng Hsuan-huai (1844—1916)
and mandarin enterprise.* Cambridge, Mass.: Harvard University Press, 1958

Feuerwerker, Albert, ed. *History in Communist China.* Cambridge, Mass.: MIT
Press, 1968

Feuerwerker, Albert. 'Handicraft and manufactured cotton textiles in China,
1871—1910'. *Journal of Economic History,* 30.2 (June 1970) 338—78

Feuerwerker, Albert. 'Industrial enterprise in twentieth-century China: the Chee
Hsin Cement Company', in *AMCH,* 304—41

Feuerwerker, Albert. *Rebellion in nineteenth-century China.* Ann Arbor: Center for
Chinese Studies, University of Michigan, 1975

Feuerwerker, Albert, Murphey, Rhoads and Wright, Mary C., eds. *Approaches to
modern Chinese history.* Berkeley: University of California Press, 1967; also cited
as *AMCH*

Fields, Lanny Bruce. *Tso Tsung-t'ang and the Muslims: statecraft in northwest China,
1868—1880.* Kingston, Ontario: The Limestone Press, 1978

Fincher, John. 'Political provincialism and the national revolution', in *CIR,*
185—226

Fleming, Peter. *The siege at Peking.* New York: Harper, 1959

Fletcher, Joseph. 'Central Asian Sufism and Ma Ming-hsin's New Teaching', in
Chieh-hsien Ch'en, ed. *Proceedings of the Fourth East Asian Altaistic Conference,*
75—96. Taipei, Dec. 1971

FO 17. China Political Correspondence, 1815—1905. London: Public Record
Office

FO 228. China Consular Correspondence, 1834—1930. London: Public Record

Office

FO 233. Chinese Secretary's Office, Legation File. London: Public Record Office

FO 371. Political Correspondence, 1906–32. London: Public Record Office

FO 405. Confidential Prints on China, 1848–1954. London: Public Record Office

FO 682. Chinese Secretary's Office, Legation File, 1839–1939. London: Public Record Office

Fo-shan chung-i hsiang chih. See Hsi Pao-kan

Folsom, Kenneth E. *Friends, guests, and colleagues: the* mu-fu *system in the late Ch'ing period.* Berkeley: University of California Press, 1968

Foreign relations of the United States, 1866– . Washington, DC: Government Printing Office

Franke, Wolfgang. *The reform and abolition of the traditional Chinese examination system.* Cambridge, Mass.: Harvard University Press, 1960

Frechtling, Louis E. 'Anglo-Russian rivalry in eastern Turkestan, 1863–1881'. *Journal of the Royal Central Asian Society*, 26.3 (1939) 471–89

Friedman, Edward. *Backward toward revolution: the Chinese revolutionary party.* Berkeley: University of California Press, 1974

Fu Tsung-mou 傅宗懋. *Ch'ing-tai chün-chi-ch'u tsu-chih chi chih-chang chih yen-chiu* 清代軍機處組織及職掌之研究 (A study of the organization and functions of the Grand Council in the Ch'ing period). Taipei: Chia-hsin, 1967

Fukuda Shōzō 福田省三. *Kakyō keizai ron* 華僑經濟論 (On the Overseas Chinese economy). Tokyo: Ganshōdō Shoten 巖松堂書店, 1939

Fukushima Yasumasa 福島安正, comp. *Rimpō heibi ryaku* 隣邦兵備略 (Military preparedness in neighbouring countries). 2nd edn. 5 vols. Tokyo: Rikugun Bunko 陸軍文庫, 1882

Fung, Edmund S. K. 'The Kung-chin hui: a late Ch'ing revolutionary society'. *Journal of Oriental Studies*, 11.2 (1973) 193–206

Fung, Edmund S. K. 'The T'ung-meng-hui Central China Bureau and the Wuchang uprising'. *Journal of the Institute of Chinese Studies of the Chinese University of Hong Kong*, 7.2 (1974) 477–96

Fung, Edmund S. K. 'Li Yuan-hung and the Revolution of 1911', *Monumenta Serica*, 31 (1974–5) 151–71

Fung, Edmund S. K. 'Military subversion in the Chinese revolution of 1911' *MAS*, 9.1 (1975) 103–23

Fung, Edmund S. K. 'Post-1949 Chinese historiography on the 1911 revolution'. *Modern China*, 4.2 (April 1978) 181–214

Furth, Charlotte, ed. *The limits of change: essays on conservative alternatives in Republican China.* Cambridge, Mass.: Harvard University Press, 1976

Gasster, Michael. *Chinese intellectuals and the Revolution of 1911: the birth of modern Chinese radicalism.* Seattle: University of Washington Press, 1969

Gerschenkron, Alexander. *Economic backwardness in historical perspective.* Cambridge, Mass.: Harvard University Press, 1962

Gipoulon, Catherine. *Qiu Jin, femme et révolutionnaire en Chine au XIXème siècle.* Paris : Editions des femmes, 1976

Godley, Michael R. 'The late Ch'ing courtship of the Chinese in Southeast Asia'. *JAS*, 34.2 (Feb. 1975) 361–85

Gordon, Charles George. Papers, British Museum

Gordon, Leonard H. D., ed. *Taiwan: studies in Chinese local history.* New York: Columbia University Press, 1970

Great Britain. Foreign Office. *Report on the native cloths in use in the Amoy consular district.* FO, Miscellaneous series, 1886, no. 19

Grimm, Tilemann. '*Shu-yuan* in the context of urbanistic research in traditional China'. Research Conference on Urban Society in Traditional China, 1968

Grimm, Tilemann. 'Academies and urban system in Kwangtung', in G. William Skinner, ed. *The city in late imperial China.* pp. 475–98. Stanford University Press, 1977

Hai-fang tang: see Chung-yang yen-chiu-yuan chin-tai-shih yen-chiu-so

Hake, Alfred E. *Events in the Taiping Rebellion.* London: W. H. Allen, 1891

Hamilton, Gary G. 'Merchants and modernization: changing views of Chinese commerce'. Paper delivered at the California Regional Seminar in Chinese Studies, University of California, Berkeley, December 1975

Hao Yen-p'ing 郝延平. 'Yu shou-chiu tao ko-hsin' 由守舊到革新 (From conservatism to reform). *Ta-lu tsa-chih* 大陸雜誌 20.7 (April 1960) 26–7

Hao, Yen-p'ing. 'The abortive cooperation between reformers and revolutionaries (1895–1900)'. *Papers on China*, 15 (1961) 91–114

Hao, Yen-p'ing. 'A study of the Ch'ing-liu tang: the disinterested scholar-offical group, 1875–1884'. *Papers on China*, 16 (1962) 40–65

Hao, Yen-p'ing. 'Cheng Kuan-ying: the comprador as reformer'. *JAS*, 29.1 (Nov. 1969) 15–22

Hao, Yen-p'ing. 'A "new class" in China's treaty ports: the rise of the comprador-merchants'. *Business History Review*, 44.4 (Winter 1970) 446–59

Hao, Yen-p'ing. *The comprador in nineteenth century China: bridge between East and West*. Cambridge, Mass.: Harvard University Press, 1970

Hart, Robert. 'Notes on Chinese matters', in Frederick W. Williams, *Anson Burlingame and the first Chinese mission to foreign powers*, 285–98. New York: C. Scribner and Sons, 1912

Hart, Robert. *These from the land of Sinim, essays on the Chinese question.* London: Chapman and Hall, 1901

Hart, Robert. Letters 1968–1907, see Fairbank, John K. *et al.* eds.

Hatano, Yoshihiro. 'The new armies', in *CIR*, 365–82

Hayes, Carlton J. H. *A generation of materialism, 1871–1970.* New York: Harper, 1941

Hedtke, C. H. 'Reluctant revolutionaries: Szechwan and the Ch'ing collapse, 1898–1911'. University of California, Ph.D. dissertation. Berkeley, 1968

Heng-feng sha-ch'ang ti fa-sheng fa-chan yü kai-tsao 恒豐紗廠的發生發展與改造 (The origin, development and reconstruction of the Heng-feng

Spinning Mill). Shanghai: Jen-min, 1958

HFHC: Wang Hsi-ch'i, comp. *Hsiao-fang-hu chai yü-ti ts'ung-ch'ao*

HFJS: Chung-yang yen-chiu-yuan chin-tai-shih yen-chiu-so, comp. *Chin-tai Chung-kuo tui Hsi-fang chi lieh-ch'iang jen-shih tzu-liao hui-pien*

HHKM: Ch'ai Te-keng *et al.* eds. *Hsin-hai ko-ming*

HHWS: Hu-pei sheng che-hsueh she-hui k'o-hsueh hsueh-hui lien-ho hui, ed. *Hsin-hai ko-ming wu-shih chou-nien lun-wen chi*

HJAS: Harvard Journal of Asiatic Studies

HMCI: Pai Shou-i, ed. *Hui-min ch'i-i*

Ho Ch'ang-ling 賀長齡. *Huang-ch'ao ching-shih wen-pien* 皇朝經世文編 (Collection of Ch'ing dynasty writings on statecraft). 120 *chüan*. 1873 edn. Taipei reproduction, Wen-hai, 1972

Ho Ch'i 何啓 and Hu Li-yuan 胡禮垣. *Hsin-cheng chen-ch'üan* 新政眞詮 (The true interpretation of new policies). Hong Kong, 1895. Reprinted in 6 *ts'e* by Chung-kuo pao-kuan 中國報館, 1900

Ho, Ping-ti. *Studies on the population of China, 1368–1953*. Cambridge, Mass.: Harvard University Press, 1959

Ho, Ping-ti. *The ladder of success in imperial China: aspects of social mobility, 1368–1911*. New York: Columbia University Press, 1962

Ho Ping-ti 何炳棣. *Chung-kuo hui-kuan shih-lun* 中國會館史論 (A historical survey of 'Landsmannschaften' in China). Taipei: Hsueh-sheng, 1966

Holcombe, Chester. *China's past and future*. London: Morgan and Scott, 1904

Hou, Chi-ming. 'Economic dualism: the case of China, 1840–1937'. *Journal of Economic History*, 23.3 (1965) 277–97

Hou, Chi-ming. *Foreign investment and economic development in China, 1849–1937*. Cambridge, Mass.: Harvard University Press, 1965

Howard, Richard C. 'K'ang Yu-wei (1858–1927): his intellectual background and his early thought', in Arthur F. Wright and Denis Twitchett, eds. *Confucian personalities*, pp. 294–316. Stanford University Press, 1962

Howard, Richard C. 'Japan's role in the reform program of K'ang Yu-wei', in Jung-pang Lo, ed. *K'ang Yu-wei: a biography and a symposium* (q.v.), pp. 288–302

Hozumi Yatsuka 穗積八束. *Kokumin kyōiku: aikokushin* 國民教育：愛國心 (National education: the spirit of patriotism). 1897. 6th edn. Tokyo, 1912

Hsi Pao-kan 冼寶榦, comp. *Fo-shan chung-i hsiang-chih* 佛山忠義鄉志 (Gazetteer of Fo-shan). 20 *chüan*. Canton, 1923

Hsi Yü-fu 席裕福 *et al.* comp. *Huang-ch'ao cheng-tien lei-tsuan* 皇朝政典類纂 (Classified compendium on the governmental documents of the Ch'ing dynasty). 500 *chüan*. Shanghai: T'u-shu chi-ch'eng, 1903; Taipei reproduction, Ch'eng-wen, 1969

Hsia-erh kuan-chen 遐邇貫珍 ('The Chinese serial' or 'A serial of foreign and domestic news'). Normally monthly. Hong Kong: *c.* 1853–8

Hsia Hsieh 夏燮. *Chung-hsi chi-shih* 中西紀事 (A record of Sino-Western affairs). 1865 edn. Taipei reproduction, Wen-hai, 1962

Hsiang-hsueh pao 湘學報 (Bulletin of Hunan learning). Changsha: Chiao-ching shu-yuan 校經書院, 1896–7

Hsiang-kang Hua-tzu jih-pao 香港華字日報 (Chinese Mail of Hong Kong, a daily), 1864–1940; also cited as *HTJP*

Hsiao-fang-hu chai yü-ti ts'ung-ch'ao. See Wang Hsi-ch'i

Hsiao I-shan 蕭一山. *Ch'ing-tai t'ung-shih* 清代通史 (A general history of the Ch'ing period). Rev. edn. 5 vols. Taipei: Commercial Press, 1962–3

Hsiao, Kung-chuan. 'Weng T'ung-ho and the reform movement of 1898'. *Ch'ing-hua hsueh-pao*, NS 1.2 (April 1957) 111–245

Hsiao, Kung-chuan. 'K'ang Yu-wei and Confucianism'. *Monumenta Serica*, 18 (1958) 88–212

Hsiao, Kung-chuan. *Rural China: imperial control in the nineteenth century*. Seattle: University of Washington Press, 1960

Hsiao, Kung-chuan. 'The philosophical thought of K'ang Yu-wei: an attempt at a new synthesis'. *Monumenta Serica*, 21 (1962) 129–93

Hsiao, Kung-chuan. 'The case for constitutional monarchy: K'ang Yu-wei's plan for the democratization of China'. *Monumenta Serica*, 24 (1965) 1–83

Hsiao, Kung-chuan. 'In and out of utopia: K'ang Yu-wei's social thought'. *The Chung Chi Journal*, 7.1 (Nov. 1967) 1–18; 7.2 (May 1968) 101–49; 8.1 (Nov. 1968) 1–52

Hsiao, Kung-chuan. 'Economic modernization: K'ang Yu-wei's ideas in historical perspective'. *Monumenta Serica*, 27 (1968) 1–90

Hsiao, Kung-chuan. 'Administrative modernization: K'ang Yu-wei's proposals and their historical meaning'. *Ch'ing-hua hsueh-pao*, NS, 8.1 and 2 (1970) 1–35

Hsiao, Kung-chuan. *A modern China and a new world: K'ang Yu-wei, reformer and utopian, 1858–1927*. Seattle: University of Washington Press, 1975

Hsiao, Liang-lin. *China's foreign trade statistics, 1864–1949*. Cambridge, Mass.: Harvard University Press, 1974

Hsiao Ling-yü 蕭令裕. *Ying-chi-li chi* 英吉利記 (On England), in *HFHC*, *ts'e* 77

Hsiao Ling-yü. *Yueh-tung shih-po lun* 粵東市舶論 (On foreign trade and shipping in Kwangtung), in *HFHC*, *ts'e* 75

Hsieh Ch'ing-kao 謝清高 and Yang Ping-nan 楊炳南. *Hai-lu* 海錄 (Records of the seas), in *HFHC*, *ts'e* 55

Hsieh Kuo-chen 謝國楨. 'Chin-tai shu-yuan hsueh-hsiao chih-tu pien-ch'ien k'ao' 近代書院學校制度變遷考 (Changes in the institutions of academy and school in the modern period), in Hu Shih 胡適 *et al.* eds. *Chang Chü-sheng ch'i-shih sheng-jih chi-nien lun-wen-chi* 張菊生七十生日紀念論文集 (A collection of essays in celebration of Chang Yuan-chi's seventieth birthday), 281–322. Shanghai: Commercial Press, 1937

Hsieh Kuo-chen. *Ming Ch'ing chih chi tang-she yun-tung k'ao* 明清之際黨社運動考 (A study of parties and societies during the transition from Ming to Ch'ing). Taipei: Commercial Press, 1967

Hsieh, Pao-chao. *The government of China 1644–1911*. Baltimore: Johns Hopkins Press, 1925

Hsieh, Winston. 'The Revolution of 1911 in Kwangtung'. Harvard University, Ph.D. dissertation. Cambridge, Mass., 1969

Hsieh, Winston. 'Triads, salt smugglers and local uprisings: observations on the social and economic background of the Waichow Revolution of 1911', in *PMSS*, 145–64

Hsieh, Winston. 'Peasant insurrection and the marketing hierarchy in the Canton delta, 1911', in *CCTW*, 119–41

Hsieh, Winston. *Chinese historiography on the Revolution of 1911: a critical survey and a selected bibliography*. Stanford: Hoover Institution Press, 1975

Hsien-hsing hsing-lü. See Shen Chia-pen

Hsin-hai shou-i hui-i lu. See Chung-kuo jen-min cheng-chih hsieh-shang hui-i Hu-pei sheng wei-yuan-hui

Hsin-min ts'ung-pao 新民叢報 (The new people miscellany). Yokohama and Tokyo, 1902–7

Hsiu-hsiang hsiao-shuo 繡像小説 (Illustrated stories). Bi-monthly. Shanghai: Commercial Press, 1903–6

Hsu Ch'ang-chih 徐昌治, comp. *P'o-hsieh chi* 破邪集 (An anthology of writings exposing heterodoxy). 1640 preface. 1855 edn (a Japanese blockprint)

Hsu Chi-yü 徐繼畬. *Ying huan chih-lueh* 瀛環志略 (A brief survey of the maritime circuit). 10 *chüan*. Foochow, 1850 edn

Hsu Chi-yü *Sung-k'an hsien-sheng ch'üan-chi* 松龕先生全集 (Complete works of Hsu Chi-yü). 10 *chüan*. 1915 preface, n.p.

Hsu I-sheng 徐義生. *Chung-kuo chin-tai wai-chai shih t'ung-chi tzu-liao, 1853–1927* 中國近代外債史統計資料 (Statistical materials on the history of China's foreign loans, 1853–1927). Peking: Chung-hua, 1962

Hsu, Immanuel C. Y. *China's entrance into the family of nations: the diplomatic phase, 1858–1880*. Cambridge, Mass.: Harvard University Press, 1960

Hsu, Immanuel C. Y. 'Gordon in China, 1880'. *Pacific Historical Review*, 23.2 (May 1964) 147–66

Hsu, Immanuel C. Y. 'The great policy debate in China, 1874: maritime defense vs. frontier defense'. *HJAS*, 25 (1965) 212–28

Hsu, Immanuel C. Y. *The Ili crisis: a study of Sino-Russian diplomacy, 1871–1881*. Oxford: Clarendon, 1965

Hsu, Immanuel C. Y. 'The late Ch'ing reconquest of Sinkiang: a reappraisal of Tso Tsung-t'ang's role'. *Central Asiatic Journal*, 12.1 (1968) 50–63

Hsu, Immanuel C. Y. *The rise of modern China*. New York: Oxford University Press, 1970

Hsu Jun 徐潤. *Hsu Yü-chai tzu-hsu nien-p'u* 徐愚齋自叙年譜 (Hsu Jun's chronological autobiography). Privately printed by the Hsu family of Hsiang-shan, *c.* 1927; Taipei reproduction, Shih-huo ch'u-pan she 食貨出版社, 1977

Hsu, Kai-yu. *Chou En-lai: China's gray eminence*. Garden City, NY: Doubleday, 1968; Anchor Books edn, 1969

Hsueh, Chün-tu. *Huang Hsing and the Chinese Revolution*. Stanford University Press, 1961

Hsueh, Chün-tu. 'Sun Yat-sen, Yang Ch'ü-yun, and the early revolutionary movement in China'. *JAS*, 19.3 (May 1960) 307–18

Hsueh Fu-ch'eng 薛福成. *Yung-an ch'üan-chi* 庸盦全集 (Complete works of Hsueh Fu-ch'eng), including *Wen-pien* 文編 (Collection of essays), *Jih-chi* 日記 (Diary), *Wai-pien* 外編 (Additional essays), *Ch'ou-yang ch'u-i* 籌洋芻議 (Preliminary proposals concerning Western affairs) and *Hai-wai wen-pien* 海外文編 (Collection of essays written overseas). Shanghai: Tsui-liu t'ang 醉六堂, 1897

Hsueh Fu-ch'eng. 'Ch'ou-yang ch'u-i' 籌洋芻議 (Preliminary proposals concerning Western affairs), in *WHPF*, 1.151–61

Hsueh-pu tsung-wu-ssu 學部總務司, comp. *Chiao-yü t'ung-chi t'u-piao* 教育統計 圖表 (Statistical charts and tables on education). Peking: Ministry of Education, 1907

'Hsueh-wu kang-yao' 學務綱要 (Guidelines for educational affairs), in Chang Po-hsi, *et al.*, Nanking 1904 edn, *ts'e* 1

HTJP: Hsiang-kang Hua-tzu jih-pao

Hu Han-min 胡漢民. 'Hu Han-min tzu-chuan' 胡漢民自傳 (Autobiography of Hu Han-min), in *KMWH*, 3 (1953) 373–442

Hu Han-min. 'Min-pao chih liu ta chu-i' 民報之六大主義 (The six great 'isms' of the *Min-pao*). *Min-pao*, 3 (April 1906) 1–22

Hu-nan chin-pai-nien ta-shih chi-shu 湖南近百年大事記述 (A chronicle of major events in Hunan in the last one hundred years). Changsha: Jen-min, 1959

Hu-nan li-shih tzu-liao 湖南歷史資料 (Historical materials on Hunan). Quarterly. Changsha: Jen-min, 1958

Hu-pei sheng che-hsueh she-hui k'o-hsueh hsueh-hui lien-ho hui 湖北省哲學 社會科學學會聯合會, ed. *Hsin-hai ko-ming wu-shih chou-nien lun-wen chi* 辛亥 革命五十周年論文集 (A collection of articles on the fiftieth anniversary of the Revolution of 1911). 2 vols. Peking: Chung-hua, 1962; also cited as *HHWS*

Hu Sheng-wu 胡繩武 and Chin Ch'ung-chi 金沖及. *Lun Ch'ing-mo ti li-hsien yun-tung* 論清末的立憲運動 (On the constitutional movement towards the end of the Ch'ing). Shanghai: Jen-min, 1959

Hua-tzu jih-pao. See *Hsiang-kang Hua tzu jih-pao*

Huang Chang-chien 黃彰健. *Wu-hsu pien-fa shih yen-chiu* 戊戌變法史研究 (Studies on the history of the reform movement of 1898). Taipei: Institute of History and Philology, Academia Sinica, 1970

Huang-ch'ao cheng-tien lei-tsuan. See Hsi Yü-fu

Huang-ch'ao ching-shih wen hsu-pien. See the two different versions under the same title, one compiled by Ko Shih-chün and the other by Sheng K'ang

Huang-ch'ao ching-shih wen-pien. See Ho Ch'ang-ling

Huang Chia-mu 黃家謨. *Chia-wu chan-ch'ien chih T'ai-wan mei-wu* 甲午戰前之 臺灣煤務 (Coalmining in Taiwan prior to the war of 1894). Taipei: IMH, Academia Sinica, 1961

Huang Chia-mu. 'Chung-kuo tien-hsien ti ch'uang-chien' 中國電線的創建 (The first installation of telegraphs in China). *Ta-lu tsa-chih* 大陸雜誌, 36.6 and 7 (combined issue, April 1968) 171–87

Huang Chia-mu *et al.* eds. *Chung-Mei kuan-hsi shih-liao* 中美關係史料 (Historical materials on Sino-American relations, 1805–1874). 3 vols. Taipei: IMH, Academia Sinica, 1968

Huang Chia-mu. *Tien hsi hui-min cheng-ch'üan ti lien-Ying wai-chiao* 滇西回民政權的聯英外交 (The diplomacy of the Muslim regime in western Yunnan towards a British alliance). Taipei: IMH, Academia Sinica, 1976

Huang Chün-tsai 黃鈞宰. *Chin-hu ch'i mo* 金壺七墨 (Seven works of Huang Chün-tsai). Shanghai: Sao-yeh shan-fang, 1929

Huang En-t'ung 黃恩彤. *Fu-i chi-lueh* 撫夷紀略 (Brief account of the pacification of barbarians). Unpublished handwritten copy, 1865 preface. Taipei: Institute of History and Philology, Academia Sinica

Huang Fu-ch'ing 黃福慶. *Ch'ing-mo liu-Jih hsueh-sheng* 清末留日學生 (Late Ch'ing students in Japan). Taipei: IMH, Academia Sinica, 1975

Huang, Philip C. *Liang Ch'i-ch'ao and modern Chinese liberalism*. Seattle: University of Washington Press, 1972

Huang, Philip C., ed. 'A symposium on the 1911 Revolution'. *Modern China: an international quarterly*, 2.2 (April 1976) 139–226; see Esherick, Joseph W.

Huang Tsun-hsien 黃遵憲. *Jih-pen kuo-chih* 日本國志 (History of the Japanese state). 40 *chüan* edn. Che-chiang shu-chü 浙江書局, 1898. Shanghai: T'u-shu chi-ch'eng yin-shu chü 圖書集成印書局, 1898; Taipei reproduction, Wen-hai, 1974

Huang Tsung-hsi 黃宗羲. *Ming-i tai-fang lu* 明夷待訪錄 (A plan for the prince). Woodblock edn printed between 1737 and 1743. A more available edn is in Hsueh Feng-ch'ang 薛鳳昌 ed. *Li-chou i-chu hui-k'an* 梨洲遺著彙刊 (Collected reprints of writings left by Huang Tsung-hsi), *ts'e* 12 of the total of 20 *ts'e*. Shanghai: Shih-chung shu-chü 時中書局, 1910, 1925

Huang Tsung-hsi. *Sung Yuan hsueh-an* 宋元學案 (Records of Sung and Yuan scholars). Ch'üan Tsu-wang 全祖望, ed. 100 *chüan*. Shanghai: Commercial Press, 1933. Taipei reproduction, Kuang-wen 廣文, 1971

Hummel, Arthur W. *Eminent Chinese of the Ch'ing period (1644–1912)*. 2 vols. Washington DC: US Government Printing Office, 1943–4; Taipei reproduction, Ch'eng-wen, 1967

Hunt, Michael H. *Frontier defense and the open door: Manchuria in Chinese-American relations, 1895–1911*. New Haven: Yale University Press, 1973

Ichiko Chūzō 市古宙三. 'Bakumatsu Nihonjin no Taihei Tengoku ni kansuru chishiki' 幕末日本人の太平天国に関する知識 (Japanese knowledge of the Heavenly Kingdom of Great Peace in late Tokugawa times), in Kaikoku Hyakunen Kinen Bunka Jigyōkai 開国百年記念文化事業会, ed. *Meiji bunkashi ronshū* 明治文化史論集 (Essays in Meiji cultural history), pp. 453–95. Tokyo: Kengensha 乾元社, 1952

Ichiko, Chūzō. 'The role of the gentry: an hypothesis', in *CIR*, 297–313

Ichiko Chūzō. *Kindai Chūgoku no seiji to shakai* 近代中国の政治と社会 (Politics and society in modern China). Tokyo University Press, 1971

Ichimata Masao 市又正雄. 'Yamaza Enjirō – Meiji jidai ni okeru tairiku seisaku no jikkōsha' 山座圓次郎—明治時代に於ける大陸政策の実行者 (Yamaza Enjirō: a practitioner of the Japanese policy on the Asian continent in the Meiji era). *Kokusaihō gaikō zasshi* 国際法外交雑誌 72.3 (Oct. 1973) 249–98

Ikei, Masaru. 'Japan's response to the Chinese Revolution of 1911'. *JAS*, 25.2 (Feb. 1966) 213–27

IMH: Institute of Modern History (Chin-tai shih yen-chiu so), Academia Sinica

Inoue Kaoru Kō Denki Hensankai 井上馨候伝記編纂会, eds. *Seigai Inoue kō den* 世外井上公伝 (Biography of Inoue Kaoru). Tokyo: Naigai Shoseki Kabushiki Kaisha 内外書籍株式会社, 1933–4

Inoue Masaji 井上雅二. *Kyojin Arao Sei (Kiyoshi)* 巨人荒尾精 (Grand old Arao Sei). Tokyo: Tōa Dōbunkai 東亜同文会, 1936

Iriye, Akira. 'The ideology of Japanese imperialism: imperial Japan and China', in Grant K. Goodman, ed. *Imperial Japan and Asia: a reassessment* , pp. 32–45. New York: Columbia University, East Asian Institute, 1967

Ishikawa, Shigeru. *Economic development in Asian perspective.* Tokyo: Kinokuniya, 1967

Ishimoda Shō 石母田正 'Kōtoku Shūsui to Chūgoku' 幸徳秋水と中国 (Kōtoku Shūsui and China), in Takeuchi Yoshimi 竹内好, ed. *Ajia shugi* アジア主義 (Asianism), vol. 9: *Gendai Nihon shisō taikei* 現代日本思想大系, pp. 384–410. Tokyo: Chikuma, 1963

IWSM: Ch'ing-tai ch'ou-pan i-wu shih-mo

Jamieson, George. 'Tenure of land in China and the condition of the rural population'. *Journal of the North China Branch of the Royal Asiatic Society*, NS, 23.6 (1889) 59–117

Jamieson, George. *Report on the revenue and expenditure of the Chinese empire.* Foreign Office, Miscellaneous series, no. 415. London: HM Stationery Office, 1897

Jane, Frederick T. *The imperial Japanese navy.* London: W. Thacker, 1904

Jansen, Marius B. *The Japanese and Sun Yat-sen.* Cambridge, Mass.: Harvard University Press, 1954

Jansen, Marius B. 'Japanese views of China during the Meiji period', in *AMCH*, 163–89

Jansen, Marius B. *Japan and China: from war to peace, 1894–1972.* Chicago: Rand McNally, 1975

Japan. Imperial General Staff. *History of the war between Japan and China.* Major Jikemura and The Revd. Arthur Lloyd, trans. vol. 1. Tokyo: Kinkodo Publishing Co., 1904

JAS: Journal of Asian Studies

Johnson, William R. 'The Revolution of 1911 in Yunnan and Kweichow'. University of Washington, Ph.D. dissertation. Seattle, 1962

Jones, Susan Mann. 'Finance in Ningpo: the "ch'ien-chuang", 1780–1880', in W.E. Willmott, ed. *Economic organization in Chinese society* (q.v.), pp. 47–77

Jones, Susan Mann. 'The Ningpo *Pang* and financial power at Shanghai', in

CCTW, 73–96

Kaigun Gunreibu 海軍軍令部, comp. *Nijūshichi-hachinen kaisen shi* 二十七八年 海戰史 (A history of the 1894–5 naval operations). 3 vols. Tokyo: Naval Ministry, 1905

Kaikoku Hyakunen Kinen Bunka Jigyōkai 開国百年記念文化事業会, ed. *Sakoku jidai Nihonjin no kaigai chishiki* 鎖国時代日本人の海外知識 (Japanese knowledge of the outside world during the era of seclusion). Tokyo: Kengensha 乾元社, 1953

Kajima, Morinosuke. *The diplomacy of Japan 1894–1922.* vol. 1, *Sino-Japanese War and Triple Intervention.* Tokyo: Kajima Institute of International Peace, 1976

Kamachi, Noriko. 'Huang Tsun-hsien (1848–1905): his response to Meiji Japan and the West'. Harvard University, Ph.D. dissertation. Cambridge, Mass., 1972

Kan Hou-tz'u 甘厚慈, ed. *Pei-yang kung-tu lei-tsuan hsu-pien* 北洋公牘類纂續編 (Categorized collection of documents from the office of the Commissioner of Trade for the Northern Ports, continued). Tientsin, *c.* 1910

K'ang Yu-wei 康有為. *Hsin-hsueh wei-ching k'ao* 新學偽經考 (An inquiry into the classics forged during the Hsin period). 8 *ts'e*, 1891. Various later edns, including 2 *ts'e* punctuated edn. Shanghai: Commercial Press, 1936; Peking: Ku-chi 古籍, 1956

K'ang Yu-wei. *K'ung-tzu kai-chih k'ao* 孔子改制考 (A study of Confucius as institutional reformer). 21 *chüan*. Shanghai: Ta-t'ung i-shu chü 大同譯書局, 1897; Peking: Wan-mu ts'ao-t'ang 萬木草堂, 1922–3; Taipei reproduction of the Peking edn, Ta-t'ung 大通, 1968

K'ang Yu-wei. *O Pi-te pien-cheng chi* 俄彼得變政記 (An account of the reform of Peter of Russia), in K'ang Yu-wei, *Nan-hai hsien-sheng ch'i shang-shu chi* 南海先生七上書記 (An account of the seventh memorial of Mr K'ang Yu-wei), appendix. Shanghai: Ta-t'ung i shu chü 大同譯書局, 1898

K'ang Yu-wei. *Jih-pen Ming-chih pien-cheng k'ao [chi]* 日本明治變政考 [記] (A study [account] of the political reforms in Meiji Japan). 16 *chüan*. Copy by hand in *K'ang Yu-wei i-kao* 康有為遺稿 (Copies of writings left by K'ang Yu-wei), microfilms made in 1947 from the K'ang family collection in Peking; available at East Asian Collection, Hoover Institution of War, Revolution and Peace or Far Eastern Library, University of Washington

Kayano Chōchi (Nagatomo). 萱野長知 *Chūka minkoku kakumei hikyū* 中華民国革命秘笈 (Private sources for the Chinese republican revolution). Tokyo: Teikoku Chihō Gyōsei Gakkai 帝国地方行政学会, 1940

Kiernan, V. G. 'Kashgar and the politics of Central Asia, 1868–1878'. *The Cambridge Historical Journal*, 11.3 (1955) 317–42

Kim, C. I. Eugene and Kim, Han-Kyo. *Korea and the politics of imperialism, 1876–1910.* Berkeley: University of California Press, 1967

Kim, K. H. *Japanese perspectives on China's early modernization: a bibliographical survey.* Ann Arbor: Center for Chinese Studies, University of Michigan, 1974

Kim, K. H. *The last phase of the East Asian world order: Korea, Japan, and the Chinese empire, 1860–1882.* Berkeley: University of California Press, 1979

Kimura Kō 木村匡. *Mori Sensei den* 森(有礼)先生伝 (Biography of Mr Mori). Tokyo: Kinkōdō 金港堂, 1899

King, H. E. *The educational system of China as recently reconstructed.* Washington, DC: US Bureau of Education Bulletin, no 15, 1911

King, Frank H. H. *Money and monetary policy in China, 1845–1895.* Cambridge, Mass.: Harvard University Press, 1965

KMWH: Ko-ming wen-hsien

Ko-chih hui-pien 格致彙編 ('The Chinese scientific magazine'). Shanghai: 1876–78 and 1880–2 (monthly); 1890–2 (quarterly)

Ko-ming wen-hsien. See Chung-kuo Kuo-min-tang chung-yang wei-yuan-hui tang-shih shih-liao pien-tsuan wei-yuan-hui

Ko Shih-chün 葛士濬, comp. *Huang-ch'ao ching-shih-wen hsu-pien* 皇朝經世文續編 (Collection of Ch'ing dynasty writings on statecraft, continued). 120 *chüan.* Shanghai: T'u-shu chi-ch'eng, 1888

Kōno Michihiro 河野通博. 'Shindai Santōshō no kansei rikujō kōtsūro' 清代山東省の官制陸上交通路 (Official overland communication routes in Shantung in the Ch'ing dynasty). *Shirin* 史林, 33.3 (May 1950) 317–36

Konoe Atsumaro 近衛篤麿. *Konoe Atsumaro nikki* 近衛篤麿日記 (Diary of Konoe Atsumaro). Tokyo: Kajima Kenkyūjō Shuppankai 鹿島研究所出版会, 1968–9

Kostiaeva, Aleksandra Sergeevna. *Narodnye dvizheniia v Kitae v 1901–1911 gg.* (Popular movements in China, 1901–1911). Moscow: Nauka, 1970

Kōtoku Shūsui 幸德秋水. *Teikokushugi* 帝国主義 (Imperialism). Tokyo: Iwanami, 1966

Krasnyi arkhiv, istoricheskii zhurnal 1922–1941 (Red archives, historical journal 1922–1941). Moscow: Izd-vo Vsesoiuznoi knizhnoi palaty, 1960

Ku-kung hsien-ts'un Chün-chi tang 故宮現存軍機檔 (Ch'ing Grand Council archives in the Palace Museum). *c.* 4,000 boxes. Taipei: Palace Museum, unpublished

Kuan T'ien-p'ei 闗天培. *Ch'ou-hai ch'u-chi* 籌海初集 (First collection of papers relating to preparation for maritime defence). 4 *chüan. c.* 1841 preface

Kuang-hsu cheng-yao. See Shen T'ung-sheng *et al.*

Kubota Bunji 久保田文次. 'Shimmatsu Shisen no daidenko, Chūgoku kisei jinushi-sei tenkai no ichimen' 清末四川の大佃戶一中国寄生地主制展開の一面 (Wealthy tenant farmers in Szechwan province in the late Ch'ing period: an aspect of the development of the parasitic landlord system in China), in Tōkyō Kyōiku Daigaku Tōyōshigaku Kenkyūshitsu 東京教育大学東洋史学研究室 *et al.* eds. *Kindai Chūgoku nōson shakaishi kenkyū* 近代中国農村社会史研究 (Studies of the history of rural society in modern China), 247–96. Tokyo: Daian, 1967

Kuhn, Philip A. *Rebellion and its enemies in late imperial China: militarization and social structure, 1796–1864.* Cambridge, Mass.: Harvard University Press, 1970

Kuhn, Philip A. 'Local self-government under the republic: problems of control, autonomy, and mobilization', in Frederic Wakeman, Jr, and Carolyn Grant, eds. *Conflict and control in late imperial China*, pp. 257–98. Berkeley: University of California Press, 1975

Kuksa p'yŏn-ch'an wiwŏnhoe 國史編纂委員會, ed. *Susinsa kirok* 修信使記錄 (Records of diplomatic envoys). Seoul: National History Compilation Commission, 1958

Kung Chun 龔駿. *Chung-kuo hsin-kung-yeh fa-chan-shih ta-kang* 中國新工業發展 史大綱 (An outline history of China's modern industrial development). Shanghai: Commercial Press, 1933

Kung-chung-tang Kuang-hsu ch'ao tsou-che 宮中檔光緒朝奏摺 (Secret palace memorials of the Kuang-hsu period, 1875–1908). 26 vols. Taipei: Palace Museum, 1973–5

Kuo-li T'ai-wan shih-fan ta-hsueh li-shih hsueh-pao 國立台灣師範大學歷史學報 (Bulletin of historical research), National Taiwan Normal University. Taipei, 1973– ; also cited as *SFLS*

Kuo, Sung-p'ing. 'Chinese reaction to foreign encroachment: with special reference to the first Sino-Japanese War and its immediate aftermath'. Columbia University, Ph.D. dissertation. New York, 1953

Kuo Sung-tao 郭嵩燾. *Kuo shih-lang tsou-shu* 郭侍郎奏疏 (Kuo Sung-tao's memorials). 12 *chüan*. 1892. Taipei reproduction, Wen-hai, 1968

Kuo Sung-tao. *Yang-chih shu-wu wen-chi* 養知書屋文集 (Collection of essays of Kuo Sung-tao). 28 *chüan*. 1892. Taipei reproduction, Wen-hai, 1968

Kuo T'ing-i 郭廷以. *T'ai-wan shih-shih kai-shuo* 台灣史事概說 (A general account of Taiwan history). Taipei: Cheng-chung, 1954

Kuo T'ing-i. *Chin-tai Chung-kuo shih-shih jih-chih* 近代中國史事日誌 (Chronology of events in modern Chinese history). 2 vols. Taipei: Cheng-chung, 1963

Kuo T'ing-i (Ting-yee Kuo) *et al. Kuo Sung-tao hsien-sheng nien-p'u* 郭嵩燾先生 年譜 (A chronological biography of Kuo Sung-tao). 2 vols. Taipei: IMH, Academia Sinica, 1971

Kuo, Ting-yee, comp. and Morley, James, ed. *Sino-Japanese relations, 1862–1927: a checklist of the Chinese Foreign Ministry Archives*. New York: Columbia University Press, 1965

Kupper, Samuel Y. 'Revolution in China: Kiangsi province, 1905–1913'. University of Michigan, Ph.D. dissertation, 1973

Kuropatkin, A. N. *Kashgaria: historical and geographical sketch of the country; its military strength, industries and trade*. Walter E. Gowan, trans. Calcutta: Thacker, Spink & Co., 1882

Kuznets, Simon. *Modern economic growth: rate, structure, spread*. New Haven: Yale University Press, 1966

Kuzuu Yoshihisa 葛生能久 *et al.* eds. *Tōa senkaku shishi kiden* 東亞先覺志士記伝 (Stories and biographies of pioneer East Asian idealists). 3 vols. Tokyo: Kokuryūkai Shuppanbu 黑龍会出版部, 1935–6. Hara Shobō 原書房 reproduction, 1966

La Faye, Jaques de (pseud.) *Histoire de l'amiral Courbet*. Paris: Bloud et Barral, 1891

Lamprey, J. 'The economy of the Chinese Army'. *Journal of the Royal United Service Institution*, 11.46 (1867) 403–33

Langer, William L. *The diplomacy of imperialism, 1890–1902*. 2nd edn. New York: Knopf, 1951, 1965

Lattimore, Owen *et al. Pivot of Asia: Sinkiang and the Inner Asian frontiers of China and Russia*. Boston: Little, Brown, 1950

LCSK: Liu Ming-ch'uan, *Liu Chuang-su kung tsou-i*

Lecomte, Ferdinand. *Lang-Son: combats, retraite et négociations*. Paris: Henri Charles-Lavauzelle, 1895

Lee [Li], En-han. *China's quest for railway autonomy, 1904–1911: a study of the Chinese railway-rights recovery movement*. Singapore University Press, 1977

Lee, Robert H. G. *The Manchurian frontier in Ch'ing history*. Cambridge, Mass.: Harvard University Press, 1970

Lee, Ta-ling. *Foundations of the Chinese Revolution, 1905–1912: the historical record of the T'ung-meng hui*. New York: St John's University Press, 1970

Legge, James, trans. *The Chinese classics*. 8 vols. Oxford: Clarendon, 1893–5; Hong Kong reproduction, Hong Kong University Press, 1960

Lei Hai-tsung 雷海宗. 'Ku-tai Chung-kuo ti wai-chiao' 古代中國的外交 (Diplomacy in ancient China). *She-hui k'o-hsueh* 社會科學 (Peiping: Tsing Hua University), 3.1 (1941)1–12

Lensen, George A., ed. *Korea and Manchuria between Russia and Japan 1895–1904: the observations of Sir Ernest Satow, British minister plenipotentiary to Japan (1895–1900) and China (1900–1906)*. Tallahassee: Diplomatic Press, 1966

Lensen, George A. *The Russo-Chinese War*. Tallahassee: Diplomatic Press, 1967

Leonard, Jane K. 'Chinese overlordship and Western penetration in maritime Asia: a late Ch'ing re-appraisal of Chinese maritime relations'. *MAS*, 6.2 (1972) 151–74

Levenson, Joseph R. *Liang Ch'i-ch'ao and the mind of modern China*. Cambridge, Mass.: Harvard University Press, 1953

Levenson, Joseph R. *Confucian China and its modern fate: the problem of monarchical decay*. Berkeley: University of California Press, 1968

Lewis, Charlton M. 'The reform movement in Hunan (1896–1898)'. *Papers on China*, 15 (1961) 62–90

Lewis, Charlton M. 'The opening of Hunan: reform and revolution in a Chinese province, 1895–1907'. University of California, Ph.D. dissertation. Berkeley, 1965

Lewis, Charlton M. *Prologue to the Chinese Revolution: the transformation of ideas and institutions in Hunan province, 1891–1907*. Cambridge, Mass.: Harvard University Press, 1976

Li Che-hou 李澤厚. *K'ang Yu-wei T'an Ssu-t'ung ssu-hsiang yen-chiu* 康有為譚嗣同思想研究 (A study of the thought of K'ang Yu-wei and T'an Ssu-t'ung).

Shanghai: Jen-min, 1958

Li Chien-nung 李劍農. *Chung-kuo chin-pai-nien cheng-chih shih* 中國近百年政治史 (A political history of China in the last hundred years). 2 vols. Shanghai: Commercial Press, 1947; Taipei reprint, Commercial Press, 1957, 1974

Li Chien-nung. *The political history of China 1840–1928.* Ssu-yü Teng and Jeremy Ingalls, trans. and eds. Princeton: Van Nostrand, 1956

Li En-han 李恩涵. *Wan-Ch'ing ti shou-hui k'uang-ch'üan yun-tung* 晚清的收回礦權運動 (The movement to recover mining rights in the late Ch'ing period). Taipei: IMH, Academia Sinica, 1963

Li En-han. *Tseng Chi-tse ti wai-chiao* 曾紀澤的外交 (Tseng Chi-tse's diplomacy). Taipei: IMH, Academia Sinica, 1966

Li En-han. 'The Chekiang gentry-merchants vs. the Peking court officials: China's struggle for recovery of the British Soochow-Hangchow-Ningpo railway concession, 1905–1911'. *CYCT*, 3.1 (1972) 223–68

Li Hung-chang 李鴻章. *Li Wen-chung kung ch'üan-chi* 李文忠公全集 (Complete papers of Li Hung-chang). Shanghai: Commercial Press, 1921 photo reprint of Nanking 1905 edn; Taipei, Wen-hai reproduction, 1962; also cited as *LWCK*

Li Hung-chang. *Li Wen-chung kung i-chi* 李文忠公遺集 (Writings of the late Li Hung-chang), in Li Kuo-chieh 李國杰 comp. *Ho-fei Li-shih san-shih i-chi* 合肥李氏三世遺集 (Writings left by three generations of the Lis of Ho-fei). 1905. Taipei reproduction, Wen-hai, 1966

Li Hung-chang. *Li Wen-chung kung p'eng-liao han-kao* 李文忠公朋僚函稿 (Li Hung-chang's letters to friends and colleagues), in Li Hung-chang, *Li Wen-chung kung ch'üan-chi* (q.v.). 20 *chüan*. Nanking, 1905; Shanghai reproduction, Commercial Press, 1921

Li Hung-chang chih P'an Ting-hsin shu-cha 李鴻章致潘鼎新書札 (Li Hung-chang's letters to P'an Ting-hsin). Nien Tzu-min 年子敏, comp. Peking: Chung-hua, 1960

Li Kuo-ch'i 李國祁. *Chung-kuo tsao-ch'i ti t'ieh-lu ching-ying* 中國早期的鐵路經營 (China's early railway enterprises). Taipei: IMH, Academia Sinica, 1961

Li Kuo-ch'i. *Chang Chih-tung ti wai-chiao cheng-ts'e* 張之洞的外交政策 (Chang Chih-tung's foreign policy proposals). Taipei: IMH, Academia Sinica, 1970

Li Kuo-ch'i, Chou T'ien-sheng 周天生 and Hsu Hung-i 許弘義. *Ch'ing-tai chi-tseng ti-fang-kuan jen-shih shan-ti hsien-hsiang chih liang-hua fen-hsi* 清代基層地方官人事嬗遞現象之量化分析 (A quantitative analysis of the careers of prefects and magistrates in the Ch'ing dynasty). 3 vols. Taipei: National Science Council, 1975

Li Pao-chia 李寶嘉. *Kuan-ch'ang hsien-hsing chi* 官場現形記 (An exposé of officialdom). Shanghai: Shih-chieh fan-hua pao 世界繁華報, 1903; Ya-tung 亞東 1927. Peking reprint, Jen-min wen-hsueh ch'u-pan-she 人民文學出版社, 1957, 1963

Li P'ei-chi 李培基. 'T'ung-meng hui yü pang-hui ti kuan-hsi tsa-i' 同盟會與幫會的關係雜憶 (Random reminiscences regarding the Revolutionary Alliance's relations with the secret societies), in Chung-kuo jen-min cheng-chih hsieh-shang hui-i ch'üan-kuo wei-yuan-hui wen-shih tzu-liao yen-chiu wei-yuan-hui, ed. *Hsin-hai ko-ming hui-i lu* (q.v.), vol. 6, pp. 83–26

Li, San-pao. 'Letters to the editor in John Fryer's *Chinese Scientific Magazine*, 1876–1892: an analysis'. *CYCT*, 4.2 (Dec. 1974) 729–77

Li Shih-yueh 李時岳. *Hsin-hai ko-ming shih-ch'i Liang-Hu ti-ch'ü ti ko-ming yun-tung* 辛亥革命時期兩湖地區的革命運動 (The revolutionary movement in the Hunan-Hupei area during the era of the 1911 Revolution). Peking: San-lien, 1957

Li Shih-yueh. *Chang Chien ho li-hsien-p'ai* 張謇和立憲派 (Chang Chien and the constitutionalists). Peking: Chung-hua, 1962

Li Shih-yueh. *Fan-yang-chiao yun-tung* 反洋教運動 (The anti-Christian movement). Peking: San-lien, 1962

Li Shou-k'ung 李守孔. *Chung-kuo chin-tai shih* 中國近代史 (China's modern history). Taipei: Hsueh-sheng, 1968

Li Shu-ch'ang 黎庶昌. *Cho-tsun-yuan ts'ung-kao* 拙尊園叢稿 (Li Shu-ch'ang's writings). Shanghai, 1893

Li Tsung-hsi 李宗羲. *K'ai-hsien Li shang-shu cheng-shu* 開縣李尚書政書 (Li Tsung-hsi's political papers). 8 *chüan*. Wuchang, 1885

Li Tsung-t'ung 李宗侗 and Liu Feng-han 劉鳳翰. *Li Hung-tsao hsien-sheng nien-p'u* 李鴻藻先生年譜 (Chronological biography of Mr Li Hung-tsao). 2 vols. Taipei: Chung-kuo hsueh-shu chu-tso chiang-chu wei-yuan-hui 中國學術著作獎助委員會, 1969

Li Tz'u-ming 李慈銘. *Yueh-man-t'ang jih-chi* 越縵堂日記 (Li Tz'u-ming's diary). 51 *ts'e*. Peking: Che-chiang kung-hui 浙江公會, 1922; Taipei reproduction, Wen-hai, 1963

Li Wen-chih, 李文治 comp. *Chung-kuo chin-tai nung-yeh shih tzu-liao ti-i chi, 1840–1911* 中國近代農業史資料第一輯 1840–1911 (Source materials on the history of agriculture in modern China, 1st collection, 1840–1911). Peking: San-lien, 1957

Li Wen-hai 李文海. 'Hsin-hai ko-ming yü hui-tang' 辛亥革命與會黨 (The Revolution of 1911 and the secret societies), in *HHWS*, 1.166–87

Li Yu-ning 李又寧 and Chang Yü-fa 張玉法, comps. *Chin-tai Chung-kuo nü-ch'üan yun-tung shih-liao* 近代中國女權運動史料 (Historical materials on the women's rights movement in modern China). 2 vols. Taipei: Chuan-chi wen-hsueh she 傳記文學社, 1975

Li Yun-lin 李雲麟. *Hsi ch'ui shih-lueh* 西陲事略 (Brief record of events on the western frontier). Fascimile reproduction of a handwritten copy of the Kuang-hsu period. Taipei: Ch'eng-wen, 1968

Liang Ch'i-ch'ao 梁啓超. *Hsi-hsueh shu-mu-piao* 西學書目表 (A bibliography of Western learning), in Chih-hsueh hui, comp. *Chih-hsueh ts'ung-shu ch'u-chi* (q.v.), *ts'e* 9–10

Liang Ch'i-ch'ao. *Yin-ping-shih wen-chi* 飲冰室文集 (Collected essays of the Ice-drinker's Studio). 80 *ts'e*. Shanghai: Chuang-hua, 1926

Liang Ch'i-ch'ao. *Yin-ping-shih ho-chi* 飲冰室合集 (Collected works and essays from the Ice-drinker's Studio). 40 vols., including *Wen-chi* 文集 (Essays), vols. 1–16. Shanghai: Chung-hua, 1936

Liang Ch'i-ch'ao. 'Nan-hai K'ang hsien-sheng chuan' 南海康先生傳 (A biography of K'ang Yu-wei), in Liang Ch'i-ch'ao, *Yin-ping-shih ho-chi, Wen-chi* (q.v.), 3.57–89

Liang Ch'i-ch'ao. *Intellectual trends in the Ch'ing period* (*Ch'ing-tai hsüeh-shu kai-lun* 清代學術概論). trans. Immanuel C.Y. Hsu. Cambridge, Mass.: Harvard University Press, 1959

Liang, Chia-pin 梁嘉彬. 'Li Hung-chang yü Chung-Jih chia-wu chan-cheng' 李鴻章與中日甲午戰爭 (Li Hung-chang and the Sino-Japanese War of 1894). *Ta-lu tsa-chih* 大陸雜誌, 51.4 and 5 (Oct. and Nov. 1975) 155–86, 227–54

Liang Chin-tung. *The Chinese Revolution of 1911*. New York: Institute of Asian studies, St John's University, 1962

Liew, K. S. *Struggle for democracy: Sung Chiao-jen and the 1911 Chinese Revolution*. Berkeley: University of California Press, 1971

Lin Ming-te 林明德. *Yuan Shih-k'ai yü Ch'ao-hsien* 袁世凱與朝鮮 (Yuan Shih-k'ai and Korea). Taipei: IMH, Academia Sinica, 1970

Lin Neng-shih 林能士. *Ch'ing-chi Hu-nan ti hsin-cheng yun-tung* 清季湖南的 新政運動 (The movement for new policies in late Ch'ing Hunan). Taipei: National Taiwan University, College of Letters, 1972

Lin Tung-ch'en (Lin Tō-shin) 林東辰. *Taiwan bōeki shi* 臺灣貿易史 (History of trade and commerce in Taiwan). Taipei: Nihon Kaikokusha 日本開國社, 1932

Liu Ch'ang-yu 劉長佑. *Liu Wu-sheng kung i-shu* 劉武慎公遺書 (Papers of the late Liu Ch'ang-yu). 28 *chüan*. Nanking, 1891; Taipei reproduction, Ch'eng-wen, 1968

Liu Chin-tsao 劉錦藻 , ed. *Ch'ing-ch'ao hsu wen-hsien t'ung-k'ao* 清朝續文獻通考 (Encyclopedia of the historical records of the Ch'ing dynasty, continued). Shanghai: Commercial Press, 1935; Taipei reproduction, Hsin-hsing 新興 , 1965

Liu Feng-han 劉鳳翰. 'Chia-wu chan-cheng shuang-fang ping-li ti fen-hsi' 甲午 戰爭雙方兵力的分析 (An analysis of the strength of both belligerents during the war of 1894). *Chung-kuo i-chou* 中國一周 , 829 (14 March 1966) 13–16; 830 (21 March 1966) 11–14

Liu Feng-han. *Hsin-chien lu-chün* 新建陸軍 (The Newly Created Army [under Yuan Shih-k'ai, 1895–1900]). Taipei: IMH, Academia Sinica, 1967

Liu Feng-han. *Wu-wei chün* 武衛軍 (The Wu-wei Army [under Jung-lu and Yuan Shih-k'ai, 1899–1901]). Taipei: IMH, Academia Sinica, 1978

Liu, Kwang-Ching. 'Two steamship companies in China, 1862–1877'. Harvard University, Ph.D. dissertation. Cambridge, Mass., 1956

Liu, Kwang-Ching. *Anglo-American steamship rivalry in China, 1862–1874*. Cambridge, Mass.: Harvard University Press, 1962

Liu, Kwang-Ching. 'British-Chinese steamship rivalry in China, 1873–1885', in C.D. Cowan, ed. *The economic development of China and Japan: studies in economic history and political economy*, pp. 49–78. London: Allen & Unwin, 1964

Liu, Kwang-Ching. 'Li Hung-chang in Chihli: the emergence of a policy, 1870–1875', in *AMCH*, 68–104

Liu, Kwang-Ching. 'Nineteenth-century China: the disintegration of the old order and the impact of the West', in Ping-ti Ho and Tang Tsou, eds. *China in crisis*, 1.1.93–178. University of Chicago Press, 1968

Liu Kwang-Ching 劉廣京. 'Cheng Kuan-ying *I-yen*: Kuang-hsu ch'u-nien chih pien-fa ssu-hsiang' 鄭觀應易言：光緒初年之變法思想. (Cheng Kuan-ying's *I-yen*: reform proposals of the early Kuang-hsu period). *Ch'ing-hua hsueh-pao* 清華學報, NS, 8.1-2 (1970) 373–425

Liu, Kwang-Ching. 'The Confucian as patriot and pragmatist: Li Hung-chang's formative years, 1823–1866'. *HJAS*, 30 (1970) 5–45

Liu, Kwang-Ching. 'The limits of regional power in the late Ch'ing period: a reappraisal'. *Ch'ing-hua hsueh-pao*, NS, 10.2 (July 1974) 176–207 (in Chinese), 207–23 (in English)

Liu Ming-ch'uan 劉銘傳. *Liu Chuang-su kung tsou-i* 劉壯肅公奏議 (Liu Ming-ch'uan's memorials). 6 *chüan*, 1906 preface. Taipei reproduction, Wen-hai, 1968; also cited as *LCSK*

Liu O 劉鶚 (Liu T'ieh-yun 鐵雲). *Lao-ts'an yu-chi* 老殘遊記 (The travels of Lao-ts'an). 20 *chüan*. Shanghai, 1906 preface, Ya-tung 亞東; 3rd edn, 1928. Hong Kong: Commercial Press, 1965. English trans. by H. Y. Yang and G. M. Taylor: *Mr. Derelict*, London: Allen and Unwin, 1948. See under Liu T'ieh-yun for the Harold Shaddick trans.

Liu Po-chi 劉伯驥. *Kuang-tung shu-yuan chih-tu yen-ko* 廣東書院制度沿革 (Institutional history of the local academies in Kwangtung). Changsha: Commercial Press, 1939; Taipei edn, Chung-hua ts'ung-shu wei-yuan-hui 中華叢書委員會, 1958

Liu, Ta-chung and Yeh, Kung-chia. *The economy of the Chinese mainland: national income and economic development, 1933–1959*. Princeton University Press, 1965

Liu T'ieh-yun. *The travels of Lao Ts'an*. Harold Shaddick, trans. Ithaca: Cornell University Press, 1952. See Liu O

Liu Yen 劉彥. *Chung-kuo wai-chiao shih* 中國外交史 (Chinese diplomatic history). Enlarged edn by Li Fang-ch'en 李方晨. Taipei: San-min shu-chü 三民書局, 1962

Lo Cheng-chün 羅正鈞. *Tso Wen-hsiang kung nien-p'u* 左文襄公年譜 (Chronological biography of Tso Tsung-t'ang). 10 *chüan*. Hsiang-yin, 1897; Taipei reproduction, Wen-hai, 1967

Lo Erh-kang 羅爾綱. *Hsiang-chün hsin-chih* 湘軍新志 (A new history of the Hunan Army). Changsha: Commercial Press, 1939

Lo Erh-kang. *Lü-ying ping-chih* 綠營兵志 (A treatise on the Green Standard Army). Chungking: Commercial Press, 1945

Lo, Hui-min. *Foreign Office confidential papers relative to China and her neighbouring countries, 1840–1914*, with an additional list, *1915–1937*. The Hague: Mouton, 1969

Lo, Jung-pang, ed. *K'ang Yu-wei: a biography and a symposium*. Tucson: University of Arizona Press, 1967

Lu Hsun. *The true story of Ah Q*. Gladys Yang and Hsien-i Yang, trans. 5th edn. Peking: Foreign Languages Press, 1972

Lu Pao-ch'ien 陸寶千. 'Wo-jen lun' 倭仁論 (On Wo-jen). *CYCT*, 2 (June 1971) 257–70

Lü Shih-ch'iang 呂實強. *Chung-kuo kuan-shen fan-chiao ti yuan-yin, 1860–1874* 中國官紳反教的原因 (Causes behind the Chinese gentry-officials' hostility towards Christianity, 1860–1874). Taipei: IMH, Academia Sinica, 1966

Lü Shih-ch'iang. *Ting Jih-ch'ang yü tzu-ch'iang yun-tung* 丁日昌與自強運動 (Ting Jih-ch'ang and the self-strengthening movement). Taipei: IMH, 1972

Lü Shih-ch'iang. 'Wan-Ch'ing Chung-kuo chih-shih fen-tzu tui Chi-tu-chiao tsai Hua ch'uan-chiao mu-ti ti i-chü, 1860–1898' 晚清中國知識份子對基督教在華傳教目的的疑懼 (Chinese intellectual's suspicion and fear of the Christian missionary's aims in the late Ch'ing period, 1860–1898). *SFLS*, 3 (Feb. 1975) 147–58

Lust, John. 'Secret societies, popular movements and the 1911 Revolution', in *PMSS*, 165–200

LWCK: Li Hung-chang, *Li Wen-chung kung ch'üan-chi*

Lyon, Chambre de Commerce de, ed. *La Mission lyonnaise d'exploration commerciale en Chine 1895–1897*. Lyon: A. Rey, 1898

Ma Chien-chung 馬建忠. *Shih-k'o-chai chi-yen* 適可齋記言 (Ma Chien-chung's essays and discourses). 1896 preface. Taipei reproduction, Wen-hai, 1968

Ma Hsiao-shih 馬霄石. *Hsi-pei hui-tsu ko-ming chien-shih* 西北回族革命簡史 (Brief history of the Muslim people's revolution in the north-west). Shanghai: Tung-fang shu-she 東方書社, 1951

Ma Te-hsin 馬德新. *Ta-hua tsung-kuei* 大化總歸 (Destiny of the universe). 1865 preface. Peking reprint, Ch'ing-chen shu-pao she 清真書報社, 1923

MacKinnon, Stephen R. 'Liang Shih-i and the communications clique'. *JAS*, 29.3 (May 1970) 581–602

MacKinnon, Stephen R. 'Yuan Shih-k'ai in Tientsin and Peking: the sources and structure of his power'. University of California Ph.D. dissertation. Davis, 1971

MacKinnon, Stephen R. 'The Peiyang Army, Yuan Shih-k'ai, and the origins of modern Chinese warlordism'. *JAS*, 32.2 (May 1973) 405–23

MacMurray, John V. A., comp. *Treaties and agreements with and concerning China, 1894–1919*. 2 vols. New York: Oxford University Press, for the Carnegie Endowment for International Peace, 1921

Maeda Katsutarō 前田勝太郎. 'Shindai no Kanton ni okeru nōmin tōsō no kiban' 清代の広東における農民闘争の基盤 (Basis of peasants' struggle in Kwangtung during the Ch'ing period). *Tōyō gakuhō* 東洋学報, 51.4 (March 1969) 1–38

Man-hua 曼華 (T'ang Tseng-pi 湯增璧). 'Tung-meng-hui shih-tai *Min-pao* shih-mo chi' 同盟會時代民報始末記 (A history of the *Min-pao* in the era of the

Revolutionary Alliance). *KMWH*, 2 (1953) 218–38

Mancall, Mark and Jidkoff, Georges. 'The Hung Hu-tzu of Northeast China', in *PMSS*, 125–34

Manchester, William. *The arms of Krupp 1587–1968*. Boston: Little, Brown, 1968

Mantetsu Chōsabu 滿鐵調查部. *Chū-Shi no minsengyō* 中支の民船業 (The junk trade of Central China). Tokyo: Hakubunkan, 1943

Marsh, Robert M. *The mandarins: the circulation of elites in China, 1600–1900*. Glencoe, Illinois: The Free Press, 1961

Martin, W. A. P. (Ting Wei-liang 丁韙良). *Wan-kuo kung-fa* 萬國公法 (Public law of all nations; translation of Henry Wheaton's *Elements of international law*). 4 *ts'e*. Peking: Ch'ung-shih kuan 崇實館, 1864

Maruyama, Masao. 'Patterns of individuation and the case of Japan: a conceptual scheme', in Marius B. Jansen, ed. *Changing Japanese attitudes toward modernization*, 489–531. Princeton University Press, 1965

MAS: Modern Asian Studies

Masui Tsuneo 增井経夫. *Taihei tengoku* 太平天國 (The Heavenly Kingdom of Great Peace). Tokyo: Iwanami, 1951

McCormack, Gavan. *Chang Tso-lin in northeast China, 1911–1928: China, Japan, and the Manchurian idea*. Stanford University Press, 1977

McAleavy, Henry. *Black flags in Vietnam: the story of a Chinese intervention*. London: Allen and Unwin, 1968; New York edn, Macmillan, 1968

Meijer, Marinus J. *The introduction of modern criminal law in China*. Batavia: De Unie, 1950

Meng Yun-sheng 夢芸生 (pseud.) *Shang-hsin jen-yü* 傷心人語 (Wounded to the soul). Shanghai: Ching-shih shu-hui 警世書會, 1906

Metzger, Thomas A. 'State and commerce in imperial China'. *Asian and African Studies*, 6 (1970) 23–46

Mi Ju-ch'eng 宓汝成, comp. *Chung-kuo chin-tai t'ieh-lu shih tzu-liao, 1863–1911* 中國近代鐵路史資料 1863–1911 (Source materials on the history of railways in modern China, 1863–1911). 3 vols. Peking: Chung-hua, 1963

Michie, Peter S. *The life and letters of Emory Upton*. New York: D. Appleton, 1885

Min-pao 民報 (The people). Tokyo, 1905–10

Ministère des Colonies. Les archives. Paris

Ministry of Industries, National Agricultural Research Bureau, Department of Agricultural Economics. *Crop reporting in China, 1934*. Nanking: Ministry of Industries, Aug. 1936

Mitchell, Peter M. 'The limits of reformism: Wei Yuan's reaction to Western intrusion'. *MAS*, 6.2 (1972) 175–204

Mito han shiryō. See Tokugawa family

Mitrano, Thomas. 'The Chinese bankruptcy law of 1906–1907: a case history'. *Monumenta Serica*, 30 (1972–3) 259–337

Miyashita Tadao 宮下忠雄. *Chūgoku heisei no tokushu kenkyū; kindai Chūgoku ginryō seido no kenkyū* 中国幣制の特殊研究；近代中国銀両制度の研究. (A monographic study of the Chinese currency system; a study of the silver tael system of modern China). Tokyo: Nihon Gakujutsu Shinkōkai 日本学術振興会, 1952

Miyazaki Ryūsuke 宮崎龍介 and Onogawa Hidemi 小野川秀美, eds. *Miyazaki Tōten zenshū* 宮崎滔天全集 (The complete works of Miyazaki Tōten). 5 vols. Tokyo: Heibonsha, 1971-6. See also Eto Shinkichi, ed. *Sanjū-sannen no yume.*

Mo Pei 墨悲 ed. *Chiang-Che t'ieh-lu feng-ch'ao* 江浙鐵路風潮 (The storm over the Kiangsu-Chekiang railway). Shanghai, 1907. Photocopy from Kuomintang Party Historical Commission, Taipei, 1968

Modern Chinese society, an analytical bibliography. (1) *Publications in Western languages, 1644-1972,* ed. G. William Skinner; (2) *Publications in Chinese, 1644-1969,* ed. G. William Skinner and Winston Hsieh; (3) *Publications in Japanese, 1644-1971,* ed. G. William Skinner and Shigeaki Tomita. 3 vols. Stanford University Press, 1973

Morgan, W. P. *Triad societies in Hongkong.* Hong Kong: Government Press, 1969

Morley, James, ed. *Japan's foreign policy, 1868-1941: a research guide.* New York: Columbia University Press, 1974

Morrison, Esther. 'The modernization of Confucian bureaucracy'. Radcliffe College, Ph.D. dissertation. Cambridge, Mass., 1959

Morse, H. B. *The trade and administration of the Chinese empire.* Shanghai: Kelly and Walsh, 1908

Morse, H. B. *The international relations of the Chinese empire.* 3 vols. London, New York (etc.): Longmans, Green and Co., 1910-18; Taipei reproduction, Wen-hsing, 1966

Mou An-shih 牟安世. *Yang-wu yun-tung* 洋務運動 (The Western affairs movement). Shanghai: Jen-min, 1956; 6th printing, 1961

Munholland, J. Kim. 'The French connection that failed: France and Sun Yat-sen, 1900-1908'. *JAS,* 32.1 (Nov. 1972) 77-95

Muramatsu Yūji. 'A documentary study of Chinese landlordism in the late Ch'ing and the early republican Kiangnan'. *BSOAS,* 29.3 (1966) 566-99

Muramatsu Yūji 村松祐次. *Kindai Kōnan no sosan: Chūgoku jinushi seido no kenkyū* 近代江南の租桟：中国地主制度の研究 (Landlord bursaries in Kiangnan in modern times: studies of landlordism in China). Tokyo University Press, 1970

Myers, Ramon H. *The Chinese peasant economy: agricultural development in Hopei and Shantung, 1890-1949.* Cambridge, Mass.: Harvard University Press, 1970

Myers, Ramon H. 'Taiwan under Ch'ing imperial rule, 1684-1895: the traditional economy'. *Journal of the Institute of Chinese Studies of the Chinese University of Hong Kong,* 5.2 (Dec. 1972) 373-411

Naba Toshisada 那波利貞. *Chūka shisō* 中華思想 (Sinocentrism), in *Iwanami kōza: Tōyō shichō* 岩波講座東洋思潮 (The Iwanami series on oriental trends of thought). Series 17. Tokyo: Iwanami, 1936

Nagai Kazumi 永井算己. 'Iwayuru Shinkoku ryūgakusei torishimari kisoku jiken no seikaku: Shimmatsu ryūgakusei no ichi dōkō' 所謂清国留学生取締規則事件の性格：清末留学生の一動向 (The nature of the so-called incident involving Ch'ing regulations for controlling overseas students: a movement among Chinese students in Japan towards the end of Ch'ing). *Shinshū Daigaku kiyō* 信州大学紀要, 2 (July 1952) 11–34

Nagai Kazumi. 'Kyoga gakuseigun o megutte' 拒俄学生軍をめぐって (Concerning the student army to resist Russia). *Shinshū Daigaku kiyō* 信州大学紀要 4 (Sept. 1954) 57–83

Nagai Kazumi. 'Kō-Setsu roji to Shimmatsu no minshū' 江浙路事と清末の民衆 (The Kiangsu-Chekiang railway and the people in late Ch'ing). *Shinshū Daigaku kiyō* 信州大学紀要, 7 (1957) 1–25

Nakada Yoshinobu 中田吉信. 'Dōchi nenkan no Sen-Kan no Kairan ni tsuite' 同治年間の陝甘の回乱について (A study of the Muslim Rebellion in Shensi and Kansu during the T'ung-chih period). *Kindai Chūgoku kenkyū*, 3 (1959) 69–159

Nakajima Masao 中島正郎, ed. *Taishi kaiko roku* 対支回顧録 (Memoirs concerning China). 2 vols. Tokyo: Dai Nihon Kyōka Tosho, 1936

Nakajima Masao, ed. *Zoku Taishi kaiko roku* 續対支回顧録 (Memoirs concerning China, supplement). 2 vols. Tokyo: Dai Nihon Kyōka Tosho, 1941

Nakamura Tadashi 中村義. 'Shimmatsu seiji to kanryō shihon: Sei Sen-kai no yakuwari o megutte' 清末政治と官僚資本：盛宣懐の役割をめぐって (Late Ch'ing politics and bureaucratic capital, with reference to Sheng Hsuan-huai's role), in Tōkyō Kyōiku Daigaku Bungakubu Tōyōshigaku Kenkyūshitsu 東京教育大学文学部東洋史学研究室, ed. *Chūgoku kindaika no shakai kōzō* 中国近代化の社会構造 (The social structure of China's modernization), pp. 21–44. Tokyo: Tōkyō Kyōiku Daigaku, 東京教育大学, 1960

Nan-k'ai ta-hsueh Ching-chi hsi, Ching-chi yen-chiu so 南開大學經濟系，經濟研究所. *Ch'i-hsin yang-hui kung-ssu shih-liao* 啓新洋灰公司史料 (Historical materials on the Chee Hsin Cement Co.). Peking: San-lien, 1963

Nan-yang hsiung-ti yen-ts'ao kung-ssu shih-liao. See Chung-kuo k'o-hsueh-yuan Shang-hai ching-chi yen-chiu-so

Nankai Institute of Economics. *Nankai index numbers, 1936*. Tientsin: Nankai University, 1936

Narochnitskii, A. L. *Kolonial'naia politika kapitalisticheskikh derzhav na dal'nem vostoke, 1860–1895* (The colonial policies of the capitalist powers in the Far East, 1860–1895). Moscow: Izd-vo Akademii nauk CCCP, 1956

National Agricultural Research Bureau. *Crop reporting in China, 1934*. Nanking, Aug. 1936. See Ministry of Industries

NCH: North-China Herald

Negishi Tadashi 根岸佶. *Shinkoku shōgyō sōran* 清国商業綜覧 (General survey of commerce of the Ch'ing dynasty). 5 vols. Tokyo: Maruzen 丸善 for Tōa Dōbunkai 東亜同文会, 1906–8

Nieh Tseng Chi-fen 聶曾紀芬. *Ch'ung-te lao-jen pa-shih tzu-ting nien-p'u* 崇德老人八十自訂年譜 (Chronological autobiography of Nieh Tseng Chi-fen at age eighty). Shanghai: The Nieh family, 1933

Nihon Shiseki Kyōkai 日本史籍協会, comp. *Kawaji Toshiakira monjo* 川路聖謨文書 (Kawaji Toshiakira documents). 8 vols. Tokyo: Nihon Shiseki Kyōkai, 1932–4; new edn, 1967–8. See Ōtsuka Takematsu

Nish, I. H. 'Japan's indecision during the Boxer disturbances'. *JAS*, 20.3 (May 1961) 449–61

Nish, Ian H. *The Anglo-Japanese alliance: the diplomacy of two island empires, 1894–1907*. London: Athlone, 1966

Nisshin Bōeki Kenkyūjo 日清貿易研究所. *Shinkoku tsūshō sōran* 清国通商綜覧 (General survey of the foreign trade of the Ch'ing dynasty). 3 vols. Tokyo: Maruzen 丸善 (vols. 1–2) and Ōkura Shoten 大倉書店 (vol. 3), 1892

Nisshin sensō jikki 日清戦争実記 (Actual record of the Japan-Ch'ing war). Issued every ten days. Tokyo: Hakubunkan, Aug. 1894–Jan. 1896

North-China Herald. Shanghai, 1850– ; also cited as *NCH*

Nozawa Yutaka 野沢豊. 'Nihon ni okeru Son Bun kankei bunken mokuroku' 日本における孫文関係文献目録 (A list of bibliographical items concerning Sun Yat-sen found in Japan). *Shisō* 思想, 1957. 6 (June) 79–93

Nung-kung-shang pu 農工商部, comp. *Nung-kung-shang pu hsien-hsing chang-ch'eng* 農工商部現行章程 (Current regulations of the Ministry of Agriculture, Industry and Commerce). 13 *ts'e*. Peking, 1908

Nung-kung-shang pu t'ung-chi ch'u 農工商部統計處, comp. *Nung-kung-shang pu t'ung-chi piao* 農工商部統計表 (Statistical tables of the Ministry of Agriculture, Industry and Commerce). Peking: *ti-i-tz'u* 第一次 (1st issue), 6 *ts'e*, 1909; *ti-erh-tz'u* 第二次 (2nd issue), 5 *ts'e*, 1910

Onogawa, Hidemi 小野川秀美. *Shimmatsu seiji shisō kenkyū* 清末政治思想研究 (Studies in political thought of the late Ch'ing). Kyoto University, 1960

Ōtaka Iwao 大高巖 and Hatano Tarō 波多野太郎, trans. *Ryūnichi kaiko – Chūgoku anakisuto no hansei* 留日回顧―中国アナキストの半生 (Recollections of a sojourn in Japan – half a life of a Chinese anarchist). Tokyo: Heibonsha, 1966. See Ching Mei-chiu, *Tsui-an*

Ōtsuka Takematsu 大塚武松, ed. *Kawaji Toshiakira monjo* 川路聖謨文書 (Kawaji Toshiakira documents), vol. 8. Tokyo: Nihon Shiseki Kyōkai 日本史籍協会, 1934

Pai Shou-i 白壽彝, ed. *Hui-min ch'i-i* 回民起義 (The Muslim uprisings). 4 vols. Shanghai: Shen-chou kuo-kuang she, 1952; also cited as *HMCI*

Pao Shih-ch'en 包世臣. *An-Wu ssu-chung* 安吳四種 (Four collections regarding peaceful government of Kiangsu). 36 *chüan*. Soochow, 1851; Taipei reproduction, Wen-hai, 1968

Pao Tsun-p'eng 包遵彭. *Chung-kuo hai-chün shih* 中國海軍史 (History of the Chinese Navy). Taipei: Naval Publication Office, 1951; Chung-hua ts'ung-shu 中華叢書, 1970

Pao Tsun-p'eng. 'Ch'ing-chi hai-chün ching-fei k'ao-shih' 清季海軍經費考實 (The truth about late Ch'ing naval funds). *Chung-kuo li-shih hsueh-hui shih-hsueh chi-k'an* 中國歷史學會史學集刊, 1 (1969) 17–55

Papers on China, annual, vols. 1–24 (1947–71). East Asian Research Center,

Harvard University

Pearl, Cyril. *Morrison of Peking*. Sydney: Angus and Robertson, 1967

Pei-chuan-chi pu 碑傳集補 (Supplement to collected epigraphs), Min Erh-ch'ang 閔爾昌 comp. Peiping: Yenching University, 1923

Pei-yang hai-chün chang-ch'eng 北洋海軍章程 (Regulations of the Pei-yang Navy). 1 *ts'e* Tientsin, 1888; reprinted in *YWYT*, 3.195–262

Pelcovits, Nathan A. *Old China hands and the Foreign Office*. New York: King's Crown Press for the Institute of Pacific Relations, 1948

P'eng Hsin-wei 彭信威. *Chung-kuo huo-pi shih* 中國貨幣史 (History of Chinese currency). 3rd edn. Shanghai: Jen-min, 1965.

P'eng Tse-chou (Hō Taku-shū) 彭沢(澤)周. *Meiji shoki Nik-Kan-Shin kankei no kenkyū* 明治初期日韓清関係の研究 (Studies on Japanese-Korean-Ch'ing relations during the early Meiji period). Tokyo: Hanawa Shobō 塙書房, 1969

P'eng Tse-chou (Hō Taku-shū). *Chūgoku no kindaika to Meiji Ishin* 中国の近代化と明治維新 (The modernization of China and the Meiji Restoration). Kyōto: Dōbōsha 同朋舎, 1976

P'eng Tse-chou (Hō Taku-shū). 'Kō Yū-i no hempō undō to Meiji Ishin' 康有為の変法運動と明治維新 (K'ang Yu-wei's reform movement and the Meiji Restoration). *Jimbun gakuhō* 人文学報, 30 (1970) 149–93

P'eng Tse-chou (Hō Taku-shū). 'Ryō Kei-chō no Meiji Ishin kan to Chūgoku henkakuron' 梁啓超の明治維新観と中国変革論 (Liang Ch'i-ch'ao's view of the Meiji Restoration and his arguments for reform in China), in Sakata Yoshio 坂田吉雄 and Yoshida Mitsukuni 吉田光邦, eds. *Sekaishi no naka no Meiji Ishin: gaikokujin no shikaku kara* 世界史のなかの明治維新：外国人の視角から (The Meiji Restoration in world history: as seen by foreigners), pp. 61–114. Kyoto University, 1973

P'eng Tse-i 彭澤益, comp. *Chung-kuo chin-tai shou-kung-yeh shih tzu-liao, 1840–1949* 中國近代手工業史資料 1840–1949 (Source materials on the history of handicraft industry in modern China, 1840–1949). 4 vols. Peking: San-lien, 1957

P'eng Tse-i. 'Shih-chiu shih-chi hou-ch'i Chung-kuo ch'eng-shih shou-kung-yeh shang-yeh hang-hui ti ch'ung-ch'ien ho tso-yung' 十九世紀後期中國城市手工業商業行會的重建和作用 (The reconstruction of urban Chinese handicraft and trade associations in the late nineteenth century and their functions). *Li-shih yen-chiu* 歷史研究 1965.1, pp. 71–102

Perkins, Dwight H. *Agricultural development in China, 1368–1968*. Chicago: Aldine, 1969

Perkins, Dwight H., ed. *China's modern economy in historical perspective*. Stanford University Press, 1975

Pi-chih hui-pien. See Ts'ai-cheng pu ch'üan-pi ssu

P'i Hsi-jui 皮錫瑞. 'Shih-fu-t'ang wei-k'an jih-chi' 師復堂未刊日記 (P'i Hsi-jui's hitherto unpublished diary). *Hu-nan li-shih tzu-liao*, 4 (1958) 65–126

Piassetsky, P. *Russian travellers in Mongolia and China*. J. Gordon-Cummings, trans. London: Chapman & Hall, 1884

PMSS: Jean Chesneaux, ed. *Popular movements and secret societies in China, 1840–1950*

P'o-hsieh chi. See Hsu Ch'ang-chih

Powell, Ralph L. *The rise of Chinese military power 1895–1912.* Princeton University Press, 1955

Prejevalsky, M. *Mongolia, the Tangut country, and the solitude of northern Tibet: being a narrative of three years' travel in eastern high Asia.* E. Delmar Morgan, trans. 2 vols. London: Sampson, Low, Marston, Searle & Rivington, 1876

Presseisen, Ernst. *Before aggression: Europeans prepare the Japanese army.* Tucson: University of Arizona Press, 1965

Price, Don C. *Russia and the roots of the Chinese Revolution, 1896–1911.* Cambridge, Mass.: Harvard University Press, 1974

Pu-hsiao sheng 不肖生 (pseud.). *Liu-tung wai-shih* 留東外史 (Unofficial history of Chinese students in Japan). 10 *ts'e*, published in 5 series. Shanghai: Min-ch'üan ch'u-pan pu 民權出版部 , 1924–5

Purcell, Victor. *The Boxer uprising.* Cambridge University Press, 1963

Puyraimond, Guy. 'The Ko-lao-hui and the anti-foreign incidents of 1891', in *PMSS*, 113–24

Rankin, Mary Backus. 'The revolutionary movement in Chekiang: a study in the tenacity of tradition', in *CIR*, 319–61

Rankin, Mary Backus. *Early Chinese revolutionaries: radical intellectuals in Shanghai and Chekiang, 1902–1911.* Cambridge, Mass.: Harvard University Press, 1971

Rawlinson, Sir Henry Creswicke. *England and Russia in the East; a series of papers on the political and geographical condition of Central Asia.* 2nd edn. London: J. Murray, 1875

Rawlinson, John L. *China's struggle for naval development 1839–1895.* Cambridge, Mass.: Harvard University Press, 1967

Remer, Charles Frederick. *Foreign investments in China.* New York: Macmillan, 1933

Report on the introduction of the gold-exchange standard into China. US Senate document, no. 128, 58th Congress, 3rd session. Washington: Government Printing Office, 1904

Report on the native cloth in use in the Amoy consular district. Foreign Office, miscellaneous series. London: 1886, no. 19

Rhoads, Edward J. M. 'Merchant associations in Canton, 1895–1911', in *CCTW*, 97–117

Rhoads, Edward J. M. *China's republican revolution: the case of Kwangtung, 1895–1913.* Cambridge, Mass.: Harvard University Press, 1975

(Rikugun) Sambōhombu （陸軍）参謀本部, comp. *Meiji nijūshichi-hachinen Nisshin senshi* 明治二十七八年日清戦史 (A history of the 1894–5 Japan-Ch'ing War). 9 vols. Tokyo: Ministry of War, 1904–7

Rinji Taiwan Kyūkan Chōsakai 臨時台湾旧慣調査会 (Temporary commission of the Taiwan government-general for the study of old Chinese customs), ed. *Shinkoku gyōseihō* 清国行政法 (Administrative laws of the Ch'ing dynasty). 5

vols., Taipei, 1905–11; 7 vols., Tokyo and Kobe, 1910–14; Tokyo: Daian 大安, 1965–7

Robinson, Ronald, Gallagher, John and Denny, Alice. *Africa and the Victorians; the official mind of imperialism.* London: Macmillan, 1961. American edn: *Africa and the Victorians: the climax of imperialism.* New York: St Martin's Press, 1961

Rosenbaum, Arthur L. 'Gentry power and the Changsha rice riot of 1910'. *JAS*, 34.3 (May 1975) 689–715

Rossabi, Morris. *China and Inner Asia from 1368 to to the present day.* London: Thames and Hudson, 1975

Rubinchak, Leonid S., comp. and trans. *A digest of Krasnyi Arkhiv: a historical journal of the Central Archive Department of the U.S.S.R.* Louise M. Boutella and Gordon W. Tgayer, eds. 106 vols. Cleveland Public Library, 1947–55

Saeki Tomi 佐伯富. *Shindai ensei no kenkyū* 清代鹽政の研究 (A study of the Ch'ing salt administration). Kyoto: Tōyōshi Kenkyūkai 東洋史研究会, 1956

Saguchi Tōru 佐口透. *Jūhachi-jūkyūseiki Higashi Torukisutan shakaishi kenkyū* 18–19 世紀東トルキスタン社会史研究 (A study of the social history of Eastern Turkestan in the 18th and 19th centuries). Tokyo: Yoshikawa Kōbunkan 吉川弘文館, 1963

Sakai, Robert K. 'The Ryūkyū (Liu-ch'iu) Islands as fief of Satsuma', in *CWO*, 112–34

Sanetō Keishū 実藤恵秀. *Chūgokujin Nihon ryūgaku shikō* 中国人日本留学史稿 (Draft history of Chinese students in Japan). Tokyo: Chūka Gakkai 中華学会, 1939; rev. edn, 1970

Sanetō Keishū. *Nihon bunka no Shina e no eikyō* 日本文化の支那への影響 (The influence of Japanese civilization on China). Tokyo: Keisetsu Shoin 螢雪書院, 1940

Sanetō Keishū. *Meiji Nisshi bunka kōshō* 明治日支文化交渉 (Cultural interchange between China and Japan in the Meiji period). Tokyo: Kōfūkan 光風館, 1943

Sanetō Keishū. *Chūgokujin Nihon ryūgaku shi* 中国人日本留学史 (History of Chinese students in Japan). Tokyo: Kuroshio Shuppan くろしお出版, 1960

Sasaki Masaya 佐々木正哉. 'Eikō shōnin no kenkyū' 営口商人の研究 (A study of the Ying-k'ou merchants). *Kindai Chūgoku kenkyū* 近代中国研究, 1 (1958) 213–67

Sauvage, Lieutenant. *La Guerre sino-japonaise 1894–1895.* Paris: Librairie Militaire de L. Baudoin, 1897

Scalapino, R. A. and Schiffrin, H. 'Early socialist currents in the Chinese revolutionary movement: Sun Yat-sen versus Liang Ch'i-ch'ao'. *JAS*, 18.3 (May 1959) 321–42

Scalapino, Robert A. 'Prelude to Marxism: the Chinese student movement in Japan, 1900–1910', in *AMCH*, 190–215

Schiffrin, Harold. 'Sun Yat-sen's land policy'. *JAS*, 26.4 (Aug. 1957) 549–64

Schiffrin, Harold Z. *Sun Yat-sen and the origins of the Chinese Revolution.* Berkeley:

University of California Press, 1968

Schiffrin, Harold Z. 'The enigma of Sun Yat-sen', in *CIR*, 443–74

Schrecker, John. 'The Pao-kuo hui: a reform society of 1898'. *Papers on China*, 14 (1960) 50–64

Schrecker, John E. *Imperialism and Chinese nationalism: Germany in Shantung*. Cambridge, Mass.: Harvard University Press, 1971

Schwartz, Benjamin. *In search of wealth and power: Yen Fu and the West*. Cambridge, Mass.: Harvard University Press, 1964

SCMP: South China Morning Post

Scott, James G. 'The Chinese brave'. *Asiatic Quarterly Review*, 1 (1886) 222–45

Seki Masaaki. 'The 1911 Revolution in Fengtien province'. Far Eastern and Russian Institute MA dissertation. Seattle: University of Washington, 1968

SFLS: Kuo-li T'ai-wan shih-fan ta-hsueh li-shih hsueh-pao

Shan Hua-p'u 單化普. 'Shen-Kan chieh-yü lu' 陝甘劫餘錄 (Legends of the Shensi-Kansu calamity), in *HMCI*, 4.303–16

Shadick, Harold, trans. *The travels of Lao Ts'an by Liu T'ieh-yun (Liu E)*. Ithaca: Cornell University Press, 1952

Shang-wu yin-shu kuan 商務印書館 (Commercial Press), comp. *Ta Ch'ing Hsuan-t'ung hsin fa-ling* 大清宣統新法令 (New statutes and decrees of the Ch'ing dynasty in the Hsuan-t'ung period). 32 *ts'e*. Shanghai: Commercial Press, 1910–11

Shang-wu yin-shu kuan (Commercial Press), comp. *Ta-Ch'ing Kuang-hsu hsin fa-ling* 大清光緒新法令 (New statutes and decrees of the Ch'ing dynasty in the Kuang-hsu period). 20 *ts'e*. Shanghai: Commercial Press, 1910

Shao Hsun-cheng 邵循正. *Chung-Fa Yueh-nan kuan-hsi shih-mo* 中法越南關係始末 (A complete account of Sino-French relations concerning Vietnam [until 1885]). Peiping: Tsing Hua University, 1935

Shao Hsun-cheng *et al*. eds. *Chung-Fa chan-cheng* 中法戰爭 (The Sino-French War). 7 vols. Shanghai: Hsin-chih-shih, 1955; Jen-min, 1957

Shao Hsun-cheng *et al*. eds. *Chung-Jih chan-cheng* 中日戰爭 (The Sino-Japanese War). 7 vols. Shanghai: Hsin-chih-shih, 1956; also cited as *CJCC*

Shao Hsun-cheng. 'Yang-wu yun-tung ho tzu-pen-chu-i fa-chan ti kuan-hsi wen-t'i' 洋務運動和資本主義發展的關係問題 (The problem of the relationship between the Western Affairs movement and the development of capitalism), in *Pei-ching-shih li-shih hsueh-hui ti-i ti-erh-chieh nien-hui lun-wen hsuan-chi* 北京市歷史學會第一第二屆年會論文選集 (Selected papers from the first and second annual meetings of the Peking Historical Association). Peking: Pei-ching ch'u-pan-she 北京出版社, 1964

Shek, Richard H. 'Some Western influences on T'an Ssu-t'ung's thought', in Paul A. Cohen and John E. Schrecker, eds. *Reform in nineteenth-century China* (q.v.), pp. 194–203

Shen Chia-pen 沈家本 *et al*. eds. *Ho-ting hsien-hsing hsing-lü* 核定現行刑律 (Current code as revised and approved). 2 *ts'e*. Peking: Fa-lü kuan 法律館, 1909–10

Shen T'ung-sheng 沈桐生 *et al*. eds. *Kuang-hsu cheng-yao* 光緒政要 (Important policies of the Kuang-hsu reign). 34 *chüan*. Shanghai: Nan-yang kuan shu chü 南洋官書局, 1909. Taipei reproduction, Wen-hai, 1969

Shen Yun-lung 沈雲龍. 'Chang-wo wan-Ch'ing cheng-ping chih I-k'uang' 掌握晚清政柄之奕劻 (Prince Ch'ing: wielder of political power towards the end of the Ch'ing period), in Shen Yun-lung, *Hsien-tai cheng-chih jen-wu shu-p'ing* 現代政治人物述評 (A critical review of some contemporary political personalities), 2.2.70–80. 2 vols. with subdivisions. Taipei: Wen-hai, 1966

Sheng Hsuan-huai 盛宣懷. *Sheng shang-shu Yü-chai ts'un-kao ch'u-k'an* 盛尚書愚齋存稿初刊 (Collected papers of ministry president Sheng Hsuan-huai, 1st issue). Lü Ching-tuan 呂景端, ed. 101 *chüan*. Shanghai, 1939

Sheng Hsuan-huai. *Sheng Hsuan-huai wei-k'an hsin-kao* 盛宣懷未刊信稿 (Unpublished letters of Sheng Hsuan-huai). Modern History Teaching and Research Center 教研室 of the Department of History, Peking University, ed. Peking: Hsin-hua shu-tien 新華書店, 1960

Sheng K'ang 盛康, comp. *Huang-ch'ao ching-shih-wen hsu-pien* 皇朝經世文續編 (Collection of Ch'ing dynasty writings on statecraft, continued). 120 *chüan*. Wu-chin, Kiangsu: Sheng-shih ssu-pu lou 盛氏思補樓, 1897

Sheng Lang-hsi 盛郎西. *Chung-kuo shu-yuan chih-tu* 中國書院制度 (The academy system in China). Shanghai: Chung-hua, 1934

Sheridan, James E. *Chinese warlord: the career of Feng Yü-hsiang*. Stanford University Press, 1966

Shih-liao hsun-k'an 史料旬刊 (Historical materials published thrice-monthly). 40 vols. Peiping: Palace Museum, 1930–1

Shih-wu pao 時務報 ('The Chinese progress'). Thrice-monthly. Shanghai, 1896–8

Shimada Kenji 島田虔次. *Chūgoku kakumei no senkusha tachi* 中国革命の先覚者たち (Forerunners of the Chinese revolution). Tokyo: Chikuma, 1965

Shimada Kenji. *Shingai kakumei no shisō* 辛亥革命の思想 (The thought behind the Revolution of 1911). Tokyo: Chikuma, 1968

Shimada Masao 島田正郎. 'Shimmatsu ni okeru min shōritsu sōan no hensan ni tsuite' 清末における民商律草案の編纂 (On the compilation of the drafts for civil and commercial codes towards the end of the Ch'ing period). *Horitsu ronsō* 法律論叢 34.6 (1962) 119–49

Shiraishi Hiroo 白石博男. 'Shimmatsu Konan no nōson shakai – ōso kankō to kōso keiko' 清末湖南の農村社会—押租慣行と抗租傾向 (Rural Hunan society in the late Ch'ing – the practice of *ya-tsu* and the tendency towards rent resistance), in Tokyo Kyōiku Daigaku Tōyōshigaku Kenkyūshitsu, ed. *Kindai Chūgoku Kindaika no shakai kōzō* (q.v.), pp. 1–19

Shisō 思想 (Thought). Monthly. Tokyo, 1921–

Shu Hsin-ch'eng 舒新城. *Chin-tai Chung-kuo chiao-yü shih tzu-liao* 近代中國教育史資料 (Materials for the history of education in modern China). 3 vols. Peking: Jen-min chiao-yü ch'u-pan she 人民教育出版社, 1962

Simon, G-Eugène. *La Cité chinoise*. Paris: Nouvelle revue, 1885

Sincere Co. *Hsien-shih kung-ssu erh-shih-wu chou-nien chi-nien ts'e* 先施公司廿五週年紀念冊 (The Sincere Co.: twenty-fifth anniversary). Hong Kong:

1924–5

Skachkov, P. E., ed. *Bibliografiia Kitaia* (Bibliography on China). Moscow: Izd-vo vostochnoi literatury, 1960

Skinner, G. William. 'Marketing and social structure in rural China, part I'. *JAS*, 24.1 (Nov. 1964) 3–43

Skinner, G. William. 'Marketing and social structure in rural China, part II'. *JAS*, 24.2 (Feb. 1965) 195–228

Skinner, G. William *et al.* eds. *Modern Chinese society: an analytical bibliography*. 3 vols. Stanford University Press, 1973. See *Modern Chinese Society*

Skinner, G. William, ed. *The city in late imperial China*. Stanford University Press, 1977

Smith, Henry D., II. *Japan's first student radicals*. Cambridge, Mass.: Harvard University Press, 1972

Smith, Richard J. 'Chinese military institutions in the mid-nineteenth century, 1850–1860'. *Journal of Asian History*, 8.2 (1974) 122–61

Smith, Richard J. 'The employment of foreign military talents: Chinese tradition and late Ch'ing practice'. *Journal of the Hong Kong Branch of the Royal Asiatic Society*, 15 (1975) 113–38

Smith, Richard J. 'Foreign training and China's self-strengthening: the case of Feng-huang-shan, 1864–1873'. *MAS*, 10.2 (1976) 195–223

Smith, Richard J. 'Reflections on the comparative study of modernization in China and Japan: military aspects'. *Journal of the Hong Kong Branch of the Royal Asiatic Society*, 16 (1976) 11–23

Smith, Richard J. *Mercenaries and mandarins: the Ever-Victorious Army in nineteenth century China*. New York: KTO Press, 1978

Smith, Thomas C. *Political change and industrial development in Japan: government enterprise, 1868–1880*. Stanford University Press, 1955; 2nd printing, 1965

Snow, Edgar. *Red Star over China*. New York: Random House, 1938. Grove Press rev. edn, 1968

'Son Bun to Nihon: Tokushu' 孫文と日本・特集 (Sun Yat-sen and Japan, a special collection of articles). *Chūgoku* 中国 (China, a monthly), Tokyo, 36 (Nov. 1966) 1–30

South China Morning Post. Hong Kong, 1903– , also cited as *SCMP*

Spector, Stanley. *Li Hung-chang and the Huai Army: a study in nineteenth-century Chinese regionalism*. Seattle: University of Washington Press, 1964

Speidel, William M. 'Liu Ming-ch'uan in Taiwan, 1884–1891'. Yale University, Ph.D. dissertation. New Haven, 1967

Speidel, William M. 'The administrative and fiscal reforms of Liu Ming-ch'uan in Taiwan, 1884–1891: foundation for self-strengthening'. *JAS*, 35.3 (May 1976) 441–59

Spence, Jonathan. 'Opium smoking in Ch'ing China', in Frederic Wakeman Jr and Carolyn Grant, eds. *Conflict and control in late imperial China* (q.v.), pp. 143–73

Stanley, Charles J. *Late Ch'ing finance: Hu Kuang-yung as an innovator*. Cambridge,

Mass.: Harvard University Press, 1961

Su Yü 蘇輿. *I-chiao ts'ung-pien* 翼教叢編 (Collection of writings for upholding sacred teachings). Wuchang 1898 edn. Taipei reproduction, T'ai-lien kuo-feng ch'u-pan she 臺聯國風出版社, 1970

Su Yun-feng 蘇雲峯. 'Wai-kuo chuan-chia hsueh-che tsai Hu-pei' 外國專家學者在湖北 (Foreign experts and scholars in Hupei). *Chung-kuo wen-hua fu-hsing yueh-k'an* 中國文化復興月刊, 8.4 (April 1975) 51–64

Su Yun-feng. *Chang Chih-tung yü Hu-pei chiao-yü kai-ko* 張之洞與湖北教育改革 (Chang Chih-tung and educational reform in Hupei). Taipei: IMH Academia Sinica, 1976

Sun, E-tu Zen. 'The Shanghai-Hangchow-Ningpo railway loan of 1908'. *FEQ*, 10.2 (1950) 136–50

Sun, E-tu Zen.'The Chinese constitutionalist mission of 1905–1906'. *Journal of Modern History*, 24.3 (Sept. 1952) 251–68

Sun, E-tu Zen. *Chinese railways and British interests 1898–1911*. New York: King's Crown Press, 1954

Sun, E-tu Zen. 'Mining Labor in the Ch'ing Period', in *AMCH*, 45–67

Sun Po-ch'un (Son Haku-jun) 孫伯醇. 'Kajuku, Dōbun Shoin, Minpōsha: Nihon ni ikiru ichi Chūgokujin no kaisō' 家塾、同文書院、民報社―日本に生きる一中国人の回想 (Family tutorial, Dōbun Shoin, the *People's Tribune*: the recollections of a Chinese resident in Japan). *Chūgoku* 中国 (Tokyo) 30 (May 1966) 24–33

Sun Po-ch'un (Son Haku-jun). 'Ryūgakusei: gakkō kyōiku, bempatsu no koto' 留学生，学校教育，辮髪のこと (Overseas Chinese students, school education, queues). *Chūgoku* 中国, (Tokyo) 31 (June 1966) 28–33

Sun Wen 孫文 (Sun Yat-sen). *Kuo-fu ch'üan-chi* 國父全集 (The complete works of the national father). 6 vols. Taipei: Kuomintang Party History Commission, distributed by Chung-yang wen-wu, 1950; rev. edn, 1957, 1961

Sun Wen (Sun Yat-sin). 'Tzu-chuan' 自傳 (Autobiography), in Sun Wen, *Kuo-fu ch'üan-chi* (q.v.), 1957 edn, vol. 1, pp. 31–49

Sun Yü-t'ang 孫毓棠, comp. *Chung-kuo chin-tai kung-yeh shih tzu-liao, ti-i chi, 1840–1895 nien* 中國近代工業史資料第一輯 1840–1895 年 (Source materials on the history of modern industry in China, 1st collection, 1840–1895). 2 vols. Peking: K'o-hsueh, 1957. See Wang Ching-yü

Sung-shih 宋史 (History of the Sung dynasty). 496 *chüan*. Ssu-pu pei-yao 四部備要 edn. Shanghai: Chung-hua, 1934; Taipei reproduction, Chung-hua, 1965

Sung Yü-jen 宋育仁. *Ts'ai-feng chi* 采風集 (Miscellaneous notes on world customs), in Chih-hsueh hui, comp. *Chih-hsueh ts'ung-shu ch'u-chi* (q.v.), *ts'e* 1

Sutton, Donald S. 'The rise and decline of the Yunnan Army, 1909–1925'. University of Cambridge, Ph.D. dissertation, 1970

Suzuki Tomoo 鈴木智夫. 'Shimmatzu gensoron no tenkai – "Sokaku" no kenkyū' 清末減租論の展開―'租覈' の研究 (The development of rent reduction theories in the late Ch'ing period – a study of 'Inquiry into rents'), in Tōkyō Kyōiku Daigaku Tōyōshigaku Kenkyūshitsu, ed. *Kindai Chūgoku nōson shakai shih kenkyū* (q.v.)

Ta-Ch'ing hsien-hsing hsing-lü. See Shen Chia-pen

Ta-Ch'ing Hsuan-t'ung hsin fa-ling. See Shang-wu yin-shu kuan

Ta-Ch'ing hui-tien. See *Ch'in-ting ta-Ch'ing hui-tien*

Ta-Ch'ing Kao-tsung shun-huang-ti shih-lu 大清高宗純皇帝實錄 (Veritable records of the Ch'ien-lung Emperor of the Ch'ing dynasty). 1,500 *chüan*. See *Ta-Ch'ing li-ch'ao shih-lu*

Ta-Ch'ing Kuang-hsu hsin fa-ling. See Shang-wu yin-shu kuan

Ta-Ch'ing li-ch'ao shih-lu 大清歷朝實錄 (Veritable records of successive reigns of the Ch'ing dynasty). Totalling 4,485 *chüan*, but with new *chüan* sequence under each reign. Mukden: Man-chou-kuo kuo-wu-yuan 滿洲國國務院, 1937–8; Taipei facsimile reproduction in 94 volumes, Hua-lien 華聯 and Hua-wen 華文, 1964. Also cited as *CSL*, followed by the title of the reign referred to

Ta-Ch'ing lü-li. See Yao Jun, comp.

Ta-Ch'ing shih-lu Hsuan-t'ung cheng-chi 大清實錄宣統政紀 (Veritable records of the Hsuan-t'ung Emperor of the Ch'ing dynasty, or the Hsuan-t'ung government records). 70 *chüan*. Also cited as *CSL-HT*. See *Ta-Ch'ing li-ch'ao shih-lu*

Ta-Ch'ing Te-tsung ching-huang-ti shih-lu 大清德宗景皇帝實錄 (Veritable records of the Kuang-hsu Emperor of the Ch'ing dynasty). 597 *chüan*. Also cited as *CSL-KH*. See *Ta-Ch'ing li-ch'ao shih-lu*

Tai Chi-t'ao 戴季陶. *Jih-pen-lun* 日本論 (On Japan). Shanghai: Min-chih shu-chü 民智書局, 1928; Taipei reprint, Chung-yang wen-wu, 1954

Takahashi Masao 高橋正雄, ed. *Nihon kindaika to Kyūshū: Kyūshū bunka ronshū* 日本近代化と九州—九州文化論集 (Kyūshū and Japanese modernization: essays on Kyūshū culture). Tokyo: Heibonsha, 1972

Takeuchi Yoshimi 竹内好. 'Asahi no koto, Takeyamasan no koto, Chūgoku o shirutameni' 朝日のこと, 竹山さんのこと, 中国を知るために (The Asahi newspaper, Mr Takeyama, and how to know China). *Chūgoku* 中国, 16 (March 1965) 34–6

Takeuchi Zensaku 竹内善作. 'Meiji makki ni okeru Chū-Nichi kakumei undō no kōryū' 明治末期における中日革命運動の交流 (Interflow in the Chinese and Japanese revolutionary movements in late Meiji years). *Chūgoku kenkyū* 中国研究, 5 (Sept. 1948) 74–95

Tamada, Noriko (Noriko Kamachi). 'Sung Chiao-jen and the 1911 Revolution'. *Papers on China*, 21 (1968) 184–229

T'an, Chester C. *The Boxer catastrophe.* New York: Columbia University Press, 1955

T'an Ssu-t'ung 譚嗣同. *Jen-hsueh* 仁學 (On humanity). Yokohama, *c.* 1899. In T'an Ssu-t'ung, *T'an Ssu-t'ung ch'üan-chi* (q.v.), pp. 3–90. Also in Chang Li-chai 章立齋 ed. *T'an Liu-yang ch'üan-chi* 譚瀏陽全集 (The complete writings of T'an Ssu-t'ung), pt 5. Taipei: Wen-hai, 1962

T'an Ssu-t'ung. *T'an Ssu-t'ung ch'üan-chi* 譚嗣同全集 (The complete works of

T'an Ssu-t'ung). Peking: San-lien, 1954

T'ang Chen 湯震. *Wei-yen* 危言 (Warnings). 4 *chüan*. Shanghai, 1890; also available in Chih-hsueh hui, *Chih-hsueh ts'ung-shu ch'u-chi* (q.v.), *ts'e* 1–2

T'ang Chih-chün 湯志鈞. *Wu-hsu pien-fa shih lun-ts'ung* 戊戌變法史論叢 (A collection of articles on the reform movement of 1898). Hankow: Jen-min, 1957

T'ang Chih-chün. *Wu-hsu pien-fa jen-wu chuan-kao* 戊戌變法人物傳稿 (Draft biographies of participants in the reform of 1898). Peking: Chung-hua, 1961

T'ang I 湯彝. *Yu-ts'un wen* 柚村文 (Essays of T'ang I). 6 *chüan*. Changsha, 1847

T'ang Ts'ai-chih 唐才質. 'T'ang Ts'ai-ch'ang ho shih-wu hsueh-t'ang' 唐才常和時務学堂 (T'ang Ts'ai-ch'ang and the School of Current Affairs). *Hu-nan li-shih tzu-liao*, 3 (1958) 98–108

Tao, L. S. (T'ao Lung-sheng 陶龍生). 'Shen Chia-pen and modernization of Chinese law'. *She-hui k'o-hsueh lun-ts'ung* 社會科學論叢, Taipei, 25 (Sept. 1966) 275–90

T'ao Ch'eng-chang 陶成章. 'Che-an chi-lüeh' 浙案紀略 (A brief account of the revolts in Chekiang), *HHKM*, 3.3–111

T'ao Chü-yin 陶菊隱. *Pei-yang chün-fa t'ung-chih shih-ch'i shih-hua* 北洋軍閥統治時期史話 (Historical anecdotes on the period of the Peiyang warlords). 7 vols. Peking: San-lien, 1957–61

T'ao Hsu 陶煦. *Tsu ho* 租覈 (Inquiry into rents). Facsimile reproduction of 1927 edn in Suzuki Tomoo, 'Shimmatsu gensoron no tenkai – "Sokaku" no kenkyū' (q.v.), appendix

Tarui Tōkichi 樽井藤吉. *Daitō gappō ron* 大東合邦論 (A proposal for a unified eastern state). Original edn, 1893. Tokyo: Daitōjuku Shuppanbu 大東塾出版部, 1963

Teng, Ssu-yü and Fairbank, John K. *China's response to the West: a documentary survey 1839–1923*. Cambridge, Mass.: Harvard University Press, 1954

Teraki Tokuko 寺木德子. 'Shimmatsu Minkoku shonen no chihō jichi' 清末民国初年の地方自治 (Local self-government in late Ch'ing and early Republican China). *Ochanomizu shigaku* お茶の水史学, 5 (1962) 14–30

TFTC: Tung-fang tsa-chih

Ti-san-tz'u chiao-yü t'ung-chi t'u-piao, Hsuan-t'ung yuan-nien 第三次教育統計圖表，宣統元年 (Statistical charts and tables on education, the third issue, for 1909). See Hsueh-pu tsung-wu ssu, comp. *Chiao-yü t'ung-chi t'u-piao*

T'ien Ju-k'ang 田汝康. 'Yu-kuan Tu Wen-hsiu tui-wai kuan-hsi ti chi-ko wen-t'i' 有關杜文秀對外關係的幾個問題 (A few problems regarding Tu Wen-hsiu's foreign relations). *Li-shih yen-chiu* 歷史研究, 1963.4, pp. 141–50

Tikhvinskii, Sergei Leonidovich. *Dvizhenie za reformy v Kitae v kontse XIX veka i Kan Iu-vei* (The reform movement in China at the end of the nineteenth century and K'ang Yu-wei). Moscow: Izd-vo vostochnoi literatury, 1959

Tikhvinskii, Sergei Leonidovich, ed. *Man'chzhurskoe vladychestvo v Kitae* (Manchu dominion in China). Moscow: Nauka, 1966

Ting Jih-ch'ang 丁日昌. *Fu-Wu kung-tu* 撫吳公牘 (Official papers of the governor of Kiangsu). 50 *chüan*. 1877 preface. Taipei reproduction, Hua-wen 華文, 1968

Ting Jih-ch'ang. 'Ting Chung-ch'eng cheng-shu' 丁中丞政書 (Political papers of Governor Ting). Manuscript copy, 36 *chüan*. New Haven, Conn.: Sterling Library, Yale University

Ting Pao-chen 丁寶楨. *Ting Wen-ch'eng kung i-chi* 丁文誠公遺集 (Collected papers of the late Ting Pao-chen). 27 *chüan*. Peking, 1893; Taipei reproduction, Wen-hai, 1967

Ting Wen-chiang 丁文江. *Liang Jen-kung hsien-sheng nien-p'u ch'ang-pien ch'u-kao* 梁任公先生年譜長編初稿 (The first draft of a documentary chronological biography of Mr Liang Ch'i-ch'ao). 3 vols. Taipei: Shih-chieh, 1959

Tōa Dōbun Shoin 東亜同文書院, comp. *Shina keizai zensho* 支那経済全書 (A comprehensive survey of China's economy). 12 vols. Osaka and Tokyo, 1907–8

Tokugawa family 徳川家蔵版. *Mito han shiryō* 水戸藩史料 (Mito han historical materials). Tokyo: Yoshikawa Kōbunkan 吉川弘文館, 1915–17

Tokyo Kyōiku Daigaku Tōyōshigaku Kenkyūshitsu 東京教育大学東洋史学研究室, ed. *Chūgoku kindaika no shakai kōzō* 中国近代化の社会構造 (Social structure in China's modernization). Tokyo: Tōkyō Kyōiku Daigaku 東京教育大学, 1960. Daian reproduction, 1966

Tōkyō Kyōiku Daigaku Tōyōshigaku Kenkyūshitsu 東京教育大学東洋史学研究室, ed. *Kindai Chūgoku nōson shakai shi kenkyū* 近代中国農村社会史研究 (Studies in modern Chinese rural social history). Tokyo: Daian, 1967

Trotter, Captain. 'Some remarks on the army of Li Hung-chang and the garrisons of the forts on the Yang-tzu-chiang'. War Office, 33/4 (1880) 127–30. Public Record Office, London

Ts'ai-cheng pu ch'üan-pi ssu 財政部泉幣司. *Pi-chih hui-pien* 幣制彙編 (Compendium of documents on the monetary system). 4 vols. Peking: Ministry of Finance, 1919

Ts'ai-cheng shuo-ming shu 財政説明書 (Reports on the financial administration). 20 vols. Peking: Ching-chi hsueh-hui 經濟學會, 1915

Ts'en Ch'un-hsuan 岑春煊. *Lo-chai man-pi* 樂齋漫筆 (Ts'en Ch'un-hsuan's autobiographical notes). Originally published in *Chung-ho yueh-k'an* 中和月刊 (Peiping) 4.5 (May 1943) 11–32. Taipei reproduction in book form together with a biography of Ts'en by Wu Hsiang-hsiang 吳相湘, Wen-hsing, 1962

Tseng Chi-tse 曾紀澤. *Tseng Hui-min kung shih-hsi jih-chi* 曾惠敏公使西日記 (Diary of Tseng Chi-tse's diplomatic mission to the West). Shanghai, 1893; also in *HFHC, ts'e* 78

Tseng Chi-tse. *Tseng Hui-min kung i-chi* 曾惠敏公遺集 (Collected papers of the late Tseng Chi-tse). Shanghai: The Kiangnan Arsenal, 1893; Taipei reproduction, Wen-hai 1966. This comprehensive collection includes *Tseng Hui-min kung wen-chi* 文集, 5 *chüan*, also found in *Tseng Hui-min kung i-chi*, Sao-yeh shan-fang edn, Shanghai 1932

Tseng Chi-tse. *Tseng Hui-min kung shou-hsieh jih-chi* 曾惠敏公手寫日記 (Tseng

Chi-tse's holograph diary). Taipei: Hsueh-sheng, 1965

Tseng Kuo-fan 曾國藩. *Tseng Wen-cheng kung (Kuo-fan) ch'üan-chi* 曾文正公(國藩) 全集 (Complete collection of Tseng Kuo-fan's papers). Amplified version, 1876 *et seq.* Taipei reproduction, Wen-hai, 40 vols. 1974; also cited as *TWCKCC*

Tseng Kuo-fan. *Tseng Wen-cheng kung shu-cha* 曾文正公書札 (Tseng Kuo-fan's letters). 33 *chüan.* Changsha: Ch'uan-chung shu-chü 傳忠書局, 1876

Tseng Kuo-fan. *Tseng Wen-cheng kung shou-hsieh jih-chi* 曾文正公手寫日記 (Tseng Kuo-fan's holograph diary). 6 vols. Taipei: Hsueh-sheng, 1965

Tseng Lien 曾廉. *Ku-an chi* 甌庵集 (Collected writings of Tseng Lien). 18 *chüan.* Tseng-shih Hui-fu-t'ang 曾氏會輔堂, 1911

Tseng Wen-wu 曾問吾. *Chung-kuo ching-ying Hsi-yü shih* 中國經營西域史 (History of China's management of the Western Region). Shanghai: Commercial Press, 1936

Tsiang, T. F. 'Sino-Japanese diplomatic relations, 1870-1894'. *Chinese Social and Political Science Review*, 17 (1933) 1–106

Tsien, Tsuen-hsuin. 'Western impact on China through translation'. *FEQ*, 13.3 (May 1954) 305–27

Tso Tsung-t'ang 左宗棠. *Tso Wen-hsiang kung ch'üan-chi* 左文襄公全集 (Complete collection of Tso Tsung-t'ang's papers). Changsha, 1890 *et seq.* Taipei, Wen-hai reproduction, 1964; also cited as *TWHK*

Tso Tsung-t'ang. *Tso Wen-hsiang kung chia-shu* 左文襄公家書 (Tso Tsung-t'ang's letters to his family). *c.* 1920. Taipei reproduction, Wen-hai, 1972

Tsou Jung. *The revolutionary army: a Chinese nationalist tract of 1903.* Introd. and trans. with nn. by John Lust. Paris: Mouton, 1968

Tsou-ting hsueh-t'ang chang-ch'eng. See Chang Po-hsi *et al.*

Ts'un-ts'ui hsueh-she 存粹學社, comp. *Chung-kuo chin-tai she-hui ching-chi shih lun-chi* 中國近代社會經濟史論集 (Collected articles on China's modern social and economic history). 2 vols. Hong Kong: Ch'ung-wen, 1971

Ts'un-ts'ui hsueh-she, comp. *Chung-kuo chin san-pai-nien she-hui ching-chi shih lun-chi* 中國近三百年社會經濟史論集 (Collected articles on China's social and economic history in the last 300 years). 2 vols. Hong Kong: Ch'ung-wen, 1972

Tsunoda, Ryusaku, DeBary, William Theodore and Keene, Donald, eds. *Sources of the Japanese tradition.* New York: Columbia University Press, 1958

Tung-a chü-shih 東阿居士 (pseud.). 'Ch'in-luan chien-wen chi' 秦難見聞記 (Diary of what I saw and heard during the Shensi calamity), in Ma Hsiao-shih, *Hsi-pei hui-tsu ko-ming chien-shih* (q.v.), pp. 85–150

Tung-fang tsa-chih 東方雜誌 (The eastern miscellany). Shanghai: Commercial Press, 1904–48; also cited as *TFTC*

Tung-hua hsu-lu. See Chu Shou-p'eng

Tung-hua lu. See Wang Hsien-ch'ien, P'an I-fu *et al.* eds. *Shih-erh ch'ao tung-hua lu*

TWCKCC: Tseng Kuo-fan, *Tseng Wen-cheng kung ch'üan-chi*

TWHK: Tso Tsung-t'ang, *Tso Wen-hsiang kung ch'üan-chi*

US Department of State. *Foreign relations of the United States.* Washington, DC: Government Printing Office, 1861–

US National Archives. *Catalogue of National Archives microfilm publications.* Washington, DC: National Archives, Records Service, 1974

Upton, Emory. *The armies of Asia and Europe.* New York: D. Appleton, 1878; Greenwood Press reproduction, 1968

Vagts, Alfred. *Defense and diplomacy: the soldier and the conduct of foreign relations.* New York: King's Crown, 1956

van Gulik, R. H. 'Kakkaron: a Japanese echo of the Opium War'. *Monumenta Serica,* 4 (1939) 478–545

Vladimir (pseud. for Zenone Volpicelli). *The China-Japan War compiled from Japanese, Chinese, and foreign sources.* London: S. Low, Marston & Co., 1896

Wakeman, Frederic, Jr. 'The price of autonomy: intellectuals in Ming and Ch'ing politics'. *Daedalus,* 101.2 (Spring 1972) 35–70

Wakeman, Frederic, Jr and Carolyn Grant, eds. *Conflict and control in late imperial China.* Berkeley: University of California Press, 1975

Wakeman, Frederick, Jr. 'Rebellion and revolution: the study of popular movements in Chinese history'. *JAS,* 36.2 (Feb. 1977) 201–37

Waley, Arthur. *The Opium War through Chinese eyes.* London: Allen & Unwin, 1958

Wallach, Richard. 'The war in the East'. *Proceedings of the United States Naval Institute,* 21.4 (1895) 691–739

Wang Ch'ao-tsung 王朝宗, comp. *Hai-wai fan-i lu* 海外番夷錄 (Collected writings on barbarians beyond the seas). 2 *ts'e.* Peking: Sou-liu-hsuan 漱六軒, 1844

Wang Chia-chien 王家儉. *Wei Yuan tui Hsi-fang ti jen-shih chi ch'i hai-fang ssu-hsiang* 魏源對西方的認識及其海防思想 (Wei Yuan's knowledge of the West and his ideas regarding maritime defence). Taipei: National Taiwan University, College of Letters, 1964

Wang Chia-chien. 'Hai-kuo t'u-chih tui-yü Jih-pen ti ying-hsiang' 海國圖志對於日本的影響 (The influence of the *Hai-kuo t'u-chih* in Japan), in *Ta-lu tsa-chih* 大陸雜誌, 32.8 (April 1966) 242–9

Wang Chia-chien. 'Ch'ing-chi ti hai-fang lun' 清季的海防論 (Opinions favouring coastal defence in the late Ch'ing period). *Shih-ta hsueh-pao* 師大學報, 12 (June 1967) 1–40

Wang Chia-chien. *Wei Yuan nien-p'u* 魏源年譜 (Chronological biography of Wei Yuan). Taipei: IMH, Academia Sinica, 1967

Wang Chia-chien. 'Ch'ing-chi ti hai-chün ya-men' 清季的海軍衙門 (The Navy Yamen of the late Ch'ing period). *Chung-kuo li-shih hsueh-hui shih-hsueh chi-k'an* 中國歷史學會史學集刊, 5 (1973) 1–32

Wang Chia-chien. 'Wen-hsiang tui-yü shih-chü ti jen-shih chi ch'i tzu-ch'iang ssu-hsiang' 文祥對於世局的認識及其自強思想 (Wen-hsiang's knowledge of world affairs and his ideas regarding self-strengthening). *SFLS,* 1 (1973) 219–39

Wang Chia-chien. 'Pei-yang wu-pei hsueh-t'ang ti ch'uang-she chi ch'i ying-hsiang' 北洋武備學堂的創設及其影響 (The Peiyang Military Academy: its creation and influence). *SFLS*, 4 (April 1976) 317–43

Wang Chia-chien. 'Lü-shun chien-kang shih-mo' 旅順建港始末 (The establishment of the Port Arthur naval base: a complete account). *CYCT*, 5 (June 1976) 223–62

Wang Ching-yü 汪敬虞, comp. *Chung-kuo chin-tai kung-yeh shih tzu-liao, ti-erh chi, 1895–1914 nien* 中國近代工業史資料第二輯, 1895–1914 年 (Source materials on the history of modern industry in China, 2nd collection 1895–1914). 2 vols. Peking: K'o-hsueh, 1957. See Sun Yü-t'ang

Wang Ching-yü and Nieh Pao-chang 聶寶璋. 'Kuan-yü Chung-kuo ti-i-tai ch'an-yeh kung-jen ti tou-cheng tzu-liao' 關於中國第一代產業工人的鬥爭資料 (Materials on the struggles of the first generation of Chinese industrial workers). *Ching-chi yen-chiu* 經濟研究, 1962.3, pp. 43–51

Wang Ching-yü. 'Shih-chiu shih-chi wai-kuo ch'in Hua ch'i-yeh chung ti Hua-shang fu-ku huo-tung' 十九世紀外國侵華企業中的華商附股活動 (Investment by Chinese merchants in the foreign firms which invaded China in the nineteenth century). *Li-shih yen-chiu* 歷史研究 1965.4, pp. 39–74

Wang Erh-min 王爾敏. *Ch'ing-chi ping-kung yeh ti hsing-ch'i* 清季兵工業的興起 (The rise of the armaments industry in the late Ch'ing period). Taipei: IMH, Academia Sinica, 1963

Wang Erh-min. 'Ch'i-ying wai-chiao' 耆英外交 (The diplomacy of Ch'i-ying). *Ta-lu tsa-chih* 大陸雜誌, 30.9 and 10 (May and June 1965) 281–7, 330–3

Wang Erh-min. *Chung-kuo chin-tai ssu-hsiang shih-lun* 中國近代思想史論 (Historical essays on modern Chinese thought). Taipei: Hua-shih ch'u-pan she 華世出版社, 1977

Wang Erh-min. 'Shang-chan kuan-nien yü chung-shang ssu-hsiang' 商戰觀念與重商思想 (The idea of trade as a weapon and the greater importance attached to commerce). *CYCT*, 5 (June 1966) 1–91

Wang Erh-min. *Huai-chün chih* 淮軍志 (History of the Anhwei Army). Taipei: IMH, Academia Sinica, 1967

Wang Erh-min. 'Lien-chün ti ch'i-yuan chi ch'i i-i' 練軍的起源及其意義 (The origins and significance of the retrained Green Standard contingents). *Ta-lu tsa-chih* 大陸雜誌, 34.6 and 7 (March and April 1967) 172–5, 216–23

Wang Erh-min. *Wan-Ch'ing cheng-chih ssu-hsiang shih-lun* 晚清政治思想史論 (Historical essays on political thought in the late Ch'ing period). Taipei: Hsueh-sheng, 1969

Wang Erh-min. 'Ch'ing-tai yung-ying chih-tu' 清代勇營制度 (The 'Brave Battalion' system of the Ch'ing dynasty). *CYCT*, 4.1 (May 1973) 1–52

Wang Hsi-ch'i 王錫祺, comp. *Hsiao-fang-hu chai yü-ti ts'ung-ch'ao* 小方壺齋輿地叢鈔 (Geographical series of Hsiao-fang-hu studio). In 3 series totalling 84 *ts'e*. Shanghai: I-shu t'ang 易書堂, 1877–97; also cited as *HFHC*

Wang Hsien-ch'ien 王先謙, P'an I-fu 潘頤福 *et al. Shih-erh ch'ao tung-hua lu* 十二朝東華錄 (Tung-hua records of twelve reigns). Facsimile reproduction of edns for Ch'ing reigns up to and including Kuang-hsu. Tainan: Ta-tung 大東, 1968

Wang Hsin-chung 王信忠. *Chung-Jih chia wu chan-cheng chih wai-chiao pei-ching* 中日甲午戰爭之外交背景 (The diplomatic background of the Sino-Japanese War of 1894). Peiping: Tsing Hua University, 1937

Wang Hsiu-ch'u 王秀楚. *Yang-chou shih-jih chi* 揚州十日記 (An account of ten days in Yang-chou) in Shen Yun-lung 沈雲龍, *Ming-Ch'ing shih-liao hui-pien* 明清史料彙編 (Compendium of Ming-Ch'ing historical sources), series 2, vol. 5. Taipei reproduction, Wen-hai, 1967

Wang Hung-chih 王宏志. *Tso Tsung-t'ang p'ing hsi-pei hui-luan liang-hsiang chih ch'ou-hua yü chuan-yun yen-chiu* 左宗棠平西北回亂糧餉之籌劃與轉運研究 (A study of the planning and transmission of food and funds in Tso Tsung-t'ang's suppression of Muslim Rebellion in the north-west). Taipei: Cheng-chung, 1973

Wang I-sun 汪詒蓀. 'Hsin-hai ko-ming shih-ch'i tzu-ch'an chieh-chi yü nung-min ti kuan-hsi wen-t'i' 辛亥革命時期資產階級與農民的關係問題 (Problem of the relationship between the bourgeoisie and the peasants during the era of the 1911 Revolution), in *HHWS*, 115-46

Wang K'ai-yun 王闓運. *Hsiang-ch'i lou wen-chi* 湘綺樓文集 (Collection of essays of Wang K'ai-yun). Taipei: Hsin-hsing 新興, 1956

Wang Ping-hsieh 王炳燮. *Wu-tzu-ch'i shih wen-chi* 毋自欺室文集 (Wang Ping-hsieh's essays). Tientsin: Kuang-jen t'ang 廣仁堂, 1885; Taipei reproduction, Wen-hai, 1968

Wang Shu-huai 王樹槐. *Wai-jen yü Wu-hsu pien-fa* 外人與戊戌變法 (Foreigners and the reform movement of 1898). Taipei: IMH, Academia Sinica, 1965

Wang Shu-huai. *Hsien-T'ung Yun-nan hui-min shih-pien* 咸同雲南回民事變 (Muslim revolts in Yunnan during the Hsien-feng and T'ung-chih reigns). Taipei: IMH, Academia Sinica, 1968

Wang Ta-hai 王大海. *Hai-tao i chih* 海島逸志 (Little-known account of the seas and islands), in Wang Ch'ao-tsung, comp. *Hai-wai fan-i lu* (q.v.), *ts'e* 2

Wang T'ao 王韜. *T'ao-yuan ch'ih-tu* 韜園尺牘 (Wang T'ao's letters). 8 *chüan*. Hong Kong: privately issued, 1876; Taipei reproduction, Ta-t'ung 大通, 1968

Wang T'ao. *T'ao-yuan wen-lu wai-pien* 韜園文錄外編 (Additional essays of Wang T'ao). 10 *chüan*. Hong Kong: T'ao-yuan (Wang's residence), 1883; *chüan* 11-12 subsequently added, n.d.

Wang T'ao, ed. *Ko-chih shu-yuan k'o-i* 格致書院課藝 (Assigned writings of students of the Shanghai Polytechnic Institute). 13 *ts'e*. Shanghai: Polytechnic Institute and Reading Room, 1886-93

Wang T'ien-chiang 王天獎. 'Shih-chiu shih-chi hsia-pan-chi Chung-kuo ti pi-mi hui-she' 十九世紀下半紀中國的秘密會社 (Chinese secret societies in the second half of the nineteenth century). *Li-shih yen-chiu* 歷史研究, 1963.2, pp. 83-100

Wang T'ien-chiang. 'T'ai-p'ing t'ien-kuo ko-ming hou Su Che Wan san sheng ti t'u-ti kuan-hsi' 太平天國革命後蘇浙皖三省的土地關係 (The agrarian relations in the three provinces of Kiangsu, Chekiang and Anhwei after the Taiping Revolution). *Hsin chien-she* 新建設, 1963.8. pp. 46-54

Wang Wen-t'ai 汪文泰. *Hung-mao-fan Ying-chi-li k'ao-lueh* 紅毛蕃英吉利考略 (Short account of the red-haired English barbarians), in Wang Ch'ao-tsung, comp. *Hai-wai fan-i lu* (q.v.), *ts'e* 2

Wang, Y. C. *Chinese intellectuals and the West, 1872-1949.* Chapel Hill: University of North Carolina Press, 1966

Wang, Yeh-chien. *Land taxation in imperial China, 1750-1911.* Cambridge, Mass.: Harvard University Press, 1973

Wang Yen-hsi 王延熙 and Wang Shu-min 王樹敏, comps. *Huang-ch'ao Tao-Hsien-T'ung-Kuang tsou-i* 皇清道咸同光奏議 (Memorials of the Tao-kuang, Hsien-feng, T'ung-chih and Kuang-hsu periods of the Ch'ing dynasty). 64 *chüan.* Shanghai: Chiu-ching chai 久敬齋, 1902. Taipei reproduction, Wen-hai, 1968

Wang Yen-wei 王彥威 and Wang Liang 王亮, comps. *Ch'ing-chi wai-chiao shih-liao* 清季外交史料 (Historical materials concerning foreign relations in the late Ch'ing period, 1875-1911). 218 + 1 *chüan* for the Kuang-hsu period (1875-1908) and 24 *chüan* for the Hsuan-t'ung period (1908-11). Peiping: Wang Hsi-yin 王希隱, 1932-5; Taipei reproduction, Wen-hai, 1963

Wang Yu-ling 王有齡. 'Shang-pu chih tse-jen' 商部之責任 (The responsibility of the Ministry of Commerce). *Shang-wu kuan-pao* 商務官報 (The commercial gazette), 7 (1906) 1-4

WCSL: Ch'ing-chi wai-chiao shih-liao

Wehrle, Edmund S. *Britain, China, and the antimissionary riots, 1891-1900.* Minneapolis: University of Minnesota Press, 1966

Wei Chien-yu 魏建猷. *Chung-kuo chin-tai huo-pi shih, i-pa i-ssu - i-chiu i-chiu* 中國近代貨幣史, 一八一四一一九一九 (History of currency in modern China, 1814-1919). Shanghai: Ch'ün-lien, 1955; Taipei: Wen-hai, 1974

Wei Yuan 魏源. *Sheng wu-chi* 聖武記 (Chronicle of the sacred dynasty's military campaigns). Ku-wei t'ang 古微堂 1842 edn. Taipei reproduction, Wen-hai, 1967

Wei Yuan. *Hai-kuo t'u-chih* 海國圖志 (Illustrated treatise on the maritime kingdoms). 100 *chüan.* Shanghai: Wen-hsien ko 文賢閣, 1898 edn. Taipei reproduction of 1847 edn, Ch'eng-wen, 1966

Wen Kung-chih 文公直. *Tsui-chin san-shih-nien Chung-kuo chün-shih shih* 最近三十年中國軍事史 (History of Chinese military affairs in the last thirty years). 2 vols. Shanghai: T'ai-ping-yang shu-tien 太平洋書店, 1930

Weng T'ung-ho 翁同龢. *Weng T'ung-ho jih-chi p'ai-yin-pen* 翁同龢日記排印本 (A typeset edition of the diary of Weng T'ung-ho). 5 vols. Taipei: Ch'eng-wen, 1970

WHPF: Chien Po-tsan *et al.* eds. *Wu-hsu pien-fa*

Wickberg, Edgar B. 'Late nineteenth century land tenure in Taiwan' in Leonard H. D. Gordon, ed. *Taiwan: studies in Chinese local history* (q.v.), pp. 78-92

Willmott, W. E., ed. *Economic organization in Chinese society*. Stanford University Press, 1972

Wilson, George M. 'Politics and the people: Liang Ch'i-ch'ao's view of constitutional developments in Meiji Japan before 1890'. *Papers on Japan*, 1 (1961) 189–226

Wilson, George M. *Radical nationalist in Japan: Kita Ikki, 1883–1937*. Cambridge, Mass.: Harvard University Press, 1969

Wilson, James Harrison. *China: travels and investigations in the 'Middle Kingdom'*. New York: D. Appleton, 1887; 2nd edn, 1894

Wing On Co. *Hsiang-kang Yung-an yu-hsien kung-ssu erh-shih-wu chou-nien chi-nien lu* 香港永安有限公司廿五週年紀念錄 (The Wing On Co. Ltd. of Hong Kong: twenty-fifth anniversary). Hong Kong, 1932

Witte, Sergei Iul'evich. *The memoirs of Count Witte*. Abraham Yarmolinsky, trans. and ed. New York: H. Fertig reproduction of 1921 edn, 1967

Wodehouse, H. E. 'Mr. Wade on China'. *The China Review*, 1.1 (July-Aug. 1872) 38–44, and 1.2 (Sept.-Oct. 1872) 118–24

Wong, Young-tsu, 'Popular unrest and the 1911 Revolution in Jiangsu [Kiangsu]'. *Modern China*, 3.3 (July 1977) 321–44

Wright, Mary C. *The last stand of Chinese conservatism: the T'ung-chih restoration, 1862–1874*. Stanford University Press, 1957

Wright, Mary C. 'The adaptability of Ch'ing diplomacy: the case of China's involvement in Korea'. *JAS*, 17.3 (May 1958) 363–81

Wright, Mary C., ed. *China in revolution: the first phase, 1900–1913*. New Haven: Yale University Press, 1968; also cited as *CIR*

Wright, Mary C. 'Introduction: the rising tide of change', in *CIR*, 1–63

Wright, Stanley F. *Hart and the Chinese customs*. Belfast: Wm Mullan, for the Queen's University, 1950

Wu-ch'ang shou-i, See Chung-hua min-kuo k'ai-kuo wu-shih-nien wen-hsien pien-tsuan wei-yuan hui

Wu Hsiang-hsiang 吳相湘. *O-ti ch'in-lueh Chung-kuo shih* 俄帝侵略中國史 (A history of the Russian imperialist aggression in China). Taipei: Kuo-li pien-i kuan 國立編譯館, 1954

Wu Hsiang-hsiang. *Wan-Ch'ing kung-t'ing shih-chi* 晚清宮廷實紀 (True account of palace politics during the late Ch'ing). Taipei: Cheng-chung, 1961

Wu Hsiang-hsiang. *Chin-tai shih-shih lun-ts'ung* 近代史事論叢 (Studies in modern historical events). Taipei: Wen-hsing, 1964

Wu, Silas H. L. *Communication and imperial control in China: evolution of the palace memorial system, 1693–1735*. Cambridge, Mass.: Harvard University Press, 1970

Wu T'ien-jen 吳天任. *Huang Kung-tu hsien-sheng chuan-kao* 黃公度先生傳稿 (A draft biography of Huang Tsun-hsien). Chinese University of Hong Kong, 1972

Wu Wo-yao 吳沃堯 (Wu Chien-jen 趼人, 繭人, or Yen-jen 研人). *Erh-shih-nien mu-tu chih kuai hsien-chuang* 二十年目睹之怪現狀 (Bizarre phenomena eyewitnessed over twenty years). 8 *chüan*. Shanghai: Hsin-hsiao-shuo shu-tien

新小説書店, 1916. Reprints include Shang-hai wen-hua ch'u-pan-she 上海文化出版社, 1957

Wu Wo-yao. *Vignettes from the late Ch'ing: bizarre happenings eyewitnessed over two decades.* Shih-Shun Liu, trans. Chinese University of Hong Kong, 1974; New York edn, St John's University, 1974

Wu, Yü-chang. *The Revolution of 1911: a great democratic revolution of China.* Peking: Foreign Languages Press, 1962

Wu Yun 吳雲. *Liang-lei-hsuan ch'ih-tu* 兩罍軒尺牘 (Wu Yun's letters). 12 *chüan.* 1884. Taipei reproduction, Wen-hai, 1968

Ya-p'ien chan-cheng. See Ch'i Ssu-ho *et al.*

Yamagata, Aritomo. 'The Japanese army', in Shigenobu Ōkuma, ed. *Fifty years of new Japan,* 1.194–217. 2 vols. London: Smith, Elder & Co., 1909

Yang, C. [Yang Tuan-liu] and Bau, H. B. [Hou Hou-p'ei] *et al. Statistics of China's foreign trade during the last sixty-five years.* Nanking: National Research Institute of Social Sciences, Academia Sinica, 1931

Yang, C. K. 'Some preliminary patterns of mass action in nineteenth century China', in Frederic Wakeman, Jr and Carolyn Grant, eds, *Conflict and control in late imperial China,* pp. 174–210. Berkeley: University of California Press, 1975

Yang Hung-lieh 楊鴻烈. *Chung-kuo fa-lü fa-ta shih* 中國法律發達史 (Chinese law: the history of its full development). 2 vols. Shanghai: Commercial Press, 1930, 1933

Yang, Lien-sheng. 'Historical notes on the Chinese world order', in *CWO,* 20–33

Yang, Lien-sheng. 'Government control of the urban merchant in traditional China'. *Ch'ing-hua hsueh-pao,* NS, 8.1–2 (1970) 186–209

Yang, Martin C. (Yang Mou-ch'un). *Chinese social structure: a historical study.* Taipei: Eurasia, 1969

Yang, Ping-nan. *Hai-lu.* See Hsieh Ch'ing-kao and Yang Ping-nan, *Hai-lu*

Yang Tuan-liu 楊端六 and Hou Hou-pei 侯厚培. *Liu-shih-wu-nien lai Chung-kuo kuo-chi mao-i t'ung-chi* 六十五年來中國國際貿易統計 (English title: *Statistics of China's foreign trade during the last sixty-five years*). Nanking: National Research Institute of Social Sciences, Academia Sinica, 1931

Yang Tuan-liu. *Ch'ing-tai huo-pi chin-jung shih kao* 清代貨幣金融史稿 (Draft history of money and money markets in the Ch'ing period). Peking: San-lien, 1962

Yang Yu-chiung 楊幼炯. *Chin-tai Chung-kuo li-fa shih* 近代中國立法史 (History of legislation in modern China). Shanghai: Commercial Press, 1936; rev. edn, Taipei, 1966

Yano Jin'ichi 矢野仁一. *Shinchō masshi kenkyū* 清朝末史研究 (Studies in late Ch'ing history). Ōsaka: Yamato Shoin 大和書院, 1944

Yao Hsi-kuang 姚錫光. *Tung-fung ping-shih chi-lueh* 東方兵事紀略 (Brief account of war in the East). 5 *chüan,* 1897. Reprinted in *CJCC,* 1.1–108

Yao Jun 姚潤 comp. *Ta-Ch'ing lü-li hsing-an hui-tsuan chi-ch'eng* 大清律例刑案彙纂

集成 (Comprehensive compilation of the Ch'ing statutes and sub-statutes, together with a conspectus of penal cases). Rev. and enlarged by Hu Chang 胡璋 . 20 *chüan*. 1865. Taipei reproduction of 1873–4 edn, Wen-hai, 1964

Yao Ying 姚瑩. *Tung-ming wen hou-chi* 東溟文後集 (Supplement to Yao Ying's collected essays). 14 *chüan*, n.p., 1867

Yeh Chung-chin 葉鍾進. *Ying-chi-li-kuo i-ch'ing chi-lueh* 英吉利國夷情紀略 (A brief account of the condition of the English barbarians), in *HFHC, ts'e* 77

Yen Chung-p'ing 嚴中平 *et al.* comps. *Chung-kuo chin-tai ching-chi shih t'ung-chi tzu-liao hsuan-chi* 中國近代經濟史統計資料選輯 (Selected statistics on China's modern economic history). Peking: K'o-hsueh, 1955

Yen Chung-p'ing. *Chung-kuo mien-fang-chih shih-kao, 1289–1937* 中國棉紡織史稿, 1289–1937 (Draft history of the Chinese cotton industry, 1289–1937). Rev. edn., Peking: K'o-hsueh, 1955; 3rd printing, 1963

Yen Fu 嚴復. *T'ien-yen lun* 天演論 (On evolution; a translation of *Evolution and ethics* by Thomas Henry Huxley 赫胥黎). Tientsin, 1897–8. In vol. 1 of Yen Fu, *Yen-i ming-chu ts'ung-k'an* 嚴譯名著叢刊 (A collection of famous works translated by Yen Fu). 8 vols. Shanghai: Commercial Press, 1931

Yen Fu. *Yen Chi-tao shih-wen ch'ao* 嚴幾道詩文鈔 (Yen Fu's poems and essays). 6 *ts'e*. Shanghai: Kuo-hua 國華, 1922

Yin Keng-yun 尹耕雲 *et al. Yü-chün chi-lueh* 豫軍紀略 (A concise history of the Honan Army). 12 *chüan* with sub-divisions. 1872 preface. Taipei reproduction, Wen-hai, 1968

Yoshida, Tadashi. 'Sakuma Shōzan as an advocate of "Eastern morality, Western science"', in *Princeton Papers in East Asian Studies* (Princeton University Program in East Asian Studies): 1 *Japan* (1972), pp. 33–56

Young, Ernest P. 'Ch'en T'ien-hua (1875–1905): a Chinese nationalist'. *Papers on China*, 13 (1959) 113–62

Young, Ernest P. 'The reformer as a conspirator: Liang Ch'i-ch'ao and the 1911 Revolution' in *AMCH*, 239–67

Young, Ernest P. 'Yuan Shih-k'ai's rise to the presidency', in *CIR*, 419–42

Young, Ernest P. *The presidency of Yuan Shih-k'ai: liberalism and dictatorship in early Republican China.* Ann Arbor: University of Michigan Press, 1977

Young, L. K. *British policy in China, 1895–1902.* Oxford: Clarendon, 1970

Yu, George T. *Party politics in Republican China: the Kuomintang, 1912–1924.* Berkeley: University of California Press, 1966

Yü En-te 余恩德. *Chung-kuo chin yen fa-ling pien-ch'ien shih* 中國禁煙法令變遷史 (The historical evolution of anti-opium statutes and decrees in China). Shanghai: CH, 1934

Yü P. K. (Ping-chüan) 余秉權, Li, Yu-ning 李又寧 and Chang, Yü-fa 張玉法, comps. *Ch'ing-chi ko-ming yun-tung ch'i-k'an hsu-mu hsuan-chi* 清季革命運動期刊 敍目選輯 ('The revolutionary movement during the late Ch'ing: a guide to Chinese periodicals'). Washington DC: Center for Chinese Research Materials, Association of Research Libraries, 1970

Yuan, Tsing. 'Yakub Beg (1820–1877) and the Moslem Rebellion in Chinese

Turkestan'. *Central Asiatic Journal*, 6 (1961) 134–67

YWYT. Chung-kuo k'o-hsueh yuan chin-tai-shih yen-chiu-so *et al.* eds *Yang-wu yun-tung*

GLOSSARY-INDEX

36; dyeing of 16, 18, 36; development of handicraft industry 17–18; in rural households 18; in urban workshops 18; effect of imported cotton on 19–22; prices of 20–1; dispersal of 22; weaving of 22–4; native v. imported 24–5; imports of 25, 48, 49, 76; consumption of 25; investment in 39; increase in manufacturing of 580, 581

Courbet, Admiral Gustave 100, 251, 575

credit, lack of 44; see also banks

crops: changes in patterns of 2, 10; size of harvests 6, 7; reports on production; annual major 9–10; size of 15; see also agriculture

Cuba 584; coolies in 584

culturalism: persistence of 181–8, 201; civilization v. barbarism 182–4; man v. beast 184–6, 188; influence of conservatism 186–8; see also Confucianism

currency: multiple local 44–5; unification of 403–5; paper 405–6; financing reform of 414

curriculum revision 331

customs duties 61; resentment of 117; see also Imperial Maritime Customs

Cyclopaedia of geography 147

Dah Sun (Ta-sheng) Mill 458–9

Dairen (Ta-lien): 55, 132, 271; railway to 56; occupied by Japanese 107, 270; coveted by Russia 109, 112

Daitō 大東 (Great East) 366

Daitō gappō ron 大東合邦論 366

Dalai Lama 達賴喇嘛, missions to Russia from 131

Danton, Georges Jacques 475

Darwin, Charles 475; see also social Darwinism

defence, Chinese: frontier v. maritime 91–2; maritime 168–9; re-

organization of Green Standard 206–9; defects of yung-ying 208–9; coastal, and Li Hung-chang 243–50; state of in Sino-Japanese War 268–9; see also coastal defence; navy

degree-holders: post-Taiping 536–9; by purchase 537; families of 537–8; regional disparities in 538; increase of 'irregulars' 539; military 539–40

democracy 309; infeasibility of 280; part of nationalism 281; K'ang Yu-wei on 286–7; Liang Ch'i-ch'ao on 295, 296–7; in study societies 333; in Sun Yat-sen's ideology 493, 494–5

Denmark 198

Dent and Company 551

Denver, Colo., Sun Yat-sen in 532

department stores 445–6

Determination Society (Li-chih hui) 477

dhikr-i jahrī (vocal recollection) 215

diplomacy, training for 162

'Discussion of Szechwanese self-protection' 522

Dōbun Shoin 同文書院, Tokyo branch of 351; see also Tōa Dōbun Shoin

Dōbunkai 同文会 367

Doctrine of the Mean 380

drought: in North China (1900) 117; as upset of geomantic forces 175; in Kiangsu and Anhwei 587

Dual Alliance 110, 130, 131; extended to East Asia 134

East Asian Socialist Party 366, 372

East India Company 150

Eastern Chou period 189

economy: and government 58–69; tradition and stability of 58–9; state of, late Ch'ing 65, 68–9; effect of indemnities on 129–30; threat of